Data Analytics for the Social Sciences

Data Analytics for the Social Sciences is an introductory, graduate-level treatment of data analytics for social science. It features applications in the R language, arguably the fastest growing and leading statistical tool for researchers.

The book starts with an ethics chapter on the uses and potential abuses of data analytics. Chapters 2 and 3 show how to implement a broad range of statistical procedures in R. Chapters 4 and 5 deal with regression and classification trees and with random forests. Chapter 6 deals with machine learning models and the "caret" package, which makes available to the researcher hundreds of models. Chapter 7 deals with neural network analysis, and Chapter 8 deals with network analysis and visualization of network data. A final chapter treats text analysis, including web scraping, comparative word frequency tables, word clouds, word maps, sentiment analysis, topic analysis, and more. All empirical chapters have two "Quick Start" exercises designed to allow quick immersion in chapter topics, followed by "In Depth" coverage. Data are available for all examples and runnable R code is provided in a "Command Summary". An appendix provides an extended tutorial on R and RStudio. Almost 30 online supplements provide information for the complete book, "books within the book" on a variety of topics, such as agent-based modeling.

Rather than focusing on equations, derivations, and proofs, this book emphasizes hands-on obtaining of output for various social science models and how to interpret the output. It is suitable for all advanced level undergraduate and graduate students learning statistical data analysis.

G. David Garson teaches advanced research methodology in the School of Public and International Affairs, North Carolina State University, USA. Founder and longtime editor emeritus of the *Social Science Computer Review*, he is president of Statistical Associates Publishing, which provides free digital texts worldwide. His degrees are from Princeton University (BA, 1965) and Harvard University (PhD, 1969).

Data Analytics for the Social Sciences

Applications in R

G. David Garson

LONDON AND NEW YORK

First published 2022
by Routledge
2 Park Square, Milton Park, Abingdon, Oxon OX14 4RN

and by Routledge
605 Third Avenue, New York, NY 10158

Routledge is an imprint of the Taylor & Francis Group, an informa business

British Library Cataloguing-in-Publication Data
A catalogue record for this book is available from the British Library

Library of Congress Cataloging-in-Publication Data
A catalog record has been requested for this book

ISBN: 978-0-367-62429-3 (hbk)
ISBN: 978-0-367-62427-9 (pbk)
ISBN: 978-1-003-10939-6 (ebk)

DOI: 10.4324/9781003109396

Typeset in Times
by KnowledgeWorks Global Ltd.

Access the Support Material: www.routledge.com/9780367624293

This book is dedicated, as I am, to my radiant Irish-American soulmate and happiness, Kathryn Kallio.

– Dave Garson, April 2021

Contents

Acknowledgments

I would like to thank the dozens of reviewers, anonymous and otherwise, who provided valuable feedback on the proposal for this work, and for the work itself, though all errors are my own, of course. The extensive R community is something all authors using R, myself included, must acknowledge and praise. Particular thanks go to Sarah Bauduin for her detailed help with the module on NetLogoR, and to Florian Pfisterer for assistance with the klr3keras package. I am also obliged to former doctoral student Kate Albrecht for her authorship of the online supplement on modeling with RSiena, and to current doctoral student Brad Johnson for his creation of the PowerPoint slides which accompany this text.

Preface

This book is intended to be an introductory graduate-level treatment of data analytics for social science. The reader may ask, "Why 'data analytics' rather than 'data science'?" When I started writing this book 2 years ago, Google searching showed "data analytics" to be the more prevalent term. Today, in Spring 2021, the tide has shifted and "data science" is more prevalent by about a 2:1 margin. However, where "data science" carries a strong connotation of computer science and programming, I feel the term "data analytics" carries a connotation of applications for social, economic, and organizational analysis. I hope one function of my work is to show that while some types of analysis benefit from a bit of programming (e.g., for looping through repetitive functions), the social science student or researcher need not feel that they need to take a career detour into computer science simply to be able to use many of the tools of data science in their dissertations and research.

The subtitle of this book is "Applications in R". R is a language which is used for statistics, data analysis, text analysis, and machine learning. R arguably is the fastest-growing and leading statistical tool for researchers. Social scientists can take advantage of thousands of cutting-edge programs for an "alphabet soup" of applications, including agent-based modeling, Bayesian modeling, cluster analysis, correlation, correspondence analysis, data management, decision trees, descriptive statistics, economics, factor analysis, forecasting, generalized linear modeling, instrumental variables regression, logistic regression, longitudinal and time series analysis, machine learning models, mapping and spatial analysis, mediation and moderation analysis, multiple linear regression, multilevel modeling, network analysis, neural network analysis, panel data regression, path analysis, partial least squares modeling, power analysis, reliability analysis, significance testing, structural equation modeling, survey research, text analytics, and visualization of data – and many more. New state-of-the-art R packages are added daily in an ever-expanding universe of research tools, many created by leading scholars in their fields.

R is free and thus liberates the researcher from dependency on the willingness of his or her institution to provide the needed software. Moreover, it is platform-independent and may be used with any operating system. Also, R is open-source, with all source code available to those inclined to look "under the hood". Statistical algorithms are not locked in proprietary "black boxes". R packages are available to import from and export to a variety of data sources, such as SPSS, SAS, Stata, and Excel, to name a few. Although R is quite full-featured in its own right, it also may be integrated with other programming environments, such as Python, Java, and C/C++. Starting with version 1.4, RStudio now offers access to Python tools and packages through its Python interpreter, the "reticulate" package, and as well as through other avenues. All of this is supported by a very large user community with a full array of mailing lists (through which help questions may be posed and answered), blogs, conferences, journals, training opportunities, and archives.

This is not a book for statisticians or advanced users. The reader will not find a forbidding mass of equations, derivations, and proofs that may rightly be associated with later courses on data analysis. Rather, to make this the introductory-level book it was intended to be, I have emphasized how to obtain output for various common types of models, how to interpret the output, assumptions underlying the interpretation, and differences among R applications packages. Among the helpful features of the book are these:

- All empirical chapters have two "Quick Start" exercises designed to allow students to immerse themselves quickly in and obtain successful results from R analyses related to the chapter topic.
- In the Support Material (www.routledge.com/9780367624293), all chapters have an abstract, which gives an overview of the contents.
- All chapters have "Review Questions" for students in the student section of the Support Material (www.routledge.com/9780367624293), with answers and comments in the instructor section.
- All chapters have text boxes highlighting the applicability of the chapter topic, and of R, to recent published examples of social science research.

- Appendix 1 provides a book-within-the-book, on "Introduction to R and RStudio".
- Data for all examples are available to the student on a Support Material (www.routledge.com/9780367624293) and are described in Appendix 1. These are listed in Appendix 2.
- The Support Material (www.routledge.com/9780367624293) also has "Command Summaries" of the runnable R code for each chapter, stripped of commentary and output in the chapters themselves.

In terms of organization of the book, I chose to start with a chapter on the uses and potential abuses of data analytics, emphasizing issues in ethics. Chapters 2 and 3 show how to implement a broad range of statistical procedures in R. I thought this to be important in order that students and researchers see data analytics in R as something having great continuity with what they already know. Chapters 4 and 5 deal with regression and classification trees and with random forests. In addition to being valuable tools for prediction and classification in their own right, these particular tools are often found desirable because they imitate the way ordinary people make decisions and because they can be visualized graphically. Chapter 6 deals with machine learning models such as support vector machines. A focus is placed on the "caret" package, which makes available to the researcher dozens of types of models and facilitates comparison of their results on a cross-validated basis. Chapter 7 deals with neural network analysis, a topic associated in the public eye with "artificial intelligence" and which also is a tool that may generate superior solutions. Chapter 8 focuses on network analysis. A very broad range of social science data may be treated as network data, and data relationships may be visualized in network diagrams. A final chapter treats text analysis, including text acquisition through web scraping and other means; showing text relationships through comparative word frequency tables, word clouds, and word maps; and use of sentiment analysis and topic analysis. In fact, topics are so numerous that for space reasons some content is placed in online supplements in the Support Material (www.routledge.com/9780367624293) to the text. Some supplements, such as agent-based modeling, are "books within the book" bonuses for the reader of this text.

Data analytics represents a paradigm shift in social science research methodology. When I took my first teaching position at Tufts University, we ran statistics, often in the Fortran language, on a "mainframe" with only 8 kilobytes of memory! The "computer lab" at my next teaching position, at North Carolina State University, was initially centered on sorting machines for IBM punch-card data. The teaching of research methods since then has been a constant process of learning new tools and procedures. As social scientists we need to ride the wave of the paradigm shift, not fear the learning curve all new things bring with them. I hope this book can be a small contribution to what can only be described as a revolution in the teaching of research methods for social science. Happy data surfing!

G. DAVID GARSON
School of Public and International Affairs
North Carolina State University
April, 2021

Chapter 1

Using and abusing data analytics in social science

1.1 Introduction

The use and abuse of data analytics (DA), data science, and artificial intelligence (AI) is of major concern in business, government, and academia. In late 2019, based on a survey of 350 US and UK executives involved in AI and machine learning, DataRobot (2019a, 2019b), itself a developer of machine learning automation platforms, issued a news release on its report, headlining "Nearly half of AI professionals are 'very to extremely' concerned about AI bias." Critics think the percentage should be even higher. This chapter has a triple purpose. First, published literature in the social and policy sciences is used to illustrate the promise of big data and DA, highlighting a variety of specific ways in which DA are useful. However, the other two sections of this chapter are cautionary. In the second section, inventory threats to good research design common among researchers employing big data and DA are discussed. The third section inventories various ethical issues associated with big data and DA. The question underlying this chapter is whether, in terms of big data and DA, we are marching toward a better society or toward an Orwellian "1984". As in all such questions, the answer is, "Some of both".

Before beginning, a word about terminology is needed. The terms "data science", "data analytics", "machine learning", and "artificial intelligence" overlap in scope. In this volume, these "umbrella" terms may be used interchangeably by the author and by other authors who are cited. However, connotations differ. Data science suggests work done by graduates of data science programs, which are dominated by computer science departments. DA connotes the application of data science methods to other disciplines, such as social science. Machine learning refers to any of a large number of algorithms which may be used for classification and prediction. AI refers to algorithms that adjust and hopefully improve in effectiveness across iterations, such as neural networks of various types. (In this book we do not refer to the broader popular meaning of artificial human intelligence as portrayed in science fiction.) The common denominator of all these admittedly fuzzy terms is what is often called "algorithmic thinking", meaning reliance on computer algorithms to arrive at classifications, predictions, and decisions. All approaches may utilize "big data", referring to the capacity of these methods to deal with enormous sets of mixed numeric, text, and even video data, such as may be scraped from the internet. Big data may magnify bias associated with algorithmic thinking but it is not a prerequisite for bias and abuse in the application of data science methods.

Official policy on ethics for information technology, including DA, is found in the 2012 "Menlo Report" of the Directorate of Science & Technology of the US Department of Homeland Security. This report was followed up by a "companion" document containing case studies and further guidance (Dittrich, Kenneally, & Bailey, 2013).

DOI: 10.4324/9781003109396-1

The Menlo guidelines contain highly generalized guidelines for ethical practice in the domain of DA. In a nutshell, it sets out four principles that are as follows:

1. *Respect for persons*: DA projects should be based on informed consent of those participating in or impacted by the project.

   The problem, of course, is that the whole basis of "big data" approaches is that huge amounts of data are collected without realistic possibility of gathering true informed consent. Even when data are collected directly from the person, consent takes the form of a button click, giving "consent" to fine print in legalese. This token consent may even be obtained coercively as failure to click may deny the person the right to make a purchase or obtain some other online benefits.

2. *Beneficence*: This is the familiar "do not harm" ethic with roots going back to the Hippocratic Oath for doctors. In practical terms, DA projects are called upon to undertake systematic assessments of risks and harms as well as benefits.

   The problem is that DA projects are mostly commissioned with deliverables set beforehand and with tight timetables. For the most part, the technocratic staff of DA projects is ill-trained to undertake true cost-benefit studies even if time constraints and work contracts are permitted. The Menlo Report itself provides a giant loophole, noting that there are long-term social benefits to having research. It is easy to see these benefits as outweighing diffuse costs which take the form of loss of confidentiality and privacy, violations of data integrity, and individual or group impairment of reputation. The reality is that few, if any, DA projects are halted due to lack of "beneficence", though placing a privacy policy on one's website or obtaining pro forma "consent" is commonplace. The costs in time and money of challenging shortcomings in "beneficence" falls of the aggrieved person, who often finds pro-business legislation and courts, not to mention the superior legal staff of corporations and governments, make the chance of success dim.

3. *Justice*: The principle of information justice means that all persons are treated equally with regard to data selection without bias. Also, benefits of information technology are to be distributed fairly.

   The problem is that on the selection side, profiling is inherent in big data analysis. Profiling, in turn, is famously subject to bias. On the fair distribution side, the Menlo Report and DA projects generally interpret fairness in terms of individual need, individual effort, societal contribution, and overall merit. These fairness concepts are subjective and extremely vague. If information justice is considered at all, it is easy to rationalize to justify DA practices without need for revision.

4. *Respect for law and the public interest*: DA projects should be based on legal "due diligence", transparency with regard to DA methods and results, and DA should be subject to accountability.

   DA projects lack "due diligence" if there is no evidence that some effort was undertaken to conform to relevant laws dealing with privacy and data integrity. The corporation or government agency which commissions a DA project is wise to have such evidence, usually in the form of an official privacy policy, a policy on data sharing, and so on. These policies are frequently posted on the web, giving evidence of "transparency". The problem is that this primarily serves for legal protection of the corporation or government entity and is rarely a constraint on what the DA project actually does.

It is common in many domains for ethical guidelines to lack impact. An illustration at this writing is the ethical standards document of the American Society for Public Administration in the era of the Trump presidency and its many challenges to ethics. Like that document, the usefulness of the Menlo Report is primarily to call attention to ethical issues, not actually to regulate DA projects.

Ostensibly, every US federal agency has appointed a "data steward" responsible for each database it maintains. While this is different from each algorithm-based program, most agencies have a data steward statement of responsibilities that often includes responsibilities in the areas of data privacy, transparency, and other values. An example is in the "Readings and References" section of the student Support Material (www.routledge.com/9780367624293) for this book.[1] There may be a Data Stewardship Executive Policy Committee to oversee data stewardship, as there is in the US Census Bureau. A literature review by the author was unable to find even a single empirical study of the effectiveness of governmental data stewards, though prescriptive articles on what makes a data steward effective abound. "The proof is in the pudding" must be the investigatory rule here. Much of this chapter is devoted to illustrations of problems with the pudding.

Petrozzino (2020), addressing the Menlo Report, has argued that formal ethical principles do make a difference. Petrozzino, a Principal Cybersecurity Engineer within the National Security Engineering Center operated by MITRE for the US Department of Defense, concluded her analysis by writing, "The enthusiasm of organizations to use big data should be married with the appropriate analysis of potential impact to individuals, groups, and society. Without this analysis, the potential issues are numerous and substantively damaging to their mission, organization, and external stakeholders" (p. 17). Like Biblical principles of morality, it is largely up to the individual to act upon ethical principles. However, it is thought better for the DA project director to have principles than not to have them!

1.2 The promise of data analytics for social science

1.2.1 Data analytics in public affairs and public policy

The Menlo Report discussed earlier specifically calls attention to the societal value of basic research based on big data. Big data and DA have been applied to address such public policy problems as diverse as making health-care delivery more efficient (Sousa et al., 2019), improving the state of the art in biomedicine (Mittelstadt, 2019), advancing the techniques of forensic accounting (Zabihollah & Wang, 2019), improving crop selection in agriculture (Tseng, Cho, & Wu, 2019), estimating travel time in transportation networks (Bertsimas et al., 2019), and identifying trucks involved in illegal construction waste dumping (Lu, 2019). Likewise, Hauer (2019: 222) is one of many who have noted the sweeping scope of algorithms, which implement DA. He wrote, "Algorithms plan flights and then fly with planes. Algorithms run factories, the bank is a vast array of algorithms, evaluating our credit score, algorithms collect revenue and keep records, read medical images, diagnose cancer, drive cars, write scientific texts, compose music, conduct symphony orchestras, navigate drones, speak to us and for us, write film scenarios, invent chemical formulations for a new cosmetic cream, order, advise, paint pictures. Climate models decide what is a safe carbon dioxide level in the atmosphere. NSA algorithms decide whether you are a potential terrorist."

In the same vein, Cathy Petrozzino has observed, "the public sector at every level – federal, state, local, and tribal – also has benefited from its creation of big data collections and applications of data science." She gave such examples as the Care Assessment Needs (CAN) system of the Veterans Health Administration (VHA), and the Office of Anti-Fraud Program of the Social Security Administration (Petrozzino, 2020: 14).

Public health and the provision of medical care is one of the domains, which have been a center of big data and DA activity. Garattini et al. (2019: 69), for instance, have noted many benefits of big data in medicine, where DA "offers the capacity to rationalize, understand and use big data to serve many different purposes, from improved services modelling to prediction of treatment outcomes, to greater patient and disease stratification. In the area of infectious diseases, the application of big data analytics has introduced a number of changes in the information accumulation models… Big data analytics is fast becoming a crucial component for the modeling of transmission – aiding infection control measures and policies – emergency response analyses required during local or international outbreaks."

1.2.2 Data analytics in the social sciences

Given the DA revolution in public and private sectors, it would be surprising not to see a rapid gravitation of the social sciences in the same direction and, indeed, this is happening quickly in the current era. The work of Richard Hendra, director of the Manpower Demonstration Research Corporation's (MDRC) Center for Data Insights (https://www.mdrc.org/), exemplifies how a social scientist can employ data analytic methods to address some of the nation's toughest social policy challenges through leveraging already collected data to derive actionable insights to help improve well-being among low-income individuals and families. Illustrative projects include a nonprofit initiative that focuses on leveraging MIS data to improve program targeting and a national effort to improve DA capacity and infrastructure in the Temporary Assistance for Needy Families (TANF) system. Other application areas include employment, housing, criminal justice, financial inclusion, and substance abuse issues. Hendra's work centers on how data science fits within long-term learning agendas, using techniques like random forests and ensemble methods to complement the causal inference studies that MDRC is known for.

1.2.3 Data analytics in the humanities

We would be remiss before closing this subsection not to mention that DA and big data open up new opportunities for scholars working in the humanities, where text analysis is paramount. Thus boyd (sic.) and Crawford (2012: 667) noted "Big Data offers the humanistic disciplines a new way to claim the status of quantitative science and objective method. It makes many more social spaces quantifiable."

1.3 Research design issues in data analytics

1.3.1 Beware the true believer

Almost a decade ago the authors boyd and Crawford (2012: 666) found "an arrogant undercurrent in many Big Data debates where other forms of analysis are too easily sidelined… This is not a space that has been welcoming to older forms of intellectual craft." This intellectual arrogance continues to the present day. For instance, this author (Garson) has experienced data science students having been taught that soon conventional statistical analysis would be a thing of the past. As boyd and Crawford noted, intellectual arrogance has the potential to "crystalize into new orthodoxies", discouraging collaboration and inhibiting rather than promoting innovation. The deserved praise for the potential of big data and DA must be tempered with recognition that there are many quantitative, qualitative, and mixed paths to knowledge. Moreover many of the "new" machine language techniques like deep learning with neural networks or text analytic content analysis antedate the rise of modern data science, and correspondingly data science texts today commonly present linear and logistic regression, cluster analysis, multidimensional scaling, and other "traditional" statistical approaches as integral to DA, albeit often done in R or Python rather than SPSS, SAS, or Stata.

Technocratic isolation encourages "true believership", diversity mitigates it. Speaking of ethics and bias in the application of machine learning and AI in response to the COVID pandemic crisis of 2020, Sipior (2020) wrote, "A diversity of disciplines is the key to success in AI, especially to minimize risk associated with rapid deployment … Team membership should be well-rounded, from a wide range of backgrounds and skill sets, for complex problem-solving with innovative solutions and for recognizing the potential for bias. To address issues such as bias, ethics, and compliance, among others, roles such as an AI Ethicist, attorney, and/or review board, may be added. She quotes Shellenbarger (2019), "The biases that are implicit in one team member are clear to, and avoided by, another… So it's really key to get people who aren't alike." Diversity in the algorithm-development team requires not only data scientists but also subject matter experts, ethicists, and, above all, representation of populations likely to be impacted. In reality, however, diversity is expensive in both time and money. While diversity in data analytic development teams is the gold standard, gold is hard to come by and is rare in nature.

1.3.2 Pseudo-objectivity in data analytics

Social science topics from education to elections have been taken up by data scientists in academia and in consulting firms with increasing frequency in recent years. Often their work is presented as reporting objective facts drawn from mountains of big data. Those from computer science and technical backgrounds are accustomed to thinking in terms of fact-based knowledge. Pseudo-objectivity replaces objectivity, however, when information is confounded with knowledge.

Kusner and Loftus (2020) discuss the "we just report the facts" problem in data science, using the example of an algorithm deployed across the United States, but found by Obermeyer et al. (2019) to underestimate the health needs of black patients. The data scientists behind the algorithm chose to use health-care costs as a measure of health needs. This failed to take into account the fact that health-care costs for black patients historically have been lower due to relative lack of access to treatment, in turn due to racism and income inequalities (Glauser, 2020). This poor research design led to wrong inferences about the health needs of the black population. Kusner and Loftus went on to note the tendency of data science algorithms to be developed by technocrats who focus on bivariate correlations at a surface level, hoping that big data washes out any research design shortcomings. However, this is a false hope. As social scientists are well aware, what is needed prior to deploying an algorithm is to have a validated model of the outcome of interest (patient health in this case), taking into account all major relevant variables and analyzing

TEXT BOX 1.1 John von Neumann on Mathematical Models

John von Neumann was a Hungarian who emigrated to the United States and helped develop the massive code-breaking first-generation computers of the WWII era. Regarded as the foremost mathematician of his time, his book, *The Computer and the Brain* (1958) was published posthumously. It is widely acknowledged that artificial intelligence and machine learning owe a great deal to his work (Findler, 1988).

Some of his insights, collected in the quotations below, remain relevant to work today in the areas of data analytics, data science, and AI.

> The sciences do not try to explain, they hardly even try to interpret, they mainly make models. By a model is meant a mathematical construct which, with the addition of certain verbal interpretations, describes observed phenomena. The justification of such a mathematical construct is solely and precisely that it is expected to work – that is correctly to describe phenomena from a reasonably wide area.
>
> It is exceptional that one should be able to acquire the understanding of a process without having previously acquired a deep familiarity with running it, with using it, before one has assimilated it in an instinctive and empirical way... Thus any discussion of the nature of intellectual effort in any field is difficult, unless it presupposes an easy, routine familiarity with that field. In mathematics this limitation becomes very severe.
>
> Truth is much too complicated to allow anything but approximations.
>
> There's no sense in being precise when you don't even know what you're talking about.
>
> Can we survive technology?
>
> John von Neumann

the data on a multivariate basis. When such a model does not exist, as is often the case, analysis is exploratory at best and is "not ready for prime time".

This example illustrates how machine learning and AI can maintain and amplify inequity. Most algorithms exploit crude correlations in data. Yet these correlations are often by-products of more salient social relationships (in the health-care example, treatment that is inaccessible is, by definition, cheaper), or chance occurrences that will not replicate.

To identify and mitigate discriminatory relationships embedded in data, we need models that capture or account for the causal pathways that give rise to them.

Information is factual. Knowledge is interpretive. As soon as the analyst seeks to understand what data mean inherently, the subjective process of interpretation has begun. Indeed, subjectivity antecedes data collection since the researcher must selectively decide what information to collect and what to ignore. Even if their topic is the same, different researchers will make different decisions about the types, sources, variables, dates, and other aspects of their intended data corpus, whether quantitative or textual, "big" or traditional. Thus David Bollier (2010: 13) observed, "Big Data is not self-explanatory". He gives the example of data-cleaning. All data, perhaps especially big data, require cleaning. Cleaning involves subjective decisions about which data elements matter. Cleaned data are no longer objective data yet data cleaning is essential. When data come from multiple sources, each with their own biases and sources of error, the problem is compounded.

1.3.3 The bias of scholarship based on algorithms using big data

1.3.3.1 Bias in access to the means of scholarly production

The old Marxian viewpoint that ownership of the means of production is the key determinant of outcomes has some relevance to bias in big data research. Large social media companies own the data and are not obligated to release it. At the same time, in-house researchers and those with direct access to the "full stream" of social media data are in a privileged position in terms of scholarship. From a scholar's perspective, such access is valuable and worth protecting and this vested interest can produce bias. Thus boyd and Crawford (2012: 674) observed, "Big Data researchers with access to proprietary data sets are less likely to choose questions that are contentious to a social media company if they think it may result in their access being cut. The chilling effects on the kinds of research questions that can be asked – in public or private – are something we all need to consider."

1.3.3.2 Bias in the tools of scholarly production

The bias of big data has also been noted by boyd and Crawford (2012: 666), who have pointed out the poor archiving and search function of such big data sources as Twitter and Facebook. Often these sources are "black boxes" with proprietary restrictions on full access by social scientists. As an example, Crimson Hexagon is a service that makes available longitudinal Twitter data, which Twitter itself does not. Its main clientele are corporations interested in following public consumer trends. To better serve this clientele, Crimson Hexagon uses an algorithm to ascribe gender to individual tweets. The algorithm is a corporate secret and is of unknown scientific validity. The social science researcher is faced with the bad alternatives of not using gender as a variable, using gender without validation, or refusing to publish research based on "black box" methods.

More generally, there is a bias toward using what is generally available, which is data that may be "scraped" from social media, blogs, websites, and other online sources. This is cited as an advantage of the big data approach: Ability to retrieve large amounts of data at costs far below the cost associated with traditional means, such as national surveys and panels. This bias focuses researchers on topics, boyd and Crawford noted (p. 666), "in the present or immediate past – tracking reactions to an election, TV finale, or natural disaster – because of the sheer difficulty or impossibility of accessing older data."

While the number of observations in large datasets drawn from social media, blogs, or websites may vastly exceed the number of observations in traditional survey research, this does not make them a better basis for interpretation, let alone make them free from error. "Large data sets from internet sources are often unreliable," boyd and Crawford (2012: 668) note, and are "prone to outages and losses, and these errors and gaps are magnified when multiple data sets are used together." With big data it is often difficult to establish the representativeness essential in the data on which an algorithm is based.

Algorithms are developed using training datasets. For instance, if an algorithm developer in the medical field has not employed random sampling for the training set, then, as Glauser (2020: E21) noted in a medical journal, "A program trained on lung scans may seem neutral, but if the training data sets include only images from patients from one sex or racial group, it may miss health conditions in diverse populations." In the same vein, Mannes (2020: 64) observed, "Many issues with algorithmic bias are the result of decisions about what data are used to train the model. Including and excluding variables, as well as errors in data curation and collection, can skew the AI's results." There is a twofold take-away from this observation:

1. Interpretation is sounder when the data sample is randomly selected from the universe to which the researcher wishes to generalize, or at least are representative of the desired sampling frame.
2. Model specification must include the proper variables. For instance, Wykstra, (2018) noted how an algorithm assigning scores predicting likelihood of recidivism was dramatically different depending on whether the predictor was past arrests or past convictions. If the true causes are not included in the model (and true causes are often unknowable or if good indicators of the true causes are not available) the reliability of the model, and hence the rate of false predictions can pose serious problems.

An example of big data bias based on scraping social media comments is given by Papakyriakopoulos, Carlos, and Hegelich (2020), who studied German users' political comments and parties' posts on social media. "We quantitatively demonstrate", they wrote, "that hyperactive users have a significant role in the political discourse: They become opinion leaders, as well as having an agenda-setting effect, thus creating an alternate picture of public opinion." The authors found hyperactive users participated in discussions differently, liked different content, and that they became opinion leaders whose comments were more popular than those of ordinary users. Other research has shown that some hyperactive users are paid political spammers or even "bots", not random individuals who happen to be more active. The bias introduced by hyperactive users translates directly into bias in recommender systems, such as those used by Facebook and all major social networks, leading to "the danger of algorithmic manipulation of political communication" by these networks.

1.3.3.3 Bias in the methods of scholarly production

A great deal of what comes out of DA may be characterized as pattern-matching. The researcher uses data analytic tools to sift through masses of data in order to show constellations of variables associated with an outcome of interest. However, correlation is not causation. The data analyst cannot escape the conundrums, which always plague social science. Intricate and difficult problems of interpretation include, to take a few examples, the problem of mutual causation (non-recursivity), the problem of causation by unmeasured variables (the endogeneity problem), and problems associated with any number of threats to model validity (e.g., making causal inferences without longitudinal data, generalizing about individuals based on aggregate data, cross-cultural differentials of meaning regarding the ostensibly same construct, etc.). Biased if not flatly erroneous interpretation arises from naïve application of pattern matching to big data. Basics of statistical research still apply, such as knowing that correlation is not causation (e.g., one researcher showed via data mining that American stock market changes correlated well with butter production in Bangladesh – an example of spurious correlation (Leinweber, 2007)). Often data scientists find themselves well advised to turn back to traditional statistical forms of modeling which address complex research problems.

To take an example, Loni Hagen commenting on big data research, which developed an algorithm purporting to flag "troll", "bot", and "Russian propaganda" messages on social media. She observed that machine learning is "good at learning biases and the majority rules of the world" but "As a consequence, minority rules can be easily ignored in the process of machine learning" (personal email to author, 2/12/2020). The machine algorithm, in essence, incorporated the reasoning that (1) Russian troll messages are highly critical of person X; (2) the message at hand is highly critical of person X; (3) therefore, the message may be classed as a troll message. In another line of reasoning, (1) user opinions are the gold standard for judging messages to be trolling; (2) a given message has received negative user comments and has sometimes been flagged as trolling; (3) therefore, the message is a troll. Hagen points out that these fallacious lines of reasoning wind up labeling minority opinion messages as "non-genuine accounts" or "trolls". The practical bias of such big data algorithms may be, in Hagen's words, "to oppress minority opinions by automatically flagging them."

In the area of medicine and AI, Parikh, Teeple, and Navathe (2019: 2377) have observed that "clinicians may have a propensity to trust suggestions from AI decision support systems, which summarize large numbers of inputs into automated real-time predictions, while inadvertently discounting relevant information from nonautomated systems – so-called automation complacency". That is, data science and AI provide a cloak of mystification and legitimacy to recommendations that might otherwise be subject to scrutiny and challenge. This is the proven tendency for complacency and bias to be associated with human use of automated technology (Parasuraman & Manzey, 2010). This bias is particularly likely to exist where AI reinforces existing biases. Parikh and his colleagues give the example of the Framingham Study, a classic study of factors in heart disease, used by doctors for decades but now known to be biased due to having been based on an overwhelmingly non-Hispanic white population. When an algorithm applies the Framingham Risk Score to populations with otherwise similar clinical characteristics, the predicted errors occurred for blacks. While this particular bias has been recognized, one must wonder how many other examples are unrecognized. Parikh gives other examples, such as AI algorithms using electronic health records (EHR) making recommendations, which wrongly fail to recommend cardiac ischemia testing for older women, or making incorrect estimates of breast cancer in black women due to treatment of missing data, not recognizing that missingness is related to race. These authors conclude, "While all predictive models may automate bias, AI may be unique in the extent to which bias is unrecognized" (p. 2377).

1.3.3.4 Bias of social media data itself

Social media users are not a random sample of the American population, let alone the world, yet some in the DA field act as if having hundreds of thousands or even millions of data points is a substitute. However, generalization made on the basis of force of numbers is not good social science. The authors boyd and Crawford (2012: 669) note of Twitter data, "Regardless of the number of tweets, it is not a representative sample as the data are skewed from the beginning." In this section, we enumerate some of the many cautions that attach to social media data, often the type of data to which data analytic methods are applied.

Based on article counts in Summon for the 2014–2019 period, Facebook and Twitter were the dominant sources of data for scholarly articles (about 280,000 articles each), followed by YouTube (116 k), Instagram (75 k), and WhatsApp (20 k). This huge number of articles reflects the relative ease with which social scientists may scrape social media data. In this section, we take Twitter data as an example, but its limitations often are similar to limitations on all social media data.

Three of the many limitations of Twitter data are those listed below.

1. *Problems in acquiring unbiased data*: Twitter is popular among scholars because it provides some tweets through its public APIs. A few companies and large institutions have access to theoretically all public tweets (those not made private by users). The great majority of researchers must be content with access to 10% or 1% Twitter streams covering a time-limited period. The sampling process is not revealed in detail to researchers. Some tweets are eliminated because they come from protected accounts. Others are eliminated because not-entirely-accurate algorithms determine they contain spam, pornography, or other forbidden content. For those that are included, there is the problem of overcounting due to some people having multiple accounts and undercounting because sometime multiple people use the same account. Then there is the much-publicized problem that a nontrivial amount of use reflects bots, which send content on an automated basis or reflects the work of banks of human agents working for some entity.
2. *Difficulty in defining users*: It is difficult to distinguish just what Twitter "use" and "participation" is. A few years back, Twitter (2011) noted that 40% of active users are passive, listening but not posting. With survey research it is possible, for example, to analyze the views of both those who voted and also the views of non-voters. In contrast, in Twitter research it is not possible to compare the sentiments of those who tweeted with sentiments of those who just listened.
3. *Dangers of pooling data*: When handing data from multiple sources, pooling issues arise. Serious errors of interpretation may well arise when different sets of data are combined, as not infrequently happens in "big data" research on social media sources. These problems are outlined, for instance, in Knapp (2013). Suffice it to say, combining social media data from multiple sources may be difficult or impossible to do without incurring bias.

1.3.3.5 Bias of big data network research

A common type of big data analysis takes the form of network analysis, sometimes presented in graphical connected-circles format called sociograms. Data may be articulated (e.g., email connections) or behavioral (e.g., proximity based on cell phone GPS data). Measures such as centrality to the network may be calculated, imputing more network importance to units with higher centrality coefficients. This is reminiscent of a line of social science researcher in which scholars such as Jacob Moreno (1934) in psychosociology and later Floyd Hunter (1969) in political sociology. But where classical sociological research focused on interpersonal and political relationships of consequence, much network research based on big data focuses on what Granovetter (1973) called "weak ties" (e.g., being "friended" on Facebook, where the user may have thousands of "friends"). As boyd and Caldwell (2012: 671) have noted, "Not every connection is equivalent to every other connection, and neither does frequency of contact indicate strength of relationship." Bias and erroneous interpretation arises when weak ties are confounded with strong ones, and when social context variables are not part of the data being analyzed.

1.3.4 The subjectivity of algorithms

When DA is engaged in support of algorithmically based decision-making, as in banking decisions about credit, insurance decisions about eligibility, or university decisions about student admittance, decisions must be made about what variables are employed by the algorithm. Even the most apparently fair-minded approach may be biased, as when available economic-based variables are included while unavailable human values variables are excluded. Bias is even more likely when the algorithm is embedded in a "black box" making assessment of the role of variables difficult or impossible, as in many AI applications. As another instance, it is common for employers to use algorithms to screen job applicants based on test scores without ever establishing that in fact those with higher test scores can perform specific job-related tasks better than, say, those with medium test scores.

In the selection and weighting of variables, biases may be introduced by the analyst creating the algorithm or by his or her employer. There is even the possibility of a politics of algorithms, in which interested parties lobby to have their interests represented. For instance, there is possible bias in the credit rating industry, as when groups lobby a credit bureau to have membership in their organization counted as a plus or when discount stores lobby to have high rates of credit card spending in their stores not count as a minus. Zarsky (2016: 125) concluded, "Lobbying obviously increases unfair outcomes of the processes mentioned because it facilitates a biased decision-making process that systematically benefits stronger and well-organized social segments (and thus is unfair to weaker segments)."

The problem of subjectivity in the development of algorithms is compounded by the tendency of data scientists and the public alike to anthropomorphize them. David Watson observed, "Algorithms are not 'just like us' and the temptation to pretend they are can have profound ethical consequences when they are deployed in high-risk domains like finance and clinical medicine. By anthropomorphizing a statistical model, we implicitly grant it a degree of agency that not only overstates its true abilities, but robs us of our own autonomy" (Watson, 2019: 435). The problem is that it is not ethically neutral to blindly accept that AI, being rooted in neural sciences of the human mind, is therefore to be seen, as human beings are seen, as agents having their own set of ethics. Rather than being like humans, AI applications are tools. Like all tools, they tend to be used in the interest of those who fund them. While it is common to observe that DA may be used for good or evil, a more accurate generalization is to say that on average, DA tends to serve powerful interests in society. Ethical vigilance by human beings is of utmost importance.

1.3.5 Big data and big noise

Social scientists have long understood that what counts is data quality, not data quantity. For instance, a scientific national survey in the United States may be accomplished with fewer than 2,000 respondents. Having 20,000 or even 2 million data points does not give a better sample. Likewise, in their classic political science study of Pearl Harbor, Wohlstetter and Schelling (1962) showed that the failure of decision in that event was not due to too little warning information but too much, combined with failure to properly analyze the data at hand.

A case in point was reported in 2020 by the Fragile Families Project, in which high-quality data were collected in a panel study with a view to undertaking predictive modeling of family outcomes as a basis for policy analysis in social and criminal justice programs. Data were collected on children at ages 1, 3, 5, 9, and 15. The panel invited a competition to predict six life outcomes (e.g., grade point average) at age 15, based only on data from the first four waves of the study. The project received 457 applications from 68 institutions from around the globe, including several teams based at Princeton University. The competitors used a variety of machine learning AI techniques. As reported by Virginia Tech, "Even after using state-of-the-art modeling and a high-quality dataset containing 13,000 data points for more than 4,000 families, the best AI predictive models were not very accurate" (Jimenez & Daniels, 2020). However, the use of large datasets may confer misplaced legitimacy and may mislead researchers and policymakers into assuming accuracy is assured.

MacFeely (2019) has made related points about big data. While acknowledging the potential benefit of big data, he noted, "Big data also present enormous statistical and governance challenges and potential pitfalls: Legal; ethical; technical; and reputational. Big data also present a significant expectations management challenge, as it seems many hold the misplaced belief that accessing big data is straightforward and that their use will automatically and dramatically reduce the costs of producing statistical information. As yet the jury is out on whether big data will offer official statistics anything especially useful. Beyond the hype of big data, and hype it may well be, statisticians understand that big data are not always better data and that more data doesn't automatically mean more insight. In fact more data may simply mean more noise." A big data researcher may brag about having 800,000 data points compared to the 800 of a survey researcher studying the same topic. However, that is no evidence at all that the former is a better basis for decision than the latter and is no evidence that the use of either dataset is appropriate and valid.

1.3.6 Limitations of the leading data science dissemination models

R and Python, along with CRAN and GitHub distribution channels, lack quality control except for virus/malware checking and checking for program error messages on multiple platforms.[2] Even the R distribution itself comes with no warranty. On this problem, Marc Schwartz observed, "Even if you narrowly define 'safe' as being virus/malware free and even if the CRAN maintainers have extensive screening in place, the burden will still be on the end users to test/scan the downloaded packages (whether in source or binary form), according to some a priori defined standard operating procedures, to achieve a level of confidence, that the packages pass those tests/scans."[3] However, the end user is typically ill-equipped to evaluate bias and error in the algorithms underlying packages the user intends to employ.

Of course, proprietary statistical and other software also may contain algorithmic errors. Moreover, unlike R and Python packages, with commercial packages source code is not available for inspection for the most part. However, companies do have paid staff to undertake quality control and vetting, and capitalist competition motivates companies to offer products which "work" lest profits suffer. In the community-supported world of R and Python, in contrast, such quality control work is unpaid, unsystematic, and idiosyncratic. For these reasons this author recommends that in the area of statistical methods that researchers cross-check and confirm critical results obtained from R and Python packages with results from major commercial packages. Even when results can be verified by forcing correct settings, the researcher may find default settings in community-supported software may be unconventional.

1.4 Social and ethical issues in data analytics

1.4.1 Types of ethical issues in data analytics

By way of introduction, La Fors, Custers, and Keymolen (2019: 217) have enumerated ten major ways in which the rise of big data and DA poses threats to ethics. These are paraphrased below:

1. *Human welfare*: Algorithm-driven decisions on matters ranging from employment to education may lead to de facto discrimination against and unfair treatment of citizens.
2. *Autonomy*: DA-driven profiling and consumer targeting can undermine the exercise of free choice and affect the news, politics, product advertising, and even cultural information to which the individual I exposed.
3. *Justice*: Algorithmic profiling can flag false positives or false negatives in law enforcement, resulting in systematic unfairness and injustices.
4. *Solidarity*: Non-transparent decisions made by complex algorithms based on big data may prioritize some groups over others without ever affording the opportunity for the mobilization of potential group solidarity in defense against these decisions.
5. *Dignity*: Algorithmic profiling can lead to stigmatization on assault on human dignity. Being treated "as a number" is inherent in algorithmic policymaking but is also inherently dehumanizing to the affected individual, who would often favor case-by-case decision by human beings. Mannes (2020: 61) thus writes about AI that it cannot only produce financial loss or even physical injury, but it also can cause "more subtle harms such as instantiating human bias or undermining individual dignity."
6. *Non-maleficence*: Non-maleficence refers to the medical principle of doing no harm, such as by a doctor's duty to end course of treatment found to be harmful. Big data analytics, however, puts non-maleficence as a value under pressure due to the prevalence of non-transparent data reuse and repurposing.
7. *Accountability*: Citizens affected by DA algorithms may well be unaware they are affected and even if aware, may not understand the implications of related decisions affecting them, and even if they do understand, citizens my well not know who to try to hold accountable or how to do so.
8. *Privacy*: Even when "opt-in" or "opt-out" privacy protections are in place, the correlations among variables in personal data in big data initiatives allow for easy re-identification and consequent intrusion on privacy. Studying verbatim Twitter quotations found in journal articles, for instance, Ayers, Nebeker, and Dredze (2018) found that in 84% of cases, re-identification was possible.
9. *Environmental welfare*: The "digitalization of everything" also has indirect environmental effects, neglect of which is an ethical issue. An example is neglecting the issue of increased lithium mining to support the

millions of batteries needed in a digital world, knowing that lithium mining is associated with chemical leakage and soil and water pollution. Impacts are not equally distributed, raising issues of environmental justice as well.

10. *Trustworthiness*: Ethically negative consequences enumerated above may well lead to diminished trust in institutions associated with these consequences. Diminished trust, in turn, is associated with diminished social capital and with negative consequences for society as a whole.

1.4.2 Bias toward the privileged

Numerous social science articles have documented the "digital divide" (access) and "second digital divide" (use) that favor higher-status groups in society. Recent research by Eszter Hargittai studied social media use, focusing on Twitter, Facebook, LinkedIn, Tumblr, and Reddit, based on a nationally representative US sample administered by NORC at the University of Chicago. This panel is noted for supplementing area probability sampling with additional coverage of hard-to-survey population segments, such as rural and low-income households. Hargittai's abstract summarized, "Those of higher socioeconomic status are more likely to be on several platforms suggesting that big data derived from social media tend to oversample the views of more privileged people. Additionally, internet skills are related to using such sites, again showing that opinions visible on these sites do not represent all types of people equally. The article cautions against relying on content from such sites as the sole basis of data to avoid disproportionately ignoring the perspectives of the less privileged. Whether business interests or policy considerations, it is important that decisions that concern the whole population are not based on the results of analyses that favor the opinions of those who are already better off" (Hargittai, 2020).

The bias toward the privileged documented by Hargittai is just the tip of the iceberg. Social media, websites, blogs, and other sources of big data are tools. Those with greater resources to use tools do so. That is, there is a multiplier effect. Not only do those higher in social status use the internet more, they also hire others to do so on their behalf. Those at the top of the status pecking order are in a position to commission websites, pay legions of blog posters, underwrite bot campaigns, fund banks of social media tweeters, and hire services which to conduct online "PR" campaigns to promote their interests, products, or candidates. With the internet landscape biased in this manner, it is all too easy for social scientists to fall prey to the same biases because "that's what the data say".

What the data say depends on for whom the data were created. Writing of advances in medicine associated with big data analytics, it has been found that "Innovators and early adopters are generally from higher-resourced environments. This leads to data and findings biased towards those environments. Such biased data in turn continue to be used to generate new discoveries, further obscuring potentially underrepresented populations, and creating a nearly inescapable cycle of health inequity" (Tossas-Milligan & Winn, 2019: 86). The same bias exists in other domains.

Virginia Eubanks (2019), author of *Automating Inequality: How High-Tech Tools Profile, Police, and Punish the Poor,* has outlined the impact of digital decision tools on the low-income populations. She observed, "At lectures, conferences, and gatherings, I am often approached by engineers or data scientists who want to talk about the economic and social implications of their designs" (p. 212). She has found all high-tech proposals from data scientists to not meet even feeble standards in terms of "dismantling the digital poorhouse" and she calls for a revolution in thinking about how digital skills might be redirected to protect human rights and strengthen human capacity, particularly with regard to poverty.

The relation of big data and DA to human rights issues has been widely recognized but what to do is an unresolved matter. Nersessian (2018: 851), for example, has noted, "Even in advanced economies, the inherently global nature of big data makes it difficult to effectively regulate at the national level, and many domestic laws and policies are behind the curve." While Nersessian, citing the United Nations' "Guiding Principles" document (United Nations, 2011), advocates using international human rights law to restrict the use of big data by "taking off the table" any use that violates human rights, at least at present this is no more an effective form of regulation than is legislation by individual nations.

Digital bias toward the privileged is not limited to matters of poverty and race. There is also a digital divide within academia as well, with privileged and deprived classes of scholars. This is expressed well by boyd and Crawford (2012: 673–674) who noted the policies of social media companies regulate access to their data and impose fees for better access. These authors wrote, "This produces considerable unevenness in the system: Those with money – or those inside the company – can produce a different type of research than those outside. Those without access can neither reproduce nor evaluate the methodological claims of those who have privileged access. It is also important to recognize that the class of the Big Data rich is reinforced through the university system: Top-tier, well-resourced universities will be able to buy access to data, and students from the top universities are the ones most likely to be invited to work within large social media companies. Those from the periphery are less likely to get those invitations and develop their skills." The result of the academic digital divide is a widening of the gap in the capacity to do scholarship with big data.

1.4.3 Discrimination

Scholarly studies have routinely found that computer algorithms, the fodder of DA, may promote bias. A 2015 Carnegie Mellon University study of employment websites found that Google's algorithms listed high-paying jobs to men at about six times the rate that the same add was displayed to women. A University of Washington study found that Google Images searches for "C.E.O." returned 11% female images whereas the percentage of CEOs who are women is over twice that (27%). Crawford (2017) gives numerous instances of discriminatory effects, such as AI applications classifying men as doctors and women as nurses, or not processing darker skin tones. Based on research in the field, Garcia (2016: 112) observed, "It doesn't take active prejudice to produce skewed results in web searches, data-driven home loan decisions, or photo-recognition software. It just takes distorted data that no one notices and corrects for. Thus, as we begin to create artificial intelligence, we risk inserting racism and other prejudices into the code that will make decisions for years to come."

The complexity of fairness/discrimination issues involving data analytics and big data are illustrated in the debate between ProPublica and the firm "equivant" (formerly Northpointe) over the COMPAS system. COMPAS, the Correctional Offender Management Profiling for Alternative Sanctions system, is widely used in the correctional community to identify likely recidivists and is advertise by the equivant company as "Software for Justice". Presumably COMPAS information is used by law enforcement for closer tracking of former inmates with high recidivism COMPAS scores. A 2016 study by the public interest group ProPublica showed that COMPAS "scored black offenders more harshly than white offenders who have similar or even more negative backgrounds" (Petrozzino, 2020: 2, referring to Angwin et al., 2016). The equivant company responded by arguing there was no discrimination since the COMPAS accuracy rate was not significantly different for whites as compared to blacks, and thus was fair. ProPublica, in turn, defended their charge of discrimination in a later article (Dressel & Farid, 2018) which argued that fairness should not be gauged by overall accuracy but by the "false positive" rate, since that reflected the area of potential discriminatory impact. By that criterion, COMPAS had a significantly higher false positive rate for blacks than for whites. Dressel and Farid concluded, "Black defendants who did not recidivate were incorrectly predicted to reoffend at a rate of 44.9%, nearly twice as high as their white counterparts at 23.5%; and white defendants who did recidivate were incorrectly predicted to not reoffend at a rate of 47.7%, nearly twice as high as their black counterparts at 28.0%. In other words, COMPAS scores appeared to favor white defendants over black defendants by underpredicting recidivism for white and overpredicting recidivism for black defendants." In this case, fairness or information justice could be defined in two ways, leading to opposite inferences. It is hardly surprising that those responsible for and heavily invested in a DA project like COMPAS chose to select a fairness definition favorable to their interests. It is not so much a case of "lying with statistics" as it is a case of data analysis resting on debatable assumptions and definitions.

A 2019 systematic literature review of big data and discrimination by Maddalena Favaretto and her colleagues at the Institute for Biomedical Ethics, University of Basel, found that most research addressing big data and discrimination focused on such recommendations as better algorithms, more transparency, and more regulation (Favaretto, De Clercq, and Elger, 2019). However, these authors found that "our study results identify a considerable number of barriers to the proposed strategies, such as technical difficulties, conceptual challenges, human bias and shortcomings of legislation, all of which hamper the implementation of such fair data mining practices" (p. 23). Moreover, the DA literature was found to have rarely discussed "how data mining technologies, if properly implemented, could also be an effective tool to prevent unfair discrimination and promote equality" (p. 24). That is, existing research focuses on avoiding discriminatory abuse of big data systems, neglecting the possible use of big data to mitigate discrimination itself.

Algorithms may enact practices which violate the law. In July, 2020, the Lawyers' Committee for Civil Rights under Law filed an amicus brief in a lawsuit against Facebook for redlining, an illegal practice by which minority groups are effectively obstructed from financing, such as for the purchase of homes in certain areas. Referring to Facebook financial services advertisements, The Lawyers' Committee for Civil Rights Under Law (2020) argued, "Redlining is discriminatory and unjust whether it takes place online or offline and we must not allow corporations to blame technology for harmful decisions made by CEOs". The lawsuit contended that digital advertising on Facebook discriminated based on the race, gender, and age of its users and then provided different services to these users, excluding them from economic opportunities. This discriminatory practice was based on profiling of Facebook users. Different users were provided different services based on their algorithm-generated profiles, resulting in "digital redlining". (At this writing the case (*Opiotennione v. Facebook, Inc.*) has not been adjudicated.)

Likewise, discrimination is inherent in big data systems, which are more effective for some racial groups than others. The MIT Media Lab, for instance, found that facial recognition software correctly identified white males 99–100% of the time, but the rate for black women was as low as 65% (Campbell, 2019: 54). The higher the rate of misidentifications, the greater the chance that actions taken on the basis of the algorithms of such software might be racially discriminatory. Concerns over misidentification using algorithms led San Francisco in May, 2019, to become the first city to ban facial-recognition software in its police department. The American Civil Liberties Union (ACLU) has demanded a ban on using facial recognition software by the government and law enforcement after finding that "Facial recognition technology is known to produce biased and inaccurate results, particularly when applied to people of color" (Williams, 2020: 11).

In a test, the ACLU ran images of members of Congress against a mug shot database, finding 28 instances where members of Congress were wrongly identified as possible criminals. Again, people of color were disproportionately represented in the false positive group, including civil rights leader John Lewis (Williams, 2020: 13). A later ACLU report headlined, "Untold Number of People Implicated in Crimes They Didn't Commit Because of Face Recognition" (ACLU, 2020). Inaccuracy, however, has not prevented its widespread and growing use and convictions based on identifications by facial recognition software. Likewise, ICE now routinely uses facial recognition software to sift through ID cards and drivers' licenses to find and deport undocumented people in a secret system largely devoid of protections for those fingered by the software (Williams, 2020: 13).

Discriminatory impacts are even more likely when the algorithm in question draws on discriminatory views in Twitter and other social media. Garcia (2016: 111) gives the example of "Tay", an AI bot created by Microsoft for use on Twitter. The intent of the algorithm was to create a self-learning AI conversationalist. The one-day Tay experiment ended in failure when, starting with neutral language, "in a mere 12 hours, Tay went from upbeat conversationalist to foul-mouthed, racist Holocaust denier who said feminists 'should all die and burn in hell' and that the actor 'Ricky Gervais learned totalitarianism from Adolf Hitler, the inventor of atheism'". That is, the Tay algorithm amplified existing extremist views of a discriminatory nature.

1.4.4 Diversity and data analytics

Sage Publications is the world's largest publisher in the field of statistics, data analysis, and research design in social science. Its "Sage OCEAN" initiative (https://ocean.sagepub.com/) seeks to support social scientists engaging with computational research methods, data science, and big data. Eve Kraicer (2019), associated with this initiative, noted, "Here at SAGE Ocean, we've been collecting data on the landscape of tools for computational social science. While looking through the data, we found an incredible variety, from resources to aid crowdsourcing to text analysis to social media analysis. Despite this diversity at the technical level of the tools, we found a persistent lack of diversity in terms of who built these tools."

Kraicer reported findings that showed that 90% of the founders, chief technical officers, and software developers were male and that a majority were white. While this is not unusual in science, technology, engineering, and mathematics (STEM) fields, it is nonetheless problematic for two major reasons:

1. *The modeling effect*: Social science research (e.g., Riccucci, Van Ryzin, and Li, 2016) has shown that when roles are representative by gender, race, or other categories, people from those categories are more likely to seek to play those roles also. In the case of DA, lack of representativeness may inhibit both being a user of

DA tools or become a developer of them. Kraicer wrote, “The gap … could limit both who we imagine as a computational social scientist, and even how computational social science should work.”

2. *Standpoint theory*: Standpoint theory research (e.g., Hekman, 1997) has shown that “where you stand” is correlated with the kinds of questions you ask and the kinds of answers you find. In part this is due to differential access to knowledge, tools, and resources, but “where you stand” also has to do with your role as a woman, a person of color, or with other life experiences. The body of DA research may be influenced by lack of representativeness in the field. Kraecer noted, “Our social position informs what and how we research, and using tools built from a single perspective may limit what we think to ask and test.”

In line with this, Frey, Patton, and Gaskell (2020) noted that “When analyzing social media data from marginalized communities, algorithms lack the ability to accurately interpret offline context, which may lead to dangerous assumptions about and implications for marginalized communities” (p. 42). Taking youth gangs as an example of a marginalized community whose social media communication can be misinterpreted by algorithms, leading to dire consequences for some and failure to provide services for others, Frey and his associates undertook an experiment in which gang members became involved in the development of algorithms for processing relevant social media messages. They found “the complexity of social media communication can only be uncovered through the involvement of people who have knowledge of the localized language, culture, and changing nature of community climate… If the gap between people who create algorithms and people who experience the direct impacts of them persists, we will likely continue to reinforce the very social inequities we hope to ameliorate” (pp. 54–55). While the likelihood of implementing the Frey experiment on a mass basis seems unlikely, to say the least, the experiment did highlight how and why algorithms for processing social media may lead to error and bias.

1.4.5 Distortion of democratic processes

“Social bots” are computer programs whose algorithms mimic the communication of human beings but whose content is dictated by whatever individual, group, or government is paying for them. These algorithms, of course, are made possible by the advance of DA methods using big data. In the 2016 presidential elections, it is estimated that 150,000,000 Americans encountered Russian disinformation on Facebook and Instagram alone (McNamee, 2020: 21). Hagen et al. (2020) studied the use of social bots in the 2020 election, concluding “Specifically, we found that bot-like accounts created the appearance of a virtual community around far-right political messaging, obscured the influence of traditional actors (i.e., media personalities, subject matter experts, etc.), and influenced network sentiment by amplifying pro-Trump messaging.”

In addition to bias in gathering and interpreting big data, data analytics suffers from another ethical problem: Withholding data from those who need it. Even if data scientists are scrupulously ethical and adhering to sound research design, their superiors may not be so. “Officials may have incentives to hide coronavirus cases. China, Indonesia and Iran have all come under scrutiny for their statistics. ‘Juking the stats’ is not unknown in other contexts in the U.S., either” (O’Neill, 2020). In June, 2020, Brazil has removed months of data on Covid-19 from a government website amid criticism of its president’s handling of the COVID outbreak. In the United States, as one of several such instances, a Florida newspaper editorialized that “The state of Florida is hiding information about coronavirus deaths from citizens. Under the direction of Gov. Ron DeSantis and the Florida Department of Health, the state has consistently refused to inform the public about deaths and infections in Florida nursing homes, prisons and now, coronavirus deaths as documented by public medical examiners” *Pensacola News Journal* (2020). Subsequently Florida’s COVID-19 data and dashboard manager was “forced to resign after voicing concerns over being told to delete coronavirus data” (CBS News, 2020).

1.4.6 Undermining of professional ethics

One dimension associated with big data and DA is the undermining of existing systems of professional ethics and accountability. In the area of medicine, for instance, Chiauzzi and Wick (2019) have written, “The availability of large data sets has attracted researchers who are not traditionally associated with health data and its associated ethical considerations, such as computer and data scientists. Reliance on oversight by ethics review boards is inadequate and, due to the public availability of social media data, there is often confusion between public and private spaces. In addition, social media participants and researchers may pay little attention to traditional terms of use." When medical professionals defer to AI and anthropomorphize its results, professional ethics may risk being compromised.

In their article, these authors presented four case studies involving commercial scraping, de-anonymization of forum users, fake profile data, and multiple scraper bots. In each case, the authors found serious violations of specific guidelines set forth by the Council for International Organizations of Medical Sciences (CIOMS). Violations, which the authors labeled forms of "digital trespass", involved "unauthorized scraping of social media data, entry of false information, misrepresentation of researcher identities of participants on forums, lack of ethical approval and informed consent, use of member quotations, and presentation of findings at conferences and in journals without verifying accurate potential biases and limitations of the data" (Chiauzzi & Wick, 2019: n.p., abstract).

While attention to ethical issues in data science has been increasing, it is also widely acknowledged that ethical training in data science has been deficient. In their article, "Data science education: We're missing the boat, again", Howe et al. (2017), for example, called for new efforts in data science classes, focusing on ethics, legal compliance, scientific reproducibility, data quality, and algorithmic bias.

The undermining of professional standards has consequences for the research result. For instance, in classic multivariate procedures such as confirmatory factor analysis and multigroup structural equation modeling, or even in exploratory factor analysis, social scientists have sought to address the common problem that different groups may attach different meanings to constructs. Chiauzzi and Wick (2019) give the example of differences over the meaning of "treatment" in medical studies, where patients routinely define treatment in broader terms than do doctors. Patients, for instance, may include not just medications but also "pets" and "handicapped parking stickers" as part of "treatment". Women more than men may attach social dimensions to "treatment". Algorithm-makers may follow the precepts of computer science without due sensitivity to the need for more subtle and appropriate development of the measurement model for multivariate analysis. Chiauzzi and Wick conclude that "Faulty data assumptions and researcher biases may cascade into poorly built algorithms that lead to ultimate inaccurate (and possible harmful) conclusions."

The worst impact on professional ethics of DA, data science, AI, and big data may be on the horizon as the automation of AI itself threatens to institutionalize poor ethical decision-making now common in the field. Dakuo Wang et al. (2019) of IBM Research USA recently surveyed nearly two dozen corporate data scientists, publishing their results in an article titled, "Human-AI collaboration in data science: Exploring data scientists' perceptions of automated AI." Though automation of the creation of AI applications is not yet widespread in business or government, Wang and his colleagues found that "while informants expressed concerns about the trend of automating their jobs, they also strongly felt it was inevitable" (p. 1). The issue for the future is what "it" is and if automated AI creation will rest on underlying assumptions that perpetuate biases and unethical practices of the past.

1.4.7 Privacy, profiling, and surveillance issues

As it is in traditional social science research, the privacy issue is a contentious one in the domain of DA, particularly with regard to "big data" of the social media variety. As the issue is still evolving, lacking consensus among social scientists, and is even subject to litigation, we cannot here set forth clear guidelines. Often commentators content themselves to note that serious ethical issues are raised and social scientists must wrestle with them and adopt research management policies they deem appropriate (e.g., boyd & Caldwell, 2012: 671–673). Speaking of information, which a citizen in earlier days would have regarded as private and protected, Chief Justice John Roberts noted, "The fact that technology now allows an individual to carry such information in his hand does not make the information any less worthy of the protection for which the Founders fought" (*Riley v. California*, 573 U.S. 373, 2014).[4]

An extreme example of data analytics gone to the dark side is provided by China, which has sold its AI-enhanced surveillance system to at least 18 other countries as of 2019. Campbell (2019: 54) reports how China "is also rolling out Big Data and surveillance to inculcate 'positive' behavior in its citizens." By combining facial, voice, and gait recognition software with intense use of cameras (one camera for every six citizens) and feeding data into computer algorithms, DA is being used to identify and penalize everything from fighting with one's neighbors to visiting a mosque to posting the wrong material online to actual crimes. After surveillance systems were installed in taxicabs, a driver sparked images of Orwell's *1984* when he told *Time* magazine that "Now I can't cuddle my girlfriend off duty or curse my bosses" (p. 54). The result is a dystopian society in which persecuted groups like the Uighurs feel compelled to be ultra-patriotic, displaying images of President Xi Jinping in their stores and making posts laudatory of the regime to social media. Over a million people have been rounded up, partly enabled by DA, and sent to "re-education centers", where dire conditions prevail.

All tools may be used for good or evil. The CEO of Watrix, one of the suppliers for surveillance systems in China, stated, "From our perspective, we just provide the technology. As for how it's used, like all high tech, it may be a double-edged sword" (Campbell, 2019: 55). This is a prevalent attitude in the big data community. Facebook, for instance, disavows any responsibility for contributing to the rise of hate groups in America, to allowing Russians to hack American and other elections via social media, or for racial bias in outcomes.

An example closer to home is Google's "Project Nightingale", an effort to digitize and store up to 50 million health-care records obtained from Ascension, a leading US health-care provider. As reported by the *Wall St. Journal*, the *Guardian*, and in a medical journal by Schneble, Elger, and Shaw (2020), a project employee blew the whistle on misconduct in failing to protect the privacy and confidentiality of personal health information. Specifically, the whistleblower charged and the *Wall St. Journal* confirmed that patients and doctors were not asked for informed consent to share data and were not even notified. Also, health data were transmitted without anonymization with the result that Google employees had full access to non-anonymous patient health-care records. All this occurred in spite of Google requiring training in medical data ethics. In her medical journal article, Schneble concludes that data science and AI should not be exempt from scrutiny and prior approval by Institutional Review Boards. The challenge, of course, is assuring IRB independence from employer interests.

Medicine provides other leading examples of privacy issues pertaining to big data and DA. Garattini et al. (2019: 69), for instance, cite four major categories of ethical issues in the medical sector:

1. Automation and algorithmic methods may restrict freedom of choice by the patient over what is done with the data that individual provides. There is great "difficulty for individuals to be fully aware of what happens to their data after collection … the initial data often moves through an information value chain: From data collectors, to data aggregators, to analysts/advisors, to policy makers, to implementers. … with the final actor/implementer using the data for purposes that can be very different from the initial intention of the individual that provided the data" (p. 74). The authors suggest that offering the freedom to opt-out of data collection or at least the option to seek a second, independent decision could be a remedy for patients, but opt-out strategies have not proved effective consumer protection in other areas and second opinions may be prohibitively costly for many patients even if possible in principle.

2. Big data analytics complexity may effectively make informed consent impossible. Garattini et al. (2019: 75–76) cite a recent Ebola outbreak in explaining the impossibility of applying informed consent in the context of viral outbreaks, for instance.

3. Data analytics may well serve as a form of profiling individual and group identities, with consequent issues for fair health access and justice. Garattini et al. (2019: 76) write, "In the case of viral diagnostics for example, the amount and granularity of information provides not only the knowledge regarding potential drug resistance parameters by the infecting organism but also the reconstruction of infectious disease outbreaks, transforming the question of 'who infected whom' into 'they infected them', i.e., from the more general to the definitive form" (cf. Pak & Kasarskis, 2015). To take another example, Lu (2019) was able to use data analytics to identify trucks engaged in illegal construction site dumping with .84 precision, meaning that 16% of trucks profiled as such were not illegal.

4. Big data analytics is normalizing surveillance of the population and changing the capabilities for and norms regarding population-wide interventions of various types. Garattini et al. (2019: 77) note that in the area of monitoring infectious diseases, big data may include information on social media, search engine search word trends, and other indirect measures such that "Algorithms can provide automated decision support as part of clinical workflow at the time and location of the decision-making, without requiring clinician initiative," as, for example, hospital-level or government-level to mount vaccination programs. The decision about vaccination is elevated from the realm of doctor-patient norms to the realm of norm pertaining to public health policy, with attendant benefits but also risks. The authors note, "The overall consequences for individuals, groups, healthcare providers and society as a whole remain poorly understood" (p. 80).

What is legal may not be ethical when it comes to DA. On the one hand there are powerful arguments in favor of treating data scraped from the web and social media as public:

1. The data are in fact publically accessible. Moreover, individuals who post do so knowing this. Journalists, law enforcement authorities, teachers, and others have frequently warned that one should not post unless one is willing for one's community, friends, workplaces, and the public to know what is posted. Users frequently use the public nature of posting to re-tweet or otherwise disseminate posted information themselves.
2. The courts have not prevented large corporations, government, and other entities from collecting web and social media data on a mass basis. For example, it is now routine for a person's posts about seeking to buy a particular automobile or other item to result in email and pop-up web advertisements directed to that person. Indeed, doing just this has become a giant business in its own right. At this writing it seems extremely unlikely that there will be a legal sea change in favor of privacy.
3. In social science, the open science movement has emphasized data availability. The ability of other scholars to replicate a researcher's work is fundamental to the scientific method. If research cannot be replicated, it is suspect. Replication requires access to the researcher's data. The National Science Foundation policy states "Investigators are expected to share with other researchers, at no more than incremental cost and within a reasonable time, the primary data, samples, physical collections and other supporting materials created or gathered in the course of work under NSF grants. Grantees are expected to encourage and facilitate such sharing" (https://www.nsf.gov/bfa/dias/policy/dmp.jsp). It is not uncommon for other research funding organizations to require the public archiving of research data they have funded. Following the replicability principle, many journals will not publish papers based on proprietary, classified, or otherwise unavailable data such that it is impossible to check the validity of the author's work. The replicability principle applies to all research data and does not make exception for data scraped from the web or social media.

On the other hand, there are strong arguments for privacy also. Most of these revolve around the Hippocratic Oath, which emphasizes the "Do no harm" principle, which is also seen as a professional obligation. What is legal is not necessarily ethical. Institutional Review Boards have long been established with the charge of promoting ethical behavior in survey and experimental research. In both of those contexts, unlike the context of social media, it is possible and expected to obtain informed consent at the individual level. Attempts have been made to apply the informed consent principle to the digital world, notably the European Union Data Directive. Its Article 7 this directive allows subjects to block usage of their personal data without consent, and its Article 12 requires that subjects receive an account of digitally-based decisions which impact them. A 2018 EU evaluation of the directive revealed considerable debate about its effectiveness.

Injury to the respondents might be incurred by release of individually identifiable information on sensitive issues such as health (employers and insurers might otherwise use this), illegal activities (law enforcement might use information on drug use), sexual views and activities (make this public could disrupt marriages), and views on race, abortion, and other sensitive issues (release of this could lead to harassment by neighbors and the community). IRBs have generally taken the view that data gathering (e.g., all survey items or interview protocols) require written consent of the individual. Applying this principle to social media and other big data may lead to a policy of not releasing data (e.g., not releasing tweets gathered from the public Twitter API) unless anonymized in order to protect individuals from possible injury.

Given the pro-public and pro-privacy arguments, social scientists are forced to do more than ponder the ethical issues. At the end of the day, decisions must be made about data access. Compromise policies must be adopted. To give one example of such compromise, the followings are guidelines from the *Social Science Computer Review* with regard to their "data availability" requirement for all articles:

- There are a variety of ways to fulfill the data availability requirement.
- Refer to the url of a public archive through which the anonymized data are available.
- State that the data are in an online supplement file hosted by the journal.
- Refer to a public source of the data, with url or contact information.

- State that data are available for use under controlled conditions by applying to a board/department/committee whose charge includes making data available for replication, giving contact information.
- State that the data may be purchased at a non-prohibitive price from a third party, whose contact information is given.
- State that the anonymized data are available from an author at a given email address.
- State that the variance-covariance matrix and variable-level descriptive statistics are available from an author at a given email address. (Many statistical procedures, such as factor analysis or structural equation modeling may be performed with such input, not requiring individual-level data.)
- In the case of data scraped from social media or the web, it is sufficient if an appendix contains detailed information that would enable a reader-researcher to reconstruct the same or a similar dataset.
- In rare cases, dataset availability is not relevant to the particular article. Check with the editor about such an exception.

This particular journal noted that the alternative to the foregoing data availability policy would not be having no data availability statement, but rather a statement from the journal that the data are unavailable for replication and consequently findings based on inference from the data should be viewed as unverifiable.

1.4.8 The transparency issue

A leading purpose of data analytics is to support policy decision-making. A prime democratic principle of policy decision-making is that it should be transparent or at least explainable to those affected by the decision. The purpose and the principle are in conflict. Tal Zarsky has outlined how automation of algorithmic-based decision-making founded on data analytics, whether it is decisions about credit-worthiness in the banking sector or life-and-death decisions about drone strikes in the military sector, inherently involves an increase in opacity. Zarsky (2016: 121) thus wrote, "Analysis based upon mined data, premised on thousands of parameters, may be difficult to explain to humans. Therefore, achieving transparency in such cases presents substantial challenges. Equally, the firm governing through such data analysis would find it difficult to adequately explain the 'real reason' for its automated response – even after making a good faith effort to do so." When data analysts use "machine learning" and "deep learning" procedures, "black boxes" are created, which undermine transparency.

That citizens tend to accept technology-based decisions as valid (Citron, 2007) only compounds the problem from the viewpoint of democratic theory. Blind and unquestioning acceptance of authoritative decisions by the public is antithetical to the premises of democracy. The mantle of data analytic technology has the capacity to cloak decisions in an aura of science. Under democratic principles, however, decision-making and governance is supposed to be founded on legitimacy, not mystery. Legitimacy, in turn, is supposed to be rooted in the will of the people, which in turn requires transparency.

Unfortunately, providing transparency is not simple and may be impossible. The citizen who wishes to challenge a decision made by algorithms may well find that there are legal and institutional restrictions (e.g., privacy laws prevent access to information on what happened to comparable patients in medicine, military, and law enforcement secrecy) may restrict information as classified, or ownership rights may lead media companies to deny access for whatever reason. Even where there is some measure of transparency, as in the credit industry or medical industry, both of which ostensibly extend a citizen right to review records and file corrections, practice undermines the theoretical benefits.

Kemper and Kolkman (2019) made the point that "one elementary – yet key – question remains largely undiscussed. If transparency is a primary concern, then to whom should algorithms be transparent? We consider algorithms as socio-technical assemblages and conclude that without a critical audience, algorithms cannot be held accountable." That is, if meaningful transparency is to exist, it must exist for an independent critical audience. Kemper and Kolkman conclude, "The value of transparency fundamentally depends on enlisting and maintaining critical and informed audiences." In other areas of public policy and governance, the critical audience might take such forms as public hearings, ombudsmen, citizen review boards, or inspectors general. However, these forms of institutionalizing a critical audience are time-intensive and do not mesh well with the production needs of algorithm-based systems and may be hamstrung by such issues as corporate property rights and governmental secrecy, not to mention their sheer cost. Moreover, the effectiveness of such remedies in other spheres has a spotty record at best, even were those commissioning algorithmic systems inclined to make trouble for themselves by institutionalizing an independent critical audience as part of their development process.

The meaningfulness of most transparency measures is questionable at present. While transparency is widely given lip service, in practice very few citizens avail themselves of the ostensible opportunities (Zarsky, 2016: 122). To the extent that people do challenge algorithmic decisions such as those related to their financial credit, this raises transactional costs for the credit-giving institution, which is apt to respond by not promoting the opportunity to challenge by making it easy but rather just the opposite. From the citizen point of view, taking advantage of transparency opportunities imposes high costs of time and sometimes even legal fees. The few who challenge may well give up after protracted dealings with the institution. The high price of implementing meaningful transparency is why, by and large, it does not exist in most settings where algorithmically-based decision-making prevails.

1.5 Summary: Technology and power

Philip Brey has argued that certain types of technology act as facilitators, enablers, and ensurers of certain types of power structures in society, sectors, and even organizations. In Brey's theoretical framework there are five types of ways in which power is exercised. Building on Brey, Mark Ryan has further shown how this works in the agricultural sector and in environmental policy specifically with regard to the technology of data analytics. In farming, agricultural big data analytics (ABDA) presents itself as a politically neutral and beneficial way of improving farming practices, improving agricultural decision-making, and creating a sustainable, environment-friendly future. However, it is not that simple. Brey's five modes of power are listed below, along with Ryan's corresponding illustrations:

1. *Manipulation*: ABDA can be used as a form of manipulative power to initiate cheap land grabs in ways farmers would not have agreed to willingly.
2. *Seduction*: ABDA can pressure farmers to install monitors on their farms, limit access to their farms, limiting the freedom of farmers and otherwise encouraging practices farmers themselves would not otherwise have chosen.
3. *Leadership*: Agricultural technology providers get farmers to agree to use of ABDA without their informed consent with regard to data ownership, data sharing, and data privacy.
4. *Coercion*: Agricultural technology providers threaten farmers with the loss of big data analytics if famers do no obey their policies, and farmers are coerced into remaining with the provider due to fear of legal and economic reprisal.
5. *Force*: Agricultural technology providers use ABDA to calculate farmer willingness-to-pay rates and then use this information to force farmers into vulnerable financial positions.

Ryan, who goes into much more detail on each of these five points in his article, makes the case that far from being neutral; data analytics is instrumental to the exercise of power. Data analytics has the proven potential to give agricultural technology providers the upper hand in the game of power, much as it does in all sectors of the economy.

In this chapter, we started with a brief account of the promise of DA, data science, and AI. As this story is prominent in the media, our account here was brief, wishing to acknowledge the positives in general and for social science specifically. However, most of this chapter has been devoted to the much-needed but less-told story of the perils and pitfalls of big data and algorithmic policymaking both in terms of research design problems and in terms of social and ethical issues.

In matters of research design this chapter called attention to the very real problem of "true believership" and disinclination of data science as a field to see the possibility that there may be multiple paths to the truth, including traditional statistics on the one hand and qualitative research on the other. Those who use data analytics must recognize pseudo-objectivity when they see it in research and recognize that progress is made not by denying bias exists but rather by acknowledging it and seeking to counterbalance it. This is an enormous challenge given the limitations in the way both big data and the tools to analyze it are created.

TEXT BOX 1.2 Data Ethics – Top Ten Checklist

10. *Does the organization restrict data collection to the necessary?* Ethical compromise often arises from collecting all data in sight. In contrast, ethical practices are better promoted by a policy of data minimization, which means collecting only data necessary to achieve organizational goals.
9. *Does the organization repurpose data?* If data authorized by the sources for one purpose are then repurposed to other goals, the principle of informed consent is violated. This problem is confounded when the repurposing is done by another entity to which the data are sold or shared.
8. *Does the organization promote data transparency?* No matter what other internal and external mechanisms the organization puts into place to assure ethical data practices, they will never be comprehensive. By making data and systems as transparent as possible, additional feedback will be forthcoming, sometimes from unexpected sources. More feedback promotes better and more ethical decision-making.
7. *Does the organization promote a culture of data ethics?* The organization must care about broader values than short-term profits or political advantage. Promoting an organizational culture of data ethics may involve embedding this culture in job descriptions, hiring processes, orientations, ongoing training, manuals and reports, and job evaluations.
6. *Does the organization reward data ethics entrepreneurs?* In every area of successful innovation, implementation of the innovation is promoted when there is an advocate promoting change. If there is such a data ethics entrepreneur, that person should be rewarded, not only for the person's sake but also as a statement of the organization's values and culture.
5. *Does the organization hire data scientists who care about ethics?* Rather than force people to change, it is better to hire the right people at the outset. Newly-hired data scientists should understand that focusing on more modest but more ethical outcomes takes precedence over constructing unbridled systems which might be technologically feasible.
4. *Does the organization seek to counter algorithmic bias?* Ethical lapses are often traced to biased and flawed model assumptions. Short of hiring better analysts to begin, giving them ethical mandates, and allowing them time to do their job, bias is also minimized if the project team includes not only technical data science staff but also subject matter experts, research methodologists from outside data science, representatives of affected groups, and peer reviewers.
3. *Are impact studies conducted prior to system deployment?* In addition to countering bias by a diverse development team, requiring a formal, independent data system impact study alerts the organization to prospective ethical problems.
2. *Does the CEO support data ethics?* Studies of technology acceptance and diffusion show many success factors, but prime among them is strong support by the chief operating officer for the innovation. This applies to introducing data ethics mechanisms into the organization.
1. *Is someone responsible for data ethics?* While all organizational members share ethical responsibilities, the organization needs (1) a named data steward for each data system deployed; (2) oversight of the data steward by an in-house Ethics Review Committee or the like; and (3) an annual independent and external data ethics audit involving a data ethicist.

There are many types of social and ethical issues in data analytics, data science, and AI. Foremost is that fact that these are tools when all is said and done. Tools may be used for good or evil. Tools may be best and most exploited by those with the resources to do so, that is why studies find a bias toward the privileged in society. Specific ethical issues such as discrimination or the undermining of privacy are becoming better known, but these issues are the tip of the iceberg. Submerged beneath the surface but posing a greater and more subtle danger to society are threats to democracy, professional standards, and the way decisions are made. Algorithmic rigidity, misleading profiling, and failure to reap the benefits of diversity are true and present dangers. It was said of those who fought despotism from within in another time, "they did what they could". It is trite but accurate to say that eternal vigilance is the price of freedom. This applies to the digital world as well. As social science scholars, we must do what we can, supporting transparency, diversity, and the public good in a problematic economic and political environment.

Endnotes

1. https://ncvhs.hhs.gov/wp-content/uploads/2014/05/090930lt.pdf
2. http://kbroman.org/pkg_primer/pages/cran.html
3. https://stat.ethz.ch/pipermail/r-help/2016-December/443689.html
4. In this case, the Supreme Court held unanimously that warrantless search and seizure of a cell phone with its digital contents during an arrest is unconstitutional.

Chapter 2

Statistical analytics with R, Part 1

PART I: OVERVIEW OF STATISTICAL ANALYSIS WITH R

2.1 Introduction

This volume is directed at readers who are new to data analytics but have familiarity with common statistical procedures and have taken the R tutorial in Appendix 1 or equivalent. By starting with coverage of statistical procedures with which the reader may already be familiar, it is hoped that readers will get a quicker start in data analysis with R as well as gain basic familiarity with procedures that arise in later chapters. This chapter is not a substitute for one of the many books teaching statistics using R but rather intends to show the reader who is already familiar with statistics as traditionally taught that what the reader already knows may be implemented easily within the R environment. This serves an auxiliary purpose as these models may serve as familiar baselines with which to compare results of machine learning procedures introduced in subsequent chapters.

2.2 Data and packages used in this chapter

2.2.1 Example data

Example data files used in this chapter are listed below. These files are all in comma-separated values (.csv) format, a common format among R users. Commands for reading these datasets into R is given in appropriate sections of this chapter. Some are read from supplied data files found in the student section of the Support Material (www.routledge.com/9780367624293). Others are supplied as modules of the R packages themselves. Fuller description of each dataset is found in "Appendix 2 – Datasets used in this book", also found in the student section of the Support Material (www.routledge.com/9780367624293). For additional practice datasets, consider those from the "ISLR" package, described in endnote.[1]

- edvars.csv – This is a subset of just four variables for 1,500 observations in the 1993 General Social Survey, used to illustrate calculation of reliability measures.
- judges.csv – *Used to illustrate reliability analysis. It contains the sports ratings of eight judges rating 300 athlete events on a scale from 0 to 10.*
- protest.csv – This survey experiment dataset focused on subjects who were asked to rate how much they liked a woman lawyer in a scenario (liking, on a 7-point scale) based on response to a protest action. The data are used to illustrate mediation and moderation analysis. Note that other versions of this dataset are in circulation and may not be equivalent to that supplied with this textbook.

DOI: 10.4324/9781003109396-2

- surveysample.csv – This is a subset of just four variables for 1,500 observations in the 1993 General Social Survey, used in this chapter to illustrate calculation of reliability measures. It is also used in later chapters.
- world.csv – This is a cleaned version of a public domain dataset on 20 variables for 212 countries of the world. It is used in this chapter to illustrate logistic regression, predicting whether a nation was above or below the mean of all national literacy rates.

2.2.2 R packages used

R is a modular language. One or more modules are required to implement any given statistical procedure. As discussed in Appendix 1, using R modules is a two-step process: (1) installing the module, usually with the `install.packages()` command; and (2) then invoking the package with the `library()` or `require()` commands. We assume the reader who wishes to follow along on their computer has already installed the required packages. Those for Chapter 2 are listed below. If following along on your computer, it may be convenient to install and invoke them now. Because many statistical procedures are being covered, there are many needed modules. Each package supports multiple commands.

```
library(car)          # Used for Levene's test in Anova and hypothesis tests
library(caret)        # Used here for logistic regression
library(cluster)      # Used for cluster analysis
library(corrplot)     # Used for visualizing correlation matrices
library(DescTools)    # Used to obtain modes
library(emmeans)      # Used for estimated marginal means
library(expss)        # Used for crosstabulation
library(fpc)          # Used for cluster analysis
library(ggplot2)      # A popular graphics package for visualization
library(gmodels)      # Used for crosstabulation
library(Hmisc)        # Used for correlation matrices
library(irr)          # Used for Krippendorf's alpha reliability
library(ISLR)         # Contains teaching datasets
library(lavaan)       # Used for structural equation modeling
library(lm.beta)      # Used for obtaining regression beta weights
library(lsr)          # Used for eta squared in Anova
library(Metrics)      # Used for root mean square error (RMSE)
library(NbClust)      # Used for cluster analysis
library(plyr)         # A utility to apply a function to subsets; used in Anova
library(polycor)      # Used for polychoric correlation
library(pROC)         # Used for ROC curve analysis in logistic regression
library(processR)     # Used for mediation and moderation analysis
library(psych)        # Used for reliability analysis
library(vcd)          # Used for measures of association
```

Other packages are also used in this chapter but are not listed above if they load automatically as part of R's system library. These include such packages as stats, graphics, MASS, and utils. For the complete list, look under the "Packages" tab of RStudio, then scroll down to "System Library". In addition, when a given package is loaded it may load other dependent packages automatically.

In this and subsequent chapters we use package prefixes before commands not coming from the system library. Unless different packages use the same command label, this is not strictly necessary but clarifies which command comes from which package. For example, consider this R code, which produces a plot of a correlation matrix for the system library dataset "mtcars" (data on automobiles):

```
data(mtcars)
M <- cor(mtcars)
corrplot::corrplot(M)
```

The `cor()` command to create the "M" correlation matrix has no command prefix because it comes from the "stats" package in the system library. The `corrplot()` command, in contrast, has the "corrplot::" command prefix comes from the "corrplot" package, which is not in the system library and must have been installed by the researcher. The prefix and the command word happen to the same in this example but often differ.

When a package loaded later uses the same command label as a command in an earlier-loaded package, a "the following objects are masked" warning will appear. If the researcher nonetheless wishes to use the command from the earlier package, it must have that package's command prefix or the command invoked will be that from the later-loaded package.

PART II: QUICK START ON STATISTICAL ANALYSIS WITH R

2.3 Descriptive statistics

"Descriptive statistics" is the first of several subsections that briefly outline how to perform traditional statistical operations using R. In the syntax below, the `read.table()` command is used to read in the "surveysample.csv" and "world.csv" data files located in the folder listed by the `setwd()` command, and the data are stored in an R data frame called "survey". The "survey" object is an R data frame. The `View()` command brings up a spreadsheet-like view of the dataset in the RStudio console (note `View()` must be upper case, unlike most R commands). The `head()` command displays the first cases of data.

Notes on the R code below:

- Variable naming is in the format "data frame$variablename" (e.g., survey$age). While the `attach(survey)` command would allow use of simple variable names, using long names is recommended for clarity and to avoid naming conflicts. If used, remember to `detach()` at the end.
- Lines starting with a hashtag (#) are comments ignored by R.
- Commands in the R system library, which includes the "stats", "graphics", "base", and "utils" packages do not require use of the `install.packages()` command.

This section uses the following functions:

- `setwd()` from the base package sets the working directory
- `read.table()` from the utils package is used to read in data
- `View()` from the utils package invokes a spreadsheet-style viewer. Note: "View" must be upper case, unlike most other R command terms
- `head()` from the utils package by default displays the first six data rows
- `mean(), min(), max(), sd()` are descriptive statistics from the base package
- `median(),sd(), var()` are descriptive statistics from the stats package
- `Mode()` from the "DescTools" package for modes
- `scale()` from the base package is used to standardize variables
- `plot()` from the graphics package is R's generic plotting program

First we declare the default directory and then read and view datasets to be used in this section

```
setwd("C:/Data")
survey <- read.table("surveysample.csv", header = TRUE, sep = ",")
world <- read.table("world.csv", header = TRUE, sep = ",")
View(survey)          # View data like a spreadsheet table
head(survey,5)        # View the first five rows of data
```

Next we get descriptive statistics for the quantitative variable age in the survey data frame.

```
mean(survey$age)                # Mean
        [1] 44.33707
median(survey$age)              # Median
        [1] 41
min(survey$age)                 # Minimum
        [1] 18
max(survey$age)                 # Maximum
        [1] 89
sd(survey$age)                  # Standard deviation
        [1] 16.60796
var(survey$age)                 # Variance
        [1] 275.8243
min(scale(survey$age))          # Standardized minimum
        [1] -1.58581
max(scale(survey$age))          # Standardized maximum
        [1] 2.689248
```

It is also possible to get descriptive statistics by group using the `aggregate()` command, which is part of the built-in stats package in R. Below, for instance, we get means grouped by node number.

```
aggregate(world$literacy, list(Region = world$region), FUN="mean")

              Region        x
1               ASIA 80.32963
2            BALTICS 99.73333
3        CWINDSTATES 98.88182
4              DQIND 97.00000
5      EASTERNEUROPE 97.48333
6       LATINAMERICA 90.30698
7           NEAREAST 79.46429
8        NORTHAFRICA 72.46667
9       NORTHAMERICA 98.20000
10           OCEANIA 90.11250
11 SUBSAHARANAFRICA 62.51000
12    WESTERNEUROPE 97.62500
```

Note above that "x" as the column variable represents whatever variable one asked for, here literacy. If one had asked for the entire world data frame, not just world$literacy, one would get means for all variables with each variable labeled (not "x"). Ignorable warnings will occur for variables which are not numeric or logical.

```
aggregate(world, list(Region = world$region), FUN="mean")
```
[Output not shown.]

Next we obtain descriptive statistics for the factor variable "litgtmean" in the world data frame. This character variable reflects national literacy rate higher or lower than the mean and has the values "High" and "Low". The `table()` command gives the frequency distribution.

```
table(world$litgtmean)
```
[Output:]
```
      High  Low
       140   72
```

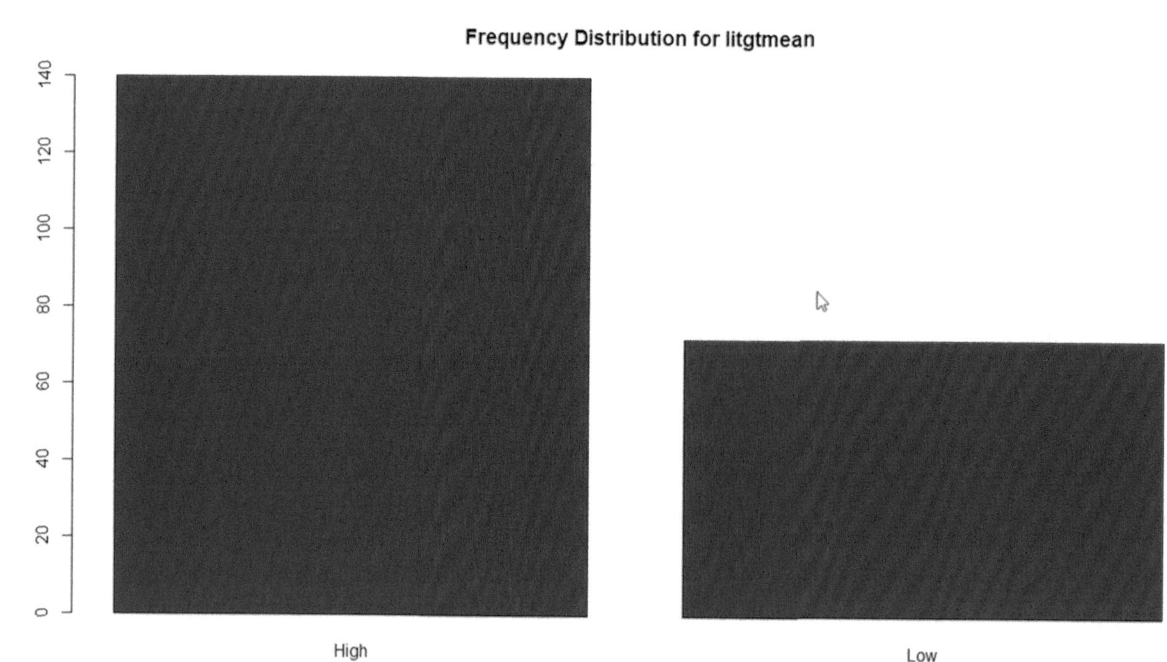

Figure 2.1 Frequency plot of litgtmean

Unfortunately, R has no built-in function for modes. However, we can obtain modes for both character and numeric variables easily using the `Mode()` command from the "DescTools" package:

```
library(DescTools)
Mode(world$litgtmean, na.rm=FALSE)
[Output:]
    [1] "High"
    attr(,"freq")
    [1] 140

Mode(world$literacy, na.rm=FALSE)
 [Output:]
     [1] 99
     attr(,"freq")
     [1] 13
```

We now create a bar chart plot for the litgtmean frequency distribution. There are many more `plot()` options than shown here. Type `help(plot)` to view them. The resulting bar chart plot is shown in Figure 2.1.

```
# Options discussed here set a color and a main title.
plot(as.factor(world$litgtmean), col="medium blue", main="Frequency Distribution for
litgtmean"))
```

2.4 Linear multiple regression

Linear multiple regression is one of the most widely used statistical procedures in social science. It is easy to implement in R. Examples in this section use the "world.csv" dataset to predict which nation are classified high or low on national literacy rate. The outcome variable is "literacy". As assumed by ordinary least squares (OLS) regression, literacy is a continuous variable with a normal distribution.

The dataset used in this and selected other chapters in this book is the "world.csv" data file, stored in comma-separated values format. This dataset, described in Appendix 1, contains 20 variables on 212 countries, including the variables "literacy" and "litgtmean". Five variables are character type: Country, regionid, region, infdeaths, and litgtmean. The first three are country and region names or abbreviations. Infdeaths and litgtmean are binary variables coded "High" or "Low". There are no missing values. In real research, of course, we would use variables thought in the literature to be important correlates of the target variable. However, for instructional purposes we can still explore prediction and classification while limiting ourselves to variables contained in the world.csv dataset. Our research purpose is to determine the relative importance of predictors of national literacy rates.

The units of analysis are nations. Nations are grouped by the variable "regionid", coded as follows:

AS = ASIA
BA = BALTICS
CW = CWINDSTATES
DQ = DQIND
EE = EASTERNEUROPE
LA = LATINAMERICA
NE = NEAREAST
NF = NORTHAFRICA
NO = NORTHAMERICA
OC = OCEANIA
SA = SUBSAHARANAFRICA
WE = WESTERNEUROPE

In OLS regression, the relative importance of predictor variables are often assessed using beta weights, which are standardized regression (b) coefficients. Therefore, as a preliminary we install and invoke the "lm.beta" package, needed for computing standardized regression weights. Also needed is the "Metrics" package, so we invoke that also. We assume both have previously been installed as in Section 2.2.2. If not, issue the commands `install.packages("lm.beta")` and `install.packages("Metrics")` now.

```
library(lm.beta)
library(Metrics)
```

We now issue other setup commands for the example just described. Specifically we set the working directory and read in the world.csv dat. Once imported, the data are in an R object of class "data.frame" under the label "world".

```
setwd("C:/Data")
world <- read.table("world.csv", header = TRUE, sep = ",")
```

We now create a regression solution, placing it in the object "OLSfit" (you could choose a different label). The command to create the OLS multiple regression model is the `lm()` command, which is part of the R system "stats" library and does not need explicit installation.

```
OLSfit <- lm(literacy ~ regionid+population+areasqmiles+ poppersqmile+coast_
arearatio+ netmigration+Infantdeathsper1k+ infdeaths+gdppercapitalindollars
+phonesper1000+arablepct+ cropspct+otherpct+birthrate+deathrate, data=world)
```

The command seems long since many predictor variables are listed. However, the command structure is simple:

- OLSfit: This is the name of the object into which we wish to put the regression solution.
- <-: This is the assignment operator. Whatever is created by commands on its right side are sent to the object named on its left side.
- lm(literacy: This is the regression command. The "lm" stands for linear model. The command specification starts with a left parenthesis and ends with a right one (after "world"). The dependent variable is the first term following the left parenthesis. Most R commands take this form.

- ~ regionid+other variables as listed: The tilde signals that a list of predictor variables is coming. If there is more than one, they are connected by plus signs, not commas or simply spaces.
- , data=world): The comma signals that a list of options is coming. Here there is only the data= option, which specifies that data are to come from the R object called "world". Most commands, including `lm()`, have multiple possible options. Type help(lm) to see them.

Next we check the class of the object we have created. The OLSfit object is of class "lm". Other commands designed for lm class objects will work with it, such as the `plot()` command illustrated below. If you cannot get a command to work with OLSfit, one common reason may be that that command expected an object of a different data class.

```
class(OLSfit)
[1] "lm"
```

Optionally, we may plot the OLSfit object to view diagnostic plots. We do this to see if we have met the assumptions of the OLS regression model, and therefore may use its predicted values in confirmatory research. The simple plot command will return a series of plots described below. The `plot()` command is from R's built-in "graphics" package and needs no installation.

```
plot(OLSfit)
```

Figure 2.2: Check for normally distributed residuals with the normal Q-Q plot. The normal distribution, of course, is a bell-shaped curve. In any well-fitting predictive procedure, regression included, we expect most predictions will be close to observed values, so residuals will be close to 0. Then high and low estimates will trail off in either direction, forming the normal curve. In a Q-Q plot, the closer the dots are to a 45-degree line, the closer to the normal distribution of residuals which characterizes a well-fitting model. OLS regression is considered robust against small to moderate deviations from normality, so most researchers would consider Figure 2.2 to suggest sufficient normality, though certain outlier cases are flagged. Case row 178, which is an outlier, is Seychelles, which had an observed literacy rate of 58 but a predicted rate of 92 – a much too high estimate.

Residuals are defined as observed minus expected (predicted), so negative residuals mean the prediction was higher than observed and positive residuals mean the prediction was lower than observed. In this figure we see that the model is tending to predict too-high values of literacy on the left and too-low values on the right, but is well-fitting for most of the range in the middle. The researcher must judge if this is "good enough" for the research purpose at hand. If the purpose focuses on average cases, the model may be acceptable. If it focuses on extreme cases, it may not be.

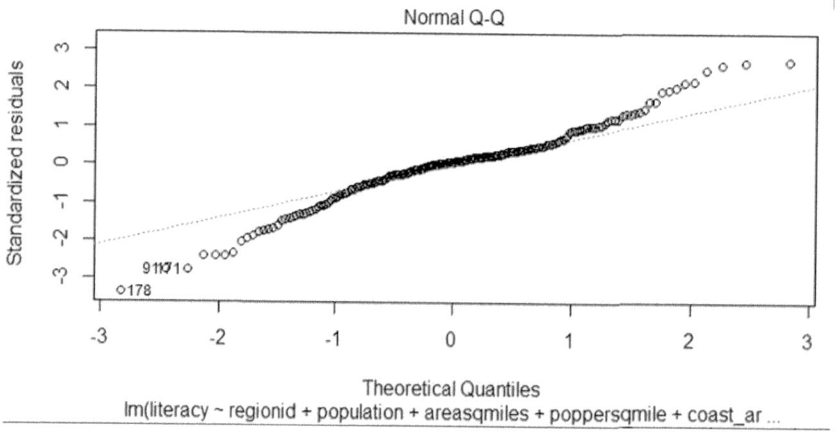

Figure 2.2 Normal Q-Q plot for OLSfit

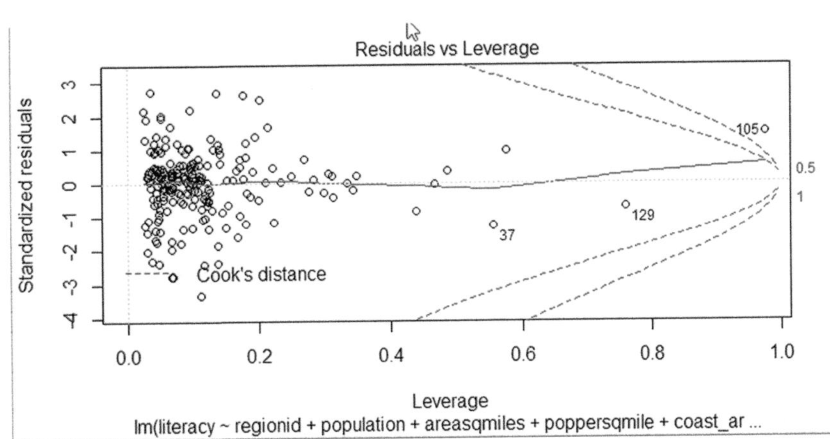

Figure 2.3 Residuals vs. Leverage plot for OLSfit

Figure 2.3: Check for outliers distorting the solution using a residuals vs. leverage plot. This plot helps spot outliers and how numerous they are. Outliers are cases with high influence on the regression line. The more to the right an observation appears, the greater its leverage. Observations outside (to the right) of the dashed lines are also high on Cook's distance, another measure of outlying-ness. Thus cases, which are to the right in the plot and outside the dashed line, are particularly outlying by leverage and Cook's D criteria, such as nation 105 in the following plot.

Figure 2.4: Check if errors seem random using a residuals vs. fitted plot. In this plot, the X-axis reflects the predicted values of literacy. The Y-axis represents the residuals (error). In a well-fitting model, points should form a random cloud centered around a horizontal line at 0 on the Y-axis (the grey dotted line). There should be no pronounced trend as predicted values increase or decrease. Here, the solid trend line shown in red shows only minor trends. OLS regression is considered robust against minor error trends. Had the trend line formed a parabola, in contrast, this would show pronounced nonlinearity, which violates a basic assumption of linear (OLS) regression. However, we can see that the model has predicted greater than 100% literacy for some nations to the right of the plot. Extrapolating beyond the possible range of real-world data values is a problem in OLS regression.

Figure 2.5: Check for heteroskedasticity using the scale-location plot. Also called a spread-location plot, the scale-location plot is used to see if the variance of residuals is constant all along the range of predicted values on the X-axis. In a well-fitting model one sees an approximately equal spread of dots from left to right in the plot (homoskedasticity, meaning the model works equally well or equally poorly for the entire predicted/fitted range). Marked heteroskedasticity would mean one might need different models for different ranges of the data. Ideally the red

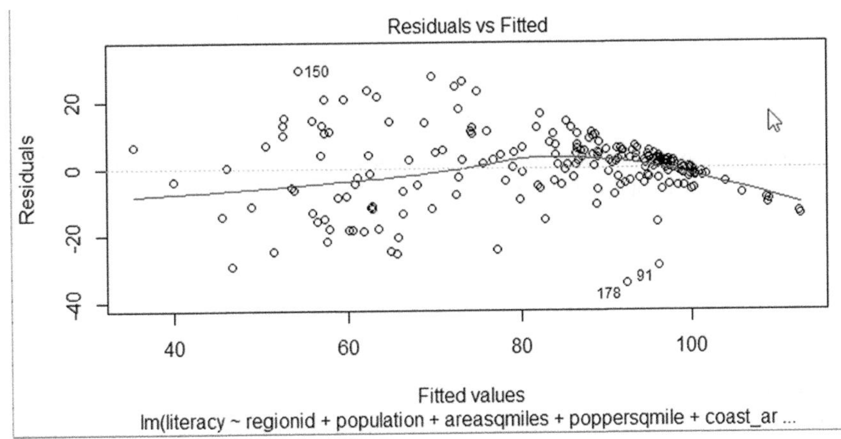

Figure 2.4 Residuals vs. Fitted plot for OLSfit

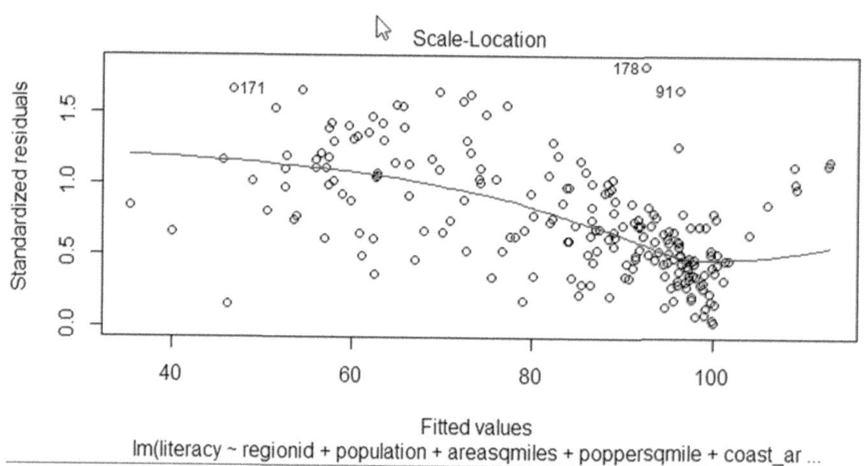

Figure 2.5 Scale-location plot for OLSfit

line, which tracks the amount of spread, should be approximately horizontal. In a poorly-fitting model, one might instead see a funnel shape with much more spread on the right than on the left, for example. Again, one is looking for pronounced departures from homoskedasticity and for the example data, most researchers would consider homoskedasticity to be adequate.

Seeing the actual regression predictions. Given that the diagnostic plots do not suggest abandoning the regression model, we now go ahead to put the predictions (also called fitted values or estimates) into an object we label "OLSpred". This is done using the `fitted()` command from R's built-in "stats" package. We see that the result (OLSpred) is of class "numeric". This means the predictions are a numeric vector. Using the `head()` command we can see the first six, which in the listing below we round to integers. Thus, the regression model predicts country 1 to have a national literacy rate of 40%, the second 62%, and so on.

```
OLSpred <- fitted(OLSfit)
class(OLSpred)
      [1] "numeric"
head(round(OLSpred,0))
       1  2  3  4  5  6
      40 62 61 91 74 67
```

To save model predictions for later used as a variable, we can add OLSpred as a column in the "world" data frame. Note that this change to the world data frame is only in memory unless world is separately saved to file as discussed in Appendix 1.

```
world$OLSpred <- OLSpred
```

The `summary()` command as shown here gives most of the rest of OLS output, including R-squared, which is the percent of variance in literacy explained by the model.

```
summary(OLSfit)
[Output:]
   Call:
   lm(formula = literacy ~ regionid + population + areasqmiles +
       poppersqmile + coast_arearatio + netmigration +
   Infantdeathsper1k +
       infdeaths + gdppercapitalindollars + phonesper1000 +
   arablepct +
       cropspct + otherpct + birthrate + deathrate, data = world)
```

```
Residuals:
    Min      1Q  Median      3Q     Max 
-34.365  -4.644   0.904   4.848  29.395 

Coefficients:
                        Estimate Std. Error t value Pr(>|t|)    
(Intercept)           -2.792e+03  9.650e+03  -0.289 0.772653    
regionidBA             1.931e+00  7.254e+00   0.266 0.790349    
regionidCW             1.742e+01  4.414e+00   3.947 0.000112 ***
regionidDQ             1.430e+01  1.138e+01   1.257 0.210411    
regionidEE             2.506e+00  4.519e+00   0.555 0.579797    
regionidLA             1.472e+00  3.262e+00   0.451 0.652247    
regionidNE            -3.073e+00  4.096e+00  -0.750 0.454079    
regionidNF            -1.292e+01  5.169e+00  -2.500 0.013272 *  
regionidNO             4.131e+00  6.652e+00   0.621 0.535407    
regionidOC             2.014e-01  4.114e+00   0.049 0.961017    
regionidSA            -3.036e+00  3.693e+00  -0.822 0.412104    
regionidWE            -1.581e+00  4.198e+00  -0.377 0.706961    
population            -1.045e-09  8.001e-09  -0.131 0.896231    
areasqmiles           -4.595e-07  5.354e-07  -0.858 0.391894    
poppersqmile          -2.661e-04  5.103e-04  -0.522 0.602609    
coast_arearatio       -2.489e-03  1.236e-02  -0.201 0.840581    
netmigration          -4.173e-02  1.914e-01  -0.218 0.827632    
Infantdeathsper1k     -2.399e-01  6.831e-02  -3.512 0.000558 ***
infdeathsLow           4.193e+00  3.495e+00   1.200 0.231729    
gdppercapitalindollars 1.517e-04  1.746e-04   0.869 0.386144    
phonesper1000         -2.802e-03  8.070e-03  -0.347 0.728823    
arablepct              2.875e+01  9.649e+01   0.298 0.766040    
cropspct               2.916e+01  9.648e+01   0.302 0.762847    
otherpct               2.889e+01  9.649e+01   0.299 0.764979    
birthrate             -5.616e-01  1.925e-01  -2.918 0.003957 ** 
deathrate              5.502e-01  2.789e-01   1.973 0.049971 *  
---
Signif. codes:  0 '***' 0.001 '**' 0.01 '*' 0.05 '.' 0.1 ' ' 1

Residual standard error: 10.93 on 186 degrees of freedom
Multiple R-squared:  0.7223,	Adjusted R-squared:  0.685 
F-statistic: 19.35 on 25 and 186 DF,  p-value: < 2.2e-16
```

The output as discussed shows there were five significant predictor variables. Indicated by asterisks. For instance, significance between 0.01 and 0.05 is one asterisk. As the data was a census of all nations, not a sample, technically significance does not apply. However, it is a common social science custom to use p values to identify important variables nonetheless. Considering only significant predictors and ranking variables by p value, the order of variable importance from most to least important was: regionid, infantdeathsper1k birthrate, and deathrate. For regionid, the most influential level was regionidCW (Russia, Ukraine, Georgia, and other former member states of the USSR; being one of these was positively associated with higher literacy) and regionidNF (being in North Africa was associated with lower literacy). In regression, importance of a variable is importance after controlling for other variables in the model.

Another way to rank variables by importance is to use beta weights, which are standardized regression coefficients. However, the R command for linear regression, `lm()`, does not automatically generate standardized regression coefficients. For this purpose we must use the `lm.beta()` function of the "lm.beta" package. Note that `lm.beta()` requires an object of class "lm", which OLSfit is.

```
library(lm.beta)
lm.beta::lm.beta(OLSfit)
```

[Output:]
```
Standardized Coefficients::
          (Intercept)                regionidBA
          0.000000000               0.011744258
           regionidCW                regionidDQ
          0.198953823               0.050462324
           regionidEE                regionidLA
          0.029818799               0.030485300
           regionidNE                regionidNF
         -0.039292653              -0.110351103
           regionidNO                regionidOC
          0.032273263               0.002738608
           regionidSA                regionidWE
         -0.066358102              -0.025785236
           population               areasqmiles
         -0.006534951              -0.043562788
         poppersqmile           coast_arearatio
         -0.023461651              -0.009375664
         netmigration        Infantdeathsper1k
         -0.010664262              -0.442277686
       infdeathsLow gdppercapitalindollars
          0.101892406               0.078687155
        phonesper1000                 arablepct
         -0.032003975              19.491994337
             cropspct                  otherpct
         11.601424752              23.875591954
            birthrate                 deathrate
         -0.324615869               0.144202568
```

The foregoing coefficients generated by the `lm()` and `lm.beta()` commands in R are the same as for other packages, such as Stata.[2] Beta weights are often used to establish the importance ranking of variables in the model based on absolute weights, with larger being more important provided the variable is significant. Since beta weights are standardized, with all variables on the same scale, for a categorical variable like region, where the listing shows each dummy variable with its own beta weight, one may add the beta weights for all regions to get an overall weight for region. This gives the importance ranking here:

Variable	Beta	Abs(beta)
otherpct	23.87559	23.87559
arablepct	19.49199	19.49199
cropspct	11.60142	11.60142
region (sum)		0.535505
Infantdeathsper1k	-0.44228	0.442278
birthrate	-0.32462	0.324616

However, some beta weights have large standard errors, meaning that, although large, they are not significant. In the discussed table, otherpct, arablepct, and cropspct are not significant. This leaves region, infantdeathsper1k, and birthrate, in descending order, as the most important variables by beta weights, after excluding nonsignificant variables.

As will be seen in later chapters, birthrate, which is usually the first or second predictor in classification and regression trees, herein OLS is ranked third. In general, OLS regression defines importance based on variance explained in the outcome variable after controlling for other variables in the model. As such, regression coefficients are semi-partial coefficients, controlling each predictor for the explanatory effect of other predictors in the model but not removing from the outcome variable the proportion of variance explained by these other predictors.

As seen in later chapters, however, this is not the only meaning of "variable importance" and other methods use other definitions.

We now determine how well OLS predictions correlate with observed values of literacy, using the `cor()` command. While there are other measures of goodness of fit, the observed-actual correlation is one which may be used to compare OLS regression with any other predictive technique. We find there is a high correlation.

```
OLSfit <- lm(literacy ~ regionid+population+areasqmiles+ poppersqmile+coast_
arearatio+ netmigration+Infantdeathsper1k+ infdeaths+gdppercapitalindollars +
phonesper1000+arablepct+ cropspct+otherpct+birthrate+deathrate, data=world)

OLSpred <- fitted(OLSfit)

cor(world$literacy, OLSpred)
[Output:]
      [1] 0.8498829
```

Another model fit metric is RMSE, a "loss metric". Lower is better model fit when comparing models.

```
# Calculate RMSE
# Assumes installation of Metrics package
library(Metrics)
pred2 <-OLSfit$fitted.values
rmse <- rmse(pred2, world$literacy)
rmse
[Output:]
      [1] 10.23507
```

In summary, predictions using the OLS model correlated at the r = .85 level with observed values of literacy. The most significant predictors were region, infantdeathsper1k, and birthrate, in descending order. RMSE was 10.235, a metric which might be compared with other models, with lower being less error.

A word of caution is in order. In OLS regression and other predictive techniques, all coefficients will change when important variables are added to or removed from the model. It is even possible that positive relationships will become negative and significant relationships will become nonsignificant. "Good fit" is relative to model specification (specifying the causes). A model fit metric is true only if the true causes of the outcome are in the model. As this is very difficult to assure, it is better not to present regression findings as "true". It is much more defensible if the researcher has two or more models and seeks to establish that fits the data best.

PART III: STATISTICAL ANALYSIS WITH R IN DETAIL

2.5 Hypothesis testing

In PART III we present the basics of several other statistical procedures in widespread use in social science. The first of these is "hypothesis testing". This term often refers to a procedure deciding if two different values are significantly different. This is the same as saying, "deciding if the difference between two values can be considered different from 0." There are many types of hypothesis tests:

- *One sample vs. two samples*: In a one-sample test, we compare some value (e.g., a mean) with a constant (e.g., 0 or some hypothesized value). We are testing whether the value observed in our sample is different from the constant, given our sample size and the variance of the variable in question.
- *Independent vs. dependent samples*: When two samples are involved, the formula for the hypothesis test is different if samples are not independent. Non-independence arises, for instance, when the samples being

compared represent the same individual sampled at different points in time. Twin studies and matched-pairs research are another type of non-independent sampling.

- *One-tail vs. two-tail*: Most tests are two-tail, referring to the right and left tails of a probability distribution. For instance, the mean age in the researcher's sample might be 43 and the mean age as reported by the Census might be 41. This is a difference of 2 years. A one-tailed test would test the likelihood of getting a sample mean age 2 years or higher than the Census mean age. A two-tailed test tests the likelihood of getting a sample mean age 2 years or more different from the Census mean age (higher or lower). In most cases the researcher will be interested in two-tail test results, testing the likelihood of obtaining a difference as great as that observed in either the positive or negative directions. In some cases, however, the researcher can rule out one direction, and then a one-tail test is appropriate.
- *What is being tested*: Typically, "hypothesis testing" refers to testing the difference between two means or two proportions, or between either a mean or proportion on the one hand and 0 on the other. Other tests, such as tests of correlation coefficients, are usually called "significance tests", not hypothesis tests, though conceptually they are the analogous.

To illustrate how hypothesis testing is done in R, we present only three of the many possible variations: (1) a one-sample test of means, (2) a test of means for two independent samples; and (3) a test of means for two dependent samples. We use variables from the "survey" dataset.

2.5.1 One-sample test of means

A one-sample test of means tests whether an observed mean is different from some constant. We use the "age" variable from the "survey" data frame to illustrate. First we compute mean age in the survey data frame, finding it is 44.34. This is actually an optional step as the `t.test()` function below also prints out the observed mean. The functions `mean()` and `t.test()` are from R's "stats" package in its system library and need no installation.

```
setwd("C:/Data")
survey <- read.table("surveysample.csv", header = TRUE, sep = ",")
mean(survey$age)
```

[Output:]

```
    [1] 44.33707
```

We then use the `t.test()` function to perform the one-sample means test. This function is part of the "stats" package, which is loaded automatically and needs no `install.packages()` command. We ask for the usual two-sided test. For one-tailed tests, set alternative = to "less" or "greater". For instance, alternative = "greater" means we are testing the alternative that mean age is larger than the comparison value.

We use the usual .95 confidence level but could have set any other level. The mu= option sets the constant used for comparison to the observed mean. Imagine that Census data showed mean age to be 42. Below we are testing if the sample mean is different from 42. We find that it is at a p-significance level better than .001. That zero is not within the 95% confidence interval also shows the sample mean is significantly different from the comparison mean of 42 years. We accept the null hypothesis that the true mean is not equal to 42.

```
t.test(survey$age, alternative="two.sided", mu=42, conf.level = 0.95)
```

[Output:]

```
        One Sample t-test
    data:  survey$age
    t = 6.3714, df = 2049, p-value = 2.307e-10
    alternative hypothesis: true mean is not equal to 42
    95 percent confidence interval:
     43.61772 45.05643
    sample estimates:
    mean of x
     44.33707
```

2.5.2 Means test for two independent samples

Below we test whether the mean ages of men and women differ in the survey data frame. This test may be performed either on the assumption that the variances are equal or that they are not. Often, as here, this makes little difference: Ages for men and women do differ in the sample whether variances are assumed to be equal or not.

Note that the first variable listed (survey$age) is a continuous variable and the second one listed (survey$sex) is a binary grouping variable. Switching their order would generate an error message.

```
t.test(survey$age~survey$sex,var.equal=FALSE,data=survey)
```
[Output:]
```
        Welch Two Sample t-test
    data:  survey$age by survey$sex
    t = -1.69, df = 2002.3, p-value = 0.09118
    alternative hypothesis: true difference in means is not equal to 0
    95 percent confidence interval:
     -2.6798316  0.1989831
    sample estimates:
    mean in group 1 mean in group 2
           43.65877        44.89920
```

The finding of nonsignificance (p = .09) above means that the difference in mean ages by sex is not significantly different from 0. This is also attested to by 0 being within the confidence limits. Put another way, we fail to reject the null hypothesis that the difference in mean ages for men and women does not differ from 0. Were we to set var.equal=TRUE, we would obtain very similar results, but the p-value would then be 0.0923.

2.5.2.1 Levene's test of equal variances/homogeneity of variances

Using Levene's test we may determine if the age variances for men and women are the same. Logically, this would be done prior to running the two-sample means test. The `leveneTest()` function is found in the "car" package, so first we install and activate this package.

```
install.packages("car")
library(car)
```

In the following command, the continuous variable (survey$age) comes before the tilde and the binary grouping variable (survey$sex) comes after. As the `leveneTest()` function wants only factor variables as grouping variables, we convert the numerically-coded sex variable into a factor. We also use the mean as the measure of central tendency but we could have used center = median.

```
car::leveneTest(survey$age ~ as.factor(survey$sex), data=survey, center=mean)
```
[Output:]
```
  Levene's Test for Homogeneity of Variance (center = mean)
          Df F value Pr(>F)
  group    1  2.1356 0.1441
        2048
```

The finding of nonsignificance (p = .14) means that variances are not significantly different from equal. Therefore, when conducting t-tests for two independent samples we would specify the option `var.equal=TRUE`.

2.5.3 Means test for two dependent samples

If samples are dependent rather than independent, as with before-after studies, then the algorithm for computing p values changes. The `t.test()` function supports this with the option `paired=TRUE`. We omitted it earlier for independent samples because FALSE is the default, corresponding to independent samples.

Though in the survey data frame the items news1 and news5 are not before-after dependent measures, for purely instructional purposes, we pretend that they are. That is we pretend that news1 is an item measured at time 1 and that news5 is the same item measured at time 2. To run a paired (dependent) sample t-test, put these variables in the t1 and t2 vectors, then run the `t.test()` program with the `paired =TRUE` option.

```
t1 <- survey$news1
t2 <- survey$news5
t.test(t1,t2, paired = TRUE, alternative = "two.sided")
[Output:]
          Paired t-test
     data:  t1 and t2
     t = -0.99846, df = 2049, p-value = 0.3182
     alternative hypothesis: true difference in means is not equal to 0
     95 percent confidence interval:
      -0.05205333  0.01693138
     sample estimates:
     mean of the differences
                 -0.01756098
```

In the output above, the mean of t1 minus the mean of t2 is –.018. Is this a significant difference? That the zero is inside the 95% confidence interval means that the difference is not significant. This corresponds to the significance level ($p = .32$) being nonsignificant. By either criterion we conclude that the difference between the t1 and t2 measures is not significant. We reject the null hypothesis that the difference differs significantly from 0, using the usual two-tailed test.

2.6 Crosstabulation, significance, and association

There are a variety of ways to do crosstabulation in R, including the simple `table()` command used for one-way tables (frequency distributions) in the previous section. Here, however, we will use the `cro()` program from the "expss" package and the `CrossTable()` program from the "gmodels" package. These versatile packages can do much more than tabulation, but here we will stick to the basics. We will also use the "vcd" package to compute measures of association for a table. A third program for crosstabulation from R's built-in "stats" package, `xtabs()`, is also mentioned at the end.

```
# Setup and data
setwd("C:/Data")
survey <- read.table("surveysample.csv", header = TRUE, sep = ",")
# Use install.packages() to install the packages below if needed
library(expss)            # A recommended crosstabulation method
library(gmodels)          # A second crosstabulation method
library(vcd)              # Used to compute measures of association
THE EXPSS METHOD

# Create a copy of survey to work with
survey2 <- survey

# Assign value labels to race
temp<- survey$race
survey2$race <- factor(temp, levels = c(1, 2, 3),labels = c("white", "black",
"other"))

# Assign value labels to degree
temp <- survey2$degree
survey2$degree <- factor(temp, levels = c(0,1,2,3,4),labels = c("< hs", "hs", "jr_
coll","bachelor","graduate"))

# Use the cro() function from the "expss" package for crosstabulation
library(expss)
expss::cro(survey2$race,survey2$degree)
```

[Output:]

```
|              |                |  survey2$degree |      |         |            |            |
|              |                |            < hs |   hs | jr_coll |   bachelor |   graduate |
|------------- | -------------  | --------------- | ---- | ------- |   -------- |   -------- |
| survey2$race |          white |             181 |  851 |     133 |        320 |        150|
|              |          black |              58 |  170 |      22 |         28 |          6|
|              |          other |              22 |   67 |      11 |         28 |          3|
|              | #Total cases   |             261 | 1088 |     166 |        376 |        159|
```

THE GMODELS METHOD

```
# Setup predictor and outcome variables in vectors x and y and define value labels
# x is race, y is educational degree
# Note the use of the c() function to combine values into a vector
temp<- survey$race
x <- factor(temp, levels = c(1, 2, 3),labels = c("white", "black", "other"))
temp <- survey$degree
y <- factor(temp, levels = c(0,1,2,3,4),labels = c("< hs", "hs", "jr_coll","bachelor
","graduate"))

# Print SPSS-style table with two decimal places, chi-square test, labels for the two dimensions

# Format could also be set to "SAS". Type help(CrossTable) to see numerous other options.
gmodels::CrossTable(x,y,digits=2,chisq=TRUE, dnn = c("race","degree"),format="SPSS")
[Output not shown]

# Print same table but with just observed, expected, and column percentages
gmodels::CrossTable(x,y,digits=2,chisq=TRUE, dnn = c("race","degree"),format="SPSS",
prop.r = FALSE, prop.c = TRUE, prop.t = FALSE, prop.chisq = FALSE, expected = TRUE)
[Output:]
   Cell Contents
|-------------------------|
|                   Count |
|         Expected Values |
|          Column Percent |
|-------------------------|

Total Observations in Table:  2050
             | degree
        race |      < hs   |         hs   |   jr_coll   |  bachelor   |  graduate   | Row Total
-------------|-------------|-------------|-------------|-------------|-------------|-----------
       white |        181  |        851  |        133  |        320  |        150  |      1635
             |     208.16  |     867.75  |     132.40  |     299.88  |     126.81  |
             |     69.35%  |     78.22%  |     80.12%  |     85.11%  |     94.34%  |
-------------|-------------|-------------|-------------|-------------|-------------|-----------
       black |         58  |        170  |         22  |         28  |          6  |       284
             |      36.16  |     150.73  |      23.00  |      52.09  |      22.03  |
             |     22.22%  |     15.62%  |     13.25%  |      7.45%  |      3.77%  |
-------------|-------------|-------------|-------------|-------------|-------------|-----------
       other |         22  |         67  |         11  |         28  |          3  |       131
             |      16.68  |      69.53  |      10.61  |      24.03  |      10.16  |
             |      8.43%  |      6.16%  |      6.63%  |      7.45%  |      1.89%  |
-------------|-------------|-------------|-------------|-------------|-------------|-----------
Column Total |        261  |       1088  |        166  |        376  |        159  |      2050
             |     12.73%  |     53.07%  |      8.10%  |     18.34%  |      7.76%  |
-------------|-------------|-------------|-------------|-------------|-------------|-----------
Statistics for All Table Factors

Pearson's Chi-squared test
------------------------------------------------------------

Chi^2 =  55.471     d.f. =  8     p =  3.575548e-09
```

```
# Get measures of association using ssocstats() a from the "vcd" package
# Put the basic table in tabl. It will be in the tabl component called tabl$t
tabl <- gmodels::CrossTable(x,y)
# Compute measures of association. These are the same values as in SPSS, for instance.
vcd::assocstats(tabl$t)
[Output:]
                    X^2 df   P(> X^2)
Likelihood Ratio 62.040  8 1.8517e-10
Pearson          55.471  8 3.5755e-09
Phi-Coefficient   : NA
Contingency Coeff.: 0.162
Cramer's V        : 0.116

# The xtabs() program from the "stats" library also does crosstabulations.
# Results are identical.
tabl <- xtabs(~race + degree, data=survey)
vcd::assocstats(tabl)
[Output:]
                    X^2 df   P(> X^2)
Likelihood Ratio 62.040  8 1.8517e-10
Pearson          55.471  8 3.5755e-09

Phi-Coefficient   : NA
Contingency Coeff.: 0.162
Cramer's V        : 0.116
```

We conclude that by the chi-square test there is a highly significant relationship between race and degree at better than the $p < .001$ level, but by the Cramer's V measure of association of 0.116, this relationship is weak.

2.7 Loglinear analysis for categorical variables

Loglinear analysis is a way of testing for interactions among categorical variables. It is a non-dependent procedure (there is no dependent variable). Interactions are two-way or higher effects in a model. Because it is a non-dependent procedure, there is no "percent explained" or other effect size measure in loglinear analysis. Rather, the purpose is to explain the distribution observed in a table with as few effects as possible (see Garson, 2012). For space reasons, this topic is presented as an online supplement in the "Readings and References" section of the student Support Material (www.routledge.com/9780367624293) for this book.

2.8 Correlation, correlograms, and scatterplots

Crosstabulation is, of course, another word for a table for categorical variables. Related to categorical data are the bivariate procedures for correlation, correlograms, and scatterplots, all of which are illustrated in this section.

The classic type of correlation is Pearson's r, which is the type meant when "correlation" is mentioned without further labeling. How is correlation calculated? Start with the concept of a deviation as a value minus its mean: x – mean. A covariance is a measure of how much the deviations of two variables match. The covariance equation is: cov(x,y) = SUM[(x – meanx)(y – meany)]. The more high positive deviations in x are matched with high positive deviations in y, high negatives with high negatives, and so on, the higher the sum in the formula above and the higher the covariance. However, one cannot easily compare the covariance of one pair of variables with the covariance of another pair of variables because variables differ in magnitude (mean value) and dispersion (standard deviation). Standardization is the process of making variables comparable in magnitude and dispersion. This is done by subtracting the mean from each variable and dividing by the standard deviation, giving all variables a mean of 0 and a standard deviation of 1. For standardized data, the covariance is the correlation. Thus, covariance is unstandardized correlation and correlation is standardized covariance. Correlation squared is the percent of variance in one variable explained by the other. As correlation is symmetric, x explains the same proportion of y as y does of x. Correlation is not necessarily causation.

There are also ordinal flavors of correlation such as Spearman's rank correlation rho and Kendall's rank correlation tau-c. These are used when both variables are ordinal. The most common social science alternative to Pearson's r, however, is polychoric correlation. Polychoric correlation was designed as the correlation between two ordinal variables each presumed to have an underlying normal distribution (bivariate normality). The exact value of the polychoric correlation coefficient may vary depending on the estimation method, the algorithms of the software package, and whether there is a continuity correction or not (continuity corrections adjust for cells with zero count). Though designed for ordinal data, it has become common in social science to use polychoric correlation when there is a mixture of binary, ordinal, and continuous variables.

Correlation matrices may be used as input into a variety of other procedures, such as factor analysis or structural equation modeling (SEM). When measured variables are all at the interval level, this is simply the Pearson correlation matrix. But when data come from a variety of levels researchers may use a polychoric correlation matrix.

Below we use R to computer Pearson's r, Spearman's rho, Kendall's tau-c, polychoric correlation, and to create Pearson and polychoric correlation matrices. Drawing from the previously-used "survey" database we select for example purposes various binary variables (sex, born), ordinal variables (polviews, cappun), and continuous variables (educ, age, income). An initial setup section sets the working directory, reads in the survey data, and invokes packages needed in this section.

```
# Setup and data
setwd("C:/Data")
survey <- read.table("surveysample.csv", header = TRUE, sep = ",")
# If needed, use install.packages() first for the packages below
library(corrplot)    # For the corrplot() command
library(Hmisc)       # For the rcorr() command
library(polycor)     # For the polychor() command
library(psych)       # For the polychoric() command
```

For Pearson's r we employ the `cor()` command from R's built-in "stats" library. In the following command, the "use" option eliminates cases with missing values, as required by the `cor()` command. We ask for two correlations and round to two decimal places.

```
r <- cor(survey$educ, survey$age, use = "complete.obs")
rsquare <- r*r
print(c(r,rsquare))
print(round(c(r,rsquare),2))
[Output:]
  [1]   -0.15  0.02
```

The output shows that older respondents have fewer years of education (hence the negative sign), but age explains only about 2% of education.

More detailed output is available with the `cor.test()` function. We again find that the Pearson correlation between age and education is –.15, significant at better than the .001 level. Pearson correlation is designed for continuous variables like age and education.

```
cor.test( ~ survey$educ + survey$age,
    data=survey,
    method = "pearson",
    continuity = FALSE,
    conf.level = 0.95)
[Output:]
        Pearson's product-moment correlation
      data:  survey$educ and survey$age
      t = -6.6778, df = 2048, p-value = 3.114e-11
```

```
alternative hypothesis: true correlation is not equal to 0
95 percent confidence interval:
  -0.1880837 -0.1033394
sample estimates:
       cor
-0.1459793
```

The `cor.test()` method option could also be "kendall" or "spearman", which are alternative versions of rank correlation. This is appropriate for ordinal (rank) variables such as "cappun" and "polviews", which are survey responses to Likert items. Note that if a rank correlation method is used on continuous variables like age and education, this is a form of measurement error in which information is lost and the effect size is attenuated (for Kendall the correlation drops to –0.06 and for Spearman it drops to –0.08). Below we compute Kendall's tau for cappun and polviews. We ask for continuity-corrected estimates. The result (–0.12) is weakly negative, meaning there is a weak tendency for those scoring higher on capon (favoring capital punishment) to score lower (toward the conservative end) on the polviews scale.

```
cor.test( ~ survey$cappun + survey$polviews,
   data=survey,
   method = "kendall",
   continuity = TRUE,
   conf.level = 0.95)
```

[Output:]

```
      Kendall's rank correlation tau
   data:  survey$cappun and survey$polviews
   z = -6.3178, p-value = 2.653e-10
   alternative hypothesis: true tau is not equal to 0
   sample estimates:
          tau
   -0.1248543
```

As mentioned, polychoric correlation is often used for variables of mixed data levels. We use the `polychor()` command from the "polycor" package and ask for the usual maximum likelihood (ML) estimation method. Below, the polychoric correlation of educ and cappun is .60. The value in parentheses (0.03) is the standard error of the correlation. As the correlation is not within 1.96 standard errors of 0, it is significant. The test of bivariate normality shows that the two variables are significantly different from bivariate normal with a probability of approximately .015.

```
polycor::polychor(survey$educ, survey$cappun, ML=TRUE, std.err=TRUE)
```

[Partial output:]

```
   Polychoric Correlation, ML est. = 0.05332 (0.0295)
   Test of bivariate normality: Chisquare = 33.36, df = 18, p = 0.01509
   . . .
     Column Threshold
     Threshold Std.Err.
        0.6004  0.02957
```

Also as mentioned, researchers sometimes wish to create correlation matrices for purposes such as input of the matrix into another program. Below we create a Pearsonian correlation matrix using the `rcorr()` function from the "Hmisc" package. This program generates three matrices: The correlation matrix, the p matrix of significance levels, and a matrix of sample sizes after listwise deletion (if any). Either Pearson or Spearman matrices may be produced. We create a Pearson correlation matrix and put it into the object labeled "Surveycorrmatrix". Note this is only in memory unless explicitly saved to file.

We start with a command which converts the "survey" data frame to character data in object "x". This is a precaution to assure any factor variables are converted properly in the ensuing step.

```
x <- sapply(survey,as.character)
```

We then run commands which create the Pearson correlation matrix.

```
# Convert x to a numeric matrix, which rcorr() wants.
surveynumeric<-data.matrix(x)
# Run rcorr() on the numeric matrix. type may be "pearson" or "spearman"
surveycorrmatrix <- Hmisc::rcorr(surveynumeric, type="pearson")
# [Output not shown for the next three commands:]
# The "r" element is the correlation matrix that may be used as input to other procedures
surveycorrmatrix$r
# The "P" element is the matrix of significance p values. Note "P" is upper case.
surveycorrmatrix$P
# The "n" element is the matrix of sample sizes for each correlation after listwise deletion
surveycorrmatrix$n
```

To view the correlation matrix, rounded to two decimals, we type:

```
round(surveycorrmatrix$r,2)
```

[Partial output:]

```
              id wrkstat marital childs   age  educ degree
id          1.00   -0.09    0.15  -0.26 -0.17  0.02   0.02
wrkstat    -0.09    1.00   -0.09   0.22  0.33 -0.24  -0.23
marital     0.15   -0.09    1.00  -0.41 -0.37  0.00  -0.05
childs     -0.26    0.22   -0.41   1.00  0.43 -0.22  -0.17
age        -0.17    0.33   -0.37   0.43  1.00 -0.15  -0.07
educ        0.02   -0.24    0.00  -0.22 -0.15  1.00   0.87
degree      0.02   -0.23   -0.05  -0.17 -0.07  0.87   1.00
```

To put the correlation matrix into an object called "mypearsonmatrix" which might be used later or saved:

```
mypearsonmatrix <- surveycorrmatrix$r
class(mypearsonmatrix)
```

[Output:]

```
[1] "matrix"
```

We could also create a Pearson correlation matrix using the simple `cor()` command but this output would not contain a matrix of p values.

```
surveymatrix <- cor(survey, use = "complete.obs")
```

[Output not shown]

A polychoric correlation matrix may be created in a variety of ways, one of which is use of the `polychoric()` command from the "psych" package. This package is only for categorical variables and will give an error message if variables have eight or more levels as it considers them continuous. Therefore, in the example below we find the index numbers for our variables and then create a subset of data in the object "surveyfinite", which contains variables with fewer than eight levels.

First create a subset of categorical variables with eight levels or fewer. The `names()` command will reveal the index numbers of all variables.

```
names(survey)
```

[Output:]

```
 [1] "id"        "wrkstat"   "marital"   "childs"    "age"
 [6] "educ"      "degree"    "sex"       "race"      "born"
[11] "income"    "polviews"  "cappun"    "happy"     "hapmar"
[16] "tvhours"   "agecat"    "childcat"  "news1"     "news5"
[21] "car1"
```

Then subset by index number, retaining numeric variables with fewer than eight levels.

```
surveycatvars <-subset(survey[,c(3, 7:10, 12:15, 17:21)])
```

The `polychoric()` command from the "psych" package then gives a polychoric correlation matric. This package also has a `tetrachoric()` program if all variables are dichotomous. In the options list, correct=TRUE, the default, requests correction for continuity for 0 values. The smooth=TRUE option, also the default, requests smoothing if the matrix is not positive definite. This may be needed because polychoric matrices can have negative eigenvalues and be not positive definite due to pairwise estimation or large sampling error (Garrido, Abad, & Ponsoda, 2013). The `na.rm=TRUE` requests that missing data be deleted. Ignorable warnings may be generated about correction for continuity and smoothing.

```
surveypolymatrix <- psych::polychoric(surveycatvars, correct=TRUE, smooth=TRUE,
na.rm=TRUE)
```

```
# The actual polychoric correlation matrix is stored in surveypolymatrix$rho
surveypolymatrix$rho
```
[Partial output:]

```
              marital       degree          sex        race
   marital  1.000000000 -0.060170929 -0.051369511  0.26415874
   degree  -0.060170929  1.000000000  0.001830497 -0.19160082
   sex     -0.051369511  0.001830497  1.000000000 -0.30402095
   race     0.264158741 -0.191600821 -0.304020953  1.00000000
```

We now turn to creating a correlogram plot with `corrplot()` from the package of the same name. We start by creating a Pearson correlation matrix for the survey data, placing it in an object named "surveymatrix". We only use observations without missing values (listwise deletion).

```
surveymatrix <- cor(survey, use = "complete.obs")
```

Having creating a correlation matrix we may visualize it in a correlogram. This is a plot with variables arranged by the angular order of eigenvectors (AOE). AOE ordering reveals clusters of variables based on correlations. For options, method gives the content format of the cells. In addition to square, method may also be "circle", "ellipse", "number", "shade", "color", or "pie". Title adds an optional title while mar= positions the title. Output is shown in Figure 2.6.

```
corrplot::corrplot(surveymatrix, method = "square",
order="AOE", title="Correlogram for Data Frame
'survey'",mar=c(0,0,1,0))
```

In Figure 2.6, darker blue shows higher positive correlations of the row and column variables. As would be expected, there are small clusters around degree/education and variables dealing with age and children. Darker red shows higher negative correlations.

Scatterplots are another way of displaying bivariate relationships, particularly between continuous variables. Often a regression line is overlaid to show the mean tendency of the relationship. The two-step process of creating the scatterplot in Figure 2.7 is to create the regression line object, then to plot the two variables (here, income and education from the survey data frame), overlaying the regression line. We use the OLS regression command, `lm()`, discussed earlier in this chapter.

```
# Create a regression object predicting education from income
regline <- lm(survey$income~survey$educ,data=survey)
```

```
# Using survey, plot income and educ, then add the regression line.
# For options, pch=16 is solid dots, lwd is line width.
with(survey,plot(survey$income, survey$educ, col="darkred", pch=16, xlab = "Income",
ylab = "Years of Education"))
abline(regline, col="blue", lwd=2)
```

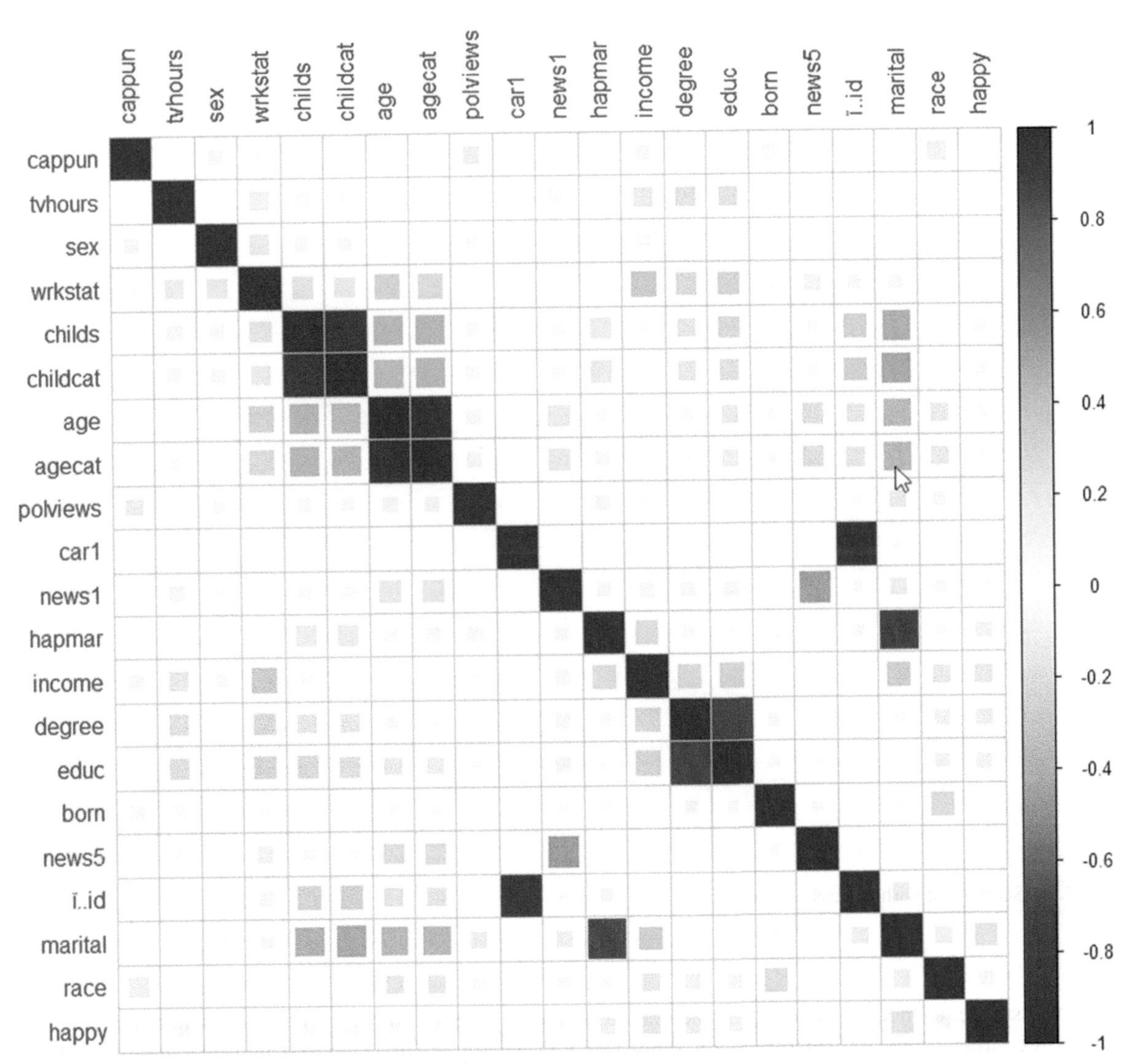

Figure 2.6 Correlogram of variables in the survey data frame

In Figure 2.7, dots for income are aligned in 12 columns because the income data were grouped into 12 ranges. That the regression line slopes upward shows that there is a small tendency for estimated income to rise as education rises. A horizontal line would suggest no relationship between education and income, provided the regression coefficient (slope) were significant.

Both `plot()` and `ggplot()` have a very large number of other options not illustrated here to add colors, symbols, styles, and more to the basic plots presented above. For that matter, almost all commands in this volume have additional options. Type `help(name _ of _ command)` to view them. In most cases there are examples in the online documentation.

2.9 Factor analysis (exploratory)

Exploratory factor analysis (EFA) is the focus of an extended example at the end of Appendix 1 (the tutorial on "Getting Started with R"), and therefore is not covered in this chapter. EFA is used to uncover a smaller number of dimensions which underlie a larger number of measured variables. As such it may be valuable for modeling. It is

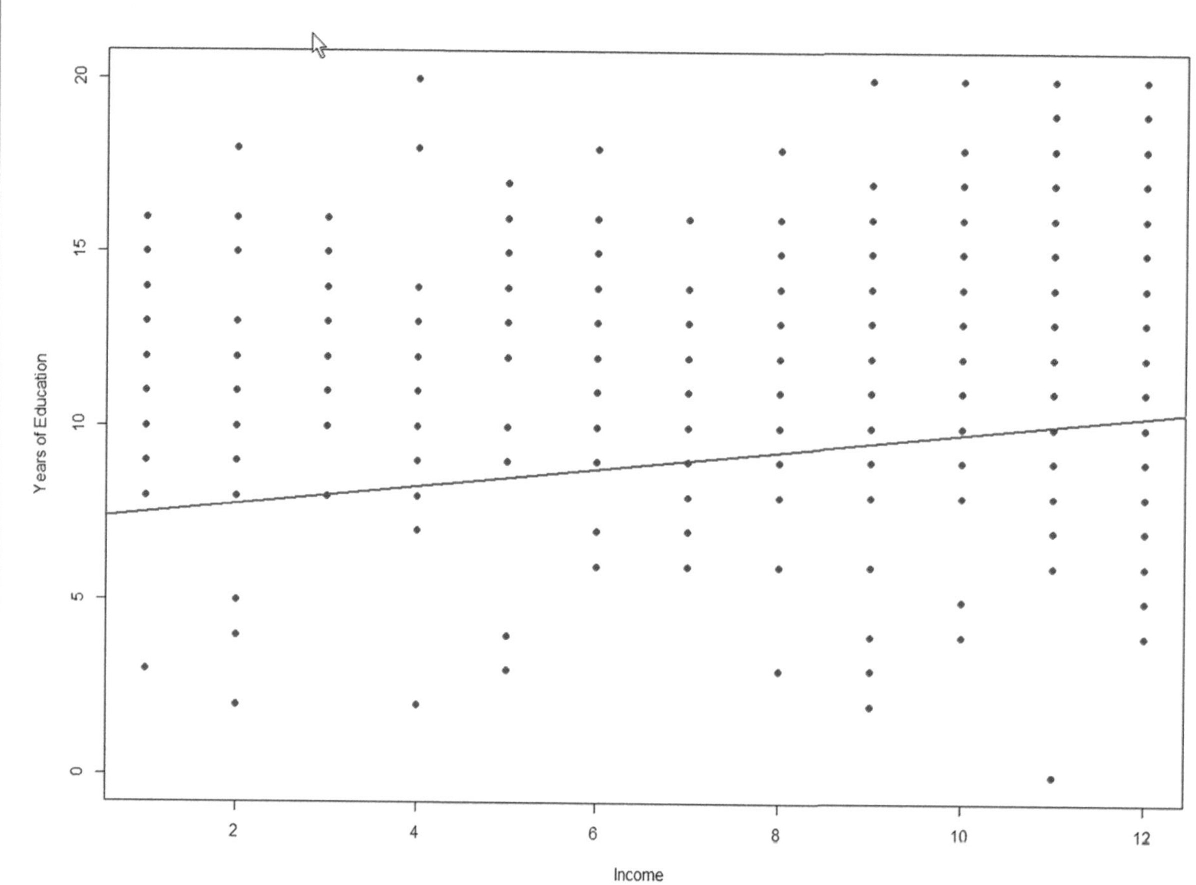

Figure 2.7 Scatterplot with regression line

easier, for instance, to model a set of seven factors that to model a set of 80 survey items on which the factors are based. EFA contrasts with confirmatory factor analysis (CFA), usually the first step in structural equation modeling, which is discussed in Chapter 3.

2.10 Multidimensional scaling

Multidimensional scaling (MDS) uncovers underlying dimensions of a set of variables based on a set of distance measures, though sometimes similarity measures are used (less preferred). The measures may be objective, such as correlations, or may be subjective, such as a series of similarity or distance judgments by subjects. Thus, one type of MDS plot depicts variables such that the higher the correlation of two variables, the closer they will be located in the map of variable space created by MDS. When measures are subjective, this is called the "perceptual map". For space reasons, this topic is presented as an online supplement in the "Readings and References" section of the student Support Material (www.routledge.com/9780367624293) for this book.

2.11 Reliability analysis

Without reliability, research results using the survey or other method of data measurement are not replicable. Reliable replicability is fundamental to the scientific method. Reliability is the correlation of an item, scale, or instrument with a hypothetical one which truly measures what it is supposed to. Put another way, the reliability coefficient squared is the percent of estimated true variance in the construct explained by the given instrument. For instance, for an instrument measuring "Altruism" with a reliability of .70, about 50% of the true variance in altruism is estimated to be accounted for.

Since the true instrument is not available, reliability is estimated in one of four ways:

- *Internal consistency*: This type of estimation is based on the correlation among the variables comprising the set. Typically, Cronbach's alpha is used. Another alternative is Guttman's lower bounds.
- *Split-half reliability*: This type of estimation is based on the correlation of two equivalent forms of the scale (typically, using the Spearman-Brown coefficient). This method is now considered outdated and is not discussed in this section.
- *Test-retest reliability*: This type of estimation is based on the correlation between two (or more) administrations of the same item, scale, or instrument for different times, locations, or populations, when the two administrations do not differ on other relevant variables (typically, also using the Spearman Brown coefficient). This method is also derogated today.
- *Interrater reliability*: This is a more specialized type of estimation based on the correlation of scores between/among two or more raters who rate the same item, scale, or instrument. Often Krippendorff's alpha is used for sub-interval data and intraclass correlation (ICC) is used for interval data. Cohen's kappa may also be employed for binary data and weighted kappa for ordinal data.

There are additional types of reliability and reliability coefficients, each reflecting different meanings of reliability. Here, however, we confine ourselves to the computation of Cronbach's alpha, Guttman's lower bounds, and Krippendorff's alpha.

All reliability coefficients return a correlation-like value that estimates the degree to which an instrument composed of the set of input variables (e.g., survey items) designed to measure a given construct (e.g., leadership) approximates an instrument which would return the true measure of the construct. Since they are all trying to do the same thing, the cutoffs are the same across all reliability coefficients. Cutoffs are arbitrary and differ among researchers. However, a common but conservative standard is:

- < .60: A poor instrument
- >= .60 to < .70: Acceptable instrument for exploratory purposes
- >= .70 to < .80: Acceptable instrument for confirmatory purposes
- >= .80: A good instrument

We again use the "survey" data frame in this section for an example. This data frame includes the following four variables:

- *childs*: Number of children from 0 to 8, where 8 is 8 or more
- *childcat*: Number of children grouped from 0 to 3, where 3 is 5 or more
- *age*: Age of respondent
- *agecat*: Age of respondent grouped from 1 – < 25 to 6 = >= 65

By conducting reliability analysis on these four items, we seek to determine if they are suitable to be combined into a scale which for purely instructional purposes we might interpret as likelihood of being child-involved.

A scale should be reliable and unidimensional (measure a single underlying construct). Therefore, even if a set of items is reliable, we would also wish to use EFA or another method to establish unidimensionality as well. If the set of items is found to be reliable and unidimensional, then it is acceptable to assemble them into a scale. The scale is accepted as a continuous/interval level of measurement even if its constituent variables are ordinal. The three most common methods for assembling items into a scale are these:

1. *Additive*: Item scores are standardized and then added to get the scale score. Standardization assures variables are comparable.

2. *Scaled additive*: The same as additive, but final scores are scaled to be in the 0–100 range.
3. *Factor score*: Factor analysis will generate factor scores for a set of items and these may be used as scale scores.

In the following example we assume that missing values have been dealt with, usually through imputation, as discussed in a later section of this chapter. We also assume that all items have been coded or recoded so that higher values all represent the "more" or "greater" direction or more of the construct being measured. The leading reliability program in R, `alpha()`, automatically reverse codes any item that correlates negatively with the overall scale. The `alpha()` command in R, also discussed below, also supports rescaling for particular variables but its options for this are not discussed here.

Likewise, we assume all items are similarity items. That is, we are testing the assumption that all measure the same thing. Not all sets of items are composed of similarity items. Some form a difficulty or composite scale, not a similarity scale. Such items are inappropriate for the reliability measures discussed below. Difficulty items are such that answering more difficult items predicts the answer to easier items (e.g., if you can solve multiplication items you can solve addition items), but the reverse is not true. Composite items compose the whole (e.g., dollars to education, dollars to environmental causes, dollars to religion, etc., compose a "philanthropy" score). Difficulty and composite items do not necessarily intercorrelate highly, even in a good scale. See Garson (2016a).

The setup for the reliability examples that follow follows the usual pattern except that we read in two data frames called "edvars" and "judges".

```
# Setup and data
setwd("C:/Data")
edvars <- read.table("edvars.csv", header = TRUE, sep = ",")
judges<- read.table("judges.csv", header = TRUE, sep = ",")

# If needed for packages below, use install.packages() first.
library(psych)      # Supports alpha() and cohen.kappa() commands
library(irr)        # Supports the kripp.alpha() command
```

2.11.1 Cronbach's alpha and Guttman's lower bounds

Cronbach's alpha (Cronbach, 1951) is the most common measure of scale reliability. It assumes interval-level continuous data because it is based on assessing shared covariance. Nonetheless Cronbach's alpha is widely used in social science for ordinal data anyway. Split-half reliability is the common-sense idea that if an instrument containing many items intended to measure the same underlying construct is randomly divided into two forms, subjects' scores on the two forms should be highly correlated. Cronbach's alpha may be interpreted as the average value of all possible spit half reliabilities when split-half reliabilities are corrected for differing test lengths.

Because Cronbach's alpha underestimates true reliability, it is considered a measure of the lower bound of reliability. That is, true reliability is at least as high as Cronbach's alpha says it is. Many researchers see underestimation not as a flaw but as a desirable conservative factor: If the scale is judged reliable by Cronbach's alpha, other more liberal reliability measures will also judge the scale reliable.

In R, the `alpha()` command in the "psych" package calculates both Cronbach's alpha and Guttman's lower bounds coefficients, discussed in next section.

2.11.2 Guttman's lower bounds and Cronbach's alpha

Guttman's lower bounds, also called Guttman's lambda 6, tries to provide a more accurate reliability measure than Cronbach's alpha by computing six reliability coefficients (L1 through L6), then reports reliability as the highest of these. Guttman's L3 is the same as Cronbach's alpha reliability. Guttman's lower bounds also assumes interval-continuous measurement, though again ordinal data are widely used in social science in spite of this assumption.

We now compute Cronbach's alpha for the edvars data frame. This data frame contains four variables which may form a potential scale: Degree, educ, madeg, and padeg. We use the `alpha()` command from the "psych" package. Its defaults include removing missing values and deleting variables with no variance. Its check.keys=TRUE option assures all items correlate positively (if not, negative items are reversed but a warning is given).

```
psych::alpha(edvars, na.rm=TRUE, delete=TRUE, check.keys=TRUE)
```

[Output:]

```
Reliability analysis
Call: alpha(x = edvars, na.rm = TRUE, check.keys = TRUE, delete = TRUE)

  raw_alpha std.alpha G6(smc) average_r S/N
       0.7      0.79    0.82      0.49 3.8
    ase mean  sd median_r
 0.0087  4.4 1.4     0.39

 lower alpha upper     95% confidence boundaries
0.68   0.7   0.72

 Reliability if an item is dropped:
          raw_alpha std.alpha G6(smc) average_r
degree         0.53      0.71    0.63      0.45
educ           0.68      0.69    0.62      0.43
madeg          0.68      0.78    0.79      0.54
padeg          0.66      0.78    0.78      0.54
       S/N alpha se var.r med.r
degree 2.4   0.0154 0.010  0.39
educ   2.3   0.0141 0.013  0.37
madeg  3.6   0.0087 0.077  0.39
padeg  3.5   0.0078 0.082  0.39

 Item statistics
          n raw.r std.r r.cor r.drop  mean   sd
degree 1496  0.77  0.83  0.82   0.81  1.41 1.18
educ   1496  0.84  0.84  0.84   0.71 13.04 3.07
madeg  1352  0.58  0.73  0.58   0.48  0.84 0.94
padeg  1207  0.62  0.74  0.59   0.48  0.93 1.19
```

Discussion of `alpha()` output:

1. Cronbach's alpha is "raw alpha" and is .70 for the education variables, which is judged an acceptable scale for confirmatory purposes by this criterion. Covariances are used for this calculation, not correlations.
2. "Reliability if an item is dropped" shows what happens to Cronbach's alpha if any item is removed from the edvars set of variables. In each case, raw alpha drops to a level lower than .70. If degree is dropped, alpha drops to the level of an unacceptable scale, even for exploratory research (i.e., it is below .60).
3. The "std. alpha" coefficient is standardized alpha, based on correlations rather than covariances. Correlations are standardized covariances. This is the reliability measure in an imagined world where every variable is comparable because it has the same mean and same variance. Standardized coefficients are used when comparing variables of different scales or variances.
4. The "G6(smc)" coefficient is Guttman's lambda 6 (L6) reliability. L6 (a.k.a. G6) is recommended when inter-item correlations are low in relation to squared multiple correlations. When all items contribute equally to the overall scale, alpha will be greater than L6. That here L6 is greater than raw alpha for three of the four variables indicates some items contribute more than other items to the scale ("lumpiness in the scale").

5. The "average r" coefficient is the average correlation between pairs of items.
6. The "S/N" value is the signal/noise ratio. Cronbach and Gleser (1964) proposed the signal/noise ratio as a measure of the quality of the scale, with higher being better. In the "Reliability if an item is dropped" section, the more important a variable is to the scale, the more dropping it will lower the S/N ratio.
7. The "alpha se" coefficient is the standard error of Cronbach's alpha.
8. The "mean" value is the mean of the scale formed by averaging or summing the items. Different cumulative options are possible.
9. The "sd" value is the standard deviation of the total scale score.
10. The "median r" coefficient is the median correlation between pairs of items. The more the "average r" and "median r" differ, the more heterogeneity (lumpiness) is flagged for the scale.
11. The "lower alpha upper" coefficients are the lower and upper confidence limits Cronbach's alpha, using the usual 95% confidence criterion. They are derived by adding or subtracting approximately 1.96 times the standard error of alpha (the "ase" column).
12. Under "Item statistics" one sees the item-scale correlations. The raw.r statistic is the correlation of the item with the entire scale. All items should correlate in the same direction. Here they do (all are positive). If some are positive and some are negative, one must reverse some so all are in the same direction. This can be done automatically with the option check.keys=TRUE.
13. Also under "Item statistics", std.r is the item-scale correlation when all items are standardized; r.cor is the item-scale correlation after correcting for item overlap by subtracting the item variance and replacing it with an estimate of common variable (the squared multiple correlation = smc); r.drop is the correlation of the item with a scale composed of the remaining items.

The bottom line: The items in the edvars dataset may be considered scalable at the confirmatory level, though the scale is heterogeneous and not up to the "good scale" level. That is, Cronbach's alpha is .70 but is not equal to or greater than .80. Actual observation-level scale scores may be computed with the `scoreItems()` command of the "psych" package, not discussed here. However, Cronbach's alpha is a lower bound on reliability. By Guttman's L6 coefficient (which R labels G6), reliability is .82 – high enough to judge that the items form a "good scale".

2.11.3 Krippendorff's alpha and Cohen's kappa

If one's data consist of raters as columns and objects rated as rows, then one wants to compute interrater reliability. This could be sports judges rating events or coders classifying text content into categories. Cohen's kappa and Krippendorff's alpha are two common measures for computing interrater reliability. Kappa is used for two raters. Krippendorff's alpha may be computed for more raters and any level of data. Since violation of the data level assumption is a measurement error, using Cronbach's alpha for ordinal data attenuates effect sizes on average, meaning that for ordinal data, Krippendorff's alpha will be higher than Cronbach's alpha on average.

One version of Krippendorff's alpha may be computed in R using the `kripp.alpha()` command from the "irr" package. The general format is: kripp.alpha(x, method= c("nominal", "ordinal","interval","ratio")). Alternatives are the `kripp.alpha()` function in the "concord" package or the `KrippAlpha()` function in the "DescTools" package.

```
# Transpose the judges data frame object so raters are rows, as kripp.alpha() wants
Judgestransposed <- t(judges)
```

Next we obtain reliability output for the judges data. The format is kripp.alpha(x, method=c("nominal","ordinal", "in terval","ratio")). By default, the method is "nominal", which here is wrong since the data are interval. This results in an alpha which is too low.

```
irr::kripp.alpha(judgestransposed)
```
[Output:]
```
Krippendorff's alpha
Subjects = 300
  Raters = 8
   alpha = 0.0487
```

Using method="interval" gives the appropriate alpha (0.678), which corresponds to a scale acceptable for exploratory research (>=.60 and < .70).

```
irr::kripp.alpha(judgestransposed,method="interval")
```
[Output:]
```
Krippendorff's alpha
Subjects = 300
  Raters = 8
   alpha = 0.678
```

However, judge #8 was a fan, not an official representative of a nation. This judge is found to be an outlier and below is removed and `kripp.alpha()` is rerun. This gives alpha = 0.715, which is acceptable for confirmatory research (>=.7 and <.8). Recall >= .8 is "good" for confirmatory research).

```
judgestransposednooutlier<-judgestransposed[1:7,]
irr::kripp.alpha(judgestransposednooutlier,method="interval")
```
[Output:]
```
Krippendorff's alpha
Subjects = 300
  Raters = 7
   alpha = 0.715
```

To illustrate Cohen's kappa, which compares two raters, we use the function `cohen.kappa()` from the "psych" package. This package wants columns to be the two raters and wants rows to be the objects/subjects which are rated. Therefore, we go back to the original judges' data frame, which is formatted this way, but we use only the first two judges as an example.

```
psych::cohen.kappa(judges[,1:2],alpha=.05)
```
[Output:]
```
Call: cohen.kappa1(x = x, w = w, n.obs = n.obs, alpha = alpha, levels = levels)

Cohen Kappa and Weighted Kappa correlation coefficients and confidence boundaries
                 lower estimate upper
unweighted kappa 0.027     0.06 0.093
weighted kappa   0.780     0.82 0.859
 Number of subjects = 300
```

This output shows that the estimated interrater reliability for the first two judges is 0.82, at the "good" level for confirmatory research.

2.12 Cluster analysis

Cluster analysis encompasses any technique that clusters variables or observations. Traditionally in social science, the clustering of variables is done through EFA, discussed earlier, and is not labeled "cluster analysis", though it is a form of it. Measured variables identified as being in the same cluster may be used to form scales or constructs called latent variables. In contrast, traditionally, "cluster analysis" referred to clustering of observations. Units of analysis identified as being in the same cluster may be assigned a cluster membership number and this membership variable may be used in crosstabulation or any other statistical procedure. Typically variables are columns in a data matrix and observations are rows. Since any matrix may be transposed, any cluster analysis technique may cluster either variables or observations, tradition notwithstanding.

There are a very large number of clustering methods, not to mention many variants within any one approach. R, in particular, has a great many clustering functions, only three of which are illustrated in this section: Hierarchical cluster analysis, k-means clustering, and nearest neighbor analysis. The setup for this section is this:

```
# Setup and data
setwd("C:/Data")
judges<- read.table("judges.csv", header = TRUE, sep = ",")

# If necessary, first use install.packages() to install the listed programs.
library(cluster)     # Has the clusplot() function for visualization
                     # Also supports silhouette analysis with the pam() function
library(FNN)         # Has the knn() function for nearest neighbor analysis
library(fpc)         # Has the cluster.stats() utility for cluster analysis
library(NbClust)     # Has methods to estimate the optimal number of clusters
```

2.12.1 Hierarchical cluster analysis

Hierarchical clustering uses information from a distance matrix (e.g., a correlation matrix or a matrix of subjects' perceived social distances from one another) to put together the two closest subjects or objects. It then looks for the pair of next-closest observations and either puts them in a second cluster or adds one to the existing cluster in which its pair resides. Later in the process, clusters may be joined to other clusters based on distance. At the end of the hierarchical process, all observations are in a single large cluster. The steps in hierarchical cluster analysis are displayed in a dendrogram.

The further one has to travel along the lines connecting clusters in a dendrogram, the greater the dissimilarity needed to join the clusters. The researcher must decide on the level of dissimilarity acceptable in his or her research context. The Y-axis measures dissimilarity. The researcher draws a horizontal cutoff line at the point on the Y-axis representing the acceptable level of dissimilarity. The solution is the number of clusters formed below this line (e.g., in Figure 2.MDS1 (this figure is in the MDS supplement at this book's Support Material (www.routledge.com/9780367624293)), variables were clustered and the distance measure was 1 minus the correlation. If the researcher sets .50 as the maximum acceptable dissimilarity, there would be four clusters of two variables each in that example (the four left-most clusters in this figure).

Note that the hierarchical clustering algorithm thus determines the number of clusters. Unlike k-means clustering, it is not necessary that the research posit the number of clusters in advance, only the acceptable level of dissimilarity. Hierarchical cluster analysis as well as other types of cluster analysis are discussed more fully in Garson (2014a).

Hierarchical clustering is most often implemented in R using the `hclust()` function from the "stats" package, which needs no explicit installation.[3] Text Box 2.1 discusses hierarchical clustering research that uses the package "pvClust". There is also a faster implementation of hierarchical clustering in the package "fastcluster", not part of the "stats" package. An example of hierarchical cluster analysis using `hclust()` was given in the section on MDS, with discussion of dendrogram diagrams, and so is not repeated here. As mentioned, the MDS section is an online supplement located on this book's Support Material (www.routledge.com/9780367624293).

2.12.2 K-means clustering

With k-means clustering, the researcher must specify in advance the desired number of clusters, K. K-means clustering tends to produce equal size clusters. Initial cluster centers are chosen randomly in a first pass of the data. Note that different initial values may affect the solution. After the initial random start, each additional iteration group's observations based on nearest Euclidean distance to the mean of the cluster. That is, the algorithm seeks to minimize within-cluster variance and maximize variability between clusters in an analysis of variance models (ANOVA)-like fashion. Cluster centers change at each iteration. The process continues until cluster means do not shift more than a given cutoff value or when the iteration limit is reached.

TEXT BOX 2.1 Social science applications of R: Hierarchical cluster analysis of depression and autism

In the field of child psychiatry, Montazeri et al. studied depression-, anxiety-, OCD-, and autism-related behaviors of 118 high-functioning individuals with autism spectrum disorders (ASD). The authors found that the ASD group had a higher rate of clinical depression and markedly higher "insomnia" and "restlessness" scores. However, hierarchical cluster analysis and network analysis for the ASD group revealed that depression and anxiety items clustered together, but separately from autism-related items. The authors concluded that depression is atypical in autism.

To reach this conclusion, the authors used the R package "Pvclust" to implement hierarchical cluster analysis. In the hierarchical clustering dendrogram (Figure 3, p. 1589) it was demonstrated that the autism cluster (ASD) was separate from the mental depression (MDD) cluster of measures. The authors also used the R package "effsize" to obtain effect size metrics (Torchiano & Torchiano, 2017). The article also contained an extensive network analysis component based on the R package "Qgraph". Other packages used in the article included "lavaan" (for structural modeling) and "WGCNA" (for weighted correlation network analysis).

Source: Montazeri, Farhad; de Bildt, Annelies; Dekker, Vera; & Anderson, George M. (2019). Network analysis of behaviors in the depression and autism realms:... *Journal of Autism and Developmental Disorders* 50(5): 1580–1595.

Suzuki, R. & Shimodaira, H. (2006). Pvclust: An R package for assessing the uncertainty in hierarchical clustering. *Bioinformatics* 22(12): 1540–1542.

Torchiano, M. & Torchiano, M. M. (2017, 2020). Package 'effsize'. CRAN-R documentation at https://cran.r-project.org/web/packages/effsize/effsize.pdf

Because cases may be shifted from one cluster to another during the iterative process of converging on a solution, k-means clustering is a type of "relocation clustering method." However, there is a variant called "agglomerative K-means clustering," where the solution is constrained to force a given case to remain in its initial cluster.

In the example below we implement k-means clustering using the `kmeans()` function of the "stats" package, which does not require installation. We also use the `clusplot()` function of the "cluster" package to plot the solution and use the `cluster.stats()` function from the "fpc" package to compare different k-means solutions. Note, however, that there are numerous other R packages available to implement k-means analysis, including the "ClusterR", "NbClust", "factoextra", and the "skmeans" packages.

For our example, which is the judges data frame, it is not necessary to standardize as the data are ratings on the same 1–10 scale. However, if we needed to make variables comparable by standardizing, we would first issue this command:

```
judgesstandardized<-scale(judges)
```

Below, we run kmeans clustering on the judges data frame, requesting five clusters. Note that `kmeans()` will return the same result only if the same seed is used each time. After storing results in the object "fit5:" We create a plot of the five clusters which cluster the 300 sports events rated by the eight judges. This plot is Figure 2.8. Above each cluster is the cluster number, 1 through 5. Clusters are numbered in the order created, not left to right.

```
set.seed(123)
fit5 <- kmeans(judges,5)

cluster::clusplot(judges, fit5$cluster, color=TRUE, shade=TRUE, labels=2, lines=0)
# View size of the five clusters, which cover 300 events.
fit5$size
[Output:]
      [1] 61 56 56 62 65
```

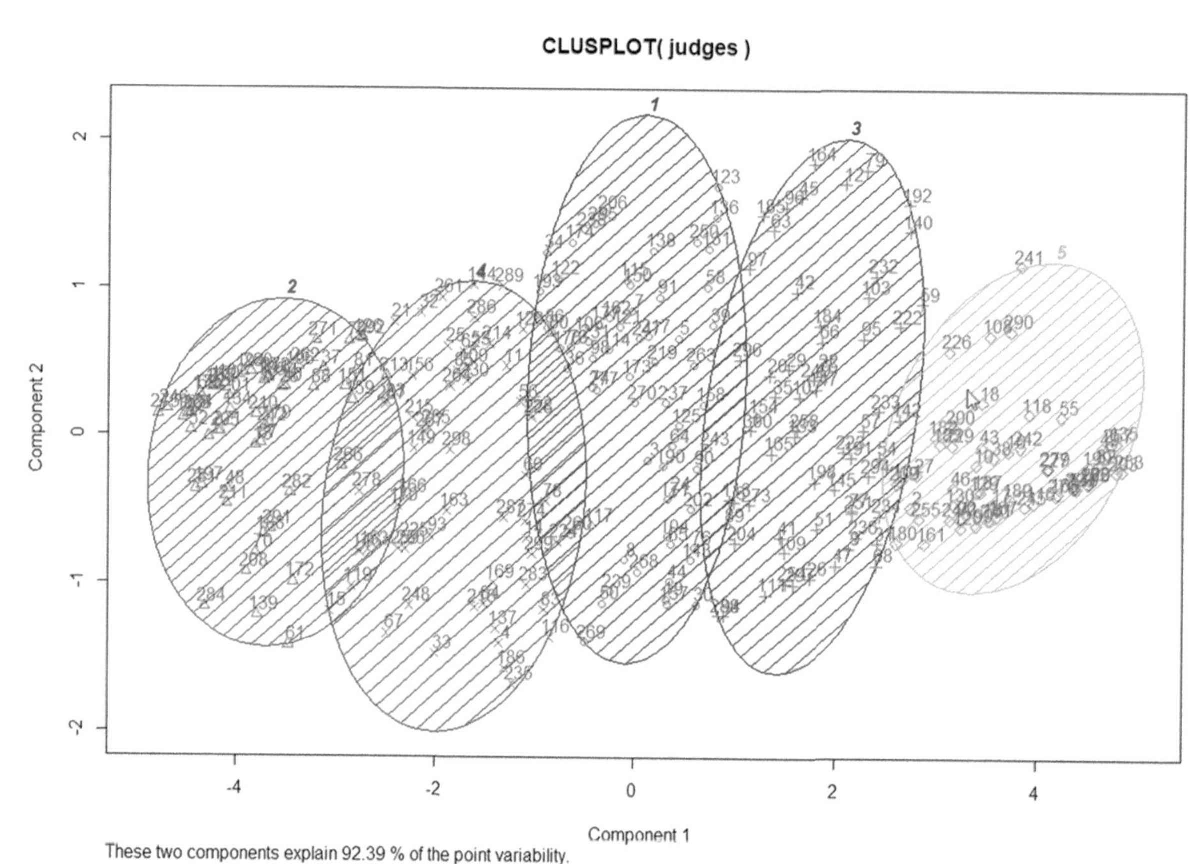

Figure 2.8 Five-cluster solution using kmeans(), judges data

```
# View cluster membership numbers of the 300 events
fit5$cluster
[Partial output:]
  [1] 1 3 5 2 5 4 5 5 4 3 2 4 1 2 1 3 3 3 5 4 1 4 2 5 2 4 3 1
 [29] 4 5 4 2 2 5 4 5 1 3 5 1 4 4 3 5 4 3 4 1 3 5 4 1 2 4 3 2
 . . .
[253] 3 4 3 2 3 4 2 2 2 1 5 2 1 1 2 5 5 5 1 1 4 2 1 3 5 1 3 1
[281] 1 1 2 1 2 2 2 4 2 3 1 1 3 4 5 4 4 2 2 4
```

The cluster membership number may be added to the judges data frame as a variable. The new clus5_num variable appears at the end of the judges data frame. It is only in memory, not file, until explicitly saved by the researcher.

```
judges$clus5_num<-fit5$cluster
```

```
# Display the average score of each judge for each of the five clusters of events
fit5$centers
[Output:]
    judge1   judge2   judge3   judge4   judge5   judge6
1 7.296721 7.555738 7.122951 7.875410 7.213115 7.318033
2 7.892857 8.457143 7.482143 8.623214 7.548214 8.242857
3 9.669643 9.862500 9.400000 9.775000 9.069643 9.937500
4 9.090323 9.527419 8.606452 9.440323 8.422581 9.577419
5 8.515385 9.093846 7.975385 9.086154 7.981538 9.118462
    judge7   judge8
```

```
1 7.057377 7.434426
2 7.333929 8.355357
3 9.635714 9.705357
4 8.851613 8.864516
5 7.944615 8.261538
```

Next we create the object "fit3" as a 3-cluster solution for comparison using fit measures discussed here.

```
set.seed(123)
fit3<-kmeans(judges,3)
```

In the next step we print the ratio of between sum of squares (BSS) to total sum of squares (TSS). The BSS/TSS ratio is a common model fit measure, with approaching 1.0 being good fit.[4] A high-value means cluster separation is high in relation to the total, which includes the within sum of squares, reflecting internal cohesion. Below, the 5-cluster solution is better since its BSS/TSS ratio is higher.

```
fit3$betweenss/fit3$totss
      [1] 0.7785121
fit5$betweenss/fit5$totss
      [1] 0.8339727
```

```
# Create a Euclidean distance matrix from judges
d <- dist(judges, method = "euclidean")
```

```
# Use the cluster.stats() function from the fpc package to compare models
library(fpc)
cstats3 <- fpc::cluster.stats(d, fit3$cluster)
cstats5 <- fpc::cluster.stats(d, fit5$cluster)
```

Above, we had placed the `cluster.stats()` output in the objects cstats3 and cstats5. These objects contain many fit values for the 3-cluster and 5-cluster solutions which we discuss next. One important fit coefficient is the Dunn Index, which is the ratio of minimum cluster separation to maximum cluster diameter. The higher the index value, the better the model by this criterion. In other words, in a good cluster model the distance between clusters is large in comparison to the diameter of the clusters. By the Dunn index, the 5-cluster solution is better than the 3-cluster solution since the index is higher, though neither is high.

```
cstats3$dunn
      [1] 0.1276765
cstats5$dunn
      [1] 0.3273268
```

Where the Dunn index is the ratio of minimum separation to maximum diameter, the Dunn2 Index is the ratio of minimum average dissimilarity between two clusters to maximum average within-cluster dissimilarity. We would like between-cluster dissimilarity to be high and within-cluster dissimilarity to be low. Therefore, higher values of Dunn2 reflect better cluster fit by this criterion. As shown below, this flips the Dunn index inference and we find the 3-cluster solution to be best.

```
cstats3$dunn2
      [1] 1.66436
cstats5$dunn2
      [1] 1.470102
```

Rather than obtain each solution separately, we may loop through cluster solutions 2 through 10, printing Dunn and Dunn2 indices. This allows us to spot the "best" solution by any of the criteria embedded in the loop. Loop output also highlights the fact that the "best" solution depends on the criteria chosen. Below, both the Dunn and

Dunn2 criteria identify as best the 2-cluster solution. Again, the `kmeans()` output would vary somewhat by random seed.

```
# In syntax below, the sep= "\t" option provides tabbed output, which is easier to read.
seed=123
for(i in 2:10) {
   set.seed(seed)
   fit <- kmeans(judges,i)
    cstats <- fpc::cluster.stats(d, fit$cluster)
   writeLines(paste(sep="\t", "Clusters = ", i, "Dunn = ",round(cstats$dunn,3),
"Dunn2 = ",round(cstats$dunn2,3)))
}
[Output:]
   Clusters =      2      Dunn =      0.447  Dunn2 =      2.097
   Clusters =      3      Dunn =      0.128  Dunn2 =      1.664
   Clusters =      4      Dunn =      0.266  Dunn2 =      1.258
   Clusters =      5      Dunn =      0.327  Dunn2 =      1.47
   Clusters =      6      Dunn =      0.104  Dunn2 =      0.775
   Clusters =      7      Dunn =      0.104  Dunn2 =      0.78
   Clusters =      8      Dunn =      0.104  Dunn2 =      0.78
   Clusters =      9      Dunn =      0.104  Dunn2 =      0.78
   Clusters =      10     Dunn =      0.141  Dunn2 =      0.972
```

For better or worse, there are over 30 criteria which have been devised to estimate the "best" cluster, and therefore the best solution. Five more criteria are listed below. Type `help(cluster.stats)` to view criteria available via the `cluster.stats()` function.

- cluster diameter ($diameter; lower values are better because points are less dispersed).
- average distance within clusters, weighted so every observation has the same weight ($average.within; lower is better because of lower dispersion).
- average distance between clusters ($average.between; higher is better because of greater cluster separation).
- Pearson's gamma ($pearsongamma; reflects the correlation between distances and a 0-1 dummy variable where 0 = same cluster and 1 = different cluster. Higher is better because higher distances should correspond to different cluster. Halkidi et al. (2002) call this normalized gamma.)
- Calinski and Harabasz index ($ch; CH uses an ANOVA-like method in which a higher score corresponds to a better model.) A squared Euclidean distance matrix is recommended, not the case here (above, use dsq<-d*d) instead.

Below we use similar loops to print out some additional goodness-of-fit criteria.

```
# Print lower-is-better criteria(diameter; average within). Output is not shown.
seed=123
for(i in 2:10) {
   set.seed(seed)
   fit<-kmeans(judges,i)
   cstats<-fpc::cluster.stats(d, fit$cluster)
   writeLines(paste(sep="\t", "Clusters = ", i, "Diameter =
",round(cstats$diameter[i],3), "Ave. within = ", round(cstats$average.within,3)))
}

# Print higher-is-better criteria (average between; gamma; CH index)
seed=123
for(i in 2:10) {
   set.seed(seed)
   fit<-kmeans(judges,i)
```

```
  cstats<-fpc::cluster.stats(d, fit$cluster)
  writeLines(paste(sep="\t", "Clusters = ", i, "Ave. between =
",round(cstats$average.between,3), "Gamma = ",round(cstats$pearsongamma,3), "CH
index = ", round(cstats$ch,3)))
}
```

[Output for higher-is-better criteria:]

```
Clusters =  2      Ave. between = 5.135  Gamma =       0.782  CH index = 516.892
Clusters =  3      Ave. between = 4.589  Gamma =       0.726  CH index = 521.965
Clusters =  4      Ave. between = 4.392  Gamma =       0.668  CH index = 448.493
Clusters =  5      Ave. between = 4.212  Gamma =       0.628  CH index = 518.866
Clusters =  6      Ave. between = 4.15   Gamma =       0.591  CH index = 436.782
Clusters =  7      Ave. between = 4.09   Gamma =       0.562  CH index = 412.157
Clusters =  8      Ave. between = 4.04   Gamma =       0.536  CH index = 394.68
Clusters =  9      Ave. between = 4.009  Gamma =       0.517  CH index = 363.027
Clusters = 10      Ave. between = 3.96   Gamma =       0.496  CH index = 390.836
```

Because criteria for "best solution" vary, the researcher may want to examine several criteria as well as to examine the cluster plots themselves in order to make a holistic judgment about which solution best serves the researcher's purposes. It is possible that the researcher will want to select a solution size in the middle for all criteria but human interpretability of the clusters trumps statistical coefficients.

Finally, the `NbClust()` function from the NbClust package supports some 26 different criteria for selecting the optimal number of clusters to request in kmeans cluster analysis. Below we request that a range of solutions from 2 to 10 be examined for all criteria. We use Euclidean distance and centroid clustering method as parameters, but different distance and method options are available and will give different results. By the parameters used here we find that two clusters are optimal since this was recommended by the largest number of criteria (9).

```
nb <- NbClust::NbClust(judges, distance = "euclidean", min.nc = 2, max.nc = 10,
method = "centroid", index ="all")
```

[Output, not showing Hubert and D index plots:]

```
[1] "Frey index : No clustering structure in this data set"
*** : The Hubert index is a graphical method of determining the number of clusters.
In the plot of Hubert index, we seek a significant knee that corresponds to a
significant increase of the value of the measure i.e the significant peak in Hubert
index second differences plot.

*** : The D index is a graphical method of determining the number of clusters. In
the plot of D index, we seek a significant knee (the significant peak in Dindex
second differences plot) that corresponds to a significant increase of the value of
the measure.

*******************************************************************
* Among all indices:
* 9 proposed 2 as the best number of clusters
* 8 proposed 3 as the best number of clusters
* 1 proposed 5 as the best number of clusters
* 4 proposed 9 as the best number of clusters
* 1 proposed 10 as the best number of clusters
                         ***** Conclusion *****

* According to the majority rule, the best number of clusters is  2
```

The `NbClust()` command generates two plots, not shown here: (1) Hubert index used to determine the optimal number of clusters based on finding a significant "knee" in the plot line corresponding to a significant increase of the value of the Hubert Statistic; and (2) D index also used in a similar manner to gauge the number of clusters.

2.12.2.1 Silhouette analysis with `pam()`

The silhouette width is a measure of how well clustered an observation is. Values approaching 1.0 are associated with observations, which are very well clustered. Observations approaching 0 lie between two clusters. A negative silhouette width flags placement of the observation in the wrong cluster. The seminal article on silhouette analysis is Rousseeuw (1987).

For a given observation (here, one of the 300 sports events), a "neighbor cluster" is the nearest cluster to which the given observation does not belong. the `silhouette()` function from the "cluster" package returns both sil_width and neighbor, as shown below. Also illustrated below, one may compute the average silhouette width by cluster and also overall, where higher width is better.

A common rule of thumb for interpreting the average silhouette width is reflected in these cutoffs:[5]

- 0.71–1.0 Strong cluster structure
- 0.51–0.70 Adequate cluster structure
- 0.26–0.50 Weak cluster structure
- < 0.25 No substantial structure

Below, the average silhouette width is 0.34, which is weak. The observed cluster structure of sports events in the judges sample may be a data-driven artifact and clusters may not generalize well to other data.

```
# Compute the average silhouette width for the 3-cluster solution
cstats3 <- fpc::cluster.stats(d, fit3$cluster)
cstats3$avg.silwidth
[Output:]
        [1] 0.4821523
```

```
# Compute a vector of cluster average silhouette widths for the 3-cluster solution
cstats3$clus.avg.silwidths
[Output:]
            1         2         3
    0.5745582 0.3571873 0.5060404
```

The "cluster" package's `pam()` function stands for "partitioning around medoids". This is simply a more robust version of the `kmeans()` clustering program but objects created by `pam()` support silhouette analysis.

```
pam3 <- cluster::pam(judges, 3)
```

Note that kmeans clustering using `pam()` tends to give better clustering for the same data than `kmeans()`. Average silhouette width for the 3-cluster solution is .48, still in the "weak clustering" category. Two of the three clusters were in the "adequate" class, not the third.

```
pam3$silinfo
[Partial output:]
  $clus.avg.widths
  [1] 0.5761753 0.5197341 0.3496981

  $avg.width
  [1] 0.4822336
```

The better clustering with `pam()` is shown in the cluster plot for the three-cluster solution (Figure 2.9).

```
cluster::clusplot(judges, pam3$cluster, color=TRUE, shade=TRUE, labels=2, lines=0)
```

We can add the pam-based cluster membership numbers to the judges data as before. The new clus3_pam variable appears at the end of the judges data frame. The cluster membership numbers for the `pam()` solution would differ from a `kmeans()` solution.

```
judges$clus3_pam <- pam3$clustering
```

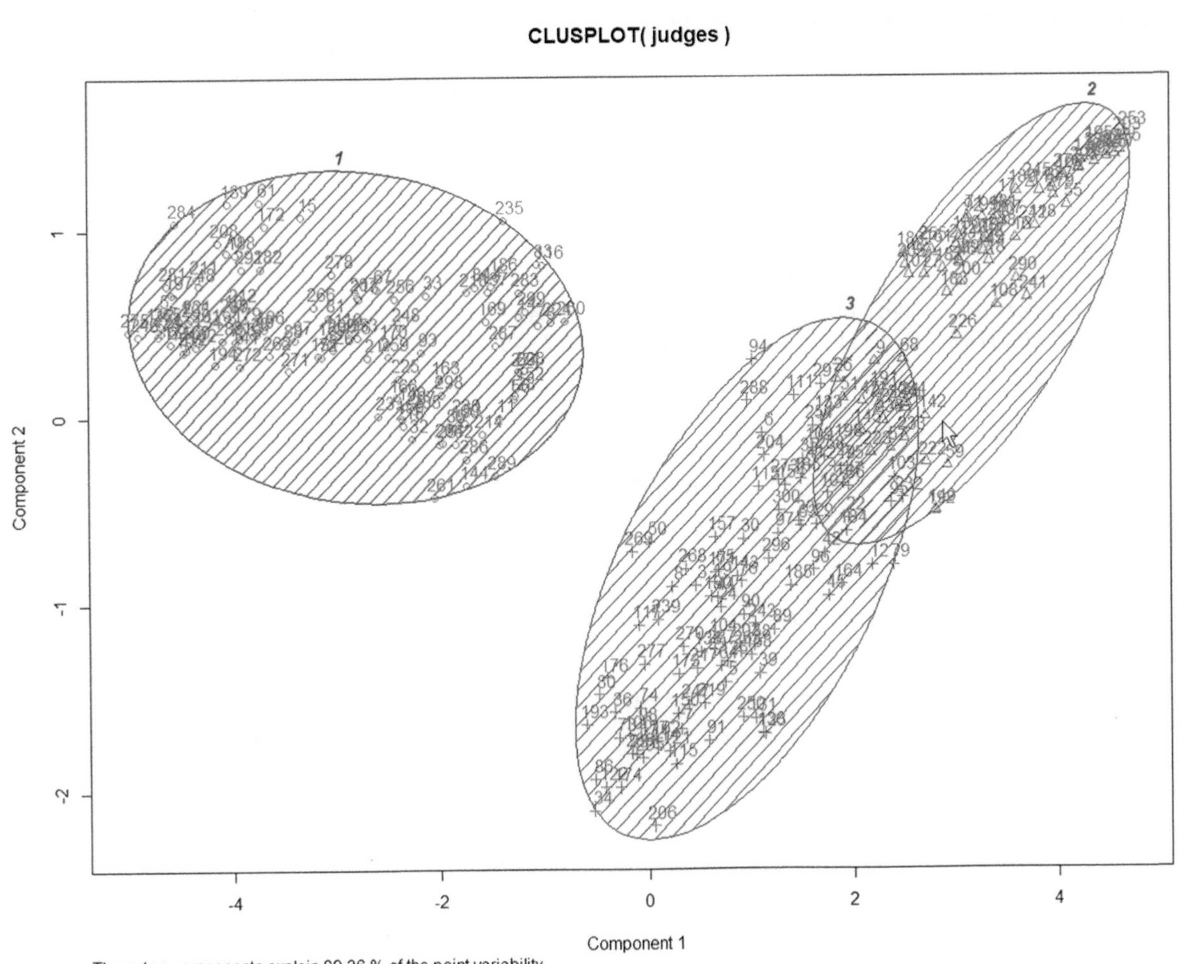

Figure 2.9 Three-cluster solution using `pam()`, judges data

We now use the `silhouette()` function from the "cluster" package. The following command puts event number, cluster number, neighbor, and silhouette width in object labeled "si3", for the three-cluster pam solution.

```
si3 <- silhouette(pam3)
si3
[Partial output:]
      cluster neighbor    sil_width
   179          1        3  0.714503791
   87           1        3  0.711303206
   . . .
   103          3        2 -0.115602966
   232          3        2 -0.123722545
   attr(,"Ordered")
   [1] TRUE
   attr(,"call")
   cluster::pam(x = judges, k = 3)
   attr(,"class")
```

Then put a summary of silhouette data into object ssi3.

```
ssi3 <- summary(si3)
ssi3
```

[Output:]

```
Silhouette of 300 units in 3 clusters from cluster::pam(x = judges, k = 3) :
Cluster sizes and average silhouette widths:
      117        78       105
0.5761753 0.5197341 0.3496981
Individual silhouette widths:
   Min. 1st Qu.  Median    Mean 3rd Qu.    Max.
-0.1237  0.3748  0.5331  0.4822  0.6587  0.7145
>
```

Finally, plot the silhouette data, yielding Figure 2.10.

```
plot(si3, col = c("red", "blue", "orange"))
```

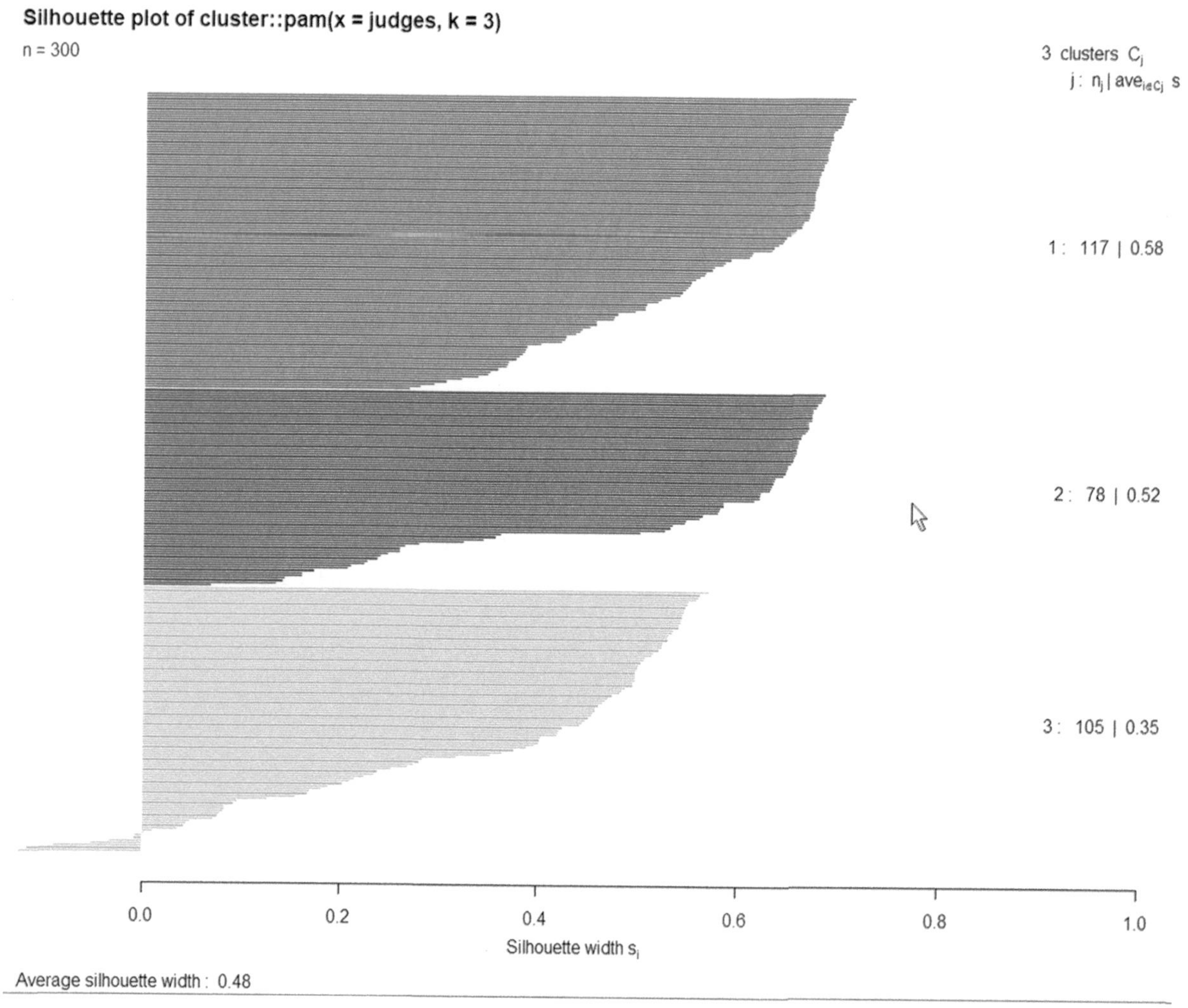

Figure 2.10 Silhouette plot of 300 events, 3 clusters, judges data

In Figure 2.10, colored plots are shown for each of the k = 3 clusters. To the right of each cluster is the cluster number, the number of events in the cluster, and the average silhouette width of the cluster. Higher is better when comparing clusters, so the first two clusters are better defined than the third. This is reflected in the plots for the first two clusters extending further to the right than the plots for cluster 3. Also, cluster 2 has the fewest observations (78) so its set of bars is a little thinner than cluster 1, which has the most observations (117). The length of lines within any cluster's set of bars reflects the distribution of silhouette widths within that cluster. The silhouette widths for clusters 1 and 2 are more likely to be in the adequate range (0.51–0.70) than those for cluster 3.

2.12.3 Nearest neighbor analysis

K-nearest neighbor (KNN) clustering classifies cases based on their similarity to other cases. The researcher sets the parameter k, which specifies how many neighbors to solve for. Below KNN is used to cluster sports events into sets of five neighbors, based on judges' ratings of events. More broadly, KNN could be used to identify sets of peer cases useful for making comparisons or setting goals or standards (e.g., peer colleges for the researcher's college). See Ripley (1996) for further discussion.

As implemented in R, KNN is a popular supervised machine learning algorithm that requires developing a model using a training portion of the data which is then applied to a test portion. The model, however, is not based on multivariate prediction but rather is based on simple distance calculations. By default "nearest" is defined in terms of Euclidean distance but other distance measurement options are possible. The procedure will be more efficient if prior to processing, low-count levels of categorical variables are collapsed into larger levels. Also, if variables are of different scales they should be rescaled by normalizing.[6]

Our example in this section is finding similar (neighbor) sports events in the judges data frame, in which 300 sports events were rated by eight judges. To illustrate nearest neighbor analysis we use the `knn()` function in the "FNN" package. We assume a classification model below, but if the data are continuous and there is a dependent (*y*) variable, the FNN package also supports the `knn.reg()` function, not discussed here. Also not treated here, note that in R there are several alternative nearest neighbor algorithms, such as the `knn()` function in the "class" package.

We start by adding an event id number for each of the 300 events. This is added to the judges data frame as "eventid". Event numbers correspond to row numbers in the judges data frame.

```
temp <- as.character(seq.int(nrow(judges)))
labels <- paste("Event", temp, sep="")
judges$eventid <- labels
```

Next we setup the training and test datasets. The training data are events 1–200 from judges (200 observations). The test data are events 291–300 from judges (100 observations). For instructional simplicity we omit randomizating observations into the two sets.

```
train<-judges[1:200,]
test<- judges[201:300,]
```

Having created the training and test dataset, we are ready to run the k nearest neighbors program. In the `knn()` syntax below, train is a matrix or data frame of training set cases. The test object is a matrix or data frame of test set cases. The labels are observation labels, not variable labels. The value k is the requested number of neighbors (here, 5). The "[,1:8]" part uses all cases only for the first eight columns, which are the eight judges. All are numeric variables. The output (knnresults) is of class factor with nearest neighbors in its attribute "nn.index".

```
trainlabels<-seq.int(nrow(train))
knnresults<- knn(train[,1:8], test[,1:8], trainlabels, k = 5,
algorithm="cover_tree")
class(knnresults)
      [1] "factor"
```

```
# We verify that knnresults is for the 100 cases in the test data, not the 200 in the test data.
length(knnresults)
       [1] 100
```

The five neighbors for any of the events in the 100 test data are containing in the "nn.index" attribute of the output (knnresults). Note that row 1 in knnressults is the first test case, corresponding to row 201 in the original judges dataset.

```
attr(knnresults,"nn.index")
```

[Partial output gives the five nearest neighbor event numbers in the training dataset for each of the 100 cases in the test dataset:]

```
        [,1] [,2] [,3] [,4] [,5]
  [1,]   134  105  175  124  178
  [2,]    89  104   19   44   24
   . . .
 [99,]    50   83  163    8    4
[100,]   154   20  158   90  165
```

We can then verify that a given cluster of neighbors has similar values. Below we do this for the first test case and its set of training set neighbors (row 1 above). Since there were 200 cases in the training dataset, the first case in the test dataset is row 201 in the original judges data frame. We use the index numbers from row 1 of the output above.

```
firsttestcase=201
judges[c(firsttestcase,134,105,175,124,178),]
```

[Output:]

```
     judge1 judge2 judge3 judge4 judge5 judge6 judge7 judge8  eventid
201     7.2    7.5    7.1    7.6    7.3    7.1      7    7.1 Event201
134     7.2    7.5    7.1    7.7    7.1    7.2      7    7.2 Event134
105     7.1    7.5    7.0    7.7    7.1    7.1      7    7.0 Event105
175     7.1    7.4    7.0    7.6    7.1    7.0      7    7.0 Event175
124     7.1    7.4    7.0    7.3    7.1    7.1      7    7.1 Event124
178     7.1    7.3    7.0    7.5    7.0    7.0      7    7.1 Event178
```

In output above we that indeed, among this set of "neighbor" events, ratings are quite similar. In this manner we have verified that this set of sports events are similar in judges' ratings for case 201 in judges and its five nearest neighbor events. These six athletic events are similar in terms of judges' ratings and may be grouped together by this criterion.

2.13 Analysis of variance

2.13.1 Data and packages used

To illustrate the ANOVA family we use as data the previously-created "survey" data frame, with income class as the outcome variable treated as continuous (it has 12 ascending levels of income). See Sections 2.2 and 2.3 regarding loading this dataset. The categorical predictors are race (coded 1 = white, 2 = black, 3 = other) and sex (coded 1 = male, 2 = female). The continuous covariate is educ, representing years of education from 0 to 20. For the multiple analysis of variance (MANOVA)/multiple analysis of covariance (MANCOVA) sections we use income and educ as outcome variables, race and sex as factors, and age as a covariate. Because there are two factors, this is a "two-way model". When no covariate is in the model and there is only one outcome, we are creating an ANOVA model. With two outcomes, it is MANOVA. When a covariate is in the model, we have either analysis of covariance models (ANCOVA) or MANCOVA. The commands below set the working directory and read in the data, the same as in earlier sections.

This section uses the `aov()` function from R's built-in "stats" package to implement both ANOVA and ANCOVA models. The `manova()` function, also from the same package, implements both MANOVA and MANCOVA. Note that the base and stats packages need no installation or invocation.

```
# Setup and data
setwd("C:/Data")
survey <- read.table("surveysample.csv", header = TRUE, sep = ",")
# If necessary, first use install.packages() to install the listed programs.
library(car)          # Used for Levene's test in Anova and hypothesis tests
library(emmeans)      # For estimated marginal means analysis
library(ggplot2)      # A popular graphics package for visualization
library(lsr)          # Has the etaSquared() command
library(plyr)         # A utility to apply a function to subsets; used in Anova
```

We also use the statistical and utility functions listed here.

- `aes()` from the ggplot2 package, to customize plot aesthetics
- `cbind()` from R's base package, used to treat multiple objects together
- `coef()` from the stats package, used to return parameter coefficients
- `ddply()` from the plyr package, used to return results (here, variances) for subsets of a data frame (here, groups formed by the sex and race factors)
- `drop1()` from the stats package to drop terms from a model (used in Type III tests)
- `factor()` from the base package, used to convert variables to class "factor" and is used in assigning labels to factor levels
- `ggplot()`from the ggplot2 package for visualization
- `levels()` from the base package reveals the levels of a factor variable
- `options()`, from the base package, used to set global options (here, to call for Type III significance tests)
- `pairwise.t.test()` from the stats package gives tests of the same name
- `plot()` from the graphics package is used to create figures
- `predict()` from the stats package is used to obtain estimates
- `relevel()` from the stats package, used to set reference levels for the factors
- `summary()` from the base package, used to summarize statistical output objects
- `tapply()` from the base package, used to compute means for each factor level
- `TukeyHSD()` from the stats package, used for multiple comparison of means
- `with()` from the base package, used to evaluate an expression for a given data frame, possibly modifying a copy of the original data

2.13.2 GLM univariate: ANOVA

Univariate general linear models include multiple regression models, ANOVA, and ANCOVA, as well as repeated measures versions of these. GLM (general linear model) modules cover both regression and ANOVA in a wide variety of research designs, which may include fixed effects, random factors, factor as well as covariate predictors, and even repeated measures with correlated error. In all GLM models, the dependent variable is continuous. The independent variables may be quantitative covariates or may be categorical (factors of either the numeric or string types). When factors are involved, the variance of the dependent variable is assumed to be the same for each cell formed by the intersection of the categories of the factors (i.e., for each cell in factor space).

Regression in GLM is simply a matter of entering the continuous independent variables as covariates. Under GLM, factors are translated into sets of dummy variables automatically. Whether a regression model is run under GLM or under a stand-alone regression module, b coefficients will be the same, as will be R-square (percent of variance explained). Advantages of doing regression via GLM include automatic coding of dummy variables, ease of adding interaction terms, computation of eta-squared (identical to R-squared when relationships are linear, but greater if nonlinear relationships are present).

Although regression models may be run easily in GLM, as a practical matter univariate GLM is used primarily to run analysis of variance (ANOVA) and ANCOVA models. To simplify, ANOVA is used to compare means of a dependent variable across levels of a factor (e.g., do pay rates differ between men and women for the same job title?) ANOVA is used to uncover the main and interaction effects of categorical independent variables (called "factors") on a continuous dependent variable. A "main effect" is the direct effect of an independent variable on the dependent variable. An "interaction effect" is the joint effect of two or more independent variables on the dependent variable. ANCOVA is simply ANOVA when one or more covariates (continuous predictors) are in the model along with possible factors (categorical predictors).

A key statistic in ANOVA is the F test of the significance of the difference of group means. If group means do not differ significantly then it is inferred that the independent variables did not have an effect on the dependent variable. If the F test shows a significant relationship, then additional "multiple comparison" and "post hoc" tests of significance are used to explore just which levels (values) of the categorical predictors have the most to do with the relationship. If repeated measures are involved, as in before-after data, the F test is computed differently but the inference logic is the same.

Note that analysis of variance tests the null hypotheses that group means do not differ. In spite of its name, ANOVA is not a test of differences in variances but rather assumes relative homogeneity of variances. Thus a key ANOVA assumption is that the groups formed by the categorical predictors have similar variances on the dependent variable. This is the crucial "homogeneity of variances" assumption. The researcher must use Levene's test to test for homogeneity of variances.

There are a very large number of ANOVA and ANCOVA programs in R, as well as many packages, options, and variations, though all have the same general logic. Other ANOVA programs, not discussed here, include `Anova()` and `Manova()` from the "car" package; `fanova.tests()` from the "fdANOVA" package; and `ezANOVA()` from the "ez" package. Moreover, `aov()` itself has many more options than can be discussed here. In the following section we limit ourselves to presenting how a basic ANOVA model is created in R using `aov()` and the programs and packages cited in Section 2.12.1.

Sex and race are of class "integer". We convert them into factor variable equivalents as a preliminary step.

```
sexf <- factor(survey$sex)
racef <- factor(survey$race)
```

We also set the desired reference categories for sex and race. A reference category is the level of a factor variable against which predictions of other levels are compared. Most packages, such as SPSS, make the highest-coded level the reference level and that is what we do also. Level 3 of race is "Other", where 1 = "White" and 2 = "Black". Level 2 of sex is "F", where 1 = "M".

```
sexf <- relevel(sexf, ref = "2")
racef <- relevel(racef,ref = "3")
```

A critical assumption for any of the ANOVA family procedures is that the variance of the outcome variable does not markedly depart from being the same in each cell of factor space. This is called the "homogeneity of variances" assumption and is checked by Levene's test. We do that here for the outcome variable income and also for educ, which is used as a second outcome in the MANOVA and MANCOVA sections. If the Levene statistic is significant at the .05 level or better, the researcher rejects the null hypothesis that the groups have equal variances. Note, however, that failure to meet the assumption of homogeneity of variances is not fatal to ANOVA, which is robust in the face of small to moderate departures from normality, particularly when groups are of equal sample size. When groups are of very unequal sample size, Welch's variance-weighted ANOVA is recommended, not discussed here (Garson, 2014b).

2.13.2.1 Levene's test of homogeneity of variances

Levene's test may be computed based on mean centering or median centering. Both are done below for the model predicting income from the main effects of race and sex plus the race*sex interaction. Either by mean or median centering, Levene' F test is highly significant. This shows that the groups formed by the factors do differ significantly on their variances on the outcome variable, income. Not shown here, we repeat for the educ variable, used as an outcome in the MANOVA/MANCOVA section further below, and find the same result.

```
with(survey, car::leveneTest(income,interaction(racef,sexf), center=median))
[Output:]
   Levene's  Test for Homogeneity of Variance (center = median)
            Df F value    Pr(>F)
   group     5  18.493 < 2.2e-16 ***
          2044
   ---
   Signif. codes:   0 '***' 0.001 '**' 0.01 '*' 0.05 '.' 0.1 ' ' 1

with(survey,car::leveneTest(income,interaction(racef,sexf), center=mean))
[Output:]
   Levene's Test for Homogeneity of Variance (center = mean)
           Df F value    Pr(>F)
   group    5  27.042 < 2.2e-16 ***
         2044
   ---
   Signif. codes:  0 '***' 0.001 '**' 0.01 '*' 0.05 '.' 0.1 ' ' 1
```

That Levene's test returns a finding of significance indicates that variances of either income or educ differ significantly in the six groups formed by race (3 levels) and sex (2 levels). That is, data are heteroskedastic, which violates the homogeneity of means assumption of the ANOVA family, all of which are, however, robust against this violation. How heteroskedastic is too much? A rule of thumb is that heteroskedasticity is acceptable if the ratio of the largest group variance to the smallest is no greater than 4:1. We can check this using the `ddply()` function of the "plyr" package as shown below. We find we do not violate the 4:1 rule and may proceed with analysis of variance procedures. Had we failed the 4:1 rule as well as Levene's test we could resort to such steps as transforming the data (e.g., log transform), applying Welch's correction to the denominator DF in the F test, using a Box-Cox transformation, using WLS (weighted least squares) estimation, or other means not demonstrated here.

```
library(plyr) # plyr must be activated in spite of being used as a command prefix

var_income <- plyr::ddply(survey,. (racef, sexf), summarize, variance = var(income))
var_income
[Output:]
     racef sexf  variance
   1     3    2  6.246278
   2     3    1  8.455085
   3     1    2  4.816934
   4     1    1  4.271955
   5     2    2 11.684251
   6     2    1  8.990117

var_educ <- plyr::ddply(survey,. (racef, sexf), summarize, variance = var(educ))
var_educ
[Output:]
     racef sexf variance
   1     3    2 5.922736
   2     3    1 8.868644
   3     1    2 8.030197
   4     1    1 8.606478
   5     2    2 6.915286
   6     2    1 5.575651
```

2.13.2.2 Parameter estimates and fitted values

The "anovaout" object, created below and containing the results of the `aov()` command, also contains information on the sum of squares, which is a measure of model error and thus also a measure model fit. Unfortunately, by default, Type I F tests are reported.[7] Type I F tests are sequential tests, assuming a causal ordering of the data and testing each effect in the order entered. A corollary is that results in Type I tests vary according to the order with which predictor variables were entered. This is not true of Type III tests. While not uncommon in experimental research, social science data almost always calls for Type III sums of squares. Therefore, it is necessary to reset the contrast options needed to get Type III F tests such as output by SPSS and other common statistical packages.

Below we set contrast options as needed to get correct b coefficients. The options statement shown is the default for `aov()` and is not actually needed unless contrasts have been set otherwise. We then run the ANOVA model and examine the coefficients, which are the same as SPSS and other statistical packages.

The listed options are for unordered and ordered factors in that order. The contr.treatment specification contrasts each level with the baseline level. The baseline level itself is omitted. These "contrasts" are not orthogonal to the intercept. The contr.poly specification returns contrasts based on orthogonal polynomials. There are other possible specifications.[8]

```
options(contrasts = c("contr.treatment", "contr.poly"))
anovaout <- aov(income ~ sexf+racef+sexf*racef,data=survey)
round(coef(anovaout),2)
```

[Output:]

```
 (Intercept)  sexf1    racef1  racef2 sexf1:racef1 sexf1:racef2
       10.20   0.25      0.64   -0.94         0.01         0.47
```

Rounding apart, the same output may be obtained by issuing the command `anovaout$coefficients`. Also, `coefficients(anovaout)` would be a synonym.

These coefficients are used to predict the value of income for each observation. We can capture these in the vector predanova (a user-created label) and add this as a variable to the survey data frame if we wish:

```
predanova<- anovaout$fitted.values
survey$predanova <- predanova
```

2.13.2.3 Type III tests of significance

The `summary (anovaout)` command will return the default Type I (sequential) F tests of sexf, racef, and the interaction of the two. As we want the usual Type III Sums of Squares F tests, we must do something different if using `aov()` to implement ANOVA. We do the following and do obtain Type III tests as in SPSS and most other packages.

```
# Reset contrast options to get Type III tests further below
options(contrasts = c("contr.sum", "contr.poly"))

# Re-run the model, creating a second output object
anovaout2 <- aov(income ~ sexf+racef+sexf*racef,data=survey)

# With contrast options set as above, use the drop1() function to ask for Type III tests.
# The results are the same as reported by SPSS and other common statistical packages.
drop1(anovaout2,. ~., test=c("F"))
```

[Output:]

```
   Single term deletions
   Model:
   income ~ sexf + racef + sexf * racef
              Df Sum of Sq   RSS    AIC F value  Pr(>F)
   <none>                  11399 3529.1
    sexf       1     31.88 11431 3532.9  5.7170 0.01689 *
```

```
racef       2    440.80 11840 3602.9 39.5211 < 2e-16 ***
sexf:racef  2     12.15 11411 3527.3  1.0891 0.33673
---
Signif. codes:
0 '***' 0.001 '**' 0.01 '*' 0.05 '.' 0.1 ' ' 1
```

The results of the Type III F tests show that race and sex are significant and the interaction of the two is not significant in predicting income.

2.13.2.4 Partial eta squared

Partial eta squared is the most common effect size measure for main and interaction effects in an ANOVA model. The `etaSquared()` function is supported by the "lsr" package and is used to obtain partial eta squared. Note we must reference anovaout2, which was the output compatible with Type III tests (anovaout is not). Below we call for Type III tests. The anova=FALSE option suppresses display of the full ANOVA table. In the full table there are additional columns for sums of squares, degrees of freedom, mean square, F, and p (significance level). The following results show that racef (the factor version of race) is the predictor with the greatest effect size and that the sexf*racef interaction has the least effect.

```
library("lsr")
etaSquared(anovaout2, type = 3, anova = FALSE )
[Output:]
                 eta.sq eta.sq.part
sexf        0.002660584 0.002789171
racef       0.036784641 0.037230592
sexf:racef  0.001013649 0.001064476
```

2.13.2.5 Raw and estimated marginal means and pairwise comparisons

We may compare levels of a factor variable such as race on some outcome variable such as income. Raw means are used to compare differences on observed income between pairs of races. Estimated marginal means are used to compare income differences also, but marginal means are means controlling for other variables in the model.

```
# Recall the levels of racef
levels(racef)
[Output:]
      [1]    "3"    "1"    "2"
```

```
# Assign value labels to racef. The factor() function is part of base R
racef <- factor(racef,levels = c(3,1,2), labels = c("Other", "White", "Black"))
```

We now get raw means for income by levels of racef. Recall that income is ranged, coded from 1 through 12. The `tapply()` function is part of base R and applies a function to each cell of an array. We also round to two decimal places. In terms of raw mean income, White has the highest income and Black has the lowest.

```
round(tapply(survey$income,racef,mean),2)
[Output:]
   Other  White  Black
   10.31  10.96   9.53
```

The `pairwise.t.test()` function outputs Bonferroni-adjusted paired t-tests on observed means. For all pairs of racef levels, all differences in observed mean income are significant, particularly White vs. Black.

```
pairwise.t.test(survey$income,racef, p.adj = "bonf", pool.sd = FALSE, alternative =
"two.sided")
```

[Output:]

```
        Pairwise comparisons using t tests with non-pooled SD
   data:   income and racef
         Other    White
   White 0.024    -
   Black 0.032    2.4e-11
   P value adjustment method: bonferroni
```

Next, we get estimated marginal means for income by levels of racef. By marginal means on income, "White" has the highest income controlling for other variables in the model. "Black" has the lowest.

```
emmeans(anovaout2,~racef)
```

[Output:]

```
   NOTE: Results may be misleading due to involvement in interactions
   racef emmean     SE   df lower.CL upper.CL
    Other  10.32 0.2071 2044     9.92     10.7
    White  10.97 0.0585 2044    10.85     11.1
    Black   9.62 0.1449 2044     9.34      9.9

   Results are averaged over the levels of: sexf
   Confidence level used: 0.95
```

As a further step we perform Tukey honestly significant difference (HSD) multiple comparison tests. These tests compare estimated marginal means assuming equal variances. SPSS, in contrast, gives slightly different coefficients because it compares raw means when Tukey HSD is requested and SPSS uses the harmonic mean sample size when group sizes are unequal. Recall that for racef, 1 = White, 2 = Black, 3 = Other race. For all pairs of racef levels, all differences in estimated marginal mean income are significant, with 2–1 (Blacks vs. Whites) the most significant.

```
TukeyHSD(anovaout2,"racef")
```

[Output:]

```
      Tukey multiple comparisons of means
        95% family-wise confidence level
   Fit: aov(formula = income ~ sexf + racef + sexf * racef, data = survey)
   $racef
              diff        lwr        upr     p adj
   1-3  0.6433160  0.1403809  1.1462510 0.0076930
   2-3 -0.7520796 -1.3370586 -0.1671005 0.0073254
   2-1 -1.3953955 -1.7514615 -1.0393295 0.0000000
```

2.13.3 GLM univariate: ANCOVA

Since loosely similar to ANOVA output, this ANCOVA section and the MANOVA and MANCOVA sections seek only to present basic elements of their respective models. ANCOVA is simply ANOVA with one or more continuous variables added as covariates. Often such covariates are conceptualized as control variables. For instance, in the previous ANOVA section we sought to determine if there was a relation of sex and race to income. In the following ANOVA model, we seek to determine if this is still true with education (educ) as a control variable.

We start by making sure that contrast options are set to obtain correct b coefficients

```
options(contrasts = c("contr.treatment", "contr.poly"))
```

```
# We then add educ as a covariate, forming an ANCOVA model.
ancovaout <- aov(survey$income ~ sexf + racef + sexf*racef + survey$educ,data=survey)
```

```
# We get the model's coefficients.
ancovaout$coefficients
round(ancovaout$coefficients,3)
```

[Output:]
```
(Intercept)      sexf1       racefWhite     racefBlack
    7.074        0.227            0.522         -0.832
survey$educ sexf1:racefWhite sexf1:racefBlack
    0.238              0.026            0.582
```

We then obtain significance tests for each model effect.
To avoid default Type I sum of squares tests, we reset contrast options to get Type III tests.
This will give results similar to SPSS and other major statistical packages.
```
options(contrasts = c("contr.sum", "contr.poly"))
```
Re-run the model, creating a second output object
```
ancovaout2<- aov(income~sexf+racef+sexf*racef+educ,data=survey)
```
Use the `drop1()` function to ask for Type III tests
```
drop1(ancovaout2,. ~., test=c("F"))
```
[Output:]
```
Single term deletions
Model:
income ~ sexf + racef + sexf * racef + educ
              Df Sum of Sq   RSS    AIC  F value     Pr(>F)
<none>                     10478 3358.5
sexf           1     34.36 10513 3363.2   6.6993   0.009714 **
racef          2    276.79 10755 3407.9  26.9838  2.711e-12 ***
educ           1    920.72 11399 3529.1 179.5190  < 2.2e-16 ***
sexf:racef     2     17.97 10496 3358.0   1.7523   0.173643
---
Signif. codes: 0 '***' 0.001 '**' 0.01 '*' 0.05 '.' 0.1 ' ' 1
```

In conclusion, we find that sex and race are still significantly related to income, even when education is controlled. The sex*race interaction effect, however, is nonsignificant.

We then ask for diagnostic plots for the ANCOVA model. Four are produced but we show only the plot in Figure 2.11.

```
plot(ancovaout)
```

The residuals vs. leverage plot in Figure 2.11 reveals cases with high leverage in the upper right and lower right of the plot. These are highly influential cases (observations 86, 92, and 1,181 in this example), removal of which would change the ANCOVA solution. Similar diagnostic plots are available for all members of the ANOVA family.

2.13.4 GLM multivariate: MANOVA

Multivariate general linear models include multivariate multiple regression (multiple regression with two or more outcomes), MANOVA and MANCOVA models, as well as repeated measures versions of these, all of which support analyses where there is more than one outcome variable explained by one or more predictors. MANCOVA is simply MANOVA where one or more continuous predictor variables (covariates) are present, often conceptualized as control variables.

MANOVA and MANCOVA are used in lieu of separate ANOVA or ANCOVA models for each dependent variable when the researcher deems it important to treat multiple outcome variables as a set because they are well-correlated. Three common purposes of GLM multivariate models are:

- *Comparing group differences*: To compare groups formed by categorical independent variables on group differences for a set of continuous dependent variables.
- *Improving model parsimony*: To use lack of difference for a set of dependent variables as a criterion for reducing them to a smaller, more easily modeled number of variables.
- *Ranking predictor variables by discriminant effect*: To identify the common independent variables, which differentiate values in a set of dependent variables the most.

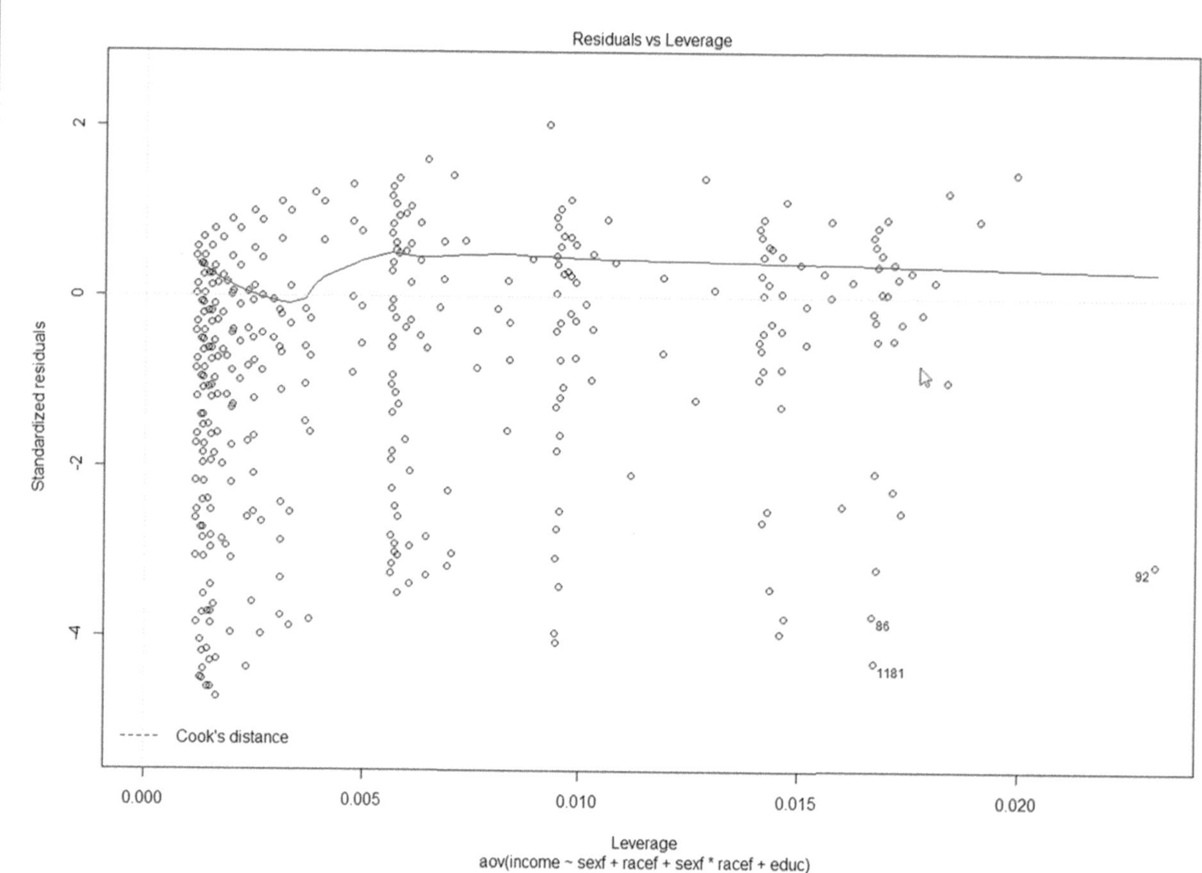

Figure 2.11 Leverage plot for the ANCOVA model

Below we create a MANOVA model similar to the ANOVA model, but we have two outcome variables rather than one. As outcome variables we use income and educ. We still use sex and race as categorical predictors (factors) and assume they have been converted to class "factor" and releveled as described earlier.

First, recall what contrast options are currently in effect.
```
options("contrasts")
```
[Output:]
```
   $contrasts
   [1] "contr.sum"  "contr.poly"
```

If needed, set options to get correct parameter estimates (b coefficients).
```
options(contrasts = c("contr.treatment", "contr.poly"))
```

With proper options set, run the MANOVA model and obtain parameter estimates. Note that by entering the factor interaction as a predictor we also get the main effects for its components, which are racef and sexf. The resulting parameter estimates are the same as in SPSS and other major packages.

```
Y <- cbind(survey$income,survey$educ)
manovaout<<- manova(Y ~ racef*sexf)

manovaout$coefficients
```

[Output:]

```
                    income          educ
(Intercept)    10.19718310 13.14084507
sexf1           0.25281690  0.10915493
racef1          0.63882608  0.49332924
racef2         -0.93875613 -0.44983383
sexf1:racef1    0.01209136 -0.05656646
sexf1:racef2    0.46988821 -0.46997749
```

Next we call for multivariate tests of effects. By default and following practice in some experimental research, `manova()` gives Type I (sequential) significance tests. This means Pillai or other test p levels differ for the factors when reordered, as shown below. The p values for the intercept and the interaction are not affected.

```
manovaout<<- manova(Y ~ racef*sexf)
summary(manovaout, test = c("Pillai"), intercept = TRUE, tol = 1e-7)
```

[Output, race first:]

```
               Df  Pillai approx F num Df den Df     Pr(>F)
(Intercept)     1 0.97134    34624      2   2043 < 2.2e-16 ***
racef           2 0.04930       26      4   4088 < 2.2e-16 ***
sexf            1 0.00504        5      2   2043  0.005755 **
racef:sexf      2 0.00233        1      4   4088  0.311134
Residuals    2044
---
Signif. codes:  0 '***' 0.001 '**' 0.01 '*' 0.05 '.' 0.1 ' ' 1
```

Show Type I significance tests differ when the order of the predictors differs.

```
manovaout<<- manova(Y ~ sexf*racef)

summary(manovaout, test = c("Pillai"), intercept = TRUE, tol = 1e-7)
```

[Output, sex first:]

```
               Df  Pillai approx F num Df den Df     Pr(>F)
(Intercept)     1 0.97134    34624      2   2043 < 2.2e-16 ***
sexf            1 0.00682        7      2   2043 0.0009247 ***
racef           2 0.04767       25      4   4088 < 2.2e-16 ***
sexf:racef      2 0.00233        1      4   4088 0.3111336
Residuals    2044
```

In either sequential order, sum of squares Type I tests show sex and race to be significant predictors and the interaction not to be. This means that by Pillai's test, sex and race are significant predictors of at least one of the outcome variables (income, educ). While Pillai's multivariate test is the default and is popular among R users, in the SPSS and SAS community, the Wilks' test is most common. Moreover, SPSS, SAS, and most commercial packages default to Type III sums of squares, which alter p values somewhat. The `summary()` command supports any of the four common tests, though as here, they usually point to the same substantive inferences. Only one test may be selected in any given `summary()` command. Possible tests are "Pillai", "Wilks", "Hotelling-Lawley", and "Roy".

The `manova()` command does not make provision for Type III multivariate tests, so p values in R will differ from SAS, SPSS, and many other packages. Moreover, the work-around using the `drop1()` function illustrated above for the `aov()` command will not work for the `manova()` command but rather returns the error message, " no 'dropl' method for 'mlm' models", meaning that the manovaout object in this section's example is not of the needed class. This author was not able to locate an R program that output Type III multivariate tests for two-way MANOVA models, though in the constantly evolving R world, some may exist. However, for one-way MANOVA (with only one factor as a predictor), the Type I tests returned by `manova()` will be almost identical to the Type III tests returned by SAS and SPSS.

2.13.5 GLM multivariate: MANCOVA

MANCOVA bears the same relation to MANOVA as ANCOVA does to ANOVA. It is simply MANOVA with one or more covariates. To illustrate MANCOVA, we simply add the covariate age to the MANOVA model. We run this augmented model, putting results in the object "mancovaout". We continue to use Y for the dependent variables, which are income and educ. The resulting parameter estimates are the same as in SPSS and other commercial programs.

```
mancovaout<<- manova(Y ~ racef*sexf + age, data=survey)
mancovaout$coefficients
```

[Output:]

```
                    income        educ
(Intercept)  10.431662205 14.14303692
racef1        0.704551302  0.77424675
racef2       -0.896418153 -0.26887623
sexf1         0.236665323  0.04012114
age          -0.006510761 -0.02782778
racef1:sexf1  0.018718919 -0.02823946
racef2:sexf1  0.484517342 -0.40745081
```

Below, the `summary()` command gives us Type I tests of model effects.

```
mancovaout <- manova(Y ~ racef*sexf + age,  data=survey)

summary(mancovaout, test = c("Pillai"), intercept = TRUE, tol = 1e-7)
```

[Output:]

```
              Df  Pillai approx F num Df den Df     Pr(>F)
(Intercept)    1 0.97183    35228      2   2042 < 2.2e-16 ***
racef          2 0.04975       26      4   4086 < 2.2e-16 ***
sexf           1 0.00504        5      2   2042   0.00577 **
age            1 0.02621       27      2   2042 1.676e-12 ***
racef:sexf     2 0.00224        1      4   4086   0.33305
Residuals   2043
---
Signif. codes:  0 '***' 0.001 '**' 0.01 '*' 0.05 '.' 0.1 ' ' 1
```

Not shown here, but if MANCOVA is run again with the order of factors reversed, tests will differ though for these data not by enough to change the finding by the sequential Type 1 Pillai's test that all main effects factors are significant at the .01 level or better, and the interaction effect is not significant. Note also that the Pillai's test statistic would differ only for the factors, not for the covariate (age) or the intercept.

We now turn to visualization of MANCOVA results using the `ggplot()` command from the ggplot2 package. This command is applicable to most forms of statistical output in R and is not at all limited to MANCOVA, which is used here merely as an example. In general, `ggplot()` allows more customizable plots than does the previously-used `plot()` command from the graphics package, which supports generic x-y plotting.

```
# Run the MANCOVA model again
mancovaout<<- manova(Y ~ sexf*racef + age, data=survey)

# Predict outcome variables (here, income and educ)
pred<- predict(mancovaout)

# Display first six predictions
head(pred)
```

[Output:]

```
      income     educ
1 10.686971 12.99717
2  9.676969 11.03016
3 10.628374 12.74672
4 10.896780 12.81425
5 11.020484 13.34298
6 10.994441 13.23167
```

Preparatory to plotting the MANCOVA model, we create "df" as a data frame containing variables of interest.

```
df<-as.data.frame(cbind(survey$income, survey$educ, survey$age, survey$sex,
survey$race))
df$predincome <- pred[,1]   ## Add income predictions
df$prededuc <- pred[,2]     ## Add educ predictions
```

```
# If needed, re-create racef and sexf as a labeled factor versions of race and sex
racef<-factor(survey$race, labels=cbind("White", "Black", "Other"))
sexf<-factor(survey$sex, labels=cbind("Male", "Female"))
```

First plot the MANCOVA model for all 2,050 observations. We do not show this plot as it is cluttered to interpret, but the reader may wish to try this at home.

```
p  <- ggplot2::ggplot(df, ggplot2::aes(predincome, prededuc))
p + ggplot2::geom_point(ggplot2::aes(colour=racef, shape=sexf, size = survey$age))
```

For simpler output we redo the MANCOVA plot of predicted income and education for just the first 100 cases. This plot is shown in Figure 2.12.

```
p  <- ggplot2::ggplot(df[1:100,], ggplot2::aes(predincome, prededuc))
p + ggplot2::geom_point(ggplot2::aes(colour=racef[1:100], shape=sexf[1:100],
size=survey$age[1:100]))
```

Figure 2.12 displays MANCOVA-based predictions for the two outcome variables, with predincome on the X-axis and prededuc on the Y-axis.

- Race is displayed by color. Higher predicted income and education (the upper right quadrant) are associated with White while lower predicted income and education are associated with Black.
- Male and female are displayed as circles and triangles respectively. In general, males are more likely to be higher in predicted income and education.
- Age is displayed by symbol sizes proportional to age, which is a covariate. In general, as one goes up in education and income, age goes down, shown by smaller symbols.

For comparison, we repeat for observed income and education. This plot is shown in Figure 2.13.

```
p2  <- ggplot2::ggplot(df[1:100,], ggplot2::aes(survey$income[1:100],
survey$educ[1:100]))

p2 + ggplot2::geom_point(ggplot2::aes(colour=racef[1:100], shape=sexf[1:100],
size=survey$age[1:100]))
```

As in any predictive model, trends in predicted values may be at variance with observed values. The weaker the MANOVA or MANCOVA model, the more different. Figure 2.13 shows the same plot for observed values of income and education. While this figure shows that Whites are higher in observed education and income, other patterns are less clear.

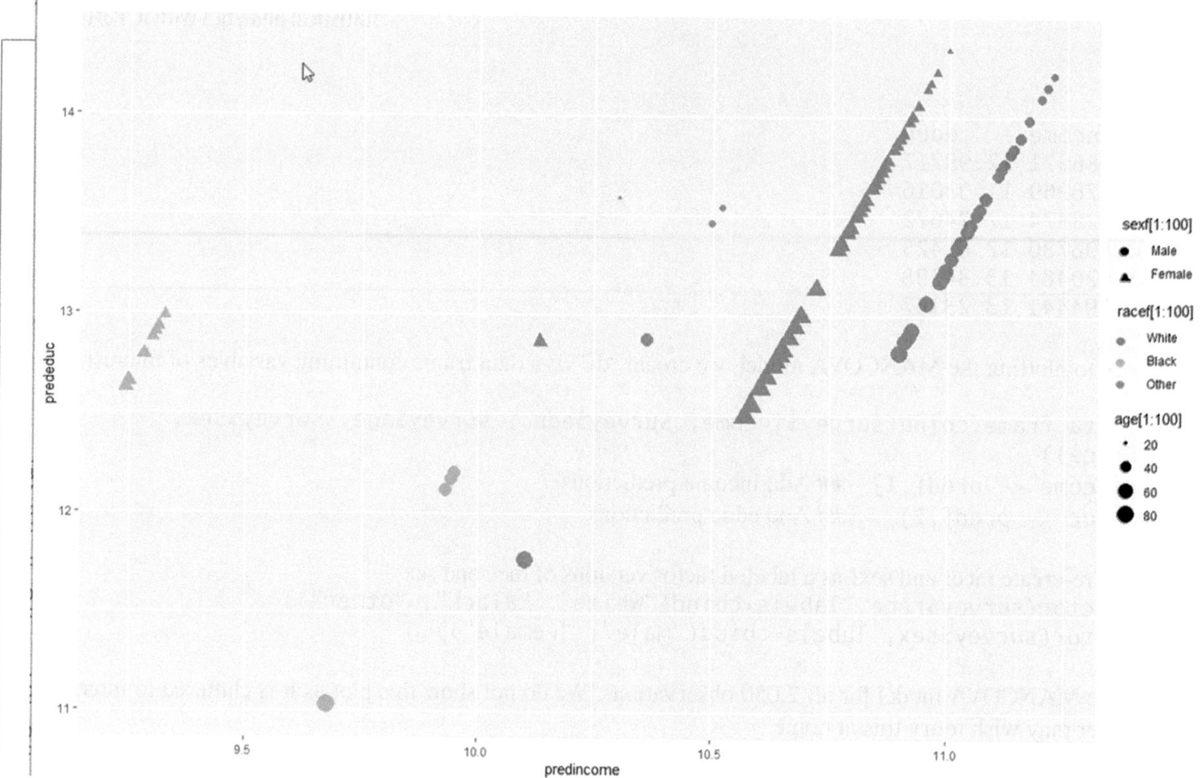

Figure 2.12 MANCOVA plot of predicted income and outcomes with race, sec, and age as predictors

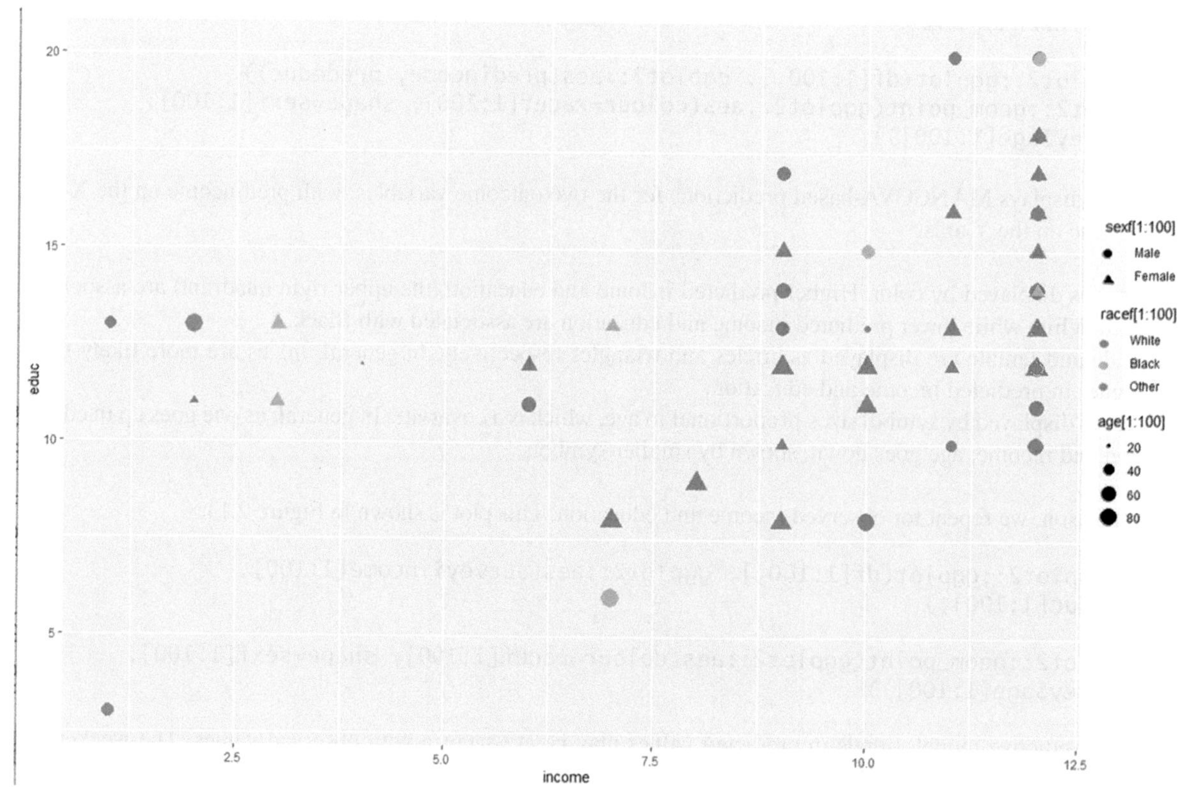

Figure 2.13 MANCOVA plot of observed income and education

Note that many other types of plots are possible than those above, such as plots of predicted means or plots of multivariate outliers.

2.14 Logistic regression

In this section, we use the "world" data as used in an earlier section of this chapter. The notable difference from OLS regression is that the dependent variable for the logistic regression example is "litgtmean", which is a binary variable coded "High" or "Low" according to whether the given nation was above or below the mean national literacy rate of all nations. Because the dependent variable is binary, we must use binary logistic regression in place of OLS linear regression. In a later chapter we use the output from the logistic model as a basis for comparison with the classification tree model for litgtmean, using the same predictor variables.

The logistic model described in this section uses the `glm()` command, specifying the binomial family. This command is also part of the R system "stats" library and does not need explicit installation. However, other needed packages require manual installation: "car", "caret", "e1071", "Metrics", and "pROC" packages. The following setup section sets the working directory, reads in the world data, and activates all of the needed packages.

```
# Setup
setwd("c:/Data")
world <- read.table("world.csv", header = TRUE, sep = ",")

# If needed, use install.packages() to first install the packages below
library(car)            # Used for recoding
library(caret)          # Used for confusion tables
library(e1071)          # Required by the caret package
library(Metrics)        # Used for root mean square error (RMSE)
library(pROC)           # Used for ROC curve analysis
```

Predictor variables remain the same as in the section on linear regression. Factor variables are again automatically treated as sets of dummy variables. The command to create the logistic regression model is below. The `glm()` command is part of the "stats" system library in R and needs no installation. It is similar to the syntax for the `lm()` command for linear regression except that the binomial family of distributions is specified. Results are put in the object "logisticFit".

The dependent variable, litgtmean, is character-coded as "Low" (1) and "High" (0). While this is acceptable for some other commands, `glm()` needs a numeric-coded binary variable. Therefore, we use the `recode()` command from the "car" package to create one, which we label "y". Results are put in the "glm" object "logisticFit".

```
library(car)
y = car::recode(world$litgtmean, "'Low'=1; 'High'=0")

logisticFit <- glm(y ~ regionid+population+areasqmiles+ poppersqmile+coast_
arearatio+ netmigration+Infantdeathsper1k+ infdeaths+gdppercapitalindollars
+phonesper1000+arablepct+ cropspct+otherpct+birthrate+deathrate, family =
'binomial', data=world)

class(logisticFit)
        [1] "glm" "lm"
```

The `summary()` command displays most of the logistic output.

```
summary(logisticFit)
[Output:]
   Call:
   glm(formula = y ~ regionid + population + areasqmiles +poppersqmile +
```

```
    coast_arearatio + netmigration + Infantdeathsper1k + infdeaths +
    gdppercapitalindollars + phonesper1000 + arablepct + cropspct +
    otherpct + birthrate + deathrate, family = "binomial", data =
    world)

Deviance Residuals:
     Min        1Q    Median        3Q       Max
-2.85284  -0.40781  -0.07774   0.27883   2.41022

Coefficients:
                         Estimate Std. Error z value Pr(>|z|)
(Intercept)             2.745e+03  8.205e+03   0.335  0.73792
regionidBA             -1.467e+01  6.173e+03  -0.002  0.99810
regionidCW             -1.953e+01  2.391e+03  -0.008  0.99348
regionidDQ             -1.808e+01  1.075e+04  -0.002  0.99866
regionidEE             -1.529e+01  3.011e+03  -0.005  0.99595
regionidLA              4.778e-01  1.022e+00   0.468  0.64002
regionidNE              1.295e+00  1.128e+00   1.148  0.25109
regionidNF              4.380e+00  1.531e+00   2.861  0.00423 **
regionidNO             -1.502e+01  4.025e+03  -0.004  0.99702
regionidOC              5.240e-01  1.211e+00   0.433  0.66508
regionidSA              1.013e+00  1.111e+00   0.912  0.36203
regionidWE              1.444e+00  1.738e+00   0.831  0.40620
population              4.317e-09  3.773e-09   1.144  0.25248
areasqmiles            -5.253e-07  5.069e-07  -1.036  0.30006
poppersqmile           -1.078e-04  4.303e-04  -0.250  0.80222
coast_arearatio        -1.981e-03  5.671e-03  -0.349  0.72686
netmigration            1.551e-02  6.274e-02   0.247  0.80480
Infantdeathsper1k       2.139e-02  2.780e-02   0.770  0.44158
infdeathsLow           -1.327e+00  1.121e+00  -1.184  0.23644
gdppercapitalindollars -3.787e-05  7.414e-05  -0.511  0.60949
phonesper1000           1.065e-03  3.117e-03   0.342  0.73267
arablepct              -2.750e+01  8.205e+01  -0.335  0.73753
cropspct               -2.752e+01  8.205e+01  -0.335  0.73730
otherpct               -2.748e+01  8.205e+01  -0.335  0.73765
birthrate               1.328e-01  6.135e-02   2.165  0.03039 *
deathrate              -1.155e-01  8.100e-02  -1.426  0.15395
---
Signif. codes:  0 '***' 0.001 '**' 0.01 '*' 0.05 '.' 0.1 ' ' 1
(Dispersion parameter for binomial family taken to be 1)

    Null deviance: 271.69  on 211  degrees of freedom
Residual deviance: 111.73  on 186  degrees of freedom
AIC: 163.73

Number of Fisher Scoring iterations: 18
```

In the output above we see that the most significant variables were regionid followed by birthrate. It is, of course, possible to run a reduced logistic model with just the significant predictors. Since when a variable is dropped from the model all coefficients change, the optimal way to do this is to run a series of logistic models, dropping the one most-nonsignificant variable each time, continuing until all predictors in the final model are significant.

To illustrate a likelihood ratio test, we create a model in which litgtmean (y) is predicted only by the GDP variable, then we use the `anova()` command to execute a likelihood ratio test comparing the full model with the reduced model. Note that the `anova()` command is part of the built-in R stats package and does not require explicit installation.

```
logisticGDP <- glm(y ~  gdppercapitalindollars, family = 'binomial', data=world)

anova(logisticGDP,logisticFit,test="Chisq")
```

[Output:]

```
   Analysis of Deviance Table
  Model 1: litgtmean ~ gdppercapitalindollars
  Model 2: litgtmean ~ regionid + population + areasqmiles + poppersqmile +  coast_
arearatio + netmigration + Infantdeathsper1k + infdeaths + gdppercapitalindollars +
phonesper1000 + arablepct + cropspct + otherpct + birthrate + deathrate
  Resid. Df Resid. Dev Df Deviance  Pr(>Chi)
  1     210     206.06
  2     186     111.73 24   94.331 2.734e-10 ***
  ---
  Signif. codes:  0 '***' 0.001 '**' 0.01 '*' 0.05 '.' 0.1 ' ' 1
```

In the output above, Model 1 is the GDP-only reduced model and Model 2 is the full model. The full model has lower residual deviance (111.73), indicating lower error. It is lower in residual deviance than the GDP model by 94.331. This difference is significant at better than the .001 probability level. We may say the full model is significantly better than the GDP-only model.

The ranking of variables by importance in logistic regression is not done with logistic b coefficients directly but rather is done using odds ratios, which are exponentiated logistic coefficients. The following command gives a list of variables sorted by odds ratio:

```
round(sort(exp(logisticFit$coefficients)),3)
```

[Output:]

```
              cropspct              arablepct               otherpct
                 0.000                  0.000                  0.000
            regionidCW             regionidDQ             regionidEE
                 0.000                  0.000                  0.000
            regionidNO             regionidBA         infdeathsLow
                 0.000                  0.000                  0.265
             deathrate        coast_arearatio           poppersqmile
                 0.891                  0.998                  1.000
gdppercapitalindollars            areasqmiles             population
                 1.000                  1.000                  1.000
         phonesper1000           netmigration      Infantdeathsper1k
                 1.001                  1.016                  1.022
             birthrate             regionidLA             regionidOC
                 1.142                  1.612                  1.689
            regionidSA             regionidNE             regionidWE
                 2.754                  3.651                  4.237
            regionidNF            (Intercept)
                79.859                    Inf
```

The higher the odds ratio above 1.0, the more the variable is associated with an increase in the outcome variable, which here means the more likely the nation is "Low" on litgtmean since that variable was coded High = 0, Low = 1. The strongest effect on Low status on litgtmean controlling for other variables in the model was region (in particular, being in NF = North Africa, followed by WE = Western Europe, NE = Near East, SA = Sub-Saharan Africa, OC = Oceania, or LA = Latin America). The second strongest effect was that higher birthrate, controlling for other variables in the model, predicted being Low on litgtmean. Only regionid and birthrate were significant. (The significance of odds ratios is the same as the significance of the logistic b coefficients on which they are based.)

The lower the odds ratio below 1.0 (i.e., closer to 0), the more the variable is associated with a decrease in litgtmean (y), which means the more likely the nation is "High" on national literacy. The three strongest variables predicting "High", controlling for other variables in the model, were the three land use variables (cropspct, arablepct, and otherpct). None of these coefficients were significant, however, and it is customary not to interpret odds ratios for nonsignificant variables.

After running the logistic model, we then put the predicted (fitted, estimated) values from the logistic regression in the object "OLSLogPred".

```
logisticPred <- fitted(logisticFit)
```

Finally, we add logisticPred as a variable to the "world" data frame. However, this is in memory only unless saved to disk explicitly by the researcher.

```
world$logisticPred <- logisticPred
```

We now determine how well logistic regression predictions correlate with observed values of litgtmean. This will be the comparison/baseline performance metric for classification trees later on. The square of the correlation is the percent of variance explained in the outcome variable, litgtmean.

```
library(car)
y = car::recode(world$litgtmean, "'Low'=1; 'High'=0")
cor(y,logisticPred)
[Output:]
        [1] 0.8061134
```

However, the correlation above is the correlation of fitted values, which are probabilities from 0 to 1 of being in a class of litgtmean, with the outcome in binary numeric form (0, 1). We might instead want the correlation of *classified* fitted values(0, 1) with litgtmean (0, 1). We convert the continuous probabilities into the "High" and "Low" outcomes they imply, putting the result in the object "logisticprobclassified". In doing so we lose information, which attenuates correlation. Both correlations are "correct". Which one is best depends on the research question.

```
logisticprobclassified <- cut(logisticFit$fitted.values, breaks = c(0, .5, 1.0),
labels = c("High", "Low"))

logisticprobclassifiednumeric <- as.numeric(logisticprobclassified)

cor(logisticprobclassifiednumeric, y)
[Output:]
        [1] 0.7550665
```

Another model fit metric is deviance. As listed in output from the `summary()` command above, we see that deviance dropped from 271.69 in the null model to 111.73 in the tested model. Lower corresponds to a better model.

```
    Null deviance: 271.69  on 211  degrees of freedom
Residual deviance: 111.73  on 186  degrees of freedom
```

The amount of the drop could be used in a likelihood ratio test to test which of two models was better, though here we have just the one model.

The `summary()` output above also generates AIC (Akaike Information Criterion), often used to compare models. The model with the lower AIC has less error and better fit. Above, the AIC was 163.73. To be a better model, its AIC would need to be lower than this amount and the difference in deviance would need to be significant by a likelihood ratio test.

Though deviance is the usual loss metric for logistic regression, it is possible to compute RMSE using the "Metrics" package. However, this is not recommended as the `rmse()` function is not appropriate for factor variables, which litgtmean may be considered. However, binary variables are sometimes treated as numeric variables even though they take on only two values. It is possible to recode litgtmean to be considered as numeric, as it is in the "y" variable.

```
predlogistic <-logisticFit$fitted.values
rmse <- Metrics::rmse(predlogistic, y)
rmse
```

[Output:]
```
[1] 0.2802471
```

In summary, predictions from the baseline logistic model correlated at the r = .806 level with observed values of litgtmean. The most significant predictors were regionid followed by birthrate.

Finally, note that there are other types of logistic regression not discussed here.:

- *Multinomial regression*: Handles nominal-level outcomes with more than two levels (categories). Use the `mlogit()` function after installing the "mlogit package.
- *Ordinal regression*: Handles categorical variables whose levels are ordered. Use the `lrm()` function after installing the "rms" package.
- *Robust logistic regression*: Recommended when data contain otherwise problematic outliers and influential cases. Use the `glmRob()` function of the "robust" package.

2.14.1 ROC and AUC analysis

A popular way to assess logistic (and other) models is through ROC curve analysis and the AUC coefficient. ROC stands for "receiver operating characteristic" and AUC stands for "area under the curve". The ROC curve is shown in Figure 2.13. The more the "elbow" of the ROC curve approaches the upper-left corner (the more it deviates from the 45-degree line), the greater the area under the curve. The greater the AUC coefficient, the better the model.

The steps in R to create the ROC plot are these:

```
# Make sure the needed package is still invoked
library(pROC)

# Create numeric vectors for the DV and the predicted values
# The "y" variable was created above as a numerically recoded version of litgtmean
actual <- y
predicted <- logisticPred

# Compute actual-predicted correlation
cor(actual,predicted)
[Output (same as earlier):]
        [1] 0.8061134
# Compute and then plot the ROC curve
# The "pROC::" Package prefix isn't needed here but reminds us of the roc() package
roc_obj <- pROC::roc(actual,predicted)
plot(roc_obj)
```

It can be seen that the ROC curve plots "sensitivity" on the Y-axis against "specificity" on the X-axis. Sensitivity is the true positive rate (TPR) of classification. Specificity is the true negative rate (TNR) of classification. (These terms are explained and illustrated in more detail in Chapter 3.) Figure 2.14 is characteristic of a well-fitting model. How well-fitting is summarized by the AUC coefficient, where higher is better fitting. Here 95% of the area is under the curve.

```
roc_obj$auc
[Output:]
    Area under the curve: 0.9523
```

2.14.2 Confusion table and accuracy

In addition to ROC/AUC, another popular performance metric for logistic binary predictions is the "confusion table" and its associated statistics, such as accuracy. The confusion table, also called the classification table or hit

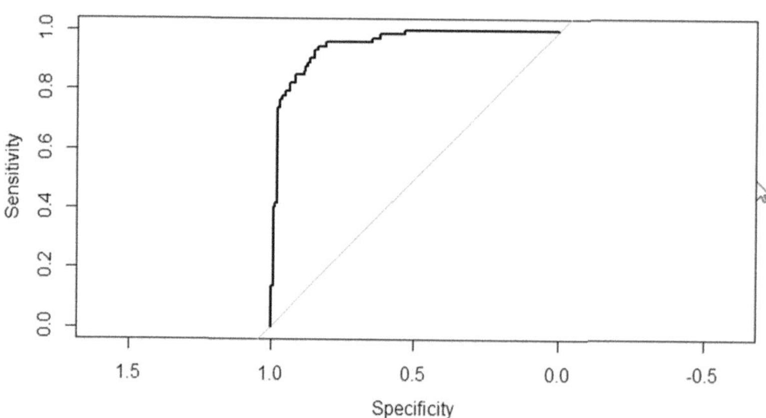

Figure 2.14 ROC curve for the logistic model

table, is a 2-by-2 table showing the number of observations correctly and incorrectly classified. "Accuracy" is simply the number of correct observations divided by *n*. We illustrate continuing to use litgtmean (y) as the binary outcome example. We also continue to use logisticFit, which was the output object created by the `glm()` command at the beginning of this section.

Recall that the logisticprobclassified object, created earlier, was the version of logisticFit with character values ("High", "Low"), corresponding to litgtmean as originally coded.

```
class(logisticprobclassified)
     [1] "factor"
head(logisticprobclassified)
     [1] Low  Low  Low  High High Low
     Levels: High Low
```

With observed and predicted being compatible (both are character type), we can create the confusion matrix with a simple `table()` command. Note predicted precedes observed in the syntax to get predicted as rows.

```
confusiontable <- table(logisticprobclassified, as.factor(world$litgtmean), dnn=c("P
redicted","Observed"))

confusiontable
```

[Output:}

```
          Observed
Predicted High Low
     High  131  14
     Low     9  58
```

The following command calculates accuracy, which is quite high at 89%.

```
accuracy = sum(diag(confusiontable))/ sum(confusiontable)
accuracy
```

[Output:}

```
     [1] 0.8915094
```

However, it is easier to use the `confusionMatrix()` command of the "caret" package. This package in turn requires that the "e1071" package be active. The syntax below computes the confusion matrix, accuracy, and many related coefficients. These coefficients are discussed in Chapter 3.

```
library(e1071)
caret::confusionMatrix(logisticprobclassified,as.factor(world$litgtmean))
```

[Output:]
```
Confusion Matrix and Statistics
          Reference
Prediction High Low
      High  131  14
      Low     9  58

               Accuracy : 0.8915
          95% CI : (0.8417, 0.93)
    No Information Rate : 0.6604
    P-Value [Acc > NIR] : 6.666e-15

                  Kappa : 0.754
 Mcnemar's Test P-Value : 0.4042
            Sensitivity : 0.9357
            Specificity : 0.8056
         Pos Pred Value : 0.9034
         Neg Pred Value : 0.8657
             Prevalence : 0.6604
         Detection Rate : 0.6179
    tection Prevalence : 0.6840
      Balanced Accuracy : 0.8706
       'Positive' Class : High
```

2.15 Mediation and moderation

Social scientists seek to understand the causal structure of variables they wish to model. In bivariate correlation the researcher posits a cause (X) and an effect (Y). Unfortunately, there are few situations in life where two variables constitute the appropriate model. As the researcher adds more variables to the model, complex questions of causation arise. Does a third variable interact with X (moderation)? Does it intervene between X and Y (mediation)? Does it mask the effect of X on Y (suppression)? Does it only seem to have an effect but the effect is not real (spuriousness)?

In this section, we will use the "processR" package developed in 2019 by Keon-Woong Moon to implement mediation and moderation analysis. There are several alternative packages including using the `mediate()` and `setCor()` functions of the "psych" package, as described by Revelle (2017). Among other related packages are also "medmod", which integrates the R modeling package "lavaan" for computational purposes (Selker, 2017); the "mediation" package (Tingley et al., 2014); and the "processr" package by Mark White (2018). Because processR uses maximum likelihood estimation, bootstrapped estimates of standard errors, and has other algorithmic differences, coefficients are not exactly the same as in SPSS, SAS, or in Hayes (2013; uses SPSS or SAS) and Garson (2017; also uses SPSS or SAS), but are substantively similar. An R version from Andrew Hayes has been announced for 2021 but was not available at this writing.

The example data file for this section is "protest", which originates from the work of Garcia et al. (2010). The "protest" dataset has been widely used to illustrate mediation and moderation analysis, as by Hayes (2013, 2018), Revelle (2017), and others. There are various versions of this dataset in circulation. Some have two levels of protest and some have three. Some include an "anger" variable and others do not. Some include variables representing interaction effects. Some center variables and others (notably Hayes) do not. Coefficients illustrating mediation and moderation may differ depending on the data version used.

In this section, we use the version of "protest.csv", which comes with this book. For this version, there are two levels of protest, variables are not centered and there are no missing values. We use this dataset to illustrate moderated mediation of Hayes's type called "Model 7". Hayes, however, used other data to illustrate this model (Hayes, 2013: 425, 432, 439). Moreover, this dataset is not identical to that used in the original Garcia et al. (2010) research nor is the model explored. The protest.csv dataset is supplied for instructional purposes only and should not be used for substantive research.

TEXT BOX 2.2 "Social science applications of R: Mediation/ moderation analysis of community cooperation"

O'Brien and Tyler (2020) studied the ability of authorities to shape community cooperation. Using the regression and the R package "mediation" (Tingley et al., 2017), built a moderated mediation model with "Cooperation" as the outcome (Y) caused by "Trust-building Strategy" (X), with "Sincerity" as the mediator (M) and "Trust-building Focus" as the moderator (W). Based on data from three experiments, the authors were able to conclude that "reconciliatory gestures (e.g., group-level initiatives by authorities to build trust with communities) emphasizing trust-building approaches to authority can increase community members' voluntary cooperation with authorities." In one experiment, for instance, it was demonstrated that African Americans were more willing to report crimes after authorities invited community involvement in forming policing strategies. The authors also used the R package "outliers" (Komsta, 2015) to first remove 19 observations deemed to be outliers.

Source: Komsta, L. (2015). Package outliers. Retrieved from https://cran.r-project.org/web/packages/outliers/outliers.pdf

O'Brien, T. C. (2019). Materials for "Authorities and Communities: Can authorities shape cooperation with communities on a group level?" Retrieved from https://osf.io/tk8us/

O'Brien, Thomas C. & Tyler, Tom R. (2020). Authorities and communities: Can authorities shape cooperation with communities on a group level? *Psychology, Public Policy, and Law* 26(1): 69–87.

Tingley, D.; Yamamoto, T.; Hirose, K.; Keele, L.; & Imai, K. (2017). Mediation: R package for causal mediation analysis. Retrieved from https://cran.rproject.org/web/packages/mediation/vignettes/mediation.pdf on 12/20/2018

```
# Setup: Declare working directory, read in data, and install needed packages
# Use install.packages() if packages are not in your user library
setwd("c:/Data")
protest <- read.table("protest.csv", header = TRUE, sep = ",")
library(processR)
library(lavaan)

# We would do this, omitting the comment hashtags,
# if we wanted the version of protest, which is in the processR package:
# data(protest)
# force(protest)
# View(protest)
```

The protest dataset consists of 129 female respondents who answered survey questions giving their reactions to a written scenario in which Catherine, a female attorney, was bypassed for a promotion by a less qualified male attorney. After reading the scenario respondents were asked to react to how Catherine responded to sexual discrimination by the senior partners at her law firm. On a random basis respondents were told Catherine told the partners the decision was unfair and asked that they reconsider (protest = 1) or that Catherine continued with the firm without taking any action (protest = 0). After receiving Catherine's response, subjects were asked to rate Catherine on six items, which were aggregated into the "liking" variable, with higher being liking more. Each subject also took the Modern Sexism Scale, a measure of how widespread the subject felt sex discrimination is in society (the sexism variable, with higher = more pervasive).

The research purpose was to see if Catherine's reaction (protest or not) affected how subjects evaluated her (liking), and if this relationship was influenced by the subject's perception of the pervasiveness of sex discrimination (sexism). The copy of protest.csv accompanying this text already contains these needed variables:

- *protest2*: X, a 2-category version of protest, similar to Hayes (2013) and Garson (2017), coded 0 = Catherine did not protest, 1 = Catherine did protest.

- *liking*: Y, the dependent variable, coded on a 7-point scale with higher being liking Catherine more.
- *respappr*: M1, the potential mediating variable, coded on a 7-point scale with higher feeling that Catherine's response was appropriate.
- *sexism*: W, the potential moderating variable, coded on an 8-point scale with higher being perceiving sex discrimination to be more pervasive in society.
- *intXW*: the interaction X*W.

We do not use centering in this example but for instructional purposes centered variables may be created by the commands below (remove the comment line hashtags). Alternative methods include the `meanCentering()` command in the processR package.

```
# cprotest <- scale(protest$protest,center=TRUE,scale=FALSE)
# csexism <- scale(protest$sexism,center=TRUE,scale=FALSE)
# crespappr <- scale(protest$respappr,center=TRUE,scale=FALSE)
# cliking <- scale(protest$liking,center=TRUE,scale=FALSE)
# Then add the centered variables to the protest data frame
# protest$cprotest <- cprotest
# protest$csexism <- csexism
# protest$crespappr <- crespappr
# protest$cliking <- cliking
# Optionally the augmented protest database to a. csv file in the working directory
# write.csv(protest, file = "protest_centered.csv", row.names = FALSE)
```

The leading work on mediation and moderation is Hayes (2013, 2018). Hayes defined dozens of such models, varying according to the number of predictors, dependents, mediators, and moderators. While his work was for the SPSS and SAS environments, the processR package brings much the same functionality to R, at this writing supporting 52 of Hayes's models. To list the model numbers, type `sort(processR::pmacro$no)`. To see all models type `processR::showModels()`, which brings up all models in a Shiny application in one's browser. Numbers in this listing correspond to model numbers used by Hayes. In the current example, we will use model 7, illustrated below.

To view a particular model such as Model 7, use the `pmacroModel()` command. The result is shown in Figure 2.15. In this model, X causes Y (protest causes liking) but there is also a mediated (indirect) path from X to Y by way of one or more mediator variables, Mi (respappr). Also, the strength of the path from X to M is moderated by W (sexism). That is, the strength of the protest -> liking path will be influenced by the level of sexism. Note that the command `showModels()` brings up a window in which all models may be viewed.

```
processR::pmacroModel(7)
```

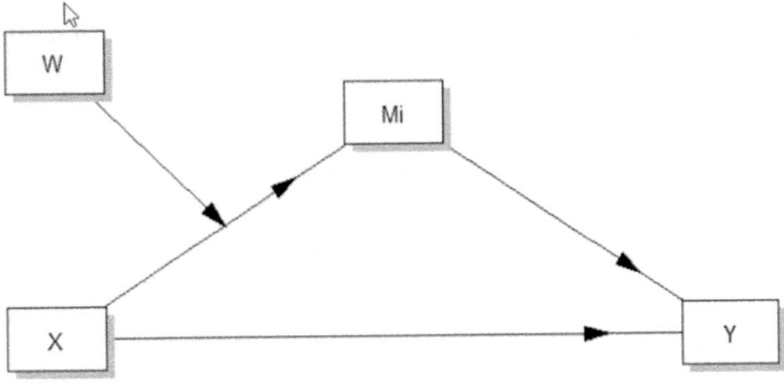

Figure 2.15 Model 7 – Mediation with moderation

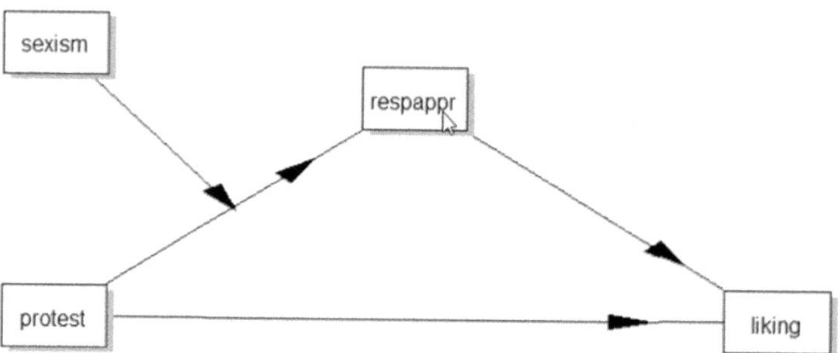

Figure 2.16 Model 7 – Variable labels

For the example in this section, the variables are:

- X protest A causal experimental condition (0 = no protest, 1 = protest)
- Y liking The DV, liking of the target (7-point Likert scale)
- M respappr A mediator, appropriateness of response (7-point Likert scale)
- W sexism A moderator, perceived pervasiveness of sex discrimination

We can diagram the same model (model 7) with actual variable names with the commands below. We use the uncentered versions of the variables. Figure 2.16 shows this diagram.

```
labels=list(X="protest",M="respappr",Y="liking",W="sexism")
processR::pmacroModel(7,labels=labels)
```

The model in Figures 2.15 and 2.16 is the conceptual model. However, the relation of the model to regression equations better seen in the statistical model shown in Figure 2.17. This model diagram is created with the following command.

```
processR::statisticalDiagram(7)
```

In the statistical model the arrow in the conceptual model connecting W (sexism) to the arrow from X (protest) to Mi (respappr) is replaced by the main effect of W on Mi plus the X*W interaction effect on Mi. If there is a moderation effect, then there is an interaction effect. Put simply, moderation is interaction. If the interaction term is significant, then there is moderation.

In the manual method below, we compute the fit of the structural equation model using the `sem()` command from the lavaan package.[9] First we define the moderator variable, which is sexism. As can be seen in Figure 2.18, the moderator variable impacts path “a” in the model.

```
# Therefore the “site” for the moderator in this Model 7 example is “a”.
# The site will differ depending on model number.
moderator = list(name="sexism", site=list(c("a")))

# The command below uses the tripleEquation() function of the processR package to create the “model” object containing the solution.
model = tripleEquation(X = "protest", M = "respappr", Y = "liking",
moderator=moderator)
```

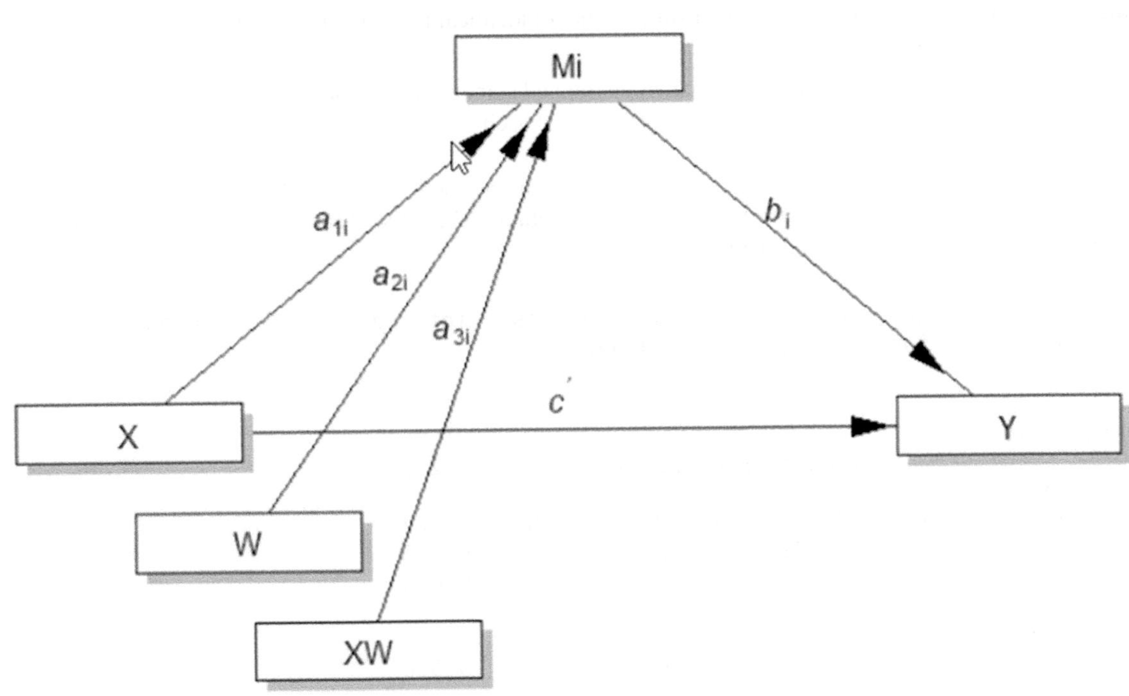

Figure 2.17 Model 7 – Statistical model

```
# Optionally, the cat() command from R's "base" package lists the model.
# The cat() command, which is optional here, is a function to concatenate and print.
cat(model)
```

[Output: Note that the user does not type the commands below into R].

```
respappr~a1*protest+a2*sexism+a3*protest:sexism
liking~c*protest+b*respappr
sexism ~ sexism.mean*1
sexism ~~ sexism.var*sexism
CE.XonM :=a1+a3*sexism.mean
indirect :=(a1+a3*sexism.mean)*(b)
index.mod.med :=a3*b
direct :=c
total := direct + indirect
prop.mediated := indirect / total
CE.XonM.below :=a1+a3*(sexism.mean-sqrt(sexism.var))
indirect.below :=(a1+a3*(sexism.mean-sqrt(sexism.var)))*(b)
CE.XonM.above :=a1+a3*(sexism.mean+sqrt(sexism.var))
indirect.above :=(a1+a3*(sexism.mean+sqrt(sexism.var)))*(b)
direct.below:=c
direct.above:=c
total.below := direct.below + indirect.below
total.above := direct.above + indirect.above
prop.mediated.below := indirect.below / total.below
prop.mediated.above := indirect.above / total.above
```

Having created the model, next the model must be fitted. The "lavaan" package (R's main SEM package) is used for this. We ask for settings which give output similar but not identical to major statistics packages:

- se='standard' asks for standard rather than bootstrapped standard errors (se's).
- information='observed' asks that se's be computed based on observed rather than expected (predicted) values.
- observed.information='h1' calls for use of an approximation based on the observed information matrix of the unrestricted (h1) model (in contrast to the "hessian" default, where the observed information matrix is based on the hessian of the objective function).

```
semfit = lavaan::sem(model = model, data=protest, information = "observed",
observed.information = "h1", se = "standard")
summary(semfit)
```
[Partial output:]
```
  Regressions:
                     Estimate  Std.Err  z-value  P(>|z|)
  respappr ~
    protest     (a1)   -2.687    1.439   -1.866    0.062
    sexism      (a2)   -0.529    0.232   -2.276    0.023
    prtst:sxs   (a3)    0.810    0.280    2.897    0.004
  liking ~
    protest      (c)   -0.101    0.202   -0.499    0.618
    respappr     (b)    0.402    0.070    5.726    0.000
```

The `summary()` command above gives the mediation/moderation output. A command with more options would add SEM fit statistics to the output: `summary(semfit, fitmeasures = TRUE)`. The summary output is much more extensive than shown in the partial listing above. Full output has sections for general model information, covariances, intercepts, variances, and more. The regression portion of the output above tells which paths in the model are significant. Standard error and p values are not identical to those in Hayes (2013) and in major packages, but are close and yield the same substantive inferences. Path labels (a1, a2, etc.) are those shown in Figure 2.17. For this example, the significant paths are a2, a3, and b. Other paths are not significant.

Next we plot the model with estimated unstandardized and standardized coefficients. The `statisticalDiagram()` function of rpocessR is used to compute these path coefficients. The unstandardized coefficients are virtually the same as those from major packages. However, because standardized coefficients are based on standard error estimates, which are a bit different in lavaan than in the algorithms of major packages, the model standardized coefficients also differ a bit, though still close.

```
# For value labeling with unstandardized b coefficients, use "est" labels.
# Recall that the "labels" object for variable names was created earlier.
processR::statisticalDiagram(7,labels=labels,fit=semfit,whatLabel="est")

# For standardized coefficients use "std" value labels:
processR::statisticalDiagram(7,labels=labels,fit=semfit,whatLabel="std")
```

In Figure 2.18 the unstandardized regression (path) coefficients are displayed. The left-most arrow (a1 = -2.687) is for the path from protest (X) to respappr(Mi) and as noted above, it is not significant. However, both the main effect of the moderator (W = sexism) and the interaction of the protest with sexism (XW = protest:sexism) were significant. Also, the path from respappr (M1) to liking (Y) was significant (b = 0.402).

The conclusion is that for the protest data, moderation by sexism was not upheld. Moderation was represented by the path from protest to respappr to liking, but in this compound path, the leg from protest to respappr was not

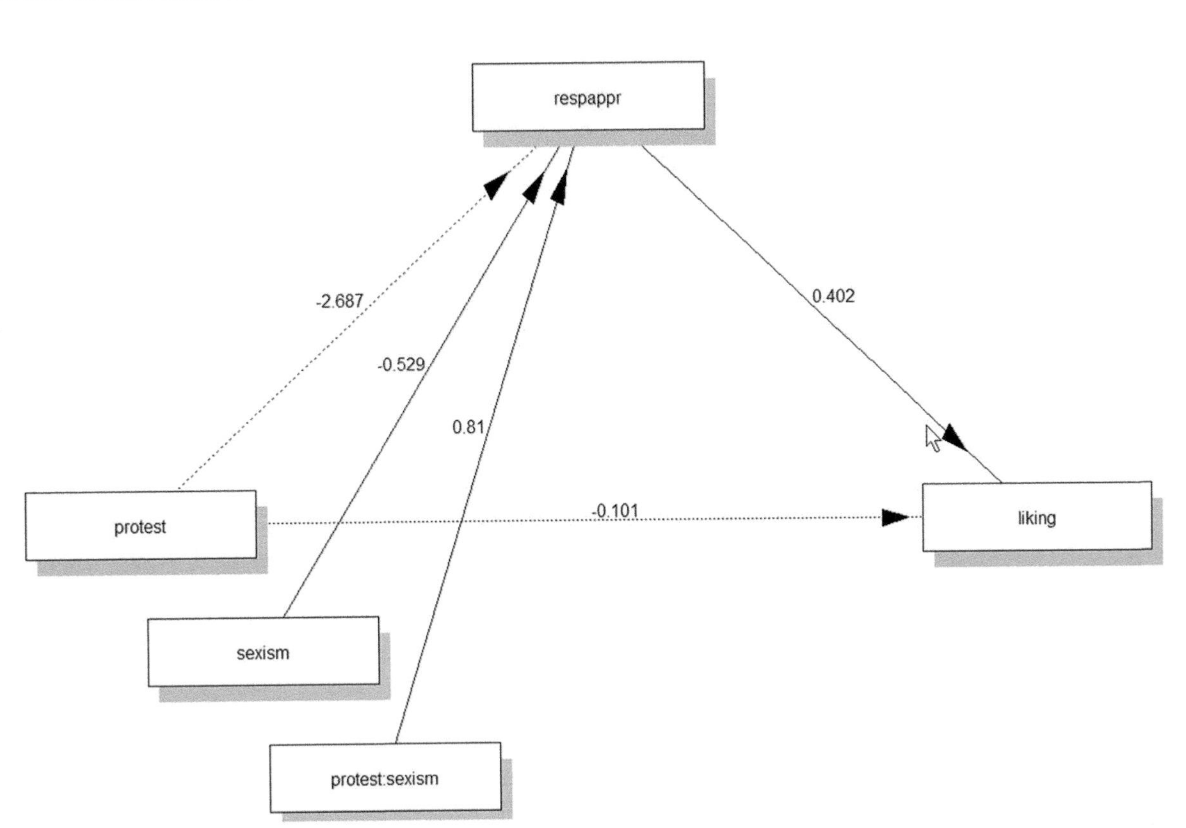

Figure 2.18 Model 7 – Unstandardized path coefficients

significant even though the second leg (from respappr to liking) was significant. Moderation of the protest-respappr relationship was upheld because the protest-sexism interaction is a significant predictor of respappr. This means that although the protest-respappr relationship is nonsignificant overall, there are some values of sexism for which this relationship is significant. Note that this means that in mediation-moderation analysis is not enough to find a moderation (interaction) effect to be significant. One must also do slope analysis, discussed further below, to show how the moderator affects the strength of relationship (slope) of the predictor variable (here, protest) for the affected path (here, path a1).

Next, the output from the `estimatesTable()` function of the processR package lists much more model information: The variables, their respective predictors, the formulas for various effects, and estimates for unstandardized b coefficients, standard errors, z values, p values, and standardized beta weights (standardized path coefficients). Note that the formulas defining some effects may differ from other packages. For instance, the indirect path from protest to liking is not the simple product of path a1 times b1. Rather it is (a1+a3*sexism.mean)*(b1). That is, the indirect path as defined in lavaan (and therefore in processR) takes the moderator into account.

Note also that the b and beta weights in the output below are the coefficients which appeared in Figures 2.18 and 2.19. Also, the significance of the direct and indirect paths linking protest to liking is shown: The indirect path is significant while the direct path is not (as we saw above in the regression table). This highlights the fact that although path a1 (protest to respappr) is not significant on a simple basis as shown in the regression table, the indirect effect (as defined in the formulas in output below) taking the moderator variable sexism into account is significant.

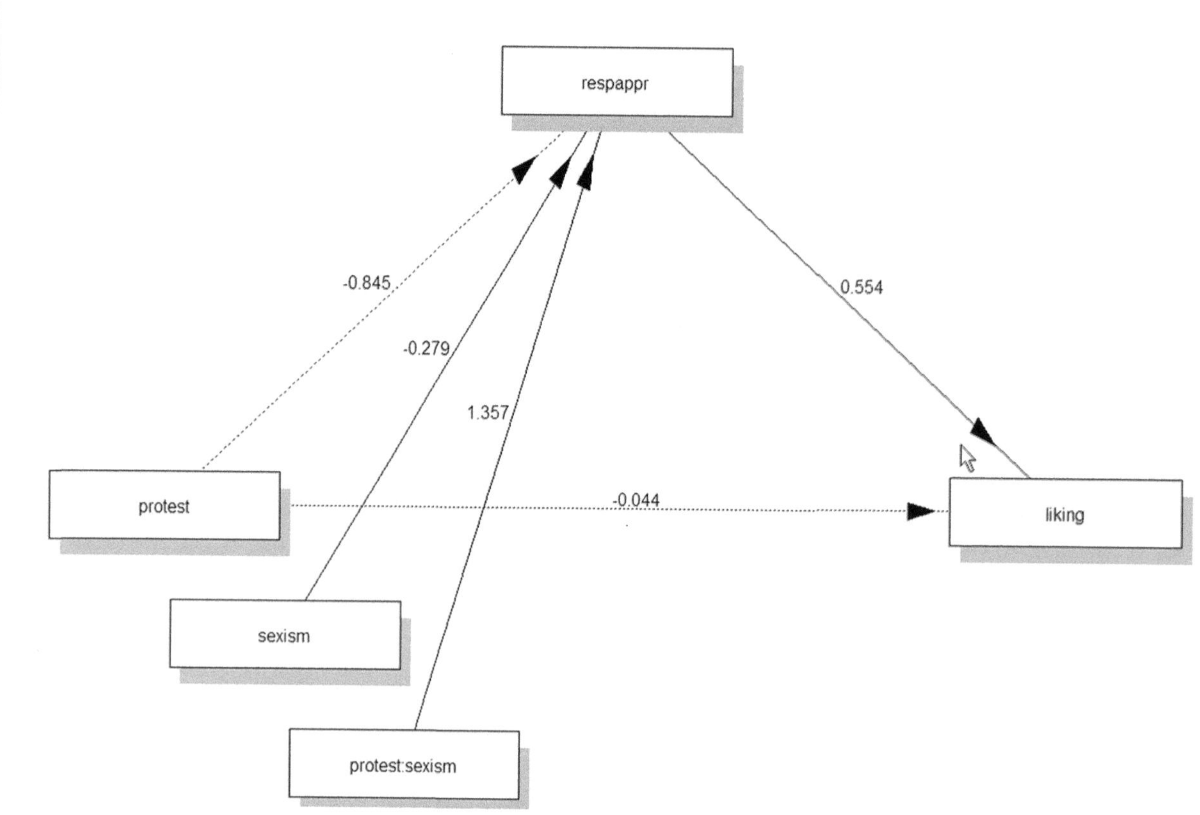

Figure 2.19 Model 7 – Standardized path coefficients

```
estimatesTable(semfit, latent = TRUE, regression = TRUE, mediation = TRUE, covar =
FALSE, ci = FALSE, standardized = TRUE, digits = 3)
```

[Output:]

```
              Variables                             Predictors               label
1              respappr                                protest                  a1
2              respappr                                 sexism                  a2
3              respappr                         protest:sexism                  a3
4                liking                                protest                   c
5                liking                               respappr                   b
6                sexism                                                 sexism.mean
7                sexism                                 sexism                sexism.var
17              CE.XonM                     a1+a3*sexism.mean
CE.XonM
18      indirect effect             (a1+a3*sexism.mean)*(b)              indirect
19      indirect effect                                 a3*b           index.mod.med
20               direct                                    c                direct
21         total effect                      direct+indirect                 total
22        prop.mediated                       indirect/total         prop.mediated
23        CE.XonM.below      a1+a3*(sexism.mean-sqrt(sexism.var))      CE.XonM.below
24      indirect effect (a1+a3*(sexism.mean-sqrt(sexism.var)))*(b)  indirect.below
25        CE.XonM.above      a1+a3*(sexism.mean+sqrt(sexism.var))      CE.XonM.above
26      indirect effect (a1+a3*(sexism.mean+sqrt(sexism.var)))*(b)  indirect.above
27         direct.below                                    c          direct.below
28         direct.above                                    c          direct.above
29         total effect          direct.below+indirect.below           total.below
30         total effect          direct.above+indirect.above           total.above
```

```
31 prop.mediated.below                     indirect.below/total.below  prop.mediated.below
32 prop.mediated.above                      indirect.above/total.above  prop.mediated.above
        B    SE      z        p      ß
1   -2.687 1.439 -1.866   0.062 -0.845
2   -0.529 0.232 -2.276   0.023 -0.279
3    0.810 0.280  2.897   0.004  1.357
4   -0.101 0.202 -0.499   0.618 -0.044
5    0.402 0.070  5.726 < 0.001  0.554
6    5.117 0.069 74.441 < 0.001  6.554
7    0.610 0.076  8.024 < 0.001  1.000
17   1.458 0.221  6.604 < 0.001  8.049
18   0.587 0.136  4.325 < 0.001  4.460
19   0.326 0.120  2.722   0.006  0.752
20  -0.101 0.202 -0.499   0.618 -0.044
21   0.486 0.200  2.428   0.015  4.417
22   1.207 0.484  2.492   0.013  1.010
23   0.826 0.308  2.682   0.007  6.692
24   0.332 0.141  2.356   0.018  3.708
25   2.090 0.318  6.579 < 0.001  9.406
26   0.841 0.187  4.496 < 0.001  5.212
27  -0.101 0.202 -0.499   0.618 -0.044
28  -0.101 0.202 -0.499   0.618 -0.044
29   0.232 0.220  1.052   0.293  3.665
30   0.740 0.223  3.318   0.001  5.169
31   1.435 1.222  1.174   0.240  1.012
32   1.136 0.300  3.791 < 0.001  1.008
```

From the `estimatesTable()` output we may make these statements:

- The indirect effect of protest on liking by way of respappr is much larger than the direct effect of protest on liking, which is nonsignificant. The indirect effect in output line 18 has a standardized (beta) weight of 4.460 compared to the direct effect in line 20 with a beta weight of -0.044.
- The proportion mediated is the indirect effect (line 18) divided by the total effect (line 21) = 4.460/4.417 = 1.01 in line 22. Because the direct effect is negative and the indirect effect is positive, there is suppression giving a value slightly larger than 1.0.
- The "above" and "below" rows present lower and upper confidence limits on other rows in the table. For example, rows 31 and 32 are the lower and upper confidence limits on the proportion mediated, which is row 22. The proportion mediated is 1.010, within the 95% confidence limits of 1.008 and 1.012.

The `modmedSummary()` and `modmedSummaryTable()` functions of the processR package support conditional analysis of effects. The effect in question is that from protest (X) to liking (Y). Conditional analysis compares the direct effect at various levels of the moderator variable, which is sexism (W). To create the conditional effects table we use the following two commands:

```
x = processR::modmedSummary(semfit,mod="sexism", boot.ci.type = "perc")
processR::modmedSummaryTable(x)
```

[Output:]

	Indirect Effect (a1+a3*W)*(b1)			**Direct Effect c1**		
sexism(W)	**estimate**	**95% Bootstrap CI**	***p***	**estimate**	**95% Bootstrap CI**	***p***
4.336	0.332	(0.056 to 0.609)	.018	-0.101	(-0.496 to 0.295)	.618
5.117	0.587	(0.321 to 0.853)	<.001	-0.101	(-0.496 to 0.295)	.618
5.898	0.841	(0.474 to 1.208)	<.001	-0.101	(-0.496 to 0.295)	.618
						boot.ci.type = perc

In the table above, the moderator, sexism, ranges from a minimum of 4.336 to 5.898, with a mean of 5.117. The direct and indirect effects protest on liking are shown at when sexism is at its mean. Note that effect estimates are shown in unstandardized form. Note also that the indirect estimate (0.587) when sexism is at its mean is the same estimate as given earlier in `estimatesTable()` output for the indirect effect.

From the conditional analysis we conclude that as sexism increases, the estimate of the indirect effect also increases. The indirect effect is significant by bootstrap methods at all three levels shown in the table. The direct effect is not significant at any level of sexism. These conditional effects are visualized in Figure 2.20, plotted with this command:

```
processR::conditionalEffectPlot(semfit, data=protest, mod="sexism")
```

Again, Figure 2.20 shows that as sexism increases, so too does the indirect effect of protest (X) on liking (Y) by way of respappr (M).

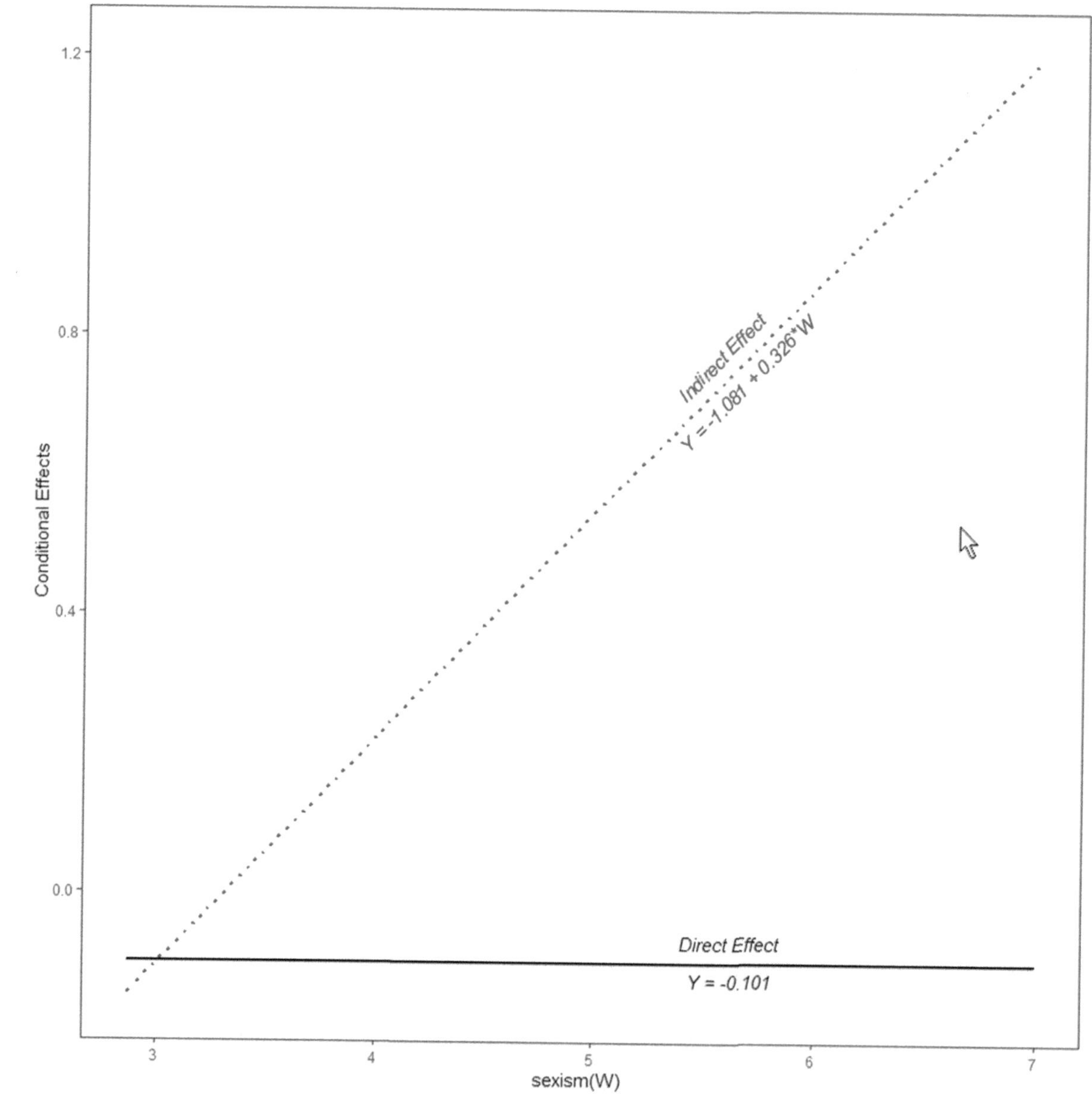

Figure 2.20 Model 7–Conditional Effects Plot

2.16 Chapter 2 command summary

For convenience for those wishing to try models out for themselves, this book's Support Material (www.routledge.com/9780367624293) contains a listing of the main commands used in Chapter 2. This listing may be handy for readers following along with the book using their home or office computers. For topics presented as online supplements (MDS and loglinear analysis), the command summary is at the end of these supplements.

Endnotes

1. The "ISLR" package from James et al. (2017) contains a number of teaching dataset.
   # Install the package "ISLR", which contains the data to be used.
   # This package contains only a collection of teaching datasets, listed below.
   # Data are from James et al. (2017).
   # If other data are to be used, it is not necessary to install this package.
   ```
   install.packages("ISLR")
   ```
   # Invoke the ISLR package.
   ```
   library(ISLR)
   ```
   # Optionally, view information about the ISLR package.
   ```
   library(help = "ISLR")
   ```
   # Declare ISLR to be the package containing the dataset to be used.
   ```
   data(package = "ISLR")
   ```
   # Load any of the datasets, such as College into a data frame.
   # Note R is case sensitive.
   # The dataset carseats will now be listed under the "Environment" tab in RStudio.
   # Double-click on it to make it appear spreadsheet-style in the View pane of RStudio.
   ```
   College <- College
   ```
   Datasets contained in James et al. (2017) and available as part of the "ISLR" package:
   Index:

Auto	Auto Data Set
Caravan	The Insurance Company (TIC) Benchmark
Carseats	Sales of Child Car Seats
College	U.S. News and World Report's College Data
Credit	Credit Card Balance Data
Default	Credit Card Default Data
Hitters	Baseball Data
Khan	Khan Gene Data
NCI60	NCI 60 Data
OJ	Orange Juice Data
Portfolio	Portfolio Data
Smarket	S&P Stock Market Data
Wage	Mid-Atlantic Wage Data
Weekly	Weekly S&P Stock Market Data

2. The corresponding Stata command is:
   ```
   regress(literacy i.regionid population areasqmiles poppersqmile coast _ arearatio netmigration Infantdeathsper1k i.infdeaths gdppercapitalindollars phonesper1000 arablepct cropspct otherpct birthrate deathrate)
   ```
   Add the option ", beta" to obtain beta coefficients.
3. See https://www.rdocumentation.org/packages/fastcluster/versions/1.1.25/topics/hclust
4. See elaboration on BSS/TSS by Luc Anselm at https://geodacenter.github.io/workbook/7bk_clusters_1a/lab7b.html
5. Source: https://www.stat.berkeley.edu/~s133/Cluster2a.html
6. If normalization is needed, use the `scale()` function in this way:
   ```
   trainscaled <-scale(judges[1:200,])
   ```
7. The output below shows Type I F test results.

   # Note `aov()` defaults to this option setting:
   ```
   # options(contrasts = c("contr.treatment", "contr.poly"))anovaout
   ```

[Output:]

```
Call:
    aov(formula = income ~ sexf + racef + sexf * racef, data = survey)
Terms:
                   sexf     racef sexf:racef Residuals
Sum of Squares   75.714   496.476     12.147 11398.943
Deg. of Freedom       1         2          2      2044
Residual standard error: 2.361521
Estimated effects may be unbalanced
```

8. The contr.SAS specification is like contr.treatment but sets the base level to be the last level of the factor. The contr.sum specification sets contrast codes which sum to zero, giving orthogonal contrasts comparing each level to the overall mean. Finally, the contr.helmert specification returns contrasts which contrast the second level with the first, the third with the average of the first two, and so on.
9. A "Shiny" app is available to avoid manual computation of the regression model. It is available at https://cardiomoon.shinyapps.io/processR/. A tutorial on the app is at https://rpubs.com/cardiomoon/468600. The app will both construct the necessary regression equations and also implement analysis, giving final output discussed further below. The app steps for the example are these:

    1. In the "Select Data" area, click "Browse" and load protest.csv as created above.
    2. In the "Select Process Macro Model Number" area, select 7 for Model 7. You may display either the conceptual or statistical diagram at this point.
    3. In the "Assign Variables" area, assign the X, Mi, Y, and W variables (protest, respappr, liking, and sexism, respectively).
    4. In the "Make Equation" area, click "make Equation". The set of appropriate equations will appear in a text box. These equations could have been typed into RStudio, but the "shiny app" automates the process. There is a "reset Equation" button which would allow the researcher to customize the set of equations. These equations also are shown at the top of output from the app.
    5. The "Options" area has a drop-down list of ways to handle missing data. Ignore this since the protest data have no missing values.
    6. In the "Analysis" area, click "Analysis". After brief computation time, statistical output, tables, and plots are printed in the user's browser (in which the app is running). There is also a button to "download PPTx" and to "select plot font". One may also select Edit > Copy from one's browser and then Home > Paste in Word, but if using this method, then one will also have to right-click on each plot and "Save image as", then select Insert > Picture in Word or another application.

    However, the app just mentioned uses default settings that cause standard errors and significance tests to be quite different from those from common packages such as SPSS and SAS. By using the manual method described in the text rather than the shiny app, we achieve results very close to output from major packages. A major way in which the app diverges from major packages is in (1) using expected rather than observed values to compute standard errors, and (2) computing standard errors based on bootstrap methods. Major packages do not use bootstrap methods. Bootstrap methods are sometimes preferred when nonparametric estimation of standard errors is needed because data cannot be assumed to be normal, and sometimes also for small sample size (here n = 129). However, bootstrap methods introduce a random factor that means estimates may well differ depending on resampling. In the processR app, one will get different bootstrapped estimates of standard errors each time the "Analyze" button is clicked. For the protest data example, this caused some paths to be significant sometimes and nonsignificant other times. For these reasons we do not use the app.

Chapter 3

Statistical analytics with R, Part 2

PART I: OVERVIEW OF STATISTICAL ANALYTICS WITH R

3.1 Introduction

In this chapter we continue an overview of implementing common social science statistical procedures using R. Five multifaceted topics are discussed: Generalized linear models (which include various types of linear and nonlinear regression), multilevel modeling (MLM) (also called hierarchical linear modeling (HLM) or linear mixed modeling (LMM)), panel data regression (PDR) (a leading method of econometric modeling), structural equation modeling (SEM, an extension of regression methods), and missing values analysis/data imputation (MVA/MI, almost always essential). The SEM and MVA/MI topics are treated in online supplements to Chapter 3, found in the student section of the Support Material (www.routledge.com/9780367624293) to this book.

3.2 Data and packages used in this chapter

3.2.1 Example data

Example data files used in this chapter are listed below. These files are all in comma-separated values (.csv) format, a common format among R users because of its universality. In addition to these files, which are supplied in the student section of the Support Material (www.routledge.com/9780367624293), other datasets are supplied as modules supplied as part of R packages. Fuller description of each dataset is found in "Appendix 2 – Datasets used in this book", also found in the student section of the Support Material (www.routledge.com/9780367624293). Datasets used in Chapter 3 supplements are listed in the supplement.

- carinsure.csv: Used for the Poisson regression model in generalized linear modeling (GZLM).
- cobb_survey.csv: This dataset is used to illustrate missing values analysis and data imputation. Later the file cobb2.csv is created from cobb_suvery.csv and saved. Missing values and data imputation are covered as a Chapter 3 supplement in the student section of the Support Material (www.routledge.com/9780367624293).
- courts.csv – This dataset is an adapted version of ICPSR Study No. 3987, "Determinants of Case Growth in Federal District Courts in the United States, 1904-2002", and is used to illustrate PDR.
- hsbmerged.csv: A version of the classic "High School and Beyond Survey" used by Raudenbush et al. (2011) in their seminal work on MLM. It is used to illustrate MLM in this chapter. Math achievement is the outcome variable.

DOI: 10.4324/9781003109396-3

- surveysample.csv – This is a subset of just four variables for 1,500 observations in the 1993 General Social Survey, used in this chapter to illustrate GZLM.
- test.csv – Used with the kind permission of NCSU doctoral student Yanan Yu, this dataset is used to illustrate handling of imported. csv files with missing data. Though this file has 408 cases, it has only 102 complete cases.[1] The dependent variable (DV) is "dpadopt", a binary variable coded 0 = did not adopt digital printing, 1 = did adopt. This dataset covered as a Chapter 3 supplement on missing values in the student section of the Support Material (www.routledge.com/9780367624293).
- world.csv – *This is a cleaned version of a public domain dataset on 20 variables for 212 countries of the world. It is used in this chapter to illustrate GZLM.*

3.2.2 R Packages used

As discussed in Appendix 1, using R modules is a two-step process: (1) installing the module, usually with the `install.packages()` command; and (2) then invoking the package with the `library()` or `require()` commands. We assume the reader who wishes to follow along on their computer has already installed the required packages. Those for Chapter 3 are listed below. Packages used in Chapter 3 supplements are listed in the supplement.

```
library(AER)          # For overdispersion tests in Poisson regression in GZLM
library(emmeans)      # Used for estimated marginal means in GZLM
library(gee)          # Used for generalized estimating equations (GEE)
library(lavaan)       # Used for structural equation modeling
library(lme4)         # Used for multilevel modeling
library(lmerTest)     # Used for multilevel modeling
library(MASS)         # Used for overdispersion in GZLM models
library(Metrics)      # Used for root mean square error in GZLM and PDR
library(multcomp)     # Used for general linear model test in regression
library(plm)          # Used for panel data regression
```

PART II: QUICK START ON STATISTICAL ANALYSIS PART 2

3.3 Quick start: Linear regression as a generalized linear modeling (GZLM)

3.3.1 Background to GZLM

In this section, we introduce a familiar topic in a new light. The familiar topic is ordinary least square (OLS) regression. The new light is implementing it as part of GZLM, which is a generalization of general linear models (GLM). Ordinarily used for nonlinear regression models, GZLM can also implement linear regression. One might wish to implement linear regression through GZLM because input and output options differ, as discussed below. Also, if you learn to do GZLM for OLS regression models, it is easy to make the switch to doing nonlinear models such as gamma regression for skewed data.

3.3.2 The linear model in `glm()`

In Chapter 2 we ran ordinary linear regression using the `lm()` command from R's "stats". In this section, we run the same linear model using the `glm()` command, which implements GZLM models. This command is also part of the "stats" package.

The following setup section sets the working directory, loads the data (we continue to use surveysample.csv to create the "survey" dataframe), and finally load needed R packages. The main command used is `glm()`, which is from the "stats" package in R's system library and thus needs no installation. In the following example, the research purpose is to predict educational level (educ) from income and race. Income is a continuous variable and may be used directly. However, race is numerically coded (1 = white, 2 = black, 3 = other) and we want it to be treated as a categorical variable (factor), so we must transform it as shown here.

```
setwd("C:/Data")
survey <- read.table("surveysample.csv", header = TRUE, sep = ",")
```

We start by transforming the integer variable "race" into the factor variable "racef." After doing this we set its highest level (3) to be the reference category. Note that this is different from the default in `glm()`, which is to use treatment coding, under which the first group in a factor is the reference level.

```
racef <- as.factor(survey$race)
racef <- relevel(racef, ref=3)
```

After these setup steps we use the `glm()` command to run linear regression model as a GZLM model. In this model educ is predicted from income and racef. By specifying a "gaussian" model we are requesting a normal distribution with an identify link function. The normal-identity model is what defines this regression as being of OLS type.

```
olsmodel <- glm(survey$educ ~ survey$income + racef, data = survey, family =
gaussian)
summary(olsmodel)
 [Output:]
   Deviance Residuals:
         Min         1Q     Median        3Q        Max
   -13.6723   -2.0093    -0.0093    1.9907    8.6865
   Coefficients:
                Estimate Std. Error t value Pr(>|t|)
   (Intercept)    9.7156     0.3522  27.585   <2e-16 ***
   income         0.3370     0.0253  13.322   <2e-16 ***
   racef1         0.2500     0.2465   1.014    0.311
   racef2        -0.3700     0.2867  -1.291    0.197
   ---
   Signif. codes:  0 '***' 0.001 '**' 0.01 '*' 0.05 '.' 0.1 ' ' 1

   (Dispersion parameter for gaussian family taken to be 7.335328)

       Null deviance: 16615  on 2049  degrees of freedom
   Residual deviance: 15008  on 2046  degrees of freedom
   AIC: 9908.7

   Number of Fisher Scoring iterations: 2
```

3.3.3 GZLM output

The GLZLM output above could be compared with the GLM output from the `lm()` command:

```
ols <- lm(survey$educ ~ survey$income + racef, data = survey)
summary(ols)
```

Output from the `lm()` command is not shown here, but this is the listing of similarities and differences:

- The "Coefficients" section of output is identical.
- The "Deviance Residuals" section is also identical, except that for the `lm()` command this is labeled "Residuals".

- Output for the `lm()` command gives the residual standard error, multiple R-squared, and the F-test of model significance. Output for the `glm()` command gives none of these as part of `summary()` output.
- Unique output for the `glm()` command gives the deviance statistic for the null model, residual deviance for the given model, and the Akaike Information Criterion (AIC) goodness-of-fit coefficient. It is this unique output which might motivate a researcher to implement OLS linear regression under `glm()` rather than `lm()`.

The reason why `lm()` computes R-Squared and `glm()` computes deviance is based on their different estimation methods. OLSs estimation supports computation of R-squared. Maximum likelihood (ML) estimation, used by `glm()`, supports computation of deviance. An attractive feature of deviance is that it lends itself to comparing model fit for the different types of regression model that one can compute with `glm()`. One measure of model fit is the AIC, which is a form of penalized deviance, where deviance is a measure of model error, with lower being better (hence lower AIC is better too when comparing models). When the researcher runs different regression models (ones with different distribution and link assumptions), `glm()` will return an AIC model fit value for each. The model with the lowest AIC coefficient is the model with the best fit.

In output above, deviance is a measure of model error. The `glm()` function reports "null deviance"[2] and "residual deviance"[3] but, unlike most statistical packages, does not by default report "model deviance". For that the `logLik()` function from R's "stats" package is used:

```
olsmodeldeviance <-  -2*logLik(olsmodel)
olsmodeldeviance
[Output:]
      'log Lik.' 9898.683 (df=5)
```

When comparing nested models, model deviance is used in "likelihood ratio (LR) tests". "Nested" means all the terms in the smaller model are found in the larger model. The LR test uses the differences in model deviance and degrees of freedom to computer a p significance value. If p is significant, the two models are significantly different in error and, all other things equal; the one with lower model deviance is preferred. Often the comparison is to the null model, which is always nested within the researcher's model.

3.3.4 Fitted value, residuals, and plots

The olsmodel object contains a large number of elements. See them all with the command `lapply(olsmodel,class)`. We can access them with the "$" operator. This is illustrated below for the elements containing residuals and predictions. We also save these back to the survey data frame.

```
# Save the residuals
olsmodelres <- olsmodel$residuals
survey$OLSresiduals <- olsmodelres

# Save the fitted (predicted, estimated) values
# The fitted values are the same as would come from the predict () command
olsmodelfitted <- olsmodel$fitted.values
survey$OLSfitted <- olsmodelfitted
```

Graphical assessment of model performance is easy in R. Three common graphs are following:

- *Plot of observed versus predicted values (Figure 3.1).* The more the pattern of the dots in the plot conforms to a 45-degree line, the better the model's predictions. Figure 3.1 shows considerable dispersion around the regression line. The line is far from the ideal 45-degree line of perfect match but the fact the line is not horizontal either does show a low-moderate correlation of observed and predicted values.
- *Plot of residuals against either observed or predicted values (Figure 3.2).* In a well-fitting model, points form a patternless cloud around a horizontal line representing residuals of 0. Figure 3.2 approximates the pattern of a well-fitting model, though there is some tendency toward heteroskedasticity in that dispersion is greater for high predicted values of educ than for low.

- *Histogram plot of residuals (Figure 3.3).* In any predictive model, estimates should center on the observed values, with most residuals at or near 0, high and low estimates trail off in either direction, forming a roughly normal distribution. Figure 3.3 shows that the OLS model comes very close to meeting this criterion.

```
# For Figure 3.1, plot fitted on X against educ on Y
plot(olsmodel$fitted.values, survey$educ)

# Then compute the OLS regression fit line and draw it
fit <- lm(survey$educ~olsmodel$fitted.values,data=survey)
lines(olsmodel$fitted.values, fitted(fit), col="red")

# Then add a horizontal line at the mean of educ (13.48)
abline(h=mean(survey$educ, col="black"))

# For Figure 3.2, plot fitted on X against residuals on Y
plot(olsmodel$fitted.values, olsmodel$residuals)

# Then add a horizontal line 0
abline(h=0, col="black")

# For Figure 3.3, create a histogram plot of OLS model residuals
hist(olsmodel$residuals)
```

It is also easy to compute a variety of quantitative model fit measures for our linear model. Two – AIC and residual deviance – were output as part of `summary(olsmodel)` above and are retrievable elements of it.

```
olsmodel$aic
[Output:]
      [1] 9908.683
```

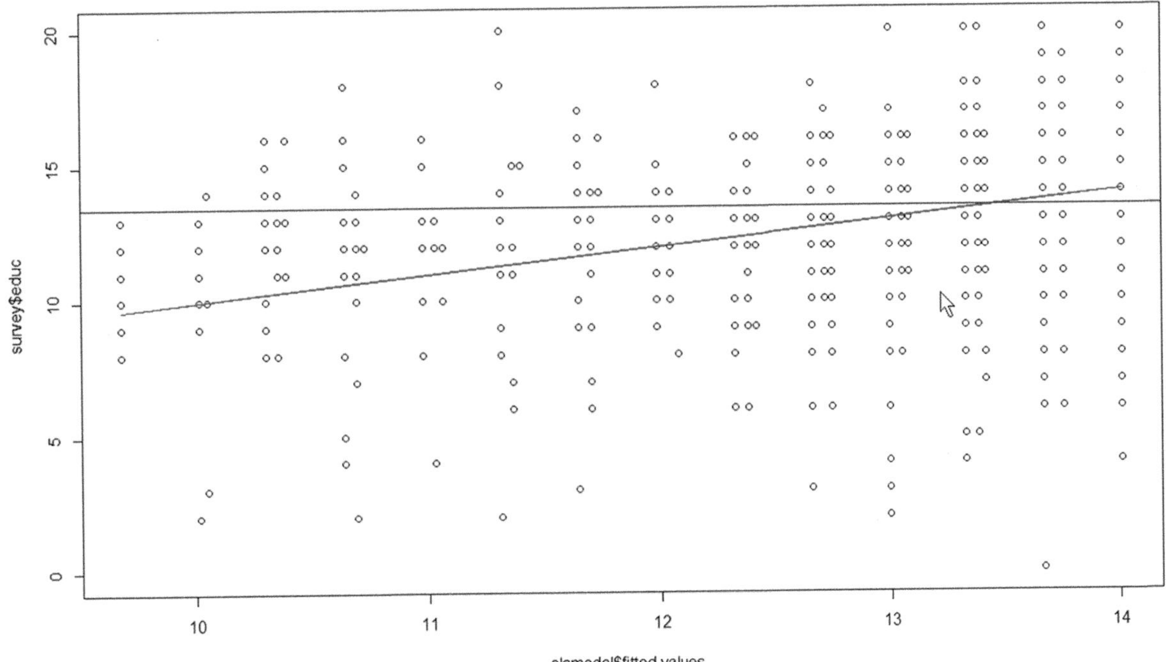

Figure 3.1 Linear Model Predicted-Observed Plot

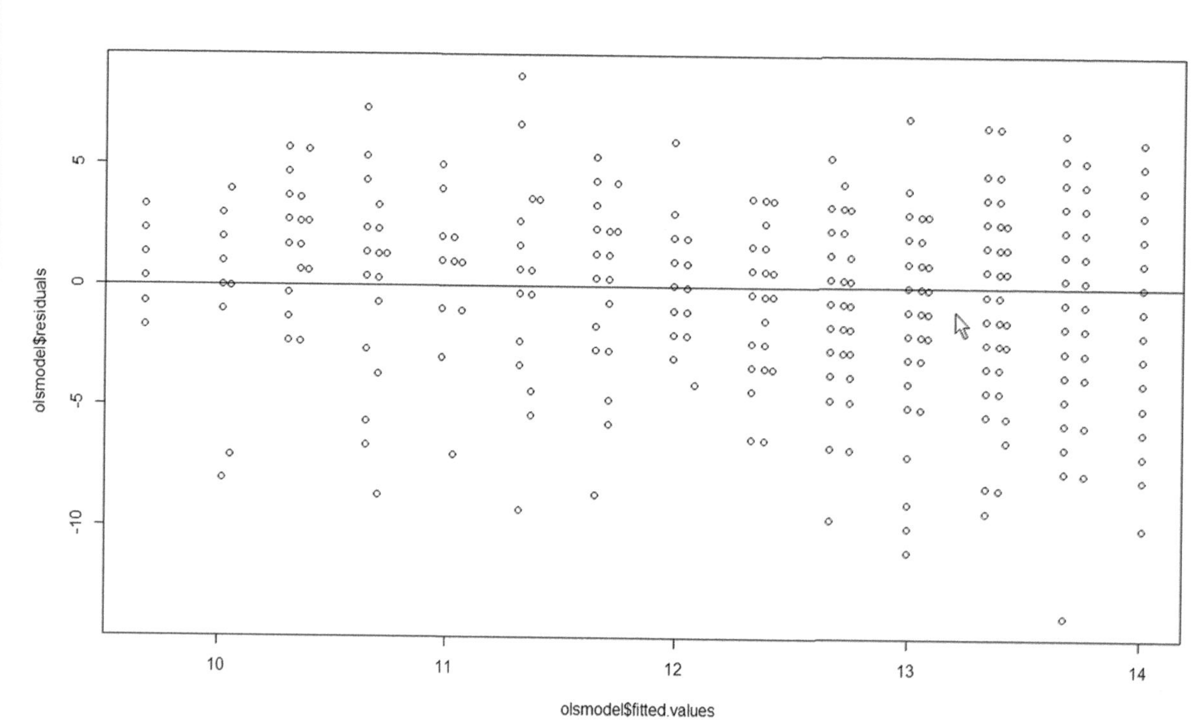

Figure 3.2 Linear Model Residuals-Observed Plot

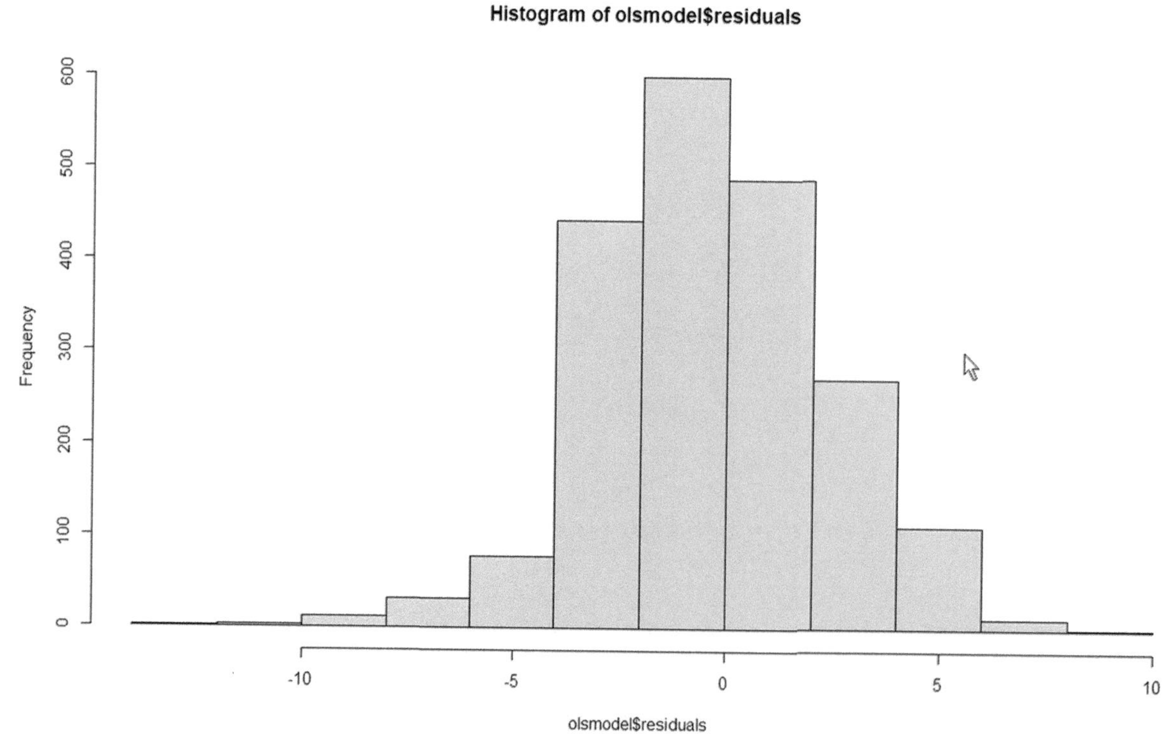

Figure 3.3 Linear Model Histogram of Residuals

```
# Recall earlier computation of model deviance:
olsmodeldeviance <-  -2*logLik(olsmodel)
olsmodeldeviance
[Output:]
        'log Lik.' 9898.683 (df=5)
        [1] 9898.683
```

AIC is a penalty on model deviance, increasing its value and thus indicating more error and worse fit than would deviance itself. This penalty is considered sufficient to allow AIC to be used for non-nested comparisons, whereas LR tests with the deviance statistic are only for nested models.

There are two other common metrics for model fit:

1. *Observed-predicted correlation*: The higher the correlation of predicted and observed values of educ, the better the model by this metric. The correlation metric can be compared across different types of regression model. Here the correlation is in the "moderate" range.

   ```
   olsmodelcor <- cor(olsmodelfitted,survey$educ)olsmodelcor
   [Output:]
           [1] 0.3110191
   ```

2. *Root mean square error*: Root mean square error is computed with the `rmse()` function from the "Metrics" package. It is used in comparing models, with lower being better. RMSE is applicable only when the DV is continuous. Thus, for example, in the binomial logistic model in a later section, "accuracy" is substituted as a performance metric.

   ```
   library(Metrics)rmse <- Metrics::rmse(olsmodel$fitted.values, survey$educ)rmse
   [Output:]
           [1] 2.705737
   ```

3.3.5 Noncanonical custom links

Returning to general discussion of the `glm()` command, note that the following `glm()` command, which spells out the identity link explicitly, gives exactly the same output as the previous `glm()` command to predict education:

```
glm(survey$educ ~ survey$income + racef, data = survey, family =
gaussian(link="identity"))
```

However, we do not have to accept the canonical link. We can customize instead. The purpose of a link function is to make the relationship of the right-hand (predictor) side of the equation linear with the left-hand (outcome) side. We might, for instance, think that our DV was normally distributed (Gaussian) but would be linear only if the square roots of the outcome, not the raw values, were predicted.

If we try to run a model with a noncanonical link, such as Gaussian with a square root link, we may well get an error message stating "`cannot find valid starting values: please specify some.`" This would happen with the command below, for instance:

```
glm(survey$educ ~ survey$income + racef, data = survey, family =
gaussian(link="sqrt"))
```

To overcome this error, we can obtain output for the noncanonical Gaussian model with a square root link by using starting values from linear regression (the `lm()` command):

```
glm(survey$educ ~ survey$income + racef, data = survey, family =
gaussian(link="sqrt"), start = coef(lm(survey$educ ~ survey$income + racef)))
```

For space reasons we do not show output of the command above, but its AIC is 9904, almost the same as AIC = 9909 for the canonical linear model. For these results, by the rule of thumb of selecting the simpler model, the researcher would probably report the canonical model, not the customized model.

3.3.6 Multiple comparison tests

By running linear regression as GZLM with `glm()`, various post-hoc multiple comparison tests are available for the model object. These tests compare levels of a factor (e.g., the three categories of racef) on mean differences on the outcome variable (educ), controlling for other main effects in the model (income). The general linear hypothesis test (`glht()`) function of the "multcomp" package is one such testing method in R.

In the R syntax below, note that the multiple comparison (`mcp()`) function is used. Within the parentheses for this function, the factor of interest is listed (racef) and the desired test (Tukey). Several tests are available though we show output only for the Tukey test. Alternative tests are discussed for R in Bretz, Hothorn, and Westfall (2010) and for other packages in Garson (2014b). For the current example, all tests result in the same substantive conclusion: Blacks differ from whites on education, but pairs involving the "other" race category are not significant.

- *"Tukey"*: The Tukey contrasts test displays all pairwise comparisons between groups. It is a conservative pairwise comparison test when group sizes are unequal. Conservative testing is often preferred when the number of groups is large, threatening to inflate Type I errors (wrongly accepting the null hypothesis of no group differences). A synonym is the Tukey-Kramer test.
- *"Dunnett"*: The Dunnett contrasts test compares each group with the mean of a reference group considered to be the control group. Output list the significance of each group's mean in relation to the reference group mean. There is no output line for the reference group. For purposes of comparing treatment groups with a control group, the Dunnett test has greater power than other tests.
- *Other supported tests* are "Sequen", "Changepoint", "AVE", "Williams", "Marcus", and "McDermott".

Below we run Tukey contrasts and find that for the model predicting education from income and race, blacks are significantly different from whites (the 2–1 row) on estimated marginal means (EMM) of education, but pairwise comparisons involving the "other" race category are not significant.[4]

```
library(multcomp)
summary(multcomp::glht(olsmodel,multcomp::mcp(racef="Tukey")))
```

[Output:]

```
        Simultaneous Tests for General Linear Hypotheses
   Multiple Comparisons of Means: Tukey Contrasts
   Fit: glm(formula = educ ~ income + racef, family=gaussian, data=survey)

   Linear Hypotheses:
              Estimate Std. Error z value Pr(>|z|)
   1 - 3 == 0   0.2500     0.2465   1.014   0.5576
   2 - 3 == 0  -0.3700     0.2867  -1.291   0.3898
   2 - 1 == 0  -0.6200     0.1778  -3.486   0.0014 **
   ---
   Signif. codes:  0 '***' 0.001 '**' 0.01 '*' 0.05 '.' 0.1 ' ' 1
   (Adjusted p values reported -- single-step method)
```

3.3.7 Estimated marginal means (EMM)

Somewhat similar inferences can be made from EMM. These are not simple means but means after controlling for other variables in the model. Below we see that on the response variable, education (educ), the EMM for whites (racef = 1) is highest, at 13.6 years of education. It is lowest for blacks (racef = 2), at 13.0 years of education. Since EMM are not raw means but are means controlling for other variables in the model, we may say that blacks on average have .6 years less education than whites, even after income is controlled.[5]

```
library(emmeans)
emm <- emmeans::emmeans(olsmodel,"racef")
summary(emm, type = "response")
[Output:]
    racef emmean     SE  df asymp.LCL asymp.UCL
    3       13.3 0.2369 Inf      12.9      13.8
    1       13.6 0.0673 Inf      13.4      13.7
    2       13.0 0.1635 Inf      12.6      13.3
   Confidence level used: 0.95
```

3.4 Quick start: Testing if multilevel modeling is needed

OLS regression makes the strong and often erroneous assumption that data are independent. That is, it assumes data do not cluster by some categorical variable. Sometimes the categorical variable represents levels in a hierarchy, such as students nested in schools and schools nested in districts. Other examples are voters nested in municipalities or employees nested within agencies. In any given research, there is a high probability that clustering occurs, making OLS regression estimates wrong. One approach to dealing with lack of data independence is MLM, also called HLM or LMM. In this section, we perform the usual statistical test to see if MLM is needed for an example dataset.

We check if MLM is needed by running a multilevel null model. In OLS regression, a null model is an intercept-only model without predictor variables. In MLM the null model is one with a single effect, which is the effect of the clustering variable. If that effect is not significant, data are independent of the clustering variable and OLS regression may be run. If it is significant, MLM is needed. The null model may also be labeled the "unconditional random intercept model".

The example data file we use is the famous "High School and Beyond" data located in a file labeled "hsbmerged.csv". This research question centered on differential schooling effects on math achievement score as the outcome variable. In MLM parlance, "level 1" is the student data on math achievement (mathach). "Level 2" is the school level (schoolid). There are no other variables in the null model. The level 2 variable is variously called the level variable, the link variable, the grouping variable, or the clustering variable. There may be other predictors at level 1 or 2, but not in a null model.

The random effects of the schoolid clustering variable at level 2 on the mathach outcome variable at level 1 are measured by a coefficient called the "variance component". If the variance component for schoolid is significant then MLM is needed. This is mathematically equivalent to determining if the intraclass correlation (ICC) is significant.

For the example in this section we import hsbmerged.csv using the `read.table()` command from the "utils" package. We run a multilevel null model using the `lmer()` command from the "lme4" package. To get p significance values we also need to install the "lmerTest" package. While utils is part of the built-in R systems library, lme4 and lmerTest are not and therefore must be installed. The MLM estimation method by is ML, not OLSs. We store results in the object "NullMLMmodel".

```
# Set the working directory
setwd("c:/Data")

# Read the data into a data frame called "hsb" and view the data
hsb <- read.table("hsbmerged.csv", header = TRUE, sep = ",")
View(hsb)

# Run the null model using the lmer () command from the "lme4" package
# To get p values, the lmerTest package must be activated
library(lme4)
library(lmerTest)
NullMLMmodel <- lme4::lmer(hsb$mathach~(1|hsb$schoolid), REML = FALSE, data = hsb)
```

Comments on `lmer()` *syntax for the null model:*

`NullMLMmodel <-`

Output is sent to an object called NullMLMmodel

`lme4::lmer(hsb$mathach)`

MLM is invoked with mathach as DV

The lme:: part is a package prefix, clarifying what package is being used.

`~(1|hsb$schoolid)`

Predictors are listed after the tilde. Here there is only the random schoolid effect.

Level 1 observations are nested within schoolid at level 2.

Note that a random effect is expressed as shown and is enclosed in parentheses.

`,`

A comma separates the list of options

`REML = FALSE,`

REML estimation is the default. FALSE invokes ML estimation.

`data = hsb)`

The data frame object hsb is named as the data source.

We now view the output using the `summary()` command. Significance (p) values for fixed effects show only if lmerTest is invoked prior to the `lmer()` command

```
summary(NullMLMmodel)
[Output:]
   Linear mixed model fit by maximum likelihood.  t-tests use
     Satterthwaite's method [lmerModLmerTest]
   Formula: hsb$mathach ~ (1 | hsb$schoolid)
      Data: hsb
        AIC       BIC    logLik deviance df.resid
    47121.8   47142.4 -23557.9  47115.8     7182
   Scaled residuals:
        Min       1Q    Median       3Q      Max
   -3.06262 -0.75365  0.02676  0.76070  2.74184
   Random effects:
    Groups       Name        Variance Std.Dev.
    hsb$schoolid (Intercept)  8.553   2.925
    Residual                 39.148   6.257
   Number of obs: 7185, groups:  hsb$schoolid, 160
   Fixed effects:
               Estimate Std. Error       df t value Pr(>|t|)
   (Intercept)  12.6371     0.2436 157.6209   51.87   <2e-16 ***
   ---
   Signif. codes:  0 '***' 0.001 '**' 0.01 '*' 0.05 '.' 0.1 ' ' 1
```

We now get p significance values for random effects with the `rand()` command from the lmerTest package

```
lmerTest::rand(NullMLMmodel)
[Output:]
   ANOVA-like table for random-effects: Single term deletions
   Model:
   hsb$mathach ~ (1 | hsb$schoolid)
                        npar logLik   AIC    LRT Df Pr(>Chisq)
   <none>                  3 -23558 47122
   (1 | hsb$schoolid)      2 -24050 48104 983.92  1  < 2.2e-16 ***
   ---
   Signif. codes:  0 '***' 0.001 '**' 0.01 '*' 0.05 '.' 0.1 ' ' 1
```

Comments on `lmer()` *summary and* `rand()` output

Significance of the schoolid random effect: The critical part of output is at the bottom, where it is shown that the random effect of the level 2 schoolid clustering variable is highly significant, with a p value better than .001 (`< 2.2e-16 ***`). This shows that student math scores do cluster by school. This in turn means that because data are not independent there is correlated error associated such that OLS regression would give incorrect estimates. Bottom line: A MLM model is needed.

AIC and fit coefficients: Near the top of the output fit statistics are printed. AIC and Bayesian Information Criterion (BIC) are information theory measures of penalized error. They may be used to compare other models, even non-nested ones, with lower AIC or BIC being less error and better fit. BIC imposes a greater penalty for model complexity than does AIC, but usually if AIC is lower for a given model, so will BIC be. The "deviance" value is minus two log likelihood (-2LL), also called model chi-square, and is used in LR tests of the significance of the difference between two nested models. The null model is always nested within the researcher's model. However, for comparing models, LR tests are preferred over AIC and BIC when models are nested.

Fixed effects: Fixed effects are the regression part of the model. However, because a null model has no predictor variables, the only fixed effect is the intercept. Note that the clustering variable schoolid is a random effect, not a fixed effect. The intercept estimate of 12.64 is the estimate of the mean mathach achievement score, controlling for schoolid.

The residual component and ICC: In the summary portion of output above, the "Variance" column shows a "Residual" component as well as an "hsb$schoolid" component. The schoolid component is the between-groups component, explaining variation in math achievement due to differences between schools. The residual component is the within-groups component, reflecting the unexplained variation in math scores due to differences among students within schools. The residual component is larger than the schoolid component by a ratio of almost 5:1. The ICC is the schoolid variance component divided by the sum of both components: `ICC = 8.553/(8.553 + 39.148) = 0.179.` Since the schoolid random effect component is significant, we can say that the ICC (which is mathematically equivalent) is also significant. Either way, significance indicates the need for MLM. That the ICC is relatively low means that unexplained variance is high, and therefore additional variables must be specified if math achievement is to be better explained. We add more effects under the section "The random coefficients (RE) model" further.

PART III: STATISTICAL ANALYSIS, PART 2, IN DETAIL

3.5 Generalized linear models (GZLM)

3.5.1 Introduction

In the "Quick Start" section of this chapter we illustrated how GZLM could be used to implement a familiar procedure, OLS linear regression. However, GZLM can implement a variety of other useful types of regression. It is not limited to models for data that are normally distributed and have an identity link function (i.e., direct prediction of raw values of the DV) like OLS regression. GZLM handles DVs with any of several non-normal distributions using any of a number of link functions. Perhaps the most common nonlinear model is binomial logistic regression, which assumes a binomial distribution and a logit link function. Other regression models supported by GZLM include gamma regression models for skewed data, Poisson models for count data, complementary log-log models for interval-censored survival data, and negative binomial regression for overdispersed data (variance larger than the mean). R supports GZLM through the `glm()` command of the "stats" package in the R system library.

Generalized estimating equations (GEE) extends GZLM even further by providing support for correlated (non-independent) data, such as repeated measures, time series, matched pairs, panel, before-after, and clustered data. As such GEE supports repeated measures logistic regression, repeated measures Poisson regression, and other models for within-subjects designs. Traditionally, most research designs were between-subjects (e.g., cross-sectional surveys) rather than within-subjects (e.g., repeated measures), so GZLM applications have been more common than those for GEE. R supports GEE in with the `gee()` command of the "gee" package and output is very similar to that for GZLM but coefficients are calculated correctly for panel and other non-independent data.

GZLM can run many types of regression within the same framework. Each type of regression assumes a given data distribution and uses a given link function. Link functions create modified versions of the raw value of the DV. For instance, binary logistic regression assumes the binomial distribution and predicts the log-odds (logit) of the DV rather than the raw value of the DV. The following bullet list summarizes some of the most common types of regression implemented under GZLM. GEE implements the same types of regression but for repeated measures data. In the following list, key output measures are noted.

- Linear regression, for normal (Gaussian) distributions use an identity link for linear solutions but log, power, or inverse links for nonlinear solutions are possible. Normally distributed continuous DVs are assumed. Independent variables (IVs) may include dummies and interaction terms.
- Poisson regression, for DVs with a Poisson distribution and a log link. Used for count data or count per unit (rate) data, where the unit is the "offset variable". The data do not have negative values for the DV since counts cannot be negative.
- Negative binomial regression, for negative binomial distributions with a log link. This is used instead of Poisson regression when there is overdispersion, which means the variance of the DV is greater than the mean. The DV should not contain negative values since this is another type of count regression.
- Binary logistic regression, for binomial distributions with a logit link. A binary DV without an underlying normal distribution is assumed (e.g., region = North/South). Logistic b coefficients can be exponentiated to obtain odds ratios, which are effect size measures.
- Binary probit regression, for binomial distributions with a probit link. The DV is binary but has an assumed underlying normal distribution (e.g., age = young/old).
- Ordinal logistic regression, for multinomial distributions with a cumulative logit link. The DV is a categorical variable with ordered levels.
- Ordinal probit regression, for multinomial distributions with a probit link. Similar to ordinal regression but frequencies are normally distributed across levels.
- Cloglog regression (complementary log-log), for binomial distributions with a cloglog link. Data are often survival time data but may be any binary or grouped data. Exponentiated coefficients are discrete time hazard ratios.
- Gamma regression, for gamma distributions usually with a log link (SPSS), though it is also possible to have an inverse power link or even an identity link. Gamma regression is used when the distribution of the DV is positively skewed (has a long tail to the right). Negative skew can be handled by flipping the data. Data cannot have negative values but this can be handled by adding a constant.
- GZLM supports many other combinations of distribution family with type of link function. Furthermore, there are variations for zero-inflated data (many 0s) and other problematic data. In this section, we treat only four of the most common generalized models: Binary logistic, gamma, Poisson, and negative binomial.

Some GZLM models require data conversions such as those discussed here, but beware that such conversions may not be justified and instead an alternate procedure not requiring such conversions may be preferable.

- Convert to eliminate values less than 0: Take the lowest negative value and add its absolute value to all values in the column. (Gamma regression, for instance, cannot have negative values).
- Convert negatively skewed data to positively skewed data: Take the highest value plus 1, then subtract all values from this number. (Note positive skew = right skew = long tail to the right. Gamma regression is for positively skewed data).

Common forms of output for GZLM models may include those on the list below.

- Deviance (-2LL, also called model chi-square): A measure of model error used in LR tests when comparing nested models.
- AIC, BIC, and other information theory measures: Penalized deviance as a measure of model error used when comparing nested or non-nested models, where lower is better.

- Odds ratios: These are effect size measures only for regression types using logit links, which transform the raw DV into its log-odds counterpart. Raising the natural log base e to the power of b gives the odds ratio. An odds ratio of 1.0 is no effect of the IV. Less than 1.0 is a negative effect; more than 1.0 is a positive effect.
- EMM tables: For factor predictor variables, these show differences on the DV by level of the IV, controlling for other effects in the model.
- Contrast coefficients: These are marginal means for particular factor contrasts, such as level Catholic vs. level Protestant for the factor Religion. Significance tests are given for each contrast but as they are independent sample tests, when there are multiple tests one must use Bonferroni, sequential Bonferroni (less stringent), or other adjustments to significance.
- Residual analysis. As in most procedures, in GZLM one may save residuals for analyzing outliers, linearity, homoscedasticity, normality, and other patterns.
- Pseudo-R^2 measures like Nagelkerke's R^2 or McFadden's R^2: Not percent of variance explained as is R^2 in OLS regression, but rather these metrics are interpreted simply as weak, moderate, or strong levels of model fit. However, these coefficients are derogated and are not output by most statistical packages.

3.5.2 Setup for GZLM models in R

To provide example variables, we start by setting the working directory and reading in both the "world" and "surveysample" data files, both described and used previously and in Appendix 2.

```
setwd("c:/Data")
survey <- read.table("surveysample.csv", header = TRUE, sep = ",")
world <- read.table("world.csv", header = TRUE, sep = ",")
```

The `glm()` command from R's built-in "stats" package is the function most commonly used to implement GZLM models. However, it is necessary to activate other packages for use with some forms of GZLM, later we will need the "Metrics", "multcomp", "emmeans", and "MASS" packages, which do need installation if not already installed. Even if installed, they should be activated with the `library()` command:

```
library(AER)          # For overdispersion tests in Poisson regression in GZLM
library(car)          # Used for recoding variables
library(emmeans)      # Used for estimated marginal means in GZLM
library(gee)          # Used for generalized estimating equations (GEE)
library(MASS)         # Used for overdispersion in GZLM models
library(Metrics)      # Used for root mean square error in GZLM and PDR
library(multcomp)     # Used for general linear model test in regression
```

The general format of the `glm()` command is this:

```
glm(formula, family = gaussian, data, weights, subset,
       na.action, start = NULL, etastart, mustart, offset,
       control = list(...), model = TRUE, method = "glm.fit",
       x = FALSE, y = TRUE, singular.ok = TRUE, contrasts =
       NULL, ...)
```

The `family =` option is the critical element for specifying which type of generalized model is being requested. In R, specifying a family specifies both the distribution and default link. For instance, specifying `family = gaussian` specifies both a Gaussian (normal) distribution and an identity link and was used for OLS regression. This default link is the "canonical" link. It can be overridden simply by specifying a different permissible link, as by specifying `gaussian(link = "log")` to get a log-normal regression.

OLS regression with canonical link:

```
olsmodelidentity <- glm(survey$educ ~ survey$income, data = survey, family =
gaussian)
```
[Partial output from `summary (oldsmodelidentity)`:]
```
            AIC: 9917.2
```

OLS regression with customized link (log, in this case)

Note that for these data, we must supply starting values for the linear predictors parameters.
We supply 0 as starting values but starting values might differ.
```
olsmodellog <- glm(survey$educ ~ survey$income, data = survey, start = c(0,0),family
= gaussian(link="log"))
```
[Partial output from `summary (oldsmodellog)`:]
```
      AIC: 9906.7
```

As AIC is lower for the log-normal regression compared to the usual OLS regression (identity-normal) model, the former is considered marginally the better model.

Possible link functions in `glm()` are these: `"logit", "probit", "cauchit", "cloglog", "identity", "log", "sqrt", "1/mu^2",` and `"inverse"`. However, not every distribution family supports every link.

The generalized types and their canonical (default) links available for `glm()` are the following:

```
family = gaussian(link = "identity")
family = binomial(link = "logit")
family = Gamma(link = "inverse")
family = inverse.gaussian(link = "1/mu^2")
family = (poisson(link = "log")
family = quasi(link = "identity", variance = "constant")
family = quasibinomial(link = "logit")
family = quasipoisson(link = "log")
```

3.5.3 Binary logistic regression example

The binary logistic model is probably the most common GZLM model, other than OLS regression. As this model was covered in Chapter 2, not much additional is added in this section. To recall the model, however, we used the "world" data frame. The outcome variable was "litgtmean", a binary character variable we choose to convert to a binary numeric variable. The litgtmean variable indicated if a nation was above or below mean national literacy rate. In the `glm()` command we specified family = 'binomial'. Output was stored in the object logisticFit. For instructional simplicity, the command below employs only three predictor variables.

First we recode the character variable litgtmean into an integer variable we label "y".

```
library(car)
y = car::recode(world$litgtmean, "'Low'=1; 'High'=0")
logisticFit <- glm(y ~ world$phonesper1000 + world$birthrate + world$infdeaths,
family = 'binomial', data=world)
```

By asking for the $family element of the output object, we can confirm the family and the link function used:

```
logisticFit$family
```
[Output:]
```
  Family: binomial
  Link function: logit
```

The model fit metrics treated in the "Quick Start" linear regression example are also available when creating a binomial logistic model using the `glm()` command. Deviance, which is used in LR tests of nested models, is one of the most important. Such tests are used to compare nested models (a model is nested if all the terms in the smaller model are present in the larger model). For instance, the null model is nested within the logisticFit model.

```
logisticmodeldeviance <- logisticFit$deviance
logisticmodeldeviance
```
[Output:]
```
        [1] 145.3737
```

In other comparisons, when models are not nested, an information theory metric such as AIC is commonly used, with lower being less error and better fit. AIC is an element of the logisticFit model as illustrated here. It is also shown in output from the `summary(logisticFit)` command.

```
logisticFit$aic
```
[Partial output:]
```
        AIC: 153.3737
```

Output is not shown for the remaining logistic model metrics, only the syntax

```
# Save the residuals to an object
logisticmodelres <- logisticFit$residuals

# Save fitted values to an object
logisticmodelfitted <- logisticFit$fitted.values

# Compute the observed-predicted correlation as a model performance metric.
# Full discussion can be seen in Chapter 2, where two types of correlation are discussed.
cor(y,logisticFit$fitted.values)
```
[Output:]
```
        [1] 0.7295797
```

```
# Compute root mean square error
library(Metrics)
Metrics::rmse(logisticFit$fitted.values, y)
```
[Output:]
```
        [1] 0.3238831
```

We now compute EMM for litgtmean (y) in the logisticFit model using infdeaths (a factor coded “High” or “Low”) as the factor of interest. Nations with either high or low infant deaths tend to be high on litgtmean because both have a prob < .5 and this corresponds to litgtmean = 1, which is the “High” code for litgtmean. However, those with low infant deaths have an even lower probability, meaning they are even more likely to be classed as 1 = “High” on litgtmean.

```
library(emmeans)
emm <- emmeans::emmeans(logisticFit,"infdeaths")
summary(emm, type = "response")
```
[Output:]
```
   infdeaths  prob     SE  df asymp.LCL asymp.UCL
    High     0.381 0.1047 Inf     0.205     0.595
    Low      0.211 0.0479 Inf     0.132     0.320
   Confidence level used: 0.95
   Intervals are back-transformed from the logit scale
```

3.5.4 Gamma regression model

3.5.4.1 Introduction

Gamma regression is often used when the response (dependent) variable is positively skewed, with a long tail to the right when portrayed in a distribution curve or histogram. That is, gamma regression is used for right-skewed data. If data have a long tail to the left, data are first converted to right skew by subtracting all values from one more than the largest original value. Gamma regression is appropriate, for example, when in a survey item, the large majority of responses are all at the extremes (e.g., mostly 1s and 2s on a 7-point Likert scale). This type of regression, like OLS regression, is for a continuous or quasi-continuous response variable. In general, gamma regression may be preferred over linear regression when the OLS normality assumption is violated by pronounced skewing of the DV.

Gamma regression assumes that the distribution family is Gamma (note R puts Gamma in upper case) and that the link function is inverse (also called inverse power or reciprocal), as it is in Stata and SAS. Other possible link functions for gamma regression are the log link (the default in SPSS) and the identity link (rare, but sometimes use in survival models, for instance). Note that when gamma regression employs an inverse link, the signs of coefficients are reversed compared to gamma with a log link.

In terms of data, gamma regression assumes that the outcome variable is continuous, or, if count data are used, that enough counts are present to form a gamma distribution. For more finite counts, Poisson or negative binomial regression is preferred. Gamma regression also assumes the response variable has no non-positive values. For survival data, all cases must be uncensored.

3.5.4.2 Setup

In this section, we assume that earlier setup operations have been performed: Setting the default directory, reading in the survey and world data frames, and installing needed packages mentioned in that section. We continue to use the `glm()` command to implement GZLM. Gamma regression requires all values be greater than 0, so below we add 1 to all values of our outcome variable, degree2. This does not affect parameter estimates or their significance.

```
degree2 = survey$degree + 1
```

Figure 3.4 illustrates that degree2 is right-skewed, and therefore appropriate for a gamma regression model. The figure is created with the following command.

```
hist(degree2)
```

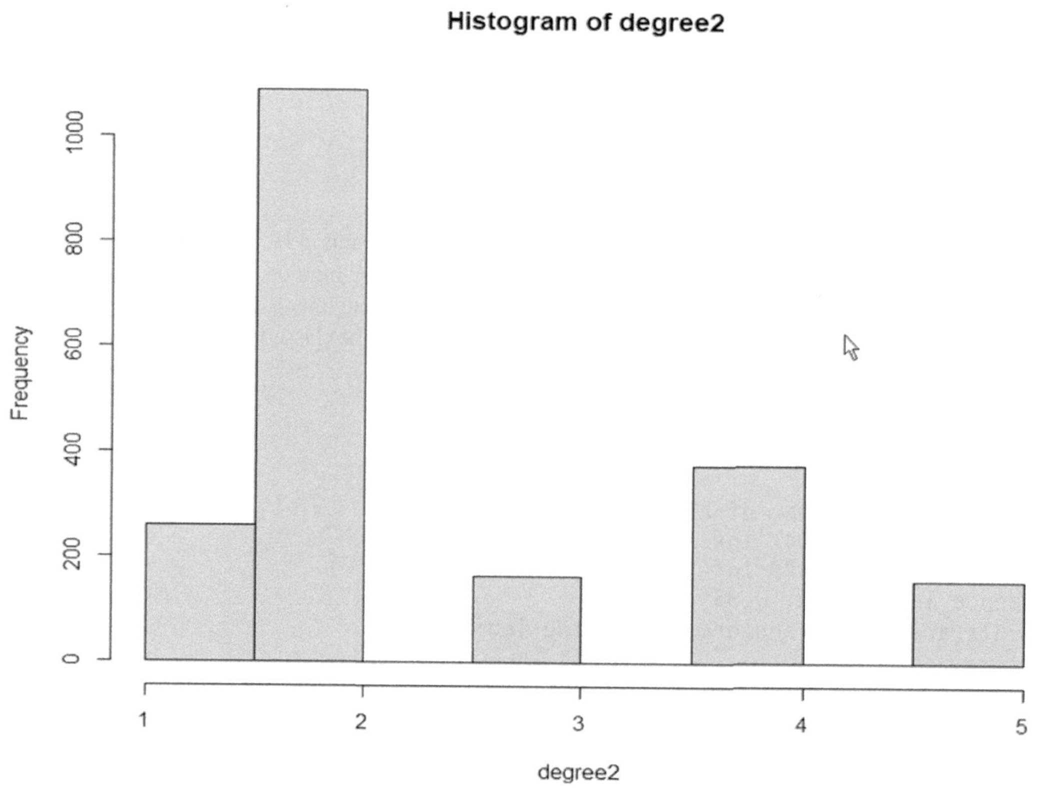

Histogram of degree2

Frequency

0 200 400 600 800 1000

1 2 3 4 5

degree2

Figure 3.4 Histogram of degree2

Also as part of setup, we create the factor variable racef using the following commands. Race = 3 (3 = "Other race") is made the reference level for racef.

```
racef <- as.factor(survey$race)
racef <- relevel(racef, ref=3)
```

3.5.4.3 The gamma regression model

Below we run the `glm()` gamma regression model specifying a Gamma distribution and an inverse link. We predict degree2 from income and race. The link="inverse" specification is not actually needed as inverse is the default for this type of model.

```
GammaFit <- glm(degree2 ~ survey$income + racef, family=Gamma(link="inverse"))
```

At this point we could issue the `summary(GammaFit)`, which would give estimates very close to those of major statistical packages. However, by calculating dispersion with the `dispersion(GammaFit)` function of the MASS package, we can get even better estimates and this is recommended.

```
library(MASS)
summary(GammaFit, dispersion = MASS::gamma.dispersion(GammaFit))
  [Output:]
  Call:
  glm(formula = degree ~ income + racef, family = Gamma(link = "inverse"))

  Deviance Residuals:
      Min        1Q    Median        3Q       Max
  -0.8805  -0.3199  -0.1847    0.3776    1.2986

  Coefficients:
               Estimate Std. Error z value Pr(>|z|)
  (Intercept)  0.715716   0.027739  25.802   <2e-16 ***
  income      -0.028219   0.002133 -13.227   <2e-16 ***
  racef1      -0.020447   0.015513  -1.318   0.1875
  racef2       0.036148   0.018906   1.912   0.0559.
  Signif. codes:  0 '***' 0.001 '**' 0.01 '*' 0.05 '.' 0.1 ' ' 1

  (Dispersion parameter for Gamma family taken to be 0.1744221)

      Null deviance: 415.76  on 2049  degrees of freedom
  Residual deviance: 367.93  on 2046  degrees of freedom
  AIC: 5794.9

  Number of Fisher Scoring iterations: 5
```

Discussion of GammaFit output

- Income is a significant predictor of degree.
- Neither level of race in comparison with the reference level is significant when "Other" is the reference level.
- However, if we were to relevel racef to make "Black" the reference level, then level 1 ("White") would be significant, as shown here.

```
            Coefficients:

               Estimate Std. Error t value Pr(>|t|)
  (Intercept)  0.751864   0.025665  29.295  < 2e-16 ***
  income      -0.028219   0.002186 -12.908  < 2e-16 ***
  racef3      -0.036148   0.019374  -1.866   0.0622.
  racef1      -0.056595   0.012584  -4.497 7.27e-06 ***
```

- The values in the "Estimate" column, the standard error column, and the significance column are the same as from SPSS for the same model. If the MASS dispersion function is not used, then `glm()` returns estimates, which are the same as SPSS but standard errors, and therefore significance values differ somewhat.
- The dispersion parameter, which is used to model skew in the response variable, is .174 when using the dispersion function from the MASS package, which is the same as what SPSS labels the scale parameter.
- The residual deviance, a measure of model error, is reported by R as 367.93 on 2046 degrees of freedom. This is the same as what SPSS labels "deviance".
- The overall model fit (model error) by AIC is 5794.9, which compares to 5794.1 in SPSS. The AIC may be used to compare nested or non-nested models, with lower being better.

The GammaFit$family, GammaFit$deviance, GammaFit$residuals, and GammaFit$fitted elements all work as described for binary logistic regression in Chapter 2. Likewise the functions for correlation, root mean square error, and EMM work similarly as well:

```
cor(degree2,GammaFit$fitted.values)
[Output:]
      [1] 0.3247171

library(Metrics)
Metrics::rmse(GammaFit$fitted.values, degree2)
[Output:]
      [1] 1.092563

library(emmeans)
emm <- emmeans::emmeans(GammaFit,"racef")
summary(emm, type = "response")
[Output:]
  racef response     SE  df asymp.LCL asymp.UCL
   3         2.42 0.0900 Inf      2.26      2.61
   1         2.55 0.0275 Inf      2.49      2.60
   2         2.23 0.0583 Inf      2.12      2.35
```

Interpretation: Whites (racef = 1) are highest on EMM degree and blacks (racef = 2) are lowest. Marginal means are means controlling for other variables in the model (here controlling for income).

3.5.5 Poisson regression model

3.5.5.1 Introduction

Poisson regression is commonly used for models for which data are counts, such as counts of health or crime events. In addition to count models, the Poisson family also supports rate and loglinear models, discussed here. All three types of models use the `glm()` command with a Poisson distribution and a log link.

If data are overdispersed then data do not form a Poisson distribution. Instead, a negative binomial distribution is commonly used. It follows that checking for overdispersion is an important early step in Poisson modeling. Overdispersion is defined as greater dispersion than would be expected by the model. If the model assumes independence, the model expectation for the outcome variable is the mean, so variance greater than the mean is sometimes used as a criterion for overdispersion. However, as independence may not be a realistic model assumption, major statistical packages commonly operationalize the overdispersion criterion as deviance (a measure of model error) per degree of freedom (a measure of model complexity). A well-fitting model has a deviance ratio (deviance/df) close to 1.0, with higher or lower values indicating overdispersion or underdispersion respectively. A manual rule-of-thumb criterion is that overdispersion exists if the variance of the DV is greater than its mean. Handling overdispersed Poisson models is treated in many texts, including Garson (2013c).

3.5.5.2 Setup

As with other GZLM models, the `glm()` function is used for Poisson models. To test for overdispersion we need the "AER" package, which requires explicit installation. Once installed, AER may be activated with the `library()` command.

```
library(AER)
```

To illustrate Poisson count and rate models the "carinsure" dataset is used, loaded with the usual `read.table()` command. This is a small teaching dataset inspired by an example in Aitkin, Anderson, Francis, and Hinde, (1989). The variables are:

- claims: number of claims, which is the count outcome variable
- clients: number of policy-holders
- lnclients: natural log of clients, used as the offset variable in rate models
- carsize: 1 = small, 2 = medium, 3 = large
- age: car age, 1 or 2 years

The research objective is to see if the number of claims or the rate of claims may be explained by car size and car age. Since rate of claims is the model of greater interest, the Poisson rate model is treated first, then the corresponding Poisson count model. We start by reading in the data.

```
setwd("c:/Data")
carinsure <- read.table("carinsure.csv", header = TRUE, sep = ",")
```

Next we create factor variables for age and carsize, which otherwise will be treated as continuous variables. Car age is coded 1 or 2, and we create agef as a factor variable with 2 as the reference level. Carsize is coded 1 = small, 2 = midsize, and 3 = large) and we create carsizef as a factor variable with 3 as the reference level.

```
agef <- relevel(as.factor(carinsure$age), ref = "2")
carsizef <- relevel(as.factor(carinsure$carsize), ref = "3")
```

3.5.5.3 The Poisson rate model

Poisson count models can be extended to rate data, such as count of crimes per 100,000 population. The denominator in the rate is the "offset variable" or "exposure variable". Typically the offset variable is entered in log form because the log link function is used in Poisson regression. The denominator variable is not used in raw form. For instance, in studying count per time unit, the log of time is entered as the offset variable. As a second example, in a study of lost luggage, the numerator is the count of luggage pieces lost and the denominator is the log of exposure, which may be the log of number of air miles traveled.

Note that, in rate models, the exposure is not a predictor but rather is an offset variable. Mathematically, the offset variable is added to the predictor side of the Poisson regression equation as a variable whose coefficient is believed to be 1. The effect is to make the expected value of the outcome variable increase in proportion to the size of the logged exposure variable.

```
PoissonRateFit <- glm(carinsure$claims ~ carsizef + agef, offset =
carinsure$lnclients, family=poisson(link="log"))

summary(PoissonRateFit)
[Output:]
   Call:
   glm(formula = claims ~ carsizef + agef, family = poisson(link
   = "log"), off\set
   = lnclients)
```

```
Deviance Residuals:
       1          2          3          4          5          6
 1.00847  -0.93383  -0.21139  -0.60484   0.71931   0.06088

Coefficients:
            Estimate Std. Error z value Pr(>|z|)
(Intercept)  -3.0810     0.2584 -11.922  < 2e-16 ***
carsizef1     1.7643     0.2724   6.478 9.32e-11 ***
carsizef2     1.0715     0.2784   3.848 0.000119 ***
agef1        -1.3199     0.1359  -9.713  < 2e-16 ***
---
Signif. codes: 0'***' 0.001'**' 0.01'*' 0.05'.' 0.1' ' 1

(Dispersion parameter for poisson family taken to be 1)

    Null deviance: 175.1536  on 5  degrees of freedom
Residual deviance:   2.8207  on 2  degrees of freedom
AIC: 40.928

Number of Fisher Scoring iterations: 4
```

Discussion of Poisson rate model output above

- In relation to the reference level (3), both levels of carsize (1 and 2) are significant predictors of claim's rate.
- Age of the car, age, is also a significant predictor.
- Standard errors and significance levels are the same as computed by SPSS.
- The residual deviance, which represents model error, is 2.8207. This is the same as what SPSS calls deviance and may be used in LR tests when comparing nested models.
- The AIC of 40.9 is also the same as SPSS and may be used on a lower-is-better basis when comparing nested or non-nested models.

Testing for overdispersion

Below we compute the deviance ratio as a test for overdispersion in the Poisson rate model. The deviance ratio is 1.41 (the same as in SPSS). A value of 1.0 represents zero overdispersion. One may ask if 1.41 is too much overdispersion, thus calling for using a negative binomial rather than Poisson rate model. One rule-of-thumb is that a deviance ratio <= 1.5 is acceptable, which it is for these data, indicating that overdispersion is not so great as to require the researcher to abandon the Poisson rate model in favor of a negative binomial model:

```
deviance <- PoissonRateFit$deviance
deviance
[Output:]
      [1] 2.820665

df <- PoissonRateFit$df.residual
df
[Output:]
      [1] 2

devianceratio <- deviance/df
devianceratio
[Output:]
      [1] 1.410333
```

Another method of testing for overdispersion is to use the `dispersiontest()` function from the "AER" package: A finding of nonsignificance, as in the following output, corresponds to finding overdispersion not to be significantly high. Thus, by either method, we retain the Poisson rate model and do not move to a negative binomial model.

```
library(AER)
AER::dispersiontest(PoissonRateFit,trafo=1)
[Output:]
      Overdispersion test
   data:  PoissonRateFit
   z = -3.2678, p-value = 0.9995
   alternative hypothesis: true alpha is greater than 0
   sample estimates:
        alpha
   -0.5092713
```

3.5.5.4 The Poisson count model

Though technically dollars of income is a count, income is a (usually) normally distributed continuous variable used in OLS linear models. OLS is appropriate for many types of counts and, indeed, has its origins in counts of agricultural products. Count models in Poisson regression are preferred over linear regression when the count is of a rare event (e.g., count of days until death, count of days between violent conflicts among nations) or the count is relatively small for discrete events (e.g., count of births of unwed mothers at a school). Count data are measured in integers and are non-negative.

Running the Poisson count model is identical to running the rate model, except the offset option is omitted.

```
PoissonCountFit <- glm(carinsure$claims~carsizef + agef, family=poisson(link="log"))
summary(PoissonCountFit)
[Output: ]
   Call:
   glm(formula = carinsure$claims ~ carsizef + agef, family = poisson(link = "log"))

   Deviance Residuals:
          1          2          3          4          5          6
   -0.10537   0.71210  -1.98923   0.06847  -0.47841    1.01992

   Coefficients:
               Estimate Std. Error z value Pr(>|z|)
   (Intercept)   2.3535     0.2613   9.008  < 2e-16 ***
   carsizef1     2.2548     0.2714   8.308  < 2e-16 ***
   carsizef2     1.9924     0.2752   7.239 4.52e-13 ***
   agef1        -0.8544     0.1335  -6.401 1.55e-10 ***
   ---
   Signif. codes:  0 '***' 0.001 '**' 0.01 '*' 0.05 '.' 0.1 ' ' 1

   (Dispersion parameter for poisson family taken to be 1)

       Null deviance: 177.341  on 5  degrees of freedom
   Residual deviance:   5.749  on 2  degrees of freedom
   AIC: 43.856

   Number of Fisher Scoring iterations: 5
```

For purposes of later comparison with other models, such as the negative binomial model, we may use the AIC model fit value, for which lower is less error and better fit.

```
PoissonCountFit$aic

[Output:]
      [1] 43.85595
```

3.5.5.5 The Poisson loglinear model

The Poisson family of model also includes loglinear analysis, where the objective is to explain the count in a table even if there is no "outcome variable". Although in Section 2.7 we illustrated loglinear analysis using the `loglm()` function of the "MASS" package, we can also use the `glm()` program as discussed here. In a Poisson loglinear model, the distribution family is Poisson and the link is log.

Loglinear analysis predicts the count in tables. Recall that in Section 2.7 on loglinear analysis we created a race by degree by sex table called "table1", using the following command.

```
table1 <- xtabs(~race+degree+sex, data=survey)
```

In this section, we use the same factor variables, which created table1 but seek only to show that the `glm()` command may be used to test the first of the models discussed in Section 2.7, the independence model.

```
# Create a flattened frequency table with the desired variables
x <- ftable(survey[c("race", "degree", "sex")])
x

# Transform it to a data frame in which the variable "Freq" is added automatically
surveydf <- as.data.frame(as.table(x))
head(surveydf,3)
[Output:]
     race degree sex Freq
  1   1       0   1   84
  2   2       0   1   23
  3   3       0   1   12
```

Given the foregoing steps, we can now run the independence (main effects only) model as in Section 2.7 but using `glm()`. "Freq" is a variable containing cell frequencies from the table implied by the predictors, which are factors.

```
LoglinearIndependenceFit<-glm(surveydf$Freq ~ surveydf$race + surveydf$degree +
surveydf$sex, family=poisson(link="log"))

# We compute the deviance, df, and p significance values.
# All are identical to Section 2.7, which used the loglm() command
deviance <- LoglinearIndependenceFit$deviance
deviance
[Output:]
      [1] 82.55919

df <- LoglinearIndependenceFit$df.residual
df
[Output:]
      [1] 22

p = 1 - pchisq(deviance, df)
p
[Output:]
      [1] 6.116095e-09
```

We may use an information theory measure such as AIC to compare other loglinear models, where lower AIC is better fit.

```
LoglinearIndependenceFit$aic
[Output:]
      [1] 248.7907
```

3.5.6 Negative binomial regression

3.5.6.1 Introduction

When count data are overdispersed, then the Poisson distribution does not apply and a negative binomial model is recommended instead. Put another way, if the deviance ratio is appreciably greater than 1.0, a negative binomial model may fit better than a Poisson regression model. Negative binomial regression is also more stable than Poisson regression for small datasets (Rogers, 1993). It may also be used as an alternative to gamma regression for skewed data.

Compared to the Poisson model, the negative binomial model has one additional term, k, representing a dispersion parameter. The dispersion criterion is reported in different ways in different statistical packages. It is the "dispersion parameter" in SPSS, labeled "Value/df" in output, where "Value" is the deviance. SAS reports it as "Value/DF". Stata reports it as "(1/df)". There are variations in algorithms causing small differences in coefficients but rarely differences in interpretation. R generates "deviance" and "df", allowing the user to easily compute deviance/df.

In all approaches, the greater the dispersion parameter is above 1.0, the greater the overdispersion. Overdispersion may reflect an incorrect data distribution specification (e.g., Poisson when the data are negative binomial), an incorrect link function, non-independent data, presence of outliers, model misspecification (important unmeasured variables), or nonlinear relationships. Uncorrected overdispersion is associated with underestimation of standard errors, and hence with Type I errors (false positive findings).

In addition to the dispersion parameter, negative binomial regression has an "ancillary parameter". By default, this is 1.0. However, the researcher may override this and insert some other value. A value of 0, for instance, is the same as assuming a Poisson distribution. Adding to the possible confusion, R calls the ancillary parameter the "dispersion parameter" in output at the bottom of the `summary()` command for a `glm()` object: E.g., "`(Dispersion parameter for poisson family taken to be 1)`". This terminology reflects disagreement in the field about labeling. In some documentation, R also calls the ancillary parameter theta (θ). Some also call it the "heterogeneity parameter". When running count and rate models, most users accept the 1.0 default set by R and major statistical packages.

3.5.6.2 Setup

At this writing and unlike GZLM modules in major statistical packages, the `glm()` command does not support negative binomial regression. Instead one uses the `glm.nb()` command from the "MASS" package. This command is a modification of `glm()` to support negative binomial regression. Note that, while not discussed here, the `glm()` command does support "quasi-Poisson" models, which do seek to adjust for overdispersion, but quasi-Poisson solutions are not identical to negative binomial solutions.

The following, in case the reader has deleted it, we again load the "carinsure" data frame. We will use this dataset to assess a count model. Thus, the outcome variable is count of insurance claims, not rate (not count per log of clients). Warning: We use this example only to compare with the Poisson count model. Be aware that in actual research negative binomial models are disparaged for small samples, which carinsure.csv is.

```
library(MASS)
setwd("c:/Data")
carinsure <- read.table("carinsure.csv", header = TRUE, sep = ",")
```

3.5.6.3 The negative binomial model

Recall that the Poisson count model for these data returned a deviance/df dispersion parameter value of 1.41. This indicates modest overdispersion below the rule-of-thumb cutoff of 1.5. Nonetheless, we run a negative binomial model to see if it returns better model fit by AIC than the Poisson count model.

The commands below run a negative binomial regression with count of insurance claims as the outcome variable and with the predictor variables carsize and age treated as factors, with reference levels of 3 and 2 respectively. Note that with the `glm.nb()` command, it is not necessary to specify the family or link.

```
car_age <- relevel(as.factor(carinsure$age),ref=2)
car_size <- relevel(as.factor(carinsure$carsize),ref=3)
```

```
NegBinomialFit <- MASS::glm.nb(carinsure$claims ~ car_size + car_age, data =
carinsure)
summary(NegBinomialFit)
[Partial output:]
    Deviance Residuals:
           1          2          3          4          5          6
    -0.10533    0.71206   -1.98921    0.06845   -0.47842    1.01991

    Coefficients:
                 Estimate Std. Error z value Pr(>|z|)
    (Intercept)    2.3535     0.2613   9.008  < 2e-16 ***
    car_size1      2.2548     0.2714   8.308  < 2e-16 ***
    car_size2      1.9924     0.2752   7.239 4.53e-13 ***
    car_age1      -0.8544     0.1335  -6.400 1.55e-10 ***
    ---
    Signif. codes:
    0 '***' 0.001 '**' 0.01 '*' 0.05 '.' 0.1 ' ' 1

    (Dispersion parameter for Negative Binomial(351916) family taken to be 1)

        Null deviance: 177.3217  on 5  degrees of freedom
    Residual deviance:   5.7489  on 2  degrees of freedom
    AIC: 45.857

    2 x log-likelihood:  -35.857
```

The coefficients above, which are the same as in major statistical packages such as SPSS and Stata, are almost identical to those for the Poisson count model. This is a tip-off that the additional term (the dispersion parameter) in the negative binomial model adds negligibly to model fit. The negative binomial model returns a model fit value of AIC = 45.86. As we saw in the Poisson count model, the AIC for that model was 43.86. Since this is lower, the Poisson count model may be said to have better fit. Also, since it has one less parameter, the researcher would prefer the Poisson model on parsimony grounds.

To conclude that the Poisson model had significantly better fit than the negative binomial model, we perform a LR test with the `anova()` command.

```
anova(PoissonCountFit, NegBinomialFit)
[Output:]
   Analysis of Deviance Table

   Model 1: carinsure$claims ~ carsizef + agef
   Model 2: carinsure$claims ~ car_size + car_age
     Resid. Df Resid. Dev Df   Deviance
   1         2     5.7490
   2         2     5.7489  0 0.00016995
```

The analysis of deviance table above is interpreted as follows:

- Model 1 is the Poisson model. This can be verified by look at PoissonCountFit$deviance, which shows a value of 5.7490.
- Model 2 is the negative binomial model. This can be verified by looking at NegBinomialFit$deviance, which shows a value of 5.7489.
- As the deviances are almost the same, the "Deviance" value, which is really the deviance difference, is almost 0.
- Moreover, as the two models have the same degrees of freedom (2), the difference in degrees of freedom is 0, so the LR test cannot be performed.
- However, we have demonstrated that the less parsimonious negative binomial model does not improve on the Poisson count model, which has slightly less error as indicated by having a lower AIC.

Note that as in other statistical procedures, factors are treated differently than continuous variables. The following command would have treated carsize and age as continuous variables and would have given different coefficients:

```
glm.nb(carinsure$claims ~ carinsure$carsize + carinsure$age, data = carinsure)
```

[Partial output:]

```
Coefficients:
      (Intercept)  carinsure$carsize      carinsure$age
           4.2515            -1.1290             0.9555
Degrees of Freedom: 5 Total (i.e. Null);  3 Residual
Null Deviance:        23.69
Residual Deviance: 7.201        AIC: 58.04
```

The NegBinomialFit object has the same statistical elements as discussed for previous GZLM models. These include NegBinomialFit$residuals, NegBinomialFit$fitted.values, and others which appear in a pop-up menu when the user types NegBinomialFit$.

3.6 Multilevel modeling (MLM)

3.6.1 Introduction

MLM is also called HLM and LMM. It is used whenever the DV clusters by levels of a categorical variable. For instance, student scores at level1 might cluster by schools at level 2. Such clustering violates the assumption of OLS regression that data be independent. That is, when there is clustering there is correlated error. MLM is a leading approach to handling correlated error, though there are alternatives such as GEEs or use of cluster-robust standard errors. If OLS regression is used in spite of the presence of correlated error, its parameter estimates will be in error, leading to possible significant errors of interpretation.

In spite of the term "hierarchical linear modeling", MLM models can handle non-hierarchical data through cross-classified models. In spite of the term "linear mixed modeling", MLM can support nonlinear generalized models. Also, MLM can handle longitudinal data. Cross-classified, generalized, and repeated measures models are not covered in this volume, however (Garson, 2020). While there are many types of MLM model, only two basic models are discussed in this chapter. The MLM null mode, used to see if MLM is needed, as presented earlier in this chapter's "Quick Start" section. In this section, the two-level RE model is presented.[6] This is one of the most-used MLM models. For coverage of other models, including in R, see Garson (2020).

All MLM models adjust estimates of the intercept (mean) of one or more DVs at level 1 based on clustering variables at level 2 or higher. RE models also adjust the slope (b coefficient) of one or more predictors at levels lower than that of the categorical clustering (level) variable. The MLM process means that not only estimates may differ from those of OLS regression but also their standard errors. In some ways this is even more important as it dictates whether an effect is seen as significant or not significant.

MLM usually employs ML estimation. ML in turn returns the "likelihood", which is a measure of model error, with lower being better. When transformed into -2LL, this statistic follows a chi-square distribution, useful for significance testing. The -2LL statistic is also called the LR, model chi-square, or the deviance (beware that there are other types of deviance in statistics). The LR (LR) test is used to compare models based on differences in -2LL in conjunction with differences in degrees of freedom. The LR test, however, is only for nested models (all the terms in the smaller model are present in the larger model when two models are compared). Forms of penalized deviance such as the AIC and BIC coefficients are used to compare non-nested models, with lower being less error and better model fit.

3.6.2 Setup and data

To illustrate MLM, we use the hsbmerged.csv dataset. We store it as a data frame called "hsb". This is a version of the classic "High School and Beyond Survey" subsample data on 7,185 student-level observations with no missing values, grouped under 160 schools, and collected in 1982. These data are used by Raudenbush et al. (2011), authors of HLM 7 software, based on their seminal work on MLM. These data were also used in the "Quick Start" section of this chapter.

While R has multiple packages for implementing MLM models; the leading package is "lme4", which requires explicit installation. The lme4 package supports the `lmer()` MLM model function. An auxiliary package, "lmerTest", is required to generate p significance values for random effects. The lme4 package is newer than another popular alternative not discussed here – the "nmle" package and its `lme()` command, which is still used due to its unique features. See Bates et al. (2015) for further information on the lme4 package.

```
library(lme4)
library(lmerTest)

# Set the working directory
setwd("c:/Data")

# Read in, view, and list variable names for the data
hsb <- read.table("hsbmerged.csv", header = TRUE, sep = ",")
View(hsb)
names(hsb)
[Output of variable names:]
   [1] "schoolid" "minority" "female"   "ses"
   [5] "mathach"  "size"     "sector"   "pracad"
   [9] "disclim"  "himinty"  "meanses"
```

In output above, the outcome variable is math achievement score (mathach) and the level 2 grouping variable is school identification number (schoolid). Other variables of interest include ses (centered student socioeconomic status), meanses (ses centered at group means at the school level), and sector (sector 0 is public schools, sector 1 is parochial schools).

3.6.3 The random coefficients model

An RC model models the intercept of the outcome variable at level 1, just like the null model. However, it also models the b coefficient of at least one lower-level predictor variable. In addition, additional predictor variables may be added at any level. Coefficients representing effects are, as in all regression models, effects "controlling for other effects in the model."

TEXT BOX 3.1 Social science applications of R: Who is more censorious of movies, the young or the old?

Chen et al. (2019) used the `lmer()` program from the lme4 package in R to implement a multilevel model of a type discussed in the text. The authors studied movie rating data to try to understand if young people or senior citizens were more censorious in their evaluations and ratings of movies. Censoriousness was the outcome variable at level 1. Age (categorized into seven age ranges) was the fixed effect. Occupation and gender were random effects. For instance, for the comedy genre the R command was:

```
Model1 <- lmer(Rating -1 + Age + (1|Occupation) + (1|Gender), comedy)
```

Illustrating the "Big Data" capabilities of the `lmer()` program, millions of movie ratings were examined in the categories of comedy, science fiction, children, adventure, and all movies. The authors found that for most genres, "When the age factor is viewed as fixed effects, the rating scores for movies are positively related to age. In general the young people tend to give lower scores than senior people."

Source: Chen, Z.; Zhu, S.; Niu, Q.; & Lu, X. (2019). Censorious young: Knowledge discovery from high-throughput movie rating data with LME4. 2019 IEEE 4th International Conference on Big Data Analytics (ICBDA), Suzhou, China, 2019, pp. 32–36, doi: 10.1109/ICBDA.2019.8713193.

In the null model, the only effect on mathach was the random effect of the level 2 link variable, schoolid. In the RC model we add a level 1 predictor, ses (a measure of students' socioeconomic status), and a level 2 predictor, meanses (the average ses level in a school). We also add a second random effect, which is the random effect of schoolid at level 2 on the b coefficient of ses at level 1. Thus, in the RC model, schoolid models both the intercept of the outcome variable (mathach) and the slope of the level 1 predictor variable (ses).

We now run the RC model using ML estimation (setting REML to FALSE does this). The double vertical bars in the random effects specification call for a random effects to be constrained to be independent. This is called a "Variance Components" or "Independence" model. The syntax for entering the two random effects is `(1+ses||schoolid)`. The two vertical bars specify a random effects (RE) model in which the random effects are independent. The "1" part gets the schoolid effect on the intercept of mathach. The "ses" part adds the random effect of schoolid on the slope of ses to the model.

We now run the model. Note that the `lmerTest::lmer()` package prefix is required to assure that fixed effect p values for fixed effects appear. The p values do not to appear if the `lme4::lmer()` package prefix is used.

```
library(lme4)
library(lmerTest)
RCMLMmodel <- lmerTest::lmer(hsb$mathach ~ hsb$ses + hsb$meanses +
(1 + hsb$ses||hsb$schoolid), REML = FALSE, data = hsb)
summary(RCMLMmodel)
```

[Output:]

```
Linear mixed model fit by maximum likelihood.  t-tests use
  Satterthwaite's method [lmerModLmerTest]
Formula: mathach ~ ses + meanses + (1 + ses || schoolid)
   Data: hsb
     AIC      BIC   logLik deviance df.resid
 46570.0  46611.2 -23279.0  46558.0     7179
Scaled residuals:
     Min       1Q   Median       3Q      Max
-3.15488 -0.72274  0.01776  0.75545  2.95298

Random effects:
 Groups     Name        Variance Std.Dev.
 schoolid   (Intercept)  2.6660  1.6328
 schoolid.1 ses          0.4676  0.6838
 Residual               36.7802  6.0647
Number of obs: 7185, groups:  schoolid, 160

Fixed effects:
            Estimate Std. Error       df t value Pr(>|t|)
(Intercept)  12.6537     0.1500 155.0738   84.34   <2e-16 ***
ses           2.1923     0.1223 184.1931   17.93   <2e-16 ***
meanses       3.7730     0.3815 185.5458    9.89   <2e-16 ***
---
Signif. codes:  0 '***' 0.001 '**' 0.01 '*' 0.05 '.' 0.1 ' ' 1

Correlation of Fixed Effects:
        (Intr) ses
ses      0.001
meanses -0.009 -0.260
```

Comments on `summary()` *output above*

- All fixed effects (ses, meanses, intercept) in the model are significant at better than the .001 level.
- Three random effects are shown: The schoolid effect on mean math achievement, the schoolid effect on the b coefficient for student ses, and the residual component reflecting otherwise unexplained variance in math

achievement. In this model random effects were constrained to be uncorrelated. Significance for random effects is given by the `rand()` command, discussed below.

- Model fit measures (log likelihood (LL), AIC, BIC) are the same as generated by the `rand()` command, discussed below.
- Unlike `rand()`, `summary()` prints the deviance, which is -2 times the LL. Deviance is a measure of model error used in LR tests of the difference between two nested models.
- The residual variance component (36.78) remains by far the largest component, showing that most of the variance in mathach is not well explained by effects specified in the model. However, an LR test may nonetheless show that the schoolid random effect is significant. If nontrivial new effects are added to the model, all coefficients will change, as they do in other forms of regression.
- The `VarCorr()` command also gives standard deviations of the random effects in the model: `lme4::VarCorr(RCMLMmodel)`

Had the random effects for the model above been specified with a single vertical bar, the model would not be constrained to have uncorrelated variance components and a "Corr" column would be in the summary table. The brief example below illustrates this. For comparison, we run a similar model, RCMLMmodel2, where random effects are allowed to covary. This is accomplished by having only a single vertical bar in the `lmer()` syntax. Only random effects output from this alternative model is shown.

```
# Comparison model
RCMLMmodel2 <- lmerTest::lmer(hsb$mathach ~ hsb$ses + hsb$meanses + (1 +
hsb$ses|hsb$schoolid), REML = FALSE, data = hsb)
summary(RCMLMmodel2)
(Partial output:)
    Random effects:
     Groups        Name        Variance Std.Dev. Corr
     hsb$schoolid (Intercept)  2.6487  1.6275
                  hsb$ses      0.4368  0.6609   -0.22
     Residual                 36.7970  6.0661
    Number of obs: 7185, groups:  hsb$schoolid, 160
```

Discussion:

- The variance component of the schoolid random effect on the ses slope is correlated at the –0.22 level with the variance component of the schoolid random effect on the intercept of mathach.
- Allowing correlated random effects changes the estimates of effects.
- This is what would happen if random effects are not constrained to be independent. For independence, use a double vertical bar when specifying random effects.

We now look at output from the `rand()` command.

```
lmerTest::rand(RCMLMmodel)
[Output:]
   ANOVA-like table for random-effects: Single term deletions
   Model:
   mathach ~ ses + means + (1 | schoolid) + (0 + ses | schoolid)
                              npar logLik   AIC     LRT Df Pr(>Chisq)
   <none>                        6 -23279 46570
   (1 | schoolid)                5 -23401 46812 243.916  1    < 2e-16 ***
   ses in (0 + ses | schoolid)   5 -23282 46574   5.851  1    0.01557 *
   ---
   Signif. codes:  0 '***' 0.001 '**' 0.01 '*' 0.05 '.' 0.1 ' ' 1
```

Comments on `rand()` *output above*

- `rand()` is a function of the lme4 package.
- The primary purpose of the `rand()` output is to show the significance of the random effects.
- The "(1|schoolid)" row is the random effect of schoolid on the intercept of mathach. This effect is significant at better than the .001 level.
- The "ses in (0 + ses|schoolid)" row is the random effect of schoolid on the slope of ses. It is significant at the .016 level.
- The "<none>" row gives the LL and the AIC for the model. These coefficients may be used when comparing nested and non-nested models respectively. The LL is multiplied by -2 for LR tests and becomes the "deviance" as shown in `summary()` output.
- Coefficients are almost identical to those from major packages such as SPSS, SAS, and Stata. R and Stata report the LL, whereas SPSS and SAS follow the more usual custom of multiplying by -2 to get the deviance (-2LL). The deviance follows a chi-square distribution and is used in LR tests of difference between nested models.

3.6.4 Likelihood ratio test

We now illustrate the LR test by comparing the NullMLMmodel output (from the "Quick Start" section) with the RCMLMmodel output. Recall NullMLMmodel contains results of the `lmer()` run of the null model and RCMLMmodel the results from the RE model. Naturally, the following syntax assumes both objects are still in the environment. The LR test assesses whether model improvement in RCMLMmodel compared to the NullMLMmodel is significant. This is done with a simple ANOVA test, using the `anova()` command from the "stats" package from R's system library.

```
anova(NullMLMmodel,RCMLMmodel)
```

[Output:]

```
Data: hsb
Models:
NullMLMmodel: hsb$mathach ~ (1 | hsb$schoolid)
RCMLMmodel: mathach ~ ses + meanses + (1 + ses || schoolid)
             Df   AIC   BIC logLik deviance  Chisq Chi Df Pr(>Chisq)
NullMLMmodel  3 47122 47142 -23558    47116
RCMLMmodel    6 46570 46611 -23279    46558 557.86      3  < 2.2e-16 ***
---
Signif. codes:  0 '***' 0.001 '**' 0.01 '*' 0.05 '.' 0.1 ' ' 1
```

The LR test shows that the RC model is significantly different from the null model at better than the .001 level. Since deviance is lower in the RC model, it is the better model. We conclude that the RC model significantly better explains math achievement compared to the null model.

3.7 Panel data regression (PDR)

3.7.1 Introduction

Panel data are cross-sectional time series data where the same subjects are measured in each time period. The "subjects" need not be people. The units could also reflect data on city governments, census tracts, or stocks, for example, but the same cities, tracts, or stocks would be measured in each time period. Panel data therefore have "between-subjects" information for any given time period and have "within-subjects" information for the same subjects across the time periods.

Having subject-level data is very important with respect to model specification and the treatment of unmeasured variables. In the usual type of multiple regression with cross-sectional data for one time period (between subjects data), the researcher wants all important variables to be explicit in the model since model misspecification can radically alter the regression coefficients. In PDR, however, one has within-subjects data for the same subjects across time, so the subjects are their own controls for unobserved variables not explicitly in the model. For models using within-subjects data the researcher does not need to know what these variables are, only assume that they affect the same individuals similarly for each time period studied. PDR uses within-subjects information across time to adjust the standard errors of variables and thereby adjust the substantive analysis of results.

Related to panel data models are "population averaged" models. These apply to repeated cross-sectional data in which the subjects are different in each time period. That is, panel data models deal with the same subjects over time and repeated cross-sectional models deal with different subjects over time. Unfortunately some textbooks, statistical package documentation, and even well-known data sources such as the "General Social Survey" confuse matters by labeling both types "panel data", but different mathematical models apply to panel data compared to repeated cross-sectional data.

OLS regression is a population-averaged (PA) model because it predicts the mean of the outcome variable (the population average) but cannot account directly for changes at the subject level. GEE is an extension of regression to handle repeated measures. In a PA model, whether OLS or GEE, the researcher cannot trace the political preference history of individuals over time but can trace group averages. For example, how white Protestant males residing in the South have changed on average in political preference over time can be analyzed with PA models.

In contrast to PA modeling, MLM models treat subject-level data at level 1 as affected by grouping factors at level 2 or higher. Like PDR, MLM can be longitudinal, as with student math scores at level 1 grouped by time periods (e.g., years tests were given) at level 2 and by schools at level 3. Also, like PDR, MLM can partition random effects into group effects (called between-group effects) and subject-level effects (called within-group effects).

Both PDR models and MLM models use the terms "fixed effects" and "random effects", but the meaning is different. Nonetheless, both PDR and MLM might be applied to the same data. Depending on the data, it may be possible to construct the same model in either PDR or MLM. However, there are three key differences:

- PDR has been developed for use in economics and incorporates features used by econometricians, such as a variety of estimation methods other than ML, support for lagged variables, and specialized tests for model selection such as the Hausman test.
- Fixed and random effects are conceptualized differently and these terms may not mean the same thing in a PDR-based analysis as in an MLM-based one.
- Unobserved heterogeneity due to unmeasured variables is treated differently.

3.7.2 Types of PDR model

PDR packages may offer both PA variants and different subject-level variants. The latter include RE models, fixed effects (FE) models, and between-effects (BEs) models. Each has distinct uses and assumptions. As described below, usage of the terms "fixed" and "random" effects differs between PDR and MLM models.

- *FE models* are used to understand the subject-level effect of variables which vary over time as well as to understand cross-sectional effects of measured variables. FE models do not shed light on the cross-sectional effects of variables which are invariant over time because FE models require assuming that unmeasured variables are constant over time and that error terms (which reflect the effect of unmeasured variables) are not correlated. If they are correlated, standard errors may not be calculated correctly and inferences may be wrong. The Hausman test, discussed below, is in part a test for correlated error. In PDR FE models, the effect of time-invariant variables is absorbed in the intercept. Contrast this usage with "fixed effects" in MLM, where the fixed effects table is simply the regression table for effects of a covariate at any level on the outcome variable at level 1, where regression coefficients and their standard errors are modeled by the clustering of the outcome within groups formed by clustering variables at level 2 and higher.

  Though not treated in this text, note that the R package "feisr" supports the function `feis()` to estimate fixed effects individual slope (FEIS) models. These models may be seen as more general version of the often-used FE panel model as implemented in the package "plm" and discussed in this chapter.

TEXT BOX 3.2 Social science applications of R: Does more external information lead to better outcomes in resource competition negotiations?

Osborne et al. used the `plm()` program from the "plm" package, discussed in this chapter, to study "Ecological interdependencies and resource competition: The role of information and communication in promoting effective collaboration in complex management situations." While it is well-established in the literature that the ability of resource users to communicate information was critical to negotiating ecological solutions, the research purpose of this study was to understand better "if, in cases when different means other than communication were available, whether they would be more effective." For instance, instead of resource users being reliant on within-group communication to acquire useful information, it might be that a public agency acting as an intermediary could provide such useful information. The authors used data from laboratory experiments to explore the relative importance of communication in managing "a complex social-ecological system characterized by common-pool resource dilemmas, ecological interdependencies, and asymmetric resource access."

The authors found, based on panel data regression with `plm()`, that the ability to communicate significantly increased individual and group performance. Surprisingly, the authors also found there was a negative effect on overall outcomes due to providing external information even when users also had the ability to communicate. Apparently the combination of providing external information combined with user communications worked jointly to increase individual cognitive load and to increase intra-group competition, leading in turn to a significant reduction of individual and group outcomes.

The appendix to the article gives `plm()` commands and output. For instance, the command below is for the panel data regression model with communication and external information, using a oneway/individual effect random effect model:

```
plm(formula = optimal_diff ~ totmsg + as.factor(round), data = Info,   na.action
= na.omit, model = "random", index = c("agame",   "round"))
```

An additional `plm()` example is Chakrabarti and Makhija (2019), who studies American advertising spending over time.

Source: Chakrabarti, Somnath & Makhija, Mayank. (2019). Exploratory study on variables impacting display advertising spend of leading advertisers in the USA. Journal of Marketing Communications. Published online: 31 Jul 2019. Doi: 10.1080/13527266.2019.1646306

Matthew Osborne, Matthew; Sundström, Emma; & Bodin, Örjan. (2019). Ecological interdependencies and resource competition: The role of information and communication in promoting effective collaboration in complex management situations. *PLoS One* 14(12): e0225903. Published online December 17, 2019; https://doi.org/10.1371/journal.pone.0225903.

- *RE models* in PDR are based on a weighted average of fixed and between effects (see below). Time-invariant variables may be specified in the model, unlike in FE models. RE models assume that cross-sectional variation due to unmeasured effects is random in any given time period and is uncorrelated with predictor variables in the model. Cross-sectional variation may be correlated with the DV and, indeed, RE models are typically used when the researcher thinks that this is the case. This means that the researcher may use an RE model if it is thought that unmeasured variables impact the DV but are uncorrelated with the predictor variables. However, on a data-driven basis, many PDR researchers use the Hausman test to choose between fixed and RE models. Contrast this usage with "random effects" in MLM, where the random effects table partitions effects, which cause correlated error into three components. In a two-level MLM model, the random effects are (1) a between-groups random component associated with the level 2 clustering variable on the mean value (intercept) of the level 1 outcome variable; (2) between-group effects of measured variables at higher levels on level 1 coefficients (if the researcher's model calls for this); and (3) a within-groups residual component reflecting unexplained variance at the subject level (e.g., due to ability variation among students within schools, where school is the random effect of the level 2 clustering variable.

- *BE models* can be used to understand the effect of variables which vary cross-sectionally but are invariant over time. Between effects models do not shed light on the longitudinal effects of variables which are invariant cross-sectionally. This is a less common type of model.
- *PA models,* discussed above, are used to model aggregate changes in a DV over time, contrasting groups. PA models address between-groups questions like, "As the ratio of cigarette smokers to non-smokers increases over time, by what factor does lung disease change?" PA models do not explain individual-level change and are sensitive to model specification (e.g., if industrial air pollution causes lung disease and is not included in the model, erroneous inferences may be made). Note that PA PDR is different from "pooled regression," where the researcher simply puts all data in a large dataset and runs an OLS regression. This treats each data row as a separate observation, artificially inflating sample size and inflating Type 1 error and ignores correlated error across time, instead assuming temporal effects are non-existent (if they aren't, estimates will be misleading. Population-averaged PDR models, in contrast, adjust coefficient estimates for possible correlation across years and do not inflate sample size, although the adjustment is on a PA rather than subject-specific basis (unlike FE, RE, and BE models). Also, pooled regression solutions have an intercept, whereas PDR population averaged solutions constrain the solution to go through the origin. Mathematically, PA models are the same as GEE models.

There are, as one might expect, literally hundreds of other econometric models, far beyond what can be illustrated here.

3.7.3 The Hausman test

The Hausman test, shorthand for the Durbin-Wu-Hausman test, is widely used to help the researcher decide if a fixed or an RE model is needed in a PDR analysis. The logic of the Hausman test rests on understanding the concepts of "consistent" and "efficient" models. "Consistent" means that the estimates are asymptotically correct. That is, a model is consistent if for large samples, its estimates are close to the actual ones. "Efficient", in the context of PDR, means that a model under consideration is not only consistent but also has lower standard errors of estimate than a comparison model. Thus, in PDR we might use the Hausman test to see if an RE model is more efficient than an equally consistent FE model. Note that the Hausman test may be used to compare other pairs of models, not just RE vs. FE.

Ideally, both FE and RE estimates would be equally good (consistent) and the RE estimate would be preferred because it yields lower standard errors (is more efficient). If both estimates are equally good, the estimates would be the same. The Hausman test tests the null hypothesis that the estimates are indeed the same. If they are, the Hausman chi-square statistic will be nonsignificant and the researcher would opt for an RE model because it is more efficient. That is, a finding of nonsignificance on the Hausman test means the estimates are not significantly different and the researcher chooses the RE model, which will have lower standard errors. However, if the Hausman statistic is significant, then the FE and RE estimates are significantly different and the researcher assumes that the FE model is the one giving more accurate estimates and selects it, even though it may have higher standard errors.

In summary, the Hausman test computes the parameter estimates for both FE and RE models. It then tests the size of the difference in estimates. A finding of significance means the estimates differ between the models and for reasons given above, an FE model may be chosen by the researcher. The "may" in the last sentence is because the researcher may take a finding of significance on the Hausman test as an indication of model misspecification. The researcher may re-specify the model by adding or deleting variables, seeking to achieve the desired finding of nonsignificance on the Hausman test, in turn leading the researcher to use an RE model with its lower standard errors.

Like all tests, the Hausman test has assumptions. It assumes that error is "exogenous" to the model, which means that error is not correlated with the predictors or with the intercept. If this assumption is violated, both FE and RE models become inconsistent and the results of the Hausman test become unreliable. Also, the Hausman test is affected by sample size. The power of the Hausman test has been shown to decrease as sample size diminishes. Consequently, the Hausman test is not recommended for small samples. Jeong and Yoon (2010: 317), for example, found that even for samples of 100, the Hausman test rejected only 13.7% of false null hypotheses. In general, the Hausman test is an asymptotic procedure appropriate for large samples and is biased for small samples. Finally, note that employing robust standard errors is inconsistent with the Hausman test because it assumes the RE model to be efficient (minimizes standard errors) without "robust" adjustment.

In R, the Hausman test is implemented by the `phtest()` command of the "plm" PDR package. The PDR package "panelr" does not have an equivalent command. As the `phtest()` command requires running both an FE and an RE models, we leave its illustration to later in this chapter.

3.7.4 Setup and data

Conceptually, in a panel dataset subjects are rows, variables are columns, and there is one such data matrix for each time period. In practice, however, for analysis purposes the usual format is to have an ID variable (representing the unit of observation, such as a city, census tract, or respondent code), a time variable (e.g., year for yearly observations), and then additional columns representing the DV and the IVs. Each unit of observation (subject, such as a respondent id) has as many data rows as there are time periods.

Put another way, time typically is nested within subject: Data are ordered by subject id, then by time period within id. It is possible, however, to sort the rows by time period so that subject is nested within time: Data are ordered by time period, then by subject within time period. The former is a "nested time" design and the latter a "nested subjects" design. Stata, for example, expects a nested time format, also called a "long form" format.

Also, most software packages will allow there to be missing time periods for any given subject. In a "balanced panel" all subjects are measured in all time periods. In an "unbalanced panel" some subjects are missing measurements for some time periods.

The following examples further used these packages, which we activate at the outset: "plm" (often cited as the leading PDR package for R, assumed to be already installed). We also activate the package "panelr" (a newer alternative PDR package by Jacob Long (2019). Finally, for PA models, we activate the "gee" package.

```
library(plm)
library(panelr)
library(gee)
```

The example in this section uses ICPSR Study No. 3987, "Determinants of Case Growth in Federal District Courts in the United States, 1904-2002", subset DS6: "Federal Court Panel Data on Drugs and Immigration, 1968-1998." This dataset is maintained and distributed by the National Archive of Criminal Justice Data (NACJD), the criminal justice archive within ICPSR. The data have been rendered suitable for PDR analysis in the example file courts.csv, read in the usual way:

```
setwd("c:/Data")
courts <- read.table("courts.csv", header = TRUE, sep = ",")
View(courts)

head(courts,5)
```

[Partial output, first 8 variables of first 5 rows only, nested time design:)

```
  year circuit district ndistrict noj pfpy totalcom totalterm
1 1968       5     AL,M         1 1.5   23      183       178
2 1969       5     AL,M         1 1.5   28      190       191
3 1970       5     AL,M         1 2.0   27      249       246
4 1971       5     AL,M         1 2.0   30      231       224
5 1972       5     AL,M         1 2.0   37      310       304
```

The data cover 90 court districts over 31 years. Each district, numerically coded by the variable "ndistrict", has one row of data per year. This should mean there are 31*90 = 2,790 rows. However, there are only 2,786 data rows because a Louisiana district (ndistrict = 35) only started recording in 1972, so there are no data for the 4 years 1968–1971. Because not all subjects (here, courts) have the same number of observations, the data are "unbalanced", something that PDR can handle. There are no missing values for the reported districts and years covered.

As usually required for PDR, data are in "long form" format, also called "nested time" or "stacked data" format. For our example, the long form format is to have data sorted first by district, then by year. Thus, rows are all years, in order, for the first district; then the same for the second district; and so on. There are other data formats.[7] If data were not in long form, the researcher would have to use data manipulation commands not discussed here to achieve long form format.

In the example below, we seek to explain variation in the number of trials terminated per judge (trialstermp) as predicted over time (year) by number of civil and criminal filings per judge (civlfpj and criminalfpj) as well as by pending cases per judge (pendingpj) and the percentage that drug and immigration cases are of all criminal cases (pdrugmm). The data file has these variables for the years 1968–1998, not counting 15 other variables not used in the example.

The time variable:

year	Year

Grouping variables:

circuit	Circuit
district	District name (a string variable)
ndistrict	District number (a numeric conversion of DISTRICT)

The DV:

trialstermpJ	Trials terminated per judge (the DV)

Predictor variables:

civilfpj	Civil case filings per judge
criminalfpj	Criminal filings per judge
pendingpj	Pending cases per judge
pdrugmm	Percentage drug & immigration cases are of all crimes

3.7.5 PDR with the plm package

3.7.5.1 Setup

The "plm" package is the leading package for implementing PDR in R. We assume that the example data have been read in and stored in the "courts" data frame and that the plm package is installed. Estimates from the models discussed below are the same as in Stata and other major packages. We start this section by activating the plm package.

```
library(plm)
```

3.7.5.2 Fixed effects model

First we run the FE model, which is the "within" model. The listed p values show all effects are significant at the .01 level or better. The "within" model is the FE model, which uses only within-district variation. Because `effect="individual"` and since "individuals" are districts in the current example, districts are treated as a fixed effect and the second index variable, year, is not used. However, had we specified `effect= twoways,` then both district and year would be treated as fixed effects. Two-way FE models are discussed further below.

The FE model is the "within" model when `effect="individual"`, which is the default. The `index=` option specifies the data structure, with the subject (ndistrict) first followed by the time variable (year).

```
PDRfixed <- plm::plm(courts$trialstermpj ~ courts$civilfpj + courts$criminalfpj +
courts$pendingpj + courts$pdrugmm, index = c("ndistrict","year"), model="within",
effect="individual",data = courts)
```

```
summary(PDRfixed)
```
[Output:]
```
Oneway (individual) effect Within Model

Call:
plm(formula = trialstermpj ~ civilfpj + criminalfpj + pendingpj + pdrugmm, data =
courts, model = "within", index = c("ndistrict", "year"))

Unbalanced Panel: n = 90, T = 27-31, N = 2786
Residuals:
      Min.      1st Qu.      Median      3rd Qu.        Max.
-1619.9056   -36.6167     -6.9595      27.4608   2484.0723

Coefficients:
               Estimate  Std. Error  t-value   Pr(>|t|)
civilfpj       0.578859    0.017441  33.1901 < 2.2e-16 ***
criminalfpj    0.681453    0.035712  19.0820 < 2.2e-16 ***
pendingpj     -0.026449    0.010041  -2.6342  0.008482 **
pdrugmm      132.120630   13.820288   9.5599 < 2.2e-16 ***
---
Signif.codes:0 '***' 0.001 '**' 0.01 '*' 0.05 '.' 0.1 ' ' 1

Total Sum of Squares:    38509000
Residual Sum of Squares: 21116000
R-Squared:      0.45166
Adj. R-Squared: 0.43271
F-statistic: 554.332 on 4 and 2692 DF, p-value: < 2.22e-16
```

In the output row above that says "Unbalanced Panel", it is reported that there are 90 subjects/entities (districts) measured for 27–31 years, for a total of 2,786 observations. If the data are balanced (all districts report all years), $N = n*T$.

Since the FE model asked for the usual `effect="individual"` option, the model is testing for individual-level (district-level) effects, not taking into account the effects of year. We could switch to `effect="time"` to get the opposite, or we could specify `effect="twoway"` to estimate the model with the effects of both district and year. For the model above, if we enter `plm::fixef(PDRfixed)` we will get a list of effects for each of the 90 districts and we can compute its mean with the command `mean(plm::fixef(PDRfixed))`. However, there is no need to do this since the mean district effect is the "overall intercept" discussed below.

Note that FE models have no intercept listed in the output above. This is because they have one intercept for each entity. The closest one can come is to get an average "overall intercept". The plm package provides the function `within_intercept()` to estimate this. The intercept, of course, is the mean value of the outcome variable (trialstermpj) controlling for other effects in the model.

```
# With ordinary standard errors
plm::within_intercept(PDRfixed)
```
[Output:]
```
              136.8944
attr(,"se")
[1] 6.129673
```

```
# With robust standard errors
plm::within_intercept(PDRfixed, vcov = function(x) vcovHC(x, method="arellano",
type="HC0"))
```
[Output:]
```
(overall_intercept)
              136.8944
attr(,"se")
[1] 46.90088
```

We can still see the year effect in an FE model by setting `effect="twoways"`. This will change the coefficients since variation by year is now taken into account and we can ask for year effects with the `fixef()` command.

```
PDRfixed2way <- plm::plm(trialstermpj ~ courts$civilfpj + courts$criminalfpj +
courts$pendingpj + courts$pdrugmm, index = c("ndistrict","year"), model="within",
effect="twoways",data = courts)
```

```
# Get the overall intercept for the fixed two-way model for comparison
plm::within_intercept(PDRfixed2way)
(Output:)
        (overall_intercept)
              194.706
        attr(,"se")
        [1] 6.861001
```

```
# Get the time (year) effects to spot which years were most discrepant from 194.706
plm::fixef(PDRfixed2way,effect="time")
[Partial output:]
      1968      1969      1970      1971      1972      1973      1974
  108.6930 111.1899 151.1631 110.8442 133.2720 137.9240 139.9660
  . . .
  1997      1998
  217.0179 230.4233
```

After having spotted two years to compare, we can compute the mean of the outcome variable for these years, say 1968 and 1998. We see below that trial terminations per judge (trialstermpj) increased dramatically between 1968 and 1998.

```
# Create 1968 and 1998 subsets of the data
y1968 <- subset(courts, year=="1968")
y1998 <- subset(courts, year=="1998")
```

```
# Compute means of trialstermpj for each year
mean(y1968$trialstermpj)
      [1] 290.6966
mean(y1998$trialstermpj)
      [1] 451.1
```

Though outside the scope of this book, average marginal effects may be obtained using the "margins" package.[8]

There are also a variety of functions in plm to retrieve specific output components. In the "Packages" tab of RStudio, click on the plm package to see all available functions. Then, for instance, to retrieve the R-squared value:

```
plm::r.squared(PDRfixed)
[Output:]
      [1] 0.451656
```

3.7.5.3 Random effects model

We now run the RE models. As with the FE model, the listed p values show all effects are significant, though here at the .001 level or better. Though both models are good, the Hausman test discussed below helps decide which of the two models to select.

The "Effects" section of output for an RE model was not present for the FE models in the previous section. Two random effects are reported, which is to say that random error is partitioned into two components:

- *individual*: This is the individual-specific error variance component. In this example, districts are the "individuals". Though not usual, the individual component is 0 for this model.

- *idiosyncratic*: This is the remaining error variance. Idiosyncratic effort is assumed to be uncorrelated with either the individual effect or with the predictor variables for any time period for the same district (individual). Note this assumption rules out lagged outcome variables.

Below these two effect components is the "theta" coefficient. It reflects the relative importance of the variance for the individual effect, which is 0 for this model.

When the individual effect component is 0, there is no estimated individual (district) effect and a pooling model is the most efficient estimator. The pooling model pools all cross-sections (years) together, without considering any individual (district) effect. The pooling model is discussed in the next section.

Note that the standard errors for the predictors are lower in the RE model than for the FE model. Moreover, the R-squared value, reflecting the percent of variance explained in the outcome variable, is also higher. For these reasons, this RE model would be preferred over the corresponding FE model, but only if it were consistent vis-à-vis the FE model.

Why select the FE model over the RE model if the Hausman test shows the two not consistent (because the estimates differ)? After all, in choosing the FE model one is selecting a model with higher standard errors and lower R-squared, which on a naïve basis seems nonsensical. The reason is that the Hausman test shows that a critical assumption of the RE model is in error, and therefore its estimates are unreliable. RE models assume that random effects are orthogonal to (uncorrelated with) the predictor variables. FE models do not make this assumption and may be seen as reliable regardless of the validity of this assumption. That is why FE estimates are the "correct standard" against which RE estimates are compared. If the orthogonality assumption is wrong, RE estimates will differ from FE estimates and will not be reliable.

```
# Random effects model
PDRrandom <- plm::plm(courts$trialstermpj ~ courts$civilfpj + courts$criminalfpj +
courts$pendingpj + courts$pdrugmm, index = c("ndistrict","year"), model="random",
effect="individual", data = courts)

summary(PDRrandom)
[Output:]
   Oneway (individual) effect Random Effect Model
      (Swamy-Arora's transformation)
   Call:
   plm(formula = trialstermpj ~ civilfpj + criminalfpj + pendingpj + pdrugmm, data =
   courts, model = "random", index = c("ndistrict", "year"))

   Unbalanced Panel: n = 90, T = 27-31, N = 2786
   Effects:
                     var std.dev share
   idiosyncratic 7843.98   88.57     1
   individual       0.00    0.00     0
   theta:
      Min. 1st Qu.  Median    Mean 3rd Qu.    Max.
        0       0       0       0       0       0

   Residuals:
         Min.     1st Qu.     Median    3rd Qu.       Max.
   -1895.7431   -37.1648    -6.0118    27.5914  2584.6414
   Coefficients:
                  Estimate  Std. Error z-value  Pr(>|z|)
   (Intercept) 105.6829693   5.2162054 20.2605 < 2.2e-16 ***
   civilfpj      0.7029279   0.0153498 45.7941 < 2.2e-16 ***
   criminalfpj   0.7992546   0.0296515 26.9549 < 2.2e-16 ***
   pendingpj    -0.0547807   0.0090602 -6.0463 1.482e-09 ***
   pdrugmm      85.9583338  10.9538647  7.8473 4.251e-15 ***
   ---
   Signif.codes:0 '***' 0.001 '**' 0.01 '*' 0.05 '.' 0.1 ' ' 1
```

```
Total Sum of Squares:    55063000
Residual Sum of Squares: 23330000
R-Squared:      0.57631
Adj. R-Squared: 0.5757
Chisq: 3782.79 on 4 DF, p-value: < 2.22e-16
```

With the first three or four predictors, the random model returns an individual (district) variance component of 0, as seen above. Does this mean district is irrelevant to explaining the outcome variable? Not exactly. Rather, the 0 individual component means there is no district effect once other effects in the model are controlled. However, with fewer or weaker predictors, there is a district effect because less is controlled. We illustrate this point below.

- As we delete predictors the coefficients change and R-squared drops. With just the first two predictors, effects portion of the output looks like this:

```
Effects:
                   var  std.dev share
idiosyncratic 8129.330   90.163 0.989
individual      88.112    9.387 0.011
```

- With just the first predictor, this is effects portion of the output:

```
Effects:
                  var std.dev share
idiosyncratic 9086.59   95.32 0.847
individual    1647.59   40.59 0.153
```

- While `plm()` does not allow us to run a null model with no predictors, we can come close by creating a variable called "nullvar", filled with all 0s except the first row is 1 since nullvar cannot be a constant.

```
# Add nullvar to courts set equal to 0
courts$nullvar <- 0
# Change the first row of nullvar to 1
courts$nullvar[1] <- 1
# Run the null PDR model
PDRrandomnull <- plm::plm(courts$trialstermpj ~ courts$nullvar, index =
c("ndistrict","year"), model="random", effect="individual", data = courts)
# View results
summary(PDRrandomnull)
# Later, to delete nullvar from courts
courts$nullvar <- NULL
```

With the near-null model, effects portion of the output looks like this:

```
Effects:
                   var  std.dev share
idiosyncratic 14277.01   119.49  0.72
individual     5556.21    74.54  0.28
```

In summary, as we drop variables, R-squared goes down (less is explained) but by the same token, the district effect goes up (district explains more of the remaining variance). This is seen in the "share" column, which rises from 0–1% to 15–28% as predictors are dropped. The original finding of no district effect did not exactly mean that district was independent of the outcome variable. Rather it meant that this was so once other predictors were controlled since these other predictors could do the work of explaining the variance in the outcome variable formerly done by district.

3.7.5.4 Pooling model

In the previous section on the RE model, it was found that there was no district effect and it was observed that in this event a pooling model is most efficient. The command for the pooling model is below. Output is not shown, however, because output is the same as that for the corresponding RE models above when, as here, there is no random effect if the individual (district) variable. Likewise, if we changed the syntax to `model="twoways"` we would also get the same results, given no district effect.

```
PDRpooling <- plm::plm(courts$trialstermpj ~ courts$civilfpj + courts$criminalfpj +
courts$pendingpj + courts$pdrugmm, index = c("ndistrict","year"), model="pooling",
effect="time", data = courts)
```

```
summary(PDRpooling)
```

[Partial output:]

```
Coefficients:
                       Estimate  Std. Error t-value  Pr(>|t|)
(Intercept)         105.6829693   5.2162054 20.2605 < 2.2e-16 ***
courts$civilfpj       0.7029279   0.0153498 45.7941 < 2.2e-16 ***
courts$criminalfpj    0.7992546   0.0296515 26.9549 < 2.2e-16 ***
courts$pendingpj     -0.0547807   0.0090602 -6.0463 1.680e-09 ***
courts$pdrugmm       85.9583338  10.9538647  7.8473 6.013e-15 ***
---
Signif. codes:  0 '***' 0.001 '**' 0.01 '*' 0.05 '.' 0.1 ' ' 1

Total Sum of Squares:    55063000
Residual Sum of Squares: 23330000
R-Squared:       0.57631
Adj. R-Squared: 0.5757
F-statistic: 945.697 on 4 and 2781 DF, p-value: < 2.22e-16
```

3.7.5.5 Population-averaged model

The plm package does not support PA PDR models but the "gee" package does. The term "gee" stands for GEEs, which is an adaptation of GZLM models for correlated data, such as repeated measures.

```
library(gee)
```

The command below gives the same PA model output as does Stata's xtreg command with the pa option. The id options declares the clustering variable, which is the numeric version of district. The family option specifies the data distribution, in effect asking here for a linear regression solution. Alternatives are `binomial`, `poisson`, `Gamma`, and `quasi`. The corstr option specifies the assumed correlation structure of the data. Following common practice for repeated measures (and Stata practice), we specify an "exchangeable" structure, also called the "compound symmetry" structure.[9] Alternatives are `"independence"`, `"fixed"`, `"stat _ M _ dep"`, `"non _ stat _ M _ dep"`, `"AR-M"` and `"unstructured"`. Note that gee assumes all variables are binomial or continuous.

```
PDRpa <- gee::gee(courts$trialstermpj ~ courts$civilfpj + courts$criminalfpj +
courts$pendingpj + courts$pdrugmm, id=ndistrict, family = "gaussian", data =
courts,corstr = "exchangeable", scale.fix = FALSE)
```

[Output:]

```
Beginning Cgee S-function, @(#) geeformula.q 4.13 98/01/27
running glm to get initial regression estimate
 (Intercept)     civilfpj  criminalfpj    pendingpj      pdrugmm
105.68296926   0.70292787   0.79925457  -0.05478067  85.95833380
```

```
summary(PDRpa)
[Output:]
   GEE:  GENERALIZED LINEAR MODELS FOR DEPENDENT DATA
   gee S-function, version 4.13 modified 98/01/27 (1998)
  Model:
   Link:                      Identity
   Variance to Mean Relation: Gaussian
   Correlation Structure:     Exchangeable
  Call:
  gee(formula = trialstermpj ~ civilfpj + criminalfpj + pendingpj +
      pdrugmm, id = ndistrict, data = courts, family = "gaussian",
      corstr = "exchangeable", scale.fix = FALSE)

  Summary of Residuals:
           Min          1Q       Median           3Q          Max
  -1718.203959  -41.552987    -6.146787    31.532898  2573.125221

  Coefficients:
                  Estimate   Naive S.E.   Naive z Robust S.E.   Robust z
  (Intercept) 125.93301428  6.294210770 20.007753 45.12320927   2.790870
  civilfpj      0.62545007  0.016545616 37.801558  0.15328960   4.080186
  criminalfpj   0.72164056  0.032960287 21.894244  0.11221849   6.430674
  pendingpj    -0.03713254  0.009616815 -3.861210  0.02686804  -1.382034
  pdrugmm     112.46482159 12.476353757  9.014238 23.64689656   4.756008

  Estimated Scale Parameter:  8493.208
  Number of Iterations:  5
```

We can now compute the p values for the estimates above, using procedures below. The ptable results show all coef ficients to be significant by either naïve (glm) or robust (robust sandwich) estimation methods. The robust version is generally preferred in gee models. The "coeftable" output contains the same coefficients as in output above.

```
coeftable <- coef(summary(PDRpa))
coeftable
                       Estimate   Naive S.E.   Naive z Robust S.E.   Robust z
(Intercept)        125.93301428  6.294210770 20.007753 45.12320927   2.790870
courts$civilfpj      0.62545007  0.016545616 37.801558  0.15328960   4.080186
courts$criminalfpj   0.72164056  0.032960287 21.894244  0.11221849   6.430674
courts$pendingpj    -0.03713254  0.009616815 -3.861210  0.02686804  -1.382034
courts$pdrugmm     112.46482159 12.476353757  9.014238 23.64689656   4.756008
```

The fifth column of coeftable contains the robust z values. The p values are computed using a normal approximation of the z values. We use `lower.tail=FALSE` to get the probability of values of z or larger. Alternatively, `lower.tail=TRUE` would give the probability of values no larger than z.

```
ptableRobust <- 2 * pnorm(abs(coeftable[,5]), lower.tail = FALSE)
ptableRobust
[Output:]
   (Intercept)     civilfpj  criminalfpj    pendingpj      pdrugmm
  5.256657e-03 4.499970e-05 1.270391e-10 1.669614e-01 1.974590e-06
```

The third column of coeftable contains the naïve z values

```
ptableNaive <- 2 * pnorm(abs(coeftable[,3]), lower.tail = FALSE)
ptableNaive
[Output:]
   (Intercept)      civilfpj   criminalfpj     pendingpj       pdrugmm
  4.714250e-89  0.000000e+00 2.947547e-106  1.128270e-04  1.982439e-19
```

3.7.5.6 Hausman test

The Hausman test is used to select between models, particularly between FE and RE models. We use the `phtest()` function from the "plm" package. Below, since the Hausman test reports a significant p value, the output shows that the fixed (FE) and RE models differ significantly in their estimates. Therefore, the researcher would assume the correctness of the FE estimates, choosing the FE model and foregoing the RE model in spite of its lower standard errors and better R-squared.

Recall the two models to be compared by the Hausman test:

```
PDRfixed <- plm::plm(courts$trialstermpj ~ courts$civilfpj + courts$criminalfpj +
courts$pendingpj + courts$pdrugmm, index = c("ndistrict","year"), model="within",
effect="individual",data = courts)
PDRrandom <- plm::plm(courts$trialstermpj ~ courts$civilfpj + courts$criminalfpj +
courts$pendingpj + courts$pdrugmm, index = c("ndistrict","year"), model="random",
effect="individual", data = courts)
```

Run the Hausman test (the order of the two models does not matter)

```
plm::phtest(PDRfixed,PDRrandom)
```

[Output:]

```
      Hausman Test
data: trialstermpj ~ civilfpj + criminalfpj + pendingpj + pdrugmm
chisq = 247.95, df = 4, p-value < 2.2e-16
alternative hypothesis: one model is inconsistent
```

3.7.5.7 Other models

- *Between model*: For the BE model, use `model="between"` in plm. Between effects models assume that unobserved variables differ over time, but are constant across subjects for the same time period. That is, BE models are based on group means (cross-sectional averages for each time period). Conceptually, this is as if the researcher took the mean of each variable for each case across time, giving a dataset where each case had one value (the mean) for each variable, and then the researcher ran regression on this collapsed dataset. BE models examine the change in effects between time periods. Because of the implausibility of assuming that unmeasured variables lack variance across subjects in the same time period and because of the loss of information in such a method, between effects models are less common in social science except insofar as they are used in RE models, discussed below, which assume a cross of fixed and between effects.
- *Pooled model*: Use `model="pooling"`. This implements a pooled OLS model. This is not the same as a PA model. Rather, the pooling model pools all cross-sections (years) together, without considering any individual (district) effect. See Example 1.1 in Croissant and Millo (2018) for an example.
- *Hausman-Taylor model*: While `model="ht"` is possible, this usage is deprecated in favor of the syntax below. This implements the Hausman-Taylor estimator, which is a type of instrumental variables estimation used to handle the correlated error effects of unmeasured exogenous variables or reciprocal causation. Below is an example of one set of options for an ht model for the example data:

```
PDRht <- plm::plm(courts$trialstermpj ~ courts$civilfpj + courts$criminalfpj +
courts$pendingpj + courts$pdrugmm, index = c("ndistrict","year"), random.method =
"ht", model = "random", inst.method = "baltagi", data=courts)
```

(Partial output:)

```
Effects:
                   var std.dev share
idiosyncratic 7832.34   88.50 0.906
individual     810.97   28.48 0.094
theta:
Min. 1st Qu.  Median    Mean 3rd Qu.    Max.
0.5126  0.5126  0.5126  0.5126  0.5126  0.5126
```

```
Residuals:
      Min.    1st Qu.     Median    3rd Qu.       Max.
-1701.4462  -38.3015    -7.4742    27.2189  2529.5572

Coefficients:
                      Estimate  Std. Error z-value  Pr(>|z|)
(Intercept)         127.8140899   6.5049081 19.6489 < 2.2e-16 ***
courts$civilfpj       0.6177975   0.0166512 37.1022 < 2.2e-16 ***
courts$criminalfpj    0.7145761   0.0333016 21.4577 < 2.2e-16 ***
courts$pendingpj     -0.0353849   0.0096681 -3.6600 0.0002523 ***
courts$pdrugmm      115.4625943  12.6471881  9.1295 < 2.2e-16 ***
---
Signif. codes:  0 '***' 0.001 '**' 0.01 '*' 0.05 '.' 0.1 ' ' 1

Total Sum of Squares:    42441000
Residual Sum of Squares: 21764000
R-Squared:      0.4872
Adj. R-Squared: 0.48646
Chisq: 2642.14 on 4 DF, p-value: < 2.22e-16
```

- *First-difference model*: Use `model="fd"`. This implements the method of first differences, which is a method for modeling change which has advantages when the model contains unmeasured, unchanging predictor variables. The `pwfdtest()` command in plm implements Wooldridge's test for errors in first-difference models.

3.7.5.8 Other effects

The `effect = "individual"` option in the fixed and RE models discussed above is the default and could have been omitted. It is the usual type of PDR model, in which plm tests for the presence of subject-level effects (here, ndistrict is the subject or "individual" and plm is testing for the presence of district effects). However, there are three other types of effects. Setting this option to another effect will change all the estimates.

- `effect="time"`: This causes plm to test for the presence of time (here, year) effects and not individual (here, district) effects.
- `effect = "twoways"`: This causes plm to test for the presence of both time (year) effects and individual (district) effects.
- `effect = "nested"`: This will give a nested error component model, also called the nested effects RE model. See Example 3-4 in Croissant and Millo (2018).

3.7.5.9 Other variations in plm

In the section above, we have used the basic `plm()` command, which uses a modified form of OLS estimation. However, the "plm" package supports a variety of other estimation models not discussed here. These commands implement different estimation methods but in general operate similarly to the `plm()` command.

- `pggls()`: Estimation by general feasible generalized least squares (GLS). This is among the most popular forms of econometric estimation.
- `pgmm()`: Estimation by generalized method of moments (GMM). Also widely used in econometrics.
- `pvcm()`: Estimation for variable coefficients models.
- `pmg()`: Estimation for mean groups (MG), demeaned MG (DMG), and common correlated effects mean groups (CCEMG) for heterogeneous panel models.
- `pcce()`: Estimation for CEMG and pooled correlated effects (CCEP), used for panel data with common factors.
- `pldv()`: Estimation for limited DVs.

An output object created by `pml()` or commands above contain various useful elements, such as residuals. For instance, to put residuals in a vector object called "fitted", use a command like this:

```
fitted <- PDRfixed$residuals
```

To see the available statistical output elements, type the name of the pml object (PDRfixed) followed by a dollar sign. A pop-up menu will show all the available elements.

Lagged variables may be integrated into a pml model using the `lag()` or `Lag()` functions from R's stats package. The case of the first letter of the command makes a huge difference! For instance, one may specify `lag(income,k=2)` or `Lag(income, k=4)`. For "lag", k is the number of time periods that the time series is shifted forward. For "Lag", k is the number of periods that the series is shifted backwards. Thus, to shift income ahead two years, one would specify `lag(income, k=2)`.

Likewise, difference variables may be integrated using the `diff()` function. For instance, one may specify `diff(income,k=2)` to convert income into two-year difference in income.

Instrumental variables (an advanced topic not discussed here) may be used through the `inst.method =` option of the `plm()` command, typically for ht models. Instrumental variables are used to handle effects of correlated error due to unmeasured exogenous variables or reciprocal causation.

3.7.6 PDR with the panelr package

For space reasons, we cannot detail the workings of the newer "panelr" package for PDR. Instead, we simply give the commands to give output for the FE and BE models discussed for the "plm" package. Output is not shown.

```
# Invoke panelr
library(panelr)

# Convert courts data frame to "long form" panel data format needed by panelr.
# The panel_data() command is from the panelr package.
courtspanel <- panelr::panel_data(courts, id = ndistrict, wave = year)
```

We now request and view the within-between model using panelr's `wbm()` command. Output has separate sections for "within" and "between" results. Had there been time-invariant predictors, these would have been listed after a vertical bar after the list of time-varying predictors. Had there been interaction effects, these would be listed after a second vertical bar. The command below gives estimates very close to those for the `plm() method=within` (fixed effects) and `method=between` (between effects) models.

```
# The within-between model, which is the default if no model is specified.
# Warning messages will suggest rescaling so all variables are on the same scale.
model <- panelr::wbm(trialstermpj ~ civilfpj + criminalfpj + pendingpj + pdrugmm,
model="w-b", data = courtspanel)

summary(model)
```

Other model options are

- `model= "within":` Just the "within" output. Can also specify `model=fixed`.
- `model= "between":` Just the "between" output. Can also specify `model=random,` but output is still BE, not RE.
- `model= "contextual":` In contextual model output, between-subjects coefficients reflect the difference between within and between effects. This implies coefficients will be 0 if there are no differences.

What about getting an RE model like the RE model in plm? Documentation for panelr states, "Thinking in a Hausman test framework – with the within-between model as described here – you should expect the within and between coefficients to be the same if an RE model were appropriate." In other words, if an RE model were consistent with the "within" FE model, then the model="between" estimates would be the same and there is no need for separate RE estimates. If an RE model were not consistent, then by Hausman criteria, the "within" FE model should be preferred and again there is no need for separate RE estimates. However, if you want separate RE estimates as provided by plm and major statistics packages, you cannot get them from panelr, at least not easily.

For PA models, the panelr package offers the `wbgee()` command, which requires having installed the "geepack" package. This author, however, could not get `wbgee()` to reproduce the same PA model estimates as `gee()` and other major statistical packages. There are many, many more options in the panelr package than can be discussed here.

3.8 Structural equation modeling (SEM)

Treatment of SEM in R is presented in an online supplement to Chapter 3, found in the student section of this book's Support Material (www.routledge.com/9780367624293).

3.9 Missing data analysis and data imputation

Treatment of missing data analysis and data imputation in R is presented in an online supplement to Chapter 3, found in the student section of this book's Support Material (www.routledge.com/9780367624293).

3.10 Chapter 3 command summary

For convenience for those wishing to try models out for themselves, this book's Support Material (www.routledge.com/9780367624293) contains a listing of the main commands used in this chapter. This listing may be handy for readers following along with the book using their home or office computers. For topics presented as online supplements (missing values and data imputation; SEM), the command summary is at the end of these supplements.

Endnotes

1. This is an instructional sample. In Yanan Yu's actual research dataset, there were many fewer missing values.
2. "Null deviance" in `glm()` output is computed as 2(LL(Saturated Model) – LL(Null Model), where the null model is the intercept-only model and the saturated model is a model where there are n estimation parameters because each data point requires its own parameters, where *n* is number of cases.
3. "Residual Deviance" in `glm()` output is computed as 2(LL(Saturated Model) – LL(Default Model)), where the default model is the researcher's model.
4. With a little more coding work, the same table can be produced with labels for race:

```
library(multcomp)
temp <- survey$race
race_labels <- factor(temp, levels = c(1, 2, 3),labels = c("white", "black", "other"))
race_labels <- relevel(race_labels,ref=3)
olsmodel_labels <- glm(survey$educ ~ survey$income + race_labels, data = survey, family =
gaussian)
summary(multcomp::glht(olsmodel_labels, multcomp::mcp(race_labels="Tukey")))
```

[Output]:

```
Linear Hypotheses:
                      Estimate Std. Error z value Pr(>|z|)
white - other == 0     0.2500     0.2465   1.014  0.55761
black - other == 0    -0.3700     0.2867  -1.291  0.38981
black - white == 0    -0.6200     0.1778  -3.486  0.00135 **
---
Signif. codes:  0 '***' 0.001 '**' 0.01 '*' 0.05 '.' 0.1 ' ' 1
(Adjusted p values reported -- single-step method)
```

5. Note, however, that the foregoing inference is for a model with no transformation (i.e., with an identify link) for the outcome variable. For instance, if we had had a log link and had created the `glm()` object logmodel (we didn't), these commands would have been necessary to display the estimated marginal means:

```
emmlog <- update(emmeans::emmeans(logmodel, "racef"), tran = "log")summary(emmlog, type =
"response")
```

Possible link types for the `tran=` option are `"identity"`, `"log"`, `"logit"`, `"probit"`, `"cauchit"`, `"cloglog"`, `"sqrt"`, `"1/mu^2"`, and `"inverse"`. See further discussion at https://cran.r-project.org/web/packages/emmeans/vignettes/transformations.html#links
6. Both "random coefficients model" and "random coefficient model" are in widespread use in the literature.
7. The long form contrasts with a "nested subjects" format, where data would have been ordered by year, then by district. There is also a "wide form", where each row is a different subject ID and columns are time-variable combinations. For instance, columns might be efficiency2020, efficiency2021, and so on for as many columns as there are years.
8. See the introductory tutorial at https://cran.r-project.org/web/packages/margins/vignettes/Introduction.html
9. Compound symmetry or exchangeable structure assumes residual correlations are not affected by time. Nearby residuals are the same as those far apart in time. The correlation of two measures adjacent in time will be the same on average as the correlation of two measures further apart in time. For repeated measures this implies that residuals have the same covariance for any pair of time periods. For random effects, it is assumed that residuals have the same covariance for any pair of units associated with the random effect (e.g., any pair of districts). That is, variances on the diagonal are assumed equal for any year or district and the covariances on the off-diagonal are also assumed to be equal.

Chapter 4

Classification and regression trees in R

PART I: OVERVIEW OF CLASSIFICATION AND REGRESSION TREES WITH R

A decision tree may be visualized as a series of branching decision points called nodes which lead to "leaves" representing alternative possible values of an outcome. These are the "terminal nodes". Nodes prior to terminal nodes represent how values of an observation on an input variable determine if the observation branches to the left or right as it traverses the tree before eventually being assigned to the "bucket", which is one of the terminal nodes or leaves. For classification trees there may be more than one path to the same terminal value of the outcome variable, a phenomenon known as "equifinality". Regression trees are not equifinal but rather show the constellations of variables associated with each range (e.g., decile ranges) of the outcome variable. For both classification and regression trees, the same input variable may be used in different branches of the tree.

The first node in a decision tree represents the "root" of the tree. At each node there are one or more test values, which are cutting points on the input variable. An observation's value relative to these cutting points determines the path to which it is assigned. To take a simplistic example, "Age" may be the origination factor in predicting whether an individual will buy an insurance policy or not. Test values may be age < 30 or age >= 30. "Marriage" may be an interior node with test values of "married" and "not married". Leaves will be the labels for the target, "buys life insurance" or "does not buy life insurance". The path age >= 30 and marriage = married may lead to the outcome leaf "buys life insurance". Many find decision trees to be intuitive, corresponding to the decision-making process of people in real life. The graphical nature of decision trees further makes them easy to explain – easier, for example, than regression equations. Moreover, from the viewpoint of causal analysis, decision tree solutions may reveal more complexity than will a simple regression equation.

This is not to say that the researcher must choose between decision trees and regression. The two can work in a complementary fashion. Decision trees may be used to select variables for inclusion in a regression model. They can also identify suitable cutting points for creating binary, dummy, or other binned variables. Decision trees are also useful to identify strata in stratified regression (Neville, 1998). And decision trees highlight subpopulations, which may require a different regression model than most cases and by the same token can be a way of identifying outliers, which are problematic for regression.

Although decision trees do incorporate prediction and even may incorporate conventional statistical techniques used for prediction, such as regression, they are better thought of as representing a set of classification procedures, which partition the sample or population into relatively homogenous groups. This is ideal when the purpose is segmentation analysis, as it is in marketing research, where decision trees are popular. For causal research, decision trees are better thought of as a different data approach, which may shed more light on the dynamics of causal systems which might be simultaneously analyzed using conventional statistical procedures as well.

DOI: 10.4324/9781003109396-4

4.1 Introduction

Decision trees go by many labels, depending on the context and algorithm used. Labels include classification and regression trees (CART), learning trees, random forests, chi-square automatic interaction detection (CHAID), and other overlapping terms. In fact, the term "decision tree analysis" is an umbrella term covering a quite wide variety of classification algorithms. Some algorithms incorporate conventional statistical procedures such as linear, multinomial, ordinal, or Cox regression. Others may incorporate refinement of the decision tree using model fit criteria familiar to users of logistic regression (e.g., using the Akaike information criterion, AIC, as a measure of model fit); using aspects of ordinary least squares (OLS) regression (e.g., using change in R-squared in regression trees); or drawing on other common procedures (e.g., using the categorical association measure Cramer's V as a fit metric). Ensemble methods, such as random forests, may improve prediction through averaging across a large number of trees. The number of algorithmic variations and options is very large and growing. The variations often lead to different tree results.

In general, "classification trees" refer to decision trees where the outcome is categorical, usually binary, as in the life insurance example above. "Regression trees", in contrast, refer to decision trees involving a continuous outcome. On the predictor side, both CART may use either categorical or binned-continuous predictor variables (i.e., grouped by use of cutting points). As cutting points and branching may be determined on an automated basis, these are considered one type of tool for "machine learning", "supervised learning", or "data mining".

Decision tree analysis is useful for a variety of purposes:

1. *Classification*: The researcher wishes to distinguish all possible values of a target based on input variables. Flower identification manuals, for instance, may contain a decision tree by which the reader may determine a flower species based on such attributes as petal length, petal width, sepal length, and other attributes.
2. *Prediction*: A decision tree model may be created using existing data and then the generated rules may be used to predict future outcomes. For instance, the banking industry may use decision tree models to assess the likelihood of loan default prior to authorizing a loan for a particular applicant.
3. *Segmentation analysis*: A decision tree model may be used to identify cases belonging to a given group. A political party may use a decision tree model to make advertising expenditure decisions in order to better target the segments of voters registered as "Independent" but likely to vote for their party.
4. *Stratification*: Decision tree analysis can be a useful exploratory technique when there is a need to bin continuous variables such as performance scores into groups, such as low, medium, and high performing employees.
5. *Model specification and data reduction*: Decision tree analysis may be a useful exploratory technique for filtering variables to include or exclude in other forms of analysis and modeling.
6. *Detection of interaction effects*: Decision trees reveal that a given predictor variable only applies to certain subgroups of the data. The branching process inherent in decision tree analysis means that values of the outcome variable are tied to an observation's values on categorical or binned continuous variables earlier in the tree. This is the definition of "interaction effect": Values of the target variable are contingent on which group the observation is in terms of the splitting variable at each node. For this reason, decision trees often arrive at a different solution from that using a conventional model, which omits interaction effects.

4.2 Advantages of decision tree analysis

While procedures in the generalized linear model family (e.g., OLS or logistic regression) sometimes provide better estimates when all their assumptions are met, in the real world of complex, nonlinear relationships among variables, decision trees may perform better. Miguel-Hurtado et al. (2016), for instance, compared decision trees with linear and logistic regression and found for their medical data that "machine learning classification algorithms outperform[ed] linear regression in most situations" (p. 1). Likewise, in the exercises later in this book on regression trees, estimates of the target variable (national literacy rates) were more correlated with observed values for some regression tree models than for OLS models. Even for linear relationships and perhaps more importantly, decision trees may provide improved insight and interpretation useful for theory development or for praxis.

There are many other advantages to use of decision trees for data analysis:

- Decision tree results are intuitive and easily communicated to the audience. Whereas some procedures such as neural network classifiers make it difficult for the researcher to see how final results were calculated due to their "black box" nature, decision trees are transparent ("white box") with the chain of calculations leading to a final result presented clearly.
- All types of categorical and continuous data may be used, even nominal (e.g., character) variables.
- Decision trees are non-parametric, not requiring normal or other particular distributions of the data. It is not necessary to standardize, normalize, or center data.
- It is not necessary that relationships be linear. Nonlinear effects are taken into account automatically.
- Interaction effects are also taken into account automatically.
- Decision tree methods are robust against multicollinearity.
- Decision tree methods scale well, handling very large datasets.
- It is not necessary to create dummy variables for categorical variables or to interpret results in terms of reference categories.
- Variable selection is built into the decision tree process, which automatically filters out inputs with less predictive power. Input variables dominated by other input variables of greater power are dropped from the final model.
- Models may be validated in a variety of ways, including cross-validation and comparison of predicted with observed values.

4.3 Limitations of decision tree analysis

Like all procedures, decision trees have analytic limitations. Due to these limitations, decision tree analysis is often used for exploratory purposes prior to modeling with conventional statistical techniques. For instance, Wim van Putten (2002), author of the CART.ado module for Stata, stated that decision trees should "Probably best be used in addition to a regression model".

Van Putten and other scholars have noted many potential disadvantages and pitfalls associated with decision tree analysis. The following list outlines some of the possible limitations of decision tree analysis.

- Decision trees can be unstable across different samples and sometimes may not generalize well. Small variations in inputs may lead to major changes in the tree representing the solution. To improve out-of-sample generalization, cross-validation is recommended when undertaking decision tree analysis. Also, ensemble methods, like random forests, may be used to seek improved out-of-sample predictions by performing a type of "averaging" across multiple decision trees. Random forests may outperform regression models (e.g., Muchlinski et al., 2016). However, random forests also may reduce the interpretability of the underlying decision trees as compared to single decision trees.
- Decision trees handle relatively few predictor variables: The greater the number of covariates and the greater the number of branches in their tests, and the more numerous the paths, which in turn may lead to leaves with few observations or singletons. On the other hand, the researcher can control the size of the minimum bucket (minimum number of observations in a terminal node) and the number of important splitting variables in a tree solution may well be greater than the number of significant predictors in a regression model for the same data and outcome variable.
- Models may not be optimally parsimonious: It is not assured that the final model will include the least number of covariates and branches needed to explain target outcomes at a model performance level set by the researcher.
- For categorical variables, decision trees are biased toward selecting as a splitting variable one with many levels. Compensating for this may require recoding for fewer levels or invoking a cardinality penalty.
- Alternative cutpoints are possible: There are differing algorithms for selecting cutpoints. Moreover, researchers may specify cutpoints manually. Alternative cutpoints lead to different solutions.
- Interactions are automatically detected but on a data-driven basis, and thus may be overfitted, increasing the likelihood of Type I error.

- Small and moderate effects may be underfitted. Weaker effects may "wash out" from the decision tree even though they would be found significant using conventional statistical methods. For these effects, Type II error is inflated.
- Decision trees do not yield a single solution. Rather, judgments must be made about such parameters as the optimum depth of the tree, the minimum size of terminal nodes, and the splitting criteria to be used.
- There is no single "decision tree algorithm". Rather, many different algorithms might be applied to the same problem, with differing results.
- There is no single goodness of fit measure for decision tree solutions. Rather, model performance may be and is gauged by multiple statistical criteria.
- In spite of built-in cross-validation in some algorithms, resulting decision trees are still subject to overfitting and solutions still may not generalize well.
- The larger the tree, the larger the sample required. Each split reduces the size of the sample available to judge splits further down the branch. This means that later splits will be based on fewer observations and will have less statistical power. It is even possible to run out of observations, forcing a premature stop to tree learning.

4.4 Decision tree terminology

Nodes are splitting points in a decision tree. These are of three types: Root nodes, parent nodes, and terminal nodes.

The *root node* in a decision tree is the starting point for the entire sample or population to be analyzed. It is associated with a splitting variable. Case values on the splitting variable determine if the case goes to the right or left when following branches of the tree to an eventual terminal point.

Parent nodes are nodes that split into further nodes, which are not root or terminal nodes in the tree.

Child nodes are sub-nodes into which a parent node is split. They may be either additional parent nodes or may be terminal nodes.

Terminal nodes, also called "leaves", form the end-points of branches in the decision tree. A terminal node represents a subpopulation or subsample, which cannot be split further. Each terminal node corresponds to a value of the target variable. In classification trees this value is the label for a level of the categorical target variable. In regression trees this value is the mean value of the continuous target variable for the observations in the terminal node.

Interior nodes are nodes between the root node and any terminal node.

The *target variable* is the variable being classified or predicted. For classification trees it is a categorical variable. For regression trees it is a numeric variable.

Splitting of a node is the work of a categorical or binned continuous predictor variable. For instance, categorical income might be "Above average" or "Below average". Continuous income would split at a cutting point, such as "<= 30000". By convention, observations that meet a given splitting criterion go to the left in the decision tree while those not meeting the criterion go to the right.

Surrogates are input variables which might be used in place of splitting variables. Surrogates are used to replace splitting variables for an observation when that observation is missing data on the splitting variable. However, in addition, since decision trees can be very sensitive to small changes in input data, examination of surrogates may be useful to the researcher when seeking to understand the dynamics of the input variables, whether competing variables might model the target just as well, and if a variable with a stronger theoretical justification might be substituted for a given splitting variable. Surrogates, when appropriate, are displayed by the `summary(tree _ object)` command, where tree_object is an object created by assignment from `rpart()` or another tree command. Surrogates are used for handling of missing values.

Pruning is the opposite of splitting, involving removal of nodes (and hence their branches). This is done in order to obtain a simpler (more parsimonious) solution which is easier to interpret. Also, low-count terminal nodes may be consolidated in order to reduce tree instability.

Branches are subsections of a decision tree. A branch may pass through multiple interior nodes before ending in a terminal node.

Edges, also called *arcs,* are the branches from a given nonterminal node. In most trees a given node splits on an input variable, resulting in an edge to the left and an edge to the right.

Binning is the process of partitioning a continuous variable into a dichotomy or into an ordinal set of ranges. There are many possible binning methods.

Cutpoints are the values of a continuous variable used to divide it into partitions.

Recursive partitioning refers to the general strategy for creating a decision tree. "Recursive" means that paths through the tree go in one direction, toward terminal nodes, and do not have feedback loops. That is, input variables are not in reciprocal relationships. The outcome of recursive partitioning occurs when a tree meets the "stopping criteria". One stopping criterion is when all cases are assigned to a terminal node, with all cases in a terminal node having the same value on the target variable. However, there may be other stopping criteria, such as stopping when a potential split would not contribute enough to reduction in model error or improvement in model fit by some measure. See Strobl, Malley, and Tutz (2009).

Predictions are the values on the target variable of observations in the terminal nodes. For classification trees, predictions are often called "classifications" and are the values of a level of the categorical target variable (e.g., candidate names in a voting preference study). For regression trees, predictions are numeric and consist of the mean of the continuous target variable for all observations in a given terminal node. Predicted values are also called "fitted values" or "estimated values". They may be saved and used to compare to observed values and, for regression trees, to undertake analysis of residuals (numeric differences between fitted and observed values).

4.5 Steps in decision tree analysis

The generic steps in decision tree analysis are simple, at least in principal. In practice, particular software programs modify or elaborate on the following steps:

1. Starting with all observations, split the group on the first (origination) nodal variable, which is the root node. Typically this is the most important classifier variable.
2. Continue using parent-node variables until groups cannot be split further. The same splitting variable may appear along different branches of the tree.
3. The end-points of each path are the terminal nodes (leaves), representing target outcomes.
4. A design choice is whether to amalgamate terminal nodes by requiring their minimum "bucket" size be larger or by other criteria. Amalgamation has the effect of simplifying the tree at the cost of losing information.
5. Display results in graphic form as a tree diagram or in tabular form. This applies only to regression trees, not regression forests.
6. Consider using cross-validation and graphical diagnostics to further refine and validate the model, as discussed in later chapters.
7. Consider using random forests, bagging, and other ensemble methods to improve out-of-sample generalization, also discussed in later chapters.

4.6 Decision tree algorithms

There is no single algorithm for creating a decision tree. For instance, algorithms for regression trees necessarily differ somewhat from algorithms for classification trees. Moreover, different statistical packages vary in their approaches and defaults. In general, where the usual classification tree splits on levels of a binary-categorical variable (e.g., high versus low income), a regression tree typically finds cutpoints in the continuous variables in the model such that a sequence of binary partitionings may be carried out. The cutpoints constitute splitting rules (e.g., if less than the cutpoint then follow path 1 through the tree, otherwise follow path 2). Splitting rules divide the feature space into regions. Splits are selected based on minimizing the some measure of error such as classification error for classification trees or one minus R-squared for regression trees. Recursive binary splitting proceeds until some stopping criterion is met, such as failure or a prospective split to reduce error greater than some specified minimum or when a split would create a terminal node whose bucket contained fewer than a specified minimum number of observations.

Because the resulting tree may be overly complex (deep), a further step may be "pruning", seeking to arrive at a more parsimonious tree, which still has an acceptable fit to the training data. The criterion used to balance depth and fit is the "tuning parameter" (alpha, α). This process may be labeled "cost complexity pruning". It is possible to select the optimal alpha parameter by using "K-fold cross-validation", which is simply a method that divides the training dataset into K groups ("folds"), calculating the error rate in the subtrees (trees in each of the K groups), then selecting the subtree associated with the lowest error rate as the basis for splitting. The prediction of the target variable for observations which have followed a given path through the decision tree, therefore having the attributes defined by the splitting variables, is the mean value of all the observations in the given terminal node. See Le (2018).

Typical classification trees, like regression trees, use recursive binary splitting. Because variables are not continuous, however, the criterion for splitting cannot be based on the residual sum of squares as in regression trees based on continuous data. Rather, classification trees must use some other error criterion. There are three major alternatives:

1. *Classification error rate*: This is simply the percent of observations incorrectly classified. For a given terminal node (leaf), let *m* be the number of observations in the node and let *c* be the number in the most widely-occurring class of the target variable for that node. The number of observations not in the most numerous class of the target variable is then 1 – (*c*/*m*). This is the classification error rate.

2. *Gini index*: Also called "Gini impurity", this is a measure similar to the classification error rate, though the formula differs. It is used for classification trees. Compared to the classification error rate, the Gini index rewards node "purity" more. The Gini index will approach 0 as the node reflects only cases from the same class of the categorical target variable, indicating 0 error. For instance, consider "gender" as a node above terminal nodes representing "High" and "Low". If using gender as a splitting variable sent all males to "High" and all females to "Low", then purity would be 100% and the Gini index would be 0 for gender. The best splitting variable is the one with the Gini index, which most closely approaches 0, by this criterion.

3. *Information gain*, also called "cross-entropy": Information gain is the value of "entropy" after a split minus entropy before the split. Entropy in turn is a coefficient from information theory which has to do with the number of bits of information needed to correctly classify an object. Entropy varies from 0 when all objects have the same target value to 1 when they are equally spit. Thus, the closer entropy is to 0, the better the classifications. Information gain is the decrease in entropy. The higher the information gain, the more the split lowered entropy and thus improved classification. Though the formula for information gain differs a bit, the information gain method yields values numerically similar to the Gini Index, with 0 indicating no error.

In general, which criterion is used may well not affect the structure of the decision tree. The Gini Index and cross-entropy may be preferred as measures of model quality. The classification error rate may be preferred if the researcher's goal is simple prediction.

Algorithms for CART often go under the label "CART", an acronym coined by Breiman et al. (1984). Among the attractions of CART is that it is an equifinal analytic approach. This means that there may be multiple paths to the same outcome and the same variables may appear in different paths, revealing interaction effects. CART is also nonparametric and may be used with any type of data distribution, and it may be less sensitive to outliers in the data. CART may be used directly to arrive at solutions for prediction and classification problems, or it may be used as the basis for exploring and selecting an appropriate set of variables to be used as inputs for other procedures (Nisbet, Elder, & Miner, 2009). Perhaps the main problem of CART is the tendency to overfit the model to noise in the data. Cross-validation, discussed in a later chapter, may mitigate this problem to some extent.

CHAID is among the most popular algorithms for quickly forming decision trees. Developed by Kass (1980), CHAID extended earlier versions going back to the 1950s and 1960s (e.g., XAID, THAID, USAID). Whereas CART handles continuous as well as categorical variables, CHAID requires categorical or binned (discrete) continuous predictors and target variables. Missing values are not imputed but rather missing values become a single class, which may or may not be merged with other classes as appropriate. CHAID is a nonparametric technique, which may be used with medium as well as large samples. However, as with other statistical techniques, larger samples may confer greater reliability and increased out of sample generalizability. The algorithm calculating branching in the decision tree utilizes Bonferroni-adjusted chi-square significance testing. Bonferroni adjustment is needed when there are multiple independent tests. This testing becomes problematic with small samples and trees with more levels of branching, since the number of observations at any node (branching point) may become insufficient. Put another way, with a large count, a split making a relatively small contribution may be judged significant while with a small count, a split may be judged nonsignificant even when its effect size is nontrivial.

The ID3 algorithm (Iterative Dichotomizer 3), authored by Ross Quinlan, remains the most widely used algorithm for solving binary decision tree problems, though Quinlan went on to author the later algorithms C4.5 and C5.0 (Quinlan, 1986, 1990, 1994; Quinlan et al., 2008). ID3 is described by Kulkarni (2017), among others, in terms of eight steps:

1. Create root node for the tree using any binary predictor
2. If all examples are positive, return leaf node 'positive'
3. Otherwise if all examples are negative, return leaf node 'negative'
4. Calculate the entropy of current state H(S)
5. For each attribute, calculate the entropy with respect to the attribute 'x' denoted by H(S, x)
6. Select the attribute which has maximum value of information gain IG(S, x)
7. Remove the attribute that offers highest IG from the set of attributes
8. Repeat until one runs out of all attributes, or the decision tree has all leaf nodes.

There are, of course, other algorithms apart from those discussed above, and more are created each year.

4.7 Random forests and ensemble methods

The term "ensemble methods" refers to the idea that if one decision tree is good, multiple trees could be combined to obtain even better predictions and classifications. The three most important ensemble procedures have to do with bagging, boosting, and random forests. We discuss each of these overlapping approaches briefly in this section.

"Bagging" is also called "bootstrap aggregation". Bootstrapping refers to resampling the training data with replacement to obtain "B" different training sets. B may be a large number in the hundreds or even thousands. Some regression or classification tree method is applied to each training set, identifying splitting variables (classifier variables). Predictions from each training set are averaged to obtain the bagged prediction. The bagged prediction may well be more robust, meaning it may generalize better to a validation dataset. Bagging may be used with any of a variety of decision tree methods. See Breiman (1996).

"Boosting" is a variant on bagging. It is also an ensemble approach, which may be used with a variety of decision tree methods, including both CART. What makes boosting different from bagging is that it incorporates a "slow learning", sequential approach to building a tree. The "boost" is that information (residuals, reflecting error) from an earlier tree is used to refine the next tree in sequence. Each tree in sequence seeks to solve for error in the previous tree, meaning that the target variable for the second and later trees is net error (residuals) in the previous tree, not the original Y variable. A series of small models may reduce error in particular regions of the tree. In boosting, misclassified observations from a prior step are weighted more in the subsequent step, seeking improved classification. This means that at any given boosting step, observations are chosen based on highest error, not based on a random bootstrap basis. A corollary is that under boosting, observations do not have an equal probability of being in the subsample for a subsequent step. At the end of the process, predictions are based on the entire sequence of trees. Put another way, predictions are an ensemble of weaker prediction models, each of which contributes to addressing some error in the model as it is sequentially constructed.

"Gradient descent" is a statistical technique, which underlies boosting. It optimizes differentiable loss functions, where loss reflects the difference between actual and predicted values. At each step in the boosting sequence the current tree attempts to recover the loss associated with the previous step. The loss function is used to select the optimal tree. The researcher will have specified such settings as the learning rate (a number between 0 and 1, which defines the learning step size; higher is faster learning at the risk of overshooting the optimal solution); the maximum number of terminal nodes per tree (higher is more precision but potentially greater overfitting); the minimum number of observations per terminal node (higher creates more parsimonious trees but there may be loss of correct classification); and the number of trees modeled (higher may improve coverage at the expense of longer training time).

"Random forests" incorporate a form of bootstrapped aggregation (bagging), but with a difference. In both bagging and random forests, the training dataset is used to generate multiple training subsets based on resampling the training sample. However, in random forests there is an additional step. The added step is that at each splitting point in the tree, random forest methods randomly sample "*m*" of the available "*p*" potential splitting variables (*m* is set by the researcher). Of the *m* splitting variables, the one is selected which gives the split with lowest error. Because different trees may be based on different randomly-selected (but error tested) splitting variables, it is sometimes said that random forests "decorrelate" the trees in the ensemble solution.

For instance, random forests may take multiple samples from the data, creating a decision tree for each sample, then synthesize across all trees to create an ensemble solution. The ensemble solution is intended to be more stable than a single tree solution and is intended to be more generalizable out of sample. Due to the averaging involved in a random forest solution, based on multiple trees, pruning is not needed. However, the ensemble solution comes at the price of being more difficult to interpret.

"Rotation forests" are a variant on random forests. "Rotation" refers to use of factor rotation in principal components analysis (PCA). Under this method, the input feature set (variable set) is randomly divided into "K" subsets of data. "K" is a researcher-set parameter. PCA is applied to each random subset. This means that K axis rotations are performed, one for each subset. PCA results in principal components (factors) for each subset. To increase accuracy, all components are retained. These may be used as new inputs when constructing a regression tree. The authors of this approach (Rodriguez, Kuncheva, & Alonso, 2006) examined 33 benchmark datasets and found the rotation forest approach resulted in improved diversity and accuracy.

4.8 Software

4.8.1 R language

This work emphasizes the use of R for decision tree models because R is the most comprehensive environment for the purpose. At this writing, a search for R functions incorporating the term "tree" returned 384 links in 165 packages. This does not even count classification-related functions not using "tree" in their nomenclature. Classification is a prolific and fast-evolving focus for R programmers. Many R packages for CART are listed in Section 4.18 and at the CRAN website.[1] We cite just a few major programs here.

- The package "rpart" is one of the most-used decision-tree packages in R and is the focus of many of the sections later in this work. Among the command functions is supports are
  - `rpart()` [Recursive Partitioning and Regression Trees program]
  - `plot.rpart()`[Plot an Rpart object]
  - `print.rpart()` [Print an Rpart object]
  - `rsq.rpart()` [Plots the approximate R-square for the different splits]
  - `summary.rpart()` [Summarize a fitted Rpart object]
  - `xpred.rpart()` [Return cross-validated predictions]
- The package "tree", which was one of the earliest and is still a widespread vehicle for creating decision trees in R, supports the command functions `tree()` and `summary.tree ()` for fitting CART. Among its several other functions is `plot.tree()` for plotting tree objects.
- The packages "party" and "partykit" support the `ctree()` command, discussed in a later section. This command incorporates stopping criteria based on permutation significance tests which arguably have superior statistical qualities.
- The package "randomForest" supports the command `randomForest(}`, and is one of several R packages which can be used to create random forest models. It is the focus of several later sections of this work.

4.8.2 Stata

In Stata, CHAID and exhaustive CHAID are supported by the `chaid` command. Random forests are supported by the `chaidforest` command. CART is supported by the `cart` command. CART is also supported by the package `crtrees.ado`, a third-party package from Ricardo Mora. Type "`findit crtrees`" and follow the directions to install, after which one may type "`help crtrees`". The `crtrees` package supports CART as well as random forest versions of either, including tree-growing, tree-pruning, and finding the "honest tree" (selecting the best tree after pruning using Gini impurity for classification trees or mean square error for regression trees). See Mora (2015).

4.8.3 SAS

Decision trees are supported by the "SAS Enterprise Miner" package, not base SAS. This decision tree module does not offer named algorithm choices for CHAID, CART, or other algorithms. However, it is possible to blend features of different algorithms, such as using CHAID-like splitting of tree nodes and CART-like retrospective pruning of branches.

4.8.4 SPSS

The "IBM SPSS Decision Trees" module supports CHAID, exhaustive CHAID (which SPSS labels "exhausted CHAID"), CART (which SPSS labels "C&RT"), and QUEST (quaternion estimation). This module is an add-on, not part of base SPSS. In addition to supporting tree-based classification analysis, SPSS supports validation tools for exploratory and confirmatory classification analysis. Another SPSS add-on, the "Answer Trees" module, supports CART models, which SPSS labels C&RT models. Also, "IBM SPSS Modeler" is the module for data science applications, which includes various machine learning models discussed in this work.

4.8.5 Python language

Python is an alternative to the R language and is one in which decision trees may be scripted using custom code. An introductory python-orient text is Smith (2017). Scikit-Learn is a python toolkit/library for machine learning, including classification solutions.[2] Scikit in turn requires the Numpy and Matplotlib libraries. The Smith text also uses the Pandas library. Python code for decision trees is also presented in Jacobs (2019: 127–140).

4.9 Data and packages used in this chapter

4.9.1 Example data

- MurderRates: Used and described in the "Quick Start" regression tree section. This data frame contains eight variables pertaining to murder rates in 44 U.S. states in 1950. The outcome variable is "rate", which is the mean murder rate. There are six other continuous variables and one binary/character variable, which may be used as predictors. The data come with the "AER" package.
- ptitanic: Used and described in the "Quick Start" classification tree section. These are data on 1,309 passengers on the ill-fated ocean liner "Titanic". The outcome variable is "survived". There are five other variables which may be used as predictors of survival. The data come with the "rpart.plot" package.
- world: Many of the examples in Part III of this chapter use the data file "world.csv". Data rows are 212 nations of the world. For classification trees, the outcome variable is "litgtmean", a binary variable indicating whether the nation is above or below the mean literacy rate for all nations. For regression trees, the outcome variable is "literacy", a continuous variable reflecting national literacy rates. Various economic and demographic variables are available as predictors. At various points in this chapter, the data frames world2, and world3 are created from world.csv. The same data file is used for the Chapter 4 online supplements for the `tree()` `and ctree() programs.`

4.9.2 R packages used

The following packages are used in this section and may need to be installed on the user's local machine using the `install_packages()` command.

```
library(AER)            # Contains the MurderRates data
library(caret)          # Supports model performance metrics and more
library(e1071)          # Required by the caret packages
library(gains)          # Supports gains plots
library(ggplot2)        # A leading graphics/visualization package for R
library(maptree)        # Supports tree visualization
library(mlr)            # The Machine Learning in R package
library(partykit)       # Has the ctree() program for decision trees
library(rattle)         # Supports fancyRpartPlot{} and asRules()
library(rms)            # Computes root mean square error
library(ROCR)           # Supports the performance() command
library(rpart)          # Has the rpart() program for decision trees
library(rpart.plot)     # Plotting for rpart and has ptitanic data
library(scales)         # Utility for data handling, labeling, and more
library(tree)           # Has the tree() program for decision trees
```

Though listed alphabetically above, due to conflicts (particularly in the `performance()` command) the following four packages should be invoked in this order for purposes in this chapter:

```
library(caret)
library(mlr)
library(scales)
library(ROCR)
```

PART II: QUICK START - CLASSIFICATION AND REGRESSION TREES

4.10 Classification tree example: Survival on the Titanic

Below we load the needed packages and read in the "ptitanic" data.[3] This is a data frame located in the "rpart.plot" package. There are data on 1,309 passengers on the Titanic ocean liner, famous for having sunk on its maiden voyage in 1912. The research objective is to discover the correlates of the variable "survived", coded in character format as "died" or "survived". Predictor variables are as follows:

- pclass: Passenger class, coded as "1st", "2nd", or "3rd". No missing values.
- sex: Gender, coded as "female" or "male". No missing values.
- age: A continuous variable with a mean of 19.88 years. There are 261 missing values.
- sibsp: Number of siblings or spouses aboard. A continuous variable varying from 0 to 8. No missing values.
- parch: Number of parents or children aboard. A continuous variable varying from 0 to 9. No missing values.

```
# Setup
library(rpart)                  # Classification and regression trees for R
library(rpart.plot)       # Plotting for rpart and has ptitanic data
library(caret)            # Supports model performance metrics

data(ptitanic)
class(ptitanic)
     [1] "data.frame"

names(ptitanic)
[1] "pclass"   "survived" "sex"      "age"      "sibsp"    "parch"
```

Below, the `rpart()` command from the "rpart" package creates the classification tree for Titanic survival. As in previous chapters, we use optional package prefixes before commands, which are not part of the R system library, to clarify the package-command connect. As illustrated below, the general format of the `rpart()` command is the name of the object to be created (classtree), the command word (rpart), the outcome variable (survived), a tilde with a list of predictor variables separated by plus signs, and a comma followed by a list of options separated by commas. In this syntax normally we would use full names like ptitanic$age but this is not necessary here and omitting the data frame prefix avoids a cluttered tree graph. The `minbucket=10` option assures that all end nodes ("died" or "survived") represent constellations of causal values with at least 10 passengers.

```
classtree <- rpart::rpart(survived ~ pclass + sex + age + sibsp + parch, method="class",
control=rpart::rpart.control(minbucket = 10), data=ptitanic)
```

We create a following basic plot. Note the two-step process: (1) create the model and display the tree structure, then (2) label the branches on the tree with the `text()` command. The example output is Figure 4.1. In the code below, setting xpd to TRUE means plotting is clipped to the figure region. The pretty=0 option requests no abbreviation of labels. That use.n = TRUE asks that counts be displayed as part of the terminal node labels. The cex option sets the magnification factor for text and symbols.

```
plot(classtree, margin = 0.05)
text(classtree, pretty=0, use.n = TRUE, xpd = TRUE, cex = 0.8)
```

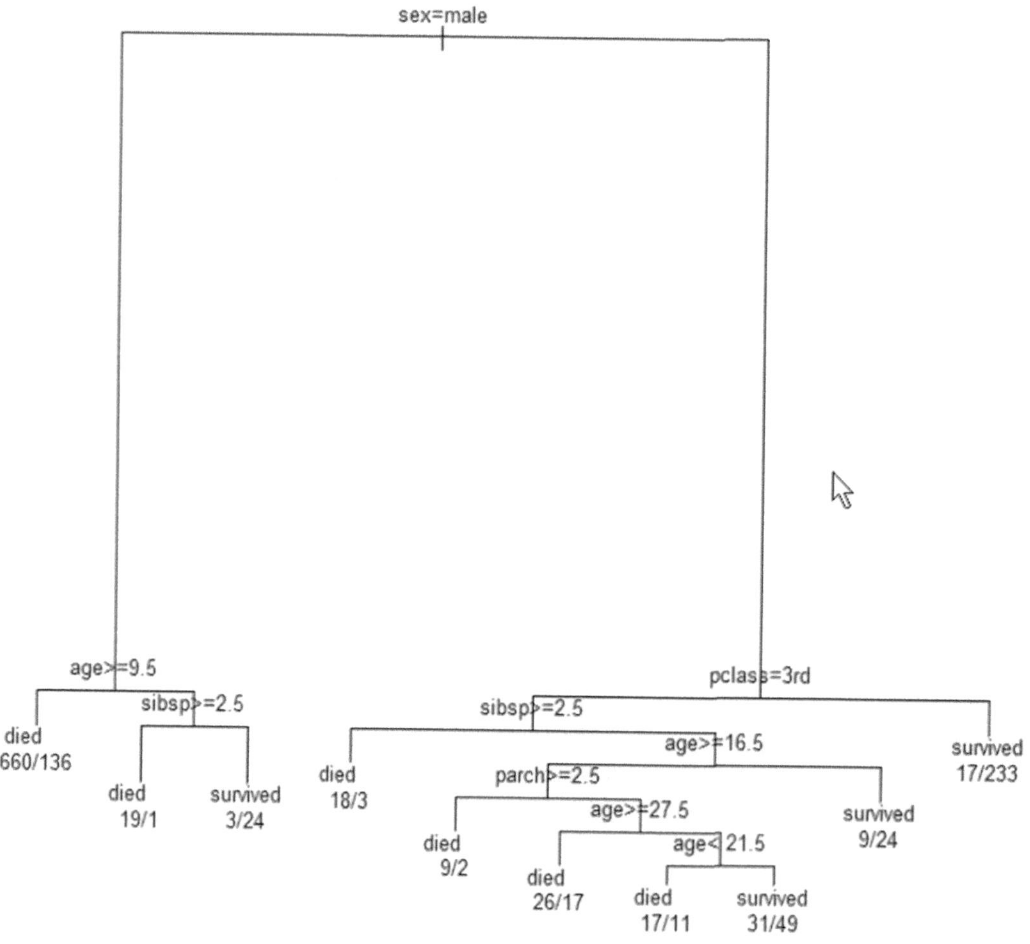

Figure 4.1 Classification tree for Titanic survival

In Part III of this chapter, we present tree graphs which go beyond the basic one here and which may be more easily read. However, reading Figure 4.1 starts at the top of the tree, called the "root" node. As explained earlier, observations that meet the term atop a split point go to the left in the decision tree while those not meeting the criterion go to the right. Consider the classification tree rules for left-most terminal node (leaf), which is "died 660/136".

1. If sex = male, go to the left.
2. If age >= 9.5, go to the left.
3. Arrive at the left-most terminal node, the value of which is "died". All those in this node are predicted to have died.

Note that in classification trees, a variable which is used (e.g., age) may appear in more than one location in the tree. Though not the case for this example, not all variables entered in the calling syntax are necessarily used at all.

To understand the pair of numbers under any terminal node it is helpful to remember how the outcome variable is coded internally, as revealed by the `levels()` command. Here the coding is 1 = "died", 2 = "survived".

```
levels(ptitanic$survived)
[Output:]
      [1] "died"     "survived"
```

Under the left-most terminal node is the term "died 660/136". This node represents 660 + 136 = 796 passengers, all of whom are predicted by the classification tree model to have died, as shown by the node label. Of these, 660 were correctly classified as outcome = 1 = died and there were 136 classification errors. Looking at the right-most terminal node, labeled "survived 17/233", there were 133 + 17 = 250 passengers in this group, of whom 233 were correctly classified as outcome = 2 = survived and there were 17 classification errors.

The `rpart.rules()` command from the rpart package reveals probability of outcomes. The first column in the output is the survival probability. For instance, when passenger class was 3rd, the probability of survival was only 26%.

```
# For sex
rpart.plot::rpart.rules(rpart::rpart(survived ~ sex, data = ptitanic))
[Output:]
      survived
      0.19 when sex is   male
      0.73 when sex is female
```

```
# For passenger class
rpart.plot::rpart.rules(rpart::rpart(survived ~ pclass, data = ptitanic))
[Output:]
      survived
      0.26 when pclass is 3rd
      0.43 when pclass is 2nd
      0.62 when pclass is 1st
```

Next we use the `predict()` command from the "stats" package in the R system library to make predictions for the outcome variable, which is "survived". We put the predictions in an object called "classtree_pred".

```
classtree_pred <- predict(classtree,type="class")
```

Model performance metrics may be computed based on the predictions. The `confusionMatrix()` command from the "caret" package uses the predictions to generate a variety of model fit metrics for a classification tree model. For instance, we see below that the classification "accuracy" metric is a relatively high 82.43%. Other performance metrics listed below are explained in Part III of this chapter.

```
caret::confusionMatrix(classtree_pred, reference = ptitanic$survived,
positive='survived')
```
[Output:]
```
  Confusion Matrix and Statistics

            Reference
  Prediction died survived
    died      749      170
    survived   60      330

                Accuracy : 0.8243
                  95% CI : (0.8026, 0.8445)
     No Information Rate : 0.618
     P-Value [Acc > NIR] : < 2.2e-16

                   Kappa : 0.6115

  Mcnemar's Test P-Value : 6.611e-13

             Sensitivity : 0.6600
             Specificity : 0.9258
          Pos Pred Value : 0.8462
          Neg Pred Value : 0.8150
              Prevalence : 0.3820
          Detection Rate : 0.2521
    Detection Prevalence : 0.2979
       Balanced Accuracy : 0.7929

        'Positive' Class : survived
```

If `positive=` is not specified (or is set to "died"), the default positive category will be the first level, which is "died". Accuracy would still be the same, but some of the other fit coefficients would change as a result.

Finally, we may wish to check for missing values in the data. While the `summary(ptitanic)` command would give the count of missing values (NAs) by variable, it also gives frequencies for categorical variables and descriptive statistics for continuous variables. The following commands give a simple count of NAs. We see missing values are concentrated in the "age" column.

```
na_count <-sapply(ptitanic, function(y) sum(length( which(is.na(y)))))
na_count
```
[Output:]
```
 pclass survived      sex      age    sibsp    parch
      0        0        0      263        0        0
```

Seeing what the correlates of missingness are is accomplished by the commands below. Values in the first output column are probabilities of missingness. The output reveals that missingness in the ptitanic data is particularly associated with being in 3rd class and having at least seven siblings or spouses aboard. Apparently the ages of the poorer passengers in 3rd class were not recorded as diligently.

```
obs.with.nas <- rowSums(is.na(ptitanic)) > 0
rpart.plot::rpart.rules(rpart::rpart(obs.with.nas ~., data = ptitanic, method =
"class"))
```

[Output:]
```
obs.with.nas
0.09 when pclass is 1st or 2nd
0.29 when pclass is        3rd & sibsp <  7
0.89 when pclass is        3rd & sibsp >= 7
```

4.11 Regression tree example: Correlates of murder

The "rpart" package works with a continuous dependent variable such as murder rate in the following example as well as with a categorical ones such as "survived" in the previous Titanic example. While regression trees generally parallel the classification tree procedure, there are differences as well. For instance, regression tree models use the "anova" method rather than the "class" method. Also, terminal nodes are levels of the continuous outcome variable (rate) and, unlike classification trees, a terminal node of a given value may only appear only once in the decision tree. That is, where classification trees are equifinal, meaning they may reveal multiple paths to the same given outcome (e.g., "died" in the Titanic example), this is not true of regression trees. Moreover, model performance measures differ (e.g., regression trees do not use confusion/classification tables with their metrics like "accuracy").

For the "Quick Start" regression tree example we use the "MurderRates" data frame, which comes with the "AER" package. This data frame contains eight variables pertaining to murder rates in 44 U.S. states in 1950. We predict "rate' from all the other variables listed below. Keep in mind that the research objective is to uncover correlates of average murder rates aggregated by state. Be cautioned that correlates are not necessarily cause and what is true at the state level is not necessarily true at the individual level. Moreover, there may be additional correlates of murder rate not present in the dataset.

- rate: Murder rate per 100,000 (FBI estimate, 1950).
- convictions: Number of convictions divided by number of murders in 1950.
- executions: Average number of executions 1946–1950 divided by convictions in 1950.
- time: Median time served (in months) of convicted murderers released in 1951.
- income: Median family income in 1949 (in 1,000 USD).
- lfp: Labor force participation rate in 1950 (in percent).
- noncauc: Proportion of population that is non-Caucasian in 1950.
- southern: Factor indicating region. This character variable is coded "yes" or "no". All other variables are continuous numeric.

```
# Setup
library(AER)                # Has the MurderRates dataset
library(rpart)              # Classification and regression trees for R
library(rpart.plot)         # Plotting for rpart

data("MurderRates")
class(MurderRates)
     [1] "data.frame"

names(MurderRates)
  [1] "rate"        "convictions" "executions"  "time"
  [5] "income"      "lfp"         "noncauc"     "southern"
```

Below, we use the `rpart()` command to create the object "regtree", which is of class "rpart" and contains the regression tree solution. For regression trees the method is set to "anova". The dot after the tilde follow rate is in lieu of a list of predictor variables. It means all other variables in the data are to be used, other than the outcome variable (rate). We require that terminal nodes have at least four observations (states). Setting the random seed is required if one wants to obtain the same exact coefficients on a subsequent run.

```
set.seed(123)

regtree <- rpart::rpart(rate ~., method="anova", control=rpart::rpart.
control(minbucket = 4), data=MurderRates)

class(regtree)
     [1] "rpart"
```

We then create a basic plot of the regression tree solution in the same manner as for classification trees, where command options were explained. Figure 4.2 shows the basic plot for the MurderRates regression tree reflects in the "regtree" object we created above. More elaborate plotting is shown in Section III.

```
plot(regtree, margin = 0.05)
text(regtree, pretty=0, use.n = TRUE, xpd = TRUE, cex = 0.8)
```

Notice that in Figure 4.2 there are five terminal nodes, each with its own mean murder rate. Unlike the "Titanic" classification tree, where an outcome like "died" appeared multiple times in the terminal nodes of the tree, in a regression tree terminal nodes do not repeat. For instance, all 17 states in the left-most leaf are predicted to have a murder rate of 1.941. All seven states in the right-most leaf are predicted to have a murder rate of 12.93. Rates are per 100,000 population. The five terminal nodes represent clusters of states with successively higher murder rates. The paths to each terminal outcome are governed by a set of rules unique to that outcome.

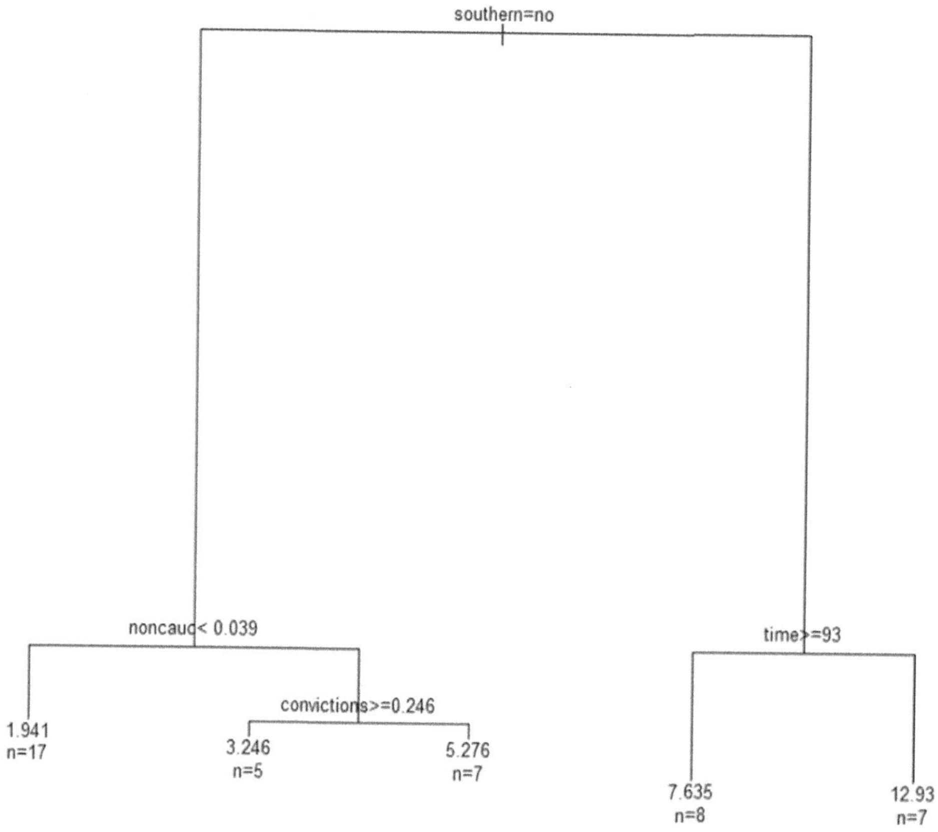

Figure 4.2 Regression tree for MurderRates

In the regression tree rules output below, there are five rows, corresponding to the five terminal nodes in Figure 4.2. The initial "rate" column is the predicted murder rate. This is the same as shown in Figure 4.2, but rounded to one decimal place. The last column, "cover", is the percent of states in each of the five terminal nodes. In between are the splitting rules associated with each node. For instance, the largest node is the first one, with 39% of the cases and a predicted murder rate of 1.9, predicted for a non-southern state with a non-Caucasian population percent below 3.9%.

```
rpart.plot::rpart.rules(regtree, cover = TRUE)
[Output:]
    rate                                                                  cover
    1.9 when southern is  no & noncauc <  0.039                            39%
    3.2 when southern is  no & noncauc >= 0.039 & convictions >= 0.25      11%
    5.3 when southern is  no & noncauc >= 0.039 & convictions <  0.25      16%
    7.6 when southern is yes & time >= 93                                  18%
   12.9 when southern is yes & time <  93                                  16%
```

Although seven predictor variables were input, only four were actually used in the regression tree. This contrasts with OLS regression, where all input variables are used for the predictions, even nonsignificant ones. In terms of number of variables, regression trees tend to provide a more parsimonious model. Variables actually used are listed in the output for the `printcp()` command.

```
printcp(regtree)
[Output:]
   Regression tree:
   rpart::rpart(formula = rate ~., data = MurderRates, method = "anova",
       control = rpart::rpart.control(minbucket = 4))

   Variables actually used in tree construction:
   [1] convictions noncauc     southern    time

   Root node error: 856.67/44 = 19.47
   n= 44
           CP nsplit rel error  xerror    xstd
   1 0.587775      0   1.00000 1.05135 0.25053
   2 0.122316      1   0.41222 0.95964 0.20016
   3 0.050888      2   0.28991 0.93103 0.19432
   4 0.014026      3   0.23902 0.81332 0.17270
   5 0.010000      4   0.22499 0.79807 0.17111
```

Model performance: A better-performing model has less error. Error is shown in the "complexity parameter" (CP) table. This table is generated by the `printcp()` command shown above and discussed in more detail in Section III of this chapter. In the CP table, the bottom row is for the final model, which has four splits.

- The "rel error" of 0.22499 is a model performance measure, with lower being better. Relative error, also called risk, is the average deviance (a measure of error) for regression tree divided by the average deviance for the null (root-only) tree. Relative error is scaled relative to the null model, so that the value for the top (root) level is always 1.0.
- The "xerror" of 0.73854 is cross-validated mean error, based on rpart's built-in tenfold cross-validation. Lower is better. One rule of thumb about what level down in the CP table is the optimal solution (optimal number of splits) is to pick the level where xerror – (rel error + xstd) is at a minimum.

As shown above, the same command also computes root node error (RNE), which is a measure of error made when cases are classified based only on the root node split (here, southern). Section III also discusses how to obtain mean square error (MSE) as another model performance measure for rpart regression trees.

There are two "R-squared" model effect values for an rpart object like regtree: One based on relative error and one based on cross-validated error (xerror). Both can be expressed as 1 minus these errors. This is accomplished by the code below. The final 4-split model is the bottom row. Though the columns are still labeled "rel error" and "xerror", they are now transformed as 1 minus these values, giving the R-square values. The information is mathematically equivalent, but in R-square format, higher is better.

```
tmp <- printcp(regtree)
rsq.val <- 1 - tmp[,c(3,4)]
rsq.val
```

[Output:]

```
  rel error      xerror
1 0.0000000 -0.05134881
2 0.5877755  0.04036433
3 0.7100917  0.06897374
4 0.7609793  0.18668177
5 0.7750057  0.20192978
```

Variable importance: The "regtree" object contains information on the relative importance of input variables, whether actually used in the regression tree or not. Calculation of variable importance is discussed in more detail in Section III of this chapter, but in general variable importance is a measure of a sum of improvement coefficients contributed by a given variable. Higher values reflect more contribution to improving the model. Variable importance coefficients may be unscaled or may be scaled to add to 100. In either form, the order of variable importance remains the same. For this example, the four top predictors by variable importance are the only ones actually used in the model. The variable "southern" is most important in predicting murder rates for the example data. In the regression tree rules output shown above, higher murder rates were associated with paths in which southern was yes.

```
# Unscaled variable importance
regtree$variable.importance
[Output:]
 southern    noncauc      income        time
503.52914  442.78704   427.02610   253.53418
      lfp executions convictions
213.48633   64.24533    56.92357
```

```
# Scaled variable importance
summary(regtree)
[Partial output:]
 Variable importance
 southern    noncauc      income        time
       26         23          22          13
      lfp executions convictions
       11          3           3
```

PART III: CLASSIFICATION AND REGRESSION TREES, IN DETAIL

4.12 Overview

In this chapter, we focus on decision trees, by which we mean single decision trees rather than random forests or other ensemble methods discussed in Chapter 5. In the subsections which follow, we create decision trees with the most popular R package used for this purpose, which is the "rpart" package already used in the "Quick Start" examples above. In online Chapter 4 supplements at this book's Support Material (www.routledge.com/9780367624293) we also explore two other widely-used R decision tree programs, `tree()` and `ctree()`. At this writing (2020), the "rpart" package is most widely used, the "tree" package second, and the "party" and "partykit" packages for the `ctree()` program rank third in usage among the R packages considered in this chapter. Yet other decision tree programs exist for R, of course.

By "single decision tree" we mean just that – one tree representing one of a larger possible set of solutions. It is universally agreed that more accurate and reliable classifications and predictions are obtained by ensemble methods which synthesize many trees using the same data. It is also well-documented that single decision trees may be unstable, with large differences in the solution resulting from small changes in inputs (Jacobucci, 2018).

Therefore we may ask, "Why use single decision tree methods at all?" The answer is that single tree solutions are more interpretable than ensemble solutions. It follows from this that single trees may well be more helpful in the exploratory phase of research when the researcher is building theory and constructing models. Moreover, single trees may be implemented under different parameters and even with different variables in a form of sensitivity analysis, which further enhances understanding of the dynamics of the elements forming a model of research interest. Finally, for the student understanding decision trees is groundwork for understanding random forests and other tree-based ensemble methods.

In this chapter, we create decision trees and cross-validate them. In Chapter 5 we will introduce ensemble methods such as random forests, bagging, and boosting. As mentioned, ensemble methods seek to improve the precision of classification or prediction by averaging across many trees. In this chapter, we also introduce the "caret" package, which adds tree-related statistical metrics useful for training, comparing, and analyzing models and which will be central to later chapters.

4.13 The `rpart()` program

4.13.1 Introduction

The rpart package contains the most widely used R programs for CART. This package supports the `rpart()` program itself, the `summary.rpart()` program for fitting CART, the `plot.rpart()` program for visualizing tree objects, and others. While the long-standing "tree" package remains very common in the literature, the "rpart" package is preferred by many, partly because `rpart()` can be faster due to its greater use of C level programming for pruning, cross-validation, and due to its many procedural options. Both implement many of the concepts found in Breiman et al. (1984).

The `rpart()` program/function/command creates either regression and classification trees depending on whether the outcome variable is continuous or categorical, or based on specifying the `method=` option. Predictor variables may be nominal, ordinal, or continuous. Nominal variables may be character type (strings) without need to recode numerically. It uses a recursive binary splitting algorithm. While the target variable for classification trees need not be binary and, indeed, even could be a continuous variable with a finite number of values, this might generate a complex tree with too many leaves (terminal nodes) to interpret usefully. Output includes the decision tree in plot or listing form. Various fit and performance measures are available, many requiring the `performance()` function in post-estimation. Survival (time-to-event) models are also supported. Below, R-language steps in the use of the `rpart()` program are explained in greater detail than in the "Quick Start" sections.

In recursive partitioning to establish branching in a tree, it is necessary to evaluate where predictor variables should be split. For instance, for the predictor variable "age" the `rpart()` algorithm must determine whether to split one incoming path into two outgoing paths by a rule such as "If age less than equal 30, go to the left, otherwise go to the right." By default, `rpart()` uses the Gini Impurity index to evaluate where to split.[4] This differs from the "Information Gain" (aka, "Entropy") method often commonly used. The Gini default may be overridden by adding the option below to the `rpart()` command

```
parms = list(split = 'information')
```

Raileanu and Stoffel (2004) compared the Gini versus Information Gain criteria, finding that 98% of the time, the choice made no difference for model performance. Also, because the formula for the Information Gain algorithm incorporates a logarithmic transformation, the Gini method will be computationally faster. Here we accept the default method (Gini).

TEXT BOX 4.1 Social science applications of R: Treating suicidal behavior of adolescents

Babeva et al. (2020) used classification trees implemented through the "rpart" package in R in conjunction with conventional statistical procedures to study the efficacy of cognitive–behavioral treatments with strong family components for reducing suicide risk among adolescents, for whom suicide is a leading cause of death. Subjects were some 50 youth with histories of suicide attempts or self-harm. The findings of the study supported the potential value of personalized treatment approaches to adolescent suicide based on pretreatment characteristics of the youth. The study also found significant sleep problems and baseline suicidal behaviors to be significant in predicting adolescents' response to treatment.

Classification tree analysis, with a correct classification rate of 93.3%, and follow-up logistic regression analyses indicated that 35% of youths reporting active suicidal behavior at baseline (pretreatment) reported active suicidal behavior at posttreatment. In contrast, posttreatment suicidal behavior was rare among youths whose active suicidality had resolved by the baseline assessment (5%). Among youths reporting baseline suicidal behavior, those reporting sleep problems were more likely to report posttreatment suicidal behavior (53%) versus those without sleep problems (0%). The authors concluded that their findings highlight the potential value of personalized treatment approaches based on pretreatment characteristics and the significance of baseline suicidal behavior and sleep problems for predicting treatment response.

The variable pool for the classification tree analysis was selected from the main domains suggested by prior research, eliminating redundant variables. It included a modestly large number of predictors, such as demographic factors (age, gender, Caucasian vs. racial/ethnic minority status, income, heterosexual vs. other); baseline suicidal behavior status; clinical measures (depression, hopelessness), PTSD, clinically significant elevation on a sleep problem scale and a parent-reported child behavior (a checklist reflecting internalizing, externalizing, and total behavior problem scales); self-reported sleep problems; youth self-reported stress; and family characteristics (parental depression, family conflict, parent hopelessness).

The classification tree method was able to correctly classify 93% of suicidal behavior at posttreatment based on only three of these variables: suicidal behavior at baseline (pretreatment), trouble sleeping, and being non-Caucasian. Cross-validated error rates for the classification tree results were calculated by sequentially excluding subsets of the data, regrowing the tree, and then classifying the held-out subjects to get an unbiased estimate of the prediction accuracy for new subjects, which was used to evaluate the stability of the resulting trees.

Commenting on their classification tree results, the authors note (p. 60), "Recursive partitioning methods are particularly useful for identifying complex interactions among predictors in a data-driven manner; handle multicollinearity, missing data, and large pools of potential covariates well; are invariant to transformations or distributional properties of the predictor variables; and provide easily interpretable clinical decision-making rules. These advantages make classification trees an attractive alternative to logistic regression and have led to these methods gaining popularity in the health sciences."

Source: Babeva, Kalina N.; Klomhaus, Alexandra M.; Sugar, Catherine A.; Fitzpatrick, Olivia B. A.; & Asarnow, Joan R. (2020). Adolescent suicide attempt prevention: Predictors of response to a… *Suicide and Life-Threatening Behavior* 50(1): 56–71.

Note also that `rpart()` is governed by parameters set in `rpart.control()`. As listed below, these parameters control such settings as when splitting is attempted and the number of observations required for a split. In the present example, all default settings were accepted. However, the researcher may use `rpart.control()` with manually-adjusted settings as in the example below the options listing. The format for `rpart.control()`, with default settings, is:

```
rpart.control(minsplit = 20, minbucket = round(minsplit/3), cp = 0.01,
              maxcompete = 4, maxsurrogate = 5, usesurrogate = 2, xval = 10,
              surrogatestyle = 0, maxdepth = 30, ...)
```

The following are the settings in `rpart.control()`:

- `maxdepth`: This is the maximum depth of any node of the final tree, counting the root node as depth 0 and the split at the root node as depth 1. The value of maxdepth must be 1 or greater. Warning: For values greater than 30 `rpart()` will give nonsense results on 32-bit machines.
- `Minsplit`: This is the minimum number of cases in a node for attempting a split.
- `Minbucket`: This is the minimum number of cases for any terminal node. If only minsplit and not minbucket is specified, then minbucket is set to minsplit/3. If neither is specified, then minsplit = 20 and minbucket = round(20/3) = 7. If only minbucket and not minsplit is specified, then minsplit is set to minbucket*3.
- `Cp`: This is the complexity parameter. To be attempted, any prospective split must decrease overall lack of fit by a factor of cp. This is a form of automatic pruning. If `method="anova"` (for regression trees) splitting is specified or is selected automatically because the outcome variable is continuous, implying that R-square must decrease by at least cp.
- `Xval`: This sets the number of cross-validations. Note that `rpart()` defaults to a built-in tenfold cross-classification.
- `Maxcompete`: This is the number of runner-up (competitor) splits printed in the output.
- `Maxsurrogate`: Surrogates refer to using an alternative splitting variable when the case is missing data on the primary (selected) splitting variable. Thus, `maxsurrogate` is the number of surrogate splits listed in the output. If set to zero, computer processing time is reduced by about half since surrogate splits will not be sought. This might be done if the data contain no missing values.
- `Usesurrogate`: If set to 0, surrogates are used for display only. If set to 1, surrogates are used for cases missing data on the primary splitting variable. If set to 2, then if all surrogates are missing, the case is assigned to the majority direction, overriding the default of not splitting the case if all surrogates are missing.
- `Surrogatestyle`: If set to 0, then the best surrogate is the one with the highest total number of correct classifications (the default). If set to 1, then the percent correct is used (number of correct classifications divided by the number of non-missing surrogate values), which is a more lenient criterion when there are many missing values.

To change settings manually, a `control=` option is added to the `rpart()` options list. For example, consider adding this option to the `rpart()` command:

```
control=rpart.control( maxdepth = 2,minsplit = 2, minbucket = 1,cp = -1)
```

This option would create a tree with only three levels (levels 0–2, counting the root node as 0), where each node to be split must have at least two cases, each terminal node need must have only one case (thereby creating a maximally complex tree), and lack of fit must decrease by at least 1.0 for the split to have occurred. For the following examples, however, we accept all `rpart()` defaults and do not change the control settings.

4.13.2 Training and validation datasets

In this chapter, we will use the "world" dataset described in the previous "Example" data section. This dataset represents all the countries of the world and the dataset is treated as a whole. In contrast to this census or enumeration of all cases, when the data are a sample, it is common to divide the available data into a training dataset and a validation dataset. The model is developed for the training dataset and if its results are satisfactory for the validation dataset, confidence is increased in the generalizability of results. When we have an enumeration, as for the world dataset, generalizability is not an issue. Nonetheless, the `rpart()` command has a form of tenfold cross-validation, as discussed further below. That is, even though we have an enumeration rather than a sample of the data, `rpart()` uses built-in cross-validation to resample the data.

Simply to illustrate the process were we to have sampled data, we now give the R commands for creating a training and validation dataset from the world data. We use the customary 70% of the sample for training and 30% for validation, but these proportions may be changed by the researcher. We create two new datasets called "train" and "validate" respectively, even though subsequent sections will use the complete "world" dataset instead.

We assume below that the world.csv dataset has been downloaded from this book's Support Material (www.routledge.com/9780367624293) and has been placed in the folder "C:\Data". We read in the data in the usual way. The last option, `stringsAsFactors=TRUE,` is not the default but is important so that character variables are read in as factors.

```
setwd("C:/Data")
world <- read.table("world.csv", header = TRUE, sep = ",", stringsAsFactors = TRUE)
```

Optionally, we first show that the world dataset has 212 observations for 20 variables by using the `dim()` dimensions command as below:

```
dim(world)
[Output:]
        [1] 212  20
```

Next we randomly select 70% of the rows in the world data frame (in the command below, "flag" is a user-named variable). Note that "flag", created below, will contain a numeric vector of randomly sampled row numbers. Setting the random number seed prior to sampling is useful to get the same sample each run. Since the process involves random selection, the reader's sample of cases will differ from the author's, if "trying this at home".

```
set.seed(99)
flag <- sort(sample(nrow(world),nrow(world)*.7))
```

We then create the training dataset, putting it in the object "train". For instructional purposes we also verify its dimensions. The flag vector sets the row numbers. That there are no columns listed after the comma means all 20 columns are to be used.

```
train <- world[flag,]
dim(train)
[Output:]
        [1] 148  20
```

Then we repeat the process for the validation dataset, putting it in the object "validate". The relevant command below uses "-flag" to get the other 30% of observations.

```
validate <- world[-flag,]
dim(validate)
[Output:]
        [1] 64 20
```

The "train" and "validate" datasets are data frames, as can be verified using the `class(train)` and `class(validate)` commands. Note that these data frames exist only in memory at this point and must be saved explicitly by the researcher if so desired. Each may be used like any other dataset, including the CART R syntax described in subsequent sections.

4.13.3 Setup for `rpart()` trees

In the following `rpart()` examples we use the "world" data as described in Section 4.9.1.

```
setwd("c:/Data")
world <- read.table("world.csv", header = TRUE, sep = ",", stringsAsFactors = TRUE)
[Output not shown]
```

The variable names list for the entire world dataset may be generated using the following command.

```
names(world)
```

```
[Output:]
     [1] "ID"                 "country"
     [3] "regionid"           "region"
     [5] "population"         "areasqmiles"
     [7] "poppersqmile"       "coast_arearatio"
     [9] "netmigration"       "Infantdeathsper1k"
    [11] "infdeaths"          "gdppercapitalindollars"
    [13] "literacy"           "litgtmean"
    [15] "phonesper1000"      "arablepct"
    [17] "cropspct"           "otherpct"
    [19] "birthrate"          "deathrate"
```

Later it turns out that regionid is a splitting variable. Since regionid is a character-type factor, it is handy to know the names associated with the regionid. This is done with the `levels()` command, which lists regionid sorted alphabetically. The `rpart()` command uses the levels of region numbered in this order. Since regionid has a one-to-one correspondence with the full region names in the variable region, we may obtain that information in the same way, listed in the same order.

```
class(world$region)
     [1] "character"
class(world$regionid)
     [1] "character"
```

Since region and region id are character variables, and since the `levels()` command wants factor variables, we use the `as.factor()` function to convert for listing purposes.

```
levels(as.factor(world$region))
 [1] "ASIA"               "BALTICS"
 [3] "CWINDSTATES"        "DQIND"
 [5] "EASTERNEUROPE"      "LATINAMERICA"
 [7] "NEAREAST"           "NORTHAFRICA"
 [9] "NORTHAMERICA"       "OCEANIA"
[11] "SUBSAHARANAFRICA"   "WESTERNEUROPE"
```

In this section's models we use regionid rather than region so as to minimize cluttering of the plotted decision tree labels.

```
levels(as.factor(world$regionid))
 [1] "AS" "BA" "CW" "DQ" "EE" "LA" "NE" "NF" "NO" "OC" "SA" "WE"
```

In contrast, the `unique()` command in R numbers regions or regionid in order as entered in the dataset. For the "world" data, the entered order is the alphabetical order, so this makes no difference here.

```
unique(world$regionid)
```

Next we install the package "rpart", which contains the decision tree program to be used. The `rpart()` program fits regression and classification trees. We assume the user has already installed the "rpart" package. The package has related statistical programs in addition to `rpart()`, listed in the endnote to this sentence.[5]

Below we install and invoke the packages used in this chapter. All are assumed to have been installed on the user's local machine. Note that the package "ggplot2" replaced the earlier "ggplot" package, and is required by the "caret" package.

```
library(rpart)
library(rpart.plot)
library(caret)
library(ROCR)
```

```
library(rattle)
library(maptree)
library(ggplot2)
```

Optionally, we may view online information about the rpart package using the `library(help=)` command. This will list all the commands and example datasets contained in the rpart package. Note also that documentation by Therneau and Atkinson (2018) is installed automatically in the researcher's local directory (e.g., C:/Program Files/R/R-4.0.2/library/rpart/doc). Contrast the command `help(rpart)`, which details the syntax of the `rpart()` command.

```
library(help = "rpart")
help(rpart)
```

4.14 Classification trees with the rpart package

While classification trees using `rpart()` were described in an earlier "Quick Start" example, in this section we provide more detail. For the example in this section, the "world" data frame is used with the outcome variable being "litgtmean", which is a binary variable that indicates if a country's literacy rate is above or below the mean for all countries. The predictors are all variables in the "world" data frame, but excluding ID, country, region, and literacy. Since binary variables may be treated as categorical or continuous, we may run this model as a classification tree (method = "class") or as a regression tree (method = "anova"), resulting in different tree solutions shown further below. In this section, the model is run as a classification tree.

To see the values of litgtmean for the first ten observations, read in the "world" data again if necessary, then type:

```
setwd("C:/Data")
world <- read.table("world.csv", header = TRUE, sep = ",", stringsAsFactors = TRUE)

head(world$litgtmean,10)
```
[Output:]
```
     [1] Low  Low  Low  High High Low  High High Low  High
     Levels: High Low
```

To see the corresponding values in numeric form, type:

```
as.numeric(head(as.factor(world$litgtmean),10))
```
[Output:]
```
     [1] 2 2 2 1 1 2 1 1 2 1
```

To see the order of coding, one may use the `levels()` command. "High" is the first level and therefore in numeric terms is 1. "Low" is the second level and in numeric terms is 2.

```
levels(as.factor(world$litgtmean))
```
[Output:]
```
     [1] "High" "Low"
```

4.14.1 The basic rpart classification tree

Before creating a classification tree using the rpart package, we first set a random seed so that if run a second time, the results will be reproducible. This is needed because the built-in cross-validation portion of `rpart()` contains a random component in its algorithm. The seed number is arbitrary and user-selected. The classification tree solution is created by the `rpart()` command below and is stored in the object called "rparttree_class". If typing this in, note that the syntax below is a single line. It assumes that the rpart package has already been installed and activated. Note that we have overridden default settings by adding the option `control=rpart.control(minbucket = 5)`, which allows terminal nodes as small as five nations to be created rather than the default value (7). Note also that the variables country, region, literacy, and ID have been omitted. The command is long, mainly because all predictor variables are listed; separated by plus signs.

```
set.seed(123)

rparttree_class <- rpart::rpart(litgtmean ~ regionid + population + areasqmiles +
poppersqmile + coast_arearatio + netmigration + Infantdeathsper1k + infdeaths +
gdppercapitalindollars + phonesper1000 + arablepct + cropspct + otherpct + birthrate +
deathrate, method="class", control=rpart.control(minbucket = 5), data=world)
```

Next we plot the rparttree_class tree using the `plot()` command. The `margin` option expands white space around the tree to prevent text truncation when labels are added later with the `text()` function. This is just a basic plot. In a later subsection, more elaborate ways of formatting the same tree are presented. However, even the basic `plot()` command has options not used here. The branching shape of the tree may be changed by adding the option `branch=d`, where *d* is a decimal which varies from 0 (default, for rectangular shoulders) to 1 (pointed V-shaped branches). Also not used here, the `uniform=TRUE` option produces equal length branches rather than default lengths scaled to the relative decrease in branch impurity.

```
plot(rparttree_class, margin = 0.05)
text(rparttree_class, pretty=0, use.n = TRUE, xpd = TRUE, cex = 0.8)
```

The tree is labeled with the `text()` command, with the following options. Figure 4.3 displays the resulting tree.

- `pretty = 0` causes actual values of a character variable like regionid to be displayed (e.g., "AS" for Asia) when used as a splitting variable, in lieu of default alphabetical character indexing (e.g., "abd" for the 1st, 2nd, and 4th regionid labels when sorted alphabetically).
- # `use.n = TRUE` causes printing of correct/incorrect classifications below terminal nodes.
- # `xpd = TRUE` keeps the labels from extending outside the plot.
- # `cex = 0.8` scales plot text and symbols to 80%. For example, `cex = 1.5` would be 50% larger, `cex=0.5` would be 50% smaller, etc.

This classification tree in Figure 4.3 has four terminal nodes. From left to right, the terminal nodes in Figure 4.3 were predicted to be High, Low, High, Low, with 12 + 1 + 2 + 7 = 22 misclassifications. The misclassification rate was thus approximately 10%: 22/212 = – .1038. The solution is "equifinal", meaning there is more than one path to the same outcome. There are two paths to each of the "High" and "Low" outcomes.

Therefore, the numbers at the bottom of Figure 4.3 are in high/low format. This ordering is because that is the order revealed above by the `levels()` command. The outcome variable (litgtmean) is coded with "High" as level 1 and "Low" as level 2. For classification trees, the number below each terminal node is the number of events for level 1/number of events for level 2.[6] The left-most node says that of the 128 + 12 = 140 nations in this node, 128 were correctly classified as "High" by the model and there were 12 misclassifications (wrongly classified "Low"). Other terminal leaves are read similarly.

The percentage of correct classifications in the rparttree_class solution, based on reading Figure 4.7, equals (128 + 4 + 4 + 54)/212 = .896. This is the "accuracy rate", which here is around 90%.

While node numbers of not printed in Figure 4.3, they are easily retrieved by asking for the rpart object's "frame" element. Terminal nodes have the variable label "<leaf>". Thus, node 4 is the left-most terminal node with 140 nations, for example.

```
rparttree_class$frame[1]
```
[Output:]

```
          var   n
1  birthrate 212
2   regionid 145
4     <leaf> 140
5     <leaf>   5
3 population  67
6     <leaf>   6
7     <leaf>  61
```

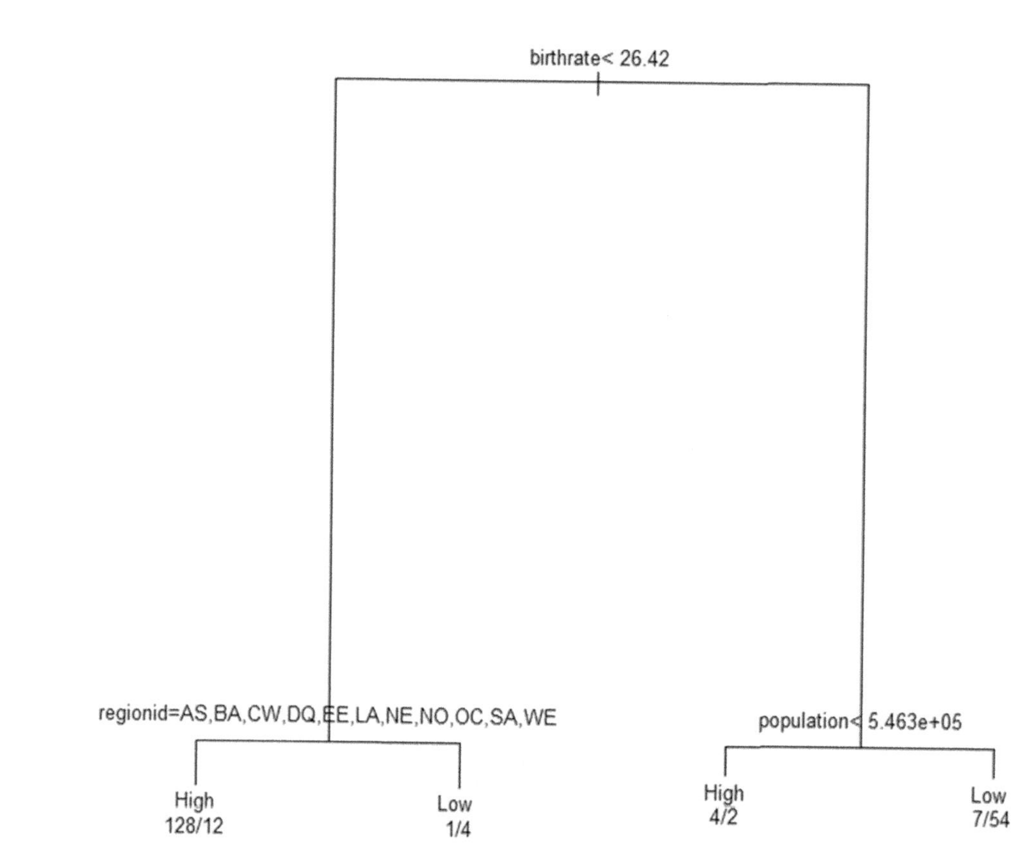

Figure 4.3 Classification tree, world data, bucket = 5

We can see there are four terminal nodes, marked "<leaf>", in the tree called rparttree_class. Their internally-assigned node numbers are 4, 5, 6, and 7. These are the nodes in Figure 4.3, from left to right. The "n" lists the number of nations in each node, whether classified correctly or incorrectly. Later we can print out the branching rules associated with arriving at each terminal node.

In terms of evaluating the classification model in Figure 4.3, we will see that there are other metrics beside the accuracy and misclassification rates. However, the question which the researcher must ask is whether the classification tree is helpful in illuminating the dynamics of literacy defined as the binary variable litgtmean. The answer to this question rests on theory and insight and cannot be answered by statistical measures alone. In understanding the dynamics of key variables identified by a decision tree, it is helpful to print out the decision tree rules embodied in the tree under consideration. That is treated in the next section.

4.14.2 Printing tree rules

The path (splitting) rules that govern an `rpart()` tree may be printed using the `rpart.rules()` command. Below, the "nn" column is the node number (4, 10, 11, 3 for this example). The "cover" coefficient is the percent of observations in the node. Note "digits=4" means there are to be four digits of accuracy, not four decimal places. The coefficient following the node number is the probability of being "Low" on litgtmean if the nation is in the given node. Nodes 4 and 10 have a low probability and thus are classed "High" since "High" was the lower-coded value, as noted earlier. Likewise, nodes 11 and 3 have a high probability and thus are classed "Low".

First we make sure the previously-installed rpart and rattle packages are active in the R environment:

```
library(rpart)
library(rattle)
```

Then, using the `asRules()` command from the "rattle" package, we request the decision rules associated with rparttree_class, which must be of class "rpart" (it is). Rules are listed by node number in an order that does not correspond to right to left order in Figure 4.3 even though the node numbers remain the same. Obtaining node numbers was presented earlier.

```
rattle::asRules(rparttree_class)
```

[Output:]

```
Rule number: 7 [litgtmean=Low cover=61 (29%) prob=0.89]
  birthrate>=26.42
  population>=5.463e+05

Rule number: 5 [litgtmean=Low cover=5 (2%) prob=0.80]
  birthrate< 26.42
  regionid=NF

Rule number: 6 [litgtmean=High cover=6 (3%) prob=0.33]
  birthrate>=26.42
  population< 5.463e+05

Rule number: 4 [litgtmean=High cover=140 (66%) prob=0.09]
  birthrate< 26.42
  regionid=AS,BA,CW,DQ,EE,LA,NE,NO,OC,SA,WE
```

We illustrate reading the table above by discussing the first node, which is node 7. We see that nations in this node are predicted to be "Low" on litgtmean. The "cover=61" term means the node contains 61 nations, telling us that the rightmost node in Figure 4.3 is Node 7. This is approximately 29% of the total population of 212 nations. Approximately 89% of the 61 nations were classified correctly (in Figure 4.3, note 54 were "Low" and 54/61 = .89). The splitting variable at the root node was birthrate. In birthrate < 26.42, nations were classed to the left, otherwise right. Here they go to the right-side path. The next splitting variable is population. If population is less than 546,300, nations were classed to the left, otherwise to the right. Node 7 was to the right. Thus, nations in node 7 were those with higher birthrate (>= 26.42) and larger population (>= 546,300). That is, a nation with a high birthrate and not a very small population is apt to be below the mean of all nations on literacy. However, node 5 is another path to low literacy, illustrating that unlike ordinary regression models, classification tree solutions are "equifinal": There can be multiple paths to the same final status.

4.14.3 Visualization with `prp()` and `draw.tree()`

Different tree visualizations are possible. The first method described in this section requires that the package "rpart. plot" be installed and activated.

```
library(rpart.plot)
```

Because we wish to add counts below terminal nodes of the tree, as a preliminary step, we first we create the function "tot_count" to add node counts. See Figure 4.4 to see the effect.

```
tot_count <- function(x, labs, digits, varlen)
{
  paste(labs, "\n\nn =", x$frame$n)
}
```

Next we print the tree using the `prp()` command. The resulting plot is shown in Figure 4.4. The options for the `prp()` command are:

- `type=5` labels each side of splits and labels leaf nodes.
- `fallen.leaves=TRUE` places terminal nodes at the bottom.
- `faclen = 0` means to use full names of the factor labels (`faclen=1` would use alphabetical index letters).
- `varlen = 0` means to use full variable names (default truncates to eight characters).

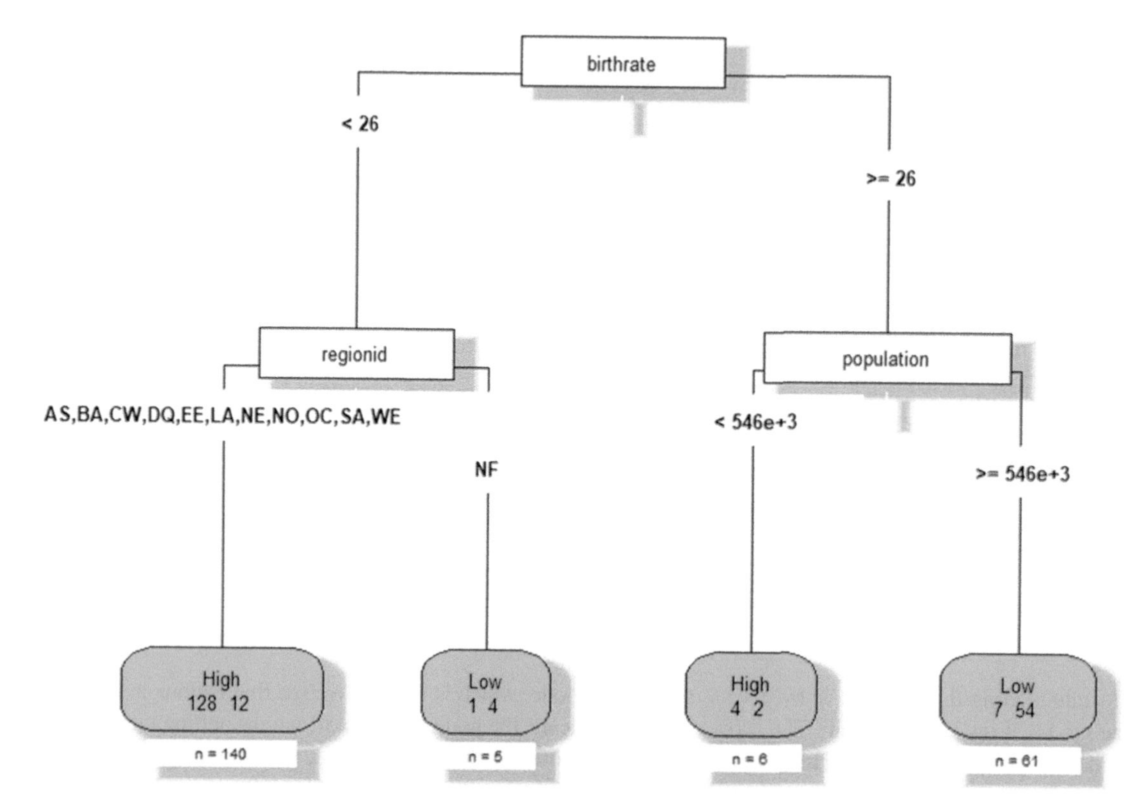

Figure 4.4 Visualization with `prp()` and the tot_count function

- `cex = 1.2` calls for scaling text labels and symbols by a factor of 120%.
- `extra = 1` adds count of correct and incorrect observations at each terminal node (equivalent to using `n = TRUE` in plot.rpart). Other possibilities are available.
- `Margin=0.1` adds a whitespace margin of 10% around the figure. Note "Margin" must be upper case.
- `box.col = 3` colors terminal nodes green.
- `shadow.col="gray"` adds a gray drop shadow for node boxes.
- `node.fun=tot_count` is the user-created function above to add node counts.
- More plotting options are available: Type `help(rpart.plot)`.
- Tip: If labels are crowded, in the Plots window select Zoom from the Plot tab. Alternatively, Export > Copy to clipboard, then uncheck "Maintain aspect ratio" and select a wider width. Also one may resize the dimensions of the plot window.

```
set.seed(123)
rpart.plot::prp(rparttree_class, type=5, fallen.leaves=TRUE, faclen = 0, varlen = 0,
cex = 0.8, extra = 1, Margin=0.1, box.col=3, shadow.col="gray", node.fun=tot_count)
```

A second alternative method of drawing the tree is to use the `draw.tree()` command from the "maptree" package. This method assumes that maptree has been installed and activated. The resulting plot appears in Figure 4.5. The following options for `draw.tree()` include:

- `cases="nations"` shows the node count with "nations" as the label.
- `print.levels=TRUE` causes display of factor levels at splits rather than just factor names (the default). The algorithm inserts a comma before each factor level (e.g., ",AS"), even the first one listed.

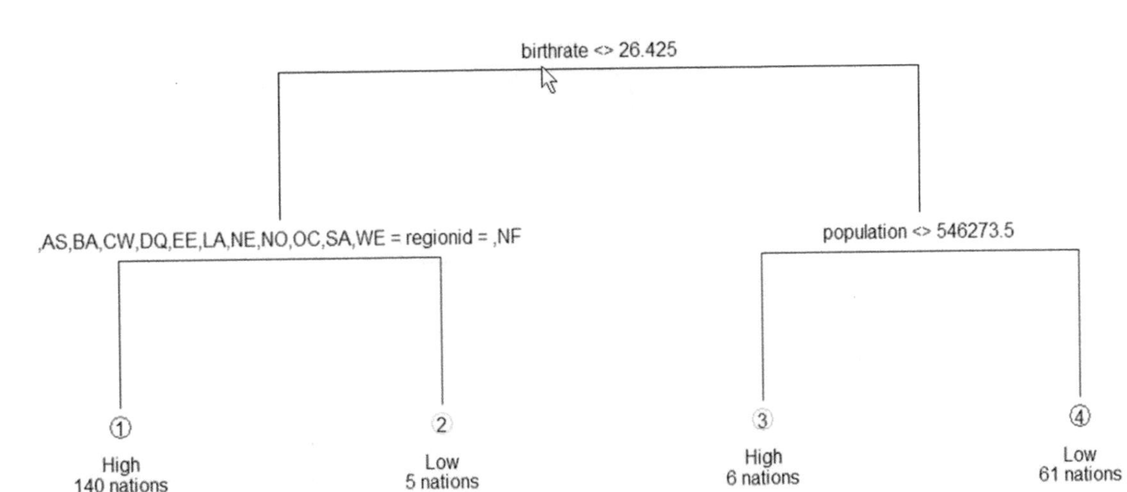

Figure 4.5 Visualization with `draw.tree()`

- `cex = 1.2` calls for scaling text labels and symbols by a factor of 120%.
- More plotting options are available: Type `help(draw.tree)`.

```
library(maptree)
maptree::draw.tree(rparttree_class,cases="nations", print.levels=TRUE, cex = 1.2)
```

4.14.4 Visualization with `fancyRpartPlot()`

Because `fancyRpartPlot()` is perhaps the most popular method of displaying an rpart tree, we give it a separate section here. The "rattle" package, which contains this function is assumed to have been installed and activated. The following options for `fancyRpartPlot()` include:

- `type=2`: Type 2 is the default layout shown in Figure 4.10, but the researcher may enter any integer from 0 through 5 to see other layouts. Note that type 2 does not support the labeling of the right side of splits (e.g., you do not see that the right-hand regionid split involves just regionid = NF = North Africa). Right-side labeling can be produced by asking for type 4 plots but then one must remove the branch.type option below, which was not supported for type 4 plots at this writing.
- `cex = 1.0`: Calls for scaling text labels and symbols by a factor of 100% rather than the default, which is smaller.
- `branch.type=5`: This option scales branch connecting lines to the size of the deviance for the node. These are the vertical gray bars in Figure 4.6. Typically this option is omitted but is shown here for instructional reasons. The default is `branch.type=3`.
- `lwd = 3`: Sets line width around nodes. This option may be omitted.
- `sub=""`: Suppresses the default subtitle below the graph.
- `main="Decision Tree"`: An optional heading above the graph (not used here).

The following command creates the fancyRpartPlot graph shown in Figures 4.4–4.6:

```
rattle::fancyRpartPlot(rparttree_class, type=2, cex=1.0, branch.type=5, lwd=3,
sub="")
```

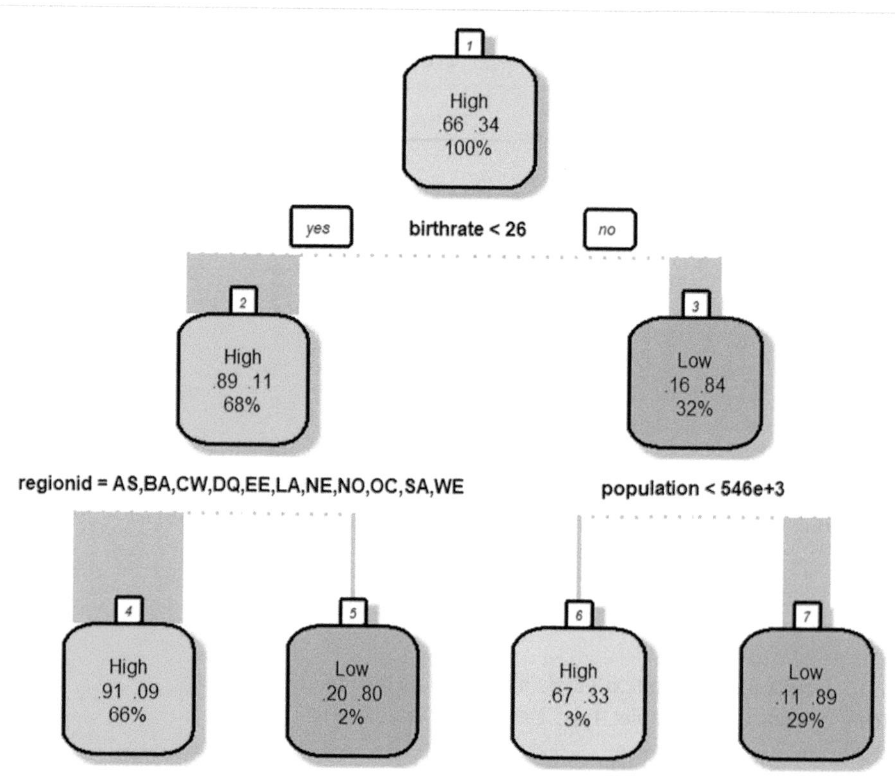

Figure 4.6 Visualization with `fancyRpartPlot()`

In the `fancyRpartPlot()` classification tree above, each shape is a node in the tree. The white box above each node shows its node number. Within each shape are three values:

1. The predicted class (here, High or Low on litgtmean). For instance, terminal node 4 (lower left) has nations predicted to be High on litgtmean (the DV). The predicted class is the most prevalent class (High). Note that predicted "High" and "Low" nodes are differentiated by color.
2. The next line down represents the conditional probability of survival of each class of the DV. For example, the conditional probability of survival for the most prevalent class (High) in node 4 is .91. There were 140 nations in node 4, all classified as "High". Of these, 128 were classified correctly, which is 128/140 = 91%, as shown in line 2 of node 4. Some 100 – 91 = 9% were classified incorrectly, also as shown.

   This percentage, 124/140 = .91, is the percentage shown in row 2 of node 4.
3. The bottom row is the percentage of observations in the node. For instance, terminal node 4 had 140 of the 212 nations, which is 66% as shown in line 3 of node 4.

4.14.5 Interpreting tree summaries

A reduced summary of the `rpart()`tree may be obtained simply by typing its name. As this is discussed in the online supplement to Chapter 4 on "The `tree()` Program", which has similar output, we concentrate in this section on reading output from the `summary()` command. This gives more detailed information on the classification tree object (here, rparttree_class).

```
summary(rparttree_class)
```

[Output is discussed below in sections]

The initial "Call:" portion simply repeats the command which generated the object and lists the sample size, which is 212 nations.

```
rpart::rpart(formula = litgtmean ~ regionid + population + areasqmiles +
poppersqmile + coast_arearatio + netmigration + Infantdeathsper1k + infdeaths +
gdppercapitalindollars + phonesper1000 + arablepct + cropspct + otherpct + birthrate
+ deathrate, data = world, method = "class", control = rpart.control(minbucket = 5))
n= 212
```

The next part of output is the "cptable". This may also be retrieved by typing `rparttree _ class$cptable`.

```
          CP nsplit rel error    xerror       xstd
1 0.62500000      0 1.0000000 1.0000000 0.09577008
2 0.04166667      1 0.3750000 0.4305556 0.07145287
3 0.02777778      2 0.3333333 0.5138889 0.07675726
4 0.01000000      3 0.3055556 0.4861111 0.07507930
```

Explanation of the complexity parameter (cptable) output above:

- Number of rows: There are four rows, indicating that the final tree is four levels deep as defined below. Figure 4.6 above displays root node numbers helpful in interpreting the cp table. Each row may be thought of as a successively more complex tree. The rows go from the smallest tree to the largest. Each tree includes the earlier splits from higher rows in the cp table. The bottom row is the final tree, which has three splits.

  1. Row 1 is the root-node-only tree with no splits (nsplit = 0).
  2. Row 2 is the tree with the root level plus the fork for the first split, which is the birthrate split, leading to the left to include node 2, where regionid is the splitting variable.
  3. Row 3 is the tree with the root level plus the other fork for birthrate, leading to the right to include node 3, where population is the splitting variable.
  4. Row 4 is the final tree with the regionid and population splits implemented, leading to the terminal nodes 4, 5, 6, and 7.

- CP: CP is the complexity parameter, also called the "threshold complexity parameter". It is interpreted as the amount by which splitting that level improved relative error. Put another way, CP is a measure of the cost of adding a split to the model. Potential splits are rejected unless the split would increase overall model fit by at least scaled CP (values in the CP column are scaled). In the CP table, the value of CP decreases as the depth of the tree increases, so that the most complex trees have the lowest CP values. The CP is used in determining optimal tree size. For more on the CP formula, see Therneau and Atkinson (2018: 12–13, 24).
- nsplit: This is the number of splits for the tree represented by the given row. The number of terminal nodes for the tree represented by the row is always nsplit + 1. For the root nsplit is 0 and the number of nodes is 1 (node 1). For the final tree, nsplit is 3 and the number of terminal nodes is 4 (nodes 4, 5, 6, and 7).
- rel error: Relative error, also called risk, is used to assess the optimal number of levels in a pruned tree. Relative error is the average deviance (a measure of error) for the given tree (given row in the CP table) divided by the average deviance for the null (root-only) tree. Relative error is scaled relative to the null model, so that the value for the top (root) level is always 1.0. If relative error is plotted on the x-axis and CP on the y-axis, this relative error plot (shown further below) gives one criterion for selecting the optimal number of levels. The relative risk curve in such a plot tends to descend markedly at first, perhaps plateau, then may even rise somewhat at the right end. By one common criterion, the best-trimmed tree will be the one with the CP with the lowest risk (the lowest point on the y-axis).

- xerror: This is cross-validated mean error, based on rpart's built-in tenfold cross-validation, as set by the xval parameter in rpart.control, discussed previously. It is a measure of how much the split for a given level contributes to model fit. The xerror value will be the highest for the first split, indicating that it improves fit the most. It does not necessarily decline in a linear fashion. Rather, some interior row in the CP table may have the lowest xerror. The lowest xerror may be retrieved with the following commands:

```
# Compute the minimum xerrror in the CP table

min(rparttree_class$cptable[,"xerror"])
[Output:]
      [1] 0.4305556

# Compute the row number with the minimum xerror
which.min(rparttree_class$cptable[,"xerror"])
[Output:]
      2

# List the row in the CP table with the minimum xerror
rparttree_class$cptable[2,]
[Output:]
        CP      nsplit  rel error      xerror        xstd
0.04166667 1.00000000 0.37500000 0.43055556 0.07145287
```

  The xerror coefficient is scaled relative to deviance in the null model, so that the value for the top level is always 1.0. The difference between xerror for a given level (row) and the next level is a measure of the contribution to fit of splitting in the next level. Whereas relative error always decreases as the tree model becomes more complex, the same may or may not be true of xerror since overfitting may well lead to it actually increasing.
- xstd: This is the standard deviation of actual (unscaled, in contrast to relative) error. It is possible for xerror to go down but for xstd to go up. One rule of thumb about what level down is the optimal solution is to pick the level where xerror – (rel error + xstd) is at a minimum. For the example data, rounding to three places for instructional purposes, this value would be .431 – (.375 + .071) = –.015 for row 2. For row 3 the value is .514 – (.333 + .077) = .104. For row 4, the value is .486 – (.306 + .075) = .1.05. Thus, xerror – (rel error + xstd) is at a minimum for row 2, which is the tree with one split. By this criterion, which is not the only one, the optimal solution is row 2.

The next part of output from the `summary()` command is the "variable importance" table. Variable importance is not causal or predictive importance. Rather it is importance in the pruning process, discussed further below. It is calculated as the sum of improvement coefficients contributed by the given variable either as an actual (primary) splitting variable or as a surrogate. Higher values reflect more contribution to improving the model. Values are then scaled to add to 100 (to view unscaled values, use the command `rparttree_class$variable.importance`). Variables with scaled importance less than 1 are omitted from the list. Note that the list of variables in the "Variable importance" list will usually include more variables, possibly many more, than are actually used in the final tree. For further discussion, see Therneau and Atkinson (2018: 12). Here, birthrate, phonesper1000, and Infantdeathsper1k (tied with gdppercapitalindollars) are the most important classifiers.

```
Variable importance
              birthrate            phonesper1000        Infantdeathsper1k
                     23                       17                       15
```

```
gdppercapitalindollars              infdeaths            regionid
                    15                     13                  13
            population        coast_arearatio            cropspct
                     2                      1                   1
```

The next part of `summary()` output gives detailed information for each node. In the following output:

- The "Node number" line marks the start of the section for each node. Node 1 is the root node.
- "P(node)=1" means there is a 100% probability of a nation being in the root node (node 1).
- For Node 1 there are 212 nations, of which 140 go to node 2 on the left in the next split; 72 go to node 3 on the right.
- Below this, primary and surrogate splits are listed. The top primary split is the one actually used in the tree (birthrate < 26.425). Lower-listed primary splits and all surrogate splits were "runners-up", which were considered but rejected because their improvement coefficients were all lower than that of birthrate. Surrogate splits are splits, which would be used if a case had missing data on the primary splitting variable (birthrate). For the "world" data, there are no missing values.

```
Node number 1: 212 observations,    complexity param=0.625
  predicted class=High  expected loss=0.3396226  P(node) =1
    class counts:   140    72
   probabilities: 0.660 0.340
  left son=2 (145 obs) right son=3 (67 obs)
  Primary splits:
      birthrate          < 26.425   to the left,  improve=48.23731, (0 missing)
      phonesper1000      < 47.3     to the right, improve=46.52058, (0 missing)
      Infantdeathsper1k  < 41.31    to the left,  improve=40.14755, (0 missing)
      infdeaths          splits as  RL,           improve=37.83093, (0 missing)
      regionid           splits as  LLLLLLRRLLRL, improve=33.98529, (0 missing)
  Surrogate splits:
      phonesper1000          < 37.8      to the right, agree=0.920, adj=0.746, (0 split)
      Infantdeathsper1k      < 49.615    to the left,  agree=0.892, adj=0.657, (0 split)
      gdppercapitalindollars < 2150      to the right, agree=0.887, adj=0.642, (0 split)
      infdeaths              splits as   RL,           agree=0.868, adj=0.582, (0 split)
      regionid               splits as   LLLLLLLLLLRL, agree=0.835, adj=0.478, (0 split)
```

Output continues with the listing for Node 2.

- "P(node)=0.6839623" means there is an approximately 68.4% probability of a nation transitioning from the root node (Node 1) to node 2.
- For Node 2 there are 145 nations, of which 129 take the path on the left toward node 4 and 16 take the path on the right toward node 5 in the next split.
- Regionid is used as the next primary splitting variable, with nations in a given regionid going left or right according to the string `"LLLLLLLRLLLL"`. Here, all regions go to the left toward Node 4 except the 8th regionid, which is NF = North Africa, which went to the right toward node 5. (To see the order of regions corresponding to this string, type `levels(world$regionid.)` Note that in some output `rpart()` lists the string levels with letters (e.g., "abcdefgijkl") rather than Ls and Rs.
- Additional rows below regionid are surrogates not actually used.

```
Node number 2: 145 observations,    complexity param=0.04166667
  predicted class=High  expected loss=0.1103448  P(node) =0.6839623
    class counts:   129    16
   probabilities: 0.890 0.110
  left son=4 (140 obs) right son=5 (5 obs)
```

```
Primary splits:
    regionid            splits as  LLLLLLLRLLLL, improve=4.926108, (0 missing)
    Infantdeathsper1k < 24.645   to the left,  improve=3.356134, (0 missing)
    birthrate         < 15.515   to the left,  improve=3.017020, (0 missing)
    phonesper1000     < 48.7     to the right, improve=2.571155, (0 missing)
    deathrate         < 5.615    to the right, improve=2.541038, (0 missing)
```

Then listing of detailed node information continues in the same fashion for the remaining nodes but for space reasons is not shown here.

Output very similar to `summary(rparttree _ class)` may be obtained from the `printcp(roarttree _ class)` command. Output will include the generating command, the sample size (n), and the CP table as for `summary()`. Below we just show the output for the "Variables actually used" list and the RNE coefficient.

```
rpart::printcp(rparttree_class)
```

[Partial output]:

```
    Variables actually used in tree construction:
    [1] birthrate  population regionid

    Root node error: 72/212 = 0.33962
```

- Variables actually used list: Only three variables were used to construct the tree: birthrate, population, and regionid. Variables actually used is one criterion for asserting these are the most important variables among all those considered.
- Root node error: This is the percent of errors made when all cases are classified based only on the root node split. At the root node one would class all nations as "High" because this is the most numerous category and would be correct approximately 66% of the time and in error approximately 34% of the time, which is what the RNE value is. This is revealed by a simple `table()` command supplemented by the `addmargins()` command to add marginal totals. This gives the values used in the RNE formula above: 72/212 = 0.33962.

```
tab1 <- table(world$litgtmean)
addmargins(tab1)
```

[Output:]

```
   High  Low  Sum
    140   72  212
```

RNE also may be calculated directly with the command below:

```
rparttree_class$frame[1, 'dev']/rparttree_class$frame[1, 'n']
```

[Output:]

```
   [1] 0.3396226
```

To view the path rules for terminal nodes, the command below is used. This lists the tree paths for all four terminal nodes in the model as shown in Figure 4.6. To see a particular one only, enter its node number after the `node=` option.

```
rpart::path.rpart(rparttree_class, node = c(4,5,6,7), pretty = 1, print.it = TRUE)
```

node number: 4

```
   root
   birthrate< 26.42
   regionid=AS,BA,CW,DQ,EE,LA,NE,NO,OC,SA,WE
```

node number: 5

```
   root
   birthrate< 26.42
   regionid=NF
```

node number: 6

```
root
birthrate>=26.42
population< 5.463e+05
```

node number: 7

```
root
birthrate>=26.42
population>=5.463e+05
```

4.14.6 Listing nodes by country and countries by node

Note that the terminal nodes are 4, 5, 6, 7 as shown in Figure 4.6 and verified below. Recall "<leaf>" signifies a terminal node.

```
rparttree_class$frame[1]
```

[Output:]

```
          var
1  birthrate
2   regionid
4     <leaf>
5     <leaf>
3 population
6     <leaf>
7     <leaf
```

Listing nodes for each case (country)
To list the node number for any country, we start by putting node numbers into the object "nodenum", which we add to the world data frame as a new variable called "node". Type `View(world)` to verify that node has been added as a last column in the data frame.

```
nodenum<- row.names(rparttree_class$frame)
world$node<- nodenum[rparttree_class$where]
```

The `table()` command reveals that the vast majority of nations are in nodes 4 and 7.

```
table(world$node)
```

[Output:]

```
  4  5  6  7
140  5  6 61
```

Countries may be listed with their node numbers by the `print()` and `paste()` commands.

```
print(paste(world$country,"Node = ",world$node))
```

[Partial output:]

```
  [1] "Afghanistan  Node =  7"
  [2] "Bangladesh  Node =  7"
  . . .
[211] "UnitedKingdom  Node =  4"
[212] "Austria  Node =  4"
```

Listing cases for a given node
The `subset()` command allows us to print the countries contained in any given node. We use node 6 since it had only six nations. Note that this requires that the "node" variables have been created as described above.

```
world6 <- subset(world,world$node==6)
world6$country
```

[Output:]
```
[1] Maldives
[2] Belize
[3] MarshallIslands
[4] Djibouti
[5] EquatorialGuinea
[6] SaoTomePrincipe
```

4.14.7 Node distribution plots

For classification trees, node distribution plots show the levels of the categorical outcome variable (here, litgtmean) on the x-axis and the terminal node number (here, 4 through 7) on the y-axis. Points are sized and colored by the number of observations (here, nations). For this example, each of the four nodes has two points, one for the number of nations classified as "Low" and one for those classified as "High". The plot is created using the `ggplot()` command from the "ggplot2" package in two steps as illustrated below. The output is shown in Figure 4.7.

```
library(ggplot2)
```

Note simple variable names may be used here
```
fig7 <- ggplot2::ggplot(world, aes(x=litgtmean, y = node)) + geom_point(size = 1) +
geom_count(aes(color =. .n.., size =. .n..))

fig7 + labs(x="Litgtmean Class", y="Node Number") + scale_x_discrete(name="Litgtmean
Class", limits=c("Low", "High")) + scale_y_discrete(name="Node Number")
```

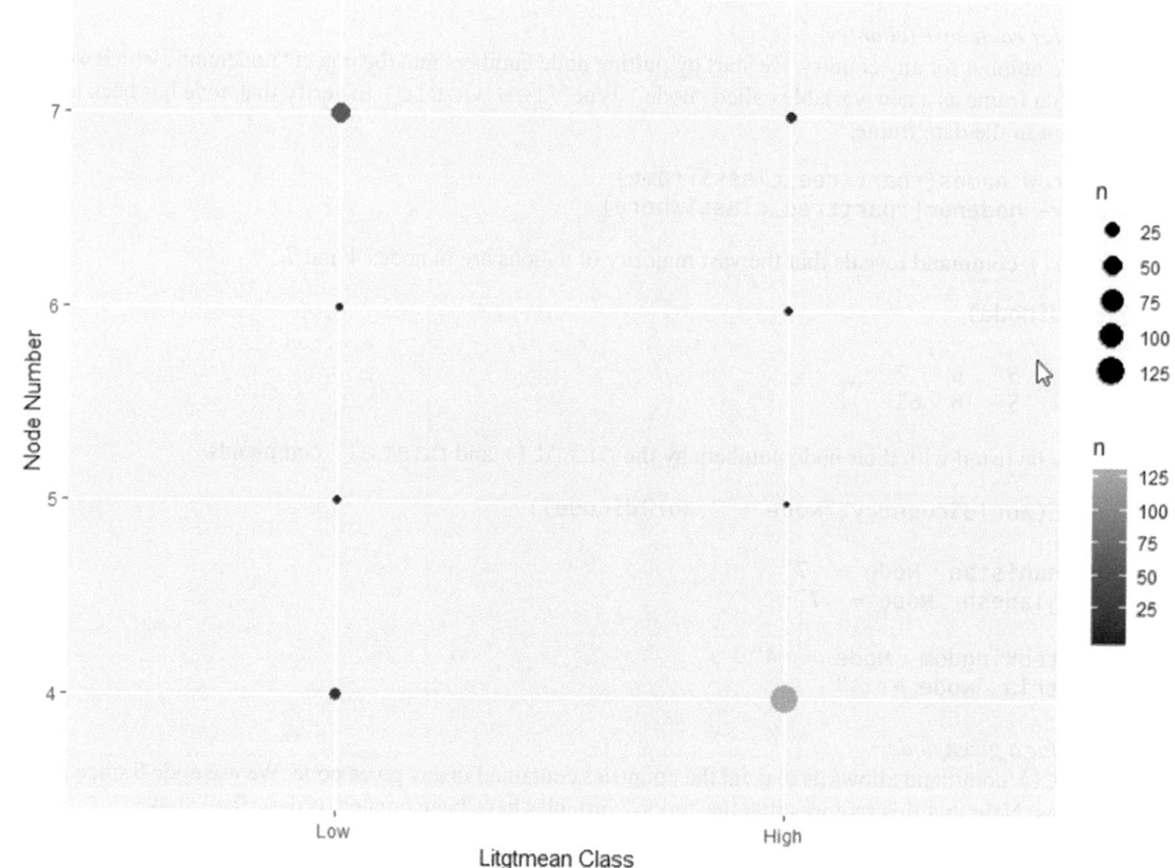

Figure 4.7 Node distribution plot for rparttree_class

Figure 4.7 shows that most nations are in nodes 4 and 7, with those in node 4 tending to be classed "High" and those in node 7 tending to be classed "Low". For instance, the USA is predicted "High" and is in Node 4 while Afghanistan is predicted "Low" and is in node 7. There are more nations in node 4 than in node 7, as shown by the circle sizes.

4.14.8 Saving predictions and residuals

Saving predictions
Below, predicted values for each nation are saved to the original world data frame. To start, predictions are put into the factor object "predclass". Then in the second command below, predclass is added to the original world data frame. Depending on the nation, world$predclass will contain the values "High" or "Low".

```
predclass <- predict(rparttree_class, type = "class")
world$predclass<-predclass
```

Similarly, we may obtain prediction probabilities rather than predicted classes by using `type = "prob"`. The `predict()` function will return a matrix with each nation having a probability of being classed "High" or classed "Low". We put results in the object "predprob", which is a user-chosen label. We then list out the first six countries. Nations 4 and 5 will be classed "High" and the others "Low".

```
predprob <- predict(rparttree_class, type = "prob")
class(predprob)
[Output:]
[1] "matrix" "array"

head(predprob)
[Output:]
       High        Low
1 0.1147541 0.88524590
2 0.1147541 0.88524590
3 0.1147541 0.88524590
4 0.9142857 0.08571429
5 0.9142857 0.08571429
6 0.1147541 0.88524590
```

The two columns are redundant since the second column is 1 minus the first column. We will save to the world data frame only the probability of being high. The "High" probability is the first column in the matrix, as demonstrated below.

```
predprob[1:6,1]
[Output:]
        1         2         3         4         5         6
0.1147541 0.1147541 0.1147541 0.9142857 0.9142857 0.1147541
```

Note that predprob[,1] is a numeric vector, which we add to the world data frame.

```
class(predprob[,1])
[Output:]
[1] "numeric"
```

We then convert predprob to a numeric variable for purposes of adding it to the world data frame. The brackets specify the first ("High") column of the matrix predprob is the probability vector to be saved.

```
world$predprob <- predprob[,1]
```

Saving residuals

A residual is the observed value of the outcome variable minus the expected (predicted) value. Below, we compare actual and predicted values for litgtmean.

1. The first line below creates a temporary data frame with the variables needed.
2. The second line sorts temp alphabetically by country using the `order()` command (not the `sort()` command, which would sort country but not keep adjacent columns in correct position).
3. To list the actual and predicted values, all that is needed is to enter the name of the sorted data frame.

```
temp <- world[c("country", "litgtmean", "predclass")]
temp <- temp[order(temp$country),]
temp
```

[Partial output:]

```
                    country  litgtmean predclass
1               Afghanistan        Low       Low
43                  Albania       High      High
....
187                  Zambia        Low       Low
188                Zimbabwe       High       Low
```

The observed and predicted values are character values. We cannot subtract the expected value from the observed value to get a residual. However, we can use the logical equality operator (==). This returns "TRUE" or "FALSE" depending on whether the equality holds for a given nation. The numeric equivalent is 1 or 0. Below, it is true that litgtmean (observed) equals predclass (expected) for the first six nations. We add the numeric vector classresid to the world data frame.

```
classresid <- as.numeric(world$litgtmean==world$predclass)
head(classresid)
```

[Output:]

```
  [1] 1 1 1 1 1 1
world$classresid <- classresid
```

All nations with a classresid of 0 have been misclassified. It is easy to list them using the `subset()` command.

```
subset(world,classresid==0, select=(c("country", "litgtmean", "predclass",
"classresid")))
```

[Output:]

```
               country litgtmean predclass classresid
9                India       Low      High          0
11                Iran       Low      High          0
38          Tajikistan      High       Low          0
39        Turkmenistan      High       Low          0
74        FrenchGuiana       Low      High          0
85           Nicaragua       Low      High          0
87            Paraguay      High       Low          0
91          SaintLucia       Low      High          0
99          GazaStrip      High       Low          0
106              Qatar       Low      High          0
110 UnitedArabEmirates       Low      High          0
116      TrinidadTobago     High       Low          0
137            Vanuatu       Low      High          0
141           Botswana       Low      High          0
145         Cape Verde       Low      High          0
150       CongoRepubof      High       Low          0
152           Djibouti       Low      High          0
161              Kenya      High       Low          0
```

```
176    SaoTomePrincipe     Low    High     0
178         Seychelles     Low    High     0
188           Zimbabwe    High     Low     0
195          Gibraltar     Low    High     0
```

Save to file
Again, the new variables added to the world data frame above are in memory only until explicitly saved with a `write.csv()` or equivalent command. We do this below, saving to "world2.csv" so as to preserve the original "world.csv". As a precaution, we first reset the working directory.

```
setwd("C:/Data")
write.csv(world, "world2.csv")
```

4.14.9 Cross-validation and pruning

One of the attractions of the `rpart()` program is that by default it implements tenfold cross-validation and outputs measures useful in assessing a model. These measures, which include CP, nsplit, rel error, xerror, xstd, and RNE, are helpful when pruning a tree to optimal size.

Cross-validation and pruning using `rpart()`centers on the CP, previously discussed in the section on "Reading tree summaries". The following listed commands are all used in evaluating a previously-created tree such as rparttree_class.

- `printcp()`: This command prints the CP table for a sequence of best trees. The CP table is the portion at the bottom of output below. Its rows indicate the final tree is three levels deep because the bottom row, which is the final tree, has three splits. These levels were created using the variables birthrate, population, and regionid (see Figure 4.6). Other portions of the CP table were discussed previously.

```
printcp(rparttree_class)
```
[Output:]
```
Classification tree:
rpart(formula = litgtmean ~ regionid + population + areasqmiles +
poppersqmile + coast_arearatio + netmigration +infantdeathsper1k + infdeaths +
gdppercapitalindollars + phonesper1000 + arablepct + cropspct + otherpct +
birthrate + deathrate, data = world, method = "class", control = rpart.
control(minbucket = 5))

 Variables actually used in tree construction:
 [1] birthrate  population regionid
 Root node error: 72/212 = 0.33962
 n= 212
          CP nsplit rel error  xerror     xstd
 1 0.625000      0   1.00000 1.00000 0.095770
 2 0.041667      1   0.37500 0.45833 0.073313
 3 0.027778      2   0.33333 0.45833 0.073313
 4 0.010000      3   0.30556 0.59722 0.081316
```

- `plotcp()`: This command produces the relative error plot shown in Figure 4.8. This plots the CP on the x-axis against relative error (rel error) on the y-axis. There are as many points on the CP axis as there are rows in the CP table (four for the example here). The CP values are not those displayed in the CP table but rather derive from the cross-validation process. Size of tree is shown on the upper horizontal axis, where size is the number of splits. This horizontal axis can be changed to size of tree by omitting the upper-option. The number of splits for this example goes from 0 to 3. Size of tree goes from 1 to 4. Either way, the axes and shape of the plot do not change.

```
rpart::plotcp(rparttree_class, upper=c("splits"))
```

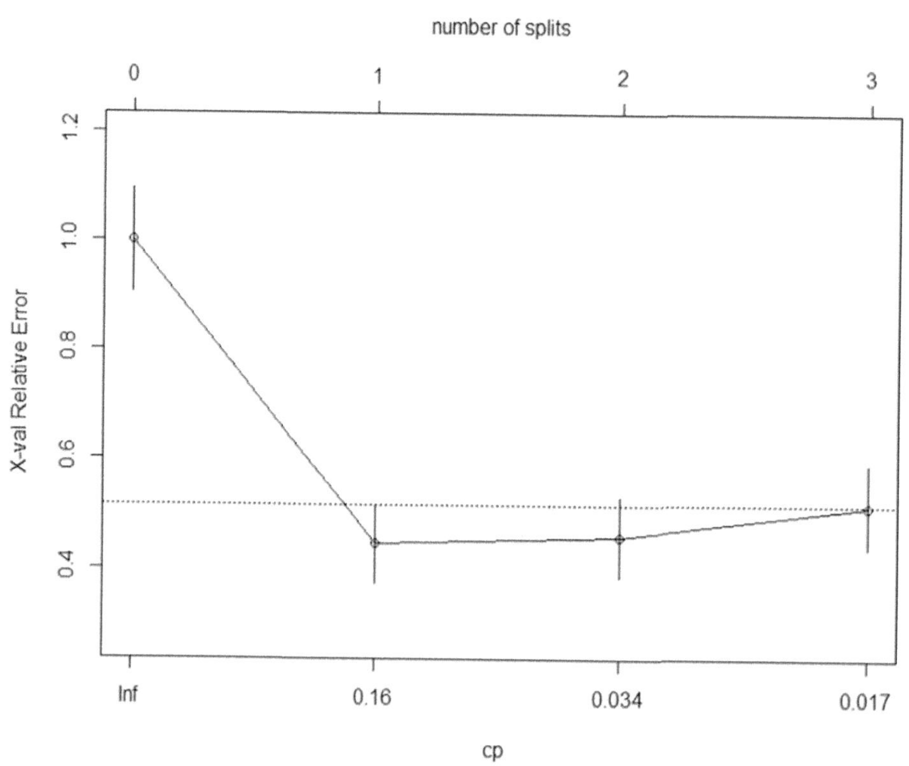

Figure 4.8 Relative error plot

In Figure 4.8, points correspond to trees of increasing depth. The relative error plot also displays error bars reflecting one standard error upper and lower limits based on the model with the smallest cross-validation error. The horizontal line is drawn by default one standard error above the upper limit of minimum point on the curve (suppress this by adding the option `minline=FALSE`). The optimal tree by common rule of thumb is the left-most value for which mean xerror lies below the horizontal line. For this example, this is the splits = 1 solution (equivalent to the size = 2 solution).

- `prune`: This command is used to prune an existing tree based on values of the cost CP. Note the take-away from Figure 4.8 was that row 2 in the CP table represented the optimal pruning solution. We do not use the CP = 0.16 value from Figure 4.8, however. Instead the most common rule of thumb for finding the optimal CP value is to use the algorithm reflected in the steps below. Of course, rules of thumb are nonbinding and the researcher should take into account such other considerations as tolerance for increased error due to pruning, the theoretical importance of splits that may be pruned, and interpretability of the results. For the example data, these are the following steps:

1. In the CP table, find the best (lowest) xerror, which is 0.45833 for either the 1-split or 2-splits solutions. However, we do not simply select the solution with the lowest xerror. Because xerror is the result of a randomized algorithm using a different random seed may result in a different sequence of xerror coefficients. Instead, the steps below use the "one standard deviation rule".
2. Add to the lowest xerror its standard deviation (xstd): .45833 + .073313 = .531643.
3. Find the smallest tree (row most toward the top of the CP table) with xerror < .531642. This is depth/row = 2, with 1 split.
4. Note the CP of this row, which is .041667.

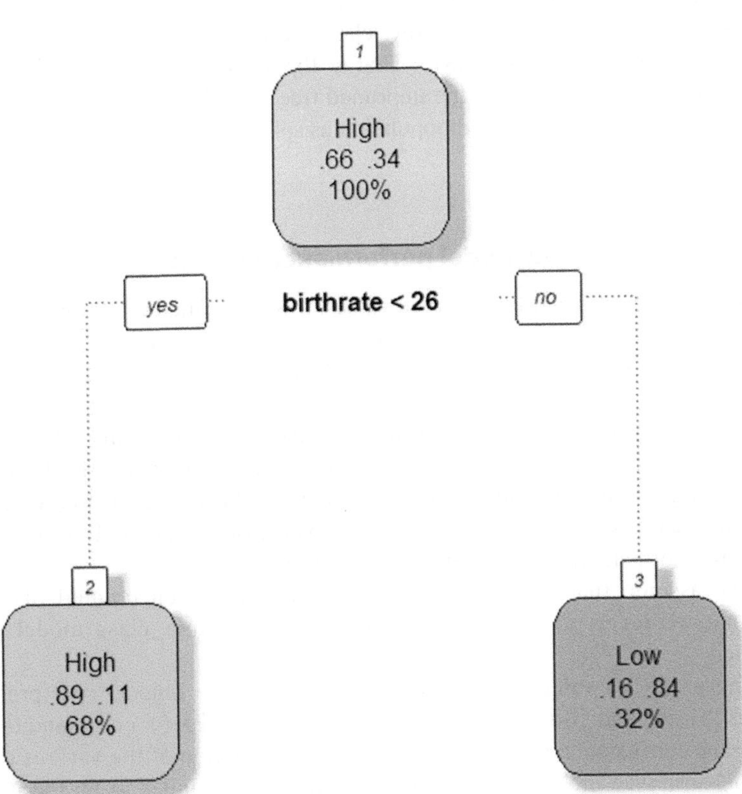

Figure 4.9 Plot of rparttree_class_pruned

5. Prune with a slightly higher CP, so we use .042.
6. Create a new data frame "rparttree_class_pruned" using the commands below, then plot it (we happen to use `fancyRpartPlot()`, described previously). The plot is shown in Figure 4.9.

```
rparttree_class_pruned <- rpart::prune(rparttree_class, cp=.042)

rattle::fancyRpartPlot(rparttree_class_pruned)
```

The pruned tree uses only one splitting variable (birthrate) rather than the three in the unpruned tree in Figure 4.6, which uses regionid and population in addition to birthrate. There are two terminal nodes, both determined by birthrate. We show the following summary output for nodes 2 and 3 only, but the command provides equivalent information for all nodes.

```
summary(rparttree_class_pruned)
[Partial output:]
Node number 2: 145 observations
  predicted class=High  expected loss=0.1103448  P(node) =0.6839623
    class counts:   129    16
   probabilities: 0.890 0.110
Node number 3: 67 observations
  predicted class=Low   expected loss=0.1641791  P(node) =0.3160377
    class counts:    11    56
   probabilities: 0.164 0.836
```

From this summary we can see that in node 2, 129 nations were predicted to be "High" on litgtmean, with 16 classification errors. In node 3, there were 56 correct "Low" classifications, with 11 errors. Thus, the accuracy (percent of correct classifications) was (129 + 56)/212 = .873. That is, the percent correctly classified by the pruned tree is 87.3%, down only modestly from the 89.6% in the unpruned tree. The difference (2.3%) is a measure of the classification improvement by retaining regionid and population as splitting variables at the cost of greater complexity/less parsimony of the solution.

4.14.10 The confusion matrix and model performance metrics

A confusion matrix is a table of predicted vs. observed values. It is also called a "hit table" or "classification table". Confusion matrix output typically includes a variety of related metrics (coefficients). For example, the "Accuracy" metric is the percent classified correctly. The confusion table and its metrics pertain to classification and not to regression tree models.

Under the usual binary splitting method, the confusion matrix is a 2-by-2 table. While there are many ways of creating it in R, use of the `confusionMatrix()` function of the "caret" package is among the easiest. Moreover, it generates a large number of model performance metrics. Which metric to use depends on its relevance to the research question at hand. Rather than report the "one best metric", it may well be more informative to report more than one. For more information, see Drozdenko and Drake (2002).

In this section, we assume that the rparttree_class object has been created, as described earlier in this chapter. Note that we revert to the using the unpruned rparttree_class model as the example, not rparttree_class_pruned.

We start by putting predicted values from rparttree_class into the object "rpartpred", which is a factor vector with the values "High" and "Low". The `confusionMatrix()` command then creates confusion matrix output. Below the confusion matrix, we provide brief explanation of the various coefficients which are produced as model performance metrics. The litgtmean variable continues to be the outcome, with "High" considered the positive value for purposes of the confusion matrix. Note that the `positive=` option in the `confusionMatrix()` command may be used to flip the focus so that "Low" is considered the positive value. Note that the `predict()` function is from the "stats" package in R's system library, not from the "rpart" package.

```
rpartpred <- predict(rparttree_class,type="class")
class(rpartpred)
[Output:]
   [1] "factor"

head(rpartpred)
[Output:]
      1    2    3    4    5    6
    Low  Low  Low High High  Low
  Levels: High Low
```

The predictions object (rpartpred) is of class "factor" while the reference object (world$litgtmean) is of class "character". Therefore, in the `confusionMatrix()` command we reconcile them by using `as.factor()`, making both of class "factor".

```
class(rpartpred)
      [1] "factor"
class(world$litgtmean)
      [1] "character"

library(caret)
caret::confusionMatrix(rpartpred,as.factor(world$litgtmean), positive='High')
```

[Output:]

```
Confusion Matrix and Statistics
          Reference
Prediction High Low
      High  132  14
      Low     8  58

               Accuracy : 0.8962
                 95% CI : (0.8471, 0.9338)
    No Information Rate : 0.6604
P-Value [Acc > NIR] : 1.547e-15

                  Kappa : 0.7639
 Mcnemar's Test P-Value : 0.2864

            Sensitivity : 0.9429
            Specificity : 0.8056
         Pos Pred Value : 0.9041
         Neg Pred Value : 0.8788
             Prevalence : 0.6604
         Detection Rate : 0.6226
   Detection Prevalence : 0.6887
      Balanced Accuracy : 0.8742

       'Positive' Class : High
```

Explanation of `confusionMatrix()` *output*

- 'Positive' Class: High: Factor levels in R are by default ordered alphabetically. The first is used as the "positive" (event present) value. Here the outcome is litgtmean, which is a two-level (High/Low) factor, with "High" as the first value. "Low" is level 2. This may be confirmed with the `levels()` command:

  ```
  levels(world$litgtmean)
  ```
  [Output]
  ```
    [1] "High" "Low"
  ```

  It happens that "High" is the most numerous class. The commands below create a "High-focus" model since High is the positive class. Though not done here, the researcher may override the default ordering. This is easily done using the `positive=` option of the `confusionMatrix()` command (e.g., for the example data, add `positive='Low'`).
- Confusion matrix: This 2-by-2 table shows observed vs. predicted (expected) classifications. Various metrics for model performance are based on it. The main diagonal (132, 58) shows the correct classifications (H, H and L, L). The off-diagonal shows the incorrect classifications (14, 8). For discussion of other measures, let n be sample size (here, 212) and let the individual cells in the confusion matrix be labeled A through D, as below. Note that the columns are the observed values and the rows are the predicted values.

  ```
  Prediction High Low
        High   A   B
        Low    C   D
  ```

  Below, these abbreviations are used, based on "High" being the positive class:

  A = TP = true positives = "hits" = 132
  B = FP = false positives = "misses" = 14

C = FN = false negatives = "false alarms" = 8
D = TN = true negatives = "correct rejections" = 58

Note that the confusion table itself also may be generated by a simple `table` command:

```
table(rpartpred,world$litgtmean)
[Output:]
rpartpred High Low
     High  132  14
     Low     8  58
```

- Accuracy (ACC): 0.8962 – This is the percent classified correctly by the rparttree_class tree model. Cell labeling (A, B, C, D) here and for other metrics assumes "High" is positive. ACC is the sum of true positives (cell A) plus true negatives (cell D), divided by n (sample or population size). Thus accuracy = sum of main diagonal/n = (A + D)/n = (132 + 58)/212 = .8962. That is, 89.62% of nations are classified correctly. Note that the "Error Rate" is simply 1 minus Accuracy = 1 – .8962 = .1038. Thus, 10.38% of nations were misclassified.

  Accuracy must be compared to the No Information Rate (NIR). That is, the baseline for comparing accuracy is not .5 but rather the NIR, which is discussed below. Note also that unlike ordinary regression models, the confusion matrix gives no model fit credit for "nearly correct" vs. "way off": A classification is either correct or it is not. In general, Kappa is preferred over Accuracy as an overall model performance measure, and there are yet other measures. ACC, the ACC confidence interval (CI), NIR, and Kappa will all be the same, regardless of whether "High" or "Low" is the positive class.
- 95% CI: (0.8471, 0.9338) – These values are the upper and lower confidence limits on Accuracy, computed using `binom.test()`. The value of NIR (below) should not be within these confidence limits, which for these data it is not. Therefore, the example data, we can say the model is significantly different at the 95% confidence level from the null (NIR) model.
- NIR: 0.6604 – NIR is the classification success rate in the null model (66.04%), which is the chance model, defining chance as always guessing the most numerous category. For the current example, "High" is the most numerous category (140 of 212 nations). NIR = (A + C)/n = (132 + 8)/212 = .6604. For the model with "Low" as positive, NIR still equals 0.6604 because the most numerous level is still "High". For the model with "High" as positive, NIR = Prevalence (discussed below), but for a model with the less numerous "Low" level as positive, the two metrics differ. The difference between ACC and NIR reflects how much the researcher's prediction model contributed to greater classification success.
- P-Value [Acc > NIR]: 1.547e-15 – This is a significance test of the difference between Accuracy for the researcher's model and Accuracy for the null model. Above, we already know this is significant since NIR is not within the confidence limits of Accuracy, but the P-Value [Acc > NIR] confirms this difference is significant at better than the .001 level. The P-Value is the same, regardless of whether "High" or "Low" is the positive level.
- Kappa: 0.7639 – Cohen's Kappa is often preferred over Accuracy as an overall measure of classification accuracy and thus of model performance. Kappa is the same, regardless of whether "High" or "Low" is positive. Arbitrary guidelines for assessing Kappa have been advanced by Landis and Koch (1977) and by Fleiss (1981). These guidelines were suggested in the context of Kappa as a measure of inter-rater agreement, not classification performance, but as Kappa may be computed for any 2-by-2 table, it is applied to confusion tables as well. Be aware that these cutoff values are common but controversial. However, for the example data, goodness of classification is "substantial" by Landis and Koch and is marginally "excellent" by Fleiss.
  - Landis and Koch: Values < 0 indicate no agreement and 0–0.20 indicate slight agreement; 0.21–0.40 = fair; 0.41–0.60 = moderate; 0.61–0.80 = substantial; and 0.81–1 = almost perfect agreement.
  - Fleiss: Values < 0.40 = poor agreement; 0.40–0.75 = fair to good; >.75 = excellent.

Kappa is defined as (totalAccuracy – randomAccuracy)/(1 – randomAccuracy), using TP, TN, FP, and FN as defined above.

totalAccuracy = (TP + TN)/n = (132 + 58)/212 = .8962
randomAccuracy = ((TN + FP)*(TN + FN) + (FN + TP)*(FP + TP))/(n*n)
= ((58 + 14)*(58 + 8) + (8 + 132)*(14 + 132))/(212*212)
= .5605

Kappa = (totalAccuracy – randomAccuracy)/(1 – randomAccuracy)
= (.8962 – .5605)/(1 – .5605) = .7638 (difference from .7639 due to rounding)

- Mcnemar's Test P-Value: 0.2864 – In the example data, the observed proportions are 140 High, 72 Low; the predicted proportions are 146 High, 66 Low. McNemar's test is testing the hypothesis that the predicted proportions are roughly equal to the observed proportions. McNemar's test will be the same regardless of whether "High" or "Low" is positive. A finding of nonsignificance (such as p = .286) means we fail to reject this equality. That is, predicted proportions are not significantly different from observed proportions, as would be expected in a well-fitting model. Computation is explained below.

```
# Put confusion matrix into the numeric object "performance"
performance1 <- matrix(c(132,8,14,58),  nrow = 2,  dimnames = list("Predicted" =
c("High", "Low"),  "Observed" = c("High", "Low")))

# List it out to make sure the confusion matrix was entered properlyperformance1
[Output:]
          Observed
 Predicted High Low
      High  132  14
      Low     8  58

# Perform McNemar's test, getting the same result (p = .286 = not significant)
# Note: mcnemar.test is part of stats package.
# The stats package is part of the system library and need not be installed
mcnemar.test(performance1)
[Output:]
McNemar's Chi-squared test with continuity correction
data:  performance
McNemar's chi-squared = 1.1364, df = 1, p-value = 0.2864
```

- Sensitivity: 0.9429 – Sensitivity is the true positive rate (TPR), also called "Recall", the "Hit rate", or the "probability of detection". Sensitivity is the percent of correctly classified cases in the positive class. For the current example, positive is "High" on litgtmean. High sensitivity indicates a high ability of the model to correctly detect nations which actually are high on the outcome (litgtmean). When sensitivity is high, the model is predicting actual positives at a higher rate (count of true positives predicted/count of observed positives). Cell A is the count of true positives (here, "High" predicted, "High" observed". C is the count of false positives ("Low" predicted, "High" observed). Sensitivity is a rate formed by dividing true positives by total positives (i.e., count of observed positives). Sensitivity = A/(A + C) = 132/(132 + 8) = 0.9429. Note that while high sensitivity means there will be few nations actually high on litgtmean which are misclassified, it does not mean that nations actually low on litgtmean will be classified correctly at a high rate (that is specificity). When the less numerous category (here, "Low") is positive, the values of Sensitivity and Specificity are flipped.
- Specificity: 0.8056 – Specificity, also called Selectivity, is the true negative rate (TNR). Specificity is the percent of correctly classified cases in the negative class. Negative for the example is litgtmean = "Low". When specificity is high, the model is predicting actual negatives at a higher rate (count of true negatives predicted/count of observed negatives). Cell D is the count of true negatives (here, "Low" predicted, "Low" observed". B is the count of false negatives ("High" predicted, "Low" observed). Specificity is a rate formed by dividing

true negatives by total negatives (i.e., count of observed negatives). Specificity = D/(B + D) = 58/(14 + 58) = 0.8056. Note that while high specificity means there will be few nations actually low on litgtmean which are misclassified, it does not mean that nations actually high on litgtmean will be classified correctly at a high rate (that is sensitivity). When the less numerous category (here, "Low") is positive, the values of Sensitivity and Specificity are flipped.

- Pos Pred Value (PPV): 0.9041 – Also called "Precision", positive predictive value is the ratio of the sum of true positives divided by the sum of predicted positives. Precision = A/(A + B) = 132/(132 + 14) = .9041. When the less numerous category (here, "Low") is positive, the values of PPV and NPV are flipped. PPV is related to sensitivity and prevalence, as shown in the following formula: PPV = (sensitivity*prevalence)/((sensitivity*prevalence)+((1 – specificity)*(1 – prevalence))) = (.9429*.6604)/((.9429*.6604) + ((1 – .8056)*(1 – .6604))) = 0.9041
- Neg Pred Value (NPV): 0.8788 – Negative predictive value is the ratio of the sum of true negatives divided by the sum of predicted negatives. NPV = D/((C + D) = 58/(8 + 58) = .8788. When the less numerous category (here, "Low") is positive, the values of PPV and NPV are flipped. NPV is related to sensitivity and prevalence, as shown in the following formula:
  NPV = (specificity*(1 – prevalence))/(((1 – sensitivity)*prevalence) + ((specificity)*(1 – prevalence)))
  = (.8056*(1 – .6604))/(((1 – .9429)*.6604) + ((.8056)*(1 – .6604))) = .8789*
  * The difference from .8788 is due to rounding.

- Prevalence: .6604. For the model with "High" as positive, Prevalence is the same as the NIR, discussed above. Prevalence is not to be confused with detection prevalence, discussed below. For the current example, "High" is the most numerous category (140 of 212 nations) and Prevalence = NIR = (A + C)/n = (132 + 8)/212 = .6604. However, for a model with the less numerous level as positive (e.g., here "Low"), Prevalence is not the same as NIR. For this model, Prevalence = (D + B)/n = (58 + 14)/212 = .3396.
- Detection Rate: 0.6226 – The detection rate is the ratio of true positives to n (sample or population size). When the most numerous category (here, "High") is positive, the detection rate = A/n = 132/212 = .6226 The detection rate is thus the percent formed by dividing the sum of correctly classified positives (cell A, here being "High" litgtmean) by the sum of cells A (representing power), B (false positives, representing Type I error), C (false negatives, representing Type II error), and D (true negatives). When the less numerous category (here, "Low") is positive, the detection rate will be different. (It will be 58/212 = .2736.)
- Detection Prevalence: 0.6887 – Detection prevalence for the model where "High" is the most numerous category and is positive, is the ratio of the sum of predicted positives divided by n (population or sample size). Detection prevalence = (A + B)/n = (132 + 14)/212 = .6887. For the model where the less numerous category is positive, detection prevalence will be (1 – .6887) = .3113.
- Balanced Accuracy: 0.8742 – Balanced Accuracy may be thought of as Accuracy adjusted for Sensitivity. It is an average of both. Balanced accuracy = (sensitivity + specificity)/2 = (.9429 + .8056)/2 = .8743 (difference due to rounding). Balanced accuracy is the same, regardless of whether "High" or "Low" is the positive class.

The following related coefficients are not displayed by `confusionMatrix()`:

- False positive rate (FPR): .1944 – The FPR is the percent of misclassified cases in the positive class. Synonyms are "fall-out" or "false alarm rate". For the model where "High" is the most numerous category and is positive, FPR is the ratio of false positives (cell B, being nations predicted "High" but observed "Low") divided by all observed negatives (B + D). FPR = B/(B + D) = 14/(14 + 58) = .1944. For the model where "Low" is the less numerous category but has been made the positive level, a false positive is predicted "Low" but observed "High". FPR = false positives/all observed negatives, where negatives are now the "High" level = 8/(132 + 8) = .0571.
- False negative rate (FNR): .0548 – The FNR is the percent of misclassified cases in the negative class. A synonym is "miss rate". For the model where "High" is the most numerous category and is positive, FNR is the ratio of false negatives (cell C, representing nations predicted "Low" but actually "High") divided by all

predicted positives (A + B). FNR = C/(A + B) = 8/(132 + 14) = .0548. For the model where "Low" is the less numerous category but has been made the positive level, FNR = false negatives/all predicted positives = 14/(8 + 58) = .2121.

- False omission rate (FOR): .1250 – The FOR is the ratio of false negatives (cell C) divided by all predicted negatives (C + D). For the model where "High" is the most numerous category and is positive, this equals C/(C + D) = 8/(8 + 58) = .1250. For the model where "Low" is the less numerous category and is the positive values, FOR = false negatives/all predicted negatives = 14/(132 + 14) = .0959. Note, since "for" or "FOR" cannot be a variable name in R, some packages label it differently (e.g., "fomr" in the `calculateROCMeasures()` command).
- False discovery rate (FDR): .0959 – For the model where "High" is the most numerous level and is positive, the FDR is the ratio of false positives (cell B) divided by all predicted positives (A + B). FDR = B/(A + B) = 14/(132 + 14) = .0959. For the model where "Low" is the less numerous category and is the positive values, FDR = false positives/all predicted positives = 8/(8 + 58) = .1212.
- Diagnostic Odds Ratio (DOR): 71.3279 – The DOR is a measure of the discriminatory performance of the model. If DOR = 1 for the present "High"-focus model example, this would mean that the model did not discriminate between nations, which are observed to be "High" and those observed to be "Low" on the outcome variable (litgtmean). The higher the DOR above 1.0, the greater the discriminatory power of the model. Note, however, that two models may have the same DOR yet be very different in sensitivity and specificity. See further discussion of DOR in Glas et al. (2003).

  Computationally, recall that Sensitivity = TPR, the true positive rate. Also, note that Specificity = TNR. For the model where "High" is the most numerous level and is positive, the positive likelihood ratio (LR+) = TPR/FPR = .9429/.1944 = 4.8503. The negative likelihood ratio (LR–) = FNR/TNR = .0548/.8056 = .0680. Then DOR = LR+/LR– = 4.8503/.0680 = 71.3279. For the model where "Low" is not the most numerous level and is positive, then LR+ = TPR/FPR = .8056/.0571 = 14.1086. Then LR– = FNR/TNR = .0548/.8056 = .0680. Then DOR = LR+/LR– = 14.1086/.0680 = 207.4794. Note that DOR is not the same for the "High"-focus and "Low"-focus models.
- F1 score: .9231. Also labeled F_1, this is the harmonic mean of sensitivity and precision. Since sensitivity and precision flip between the "High"-focus and "Low"-focus models, the F1 score will be the same under either model. F1 is one of the several metrics available to evaluate model performance. In terms of the "High"-focus model, the F1 formula is 2 divided by the sum of the inverse of sensitivity and the inverse of precision. Sensitivity is also labeled "Recall" or "TPR" and its formula is TPR = (A/(A + C)), being true positives as a percent of all observed positives. Precision is the PPV = (A/(A + B)), being true positives as a percent of all predicted positives. Because F1 is looking only at the positives, it is sensitive to the threshold. The threshold by default is 0.5, meaning that this is the cutting point for splitting: If the count in class "High" is more than 50%, the case goes to the left in the tree, otherwise to the right. If "High" were rare and never more than 50%, no case would ever be predicted to be "High". For this reason, when interest is in classes which are small, the researcher may need to tune the threshold value. On this advanced topic, see Kuhn and Johnson (2016). Here we only say that under the default threshold, F1 reflects the misclassification of positives and must be interpreted relative to the threshold value (0.5 by default).

  To compute F1:

  $$\begin{aligned} F1 &= 2/(1/(A/(A + C)) + 1/(A/(A + B))) \\ &= 2/(1/(132/(132 + 8)) + 1/(132/(132 + 14))) \\ &= 0.9231 \end{aligned}$$

  An easier mathematically equivalent computational formula is:

  $$\begin{aligned} F1 &= (2*A)/(2*A + B + C) \\ &= (2*132)/(2*132 + 14 + 8) \\ &= 0.9231 \end{aligned}$$

Below we store the `rpart()` `confusionMatrix()` results for rparttree_class in the object CMresult. The F1 score is the 7th of the stored metrics and can be retrieved by this command:

```
CMresult <- caret::confusionMatrix(rpartpred,as.factor(world$litgtmean))
CMresult$byClass[7]
[Output:]
              F1
     0.9230769
```

4.14.11 The ROC curve and AUC

The ROC curve, where ROC stands for "receiver operating characteristic", and its associated area under the curve (AUC) coefficient are important additional model performance metrics. The larger the AUC, the better the performance of the model by this criterion. Thus, when comparing models to see which classifies the outcome best, the model with the larger AUC is preferred. The curve itself plots the TPR (TPR = Sensitivity) on the y-axis against the FPR (FPR = 1 – TNR = 1 – Specificity) on the x-axis.

We will use the four packages listed below. The ROCR package has the `prediction()` function to create prediction objects and also has the `performance()` function needed to get performance metrics. These will be used by the `plot()` command to get the ROC curve and related plots (ROCR is authored by Sing et al., 2005). See also Fawcett (2003) and Flach (2003). Unfortunately, both the `mlr` and `ROCR` packages invoked below contain a `performance()` function but these are not quite identical. The former wants predictions of class "Prediction" and the latter wants predictions of class" prediction". We want to make sure we use the `ROCR` version and do so by employing the ROCR:: package prefix with the `performance()` command.

```
library(caret)
library(mlr)
library(scales)
library(ROCR)
```

As a next step we store predictions in object "pred", which is of class type "matrix". Then we convert pred into a new variable, pred_val, which is of class type "prediction", as needed by the ROCR package's `performance()` function.

```
pred <- predict(rparttree_class, world, type = "prob")
pred_val <- prediction(pred[,2],world$litgtmean)
```

Next we put the TPR and FPR metrics into the "perf" object, making sure to use the ROCR:: package prefix. These two metrics are the ones needed by the ROC and AUC algorithms.

```
perf <- ROCR::performance(pred_val,"tpr","fpr")
```

Finally, we are ready to plot the ROC curve for rparttree_class. This plots as a red line the FPR on the x-axis and the TPR on the y-axis. The `abline()` command adds a 45-degree reference line in blue. The resulting ROC curve is shown in Figure 4.10.

```
plot(perf, col="red", main="ROC Curve")
abline(0,1, lty = 1, col = "blue")
```

How is the ROC curve drawn? To simplify, think of a red pencil that starts at the 0, 0 position and considers all the true positive and false positive cases. When it encounters a true positive observation, the pencil moves up one scaled step on the y-axis. Likewise, when a false positive is encountered, the pencil moves to the right by one scaled step. Scaling assures that when all cases have been considered, the pencil will be at the 1, 1 position on the plot. The area

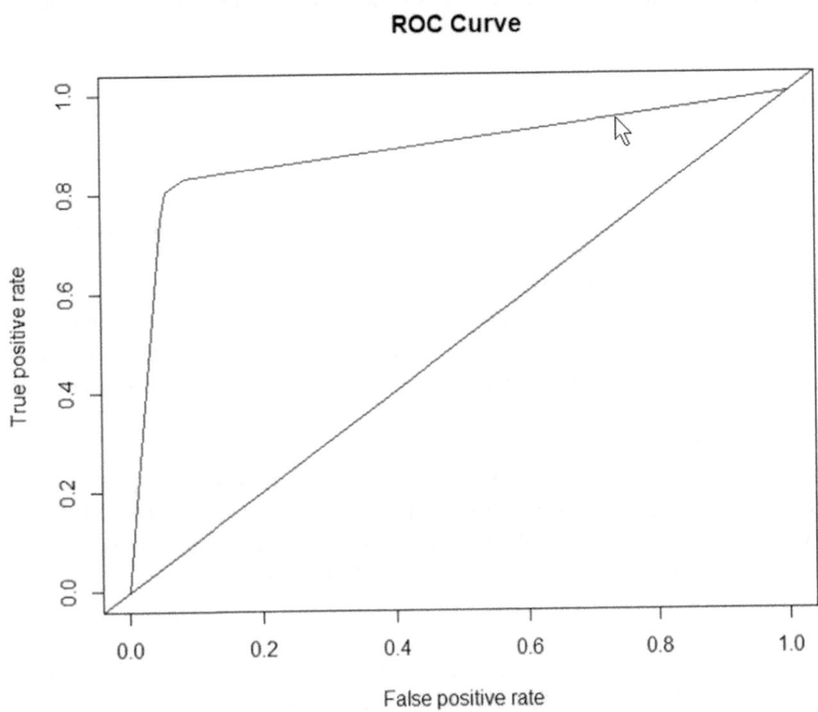

Figure 4.10 The ROC curve for rparttree_class

under the red curved line drawn by the pencil reflects correct classifications. The area above the 45-degree blue line reflects the maximum area that could be under the red line. Put another way, in a perfect model, the "red pencil" moves all the way to the top of the y-axis before moving at all to the right (along the x-axis) and the AUC is at its maximum.

The AUC is the area under the ROC curve as a percentage of the maximum area. The AUC may be used to compare performance between groups in a model, with higher AUC being better. The AUC may also be used to compare a given model's performance among groups formed by a categorical variable, again with higher being better.

As just discussed, the AUC value is a common metric for model performance used to compare models. The `ROCR::performance()` command below puts AUC information into an object called auc.tmp. This object is of class "performance". While it does contain the AUC value, listing it generates a cluttered list with many elements. Therefore, we separate out the AUC value, putting it in the object "auc", which is of class "numeric". Typing auc lists the AUC coefficient.

```
auc.tmp <- ROCR::performance(pred_val,"auc")
auc <- as.numeric(auc.tmp@y.values)
auc
```

[Output:]

```
[1] 0.8858135
```

By the AUC definition of model performance, we may say the example model has a performance rate which is 89% of maximum performance. Note, however, that there are many other model performance metrics, each with their own definition of model performance. In particular note that AUC only deals with the true and false positive classifications. If the research focus is on the negative class of the binary outcome (or some other class for multinomial outcomes), then for purposes of ROX analysis the class of interest must be made the positive class as explained earlier.

4.14.12 Lift plots

"Lift" is a performance coefficient which compares predictions made by the researcher's model with predictions, which are randomly generated. Lift varies from 0 to infinity. Lift is interpreted relative to a baseline value, which typically reflects results using no model (using the null model). Note that lift is not necessarily highly correlated with model accuracy. Lift, as illustrated below, is usually computed by the `performance()` function of the ROCR package and is retrieved as its "lift" result.

Let "Yhat = +" refer to predicted positives. The `performance()` function defines lift as in the first bullet below. The next three bullets are equivalent. Note that the formula for lift defines it in terms of predicted and observed positives. Predicted and observed negatives do not directly figure into the calculation of lift.

- lift = P(Yhat=+|Y=+)/P(Yhat=+)
- lift = (positive correct predictions as % of observed positives)/(total predicted positives as % of population). The numerator reflects the researcher's model while the denominator reflects the null or random model.
- lift = (A/(A + C))/((A + B)/n), in terms of the lettered cells in the confusion matrix.
- lift = sensitivity/detection prevalence (recall sensitivity = TPR = true positive rate; detection prevalence = the sum of predicted positives divided by n).

Relative lift is lift relative to a threshold value (by default, threshold = .5). Different threshold values will give different computed relative lift. The formula for relative lift is the same as for lift, except the threshold (e.g., .5) is subtracted from both the numerator and the denominator. We do not use relative lift here.

Lift charts involve comparing models. The term "lift plot" or "lift chart" may refer to different combinations of what is plotted on the x and y axes. Here we use the common definition which put lift on the y-axis and puts percent of population responding positively (RPP = rate of positive response) on the x-axis. There are three contexts, enumerated below. Lift plots for each are labeled Types 1, 2, and 3 (this labeling is for convenience here and is not part of general classification terminology):

1. Type 1: For a single, unsegmented dataset, lift may be used to compare the performance of a single model (e.g., an `rpart()` model) with a baseline, typically lift = 1. Since lift = (expected correct classifications in the researcher's model/expected correct classifications with no model (random basis for classification)), a value of 1 means the researcher's model is no better than a random model. A lift curve may be plotted reflecting the researcher's model and the baseline represented by a horizontal line at lift = 1, where lift is on the y-axis. This is the usage in the example further below.

2. Type 2: For a single, unsegmented dataset, lift may be used to compare models, such as comparing classification with `rpart()` with classification using `glm()`. In social science research, both models may be compared to the lift = 1 baseline but the model with the higher lift curve is the better model by this model performance metric.

3. Type 3: For a dataset divided into segments, lift will indicate the segments with the highest percentage of true positive classifications as reflected in the rate of positive predictions (RPPs). In marketing research, where lift charts are widely used, one might market to the segments with the highest lift on the assumption that these segments have the greatest payoff for advertising investment.

Lift plot example

Figure 4.11 displays the lift plot for the rparttree_class model, discussed in earlier examples. This model is compared with a baseline (here, lift = 1). As discussed above, when lift = 1 the researcher's model is no better than a random (null) model. A lift curve may be plotted reflecting the researcher's model and the baseline represented by a horizontal line at lift = 1, where lift is average lift value on the y-axis. The higher the lift curve from the baseline, the better the model performance. Though computed here for the original dataset (world), lift may be more informative regarding model performance when computed using the same model for a validation (hold-out or future) dataset, thereby giving an indicator of performance generalizability.

```
# Compute and plot lift chart Type 1, shown in Figure 4.11
# lwd is line width; lty is line type
perf_lift <- ROCR::performance(pred_val,"lift", "rpp")
plot(perf_lift, col="red", lwd=2,main="Lift Curve", xlab="Population %",
ylab="Lift")
#Add horizontal grid (use plot tick marks as h= and v= grid values)
abline(h = c(1,1.5,2,2.5),  lty = 2, col = "grey")
#Add vertical grid
abline(v = c(.3,.4,.5,.6,.7,.8,.9,1),  lty = 2, col = "grey")
# Draw blue baseline at 1.0, indicating random performance in the null model
abline(1,0,col="blue", lwd=2)
```

The x-axis in the lift plot is formed by the RPP, which is the prediction success rate. This may also be interpreted as the predicted population response rate, such as the percent of the population giving a positive response to a marketing campaign. The x-axis thus may have such equivalent labels as "RPPs", or "Population %". Put another way, RPP is the average percent of positive predictions for a given percent of the population when sorted in descending order of positive response.

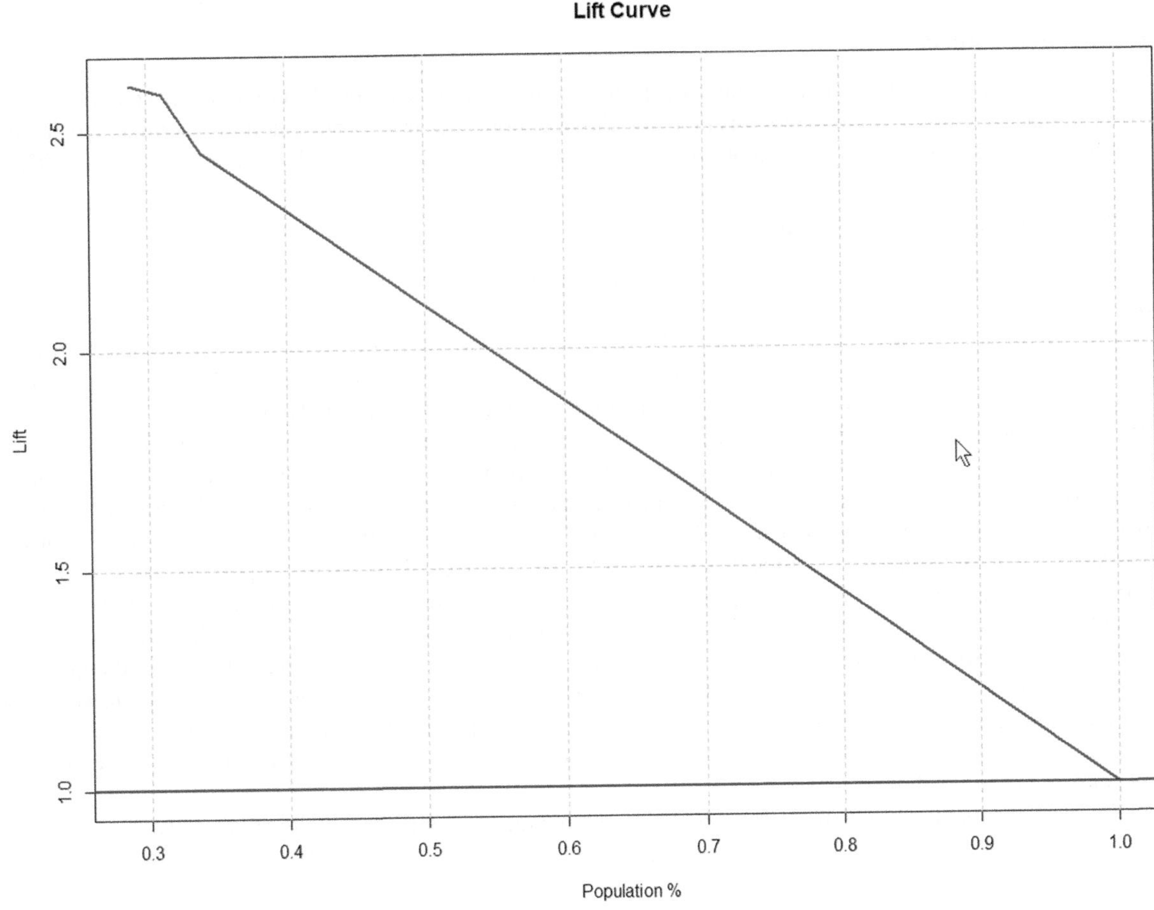

Figure 4.11 Lift curve

To form the lift curve, shown in red in Figure 4.11, cases (here, nations) are ordered along the x-axis in descending order of probability of classifying the nation as positive (here, as "High"). That is, the classification algorithm computes a probability value from 0 to 1.0 that the nation under consideration is a positive ("High" in this example). The horizontal line at lift = 1.0 is sometimes called the "naive prediction rate" and is the baseline against which the researcher's model is compared.

The y-axis (the lift axis) reflects the ratio of how "rich" (how high a proportion of positive classifications) that the portion of the population shown on the x-axis is compared to the response level for the population as a whole. Above, when 50% of the population is considered (the 0.5 tick on the "Population %" x-axis), lift is approximately 2.15, meaning that the richness of the model for the 50% of nations with the highest probabilities of being classified as positive ("High") is a little over twice as good as the richness of the null model, defined as the model for the general population. All lift curves reach the coordinates of x = 1, y = 1 on the far lower right since the population as a whole has the general response rate.

The lift plot is useful where the interest is in response rate. This does not really apply to classifying nations as "High" or "Low" literacy. Consider instead if data were on consumer response to a sales campaign or citizen response to a recycling campaign. Imagine also a lift curve that descended sharply then leveled off near the base rate, forming a concave curve. Such a lift chart might reveal that by targeting a much smaller percentage of the population, rather than the entire population, the campaign could reap much of the "lift" (positive response) without the cost of targeting the entire population. Also, if one had data on response by political campaign mode (advertising by television vs. newspaper vs. social media, for instance), one could have lift curves for each mode superimposed on the same plot. The mode with the highest lift curve would be the one providing the most "lift". Likewise, lift could be compared by geographic, religious, racial, or other groups formed by categorical variables in the dataset, thereby showing the differential response of each group.

4.14.13 Gains plots

Gains plots provide another basis for assessing model performance, analogous to but different from lift plots described above. For space reasons, treatment of gains plots for classification trees in R is presented in an online supplement to Chapter 4, found in the student section of this book's Support Material (www.routledge.com/9780367624293).

4.14.14 Precision vs. recall plot

Precision/recall plots are used to assess the performance of the model for positive predictions. Higher values for precision and recall correspond to better models. For instance, Model 1 might have 95%+ precision (almost all predicted as "High" actually are "High"). Likewise Model 1 also might have 95%+ recall (almost all observed to be "High" were predicted to be "High"). Model 2, in contrast might have 95%+ precision like Model 1, but would not be as good a model if it had only 50% recall (the model misclassifies half of actual "High" cases).

Precision is the same as the PPV, which is the sum of true positives (those both predicted and observed to be positive, which is cell A in the earlier confusion table) as a percent of the sum of all predicted positives (both correctly and incorrectly classified predicted positives = (A + B). Put another way, precision answers the question, "Of observations predicted as positive (e.g., 'High'), what proportion actually are 'High'?" The answer is in the precision equation: True Positives/(True Positives + False Positives). Precision thus measures the performance of the model for positive predictions where performance is defined in terms of predicted positives. Precision is placed on the y-axis in a precision/recall plot.

Recall, also called "Sensitivity", is the same as the TPR, which is the number of correctly classified cases in the positive class (cell A) as a percent of all observed positives (A + C). Put another way, recall answers the question, "Of observations that were observed to be 'High', what proportion were predicted as 'High'?" The answer is the recall equation: True Positives/(True Positives + False Negatives). Recall thus measures the performance of the model for positive predictions where performance is defined in terms of observed positives. Recall is placed on the x-axis in a precision/recall plot.

It may be noted that the F statistic is the weighted harmonic mean of precision and recall (van Rijsbergen, 1979). Not illustrated here, the F (a.k.a, F1) value may be plotted with this code, based on the `performance()` and `plot()` commands:

```
f1val<- ROCR::performance(pred_val, "f", "rec")
plot(f1val, col="red", lwd=2)
```

[Plot not shown here]

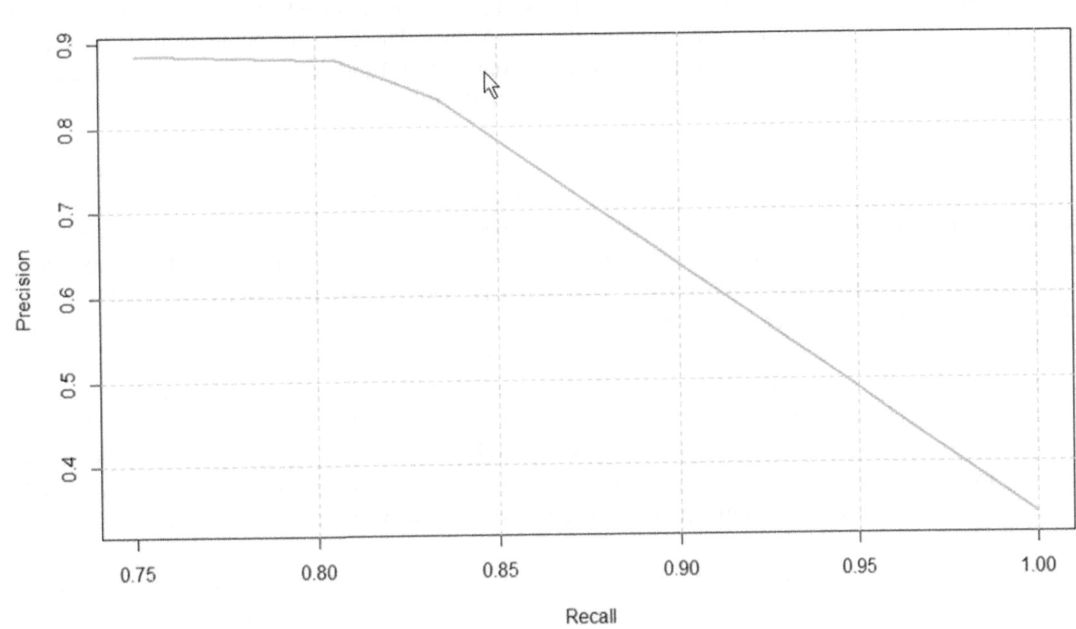

Figure 4.12 Precision vs. Recall plot

We now create the precision-recall plot. Because there is a `performance()` command in both the ROCR and mlr packages, one must use the ROCR:: package prefix when creating the rpcurve2 object below. The `abline()` commands create a grey grid in the background of the plot.

```
library(ROCR)
rpcurve2 <- ROCR::performance(pred_val,"prec","rec")
plot(rpcurve2, col="orange", lwd=2)
abline(v = c(.8, .85, .90, .95, 1),  lty = 2, col = "grey")
abline(h = c(.4,.5,.6,.7,.8),  lty = 2, col = "grey")
```

The precision/recall plot in Figure 4.12 is constructed based on x values for the Recall axis, y values for the Precision axis, and alpha values for cutoffs used. These values can be seen by listing the contents of the precision/recall object, which was rpcurve:

```
rpcurve2
[Output:]
      An object of class "performance"
      Slot "x.name":
     [1] "Recall"
      Slot "y.name":
      [1] "Precision"
      Slot "alpha.name":
      [1] "Cutoff"
      Slot "x.values":
      [[1]]
      [1] 0.0000000 0.7500000 0.8055556 0.8333333 1.0000000
      Slot "y.values":
      [[1]]
      [1]       NaN 0.8852459 0.8787879 0.8333333 0.3396226
      Slot "alpha.values":
      [[1]]
      [1]        Inf 0.88524590 0.80000000 0.33333333 0.08571429
```

Recall and precision values are calculated for each of the threshold (alpha, cutoff) values selected by the ROCR algorithm. There are four x values and four y values, not counting the 0/NaN ones. These are the points plotted on the precision/recall plot, with connecting lines. Left to right, the x-axis goes from .75 to 1.0 and the y-axis goes from .8852 to .3396.

A number of possible patterns may appear on a precision/recall (P/R) plot.

- *Random classifier*: If the ratio of positives to negatives in the data is 1:1, then when using a random classifier as a model, the P/R curve will be a horizontal line at Precision = .50. If the ratio is 1:3, the horizontal line will be at Precision = .25. Area above the line represents good performance and area below the line represents poor performance.
- *Perfect classifier*: A perfect classifier will have 1.0 precision for all levels of recall. The curve formed is a horizontal line with a downward drop at x = 1. That is, a horizontal line extends from x = 0, y = 1 to x = 1, y = y, but then there plot line goes vertically down to the baseline. The baseline represents the random classifier (e.g., for the 1:1 distribution discussed above, the plot line drops to the x = 1, y = .5 point.
- *Comparing classifiers*: Since the P/R plot line for the perfect model is a horizontal line at the top of the plot, for an imperfect classifier (the researcher's model in the real world), the higher the plot line, the better the performance of the model. When two plot lines are plotted in the same graph (e.g., one for "developed nations" and one for "other nations", the higher plot line represents the better-performing model. Keep in mind, however, that precision/recall plots define performance in terms of the positive side of the data.

It is possible to compute a type of AUC for precision/recall plots. This AUC value will be different from the AUC for ROC curves discussed above, though related. The precision/recall AUC is the AUC down to the random model baseline. As noted, the baseline is defined by the ratio of observed positives to negatives. The lower the curve, the lower the AUC score. But also, the lower the baseline, the greater the AUC score. Therefore, a maximum AUC score will be computed for a perfect model with a highly imbalanced dataset whose baseline approaches 0. Such a case would be trivial, however.

TEXT BOX 4.2 Social science applications of R: Do early adolescent sexual behaviors predict sexual orientation?

Li and Davis (2019) studied the sexual behaviors of over 5,000 British youth ages 11–15. Much of their work was reflected in separate classification tree analyses using the "rpart" package in R. At issue was the question of whether sexual activities of young teens are a good predictor of self-reported sexual orientation at age 15 (heterosexual, bisexual, gay or lesbian, questioning). Sexual activities used for classification included holding hands, kissing, cuddling, and touching private parts with members of the same or opposite sex. If parents find early adolescents engaging in these activities with another youth of the opposite sex, should this be taken as a good indicator of sexual orientation? Or are such activities a widespread aspect of growing up?

The authors found that such low-intensity sexual activities did not reliably distinguish among adolescents' sexual orientation identities at age 15. This was true for both genders, although there was a slight tendency for girls to engage in more sexual exploration. The classification tree models correctly classified sexual orientation at 15 some 65% of the time for girls and only 49% of the time for boys. For both genders, the most salient predictor of sexual orientation at age 15 was kissing same-sex individuals at age 15.

In their analysis, the authors found that for both boys and girls it often took more than two tree branchings to reach an end node (which was predicted sexual orientation at age 15). This suggested, the authors noted, that the same sexual activities were often practiced by adolescents with different sexual orientation identities. Likewise, there were repeated end nodes representing prediction of a given sexual orientation on parallel tree branches, suggesting large variations in the types of sexual activities practiced by adolescents with the same sexual orientation identity (Li & Davis, 2019: 433).

In summary, while correlations do exist, sexual activities of early adolescents short of intercourse are not reliable as predictors of sexual orientation at age 15, at least for this sample of British youth. Classification trees produced by the "rpart" package for these data were shown in Figures 4.2 and 4.3.

Source: Li, Gu & Davis, Jacqueline T. M. (2019). Sexual experimentation in heterosexual, bisexual, lesbian/gay, and questioning adolescents from ages 11 to 15. *Journal of Research on Adolescence* 30(2): 423–439.

4.15 Regression trees with the rpart package

We now turn to the creation of single decision trees using `rpart()` with the `method = "anova"` option, which creates regression rather than classification trees. Regression trees are similar to classification trees, with some crucial differences. Both use binary branching to create the decision tree. The primary difference is that the outcome variable is continuous and therefore the primary model performance measure is mean square error (mse) rather than the misclassification rate. In terms of syntax, the main difference in `rpart()` involves specifying `method = "anova"` rather than `method = "class"`.

The regression tree section here has the same subsections as the previous classification tree section. We assume that the reader has read the classification section above and/or is familiar with `rpart()` classification trees. Therefore, discussion which would be repetitive is omitted or minimized (e.g., the nature of a confusion matrix is not re-explained, nor are performance measures redefined). Instead, the subsections below are devoted to highlighting what is different about regression trees or their interpretation.

We continue to use the "world" dataset, but in the regression tree section we use "literacy" as the outcome variable (the DV = dependent variable). This is the continuous version of litgtmean, used above as the DV for classification trees. By using a continuous outcome and avoiding dichotomization, we retain more information. Losing information through dichotomization is a form of measurement error. Measurement error in turn inflates standard errors and attenuates effect sizes, on average, increasing the chance of Type II error (false negatives). If the DV may be measured as a continuous variable, regression trees are preferable to classification trees for these reasons, among others.

4.15.1 Setup

For this section we want to declare the working directory and read in the data, the same as for classification trees/

```
setwd("C:/Data")
world <- read.table("world.csv", header = TRUE, sep = ",", stringsAsFactors = TRUE)
```

Also make sure the needed R libraries listed below are active (if necessary use `install.packages()` to install them prior to using the `library()`command). All were discussed in the classification trees section. As elsewhere in R, if at some point a function known to exist is not working, try issuing its `library()` command again.

```
library(mlr)
library(scales)
library(ROCR)
library(gains)
library(rpart)
library(rpart.plot)
library(rattle)
library(caret)
library(e1071)
```

4.15.2 Creating an rpart regression tree

The regression tree to be created predicts the variable literacy. This is a continuous variable representing the national literacy rate of a nation. It is from the same "world" data frame used for the classification tree example earlier. The same predictor variables are available. For this section we assume that the default directory has been set and the world data read in, as described earlier. For the regression solutions we set the "minbucket" control parameter for `rpart()` to set the minimum number of observations for any terminal node in the tree to seven. Thus, in the tree diagram in Figure 4.13, all leaves have seven or more observations. Setting minimum bucket size is one type of pruning which is built into `rpart()` regression trees, helping assure they are not overfitted to noise in the data. Nonetheless, we shall call the result the "unpruned tree" as additional explicit pruning is possible based on cross-validation, as discussed in a later subsection.

The default control parameter determining the minimum size of terminal nodes is rpart.control(minsplit = 20, minbucket = round(minsplit/3)), where minsplit is the minimum number of observations that must exist in a node in order for a split to be attempted, and minbucket is the minimum number of observations in any terminal node. Thus by default, the smallest node will have no fewer than seven observations. The rpart.control parameters may be overridden by the user by inserting into the `rpart()` command an option such as control = rpart.control(minbucket = 10), which would allow terminal nodes with a count of 10 or more.

First we create the regression tree, storing it in the object "rparttree_anova". The crucial difference from classification trees is the option method = "anova", which calls for a regression. The `rpart()` command below creates the regression tree solution and the `plot()` command creates a basic visualization for it. The `text()` command simply adds the labels. The resulting regression tree is shown in Figure 4.13.[7]

```
set.seed(123)

rparttree_anova <- rpart::rpart(literacy ~ regionid + population + areasqmiles +
poppersqmile + coast_arearatio + netmigration + Infantdeathsper1k + infdeaths +
gdppercapitalindollars  + phonesper1000 + arablepct + cropspct + otherpct +
birthrate + deathrate, method = "anova", data = world)

plot(rparttree_anova, margin = 0.05)

text(rparttree_anova, pretty=0, use.n = TRUE, xpd = TRUE, cex = 1.0)
```

As seen in Figure 4.13, the regression tree has many more terminal nodes than the corresponding classification tree (9 rather than 4). The number of nations in each leaf is listed below it. The smallest terminal node has seven nations, as dictated by the minbucket parameter. The number at the leaf (e.g., 39.47 for the left-most leaf) is the predicted value for literacy. Note that the nodes are arranged from lowest literacy (39.47%) to highest (97.2%). For purposes of comparison with the classification tree, mean literacy = 83.28, so therefore only the 7 + 48 + 79 = 134 nations in the three right-most terminal nodes correspond to "High" as labeled by the classification tree scheme. The observed

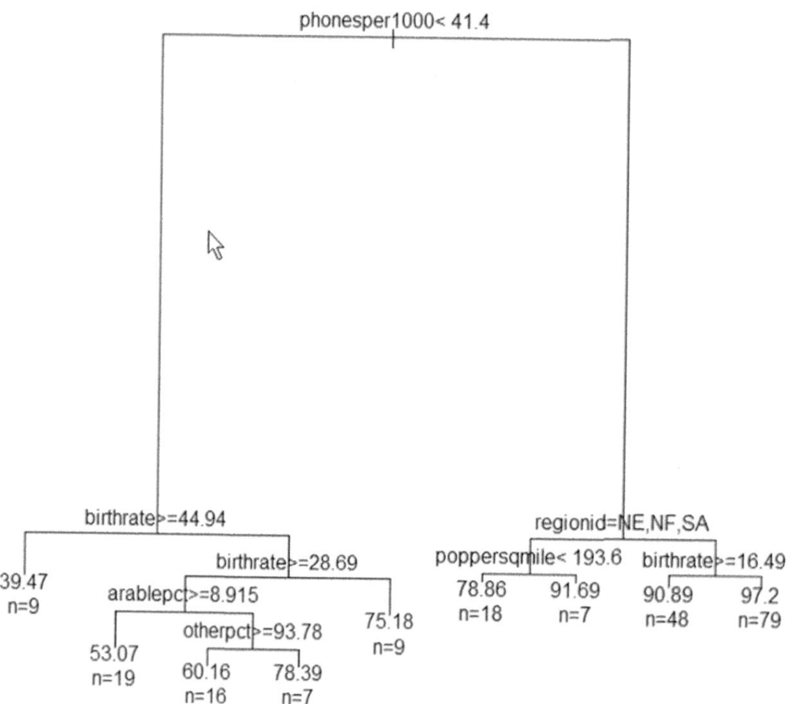

Figure 4.13 Rpart regression tree for national literacy rate

count of "High" nations was 140. By way of comparison, the classification tree predicted 132 nations to be "High", yielding two more errors than the regression tree.

The order of branching does not represent a causal sequence. For instance, the root node is phones per 1,000 population, a measure of communications infrastructure. It is impossible that this variable caused either of those next in sequence (birthrate and regionid). Also, even though regression is used to construct the tree, the variables do not represent semi-partial effects as in ordinary regression (not effects controlling for other variables in the model). Rather, the variables encountered in the path from the root node (phonesper1000) to any terminal node may be viewed as a constellation of factors which suffice to predict that all nations in the node have a particular value of literacy. That is, all nations in a given node are predicted to have this same value (e.g., a national literacy rate of 39.47 for the nine nations in the left-most node). This clustering of predicted values by node introduces a smoothing effect for the predictions. Predicted values from regression trees may or may not be more correlated with observed values than would be predicted values from OLS regression for the same data. Typically the difference is small. The primary value of regression tree analysis compared to OLS regression is not superior prediction per se, though that may occur, but rather utility for theory construction based on identifying underlying configurations of variables and typically doing so in a more parsimonious way.

Because the variables in Figure 4.13 represent constellations or configurations of levels of classifier variables associated with outcomes reflected in the terminal nodes, decision trees are more analogous to other configurational approaches such as qualitative comparative analysis (QCA) (Garson, 2016c) than they are to OLS regression models. Configurational analysis does not result in a "percent of DV variance explained" coefficient like R^2 in regression. Rather it results in identification of configurations associated with outcomes.

Thus, the outcome of configurational analysis is identification of commonly occurring clusters of value classes or ranges of classifier variables associated with outcomes of interest. While classifier variables are often called "predictors" and while the `predict()` command is integral to the tree-building process, they are not predictor variables in the regression or causal sense. Commonly occurring clusters represent "paths" through the decision tree to an outcome of interest, but no causal sequence is implied by this use of the term "path". In classification tree analysis there may be paths to multiple terminal nodes all having the same outcome value, such as "High" literacy. This "equifinality of paths" often reveals complexity not easily uncovered when using multinomial regression models. Regression trees, however, are not equifinal. There is only one path to each terminal value.

The configurations in CART also may be called paths, patterns, constellations, or simply sets of classification variables and cutting points. In Figure 4.13, by far the largest configuration is that for the 79 nations in the right-most terminal node, representing the highest-literacy nations. When interpreting the tree, keep in mind that for the criterion printed above the node, nations go to the left if the criterion is true for that nation. A nation being in this largest cluster is predicted by its not having fewer phones per 1,000 population than 41.4, not being in the NE/NF/SA regions (Near East, North Africa, sub-Saharan Africa), and not having a birthrate greater or equal to 16.49. Simplifying, very high literacy is associated with being in certain regions with lower birthrates and better communications infrastructure (as measured by higher phones per 1,000). Simply having high phone prevalence and being in certain regions accounts for another 48 nations even though these did have higher birthrates.

Regression tree analysis is especially useful in two situations:

1. *Data-driven prediction*: In some circumstances, the objective is not causal analysis but simply coming up with a model which classifies well. This is the typical case in marketing research, for instance, where the objective is to segment the population of consumers in order to determine the segment or segments which are apt to be most responsive to an advertising campaign. The classification variables may or may not be "causes", but this is largely irrelevant to the research objective. Regression tree analysis is therefore popular in the marketing discipline.
2. *Causal theory construction*: Social scientists are often interested in causal analysis. Using regression trees alone for this purpose is insufficient for a variety of reasons, including that the classifier variables selected are not based on their predictive effect after controlling for other variables in the model, do not take into account possible mediation and moderation effects, and do not take into account multilevel (random) effects. However, as part of a multipronged attack on the tangled ball of effects which is "causality", regression trees can add important insights such as better selection of variables to model and better understanding of heterogeneity in the data.

In the foregoing regression tree analysis, some 14 possible predictor variables were entered into the model. The tree in Figure 4.13 has reduced this number to only 6, of which only 2 (region and communications infrastructure represented by phones per 1,000) are required to classify most nations. Of course, some terminal nodes will be shown to have a higher rate of correct predictions than others. This can be explored just as researchers would explore residuals in regression analyses. It is also possible to see the effect on the structure of the calculated tree with and without a given predictor/classifier variable in the model. At a minimum, however, regression tree analysis (1) suggests variables which *may* play a causal role and which should be considered in other forms of modeling, and (2) suggests how causation may be heterogeneous, with different clusters of nations associated with different configurations of variables.

Also, regression tree analysis may suggest theories and hypotheses to be explored. For instance, the tree in Figure 4.13 suggests that literacy may be promoted by having a good communications infrastructure combined with supportive regional culture, but in other regions, high birthrate and rural life may be determinative. Regression tree analysis, it should be emphasized, merely suggests theories and hypotheses which may be useful in the exploratory stage of causal research. It is an exploratory, not a confirmatory analytic technique, when the research purpose is causal analysis.

4.15.3 Printing tree rules

Tree rules may be printed in the same manner as for classification trees earlier. This requires the `asRules()` function of the "rattle" package. Below we display output for the right-most and left-most nodes only, though the command prints rules for all nodes. In output below, note that the "cover = " segment lists the count for the given nod. For instance, node 15 has a count of 79 nations, which is 37% of the sample. It is the right-most node in Figure 4.13 and is the one with the highest average literacy (97.2). The path rules show that the nations in node 15 and ones which are high on telecommunications infrastructure (phonesper1000 >= 41.4); low birthrate (< 16.49); and located in the listed regions (which include North America and Western Europe, among others).

```
library(rattle)
rattle::asRules(rparttree_anova)
```

[Partial output for nodes 15 and 4 only:]

```
    Rule number: 15 [literacy=97.2012658227848 cover=79 (37%)]
      phonesper1000>=41.4
      regionid=AS,BA,CW,DQ,EE,LA,NO,OC,WE
      birthrate< 16.49

    Rule number: 4 [literacy=39.4666666666667 cover=9 (4%)]
      phonesper1000< 41.4
      birthrate>=44.94
```

4.15.4 Visualization with `prp()` and `fancyRpartPlot()`

An alternative way to visualize the regression tree is to use the `prp()` function of the `rpart.plot` library, as was discussed above for classification trees. The result is displayed in Figure 4.14. While similar to Figure 4.13, it usefully displays values for both sides of any split in the tree.

```
rpart.plot::prp(rparttree_anova, type=5, fallen.leaves=TRUE,faclen = 0, varlen = 0,
cex = 0.8, extra = 1, Margin=0.1, box.col=3, shadow.col="gray")
```

As discussed for the classification tree example, perhaps an even more popular alternative tree display method uses the `fancyRpartPlot()` command from the `rattle` package. The plot shows clearly that the regression tree algorithm has clustered outcomes into nine ranges of the continuous dependent variable (literacy).

```
require(rattle)
rattle::fancyRpartPlot(rparttree_anova, type=4, cex=1.1, branch.lwd=3, sub="")
```

In Figure 4.15, the bottom row depicts the terminal nodes. The number in a white box on the top of each shape is the internally-assigned node number. The top number inside the green shape is the estimated literacy rate for nations

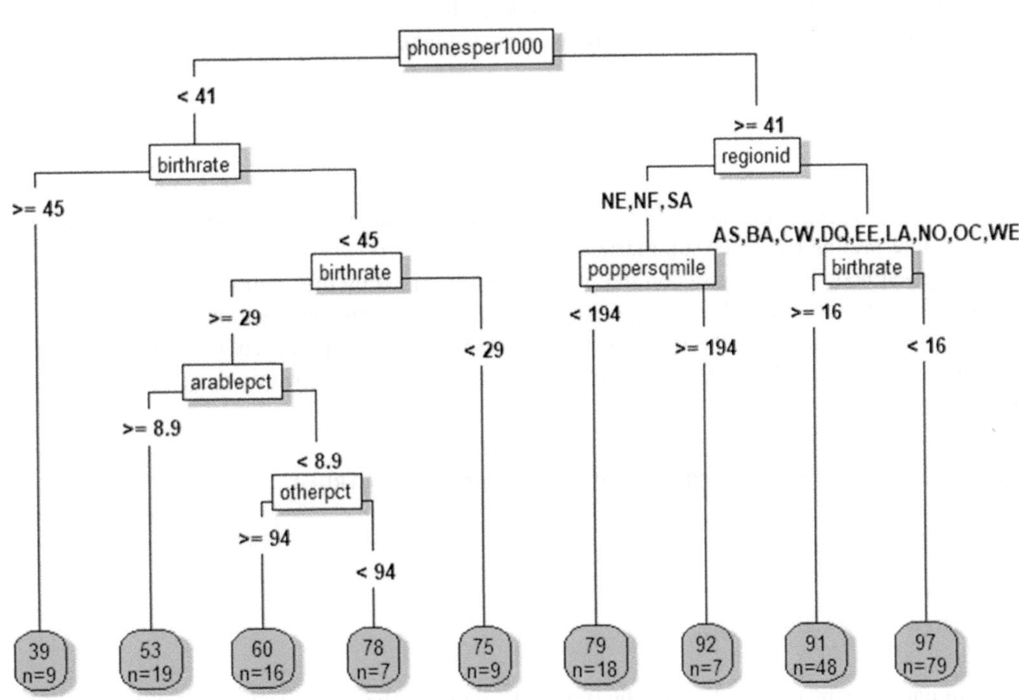

Figure 4.14 `Prp()` visualization of the regression tree for literacy

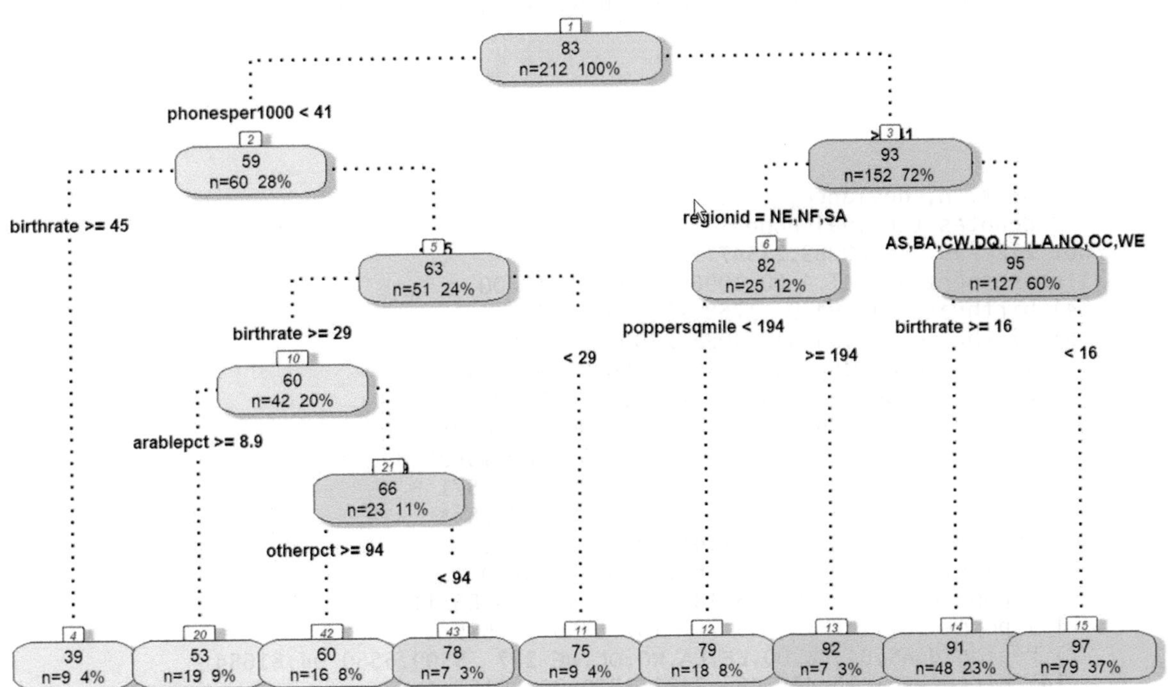

Figure 4.15 `fancyRpartPlot()` visualization of the regression tree

in that node, rounded to integers. The bottom figures inside each shape are the count of nations in the node and the corresponding percent share of the total of 212 nations in the sample.

4.15.5 Interpreting tree summaries

In this section on `rpart()` regression trees, we briefly discuss how to interpret tree summaries of the "rparttree_anova" object containing the results of the `rpart()` command. See the previous section on classification trees for more on interpreting rpart tree summaries.

The path to a given node in the regression tree may be summarized by this command, here specifying node 4. The path to node 4 starts at the root. If phonesper1000 is less than 41.4, the observation (nation) goes to the left. If birthrate is more than or equal to 44.94, the observation again goes to the left, arriving at a terminal node (leaf). Further splitting would reduce the goodness of fit measure (R-squared in anova models) by less than the default value (0.01).

```
rpart::path.rpart(rparttree_anova,4,pretty=0,print.it=TRUE)
[Output:]
       node number: 4
         root
         phonesper1000< 41.4
         birthrate>=44.94
```

A basic tree summary may be obtained simply by typing the name of the tree object, here rparttree_anova. See the earlier corresponding discussion for classification tree sections, where the meaning of listed elements (node, split, n, deviance, yval) was discussed. In output below, a node is a terminal node if there is an asterisk at the end of its row. As seen in Figure 4.15, the first node in the lower left is internally labeled node 4. It represents nine nations (4% of the total of 212). It has a y-value (literacy rate) of approximately 39.47. This is shown in output below, in line "4)". Starting at the root node, node "4)" is arrived at when phonesper1000 is less than 41.4 (line 2) and birthrate is more than or equal to 44.94 (line 4). The last line in this output refers to node 15 (this is the right-most terminal node in Figure 4.15).

```
rparttree_anova
[Output:]
   n= 212
   node), split, n, deviance, yval
         * denotes terminal node
   1) root 212 79972.9700 83.27547
      2) phonesper1000< 41.4 60 19969.9700 59.19000
        4) birthrate>=44.94 9  1768.7800 39.46667 *
        5) birthrate< 44.94 51 14082.2700 62.67059
         10) birthrate>=28.685 42 10456.5600 59.99048
           20) arablepct>=8.915 19  2920.0370 53.07368 *
           21) arablepct< 8.915 23  5876.6100 65.70435
             42) otherpct>=93.78 16  2977.4590 60.15625 *
             43) otherpct< 93.78 7  1280.9290 78.38571 *
         11) birthrate< 28.685 9  1916.1560 75.17778 *
      3) phonesper1000>=41.4 152 11456.9600 92.78289
        6) regionid=NE,NF,SA 25  2663.9820 82.45200
         12) poppersqmile< 193.55 18  1677.4430 78.86111 *
         13) poppersqmile>=193.55 7   157.6086 91.68571 *
        7) regionid=AS,BA,CW,DQ,EE,LA,NO,OC,WE 127  5599.5550 94.81654
         14) birthrate>=16.495 48  3481.2770 90.89167 *
         15) birthrate< 16.495 79   929.5899 97.20127 *
```

A different listing of nodes can be obtained by asking for the "frame" element of the `rpart()` object:

```
rparttree_anova$frame
```

[Output:]

```
             var   n  wt        dev     yval  complexity ncompete    nsurrogate
1  phonesper1000 212 212 79972.9725 83.27547 0.607030618        4             5
2      birthrate  60  60 19969.9740 59.19000 0.051504002        4             5
4         <leaf>   9   9  1768.7800 39.46667 0.010000000        0             0
5      birthrate  51  51 14082.2659 62.67059 0.021376649        4             5
10     arablepct  42  42 10456.5562 59.99048 0.020755885        4             5
20        <leaf>  19  19  2920.0368 53.07368 0.010000000        0             0
21      otherpct  23  23  5876.6096 65.70435 0.020234606        4             5
42        <leaf>  16  16  2977.4594 60.15625 0.010000000        0             0
43        <leaf>   7   7  1280.9286 78.38571 0.010000000        0             0
11        <leaf>   9   9  1916.1556 75.17778 0.010000000        0             0
3       regionid 152 152 11456.9555 92.78289 0.039931214        4             4
6    poppersqmile  25  25  2663.9824 82.45200 0.010365140        4             5
12        <leaf>  18  18  1677.4428 78.86111 0.010000000        0             0
13        <leaf>   7   7   157.6086 91.68571 0.010000000        0             0
7      birthrate 127 127  5599.5553 94.81654 0.014863631        4             5
14        <leaf>  48  48  3481.2767 90.89167 0.007136589        0             0
15        <leaf>  79  79   929.5899 97.20127 0.001799038        0             0
```

In the frame listing above, the first column lists the internally-assigned node numbers. The second column (var) lists the classifier variables actually used in the solution, except "<leaf>" designates a terminal node. In node 4 there are nine nations (the "n" column). The data are unweighted because the "wt" column is identical to the "n" column. Other columns are as follows:

- The "dev" column is the deviance value for the node, representing error. This is the same value as shown in output when a listing of `rparttree _ anova` is requested.
- Nodes with lower deviance have less error. A deviance value of 0 reflects no error.
- The "yval" column is the fitted value of the outcome variable. For node 4, the predicted literacy rate is 39.47%.
- The "complexity" column is the CP, which is the value at which the given split will collapse. That is, all prospective splits must decrease the lack of fit measure (R-squared in anova regression trees) by at least the CP amount. By default, the minimum amount is .01.
- The "ncompete" column is the number of recorded competitor splits. The "nsurrogate" value is the number of surrogate splits for the given node. These values are 0 for all terminal nodes since the input data contained no missing values. Surrogates were discussed earlier in the section on "Decision tree terminology".
- Note that for certain other types of tree, other columns will be present. For Poisson trees, "yval2" contains the number of events at the given node. For classification trees, there will be class probabilities and node probabilities.

The `summary()` command provides a listing of the CP table, the "Variable importance" list, and a third section which (1) lists the mean square error (mse) and predicted value for each terminal node, or (2) for nonterminal nodes, lists alternative and surrogate splits which were considered.

- The CP table is discussed in the next section.
- The variable importance list (see discussion in the corresponding classification tree section):

```
Variable importance
         phonesper1000    birthrate       Infantdeathsper1k
                    20           18                      16
gdppercapitalindollars    infdeaths                regionid
                    14           14                      12
           poppersqmile    otherpct               arablepct
                     1            1                       1
            areasqmiles   deathrate
                     1            1
```

- Summary output for terminal nodes (we list them left to right in Figure 4.15). The least mean square error is in node 15, which is the largest node (79 nations) and is right-most in the tree.

```
Node number 4: 9 observations
  mean=39.46667, MSE=196.5311
Node number 11: 9 observations
  mean=75.17778, MSE=212.9062
Node number 12: 18 observations
  mean=78.86111, MSE=93.19127
Node number 13: 7 observations
  mean=91.68571, MSE=22.51551
Node number 14: 48 observations
  mean=90.89167, MSE=72.5266
Node number 15: 79 observations
  mean=97.20127, MSE=11.76696
Node number 20: 19 observations
  mean=53.07368, MSE=153.6861
Node number 42: 16 observations
  mean=60.15625, MSE=186.0912
Node number 43: 7 observations
  mean=78.38571, MSE=182.9898
```

- Summary output for other nodes. We list only output for node 1, which is the split at the root node. As the most improvement was for phonesper1000 < 41.4, this is the split actually used. Other splits were considered. Surrogate splits would be used if there were missing values on phonesper1000, but the data do not have missing values.

```
Node number 1: 212 observations,    complexity param=0.6070306
  mean=83.27547, MSE=377.231
  left son=2 (60 obs) right son=3 (152 obs)
  Primary splits:
      phonesper1000          < 41.4     to the left,  improve=0.6070306, (0 missing)
      birthrate              < 29.35    to the right, improve=0.5567432, (0 missing)
      Infantdeathsper1k      < 41.6     to the right, improve=0.5194770, (0 missing)
      infdeaths              splits as  LR,           improve=0.4970423, (0 missing)
      gdppercapitalindollars < 2150     to the left,  improve=0.4464908, (0 missing)
  Surrogate splits:
      Infantdeathsper1k      < 41.6     to the right, agree=0.934, adj=0.767, (0 split)
      birthrate              < 29.35    to the right, agree=0.934, adj=0.767, (0 split)
      infdeaths              splits as  LR,           agree=0.920, adj=0.717, (0 split)
      gdppercapitalindollars < 2350     to the left,  agree=0.915, adj=0.700, (0 split)
      regionid               splits as  RRRRRRRRRRLR, agree=0.877, adj=0.567, (0 split)
```

4.15.6 The CP table

The CP table may be printed as an element of the rparttree_anova object:

```
rparttree_anova$cptable
```
[Output:]
```
          CP nsplit rel error    xerror       xstd
1 0.60703062      0 1.0000000 1.0215919 0.11205498
2 0.05150400      1 0.3929694 0.4315248 0.05567084
3 0.03993121      2 0.3414654 0.4436655 0.05605471
4 0.02137665      3 0.3015342 0.4042181 0.05448523
5 0.02075588      4 0.2801575 0.3894130 0.05033936
6 0.02023461      5 0.2594016 0.3812970 0.05013834
7 0.01486363      6 0.2391670 0.3888834 0.05510100
8 0.01036514      7 0.2243034 0.4008172 0.05539662
9 0.01000000      8 0.2139383 0.4062411 0.05646228
```

The CP table has nine rows, representing trees with successively more splits. To be attempted, any prospective split must decrease overall lack of fit by a factor of cp. For method="anova" regression trees, R-squared must decrease by at least CP, set by default to .01. By default, the CP value decreases until additional splitting would cause the CP value to drop below 1%. The highest CP contribution occurs in the first row, dropping off markedly after that.

In the CP table, "nsplit" is the number of splits for the tree represented by the given row. The number of nodes for the tree represented by the row is always nsplit + 1. That is, row 1 is the tree with only 0 + 1 = 1 split. Row 2 is the tree with 1 + 1 = 2 splits, and so on.

The "rel error" column is relative error (risk), used along with other criteria to assess the optimal number of tree levels. In regression models, relative error is equal to the sum of squares within nodes divided by the sum of squares of the root node. Relative error is always scaled so the top row has a value of 1.0. This value typically falls off sharply as tree complexity increases. Figure 4.16 shows the resulting relative error plot, invoked by this command. This figure may be compared to Figure 4.8, which was for the classification tree version. Here, it is shown that a tree pruned to a depth of 2 captures most of the information.

```
rpart::plotcp(rparttree_anova, upper=c("splits"))
```

The "xerror" value is the cross-validated mean error for the tree for the given row, based on a built-in cross-validation procedure. The difference between xerror for a given level (row) and the next level is a measure of the contribution to fit of splitting in the next level. While xerror usually decreases with each additional level, overfitting may lead to it actually increasing. The "xstd" value is the standard deviation of actual error (unscaled, in contrast to relative error). See discussion in the classification tree section on how relative error and xstd are used to select the optimal tree.

The variables actually used list. The `printcp()` command returns a convenient list of variables actually used in the unpruned tree shown in Figures 5.20–5.22. Here, six variables are used out of the input set of 15 variables. This command is also another way to print out the CP table discussed above, though this portion of the output is not shown below.

```
printcp(rparttree_anova)
```
[Partial output:]
```
Variables actually used in tree construction:
[1] arablepct     birthrate     otherpct    phonesper1000
[5] poppersqmile  regionid

Root node error: 79973/212 = 377.23
n= 212
```

For a regression tree, RNE represents error made when cases are classified based only on the root node split. RNE has a different meaning for regression trees compared to classification trees. In a regression tree, RNE is

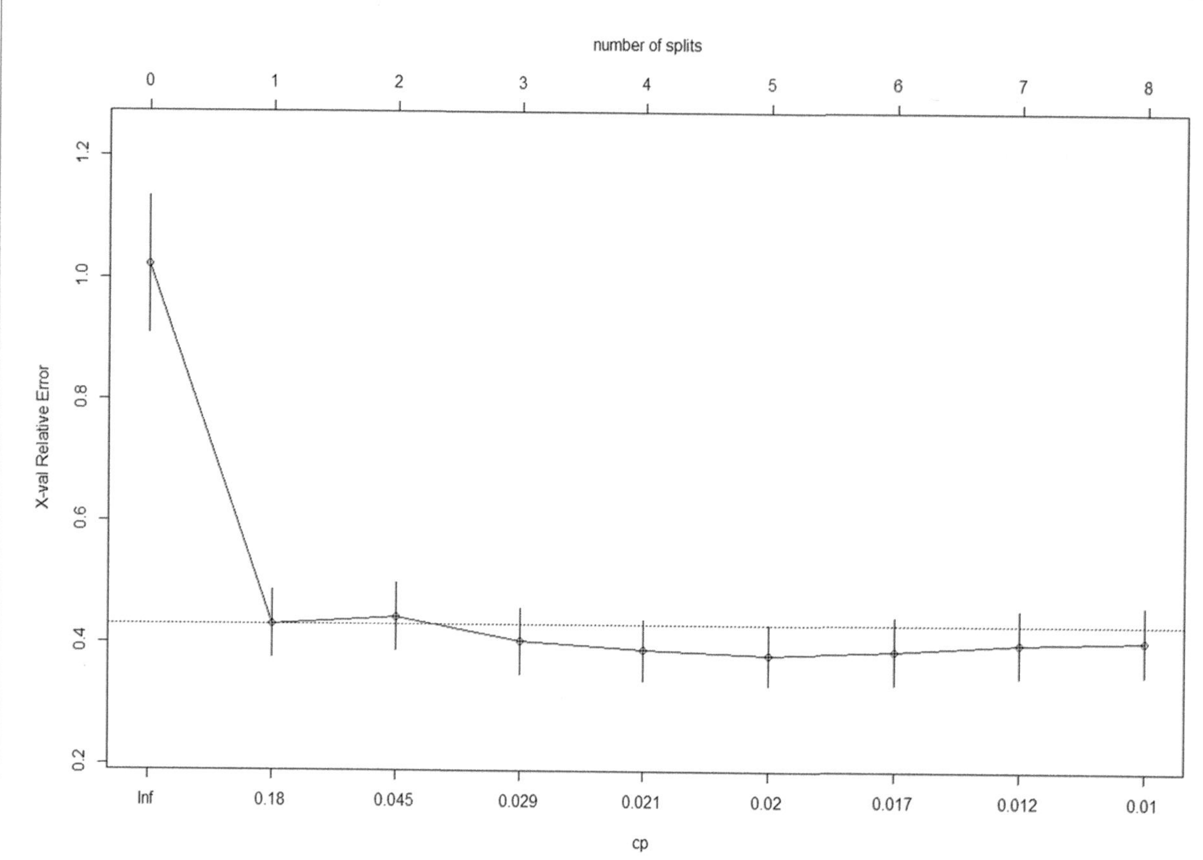

Figure 4.16 Relative error plot

the variance of the root node and is calculated as the sum of squares of the root node (representing absolute error) divided by the number of observations. RNE multiplied by xerror equals the cross-validation variance (the cross-validation error rate).

4.15.7 Listing nodes by country and countries by node

This section parallels the corresponding section for classification trees. Node numbers are part of the frame element, with rows labeled "<leaf>" being terminal nodes.

```
rparttree_anova$frame[1]
```

[Output:]

```
                var
1   phonesper1000
2       birthrate
4          <leaf>
5       birthrate
10      arablepct
20         <leaf>
21       otherpct
42         <leaf>
43         <leaf>
11         <leaf>
3        regionid
6    poppersqmile
12         <leaf>
```

```
13        <leaf>
7      birthrate
14        <leaf>
15        <leaf>
```

Listing nodes by observation (country)
To list the node number for any country, we start by putting node numbers into the object "nodenum", which we add to the world data frame as a new variable called "node". Warning: This will overwrite the world$node values from the classification tree section.

```
nodenum <- row.names(rparttree_anova$frame)
world$node <- nodenum[rparttree_anova$where]
```

Countries may be listed with their node numbers by the `print()` and `paste()` commands.

```
print(paste(world$country,"Node = ",world$node))
[Partial output:]
     [1] "Afghanistan  Node =  4"
     [2] "Bangladesh  Node =  20"
   . . .
   [211] "UnitedKingdom  Node =  15"
   [212] "Austria  Node =  15"
```

Listing observations (countries) by node
The `subset()` command allows us to print the countries contained in any given node. We use node 4 as an example. Note that this requires that the "node" variable have been created as described above. For node 4, all nations are from sub-Saharan Africa plus Afghanistan.

```
worldnode4 <- subset(world,world$node==4)
worldnode4$country
[Output:]

   [1] "Afghanistan " "Angola "
   [3] "BurkinaFaso " "Chad "
   [5] "Mali "        "Niger "
   [7] "SierraLeone " "Somalia "
   [9] "Uganda
```

To save to file the world data frame, which now includes world$node as the node number variable, optionally we may use the usual method below. We save to "world3.csv" to avoid overwriting the original world.csv file or the world2.csv file created in the classification tree section.

```
write.csv(world, file = "world3.csv", row.names = FALSE)
```

4.15.8 Saving predictions and residuals

Below, we save predictions to the original world data frame. First, predictions are put into the numeric object "predanova", which is a numeric variable containing the predicted literacy rates for each nation. The world$literacy variable is also numeric. Then below, predanova is added to the original world data frame:

```
predanova <- predict(rparttree_anova, type = "matrix")
class(predanova)
     [1] "numeric"
class(world$literacy)
     [1] "numeric"
world$predanova <- predanova
```

For clarity, we use the multistep process below to save raw residuals to the world data frame under the label "anovaresid".

```
observed <- world$literacy
predicted <- predanova
anovaresid <- observed - predicted
world$anovaresid <- anovaresid
```

4.15.9 Plotting residuals

In the previous subsection we saved raw residuals to the world data frame under the label "anovaresid". A simple plot of residuals may be produced using observed values on the x-axis against predicted values on the y-axis. This scatterplot is shown in Figure 4.17. In a perfect prediction, all points would be on a 45-degree line. That points very roughly follow the 45-degree reference line is indicative of good but far from perfect prediction. Note that points are in nine rows (some pairs of rows are close together), corresponding to the nine nodes in the regression tree. Recall all nations in a given node have the same predicted literacy value. The tighter (less dispersion) the range in any row,

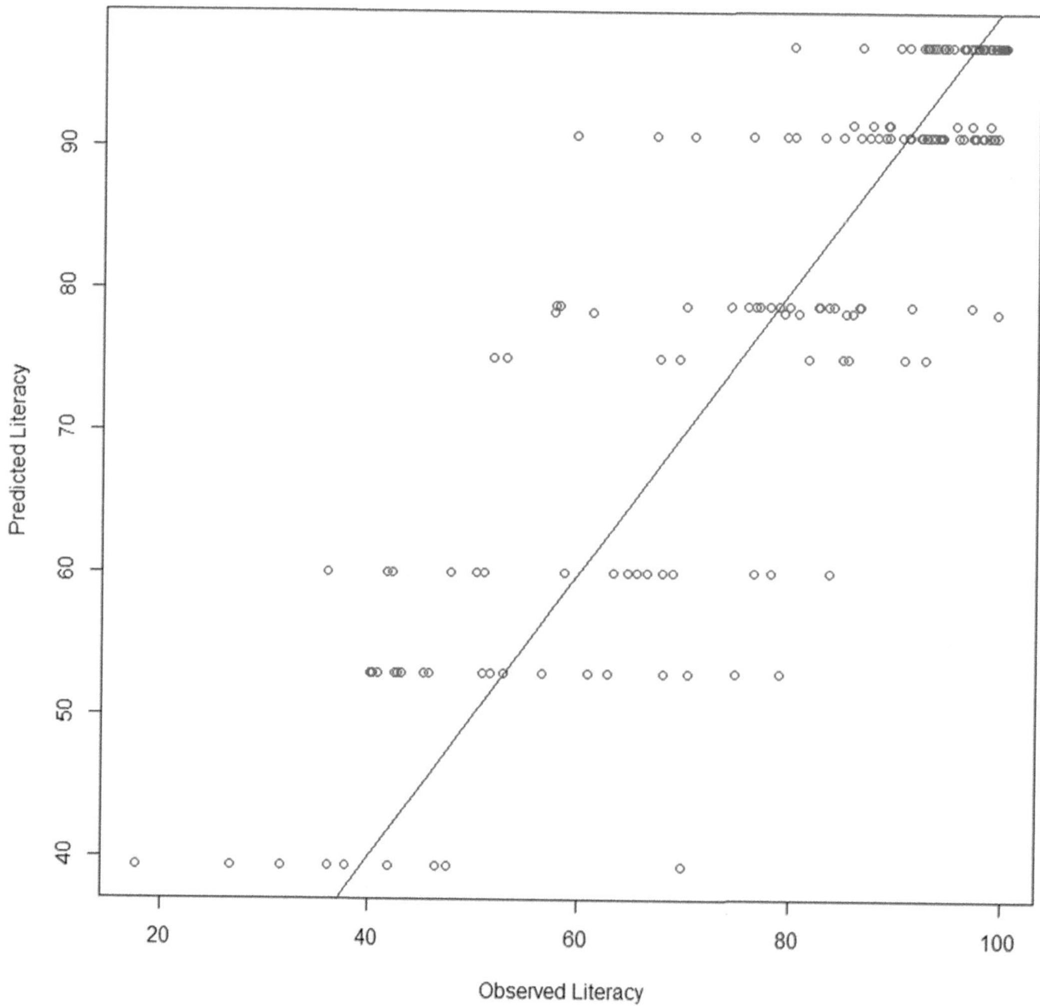

Figure 4.17 Observed vs. Actual plot, regression tree example

the lower the residuals are for that node. For instance, for the node cluster of observations with highest predicted literacy, the dispersion of high and low residuals is less than for the node predicted to have approximately 60% literacy. Prediction is better for the former node than the latter.

```
plot(world$literacy, world$predanova, col="red", xlab="Observed Literacy",
ylab="Predicted Literacy")

# Add the reference line.
abline(0,1, lty = 1, col = "blue")
```

4.15.10 Cross-validation and pruning

By default the rpart package implements tenfold cross-validation and also outputs measures (e.g., CP, nsplit, rel error, xerror, xstd, and RNE) useful for pruning a tree to optimal size. For regression trees, the `prune()` command may be used to simplify the initial untrimmed tree. This will make the tree more interpretable but at a trade-off of somewhat diminished model fit. The common rule of thumb for finding the optimal level of pruning is to prune based on the CP, though the researcher should consider tolerance for increased error due to pruning, the theoretical importance of splits which may be pruned, and interpretability of the results.

1. Recall the CP table:

```
rparttree_anova$cptable
[Output:]
          CP nsplit rel error    xerror       xstd
1 0.60703062      0 1.0000000 1.0215919 0.11205498
2 0.05150400      1 0.3929694 0.4315248 0.05567084
3 0.03993121      2 0.3414654 0.4436655 0.05605471
4 0.02137665      3 0.3015342 0.4042181 0.05448523
5 0.02075588      4 0.2801575 0.3894130 0.05033936
6 0.02023461      5 0.2594016 0.3812970 0.05013834
7 0.01486363      6 0.2391670 0.3888834 0.05510100
8 0.01036514      7 0.2243034 0.4008172 0.05539662
9 0.01000000      8 0.2139383 0.4062411 0.05646228
```

2. In the CP table, find the lowest xerror, which is 0. 3812970 in row 6.
3. Add its standard deviation (xstd) = 0. 3812970 + 0.05013834 = 0.43143534.
4. Find the smallest tree (row most toward the top of the CP table) with xerror < 0.43143534. This is depth/row = 4, with xerror = 0.4042181 (though row 2 is very close).
5. Note the CP of this row, which is 0.02137665.
6. Prune with a slightly higher CP, so we use .03.
7. Create a new data frame "rparttree_anova_pruned" using the commands below, then plot it (we happen to use `fancyRpartPlot()`, described previously). The plot is shown in Figure 4.18.

```
rparttree_anova_pruned <- rpart::prune(rparttree_anova,cp=.03)
rattle::fancyRpartPlot(rparttree_anova_pruned, type=4, cex=1.0, branch.lwd=3,
sub="")
```

The pruned regression tree is shown in Figure 4.18. Unlike the pruned classification tree in Figure 4.9, the pruned regression tree is three rather than two levels deep. Where the pruned classification tree was based on splitting the root node by birthrate, the pruned regression tree is based on splitting by phonesper1000, an indicator of telecommunications infrastructure, and then by birthrate, but only for the nations low on phonesper1000. The phonesper1000 variable was also the root-level split for the unpruned regression tree shown in Figure 4.13.

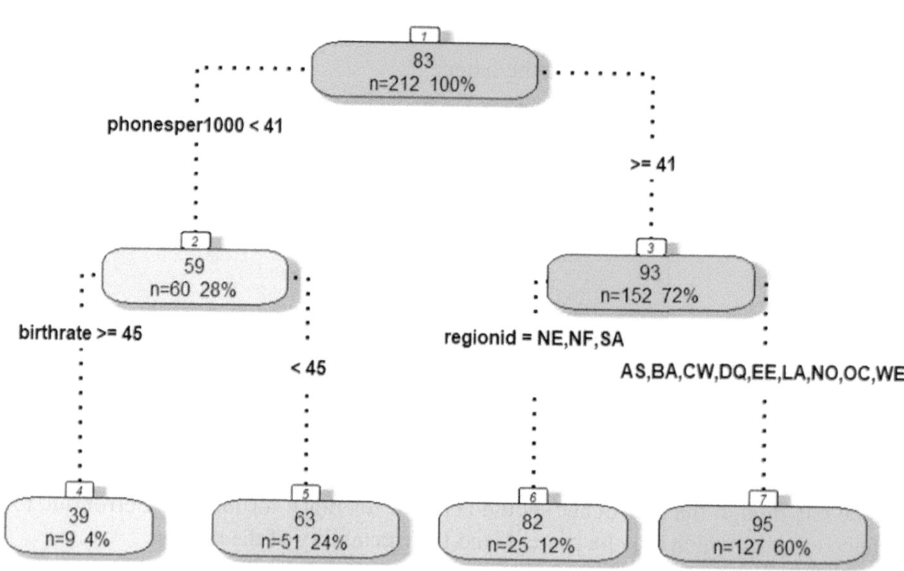

Figure 4.18 The pruned regression tree

4.15.11 R-squared for regression trees

Regression trees generate two versions of an R-squared measure.

- "Apparent R-squared" is unadjusted R-squared. It equals 1 – relative error, where relative error is listed in the CP table discussed above.
- "X-relative R-squared" is cross-validated R-squared. It equals 1 – xerror, as also listed in the CP table.

For reading convenience, we reproduce the cp table below.

```
rparttree_anova$cp
[Output:]
          CP nsplit rel error    xerror       xstd
1 0.60703062      0 1.0000000 1.0215919 0.11205498
2 0.05150400      1 0.3929694 0.4315248 0.05567084
3 0.03993121      2 0.3414654 0.4436655 0.05605471
4 0.02137665      3 0.3015342 0.4042181 0.05448523
5 0.02075588      4 0.2801575 0.3894130 0.05033936
6 0.02023461      5 0.2594016 0.3812970 0.05013834
7 0.01486363      6 0.2391670 0.3888834 0.05510100
8 0.01036514      7 0.2243034 0.4008172 0.05539662
9 0.01000000      8 0.2139383 0.4062411 0.05646228
```

Since each row in the CP table lists both "rel error" and "xerror", there is an apparent and an x-relative R-squared value for each row also, which are 1 minus these values. Rows represent increasingly deep tree solutions with more splits. If the bottom row is the researcher's solution, then the apparent R-squared for the full tree would be 1 minus relative error for the bottom row.

"Apparent" refers to model fit prior to cross-validation. "Relative" refers to model fit based on cross-validation. Relative R-squared is always lower than apparent R-squared. Pruning involves loss of information, so the apparent R-squared for the pruned tree will be lower than for the unpruned tree. The same is not true for relative (cross-validated) R-squared. For these data, for instance, relative R-squared is actually higher for the pruned tree compared to the original unpruned tree.

We now illustrate how to print out the relative error and xerror and the corresponding R-squared values for the rparttree_anova. The procedure is the same for rparttree_anova_pruned but for space reasons is omitted here.

Step 1: Send the CP table to the object "temp". Put columns 3 and 4, which are rel error and xerror, into the object "val". Print out the bottom row, which is usually the preferred solution. The bottom row is the same as `nrow()`. Therefore, the third command is equivalent to `val[9,]` for the current example. If a different row represents the desired solution, such as row 2, let the third command be `val[2,]`.

```
temp <- rpart::printcp(rparttree_anova)
val <- temp[,c(3,4)]
val[nrow(val),]
[Partial output:]
   rel error    xerror
   0.2139383 0.4062411
```

Step 2: Put 1 minus rel error and 1 minus xerror into the object rsq.val. Get rid of the names of rsq.val, which is a named numeric vector (the names are "rel error" and "xerror"). Bind the R-square coefficients into a data frame called "df". Replace the column names with the desired ones instead of the default "V1" and "V2". Then list the df data frame. Note that in the second command, `nrow(rsq.val)` evaluates to 9, the bottom row. If the preferred solution is row 2, for example, then the second command becomes `rsq <- unname(rsq.val[2,])`.

```
rsq.val <- 1 - temp[,c(3,4)]
rsq <- unname(rsq.val[nrow(rsq.val),])
df <- as.data.frame(cbind(round(rsq[1],3), round(rsq[2],3)))
colnames(df) = c("Apparent R2", "x-Relative R2")
df
[Output:]
     Apparent R2 x-Relative R2
   1       0.786         0.594
```

In the same way we can calculate R2 for the pruned tree (rpart_anova_pruned), getting the coefficients below. Pruning leads to some loss of percent explained but does so with a more parsimonious model. The researcher may feel the latter compensates for the former.

```
temp <- rpart::printcp(rparttree_anova_pruned)
rsq.val <- 1 - temp[,c(3,4)]
rsq <- unname(rsq.val[nrow(rsq.val),])
df <- as.data.frame(cbind(round(rsq[1],3), round(rsq[2],3)))
colnames(df) = c("Apparent R2", "x-Relative R2")
df
[Output:]
     Apparent R2 x-Relative R2
   1       0.698         0.596
```

For the rparttree_anova, we may say that 78.6% of the variance in national literacy rate is explained by the model, not taking cross-validation into account. On a cross-validated basis, 59.4% of the variance in literacy is explained because x-Relative R-squared is based on xerror, which reflects cross-validation. On a cross-validated basis, the pruned model performs as well as the original, less parsimonious model.

The rpart package provides a way to plot R-squared. The commands below each produce two plots:

- R-squared (apparent and apparent from cross-validation) versus the number of splits.
- Relative Error (cross-validation) +/– 1-SE from cross-validation versus the number of splits.

Figure 4.19, however, only displays the R-square plots, not the relative error plots. Two R-squared plots are shown, one for rparttree_anova and one for rparttree_anova_pruned. Note that each command below produces two plots,

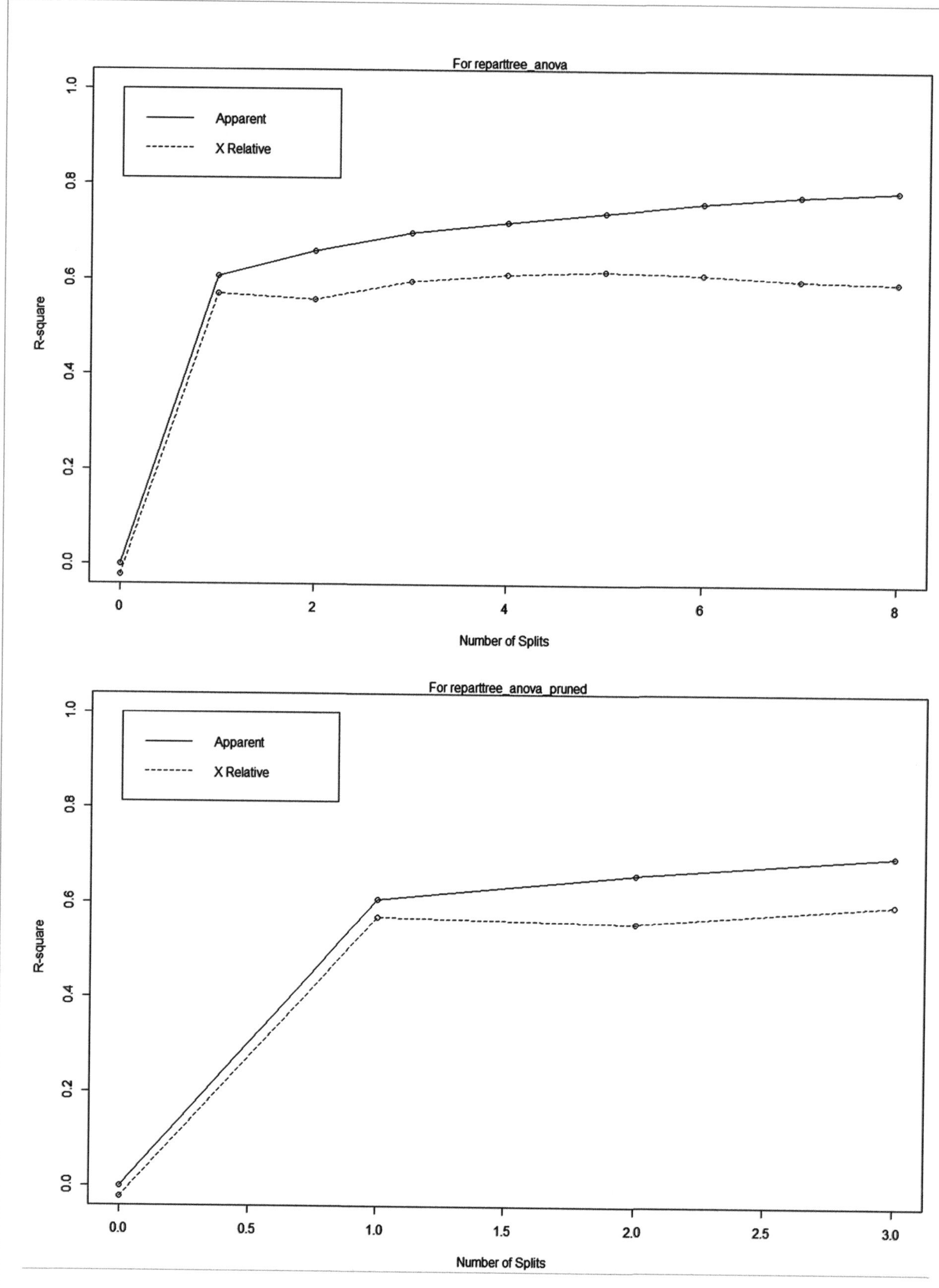

Figure 4.19 R-Squared plots for unpruned and pruned regression trees

of which we use only the first. Each plot has been labeled with its object name using the `mtext()` command. The plots show that for each model, most of the R-squared gain comes at the first split. One also sees that apparent R-square increases, albeit slowly, as models have more splits, the same is not true of relative R-square.

```
rpart::rsq.rpart(rparttree_anova)
mtext("For reparttree_anova", side=3)
rpart::rsq.rpart(rparttree_anova_pruned)
mtext("For reparttree_anova-pruned", side=3)
```

4.15.12 MSE for regression trees

Mean square error (MSE) is a leading model performance metric for regression trees. As discussed in the section on "Interpreting tree summaries" for regression trees, MSE is printed for each terminal node as part of output for the `summary(rparttree _ anova)` command. However, the rpart package does not produce an MSE value for the model as a whole. This is produced by the `validate()` function of the package "RMS".

For purposes of the `validate()` command, when producing the regression (anova) model using `rpart()`, the `model=TRUE, x=TRUE, y=TRUE` options must be used. In the command below, these are the final options in the `rpart()` command:

```
library(rms)

rparttree_anova2 <- rpart(literacy ~ regionid + population + areasqmiles +
poppersqmile + coast_arearatio +  netmigration + Infantdeathsper1k + infdeaths +
gdppercapitalindollars  + phonesper1000 + arablepct +  cropspct + otherpct +
birthrate + deathrate, method="anova", data=world, model=TRUE, x=TRUE, y=TRUE)
```

We can simplify discussion in this section by copying the rpart object to "df" (for data frame).

```
df <- rparttree_anova2
```

Below, the `set.seed()` command assures the same results are obtained on each run. Otherwise cross-validation estimates would differ each time. The `rms:validate()` command assures that the `validate()` function from the rms package is used.

```
set.seed(123)
out <- rms::validate(df, method="boot", rule="p", pr=FALSE)
out
```

[Output:]

```
  10-fold cross-validation
           k size Dxy.apparent   Dxy.val MSE.apparent  MSE.val
  1 0.60703062    0    0.1503648 0.1232378    284.07396 305.9480
  2 0.05150400    1    0.3856959 0.3546554    138.63976 192.2582
  3 0.03993121    2    0.4497417 0.3191884    118.14648 185.5328
  4 0.02137665    3    0.5077328 0.3043595    103.30910 208.2810
  5 0.02075588    4    0.5110803 0.3045759     99.30073 212.6737
  6 0.02023461    5    0.5110803 0.3045759     99.30073 212.6737
  7 0.01486363    6    0.5940189 0.3617013     87.66521 211.4259
  8 0.01036514    7    0.6111172 0.3886422     81.78519 209.2311
  9 0.01000000    8    0.6126954 0.3886422     81.39263 209.0102
```

In tenfold cross-validation, for the first cross-validation, the first 10% of data rows are set aside for validation and the other 90% used for training. In the second cross-validation, the second 10% of cases are set aside and the rest used for validation. And so on. On the final cross-validation, the last 10% are used for validation. At each step the mean square error is calculated for the training set and for the test set.

The `out$mse.val` element contains the MSE values for the validation set in each fold. That is, "val" MSE refers to validated accuracy on the test (validation) samples, which some might label the cross-validated MSE.

```
out$mse.val
[Output:]
   [1] 305.9480 187.8105 161.9997
   [4] 171.3401 175.7328 175.7328
   [7] 176.2515 174.3824 174.0186
```

The `out$mse.app` element contains the MSE values for the training set in each of the folds. That is, "app" refers to apparent accuracy on training samples, which some might label apparent MSE. Apparent MSE is always lower than cross-validated MSE.

```
out$mse.app
[Output:]
   [1] 284.07396 138.63976 118.14648
   [4] 103.30910  99.30073  99.30073
   [7]  87.66521  81.78519  81.39263
```

What is "the" mse? It is most common to use the mean MSE for the validation sets, though the median might be used. The former is the most common value and is appropriate for sample data. Typically error is greater for cross-validation (mse.val) than for the non-cross-validated model (mse.app), as here.

```
mean(out$mse.app)
 [1]  121,5126
mean(out$mse.val)
 [1]  189.2463
```

When comparing models, lower mean square error is better. There is no rule-of-thumb cutoff for a "good model". It is simply the lower the MSE, the better, with MSE = 0 reflecting a perfect model.

4.15.13 The confusion matrix

Confusion matrices and related coefficients discussed with regard to classification trees assume a binary dependent variable and an associated 2-by-2 table of actual versus predicted responses. As regression trees have more response categories (9 in the current example), regression trees with rpart's `method=anova` do not output a confusion matrix. It is still possible, however, to output an observed-by-predicted scatterplot. This was done for the current example in Figure 4.17.

4.15.14 The ROC curve and AUC

For the same reasons as for the confusion matrix, ROC curves, AUC coefficients, lift plots, and gains plots based on the `performance()` command, and precision/recall plots are not available for regression trees created by `rpart()` with `method=anova` as they were for classification trees.

4.15.15 Gains plots

Gains plots are commonly implemented by the "gains" package in R, which requires a vector of predicted values and a vector of observed values. For the current example, these are predanova and world$literacy, both treated previously. Implementation uses the `gains()`command of the "`gains`" package. The syntax of the `gains()` command requires, at a minimum, specifying an `rpart()` object (rparttree_anova), a vector containing observed values of the outcome (world$literacy), a vector containing predicted values (predanova), and the number of groups (nine terminal nodes for the rparttree_anova solution).

For reading convenience, we recreate the rparttree_anova and predanova objects. The predanova object was added to the world data frame with the column name "predanova".

```
set.seed(123)

rparttree_anova <- rpart(literacy ~ region + population + areasqmiles + poppersqmile +
coast_arearatio +  netmigration + Infantdeathsper1k + infdeaths +
gdppercapitalindollars + phonesper1000 + arablepct + cropspct + otherpct + birthrate +
deathrate, method="anova", data=world)

predanova <- predict(rparttree_anova, type = "matrix")
world$predanova <- predanova
```

We now issue the `gains()` command, placing results in the "gainsobj2" object. Setting the random seed assures that the same (but arbitrary) confidence limits will be computed for each run of the syntax. Also note that the number of groups is 9, which is the number of terminal nodes in rparttree_anova. Below, the settings for the CI may be "none", "normal", "t", or "boot". If it is "boot" then CI will vary for each run due to random resampling.

```
library(gains)
set.seed(123)

gainsobj2 <- gains::gains(actual=as.numeric(world$literacy), predicted=predanova,
groups=9, conf=c("normal"), boot.reps=1000, conf.level=0.95)
```

The gains table. The just-created gainsobj2 object is of class "gains". Its contents are listed simply by typing its name, giving the gains table:

```
gainsobj2
```

[Output:]

Depth of File	N	Cume N	Mean Resp	Cume Mean Resp	Cume Pct of Total Resp	Lift ndex	Cume Lift	Mean Model Score	CI for Mean Resp Lower	CI for Mean Resp Upper
37	79	79	97.20	97.20	43.5%	117	117	97.20	96.44	97.96
41	7	86	91.69	96.75	47.1%	110	116	91.69	87.89	95.48
63	48	134	90.89	94.65	71.8%	109	114	90.89	88.46	93.33
72	18	152	78.86	92.78	79.9%	95	111	78.86	74.27	83.45
75	7	159	78.39	92.15	83.0%	94	111	78.39	67.56	89.21
79	9	168	75.18	91.24	86.8%	90	110	75.18	65.07	85.29
87	16	184	60.16	88.54	92.3%	72	106	60.16	53.25	67.06
96	19	203	53.07	85.22	98.0%	64	102	53.07	47.35	58.80
100	9	212	39.47	83.28	100.0%	47	100	39.47	29.75	49.18

In output above there are nine rows, corresponding to the nine terminal nodes in the rparttree_anova regression tree. The rows are sorted by descending mean response, from node 15 = 97.20% predicted literacy in row 1 to node 4 = 39.47% predicted literacy in the bottom row. For more detailed explanation of columns in this table, see the discussion in the online supplement "Gains Plots for Classification Trees" located in readings for Chapter 4 in the Support Material (www.routledge.com/9780367624293) for this book.

The contents of any column may be listed as shown below for column 4, which is mean response. This command is equivalent to the command `gainsobj2$mean.resp`. The contents of all columns may be listed by the command `gainsobj2[]` (output not shown here).

```
gainsobj2[4]
```

[Output:]

```
$mean.resp
[1] 97.20127 91.68571 90.89167
[4] 78.86111 78.38571 75.17778
[7] 60.15625 53.07368 39.46667
```

The gains plot (also called the "gains chart") contains a graphical version of the gains table information. It is obtained using the `plot()` command in conjunction with an object of class "gains", here gainsobj2. The plot is shown in Figure 4.20. Type `help(plot.gains)`for more information on plotting options.

The following plotting options are used:

- type: Type of plot. The default is "b" for points and lines.
- pch: Vector of length 3 specifying the plotting characters for the series of mean response rates, cumulative mean response rates, and mean predicted response rates, respectively.
- lwd: Sets line width.
- cex: Sets the size of symbols.

```
plot(gainsobj2, y=NULL, xlab="Depth of File", ylab="Mean Response", type="b",
pch=c(1,2,3), legend=c("Mean Response","Cum Mean","Mean Predicted"), lwd=2,
cex = 2.5)
```

In Figure 4.20 the y-axis, labeled "mean response", is the national literacy rate. The "Mean Response" red line has 9 symbols, one for each terminal node in the regression tree solution. Nodes are ordered descending by predicted literacy rate, ranging from 97.2% for the highest node to 39.5% for the node with the lowest estimated literacy.

The x-axis in Figure 4.20 "depth of file", drawn from the first column in the gains table shown above. Depth of file represents the cumulative percent of nations associated with each row (each terminal node). The right-most point is always 100% of the sample. As 37% of observations are associated with row 1, the range of the x-axis is from 37 to 100, with some margin.

The gains plot has three lines, though in this instance two of the lines overlay each other.

- Mean response: The mean response line is simply the line plot of the "Mean Resp" column in the gains table.
- Predicted mean response: The predicted mean response in a regression tree is the same as the mean response when the "predicted" vector is, like predanova, the result of applying `predict()` to an rpart object such

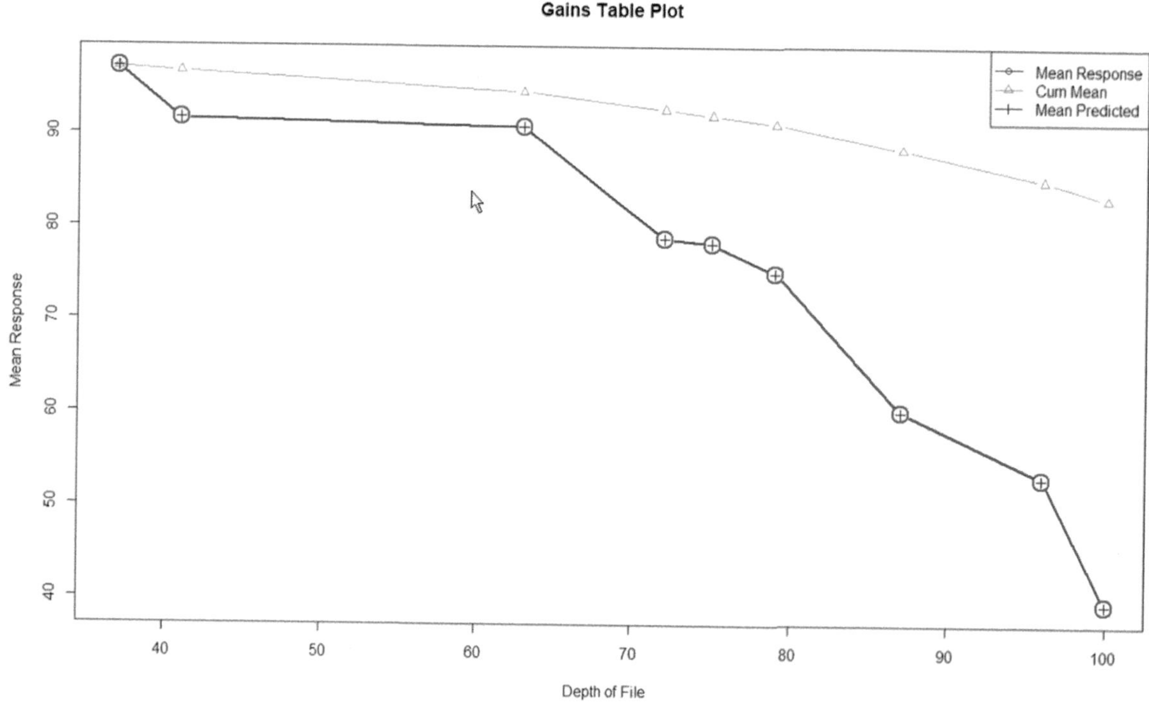

Figure 4.20 Gains plot for rparttree_anova

as rparttree_anova. This is why the gains table has no column for it. The `plot.gains` module, however, automatically creates a line for it. In Figure 4.20, this line overlays the mean response line. However, if the "predicted" vector is based on something else, such as OLS multiple regression, the predicted mean response line will differ from the mean response line.

- Cumulative mean response: This is a plot of the "Cume Mean Resp" column in the gains table. At the top-most node we are considering 79 nations and estimating a mean literacy rate of 97.20%. By the time we reach the bottom row in the gains table, we have considered 100% of the 212 nations and are estimating a mean literacy rate of 83.28%.

The gains plot shows, for instance, that roughly two-thirds of the nations as shown on the x-axis have a national literacy rate (response) of about 90% or higher as shown on the y-axis.

4.15.16 Gains plot with OLS comparison

Gains plots are one way to compare models. In this section we compare mean response in the rparttree_anova solution with predicted means in a solution based on OLS regression. That is, we create a gains table in which the "predicted" vector consists of fitted values from OLS. The resulting gains table is shown in Figure 4.21.

In R, multiple regression is implemented with the `lm()` linear model function, which is part of the system stats library. Figure 4.21 compares estimates using `rpart()` with estimates using OLS multiple regression. Though `rpart()` regression trees and OLS multiple regression both use the term "regression", the estimates are not the same. In the example below, OLS regression computes slopes (b coefficients) using all the input variables on a population-averaged basis and then computes an estimated literacy value for each nation. The `rpart()` estimate is based on a more parsimonious model using only a few of the input variables to cluster the nations into nine nodes, with any specific nation's estimated literacy being the average for all nations in its node.

Prior to creating the gains table we use the `lm()` command to create an output object called "OLSfit", containing OLS predictions. The variables in the model are the same as for rparttree_anova. After creating OLS fit, we put the predicted (a.k.a., fitted or estimated) values in an object called "OLSpred".

```
OLSfit <- lm(literacy ~ regionid + population + areasqmiles +  poppersqmile + coast_
arearatio + netmigration + Infantdeathsper1k + infdeaths + gdppercapitalindollars +
phonesper1000 + arablepct + cropspct + otherpct + birthrate + deathrate, data=world)
OLSpred <- fitted(OLSfit)
```

We use OLSpred as the "predicted" vector in `the gains()` command to create the object called gainsobj3.

```
library(gains)

gainsobj3 <-gains::gains(actual = as.numeric(world$literacy),predicted=OLSpred,
groups=10,conf=c("normal"), boot.reps=1000, conf.level=0.95)
```

Note that gainsobj3 is different in nature from gainsobj2. Gainsobj3 divides the population into deciles (hence 10 groups), whereas gainsobj2 divided the population as grouped into nine nodes. Therefore, the gains table differs as well. The cumulative mean response for 100% of the population of nations is the same (83.28% literacy) but the mean response is different since the rows represent different groups (deciles rather than nodes).

```
gainsobj3
```

[Output:]

```
 Depth                              Cume    Cume Pct                        Mean          CI for
  of               Cume    Mean     Mean    of Total   Lift    Cume        Model        Mean Resp
 File      N        N      Resp     Resp        Resp   Index   Lift        Score      Lower Upper
--------------------------------------------------------------------------------------------------
   10     21       21     98.47    98.47       11.7%    118     118       103.20      97.70 99.24
   20     21       42     97.98    98.22       23.4%    118     118        98.37      97.03 98.94
```

```
 30   21    63   95.31   97.25    34.7%   114   117    96.45   91.94 98.69
 40   21    84   94.15   96.48    45.9%   113   116    94.24   90.34 97.96
 50   22   106   91.90   95.53    57.4%   110   115    90.57   89.57 94.22
 60   21   127   91.36   94.84    68.2%   110   114    86.70   89.00 93.72
 70   21   148   81.37   92.93    77.9%    98   112    80.51   76.91 85.82
 80   21   169   74.81   90.68    86.8%    90   109    70.68   67.31 82.31
 90   21   190   56.50   86.90    93.5%    68   104    61.40   49.83 63.16
100   22   212   52.00   83.28   100.0%    62   100    51.78   44.67 59.32
```

The following table may be helpful to recap the objects involved in the comparison of rpart with linear regression:

Regression tree			**Linear regression**
Object	**Result of**	**Object**	**Result of**
rparttee_anova	`rpart()`	OLSfit	`lm()`
predanova	`predict()`	OLSpred	`fitted()`
gainsobj2	gains(0 with predicted = predanova	gainsobj3	`gains()` with predicted = OLSpred

To proceed to the gains plot itself, we use the following command. The plot is shown in Figure 4.21. Note that the pch option selects the symbol set; lwd sets line width; cex sets symbol size; and asp sets aspect ratio

```
plot(gainsobj3, y=NULL, xlab="Depth of File", ylab="Mean Response", type="b",
pch=c(1,2,3), legend=c("Mean Response","Cum Mean","Mean OLS"), lwd=2, cex=1.5, asp=.75)
```

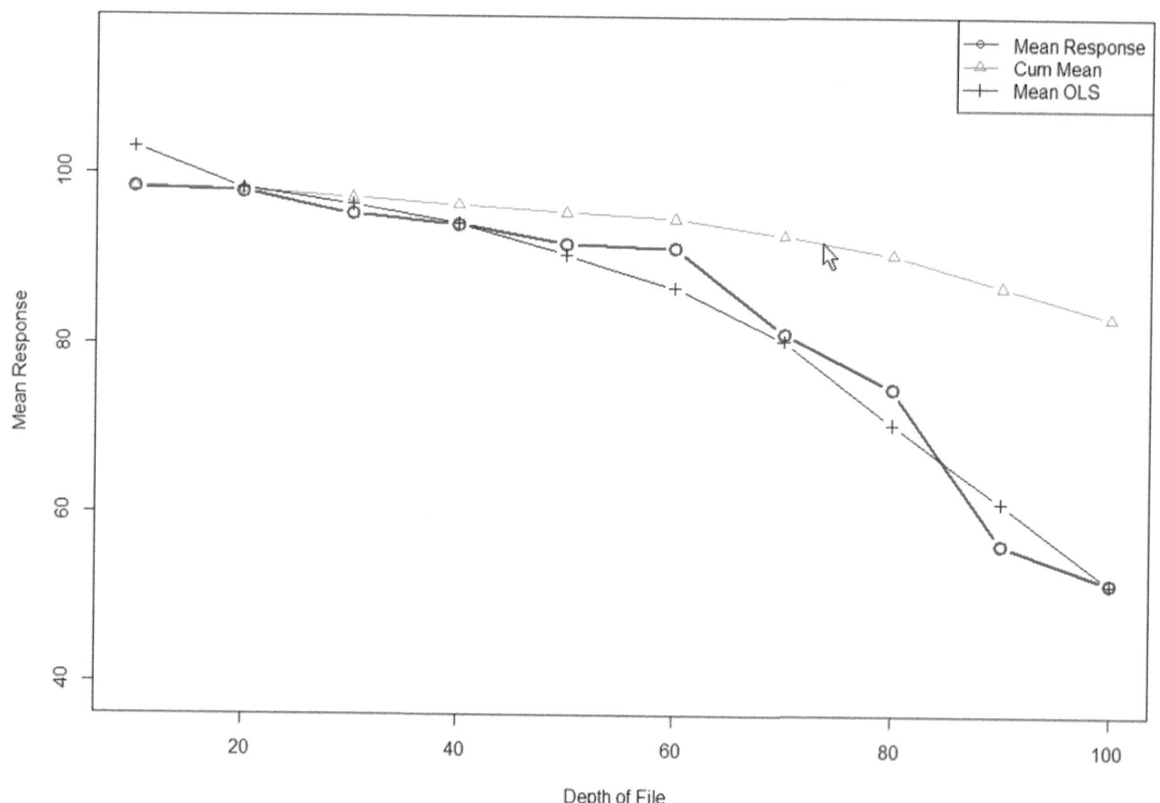

Figure 4.21 Gains plot, regression tree vs. OLS prediction

In Figure 4.21, the red line with circle symbols is mean response from the rpart regression tree solution. Points are regression tree predictions for nodes in descending order of mean response, which is descending order of estimated literacy. The blue line with plus symbols are predictions from OLS regression. However, differences exist by decile. For example, for the 10% of nations with highest literacy, the OLS model predicts over 100% literacy, which is outside the valid range, whereas the `rpart()` prediction is 98.56% literacy. For the next cumulative 40% of the population, OLS and `rpart()` estimates are very similar. For the half of nations in the lower literacy deciles, OLS and `rpart()` predictions usually differ somewhat until depth of file = 100, when the two converge.

The gains plot shows us that the regression tree and OLS regression solutions differ, though they are broadly similar. The plot does not tell us whether one is better than the other. One way to answer this question is to see which predictions correlate more highly with observed values of literacy. As literacy, predanova, and OLSpred are all continuous numeric variables, we may use the `cor()` command, which implements the usual Pearson correlation coefficient. To do this we first add OLSpred into the world data frame, which already has a column for predanova.

```
world$OLSpred<-OLSpred
```

Then we may see how observed values (world$literacy) correlate with the predictions from OLS regression (world$OLSpred) and from rpart regression tree predictions (predanova).

```
cor(world$literacy, world$predanova)
        [1] 0.886102
cor(world$literacy, world$OLSpred)
        [1] 0.8498829
```

The rpart regression tree predictions are better, at r = .89 compared to r = .85 for OLS regression. As this is a census of all nations of interest, significance testing of this difference is not appropriate. Perhaps more noteworthy, the rpart solution was much more parsimonious, using only six predictors compared to a much larger number (all) predictors, as shown below. While normally a researcher would report a more parsimonious solution that arrived at better predictions, the real question is the non-statistical one of which model provided more insight for purposes of theory construction and explanation. It is not necessary to choose between regression trees and linear regression. Rather, the researcher should glean as much insight as is possible from both models.

Variables in the regression tree solution

```
printcp(rparttree_anova)
[Partial output:]
      Variables actually used in tree construction:
      [1] arablepct     birthrate     otherpct
      [4] phonesper1000 poppersqmile  regionid
```

Variables in the OLS solution

```
OLSfit
[Partial output:]
 Coefficients:
(Intercept)            regionidBA    regionidCW                regionidDQ
    -2.792e+03           1.931e+00      1.742e+01                 1.430e+01
    regionidEE          regionidLA     regionidNE                 regionidNF
     2.506e+00           1.472e+00     -3.073e+00                -1.292e+01
    regionidNO          regionidOC     regionidSA                 regionidWE
     4.131e+00           2.014e-01     -3.036e+00                -1.581e+00
    population         areasqmiles   poppersqmile           coast_arearatio
    -1.045e-09          -4.595e-07     -2.661e-04                -2.489e-03
  netmigration   Infantdeathsper1k   infdeathsLow  gdppercapitalindollars
    -4.173e-02          -2.399e-01      4.193e+00                 1.517e-04
```

```
honesper1000      arablepct     cropspct          otherpct
  -2.802e-03      2.875e+01     2.916e+01         2.889e+01
   birthrate      deathrate
  -5.616e-01      5.502e-01
```

4.16 The tree package

Treatment of the `tree()` program for decision trees in R is presented in an online supplement to Chapter 4, found in the student section of this book's Support Material (www.routledge.com/9780367624293).

4.17 The `ctree()` program for conditional decision trees

Treatment of conditional decision trees with the `ctree()` program in R is presented in an online supplement to Chapter 4, found in the student section of this book's Support Material (www.routledge.com/9780367624293). Conditional trees are notable for incorporating significance testing.

4.18 More decision trees programs for R

As mentioned earlier, the R community is prolific in generating new and diverse programs for implementing classification trees, regression trees, and related forms of machine learning. Many of these have been inventoried, with Internet links, by Torsten Hothorn (2018), a biostatistician at the University of Zurich.[8] Below we mention just a few of the much larger number of additional R programs for single decision trees. A full listing of R packages by name is at: https://cran.r-project.org/web/packages/available_packages_by_name.html

A partial alphabetical list of packages includes the following packages. More are added regularly.

- "BART", "bartMachine", and "BayesTree" create Bayesian additive regression trees.
- "boostmtree" is for boosted multivariate trees for longitudinal data.
- The "C50" package can fit C5.0 classification trees, rule-based models, including boosted versions.
- The "collapsibleTree" package supports interactive collapsible tree diagramming, allowing the researcher to click on any node to expand or collapse it. Works with the "d3Tree" package and the JavaScript Library.
- The "Cubist" package fits tree-like rule-based models using linear regression models in the terminal leaves, instance-based corrections and boosting.
- "DIFtree" is used for item-focused trees in item analysis. See also the "irtrees" and "ItemResponseTrees" packages for item analysis.
- "DStree" is for recursive partitioning of discrete-time survival trees. See also "MST" for multivariate survival trees.
- The "dtree" package integrates rpart, party, partykit, evtree, rf, lm, and caret methods into one package.
- The "extraTree" package is for the extremely randomized tree method for regression and classification problems.
- The "ggtree" package creates dendrograms and tree diagrams using ggplot2.
- The package "glmertree" is for generalized linear mixed model trees.
- The package "glmtree" is for logistic regression trees.
- The package "LTRCtrees" implements survival trees, including left-truncation and interval-censoring in addition to right-censoring.
- The package "maptree" provides graphical tools for tree visualization.
- The package "model4you" can be used for stratified and other complex tree and forest designs, including for treatment effects.
- "MplusTrees" is for decision trees in conjunction with structural equation models using Mplus. See also the "semtree" package.
- The package "networktree" is for recursive partitioning of network models.
- The package "outliertree" is for explainable outlier detection through decision trees.

- "ParallelTree" is for visualizing multilevel data.
- The "policytree" package is for policy learning via doubly robust empirical welfare maximization over trees.
- The "psychotree" package is for recursive partitioning for psychometric models.
- The package "REEMtree" provides tree-based modeling for longitudinal and panel data incorporating random effects.
- The "rpartScore" package is for rpart classification trees with ordinal data.
- The package "RPMM" supports recursively partitioning mixture models for heterogeneous data.
- The "RWeka" package is a toolbox of partitioning algorithms, including interfaces for new variants of algorithms like C4.5 and M5. It includes the `JRip()` command to implement the "RIPPER" propositional rule learner.
- The "splinetree" package is for longitudinal CART.
- The package "structree" is for tree-structured clustering.
- The package "tbmf" is for tree-based moving average forecasting models.
- The package "TimeVTree" supports functions for a tree-based approach to survival data, including `coxph.tree()` and `plot_coxphtree()`
- The package "trtf" implements transformation trees for discrete and continuous predictive distributions and also supports censoring and truncation.
- The package "vcrpart" implements tree-based varying coefficient regression for generalized linear and ordinal mixed models.
- The package "visTree" visualizes decision tree subgroups.

4.19 Chapter 4 command summary

For convenience for those wishing to try models out for themselves, this book's Support Material (www.routledge.com/9780367624293) contains a listing of the main commands used in Chapter 4. This listing may be handy for readers following along with the book using their home or office computers. For topics presented as online supplements (the `tree()` and `ctree()` programs), the command summary is at the end of these supplements.

Endnotes

1. https://cran.r-project.org/web/views/MachineLearning.html
2. http://scikit-learn.org/stable/
3. The "ptitanic" data are a data frame located in the "rpart.plot" package. This is not to be confused with the "Titanic" data in the "datasets" package in R. The two have different variables.
4. https://gormanalysis.com/magic-behind-constructing-a-decision-tree/
5. Index of `rpart` package components:

```
car.test.frame        Automobile Data from 'Consumer Reports' 1990
car90                 Automobile Data from 'Consumer Reports' 1990
cu.summary            Automobile Data from 'Consumer Reports' 1990
kyphosis              Data on Children who have had Corrective Spinal Surgery
labels.rpart          Create Split Labels For an Rpart Object
meanvar.rpart         Mean-Variance Plot for an Rpart Object
na.rpart              Handles Missing Values in an Rpart Object
path.rpart            Follow Paths to Selected Nodes of an Rpart Object
plot.rpart            Plot an Rpart Object
plotcp                Plot a Complexity Parameter Table for an Rpart Fit
post.rpart            PostScript Presentation Plot of an Rpart Object
predict.rpart         Predictions from a Fitted Rpart Object
print.rpart           Print an Rpart Object
printcp               Displays CP table for Fitted Rpart Object
prune.rpart           Cost-complexity Pruning of an Rpart Object
residuals.rpart       Residuals From a Fitted Rpart Object
rpart                 Recursive Partitioning and Regression Trees
rpart.control         Control for Rpart Fits
```

```
rpart.exp               Initialization function for exponential fitting
rpart.object            Recursive Partitioning and Regression Trees  Object
rsq.rpart               Plots the Approximate R-Square for Different Splits
snip.rpart              Snip Subtrees of an Rpart Object
solder                  Soldering of Components on Printed-Circuit Boards
stagec                  Stage C Prostate Cancer
summary.rpart           Summarize a Fitted Rpart Object
text.rpart              Place Text on a Dendrogram Plot
xpred.rpart             Return Cross-Validated Predictions
```

6. For regression trees `(method="anova")`, the count (n) is listed. For Poisson, #events/n is listed.
7. Had one wanted to see the full tree with the maximum number of splits, simply add the control parameter `control=list(cp=0)` to the `rpart()` command, revealing a tree with 17 terminal nodes rather than 9.
8. See https://cran.r-project.org/web/views/MachineLearning.html.

Chapter 5

Random forests

PART I: OVERVIEW OF RANDOM FORESTS IN R

5.1 Introduction

Ensemble techniques like random forest (RF) often outperform decision trees discussed in Chapter 4. Random forest algorithms may be applied to both classification and regression problems. Like all statistical procedures, there are pros and cons to random forests. These pros and cons are discussed below. First, however, we seek to suggest the value of RF for social scientists by drawing a few recent examples from the literature.

5.1.1 Social science examples of random forest models

The following cited research examples are only a few arbitrary selections from a much, much larger literature applying RF to social science topics.

In Anthropology

- Marcin Bugdol et al. (2019) used RF in their study evaluating the menarcheal status of girls on the basis of their voice features and measurements of 20 anthropological features. Menarcheal status, which has to do with girls' first menstruation, is important in anthropological understanding of status relationships but requires unobtrusive measurement. The authors compared RF with linear discriminant analysis (LDA) and support vector machine (SVM) regression in a tenfold cross-classification process. They found RF to provide classification accuracy superior to LDA or SVM and concluded that their method could "be used for automatic recognition of girls' menarcheal status using voice signal" (p. 296).

In Economics

- Ciner (2019) studied the ability of random forests to predict industry stock market returns, finding RF to yield "statistically and economically significant predictive power" and to reveal "interdependencies among industry returns" (p. 58). In contrast, when "several other methods are used for regression, including the conventional OLS, the forecast accuracies are poor" (p. 58). In general, Ciner found that RF's inherently nonlinear models combined with validating results through out-of-sample testing outperformed traditional models and pointed up the fact that in traditional models, "sample statistical significance does not always translate into out of sample predictive accuracy" (p. 58).

DOI: 10.4324/9781003109396-5

In Geography

- Reades, De Souza, and Hubbard (2019) studied the process of gentrification by using RF methodology to "tease out the trajectories of 4,835 London neighborhoods between 2001 and 2021, based on analysis of social, economic and environmental variables" (p. 924). In addition to making substantive predictions about which neighborhoods were on the "uplift", the authors compared methods, finding that their tuned RF model outperformed multiple regression by over 10% across all performance measures (R-squared, mean square error (MSE), and other metrics).

In Political Science

- Focusing on predicting the onset of civil wars, Wang (2019) used a type of RF to improve upon the work of Muchlinski et al. (2016), whose RF model outperformed three leading logistic regression models previously used for this type of analysis. Wang noted that the Muchlinski et al. paper "has quickly established itself in the machine learning/prediction-inclined community in our discipline" (p. 107). Wang's contribution was to use out-of-sample cross-validation in conjunction with AdaBoosted trees and gradient boosted trees (Hastie, Tibshirani, & Friedman, 2013), showing that this refined/corrected model's improvement from logistic models to RF models was "dramatic" (p. 109).

In Psychology

- Balakrishnan et al. (2019) used RF methods to detect cyberbullying automatically, based on user personalities profiled by classic "Big Five" personality scales and as well as based on Twitter features. RF was used to classify Twitter users into four roles: Bully, aggressor, spammer, and normal. In terms of predicting the bully role, the authors found extraversion, agreeableness, neuroticism, and psychopathy had the largest impacts on cyberbullying compared to other psychological traits, and that these provided the best models for predicting cyberbullying from among all models tested. RF has become a well-established method in psychology for the study of cyberbullying and this disciplinary popularity was stated by the authors as the reason for its selection as a methodology (p. 254).

In Sociology

- Baćak and Kennedy (2019) sought to predict prison violence and to rank predictor variables by their importance. In doing so they compared some 25 models, including not only RF but also parametric multiple regression spline regression, Bayesian regression, generalized regression, logistic regression, k-nearest neighbors, and simple mean substitution predictions. They found the single best algorithm to be RF, matching the performance of the authors "Super Learner" algorithm-search software. In particular, the authors found "there was much predictive accuracy to be gained over logistic regression, which is the most commonly used prediction method in practice" in past prison violence research (p. 725).

5.1.2 Advantages of random forests

Often-cited desirable features of random forests are listed here.

- Random forests address a wide range of problems, including prediction of outcomes; organizing observations into classes; selection of the most important predictor variables with respect to a given target variable; and survival analysis problems.
- As an ensemble method, random forests average across a large number of individual solutions, increasing the chance that results will be stable and generalizable.
- Both categorical and continuous predictors may be used, and likewise the outcome variable may be categorical or continuous. For categorical predictors, character coding is supported.
- Random forests take nonlinearities into account automatically.
- Random forests take interaction effects into account automatically.

- Random forests take multilevel effects into account automatically.
- Random forests are a nonparametric procedure.
- Random forests are robust against multicollinearity of the predictors.
- Random forests handle missing data automatically.
- Random forests support a very large number of predictor variables (even thousands) without the need for pre-determined variable selection. Predictor variables may be of any data level/type.
- For classification models, the solution is equifinal rather than monofinal (i.e., it will reveal multiple paths through a constellation of predictor variables to arrive at the same outcome class of the categorical target variable.

5.1.3 Limitations of random forests

Often-cited disadvantages of random forest methods are likewise listed here.

- For random forests, a random factor is built in, so unless the same random seed is used, a different solution will be returned on each run of the model. The differences in the solution may be non-trivial. Having a very large forest does not completely eliminate instability in random forest methods.
- Unlike classification and regression tree methods, in random forests no graphical decision tree is returned, making the random forest solution less readily interpretable by a lay audience. Output does not include a "typical tree".
- Predictions become unreliable if the OOB (out-of-bag) validation set contains values of variables, which are out of the range of the same variables within the training/test/in-bag set.
- Random forest methods are computer-intensive. For "big data", computing time may be an issue, especially for very large forests.

5.1.4 Data and packages

5.1.4.1 Example data

Example datasets used in this chapter are listed here.

- Boston: Boston housing data contained in the "MASS" package, with 506 observations on 14 variables listed below. There are no missing values and no variables are factors. Source: Harrison, D. & Rubinfeld, D.L. (1978). Hedonic prices and the demand for clean air. *Journal of Environmental Economics and Management* 5: 81-102.

  Variable list

  age: proportion of owner-occupied units built prior to 1940.
  black: 1,000(Bk – 0.63)^2 where Bk is the proportion of blacks by town.
  chas: Charles River dummy variable (= 1 if tract bounds river; 0 otherwise).
  crim: per capita crime rate by town.
  dis: weighted mean of distances to five Boston employment centers.
  indus: proportion of non-retail business acres per town.
  lstat: lower status of the population (percent).
  medv: median value of owner-occupied homes in $1,000s.
  nox: nitrogen oxides concentration (parts per 10 million).
  ptratio: pupil-teacher ratio by town.
  rad: index of accessibility to radial highways.
  rm: average number of rooms per dwelling.
  tax: full-value property-tax rate per $10,000.
  zn: proportion of residential land zoned for lots over 25,000 sq. ft.

- Gssdata: In the "Quick Start" sections, the data file gssdata.csv is used. This contains a small subset of 24 variables from the 2012 General Social Survey. Variables with few missing cases were selected. Nonetheless, remaining missing cases were dropped listwise, resulting in a data frame of 1,785 observations on 24 variables. While useful for instructional purposes, this dataset is not intended for research. For the 2012 or other GSS data sets, go to http://www.gss.norc.org/Get-The-Data. Variables in gssdata include adults, age, attend, babies, bible, born, childs, class, degree, fund, genderl, happy, hhrace, Hispanic, marital, partyid, relig, respnum, satfin, sex, vetyears, and wrkstat. These labels are explained when used below.

- World: Most random forest illustrations in this chapter use the same "world.csv." data file as in Chapter 4. Data rows are 212 nations of the world. For classification trees, the outcome variable is "litgtmean", a binary variable indicating whether the nation is above or below the mean literacy rate for all nations. For regression trees, the outcome variable is "literacy", a continuous variable reflecting national literacy rates. Various economic and demographic variables are available as predictors.

5.1.4.2 R packages used

The following packages are used in this chapter. They may need to be installed on the user's local machine using the `install _ packages()` command.

```
library(corrplot)                    # Used for visualizing correlation matrices
library(factoextra)                  # Visualization for multivariate procedures
library(foreach)                     # Utility for looping without a counter
library(lm.beta)                     # Provides beta weights for regression
library(mlbench)                     # Benchmark data and utilities
library(nnet)                        # Has the multinomial regression program
library(randomForest)                # The leading random forest package in R
library(randomForestExplainer)       # Supplementary statistics for randomForest
library(REAT)                        # Nonlinear curve fitting for scatterplots
library(rpart)                       # Has the rpart() program for decision trees
library(RColorBrewer)                # A color management utility for visualization
```

PART II: QUICK START – RANDOM FORESTS

5.2 Classification forest example: Searching for the causes of happiness

In this example, we use the data file "gssdata.csv:, described in Section 5.1.4.1. The outcome variable of interest is "happy", intended to measure "general happiness", and coded as below:

1. = Very happy
2. = Pretty happy
3. = Not too happy

The predictors of happiness are ten variables commonly asserted to be associated with happiness. Those with an asterisk were coded as factor variables. Binary, ordinal, and continuous variables were treated as numeric.

- age: Age of respondent
- Attend: How often respondent attends religious services
- Bible: Feelings about the Bible*
- Born: Was respondent born in this country?
- Class: Subjective class identification
- Degree: Respondent's highest degree
- Marital: Marital status*
- Satfin: Satisfaction with financial situation

- Sex: Gender
- Wrkstat: Labor force status*

The research question is whether these plausible predictors of happiness can actually serve to correctly predict the level of self-reported happiness, as many would expect. We also show how to compare random forest (RF) predictions with those from multinomial regression (MR).

After setting the working directory, we read in the data. As some variables are numeric (binary, ordinal, or continuous) and some are factors, we use the `colClasses=` option to assign the proper data types.

```
setwd("C:/Data")

# Read in the data, assigning columns their appropriate data classes.
# For instance, the first 6 columns are numeric, then 1 is factor, then y are numeric,
# then 5 are factor, then 4 are numeric, then 1 is factor, for a total of 24 columns.
gssdata <- read.csv("C:/Data/gssdata.csv", header=TRUE, sep = ",", stringsAsFactors =
TRUE, colClasses=c(rep("numeric",6),"factor", rep("numeric",6), rep("factor",6),
rep("numeric",4),"factor"))

# Verify data classes of all columns
sapply(gssdata, class)
[Output:]
       year         id     adults        age     attend
  "numeric"  "numeric"  "numeric"  "numeric"  "numeric"
     babies      bible       born     childs      class
  "numeric"   "factor"  "numeric"  "numeric"  "numeric"
     degree       fund    gender1      happy     hhrace
  "numeric"  "numeric"  "numeric"   "factor"   "factor"
   hispanic    marital    partyid      relig    respnum
   "factor"   "factor"   "factor"   "factor"  "numeric"
     satfin        sex   vetyears    wrkstat
  "numeric"  "numeric"  "numeric"   "factor"

  # Invoke needed packages
  library(randomForest)
```

There is a random variable selection process used at each branch in the random forest to select a finite number (mtry) of predictors. The random seed is used as the starting point and also can make a difference in results. Tuning the RF model for the optimal random seed, value of mtry, and other parameters is discussed in Part III of this chapter.

```
# Set the random seed
set.seed(66)

# Predict "bible" from 10 other variables.
GSSclass <- randomForest::randomForest(happy ~ age+ attend + bible + born + class +
degree + marital + satfin + sex + wrkstat, control=rpart.control(minbucket = 20),
ntree=1501, mtry=3, importance=TRUE, proximity=TRUE, oob.prox=TRUE, data=gssdata)

class(GSSclass)
[Output:]
  [1] "randomForest.formula" "randomForest"

GSSclass
[Partial output:]
                    Type of random forest: classification
                          Number of trees: 1501
      No. of variables tried at each split: 3
              OOB estimate of  error rate: 42.91%
```

```
Confusion matrix:
    1   2  3 class.error
1 188 347 10   0.6550459
2 170 791 31   0.2026210
3  23 185 40   0.8387097
```

Another model performance metric is accuracy, defined as the sum of the confusion matrix diagonal (correct predictions) divided by the number of observations.

```
# Compute accuracy for the RF model based on the confusion matrix.
sum(diag(GSSclass$confusion))/nrow(gssdata)
[1] 0.5708683
```

Thus, for the random forest classification model for the "happy" variable using "gssdata", the accuracy of prediction is 57.09%, with a cross-validated (OOB) error rate of 42.91%. In the formula above we used ten of the available variables as predictors. If we used all available predictors, accuracy would increase further by a small amount. While happy = 2 = "Pretty Happy" is predicted somewhat better than other values of "happy", there is considerable room for improvement. In further analysis we would try to improve upon the accuracy and OOB error through better model specification and optimization, most likely involving the need to add additional variables to gssdata. Put another way, weak results suggest the need for better model specification.

Actual predictions are in the "predicted" element of GSSclass. This vector could be added to the dataset if desired.

```
head(GSSclass$predicted,30)
[Predicted value of "happy" for the first 30 observations:]
  1  2  3  4  5  6  7  8  9 10 11 12 13
  1  1  1  1  3  1  2  1  2  2  2  1  3
 14 15 16 17 18 19 20 21 22 23 24 25 26
  2  2  2  3  2  2  1  2  1  1  2  2  2
 27 28 29 30
  1  2  2  2
 Levels: 1 2 3
```

```
# Add predictions to data frame in memory
gssdata$GSSclasspreds <- GSSclass$predicted
```

By way of comparison, we may now see how a traditional regression method would perform on the same problem. We use MR, which is designed for categorical outcome variables such as "happy". We employ the `multinom()` command from the "nnet" package.

```
library(nnet)
GSSclass_mr <- nnet::multinom(happy ~ age+ attend + bible + born + class + degree +
marital + satfin + sex + wrkstat, data = gssdata)
```

Below, the `multinom()` procedure outputs two model performance measures, residual deviance and AIC. These may be used to compare other models, with lower being less error and better model fit. However, both measures are based on maximum likelihood estimation, which is not used by the `randomForest()` program, so these measures are not appropriate for our comparison of MR with the RF solution.

```
GSSclass_mr
[Partial output:]
  Residual Deviance: 3087.075
  AIC: 3175.075
```

Instead, we use "accuracy" as the performance measure. As for the RF solution, this is based on the confusion table, which is a classification table of observed versus predicted values of "happy" as the outcome variable.

```
# Compute predicted "happy" based on the MR model
preds <- predict(GSSclass_mr)
# Construct the confusion table
GSStable <- table(preds,gssdata$happy)
GSStable
[Output:]
   preds   1   2   3
       1 146 109   8
       2 392 863 209
       3   7  20  31

# Compute accuracy for the MR model based on the confusion table.
sum(diag(GSStable))/nrow(gssdata)
[Output:]
   [1] [1] 0.5826331
```

Discussion: The MR model marginally outperforms the RF model based on accuracy as a performance measure, by 58.3% to 57.09%. We cannot test for significance of this small difference. Both results are marginally better than the null model, under which one would always predict the most numerous category (happy = 2 = 992 count), giving an accuracy of 992/1,785 = 55.6%. The similarity of the RF and MR models leads to the inference that relationships of the predictors with happy are weak and do not involve striking nonlinearities, interaction effects, or multilevel effects which might differentiate the RF model.

While further tuning of the RF model might improve its accuracy, the better interpretation of these results is that the model needs to be better specified because the true causes of "happy" are not in the set of predictors. In the set of predictors were one's age, church attendance, Bible beliefs, whether being born in the United States, one's self-reported social class, one's highest educational degree, one's marital status, being satisfied with one's financial situation, and one's work status. It is not implausible to think that any or all of these might determine one's level of happiness. However, the finding of this exercise is that happiness is not so easily predicted and popular beliefs about the causes of happiness may be wrong.

5.3 Regression forest example: Why so much crime in my town?

In this example, we use the "Boston Housing Study" data on 14 variables for 506 towns in the Boston area. We will use a random forest procedure to predict the variable "crim", which is per capita crime rate by town. The "crim" variable is numeric. Just as the `randomForest()` command will create a classification forest if the outcome variable is a factor, likewise here it will create a regression forest since the outcome is numeric. The remaining 13 variables, described in Section 5.1.4.1 are used as predictors.

```
# Setup
setwd("C:/Data")
library(corrplot)          # Produces correlation plots
library(MASS)              # Has the "Boston" example dataset
library(ggplot2)           # Commands for visualization
library(randomForest)      # The leading random forest package in R
library(REAT)              # Nonlinear curve fitting for scatterplots

# Load in and view "Boston" data
attach(Boston)
View(Boston)
```

List variable names, whose meanings are described in Section 5.1.4.1.
```
names(Boston)
```
[Output:]
```
    [1] "crim"      "zn"        "indus"     "chas"      "nox"
    [6] "rm"        "age"       "dis"       "rad"       "tax"
   [11] "ptratio"   "black"     "lstat"     "medv"
```

Confirm that there are no missing values.
```
any(is.na(Boston))
```
[Output:]
```
   [1] FALSE
```

The correlation matrix plot in Figure 5.1 shows that the highest correlates of “crim” are “rad” and “tax” followed by “lsat; “nox”, “indus”, and “age”. “Rad” is the index for accessibility to radial highways, which tends to be higher for inner city towns. Also radial highways are a get-away factor for crime. “Tax” is property tax per $10,000 and tends to be higher in inner city towns, as does “lsat” (percent of population classes as lower status), “nox” (pollution), “indus” (proportion of non-retail business acres), and “age” (proportion of older homes).

```
Boston_corr_matrix <- cor(Boston)
corrplot::corrplot(Boston_corr_matrix, type="upper", tl.cex=1.6, tl.col="black")
```

In order to see the actual correlation coefficients, we obtain the correlation of crim with all other variables in two steps:

Step 1: Create temp as data frame of all variables except the first, which is crim
```
temp <- Boston[,-1]
```

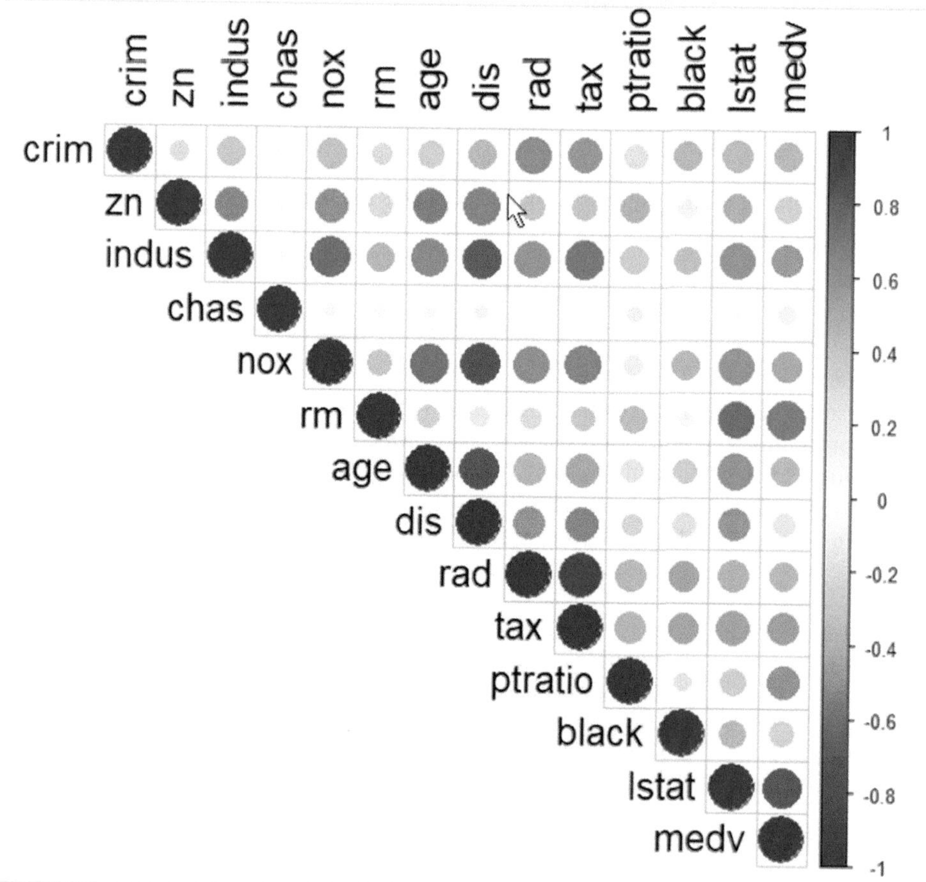

Figure 5.1 Correlation matrix plot for the Boston data frame

```
# Step 2: Correlate Boston$crim with all other variables (which are in temp).
cor(Boston$crim, temp)
              zn     indus        chas       nox         rm
  [1,] -0.2004692 0.4065834 -0.05589158 0.4209717 -0.2192467
             age        dis        rad       tax   ptratio
  [1,] 0.3527343 -0.3796701 0.6255051 0.5827643 0.2899456
           black     lstat       medv
  [1,] -0.3850639 0.4556215 -0.3883046
```

The "REAT" package can demonstrate nonlinearities in the data. If there are nonlinearies, one would expect on this basis alone that the RF model would outperform the OLS model. Below in either the R squared or adjusted R-squared column of `REAT::curvefit()` output, we see that the linear model underperforms all nonlinear models for a model in which "crim" is predicted from "age" of housing. While this only demonstrates nonlinearity in a bivariate model with one predictor (this is the only type of model supported by `curvefit()`), it is quite possible that tests of other variables would show further nonlinearities in the data. Figure 5.2 plots the linear, power, exponential, and logistic solutions for the crim by age model. Note also that the linear regression solution predicts "crim" to be below 0 for age of housing below about 23, which is out of bounds. This does not occur with the nonlinear models.

```
library(REAT)
REAT::curvefit(x=Boston$age, y=Boston$crim, xlab="age", ylab="crim", plot.curves =
TRUE)
[Output:]
   Curve fitting
                           a           b Std. Error a Std. Error b
   Linear      -3.7779063180  0.10778623    0.9439847  0.012736436
   Power        0.0001488556  1.96345267    0.2356865  0.131209214
   Exponential  0.0142975032  0.05056127    0.1908838  0.002575443
   Logistic     8.8019548106 -0.05237688    0.2057723  0.002776322

                 t value a  t value b     Pr(>|t|) a   Pr(>|t|) b
   Linear        -4.002084   8.462825  7.221718e-05 2.854869e-16
   Power        -16.238667  14.964290  5.320670e-48 3.719667e-42
   Exponential  -22.252651  19.632064  6.372400e-77 3.705048e-64
   Logistic      42.775214 -18.865560 7.368277e-170 1.867595e-60

               R squared Adj. R squared  F value       Pr(>F)
   Linear      0.1244215      0.1226842  71.6194 2.854869e-16
   Power       0.3076257      0.3062519 223.9300 3.719667e-42
   Exponential 0.4333373      0.4322129 385.4179 3.705048e-64
   Logistic    0.4138917      0.4127288 355.9093 1.867595e-60
```

We now compute the OLS linear regression model for later comparison with the random forest model. Computation is based on pooled data on all observations in the Boston data frame.

For the OLS regression model, use the `lm()` linear modeling command from R's built-in "stats" package. The dot is shorthand for "all other variables". This model explains about 45.40% of the variance in crime.

```
OLSmodel <- lm(crim~., data=Boston)
OLSfit <- OLSmodel$fitted.values
r_OLS <- cor(Boston$crim, OLSfit)
r_OLS
[Output:]
   [1] 0.6738029
R2_OLS <- r_OLS*r_OLS
R2_OLS
[Output:]
   [1] 0.4540104
```

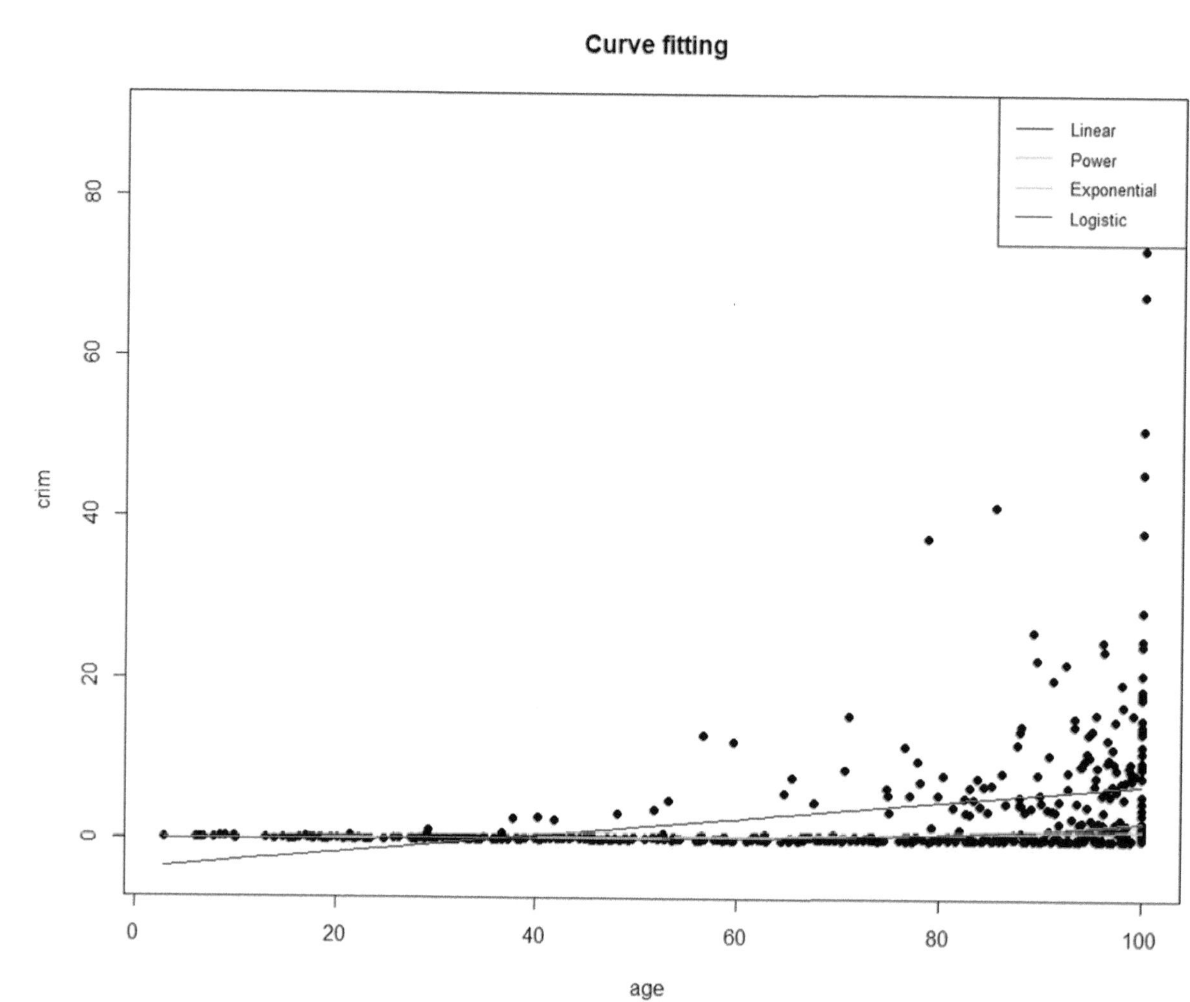

Figure 5.2 Exploring nonlinearity for "crim" as outcome

The R-squared value may be confirmed by using the `summary(OLSmodel)` command. Unfortunately, however, `summary()` does not give equivalent information for RF model.

```
summary(OLSmodel)
[Partial output:]
   Residual standard error: 6.439 on 492 degrees of freedom
   Multiple R-squared:  0.454,    Adjusted R-squared:  0.4396
   F-statistic: 31.47 on 13 and 492 DF,  p-value: < 2.2e-16
```

We now apply the corresponding random forest procedure to the same data.

```
set.seed(123)
RFmodel  <-  randomForest::randomForest(crim ~. , control=rpart.control(minbucket =
10), ntree=1501, mtry=3, importance=TRUE, proximity=TRUE, oob.prox=TRUE,
data=Boston)
RFfit <- RFmodel$predict
```

```
r_RF <- cor(Boston$crim, RFfit)
r_RF
[Output:]
   [1] 0.7441445
R2_RF <- r_RF*r_RF
R2_RF
   [1] 0.5537511
```

The random forest model is shown to account for more of the variance explained (55.38%), as expected based on known nonlinearities in the data. Note that these results are without tuning the RF model and without cross-validation – topics discussed in Part III of this chapter.

There are various criteria for assessing the relative importance of predictors in the RF model. Two of the most common metrics are percent increase in mean square error (%IncMSE) and increase in node purity (IncNodePurity). Both are easily retrieved as the "importance" element of RF model, as shown below. However, the variable importance plots in Figure 5.3 are helpful in visualizing these importance metrics. These metrics, which are only for regression models, are discussed in more detail in Section 5.5.3. In brief, however, the %IncMSE metric is the amount error increases in a given variable if its values are permuted, so that the larger the %IncMSE, the more important the variable (the more important to use the original values, not randomized values). The IncNodePurity metric measures purity, which is small intra-node variance and high inter-node variance. As IncNodePurity has known biases, %IncMSE is the preferred variable importance measure.

```
RFmodel$importance
[Output:]
              %IncMSE IncNodePurity
zn         0.03260431       4.53027
indus      4.27031455    1452.93343
chas       0.11019544      40.36238
nox        5.44751778    2413.19748
rm         9.26865465    2651.90775
age        2.21666565    1609.72443
dis        5.15069050    4247.40222
rad       13.87318194    4497.47790
tax        9.02398219    3603.66819
ptratio    2.45007701     641.15445
black     -0.07100696    2193.70624
lstat      9.80166385    2306.14905
medv      11.43720832    7109.73682

randomForest::varImpPlot(RFmodel)
```

Using %IncMSE as the measure of variable importance, the following four most important variables, in descending order, are:

- rad: Access to radial highways is a surrogate for being in the inner city, where radial highways converge. This is also access to post-crime escape routes.
- tax: Higher property taxes per $10,000 value. The correlation plot showed an inverse relationship: Homes in high crime towns are worthless but taxed at a higher rate.
- indus: High crime towns have a higher proportion of non-retail business acreage.
- lstat: High crime towns have a higher proportion of their population classed as lower status.

To return to this section's heading, "Why so much crime in my town?", put bluntly, if you are living in an inner city town with high tax rates, a lot of land devoted to industry, and a lot of lower status residents, it is predicted that your town will have more crime than average.

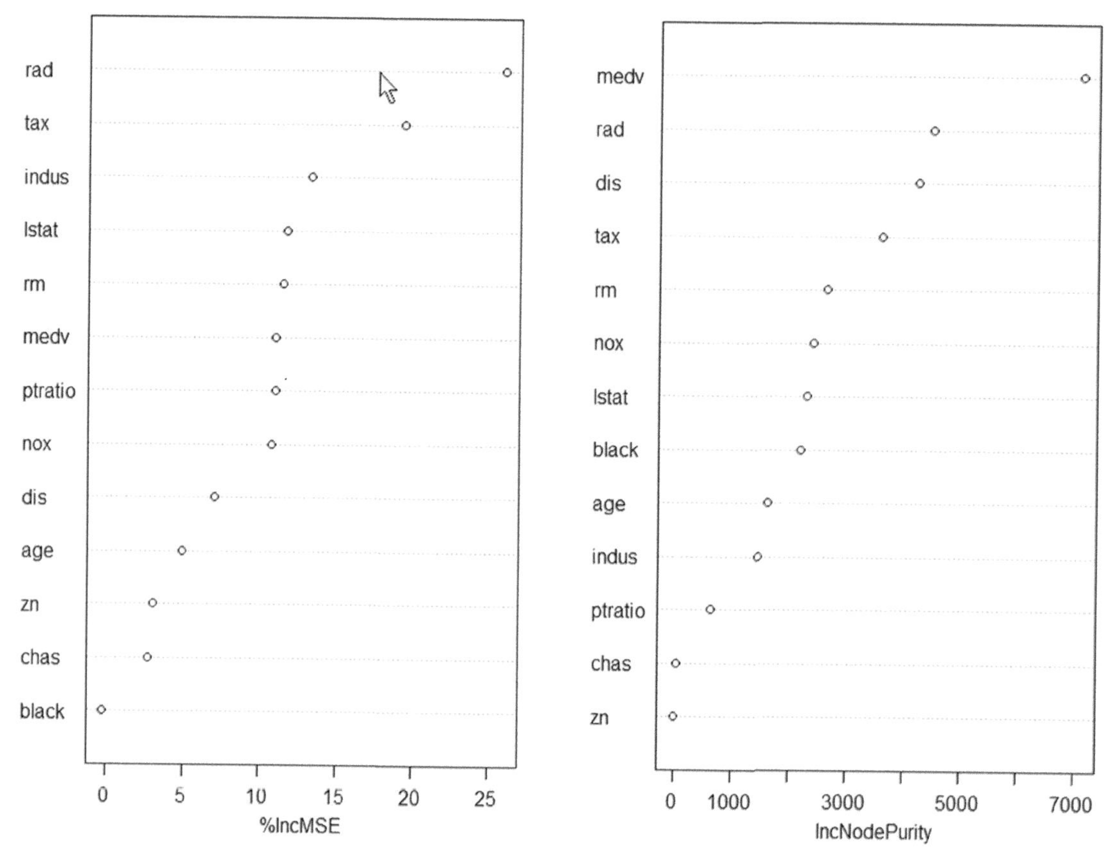

Figure 5.3 Variable importance plots for the RFmodel

PART III: RANDOM FORESTS, IN DETAIL

5.4 Classification forests with `randomForest()`

In this section, we provide more detail on classification forests. We use the 212-nation "world" data treated in Chapter 4. The categorical outcome variable is again "litgtmean", coded "High" if the nation has a national literacy rate above the mean for all nations and coded "Low" if below the mean. No nation is exactly at the mean. As in the "Quick Start" examples above, we use the "randomForest" package. This is by far the leading R package for implementing random forests. The random forest technique is a long-established approach attributed to the work of Leo Breiman and Adele Cutler, based on an algorithm originally written in Fortran (Breiman, 2001).

5.4.1 Setup

First, after setting the working directory we invoke the previously-installed randomForest package. After issuing the `library()` command, one may type `help(randomForest)` for additional information or type `rfNews()` for information on updates. We then read in the world.csv data into the data frame "world", view it, and check for missing values.

```
# Setup
setwd("C:/Data")
library(randomForest)
help(randomForest)
rfNews()
```

```
# Read in data
world <- read.table("world.csv", header = TRUE, sep = ",", stringsAsFactors = TRUE)
View(world)

# Confirm that there are no missing values.
any(is.na(world))
[Output:]
   [1] FALSE

# Set the max.print option to maximum print queue size
options("max.print"=.Machine$integer.max)
```

5.4.2 A basic classification model

Before actually creating a basic classification forest, we go over its most-used options. Options are separated by commas in the `randomForest()` command line. Note that there is no `method=` option as `randomForest()` will automatically select a classification model if the outcome variable is a factor and will select a regression model if the outcome is numeric.

`ntree=1501`	Specify number of trees; 500 is the default. There is a random process underlying random forests such that if the same model is run again, error may vary somewhat. The larger the specified ntree, the less the variation and the more the solution will, on average, represent a stable solution. Many prefer a larger number than the default 500. Also preferred is an ntree with an odd number of trees, in order to break ties (e.g., `ntree = 1501`). If predictor variables have interactions, a large number of trees are recommended.
`mtry=4`	Specify the number of predictors to randomly sample as candidate splitting variables at each split. For classification trees, the default is sqrt(p), where *p* is number of predictor variables. For regression trees, the default is (*p*/3). Or the researcher may enter an integer larger than 0 and no larger than *p*. If mtry is specified as *p* (the number of all the predictor variables) then all variables are used and the benefit of random sampling is lost, resulting in greater error on average. A common strategy is using the highest integer less than the square root of the number of variables in the data frame. For the example data, `mtry=floor(sqrt(ncol(world)))` = 4. The mtry value is one of the parameters that may be adjusted when tuning an RF model. Typically, however, varying mtry has little effect.
`importance=TRUE`	Asks that importance coefficients for input variables be output; FALSE is the default.
`localImp=FALSE`	Computes a casewise importance measure. The default is FALSE. Setting this to TRUE overrides the `importance=` option.
`proximity=TRUE`	Asks for a matrix of proximity measures among the input variables based on the frequency that pairs of data points are in the same terminal nodes. The default is FALSE. We set proximity to TRUE later in order to use proximity information to construct clusters.
`oob.prox=TRUE`	The default is TRUE, meaning that proximity coefficients are computed based on the OOB (out-of-bag = validation = test) subsets. If FALSE, all observations are the basis for the solution.
`do.trace=FALSE`	Gives more verbose output as `randomForest()` runs if set to =TRUE. If set to an integer, verbose output if given for every nth tree (e.g., every 100th tree if the integer is 100). The default is =FALSE, which gives no trace output. Setting to TRUE may be useful for debugging.

There are several other possible input options, including ones dealing with how observations are sampled (with replacement is the default), how many observations are to be sampled, and if sampling is stratified by some categorical variable. Some input settings differ for classification trees compared to regression trees. Type `help(randomForest)` for details.

As `randomForest()` contains a random element, it is possible to get slightly different results each time it is run. Before issuing the `randomForest()` command, however, one can issue the `set.seed()` command as below. To get the same results each time, simple set the seed to the same value prior to running `randomForest()`.

The format for the `randomForest()` command for the classification forest example uses the same model as and follows the format of the `rpart()` classification trees discussed in Chapter 4. We input the same predictor variables as in Chapter 4, except now we are creating a random forest rather than a single classification tree. Note that `rpart()` controls, discussed in Chapter 4, may be used, such as setting the minimum bucket size for terminal nodes (here constraining terminal nodes to have a count of at least 5). The following command creates the output object "RFclass", which is a "randomForest.formula" object of class "randomForest".

```
set.seed(123)

RFclass <- randomForest::randomForest(litgtmean ~ regionid + population +
areasqmiles + poppersqmile + coast_arearatio + netmigration + Infantdeathsper1k +
infdeaths + gdppercapitalindollars + phonesper1000 + arablepct + cropspct + otherpct +
birthrate + deathrate, control=rpart.control(minbucket = 5), ntree=1501, mtry=4,
importance=TRUE, proximity=TRUE, oob.prox=TRUE, data=world)
class(RFclass)
[Output:]
     [1] "randomForest.formula" "randomForest"
```

We list the contents of RFclass below. We see that the error rate is higher for "Low" litgtmean nations than for "High". The overall cross-validated error rate is 15.09%. Later we will investigate whether tuning the RF classification model would improve results. Note that in output below, "OOB" stands for "out of bag" validation, where the "bag" is the training set and OOB refers to the test or validation set. Cross-validation is built into the RFclass algorithm.

```
RFclass
(Partial output)
        Type of random forest: classification
        Number of trees: 1501
        No. of variables tried at each split: 4

                OOB estimate of  error rate: 15.09%
        Confusion matrix:
             High Low class.error
        High  124  16   0.1142857
        Low    16  56   0.2222222
```

The following `summary()` command lists all the components, also called elements, of the RFclass object resulting from the `randomForest()` program. Some elements apply only to classification trees, Type `help(randomForest)` to view the meaning of each component. To view any component, type the `randomForest()` object name (here, RFclass) then a dollar sign followed by the component name. For instance, `RFclass$call` will output the original generating command that created RFclass. Entering `RFclass$predicted` will return a vector of estimates of whether a nation is "High" or "Low" on litgtmean. Other output components are discussed in later sections.

```
summary(RFclass)
[Output:]
                    Length Class  Mode
   call                9   -none- call
   type                1   -none- character
   predicted         212   factor numeric
   err.rate         4503   -none- numeric
```

```
confusion             6   -none- numeric
votes               424   matrix numeric
oob.times           212   -none- numeric
classes               2   -none- character
importance           60   -none- numeric
importanceSD         45   -none- numeric
localImportance       0   -none- NULL
proximity         44944   -none- numeric
ntree                 1   -none- numeric
mtry                  1   -none- numeric
forest               14   -none- list
y                   212   factor numeric
test                  0   -none- NULL
inbag                 0   -none- NULL
terms                 3   terms  call
```

The plot of the RFclass solution is shown in Figure 5.4. Note that the `legend()` command is separate from the `plot()` command even though results of both end up in the same figure.

```
plot(RFclass, col=c("black", "blue","red"), lwd=2)

legend("topright", text.col=c("black", "blue", "red"), legend = c("Mean Error",
"Error for High","Error for Low") )
```

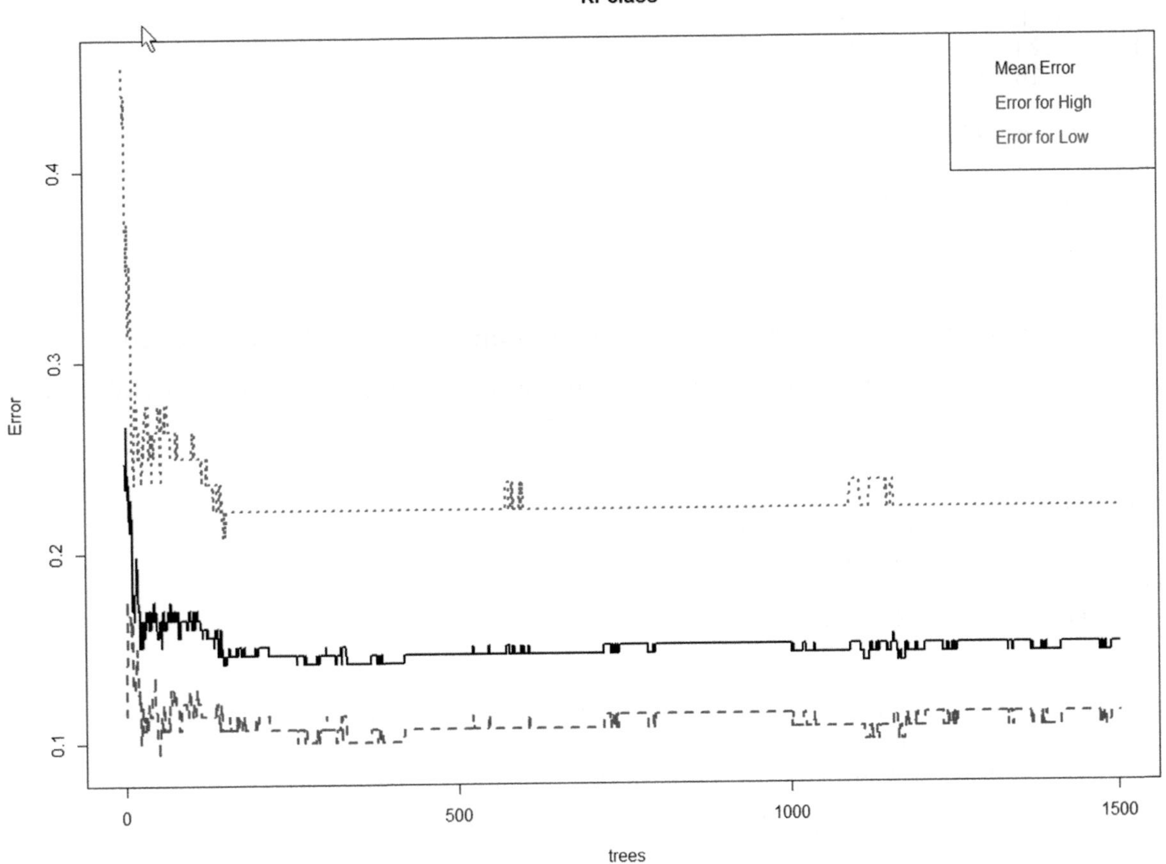

Figure 5.4 Error rates for RFclass by number of trees

In the Figure 5.4 plot, the black line represents the mean error rate across all levels of the outcome variable (i.e., both "High" and "Low" litgtmean). The red and blue lines above and below the mean, respectively, are the class-specific error rates for litgtmean = "Low" and "High" respectively. The x-axis is the number of trees in the solution. The error rates in the plot are the "stabilized" rates, with the right-hand side of the plot showing the rates for the full 1501-tree solution. There is greater error when classifying "Low" than "High". For further information on the `plot()` command, type `help(plot.randomForest)`.

The error rate plot is helpful in estimating the minimum number of trees needed. Here, to minimize error for both "High" and "Low" predictions, no more than 501 trees are needed, not the 1501 requested. In fact, if ntree is set to 501 rather than 1501, OOB mean error drops from 15.09% to 13.65%. On the basis of Figure 5.4 we rerun the model for 501 trees rather than 1501, putting the model in the object "RFclass2".

```
set.seed(123)

RFclass2 <- randomForest::randomForest(litgtmean ~ regionid + population +
areasqmiles + poppersqmile + coast_arearatio + netmigration + Infantdeathsper1k +
infdeaths + gdppercapitalindollars + phonesper1000 + arablepct + cropspct + otherpct +
birthrate + deathrate, control=rpart.control(minbucket = 5), ntree=501, mtry=4,
importance=TRUE, proximity=TRUE, oob.prox=TRUE, data=world)
```

The confusion tables for RFclass and RFclass2 show that the smaller number of trees converged on a solution in which one additional "High" case was classified correctly.

```
RFclass$confusion
```
[Output:]
```
     High Low class.error
High  124  16   0.1142857
Low    16  56   0.2222222
```

```
RFclass2$confusion
```
[Output:]
```
     High Low class.error
High  125  15   0.1071429
Low    16  56   0.2222222
```

5.4.3 Output components of `randomForest()` objects for classification models

The `summary()` command lists a large number of output components for objects created with the `randomForest()`command, such as RFclass or RFclass2.

```
summary(RFclass2)
```
[Partial output:]
```
                Length Class  Mode
call              9    -none- call
type              1    -none- character
predicted       212    factor numeric
```
...

Any components may be listed by using the "$" operator and sent to another object, if desired, using the "<-" operator. For instance, the following command sends model predictions to the factor vector "RFclass2preds". It is of class "factor" because the outcome was a factor and predictions are its strings "High" or "Low".

```
RFclass2preds <- RFclass2$predicted
```

Below we illustrate only a few of the most useful components. Type `help(randomForest)` for a complete list.

TEXT BOX 5.1 Social science applications of R: Predicting Time to Justice

"The quality of the judicial system of a country can be verified by the overall length time of lawsuits, or the lead time," argued Lúcia and Guilherme (2018). Lead time is the time between arraignment in the judicial system and disposition of the case. As such lead time does not measure justice but rather time to justice, or at least time to final adjudication. The authors used Brazilian data on judicial lead time as the outcome variable of their study of time to disposition.

Of particular interest to this textbook, Lúcia and Guilherme compared four forms of modeling: random forest (RF), support vector machines (SVM), naïve Bayes (NB), and neural networks (NN) models. RF models are treated here in this chapter, SVM and NB models in Chapter 6, and NN in Chapter 7. Five different measures of model performance were used: accuracy, sensitivity, specificity, precision, and the F1 measure. As the outcome variable was measured in days and then binned into ranges, the analysis was cast as a classification rather than regression problem.

The evaluation of the models was made using k-fold cross-validation. The authors' comparison among the models showed that the RF and SVM approaches were both very close to each other and were superior to estimates by NN and NB methods. An advantage of RF, the authors noted, was that "Overfitting is not a problem as the generalization error for a forest converges when the number of trees in the forest is large." Performance data comparing methods may be found at https://journals.plos.org/plosone/article/figure?id=10.1371/journal.pone.0198122.t003

Source: Lúcia Adriana Dos Santos Gruginskie & Guilherme Luís Roehe Vaccaro (2018). Lawsuit lead time prediction: Comparison of data mining techniques based on categorical response variable. *PLoS One* 13(6): 1–26. doi:http://dx.doi.org.prox.lib.ncsu.edu/10.1371/journal.pone.0198122

5.4.3.1 Confusion matrix output

The `RFclass2$confusion` component was illustrated at the end of Section 5.4.2, This gives the confusion matrix (the classification table) of correctly and incorrectly classified cases. Below we send this to the object "confusionmatrix" and then list it. In the confusion matrix, columns are the "Observed" and rows are the "Predicted". Below, for instance, 140 nations were predicted to be "High" on litgtmean, of which only 125 actually were.

```
confusionmatrix <- RFclass2$confusion
confusionmatrix
[Output:]
      High Low class.error
  High  125  15   0.1071429
  Low    16  56   0.2222222
```

Using the `summary()` command, however, yields quartile results, not the confusion matrix itself. The litgtmean variable was coded with "High" being the first or lower value.

```
levels(world$litgtmean)
[1] "High" "Low"
```

Therefore, in the class.error column, the 0.1071 is the class error for the minimum or lowest level, which is "High". The "Max." value is 0.2222, which is the classification error for the maximum level, which is "Low". These are the values showing in the confusion table itself.

```
summary(confusionmatrix)
[Output:]
       High             Low           class.error
  Min.   : 16.00   Min.   :15.00   Min.   :0.1071
  1st Qu.: 43.25   1st Qu.:25.25   1st Qu.:0.1359
```

```
Median : 70.50   Median :35.50   Median :0.1647
Mean   : 70.50   Mean   :35.50   Mean   :0.1647
3rd Qu.: 97.75   3rd Qu.:45.75   3rd Qu.:0.1935
Max.   :125.00   Max.   :56.00   Max.   :0.2222
```

5.4.3.2 Variable importance output

For classification trees, the "$importance" component of a `randomForest()` object like RFclass2 is a matrix. Below, there are five columns in the matrix: Variable name, columns for the number of classes of the categorical outcome variable (here, two, for "High" and "Low" respectively), MeanDecreaseAccuracy, and MeanDecreaseGini. For regression trees the variable importance plots have different columns, as discussed later.

Variable order: Variables in the importance table are not listed in order of importance. The order is simply the order as entered into the generating `randomForest()` command, which may be arbitrary.

- High and Low columns: These are the class-specific coefficients for MeanDecreaseAccuracy. For the current example, the overall MeanDecreaseAccuracy is in between the values shown in the "High" and "Low" columns below.
- MeanDecreaseAccuracy: This is a measure of variable importance by one definition of importance discussed previously. It is the percent of observations classified correctly. To give an idea of the algorithm, let gender be the splitting variable for a non-terminal node, then compute accuracy. Then create a new variable, "gender_random", which has the same proportion of males and females but where gender is assigned randomly to rows in the data frame. Again, compute accuracy. The accuracy for the gender variable will be higher than for the gender_random variable. The decrease in accuracy is a measure of how much greater the predictive accuracy of the row variable in the variable importance table is compared to prediction with a random (but proportional) variable. This coefficient may be taken as a measure of the importance of the row variable as a predictor (as a parent node). Note that this criterion compares the importance of the variable with a proportional random variable, not with other variables in the model. That is, MeanDecreaseAccuracy may be taken as a measure of how good the row variable is as a predictor (as a parent node). Better splitting variables have higher MeanDecreaseAccuracy. In the importance table below, the birthrate variable has the highest MeanDecreaseAccuracy coefficient (.088) and by this criterion is the most important predictor variable.
- MeanDecreaseGini: This is a measure of variable importance by a different criterion. The Gini index, which measures purity resulting from the splitting process, was discussed earlier. The higher the MeanDecreaseGini coefficient, the more important the predictor variable is by this alternative criterion. In the importance table below, the birthrate variable has the highest MeanDecreaseGini coefficient (17.643) and also by this criterion is the most important predictor variable.

Note that the decrease in accuracy and the decrease in Gini criteria do not always agree on the importance of a variable as they did here on birthrate for the example data. For that matter, different runs of `randomForest()` using different random seeds may not agree completely on rankings by variable importance measures.

```
RFclass2$importance
```

[Output:]

```
                                High          Low MeanDecreaseAccuracy MeanDecreaseGini
regionid                2.981890e-02 0.0167649330          0.025227639         9.554643
population             -2.259153e-03 0.0083340511          0.001318891         2.513385
areasqmiles             1.228305e-05 0.0086681128          0.003045796         2.982449
poppersqmile            1.326414e-03 0.0046317911          0.002358316         2.697294
coast_arearatio         3.741435e-03 0.0054390466          0.004374943         3.041380
netmigration            1.445054e-03 0.0099197252          0.004337542         2.856393
Infantdeathsper1k       3.433666e-02 0.0712556889          0.046190607        10.481324
infdeaths               1.480588e-02 0.0214373152          0.016950960         4.048968
gdppercapitalindollars  8.224080e-03 0.0474492500          0.021633373         5.972855
phonesper1000           4.429984e-02 0.1060936514          0.064656229        16.449972
arablepct               2.694507e-03 0.0060962825          0.003779420         3.258193
cropspct                3.009402e-03 0.0007765463          0.002181457         2.527426
```

```
otherpct          1.852862e-03 0.0111265940    0.004849998     3.258100
birthrate         6.623289e-02 0.1523912593    0.095243605    19.581744
deathrate         2.443895e-03 0.0175797146    0.007592632     4.915500
```

Variable importance plots are the easiest way to view the relative importance of predictor variables by either importance criterion, as shown in Figure 5.5. Importance by accuracy is shown on the left and importance by Gini purity is shown on the right. While the rankings are similar, they are not identical. The command to generate Figure 5.5 is as follows.

```
# If there are more than two outcome levels, the color= option must be changed to fit.
randomForest::varImpPlot(RFclass2, color = c("red","brown"), pt.cex=2, pch=16,
frame.plot=TRUE, main="Variable Importance Plots for RFclass")
```

It is also possible to get separate plots, though graphical output is not shown here.

```
#Get a basic plot of importance by accuracy
randomForest::varImpPlot(RFclass2, type=1)

# Get a basic plot of importance by Gini purity
randomForest::varImpPlot(RFclass2, type=2)
```

Finally, it is possible to create an object that lists variables in order of importance by either criterion. Exact importance values are shown, difficult to discern in the plot. Below we get variable importance by accuracy. Output is not sorted and therefore is not displayed.

```
varImpAccuracy2 <- randomForest::varImpPlot(RFclass2, type=1)
varImpAccuracy2
[Output not shown]
```

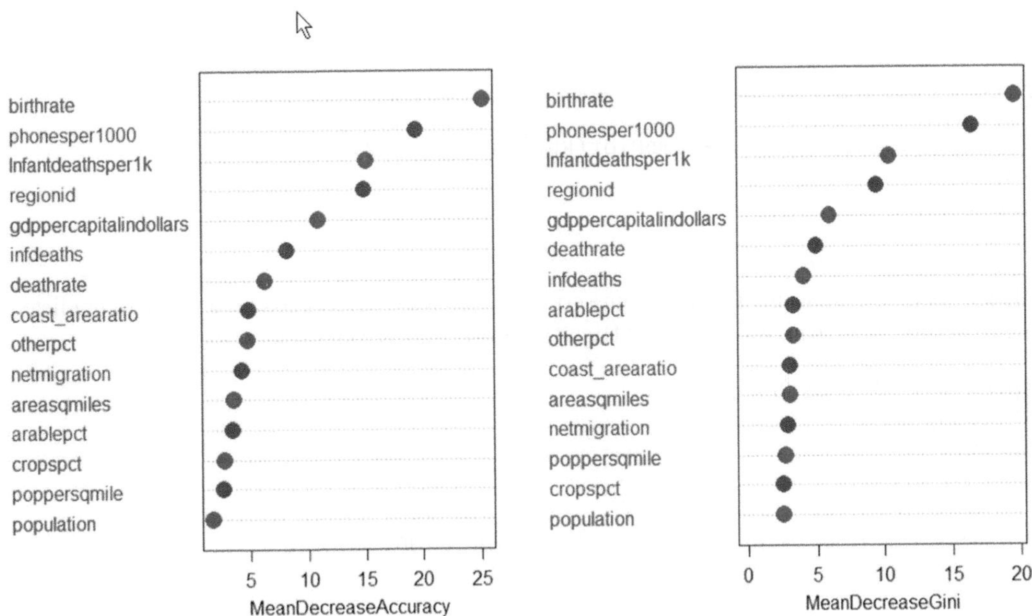

Figure 5.5 Variable importance plots for RFclass

Below, we add the `sort()` command and ask for descending order by using the "–" minus sign before the varImpAccuracy2 object.

```
sort(-varImpAccuracy2[,1])
```
[Output:]
```
              birthrate
             -25.199022
         phonesper1000
             -19.470123
     Infantdeathsper1k
             -15.079242
               regionid
             -14.913440
gdppercapitalindollars
             -10.905115
              infdeaths
              -8.217784
              deathrate
              -6.330634
       coast_arearatio
              -4.836365
               otherpct
              -4.777265
           netmigration
              -4.276232
             areasqmiles
              -3.522131
              arablepct
              -3.402056
               cropspct
              -2.769496
           poppersqmile
              -2.672027
             population
              -1.714581
```

Similar results for importance by Gini purity are obtained with the commands below.

```
varImpGini <- randomForest::varImpPlot(RFclass, type=2)
sort(-varImpGini[,1])
```
[Output not shown]

5.4.3.3 Predictions output

The "predicted" output component of a `randomForest()` object like RFclass2 is a vector of predicted values. As the target variable, litgtmean, was coded as "High" or "Low", this is a character vector.

```
RFclasspreds2 <- RFclass$predicted
class(RFclasspreds2)
RFclasspreds2
```
[Partial output:]
```
    1    2    3    4    5    6    7    8    9   10
  Low  Low  Low High  Low  Low High High High High
  . .
  High High
   211  212
  High High
  Levels: High Low
```

Finally (and optionally) we now place predicted values in the data frame as a variable called "RFclasspred". This saves to memory, not to file, which must be done separately if desired.

```
RFclasspred2 <- RFclass2$predicted
world$RFclasspred2 <- RFclasspred2
```

Andy Liaw, author of the randomForest package, cautioned, "One thing people should keep in mind about the "predicted" component of the randomForest object (and the confusion matrix for the training data), as well as "`predict(rf.object)`" without giving the newdata for prediction: That prediction is based on out-of-bag samples, so is *NOT* the same as the usual prediction on training data. It is closer to the out-of-sample prediction as in, e.g., cross-validation" (Liaw, 2003). That is, predictions are based on cross-validation but are returned for all cases, not just the OOB sample.

5.4.3.4 Proximities and the proximity plot

Proximity coefficients may be used to detect outliers. A proximity matrix is returned if the generating `randomForest()` command contained the option `proximity=TRUE`. The resulting proximity component (RFclass2$proximity) has a table of proximities relating each observation to each other observation. For the current data observations are 212 nations, so the output is a 212×212 matrix, too large to print here.

The proximity coefficient is a symmetrical one (the proximity of case 1 with case 2 is the same as case 2 with case 1), so the upper triangle of the matrix is redundant with the lower triangle, while the main diagonal contains the proximity of an object with itself, which is 1.0. For example, in the output below, the proximity coefficient of nation 1 with nation 2 is approximately 0.34. The proximity coefficient reflects the frequency that pairs of nations follow the same path and wind up in the same terminal node. Note this is not the same as ending up with the same value of the target variable (e.g., there are multiple paths to "High" on litgtmean and thus multiple "High" terminal nodes).

```
RFclass2$proximity
```

[Partial output:]

```
           1          2          3          4          5
1 1.00000000 0.33898305 0.53731343 0.01724138 0.20833333
2 0.33898305 1.00000000 0.23376623 0.00000000 0.39705882
3 0.53731343 0.23376623 1.00000000 0.00000000 0.20588235
4 0.01724138 0.00000000 0.00000000 1.00000000 0.00000000
```

In the proximity plot in Figure 5.6, the researcher will want to label the points in order to see just which nations are outliers. Labeling by country name will clutter the plot too much so we use country index number instead. Countries may be listed by index number by the following simple command.

```
world$country
```

[Partial output listing countries of interest in Figure 5.6:]

```
 [1] Afghanistan
...
 [5] Burma
 [6] Cambodia
 [7] China
 [8] HongKong
...
[12] Japan
...
[14] KoreaSouth
...
[18] Maldives
...
[38] Tajikistan
...
```

```
 [41] Uzbekistan
...
 [87] Paraguay
...
 [99] GazaStrip
...
[122] USA
...
[128] MarshallIslands
[129] Micronesia
...
[162] Lesotho
...
[170] Namibia
...
[211] UnitedKingdom
[212] Austria
212 Levels: Afghanistan ...
```

The country number can be made into an id variable for purposes of forming the x-axis in Figure 5.6.

```
id <- seq_len(nrow(world))
```

In output above we see that the USA has an index number of 122. We can get the proximities of the USA with all other countries by the command below. The higher the proximity, the more similar the USA is to that country. We can see that for the first 15 nations, the USA is most similar to nations 7, 8, 12, and 14. These are China, Hong Kong, Japan, and South Korea – all nations are more developed than others among the first 15.

```
RFclass2$proximity[,122]
[Partial output:]
         1          2          3          4          5
0.01282051 0.00000000 0.00000000 0.19354839 0.08108108
         6          7          8          9         10
0.00000000 0.78125000 0.57954545 0.32183908 0.29032258
        11         12         13         14         15
0.36000000 0.74698795 0.28378378 0.62068966 0.00000000
...
```

Though also used to create clusters, as discussed further below, proximities may be used to plot outliers. Below, a measure of outlier-ness is created. This outlier index is plotted on the y-axis against country id on the x-axis (nations 1 through 212). By one common rule of thumb, a nation is an outlier if its outlier index exceeds 10. A dozen or so nations are outliers by this criterion in the plot shown in Figure 5.6, including nation #5 (Burma) in the upper left of Figure 5.6.

The `outlier()` function from the randomForest package creates an outlier index coefficient for each observation. We label this vector "outlier1". This outlier coefficient equals n/sum (squared proximity), normalized by subtracting the median and dividing by the median absolute deviation (MAD),[1] within each class of the target variable as specified by the cls = option. If there is no cls = specification or if cls = NULL, a single class is assumed for all observations. Other definitions of being an outlier are also found in the literature.[2]

```
# Create a numeric vector of outlier-ness to use for the y-axis
outlier1 = randomForest::outlier(x = RFclass2$proximity, cls = world$litgtmean)

# Plot outliers based on proximities. The pch=16 option is for filled circles.
# Colors of points are set the levels of litgtmean (two levels, High and Low)
plot(outlier1, col=world$litgtmean, pch=16, ylab="Outlier Index", xlab="Country ID")
```

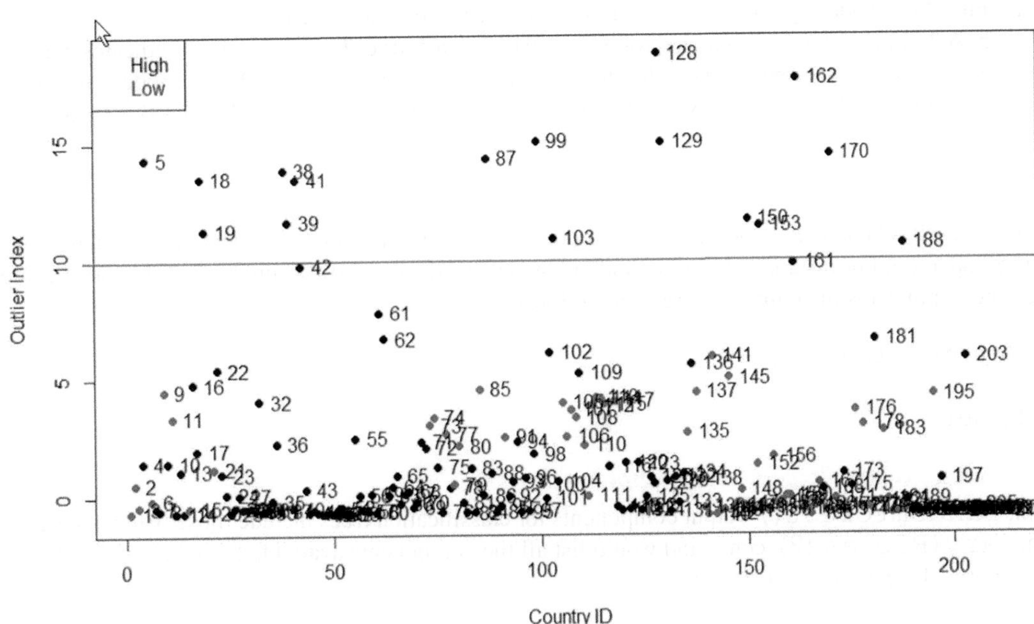

Figure 5.6 Proximity outlier plot for RFclass2

```
# Label the points with observation numbers, producing Figure 5.3
with(world[1:212,], text(outlier1 ~ id, labels = row.names(world[1:212,]), pos = 4))

# Draw the horizontal cutoff line for being an outlier.
abline(h=10, col="red")

# Add a legend to explain the color coding. Recall the order of levels was High, Low.
legend("topleft", text.col=c("black", "red"), legend = c("High", "Low") )
```

In Figure 5.6 we note that all outliers are from the "High" group on observed litgtmean. These are nations we would not expect to be above the world mean in literacy but actually are (or at least self-report as such). The most outlying nations is id = 128. We can look up the name of the country easily. It is the Marshall Islands, which is an "Associated state" of the United States, though also a sovereign nation. Although a less developed nation, the Marshall Islands receives financial aid from the United States, in part for education, which of course has increased its literacy rate beyond what one might otherwise expect. Foreign aid for education was not one of the predictor variables in RFclass2 but might be in a different model.

```
world$country[128]
[Output:]
   [1] MarshallIslands
```

5.4.3.5 The complete forest

The "forest" component of a randomForest object will output a potentially huge amount of information on the entire forest object (here, RFclass2$forest). This output is not generally reported but instead is primarily useful for debugging the randomForest model. This output has sub-components as listed below, with explanations by Andy Liaw (2003), the author of the randomForest package. For each tree:

- nrnodes: The maximum number of nodes a tree can have.
- ndbigtree: A vector of length ntree containing the total number of nodes in the trees.

- nodestatus: An nrnodes by ntree matrix of indicators: –1 if the node is terminal.
- treemap: A 3-D array containing a two-column matrix for each tree. The first column indicates which node is the "left descendent" and the second column the "right descendent". Both are 0 if the node is terminal.
- bestvar: An nrnodes by ntree matrix that indicates, for each node, which variable is used to split that node. 0 for terminal nodes.
- xbestsplit: The same as "bestvar" except it tells where to split.

The contents of each subcomponent of the forest component for a classification tree object may be viewed by double use of the "$" operator. For instance, the command below returns the ntree subcomponent of the forest component. The ntree subcomponent is the number of trees in the forest.

```
RFclass2$forest$ntree
[Output:]
      [1] 501
```

5.4.3.6 Other `randomForest()` components

In addition, `randomForest()` output components for classification trees include those listed below. Note that the `summary(RFclass2)` command would list all the components available for a `randomForest()` classification tree object such as RFclass2:

`RFclass2$call`	Reprints the command creating RFclass
`RFclass2$classes`	Prints the levels of the categorical target variable in the classification tree (here, "High" or "Low" litgtmean)
`RFclass2$err.rate`	Prints the classification error rate (accuracy) for each tree in the forest (500 by default). The "OOB" value is the out-of-bag cross-validation error rate while for this example the "High" and "Low" columns give the class-specific error rate
`RFclass2$mtry`	Prints the number of variables sampled at each splitting node (4 in the example)
`RFclass2$ntree`	Prints number of trees in the forest (default = 500)
`RFclass2$type`	Gives the type of tree, which can be classification, regression, or unsupervised. Note this is different from the `class()` function

```
RFclass2$type
[Output:]
   [1] "classification"

class(RFclass2)
[Output:]
   [1] "randomForest.formula" "randomForest"

RFclass2$oob.times
[Output not shown. For each observation (here, 212 nations)
gives the number of times it was used for OOB validation
in the forest.
```

5.4.4 Graphing a randomForest tree?

The `randomForest()` program does not have a module to plot a "typical" tree. Some view the idea of attempting to do so to be heretical on the grounds that the whole point of an ensemble method like `randomForest()` is to average across a large number of trees, not to come up with one tree. Any such single tree would not capture the diversity of the large number of trees in the random forest. Andy Liaw, author of the randomForest package, has said, "I don't see much use in 'looking' at the trees except for debugging purposes. If you really want to see what a tree looks like [just] look at the 'forest' component (Liaw, 2003)". The forest component was just described in the previous section.

While the `getTree()` function in the randomForest library does not graph a "typical" `randomForest()` tree, it does list the paths for any given tree among the trees in the forest. The output below shows paths for the RFclass2 object discussed above. Below, output is requested for the first tree (hence k = 1). In the "prediction" column of output below, rows with "High" or "Low" are terminal nodes predicting nations which are above-mean or below-mean on national literacy rates respectively. Rows labeled "<NA>" are parent nodes earlier along paths in the tree. Terminal nodes have a status of –1 while parent nodes have a status of 1.

To read row 1 of the output below,Infantde3athsperlk is the splitting variable at the root node, splitting at 50.215, and sending nations less than or equal to that amount to the left to node 2 and sending nations which are higher to the right to node 3. Taking row 2, which is node 2, birthrate is the splitting variable, splitting at 25.93, with nations with a lower rate sent to the left to node 4 and those which are higher are sent to the right toward node 5, and so on. The entire random forest solution for tree 1 is very complex, with 31 nodes in all. Tree 2 (k = 2), of course, might look quite different.

```
randomForest::getTree(RFclass2, k=1, labelVar=TRUE)
```

[Output:]

```
   left daughter right daughter              split var split point status prediction
1              2              3     Infantdeathsper1k      50.215      1       <NA>
2              4              5             birthrate      25.930      1       <NA>
3              6              7         phonesper1000      58.650      1       <NA>
4              8              9             deathrate       5.255      1       <NA>
5             10             11              otherpct      53.040      1       <NA>
6             12             13      coast_arearatio        0.100      1       <NA>
7              0              0                  <NA>       0.000     -1       High
8             14             15     Infantdeathsper1k      23.485      1       <NA>
9              0              0                  <NA>       0.000     -1       High
10             0              0                  <NA>       0.000     -1       High
11            16             17         phonesper1000      58.350      1       <NA>
12            18             19         phonesper1000      21.550      1       <NA>
13            20             21           areasqmiles   32085.500      1       <NA>
14            22             23 gdppercapitalindollars   21250.000      1       <NA>
15             0              0                  <NA>       0.000     -1        Low
16             0              0                  <NA>       0.000     -1       High
17            24             25            population 3094242.000      1       <NA>
18            26             27      coast_arearatio        0.085      1       <NA>
19             0              0                  <NA>       0.000     -1       High
20            28             29             arablepct      14.815      1       <NA>
21             0              0                  <NA>       0.000     -1       "Low
22             0              0                  <NA>       0.000     -1       High
23             0              0                  <NA>       0.000     -1        Low
24             0              0                  <NA>       0.000     -1       High
25             0              0                  <NA>       0.000     -1        Low
26             0              0                  <NA>       0.000     -1        Low
27            30             31 gdppercapitalindollars     950.000      1       <NA>
28             0              0                  <NA>       0.000     -1       High
29             0              0                  <NA>       0.000     -1        Low
30             0              0                  <NA>       0.000     -1        Low
31             0              0                  <NA>       0.000     -1       High
```

An object created by the `getTree()` command is a data frame, not a randomForest object, and cannot be plotted as a tree.

5.4.5 Comparing randomForest() and rpart() performance

For the `rpart()` classification tree discussed in Chapter 4, there were 22 classification errors when predicting litgtmean for the 212 observations in the "world" dataset (error rate = 10.38%). Above, in Section 5.4.2, the randomForest RFclass2 model resulted in 31 classification errors (error rate = 14.62%), a higher number. Why is this, given that random forests are supposed to be more accurate?

Apart from the need for tuning the model as discussed in the next section, the primary answer is that the estimates from randomForest are "out-of-bag" (OOB) or "out-of-sample" (OOS) estimates based on built-in cross-validation. The `rpart()` estimates, if no training and validation sets are involved, represent a data-driven solution for the entire sample. On average, this solution does yield lower error, but at the expense of overfitting and less generalizability to other samples. For an enumeration of all cases, as for the "world" dataset, there is no "other sample" and the `rpart()` solution is sensible. Where the data are a sample, however, overfitting is a real problem. Put another way, the rpart error rate will be overly optimistic.

For instructional purposes, to compare rpart with randomForest we must divide the "world" data into training and validation sets. We will refer to these the "train" subset for the training cases and "-train" subset for all other observations, which are used for validation. We treating the training set as "the sample" and the results for the validation set as the OOB results, making them more comparable to `randomForest()`'s OOB results. We wish to compare error in the validation set for `rpart()` with error in randomForest's RFclass2 model, which reflects built-in cross-validation across 501 trees. This involves the five-step process described below.

Below, in Step 1 of this process, we create an integer vector of 127 (60% of n = 212) random observation id numbers. Later we can use this vector to specify `subset=train` for the training set and `subset=-train` for the validation set, which will contain the other 85 (40%) nations.

```
set.seed(1723)
train <- sample(1:nrow(world), 127)
```

In Step 2, we run the `rpart()` classification model for the training set, placing the results in the object "rpart_train".

```
library(rpart)

set.seed(123)
rpart_train <- rpart::rpart(litgtmean ~ regionid + population + areasqmiles +
poppersqmile+coast_arearatio + netmigration + Infantdeathsper1k + infdeaths +
gdppercapitalindollars + phonesper1000 + arablepct + cropspct + otherpct + birthrate +
deathrate, method="class", data=world, subset = train)
```

In Step 3, we also place predictions based on this model in the object "rpart_trainPred". These are predictions for the `rpart()` classification model for the training subset.

```
rpart_trainPred <- predict(rpart_train, world[train,], type="class")
```

In Step 4, we compute the classification table, also for the training subset. The misclassification rate is (10 + 6)/127 = 12.60%. Note if the random seed differs then the misclassification rate will also differ due to random factors built into the `rpart()` procedure.

```
with(world[train,], table(rpart_trainPred, litgtmean))
```

[Output for the 127 cases in the training set:]

```
                 litgtmean
rpart_trainPred High Low
           High   75   6
           Low    10  36
```

In Step 5, we repeat for the validation set, referenced as "-train" (the anteceding minus sign signifies all cases minus those in the train subset). We save results in the objects "rpart_validate" and "rpart_validatePred", and then display the validation set confusion table.

```
set.seed(123)
rpart_validate <- rpart::rpart(litgtmean ~ regionid + population + areasqmiles +
poppersqmile + coast_arearatio + netmigration + Infantdeathsper1k + infdeaths +
```

```
gdppercapitalindollars + phonesper1000 + arablepct + cropspct + otherpct + birthrate +
deathrate, method="class", data=world, subset = -train)

rpart_validatePred <- predict(rpart_train, world[-train,], type="class")
with(world[-train,], table(rpart_validatePred, litgtmean))
```

[Output for the 85 cases in the validation set:]

```
   litgtmean
   rpart_validatePred High Low
                 High    47   9
                 Low      8  21
```

The misclassification rate for the validation set is (8 + 9)/85 = 20.0%. On a cross-validated basis, the `rpart()` training model does not generalize well to the validation sample.

In summary, the cross-validated (OOB) error rate is 20.0% for the `rpart()` classification tree. This is higher than for the rpart tree without cross-validation (10.38%). Further, it is higher than the randomForest rate of (14.62%), even before tuning the randomForest model. Thus the random forest procedure, as it usually does, returns a lower OOB error rate than generalization from a single `rpart()` tree. While the best rate (10.38%) is for the whole-sample rpart tree, that solution is apt to overfit the data and not generalize well. However, generalization may not be an issue if the "sample" is actually a census of all cases (here, nations) of interest.

5.4.6 Tuning the random forest model

It is possible that random forest results can be made even better by "tuning" the model. Tuning may mean many things, only two of which are discussed in this section:

1. Selecting the optimal value for the mtry and ntree parameters
2. Removing outliers

5.4.6.1 Optimizing the mtry and ntree parameters

The mtry parameter in the `randomForest()` command is used to specify the number of predictors to randomly sampled as candidate splitting variables at each split. The ntree parameter sets the size of the forest. While it is often noted that varying either may have little effect on interpretation of a decision tree, this is an empirical matter which will vary with the data at hand. The approaches below define "optimal" in terms of classification error (accuracy). Note these are data-driven tuning processes for which different random seeds might give different results. Also, as with many tasks in R, there are many other tuning strategies and algorithms not discussed here.[3]

A whole-sample approach to optimizing mtry

In an approach based on the entire sample rather than out-of-bag estimates, we can run the random forest model with a sequence of mtry values to see what empirical difference is made in classification error. By invoking the same `set.seed()` command prior to each run of `randomForest()`, the same results are output unless other parameters like mtry are varied.

Step 1: Below we create a for-loop to cycle through possible values of mtry from 1 through 10. Of course, another range may be used as long as one does not ask for more predictor variables than exist in the model. The "i" variable is used as a counter. Note mtry is set to i in each loop. Normally loops suppress printing but the `writeLines(paste())` syntax prints to the console anyway. Also, `RFclassTemp$confusion[, 3]))` refers to the third component of the RFclassTemp$confusion matrix, which consists of the class error values.

```
for(i in 1:10) {
set.seed(76543)
RFclassTemp <- randomForest::randomForest(litgtmean ~ regionid +  population +
areasqmiles + poppersqmile + coast_arearatio + netmigration + Infantdeathsper1k +
infdeaths + gdppercapitalindollars + phonesper1000 + arablepct + cropspct + otherpct +
birthrate + deathrate, control = rpart.control(minbucket = 5), ntree=501, mtry=i,
importance=TRUE, proximity=TRUE, oob.prox=TRUE, data=world)
```

```
writeLines(paste("class errors for mtry = ", i,
RFclassTemp$confusion[, 3]))
}
```

[Output, with two lines per mtry value, for High and Low class error respectively:]

```
class errors for mtry =  1 0.0857142857142857
class errors for mtry =  1 0.291666666666667
class errors for mtry =  2 0.0857142857142857
class errors for mtry =  2 0.222222222222222
class errors for mtry =  3 0.0928571428571429
class errors for mtry =  3 0.222222222222222
class errors for mtry =  4 0.114285714285714
class errors for mtry =  4 0.222222222222222
class errors for mtry =  5 0.0928571428571429
class errors for mtry =  5 0.222222222222222
class errors for mtry =  6 0.121428571428571
class errors for mtry =  6 0.222222222222222
class errors for mtry =  7 0.107142857142857
class errors for mtry =  7 0.222222222222222
class errors for mtry =  8 0.121428571428571
class errors for mtry =  8 0.222222222222222
class errors for mtry =  9 0.107142857142857
class errors for mtry =  9 0.236111111111111
class errors for mtry =  10 0.135714285714286
class errors for mtry =  10 0.25
```

Inspecting this table we see that mtry = 1 or 2 gives the lowest error for the first (High) class of litgtmean, followed closely by mtry = 3 or 5. For the second (Low) class of litgtmean, mtry = 2 through 8 are tied for the lowest error. Thus selecting mtry = 2 gives the lowest error for both classes of the outcome variable. Note that the same looping process could be used to select optimal values for minbucket, ntree, or other `randomForest()` parameters.

Optimizing mtry with `tuneRF()`: an OOB approach

The whole-sample approach above is appropriate when the data are an enumeration (census) of all data. In the more typical case where the data are a sample, an OOB (out-of-bag) approach is more appropriate. OOB refers to focusing on classification error for validation (test) data after having developed the model using a training (development) subset of the sample. In the randomForest package, the `tuneRF()` function optimizes mtry based on OOB estimates. This gives both tabular and graphical output, but below we display only the former.

The template below shows the syntax for the `tuneRF()` function.

```
randomForest::tuneRF(x, y, mtryStart, ntreeTry=50, stepFactor=2, improve=0.05,
trace=TRUE, plot=TRUE, doBest=FALSE, ...)
```

Parameters for this function are listed below.

`x`	A matrix or data frame containing the predictor variables. All variables will be used to construct random forests. If the researcher's model contains only a subset of variables of a data frame (e.g., not all variables in the world data frame) then a subset data frame must be created.
`y`	A vector containing the categorical response variable (e.g., litgtmean).
`mtryStart`	Specifies the starting value of mtry. If omitted, the default is the same as for randomForest (see discussion in Section 5.2.2).
`ntreeTry`	Sets the number of trees in the forest. The default is 50 but it is usual to specify the same number as for the `randomForest()` command itself (e.g., 501 or higher).

`stepFactor`	An integer specifying how much mtry is increased (or decreased if a negative integer is entered) at each iteration. When mytryStart = 1 and stepFactor = 2, OOB error will be plotted for mtry values or 1, 2, 4, 8, etc., will be returned; for stepFactor = 3, mtry values of 1, 3, 9, etc., will be plotted; when stepfactor = 2.5, mtry values of 1, 2, 5 will be plotted.
`improve`	The iterative search stops when OOB error improvement falls below the value of improve (default = 0.05).
`trace`	If TRUE (the default), progress of the iterative search is displayed.
`plot`	The default (TRUE) returns a plot of a sequence of mtry values on the x-axis against OOB error on the y-axis. If FALSE, the plot is suppressed.
`doBest`	If doBest = TRUE then only the best model is returned, not full results. The default is FALSE. When doBest=FALSE (default), a matrix is returned whose first column contains the mtry values searched, and the second column the corresponding OOB error. When doBest=TRUE, the randomForest object produced with the optimal mtry is returned.

The commands below run the `tuneRF()` program. In the next step we specify the predictor (x) and outcome (y) objects. The "x" object contains columns 5:12 and 15:20 from the world data frame. These columns are the same variables specified for earlier randomForest classification models. These variable index numbers may be viewed by typing `names(world)`.

As before, the y variable is the categorical outcome variable, litgtmean, which is the column 14 in the world data frame. Warning: Factor variables with more than 53 levels are not allowed (e.g., not country, which has 212 levels, which are nation names, in the world data frame). Note that setting a different random seed may lead to slightly different results.

```
x <- world[, c(5:12,15:20)]
y <- world[,14]
set.seed(123)

tunedRFout <- randomForest::tuneRF(x, y, mtryStart=1, ntreeTry=501, stepFactor=2,
improve=0.001,trace=TRUE, plot=TRUE, doBest=FALSE)

print(tunedRFout)
```

[Output for stepFactor = 2. The same data also appears in graph form, not shown.]

```
      mtry  OOBError
1.OOB    1 0.1792453
2.OOB    2 0.1320755
4.OOB    4 0.1603774
```

```
set.seed(123)
tunedRFout <- randomForest::tuneRF(x, y, mtryStart=1, ntreeTry=501, stepFactor=3,
improve=0.001,trace=TRUE, plot=TRUE, doBest=FALSE)

print(tunedRFout)
```

[Output for stepFactor = 3:]

```
mtry  OOBError
1.OOB    1 0.1792453
3.OOB    3 0.1509434
9.OOB    9 0.1603774
```

From the OOBError coefficients above, mtry = 2 minimizes OOB error the values of mtry explored. Be warned, however, that different random seeds might lead to different choices for the optimal mtry.

Welling approach to optimizing mtry using OOB error rates

An alternative routine for tuning mtry for minimum OOB error was developed by Soren Havelund Welling.[4] This approach prints out all levels of mtry and does so showing 1 standard deviation confidence limits around OOB error, as shown in Figure 5.7. We have adapted the code to our classification tree example predicting litgtmean from other variables in the world data frame. Below we assume that the mlbench and randomForest packages have been installed previously.

```
# Invoke needed libraries
library(mlbench)
library(randomForest)

# Define x as data frame with predictors, as discussed in the previous section.
# Define y as a factor vector for the response variable (here litgtmean).
x <- world[, c(5:12,15:20)]
y <- world[,14]

# Set a random seed, number of variables, number of repetitions, and forest size.
set.seed(123)
nvar = ncol(x)
nrep = 25
forestsize=501

# Run the model; This can take a couple of minutes, more for very large forests.
rf.list = lapply(1:nvar,function(i.mtry) {
oob.errs = replicate(nrep,{
oob.err = tail(randomForest::randomForest(x,y,mtry=i.mtry,ntree=forestsize)$err.
rate[,1],1)})
})

# Create the plot of OOB error by mtry with 1 standard deviation limit lines.
plot(replicate(nrep,1:nvar),do.call(rbind,rf.list),col="grey",  pch=16,
xlab="MTRY",ylab="OOB Error",main="Tuning mtry by oob.err")
rep.mean = sapply(rf.list,mean)
rep.sd = sapply(rf.list,sd)
points(1:nvar,rep.mean,type="l",col=4, lwd=3)
points(1:nvar,rep.mean+rep.sd,type="l",col=2, lwd=1.5)
points(1:nvar,rep.mean-rep.sd,type="l",col=2, lwd=1.5)
```

Figure 5.7 shows that, given a forest size of 501 trees, the lowest point on the blue line flags the optimal mtry value as 3. Warning: There are random processes in any OOB approach. Therefore, setting the random seed may make a difference. Here, for instance, `set.seed(12)` will specify an optimal mtry value of 2, not 3. Type `rep.mean` to list the actual oob.err error rates based on `set.seed(123)`. Note the error rates for, try values of 2 and 3 are close, so it is not surprising a different random seed might flip which is flagged as optimal.

```
rep.mean
[Output:]
  [1] 0.1579245 0.1449057 0.1428302 0.1507547 0.1526415
  [6] 0.1549057 0.1545283 0.1549057 0.1566038 0.1556604
 [11] 0.1560377 0.1522642 0.1564151 0.1558491
```

Optimizing both mtry and ntree using OOB error rates

Another tuning approach tunes for both mtry and ntree simultaneously. Self-explanatory comments head each section of the code, which is run as a block. As in previous sections, the classification tree model for the world data frame is used as the example.

```
# Invoke needed packages
library(foreach)
library(randomForest)
```

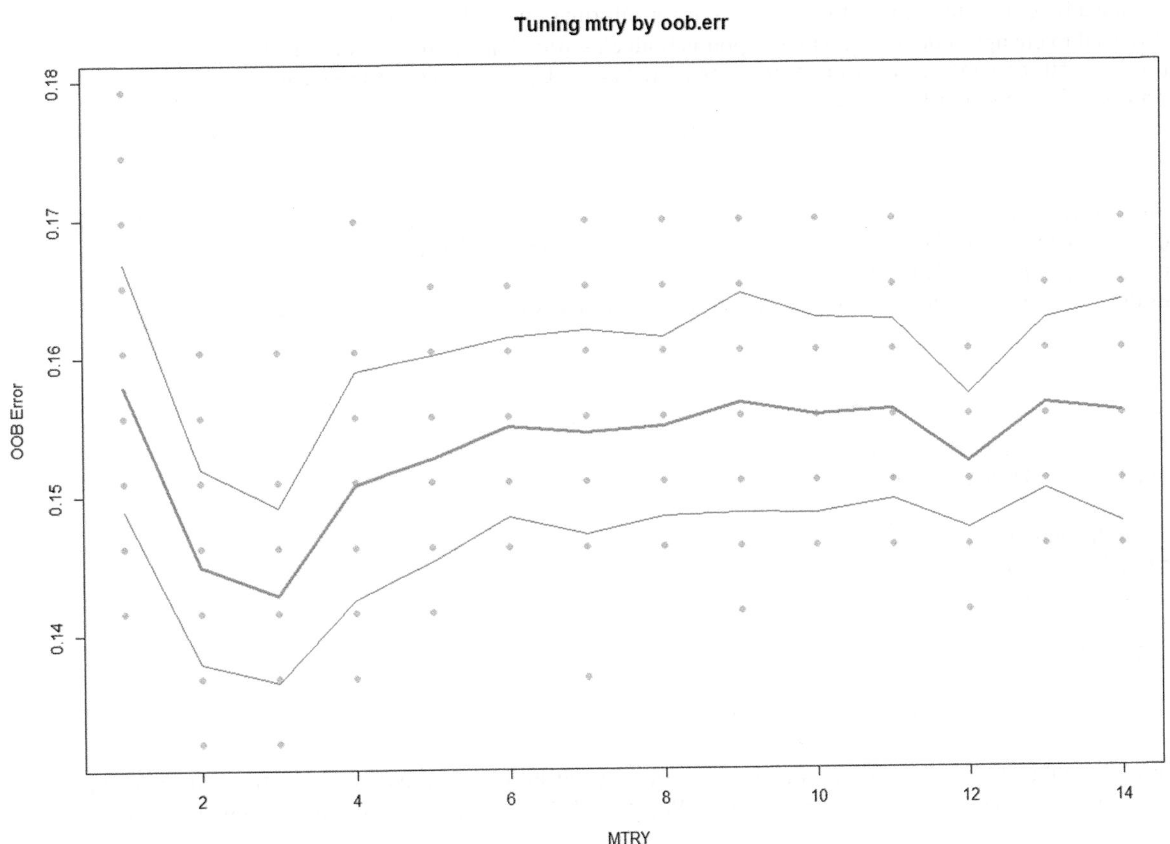

Figure 5.7 Mtry by OOB error, Classification model, Welling method

```
# Create an iteration function (mtryiter) to search over different values of mtry.
# This section of code is left "as is" unless the researcher wishes a different stepFactor.
mtryiter <- function(from, to, stepFactor=1.05) {
nextEl <- function() {
if (from > to) stop('StopIteration')
i <- from
from <<- ceiling(from * stepFactor)
i
}
obj <- list(nextElem=nextEl)
class(obj) <- c('abstractiter', 'iter')
obj
}

# Create a vector of ntree values of interest
vntree <- c(51, 101, 501, 1001, 1501)

# Specify the predictor (x) and outcome (y) objects as previously
x <- world[, c(5:12,15:20)]
y <- world[,14]

# Specify a random seed. This random starting point will affect results and may not be optimal.
set.seed(123)
```

```
# Create a function (tune) to get random forest error information for different mtry values.
# No need to change code below, which supports both classification and regression forests.
tune <- function(x, y, ntree=vntree, mtry=NULL, keep.forest=FALSE, ...) {
comb <- if (is.factor(y))
function(a, b) rbind(a, data.frame(ntree=ntree, mtry=b$mtry, error=b$err.rate[ntree,
1]))
else
function(a, b) rbind(a, data.frame(ntree=ntree, mtry=b$mtry, error=b$mse[ntree]))
foreach(mtry=mtryiter(1, ncol(x)),. combine=comb,. init=NULL,
.packages='randomForest') %dopar% {
randomForest::randomForest(x, y, ntree=max(ntree), mtry=mtry, keep.forest=FALSE,
...)
}
}

# Create randomForest() results
results <- tune(x, y)

# Print the output
print(results)
[Partial output:]
     ntree        mtry     error
  1  51           1        0.1603774
  ...
  70 1501         14       0.1509434
```

With 70 combinations of forest sizes and mtry values, spotting the "optimal" combination can be complex. For easier interpretation, we sort ascending on error. Was "results" is a data frame, we may follow these steps.

1. View(result)
2. Click on the "error" column header to sort ascending (this is a toggle: lowest values should wind up at the top), as illustrated in Figure 5.8.

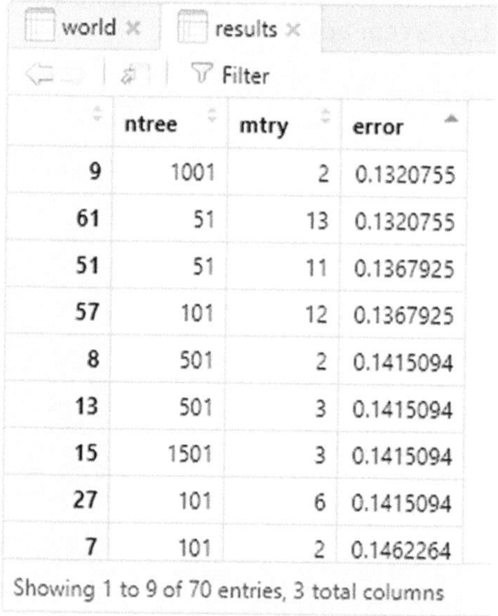

world × results ×

Filter

	ntree	mtry	error
9	1001	2	0.1320755
61	51	13	0.1320755
51	51	11	0.1367925
57	101	12	0.1367925
8	501	2	0.1415094
13	501	3	0.1415094
15	1501	3	0.1415094
27	101	6	0.1415094
7	101	2	0.1462264

Showing 1 to 9 of 70 entries, 3 total columns

Figure 5.8 Error for mtry and ntree

Assuming a random seed of 123 and limiting ourselves to consideration of selected ntree sizes, the lowest OOB error (0.1320755) was achieved by having 1,001 trees and setting mtry = 2, on iteration 9. By comparison, having 501 trees and mtry = 2 achieved an error rate of .1415094 and was the fifth best, achieved on iteration 8. In general, larger forests and smaller mtry values do better but there can be so many exceptions to this generalization that empirical optimization using one of the methods in this section is recommended.

Running the tuned model

By using similar grid search (looping) methods, we could also seek to optimize the random seed starting point or the minbucket size, either of which could further optimize the model. However, for space reasons we do not do that here. The foregoing optimization methods disagree slightly. The author's recommendation is to explore manually the most-recommended settings, which are mtry of 2 or 3 and ntree of 501 or 1,001. Below, we decide to use mtry = 3 with ntree = 501, obtaining an OOB error rate of 13.68%.

```
set.seed(123)

RFclass_tuned <- randomForest::randomForest(litgtmean ~ regionid + population +
areasqmiles + poppersqmile + coast_arearatio + netmigration + Infantdeathsper1k +
infdeaths + gdppercapitalindollars + phonesper1000 + arablepct + cropspct + otherpct +
birthrate + deathrate, control = rpart.control(minbucket = 5), ntree=501, mtry=3,
importance=TRUE, proximity=TRUE, oob.prox=TRUE, data=world)

RFclass_tuned
```

[Partial output:]

```
           Type of random forest: classification
                 Number of trees: 501
No. of variables tried at each split: 3
         OOB estimate of  error rate: 13.68%
Confusion matrix:
     High Low class.error
High  128  12  0.08571429
Low    17  55  0.23611111
```

Conclusion

The error rate for the RFclass_tuned model with mtry = 3 and ntree = 501 is 13.68%, reflecting 29 classification errors out of 212 nations. By comparison, the original error rate in RFclass with mtry = 4 and ntree = 1501 was 15.09%, with 32 classification errors. In the improved RFclass2 model with mtry = 4 but ntree = 501, the error rate was 14.62%, with 31 misclassifications.

In general, tuning often leads to modest improvement in model accuracy such as those here but is not guaranteed to do so. Using tuned parameters on average will be better than using arbitrary parameters, and therefore tuning is still recommended. However, tuning results should be treated as exploratory. The researcher may still want to vary the values of settings as part of sensitivity analysis of the model at hand.

5.4.6.2 Outliers: Identifying, plotting, and removing

Identifying outliers has two main uses:

1. Diagnostics: Outliers reflect where the model is not working well. Too many outliers suggest a weak model.
2. Dropping cases: Outlying cases affect results disproportionately.

Dropping outliers is a strategy for seeing results for "ordinary cases". Sensitivity analysis may be performed by varying the outlier score threshold for a case being considered to be "an outlier". First, however, the researcher should determine if cases flagged as strong outliers actual represent some form of miscoding or data entry error. After possible data cleaning due to errors, analysis may be run for the entire data frame and for a data frame in which outliers have been removed. This dual approach satisfies both the need to look at all valid cases and also the need to consider "ordinary" cases. Simply dropping outliers is disparaged. If cases which are dropped represent a pattern, then any generalization made must be adjusted to state that the generalization does not apply to the pattern which is dropped.

The randomForest package can compute an outlier score, which reflects the distance of the observation from the cluster centroids of each class. This is applicable to classification trees but not regression trees. The `outlier()` function returns a numeric vector containing the outlier scores for each observation. As discussed previously in Section 5.2.3.4, on `randomForest()` output components, the outlying score is computed as n/sum(squared proximity), normalized by subtracting the median and divided by the MAD, within each class.

An outlier is an observation whose proximity to the centroid of its class is small. Recall that small values of proximity are associated with greater distance. The outlier score reverses this, such that outlier scores are high when average proximity is low. Therefore, in Figure 5.9, tall vertical bars represent greater outlier-ness. By common rule of thumb, an outlier score of 10 or higher flags the observation as an outlier.[5]

```
# Obtain a numeric vector of outlier scores for each observation
RFoutliers <- randomForest::outlier(RFclass_tuned)

# Optionally, view outlier scores (output not shown)
RFoutliers

# Optionally, add outliers as column in the world data frame
world$outlierscore <- RFoutliers

# Simple scatterplot of outlier scores (output not shown)
plot(RFoutliers)

# Plot and label by country name (more cluttered), shown in Figure 5.9.
# As litgtmean has two values, High and Low, these are numerically coded as 1,2
# and their respective colors in the vertical line histogram (type "h") will be red and blue.
# A green line is drawn at outlier score = 10, to demarcate outliers.
plot(outlier(RFclass_tuned), type="h", col=c("red", "blue")[as.
numeric(world$litgtmean)])
with(world[1:212,], text(RFoutliers, labels = world$country[attr(world,"row.
names")], cex=1,pos = 4))

legend("topright", title = "litgtmean", legend = levels(world$litgtmean),
fill=(c("red","blue")))

abline(10,0,col="darkgreen")
```

In Figure 5.9, 15 nations are flagged as outliers. All were observed to be (actually self-reported to be) in the "High" litgtmean group.

Next we print out the outlier nations sorted descending on their outlier scores. The x1 data frame contains just the outlier nations. The x2 data frame contains just the columns of interest. In the order command, the minus sign asks for descending (the default is ascending). Keep in mind that one could use other definitions of outlierscore than that here, which is based on the `outlier()` function of the randomForest package.

```
x1 <- subset(world, world$outlierscore > 10)
x2  <-  x1[,c("country","outlierscore")]
x2[order(-x2$outlierscore),]
```

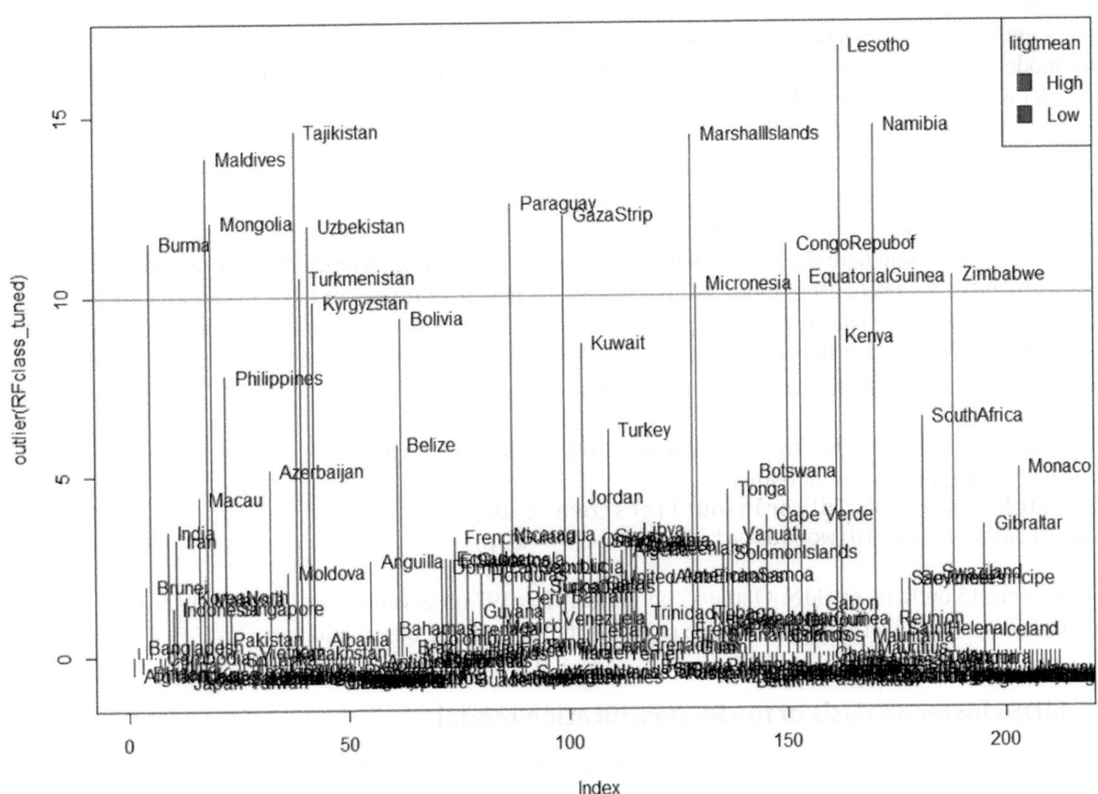

Figure 5.9 Plot of outlier scores by country

[Output:]

```
              country outlierscore
162           Lesotho     16.86583
170           Namibia     14.67718
38         Tajikistan     14.58408
128   MarshallIslands     14.44907
18           Maldives     13.85460
87           Paraguay     12.53921
99          GazaStrip     12.21567
19           Mongolia     12.05196
41         Uzbekistan     11.96409
5               Burma     11.50601
150      CongoRepubof     11.35966
39       Turkmenistan     10.51128
188          Zimbabwe     10.48976
153  EquatorialGuinea     10.46298
129        Micronesia     10.27375
```

Alternatively, for a less cluttered look, we may create the same plot but labeled by nation ID (row) number:

```
plot(outlier(RFclass), type="h", col=c("red", "blue")[as.numeric(world$litgtmean)])
with(world[1:212,], text(RFoutliers, labels = row.names(world[1:212,]), cex=1,pos = 4))
legend("topright", title = "litgtmean", legend = levels(world$litgtmean),
fill=(c("red","blue")))
abline(10,0,col="darkgreen")
```

[Plot not shown]

Removing outliers

Removing outliers from the data frame is controversial. On the one hand, removing exceptional observations may improve model fit for the remaining ones, possibly with a different model. On the other hand, the population included in the model is changed. For our classification tree model for 212 nations of the world, for instance, we would have to stop discussing correlates of high/low national literacy in general and discuss correlates for nations of the world excluding a list of outlying nations. That is, removing outliers will have changed our research purpose, which may well not be desirable. For this reason many researchers oppose dropping outliers, preferring instead to examine them and discuss why they are exceptional cases.

Nonetheless, we present here the simple step to create a new data frame stripped of outlying cases, defining these as those with outlier scores of 10 or more. We put this in the new data frame we label worldNoOutliers. We do the same for worldOutliers, for later use. It is important to note that while the new data frame does not have any of the nations which were outliers in the original model, if `randomForest()`is run on the reduced data frame, this will be a different model which is likely to have its own set of outliers.

```
# We assume that outlierscore has been added to the world data frame, as above.
# Create a new data frame without outliers.
worldNoOutliers <- world[world$outlierscore < 10,]
worldOutliers <- world[world$outlierscore >= 10,]
```

Since there were 15 outliers, worldNoOutliers contains 21–15 =197 observations/nations. It may be used for any data frame operation, as may worldOutliers, which contains the 15 outlying observations.

5.4.7 MDS cluster analysis of the RF classification model

We now create multidimensional scaling (MDS) plots in which nations are clustered based on proximities. We first obtain the basic MDS plot without the original outliers in Figure 5.10, then we apply k-means clustering to create the clustered MDS plot in Figure 5.11. Both employ the randomForest package's `MDSplot()` function. In order to obtain more well-defined, differentiated clusters, we use worldNoOutliers, which lacks the 15 outlier nations.

First we run `randomForest()` on worldNoOutliers, created in the previous section. We label the resulting object (model) as "RFclassNoOutliers". This is the same `randomForest()` model as for RFclass_tuned earlier.

```
set.seed(123)

RFclassNoOutliers <- randomForest::randomForest(litgtmean ~ regionid + population
+areasqmiles + poppersqmile + coast_arearatio + netmigration + Infantdeathsper1k +
infdeaths + gdppercapitalindollars + phonesper1000 + arablepct + cropspct + otherpct +
birthrate + deathrate, control = rpart.control(minbucket = 5), ntree=501, mtry=3,
importance=TRUE, proximity=TRUE, oob.prox=TRUE, data=worldNoOutliers)
```

Below, needed libraries are invoked, the random seed is set, and we create a plot with MDS clustering but without cluster boundaries. Since the outcome variable has two classes (High, Low) we ask for two clusters in the k=2 option. This is Figure 5.14.

```
library(randomForest)
library(RColorBrewer)
set.seed(123)

n=seq(1:2)
plot2 <- randomForest::MDSplot(RFclassNoOutliers, worldNoOutliers$litgtmean, k=2,
palette=rep(n, 2))
text(plot2$points,labels=attr(plot2$points,"dimnames")[[1]], cex=1, pos=4)
legend("bottomleft", title = "litgtmean", legend = levels(RFclassNoOutliers$predicted),
fill = RColorBrewer::brewer.pal(length(levels(RFclassNoOutliers$predicted)), "Set1"))
```

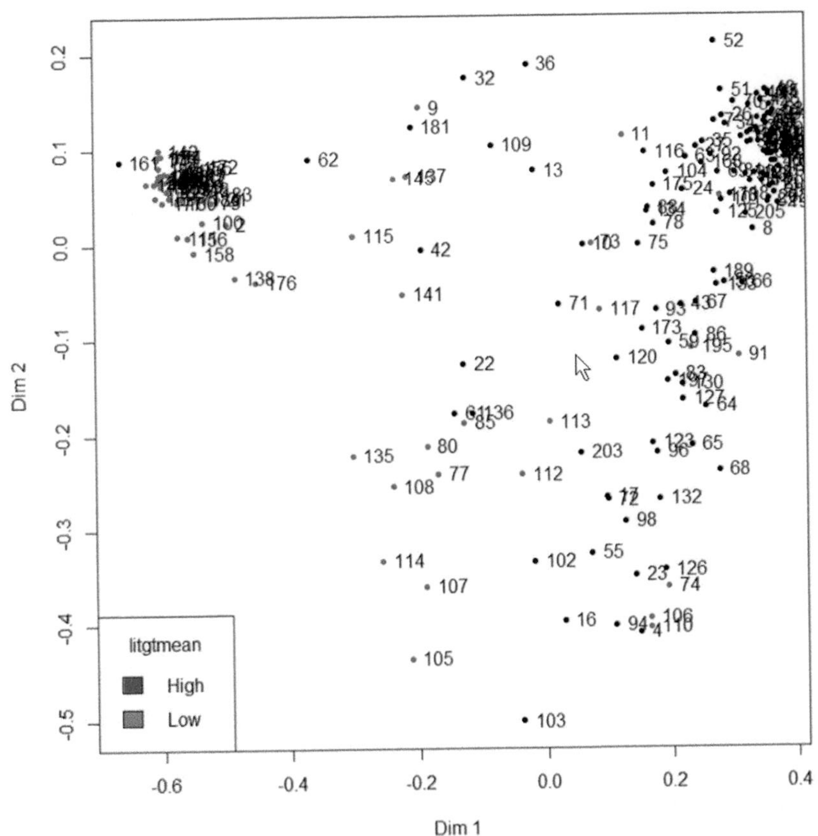

Figure 5.10 MDS clustering for worldNoOutliers

Figure 5.10 depicts two clusters – one mostly "Low" in blue and one mostly "High" in red, but with many nations not clearly in either cluster. We can improve interpretability and analysis in two ways:

1. Calculate the optimal number of clusters to request, which may not be 2.
2. Add cluster boundaries using functions from the "factorextra" package.

The optimal number of clusters can be determined using the gap statistic as visualized for various number of clusters (k) by the `fviz _ nbclust()` command of the factoextra package. The optimal number turns out to be 3, as visualized in Figure 5.11.

```
# Recall that plot2 was the MDSplot() object created above, One of its elements is $points.
library(factoextra)
temp <- plot2$points
factoextra::fviz_nbclust(temp, kmeans, method = "gap_stat")
```

Having decided that the optimal number of clusters is 3, we a 3-cluster solution using `kmeans()` from the "stats" package in R's system library. We visualize cluster boundaries with the `fviz _ cluster()` program from the factoextra package. The result is Figure 5.12.

```
ktemp3 <- kmeans(temp,3)
factoextra::fviz_cluster(ktemp3, data = temp, ellipse.type = "convex") +
theme_minimal()
```

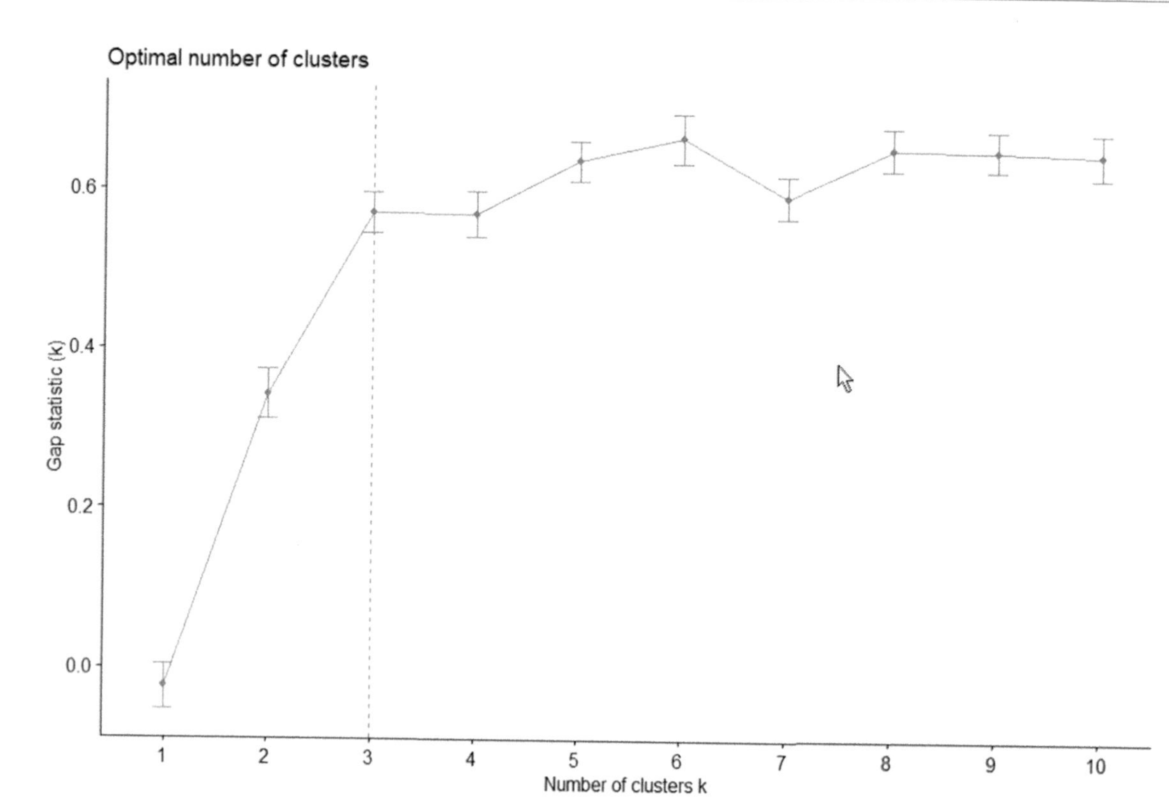

Figure 5.11 Optimal number of clusters (k)

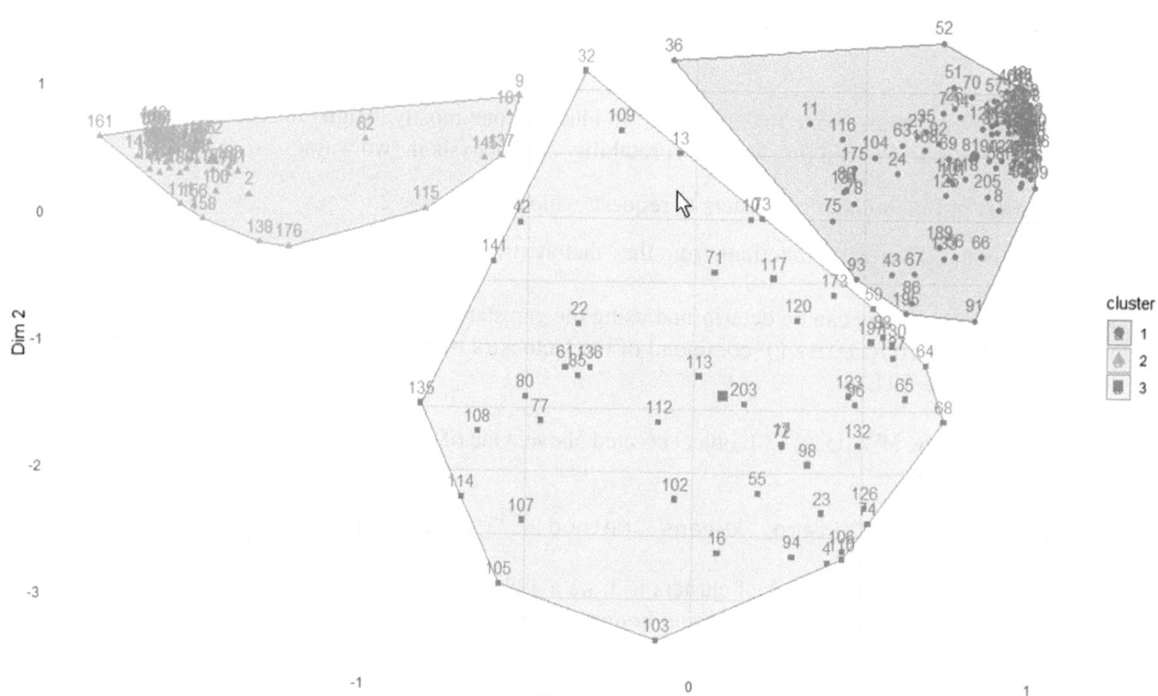

Figure 5.12 MDS plot with K-means clustering

Cluster membership numbers (here 1–3) may be added to the world data frame. The cluster membership numbers are contained in the $cluster element of the ktemp3 object created above by `kmeans()`. The following command adds these cluster membership numbers to the worldNoOutliers data frame.

```
worldNoOutliers$cluster <- ktemp3$cluster
```

The cluster membership variable may be then used in any other statistical procedure that supports nominal variables, such as tabulation or multinomial logistic regression.

It is also possible to combine worldNoOutliers with worldOutliers to generate worldWithClusters, containing all 212 nations in sorted order. Along the way we add a "cluster" column to worldOutliers and initialize it to 4. In worldWithClusters, nations with cluster values of 1 through 3 reflect a cluster membership number created above by the `kmeans()` command with k=3 clusters specified. Nations coded 4 are outliers grouped in their own cluster for analysis purposes. All objects are only in memory unless explicitly saved to file.

```
x1 <- worldNoOutliers
x2 <- worldOutliers
x2$cluster <- 4
x3 <- rbind(x1, x2)
worldWithClusters <- x3[order(x3$ID),]
```

5.5 Regression forests with `randomForest()`

5.5.1 Introduction

The primary difference between regression forest and classification forest models is that the outcome variable (also called the response, target, dependent variable, or DV) is continuous rather than categorical. Having a continuous outcome means that the terminal nodes of the tree can be a sequence of ranges of the DV and that model performance can be measured by MSE. Regression models for `randomForest()` follow much the same R syntax as `randomForest()` classification models described in the previous section. For this reason, treatment in this section focuses on what is different, assuming that the reader has read the previous classification forest section.

In simplified form, the algorithm for a random forest regression model follows five general steps:

1. The data frame is divided into a training set and OOB (out-of-bag) validation set, with roughly two-thirds of the sample being in the training set and one-third in the OOB validation set.
2. Many subsamples of the training set are taken, sampling with replacement.
3. For each subsample a tree is grown with the splitting criterion being maximizing the reduction in variance of the estimated continuous outcome variable. That is, variables (columns) are selected based on the highest reduction in residual sum of squares (error) and splitting rules are based on a variable's contribution to the purity and homogeneity of child nodes. Not all variables are considered at each node, only a randomly-selected subset (defaulting typically to p/3, where p is the number of predictor variables in the data; this is the mtry parameter). Error is based on results for the OOB validation set. There is no pruning and cross-validation is built in based on the OOB sample.
4. For each completed tree, its prediction is the mean estimated value of the outcome variable for each of its terminal nodes, which represent ranges of the continuous outcome variable. All cases in a node are predicted to have the same mean value.
5. The prediction for the forest is the average across all tree predictions.

Note that the random forest algorithm above is different from simple bagging. In simple bagging one would average many trees grown in the same manner. If there were a single strong predictor, that would dominate the solution for all trees in the bag, with little variation. That is, trees being averaged (bagged) would be correlated. The random forest algorithm decorrelates the trees being averaged by randomly considering a subset of predictors at each node for each tree.

5.5.2 Setup

Basic setup for random forests is identical to that for classification forests::

```
setwd("C:/Data")
options("max.print"=.Machine$integer.max)
library(randomForest)

world <- read.table("world.csv", header = TRUE, sep = ",", stringsAsFactors = TRUE)
```

5.5.3 A basic regression model

Running a basic `randomForest()` regression model closely parallels syntax for classification trees. See Section 5.4 for additional treatment of input settings. The critical difference is that a continuous variable, literacy, is substituted for the categorical variable litgtmean, thus leading to a regression forest model. The model uses the same ntree and mtry settings as the initial classification forest model in Section 5.4.2. It is not yet tuned (tuning is discussed later in Section 5.5.9).

```
set.seed(123)
RFreg <- randomForest::randomForest(literacy ~ regionid + population + areasqmiles +
poppersqmile + coast_arearatio + netmigration + Infantdeathsper1k + infdeaths +
gdppercapitalindollars + phonesper1000 + arablepct + cropspct + otherpct + birthrate +
deathrate, control = rpart.control(minbucket = 5), ntree = 1501, mtry=4,
importance=TRUE, proximity=TRUE, oob.prox=TRUE, data=world)
```

View the RFreg model simply by typing its name. Notice that output differs for regression forests compared to classification forests:

- Type is now "regression" rather than "classification".
- Error is measured by mean square residual (MSE) rather than OOB estimate of error rate in the confusion table. No confusion table is output.
- A percent of variance explained measure ("% var explained") is output as an overall effect size measure for the model.

```
RFreg
```

{Partial output:}

```
   Type of random forest: regression
                     Number of trees: 1501
   No. of variables tried at each split: 4
              Mean of squared residuals: 131.8804
                        % Var explained: 65.04
```

Not the case above, but it is possible that "% Var explained" may be negative. This occurs when there are many pairs of variables which are uncorrelated or nearly so. If that happens, the researcher should respecify the model, dropping such "noise" variables. Put another way, negative percent explained in a random forest regression model flags overfitting.

The `plot()` command for the RFreg model does not plot a typical tree within the forest (there is no such thing). Rather it displays the OOB error rate for forests of sizes 0 through ntree (here, 1501). This is Figure 5.13.

```
plot(RFreg)
```

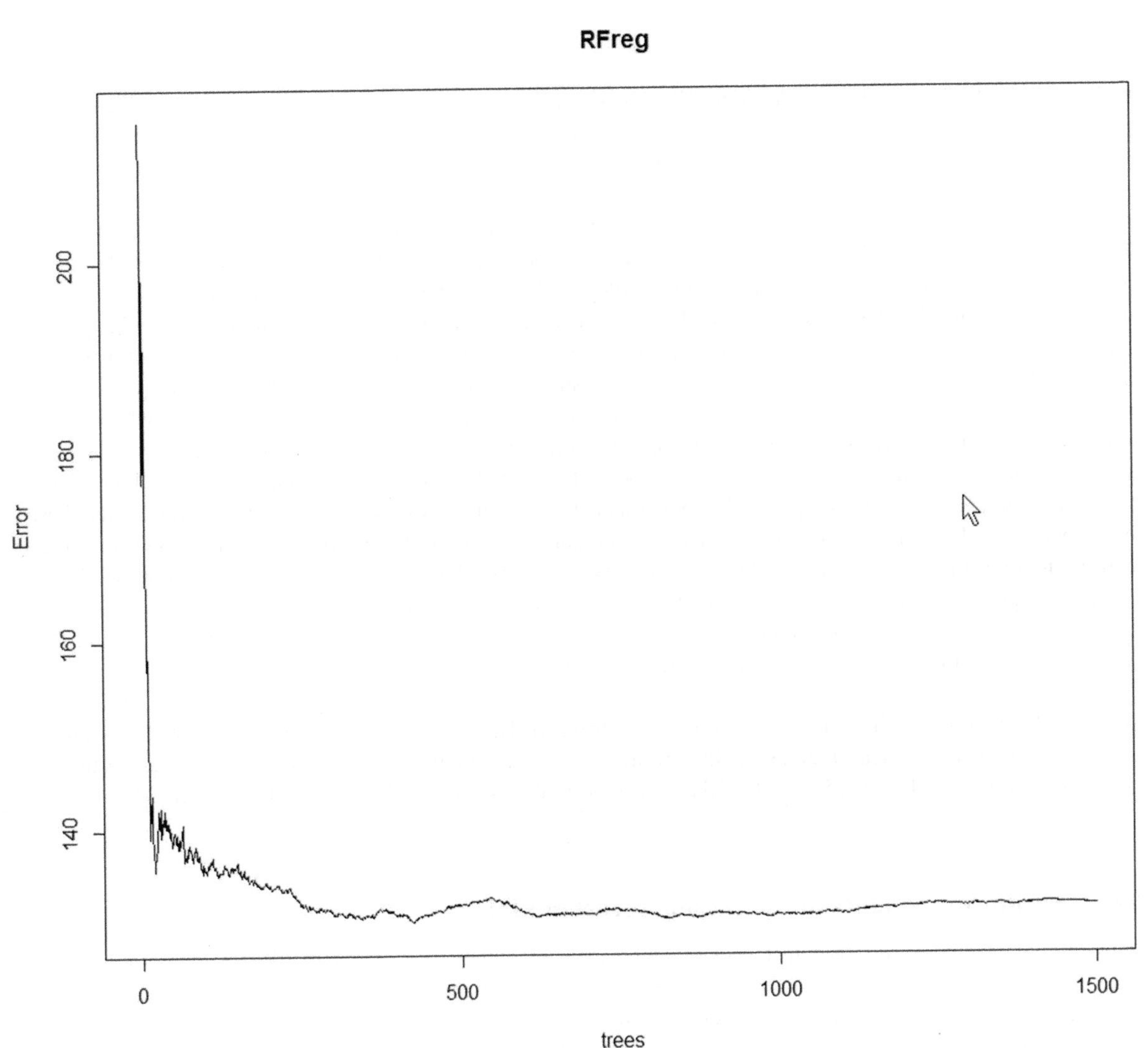

Figure 5.13 Error rate for RFreg by number of trees

In the Figure 5.13 plot, the black line represents the mean error rate when predicting literacy for forests up to ntree (1501). The error rates in the plot are the "stabilized" rates, with the right-hand side of the plot showing the rates for the full 1501-tree solution. We can see that a much small number of trees would have sufficed to return similar error.

We can use the `min()` and `which.min()` functions to find the minimum error point. We do this by copying plot information to the object "x", then getting its minimum value and the index number for it.

```
x <- plot(RFreg)
min(x)
     [1] 130.1875
which.min(x)
     [1] 422
```

The lowest error was 130.1875, which occurred when ntree was 422, assuming the random seed starting point and other parameters such as mtry are as specified. While one could rerun the model with ntree = 422, we leave tuning the model to a later section.

TEXT BOX 5.2 Social science applications of R: Global Warming and Wildlife Endangerment

Griffin et al. (2019) used the "randomForest" package in R to analyze sea surface temperature (SST) data in relation to mortality of Kemp's ridley sea turtles due to cold-stunning in the Cape Cod bay area of the Atlantic Ocean. The Kemp's ridley sea turtle is the rarest species of sea turtle and is critically endangered. In this environmental impact study, the authors used the randomForest package in R to identify leading correlates of sea turtle mortality in order to specify variables for a predictive model (a Bayesian count model) which forecast increasing mortality through 2034. The authors found that the minimum of daily mean SSTs, alone best explained the magnitude of annual Kemp's ridley cold-stunning events in Cape Cod Bay.

The authors outlined the steps in their analysis, noting that the random forest (RF) model was used to generate 2,000 decision trees, each being a bootstrap sample of the entire data set. At each branching point in a decision tree, the RF algorithm searched through a random subset of the predictor variables. In the RF process, the best predictor variable for a specific node is chosen and the decision tree proceeds to the next node where a new random subset of predictor variables is evaluated. The importance of each predictor variable is evaluated by using "mean decrease in accuracy", a measure which reflects the how accuracy decreases when each predictor variable is removed. After running the RF model on all 11 explanatory variables, the top two variables that best explained the cold-stunning count were selected. The authors then used the top non-collinear SST variables (minimum and standard deviation of daily mean SSTs, number of days with daily mean SST below 10°C, and number of days with daily mean SST above 20°C) in their model (Griffin et al., 2019: 5).

As a result of these steps, the authors were able to provide cogent evidence of the harmful effects of global warming on sea life, at least for the Kemp's ridley sea turtle.

Source: Griffin, L. P.; Curtice, R. G.; Finn, J. T.; Prescott, R. L.; Faherty, M.; Still, B. M.; & Danylchuk, A. J. (2019). Warming seas increase cold-stunning events for Kemp's ridley sea turtles in the northwest Atlantic. *PLoS One* 14(1): 1–15. doi:http://dx.doi.org.prox.lib.ncsu.edu/10.1371/journal.pone.0211503

5.5.4 Output components for regression forest models

Output components for regression forest models, such as RFreg, may be listed by using the "$" operator and sent to another object, if desired, using the "<-" operator. Subsections below illustrate a few of the most useful components and note differences from classification model random forests.

The following `randomForest()` output components apply only to regression models:

$mse Generates a vector of MSEs, which are the sum of squared residuals divided by n. A residual is the observed value minus the OOB prediction. MSE is the sum of the squares of these residuals, with the sum divided by n. Note this is computed cumulatively per tree such that the ith element in the vector is the MSE for a forest consisting of the first i trees. The last element in the vector is therefore the MSE for the forest as a whole. The $mse values are not MSE estimates for each tree.

$rsq Generates "pseudo R-squared", defined as 1 – (mse/Var(y)). Note that $rsq reflects estimation based on the OOB sample, not the entire dataset. As with MSE, R-squared (rsq) is computed cumulatively per tree such that the ith element in the vector is the rsq for a forest consisting of the first i trees. The last element in the vector is therefore the rsq for the forest as a whole. The $rsq values are not rsq estimates for each tree.

5.5.4.1 Confusion matrix output

A regression tree or regression forest, not having a categorical outcome variable, do not generate a confusion matrix.

5.5.4.2 Variable importance output

Invoked by calling `RFclassreg$importance`, the importance component has a different basis for regression models compared to classification models. For regression, the importance component is a matrix with two columns whereas for classification models the matrix has nclass + 2 columns, with the nclass + 1st column being the mean decrease in accuracy over all classes and the last column being the mean decrease in the Gini index. However, for regression models the two columns represent, in order, the percentage improvement in MSE and the increase in node purity. Even if the call specifies `importance=FALSE`, the MSE measure is still returned as a vector

%IncMSE — This is the more robust of the two variable importance measures and is preferred. The higher the %IncMSE for a variable, the greater its variable importance. The %IncMSE measure represents the increase in MSE of predictions based on OOB (out-of-bag) cross-validated estimates. In the estimation process, values of a given variable are randomly shuffled (permuted) in three steps:

- A random forest is grown, computing OOB MSE. Call this mse0.
- For each variable j, the values in its column are permuted and an OOB MSE is computed. Call this mse(j).
- For the jth variable, %IncMSE = (mse(j) – mse0)/mse0 * 100%. That is, %IncMSE takes mse0 as a denominator (baseline) constituted by permutation. The numerator is the amount the actual (non-permuted) variable reduces the larger MSE of the permuted version of itself.

IncNodePurity — Purity is small intra-node variance and high inter-node variance. A given variable is rated as more important (useful) than another if it results in greater increases in node purities. A variable with higher IncNodePurity is more important by this definition than one with a lower value of IncNodePurity. Node purity is the basis of the loss function by which splits in a regression tree are made. However, IncNodePurity is a biased measure of importance and for this reason when it conflicts with variable importance ranking by %IncMSE, the latter is preferred. Typically, only in huge problems where the greater computational burden of %IncMSE becomes problematic is IncNodePurity employed.

Note that the classification model measures of variable importance (MeanDecreaseAccuracy and MeanDecreaseGini) are not appropriate nor output for regression models.

```
round(RFreg$importance,3)
```

[Output:]

```
                         %IncMSE IncNodePurity
regionid                  40.527      5936.123
population                 1.611      1756.168
areasqmiles                0.019      1617.171
poppersqmile               1.833      1596.715
coast_arearatio            0.563      1641.922
netmigration               5.174      1635.725
Infantdeathsper1k         59.118     11449.548
infdeaths                 30.917      5362.225
gdppercapitalindollars    17.496      5997.351
phonesper1000            123.891     17912.257
arablepct                  2.847      1569.842
cropspct                   1.985      1944.250
otherpct                   3.995      1509.987
birthrate                 86.388     14022.798
deathrate                 12.463      3849.436
```

As the simple listing above is not in order of variable importance, it may be more helpful to use the `varImpPlot()` command of the randomForest package. Output is shown in Figure 5.14.

```
randomForest::varImpPlot(RFreg, color = c("red","brown"), pt.cex=2, pch=16, frame.
plot=TRUE, main="Variable Importance Plots for RFreg")
```

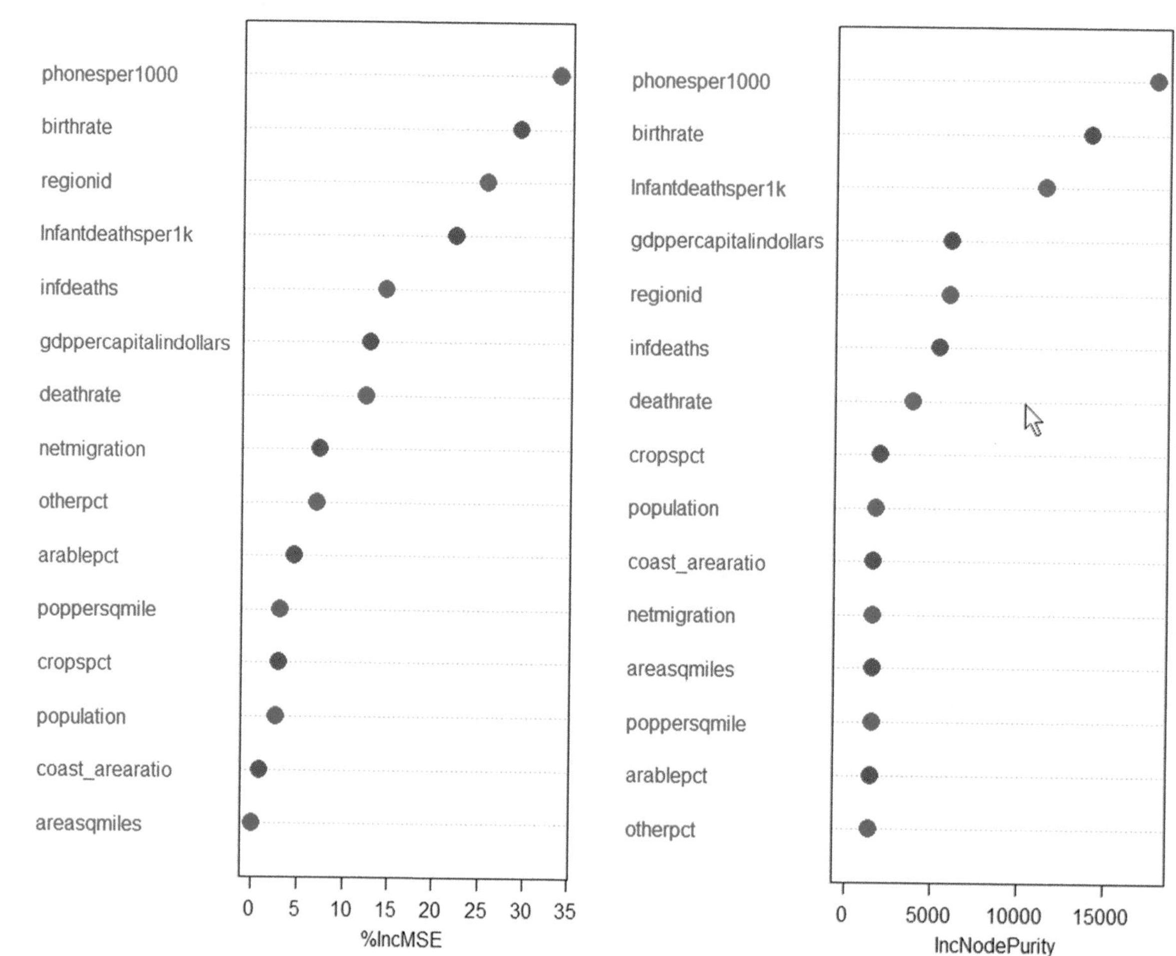

Figure 5.14 Variable importance for RFreg

Using the MSE rather than the purity definition of "importance", Figure 5.14 shows that the most important three variables in the regression model are phonesper1000, birthrate, and regionid. This is slightly different were we to use IncNodePurity as the importance measure.

It is also possible to get separate plots. Below, basic plots are requested but not displayed here.

```
# Basic plot by MSE
varImpPlot(RFreg, type=1)

# Basic plot by node purity
varImpPlot(RFreg, type=2)
```

Finally, it is possible to create an object that lists variables in order of importance by either criterion. In the following example, type 1 is the %IncMSE criterion. Exact importance values are shown in the resulting listing, difficult to discern in the variable importance plot. Note that in the `sort()` command, "-" asks for descending order. Note that as impByMSE is a variable-level rather than an observation-level measure, it cannot be added to the world data frame.

```
impByMSE <- varImpPlot(RFreg, type=1)
impByMSE
sort(-impByMSE[,1])
```

[Output:]

```
        phonesper1000              birthrate                 regionid
         -33.78744591           -29.37820278             -25.72230438
    Infantdeathsper1k              infdeaths gdppercapitalindollars
         -22.34248974           -14.48868783             -12.79029909
            deathrate           netmigration                 otherpct
         -12.30323373            -7.27458304              -6.97517257
            arablepct           poppersqmile                 cropspct
          -4.54210158            -3.10272289              -2.95927372
           population       coast_arearatio               areasqmiles
          -2.70867983            -0.92498537              -0.03568421
```

5.5.4.3 Predictions output

The $predicted output component of a randomForest object like RFclass contains the predicted (fitted) values. As the target variable, literacy, is a continuous variable, the predictions are numeric estimates for each of the 212 nations in the world data frame. As noted earlier, these are predictions based on OOB cross-validation samples, not on the entire population directly. (Recall whole-sample error rates may be obtained by setting oob.prox=FALSE in the `randomForest()` command.)

```
RFreg$predicted
```

[Partial output:]

```
       1        2        3        4        5        6        7        8
44.33889 63.92147 61.80042 89.66693 66.22535 63.27925 93.05631 95.21886
...
     209      210      211      212
98.82980 98.78469 98.36260 98.91092
```

Predicted values may be put into a numeric vector (RFregpred) and added to the world data frame. This saves to memory, not to file, which must be done explicitly.

```
RFregpred<-RFreg$predicted
world$RFregpred<-RFregpred
```

It should be emphasized that there is an intrinsic bias in `randomForest()` predictions when it comes to predicting extreme values. Predicted values are assigned based on terminal node averages. Averaging in turn may "wash out" outlying extremes. When the researcher's interest is in extreme values, a "model-in-leaf" approach may return better results. This is implemented by the `mob()` function of the "party" package, an advanced topic not covered here.[6] Whereas a `randomForest()` solution simplifies predictions to a single value per terminal node, the model-in-leaf solution bases predictions on a linear (or nonlinear) relation between the target variable and its predictors, preserving the potential to predict extreme values. See Zeileis, Hothorn, and Hornik (2008).

5.5.4.4 Proximities output

In classification models, the proximity coefficient is a coefficient which reflects the frequency that pairs of data points are in the same terminal nodes. For regression trees, this frequency will be very low since a regression tree will have a very large number of discrete terminal nodes. This in turn is why the proximity method and resulting outlier scores are not recommended as a way of identifying outliers in regression models.

5.5.4.5 The complete forest

The RFreg$forest component will output a potentially huge amount of information on the entire forest object, while the forest component is used internally for predictions. This output has subcomponents as listed below.[7]

```
summary(RFreg$forest)
```
[Output:]
```
                Length Class  Mode
  ndbigtree       1501 -none- numeric
  nodestatus    253669 -none- numeric
  leftDaughter  253669 -none- numeric
  rightDaughter 253669 -none- numeric
  nodepred      253669 -none- numeric
  bestvar       253669 -none- numeric
  xbestsplit    253669 -none- numeric
  ncat              15 -none- numeric
  nrnodes            1 -none- numeric
  ntree              1 -none- numeric
  xlevels           15 -none- list
```

Elements are nested, with levels of nesting connected by dollar signs. For instance, the term below displays the forest element, xlevels component, for the variable region.

```
RFreg$forest$xlevels$region
```
[Output:]
```
 [1] "AS" "BA" "CW" "DQ" "EE" "LA"
 [7] "NE" "NF" "NO" "OC" "SA" "WE" [Output:]
```

5.5.4.6 Other components for `randomForest()` regression models

The `summary(RFreg)` command lists all the components available for a `randomForest()` regression forest object such as RFreg. Most components are common to classification forests as well. Unique to regression forests are the components mse, rsq, and coefs. Absent from this listing are the classification forest components err.rate, confusion, votes, and classes. Type `help(randomForest)` for more information.

The meaning of components unique to regression forests is described below:

mse A vector of MSEs, representing the sum of squared residuals divided by n. `RFreg$mse` will list the MSE for every tree in the forest.

rsq Not to be interpreted as R-squared in regression, this is a "pseudo R- squared" measure, calculated as 1 – (mse/Var(y)). R-squared in OLS regression is percent of variance explained in the DV. The "rsq" measure here is an approximation of what R-squared would be if OLS estimation applied directly, which it does not in regression trees and regression forests. Thus, it is a controversial measure. This author recommends viewing it as an effect size measure for the model while avoiding use of the phrase "percent of variance explained". `RFreg$rsq` will list the pseudo-R-squared for every tree in the forest.

coefs Always "NULL" as regression-type slope (b) coefficients are not used in random forests. Use $importance instead to gauge variable importance, as discussed in an earlier section.

5.5.5 Graphing a randomForest tree?

The `randomForest()` program does not have a module to plot a "typical" regression tree, nor is there one. See the corresponding discussion for classification trees in Section 5.4.4.

5.5.6 MDS plots

While it is possible to create an MDS plot for a random forest regression model, unlike MDS for classification forests, this is rarely done and is not recommended. The categorical outcome variable in classification models will have a limited number of outcome values (e.g., two for litgtmean). Since the target variable in a regression model is continuous (e.g., literacy), however, the number of distinct outcomes can be very large and the probability of two nations arriving at exactly the same terminal value is very sharply diminished. Consequently, in a regression model the proximity coefficients are apt to be tiny and not very useful for clustering purposes. Nonetheless, proximity is still calculated for random forests and is available for an analysis.

5.5.7 Quartile plots

A quartile plot depicts any two predictor variables of interest as axes and color-codes point by the interquartile range of the outcome variable (literacy). Quartile plots do not use information from the `randomForest()` command but are useful in understanding the dynamics of the two most important variables from that command (or any pair of variables). We plot birthrate (the 19th column in the world data frame) against phonesper1000 (the 15th column). Birthrate, being listed first, forms the x-axis while phonesper1000 forms the y-axis. To color-code by quartile ranges of literacy, we first obtain them using the `summary()` command and store corresponding colors in the new variable "Color", placed in the world data frame. We then issue the `plot()` command using these colors.

```
# Note the quartile cutpoint values for literacy to insert below
summary(world$literacy)
[Output:]
   Min. 1st Qu.  Median    Mean 3rd Qu.    Max.
  17.60   75.55   92.50   83.28   98.00  100.00

# Create a new column in world initialized to "blue", then set bottom and top quartile colors.
world$Color="blue"
world$Color[world$literacy < 75.55]="green"
world$Color[world$literacy >= 98.00]="red"

# Plot all points using these colors. This is the basis for Figure 5.15.
plot(world[,19], world[,15], pch=21, xlab="Birth Rate", ylab="Phones per 1000
Population", col=world$Color)

# Draw lines at means
xmean <- mean(world$birthrate)
abline(v=xmean, col="gray50")
ymean <- mean(world$phonesper1000)
abline(h=ymean, col="gray50")

# Add a legend
# The RColorBrewer color management package was discussed in Section 5.4.7
library(RColorBrewer)
legend("topright", legend=c("Upper Quartile: > 98","Interquartile Range: 77-97",
"Lower Quartile: 0-76"), fill=brewer.pal(length(3), "Set1"))

# To minimize clutter, we just label the point for the USA.
# This involves creating a USAonly subset of the world data frame.
USAonly<-subset(world, world$country=="USA")
text(USAonly[,19], USAonly[,15], USAonly$country, cex=1.0, pos=3, col="black")
```

The resulting plot is shown in Figure 5.15. Phonesper1000 and birthrate were chosen because these were the two most important predictors by %IncMSE (recall Section 5.5.4.2). The x-axis is the nation's reported birth rate and the y-axis is the reported number of telephones per 1,000 population. The color of the points reflects the quartile range in which the nation's reported literacy rate falls, with red being the upper quartile, green being the lower quartile, and blue representing nations falling in the interquartile range. The point representing the USA is labeled.

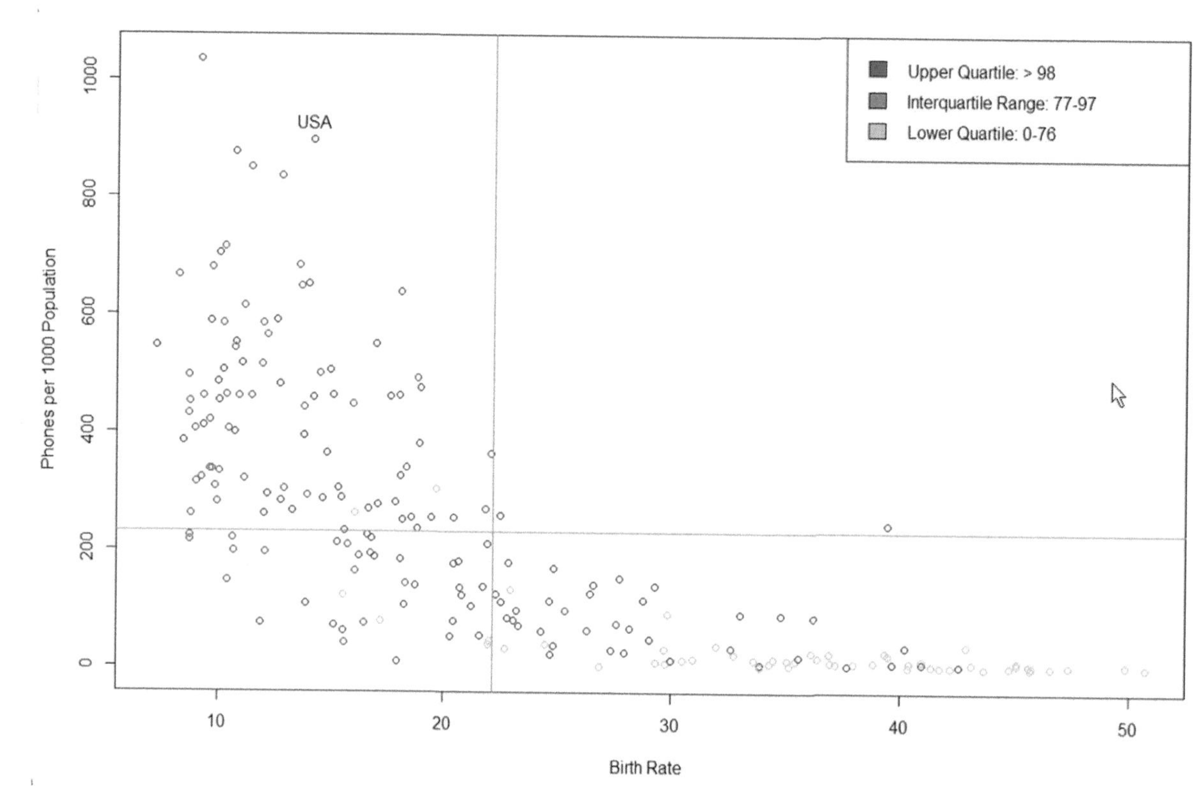

Figure 5.15 Literacy quartile plot for birthrate by phonesper1000

With a reported national literacy rate of 97.0, the USA is within the interquartile range. In general, low literacy (shown as green points for the lower quartile) is associated with high-birth rate and low-communications infrastructure (as reflected in fewer phones per 1,000 population).

However, we could have labeled all points by their index (row) numbers or by their country names using the following commands.

```
# Label all points by country index (row) number (not run)
text(world[,19], world[,15], labels = row.names(world[1:212,]), cex=0.6, pos=3,
col="gray50")
# Label all points by country names (more cluttered; not run)
text(world[,19], world[,15], world$country, cex=0.6, pos=3, col="gray50")
```

5.5.8 Comparing `randomForest()` and `rpart()` regression models

In Section 5.4.5, we compared `randomForest()` and `rpart()` classification models. In this section, we do the same for regression models. Many of the same considerations, procedures, and even relevant R commands apply.

For the `rpart()` model in Chapter 4, Section 4.15.11 discussed R-squared values for the rparttree_anova regression model solution. There were four versions of R-squared: Apparent R-squared (1 – rel error) and R-squared based on cross-validation (1 – xerror), with each being calculated for the unpruned `rpart()` tree and for the pruned tree. All are calculated on an OOB basis. For these measures, higher is better.

Apparent R-squared, unpruned:	0.786
Cross-validated R-squared, unpruned:	0.623
Apparent R-squared, pruned:	0.659
Cross-validated R-squared, pruned:	0.531

Another model performance measure for the regression tree model in Chapter 4 was MSE, which also comes in apparent and cross-validated flavors. For these measures, lower is better.

Apparent MSE	121.513
Cross-validated MSE	189.246

The central problem with `rpart()` regression trees is the danger of overfitting and consequent instability of the model when applied to new samples. Both cross-validation and pruning are intended to stabilize `rpart()` models. For this reason, for comparison with the random forest model, the cross-validated R-squared for the pruned model (0.531) and the cross-validated MSE (189.246) coefficients are used here for the regression tree solution.

We now look at model performance metrics for the `randomForest()` regression solution. To make this comparison we need to obtain the R-squared value from OOB estimates for the `randomForest()` regression model. The OOB estimates are cross-validated ones, output by default. Pruning is irrelevant as random forest solutions employ random selection of a number (the mtry parameter) of predictor variables at each node in lieu of pruning. There is an R-squared estimate for each tree in the random forest. The last element of the RFreg$rsq vector is the overall forest value of R-squared.

```
round(RFreg$rsq[1501],3)
[Output:]
   [1] 0.650

round(RFreg$mse[1501],3)
[Output:]
   [1] 131.880
```

Thus, the `randomForest()` regression model returns an R-squared estimate of 0.650, higher than the `rpart()` regression model R-squared estimate of 0.531. Moreover, the random forest solution has less error (131.880) compared to the regression tree solution (189.246). The `randomForest()` procedure, as it usually does, returns better results than does a regression tree using a pruned, cross-validated solution.

5.5.9 Tuning the `randomForest()` regression model

For some `randomForest()` regression models, failure to tune mtry may result in bias (overestimating some ranges and underestimating others). Results may be improved by tuning the model. In Section 5.4.6 on classification forests, several methods of optimizing the mtry and ntree parameters of a `randomForest()` classification forest model were presented. Much of the discussion there applies to regression forest models as well. The essential difference is that whereas classification models seek to tune on the basis of classification error (e.g., accuracy in confusion matrices), regression models seek to tune on the basis of minimizing MSE or maximizing pseudo-R-squared (whose formula reflects MSE).

A whole-sample approach to optimizing mtry

In an approach based on the entire sample rather than OOB estimates, we can run the random forest model with a sequence of mtry values to see what empirical difference is made in classification error.

Step 1: First we replicate the model as run in Section 5.5.3 using are mtry = 4 and ntree = 1501. This gives us the two baseline model performance measures we hope to surpass through tuning: MSE = 131.8804 and "% Var explained" (pseudo-R-squared) = 65.0399. Below, "Mean of squared residuals" and "% Var explained" are discussed further.

```
# Run the same model as in Section 5.5.3, with literacy as the outcome variable
set.seed(123)

RFregTemp <- randomForest::randomForest(literacy ~ regionid + population +
areasqmiles + poppersqmile + coast_arearatio + netmigration + Infantdeathsper1k +
```

```
infdeaths + gdppercapitalindollars + phonesper1000 + arablepct + cropspct + otherpct +
birthrate + deathrate, control = rpart.control(minbucket = 5), ntree = 1501, mtry=4,
importance=TRUE, proximity=TRUE, oob.prox=TRUE, data=world)
```

Get MSE and pseudo-R-squared
Note use of pound (#) sign below to get output summation shown below

```
RFregTemp#mse
```

[Partial output:]

```
  Type of random forest: regression
  Number of trees: 1501
  No. of variables tried at each split: 4
  Mean of squared residuals: 131.8804
  % Var explained: 65.04
```

Note that "Mean of squared residuals" is MSE for the entire forest, which is shown in the last (for these data, the 1501th) mse entry in the RFregTemp$mse vector. Similarly, "% Var explained" is the pseudo-R-squared value for the last rsq entry in the RFregTemp$rsq vector.

```
RFregTemp$mse[1501]
```

[Output:]

```
   [1] 131.8804
```

[Output:]

```
   [1] 0.6503988
```

As in the classification section, we now create a for-loop to cycle through possible values of mtry from 1 through 14. The code differs for the performance criterion. Recall that the mse value for the model is the last entry in the RFregTemp$mse vector (`RFregTemp$mse`[1501]).[8] Note that the same grid search looping strategy could be used to optimize ntree, mbucket, and set.seed.

```
ntree = 1501
for(i in 1:14) {
  set.seed(123)
  RFregTemp <- randomForest::randomForest(literacy ~ regionid + population +
  areasqmiles + poppersqmile + coast_arearatio +  netmigration + Infantdeathsper1k +
  infdeaths + gdppercapitalindollars + phonesper1000 + arablepct + cropspct +
  otherpct + birthrate + deathrate, control=rpart.control(minbucket = 5),
  ntree=1501, mtry=i, importance=TRUE, proximity=TRUE, oob.prox=TRUE, data=world)
  writeLines(paste("mse error for mtry = ", i, RFregTemp$mse[ntree]))
}
```

[Output, with one line per mtry value, for the MSE. These aren't OOB estimates.]

```
   mse error for mtry =  1 140.949878013738
   mse error for mtry =  2 132.515108754086
   mse error for mtry =  3 130.8878780641
   mse error for mtry =  4 131.880413399034
   mse error for mtry =  5 131.227376527367
   mse error for mtry =  6 131.467214203566
   mse error for mtry =  7 134.036086442934
   mse error for mtry =  8 134.177696823633
   mse error for mtry =  9 137.307571894437
   mse error for mtry =  10 136.820222348184
   mse error for mtry =  11 137.702360253306
   mse error for mtry =  12 141.000758817817
   mse error for mtry =  13 140.904294026317
   mse error for mtry =  14 143.046263570334
```

Setting mtry = 3 gives the lowest MSE, holding other parameters the same. However, due to random factors in the algorithm, a different result might be reached using a different random seed. Moreover, this tuning of mtry is based on the entire sample, whereas methods below tune based on the out-of-bag (OOB) sample, which is more common. The entire-sample approach is appropriate when the data are an enumeration or census of all cases. OOB approaches are appropriate when the data are a sample of all cases.

Optimizing mtry with `tuneRF()`: an oob approach
The syntax and parameters for the `tuneRF()` function were given in Section 5.4.6.1 for the classification model. We again specify the predictor (x) and outcome (y) objects. The "x" object contains the variables in columns 3 (regionid), 5:12 and 15:20 from the world data frame (view variable index numbers by typing `names(world)`). The outcome variable in the regression model is literacy and is the 13th column in the world data frame.

```
# In the first run of tuneRF(), the stepFactor is 2, giving results for mtry = 1, 2, and 4.
library(randomForest)
x <- world[, c(3,5:12,15:20)]
y <- world[,13]
set.seed(5664)
tunedRFout2 <- randomForest::tuneRF(x, y, mtryStart=1, ntreeTry=1501, stepFactor=2,
improve=0.001,trace=TRUE, plot=TRUE, doBest=FALSE)
[Output]
   mtry = 1  OOB error = 141.4669
   Searching left ...
   Searching right ...
   mtry = 2  OOB error = 132.5212 0.06323529 0.001
   mtry = 4  OOB error = 132.6842 -0.001230074 0.001
```

Unfortunately, `tuneRF()` will not step by 1, so above we have solutions for mtry = 1, 2, and 4. We repeat with stepfactor = 3, giving solutions for mtry = 1, 3, and 9. We could try other values of stepfactor but stop here for space reasons, but these would give higher error values.

```
   mtry = 1  OOB error = 141.4669
   Searching left ...
   Searching right ...
   mtry = 3  OOB error = 131.5394 0.07017504 0.001
   mtry = 9  OOB error = 134.3649 -0.02147973 0.001
```

By the `tuneRF()` method, for the values of mtry explored, mtry = 3 gives the lowest error, measured as MSE on an OOB basis. Again, random factors in the algorithm might lead to a different solution if a different random seed is used.

A second approach to optimizing mtry using OOB error rates
The Welling method checks all levels of mtry with error confidence limits, with graphical output. This was applied to the classification model as shown in Figure 5.7.

```
# Invoke needed libraries
library(mlbench)
library(randomForest)

# Define x as data frame with predictors, as discussed in the previous section.
# Define y as a factor vector for the response variable (here literacy, the 13 column in world).
x <- world[, c(3,5:12,15:20)]
y <- world[,13]

# Set a random seed, number of variables, number of repetitions, and forest size.
# A different random seed will cause results to differ.
set.seed(123)
nvar = ncol(x)
nrep = 25
forestsize=1501
```

```
# Run the model. The larger the forest, the longer the runtime.
# This took almost 5 minutes on the author's computer.
forestsize=1501
rf.list = lapply(1:nvar,function(i.mtry) {
oob.errs = replicate(nrep,{
oob.err =
tail(randomForest(x,y,mtry=i.mtry,ntree=forestsize)$mse,1)})
})

# Create the plot of oob error by mtry with 1 standard deviation limit lines.
plot(replicate(nrep,1:nvar),do.call(rbind,rf.list), col="grey", pch = 16,
xlab="MTRY", ylab="OOB Error", main="Tuning mtry by oob.err")
rep.mean = sapply(rf.list,mean)
rep.sd = sapply(rf.list,sd)
points(1:nvar,rep.mean,type="l",col=3, lwd=3)
points(1:nvar,rep.mean+rep.sd,type="l",col=2, lwd=2)
points(1:nvar,rep.mean-rep.sd,type="l",col=2, lwd=2)
```

The resulting figure is shown in Figure 5.16, where we can see that mtry = 3 has the lowest error. To see the actual mean mse values used in the plot, type:

```
rep.mean
[Output:)]
   [1] 141.4478 133.6505 131.2220 131.5471 131.7462
   [6] 132.5776 133.5494 134.9577 136.5935 137.8947
   [11] 139.0863 140.2909 141.5022 143.6883 144.2464
```

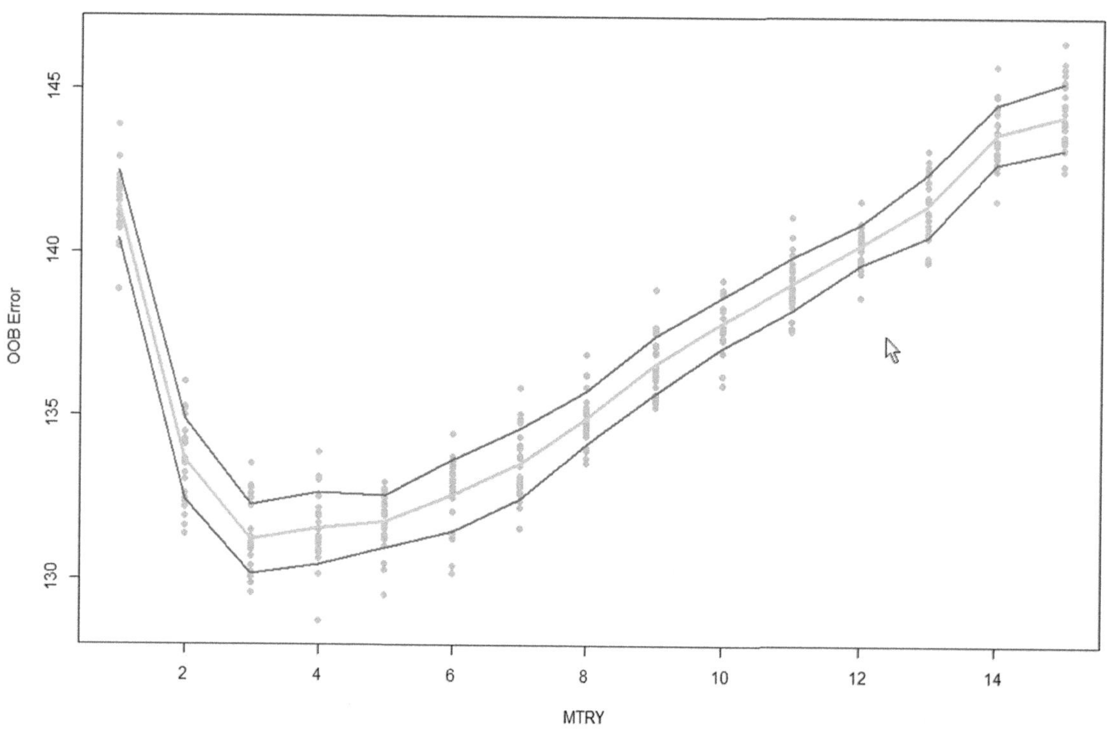

Figure 5.16 Mtry by OOB error, Regression forest, Welling method

Optimizing both mtry and ntree using OOB mse error rates

A method described for classification forests in Section 5.4.6.1 tunes for both mtry and ntree simultaneously. The code below only slightly differs from that for classification models.

```
# Invoke needed packages and set the random seed
set.seed(123)
library(foreach)
library(randomForest)

# Create an iteration function (mtryiter) to search over different values of mtry
mtryiter <- function(from, to, stepFactor=1.05) {
nextEl <- function() {
if (from > to) stop('StopIteration')
i <- from
from <<- ceiling(from * stepFactor)
i
}
obj <- list(nextElem=nextEl)
class(obj) <- c('abstractiter', 'iter')
obj
}

# Create a vector of ntree values of interest
vntree <- c(51, 101, 501, 1001, 1501)

# Specify the predictor (x) and outcome (y) object
# x contains columns 3, 5:12 and 15:20 as predictor variables
# Type names(world)to see column index numbers
# The 13th column is literacy, the outcome variable
x <- world[, c(3,5:12,15:20)]
y <- world[,13]

# Create a function (tune) to get random forest error information for different mtry values.
# Note this function handles both classification and regression forests.
tune <- function(x, y, ntree=vntree, mtry=NULL, keep.forest=FALSE, ...) {
comb <- if (is.factor(y))
function(a, b) rbind(a, data.frame(ntree=ntree, mtry=b$mtry, error=b$err.
rate[ntree, 1]))
else
function(a, b) rbind(a, data.frame(ntree=ntree, mtry=b$mtry, error=b$mse[ntree]))
foreach(mtry=mtryiter(1, ncol(x)),. combine=comb,. init=NULL,
.packages='randomForest') %dopar% {
randomForest(x, y, ntree=max(ntree), mtry=mtry, keep.forest=FALSE, ...)
}
}

# Create and print randomForest() results
results <- tune(x, y)
```

The "results" object is a data frame with the columns ntree, mtry, and error. With five levels of mtry considered and with 14 predictor variables in the model, making for 70 combinations of forest sizes and mtry values, spotting the "optimal" combination can be complex. For easier interpretation, we sort decreasing on mse error. Viewing the results data frame and clicking on the header for the "error" column will sort the data frame by ascending or descending error (the header functions as a toggle).

Alternatively, the function below lists the ten best (lowest) OOB error rates for various levels of ntree and mtry.

```
head(results[order(results$error,decreasing=FALSE),],10)
[Output:]
   13   501     3 127.3821
   14  1001     3 129.7531
   15  1501     3 130.2869
   28   501     6 130.3783
   29  1001     6 131.2330
   18   501     4 131.7738
   20  1501     4 131.7815
   19  1001     4 132.0518
   30  1501     6 132.1243
   35  1501     7 132.7898
```

By this method, the top three results all use mtry = 3, with smaller forests doing a bit better. Note, however, that results will differ if the random seed or other parameters are changed.

Running the tuned model

We may now rerun the `randomForest()` model tuned to ntree = 501 and mtry = 3. The original model used ntree = 1501 and mtry = 4. The commands below set the random seed run an otherwise identical model. We print the last results.

```
set.seed(123)
RFreg_tuned <- randomForest::randomForest(literacy ~ regionid +  population +
areasqmiles + poppersqmile + coast_arearatio + netmigration + Infantdeathsper1k +
infdeaths + gdppercapitalindollars + phonesper1000 + arablepct + cropspct + otherpct +
birthrate + deathrate, control=rpart.control(minbucket = 5), ntree=501, mtry=3,
importance=TRUE, proximity=TRUE, oob.prox=TRUE, data=world)
```

```
# View results
RFreg_tuned
[Partial output:]
   Type of random forest: regression
   Number of trees: 501
   No. of variables tried at each split: 3
   Mean of squared residuals: 129.734
   % Var explained: 65.61
```

The tuned model was only slightly better than the original model in Section 5.5.3 by the metric of MSE (129.734 vs. 131.880). However, by the percent of variance explained metric the tuned model was marginally worse at 65.61% vs. 65.02%. Likewise, variable importance is very similar though not identical in the untuned and tuned models, as illustrated in Figure 5.17.[9] The results of tuning, as happens not infrequently, were marginal and might well not affect substantive analysis. Nonetheless, tuning often leads to modest improvements though is not guaranteed to do so, and so is recommended. Note also we have not tuned for mbucket or set.seed, which might have made a further difference.

5.5.10 Outliers: Identifying and removing

For classification forests, outliers were defined in terms of an outlier score (RFclass$outlier), which was the distance of the observation from the cluster centroids of each class. However, this is not applicable to

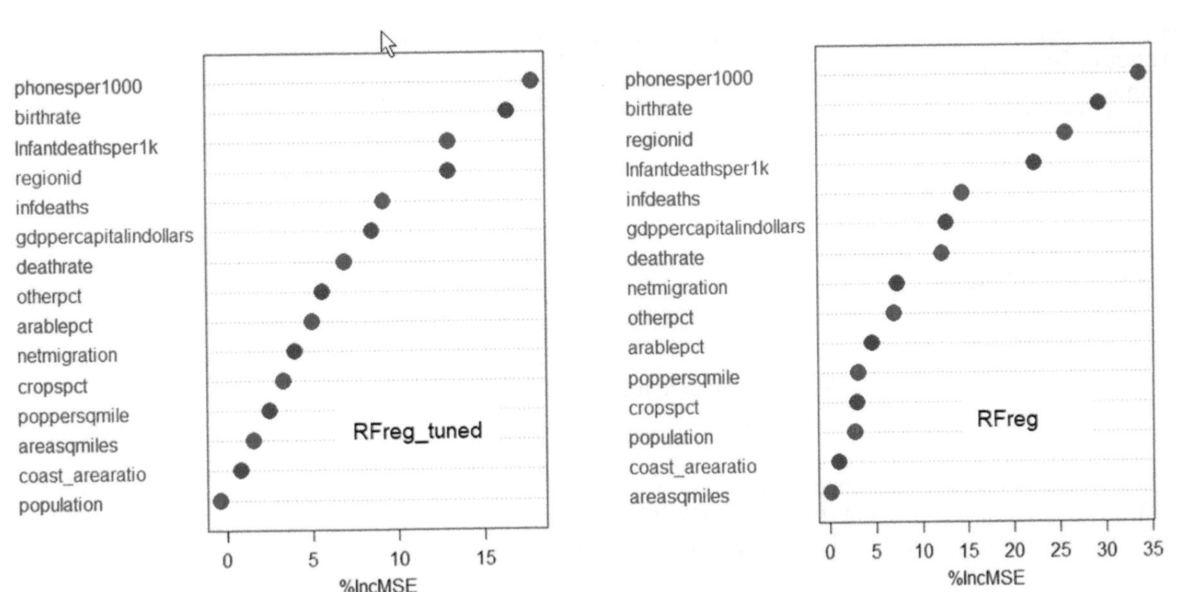

Figure 5.17 Variable importance for the Tuned and Untuned models

regression trees, which, not being categorical, have no "classes" of the outcome variable. Instead we may use residuals, being the difference of observed and predicted (expected) values (O – E), storing them in the object "residuals".

```
expected <- RFreg_tuned$predicted
observed <- world$literacy
residuals <- (observed-expected)
```

Optionally, we may view the first five residuals:

```
head(residuals, 5)
[Output:]
          1          2          3          4         5
  -9.932051 -22.129722 -17.670414   4.024936  14.644462
```

Now add residuals as a column called residuals in the world data frame

```
world$residuals <- residuals
```

Below we compute the mean and standard deviation for residuals, and the cutpoints for high and low outlier status, defining that as plus or minus 1.96 standard deviations from the mean or greater.

```
mean(world$residuals)
[Output:]
   [1] [1] 0.3913246

sd(world$residuals)
[Output:]
   [1] 11.4103
```

```
highOutlier = mean(world$residuals)+1.96*sd(world$residuals)
highOutlier
[Output:]
   [1] 22.75551

lowOutlier = mean(world$residuals)-1.96*sd(world$residuals)
lowOutlier
[Output:]
   [1] -21.97286

# Create the color codes.
# First create the new column "Color" and initialize it to white.
world$Color="white"

# Then set colors for lower and upper outliers.
world$Color[world$residuals < -21.97286]="blue"
world$Color[world$residuals >= 22.7551]="red"

# Plot all points using these colors. This is the basis for Figure 5.18.
# literacy is column 13 and residuals is column 25 (check using names(world)).
# Optionally we store the plot in the object "plot3reg" for later use.
plot3reg <- plot(world[,"literacy"], world[,"residuals"], pch=19, lwd=4,
xlab="Observed Literacy", ylab= "Raw Residual", col=world$Color)
# We then draw a line at the mean of residuals, which is always 0:
abline(h=0, col="gray50")

# Add a legend for the high and low outliers ranges.
# The RColorBrewer color management package was discussed earlier.
library(RColorBrewer)
legend("bottomright", legend=c("High Outliers","Low Outliers"), fill=brewer.
pal(length(3), "Set1"))
```

We now label the outliers by country name. This involves creating an OutliersOnly subset of the world data frame. As with the plot, we use as coordinates the values in the 13th (literacy) and 25th (residuals) column of the world database.

```
OutliersOnly <- subset(world, world$Color!="white")

text(OutliersOnly[,"literacy"], OutliersOnly[,"residuals"], OutliersOnly$country,
cex=1.0, pos=3, col="grey40")
```

Removing outliers from the data frame is controversial for reasons given in Section 5.4.6.2. However, it is easy to create a subset of the world dataframe in a manner similar to creating the OutliersOnly data frame above. Recall that nations that were not outliers were assigned the world$Color value of "white", so this may be used as a selection criterion. The resulting data frame, NoOutliers, contains the 194 nations which were not outliers.

```
NoOutliers <- subset(world, world$Color=="white")
nrow(NoOutliers)
[Output:]
     [1] 194
```

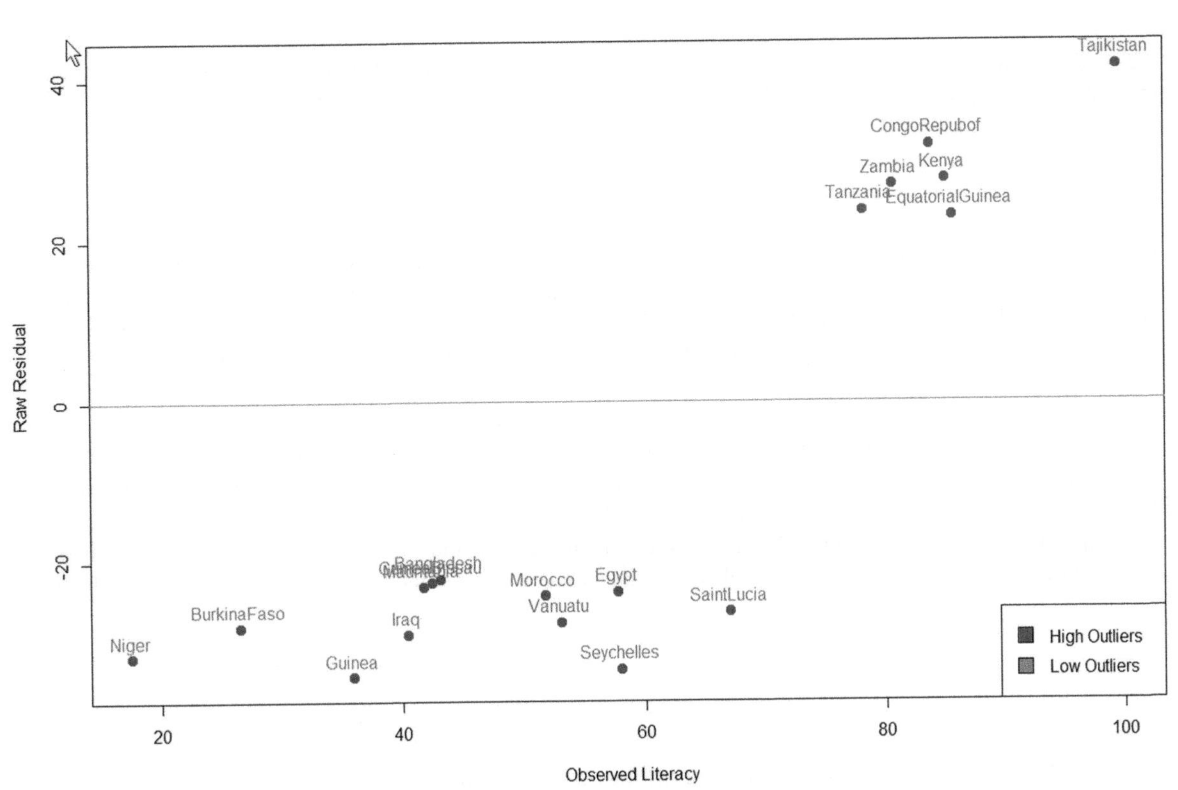

Figure 5.18 Outliers for the Regression forest model

TEXT BOX 5.3 Social science applications of R: Risk factors for corporal punishment

Fritsch et al. (2019) used the randomForest package in R to study aggressiveness, dysfunctional parent-child interactions, and other risk factors for corporal punishment of children by their fathers. In the study, the authors compared the random forest (RF) method with quantile regression (QR). Noting the possibility of complex multilevel interactions among risk factors, the authors viewed RF as a valuable check on the validity of QR models.

As discussed in the literature review portion of their article, the use of regression trees and random forests in psychological research has been common. They note that a reason for its use is that RF enables the researcher to avoid imposing a priori assumptions on the model, such as specifying a particular functional form (e.g., linear vs. nonlinear link functions relating the predictors to the outcome) or specifying exactly which predictors affect the outcome variable. This is particularly appropriate where researchers lack clear guidance from psychological theory or literature, as is not infrequently the case. Where regression trees may be unstable and exhibit low predictive performance due to overfitting, random forests do not suffer the same drawbacks due to their averages over a forest of regression trees. By fitting a model on bootstrap samples from the original data, RF decorrelates individual tree results by reducing the overlap of the data based on which the trees are fit and by using only a subset of predictors to make any particular split.

In the empirical portion of their paper, the authors compared RF results with QR-based results of Haupt et al. (2014). In the main, RF was able to replicate the main results of the 2014 study but varied in the choice of predictors chosen on a data-driven basis by RF as compared to those chosen based on a priori assumptions by QR. Both models were found to reveal similar facts: (1) in- and out-of-sample error measures were comparable; and (2) in agreement with the QR approach, the authors found different effects at different levels of the predictors (e.g., with regard to SES). In contrast, both RF and QR models demonstrated that conventional multiple linear regression (OLS) might not be adequate to capture complex dynamics among the predictor variables.

The RF approach, which may be more parsimonious than regression, revealed a small number of risk factors that were relevant for fathers' corporal punishment of children. The RF model suggested that corporal punishment was most prevalent where there was dysfunction interaction between parents and children and the fathers had enhanced levels of physical health complaints. The key findings were consistent with the international literature on risk factors for corporal punishment and physical abuse. Perhaps because data was from a "normal" population without many families at high risk for corporal punishment, effect sizes were small. The authors speculate that an oversampling of high-risk families would probably have led to more extreme cases and stronger correlations.

Source: Fritsch, M.; Haupt, H.; Lösel, F.; & Stemmler, M. (2019). Regression trees and random forests as alternatives to classical regression modeling: Investigating the risk factors for corporal punishment. *Psychological Test and Assessment Modeling* 61(4): 389–417.

Haupt, H.; Lösel, F.; & Stemmler, M. (2014). Quantile regression analysis and other alternatives to ordinary least squares regression: A methodological comparison on corporal punishment. *Methodology* 10(3): 81–91.

5.6 The randomForestExplainer package

The "randomForestExplainer" package is a set of utilities which accepts objects from the `randomForest()` command and provides output beyond that of the randomForest package itself. To illustrate this additional output, in this section we follow the work of Aleksandra Paluszyńska (2017a,2017b), coauthor with Biecek Przemyslaw of the randomForestExplainer package.[10]

5.6.1 Setup for the randomForestExplainer package

In Section 5.4.1, we start by making sure needed objects are still in the R environment. The following commands have been used in previous sections to clear the environment, set the working directory, read in the "world" data frame, set print options to maximum machine size, and call the randomForest package. We also call the randomForestExplainer package. Note that installation of the latter also automatically installs a large number of dependent packages, such as ggplot2.

```
setwd("C:/Data")
world <- read.table("world.csv", header = TRUE, sep = ",", stringsAsFactors = TRUE)
options("max.print"=.Machine$integer.max)

library(randomForest)
library(randomForestExplainer)
```

We rerun the command creating RFreg_tuned, the tuned regression forest model created in Section 5.5.9. However, the option `importance=TRUE` is replaced with `localImp=TRUE`, which calls for computation of casewise importance measures. This substitution is essential for randomForestExplainer.

```
set.seed(123)
RFreg_tuned <- randomForest::randomForest(literacy ~ regionid +  population +
areasqmiles + poppersqmile + coast_arearatio + netmigration + Infantdeathsper1k +
infdeaths + gdppercapitalindollars + phonesper1000 + arablepct + cropspct + otherpct +
birthrate + deathrate, control=rpart.control(minbucket = 5), ntree=501, mtry=3,
localImp=TRUE, proximity=TRUE, oob.prox=TRUE, data=world)
```

Below, we verify that basic performance data are the same as in Section 5.5.9.

```
RFreg_tuned
```
[Partial output:]
```
   Type of random forest: regression
   Number of trees: 501
   No. of variables tried at each split: 3
   Mean of squared residuals: 129.734
   % Var explained: 65.61
```

5.6.2 Minimal depth plots

The minimal depth plot provides another basis for evaluating variable importance. "Depth" for a variable is how many nodes down in the tree are located, starting numbering at 0 for the root node. "Minimal depth" is the lowest depth value (hence highest in the tree) for the first instance of a given splitting variable. "Mean minimal depth" is minimal depth for a variable averaged across all the trees in the forest.

Variables with similar minimal depth are closely related to each other within the forest. Moreover, mean minimal depth is an indicator of variable importance since variables with lower mean minimal depth are higher in the tree, and thus serve to sort more observations. Put another way, the lower the mean minimal depth of a variable across trees in a forest, the greater the influence of that variable. Note that some authors use "minimal depth" as shorthand for "mean minimal depth". See Ishwaran et al. (2010).

To analyze minimal depth by variable, we use two randomForestExplainer programs: `min_depth_distribution()` and its plotting companion, `plot_min_depth_distribution()`. The nature of minimal depth analysis is best understood when the reader can view the distribution plot. Therefore, we first create the plot in Figure 5.19, then interpret it.

```
# Compute a data frame for minimal depth (may take a long time for large forests).
min_depth_frame <- randomForestExplainer::min_depth_distribution(RFreg_tuned)

# Optionally we can save and load this data frame from/back to memory.
# We do this because large forests take a long time to create min_depth_frame.
save(min_depth_frame, file = "min_depth_frame.rda")
load("min_depth_frame.rda")
```

In the plot command below, the "relevant trees" option calculates mean minimal depth excluding missing values. Missing values occur when a variable is not used for splitting. The alternative "all_trees" fills in missing values with the mean depth of trees. The alternative "top_trees" is the default and penalizes missing values.

```
# Plot minimal depth of variables. This produces Figure 5.19.
# k=15 asks for 15 variables; leaving the k= option out defaults to the top ten variables.
# If k is more than the number of predictors, all variables will be plotted.
randomForestExplainer::plot_min_depth_distribution(min_depth_frame, mean_sample =
"relevant_trees", k = 15)
```

Interpretation of the minimal depth plot. In Figure 5.19, the x-axis is the number of trees (0 to 501) and the y-axis are rows for the 15 predictor variables, ordered by mean minimal depth. The higher the variable is in this plot, the greater its influence in the model. Influence here is defined in terms of splitting. The lower the mean minimal depth, the closer that variable was on average to the root of trees in the forest and consequently the higher the number of observations (nations) were affected by it. The birthrate variable was the most influential by this criterion and otherpct the least influential. Since reds and oranges corresponded to depths of 0 and 1, the more red and orange in a given variable's row, the lower its mean minimal depth and the greater its influence. Put another way, the color bar for a variable shows its distribution on minimal depth, giving more information than mean minimal depth alone.

Note that there are multiple ways to measure variable influence or importance. Previously, for instance, variable importance plots were shown for regression forests, where node MSE and node purity were used as criteria to rank

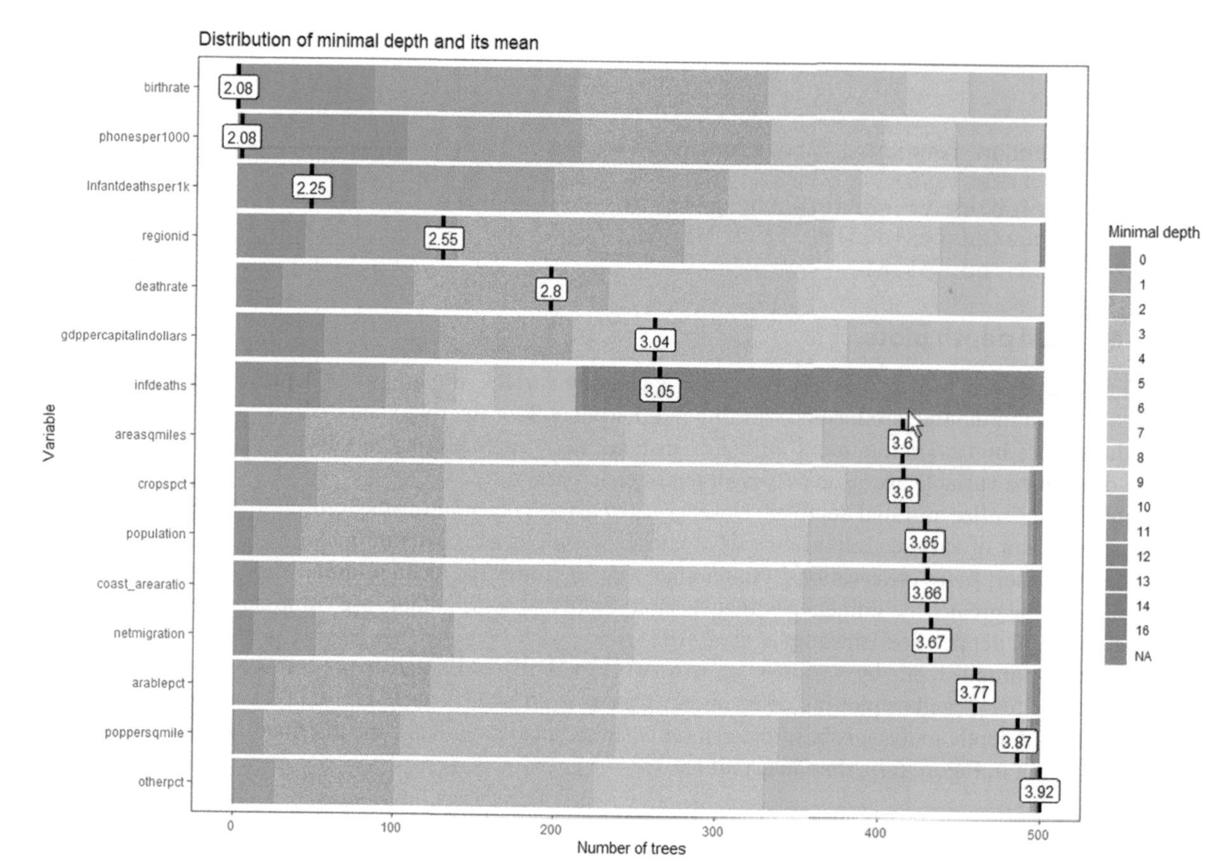

Figure 5.19 Minimal depth plot for RFreg_tuned

variables by importance. These alternative criteria led to slightly different rankings of variables. One of the advantages of randomForestExplainer is that it supports a variety of variable importance criteria, as discussed below. The researcher may prefer one criterion over another or may wish to look at rankings by all criteria to best assess the role of a given predictor variable.

5.6.3 Multiway variable importance plots

The randomForestExplainer packages supports analysis of variable importance by up to seven separate criteria for "importance." Moreover, criteria may be applied jointly. The `measure_importance()` command in the randomForestExplainer package creates an "importance frame", which is the foundation for multiway importance plots. This command assumes that the `randomForest()` call that created the randomForest object (here, RFreg_tuned) included the option `localImp=TRUE`, as specified above. Due to the time involved for large forests, we save this frame for future reuse and then reload it.

```
importance_frame <- randomForestExplainer::measure_importance(RFreg_tuned)
```

Due to the time involved for large forests, the measure_importance frame may be saved and then reloaded later as needed (not run here).

```
save(importance_frame, file = "importance_frame.rda")
load("importance_frame.rda")
```

The `head()` command below provides a listing of first six rows (variables) in the importance_frame, with seven importance criteria as columns.

```
head(importance_frame)
[Output:]
         variable mean_min_depth no_of_nodes mse_increase
1       arablepct       3.798287        2366    5.1563372
2     areasqmiles       3.638383        2425    1.6472192
3       birthrate       2.088096        2967   84.7996981
4 coast_arearatio       3.740862        2086    0.8347313
5        cropspct       3.640383        2485    4.0952563
6       deathrate       2.800000        2840   11.1017964
  node_purity_increase no_of_trees times_a_root      p_value
1             1757.688         497            1 2.943672e-01
2             1810.682         496            9 3.640109e-02
3            13327.779         499           85 2.219033e-38
4             1885.237         491           16 1.000000e+00
5             2088.935         496            1 1.110183e-03
6             4220.937         500           29 1.894728e-25
```

The object importance_frame contains as many rows as there are predictor variables. The eight columns (not counting the row index number column) contain the variable names and seven variable importance measures, which are listed here.

- `mean_minimal_depth`: mean minimal depth, as discussed in Section 5.4.3. Lower is more influential.
- `no_of_nodes`: total number of nodes that use XjXj for splitting. Higher is more influential.
- `mse_increase` (regression trees only): mean increase of mean squared error after splitting of the given variable is permuted (shuffled). Higher is more influential. See discussion of %IncMSE in Section 5.3. For classification trees, accuracy_decrease, which is the mean decrease of prediction accuracy after splitting, is shown.
- `node_purity_increase` (regression trees only): mean node purity increases by splits on the given variable, as measured by the decrease in sum of squares. Higher is more influential. For classification trees, gini_decrease, which is the mean decrease in the Gini index of node impurity (equivalent to an increase of node purity) after splitting, is shown.
- `no_of_trees`: total number of trees in which a split on the given variable occurs, Higher is more influential.
- `times_a_root`: total number of trees in which the given variable is used for splitting the root node, thus applying to the whole sample. Higher is more influential.
- `p_value`: the p value indicates the number of nodes in which the given variable was used for splitting divided by the theoretical number if splits were random, based on a binomial distribution. A low p value means there is strong evidence against the null hypothesis that the number of nodes in which the given variable was used for splitting is no greater than would be expected by chance. Lower is more influential.

The `plot_multi_way_importance()` function in the randomForestExplainer package produces plots for any pair of these importance criteria. This function uses the importance_frame object discussed above. We present only two of the many possible plots. Since dot size can be used to represent a third importance criterion in addition the x-axis and y-axis criteria, it is possible in any given plot to represent all modeled variables in terms of three definitions of importance.

In the first plot we show all variables in terms of mse_increase on the x-axis, mean_min_depth on the y-axis, using node_purity _increase as dot size. By specifying `no_of_labels = 15` we ask that all 15 predictor variables be plotted. (Ten is default, though if there is a tie, then 11 might be plotted.)

```
randomForestExplainer::plot_multi_way_importance(importance_frame, size_measure =
"node_purity_increase", x_measure="mse_increase", y_measure="mean_min_depth",
no_of_labels=15)
```

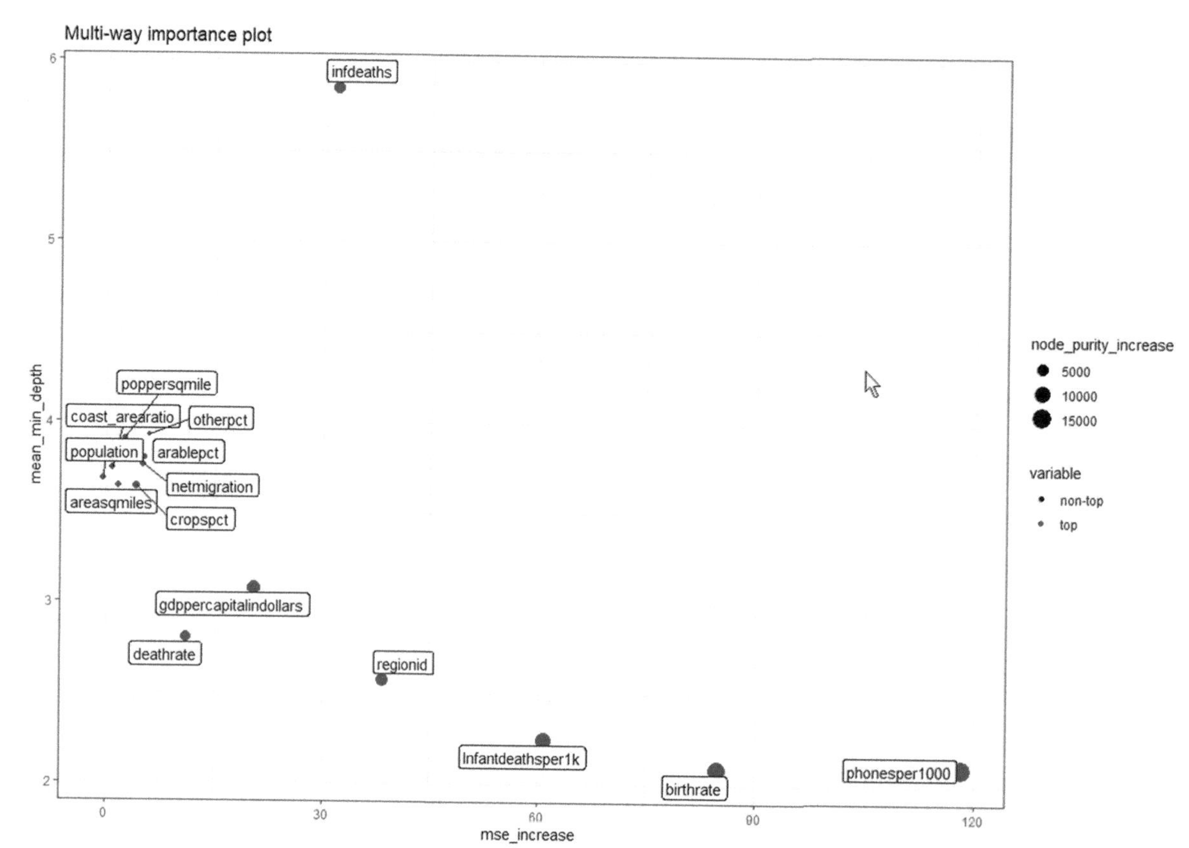

Figure 5.20 Multiway variable importance plot 1

Figure 5.20 shows that phonesper1000 is most influential in predicting literacy by the mse_increase criterion and also by the mean_min_depth criterion. Birthrate is second.

In the second plot, we show all variables in terms of p_value on the x-axis, mean_min_depth on the y-axis, using mse_increase as dot size.

```
randomForestExplainer::plot_multi_way_importance(importance_frame, size_measure =
"mse_increase", x_measure="p_value", y_measure="mean_min_depth", no_of_labels=15)
```

Figure 5.21 shows that birthrate closely followed by phonesper100 is most influential in predicting literacy by the mean_minimum_depth criterion. By the p_value criterion, both are also highly significant, though so are six other variables. However, by the mse_increase criterion, phonesper100 is the most influential variable, closely followed by birthrate and infantdeathsper1k.

The reader may be wondering what the "Variable" portion of the legend is in the previous two figures. Here this is irrelevant if, as above, we specify that all variables be labeled. However, if we ask for fewer, say 5, then the plot will depict the 5 variables, which are most important on the combined multiple importance criteria. These variables will be shown in blue as the "top" variables, while all other variables are plotted in black without labels. "Top" variables are selected based on the sum of rankings by the three specified importance criteria.

In conclusion, which variables are most important or influential depends on which definition (which criterion) of "importance" one uses, though it is clear for the present example that by any criterion, some variables are more important than others in predicting literacy. In the following section (Section 5.6.4), we see that randomForestExplainer allows us to rank predictor variables on importance across multiple combined criteria.

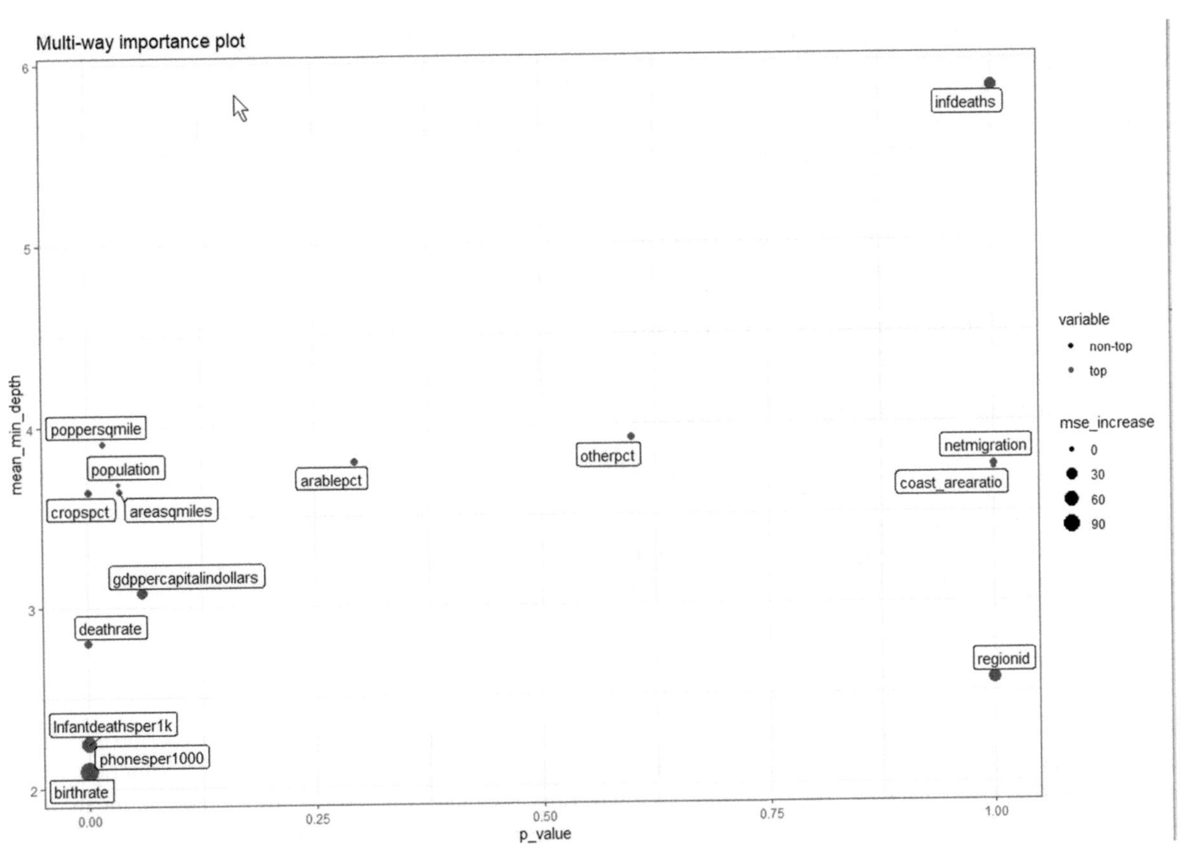

Figure 5.21 Multiway variable importance plot 2

5.6.4 Multiway ranking of variable importance

In this section, we rank variables by importance using from 1 to all 7 importance criteria. First, however, it is useful to keep in mind the list of possible importance criteria as we will need to use their index numbers in the `important _ variables()` function, which will return the ranking of variables. The `names()` function can provide this listing.

```
names(importance_frame)
[Output:]
    [1] "variable"
    [2] "mean_min_depth"
    [3] "no_of_nodes"
    [4] "mse_increase"
    [5] "node_purity_increase"
    [6] "no_of_trees"
    [7] "times_a_root"
    [8] "p_value"
```

Note that no_of_trees and p_value all share similar information with no_of_nodes since all reflect the number of nodes that use a given variable for splitting.

If we are interested in ranking predictors by a single criterion, such as mse_increase, this is simply a matter of sorting the importance_frame by that criterion into a new data frame, then calling the columns in that new data frame corresponding to the variable name (1) and the criterion (4 for mse_increase). Since higher is better for the mse criterion, we sort descending by adding a minus sign before `importance _ frame$mse _ increase`. The syntax below provides a listing of all 15 predictor variables ranked in descending order by the mse_increase criterion for variable importance. A similar listing could be provided for any of the seven importance criteria in the same manner.

```
Iframe_sorted_on_mse <- importance_frame[order(-importance_frame$mse_increase),]

Iframe_sorted_on_mse[,c(1,4)]
```

[Output:]

```
                     variable mse_increase
12              phonesper1000  118.3072516
3                   birthrate   84.7996981
8           Infantdeathsper1k   60.8514470
15                   regionid   38.3416873
9                   infdeaths   31.7439324
7     gdppercapitalindollars   20.3872234
6                   deathrate   11.1017964
11                   otherpct    5.9280515
1                   arablepct    5.1563372
10               netmigration    5.0264190
5                    cropspct    4.0952563
13               poppersqmile    2.5346831
2                 areasqmiles    1.6472192
4             coast_arearatio    0.8347313
14                 population   -0.4640539
```

However, what if we wish to rank variables by importance using more than one importance criterion simultaneously? This can be implemented easily using the `important _ variables()` function of the randomForestExplainer package. As an example, we will rank predictor variables on three criteria: mean_min_depth (index number 2 in importance_frame), mse_increase (4), and node_purity_increase (5). We then run the `important _ variables()` function for the selected criteria. The output is the ranking of predictor variables by the combined three importance criteria.

```
randomForestExplainer::important_variables(importance_frame, k = 15,  measures =
names(importance_frame)[c(2,4:5)], ties_action = "all")
```

[Output:]

```
 [[1] "phonesper1000"
  [2] "birthrate"
  [3] "Infantdeathsper1k"
  [4] "regionid"
  [5] "gdppercapitalindollars"
  [6] "deathrate"
  [7] "infdeaths"
  [8] "cropspct"
  [9] "netmigration"
 [10] "areasqmiles"
 [11] "arablepct"
 [12] "coast_arearatio"
 [13] "population"
 [14] "otherpct"
 [15] "poppersqmile"
```

5.6.5 Comparing randomForest and OLS rankings of predictors

In this section, we use the same predictor variables in an OLS regression and use the standardized regression coefficient weights (beta weights) to rank the predictors by importance, where a higher beta reflects more importance for variables, which are significant. We demonstrate that the ranking of variables by OLS is different from that using a random forest approach.

Because the ranking of variables by importance in the OLS regression model was treated in detail in Section 2.3, that R code and output is not repeated here. Instead we take the opportunity to illustrate a different approach using the lm.beta package (in Section 2.3, the betas package was used).

```
# Install and activate a package to add beta weights to lm() objects
library(lm.beta)

# Compute linear regression using same variables as for the regression forest model.
regOut <- lm(literacy ~ regionid + population + areasqmiles + poppersqmile + coast_
arearatio + netmigration + Infantdeathsper1k + infdeaths + gdppercapitalindollars +
phonesper1000 + arablepct + cropspct + otherpct + birthrate + deathrate, data=world)

#Apply the lm.beta() function to add beta weights
regOut_beta <- lm.beta::lm.beta(regOut)
```

The estimated beta weights below are the same as computed by Stata or other statistical packages, provided regionid is designated as a categorical variable (in Stata, i.regionid). In R the intercept is given a beta value of 0, whereas most statistical packages do not compute beta for the intercept and assign it a blank entry.

```
# Put beta weights into an object labeled "betas".
betas <- coef(regOut_beta, standardized=TRUE)
# Sort betas on the absolute value of beta weights, from highest to lowest
sorted <- sort(abs(betas),decreasing=TRUE)

# Loop through to print out the sorted beta weights
# Note there are now more variables (26) than in randomForest (16) because the regression function converts
factors like regionid into dummy variables.
# The sep="\t" option provides tabbed output, which is easier to read.
maxvars = length(sorted)
labels<-names(sorted)
   for(i in 1:maxvars) {
   sorted[i]
   writeLines(paste(sep="\t", "absolute beta weight rank ", i,
labels[i], sorted[i]))
}
[Output:]
   absolute beta weight rank     1     otherpct     23.8755919539934
   absolute beta weight rank     2     arablepct    19.4919943373246
   absolute beta weight rank     3     cropspct     11.6014247519024
   absolute beta weight rank     4     Infantdeathsper1k     0.442277686429311
   absolute beta weight rank     5     birthrate    0.324615869450487
   absolute beta weight rank     6     regionidCW   0.198953823142167
   absolute beta weight rank     7     deathrate    0.144202568217321
   absolute beta weight rank     8     regionidNF   0.110351102641437
   absolute beta weight rank     9     infdeathsLow 0.101892405739812
   absolute beta weight rank     10    gdppercapitalindollars     0.0786871553704361
   absolute beta weight rank     11    regionidSA   0.0663581020539736
   absolute beta weight rank     12    regionidDQ   0.0504623242952434
   absolute beta weight rank     13    areasqmiles  0.0435627876823107
   absolute beta weight rank     14    regionidNE   0.0392926531656823
   absolute beta weight rank     15    regionidNO   0.0322732629612451
   absolute beta weight rank     16    phonesper1000 0.0320039749648959
   absolute beta weight rank     17    regionidLA   0.0304852998775114
   absolute beta weight rank     18    regionidEE   0.0298187985778859
   absolute beta weight rank     19    regionidWE   0.0257852364357545
   absolute beta weight rank     20    poppersqmile 0.023461651473014
```

```
absolute beta weight rank      21     regionidBA     0.0117442579634847
absolute beta weight rank      22     netmigration 0.0106642623692867
absolute beta weight rank      23     coast_arearatio      0.00937566427235431
absolute beta weight rank      24     population     0.00653495096501433
absolute beta weight rank      25     regionidOC     0.0027386083454321
absolute beta weight rank      26     (Intercept)   0
```

Discussion: Identification of the most important predictors differs.

- OLS model: In OLS regression, the top three predictors were otherpct, arablepct, and cropspct, but these were all nonsignificant. The land use variables could not be seen as surrogates for GDP since GDP was in the model and was not among the important predictors. For significant variables, the top three predictors in the OLS model were infantdeathsper1k, birthrate, and regionidCW (where regionidCW was Russia, Ukraine, Georgia, and other now-independent former USSR entities).
- RF model: By almost any combination of importance criteria, the top three predictors of literacy in the random forest procedure were phonesper1000, birthrate, and infantdeathsper1k. Thus, the random forest procedure focused on communications infrastructure (measured by phonesper1000) and demographic factors related to birthrate and infant deaths.

Selecting the optimal listing of variables by importance is not a statistical question, though some orderings are inconsistent with the data (e.g., net migration is not an important predictor under any model). As is often the case, different procedures call attention to different dynamics within a constellation of causes and effects. Some valuable information is to be gained from each approach. Relying on only one approach might well obscure the dynamics involved. Whether random forest regression or OLS regression is suggestive of more important aspects of the dynamics of national literacy and thus more useful for theory building, this writer leaves to the reader to decide. At a minimum, it can be said that random forest regression provides different insights of a more complex nature. Methodologically these insights are based on nonparametric, nonlinear modeling with automatic handling of factor variables and interactions, aspects of random forest regression that some researchers will find compelling arguments for its use at least as a complement to linear regression if not a replacement for it.

5.6.6 Which importance criteria?

In random forest analysis, although criteria used for ranking variables by importance are best based on theory and appropriateness to the specific research subject at hand, Paluszyńska (2017a: 9) suggests that the criterion of selecting "three that least agree with each other and use them in ... `plot _ importance _ ggpairs()`." This randomForestExplainer function returns correlations and scatterplots relating each pair of five importance criteria.

```
randomForestExplainer::plot_importance_ggpairs(importance_frame)
```

This plot is not shown here but is left to the reader. Instead a simple correlogram is recommended, in part because it shows the correlation of all seven importance measures, not just five.

```
# Load the corrplot package
library(corrplot)

# Place importance variables in the data frame "temp".
# The first column of the importance_frame (variable) is not numeric.
temp <- importance_frame[2:8]

# Create a correlation matrix of the importance variables.
temp2 <- cor(temp)

# Produce a correlogram of the correlation matrix. This is Figure 5.22.
corrplot(temp2,method="number")
```

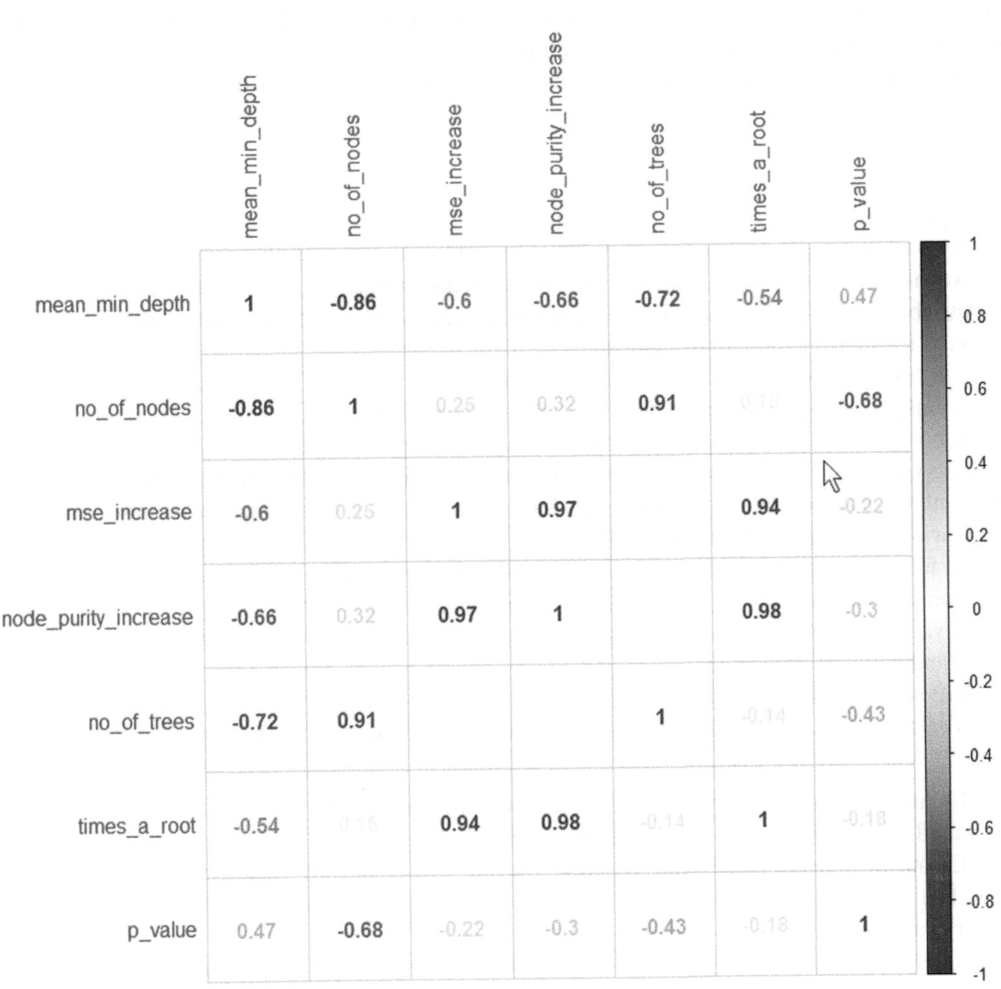

Figure 5.22 Correlation among importance measures

In Figure 5.22, positive correlations use a blue color ramp and negative correlations use a red one. Note that by default, correlations near 0 are printed in white, making the given cell appear empty.

As an example of using the correlogram in Figure 5.22, a researcher might be committed to using mse_increase as one of three importance criteria. For the other two, picking node_purity or times_a_root would be virtually redundant. Instead, picking no_of_nodes (or no_of_trees) and p_value would add diversity to the elements of combined importance.

5.6.7 Interaction analysis

In ordinary linear regression, an interaction is the joint effect of two (or more) variables, typically represented as the product of the two variables. If the two constituent variables are also in the model, then if this product term is significant then there is a non-zero joint effect of the interaction even after controlling for the two individual effects. Such a significant interaction means there is a moderating effect in the model.

In contrast, in random forest models, an interaction is defined by two criteria:

1. Maximal subtree: The maximal subtree for a given variable is the largest subtree whose root node splits on that variable. This might be the root node for the whole tree if the given variable is a root node variable. Otherwise the given variable forms the root node of a subtree and the maximal subtree is the largest such subtree.

2. Conditional minimal mean depth: The conditional minimal mean depth of a given variable is its minimal mean depth for the maximal subtree of the conditioning variable. The relation of the given variable to the conditioning variable, expressed as conditional minimal mean depth, defines its interaction with the conditioning variable.

Interaction in random forest regression thus has the same general meaning as in linear regression: The strength of the relationship of a given variable to the outcome variable depends on a conditioning variable. For instance, strength of relationship may be defined by a variable's unconditional mean depth across the trees in the forest. For interactions, we may look at the conditional mean depth, referring to mean depth when a given important variable is the splitting variable. By this criterion, variables higher in the tree have lower depth and are more important because they are the basis for splitting more of the sample.

If we were to take some of the unconditionally most important variables in the study, selecting them based on any of the previously-discussed multiple criteria for "importance", these could be treated as conditioning variables. We could then compute the conditional mean minimal depth of any variable the study with respect to any one of the conditioning variables. Conditionally, the mean minimal depth of a given variable would depend not on how far it was beneath the unconditional root of the tree, but rather how far it was beneath the split associated with the conditioning variable in its maximal subtree. By comparing the unconditional mean minimal depth of a variable (the same value for all conditioning variables) with its conditional mean minimal depth for each of the conditioning variables, we can see the effect of any conditioning variable on the strength of the relationship of the given variable to the outcome variable, thus revealing the interaction effect of the conditioning variable with the given variable in the context of random forest procedures.

The randomForestExplainer package is setup to use mean_min_depth as the importance criterion for the y-axis in the graph of interactions shown further below. The general procedure follows these steps:

- Step 1: Create "vars" as an object containing the result of the `important_variables()` function for a limited number of predictor variables (e.g., k = 5).
- Step 2: Create an "interactions_frame" based on the `min_depth_interactions()` function.
- Step 3: The `plot_min_depth_interactions()` function is used to create the interactions bar chart plot.
- Step 4: Interactions may also be plotted on a color grid using the `plot_predict_interaction()` function.

Step 1: In the first step we create an object labeled "vars" to contain the list of important variables, based on the "importance_frame" object created in Section 5.6.3 on the basis of RFreg_tuned, which was the tuned random forest model. In this section, we look at interactions involving these important variables. We select as importance measures mean_min_depth and mse_increase. Though we ask for the five most important variables, we get six due to a tie. The vars object is created by the `important_variables()` function of the randomForestExplainer package.

```
vars <- randomForestExplainer::important_variables(importance_frame, k = 5, measures =
c("mean_min_depth", "mse_increase"))

vars
```

[Output:]

```
  [1] "birthrate" "deathrate" "gdppercapitalindollars"
  [4] "Infantdeathsper1k" "phonesper1000" "regionid"
```

Step 2: The next step in analysis of interactions is to create an "interactions_frame" data frame based on the `min_depth_interactions()` function of randomForestExplainer. The interactions_frame object contains the information needed to compute the conditional minimal depth of variables in relation to each important variable contained in vars. If vars were omitted, then the vector of conditioning variables would by default be based on the nested functions in this command (not run here): `randomForestExplainer::important_variables(measure_importance(RFreg_tuned))`

However, for the current example, we create interactions_frame using the `min_depth_interactions()` function. This function computes conditional minimal depth in all trees (labeled mean_min_depth in output below) and also unconditional minimal depth (labeled uncond_mean_min_depth).

The commands below create the interactions_frame object for the current example. Note that we use the "relevant_trees" sample, which calculates mean minimal depth excluding missing values. Alternatives are "all_trees" (fills in missing values with the mean depth of trees) or "top_trees" (the default, which penalizes missing values). Be patient: For a large forest, this can take a long time (about 5 minutes on the author's machine). Optionally, we save and then reload this data frame so it does not need to be recreated in the future.

```
interactions_frame <- randomForestExplainer::min_depth_interactions(RFreg_tuned,
vars,mean_sample="relevant_trees")

save(interactions_frame, file = "interactions_frame.rda")
load("interactions_frame.rda")
```

We may view the six most-frequently occurring interactions using the `head()` function:

```
head(interactions_frame[order(interactions_frame$occurrences, decreasing = TRUE), ])
[Output:]
             variable root_variable mean_min_depth occurrences
7         areasqmiles     birthrate       2.329577         355
31          deathrate     birthrate       2.219020         347
43 Infantdeathsper1k     birthrate       1.962536         347
47 Infantdeathsper1k phonesper1000       2.078488         344
13          birthrate     birthrate       2.113703         343
71      phonesper1000 phonesper1000       2.452941         340
                    interaction uncond_mean_min_depth
7         birthrate:areasqmiles              3.602823
31          birthrate:deathrate              2.800000
43      birthrate:Infantdeathsper1k          2.246000
47 phonesper1000:Infantdeathsper1k          2.246000
13          birthrate:birthrate              2.076152
71      phonesper1000:phonesper1000          2.084168
```

Interpretation of the output above. The interactions_frame object for the example data has 90 rows – six conditioning variables (the six important variables) times all 15 variables in the model. Each row represents a pairwise interaction of two variables (three-way and higher interactions cannot be computed by the `min_depth_interactions()` function). Note that for the pair of variables, coefficients will differ depending on which is the conditioning variable and which is the given variable of interest.

The output above lists the six most frequently-occurring interactions. The most frequent, found in the row whose index number is 7 (the top row), was the "birthrate:areasqmiles" interaction. For this interaction, the conditioner (root_variable) was birthrate and the variable was areasqmiles. The interaction occurred 355 times out of the 501 trees in the forest. The mean minimal depth of areasqmiles conditional on birthrate was approximately 2.3 and the unconditional minimal depth of areasqmiles was approximately 3.6. This indicates that the mean minimal depth for areasqmiles was lower (recall lower means more important) in subtrees where birthrate was the splitting variable for the maximal subtree containing areasqmiles as compared to its mean minimal depth for the forest as a whole (the unconditional depth). This differential is the interaction labeled "birthrate:areasqmiles".

What may more informative is to look at the mean minimal depth for a given variable such as areasqmiles, conditional on each of the important conditioning variables. In the "interactions_frame$root_variable" element, variables 1–6 are the important/conditioning variables. Rows 7:12 are for areasqmiles as the variable, for each of six root variables. Type `View(interactions_frame)` to verify this. Among the six important variables, which were selected based on mean_min_depth and mse_increase, the Infantdeathsper1k:areasqmiles interaction has the highest mean minimal depth, and the gdppercapitalindollars:areasqmiles interaction has the lowest. Since low corresponds to more important, we can say that the interaction of area with gdp, among the six important variables, is the most important. That is, this interaction is associated with lower mean minimal depth.

```
writeLines(paste(sep="\t",interactions_frame$root_variable[1:6],interactions_
frame$mean_min_depth[73:78],interactions_frame$occurrences[7:12],
interactions_frame$interaction[7:12]))
```

[Output:

```
conditioning var., mean min. depth, no. of occurrences, interaction
birthrate        2.57878787878788    355    birthrate:areasqmiles
deathrate        2.33217993079585    289    deathrate:areasqmiles
gdppercap…lars 2.28735632183908    245    gdppercapitalindollars:areasqmiles
Infantdeath…1k 2.5981308411215     319    Infantdeathsper1k:areasqmiles
phonesper1000    2.52                333    phonesper1000:areasqmiles
regionid         2.55891238670695    317    regionid:areasqmiles
```

Step 3: Interaction information is visualized using the `plot _ min _ depth _ interactions()` function to create the interactions bar chart plot.

```
# The k=10 option asks for the ten best interactions.
randomForestExplainer::plot_min_depth_interactions(interactions_frame,k=10,main="Ten
Most Frequent Interactions")
```

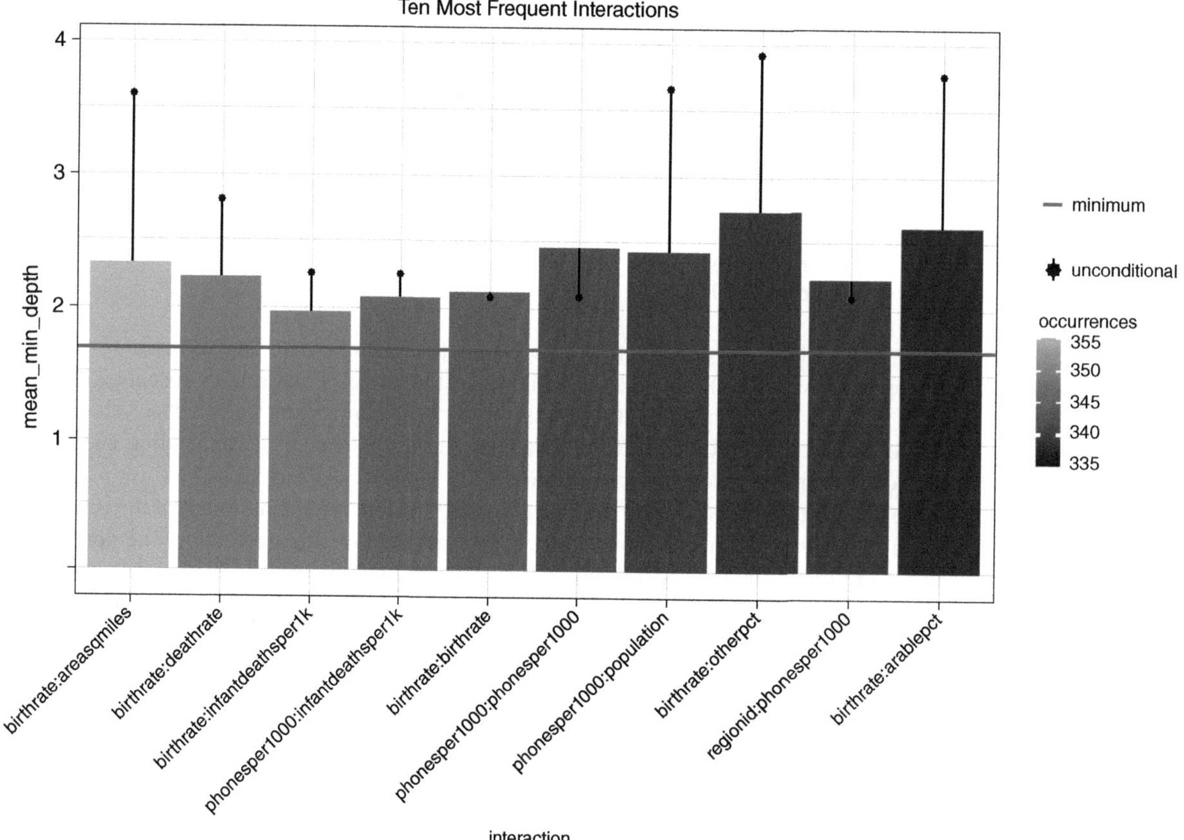

Figure 5.23 Ten most frequent interactions

Interpretation of Figure 5.23. The interactions are shown in order of decreasing occurrence, from bright blue on the left to fewer occurrence shows in black on the right. Interactions are labeled below the bars, with the first interaction being birthrate:areasqmiles, where areasqmiles is conditioned by birthrate. The height of the bar corresponds to the conditional mean minimal depth for that interaction. The red line represents the mean minimal depth across all interactions. These may be compared to the unconditional mean minimal depth for a given interaction, represented by the black "lollipop", which is the point at the end of the line above the bar. For the first bar, this is the unconditional mean minimal depth for areasqmiles. Note that it is possible for the unconditional mean minimal depth to be higher or lower than the conditional depth.

Step 4: Interactions may also be plotted on a color grid using the `plot _ predict _ interaction()` function. Below we use this function to explore the phonesper1000:Infantdeathsper1k interaction as an example, illustrated in Figure 5.24.

In Figure 5.24, the `plot _ predict _ interaction()` function of the randomForestExplainer package is used to show the interaction effect of phonesper1000 and Infantdeathsper1k when predicting literacy.

```
plot_predict_interaction(RFreg_tuned,world, "phonesper1000","Infantdeathsper1k")
```

With a very strong interaction effect, the corner quadrants of the graph would contrast markedly, with blues in the upper left and reds in the lower right, for these variables. Though here the interaction is not strong, it can be seen that when phonesper1000 is less than about 50 and Infantdeathsper1k is high, there is a tendency to predict low national literacy rates (blue). When phonesper1000 are greater than about 50 there is tendency to predict higher literacy (red). When phonesper1000 are greater than about 50 and Infantdeathsper1k are less than about 25, there is a tendency to predict even higher national literacy rates (more dark red).

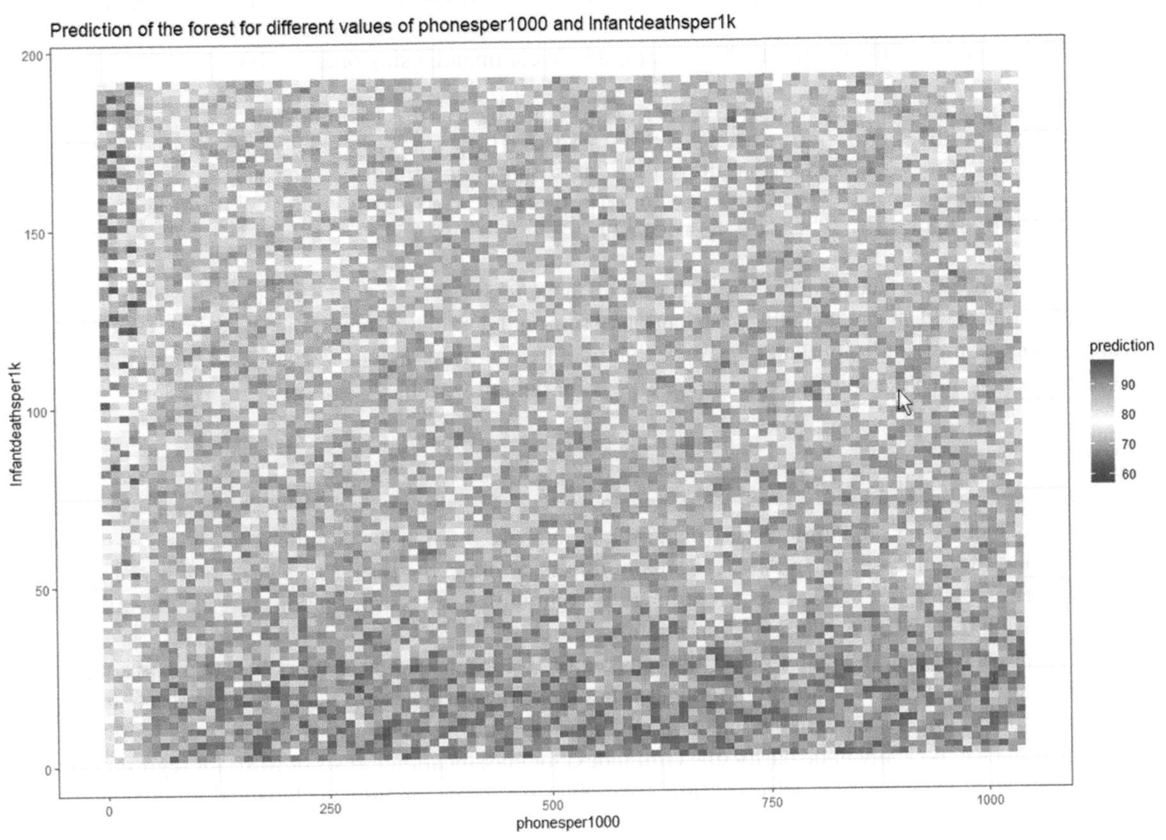

Figure 5.24 The phonesper1000: deathsper1k interaction

5.6.8 The explain_forest() function

The explain_forest() function of the randomForestExplainer package is intended by its author to be the "flagship function" of the package. It produces an html report summarizing the basic results possible with the various other functions of the package. The basic command for the example data is below. Output is sent to an html file in the user's working directory by default titled "Your_forest_explained.html". This file is readable by web browsers. While it may be opened by most word processors, including Microsoft Word, figures may not be viewable by this method.

These are the options for the explain_forest() function:

forest	A randomForest object created with the option localImp = TRUE
interactions	Logical value = TRUE if variable interactions be considered
data	The data frame on which forest was trained
vars	A character vector with variables with respect to which interactions will be considered if NULL then they will be selected using the important_variables() function
no_of_pred_plots	The number of most frequent interactions of numeric variables to plot predictions for
pred_grid	The number of points on the grid of plot_predict_interaction decreases if memory problems occur
measures	A character vector specifying the importance measures to be used

The basic explain_forest() command for the example data is:

```
randomForestExplainer::explain_forest(RFreg_tuned,interactions=TRUE,data=world)
```

A more elaborate version of the explain_forest() command, using options above, is:

```
randomForestExplainer::explain_forest(RFreg_tuned,interactions=TRUE, data=world,
vars = NULL,  no_of_pred_plots = 3, pred_grid = 100, measures = if (RFreg_tuned$type
== "classification") c("mean_min_depth", "accuracy_decrease", "gini_decrease", "no_
of_nodes", "times_a_root") else c("mean_min_depth", "mse_increase","node_purity_
increase", "no_of_nodes", "times_a_root"))
```

Though output is not reproduced here, key sections of the explain_forest() report parallel earlier tables and plots discussed above, including distribution of minimal depth, the Importance measures table, multiway importance plots, comparing importance measures and comparing rankings of variables,[11] conditional minimal depth for interactions, and grid plots of interaction effects for default variables.

5.7 Summary

This chapter has focused on random forests, which seek to improve predictions of either categorical or continuous outcome variables through ensemble methods. Random forests combine the results of a large number of individual classification or regression trees. Because this strategy is commonly successful, random forests are routinely preferred over decision trees when prediction is paramount.

There are many flavors of random forest but all types require selection of splitting variables to use in constructing the decision trees in the forest. A major divide concerns how splitting variables are selected. The most common type of random forest algorithm bases variable selection on choosing splitting variables, which optimize some measure of model performance, typically node purity (the Gini index) for classification forests or MSE for regression forests. A second, increasingly popular type selects splitting variables based on conditional statistical inference, selecting variables with the best significance (p) values. The cforest() program is of this type, described in an online supplement to Chapter 5.

Classification forests deal with categorical response variables and lend themselves to some forms of analysis, which regression forests do not. A notable illustration described in Section 5.4.7 was MDS plots showing the clustering of observations. Likewise, regression forests have their own unique forms of analysis, such as quartile plots (Section 5.5.7).

In summary, random forests are a powerful analytic tool for research. The researcher's goals may include prediction, classification, and variable selection. Its ensemble methods typically lead to better results than those of single decision trees. The fact that random forests automatically handle nonlinearity means random forests routinely outperform linear regression. Moreover, the random forest approach does so using both categorical and continuous variables, is robust against multicollinearity, works with large numbers of variables, can be used with small samples, and is nonparametric.

For data exploration and theory-construction with a categorical outcome variable, classification forests have the advantage of being equifinal, meaning this procedure can reveal multiple constellations of classes (categorical variables) or value ranges (continuous variables) leading to the same prediction for a given class of the outcome variable. In contrast with OLS regression's focus on beta weights as a measure of variable importance, in regression forests there are multiple possible definitions of and metrics for variable importance. These give different rankings of variable importance by different definitions of that term. For reasons such as these, random forests are among the most widely used of data science techniques.

5.8 Conditional inference forests

Treatment of conditional inference forests `cforest()` program is presented in an online supplement to Chapter 5, found in the student section of this book's Support Material (www.routledge.com/9780367624293). Conditional forests are notable for incorporating significance testing.

5.9 MDS plots for random forests

Treatment of MDS plots for random forests is presented in an online supplement to Chapter 5, found in the student section of this book's Support Material (www.routledge.com/9780367624293). MDS plots use proximity information from random forest solutions to cluster observations, as shown in the Figure 5.25. Explanation of the figure is contained in the supplement.

5.10 More random forest programs for R

As mentioned earlier, the R community is prolific in generating new and diverse programs for many procedures, including random forests. Below we mention just a few of the much larger number of additional R programs for random forests. By "additional" we mean beyond the randomForest and randomForestExplainer packages, which are by far most widely used and are the focus of in this chapter, and beyond the party and partykit packages which contain `cforest()`, the second most widely used package and the focus of an online supplement to this chapter. A full listing of R packages by name, with links, is at: https://cran.r-project.org/web/packages/available_packages_by_name.html

Among the most popular packages listed are these:

- extraTrees: Extremely Randomized Trees (ExtraTrees) Method for Classification and Regression.
- randomForestSRC: Fast Unified Random Forests for Survival, Regression, and Classification (RF-SRC).
- ranger: A Fast Implementation of Random Forests. See also tuneRanger: Tune Random Forest of the 'ranger' Package
- Rborist: Multiple Imputation using Chained Random Forests.
- rotationForest: Fit and Deploy Rotation Forest Models.
- RRF: Regularized Random Forest.
- wsrf: Weighted Subspace Random Forest for Classification.

Figure 5.25 Illustration of an MDS plot for random forest proximities

Other relevant random forest packages are these:

- abcrf: Approximate Bayesian Computation via Random Forests
- AUCRF: Variable Selection with Random Forest and the Area Under the Curve
- binomialRF: Binomial Random Forest Feature Selection
- blockForest: Block Forests: Random Forests for Blocks of Clinical and Omics Covariate Data
- Dforest: Decision Forest
- drf: Distributional Random Forests
- forestError: A Unified Framework for Random Forest Prediction Error Estimation
- ggRandomForests: Visually Exploring Random Forests
- grf: Generalized Random Forests
- h2o: R Interface for the 'H2O' Scalable Machine Learning Platform. For Big Data.

- IntegratedMRF: Integrated Prediction using Univariate and Multivariate Random Forests
- iRF: Iterative Random Forests
- JRF: Joint Random Forest (JRF) for the Simultaneous Estimation of Multiple Related Networks
- KnowGRRF: Knowledge-Based Guided Regularized Random Forest
- LongituRF: Random Forests for Longitudinal Data
- metaforest: Exploring Heterogeneity in Meta-Analysis using Random Forests
- miceRanger: Multiple Imputation by Chained Equations with Random Forests
- missForest: Nonparametric Missing Value Imputation using Random Forest
- mobForest: Model Based Random Forest Analysis
- moreparty: A Toolbox for Conditional Inference Random Forests
- MultivariateRandomForest: Models Multivariate Cases using Random Forests
- obliqueRF: Oblique Random Forests from Recursive Linear Model Splits
- obliqueRSF: Oblique Random Forests for Right-Censored Time-to-Event Data
- orf: Ordered Random Forests
- pRF: Permutation Significance for Random Forests.
- randomUniformForest: Random Uniform Forests for Classification, Regression, and Unsupervised Learning
- Rfinterval: Predictive Inference for Random Forests
- rfUtilities: Random Forests Model Selection and Performance Evaluation
- rfVarImpOOB: Unbiased Variable Importance for Random Forests
- rfviz: Interactive Visualization Tool for Random Forests
- SoftRandomForest: Classification Random Forests for Soft Decision Trees
- Sstack: Bootstrap Stacking of Random Forest Models for Heterogeneous Data
- tree.interpreter: Random Forest Prediction Decomposition and Feature Importance Measure
- trimTrees: Trimmed Opinion Pools of Trees in a Random Forest.
- varSelRF: Variable Selection using Random Forests
- VSURF: Variable Selection using Random Forests
- xgboost: Extreme Gradient Boosting

5.11 Command summary

For convenience for those wishing to try models out for themselves, this book's Support Material (www.routledge.com/9780367624293) contains a listing of the main commands used in this chapter. This listing may be handy for readers following along with the book using their home or office computers. For topics presented as online supplements (conditional inference forests with `cforest()`; MDS plots), the command summary is at the end of these supplements.

Endnotes

1. The median absolute deviation is found by identifying the median value, then computing a vector of deviations from that median, then taking the median of this vector.
2. For example, a different definition of outlier-ness is: `outlier2 = apply(RFclass$proximity, 1, function(x) 1/(sum(x^2)-1))`
   Different definitions identify different cases as outliers. Also the "10 or more" cutoff does not apply.
3. Many tuning strategies are discussed, for example, at https://machinelearningmastery.com/tune-machine-learning-algorithms-in-r/
4. https://stackoverflow.com/questions/34033249/r-tunerf-unstable-how-to-optimize
5. Using 10 as the cutoff follows Breiman. See https://www.stat.berkeley.edu/~breiman/RandomForests/cc_home.htm#outliers
6. https://cran.r-project.org/web/packages/party/vignettes/MOB.pdf
7. Elements are explained below:
   - ndbigtree Vector of length ntree containing the total number of nodes in each tree.
   - nodestatus A nrnodes-by-ntree matrix in which terminal nodes are coded –1.
   - leftDaughter Row where the left daughter node is; 0 if the node is terminal.

- nodepred — A nrnode-by-ntree matrix of average estimates at each node of each tree.
- bestvar — A nrnode-by-ntree matrix shoqing for each node, which variable is used to split that node. Coded 0 for terminal nodes.
- xbestsplit — A nrnode-by-ntree matrix paralleling "bestvar", except for regression models it gives the cutting points at which to split.
- ncat — For each variable the number of levels for factors or 1 for continuous.
- nrnodes — Maximum number of nodes a tree may have.
- ntree — Number of trees in the random forest.
- xlevels — Lists all variables names. For categorical variables, the labels for each level are listed. Continuous variables are coded 0.

8. Initialization of ntree is needed for RFregTemp$mse because it is a numeric vector of length ntree, whereas initialization is not needed for RFclassTemp$confusion since it is a matrix of size 2 by 3 (the size of the confusion table).
9. Figure 5.17 was produced by these following commands:

```
randomForest::varImpPlot(RFreg_tuned, color = c("red","brown"), pt.cex=2, pch=16, frame.
plot=TRUE)

randomForest::varImpPlot(RFreg, color = c("red","brown"), pt.cex=2, pch=16, frame.
plot=TRUE)
```

10. **More information is at** https://cran.r-project.org/web/packages/randomForestExplainer/randomForestExplainer.pdf
11. https://rawgit.com/geneticsMiNIng/BlackBoxOpener/master/examples/Boston_forest_explained.html

Chapter 6

Modeling and machine learning

PART I: OVERVIEW OF MODELING AND MACHINE LEARNING

6.1 Introduction

The "caret" package in R supports comparison of 238 modeling approaches. Those are called "machine learning" models, which have the capacity to learn from input data to improve their own performance. Which procedures are "modeling" and which are "machine learning" is a semantic debate that we prefer to ignore in this chapter. As a set of procedures, those supported by the "caret" package in R range from traditional statistical approaches such as linear modeling to those which incorporate artificial intelligence learning algorithms, such as neural networks (NNs) (treated in Chapter 7). The main message of this chapter is that the "caret" package is an example of an R resource, which places a very large number of modeling techniques into the researcher's toolbox and, in addition, allows the researcher to compare model performance among them for the researcher's particular data and research questions. Another newer package for these purposes is "mlr3". See Chapter 6's online supplement "Modeling Procedures Supported by the caret and mlr3 Packages", located in the Student Resources section of this book's Support Material (www.routledge.com/9780367624293), for more helpful information about both packages and tutorials for them.

Obviously a single chapter cannot cover the hundreds of modeling approaches supported by the "caret" package alone. Therefore, in this chapter we will focus in this chapter on one widely popular approach, support vector machine (SVM) regression. Then we will use caret functions to compare SVM with two selected other modeling methods: Gradient boosting machine (GBM) and learning vector quantization (LVQ) models. The former extends decision tree methods while the latter is a type of neural model, prefiguring Chapter 7 on NN models and deep learning in R. In addition, one of the "Quick Start" examples treats Naïve Bayes modeling, also a procedures supported by the "caret" package, while the other "Quick Start" example illustrates use of the "mlr3" package.

Because of its popularity, we focus in this chapter on survey vector machine regression (SVR) as reflected in the `svm()` command. The code behind this command was developed by David Meyer based on C/C++-code by Chih-Chung Chang and Chih-Jen Lin. Originally intended for and still widely used for binary classification problems (e.g., is a person likely to be a survey respondent or a nonrespondent?), survey vector machine (SVM) methods have since been generalized for categorical classification as well as regression problems involving continuous outcome variables.

SVM has two variants: (1) SVR-SVM models (Drucker et al., 1997) and (2) least-squares support vector machine (LS-SVM) models. LS-SVM uses a different algorithm (Suykens, Johan, & Vandewalle, 1999) and has been found useful when working with longitudinal data (Seok et al., 2011). However, SVR-SVM is the more prevalent approach and is what is used in this chapter. That is, in this chapter we use "SVM" to refer to SVR-SVM, a usage which

DOI: 10.4324/9781003109396-6

conforms to documentation for the `svm()` command from the "e1071" package. This popular package supports four major functions related to SVM:

`svm()`
This function is used to train and create an SVM model, either of the classification or the regression type, depending on whether the outcome variable is categorical or continuous.

`predict()`
This function serves to generate predicted values of the outcome variable, based on the SVM model.

`plot()`
This function serves to visualize the data and predictions, including the support vectors and decision boundaries as provided.nu the model.

`tune()`
This function is used to tune the model, finding optimal input parameters using a grid search over parameter ranges specified by the researcher. This process is called "hyperparameter tuning" of the SVM model.

The "e1071" package supports SVM for binary, categorical, and regression problems. It supports a variety of popular kernels (use of kernels to optimize SVM predictions is discussed further below) as well as various functions for tuning SVM models through cross-validation. A second popular package for SVM modeling in R is the "kernlab" package, which implements the `ksvm()` command. It supports a broad range of kernels, not all of which are available in e1071 (e.g., LaPlacian and hyperbolic tangent kernels). It also may be used for binary, categorical, and regression problems. See Karatzoglou, Meyer, and Hornik (2006).

The "caret" package is of a different nature. Caret stands for "Classification And REgression Training" and at this writing supports some 238 machine learning methods, including various SVM flavors. The caret package creates SVM models based on e1071 or kernlab, but adds functions for parameter tuning, cross-validation, and model calibration. It is particularly fast for cross-validation since it automatically detects and takes advantage of parallel environments created for that purpose. For further reading, see the popular introductions by Bennet and Campbell (2000) and James et al. (2013).

6.1.1 Social science examples of modeling and machine learning in R

To take SVM as a focus for this chapter, the following research examples cited are only a few arbitrary selections from a much larger literature applying SVM to social science topics.

In Anthropology
A *Journal of Physical Anthropology* article by Barbara Fliss et al. (2019) sought to identify the gender of decomposed corpses and skeletal remains using linear logistic regression and SVM models. Using linear logistic regression the authors were able to correctly classify 80% of remains but using nonlinear SVMs increased the rate of correct classifications to 87%.

In Economics
Ghoddusi, Creamer, and Rafizadeh (2019) reviewed over 130 studies, which had applied machine learning, including SVM, to topics in energy economics and finance. They found SVM, along with NN models to be the most popular machine learning techniques in this field, with the most common research objectives being prediction of crude oil and electricity prices. Synthesizing across studies Ghoddusi, Creamer, and Rafizadeh found the merits of SVM to include accuracy, speed of classification, robustness against irrelevant or redundant attributes, tolerance to high interdependency among predictor attributes, and, of course, nonlinear modeling (p. 717).

In Geography
Karimi et al. (2019) used SVM to model urban expansion, a phenomenon characterized by non-normal data, nonlinear relationships, and dynamic convoluted patterns. Studying Guilford County (Greensboro area), North Carolina, for the period 2001–2011, the authors found SVM "demonstrated highly accurate and reliable results" (p. 61), with accuracy of 98% in the training sample associated with 85% accuracy in the test (validation) sample. The authors concluded that

their "urban expansion model based on SVM method can substantially improve the prediction accuracy and would be helpful for making appropriate plans and policies to mitigate the adverse impacts of urban expansion" (p. 61).

In Political Science
Adam Bonica (2018) used SVM as well as random forests (RFs) to predict from campaign contributions the roll-call scores of members of Congress. Both SVM and RF yielded excellent predictions (R for SVM was .97 and for RF was .98). Bonica noted that the performance of machine learning algorithms "demonstrates that it is possible to infer legislators' DW-NOMINATE scores from their contribution records just as accurately as we can from observing how they vote during their first 2 years in Congress" (p. 838). (DW-NOMINATE scores are ideological ratings by interest groups based on members' voting records).

In Psychology
Di et al. (2019) used SVM to detect Internet Addiction (IA) Disorder and to identify the best personality scales for detection, achieving a detection accuracy of 96.3%. The authors, following the lead of other personality researchers who had also used SVM, concluded "that SVM is a reliable method for the assessment of IA" based on analysis of personality questionnaires.

TEXT BOX 6.1 The role of machine learning in personality psychology

"As of this writing, the caret package within the R programming language contains 238 machine learning algorithms for prediction, a huge number that only keeps growing ... Although the algorithms differ widely, they share the central goal of achieving robust prediction by doing two things not typically found in traditional statistical analyses of personality data:

1. *Disturb the model*: Certain machine learning algorithms tend to combine predictive results across hundreds of weak models to result in a stronger prediction (e.g., averaging across hundreds of trees in an RF). Or in a similar vein, other algorithms might examine a grid of possible model parameters (hyperparameters) to 'tune' the model in the search for complex yet robust relationships (e.g., the learning rate parameter in gradient boosted machines; the cost parameter in SVMs).
2. *Disturb the data*: Virtually all machine learning models are concerned with some form of cross-validation that keeps the data for model development and the data for prediction separate.

Machine learning algorithms can also be considered in terms of their interpretability... Some algorithms are more interpretable than others. For example, it is relatively straightforward to explain the personality profiles of cluster means (centroids) in k-means clustering or k-nearest-neighbor prediction... By contrast, there are many black-box algorithms that, as the name suggests, are relatively opaque.(e.g., artificial NNs tune network weights within arbitrary layers of hidden nodes; RFs average across hundreds of trees of variables; SVMs use nonlinear profile matching along classification and prediction boundaries)....

Given this challenge of interpretability, why should one even consider using machine learning algorithms in personality measurement with big data? There are two very practical reasons worth emphasizing:

i. the number of variables exceeds the number of cases in a data set (e.g., because text, audio, and social media data sets are vast), meaning that traditional analyses such as multiple linear regression are impossible (i.e., the matrix will not be invertible); and

ii. the researcher seeks to go beyond traditional analyses, to see whether robust complex relationships (ones that may not be specified a priori) can be located, and prediction can improved without overfitting the data...

Concluding, ...personality psychologists must continue to build and play a part in multidisciplinary communities of interest focused on future developments, applications, and evaluations of big data and machine learning."

Source: Alexander, L.; Mulfinger, E.; & Oswald, F. L. (2020). Using big data and machine learning in personality measurement: Opportunities and challenges. *European Journal of Personality* 34(5): 632–648.

In Sociology
Sociologist Kirchner and Signorino (2018), in their article "*Using Support Vector Machines for Survey Research*", noted of SVM models that "Their versatility in combination with the fact that they perform well in the presence of a large number of predictors, even with a small number of cases, makes them very appealing for a wide range of problems, including character recognition and text classification, speech and speaker verification, as well as imputation problems and record linkage" compare to a traditional logistic regression. The authors then tested whether SVM or logistic regression better predicted survey response status (respondent vs. nonrespondent), finding that the SVM model outperformed the main effects logistic regression model, correctly classifying 78% of cases compared to only 70% for the logistic model.

6.1.2 Advantages of modeling and machine learning in R

There are many commonly-cited advantages to the use of SVMs to solve social science problems.

- The outcome variable may be categorical or continuous, meaning that both classification and regression problems may be addressed. Predictor variables may be binary, categorical, or continuous.
- The SVM decision function uses a subset of the data for training the model and it is common for SVM algorithms to employ cross-validation automatically. For this reason, overfitting is less of a problem in SVM than in some other approaches.
- Not only may the solution be nonlinear but the researcher can model the nature of nonlinearity through experimentation with and selection of the kernel function used in training the model.
- Though often effective with default settings, a number of the parameters of SVM models, such as the value of gamma, may be adjusted and the model may be optimized to achieve even better results.
- For nonlinear solutions, SVM maps the raw data into multidimensional space in order to achieve better separation of sets of data points based on values of the outcome variable. SVM is effective when the solution requires high dimensionality (many predictors). Moreover, SVM is effective even when the number of dimensions is greater than the number of observations.
- SVM incorporates some aspects of NN solutions but is easier to use.
- SVM is robust against irrelevant or redundant predictors. It is also relatively robust against noisy data.
- SVM is generally fast and accurate. In data mining competitions, SVM has frequently emerged as the winner.

6.1.3 Limitations of modeling and machine learning in R

SVM approaches (like all methodologies) have disadvantages as well. Some commonly-cited drawbacks are listed here.

- Like NN approaches, SVM has "black box" aspects which make it less transparent than conventional regression, for example. The "black box" aspect makes SVM more useful for prediction and classification than for causal explanation of processes, though determination of variable importance is still possible.
- Selection of the best kernel function and tuning other model parameters can be a matter of trial and error, working through many combinations of settings. Different researchers may make different choices and arrive at different solutions for the same data problem.
- At this writing, though longitudinal SVM is possible, it is not integrated into packages explained in this volume, making implementation less user-friendly.
- Because SVM involves mapping data into high dimensional feature space, inferences from the data may be more general.
- While somewhat robust against overfitting, it is still possible to overfit SVM models to noise in the data. This is particularly true when the number of predictor variables exceeds the number of observations.

- The probabilities generated by SVM are not based on ordinary statistical inference but rather on cross-validation. Multifold cross-validation can be time- and computer-intensive with large datasets. That is, SVM can be slow for very large datasets.
- SVM regression is only moderately robust against noise in the data.
- Like ordinary least squares (OLS) regression, SVM is not robust against missing data.

6.1.4 Data, packages, and default directory

Data

- `covid19.csv` is used in the "Quick Start Example 1" section to illustrate Bayesian and other machine learning models. The outcome variable is SES, representing a measure of the poverty level of a county, based on percentages below the poverty line, unemployed, and lacking a high school diploma. As SES is a continuous outcome variable, analysis is of the regression rather than classification type. Variables in the dataset are as follows:

1. "State"
2. "StateCode"
3. "County"
4. "FIPScode"
5. "SES"
6. "Household"
7. "Minority"
8. "HouseTransp"
9. "Epidemiology"
10. "Healthcare"
11. "VScore"

There are six predictor variables (variables 5 through 10 above), each representing multiple items in six themes. Variables are composite numeric indexes varying from 0 to 1.0. Themes are described in the CCVI methodology document.[1]

- Epidemiology: Health-care demand factors measured by estimates of percent of adults diagnosed with high blood pressure, percent of adults diagnosed with high cholesterol, percent of adults diagnosed with a stroke, percent of adults reporting to have asthma, percent of adults diagnosed with chronic obstructive pulmonary disease, emphysema, or chronic bronchitis, percent of adults reporting to smoke cigarettes, annual cancer incidence per 100,000 persons, rate of persons living with an HIV diagnosis per 100,000 people, percent of adults reporting to be obese (a body mass index of 30 or greater), percent of adults ever diagnosed with diabetes, total number of people per area, number of deaths due to influenza and pneumonia per 100,000 people.
- Healthcare: Health-care supply factors measured by estimates of proportion of Hospital Beds; proportion of Intensive Care Unit (ICU) Beds; proportion of Epidemiologists; Agency for Healthcare Research and Quality – Prevention Quality Indicator Overall Composite: Admission rates for preventable conditions (via good outpatient care); Health Spending per Capita; Total Public Health Emergency Preparedness (PHEP) Funding Per Capita; proportion of Health Labs; proportion of Emergency Services.
- Household: Measured by estimates of persons aged 65 and older, persons aged 17 and younger, civilian non-institutionalized population with a disability, single parent households with children under 18.
- HouseTransp: Measured by estimates of housing with structures with 10 or more units, mobile homes, households with more people than rooms, households with no vehicle available, and persons in institutionalized group quarters.

- Minority: Measured by estimates of all persons except white, non-Hispanic; persons (age 5+) who speak English "less than well".
- SES: Measured by estimates if persons below poverty, civilian (age 16+) unemployed, per capita income, and persons with no high school diploma (age 25+).
- VScore is the COVID-19 vulnerability score of a country. As VScore is based on the foregoing measures, it is multicollinear with them and for this reason is not used as a predictor variable.

The data used here represent 3,141 U.S. counties (all of them after deleting Rio Arriba County, NM, due to missing data). Data were sourced from the CDC, Centers for Medicare & Medicaid Services (CMS), the Harvard Global Health Institute, PolicyMap, the US Bureau of Labor Statistics (BLS), the US Census Bureau (USCB), and the Association of Public Health Laboratories. Data used in the CCVI model were compiled and released in March, 2020.

- The "iris" data frame contained in R's built-in "datasets" package is used to illustrate multinomial SVM. This coverage is in the Chapter 6 supplement titled "Multinomial SVM", found in the Student Resources section of the Support Material (www.routledge.com/9780367624293).
- The "pima" data set is contained in the "pima" task of the mlr3 package. It is used to illustrate various modeling methods in Section 6.3, which is "Quick Start" example 2, seeking to predict diabetes among Pima Indians.
- senateratings05.csv is used to illustrate binary classification with the `svm()` command and also for comparing SVM with LVQ and GBM models using the "caret" package. The outcome variable is PARTY, coded as "Dem" or "GOP".
- `world.csv` is use to illustrate SVM regression with the `svm()` command from the e1071 package; to illustrate SVM regression with the `ksvm()` command via the caret package; and to illustrate tuning both SVM commands. The outcome variables are "litgtmean" (coded 0 = at or below mean of all nations on national literacy ratel; 1 = above mean, to illustrate SVM classification) and "literacy" (the continuous version of national literacy rate, to illustrate SVM regression). The world data frame is also used in the chapter appendix to further illustrate variable importance ranking.

Packages
If the reader is following along on the computer, the `install.packages()` command should be used to install the packages below if needed. Note also that when packages are installed other dependent packages may be installed automatically.

```
library(arm)                  # For method= "bayesglm" in caret
library(caret)                # Most popular modeling and training integration package
library(corrplot)             # Supports corrplot() command
library(e1071)                # Contains the svm() command and more
library(gbm)                  # Supports the gbm() command
library(kernlab)              # Supports method="svmRadial" in caret
library(kknn)                 # For the k-nearest-neighbor learner
library(lattice)              # Supports dot plots
library(lvq)                  # Supports the lvq() command
library(MCMCpack)             # Supports the MCMCregress() command
library(Metrics)              # Contains the RMSE() command and other metrics
library(mlr3)                 # The core of the mlr3 suite for modeling
library("mlr3learners")       # Supports about almost two dozen mlr3 learners2
library(mlr3oml)              # Used when imputing missing data
library("mlr3proba")          # Adds supervised probabilistic and survival learners
library(modEvA)               # Supports the Dsquared() command for glm objects
library("NADIA")              # For imputation of missing values
library(rpart)                # For the classification tree learner
```

Default directory
Setup requires declaring the default directory, which is where the data are located. The folder used by the reader may differ.

```
setwd("C:/Data")
```

PART II: QUICK START – MODELING AND MACHINE LEARNING

6.2 Example 1: Bayesian modeling of county-level poverty

6.2.1 Introduction

Bayesian analysis seeks better statistical inferences by incorporating prior information into the model, as explained further below. To provide an example, this section models "SES" as a measure of U.S. county-level poverty, using the "covid19.csv" data file. As discussed in Section 6.1.4, SES measures such factors as percentage of people in a county who are below the poverty line, unemployed, or lack a high school diploma. There are five predictor variables: Household, Minority, HouseTransp, Epidemiology, and Healthcare, also explained in Section 6.1.4. The "caret" package supports nine Bayesian analysis methods,[3] of which in this section we consider the Bayes generalized linear model (the `bayesglm()` method). However, note that the number of R packages for Bayesian analysis is very large, going well beyond what can be discussed here.[4] For this section, the main point of the `bayesglm()` method is not so much better outcome predictions as it is better parameter inferences (better inferences about the b coefficients of the predictor variables).

6.2.2 Setup

The following packages are needed for Quick Start Example 1.

```
library(arm)            # For method= "bayesglm" in caret
library(caret)          # For modeling and training, including Bayesian
library(corrplot)       # Supports the corrplot() command
library(kernlab)        # Supports method="svmRadial" in caret
library(MCMCpack)       # Supports the MCMCregress() command
library(modEvA)         # Supports the Dsquared() command for glm objects

# Declare the working directory
setwd("C:/Data")

# Read the data into the "covid19" data frame and list its column names
covid19 <- read.csv("c:/Data/covid19.csv", header=TRUE, sep = ",",
stringsAsFactors=TRUE)

View(covid19)
names(covid19)
[Output:]
  [1] "State"         "StateCode"     "County"
  [4] "FIPScode"      "SES"           "Household"
  [7] "Minority"      "HouseTransp"   "Epidemiology"
 [10] "Healthcare"    "VScore"
```

Some of these variables are character-type factors and some are continuous numeric variables. We can tell the data class of each variable with the following command.

```
# Verify data classes of variables (columns)
sapply(covid19, class)
```

[Output:]

```
        State        StateCode          County
     "factor"        "factor"         "factor"

     FIPScode             SES        Household
    "integer"       "numeric"        "numeric"

     Minority  HouseTransp Epidemiology
    "numeric"       "numeric"        "numeric"

   Healthcare          VScore
    "numeric"       "numeric"
```

Note that the outcome variable (SES) and all predictor variables are numeric, making this a regression rather than a classification problem. To simplify the data frame, we select the first six numeric variables (SES, Household, Minority, HouseTransp, Epidemiology, and Healthcare) and put them in the data frame labeled "df". The variables are selected by their index (column) number. Index numbers were seen above in the output from the `names()` command. SES, for example, is index 5. The "df" data frame is used for the remainder of this example.

```
df <- covid19[5:10]
View(df)
```

The `summary()` command shows that all the variables in the df data frame are numeric and on the same scale, varying from 0 to 1.0.

```
summary(df)
```

[Output:]

```
      SES              Household           Minority
 Min.   :0.0000   Min.   :0.0000   Min.   :0.0000
 1st Qu.:0.2500   1st Qu.:0.2500   1st Qu.:0.2500
 Median :0.5000   Median :0.5000   Median :0.5000
 Mean   :0.4998   Mean   :0.4999   Mean   :0.4999
 3rd Qu.:0.7500   3rd Qu.:0.7500   3rd Qu.:0.7500
 Max.   :1.0000   Max.   :1.0000   Max.   :1.0000

  HouseTransp      Epidemiology       Healthcare
 Min.   :0.0000   Min.   :0.0000   Min.   :0.0000
 1st Qu.:0.2500   1st Qu.:0.2500   1st Qu.:0.2500
 Median :0.5000   Median :0.5000   Median :0.5000
 Mean   :0.4999   Mean   :0.5001   Mean   :0.5001
 3rd Qu.:0.7500   3rd Qu.:0.7500   3rd Qu.:0.7500
 Max.   :1.0000   Max.   :1.0000   Max.   :1.0000
```

6.2.3 Correlation plot

It is helpful in the exploratory phase to view the bivariate correlations among numeric variables. This may be visualized by the `corrplot()` command, as shown in Figure 6.1.[5] Type `help(corrplot)` for discussion of the parameters used.

```
library(corrplot)

col1 = colorRampPalette(c("lightskyblue","deepskyblue", "darkblue"))(10)

corrplot::corrplot(abs(cor(df)), method="color", col=col1, diag=FALSE,type="lower",
order="alphabet", addCoef.col = "grey", tl.pos="ld", tl.col="black", tl.cex=1.3,
cl.lim=c(0,1))
```

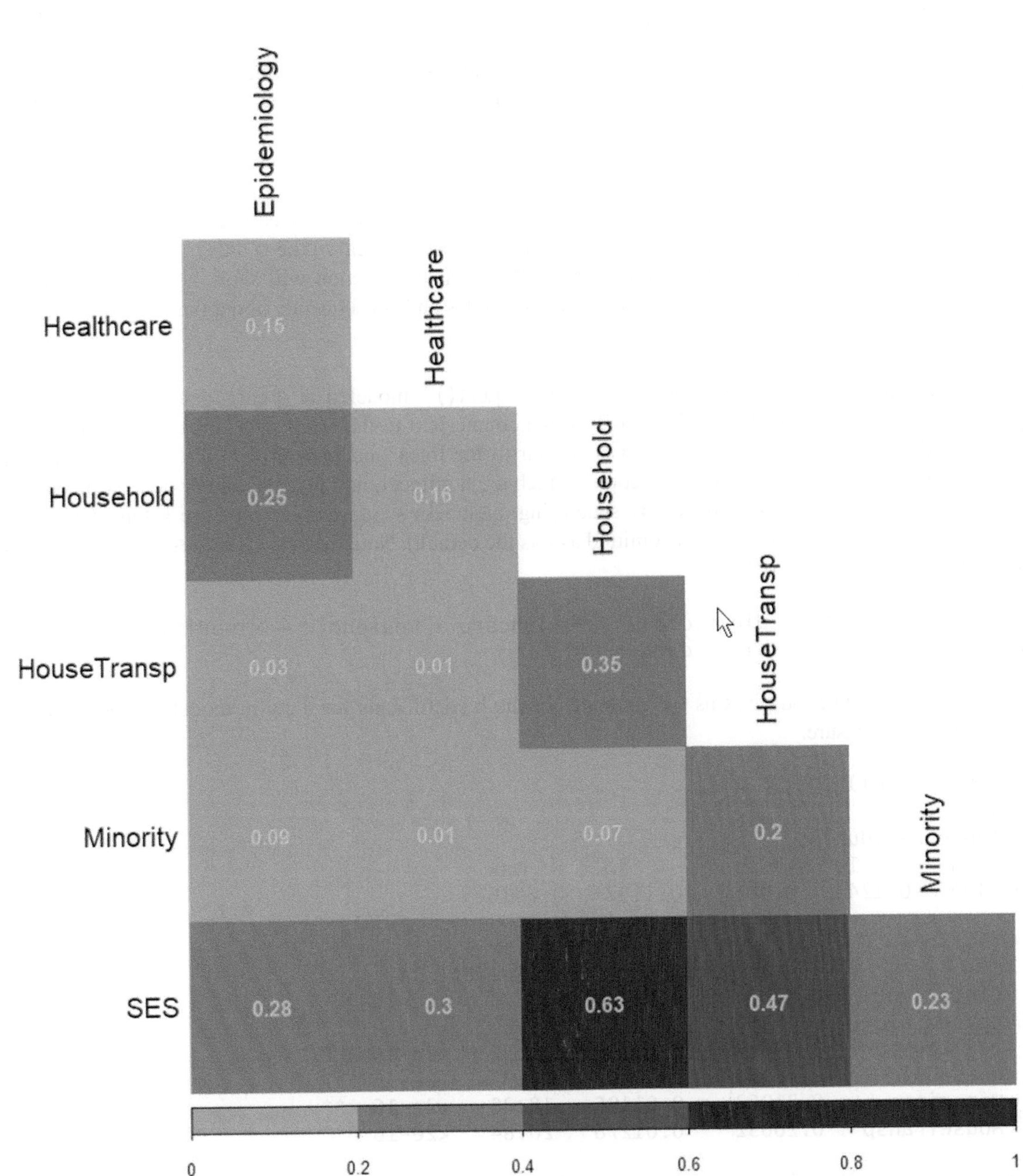

Figure 6.1 Correlation matrix, df dataframe

The correlogram above suggests that the most important predictor of the poverty of a county as measured by SES is "Household" (higher on old, young, disabled, and institutionalized persons), followed by "HouseTransp" (poor housing and transportation). Though not the focus of this example, it is interesting to note that health demand factors (Epidemiology) have a low correlation (0.15) with health supply factors (Healthcare), indicating an important aspect of the problematic American healthcare system. However, these inferences are on a bivariate basis, which in general is less informative than multivariate analysis pursued below.

6.2.4 The Bayes generalized linear model

The Bayes generalized linear model implements Bayesian models for either continuous or categorical outcome variables. In spite of "linear" being in the title, "generalized" means that logistic and other nonlinear models may be swapped for the default linear model. It is implemented in the "caret" package as `method = bayesglm`. The caret package in turn relies on the implementation of bayesglm in the "arm" package.

The point of Bayesian analysis is to improve inferences about estimates by incorporating prior information. When `bayesglm()` is run with default settings, the `prior.mean=` and `prior.mean.for.intercept parameters=` are set to 0 and the results are estimates almost identical to the `glm()` or the `lm()` commands from the "stats" package in R's system library. However, this section will show how Bayesian analysis improves inferences about the b coefficients of predictor variables and consequently about their significance.

The glm model (non-Bayesian)

To provide a baseline for comparison, below we run the `glm()` model. The `glm()` command is from the stats package in R's system library. It is the non-Bayesian counterpart to the `bayesglm()` command. It stands for "generalized linear model", which means it is similar to the linear model with the `lm()` command but is capable of supporting models, which have outcomes which are nonlinear, non-normal, and/or noncontinuous, such as `family=Gamma` for skewed data.[6] By specifying `family=gaussian` we are asking for a simple linear model (however, this option could be omitted as it is the default). Note that the `bayesglm()` command also supports the `family=` option.

```
glm_model <- glm(SES ~ Epidemiology + Healthcare + Household + Minority +
HouseTransp, family=gaussian, data = df)
```

The `summary()` command gives us the estimates of the b coefficients for the glm model as well as the AIC model performance measure.

```
summary(glm_model)
```

[Partial output:]

```
   Deviance Residuals:
       Min        1Q    Median       3Q      Max
   -0.7400  -0.1244  -0.0057   0.1197   0.6016

   Coefficients:
                   Estimate Std. Error t value Pr(>|t|)
      (Intercept)  -0.16035    0.01170  -13.71   <2e-16 ***
      Epidemiology  0.15758    0.01212   13.00   <2e-16 ***
      Healthcare    0.19482    0.01179   16.52   <2e-16 ***
      Household     0.48216    0.01304   36.97   <2e-16 ***
      Minority      0.21963    0.01195   18.38   <2e-16 ***
      HouseTransp   0.26632    0.01278   20.84   <2e-16 ***
      ---
Signif. codes:  0 '***' 0.001 '**' 0.01 '*' 0.05 '.' 0.1 ' ' 1

(Dispersion parameter for gaussian family taken to be 0.03490368)

    Null deviance: 261.75  on 3140  degrees of freedom
Residual deviance: 109.42  on 3135  degrees of freedom
AIC: -1616.8
```

As `glm()` is not based on OLS estimation it does not output an R-squared measure. The equivalent is D-squared, which is the adjusted amount of deviance accounted for by a generalized linear model.

```
modEvA::Dsquared(model=glm_model)
```

[Output:]

```
      [1] 0.5819534
```

The Bayes general linear model with default settings

In this section, we run the bayesglm() command, accepting its defaults. As noted by Gelman et al. (2008: 1361), the method embedded in bayesglm() differs from some related Bayesian approaches "in using a generic prior constraint rather than information specific to a particular analysis. As such, we would expect our prior distribution to be more appropriate for automatic use." The estimates from bayesglm() are almost identical to the glm model. However, "credible intervals", a Bayesian counterpart to frequentist "confidence intervals", are different. This in turn leads to possible differences in statistical inference and assessment of the significance of predictor variables. Along the way, we demonstrate how a model like bayesglm() is run from within the caret package.

Setup

Running bayesglm() under caret provides for cross-validated estimates. The following command prefix "caret::" has been added for instructional reasons. It is not needed here but reminds the researcher that the command it references requires installation and loading of the "caret" package, typically using a simple install.packages("caret") command.

The caret process calls for two main steps: (1) setting control parameters, and (2) running the selected model. The trainControl() command sets the parameters. Under it, the method= parameter is set to repeated cross-validation. (If method="none" then no cross-validation is performed). The number= parameter sets the number of iterations in a fold of cross-validations (10 is the default). The repeats= parameter sets the number of times that folds are repeated (1 is the default). The p= parameter gives the proportion of observations to be used for the training sample in the cross-validation process. The classProbs=FALSE setting does not call for computation of class probabilities, appropriate only for binary and factor variables. The default summary function is used.

```
ctrl <- caret::trainControl(
method = "repeatedcv",
number = 20,
repeats = 2,
p = .70,
  classProbs = FALSE,
  summaryFunction = defaultSummary
)
```

We now run the bayesglm() model, which is supported by caret. Thus, method= is set to the "bayesglm" method, which corresponds to Bayes generalized linear model. We use the "df" data frame created above for SES predicted by five other variables. As all variables are on the same 0.0 to 1.0 scale, there is no need to rescale the data. The trControl parameter is set to the "ctrl" object created above. The performance metric is set to "RMSE" (for classification models, "Accuracy" is usual). The settings below are largely defaults except prior.scale and prior.df are set to infinite ("Inf") as recommended for regression models in lieu of the NULL and 1 default (this made very little difference). Setting the random seed is recommended for model reproducibility purposes. Type help(train) to see all the many available parameters and settings. Note that output pauses while cross-validation iterations are performed.

```
set.seed(123)

bayesglm_model <- caret::train(
  SES ~ Epidemiology + Healthcare + Household + Minority +
HouseTransp,
  data = df,
  family = gaussian,
  method = "bayesglm",
  scaled = TRUE,
  keep.order=TRUE,
  model = TRUE,
  prior.mean = 0,
  prior.mean.for.intercept = 0,
  prior.scale = Inf,
  prior.df = Inf,
```

```
    prior.scale.for.intercept = NULL,
    prior.df.for.intercept = 1,
    min.prior.scale=1e-12,
    trControl = ctrl,
    metric = "RMSE"
)
```

To see the cross-validated model results, simply type the name of the model. The bayesglm method has no parameters to set but had there been any, that caret would have attempted to pick optimal values automatically. The Bayes generalized linear model has an R-squared that explains 58.3% of the variance in SES across counties. This compares to a D-squared of 58.2% in the glm comparison model.

```
bayesglm_model
[Output:]
   Bayesian Generalized Linear Model

   3141 samples
      5 predictor

   No pre-processing
   Resampling: Cross-Validated (20 fold, repeated 2 times)
   Summary of sample sizes: 2984, 2983, 2983, 2985, 2984, 2985,
   ...
   Resampling results:

     RMSE       Rsquared   MAE
     0.1865323  0.5830577  0.1469327
```

Additional related information is in the model's $results element:

```
bayesglm_model$results
[Output:]
   parameter       RMSE  Rsquared       MAE
   1       none 0.1865323 0.5830577 0.1469327

          RMSESD RsquaredSD        MAESD
   1 0.01255471 0.05554544 0.008940449
```

The $finalModel element of bayesglm_model gives the b coefficients and the AIC value. These are virtually identical to the glm model. While almost identical, note that the `bayesglm()` estimates are cross-validated whereas the `glm()` ones are not.

```
bayesglm_model$finalModel
[Output:]
   Call:  NULL
   Coefficients:
    (Intercept)  Epidemiology    Healthcare     Household
        -0.1603        0.1576        0.1948        0.4822
       Minority   HouseTransp
         0.2196        0.2663

   Degrees of Freedom: 3140 Total (i.e. Null);  3135 Residual
   Null Deviance:       261.7
   Residual Deviance: 109.4     AIC: -1617
```

Setting other priors might change results. Defaults for prior settings are described in the endnote to this sentence.[7] The classic reference on setting priors for `bayesglm()` is Gelman et al. (2008), who focused on logistic models.

Alternatively, one might run a non-cross-validated model using the `bayesglm()` command outside of caret by employing the syntax below. Results for the parameter estimates, deviance values, and AIC are almost identical. However, the near-identity of results with the same model run under caret shows that its results conform to cross-validated ones. For the remaining treatment, we use the bayesglm_model2 object.

```
bayesglm_model2 <- arm::bayesglm(SES ~ Epidemiology + Healthcare + Household +
Minority + HouseTransp, family=gaussian, prior.mean=0, prior.scale=Inf, prior.
df=Inf, data = df)

summary(bayesglm_model2)
```

[Partial output:]

```
   Deviance Residuals:
       Min        1Q    Median        3Q       Max
   -0.7400  -0.1244  -0.0057   0.1197   0.6016

   Coefficients:
                Estimate Std. Error t value Pr(>|t|)
   (Intercept)  -0.16035    0.01170  -13.71   <2e-16 ***
   Epidemiology  0.15758    0.01212   13.00   <2e-16 ***
   Healthcare    0.19482    0.01179   16.52   <2e-16 ***
   Household     0.48216    0.01304   36.97   <2e-16 ***
   Minority      0.21963    0.01195   18.38   <2e-16 ***
   HouseTransp   0.26632    0.01278   20.84   <2e-16 ***
   ---
   Signif. codes:  0 '***' 0.001 '**' 0.01 '*' 0.05 '.' 0.1 ' ' 1

   (Dispersion parameter for gaussian family taken to be 0.03490368)

       Null deviance: 261.75  on 3140  degrees of freedom
   Residual deviance: 109.42  on 3135  degrees of freedom
   AIC: -1616.8
```

There is a crucial difference between bayesglm_model (caret package) and bayesglm_model2 (arm package). The latter is a glm object with a coefficients element. This is critical for the next step.

```
class(bayesglm_model)
     [1] "train"          "train.formula"
bayesglm_model$coefficients
     NULL

class(bayesglm_model2)
     [1] "bayesglm" "glm"       "lm"
bayesglm_model2$coefficients
     (Intercept) Epidemiology   Healthcare     Household
     -0.1603460     0.1575754   0.1948152     0.4821571
     Minority   HouseTransp
     0.2196264     0.2663192
```

In Bayesian analysis, a posterior distribution is the distribution of possible unobserved values (e.g., values of regression coefficients) conditional on the observed values. The posterior distribution for the `bayesglm()` model is obtained using the `sim()` command from the "arm" package.[8] This operates on objects of class "glm", which bayesglm_model2 is and bayesglm_model is not. Posterior distributions yield the "credible interval", which is similar to but also critically different from the usual "confidence interval" from, say, OLS regression.

Let a b coefficient be .50. In traditional (frequentist) statistics, if the 95% confidence interval is plus or minus .10, then this means that if a large number of samples are taken from the population, 95% of b coefficient values would be between .40 and .60. There is no implication that the true b coefficient value is within the confidence interval, only that the b coefficients from most samples are. Contrast this with the "credible interval" in the Bayesian approach. The corresponding causal inference is that there is a 95% chance that the true parameter value (b) is within the computed credible interval. The Bayesian approach, in contrast to the traditional frequentist approach, is able to do this because it relies on information from the distribution of posterior results. To visualize this, below we graph the posterior distribution for one variable, "Household", which is a composite predictor variable measured by estimates of persons aged 65 and older, persons aged 17 and younger, civilian noninstitutionalized population with a disability, and single parent households with children under 18.

Getting the posterior distribution

First we get the posterior distribution of coefficients. Note that in syntax below, `coef()` is a function in the stats library to retrieve coefficients. The `sim()` function is from the "arm" package. The `n.sims=` option is the requested number of simulations (default = 100).

```
set.seed(123)
simulates <- coef(arm::sim(bayesglm_model2,n.sims=100))
head(simulates,5)
```

[Output of parameter estimates for the first five simulations:]

```
      (Intercept) Epidemiology Healthcare Household  Minority HouseTransp
[1,]  -0.1626680     0.1730682  0.1713665 0.4926820 0.2304329   0.2612867
[2,]  -0.1540155     0.1581689  0.1746828 0.4836974 0.2267559   0.2715591
[3,]  -0.1723488     0.1608487  0.1959388 0.4724593 0.2173602   0.2900690
[4,]  -0.1666863     0.1617631  0.1855596 0.4886395 0.2194794   0.2721680
[5,]  -0.1708533     0.1639842  0.2032589 0.4920241 0.2215783   0.2692554
```

Key output values are as follows:

`simulates`

A matrix of dimensions 100 simulate rows by six columns, where column 1 is the intercept and the others are coefficients for the five predictors, based on random draws.

`simulates[,1]`

Simulated parameter values for the intercept

`simulates[,2:6]`

Simulated coefficient values for the five predictor variables

We now list the posterior distribution of estimated b coefficients for Household, which is in column 4.

```
posterior_Household <- simulates[,4]
head(posterior_Household,5)
```

[Output for first five simulations:]

```
  [1] 0.4926820 0.4836974 0.4724593 0.4886395 0.4920241
```

Posterior results may be visualized in a plot with a histogram of the posterior distribution for the estimated b coefficients for Household, with a density curve overlay. The # `plot()` function is from the "graphics" package in R's system library. The `par()` function is also from the graphics package and here causes the plot to be overlaid. The `density()` function is from the "stats" package, also in R's system library. The plot is shown in Figure 6.2.

```
hist(posterior_Household, col = "pink", main="Histogram of Household Posterior
Distribution with Density Curve")
par(new=TRUE)
plot(density(posterior_Household),main="", xlab="", ylab = "",axes = FALSE)
```

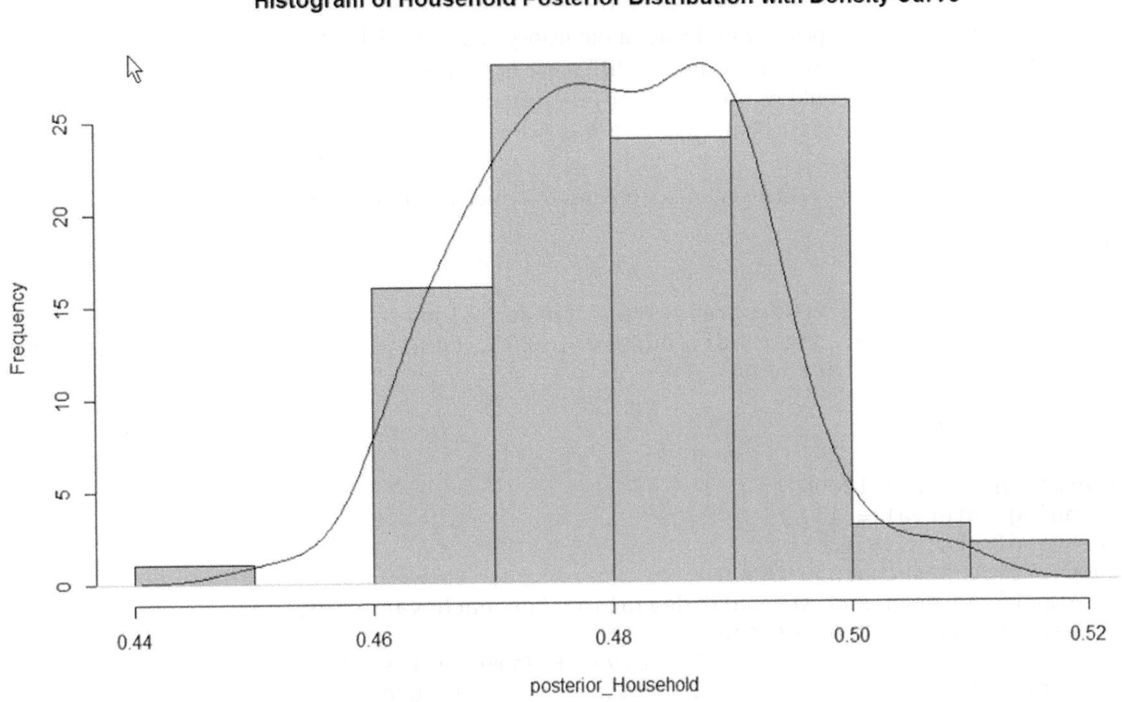

Figure 6.2 Histogram of household posterior distribution, with density curve

We may use the `quantile()` program from the "stats" package to compute the credible interval for Household at the 95% level. Using the `sim()` method which created posterior_Household, we can say at the 95% level that the true b coefficient for Household lies between 0.4606 and 0.5049. We may also say that Household is significant as a predictor as 0 is not within the credible interval.

```
quantile(posterior_Household,c(.025, .975))
[Output:]
      2.5%     97.5%
 0.4605863 0.5048633
```

The foregoing `sim()` method uses simulates as a proxy for constructing an empirical distribution based on draws from the posterior distribution of parameter estimates. When reporting Bayesian inferences, however, it is preferable to create such an empirical distribution. This may be done with the `MCMCregress()` command from the "MCMCpack" package.

The `MCMCregress()` function generates a sample from the posterior distribution of a linear regression model with Gaussian errors.

The MCMCregress package constructs the Markov Chain Monte Carlo simulations used to create the desired empirical distribution. "Empirical" means that the distribution draws from the original data frame (df), not from the simulates object as in the previous method. These are the following options in the syntax:

data = *df*: This was the original data frame.
burnin = *3000*: The MCMC method is unreliable for the early iterations, so here we ask to discard the first 3,000.
mcmc =*10000*: We ask for 10,0000 iterations of the MCMC algorithm, beyond the 3,000 burn-in iterations.

thin = 1: This can be used for thinning the process. The number of MCMC iterations must be divisible by this value.
verbose = 0: This suppresses printing of the iteration history and is the default.
seed = 123: The random seed will make a small difference in results.
beta.start = NA: The user could provide a vector of the starting values of the beta values (standardized b values) for all predictors. The default value of NA uses the OLS estimates of beta as the starting values.

While default priors are used here, there are other options by which the user may supply priors.

```
library(MCMCpack)

MCMC_model <- MCMCpack::MCMCregress(SES ~ Epidemiology + Healthcare + Household +
Minority + HouseTransp, data = df, burnin = 3000, mcmc = 10000, thin = 1, verbose =
0, seed = 123,  beta.start = NA)

summary(MCMC_model)
```

[Output:]

```
Iterations = 3001:13000
Thinning interval = 1
Number of chains = 1
Sample size per chain = 10000
1. Empirical mean and standard deviation for each variable,
   plus standard error of the mean:
                  Mean        SD  Naive SE Time-series SE
(Intercept)  -0.16047 0.0118133 1.181e-04      1.163e-04
Epidemiology  0.15770 0.0120213 1.202e-04      1.202e-04
Healthcare    0.19478 0.0117177 1.172e-04      1.172e-04
Household     0.48206 0.0131782 1.318e-04      1.318e-04
Minority      0.21990 0.0118907 1.189e-04      1.189e-04
HouseTransp   0.26640 0.0127430 1.274e-04      1.274e-04
sigma2        0.03493 0.0008891 8.891e-06      8.891e-06

2. Quantiles for each variable:

                 2.5%      25%      50%      75%    97.5%
(Intercept)  -0.18377 -0.16840 -0.16054 -0.15260 -0.13730
Epidemiology  0.13389  0.14969  0.15767  0.16587  0.18110
Healthcare    0.17206  0.18682  0.19479  0.20260  0.21777
Household     0.45635  0.47317  0.48206  0.49085  0.50785
Minority      0.19648  0.21206  0.21996  0.22796  0.24307
HouseTransp   0.24096  0.25774  0.26660  0.27523  0.29088
sigma2        0.03324  0.03431  0.03493  0.03552  0.03673
```

Credible intervals for the intercept and the predictor variables are shown in Part 2 of output above, in the "Quantiles for each variable" section. Recall that with the `sim()` method we inferred that at the 95% level that the true b coefficient for Household lies between 0.4606 and 0.5049. Using the empirical distribution of posteriors above, we more reliably may say that at the 95% probability level that the true (population) b coefficient for Household lies between 0.45635 and 0.50785. Again, Household is significant since 0 is not within the credible interval.

In summary, advocates of Bayesian analysis argue that its approach to credible intervals and significance testing utilizes more information and is superior to traditional frequentist approaches to confidence intervals and significance testing. The caret package supports a variety of Bayesian approaches, including the Bayes generalized linear model illustrated in Example 1. The bayesglm method in caret gives cross-validated estimates equivalent to those of non-Bayesian glm. However, Example 1 also showed how Bayesian statistical inference draws on prior information to produce posterior distributions of parameter estimates, which is the basis for Bayesian statistical inference.

6.3 Example 2: Predicting diabetes among Pima Indians with mlr3

6.3.1 Introduction

There are a very large number of modeling and machine learning methods available in R. This has given rise to modeling integration packages which provide a unified framework for using R modeling packages. These also provide useful model training and evaluation functions. The two leading modeling integration packages are "caret" and "mlr3". While most of this chapter illustrates the "caret" package, a purpose of Example 2 is to illustrate the "mlr3" package. The "mlr3" package is faster than caret and better supports Big Data. We use the example of predicting diabetes among Pima Indians.

6.3.2 Setup

As usual, setting the default directory where the data are stored is a first step, followed by loading the needed packages. Installing and loading packages is best done after closing and restarting a new RStudio session.

```
setwd="C:/Data"
```

The following packages may be installed with the usual `install.packages()` command.

```
library(kknn)                # For the k-nearest-neighbor learner
library(mlr3)                # The core of the mlr3 suite for modeling
library("mlr3learners")      # Supports about almost two dozen mlr3 learners9
library(mlr3oml)             # Used when imputing missing data
library("mlr3proba")         # Adds supervised probabilistic and survival learners
library("NADIA")             # For imputing missing values
library(rpart)               # For the classification tree learner
```

6.3.3 How mlr3 works

Modeling under mlr3 involves six not-necessarily-sequential steps:

1. Load the needed packages, as in Section 6.3.2.
2. Select the desired "learner". Learners are simply the possible statistical methods.
3. Create or select the desired "task". Tasks define the data to be used and what is to be done to it. Data should be checked for missings and imputed if needed.
4. Run the model. Typically the model is trained on a training subset of the data and then predictions are made on the remaining data (the test or validation subset).
5. Evaluate the model. Evaluation metrics vary by type of model, but may include "Accuracy" for classification models or "RMSE" for regression models. Multiple metrics may be available for a given model.
6. Consider changing the default model parameters. Learners have parameters, which are settings dependent on the method being used. For instance, in decision tree models, "minbucket", which sets the minimum number of cases in each terminal node, may be a parameter. We may wish to rerun the model with other than the default parameters.
7. Cross-validate the model using resampling. Different types of resampling are available and the researcher may set the number of iterations (e.g., tenfold cross-validation).
8. Comparing multiple learners for the same task can be accomplished by mlr3's `benchmark()` command.

A free book on the "mlr3" package is found at https://mlr3book.mlr-org.com. Cases and examples are found at https://mlr3gallery.mlr-org.com.

6.3.3.1 Learners for mlr3

"Learners" for mlr3 are like "methods" for caret: They are the analytic procedures which may be implemented. The following command lists recommended mlr3 learners. Other learners are found in related packages such as "mlr3proba" and yet others may be added by the researcher.

```
print(as.data.table(mlr_learners)[, c("key", "packages")])
[Output:]
                    key              packages
 1:    classif.cv_glmnet               glmnet
 2:        classif.debug
 3: classif.featureless
 4:       classif.glmnet               glmnet
 5:         classif.kknn                 kknn
 6:          classif.lda                 MASS
 7:      classif.log_reg                stats
 8:     classif.multinom                 nnet
 9:  classif.naive_bayes                e1071
10:         classif.nnet                 nnet
11:          classif.qda                 MASS
12:       classif.ranger               ranger
13:        classif.rpart                rpart
14:          classif.svm                e1071
15:      classif.xgboost              xgboost
16:            dens.hist               distr6
17:             dens.kde               distr6
18:       regr.cv_glmnet               glmnet
19:     regr.featureless                stats
20:          regr.glmnet               glmnet
21:            regr.kknn                 kknn
22:              regr.km          DiceKriging
23:              regr.lm                stats
24:          regr.ranger               ranger
25:           regr.rpart                rpart
26:             regr.svm                e1071
27:         regr.xgboost              xgboost
28:           surv.coxph      survival,distr6
29:       surv.cv_glmnet               glmnet
30:          surv.glmnet               glmnet
31:          surv.kaplan      survival,distr6
32:          surv.ranger               ranger
33:           surv.rpart rpart,distr6,survival
34:         surv.xgboost              xgboost
```

A more detailed description of mlr3 learners is at https://cran.r-project.org/web/packages/mlr3learners/mlr3learners.pdf.

6.3.3.2 Tasks in mlr3

An mlr3 task specifies the data to be used and other information, such as specifying the dependent variable. The mlr3 package comes with a number of predefined tasks. To see a list, type the expression below. For this example we use the predefined "pima" task, which deals with detecting diabetes among Pima Indians. Section 6.3.4 provides more detail on tasks in mlr3.

```
mlr3::mlr_tasks
[Output]
<DictionaryTask> with 20 stored values
Keys: actg, boston_housing, breast_cancer, faithful, gbcs, german_credit,grace, iris,
lung, mtcars, oml, pima, precip, rats, sonar, spam,unemployment, whas, wine, zoo
```

6.3.4 The Pima Indian data

6.3.4.1 Select the learner

Below we create two learners by retrieving them from the mlr3learners dictionary. These are for the k-nearest-neighbors method (implemented by the "kknn" package) and the classification tree method (implemented by the "rpart" package discussed in Chapter 4).

```
learner_kknn = mlr_learners$get("classif.kknn")
learner_rpart = mlr_learners$get("classif.rpart")
```

The printout below says that kknn may be used for multiclass or twoclass classification problems. "Features" are predictors, which may be any of the types listed.

```
print(learner_kknn)
<LearnerClassifKKNN:classif.kknn>
* Model: -
* Parameters: list()
* Packages: kknn
* Predict Type: response
* Feature types: logical, integer, numeric, factor, ordered
* Properties: multiclass, twoclass
```

The printout for the rpart learner is similar:

```
print(learner_rpart)
<LearnerClassifRpart:classif.rpart>
* Model: -
* Parameters: xval=0
* Packages: rpart
* Predict Type: response
* Feature types: logical, integer, numeric, factor, ordered
* Properties: importance, missings, multiclass, selected_features, twoclass, weights
```

6.3.4.2 Create the task

We will use the "pima" task as an example. This deals with diabetes among Pima Indians. We define "task" as an object name for the pima task. We see that the pima dataset has 768 observations (rows) for nine variables (columns). The dependent variable is predefined as "diabetes". Possible predictor variables are listed under "Features". The "Properties: twoclass" portion of the listing means that diabetes has two classes. The "TaskClassif" portion means this is a classification problem, requiring a learner appropriate for classification. Other tasks will have other listings, such as "TaskRegr" for the boston_housing task, which is a regression problem, or "TaskSurv" for the unemployment task, which is a survival analysis problem.

```
task = mlr3::tsk("pima")
print(task)
[Output]
   <TaskClassif:pima> (768 x 9)
   * Target: diabetes
   * Properties: twoclass
   * Features (8):
     - dbl (8): age, glucose, insulin, mass, pedigree, pregnant, pressure, triceps
```

6.3.4.3 Check missings and impute if needed

```
# Check if there are missings
sum(task$missings())
[Output:]
      [1] 652
```

```
# Show where missings are
task$missings()
[Output:]
   diabetes       age  glucose  insulin     mass
          0         0        5      374       11
   pedigree pregnant pressure  triceps
          0         0       35      227
```

We now impute missing values using the "NADIA" package, which has multiple imputation methods.[10] We use the "mice" package method to create "task2" as the imputed version of "task". The "task2" task is used for the remainder of the example. For further information on the NADIA package, see https://cran.r-project.org/web/packages/NADIA/vignettes/NADIA_examples_and_motivation.html.

```
pipe_imp <- NADIA::PipeOpMice$new()
task2 <- pipe_imp$train(list(task))$output

#Check output task, no missings!
sum(task2$missings())
[Output:]
      [1] 0
```

Note that mlr3 works with what are called R6 objects, not data frames like most procedures in R. The "task" object is an R6 object. The "pima" data are not a data frame or even an object at all, which is why the `class(pima)` command below does not work. By using R6 objects, mlr3 bypasses R's usual data structures and instead uses object-oriented programming, which is faster and scales to very large data much better. Online documentation for mlr3 states that it "provides 'R6' objects for tasks, learners, resamplings, and measures. The package is geared towards scalability and larger datasets by supporting parallelization and out-of-memory data-backends like databases."

```
class(task2)
     [1] "TaskClassif"    "TaskSupervised" "Task"           "R6"
class(pima)
     Error: object 'pima' not found
```

It is easy to export from "task2" (the task with imputed data) to a conventional R data frame:

```
pima_df <- task2$data()
class(pima_df)
[Output]
   [1] "data.table" "data.frame"
```

To be clear what kind of problem task addresses, use the element $task_type:

```
task2$task_type
[Output]
      [1] "classif"
```

Also, the $backend element of task reveals the first several rows of the data. Because we imputed missing values, no "NAs" appear:

```
task2$backend
[Output]
   <DataBackendDataTable> (768x10)
   pregnant glucose pressure triceps insulin mass pedigree age diabetes. .row_id
          6     148       72      35     495 33.6    0.627  50      pos       1
          1      85       66      29      90 26.6    0.351  31      neg       2
```

```
8      183      64      20      321 23.3     0.672  32      pos      3
1       89      66      23       94 28.1     0.167  21      neg      4
0      137      40      35      168 43.1     2.288  33      pos      5
5      116      74      12      215 25.6     0.201  30      neg      6
```

Likewise, the $col_info element of task lists the variables, their data types, and gives the level labels for categorical variables such as "diabetes":

```
task2$col_info
[Output]
            id    type  levels
  1:. .row_id integer
  2:      age numeric
  3: diabetes  factor pos,neg
  4:  glucose numeric
  5:  insulin numeric
  6:     mass numeric
  7: pedigree numeric
  8: pregnant numeric
  9: pressure numeric
 10:  triceps numeric
```

There are many other elements of the "task" object. For instance, other elements of task list the dependent variable and the predictors:

```
task2$target_names
[Output]
      [1] "diabetes"

task2$feature_names
[Output]
      [1] "age"      "glucose"  "insulin"  "mass"     "pedigree" "pregnant"
"pressure" "triceps"
```

Note that we do not have to use mlr3's built-in tasks. We may create them from existing data frames. Below we read in the "world" data, used in previous chapters. World has the categorical variable "litgtmean" (above or below world mean literacy) and the continuous variable "literacy" (national literacy rate). Note this is presented to explain importing data frames to mlr3 tasks. We do not use the world data in the remainder of the example.

```
# Read world.csv data into the data frame "world".
world <- read.csv("C:/Data/world.csv", header=TRUE, sep = ",",
stringsAsFactors=TRUE)

# Create taskworld1 as a classification task
taskworld1 = mlr3::TaskClassif$new(id = "world", backend = world, target =
"litgtmean")
# Create taskworld2 as a regression task
taskworld2 = mlr3::TaskRegr$new(id = "world", backend = world, target = "literacy")
```

6.3.4.4 Train and predict the models

The next step of the mlr3 process is to train the models for one subset of the data (the train or development set) and to predict another subset (the test or validation set). Specifically, the prediction model will be trained using the first

70% of observations, which are rows 1 through 538. Then the prediction will be made on all 768 cases, or we could just predict for the test cases in rows 538–768. For this exercise, we do the former.

To train learner_knn on the "task" problem:

```
learner_kknn$train(task2, row_ids = 1:538)

print(learner_kknn$model)
```
[Output not shown]

Below we predict diabetes for all 768 observations in task2. We see that most the predictions (response) match the observed values (truth).

```
preds_kknn = learner_kknn$predict(task2)

preds_kknn
```
[Output:]
```
<PredictionClassif> for 768 observations:
    row_id truth response
         1   pos      pos
         2   neg      neg
         3   pos      pos
---
       766   neg      neg
       767   pos      neg
       768   neg      neg
```

The $confusion element of preds_kknn shows the classification table for model results. Accuracy is (198 + 456)/768 = 0.8516. The k-nearest-neighbors method correctly predicted diabetes for 85% of the Pima Indians in the sample.

```
preds_kknn$confusion
```
[Output:]
```
          truth
response pos neg
     pos 198  44
     neg  70 456
```

Accuracy may be computed using the expression below.

```
preds_kknn$score(msrs("classif.acc"))
```
[Output:]
```
classif.acc
0.8515625
```

6.3.4.5 Evaluate the model

Accuracy is just one possible model performance metric. Appropriate metrics will vary by task. To see 98 possible metrics, use the following command.

```
as.data.table(mlr_measures)
```
[Partial output:]
```
                 key task_type     packages predict_type task_properties
 1:      classif.acc   classif mlr3measures     response
 2:      classif.auc   classif mlr3measures         prob       twoclass
.. .
```

```
22:      classif.recall  classif mlr3measures      response        twoclass
...
43:           regr.rmse     regr mlr3measures      response
...
47:            regr.rsq     regr mlr3measures      response
...
78:           surv.rmse     surv                   response
...
98:          time_train     <NA>                   response
```

For a given prediction like preds_kknn, we may only use metrics of the correct task_type (classif) and correct predict_type (response). For instance, we could use accuracy (classif.acc) or recall (classif.recall) but not area under the curve (classif.auc). Accuracy, recall, and other classification metrics were discussed in Chapter 4.

```
preds_kknn$task_type
[Output:]
      [1] "classif"

preds_kknn$predict_types
[Output:]
      [1] "response"
```

The following command prints both the Accuracy and Recall metrics for the preds_kknn predictions.

```
preds_kknn$score(msrs(c("classif.acc", "classif.recall")))
[Output:]
      classif.acc classif.recall
        0.8515625      0.7388060
```

Below, we now repeat the foregoing process for the learner_rpart classification tree learner and get the same model evaluation metrics for comparison. Note that all that is needed is to change the learner, not the task (which includes the data).

```
learner_rpart = mlr_learners$get("classif.rpart")
learner_rpart$train(task2, row_ids = 1:538)
preds_rpart = learner_rpart$predict(task2)
preds_rpart$confusion
[Output:]
            truth
   response pos neg
        pos 195  74
        neg  73 426

preds_rpart$score(msrs(c("classif.acc", "classif.recall")))
[Output:]
      classif.acc classif.recall
        0.8085938      0.7276119
```

We see that the k-nearest-neighbors algorithm predicted diabetes among Puma Indians better than did the classification tree algorithm, both in terms of the accuracy rate and, to a lesser degree, the hit rate (recall).

6.3.4.6 Consider changing model parameters

Almost all procedures have parameters (which mlr3 documentation calls "hyperparameters"), which are settings which the researcher might specify. This is an advanced topic requiring understanding of what each parameter does. However, in this section, we briefly illustrate the process. The first step is using the $param_set element of the learner to list what the parameters are.

```
print(learner_kknn$param_set)
[Partial output:]
           id    class lower upper
   1:       k ParamInt     1   Inf
   2: distance ParamDbl     0   Inf
   3:   kernel ParamFct    NA    NA
   4:    scale ParamLgl    NA    NA
   5:  ykernel ParamUty    NA    NA
```

```
print(learner_rpart$param_set)
[Output:]
                  id    class lower upper      levels        default value
   1:       minsplit ParamInt     1   Inf                         20
   2:      minbucket ParamInt     1   Inf             <NoDefault[3]>
   3:             cp ParamDbl     0     1                       0.01
   4:     maxcompete ParamInt     0   Inf                          4
   5:   maxsurrogate ParamInt     0   Inf                          5
   6:       maxdepth ParamInt     1    30                         30
   7:   usesurrogate ParamInt     0     2                          2
   8: surrogatestyle ParamInt     0     1                          0
   9:           xval ParamInt     0   Inf                         10     0
  10:     keep_model ParamLgl    NA    NA  TRUE,FALSE          FALSE
```

Any of these parameters might be changed. Using the classification tree (rpart) learner as an example, both commands below specify that the "maxdepth" parameter (which sets the maximum tree depth) be 10. The first command makes this change when the learner is being created (here learner_rpart2 is created). The second alternative method makes the change to an existing learner (learner_rpart) through "active binding".

```
learner_rpart2 = lrn("classif.rpart", predict_type = "prob", maxdepth = 5)
```

```
learner_rpart$param_set$values$maxdepth=5
```

After changing a parameter, we may see what difference it made for performance metrics. Below, if we restrict the maximum depth of the classification tree to 5, classification accuracy drops from 0.8085930 to 0.7851562. This is the price of forcing the solution to have a more parsimonious tree. Of course, change a parameter may improve as well as diminish model performance.

```
learner_rpart2 = lrn("classif.rpart", predict_type = "prob", maxdepth = 5)
learner_rpart2$train(task2, row_ids = 1:538)
preds_rpart2 = learner_rpart2$predict(task2)
preds_rpart2$score(msrs(c("classif.acc", "classif.recall")))
[Output:
    classif.acc classif.recall
     0.7851562      0.7500000
```

6.3.4.7 Cross-validate the model

```
# Perform 10-fold resampling on learner_kknn for task2 (pima).
set.seed(123)
cv10 = mlr3::rsmp("cv", folds = 10)
r_kknn = mlr3::resample(task2, learner_kknn, cv10)
print(r_kknn)
```

[Output:]
```
<ResampleResult> of 10 iterations
* Task: pima
* Learner: classif.kknn
* Warnings: 0 in 0 iterations
* Errors: 0 in 0 iterations
```
```
class(r_kknn)
```
[Output:]
```
[1] "ResampleResult" "R6"
```

The train-predict-score loop is repeated 10 times for the Accuracy and Recall metrics.
The `msrs()` function retrieves measures from the r_kknn created in the previous step.
The result is a set of 10 Accuracy measures and 10 Recall measures, one per cv fold.
```
r_kknn$score(mlr3::msrs(c("classif.acc", "classif.recall")))
```
[Partial output:]
```
                    task task_id                    learner   learner_id
  1: <TaskClassif[45]>    pima <LearnerClassifKKNN[31]> classif.kknn
 . . .
 10: <TaskClassif[45]>    pima <LearnerClassifKKNN[31]> classif.kknn
               resampling resampling_id iteration              prediction
 1: <ResamplingCV[19]>              cv         1 <PredictionClassif[19]>
 . . .
10: <ResamplingCV[19]>              cv        10 <PredictionClassif[19]>
   classif.acc classif.recall
 1:   0.7402597      0.7586207
 2:   0.7662338      0.6190476
 3:   0.7142857      0.6071429
 4:   0.8181818      0.7000000
 5:   0.7532468      0.5806452
 6:   0.6753247      0.5000000
 7:   0.7272727      0.5172414
 8:   0.8051948      0.7500000
 9:   0.6315789      0.3448276
10:   0.7368421      0.4285714
```

We now put overall cross-validated predictions using kknn into preds_kknn
If we wanted predictions for each of the 10 cv folds, substitute `r _ kknn$predictions()`
```
preds_kknn = r_kknn$prediction()
print(preds_kknn)
```
[Partial output:]
```
<PredictionClassif> for 768 observations:
    row_id truth response
        16   pos      neg
        23   pos      pos
        24   pos      pos
 ---
       761   neg      neg
       763   neg      neg
       768   neg      neg
```

Print out the cross-validated classification table for the kknn method
```
kknn_table = preds_kknn$confusion
print(kknn_table)
```
[Output:]
```
          truth
response pos neg
     pos 156  90
     neg 112 410
```

Printing the chosen cross-validated metrics for the kknn method is done in the next section, on benchmarking the model.

We do not show the output, but we may repeat the cross-validation process for the rpart method using almost identical commands:

```
# Perform 10-fold resampling on learner_rpart for task2 (pima).
# Note that the cv10 object remains the same as for the kknn method above.
# Note that different random seeds return different truth tables
set.seed(123)
r_rpart = mlr3::resample(task2, learner_rpart, cv10)

r_rpart$score(mlr3::msrs(c("classif.acc", "classif.recall")))
preds_rpart = r_rpart$prediction()

rpart_table = preds_rpart$confusion
print(rpart_table)
[Classification table output:]
            truth
    response pos neg
         pos 174  97
         neg  94 403
```

6.3.4.8 Benchmark the model against other learners

The `benchmark()` function in mlr3 conveniently compares the selected methods (kknn, rpart) on the selected performance metrics (Accuracy, Recall), on a cross-validated basis. It is easy to add an additional learner in the benchmark process. Below we add the SVM method, using its mlr3 label of "classif.svm". Though differences are small, we find that by the Accuracy metric, the SVM method is best. By the Recall metric, the classification tree method (rpart) is best.

```
learners = list(learner_kknn, learner_rpart, lrn("classif.svm"))

set.seed(123)
bm_grid = benchmark_grid(task2, learners, cv10)

bm = benchmark(bm_grid)

print(bm$aggregate(measures = msrs(c("classif.acc", "classif.recall"))))
[Output:]
   nr      resample_result task_id    learner_id
1:  1 <ResampleResult[21]>    pima  classif.kknn
2:  2 <ResampleResult[21]>    pima classif.rpart
3:  3 <ResampleResult[21]>    pima   classif.svm
   resampling_id iters classif.acc classif.recall
1:            cv    10   0.7368421      0.5806097
2:            cv    10   0.7513158      0.6417380
3:            cv    10   0.7538619      0.5356460
```

PART III: MODELING AND MACHINE LEARNING IN DETAIL

6.4 Illustrating modeling and machine learning with SVM in caret

As it is impossible to in one chapter to treat the hundreds of modeling and machine learning methods available in R, in this Part III we illustrate by focusing on one of the most widely used methods, SVM models as implemented under the leading modeling integration package, caret, which is an older but still more widely used alternative to the mlr3 package discussed in Section 6.3. While we focus on SVM, in a later section we compare it with two other methods: gradient boosting machines (GBM) and learning vector quantization (LVQ).

6.4.1 How SVM works

The SVM algorithm attempts to find a hyperplane that will classify observed data points into distinct and separate classes. For instance, consider the case where the outcome is coded 0 or 1, such as Republicans = 0 and Democrats = 1. To simplify, if there are only two input variables, such as two opinion scales on environmental policy and labor union policy, then these can form the axes of a scatterplot. Democrats, being more in favor of environmental regulation and policies favoring unionism, will fall in the upper right with Republicans in the lower left. In this two-dimensional example, the hyperplane is a line best separating the 0s from the 1s. With three predictors a third orthogonal axis is added and the hyperplane is a two-dimensional surface. As the number of inputs increases, it becomes difficult or impossible for the human mind to visualize, but mathematics handles n-dimensional space without a problem.

The SVM solution also tries to maximize the separation, called the "margin", between classes being predicted. That is, SVM seeks the "maximum margin hyperplane" (MMH). Maximum margins are not the only hyperplanes separating classes of the outcome variable but maximum width is desirable because then the chances of an observation being on the wrong side of the hyperplane are minimized.

Margins may be "hard" or "soft", depending on whether exceptions are allowed (soft margins allow some misclassified observations on the wrong side of the margin). To create a hard margin, simply set the cost to a high value (e.g., cost = le10). Cost is discussed below. The default value of cost is 1 in the e1071 package to be used in the example.

"Support vectors" are the data points which are closest to the margin (i.e., to the MMH). There must be at least one support vector per class of the outcome variable. There may be more than one if two points are equally close to the margin for a given class. Eliminating a support vector will change the position of the hyperplane and the width of the margin. Note that the number of support vectors may be very small even if the number of observations is very large. Thus, by using support vectors, SVM is able to store a classification model very compactly. For an introduction to the vector geometry underlying SVM, see Bennet and Campbell (2000).

"Cost" is a parameter needed to calculate some hyperplanes. If data are linearly separable, the hyperplane may be solved using quadratic optimization without invoking nonlinear kernels (also discussed below). However, if the data are separable only on a nonlinear basis, the margin is created through an algorithm that attaches a "cost" to points which fall on the wrong side of the hyperplane. The researcher can set the cost parameter. Too high a cost and the algorithm will work toward 100% separation but at the price of a complicated hyperplane, which may not generalize well to other data in the future. Such a model has narrow margins and is "overfitted", meaning it is responsive even to noise in the data. If cost is too low then the margin will be wide, allowing more error in the model.

6.4.2 SVM algorithms compared to logistic and OLS regression

SVM regression seeks a solution with maximally wide margins. In contrast, OLS regression seeks a solution minimizing mean squared error. Logistic regression seeks a solution maximizing likelihood or minimizing deviance (-2 log likelihood), using maximum likelihood estimation.

SVM regression measures error differently from linear regression, whether of the OLS or logistic variety. In statistical jargon, SVM has a different "loss function", also called a "cost function". The loss function in SVM regression is a "hinge loss function". To simplify, for the case where the outcome values are 0 and 1 and the true value of a given case is 1, then predictions of >= 1 are assigned an error value of 0, but predictions < 1 are penalized and are assigned a linearly higher error value the further the prediction is below 1, which is the hinge. In contrast, in linear regression, predictions > 1 will receive an error value greater than 0 just as do predictions < 1. In logistic regression, predictions will be in the 0 to 1 range and error is reflected in how far predicted probabilities deviate from 1 (for predictions >=.5, which causes the case to be classified as 1) or from 0 (for probabilities <.5, which causes the case to be classified as 0).

Put another way, a "loss function" is a measure of how well a model's predictions or classifications are working. In OLS regression, for instance, a common loss function metric to evaluate alternative models is mean square error

(MSE) or its root mean square error (RMSE), with lower error being a better model. In logistic regression, using a logistic loss function, a common metric is log likelihood error (usually transformed as deviance, which is –2 log likelihood). In SVM regression the most common loss function metric is MSE, but as noted above, error is calculated differently, using a hinge loss function. For a more technical but brief discussion of loss functions in linear versus SVM regression, see Bonica (2018: 835–836).

6.4.3 SVM kernels, types, and parameters

"Kernels" are important in SVM because they linearize nonlinear problems and make a solution possible. As nonlinear problems are commonplace in the real world and as the researcher may well not know beforehand if the problem at hand is nonlinear, selecting a kernel is an early step. A kernel is a transformation that projects the data to a higher dimensional space where linearity may become apparent. The projection process is called the "kernel trick". Different kernels invoke different kinds of projection, some of which may linearize a given problem better than others. Kernel selection is not automatic but is an explicit choice made by the researcher, unless the researcher accepts the software's default kernel.

What are the "higher dimensions" involved in the "kernel trick"? A dimension is an axis on which the data are plotted, such as environmental and unionism scales in the earlier political party example. If an additional input (predictor) is added, that is a third dimension. What the kernel algorithm does is create a new input which was not a variable in the original data. This new input is the "higher dimension" and is constructed as a mathematical function of existing data vectors. This mathematical function is usually denoted by the Greek letter phi (ϕ).

Further below is a list of kernel functions available in the e1071 package, which contains the `svm()` command. Not all of which are available in all SVM software implementations. The best kernel to select is often based on trial and error though the literature in a given field may suggest what has worked well in the past. Often the choice of kernel does not greatly affect model performance but that cannot be assumed.

Kernels

Kernel specifications are used in both SVM tuning and predicting. A kernel transforms and projects data onto a higher space, enabling a solution (fit), after which fitted values are mapped back to the original data space. Put a second way, SVM uses kernel methods, meaning that data are mapped to a higher dimension in which it is hoped separation of the data by outcome will be easier and a solution more readily obtained. Put a third way, the kernel function operates as a sort of "sunglass" filter that highlights possible separation of the raw data which is difficult to perceive on an unfiltered basis. Good separation allows similar data points to be seen as being together. In this sense it may be said that a kernel is a form of similarity measurement algorithm.

It is important that the researcher select the kernel function appropriate to the particular data at hand. While it is possible to select the type of kernel and parameters through some automated process, such as grid search, this data-driven approach can easily lead to over-fitting of the model. The effect of alternative kernels is illustrated in later sections. Below we list the four kernel types supported by the e1071 package.

- `kernel = "radial"`: Also called the radial basis function (RBF) or Gaussian kernel, this type of kernel has similarities to the algorithm for RBF NNs. This is the default kernel in the `svm()` command of the e1071 package used here. Radial kernels can create complex regions in feature space, such as closed polygons in two-dimensional space. This kernel requires setting the gamma parameter, discussed later with regard to tuned SVM models. In using a radial model, the researcher is assuming that there may be some nonlinearity in the data, making the data not linearly separable, something which is more often the case than not. That is, the researcher is assuming that data may be separated better by circles and hyperspheres than by straight lines and hyperplanes.
- kernel="linear": This is equivalent to not applying a kernel. The researcher is assuming the problem is linear, not nonlinear. That is, data separation is assumed to be achievable by lines or hyperplanes. A linear kernel is recommended by some authors for text classification problems. However, based on demonstration by Keerthi and Lin (2003) that the linear kernel is essentially a special case of the RBF kernel, experimental studies by Lin and Lin (2003: 27) led to the conclusion that "among existing kernels, RBF should be the first choice for general users" (p. 27).

- kernel="polynomial": This is the simplest type of nonlinear transformation. It requires setting the gamma, degree, and coef0 parameters, or accepting their default values. By default degree is 3, which is a cubic polynomial. Third degree polynomials have one inflection point, point symmetry about the inflection point, and come in three basic shapes: (1) up-down-up; (2) up-over-up; and (3) up more steeply – up less steeply – up more steeply. One may override this by specifying degree to be equal to some other value if other polynomial line shapes known to characterize the data. A polynomial kernel may work best when the training data are normalized. In addition to specifying the polynomial degree, the researcher may also specify the constant term (coef0) and the slope (gamma).
- kernel="sigmoid": This type of kernel has similarities to the type of activation function used by NN algorithms. This kernel requires setting the degree and coef0 parameters, or accepting their default values. Also called the hyperbolic tangent or multilayer perceptron (MLP) kernel, the sigmoid kernel is used in certain classes of NN. The sigmoid function is also the function used in logistic regression when analyzing binary outcomes. An SVM model with a sigmoid function is equivalent to a two-layer perceptron NN. The researcher may set the slope (gamma in the terminology of package e1071 but more often called alpha or just the slope parameter) and the constant (coef0). The sigmoid kernel has been found to perform well in image recognition problems.[11] However, Lin and Lin (2003: 1) found that "the sigmoid kernel is not better than the RBF kernel in general" (p. 1) and "in general we do not recommend the use of the sigmoid kernel" (p. 27).

Parameters

As alluded above, different kernels have different parameter settings. The researcher may accept default settings or may override them to set other values in an attempt to improve model performance.

- `gamma`: This parameter is needed for the radial, polynomial, and sigmoid kernels. Let x be a data matrix or vector. Typically x is a data frame, which is a matrix. The default is gamma = if `(is.vector(x)) 1 else 1 / ncol(x)`. Translated, this means that the default value of gamma is 1 if x is a vector but if it is a matrix, then gamma is the 1 divided by the number of columns (fields, dimensions).
- `Degree`: This parameter is needed for polynomial kernels. The default value is 3. This specifies a third-degree polynomial, also called a cubic polynomial. If degree is set to 1, this is equivalent to using a linear kernel. If degree is set to 2, one is specifying a quadratic polynomial, which has a parabola-shaped form. Third degree polynomials can take multiple shapes.[12]
- `coef0`: This parameter is needed for polynomial and sigmoid kernels. The default value is 0.
- `Nu`: This parameter is needed if one of the "nu" type models is specified. The default is `nu = 0.5`. See discussion above in the section on types.

6.4.4 Tuning SVM models

One reason for the popularity of SVM models is precisely that acceptable results may be obtained with little or no tuning. Nonetheless, tuning is strongly recommended and may make a significant difference. Using SVM as implemented in the e1071 package, tuning may be accomplished using the `tune.svm()` function, which will perform a tenfold cross-validation search for the best values of the gamma and cost parameters. To discuss this for a specific example requires an SVM model to have been run. Therefore, tuning is illustrated when the SVM model is applied in later sections of this chapter.

6.4.5 SVM and longitudinal data

SVM may be used with longitudinal, panel, and repeated measures data, though there is controversy on this point. Traditional predictive methods like OLS and logistic regression assume data are "IID" (independent and identically distributed). Independence means knowing one data point should not affect your prediction of the next data point. Longitudinal data are not independent. For instance, knowing a student's math score in year 1 does affect what one expects that student's math score would be in year 2. The predictability of a later score in a longitudinal sequence means that error of prediction will correlate. To pool all the data across years assumes that correlated error does not matter. This is not an acceptable assumption for traditional predictive methods.

However, SVM (and many other machine learning approaches) do not make the usual assumptions about data being independent, linear, devoid of multicollinearity, and other requirements of traditional predictive methods (Tan, 2020). Rather SVM is a nonparametric method that takes data "as is" and does not require any particular assumption be made about it. It treats longitudinal data as pooled data but it is not affected in its results by the presence of correlated error. Rather, data are separated in a data-driven manner based on empirically-derived vector points and margins. If an observation is measured at, say, 10 time points, it will be treated as 10 observations. Since every other observation is also treated the same way, weighting of observations is not affected. The SVM model may classify or predict as well as or even better than traditional methods, which do correct for correlated error.

Nonetheless, this is not the end of the story. Pooling longitudinal data throws away sequence information. It may be that better classifications and predictions could be made by adapting the SVM model to take advantage of the full information presented by longitudinal data. This advanced topic, however, is not covered in this volume, in part because it is not yet supported by packages we discuss here. There is some evidence that longitudinal SVM models are best tuned using a "Fisher kernel", not offered in all packages. See Lu, Leen, and Kaye (2009) on longitudinal SVR-SVM for categorical outcomes.

As an alternative, SVR for longitudinal continuous data was implemented by Azamathulla and Wu (2011), who used *Neurosolutions* software (www.neurosolutions.com) for the purpose. For longitudinal analysis of continuous outcomes using LS-SVM, see Seok et al. (2011). Because LS-SVM uses regression estimators from a straightforward linear equation system, it is easier to apply to longitudinal regression problems than is SVR-SVM. For applications of LS-SVM to longitudinal data, see Luts et al. (2012) and Du et al. (2015).

6.5 SVM versus OLS regression

Comparing SVM models with traditional OLS models is presented in an online supplement to Chapter 6, found in the student section of this book's Support Material (www.routledge.com/9780367624293), under the supplement title "SVM versus OLS".

6.6 SVM with the caret package: Predicting world literacy rates

The caret package supports hundreds of modeling methods, including a dozen SVM methods. This is convenient if we wish to compare an SVM model with some other types of models. To get a list of all possible methods, type:

```
library(caret)
names(caret::getModelInfo())
[Output:]
    [1] "ada"
    [2] "AdaBag"
  . . .
  [237] "xgbTree"
  [238] "xyf"
```

More information about caret is in the online supplement, "Modeling Procedures Supported by the caret and mlr3 Packages", located in the Student Resources section of this book's Support Material (www.routledge.com/9780367624293).

The main listed SVM methods correspond to different types of kernels, discussed in Section 6.4.3: "svmRadial", "svmLinear", "svmPoly", and "svmRadialSigma". Others include "svmBoundrangeString", "svmExpoString", "svmLinear2", "svmLinear3", "svmLinearWeights", "svmLinearWeights2", "svmRadialCost", "svmRadialWeights", and "svmSpectrumString". In this section, we use the most common SVM model, which is "svmRadial". This is often the default model in statistical software for SVM.

Note that by default, to implement SVM models, caret uses the "kernlab" package's `ksvm()` command, to be discussed in section, not the `svm()` command of the "e1071" package used in other examples. It is possible, however, to force caret to use e1071, as discussed in Section 6.6.8.

TEXT BOX 6.2 Predicting informed consent in social research

Norval and Henderson (2020) conducted an experiment to investigate the controversial issue of harvesting social media data in the process of conducting analyses in health research. They noted that "the use of such data raises significant ethical questions about the need for the informed consent of those being studied. Consent mechanisms, if even obtained, are typically broad and inflexible, or place a significant burden on the participant" (p. 187). Their research question centered on whether machine learning algorithms might be used to predict and automate consent decisions.

The authors explained their experiment, noting, "Our research hypothesis is that we can predict whether or not a given bit of social data should be shared (dependent variable) based on attributes of the social data itself and of its author (independent variable). This prediction might factor in, for example, the kind of social content in question (e.g., a picture, status update, page like), with whom it would be shared (the receiving audience), and how willingly the individual has approved similar requests in the past. To create and evaluate a predictive consent model for the above task, we first designed a web-based study to collect a corpus of data. Participants were repeatedly asked whether they would find it appropriate to have different types of their social data shared with different hypothetical audiences within a medical context. From this data set, we went on to train models to predict the appropriate flow of such data, and explored how the different factors of the model each influenced the consent decision" (pp. 189–190).

Norval and Henderson (2020) performed all their analysis using the "caret" package in R to evaluate six machine learning models: Naïve Bayes, SVM with a radial kernel, logistic regression, multilayer perceptron NN, RF, and k-nearest-neighbor. They used four model performance metrics, all discussed in Chapter 4:

- Accuracy: percent classified correctly
- Precision: number correctly classified high as percent of all predicted high
- Sensitivity: number correctly classified high as percent of all observed high
- Specificity: number correctly classified low as percent of all observed low

The authors found the highest accuracy for the SVM model. However, the Naïve Bayes classifier has the highest precision and specificity. Logistic regression had the highest sensitivity. Though accuracy is the most common model performance metric for classification, the researcher should select the metric which fits her or his particular research question, which may vary.

Source: Norval, Chris; & Henderson, Tristan (2020). Automating dynamic consent decisions for the processing of social media data in health research. *Journal of Empirical Research on Human Research Ethics* 15(3): 187–201.

6.6.1 Setup

The recommended install command assures all of caret's dependent packages are also installed. However, this full installation takes a long time:

```
install.packages("caret", dependencies = c("Depends", "Suggests"))
```

The researcher may well be able to get by with the faster usual install command:

```
install.packages("caret")
```

Either way, then load the caret and other needed packages and set the working directory:

```
library(caret)          # A leading package for training models
library(e1071)          # Supports the svm() command
library(kernlab)        # Supports the ksvm() command
library(Metrics)        # Supports the rmse () command
```

```
setwd("C:/Data")              # Declares the working directory
```

Also, read in the "world" example data:

```
world <- read.csv("C:/Data/world.csv", header=TRUE, sep = ",",
stringsAsFactors=TRUE)
```

6.6.2 Constructing the SVM regression model with caret

The caret package is designed for selecting models, tuning and training them through cross-validation, and evaluating the trained models. We leave discussion of tuning and training to a later section. Instead, in this section, we simply present how to run an SVM regression model for all cases in a data frame. For example data we use the same "world" data frame as in previous chapters. The world data frame file is "world.csv"; literacy is the continuous outcome variable (DV); predictors are Infantdeathsper1k, poppersqmile, gdppercapitalindollars, phonesper1000, and birthrate. The research objective is to predict why some nations are higher than others in national literacy rate.

In the first step of a two-step caret process, create an object called "ctrl", which contains control parameters for the model we are about to create. Below, by setting method="none" we ask for the entire sample without cross-validation. The classProbs setting is "FALSE" because class probabilities are only for classification models, not regression models for continuous variables such as literacy. We use the default summary function. Type `help(trainControl)` for more information about these and other settings.

```
ctrl <- caret::trainControl(
  method = "none",
  classProbs = FALSE,
  summaryFunction = defaultSummary
)
```

In the second caret step we run the SVM model using the `train()` command. In the `train()` function we list the DV (literacy) and our five predictors, declare world to be our data frame, specify svmRadial to be the kernel method (this is actually the default and may be left out), ask for centering of variables (optional; note we do not standardize), declare the ctrl object created above to contain the control parameters, and ask that RMSE be the model performance metric. The result is put into the "SVMfit1" object. Setting the random seed is mainly useful later, when we ask for cross-validation, which involves a random element. Type `help(train)` for more information.

```
set.seed(123)
SVMfit1 <- caret::train(
  literacy ~ Infantdeathsper1k + poppersqmile + gdppercapitalindollars +
phonesper1000 + birthrate,
  data = world,
  method = "svmRadial",
  preProc = "center",
  trControl = ctrl,
  metric = "RMSE"
)
```

Typing the name of the results object verifies basic information about the model we have just run.

```
SVMfit1
```

[Output:]

```
Support Vector Machines with Radial Basis Function Kernel
212 samples
  5 predictor
Pre-processing: centered (5)
Resampling: None
```

The `summary()` command verifies that we have just created an SVM output object using the caret package, which by default uses the kern package's `ksvm()` command to implement SVM. However, the object is of class "train", not class "ksvm", so only `train()` and not `ksvm()` output elements are available. For instance, the `ksvm()` element SVMfit2$error is not available as it would be if we used the `ksvm()` command directly rather than via caret's `train()` function.

```
class(SVMfit1)
[Output:]
      [1] "train"          "train.formula"
summary(SVMfit1)
[Output:]
   Length  Class   Mode
        1   ksvm     S4
```

6.6.3 Obtaining predicted values and residuals

Predicted values are produced in the usual manner by the `predict()` command:

```
SVM1fitted <- predict(SVMfit1, data=world)
```

To add predicted/fitted values to the world data frame (remember to resave world if desired):

```
world$SVM1pred <- SVM1fitted
```

Residuals are observed minus predicted values. Below we place them in the object "SVM1resid", which we then add to the world data frame.

```
SVM1resid <- world$literacy - SVM1fitted
world$SVM1resid <- SVM1resid
```

6.6.4 Model performance metrics

The "caret" package comes with a number of its own convenient model performance functions. `R2()` is to obtain R-squared; `RMSE()` is for RMSE; and `MAE()` is for mean average error.

```
caret::R2(SVM1fitted,world$literacy)
[Output:]
      [1] 0.6559676

caret::RMSE(SVM1fitted,world$literacy)
[Output:]
      [1] 12.04565

caret::MAE(SVM1fitted,world$literacy)
[Output:]
      [1] 7.707253
```

To compare R-squared from the default-tuned, non-cross-validated SVM model, we may use the commands below, which implement an OLS model. We see that the SVM model is only marginally better. That the difference is very small implies that the data relationships are largely linear, fitting OLS assumptions.

```
OLSfit1 <- lm(literacy ~ Infantdeathsper1k + poppersqmile + gdppercapitalindollars +
phonesper1000 + birthrate,data = world)
summaryOLSfit1 <- summary(OLSfit1)
summaryOLSfit1$r.squared
[Output:]
   [1] 0.6473269
```

Below we create a vector of fitted values (OLSfit1_fitted) and use the "Metrics" package to compute the RMSE, a common model performance measure used later for model comparisons.

```
OLSfit1_fitted <- predict(OLSfit1)
Metrics::rmse(OLSfit1_fitted,world$literacy)
   [1] 11.53426
```

6.6.5 Variable importance

The caret package provides the `varImp()` function for assessing variable importance. For regression models, when `nonpara = FALSE` in the `varImp()` command, a linear model is fit and the absolute *t*-value for the b coefficient of the given predictor variable is used as the importance criterion. If `nonpara=TRUE` (the default) is the option, a LOESS smoothing line is fit between the outcome variable and the given predictor variable and then R-squared for this model is compared to the null (intercept only) model and what is returned is a measure of variable importance in the researcher's model relative to the null model. Which method is "right" depends on how the researcher wishes to define "variable importance".

```
caret::varImp(SVMfit1, nonpara = FALSE, scale = TRUE)
[Output:]
   Linear model variable importance
                           Overall
   birthrate                100.00
   Infantdeathsper1k         94.41
   phonesper1000             53.97
   gdppercapitalindollars    42.54
   poppersqmile               0.00
```

Alternatively, we may set `nonpara = TRUE` to obtain a LOESS R-squared variable importance ranking:

```
caret::varImp(SVMfit1, nonpara = TRUE, scale = TRUE)
[Output:]
                           Overall
   birthrate                100.00
   phonesper1000             99.02
   Infantdeathsper1k         96.43
   gdppercapitalindollars    76.97
   poppersqmile               0.00
```

In the output above, the variable importance order is similar for the two ranking methods, though the second and third ranked predictors are flipped, swapping the order of importance of phonesper1000 and Infantdeathsper1k. Under both methods birthrate still emerges as the most important predictor variable.

Treatment of a more complex example of computing variable importance for SVM models is presented in an online supplement to Chapter 6, found in the student section of this book's Support Material (www.routledge.com/9780367624293), under the supplement title "SVM Variable Importance".

6.6.6 Other output elements

SVMfit1, the object created by caret's `train()` command, has several output elements, the most useful of which are presented below. Note that no "$fitted.values" element or "$residuals" element is returned.

Elements spelling out the model that was used

SVMfit1$method: Reminds the user that the SVM method is "svmRadial"

SVMfit1$modelType: Reminds the user that the model type is "Regression"

SVMfit1$metric: Reminds the user that the model evaluation metric was RMSE in this example

SVMfit1$bestTune: Lists the caret-selected optimal tuning parameters.

```
SVMfit1$bestTune
```
[Output:]
```
sigma    C
1 0.7903274 0.25
```

Elements summarizing model inputs
SVMfit1$call: Reminds the user what the `train()` command was
SVMfit1$coefnames: Returns predictor variable names
SVMfit1$trainingData: Lists the data frame for the training cases (all cases in this example)
SVMfit1$control: Lists all control parameters for the model, including default settings
SVMfit1$preProcess: Lists any pre-processing operations such as centering in this example

Elements summarizing model results
SVMfit1$finalModel: Gives a summary of the final model, with final tuning values

```
SVMfit1$finalModel
```
[Output:]
```
Support Vector Machine object of class "ksvm"
SV type: eps-svr  (regression)
parameter : epsilon = 0.1  cost C = 0.25
Gaussian Radial Basis kernel function.
Hyperparameter : sigma =  0.790327361037867
Number of Support Vectors : 153
Objective Function Value : -19.4224
Training error : 0.382824
```

SVMfit1$yLimits: Give the range of estimates of the outcome variable for the training set. For this example, the training set is all nations. Note SVM predictions exceed 100, which is the actual upper limit of observed literacy, showing that as in OLS predictions, estimates may be outside the valid range of the data.

```
SVMfit1$yLimits
```
[Output:]
```
1]  13.48 104.12
```

Elements pertinent only if cross-validation is used
SVMfit1$resample: Returns a data frame with columns for each performance metric and rows for each resample.

6.6.7 SVM plots

Given the SVMfit1 object created with caret, and given the SVM1fitted and SVM1resid objects created from it previously, various diagnostic plots may be created. For instance, simple plots of literacy on the Y-axis may be plotted against SVM fitted values on X or against SVM residuals on X by the commands below. The `par()` command creates stacked plots (the last command resets to single plots). The result is shown in Figure 6.3.

```
par(mfrow=c(2,1))

plot(SVM1fitted,world$literacy, col="blue",ylab="National Literacy Rate", xlab="SVM
Fitted Values")

plot(SVM1resid,world$literacy, col="blue",ylab="National Literacy Rate", xlab="SVM
Residuals")

par(mfrow=c(1,1))
```

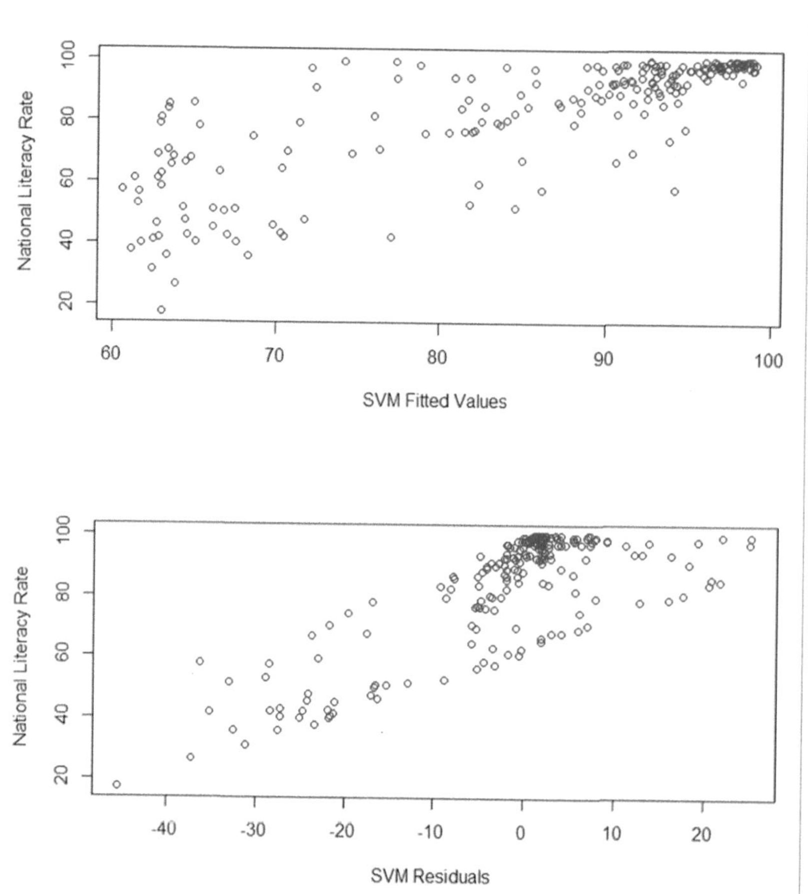

Figure 6.3 National literacy by fitted values and residuals, SVM1 model

In Figure 6.3 we see that predictions from the SVM1 model are moderate. Lower observed and predicted values tend to go together and likewise with higher values. However, the correspondence is far from linear and lower fitted values are very heteroskedastic. The residuals plot does not show the desired patternless cloud but instead lower observed values of literacy tend to have negative residuals (observed is lower than predicted) and the opposite is true for higher observed values. Real-world predictions are often of this moderate strength type.

6.7 Tuning SVM models

Like other R commands, the `train()` command from the caret package, which by default uses the kern package's `ksvm()` command, as well as the `svm()` command from the e1071 package have many options. In both cases it is possible to refine the SVM model by optimizing various input parameters in a process called "tuning". The generic syntax listings below show tuning-related options, with default values. In each case, the list of options is long. While the researcher is apt to accept many default values for these options, thereby avoiding the need to make them explicit in the calling command, this is not always wise. Tuning is simply seeking whether there are better settings values for the model than the default ones.

As a prefatory caution, the reader is warned that there are many approaches to tuning models, including other possible settings and even use of other packages not discussed here. Type `help(svm)`or `help(train)` to see further explanation of some of these options. The default `train()` and default `svm()` generic command syntax is below. The syntax for each command shows default values for various settings. These are the settings which may be "tuned".

```
# Default train() generic command syntax:
caret::train(x, y, method = "rf", preProcess = NULL, ...,weights = NULL, metric =
ifelse(is.factor(y), "Accuracy", "RMSE"),  maximize = ifelse(metric %in% c("RMSE",
"logLoss", "MAE"), FALSE, TRUE), trControl = trainControl(), tuneGrid = NULL,
tuneLength = ifelse(trControl$method == "none", 1, 3))
```

```
# Default svm() generic command syntax:
# The gamma expression is equivalent to 1/data dimensions.
caret::svm(x, y = NULL, scale = TRUE, type = NULL, kernel = "radial", degree = 3,
gamma = if (is.vector(x)) 1 else 1 / ncol(x), coef0 = 0, cost = 1, nu = 0.5,class.
weights = NULL,
cachesize = 40, tolerance = 0.001, epsilon = 0.1,
shrinking = TRUE, cross = 0, probability = FALSE, fitted = TRUE,
..., subset, na.action = na.omit)
```

6.7.1 Tuning for the `train()` command from the caret package

The `train()` command from the caret package implements tuning on a built-in basis. "Behind the scenes" by default it uses the version of SVM from the "kern" package, which is the `ksvm()` command. Earlier the `train()` command was used on the world data frame with literacy as the outcome, storing results in the object SVMfit1. Using the `predict()` command on SVMfit1 then created the predictions output object SVM1fitted. Various model performance metrics were then computed. R-squared for this model was 0.656, a bit higher than for the OLS model (0.647).

The SVMFit1 reflects default caret tuning parameters. While SVMfit1 is not an "untuned" model, there is a question as to whether the default tuning parameters below are optimal. The default tuning parameters may be viewed by the following command.

```
<CDTX>SVMfit1$bestTune
[Output:]
       sigma    C
  1 0.7903274 0.25
```

It can be seen that the `train()` command tunes for two parameters: cost (C) and sigma. Sigma is a parameter based on the `sigest()` function of the kernlab package, which is also the package supporting the `ksvm()` function, which caret uses for SVM models. When `method = "svmRadial"` in caret's `train()` command, tuning is done for the cost parameter for a single value of sigma as based on `sigest()` output. The number of cost values searched was the default for our example but this can be changed by adding a `tuneLength =` specification to the `trainControl()` function. Type `help(sigest)` for more information on the sigma parameter.

One way to tune the model is to change the SVM method. The default tuned model will differ if the SVM method differs. For instance, one could specify `method = "svmRadialSigma"` in caret's `train()` command instead of `method = "svmRadial"`. This will invoke a tuning grid search over values of both cost and sigma. When implemented for the same example, different optimal tuning parameters are returned, which result, for these data, in a somewhat lower (worse) R-squared performance metric. Below, SVMfit2 is the object created by the svmRadialSigma method and SVM2fitted is the corresponding prediction object.[13] The generating commands are identical to those above for SVMfit1 and SVM2fitted except for changing the method to svmRadialSigma. This method gives different tuning parameters and a slightly lower R-squared values. Other SVM methods fare even more poorly.

```
SVMfit2$bestTune
[Output:]
          sigma    C
     1 0.04061206 0.25
```

```
caret::R2(SVM2fitted,world$literacy)
[Output:]
      [1] 0.6472629
```

6.7.2 Tuning for the `svm()` command from the e1071 package

SVM is also available in the "e1071" package, which also supports a `tune()` command. In online help documentation, David Meyer, developer of the `svm()` program, warns, "Parameters of SVM-models usually must be tuned to yield sensible results!" In this section, we tune and then rerun a model based on the `svm()` command, finding that the tuned model indeed has better model performance. In actual research we would then cross-validate the model and use the tuned model to obtain measures of model performance, variable importance rankings, plots, and other output described in earlier sections but do not do so here for space reasons.

The parameters to be tuned are cost, gamma, and in the case of regression models, epsilon:

1. cost: Cost is the cost of estimation errors in the training set, where errors are data points on the "wrong" side of the separations formed by the support vectors created by the kernel algorithm. Called the "regularization parameter" and labeled "C", cost balances correct estimation against overfitting. One could also say that cost balances misclassification against model parsimony. High cost causes the SVM algorithm to create separations that have few errors, improving correct estimation, but this comes at the expense of possibly creating an overly complex, unparsimonious model, which is overfitted. Small cost reduces overfitting but increases errors of estimation, though the reduction in overfitting may mean the model is more stable when generalized to other data.
2. gamma: Called the "kernel parameter" and labeled "γ", this balances correct estimation and overfitting in a different way. Large gamma reduces the radii of support vectors and increases the chances of overfitting by increasing granularity. Small gamma increases the radii of influence of support vectors and may increase mis-estimation by lacking the needed granularity. Put another way, too low a gamma will lead to overfitting while too high a gamma will force a too-linear solution and the model will lack power to reflect nonlinearity in the data.
3. epsilon: Called "parameter epsilon" and labeled "ε", this is a tolerance parameter applicable only to regression models. In an SVM model, there is a margin of tolerance within which errors do not receive a penalty. Large epsilon penalizes less error in the model and smaller epsilon penalizes more. When epsilon is zero, all errors are penalized and the number of support vectors may approach the number of observations in the data frame. The default value is usually epsilon= 0.1 (10%).

The syntax for the `tune()` command from the e1071 package is below. We place its results in an object labeled "SVMtuningObject". Explanation of terms is given below the commands. We start by setting ranges of values for the tuning parameters. Ranges for gamma and cost are based on `tune()` help documentation but could be anything (e.g., `gammas=2^(-8:3)`). Many sources, including help documentation, omit epsilon, accepting the default of value of 0.1. Below, with 3 grid values each for gamma and cost and 4 for epsilon, 3*3*4 = 36 models will be searched.

```
# Set parameter ranges for grid search
gammas <- 2^(-1:1)  # gives grid values of 0.5 1.0 2.0
costs <- 2^(2:4)    # gives grid values of 4 8 16
epsilons <- c(1,0.1,0.01,0.001)

# Set random seed for tuning
# Tuning selection involves a random factor and results may differ by random seed
set.seed(123)

# SVMtuningObject is of class "tune"
SVMtuningObject <- e1071::tune(svm,
```

```
    literacy ~ Infantdeathsper1k + poppersqmile + gdppercapitalindollars +
phonesper1000 + birthrate,
    type = "eps-regression",
    kernel = "radial",
    scale = FALSE,
    fitted = TRUE,
    ranges = list(gamma = gammas, cost = costs, eps1lon = epsilons),
    tunecontrol = tune.control(sampling="fix"),
    data=world
)
```

Verify class
```
class(SVMtuningObject)
```
[Output:]
```
    [1] "tune"
```

```
# View best tuning parameters
SVMtuningObject$best.parameters
```
[Output:]
```
    gamma cost eps1lon
  7   0.5   16       1
```

Then use best parameters to display performance of the best model, which was Model 7
```
perf <- SVMtuningObject$performances
perf[7,]
```
[Output:]
```
    gamma cost   eps1lon    error       dispersion
  7   0.5   16   1          514.6231    NA
```

Run the best model based on tuned parameters from `svm::tune()`
```
SVMfit3_tuned <- e1071::svm(
    literacy ~ Infantdeathsper1k +poppersqmile+ gdppercapitalindollars+phonesper
1000+birthrate,
    type = "eps-regression",
    kernel = "radial",
  scale = FALSE,
  cost = 16,
  gamma = 0.5,
  epsilon = 1,
  data=world
)
```

Verify class
```
class(SVMfit3_tuned)
```
[Output:]
```
    [1] "svm.formula" "svm"   "
```

Get predicted values for tuned model
SVM3fitted_tuned holds the results of the `predict()` command
It is a vector of class "numeric"

```
SVM3fitted_tuned <- predict(SVMfit3_tuned,world)
class(SVM3fitted_tuned)
```
[Output:]
```
    [1] "numeric"
```

```
# Get model performance metrics
# Note: AIC and BIC metrics are not available as SVM does not use ML estimation
# First get the predicted-observed correlation
SVMcor <- cor(world$literacy,SVM3fitted_tuned)
SVMcor
[Output:]
   [1] 0.9257805

# Then get root mean square error
rmse <- Metrics::rmse(SVM3fitted_tuned, world$literacy)
rmse
[Output:]
   [1] 11.2206
```

Comparing results:
It is common to use RMSE to compare models. Lower RMSE reflects a model with less error.

Model	RMSE
OLSfit1	11.53426
SVM1fitted from caret, method = SVMRadial	12.04565
SVM2fitted from caret, method = SVMRadialSigma	11.96992
SVM3fitted_tuned from e1071, kernel = radial	11.2206

Note that the OLS fit1 RMSE coefficient is not cross-validated. The ones from caret normally default to caret's built-in tenfold cross-validation but because method = "none" in the "ctrl" object, there was no cross-validation, making results more comparable to the OLS solution. The SVM3fitted_tuned from el071 used cross-validation from a single training to a single validation set. Cross-validation is discussed further in the next section.

By the RMSE criterion, the SVM3fitted_tuned model from e1071 performed best and the SVM1fitted model from default caret settings with radial SVM performed least well. However, differences in error are small, even for comparison with the OLSfit1 model. The more nonlinearity in the data, the more tuned SVM will out-perform OLS. However, not infrequently, as here, linear models (or weaker models with no clear nonlinear pattern) may fit almost as well in terms of RMSE.

Also note that tuned SVM results may vary depending on the grid search specifications and the random seed. For instance, setting the random seed to 17 rather than 123 reduces RMSE for the SVM1fitted model from 12.046 to 11.868. This is because random seeds set the starting point for the computational algorithm and some starting points are better than others. As here, the difference is usually small.

Additional things to know about SVM modeling with the e1071 package are listed in an endnote.[14] There are other options for the `svm()` command not discussed here. Type `help(svm)` to view them.

6.7.3 Cross-validating SVM models

Previously, the ctrl control object set method to "none", which meant no cross-validation for the SVMfit1 model. Below we create SVMfit4 with 20-fold cross-classification and with tuneLength set to adjust tuning granularity. We continue to use caret's `train()` command and hence also its default kernlab `ksvm()` method. The result is a somewhat higher level of explanation (R-squared = .718). Improvement in R-squared, it should be noted, is not guaranteed.

```
# Set controls for 20 fold cross-classification repeated 3 times
ctrl2 <- caret::trainControl(
   method = "repeatedcv",
   number = 20,
   repeats = 3,
   classProbs = FALSE,
   summaryFunction = defaultSummary
)
```

```
# Parameters vary by method and by tuneLength, which sets grid parameter search granularity.
set.seed(123)
SVMfit4 <- caret::train(
  literacy ~ Infantdeathsper1k + poppersqmile + gdppercapitalindollars + phonesper1000 +
birthrate,
  data = world,
   method = "svmRadial",
   preProc = "center",
   trControl = ctrl2,
   metric = "RMSE",
   tuneLength = 3
)
```

Note that tuning has led the cost parameter (C) to change from, .25 to 1.

```
SVMfit4$bestTune
[Output:]
         sigma C
  3 0.7903274 1
```

Note that in the cross-validated, tuned SVM model the R-squared for SVMfit4 has increased to .7181556 from .6559676 for SVM1fitted in Section 6.6.4.

```
SVM4fitted <- predict(SVMfit4, data=world)
caret::R2(SVM4fitted,world$literacy)
[Output:]
      [1] 0.7181556
```

Likewise there is less error by the RMSE metric. RMSE drops from 12.04565 for SVM1fitted to 10,47707 for SVM4fitted.

```
Metrics::rmse(SVM4fitted, world$literacy)
[Output:]
      [1] 10.47707
```

6.7.4 Using e1071 in caret rather than the default kern package

As mentioned earlier, the caret package relies on the "kern" package to implement SVM. At this writing, caret has several methods for kern-based SVM modeling but only has one for e1071-based SVM models. That is the "svm-LinearWeights" model, which is for classification (not regression) models. Its use with the "world" data is treated in this section and with the "senate" data in Section 6.9.4.

Before turning to the svmLinearWeights method in caret, it should be noted however that it is possible to create a custom model in caret. This somewhat elaborate process is not treated here but is documented at http://topepo.github.io/caret/using-your-own-model-in-train.html. Various online sources have further documented how to apply customized caret models to emulate the e1071 package's `svm()` command.[15]

We now compare creating a linear classification model with e1071's `svm()` command independently and then with caret. The former model is labeled "SVMfit_e1071" and the latter model is labeled "SVMfit_caret". Note that to make models comparable, the cost parameter must be same in both models and the `scale=TRUE` option must match. It is assumed that the setup steps in Section 6.6.1 have been completed.

```
# Create SVM linear model in e1071
set.seed(123)
SVMfit_e1071 <- e1071::svm(litgtmean~ Infantdeathsper1k + poppersqmile +
gdppercapitalindollars + phonesper1000 + birthrate, kernel="linear",cost=.25,scale=
TRUE, data=world)
```

```
summary(SVMfit_e1071)
```
[Partial output:]
```
   Parameters:
      SVM-Type:  C-classification
    SVM-Kernel:  linear
          cost:  0.25
   Number of Support Vectors:  81
    ( 40 41 )
   Number of Classes:  2
   Levels:
    High Low
```

For comparison we create a linear classification model with caret's `train()` command using the option `method = "svmLinearWeights"`. Note that `classProbs = TRUE` since classification models have classes and use class probabilities.

```
# Create SVM linear model in caret
set.seed(123)
ctrl4 <- caret::trainControl(
  method = "none",
  classProbs = TRUE,
  summaryFunction = defaultSummary
)

SVMfit_caret <- caret::train(
  litgtmean ~ Infantdeathsper1k  + poppersqmile + gdppercapitalindollars +
phonesper1000 + birthrate,
  data = world,
  method = "svmLinearWeights",
  preProc = "scale",
  trControl = ctrl4,
  metric = "ROC"
)

# Summary output shows the caret mode creates the same model as using e1071 directly.
summary(SVMfit_caret)
```
[Partial output:]
```
   Parameters:
      SVM-Type:  C-classification
   SVM-Kernel:  linear
         cost:  0.25
   Number of Support Vectors:  81
    ( 40 41 )
   Number of Classes:  2
   Levels:
    High Low
```

From their classification (confusion) tables below, we can also see that the two models are identical, demonstrating that the SVM linear model may be run under caret as well as under e1071.

```
predse1071 <- predict(SVMfit_e1071)
confusiontable <- table(predicted = predse1071, observed = world$litgtmean)
confusiontable
```
[Output for e1071 model:)
```
              observed
   predicted High Low
```

```
        High  129  22
        Low    11  50

predscaret <- predict(SVMfit_caret)
confusiontable <- table(predicted = predscaret, observed = world$litgtmean)
confusiontable
```

[Output for caret model:)

```
            observed
   predicted High Low
        High  129  22
        Low    11  50
```

6.8 SVM classification models: Classifying U.S. Senators

The SVM method may be used for classification as well as regression problems. In this section, we explore SVM classification models using what has been their classic use, which is to classify binary variables. Classification models in SVM are an alternative to discriminant function analysis (DA) or logistic regression. If nonlinearity is present, SVM might perform better than either of these since it does not require linearity in the raw data as does DA nor linearity in the logit as does logistic regression. Moreover, SVM is nonparametric, handles interaction effects automatically, and has other advantages cited earlier in this chapter. In addition to creating an SVM classification model, in this section we also explore in greater depth issues pertaining to alternative kernels and tuning diagnostics.

6.8.1 The "senate" example and setup

In this section, we use a different example, the "senate.csv" data file. This file contains data on 99 U.S. Senators. The variable to be classified is "PARTY", coded as the strings "Dem" or "GOP". There are two predictor variables, ACLU and NAACP. These variables contain the interest group ratings of senators' votes in 2005. The research question is whether interest group ratings suffice to classify U.S. Senators by political party. To make this a binary problem, the one Senator (Jeffords, VT-Ind) who was not classified as Dem or GOP was dropped from the dataset. Note that, while the outcome variable (PARTY) may be numeric or alphanumeric, the predictor variables must be numeric. The data file is stored in comma-separated values format, which R reads easily with the following command.

```
senate <- read.csv("C:/Data/senateratings05.csv", header=TRUE, sep = ",",
stringsAsFactors=TRUE)
```

We also load the needed packages and set the working directory.

```
library(caret)          # A leading package for training models
library(e1071)          # Supports the svm() command
setwd("C:/Data")        # Declares the working directory
```

6.8.2 SVM classification with alternative kernels: Senate example

The initial SVM model in this section is created by the `svm()` command from the e1071 package. The model is put into the object "svmlinear". Though this particular model uses a linear kernel, subsequently we use the three other main types of kernel. Plots further below illustrate differences among kernels. Because these plots can have only two dimensions, the data file must be constructed to have exactly three columns. For the "senate" example, the columns are PARTY, ACLU, and NAACP. These measure the Senator's political party and his or her two interest group ratings. PARTY is coded "Dem" or "GOP" and is the variable to be classified by SVM. The two predictors must be numeric. If the data have over two columns, one may select two using the `formula=` option of plot.svm.[16]

The command below creates the "svmlinear" svm object in which PARTY is predicted for all other variables in senate.csv (the "." following the tilde signifies all other variables). By typing the name of this object, we can see it is an svm classification model with a linear kernel and 11 support vector points. Note that the `svm()` command detected that the outcome variable, PARTY, was categorical and automatically implemented a classification rather than regression model.

```
set.seed(123)
svmlinear <- e1071::svm(PARTY~., data = senate, kernel="linear")
svmlinear
```

[Partial output:]

```
   Parameters:
      SVM-Type:  C-classification
    SVM-Kernel:  linear
          cost:  1
   Number of Support Vectors:  11
```

The `plot()` command below may be used to show the linear separation created by svm with a linear kernel. The plot is shown in Figure 6.4. The support vector points are marked by "L" (for linear support vector) and the data points by "*". The figure shows the support vectors create good separation of the data points.[17]

```
plot(svmlinear, senate, col = c("lightblue","pink"), svSymbol = "L",
dataSymbol = "#")
```

Below we use the `predict()` command to get the `svm()` prediction of PARTY using a linear kernel. The `head()` command displays the first five predictions.

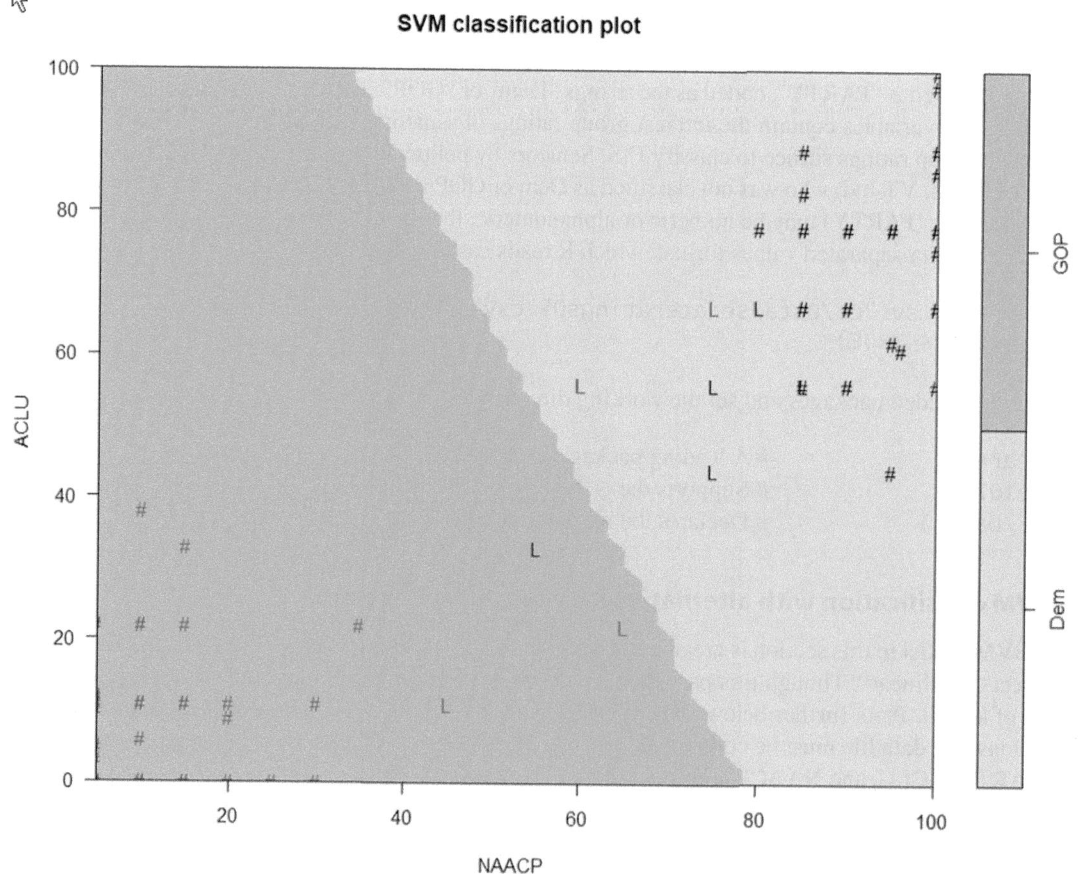

Figure 6.4 Senate separation with a linear kernel

```
# Obtain linear svm predictions, storing them in the object "predlinear"
predlinear <- predict(svmlinear,senate)

#Display first five predictions
head(predlinear,5)
[Output:]
    1   2   3   4   5
  Dem Dem Dem Dem Dem
  Levels: Dem GOP Ind

# If desired, store the predictions in the senate data frame
# As senate will now have > 3 columns, the plot command for Figure 6.4 will no longer work
# Likewise the plot commands used for Figure 6.5 will not work either, so we comment it out.
# senate$svmlinearpred<-predlinear
```

Having created the predictions for the linear kernel model, we can create some performance metrics for it. As a performance measure, we compute the correlation of linear predictions with observed PARTY, finding the correlation to be high.

```
cor(as.numeric(predlinear),as.numeric(senate$PARTY))
[Output:]
  [1] 0.9193147
```

As a second performance measure, we compute the confusion table and misclassification rate. This metric only applies to classification problems, not regression.

```
confusionTable <- table(predicted = predlinear, observed = senate$PARTY)
confusionTable
[Output:]
           observed
  predicted Dem GOP
        Dem  43   3
        GOP   1  52

# Compute the misclassification (error) rate
misclassificationRate <- 1- sum(predlinear == senate$PARTY)/length(predlinear)
misclassificationRate
[Output, equivalent to 4 errors/99 Senators:]
  [1] 0.04040404
```

In a like manner we may create SVM models for similar models but using the radial, sigmoid, and polynomial kernels.

```
# Run the three models
svmradial <- e1071::svm(PARTY~., data = senate, kernel="radial")
svmsigmoid <- e1071::svm(PARTY~., data = senate, kernel="sigmoid")
svmpolynomial <- e1071::svm(PARTY~., data = senate, kernel="polynomial")
```

After running the models, we plot them and combine the plots in Figure 6.5.[18] We use the symbols R, S, and P for support vector points in the radial, sigmoid, and polynomial models, respectively.

```
#Plot the three models
plot(svmradial, senate, col = c("lightblue","pink"), svSymbol = "R", dataSymbol = "#")
plot(svmsigmoid, senate, col = c("lightblue","pink"), svSymbol = "S", dataSymbol = "#")
plot(svmpolynomial, senate, col = c("lightblue","pink"), svSymbol = "P", dataSymbol
= "#")
```

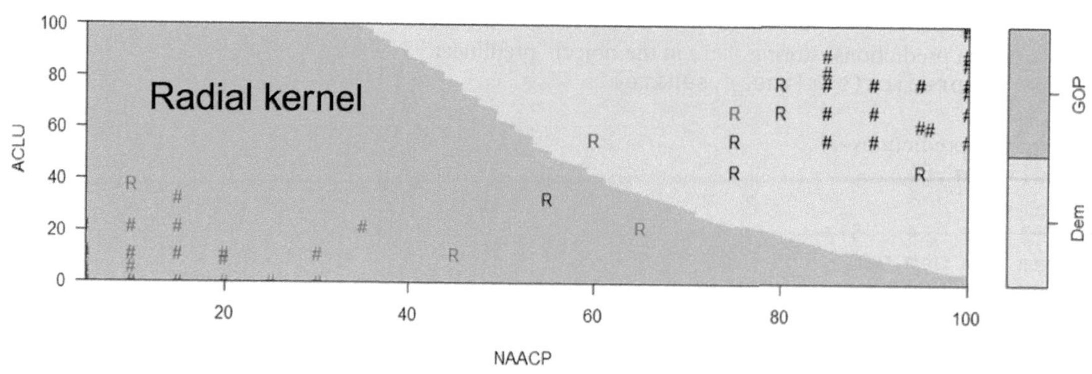
SVM classification plot
Radial kernel
ACLU
NAACP
GOP
Dem

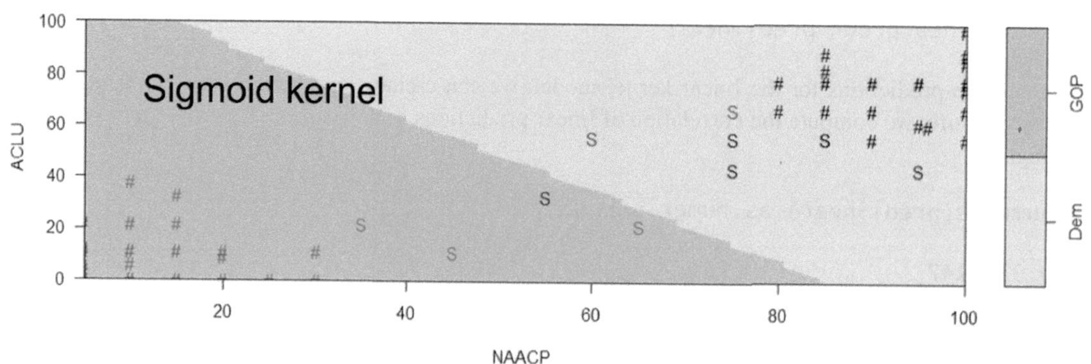
SVM classification plot
Sigmoid kernel
ACLU
NAACP
GOP
Dem

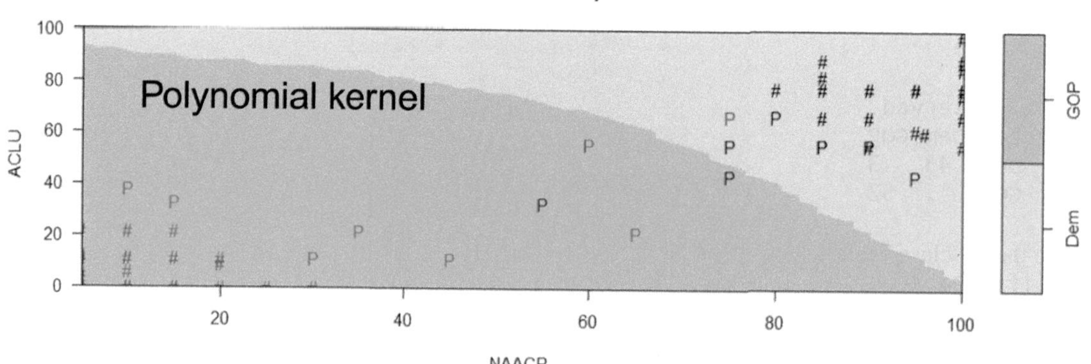
SVM classification plot
Polynomial kernel
ACLU
NAACP
GOP
Dem

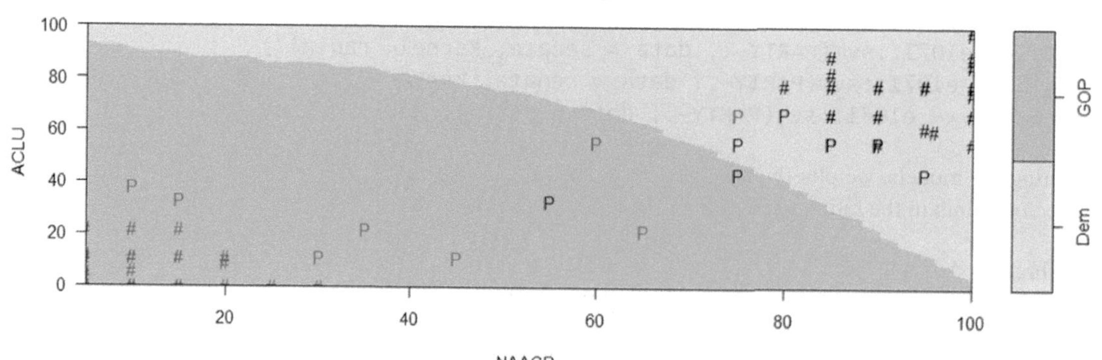
SVM classification plot
ACLU
NAACP
GOP
Dem

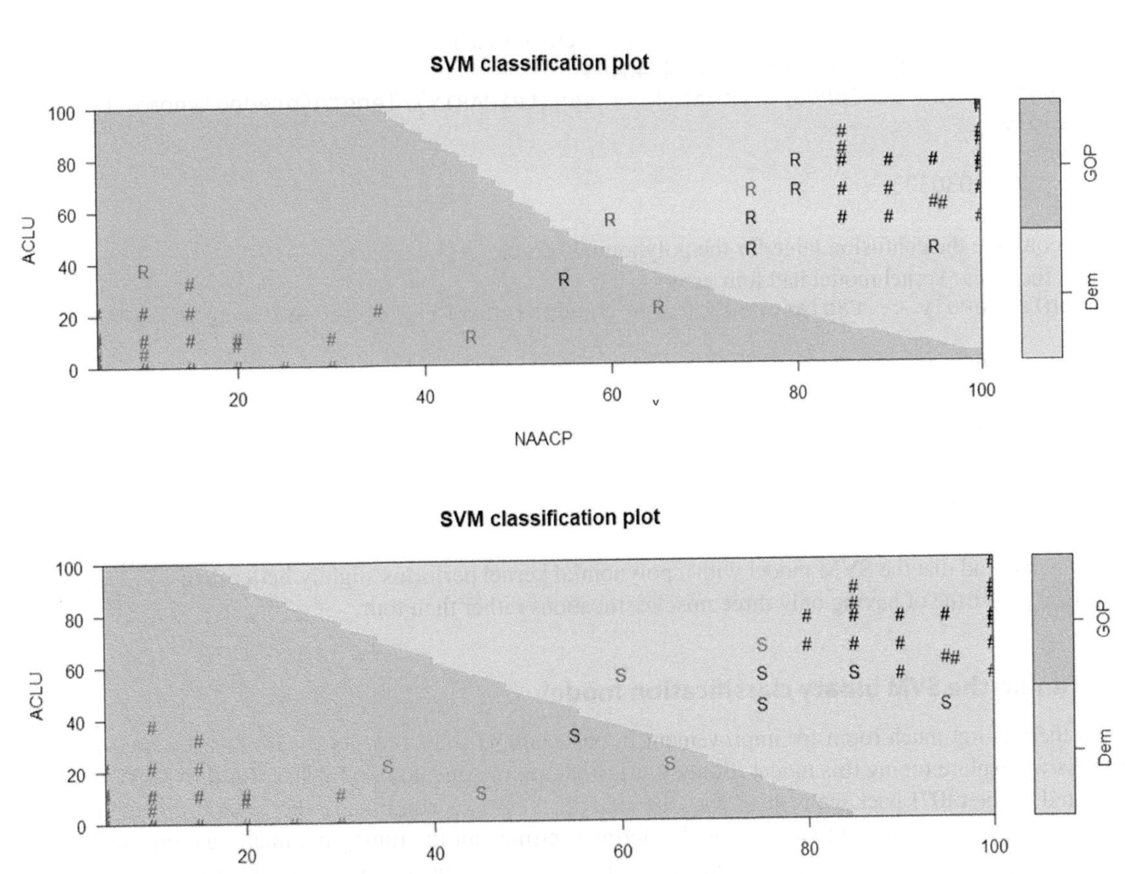

Figure 6.5 SVM classification with alternative kernels

We repeat the model metrics for the polynomial, sigmoid, and radial kernel models below. We find that the polynomial model was able to classify correctly one additional Senator compared to the other models, yielding a slightly higher correlation and slightly lower misclassification rate. Other kernels performed the same as the linear kernel model.

```
# Compute the observed-actual correlation for the three models
# Recall the correlation was 0.9193147 for the linear kernel
predradial <- predict(svmradial,senate)
cor(as.numeric(predradial),as.numeric(senate$PARTY))
[Output]:
      [1]  0.9193147

predsigmoid <- predict(svmsigmoid,senate)
cor(as.numeric(predsigmoid),as.numeric(senate$PARTY))
[Output]:          [
      1] 0.9193147

predpolynomial <- predict(svmpolynomial,senate)
cor(as.numeric(predpolynomial),as.numeric(senate$PARTY))
[Output]:
      [1] 0.9386939
```

```
# Compute the misclassification rate for the polynomial kernel model
# Recall that the rate for the linear kernel was .04040404
misclasspoly <- 1- sum(predpolynomial == senate$PARTY)/length(predpolynomial)
misclasspoly
[Output]:
      [1] 0.03030303

# We now compute the confusion table for the polynomial kernel
Recall that the linear kernel model had four errors.
confusionTablePoly <- table(predicted = predpolynomial, observed = senate$PARTY)

confusionTablePoly
[Output]
            observed
   predicted Dem GOP
         Dem  42   1
         GOP   2  54
```

In summary, we find that the SVM model with a polynomial kernel performs slightly better than SVM models with other kernels, by virtue of having only three misclassifications rather than four.

6.8.3 Tuning the SVM binary classification model

Although there is not much room for improvement in our example since polynomial SVM had only three errors, nonetheless we explore tuning this model if only to illustrate tuning diagnostics further. Tuning the SVM model as implemented in the e1071 package is done with the `tune.svm()` command. The general procedure is to use the `tune.svm()` command to determine the optimal settings for the tuning parameter gamma and cost, then insert these values into an `svm()` command for the kernel model we want. Since it was found slightly better in the previous section, we illustrate tuning for the polynomial kernel model but the same method would apply to models based on other kernels.

The `tune.svm()` function has built-in tenfold cross-validation, which in turn involves a random factor. For this reason, "best performance" will vary slightly each time the function is run. To obtain the same performance settings and metrics each time, precede the `tune.svm()` command by issuing the `set.seed()` command.

6.8.3.1 Step 1: Find the best tuning parameters

The tuning grid specified in the `tune.svm()` command below is illustrative but values of gamma and cost could be changed. The command will report the best parameters for values found in the grid.

```
# Do a grid search for the best parameters
set.seed(123)

obj1 <- e1071::tune.svm(PARTY~., data = senate, sampling = "fix", gamma = 2^c(-8,-4,
0,4), cost = 2^c(-8,-4,-2,0))

# Print the best parameters and corresponding error rate
obj1
[Output:]
   Parameter tuning of 'svm':
   - sampling method: 10-fold cross validation
   - best parameters:
    gamma cost
       16    1
   - best performance: 0.03111111
```

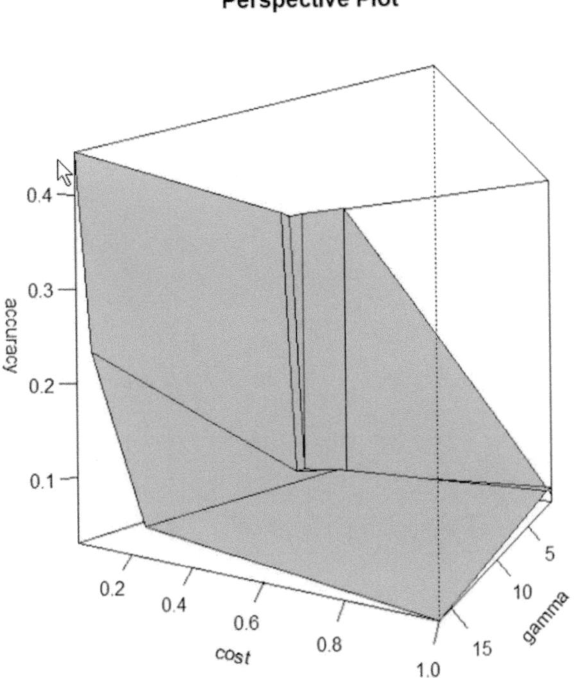

Figure 6.6 Perspective plot of SVM tuning parameters

It is possible to retrieve the best gamma and cost visually by using a perspective plot. In the plot below, note that the performance measure "Accuracy" is the "best performance" value from the printed output above. In Figure 6.6, one can see that the best performance (misleadingly labeled accuracy, but actually lowest misclassification) is when cost = 0 and gamma = 16. The perspective plot also allows us to understand the effect on performance of other values of cost and gamma as tuning parameters.

```
# Perspective plot for tuning parameters for senate example
# theta and phi define the viewing direction and angle.
plot(obj1, type = "perspective", theta = 120, phi = 0, col = "green3",
main="Perspective Plot")
```

6.8.3.2 Step 2: Apply the best tuning parameters to the model

The best model in the previous section was the one with the polynomial kernel, which reduced errors in classifying U.S. Senators from 4 to 3 compared to other SVM kernels. We now take that model and rerun it with the tuned parameters above (gamma = 16, cost = 1). As the performance of the untuned model was already very high, one would not expect much improvement. For other data, tuning may bring noticeable optimization. Nonetheless, tuning the polynomial model succeeded in reducing errors from 3 to only 1. This is illustrated in the code and output below. The plot for the tuned polynomial kernel model is shown in Figure 6.7.

```
# Run the polynomial SVM model with tuned parameters
svmpolynomialtuned <- e1071::svm(PARTY~., data = senate, kernel="polynomial",
gamma=16, cost=1)

# Plot the solution
plot(svmpolynomialtuned, senate, col = c("lightblue","pink"), svSymbol = "P",
dataSymbol = "#")
```

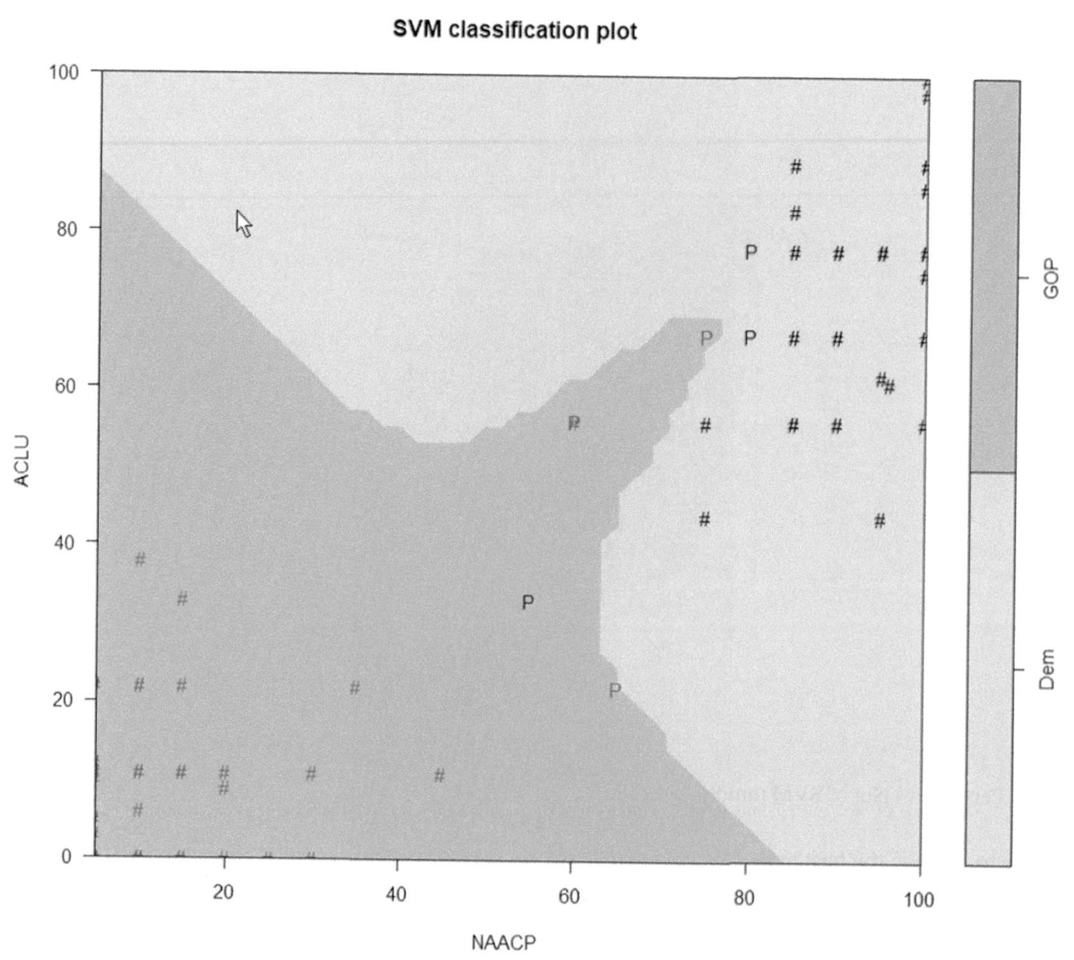

Figure 6.7 SVM solution, tuned polynomial kernel

The plot of the tuned polynomial kernel solution shows the support vector points with the symbol "P" (for "Polynomial"). To evaluate it we compute two model performance metrics: The observed-actual correlation and the misclassification rate. The correlation is approximately .98 and the misclassification rate is approximately .01. The confusion table shows that only one Senator was misclassified, predicted as Democratic but actually GOP, down from three misclassifications in the untuned polynomial SVM model.

```
predpolynomialtuned <- predict(svmpolynomialtuned,senate)
cor(as.numeric(predpolynomialtuned),as.numeric(senate$PARTY))
[Output:]
   [1] 0.9797048

misclassificationRate <- 1- sum(predpolynomialtuned == senate$PARTY)/
length(predpolynomialtuned)

misclassificationRate
[Output:]
   [1] 0.01010101

confusionTable <- table(predicted = predpolynomialtuned, observed = senate$PARTY)
```

```
confusionTable
```
[Output:]
```
confusionTable
        observed
predicted Dem GOP
      Dem  43   0
      GOP   1  55
```

One might wonder why only the gamma and cost parameters were tuned and not degree or coef0. The tuning process above performed a grid search and found the best model was one with cost = 1 and gamma = 16. However, the researcher might have extended the grid search to cover the degree and coef0 parameters as well, using code like that below. However, we do not run this code here and note only that it did not improve classification.

```
# Grid search for gamma, costs, degree, and coef0.
set.seed(123)
obj2 <- caret::tune.svm(PARTY~., data = senate, sampling = "fix", gamma = 2^c(-8,-4,
0,4), cost = 2^c(-8,-4,-2,0), degree=c(1,2,3,4), coef0=c(-1,0,1))

# Then compute a polynomial solution with degree and coef0 parameters also.
# Other steps are as before.
svmpolynomialtuned2 <- e1071::svm(PARTY~., data = senate, kernel="polynomial",
gamma=16, cost=1, degree=1, coef0 = -1)
```

6.9 Gradient boosting machines (GBM)

6.9.1 Introduction

In this section, we introduce another modeling methodology, GBM, and compare it with SVM. The "caret" package is capable of implementing a very large number of models apart from SVM models and GBM is one of them. GBM models support a variety of learning models, including decision tree or RF models, discussed in Chapters 4 and 5 respectively. "Boosting" refers to weighting cases and "gradient" refers to boosting in a gradual manner. In R, a commonly used GBM program is the `gbm()` function from the "gbm" package, but there are others. The caret package, implemented below, uses the gbm package version of GBM.

"Boosting" is a method of improving tree performance by differentially weighting the input cases. There are multiple possible algorithms for boosting, of which GBM is a popular one. Initially, all cases are weighted equally. In an iterative process, weights are increased for difficult-to-classify cases and decreased for easy-to-classify ones. In a second iteration, an ensemble of solutions is calculated based on the revised case weights from the first iteration. Iterations are repeated for a researcher-specified number of iterations or until some stopping criterion is met. Put another way, at each iteration a new "base-learner" model is trained, which focuses on error as learned from previous iterations. Base-learners, like neurons in a NN, function as a memory medium, sequentially capturing patterns in the data and "gradually increasing the level of pattern detail" (Natekin & Knoll, 2013: 2).

GBM supports a variety of base-learner models. Decision tree/RF models are only one type. Other types include ones based on OLS regression, ridge regression, random effects regression, Markov models, RBF models, and others. Moreover, several types of leaner models may be specified in a complex GBM model. In essence, different boosted base-learner models may be fit simultaneously for different data sub-spaces.

Predictions in GBM are the weighted sum of predictions for the base-learner model at each iteration. Where predictions in RF models simply average across the ensemble of trees, predictions in tree-based GBM models average across iterations of ensembles, where at each iteration the algorithm maximizes correlation with the negative gradient of the loss function. In practical terms, this often means that GBM models outperform RF models but may run the risk of overfitting, discussed further below.

"Gradient" refers to training the models involved in boosting in a gradual, sequential manner. In GBM, a "loss function" is defined, representing how well estimated coefficients fit the input data. That is, the loss function is a model performance metric. Gradients in the loss function are used as the basis for weighting cases. In general, loss functions go by type of outcome variable (e.g., categorical, continuous, count, survival; see Natekin & Knoll, 2013: 4–6.). A loss function for a regression problem might be mean squared error, where error is observed minus predicted values. A loss function for a classification problem might be the misclassification rate. An advantage of GBM is that it allows the user to select a loss function which matches her or his research problem rather than having to accept a "one size fits all" default performance metric.

A number of steps may be needed to address overfitting in GBM models. Of course, a primary method is cross-validation, which is built in for training models under the caret package. Other tactics, some of which apply only to tree-based GBM learning models, include the following:

- Increasing the number of training cases
- Reducing the maximum tree depth
- Increasing the minimum loss reduction to allow a node to be split (the gamma parameter)
- Increasing the bucket size (the minimum number of cases in a child node before a split is allowed)
- Reducing the number of input features (e.g., dropping nonsignificant ones)
- Specifying a smaller value for the learning rate
- Limiting the number of base-learner iterations
- GBM software may offer regularization parameters (e.g., L1 and L2), which smooth the loss gradient, reducing variance in the cost function
- Using stochastic gradient boosting (the training data are subsampled at each iteration)

Note that for more complex models, the memory-intensive nature of the GBM algorithm may mean a longer time to reach a solution. For further information on GBM, see Friedman (2001); Natekin and Knoll (2013); and Golden, Rothrock, and Mishra (2019).

The foregoing suggests that coverage of GBM modeling could be a book in its own right. However, while GBM modeling lends itself to many complex variations, in the simple GBM model below we present a basic example using caret default settings. Such a basic, default GBM model may still outperform other types of machine learning models.

6.9.2 Setup and example data

For GBM we continue to use the "senate" binary outcome data. In this example, the political party of U.S. Senators (PARTY = "Dem" or "GOP") is classified based on interest group ratings entered as continuous variables (ACLU, NAACP). The data file is read in as before:

```
senate <- read.csv("c:/Data/senateratings05.csv", header=TRUE, sep = ",",
stringsAsFactors=TRUE)
```

Setup also includes declaring the working directory and loading needed packages.

```
# Declare the working directory
setwd("C:/Data")

# Load needed packages (use install.packages() first if needed, as usual).
library(caret)            # For modeling and training, including Bayesian
library(gbm)              # Supports the gbm() command
library(lattice)          # Supports dotplots of results
```

Note that a major difference from Section 6.8 is that in Section 6.9 we use the "caret" package's `train()` program to execute and then compare models. This program assumes that the data frame may be partitioned into training and validation subsets. The training set is selected by a random process, which means estimates may vary with different random seeds.

6.9.3 Metrics for comparing models

To compare models, we must select model performance metrics. For the classification problem in the "senate" example, we use accuracy and Kappa. Accuracy is the percent of observations classified correctly. Kappa is a performance measure for binary outcomes, often preferred over accuracy as a metric. It is defined as (totalAccuracy – randomAccuracy)/(1 – randomAccuracy). Arbitrary guidelines for assessing Kappa have been advanced by Landis and Koch (1977) and by Fleiss (1981). For Landis and Koch, Kappa < 0 indicates no agreement and 0–0.20 indicates slight agreement; 0.21–0.40 = fair; 0.41–0.60 = moderate; 0.61–0.80 = substantial; and 0.81–1 = almost perfect agreement. For Fleiss, Kappa < 0.40 = poor agreement; 0.40–0.75 = fair to good; >.75 = excellent.

While the example here is for a categorical outcome (PARTY), if the outcome is a continuous variable, caret's `train()` algorithm will substitute RMSE and R-square for accuracy and Kappa. In this context, R-square is the square of the correlation between predicted and observed values of the outcome.

6.9.4 The caret control object

Training modeling procedures in caret is a two-step process. The first step is creating the caret control object, which we here label "ctrl". This object contains parameters to be used by the `train()` command below. Recall this was done in Section 6.2 in the "Quick Start" example on Bayesian modeling. For the current "senate" example with GBM or LVQ methods, we ask below that resampling by the `train()` command use tenfold cross-validation, repeated for three sets. The `p= parameter` specifies that 67% of observations be used for the training sample in the cross-validation process. Other resampling methods are available. Type `help(trainControl)` for further information on the extensive list of other control parameters which may be implemented. Note that the same control object may be used for training other models, as it is in Section 6.10 for LVQ models.

```
ctrl <- caret::trainControl(
  method = "repeatedcv",
  number = 10,
  repeats = 3,
  p = .67,
  classProbs = TRUE,
  summaryFunction = defaultSummary
)
```

In Step 2 we train the models. In the next section we will create the object GBMmodel under caret. For later comparison of GBMmodel with SVM, we used the commands below to create SVMpolymodel, based on SVM with a polynomial kernel. Note that the control parameters in the "ctrl" object are invoked by `trControl=` option of caret's `train()` command. Training may take noticeable computing time depending on the data and method. Also, be aware that different random seeds will lead to different estimated coefficients.

```
set.seed(123)

SVMpolymodel <- caret::train(PARTY~.,
     data=senate,
     method="svmPoly",
     trControl=ctrl,
     verbose=FALSE,
     metric = "Accuracy",
     tuneGrid = NULL,
)
```

To view results, we need only type the name of the model. The grid search for best tuning parameters is printed. If there are ties, caret picks the first set of parameters with the best performance metric. For the SVMpolymodel, Accuracy was 0.9598653 and Kappa was 0.9194410.

```
SVMpolymodel
```

[Partial output:]

```
Support Vector Machines with Polynomial Kernel
99 samples
 2 predictor
 2 classes: 'Dem', 'GOP'
No pre-processing
Resampling: Cross-Validated (10 fold, repeated 3 times)
Summary of sample sizes: 88, 88, 90, 90, 90, 89, ...
Resampling results across tuning parameters:
  degree  scale  C     Accuracy   Kappa
  1       0.001  0.25  0.9594949  0.9197087
. . .
  1       0.100  0.25  0.9598653  0.9194410
  1       0.100  0.50  0.9598653  0.9194410
. . .
  3       0.100  1.00  0.9598653  0.9194410

Accuracy was used to select the optimal model using the largest value.
The final values used for the model were degree = 1, scale = 0.1 and C = 0.25.
```

6.9.5 Training the GBM model under caret

In Step 2 we train the GBM model in caret. Caret training includes tuning and cross-validation automatically. Note that different random seeds may lead to small differences in results.

```
set.seed(123)

GBMmodel <- caret::train(PARTY~.,
     data=senate,
     method="gbm",
     trControl=ctrl,
     verbose=FALSE,
     metric = "Accuracy",
     tuneGrid = NULL
)
```

Below we view the model. Accuracy for GBMmodel is 97.99%, higher than for the SVMpoly model, which was 95.99%. Kappa is .9594 for the GBMmodel. Note in the last line, caret has set optimal tuning values. These parameters are also in the model's $bestTune element:

```
GBMmodel$bestTune
```

[Output:]

```
    n.trees interaction.depth shrinkage n.minobsinnode
  7      50                 3       0.1             10
```

Note that it is not necessary to rerun the model with these tuning parameters since tuning is a built-in feature of the `train()` command. The initial column, here with a value of 7, refers to the row number of the optimal solution in the listing of iterations in "Resampling results" below. There may be ties.

```
# Print out GBMmodel
GBMmodel
```

[Output:]
```
Stochastic Gradient Boosting
99 samples
 2 predictor
 2 classes: 'Dem', 'GOP'
No pre-processing

Resampling: Cross-Validated (10 fold, repeated 3 times)
Summary of sample sizes: 88, 88, 90, 90, 90, 89, ...
Resampling results across tuning parameters:
  interaction.depth  n.trees  Accuracy   Kappa
  1                   50      0.9765993  0.9527597
  1                  100      0.9769024  0.9532116
  1                  150      0.9701684  0.9402813
  2                   50      0.9732660  0.9460930
  2                  100      0.9799327  0.9594263
  2                  150      0.9799327  0.9594263
  3                   50      0.9799327  0.9594263
  3                  100      0.9799327  0.9594263
  3                  150      0.9769024  0.9532116

Tuning parameter 'shrinkage' was held constant at a value of 0.1
Tuning parameter 'n.minobsinnode' was held constant at a value of 10
Accuracy was used to select the optimal model using the largest value.
The final values used for the model were n.trees = 50, interaction.depth= 3,
shrinkage = 0.1 and n.minobsinnode = 10.
```

Below we get PARTY values as predicted by the GBM model. The GBMpreds object is a factor vector with "GOP" or "Dem" values for each of the 99 Senators. This is percent of variance explained, which is a different and for these data lower metric than Accuracy, which was percent classified correctly.

```
GBMpreds <- predict(GBMmodel, newdata=senate, type="raw")
```

To use the predictions in a procedure like correlation, we must convert variables temporarily to numeric form. We see that when PARTY is predicted by the GBMmodel, the R-squared value is 91.99%.

```
cor(as.numeric(GBMpreds), as.numeric(senate$PARTY))^2
```
[Output:]
```
[1] 0.9198554
```

6.10 Learning vector quantization (LVQ)

6.10.1 Introduction

Finally, in this section, we introduce yet another modeling methodology, LVQ, and we compare results with SVM. LVQ models are the supervised version of vector quantization (VQ) systems. They are a common type of classification algorithm in computer science and are a type of artificial neural network (ANN). LVQ models, invented by Teuvo Kohonen (1997), are related to Kohonen self-organizing maps (KSOM), a type of ANN. Kohonen has also put forward a number of LVQ variants (LVQ2, LVQ2.1, and LVQ3). Note that LVQ is a classification algorithm, not designed for regression problems. It can classify categorical outcome variables with multiple levels, though below we use a binary outcome. "Supervised" means that the researcher must input a set of training patterns (data rows) for which the correct value of the output variable to be classified is known. In R, a commonly used LVQ program is the `lvq1()` function from the "class" package, but there are others, including others within the class package itself and in the "LVQTools" package.

As a type of ANN, LVQ involves an iterative process in which inputs influence intermediary variables called "prototypes". These in turn predict the categorical outcome variable. That is, simple LVQ may be thought of as a three-layer model having input, prototype, and output layers. Prototypes are points in feature data space, typically selected automatically by use of class means (the means of each outcome category [class] for each input feature [variable, vector]). Prototypes are initialized to some weight, usually class means. In ANN terminology, prototypes function as neurons. There may be one prototype per outcome class or there may be more.

In an iterative process of model updating, weights are adjusted up or down according to whether the prototype makes the correct classification. Each input feature vector (variable) is examined in turn for each data row. The distance of the input (case) to the prototype is assessed for that vector. The weights are updated only for the closest prototype (called the "winner"), increasing its weight for that vector if the prototype's label for the outcome class with which is associated is the same as the output class label for the given training set data row being considered. If class labels differ, the weight for the winning prototype is decreased. An "epoch" is one iteration through all cases in the training sample. Typically multiple epochs of iterations are needed before weights stabilize (reach convergence).

The amount of the adjustment in a given iteration is determined by the "learning rate", which the researcher may set. Unlike KSOM, LVQ is a "winner-take-all" algorithm with adjustments made on the winning prototype, which is the one closest to the training set input's correct class. Unlike KSOM, no "neighborhoods" are defined around the winning algorithm and no adjustments are given to nonwinning prototypes.

To achieve best results, LVQ might require centering or even normalization of input data as a pre-processing step. In some cases, reduction in data dimensions, as through input of factor scores rather than raw indicator scores, may also improve performance. The researcher may also wish to explore alternative distance measures other than the default, which is Euclidean distance. There are even "adaptive" LVQ models in which the distance measure changes over the course of training. However, in the simple LVQ model below we implement none of these possible refinements. Rather, we present a "vanilla" approach using caret's default settings. For more about LVQ models, see also Hammer and Villman (2002); Somervuo and Kohonen (2004); and Nova and Estévez (2014).

6.10.2 Setup and example data

As for GBM, for LVQ we continue to use the "senate" binary outcome data. In this example, the political party of U.S. Senators (PARTY = "Dem" or "GOP") is classified based on interest group ratings entered as continuous variables (ACLU, NAACP). The data file is read in as before:

```
senate <- read.csv("C:/Data/senateratings05.csv", header=TRUE, sep = ",",
stringsAsFactors=TRUE)
```

Setup also includes declaring the working directory and loading needed packages.

```
# Declare the working directory
setwd("C:/Data")

# Load needed packages (use install.packages() first if needed, as usual).
library(caret)          # For modeling and training
library(lattice)        # Supports dotplots of results
library(lvq)            # Supports the lvq() command
```

6.10.3 Metrics for comparing models

We use accuracy and Kappa as model performance metrics. See discussion in Section 6.9.3.

6.10.4 The caret control object

Step 1 of the caret training process requires creating a control object, here labeled "ctrl". We use the same ctrl object created and discussed for GBM in Section 6.9.4. We also assume that the SVM comparison model, SVMpolymodel, created in that section is still in the R environment.

6.10.5 Training the LVQ model under caret

Training the LVQ model parallels training for the GBM model in the previous section.

```
set.seed(123)
```

```
LVQmodel <- train(PARTY~.,
   data=senate,
   method="lvq",
   trControl=ctrl,
   metric = "Accuracy",
   tuneGrid = NULL
)
```

Below we view the model. Accuracy for the model is 96.29%, higher than for the SVMpoly model, which was 95.99% but lower than the GBMmodel, which was 97.99%. Kappa is .9245 for the LVQmodel. Be aware that these results may differ if the random seed is changed. Note in the last line, caret has set optimal tuning values. These parameters are also in the model's $bestTune element:

```
LVQmodel$bestTune
[Output:]
     size k
   5    3 6

# View the model
LVQmodel
[Output:]
   99 samples
    2 predictor
    2 classes: 'Dem', 'GOP'
   No pre-processing
   Resampling: Cross-Validated (10 fold, repeated 3 times)
   Summary of sample sizes: 88, 88, 90, 90, 90, 89, ...
   Resampling results across tuning parameters:
     size  k   Accuracy   Kappa
     2      1  0.9598653  0.9196448
   . . .
     3      6  0.9628956  0.9254520
   . . .
     4     11  0.9598653  0.9196448

   Accuracy was used to select the optimal model using the largest value.
   The final values used for the model were size = 3 and k = 6.
```

6.11 Comparing models

The foregoing sections have created three models: SVMpolymodel, GBMmodel, and LVQmodel. The `resamples()` program in caret may be used to collate these models into a single object, here given the name "results". Then the `summary()` command (part of R's built-in "base" package) may be used to display the model performance results.

```
# More than three models might be compared.
results <- caret::resamples(list(SVMPoly=SVMpolymodel, LVQ=LVQmodel, GBM=GBMmodel))

# Summarize the results object:
summary(results)
[Partial output:]
   Models: SVMPoly, LVQ, GBM
   Number of resamples: 30
   Accuracy
                Min. 1st Qu. Median      Mean 3rd Qu. Max. NA's
   SVMPoly 0.7777778     0.9      1 0.9598653       1    1    0
   LVQ     0.7777778     0.9      1 0.9628956       1    1    0
   GBM     0.8888889     1.0      1 0.9799327       1    1    0
```

```
Kappa
              Min. 1st Qu. Median      Mean 3rd Qu. Max. NA's
SVMPoly 0.5500000     0.8      1 0.9194410       1    1    0
LVQ     0.5500000     0.8      1 0.9254520       1    1    0
GBM     0.7692308     1.0      1 0.9594263       1    1    0
```

Above, results are displayed for all three models, using two model performance metrics.

- "Accuracy" is 1 minus the misclassification rate. The GBM model had the highest mean accuracy, followed in descending order by the LVQ and SVMPoly models.
- "Kappa" is the percent by which the researcher's mode is better than random. Here, the ranking of models was the same on mean Kappa as for mean Accuracy, with the GBM model performing best. Kappa reflects performance in the given model compared to what would be expected by chance if cases were allocated to outcome classes at random, but preserving margins (proportions in each class). The greater the difference between model classifications and random classifications, the higher the kappa coefficient and the better the model. By the same token, a kappa of 0 means the model is no better than chance. Kappa is always lower than Accuracy and as such is a more conservative measure of model performance. Some derogate the use of kappa because it underestimates accuracy (e.g., Pontius & Millones, 2011).

Results may be visualized as dot or boxplot plots. The commands used below (`dotplot()` and `bwplot()`) are from the "lattice" package (Trellis Graphics for R), which is a built-in System Library package in R.

```
# Create a dot plot, shown in Figure 6.8
lattice::dotplot(results)
```

Recall that when we defined ctrl for caret training in Section 6.9.4, we asked asking for tenfold cross-validation repeated three times. What the dot plot in Figure 6.8 shows is the distribution of results for each model for all of its trials. The wings show the range of results and the dot shows the mean of the range. The GBM model, being farthest

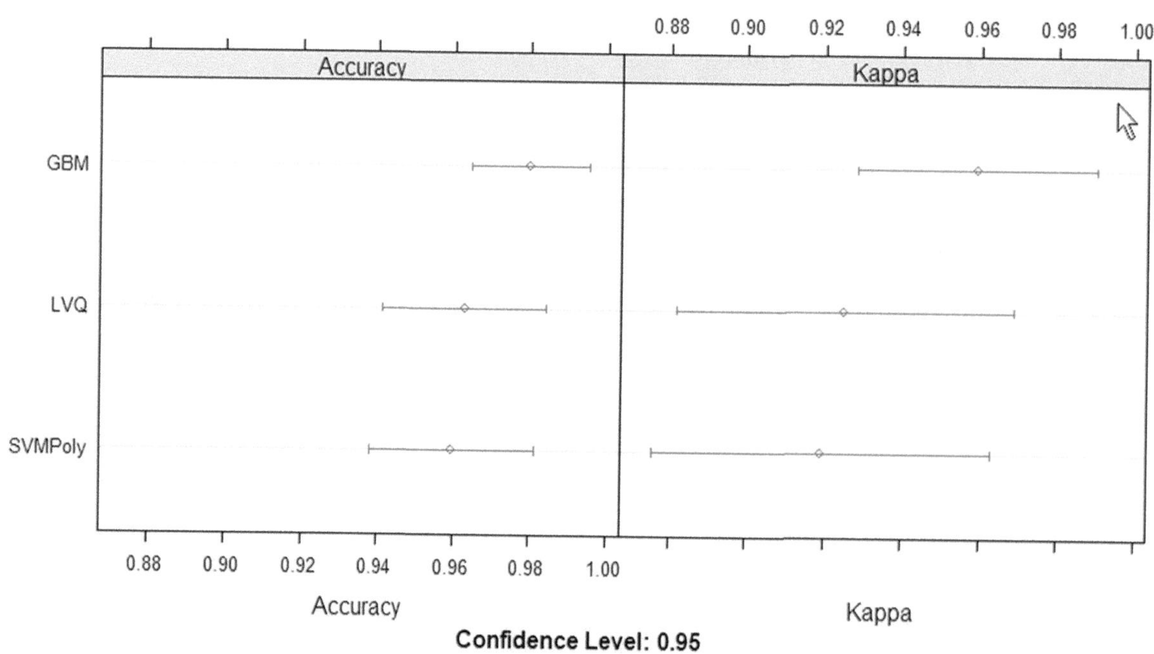

Figure 6.8 Comparison of models with caret

toward the high end (to the right), is shown to be the best model. The worst models are shown farthest toward the low end (to the left).

Boxplots may also be created in the same manner, to generate box-and-whiskers plots of the same results (not shown).

```
lattice::bwplot(results)
```

In summary, all three models performed the classification task (classifying members of the Senate by their political party) very well, though the GBM model had a slight edge.

6.12 Variable importance

While machine learning models like SVM are sometimes described as "black box" procedures, it is possible to rank by importance the variables used for prediction or classification. There are two main rationales for ranking variables by importance: Feature selection and variable effect ranking.

The concept behind feature selection is often that a model would be improved if prior to running it the researcher would eliminate or reduce noise by dropping variables with little or no apparent effect on the outcome variable. This is also a common research design principle in conventional statistical modeling, such as OLS regression. However, in machine learning approaches like SVM regression, following this wisdom may defeat some of the purposes of such approaches, an advantage of which is precisely the ability to sift through large numbers of input variables to arrive at high accuracy classifications or predictions. As discussed previously, SVM incorporates regularization to guard against over-fitting. That is, good model performance does not require prior feature selection. In fact, prior feature selection may actually worsen performance (Millar, 2002).

The second purpose of variable importance is to aid the process of explanation and exploratory theory construction. For both it is critical to understand whether the data at hand are or are not consistent with viewing a given variable as a determinant of the outcome of interest. There are several approaches, two of which are discussed below: "leave-one-out" modeling and "recursive feature selection".

While below we use SVM as an example, using the `svm()` command from the e1071 package, leave-one-out modeling and recursive feature selection apply to many other machine learning approaches as well. Also, note that a more complex example of assessing variable importance is presented in the online supplement to this chapter titled "SVM Variable Importance". This is found on this book's Support Material (www.routledge.com/9780367624293).

6.12.1 Leave-one-out modeling

It is possible to run a model with all inputs to obtain a baseline performance metric (e.g., the misclassification rate, observed-actual correlation, or RMSE), then run a series of models leaving out one input in each model. Variables, which worsen performance more when left out of the model, are the most important by this criterion. This method works regardless of model and can be automated to handle models with many predictors. This method is illustrated below using an SVM radial kernel model.

To implement the leave-one-out method of determining variable importance, we create a for-loop to cycle through the predictor variables. In this example, there are only two: ACLU and NAACP. For other models there may be more predictors. The "i" variable is used as a counter. The predictor to leave out is set to i in each loop. Normally loops suppress printing but the `writeLines(paste())` syntax prints to the console anyway. We start by creating a data frame for the outcome variable (PARTY) and a data frame for the predictor variables. We label these objects y and x respectively.

```
# Outcome variable (the factor PARTY) is put in y as numeric
# The two-step process below assures the label will be PARTY rather than senate$PARTY
PARTY <- senate$PARTY
y <- as.data.frame(PARTY)

# Put predictors in x (numeric variables ACLU and NAACP, which are columns 2 and 3 in senate)
x <- senate[2:3]
```

```
#Define maxcols as number of predictors to cycle through and store labels in predlabels
maxcols = ncol(x)
predlabels <- colnames(x)

# Start loop through the predictors
   for(i in 1:maxcols) {
   # Set same random seed each loop
   set.seed(1)
   # Create a predictor data frame called temp without variable i
   temp<-x[-c(i)]
   # Add the outcome variable (PARTY) in y back in; temp2 has PARTY plus all but column i
   temp2<-cbind(temp,y)
   # Run the SVM model; we use a radial kernel but any could be used
   svmradialtemp <- e1071::svm(PARTY~., data = temp2, kernel="radial")
   # Get radial SVM predictions
   predradialtemp<-predict(svmradialtemp,temp2)
   # Compute predicted/actual correlation
   r <- cor(as.numeric(predradialtemp),as.numeric(temp2$PARTY))
   # Compute misclassification rate
   misclassificationRate <- 1- sum(predradialtemp == temp2$PARTY)/
   length(predradialtemp)
   # Print out results to three decimal places for model without variable i
   writeLines(paste("Predicted/observed r when dropping", predlabels[i],
   round(r,3)))
   writeLines(paste("MisClassification rate when dropping", predlabels[i],
   round(misclassificationRate,3)))
   writeLines(" ")
   }
# End of loop through the predictors.
```

Output is shown below, with two lines per predictor, for correlation and misclassification rate respectively:

```
Predicted/observed r when dropping ACLU 0.939
MisClassification rate when dropping ACLU 0.03

Predicted/observed r when dropping NAACP 0.9
MisClassification rate when dropping NAACP 0.051
```

We see that of the two predictors, NAACP is the stronger since the predicted/observed correlation drops more and the misclassification rate is higher when NAACP is not in the model.

This method works fine when there are two predictors, identifying the more important of the two. However, when there are more predictor variables considered, the ranking of variables by the leave-one-out method identifies only the most important of the various potentially "most important" predictors. It does *not* yield a ranking which conditionally identifies the second most important variable given the most important one, and so on conditionally down the line. If the researcher's purpose is to rank predictors by importance using the leave-one-out method, then a conditional approach must be taken. This is discussed in the supplement to Chapter 6 titled "SVM Variable Importance".

6.12.2 Recursive feature elimination (RFE) with caret

RFE is a backward stepwise procedure, also called backward selection, which eliminates the weakest input first and then continues in this fashion until a researcher-specified number of inputs remains. Variable importance corresponds inversely to order of elimination, though full ranking would require specifying the number of final inputs to be one. Ideally, at each step there is recalibration of model parameters and cross-validation, though the random factor in cross-validation can alter variable rankings, particularly in small datasets. RFE is not implemented by the e1071 or kernlab packages but is available in the caret package.

In this section, we use caret to perform RFE to identify the "best" predictor variables and to list features by importance. We do so for the SVM radial kernel model, but the same approach could be used for other models discussed in this chapter. Note that the code below may take noticeable processing time and the program may appear to "hang" (two minutes on the author's computer): be patient.

First we declare control parameters using caret's `rfeControl()` command. These parameters are then used by caret's `rfe()` command, which implements RFE. For control parameters we specify tenfold repeated cross-validation three times. The training sample is specified as 75% of the input data rows (cases). We also specify that predictions and variable importance should be saved.

```
control<- caret::rfeControl(functions = caretFuncs, rerank = FALSE, method =
"repeatedcv", number = 10, repeats = 3, p = 0.75, saveDetails=TRUE)
```

Next we use `rfe()` for an SVM radial kernel model, putting results in svmProfile. The x and y objects were declared in earlier command statements. Thus x is a data frame with the predictor variables ACLU and NAACP and y is a data frame with the factor outcome variable PARTY as its first and only variable. The `sizes` object defines the sizes of the models to be examined (here, 1 or 2 variable models, given there are only two predictors). The method parameter is passed to `train()` on which `rfe()` relies

```
set.seed(123)

svmProfile <- caret::rfe(x, y[[1]],
  sizes = c(1:2),
rfeControl = control,
  method = "svmRadial")
```

To print results, simply type the name of the rfe object:

```
svmProfile
```

[Output:]

```
   Recursive feature selection
   Outer resampling method: Cross-Validated (10 fold, repeated 3 times)
   Resampling performance over subset size:
    Variables Accuracy  Kappa AccuracySD KappaSD Selected
            1   0.9711 0.9416    0.06208  0.1253        *
            2   0.9574 0.9152    0.06649  0.1315

   The top 1 variables (out of 1):
      NAACP
```

The model selected by the RFE algorithm is indicated by the asterisk in its row. For the current example this is the one-variable model, which has a higher accuracy and higher Kappa than does the two-variable model, using SVM with a radial kernel. The one variable is NAACP. In a model with many predictors, RFE would select the model having the best subset of predictors and list them as the top variables. The list of best variables is retained in the optVariables component (for this example, in `svmProfile$optVariables`) or may be obtained by the function `predictors(svmProfile)`.

Finally, it is easy to save predictions to a variable object, here one called predPARTY. The predict command implements predictions based on the class of the first term, so here predict.rfe is used.

```
class(svmProfile)
```

[Output:]

```
   [1] "rfe"
```

We now create the object predPARTY, containing model predictions. Again, x is the data frame containing the predictor variables. Has we used `newdata=senate` we would obtain the same result as it has the same predictors.

Warning: `svmProfile$pred` has predictions for every cross-validation fold for each model for each repetition, not one prediction per senator. The predPARTY object, created below, is the object with one prediction per senator.

```
predPARTY <- predict(svmProfile,newdata=x)
predPARTY
```
[Partial output for the 99 senators:]
```
 [1] Dem Dem Dem Dem Dem Dem Dem Dem Dem Dem Dem Dem Dem Dem Dem
 . . .
[91] GOP GOP GOP GOP GOP GOP GOP GOP GOP
Levels: Dem GOP
```

6.12.3 Other approaches to variable importance

There are various other approaches to identifying variable importance, two of which are mentioned below:

- Permutation: This is a similar automated approach, which runs multiple models, cycling through the input variables. In each cycle one of the inputs is permuted, which means that random values are substituted. The logic is the same as for leave-one-out modeling: The variable whose permutation worsens performance the most is the most important variable. With smaller datasets there is a chance that the random factor in permutation may affect the ranking of input variables (different random seeds may affect order).
- The Java package weka.attributeSelection in its SVMAttributeEval module has the capability to evaluate variable importance based on SVM classification, but this is outside the scope of this book. In general, however, one might convert an R data frame to a. csv file, then use it in SVMAttributeEval to obtain variable importance rankings.

6.13 SVM classification for a multinomial outcome

Use of SVM modeling with multinomial outcome data is presented in an online supplement to Chapter 6, found in the student section of this book's Support Material (www.routledge.com/9780367624293), under the supplement title "Multinomial SVM".

6.14 Command summary

For convenience for those wishing to try models out for themselves, this book's Support Material (www.routledge.com/9780367624293) contains a listing of the main commands used in this chapter. This listing may be handy for readers following along with the book using their home or office computers. For topics presented as online supplements ("SVM versus OLS", "Multinomial SVM", "SVM Variable Importance"), the command summary is at the end of these supplements.

Endnotes

1. https://docs.google.com/document/d/1aN9BcOYoJcr7p9zRnwBHYJ_02fKDyJJavnjTl3A0JT0/edit#
2. https://cran.r-project.org/web/packages/mlr3learners/mlr3learners.pdf
3. The nine methods are:

• bayesglm	Bayes generalized linear model
• brnn	Bayesian regularized neural networks
• bartmachine	Bayesian additive regression trees
• bridge	Bayesian ridge regression
• blassoAveraged	Bayesian ridge regression (model averaged_
• nb	Naïve Bayes (classification) via the klaR package
• naïve_bayes	Naïve Bayes (classification) via the naivebayes package

- nbDiscete Naïve Bayes Classifier
- awnd Naïve Bayes Classifier with attribute weights

4. See https://cran.r-project.org/web/views/Bayesian.html
5. The "arm" package also has a `corrplot()` command.
6. Available families and their usual link functions are:

   binomial(link = "logit")
   gaussian(link = "identity")
   Gamma(link = "inverse")
   inverse.gaussian(link = "1/mu^2")
   poisson(link = "log")
   quasi(link = "identity", variance = "constant")
   quasibinomial(link = "logit")
   quasipoisson(link = "log")

7. Settings and their defaults for priors in `bayesglm())` are listed below.

   prior.mean
   Prior mean for the coefficients: Default is 0 but a vector of length equals to the number of predictors (not counting the intercept, if any) may be specified. T
   prior.mean.for.intercept
   Prior mean for the intercept. The default is 0.
   prior.scale
   Prior scale for the coefficients: The default is NULL for a model without priors. For models with priors, set to 2.5. A vector of length equals to the number of predictors (not counting the intercept) may be specified. Gelman notes, "Changing the values of x can change the correlation, and thus the implicit prior distribution, even though the regression is not changing at all (assuming an underlying linear relationship). That said, this is the cost of having an informative prior distribution: Some scale must be used, and the scale of the data seems like a reasonable default choice" (Gelman et al., 2008: 1380).
   prior.df
   Prior degrees of freedom for the coefficients. For t distribution, the default is 1 (Cauchy). Set to Inf to get normal prior distributions. A vector of length equals to the number of predictors (not counting the intercept) may be specified. I
   prior.scale.for.intercept
   Prior scale for the intercept. The default is NULL without priors and 10 to model with priors.
   prior.df.for.intercept
   Prior degrees of freedom for the intercept. The default is 1.
   min.prior.scale
   Minimum prior scale for the coefficients. The default is near 0 (1e-12).

8. This section follows Jon Startkweather, https://it.unt.edu/sites/default/files/bayesglm_jds_jan2011.pdf
9. https://cran.r-project.org/web/packages/mlr3learners/mlr3learners.pdf
10. The mlr3 package also provides a different, more complex method of imputation. See https://mlr3gallery.mlr-org.com/posts/2020-01-30-impute-missing-levels/.
11. http://perso.lcpc.fr/tarel.jean-philippe/publis/jpt-icme05.pdf
12. For example, see https://math.usask.ca/emr/examples/grpo_eg3.html
13. The syntax parallels SVMfit1:

```
ctrl <- caret::trainControl(
  method = "none",
  classProbs = FALSE,
  summaryFunction = defaultSummary
)

set.seed(123)
SVMfit2 <- caret::train(
  literacy ~ Infantdeathsper1k + poppersqmile + gdppercapitalindollars + phonesper1000 +
birthrate,
  data = world,
  method = "svmRadialSigma",
  preProc = "center",
  trControl = ctrl,
  metric = "RMSE"
)
```

```
SVM2fitted <- predict(SVMfit2, data=world)
Metrics::rmse(SVM2fitted, world$literacy)
```

14. Additional things to know about SVM modeling with the e1071 package:
    - By default the `svm()` algorithm automatically scales both x and y variables internally to have a mean of 0 and a standard deviation of 1. That is, data are standardized. Set `scale = FALSE` if an unstandardized model is preferred, as in the example above (most uses of OLS models, for example, are unstandardized) or if data are already standardized. It is also possible to specify that some variables are to be scaled and others not. Standardization equalizes the means and variances of predictor variables. This is desirable for ranking and comparing variables but is undesirable when real-world predicted values are important.
    - The `svm()` command only supports one response variable.
    - The `tune()` command may also be used with `nnet()`, `randomForest()`, `rpart()`, and `knn()` objects, not just `svm()` objects.
    - Above, `tune.control()` specified the sampling scheme. The "fix" scheme asked for a single split into training and validation sets. Alternatives are "cross" and "boot".
    - The default value of `cross = 0` suppresses cross-validation of the model. If an integer value of k > 0 is specified, a k-fold cross validation on the training data is performed, using accuracy rate for classification models or mean squared error for regression models.
    - The `na.action` option, not used in this example, specifies what to do about missing (NA) values. The default action is na.omit, which drops observations which have a missing value on any required variable. An alternative is na.fail, which causes an error if NA cases are found.
    - A logical value of `probability = TRUE` or `FALSE` specifies whether the model should allow for probability predictions. This might be set to TRUE in classification models. If so, for each observation, a probability would be returned for the chance of the given observation being in each class of the categorical outcome variable.
15. E.g., see https://stackoverflow.com/questions/29449639/svm-in-r-with-caret-using-e1071-instead-of-kernlab
16. Note that if the data were to have additional variables, the researcher could select the desired variables using the formula option of plot.svm. This is required if there are more than two predictors. Type `help(plot.svm)` for more information.
17. In the plot, some support vectors are overwritten. Also, the title and location of the legend are hard-coded into plot.svm. Setting fill=FALSE eliminates the legend and may show more support vector points.
18. Combining plots was done in Photoshop.

Chapter 7

Neural network models and deep learning

PART I: OVERVIEW OF NEURAL NETWORK MODELS AND DEEP LEARNING

7.1 Overview

When the public thinks of the power of modern computing, the phrase "artificial intelligence" (AI) is apt to come to mind. AI is a broad term encompassing a large variety of methods and applications, but a central one is artificial neural network (ANN) methods, which is the focus of this chapter. ANNs are inspired by neurobiology, with components loosely analogous to the axons, dendrites, and synapses of a living creature. In neurobiology, dendrites in neural networks collect signals, which are fed to neurons. Neurons process a signal by sending a spike of electrical current along an axon, discharging at a synapse connected to other neurons, which in turn are excited or inhibited as a result. In ANNs, input signals are sent to a digital neural processing entity, also called a neuron. After a digital neuron processes an input signal, it sends an output signal on to later neurons in the network. While ANN processing speed is astonishingly fast, by comparison the human brain has some 10 billion neurons and perhaps 60 trillion synapses, giving it a complexity about ten orders of magnitude greater than current ANNs.

Where ordinary statistical procedures are based on instruction sets (programs), ANNs are not. Instead ANNs pass data through multiple intermediary digital processing entities (neurons) on the way to output entities (neurons in the terminal layer). Intermediary neurons "learn" through shifting patterns of weights based on input signals. Shifting weights reflect better or worse predictions or classifications at the terminal output layer. In ANNs, no "solution" or "answer" is ever stored at a particular computer memory address. Rather, the solution takes the form of weighted connections along linkages from the input layer through one or more processing layers to an output layer of neurons. ANNs still predict outputs, often better than classical statistical procedures, but the process by which they arrive at a solution is not embedded in a formula and may seem to researchers to be a "black box". The "black box" reputation of ANNs is exaggerated; however, as it is still possible to measure model performance and to make inferences about the relative importance of input variables.

While there are many types of ANN, there are three common components:

1. Signal-processing digital entities called "neurons"
2. The pattern of interconnections, called the "topology"
3. Rules pertaining to the shifting of weights, referred to as the "learning scheme"

While all ANNs have all these three components, individual elements may differ. For instance, one type of ANN may have a topology with only one processing layer while another type may have multiple processing layers. Topologies also may involve parallel processing and feedback loops and they may differ in the number and complexity of

DOI: 10.4324/9781003109396-7

interconnections. The constellation of elements in the three ANN components may be called the "network paradigm" for a particular ANN.

"Learning" in neural networks refers to the matching of incoming inputs with past patterns and past outcome results. That is, ANN learning operates through a type of associative recall. One aspect of learning is that inputs need not be complete data. Neurons may generate output signals based on whatever input signals are received even if incomplete by the standards of conventional statistics. Incomplete information is still information and the outcome of learning based on partial data may still be a level of prediction or classification, which meets research purposes.

7.2 Data and packages

Data and R packages used in this chapter are listed in this section.

Data

- boston_c.csv: The "boston_c" dataset is a corrected version of the "Boston" data frame found in the "MASS" package and is almost identical to the "BostonHousing2" data frame found in the "mlbench" package.[1] The original data were found in Harrison and Rubinfeld (1978). The dataset contains 21 variables (columns) for 506 rows (observations). Each observation is a Census tract in the Boston area. A given town may have multiple tracts. In examples later in this chapter these data were read into a data frame labeled "BostonHousing". This data file is used in Sections 7.8–7.10. Variables, which are upper case, are listed below by column number:

  1. OBS — the observation id number
  2. TOWN — the name of the town (a character variable)
  3. TOWN.1 — the id of the town in numeric form
  4. TRACT — the tract number of the observation
  5. LON — the longitude of the tract centroid
  6. LAT — the latitude of the tract centroid
  7. MEDV — the median value of owner-occupied homes in $1000s
MEDV is censored: all values > 50 are set to 50
  8. CMEDV — corrected MEDV (very minor corrections)
  9. CRIM — the town's per capita crime rate
  10. ZN — the percent or residential land zone for large lots (> 25k sq. ft.)
  11. INDUS — the percent of non-retail business acres in a town
  12. CHAS — dummy variable coded 1 = tract bounds Charles River, 0 = doesn't
  13. NOX — nitrogen oxides concentration in parts per 10 million
  14. RM — mean number of rooms per dwelling
  15. AGE — percent owner-occupied units built prior to 1940
  16. DIS — weighted mean of distances to five Boston employment centers
  17. RAD — an index of accessibility to radial highways
  18. TAX — the full-value property tax rate per $10,000
  19. PTRATIO — the town's pupil-teacher ratio
  20. B — 1000(Bk – 0.63)^2 where Bk is the proportion of blacks by town
  21. LSTAT — percent of population classed lower status

- boston_housing: The mlr3 package revolves around "tasks", one of which is the predefined "boston_housing" task. This is a variant on the previous dataset. As it is built into mlr3, there is no. csv file to load. We use it in Section 7.12, where it is transformed into the bostoncrim data frame and the boston_crim_task object.
- Iris: The iris dataset is used to illustrate nnet classification models. It is a data frame in the "datasets" package, which loads automatically when R is loaded. This classic classification problem is to classify three types of

iris flower (setosa, versicolor, virginica) based on the four measurement features (Sepal.Length, Sepal.Width, Petal.Length, Petal.Width).

- nycflights.csv: The nycflights dataset contains data on 897,629 flights by American Airlines (AA) and United Airlines (UA) in 2013. The outcome variable is arrival delay (arr_delay). Predictor variables are dep_delay, dep_time, arr_time, air_time, and distance. The data are modified and selected from the original "flights" dataset that is contained in the "nycflights13" package, which is available on CRAN. The nycflights.csv data are used in Quick Start Example 1 in this chapter.
- nycflights_scaled.csv: This is the same dataset as nycflights.csv above, except the outcome variable is rescaled to range from 0 to 1 and all other variables are normalized to make them of comparable scale. The nycflights_scaled.csv data are also used in Quick Start Example 1 in this chapter.
- surveysample.csv: This data frame contains data on 21 social variables for 2,050 U.S. individuals. The data are a subset from which missing values have been eliminated, adapted from but different from a General Social Survey sample provided by IBM SPSS for instructional purposes. It is used in this chapter to illustrate classification models under the nnet package.

Packages
This chapter assumes that if following along, the reader has installed and loaded the following packages used in this chapter.

```
library(caret)              # Provides a training shell for nnet
library(corrplot)           # Supports the corrplot() command
library(plyr)               # Supports the revalue() command
                            # plyr must be loaded before dplyr
library(dplyr)              # Supports the %>% assignment operator
library(ggplot2)            # For graphic and visualization
library(keras)              # See Section 7.12 on installation; used with mlr3keras
library(lm.beta)            # Used to compute beta weights for linear regression
library(mlr3)               # A modeling integration package
library(mlr3keras)          # Adds Keras-derived learners to mlr3
library(mlr3learners)       # Provides additional learners for
library(mlr3pipelines)      # Preprocessing operators and pipelines for 'mlr3'
library(neuralnet)          # One of the major neural network packages in R
library(NeuralNetTools)     # Visualization tools for nnet, neuralnet, & other packages
library(nnet)               # A second leading neural network package in R
library(nycflights13)       # Contains NYC airline flight data
library(remotes)            # Utility for installing packages from remote repositories
library(reshape2)           # Contains the melt() function for names for violin plots
library(reticulate)         # See Section 7.12 on installation; used with mlr3keras
library(tensorflow)         # See Section 7.12 on installation; used with mlr3keras
```

7.3 Social science examples

In Anthropology
The analysis of skeletal remains is an important topic in forensic and physical anthropology. Etli et al. (2019) compared four statistical methods for identification of sex from skeletal remains based on sacral and coccygeal measurements: Univariate discriminant analysis (67% accuracy), stepwise discriminant analysis (79% accuracy), linear discriminant function analysis (83% accuracy), and multilayer perceptron (MLP) neural networks (86% accuracy). The authors concluded that sex estimation with neural networks is a promising field of research in forensic anthropology as applied to corpses where identification is otherwise not possible.

In Economics
As neural networks are often sought out as a methodology for forecasting when causal factors are complex and the model of causation is not well known, it is not surprising that in economics, neural networks have been used to

predict stock market prices, as in the work of Yu et al. (2020). The authors compared forecasting procedures: (1) a traditional ARIMA model, (2) a back-propagation neural model using principle components analysis for dimension reduction of factors affecting stock prices (the BP-PCA model), and (3) a back-propagation neural model using a local linear embedding dimensional reduction algorithm (the LLE-BP model). They concluded, "The results show that LLE-BP neural network model has higher prediction accuracy in stock price prediction, and it is an effective and feasible stock price prediction method" (from abstract).

In Geography

Shatnawi and Qdais (2019) used satellite imagery data in conjunction is ANNs to predict the changes in land surface temperature (LST) in the North of Jordan. The authors hypothesized that increased influxes of refugees, starting from 2003, had led to urban expansion, which might be reflected on the climatic conditions and affect LST values. Their analysis revealed an average increase of 1.1°C in average LST, considered a significant increase compared with prior studies.

In Political Science

In the field of global conflict studies, Felix Ettensperger (2020) of the Department of Political Science, Albert-Ludwigs-University Freiburg, Germany, compared neural network methods with other machine learning procedures to predict conflict intensity. He concluded that while results varied by the nature of the dataset, in general, "The argument derived from this study is that researchers should combine Supervised Learning Algorithms and Deep Learning Networks as a general approach". That is, Ettensperger recommended ANN as a "powerful complement" to but not a replacement for other machine language tools for prediction such as random forests.

In Psychology

Durstewitz et al. (2019) surveyed the literature on the use of neural networks in psychiatric research. In this study, which referenced some 180 articles, the use of ANNs was found to be diverse. They concluded, "In summary, although in past years NNs have been mainly used as sophisticated nonlinear tools for classification, regression, and prediction, a very exciting development is to employ them to also to gain insight into physiological, computational, and cognitive mechanisms."

In Sociology

Han Zhang, a sociology doctoral student at Princeton University, and Jennifer Pan of the Department of Communication, Stanford University, used two types of neural networks to analyze text and image data respectively in a study of collective action based on social media. They studied 100,000 Chinese collective action events in a form of protest event analysis. The primary purpose of the study was the creation of large baseline protest event dataset using deep learning. This was judged particularly import for China since "Social media data provide unique benefits in detecting collective action events in authoritarian regimes because they provide information when other sources, such as traditional media, are silent" (Zhang & Pan, 2019: 42–43).

7.4 Pros and cons of neural networks

Like all procedures, ANNs have advantages and disadvantages. In this section, we list commonly-cited pros and cons.

Pros

- ANNs automatically handle nonlinearities and interaction effects in the data. Put another way, it is not necessary that causal dynamics in the field be well-enough understood that nonlinearity and interactions can be identified and explicitly incorporated in the model, as traditional statistical methods would require.
- Handles any type of numeric data and is a nonparametric procedure.
- Can handle a very large number of input/predictor variables/signals (columns), even pixel-level image data. ANNs are often preferred when pattern recognition is needed in spite of incomplete data and lack of knowledge about how input variables relate to one another. Likewise, ANNs are particularly appropriate when the inputs and outputs are known and clearly defined but the relationship of inputs to outputs is not well understood. Many social science problems are of this type.
- Can handle and works best for a large number of data points (rows), in the thousands or even millions. ANNs can keep improving with additional data inputs whereas many other machine language procedures do not improve in performance after the number of data points reaches a performance plateau level.
- Handles both classification and regression problems.

- Can predict well at the extremes (in contrast, linear regression [ordinary least squares, OLS] predicts at the mean), given appropriate training data.
- Is robust against missing data provided this does not affect the representativeness of the training examples provided.
- Trained neural models can make quick predictions.
- There is an appeal to mimicking neural processes in the human mind. Some may feel this gives greater legitimation to results achieved by ANN processes.
- The academic and practitioner literature on ANN models is very large, going back to the 1940s, and is now expanding rapidly. Also, the number of different software implementations in R alone is very large, providing many options that can be tailored to the local research setting.

Cons

- Specification of the ANN structure (number of layers, number of neurons, and other parameters) requires trial and error. Structure cannot be set by predetermined rules. Training requires optimizing a number of parameters and is more complex, requires more expertise, and is more time-consuming than for training, say, a linear regression model.
- It is difficult to assess the relative importance of input variables. Therefore, it is difficult to explain to clients why a neural network-based decision was made. By the same token, it is difficult to employ ANNs in causal modeling in social science. However, the alleged "black box" nature of neural networks can be exaggerated, as discussed later in this chapter.
- Results are probabilistic, not determined by a single accepted equation. Error is possible. The amount of error is affected by many parameters and, of course, by the training data.
- Training time can be long for larger problems.
- While neural models may work well with small to medium datasets (e.g., under 1,000 data points), they are less likely to outperform other machine language procedures for such data. Alternatives such as decision trees, SVM, and even linear (OLS) regression are simpler and may perform better, though this depends of the particular dataset at hand.
- Overfitting can be a problem and therefore cross-validation is required.
- Results are dependent on the training examples put in.
- Results are dependent on starting points set by the random seed. Some random seeds give much better starting points than others, requiring trial and error or grid search. Failure to set the random seed means results will differ for each run, even for the same data and model.
- In terms of R limitations, more complex neural network models require other programming environments associated with Python, Keras, and Tensorflow.

7.5 Artificial neural network (ANN) concepts

7.5.1 ANN terms

In this section, we present explanations of common terms encountered in neural network analysis. Note, however, that not all design constructs mentioned below are applicable to all ANN programs and models. Moreover, different software packages use different terminologies.

- *Neural networks*: ANNs are various types of parallel distributed processing systems composed of an input layer, one or more layers of processing entities called neurons, and a terminal or output layer. Depending on the program, inputs may be numbers, text, or images (pixel arrays). Weighting rules are used to adjust connection strengths between inputs and outputs based on experiential knowledge about outcomes in prior iterations. Neural networks may be used for either regression or classification problems.
- *Iterations, epochs, and cross-validation*: Training a neural model is an iterative process involving setting starting weights (typically at random), feeding inputs through the network, and feeding error back for the next iteration. Testing of a model is done on a hold-out validation or test dataset not used in training, thereby building in cross-validation. An epoch is usually defined as one pass through the entire set of inputs, including updating of weights. In some software, specifying the number of "repetitions" is specifying the number

of epochs. Training almost always involves multiple epochs. Others define an epoch as a pass through all the inputs in the training data plus comparing results for the training model applied to the validation (test) data. Cross-validation of the training model with the test data is usually performed multiple times. For instance, tenfold cross-validation is cross-validation performed ten times, with final estimates derived only at the end.

- *Perceptrons*: Neural network models are sometimes called "multilayer perceptrons", particularly in earlier literature. Early ANNs often used perceptron as a term referring to simple models simulating biological neural activity.
- *Neurons*: Neurons are digital processing entities which are sometimes also called nodes or cells. Neurons pass information to other neurons, adjusting weights based on learning from past iterations.
- *Layers*: A layer is a set of neurons, which serve some type of purpose. The three main types are input, middle (also called "hidden"), and output. There may be more any number of hidden layers but this does not necessarily assure a better model. Three to five layers is common. The hidden layer will typically have more neurons than the output layer. The number of neurons in the output layer varies by what is being predicted. A binary classification problem, for instance, will have only one output neuron, which will have a weight representing a probability which, if more than or equal to .5, will predict a value of 1. A "single-layer network" has no hidden layers but rather transmits data inputs directly to output nodes. While simple problems with linearly separable data may work well with single-layer networks, most problems require one or more hidden layers. A network with one or more hidden layers is a "multilayer network" or a "deep neural network". Thus "deep learning" refers to using multilayer networks.
- *Neighborhoods*: An adjacent set of neurons in a given layer is a neighborhood. Some neural modes use neighborhood neurons in their weight updating algorithm (e.g., Kohonen self-organizing models).
- *Weights*: In a system with n inputs, each neuron can accept up to n – 1 inputs. Weights, after being initialized to random values, are assigned to each path. Then, in each iteration of the neural algorithm, weights are adjusted based on learning. Weights determine the relative strength of each connection path. The rectangular array of weights is called the "connection matrix" or "decision matrix".
- *Gradient descent*: The adjustment of weights at each iteration is usually based on a gradient descent algorithm. This algorithm estimates how steeply error will be reduced or increased by a given change in a weight, and then selects the change corresponding to the estimated steepest decline in error. The amount estimated by gradient descent is the "learning rate". While this process usually works well, gradient descent can lead to locally suboptimal minimization of error. To avoid suboptimal solutions, some software incorporates noise (discussed below) to jog the algorithm out of local minima.
- *Learning*: Learning is the process of updating weights in a neural network. Learning is the second of two phases of neural modeling. The first phase is "recall," which is the passing of signals from the input layer to the output layer. "Learning", is the second phase, which is the adjustment of neural weights, usually in response to the error arising in the recall phase. During learning, "saturation" may occur, meaning that reinforcing weights above a certain level may no longer affect the output value.
- *Learning and recall schedule*: The "learning and recall schedule" is the set of parameters, which may affect recall and learning. As in other procedures, default parameters may be defined by the software but some or all may be researcher-specified. The learning rate is a parameter, which set the magnitude of weight adjustments in response to error. The default learning rate is typically 1.0, but may range from .1 to 1. In some neural software a "learning schedule" governs changes in the learning rate during training.
- *Supervised learning*: Supervised learning is the usual form, in which input data in the training set includes the correct output values for each presented input pattern. "Unsupervised learning", in contrast, takes input examples and classifies them inductively without reference to correct classifications. In unsupervised learning, the researcher may specify the desired number of clusters and then observations are clustered based on similarity across all input variables. Another label for unsupervised models is "self-organizing networks", of which Kohonen networks are the leading example.
- *Weight types*: Most weights are variable, varying based on learning adjustments. However, there are other types. Fixed weights are constants for all iterations. Modified weights are fixed in the sense of not being adjusted for learning but instead are different constants for different training phases. Set weights are modified weights that are multiplied by an input clamp, which is a coefficient in the learning and recall schedule. Clamping assures current activation levels are retained rather than being adjusted during learning. Weights may also be subject to pruning, as when weights below a given threshold value are eliminated.
- *Summation function*: In any given iteration, a neuron receives multiple weighted inputs, which must be combined. The summation function is the set of linear combiner rules which compute net input. In simplest form,

the summation function is the sum of path weights from all inputs times the signal (output) of these inputs. Alternative summation rules may involve taking the maximum input, minimum, majority, product, normalized value, or other function. Also, a summation function may be applied only to certain weights.

- *Noise*: In some neural models, random noise may be added during summation, either to all weights or to a subset. Noise may be uniform or Gaussian (random-normal) across weights. The noise level may be set through the "temperature" parameter of the learning and recall schedule. Noise signals serve as "jog weights" to help a model get beyond some local minima and converge toward an optimal solution.
- *Activation function*: Summed weights are forwarded to later neurons by an activation function. The activation function combines input signals and emits a single output signal. Synonyms are transfer or squashing functions. The activation function is a form of learning rule. This function converts the summed weighted inputs into an activation value or transfer weight. "Squashing" means that the activation function may truncate the weight to be within permitted bounds. The activation function typically introduces nonlinearity into the neural network model by transforming weights by some nonlinear function.

  Nonlinearity functions include sigmoidal (s-shaped, a common form, squashes from 0 to 1 but is not 0-centered, which can hurt performance), tanh (hyperbolic tangent, squashes to -1 to +1, and is 0-centered), rectified linear unit (ReLU, squashes to 0 or 1 and is 0-centered, which usually aids performance and thus may be preferred to sigmoid for classification problems), leaky ReLU (has a small positive rather than 0 slop for negative values, hence may handle negative input data better), Softmax (akin to sigmoidal but handles multiple classes, constraining outputs to sum to 1 such that weighting one class more must weight others less), stepped, linear, Gaussian (normal, which is used in radial basis function [RBF] networks), logistic, and other generalized forms. Different layers may use different activation functions. For instance, a not-uncommon choice is to use ReLU for the hidden layers and Softmax for the output layer. ReLU was found superior, for instance, in a comparative study of activation functions by Ertam and Aydin (2017). Usually activation, transfer of weights (signal propagation), and summation are all calculated simultaneously across all neurons in the entire network.
- *Firing thresholds*: If the activation value is above some threshold, the neuron will "fire". Firing means the neuron will generate an output (commonly a value of 1). The "parent node" is the firing node and the "child node" receives the weighted signal. A "firing rate" may be specified. For instance, a firing rate of .5 means the neuron would only fire half the time, at random. Also, an "input bias" value may be added to change the threshold level for firing. Firing may also be affected by a "momentum" term, which gives inertia to prior weights in the given neuron.
- *Gain factor*: A gain factor, also specified in the learning and recall schedule, may serve as a multiplier of the summed weights. Also, weights may be scaled, which is multiplying weights by an "offset value".
- *Output function*: The output function is the rule which sets the nature of the transfer of a weight. The rule may permit direct transfer of the weight, transfer of only the highest weight in a layer, transfer of only the two highest weights, or other "competition" rules.
- *Network topology*: The network topology is the overall design of the neural network as an input-output model. A synonym is "network architecture". The topology always includes an input layer of neurons and an output layer, and always has at least one processing layer in between input and output. The network's "framework" is its number of layers and number of nodes per layer. The framework and its connection patterns (see below) is the network's topology. Thus, the topology has three main components: (1) number of layers, (2) number of neurons, and (3) rules governing connections, such as whether information may be fed backward. Unfortunately, selecting the optimal number of layers, nodes, and connection parameters cannot be reduced to simple rules and is often a matter of trial, error, and experience with given types of problems and data. The scientific principle of parsimony still applies: For the same level of model performance, choose the simpler model (fewer layers, fewer neurons, and/or simpler connection rules).
- *Connections*: Neurons can be connected in several ways. Typically there is a "forward connection", transferring a weight from the neuron in one layer to a neuron in the next layer. However, it is also possible to have lateral connections connecting neurons in the same layer. Connections are usually "excitatory", meaning they cause the neuron to fire, but they can also be "inhibitory", preventing firing. A "jump connection" is one directly connecting an input neuron to an output neuron, jumping over middle layers. If connections all go forward or laterally, it is a "feed-forward model".
- *Backpropagation models*: Backpropagation models, in spite of their name, are feed-forward networks. This is the most common type of neural model. In any given iteration, there is a feed-forward process sending weights from input to middle to output neurons. The "back" in backpropagation means information on output

error (the difference between predicted values based on the training set and observed values based on the test set) is fed back to neurons in earlier layers so that learning occurs (weights are adjusted) in the next iteration.

- *Feedforward versus recurrent networks*: Feedforward networks allow signals only to be passed in one direction. Recurrent networks, also called feedback networks, allow signals to be passed both forward and backward. Use of feedforward models greatly exceeds use of recurrent networks. Most common models, such an MLPs and backpropagation models, are of the feedforward type. Backpropagation models (Rumelhart, Hinton, & Williams, 1986) feed signals forward in one iteration, compare predictions with observed training data, then back-propagate measures of error for the next iteration.

  The less common recurrent model, such as Hopfield networks, sends information backward in a type of delay loop in which a node's output is dependent on the previous state of the network. A corollary is that recurrent networks are less influenced by the input of new data in a subsequent iteration. However, they may have more difficulty in converging on a stable solution. This is a major reason why feedforward neural models are more common than feedback models. Selecting a feedback model versus a backpropagation or some other algorithm is part of the selection of "network architecture".
- *Competition*: Competition refers to selecting which neurons fire. Lateral connections are often inhibitory, for example, reducing the number of neurons firing in a given layer. Competition often means only one neuron in a layer is allowed to fire. Alternatively, multiple neurons may be allowed to fire but the sum of their weights is constrained to 1. "Normalization" is the opposite of competition, allowing all neurons to fire.
- *Training and test datasets*: Typically, the neural model is developed on a "training" dataset and then tested on a "test" or "validation" dataset. Frequently the neural software being used will divide the input dataset into training and test subsets automatically, assigning observations at random. The test subset is usually smaller than the training set, such as in a 2:1 proportion. Also commonly, this process may be repeated. For instance, "tenfold cross-validation" refers to employing ten rounds of random sampling into training and test subsets. Cross-validation is a guard against overfitting the data. It is mainly applicable to sampled data but could be used on census (all relevant cases) data. Part of training is setting the "training tolerance", a parameter which defines the degree of difference between predicted and observed values in the training set, which can be treated as small enough to be equivalent to no difference (i.e., to a correct estimate).
- *Training algorithm*: The training algorithm is the set of rules, which governs how input signals are processed to enhance (excite) or inhibit the connection weights used by given neurons to transmit to connected neurons later in the network architecture.
- *Convergence*: When the iterative process of a neural model has arrived at a stable set of weights, which meet some stopping criterion, convergence is said to have been achieved. Convergence also refers to the speed with which a model arrives at such a stable set of weights. Fast convergence, of course, is not equivalent to model performance in terms of accuracy of estimation (correct predictions or classifications) and generalization (effectiveness in the test/validation datasets). The researcher seeks convergence without overfitting, which is fitting the model even to noise in the data. With enough hidden nodes one can always achieve perfect fit in the training set but overfitting is likely. Some neural software algorithms seek to stop model iterations before overfitting occurs. If a model converges, estimates, and generalizes well, it may be saved as a "pretrained network" for use with other, new datasets. Strategies for dealing with failure to converge are enumerated in Section 7.9.

7.5.2 R software programs for ANN

As in other statistical areas, R offers a variety of programs to implement ANNs. Among the most widely used programs are as follows:

- `neuralnet ()` from the "neuralnet" package, developed by Stefan Fritsch and Frauke Guenther with other contributors. This is one of the most popular packages and supports multiple processing (hidden) layers with alternative neural methods.
- `nnet()` from the "nnet" package, developed by Brian Ripley and William Venables, is a simpler package supporting only one processing layer, but ease of use has meant wide application. It uses a modified version of backpropagation.
- `train ()` with `method = "nnet"` from the "caret" package, which makes it easier to compare nnet models with other machine language models (caret supports 283 models!).

- `nntrain ()` and other programs from the "deepnet" package, developed by Xiao Rong.
- `mlp ()` and other programs for a variety of types of neural network. The acronym "mlp" stands for multilayer perceptrons using backpropagation. It is from the RSNNS package (R version of the Stuttgart Neural Network Simulator, SNNS), developed by Christoph Bergmeir, José M. Benítez, and associates.
- `ANN ()` from the "ANN" package, developed by Francis Roy-Desrosiers. This package, which incorporates a unique "genetic algorithm" involving mutation and crossover, also supports the commands `ANNGA ()` for optimizing models and `predictANN ()` for predictions. Not to be confused with the less widely used `ann()` program from the "validann" package. At this writing, ANN is no longer being updated by the author; however, though its use may still be found in the literature.

The listing above is far from comprehensive and even this relatively short list is too extensive to allow illustration of each package in this chapter. Moreover, ANNs are computationally intensive and for speed reasons Python or C++ are often preferred for larger and more complex models, giving more choices. Related Python libraries include pylearn2 and PyBrain.

7.5.3 Training methods for ANN

There are many algorithms for training neural models. Selection of an algorithm may make a large or small difference. This is something to be explored by the researcher on an empirical basis and optimal selection will depend on the data at hand and on parameter settings dictated by the researcher. Moreover, for a given problem, one algorithm may converge on a solution and another may not be able to. Below we list the algorithms available in R packages discussed in this chapter.

7.5.4 Algorithms in neuralnet

A major advantage of the neuralnet package is that it offers five alternative training methods. The `algorithm=` parameter in the `neuralnet()` command sets the method. For further discussion of the pros and cons of each, see Bailey (2015).

- backprop: Backpropagation is the classic, time-honored method of training neural models. It often performs satisfactorily but can be slow and may fail to converge. It is also highly sensitive to various parameters, which are not intuitive. For tips on achieving efficient backpropagation models (e.g., shuffle the order of your examples, normalize your data), see LeCun et al. (1998).
- rprop+: This method is the default in neuralnet. Its name stands for resilient backpropagation with weight backtracking. See Riedmiller (1994). The rprop algorithm is known to get stuck in loops and fail to converge sometimes (Bailey, 2015).
- rprop: This is resilient backpropagation without weight backtracking. See Riedmiller and Braun (1993).
- sag: The sag algorithm incorporates GRprop, a globally convergent version of backpropagation, which modifies the learning rate associated with the smallest absolute gradient (hence "sag"). "Globally convergent" means that this algorithm is intended to always converge, but see Bailey (2015), who proposes ARCprop as a truly globally convergent algorithm. The ARCprop algorithm is not yet implemented in neuralnet. On the original sag algorithm, see Anastasiadis et al. (2005).
- slr: The slr algorithm also incorporates GRprop but modifies the learning rate associated with the smallest learning rate (hence "slr").

7.5.5 Algorithms in nnet

The nnet package only supports the BFGS algorithm (the Broyden–Fletcher–Goldfarb–Shanno algorithm). The `nnet()` command draws on the `optim()` function in R's base package, which implements a version of BFGS. The BFGS algorithm is a much less common one than backpropagation variants but is among the most popular in the class known as quasi-Newton methods. BFGS calculates new search directions for each iteration based on solutions in the initial and previous iterations. Its performance is affected by the decay parameter, among others. For further discussion see Fletcher (1987).

7.5.6 Tuning ANN models

A neural model is not an equation with a "result". Rather it is an iterative algorithm governed by many possible parameters. The parameter settings can make all the difference in the neural model's performance. Settings include the number of layers, the number of neurons, the starting values for weights, the selection of the error function, and more. There is not a priori method of tuning a neural model to be optimal. In the sections which follow, the search for best parameter settings is discussed. Sometimes this is a matter of trial and error, sometimes grid search of the range of alternatives, and sometimes packages provide optimization utility programs.

PART II: QUICK START - MODELING AND MACHINE LEARNING

7.6 Example 1: Analyzing NYC airline delays

7.6.1 Introduction

In this exercise, we use the "nnet" neural network analysis package to predict airline flight delays in New York City. The target variable is arrival delay (arr_delay). Since this is a continuous variable, this is a regression rather than classification problem. Predictors are departure delay, departure time, arrival time, air time, and distance. The data are described in Section 7.2. In part we selected this example because is based on the same source data as Beck (2018).[2] This example has added importance because it illustrates the capabilities of the "NeuralNetTools" package. This package enables easy ranking of predictor variables by importance, thereby helping overcome neural network analysis's image as a "black box" procedure.

7.6.2 General setup

The setup for this exercise involves the usual setting of the working directory and loading of needed packages. For the reader following along, packages were already loaded in Section 7.2. In addition, for replicability purposes, a random seed is set.

```
set.seed(123)
setwd("C:/Data")

library(corrplot)           # Supports the corrplot() command
library(dplyr)              # Supports the %>% assignment operator
library(neuralnet)          # A leading neural network analysis package
library(nnet)               # Another popular neural network analysis package
library(NeuralNetTools)     # Visualization tools for nnet, neuralnet, & other packages
library(nycflights13)       # Contains NYC airline flight data
```

7.6.3 Data preparation

This text provides the data file for this exercise: "nycflights.csv". The reader could skip ahead to Section 7.6.4 and use this file directly. However, here in this section we present the steps, which were used to create the example file.

The unmodified source data is contained in the package "nycflights13", which includes the "flights" data frame as well as data frames for "airlines", "airports", "weather", and "planes". Only "flights" is used in the exercise, but in modified form. It is immediately accessible simply by virtue of loading the nycflights13 library.

```
library(nycflights13)
```

As "flights" is a huge data frame with 336,776 rows, we begin modification by subsetting it to consider only flights by United Airlines (UA) and American Airlines (AA). Airline codes are in the "carrier" column. In syntax below, the %in% operator is from R's base package (type `help("%in%")`) for more explanation.

```
nycflights <- flights[flights$carrier %in% c("UA", "AA"), ]
```

We further reduce the size of the nycflights data frame by retaining only the columns we will actually use. Note that "arr_delay" will be the target (DV). The "nycflights" object is a data frame.

```
nycflights <- nycflights[,c("arr_delay", "dep_delay", "dep_time", "arr_time", "air_
time", "distance")]
```

Next we check that all variables are numeric or integer, as some neural network prediction programs want. All columns are numeric or integer.

```
lapply(nycflights, class)
```

[Output:]

```
$arr_delay
[1] "numeric"
$dep_delay
[1] "numeric"
$dep_time
[1] "integer"
$arr_time
[1] "integer"
$air_time
[1] "numeric"
$distance
[1] "numeric"
```

Then we check for missing values. The command below, whose output is not shown here, reveals that there are missing values. While data imputation as discussed in Chapter 3 would be a better approach, we simplify by dropping cases listwise for rows with missing values.

```
# Check for missing listwise
sapply(nycflights, function(x) sum(is.na(x)))
# Retain only complete cases
nycflights <- na.omit(nycflights)
# Verify missing values are now gone
sapply(nycflights, function(x) sum(is.na(x)))
```

[Output:]

```
arr_delay dep_delay  dep_time  arr_time  air_time  distance
        0         0         0         0         0         0
```

```
# Show that the nycflights data frame was reduced from 91,394 data rows to 89,729.
nrow(nycflights)
```

[Output:]

```
[1] 89729
```

Having created "nycflights", we end the data preparation process by saving it as a comma-separate values (.csv) file. The file is saved to the default working directory set by the researcher.

```
write.csv (nycflights, file = "nycflights.csv", row.names=FALSE)
```

7.6.4 Modeling NYC airline delays

7.6.4.1 Setup

If the reader has skipped the previous "Data preparation" section, it is necessary to read "nycflights" in from file.

```
nycflights <- read.csv("nycflights.csv", header=TRUE, sep = ",",
stringsAsFactors=TRUE)
```

Next we create a model of NYC flight delays, based on the "nnet" package, which supports the `nnet()` command. For comparison, we also create a model using linear regression. In the syntax below, arr_delay is declared as the target variable.

Warning: As this is a very large dataset, computation can be very time-consuming. Therefore, for instructional purposes, we take a 1% random sample of the 89,729 rows of data in nycflights and put it in the data frame "df" and then use "df" instead of "nycflights" in the remainder of the exercise. The df data frame has 897 observations.

```
set.seed(123)
samp_pct <- .01
df <- nycflights %>% dplyr::sample_frac(samp_pct)
nrow(df)
```
[Output:]
```
    [1] 897
```

It is useful to look at the bivariate correlations among the variables. In particular we note the high correlation, as expected, between departure time and arrival delay. The correlation plot in Figure 7.1 shows that arrival delay is highly correlated with departure delay and is little correlated with air time or distance.

```
# Create a correlation matrix, here called "M"
M <- cor(df)

# Visualize M in a correlation plot
# Options: lower triangle only, no diagonal, set sizes for the labels/legend, set coefficient color
corrplot(M, type="lower", diag=FALSE, tl.cex=1.5, cl.cex=1.1, addCoef.col = "grey60" )
```

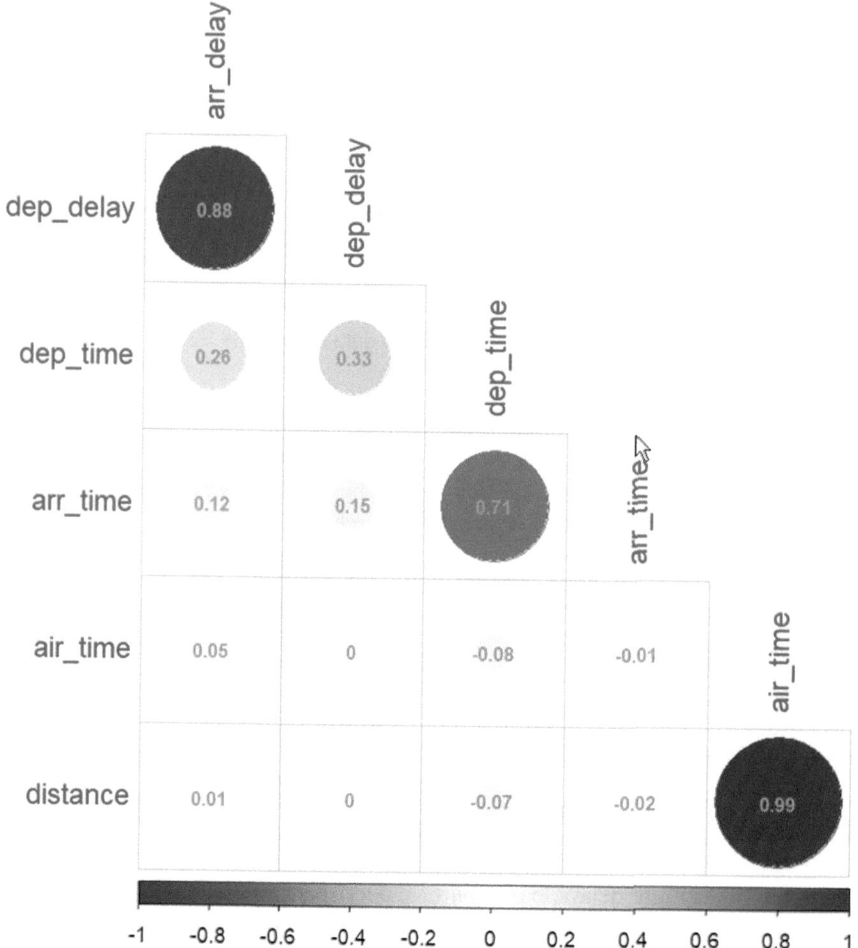

Figure 7.1 Correlation plot of the NYC airflights variables

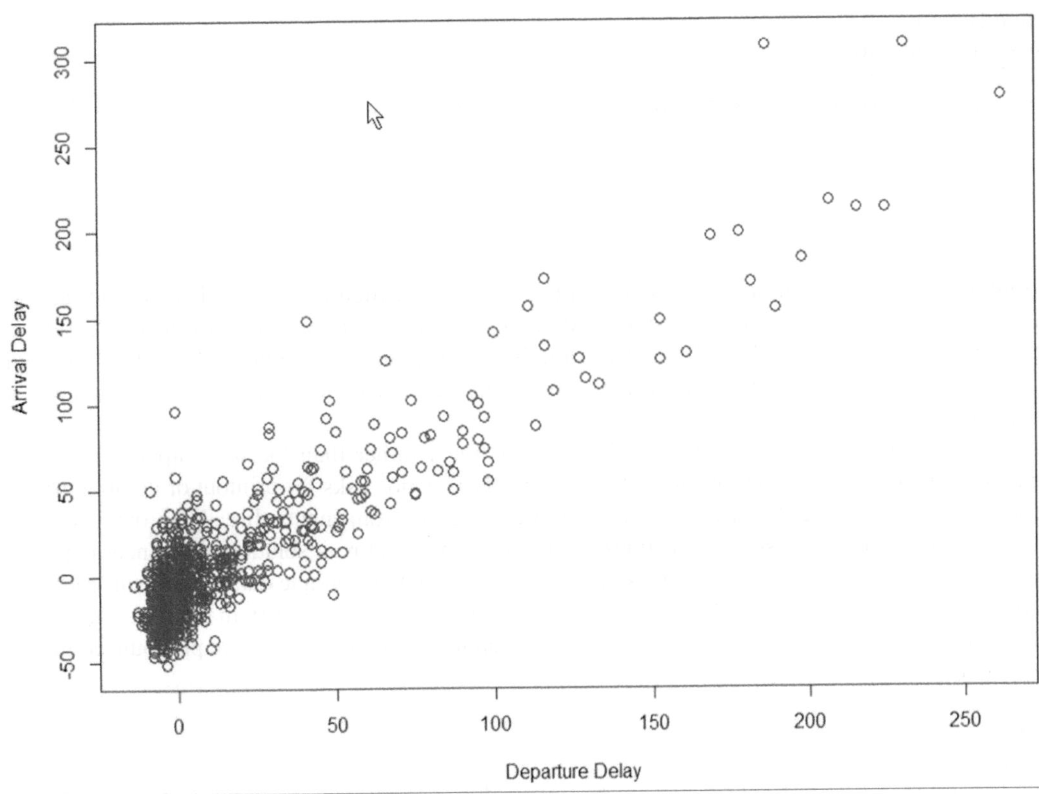

Figure 7.2 Arrival delay by departure delay

The bivariate correlations in Figure 7.1 suggest that the outcome variable, arr_delay, may be linearly related to dep_delay. We can check this visually with the simple bivariate plot in Figure 7.2. This figure confirms rough linearity, which means that a linear regression model should do quite well. There will not be a great deal of room for improvements by nonlinear procedures such as neural networks. Nonetheless, the simplicity of the example can serve instructional purposes.

```
plot(df$dep_delay,df$arr_delay, col= "blue", cex = 1.2, ylab = "Arrival Delay", xlab
= "Departure Delay")
```

7.6.4.2 Airline delays: The lm method

To get the linear regression baseline for comparison, we run the linear ("lm") model via the previously-illustrated "caret" package so that the result is cross-validated. As the relationships of the predictors to the target variable (arr_delay) are largely linear, the simple linear regression model does quite well, explaining a little over 84% of the variance in arrival delays, using all other variables as predictors. (Other metrics shown in output are root mean square error and mean absolute error.)

```
# The lm model via caret
model_caret_lm <- caret::train(arr_delay ~ dep_delay + dep_time + arr_time + air_
time + distance, df, method="lm", linout=TRUE, trace = FALSE)

# The cross-validated R-squared for the lm model is 0.8442
model_caret_lm
  Linear Regression
```

```
897 samples
  5 predictor
No pre-processing
Resampling: Bootstrapped (25 reps)
Summary of sample sizes: 897, 897, 897, 897, 897, 897, ...
Resampling results:
  RMSE     Rsquared   MAE
 15.5167  0.8441853  11.30444
```

7.6.4.3 Airline delays: The nnet method

To illustrate a neural network model, we use the "nnet" package, which is discussed further in later sections of this chapter. As with the linear regression model, we run nnet as a method within the "caret" package in order to obtain cross-validated results and to tune hyperparameters automatically. (The "lm" regression method did not have tuning parameters but nnet does: The number of neurons in the hidden layer and the decay parameter.)

In the command syntax below, linout = TRUE asks for linear rather than logistic output units, as usual for regression rather than classification problems. The trace = TRUE option asks for printout of iteration progress and convergence. That skip = is set to TRUE creates a skip connection from inputs directly to outputs (see Section 7.10.4). To simplify, a model with skip connections is one which melds a linear solution with a neural network solution, creating better results when linear relationships are strong, as in the example data. The R-squared for the nnet model is 0.8591, up only slightly from the lm model at 0.8442. Given strong linearity in the data, this outcome was expected. Later in this chapter, another nnet model with different data will show a more pronounced improvement over linear regression.

```
#Fit model
set.seed(123)
model_caret_nnet <- caret::train(arr_delay ~ dep_delay + dep_time + arr_time + air_
time + distance, df, method="nnet", linout=TRUE, skip=TRUE, trace = FALSE)

#Display model
model_caret_nnet
[Output, with final result highlighted in red:]
  Neural Network
  897 samples
    5 predictor
  No pre-processing
  Resampling: Bootstrapped (25 reps)
  Summary of sample sizes: 897, 897, 897, 897, 897, 897, ...
  Resampling results across tuning parameters:
    size  decay   RMSE      Rsquared   MAE
    1     0e+00   15.62339  0.8491592  11.28898
    1     1e-04   15.60907  0.8491136  11.30416
    1     1e-01   15.57927  0.8497549  11.22831
    3     0e+00   18.50286  0.8256811  11.34911
    3     1e-04   15.29219  0.8544389  11.14542
    3     1e-01   15.20761  0.8574098  10.86338
    5     0e+00   24.90506  0.8203394  11.85339
    5     1e-04   15.44504  0.8521085  11.04991
    5     1e-01   15.19003  0.8591250  10.85460
  RMSE was used to select the optimal model using the smallest value.
  The final values used for the model were size = 5 and decay = 0.1.
```

The "NeuralNetTools" package allows us to visualize the results. In Figure 7.3 we simply view the neural model. In the commands below, the `par()` command stacks the two plots and then restores the graphic environment at the

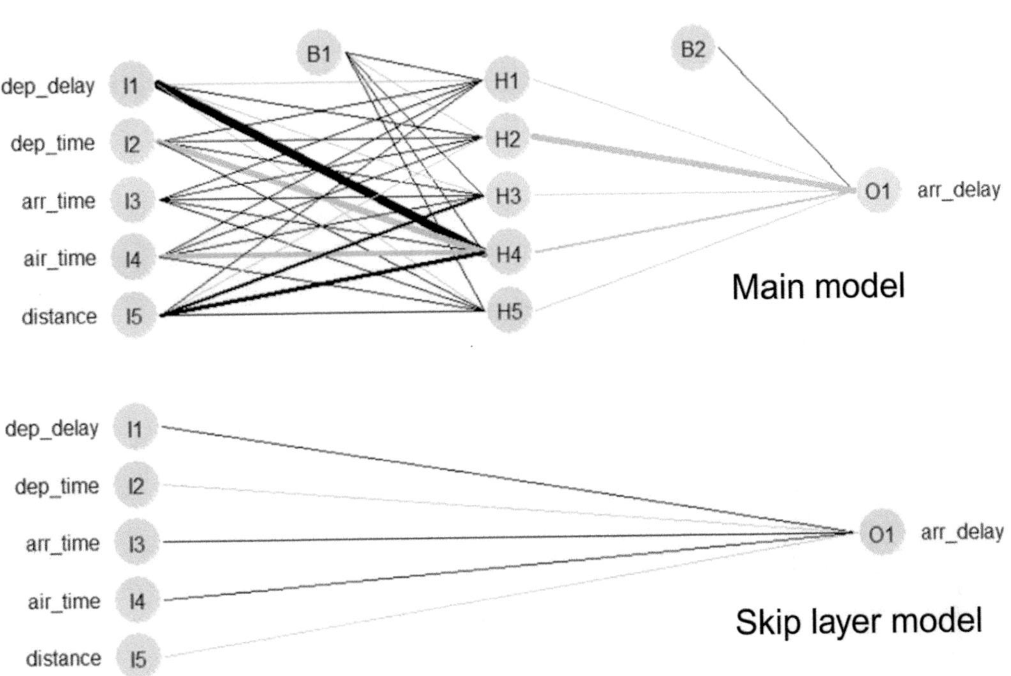

Figure 7.3 Arrival delay models using nnet via caret

end. The first `plotnet()` plot is of the main nnet model. The second is of the skip layer model. The thickness of lines reflects their importance.

```
par(mfrow=c(2,1))
NeuralNetTools::plotnet(model_caret_nnet)
NeuralNetTools::plotnet(model_caret_nnet,skip=TRUE)
par(mfrow=c(1,1))
```

The "NeuralNetTools" package also allows us to view the relative importance of predictor variables, as shown in Figure 7.4. The algorithm by Olden and Jackson (2002) is used for ranking. Figure 7.4 shows that departure delay is the most important predictor of arrival delay, in a negative direction, while departure time is second, in a positive direction.

```
NeuralNetTools::olden(model_caret_nnet)
```

Finally, the NeuralNetTools supports a form of sensitivity analysis of the predictor variables. The `lekprofile()` command allows the researcher to partition the data in quantiles (here five) and then display the response (here predicted arrival time) in chart form. For space reasons and to keep Example 1 simple, only the commands are given here. See Beck (2018: Sec. 3.3) for further discussion of the `lekprofile()` command.

```
# Group_vals are quantile values at which to hold other explanatory variables constant
# Parallel lines suggest similarity of response across quantiles.
NeuralNetTools::lekprofile(model_caret_nnet, group_vals = 5, group_show = FALSE)
# The bar plot shows values at which each explanatory variable was held constant
# while not being evaluated (while another variable was the variable of current interest).
NeuralNetTools::lekprofile(model_caret_nnet, group_vals = 5, group_show = TRUE)
```

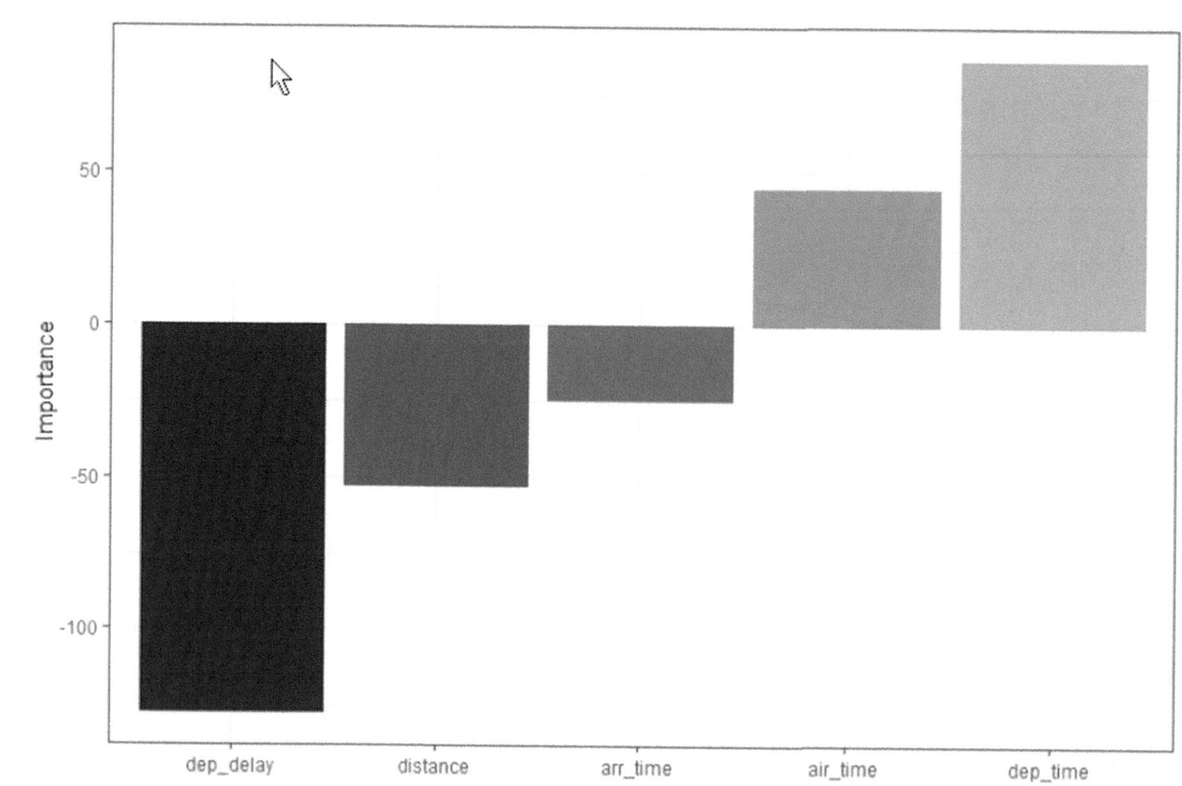

Figure 7.4 Relative predictor importance by the olden method

Though omitted here for space reasons, also note that the `NeuralNetTools::plotnet()`, `NeuralNetTools::olden()`, and `NeuralNetTools::lekprofile()` procedures may also be used with "nn" objects from other packages, such as the "neuralnet" package, neural networks created under "caret" (the `train()` procedure), or "mlp" objects from the "RSNNS" (Stuttgart Neural NetworkSimulator) package.

7.7 Example 2: The classic iris classification example

The previous "nnet" example was a regression problem. In "Quick Start Example 2" we use nnet (outside caret) for a classification problem. Specifically, we apply nnet to the classic "iris" dataset. The classification problem is to classify three types of iris flower (setosa, versicolor, virginica) based on the four measurement features (Sepal.Length, Sepal.Width, Petal.Length, Petal.Width).

7.7.1 Setup

The working directory should be set and the five packages below should be loaded.

```
setwd("C:/Data")
library(nnet)        # the neural network package used in this section
library(caret)       # provides a training shell for nnet
library(ggplot2)     # creates the violin plot below
library(dplyr)       # supports the %>% operator (for violin plots)
library(reshape2)    # contains the melt()  command to get labels for violin plots
```

As the iris dataset is contained in the "databases" package of R, which is installed by default, it may be read in with the `data()` and `View()` commands. The `names()` command shows the variable (column) names. The `dim()` command shows there are 150 observations for the five variables.

```
data("iris")
View(iris)
names(iris)
[Output:]
   [1] "Sepal.Length" "Sepal.Width"  "Petal.Length" "Petal.Width"  "Species"

dim(iris)
[Output:]
   [1] 150   5
```

7.7.2 Exploring separation with a violin plot

We can use data visualization on the target character variable (Species) to obtain graphical insight into how separable the three classes of Species are on the four predictor variables. Below, we visualize for the entire, non-normalized dataset (iris). In the violin plot shown in Figure 7.5, each species is shown as different colored dots. Each predictor variable is a column. If separability were going to be a problem, the colored dots would be random within each column. In this case, good separability may be anticipated.

This visualization requires the ggplot2, dplyr, and reshape2 libraries. The ggplot package allows fine tuning of all aspects of a plot. To accomplish this, it may need to specify many graphical parameters. The example below has several ggplot2 components, but many more might have been specified. Type `help(ggplot2)` for more information on ggplot2 options or enter "tutorial on ggplot2" in your browser.

```
# The melt() converts wide format data into a single data column
exploratory_iris <- reshape2::melt(iris)

# The melted iris data is then fed into ggplot2
exploratory_iris %>%
ggplot2::ggplot(aes(x = factor(variable), y = value)) +
ylab("Centimeters") +
xlab("Predictor Variables") +
ggplot2::geom_violin() +
ggplot2::geom_jitter(height = 0, width = 0.1, aes(colour = Species), alpha = 0.7) +
ggplot2::theme(axis.text = element_text (size=14)) +
ggplot2::theme(legend.text = element_text (size=16)) +
ggplot2::theme(axis.title.y = element_text(size = 16)) +
ggplot2::theme(axis.title.x = element_text(size =16))+
ggplot2::theme(panel.background = element_rect(fill = "lightblue", colour =
"lightblue", size = 0.5, linetype = "solid")) +
# Make the size of the points & lines in the legend larger
guides(color = guide_legend(override.aes = list(size = 4)))
```

7.7.3 Normalizing the data

Optionally we pre-process the data by normalizing the continuous variables (columns 1:4), such that "iris" is the original, non-normalized data and "iris_n" is the normalized data. Both have 150 observations. Normalization is often recommended when the scales of the predictor variables are very different. This is not the case for the iris data and below we find that the original non-normalized iris data and the normalized data lead to almost identical results.

```
iris_n <- as.data.frame(scale(iris[,1:4], center = TRUE, scale = TRUE))
```

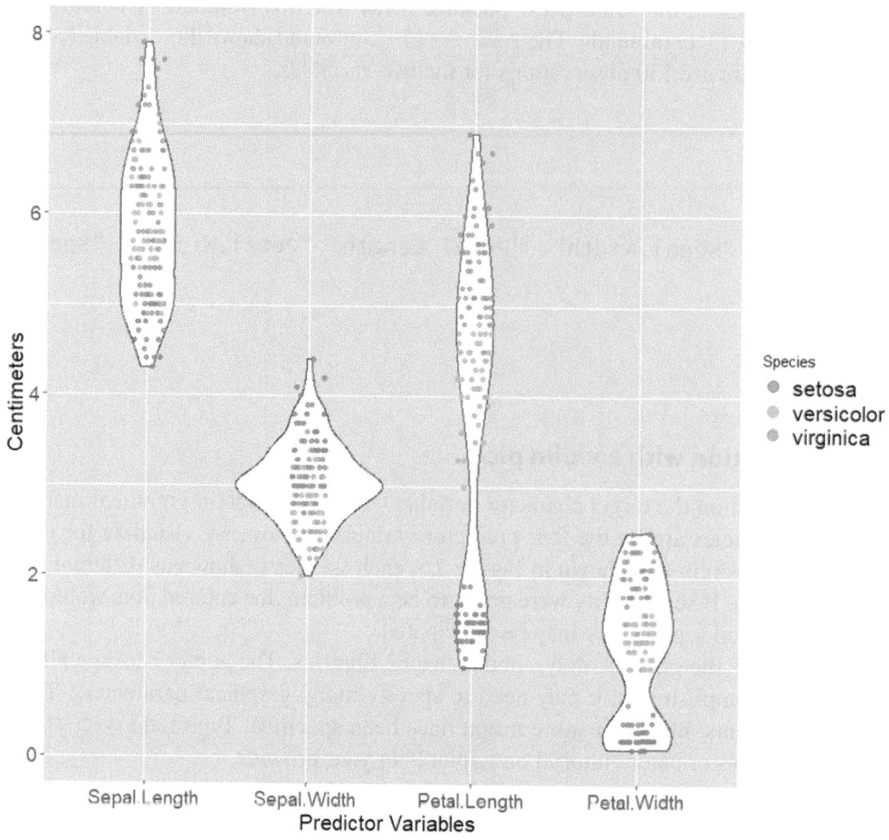

Figure 7.5 Violin plot of species by predictor

Then add the character variable "Species" back into the "iris_n" object, which is a data frame. (Species is upper case in the original data and we retain that usage.)

```
iris_n$Species<- iris$Species
# View result
View(iris_n)
```

7.7.4 Training the model with nnet in caret

We can now train a neural network for the training data. We use the caret package's `train()` command with "nnet" method. The advantages of running nnet in caret is that caret provides automatic cross-validation and automatic tuning of parameters. Other options are as follows:

- linout = TRUE: asks for linear output units. If set to FALSE, logistic output units would be used, suitable for a binary outcome variable, which is not the case in the iris example.
- Entropy = FALSE option is the default, asking for least-squares estimation. If set to TRUE, maximum conditional likelihood estimation would be used.
- skip = FALSE requests no skip layer (no direct connection of inputs to outputs).
- trace = FALSE suppresses the printout of iteration information.
- trControl = trainControl("cv") asks for tenfold cross-validation. By default, 90% of the cases (n = 135) are used for training in each fold and 10% (m = 15) for testing.

Results of training are here placed in the nnet object labeled "model1", which is based on the non-normalized "iris" data.

```
#Fit the nnet model for the iris data
set.seed(123)
model1 <- caret::train(Species ~ Sepal.Length + Sepal.Width + Petal.Length + Petal.
Width,data=iris, method="nnet", linout=TRUE, entropy=FALSE, skip=FALSE, trace =
FALSE, trControl= trainControl("cv"))

model1
[Output, with best solution in red font:]
   Neural Network
   150 samples
     4 predictor
     3 classes: 'setosa', 'versicolor', 'virginica'
   No pre-processing
   Resampling: Cross-Validated (10 fold)
   Summary of sample sizes: 135, 135, 135, 135, 135, 135, ...
   Resampling results across tuning parameters:

     size  decay  Accuracy   Kappa
     1     0e+00  0.6933333  0.54
     1     1e-04  0.8000000  0.70
     1     1e-01  0.9666667  0.95
     3     0e+00  0.8133333  0.72
     3     1e-04  0.9733333  0.96
     3     1e-01  0.9733333  0.96
     5     0e+00  0.9666667  0.95
     5     1e-04  0.9733333  0.96
     5     1e-01  0.9733333  0.96

   Accuracy was used to select the optimal model using the largest value.
   The final values used for the model were size = 3 and decay = 0.1.

#Fit the nnet model for the normalized iris_n data
set.seed(123)
model2 <- caret::train(Species ~ Sepal.Length + Sepal.Width + Petal.Length + Petal.
Width,data=iris_n, method="nnet", linout=TRUE, entropy=FALSE, skip=FALSE, trace =
FALSE, trControl= trainControl("cv"))

model2
[Partial output:]
   Resampling results across tuning parameters:
   size  decay  Accuracy   Kappa
   1     1e-01  0.9666667  0.95

   Accuracy was used to select the optimal model using the largest value.
   The final values used for the model were size = 3 and decay = 0.1.
```

Above, for both the original iris dataset and the normalize iris_n dataset, caret's `train()` program has optimized the size and decay parameters. In each case the optimum is size = 3 and decay = 0.1. In the output shown above, model performance is almost but not quite identical for the two models. The non-normalized iris data has a classification accuracy of 97.33%, fractionally higher than for the normalized data in model2. Another measure of model performance, kappa, is also reported and is also highest for model1.

7.7.5 Obtain model predictions

```
model1Preds<- predict(model1, data=iris, type="raw")
```

We now compute the "confusion table" for model1, which was for the non-normalized iris data. This table shows the correspondence of observed and predicted Species. To create the table we use the `confusionMatrix()` command from the caret package, assumed to have been loaded. This program was discussed in Chapter 3, along with the meaning of associated statistics listed below. Here, this output shows 97.33% classification accuracy for model1.

```
caret::confusionMatrix(model1Preds, iris$Species)
```

[Output:]

```
    Confusion Matrix and Statistics
                Reference
   Prediction    setosa versicolor virginica
     setosa          50          0         0
     versicolor       0         47         1
     virginica        0          3        49

   Overall Statistics


                  Accuracy : 0.9733
                    95% CI : (0.9331, 0.9927)
       No Information Rate : 0.3333
       P-Value [Acc > NIR] : < 2.2e-16

                     Kappa : 0.96

   Mcnemar's Test P-Value : NA

  Statistics by Class:
                       Class: setosa Class: versicolor Class: virginica
  Sensitivity                 1.0000            0.9400           0.9800
  Specificity                 1.0000            0.9900           0.9700
  Pos Pred Value              1.0000            0.9792           0.9423
  Neg Pred Value              1.0000            0.9706           0.9898
  Prevalence                  0.3333            0.3333           0.3333
  Detection Rate              0.3333            0.3133           0.3267
  Detection Prevalence        0.3333            0.3200           0.3467
  Balanced Accuracy           1.0000            0.9650           0.9750
```

Optionally, we may save the predictions to the iris data frame and may save it to a. csv file for later use.

```
# Save to iris_n as a variable named "nnet_preds"
iris$model1Preds<- model1Preds

# Save to file on the current setwd() location under the new filename of iris2.csv
write.csv(iris, file = "iris2.csv", row.names = FALSE)
```

Once the prediction variable (model1Preds) is saved to the iris data frame (even if not saved to disk), the following command will list the row numbers of the misclassified cases.

```
which(iris$Species != iris$model1Preds)
```

[Output:]

```
  [1]  71  73  84  134
```

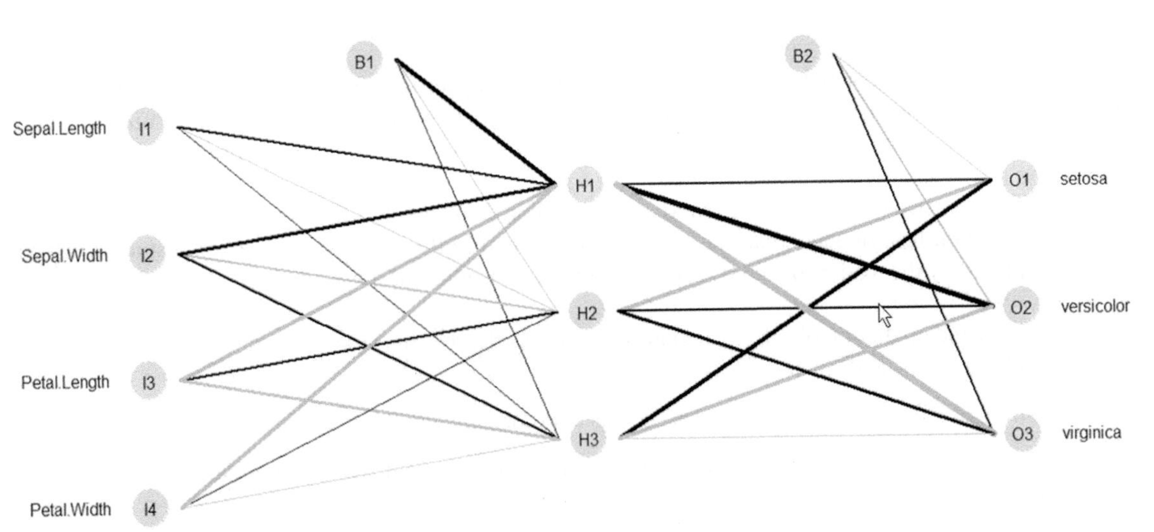

Figure 7.6 Modell Neural Network, Quick Start Example 2

7.7.6 Display the neural model

Optionally, one may display model1 using NeuralNetTools, as in Quick Start Example 1.

```
# Get levels of the DV, in order, label the plot
levels(iris$Species)
[Output:]
   [1] "setosa"      "versicolor" "virginica"

# Use plotnet() to plot the model1 neural network, shown in Figure 7.6.
NeuralNetTools::plotnet(model1, y_names=c("setosa",   "versicolor", "virginica"))
```

PART III: NEURAL NETWORK MODELS IN DETAIL

7.8 Analyzing Boston crime via the neuralnet package

In this section, we use the "neuralnet" package to model crime in Boston municipalities. The outcome variable is "CRIM" and there are several predictor variables, already described in Section 7.2.[3] Previous sections of this chapter ("Quick Start" examples 1 and 2) used the "nnet" package for other examples of neural network analysis. In this section, we explore neuralnet as a more versatile package. The neuralnet package is associated with the work of Frauke Günther and Stefan Fritsch (2010), who designed it for regression problems. However, it is capable of handling classification problems as well.

Advantages of neuralnet compared to nnet:

- Neural models are not limited to a single hidden layer as in nnet.
- More algorithmic methods are available. The nnet package is limited to a single algorithm (BFGS, the Broyden–Fletcher–Goldfarb–Shanno method – even backpropagation is not available).
- More activation functions are supported; whereas the nnet package is limited to the logistic sigmoid function (the popular hyperbolic tangent function is not available, for example).
- In general, there are many more options for tuning the neural model and this may be associated with better model performance compared to nnet.

TEXT BOX 7.1 Applying artificial intelligence to the behavioral and social sciences

Robila and Robila (2020) conducted a systematic examination of peer-reviewed research articles (2010–2019) that used AI methodologies in the social and behavioral sciences with a focus on children and families. Among these methods, neural network analysis was frequently mentioned and the neuralnet package in R, discussed in this chapter, was specifically cited.

Their comprehensive review revealed that that AI has been employed for three main purposes in the study of children and families. In each area, the source articles cited in this test box lists specific studies, which could be explored by the reader (p. 2963). The following three leading purposes were:

1. Diagnosis and prediction of different conditions such as depression, stress, substance abuse, impulsive-compulsive issues, and suicide
2. The study of human development issues such as child obesity and the transition to fatherhood
3. The investigation of social and human services issues such as child welfare and maltreatment, and the quality of nursing services

Robila and Robila (2020: 2964) concluded, "AI has the potential to greatly contribute to science and society and developing partnerships between computer scientists and scholars in behavioral and social sciences to solve complex problems. The increased opportunities for stimulating interdisciplinary work have the potential for developing creative solutions which could result in improved services and improved quality of life."

Source: Robila, M. & Robila, S.A. (2020) Applications of artificial intelligence methodologies to behavioral and social sciences. *Journal of Child and Family Studies* 29: 2954–2966.

Disadvantages or neuralnet compared to nnet:

- Greater complexity and therefore lower ease of use
- Lower computational speed

7.8.1 Setup

As usual, we load the needed packages, set the working directory, and read in the data. Data are read from the "boston_c.csv" data file supplied with this book. The filename stands for corrected Boston data.

```
library(lm.beta)
library(neuralnet)
library(NeuralNetTools)

setwd ("C:/Data")
boston_c <- read.table ("boston_c.csv", header = TRUE, sep = ",", stringsAsFactors =
TRUE)
```

Though for space reasons we do not show output, it may be helpful to view column (variable) names. See Section 7.2 for a listing.

```
names (boston_c)
```
[Output not shown]

For compatibility with neuralnet, we next keep only numeric variables. In addition, we keep CMEDV (corrected median house values) but not the multicollinear MEDV. The retained variables are stored in the data frame labeled "data". This is the data frame used for the remainder of the example.

```
keepvars <- boston_c[,8:21]
# Copy into "data" for convenience
data <- keepvars

# Check for missing (there are none)
apply(data,2,function(x) sum(is.na(x)))
[Output:]
   CMEDV     CRIM       ZN    INDUS     CHAS      NOX       RM
       0        0        0        0        0        0        0
     AGE      DIS      RAD      TAX  PTRATIO        B    LSTAT
       0        0        0        0        0        0        0
```

For cross-validation purposes, we also create "train" and "test" subsets of the data. The model is, of course, trained on the train data and then validated on the test data. Using a different random seed will affect the subsampling process and thus the results. Some 75% of the data are used for training and 25% for testing. Practice in the field, however, varies considerably, typically ranging from 60:40 to 90:10 splits. Here the train set winds up with 380 observations (Boston jurisdictions) and the test set winds up with 126.

```
# Create train and test datasets
set.seed(123)
index <- sample(1:nrow(data),round(0.75*nrow(data)))
train <- data[index,]
nrow(train)
    [1] 380
test <- data[-index,]
nrow(test)
    [1] 126
```

7.8.2 The linear regression model for unscaled data

As a baseline for comparison with the later neuralnet model, we start by creating the "lm model". This refers to R's `lm(()` command for implementing OLS linear regression. The lm model for unscaled data, based on the train data, is put in the object labeled "lm.fit".

```
# "lm.fit" is the lm model. It is based on the train data.
# Using the glm() command would give the same results.
lm.fit <- lm(CRIM~., data=train)
summary(lm.fit)
[Output not shown]
```

Next we compute predicted values for the test data (n = 126), based on the lm.fit model, which in turn is based on training observations in the train subset. The output is placed in the prediction object "pr.lm.test" and is a numeric vector of predictions for the 126 validation observations in the test subset.

```
pr.lm.test <- predict(lm.fit, test)
class(pr.lm.test)
[Output:]
      [1] "numeric"
length(pr.lm.test)
[Output:]
      [1] 126
```

Having developed the model, we then compute its model performance measures when the model is based on the unscaled data in test. The metrics we choose to compute are mean square error (MSE), root mean square error (RMSE), and R-squared (R2). Later we will compare these metrics with those from the neuralnet model.

```
# Mean square error for the test data for the lm model
# Below, pr.lm.test are the predicted values, test$CRIM are the observed values.
# The differences are summed and squared, then divided by the number of observations,
# giving MSE.
MSE.lm.test <- round(sum((pr.lm.test - test$CRIM)^2)/nrow(test),3)
# RMSE for test data, which is simply the square root of MSE.
RMSE.lm.test <- round(sqrt(MSE.lm.test),3)
# R2 for test data for the lm model, which is
# the square of the correlation of predicted and observed values.
predicted_lm <- pr.lm.test
observed_lm <- test$CRIM
R2.lm.test <- round(cor(observed_lm,predicted_lm)^2,3)
# Finally, display all three model performance measures for the test data for the lm model
cat("LM model, unscaled test data:","\n","MSE:", MSE.lm.test, "\n", "RMSE:", RMSE.
lm.test,"\n", "R-square:",R2.lm.test, "\n")
[Output:]
   LM model, unscaled test data:
    MSE: 19.254
    RMSE: 4.388
    R-square: 0.579
```

The lm model metrics above are for the test data. However, the researcher may be interested in obtaining the corresponding measures as applied to the lm model for whole dataset (n = 506). Recall the entire unscaled dataset was copied into the "data" object created above. The process is analogous, where the "data" data frame is substituted for the "test" data frame.

```
# Get predicted values for the entire data
pr.lm.all <- predict(lm.fit, data)
class(pr.lm.all)
[Output:]
      [1] "numeric"
length(pr.lm.all)
[Output:]
      [1] 506

# Mean square error for all observations for the lm model
MSE.lm.all <- round(sum((pr.lm.all - data$CRIM)^2)/nrow(data),3)
# RMSE for test data
RMSE.lm.all <- round(sqrt(MSE.lm.all),3)
# Compute R2 for test data for the lm model
predicted.lm <- pr.lm.all
observed.lm <- data$CRIM
R2.lm.all <- round(cor(observed.lm,predicted.lm)^2,3)
# Print all three model performance measures for all data for the lm model,
# which was based on the train subset
cat("LM model, entire unscaled data:","\n","MSE:", MSE.lm.all, "\n", "RMSE:", RMSE.
lm.all,"\n", "R-square:",R2.lm.all, "\n")
[Output:]
 LM model, entire unscaled data:
  MSE: 40.69
  RMSE: 6.379
  R-square: 0.453
```

7.8.3 The neuralnet model for unscaled data

The corresponding neuralnet model for the same unscaled data did not converge on a solution, instead giving the error message below. It is often possible to overcome such failure-to-converge problems by changing command options. For instance, something as simple as changing the random seed may suffice. Because the model did not converge and in order to illustrate the benefits of scaling, rather than adjusting options instead we followed the usual recommended procedure, which is to scale the data (see Section 7.8.4). Scaled data often work better for neural models.

```
library(neuralnet)
set.seed(123)
nn_model_unscaled <- neuralnet::neuralnet(CRIM ~ CMEDV + ZN + INDUS + CHAS + NOX +
RM + AGE + DIS + RAD + TAX + PTRATIO + B + LSTAT, data = train, hidden =
c(5,3),linear.output = TRUE)
```

[Output:]

```
  Warning message:
  Algorithm did not converge in 1 of 1 repetition(s) within the stepmax.
```

7.8.4 Scaling the data

Recall "data" is the original boston_c data read from a. csv file and train and test are subsets used for training and validation respectively. In this section, we scale the data, test, and train data frames into their scaled equivalents, labeled data_s, test_s and train_s. We use min-max scaling (see the next paragraph on types of scaling).

```
# Get the maximum and minimum values for all variables in the unscaled "data" data frame.
maxs <- apply(data, 2, max)
mins <- apply(data, 2, min)
# Create the scaled data frame, "data_s".
data_s <- as.data.frame(scale(data, center = mins, scale = maxs - mins))
# Create the scaled versions of train and test
train_s <- data_s[index,]
test_s <- data_s[-index,]
```

There are two types of scaling: min-max scaling and z-normalization scaling, also just called "normalization" of data. Below, x1 reflects min-max scaling and is what was done above. Min-max scaling centers the data to range from 0 to 1, which often gives better neural results.

```
x1 <- scale(data, center = mins, scale = maxs - mins)
summary(x1[,"CRIM"])
```

[Output:]

```
     Min.    1st Qu.    Median      Mean   3rd Qu.      Max.
0.0000000 0.0008511 0.0028121 0.0405441 0.0412585 1.0000000
```

Below, x2 reflects the more common normalization scaling in other statistical contexts. This type of scaling centers the data to have a mean of 0 and a standard deviation of 1.

```
x2 <- scale(data, center = TRUE, scale = TRUE)
summary(x2[,"CRIM"])
```

[Output:]

```
 Min.       1st Qu.    Median     Mean      3rd Qu.   Max.
 -0.419367 -0.410563 -0.390280  0.000000  0.007389  9.924110
```

7.8.5 The linear regression model for scaled data

This section presents in abbreviated form the same linear regression analysis as in Section 7.8.2, except using scaled rather than unscaled data. The analysis is for the lm model for the entire scaled dataset (n = 506) located in the "data_s" data frame created previously. The purpose is to provide a comparable baseline to which to compare the subsequent neuralnet model.

```
# Create the lm model for the scaled data
lm.scaled.fit <- lm(CRIM ~ CMEDV + ZN + INDUS + CHAS + NOX + RM + AGE + DIS + RAD +
TAX + PTRATIO + B + LSTAT, data = train_s )
# Get predicted values for the entire data
pr.lm.all.scaled <- predict(lm.scaled.fit, data_s)
# Mean square error
MSE.lm.all.scaled <- round(sum((pr.lm.all.scaled - data$CRIM)^2)/nrow(data),3)
# RMSE
RMSE.lm.all.scaled <- round(sqrt(MSE.lm.all.scaled),3)
# R-squared
predicted.lm.scaled <- pr.lm.all.scaled
observed.lm.scaled <- data_s$CRIM
R2.lm.all.scaled <- round(cor(observed.lm.scaled,predicted.lm.scaled)^2,3)
# Print all three model performance measures.
cat("LM model, entire scaled data:","\n","MSE:", MSE.lm.all.scaled, "\n", "RMSE:",
RMSE.lm.all.scaled,"\n", "R-square:",R2.lm.all.scaled, "\n")
[Output:]
  LM model, entire scaled data:
   MSE: 85.773
   RMSE: 9.261
   R-square: 0.453
```

Because the scale has changed, MSE and RMSE change but R-squared is the same as for the lm model for unscaled data.

7.8.6 The neuralnet model for scaled data

In this section, we now fit the corresponding neuralnet model. The scaled training data (train_s) are used to train the model. The resulting "nn.scaled.fit" neuralnet model converges quickly without error messages. Note that unlike the formula-based linear regression model, random processes are involved in the iterative neural model, and therefore it is necessary to set the random seed. Different random seeds may affect the results, usually just to a small degree.

```
set.seed(123)
nn.scaled.fit <- neuralnet::neuralnet(CRIM ~ CMEDV + ZN + INDUS + CHAS + NOX + RM +
AGE + DIS + RAD + TAX + PTRATIO + B + LSTAT, data = train_s, hidden = c(5,3),linear.
output = TRUE)
```

Observe that the nn.scaled.fit model is a list data type. The lm.scaled.fit object, in contrast, was of data type "lm". Both contain the predictions but the difference in data types will affect how we retrieve them.

```
class(nn.scaled.fit$net.result )
[Output:]
   [1] "list"
```

We now retrieve predicted values for the entire scaled dataset for the neuralnet model. For space reasons we do not analyze predicted values for the test set but for that purpose one would substitute test_s for data_s. For convenience, we put the neuralnet predictions in an object labeled "x".

```
x <- predict(nn.scaled.fit, data_s)
class(x)
[Output:]
   [1] "matrix" "array"
```

Where the results of `predict()` for the lm model were a simple numeric vector of predictions, the corresponding results for the neuralnet model are a matrix. This is because nn.scaled.fit is of "list" type, not "lm" type. However, "x" may be converted into a numeric vector of predictions which we label "pr.nn.all.scaled".

```
pr.nn.all.scaled <- x[,1]
class(pr.nn.all.scaled)
[Output:]
   [1] "numeric"
```

Optionally, we use the `length()` command to verify this is for all 506 cases in the dataset.

```
length(pr.nn.all.scaled)
[Output:]
   [1] 506
```

We are now ready to compute performance measures for the neuralnet model for all observations for the scaled data. This is done in the same manner as for previous models discussed above. Note that this model was based (trained) on train_s but the predictions we discuss here are for the entire data_s data frame.

```
# Compute mean square error
MSE.nn.all.scaled <- round(sum((pr.nn.all.scaled - data_s$CRIM)^2)/nrow(data_s),3)
# RMSE for neuralnet for the entire scaled dataset
RMSE.nn.all.scaled <- round(sqrt(MSE.nn.all.scaled),3)
# Compute R2 also
predicted.nn.all.scaled <- pr.nn.all.scaled
observed.nn.all.scaled <- data_s$CRIM
R2.nn.all.scaled <- round(cor(observed.nn.all.scaled,predicted.nn.all.scaled)^2,3)
# Print all three model performance measures for the neuralnet model
cat("The neuralnet model, entire scaled dataset:","\n","MSE:", MSE.nn.all.scaled,
"\n", "RMSE:", RMSE.nn.all.scaled,"\n", "R-square:",R2.nn.all.scaled, "\n")
[Output:]
   The neuralnet model, entire scaled dataset:
    MSE: 0.001
    RMSE: 0.032
    R-square: 0.885
```

The output above shows that the neuralnet model had markedly lower error and higher R-squared than the lm model, where both were based on scaled data. The neuralnet model explains over 88% of the variance in Boston crime, whereas the linear regression model explained only a little over 45%.

7.8.7 Neuralnet results for the training data

Usually the researcher's interest is in predictions for the entire dataset or for the test data. However, results for the training data may be used to help assess how well training is working. The syntax below relies on two elements of the training model:

- nn.scaled.fit$net.result has the predictions for the 380 cases in the train or train_s data
- nn.scaled.fit$response has the observed values

```
# Get predictions
x <- nn.scaled.fit$net.result
class(x)
     [1] "list"
```

```
# Extract the vector of predictions for CRIM for the training set
predicted <- unlist(x)
class(predicted)
        [1] "numeric"

# Get the observed values
y <- nn.scaled.fit$response
class(y)
        [1] "matrix" "array"
# Extract the vector of observed (response) values for CRIM
observed <- unname(y[,1])
class(observed)
        [1] "numeric"
# Verify that this is for the 380 cases in the scaled train set
length(observed)
        [1] 380
length(predicted)
        [1] 380

# Compute R-squared for the scaled training data, based on the neuralnet model.
R2 <- cor(predicted, observed)^2
R2
[Output:]
        [1] 0.9171628
```

Thus, the neuralnet model explained 91.7% of the variance in Boston crime for the training sample. When this model is generalized to the entire scaled Boston dataset (data_s), we saw earlier that the model explained 88.5%. As here, performance on the training data is usually better than for the test data or than for the entire dataset. If performance on the training sample is poor (not the case here), the model will not generalize well.

7.8.8 Model performance plots

In this section, we plot observed versus predicted values of crime for both the neuralnet (NN) and the linear regression (LM) models. The plot is shown in Figure 7.7.

```
# Setup for 1 column of 2 stacked plots (2 rows):
par(mfrow=c(2,1))
# Plot 1 for LM predictions (blue)
# In R, the "\n" expression inserts a linefeed, here breaking a label into two lines.
# In R, pch is the plotting character type and cex is the character size.
plot(data_s$CRIM, pr.lm.all.scaled,col='blue', xlab="OBSERVED CRIME (SCALED)\nEntire
Dataset", ylab="PREDICTED BY LM", main = "LM Model", pch=18, cex=0.7)
abline(0,1,lwd=2)
legend('bottomright',legend='LM',pch=18,col='blue', bty='n', cex=.95)
# Plot 2 for NN predictions (red)
plot(data_s$CRIM,pr.nn.all.scaled,col='red', xlab="OBSERVED CRIME (SCALED)\nEntire
Dataset", ylab="PREDICTED BY NN", main= "NN Model", pch=18,cex=0.7)
abline(0,1,lwd=2)
legend('bottomright',legend='NN',pch=18,col='red', bty='n')
# Reset graphics
par(mfrow=c(1,1))
```

Figure 7.7 makes visually clear why the neuralnet model (NN) has so much better model performance than the linear regression model (LM). The major reason is that nonlinearity in the data is not captured by the LM method,

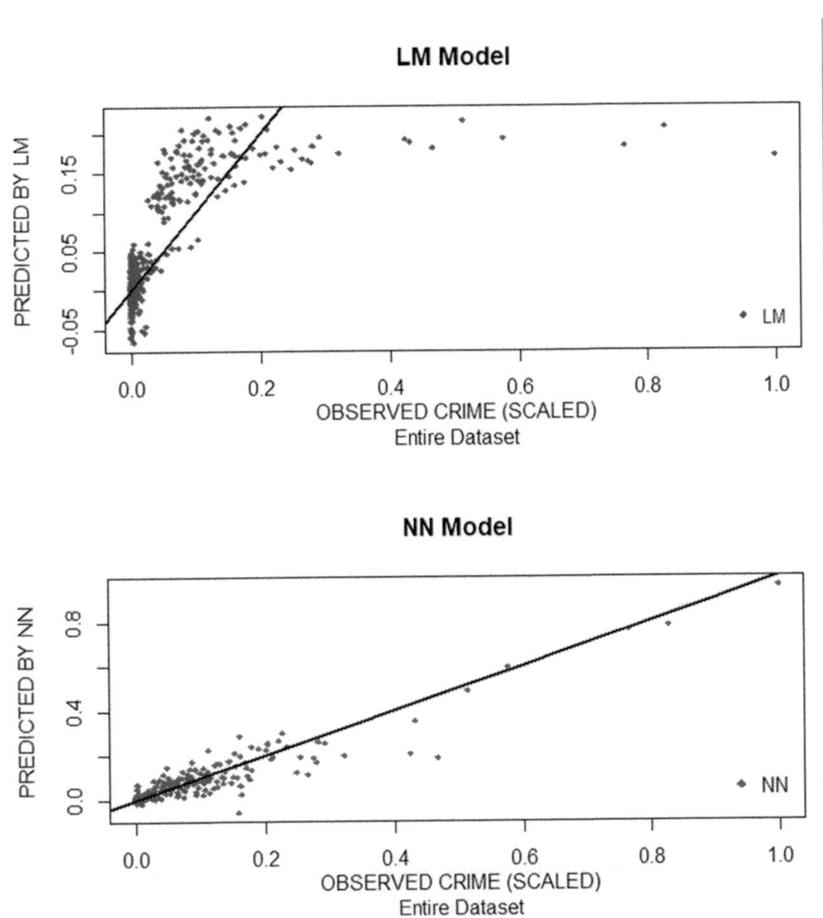

Figure 7.7 Predictions for the LM and NN models

which in effect draws a straight line through a curved pattern of dots. Neural network models automatically capture not only nonlinearities but also interaction effects, causing them to typically outperform linear regression.

7.8.9 Visualizing the neuralnet model

The default method of visualizing the neuralnet model produces a somewhat cluttered plot with path weights shown on the arrows connecting neurons. A more visually pleasing plot is created by the `plotnet()` command from the NeuralNetTools package. In this plot, path weights are represented by varying thickness of lines. The visualization of the neuralnet model is shown in Figure 7.8.

```
# Using the NeuralnetTools package for the model based on scaled data:
NeuralNetTools::plotnet(nn.scaled.fit, pos_col = "blue", neg_col = "red")
# Plots the legend
# pch is the plotting character and pt.cex is its size; cex is the label font size; bty is for no border
legend('bottomright',legend=c("Positive connection","Negative connection"), pch="-",
pt.cex=4, cex=1.2, col=c("blue", "red"), bty='n')

# Using the neuralnet package, for the same model:
# For space reasons, this cluttered plot is not shown. It shows path weights on the arrows.
plot(nn.scaled.fit)
```

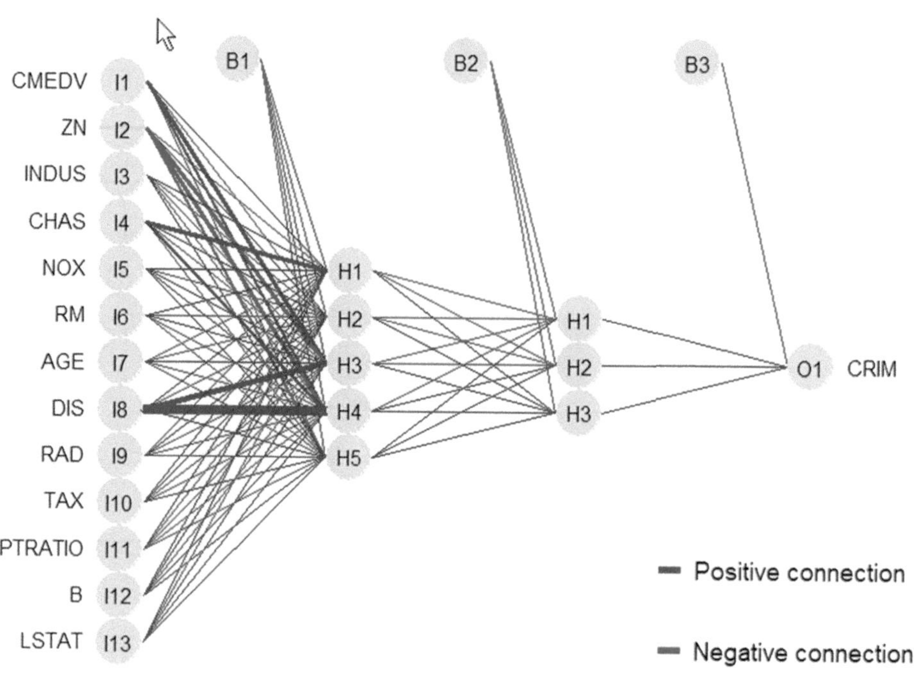

Figure 7.8 The neuralnet model

In Figure 7.8, the first column represents the 13 input variables. The next two columns represent the hidden layers of 5 and 3 neurons respectively. The final layer is the output layer. For regression problems, the output layer has just one neuron, which captures the prediction. In this NeuralNetTools plot, thicker lines represent stronger connection weights. Positive and negative connections are color-coded (the default positive connection color is black, negative is gray, but we use blue and red instead).

7.8.10 Variable importance for the neuralnet model

While neural network models are sometimes described as based on a "black box" method, in fact the relative importance of predictor variables may be calculated. The NeuralNetTools package's `olden()` command, named after the algorithm's author, creates a histogram plot of the importance of predictor variables in the neuralnet model. The Olden et al. (2004) method uses the connection weights between neurons in successive layers for determining variable importance. Specifically, the Olden method calculates variable importance as the product of the raw input-hidden and hidden-output connection weights between each input and output neuron and sums the product across all hidden neurons. The actual values should only be interpreted based on relative sign and magnitude between explanatory variables in the same model. Comparisons between different models should not be made. When there is more than one outcome variable, the results are shown only for the first one but the outcome variable can be changed by specifying the "out_var" option. The resulting plot for the current example is shown in Figure 7.9.

The `olden()` command will generate a listing of the importance coefficient if bar_plot is set to FALSE (TRUE is the default).

```
NeuralNetTools::olden(nn.scaled.fit, bar_plot=FALSE)
[Output (not sorted by importance: use the importance coefficient to rank or use the
bar chart below, which is sorted):]
          importance
CMEDV    -789.116528
```

```
ZN          328.077369
INDUS        47.878322
CHAS       -951.150690
NOX         -33.402038
RM           12.664566
AGE          25.463041
DIS       -2316.329865
RAD         209.320869
TAX          58.449640
PTRATIO       0.372822
B           -70.174195
LSTAT      -155.668700
```

Above, for variable importance by the Olden method for the neuralnet scaled model, it can be seen that the two largest importance effects in a negative direction are DIS and CHAS. The two largest in a positive direction are ZN and RAD.

We now obtain the bar plot for the importance coefficients. This is Figure 7.9.

```
NeuralNetTools::olden(nn.scaled.fit, bar_plot=TRUE)
```

Discussion:

- The largest absolute effect, which is in a negative direction, is between DIS and CRIM. DIS is the weighted mean distance to five Boston employment centers. It appears that the closer to employment centers, the less the crime.
- The second largest absolute effect, also in a negative direction, is between CHAS and CRIM. CHAS is a dummy variable coded 1 = tract bounds the Charles River, 0 = does not. In general, tracts along the Charles River include Back Bay, Cambridge, and more desirable communities, which also are lower in crime.
- The third largest absolute effect, again in a negative direction, is between CMEDV and CRIM. CMEDV is corrected median value of owner-occupied homes. Where homes are more valuable, crime is less.

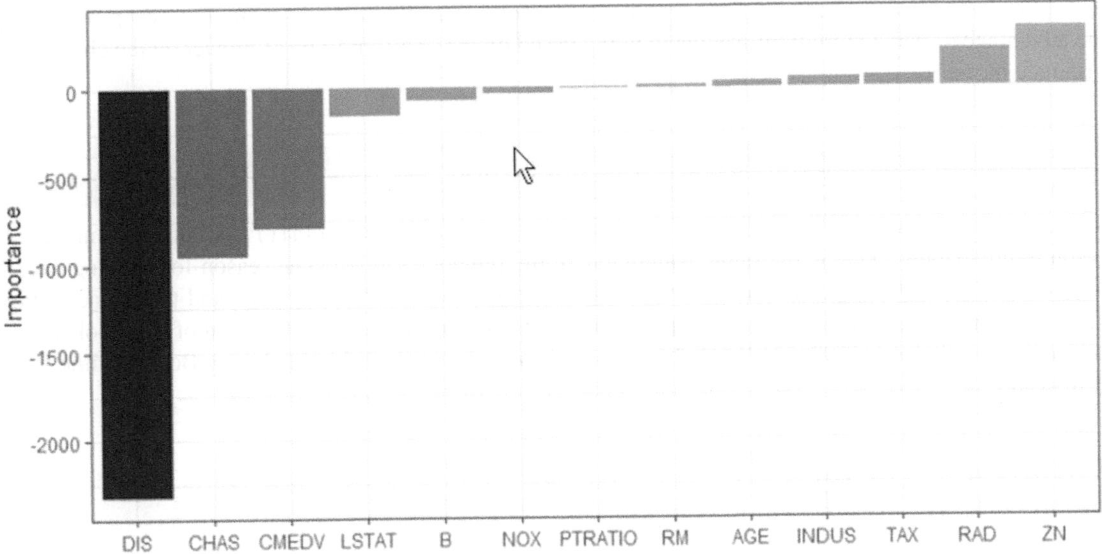

Figure 7.9 Variable importance for the neuralnet model

- The largest effect in a positive direction is between ZN and CRIM. ZN is the percent of residential land zoned for large lots of more than 25,000 square feet. It appears these less dense tracts have more crime.
- The second largest effect in a positive direction is between RAD and CRIM. RAD is an index of accessibility to radial highways. Such accessibility is related to being more central within the city of Boston. Also, radial highways are escape routes for crime. Being closer to radial highways is related to more crime.

In way of comparison, for linear regression the size of the beta weights (printed below; see Chapter 2) is commonly interpreted to reflect the relative importance of the predictor variables. The sign of the beta weights for all five variables found most important in the neural network model matches the direction in the neural model, though this correspondence does not hold for all variables. The order of variable importance in the linear regression model differs, however. The order of the five most important variables based on absolute beta weight in the LM model was RAD, DIS, CMEDV, NOX, and ZN, in that order. However, as the LM model explained much less variance in CRIM than did the NN model, the latter may be preferred as a basis for interpreting variable importance.

```
library(lm.beta)
lm.beta::lm.beta(lm.scaled.fit)
[Output:]
   Standardized Coefficients::
   (Intercept)         CMEDV            ZN         INDUS          CHAS
   0.000000000  -0.226289184   0.129934539  -0.037382272  -0.009477275
           NOX            RM           AGE           DIS           RAD
  -0.144195285   0.038636279   0.019788429  -0.232083956   0.601998456
           TAX       PTRATIO             B         LSTAT
  -0.083502266  -0.073581489  -0.083422700   0.086797232
```

Though we do not do so here, note there is a different way of calculating variable importance for any predictive model, including both neural network models and linear regression models. That is the "drop one" method described in Section 6.12.1. In this method a loop is established that runs the model repeatedly, dropping one of the predictor variables each time. The variable that adversely affects the performance measure (e.g., R-squared, RMSE) the most is judged the most important variable. That variable is set aside and the process repeated with the remaining variables to determine the second-most important variable. And so on. The "drop one" method has the advantage of being more intuitive due to being based on the "bottom line" of impact on the chosen model performance measure.

7.9 Analyzing Boston crime via neuralnet under the caret package

In this section, we use the "neuralnet" package under the "caret" package's `train()` command to model crime in Boston municipalities. This is the same example as in the previous section. The reason for running neuralnet under caret is to take advantage of caret's built-in tenfold cross-validation of the model, and to take advantage of caret's model tuning (optimization) functionality. Section 7.9 is found in the student section of this book's Support Material (www.routledge.com/9780367624293), as a supplement under the title "Analyzing Boston crime via neuralnet with caret".

7.10 Analyzing Boston crime via nnet in caret

In this section, we analyze the same Boston crime dataset as in the previous section. The difference is that we use the "nnet" package rather than "neuralnet" and we do so under the "caret" package, which provides model optimization and cross-validation.

TEXT BOX 7.2 Studying inmate psychopathology with nnet

Do women convicted of drug-related violent crime differ on individual-level risk factors from women convicted of a nondrug-related violent crime and women convicted of nonviolent crimes? To answer this question, Nicholas Thomson (2020) studied the likelihood of a woman prison inmate belonging to a crime group based on levels of psychopathic traits. To do this Thomson used R's "nnet" package in RStudio and other statistical procedures.

While the "nnet" packages is best known for its `nnet()` program to fit neural network solutions, as discussed in this chapter, it also offers a `multinom()` program to fit multinomial log-linear models. In the case of his analysis, Thomson used the `multinom()` procedure. Log-linear analysis was discussed in Sections 3.7 and 3.5.5.5.

The rationale for this text box, however, is to point up the multiplicity of supporting programs for any given R procedure. Thus, there are many supplementary supporting programs for each of the `nnet()` and `multinom()` commands. The reader may find valuable additional functions not part of introductory discussions of the main commands associated with any package. In RStudio, click on the "Packages" tab, then on "nnet" or "multinom", then on any of the programs listed below to see what each does.

Fit neural networks	**Fit multinomial log-linear models**
nnet	multinom
add.net	add1.multinom
coef.nnet	anova.multinom
eval.nn	coef.multinom
nnet.default	drop1.multinom
nnet.formula	extractAIC.multinom
nnetHess	logLik.multinom
norm.net	model.frame.multinom
predict.nnet	predict.multinom
print.nnet	print.multinom
print.summary.nnet	print.summary.multinom
summary.nnet	summary.multinom
	vcov.multinom

Thomson's analysis indicated that female "inmates higher in antisocial psychopathic traits and low level of educational attainment were more likely to be in the drug-related violent crime group. In comparison, inmates higher in callous psychopathic traits were more likely to be in the nondrug-related violent crime group" (p. 794).

Source: Thomson, Nicholas D. (2020). An exploratory study of female psychopathy and drug-related violent crime. *Journal of Interpersonal Violence* 35(3–4): 794–808.

7.10.1 Setup

For purposes of this section, we assume that all the setup steps for Section 7.8 have been completed. However, for convenience, the relevant commands are shown below with a minimum of comments.

```
# Load needed libraries (caret and nnet differ from the previous section)
library(caret)
library(lm.beta)
library(nnet)
library(NeuralNetTools)
```

```
# Set the working directory and load the data
setwd ("C:/Data")
boston_c <- read.table ("boston_c.csv", header = TRUE, sep = ",", stringsAsFactors =
TRUE)
keepvars <- boston_c[,8:21]
# Copy into "data" for convenience
data <- keepvars
# Create the train and test datasets
set.seed(123)
index <- sample(1:nrow(data),round(0.75*nrow(data)))
train <- data[index,]
test <- data[-index,]
# Create the scaled versions: data_s, train_s, and test_s
# Get the maximum and minimum values for all variables in the unscaled "data" data frame.
maxs <- apply(data, 2, max)
mins <- apply(data, 2, min)
# Create the scaled data frame, "data_s".
data_s <- as.data.frame(scale(data, center = mins, scale = maxs - mins))
# Create scaled versions of train and test
train_s <- data_s[index,]
test_s <- data_s[-index,]
```

The commands above created, among other objects, the data_s, train_s and test_s scaled data frames for the crime data on 506 Boston-area jurisdictions, with 380 in the training data frame and 126 in the test (validation) data frame.

7.10.2 The nnet/caret model of Boston crime

The first step in creating a model using nnet is to set a random seed. The caret package does not attempt to optimize for seed (which sets starting values) or for the "rang" parameter (which sets the range for starting values). However, setting the seed only makes a relatively small difference when nnet is implemented in caret due to the other optimization algorithms built into caret's `train()` procedure.

In a two-step process, we define the parameters for the `train()` command, then we fit the model for the training data, which are in the object train_s. Specifically, we ask for tenfold cross-validation repeated three times. We also use lowest error as measured by RMSE as the fitting metric.

```
# 1. Define caret control parameters
ctrl = caret::trainControl(method = "repeatedcv",
    number = 10,
    repeats = 3,
    returnResamp = "all",
    savePredictions = "all")

# 2. Fit the model
set.seed(123)
metric = "RMSE"
nnet_model = caret::train(CRIM ~ CMEDV + ZN + INDUS + CHAS + NOX + RM + AGE + DIS +
RAD + TAX + PTRATIO + B + LSTAT,
     data = train_s,
     method = "nnet",
     linout=TRUE,
     metric = metric,
     trControl = ctrl,
     trace = FALSE)
```

```
# This returns an ignorable warning message.
[Output:]
   Warning message:
   In nominalTrainWorkflow(x = x, y = y, wts = weights, info = trainInfo,  :
     There were missing values in resampled performance measures.
```

To understand the error message, look at some of the resamplings:

```
head(nnet_model$resample,10)
[Partial output:]
           RMSE   Rsquared        MAE size decay   Resample
   1  0.03266987 0.75150165 0.01636129    1 0e+00 Fold01.Rep1
   2  0.05323102 0.52561549 0.02828762    3 0e+00 Fold01.Rep1
   3  0.03511574 0.76724029 0.01800894    5 0e+00 Fold01.Rep1
   4  0.04460567 0.62181928 0.03117211    1 1e-01 Fold01.Rep1
   5  0.04502770 0.61842529 0.03175750    3 1e-01 Fold01.Rep1
   6  0.04494167 0.61949626 0.03166817    5 1e-01 Fold01.Rep1
   7  0.03389096 0.73121669 0.01774392    1 1e-04 Fold01.Rep1
   8  0.04251004 0.58111710 0.02158542    3 1e-04 Fold01.Rep1
   9  0.03774431 0.73668093 0.01812228    5 1e-04 Fold01.Rep1
   10 0.05768540         NA 0.04871070    1 0e+00 Fold02.Rep1
```

Above, the "NA" for resample 10 is the only resampling among a large number where the problem occurred. The algorithm is still able to compute stable performance measures across many resamplings (RMSE, Rsquared, MAE), so the warning may be ignored.

We can view nnet's results in the $results element:

```
nnet_model$results
[Output:]
     size decay       RMSE  Rsquared        MAE
   1    1 0e+00 0.07036369 0.5887109 0.03176398
   2    1 1e-04 0.06707024 0.6494515 0.02766113
   3    1 1e-01 0.07151120 0.5638511 0.03267990
   4    3 0e+00 0.10712251 0.6010540 0.03339339
   5    3 1e-04 0.09213301 0.5733979 0.03057702
   6    3 1e-01 0.07175691 0.5617129 0.03297293
   7    5 0e+00 0.22625801 0.5578640 0.05291948
   8    5 1e-04 0.09770188 0.5891441 0.03219969
   9    5 1e-01 0.07182370 0.5603808 0.03301601

         RMSESD RsquaredSD       MAESD
   1 0.03613032  0.2394380 0.013430358
   2 0.03418331  0.1970791 0.009993502
   3 0.03805732  0.1847752 0.008160216
   4 0.17078604  0.2374112 0.028969370
   5 0.05894054  0.2402197 0.012345703
   6 0.03792679  0.1849597 0.008214108
   7 0.42732018  0.2782147 0.075374520
   8 0.07915669  0.2339964 0.016488848
   9 0.03801777  0.1856148 0.008235438
```

At the bottom of the listing for the nnet_model object, the `train()` algorithm shows its optimization of the model. Note the coefficients pertain to the 380 observations in the train_s training sample.

```
nnet_model
[Partial output:]
   Neural Network
   380 samples
```

```
 13 predictor
No pre-processing
Resampling: Cross-Validated (10 fold, repeated 3 times)
Summary of sample sizes: 341, 342, 342, 343, 342, 342, ...
Resampling results across tuning parameters:
  size  decay  RMSE        Rsquared   MAE
  1     0e+00  0.07036369  0.5887109  0.03176398
  1     1e-04  0.06707024  0.6494515  0.02766113
  1     1e-01  0.07151120  0.5638511  0.03267990
  . . .
  5     1e-01  0.07182370  0.5603808  0.03301601
RMSE was used to select the optimal model using
 the smallest value.
The final values used for the model were size =
 1 and decay = 1e-04.
```

Above, the `train()` algorithm, based on resampling and using the "nnet" method with lowest error as measured by RMSE as the evaluation criterion, has selected as optimal the model with size = 1 and decay = 0.0001. We have shown the row for this solution in red. The nnet method supports only one hidden layer, and `train()` is recommending one neuron in that layer. The R-squared for this solution shows a model which explains 64.9% of the variance in Boston crime in the scaled training subset of 380 observations (in train_s).

Based on the caret/nnet model, we can predict CRIM for the 126 cases in the test_s data:

```
nnet_preds <- predict(nnet_model, newdata=test_s)
length(nnet_preds)
```

[Output:]

```
  [1] 126
```

To get a comparison with linear regression (lm), we next get the caret/lm model based on the 380 cases in the scaled train_s data. In code below, note that linear regression doesn't need the linout= or trace= settings used earlier for the nnet_model.

```
set.seed(123)
metric = "RMSE"
lm_model = caret::train(CRIM ~ CMEDV + ZN + INDUS + CHAS + NOX + RM + AGE + DIS +
RAD + TAX + PTRATIO + B + LSTAT,
     data = train_s,
     method = "lm",
     metric = metric,
     trControl = ctrl)
lm_model
```

[Partial output:]

```
  Linear Regression
  380 samples
```

We then get predictions of CRIM using the caret/lm model. These predictions are for the 126 cases in the test_s data.

```
lm_preds <- predict(lm_model, newdata=test_s)
length(lm_preds)
```

[Output:]

```
  [1] 126
```

Having obtained the predictions both for the nnet model (nnet_preds) and the linear regression model (lm_preds), we create comparison plots of the nnet and lm solutions. This is shown in Figure 7.10. For the linear regression portion, the straight line represents the linear prediction, which fails to capture curvilinearity in the data. For the nnet portion, the lowess smoothing line represents the curvilinearity in the data. It can be seen that nnet predictions roughly follow the lowess line, capturing more of the curvilinearity in the data.

```
# Set graphics for two side-by-side plots
par(mfrow=c(1,2))
# Plot the linear regression (lm) solution for the test_s validation data
plot(lm_preds, test_s$CRIM, col="red", xlab="LM Predictions", ylab= "Observed CRIM")
abline(lm(test_s$CRIM ~ lm_preds),col="darkred")
# Plot caret's nnet solution with both linear trend and loess smoothing lines
plot(nnet_preds, test_s$CRIM, col="blue", xlab="NNET Predictions", ylab= "Observed
CRIM")
abline(lm(test_s$CRIM ~ nnet_preds),col="darkred")
loessline <- loess(test_s$CRIM~nnet_preds,data=test_s)
j <- order(nnet_preds)
lines(nnet_preds[j],loessline$fitted[j],col="darkblue",lwd=3)
# Reset for single plotting in the future
par(mfrow=c(1,1))
```

We now compute R-squared for the nnet via caret model and for the linear regression (lm) models. Both are for the test_s validation data. As elsewhere in this chapter, R-squared is defined as the square of the correlation of predicted and observed values.

```
# For nnet
R2_nnet <- (cor(nnet_preds,test_s$CRIM))^2
R2_nnet
[Output:]
    [1] 0.7554375

# For lm
R2_lm<- (cor(lm_preds,test_s$CRIM))^2
R2_lm
[Output:]
      [1] 0.5791103
```

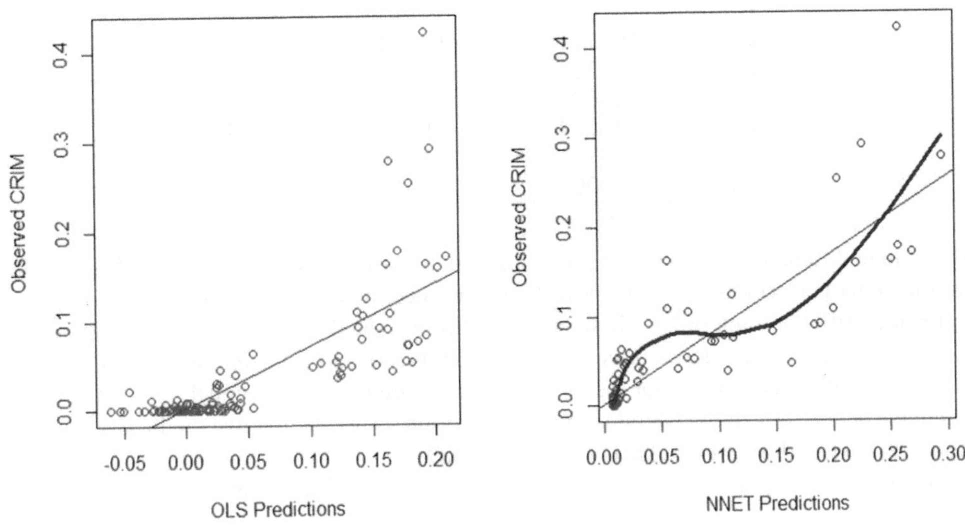

Figure 7.10 NNET and LM solutions, Boston Crime Test Subset

We see above that the nnet neural network solution under caret accounts for a higher percentage of the variance in Boston crime than does linear (OLS) regression, on a cross-validated basis (i.e., using the model trained on the train_s data to predict the validation cases in the test_s data). This follows in part from the fact that there is nonlinearity in the data, as highlighted by the lowess smoothing line in Figure 7.10. The R-squared for the nnet solution for these data was 0.755, higher than for the lm solution (0.579).

7.10.3 Variable importance for the nnet/caret model

Descriptions of neural network models as "black boxes" notwithstanding, it is easy to obtain a ranking of variable importance for the nnet model (the nnet_model object) compared to the lm model (lm_model) using the `varImp()` command. This object was the nnet model created in the previous section based on the train_s data frame, and it is the same model later applied to the test_s data by the `predict()` command. The object lm_model was the `lm()` object created based on the train_s data and predicted for the test_s data. In Section 7.10.1, data_s, train_s, and test_s were created. In Section 7.10.2, lm_model and nnet_model were created.

The `varImp()` command is part of the previously-loaded "caret" package. It computes variable importance for a wide variety of types of models, including those generated by the lm and nnet methods. For linear models the reported coefficient is the absolute value of the t-statistic for each model parameter. For nnet models the criterion is based on Gevrey, Dimopoulos, and Lek (2003), which employs combinations of the absolute values of the weights. While the lm and nnet values reported below are not comparable, the point is to compare the variable importance rankings of each predictor in the two models.

```
caret::varImp(object= nnet_model)
caret::varImp(object= lm_model)
```

[Output for nnet:]	Overall	[Output for lm:]	Overall
DIS	100.000	RAD	100.0000
CMEDV	41.690	CMEDV	47.7699
RAD	31.863	DIS	45.2207
ZN	19.138	ZN	33.4148
AGE	13.874	B	28.4094
LSTAT	11.840	NOX	26.6348
PTRATIO	11.105	PTRATIO	19.6878
TAX	10.182	LSTAT	16.1787
NOX	6.254	TAX	8.3243
CHAS	4.639	RM	7.8672
B	3.054	INDUS	4.0307
RM	1.391	AGE	0.9335
INDUS	0.000	CHAS	0.0000

The rankings are quite different between the nnet and lm models, based on scaled data in each case. They are also different from the better-performing neuralnet model. For instance, while the top four predictors are the same in both models, albeit in different rank order. These four are DIS (weighted mean distances to employment centers), CMEDV (median value of housing), RAD (access to radial highways), and ZN (zoning). After this there is greater variation in variable importance ranking for the NN model compared to the lm model. For comparison of importance rankings in the better-performing neuralnet model in Section 7.8.10, the top five predictors in order were DIS, CHAS (adjacency to the Charles River), CMEDV, ZN, and RAD.

Though not shown here for space reasons, nnet variable importance rankings may be visualized by the `plot()` command below.

```
plot(varImp(object = nnet_model),main="NNET - Variable Importance")
```

Naturally, nnet predictions may be saved to the data frame and the data frame can be saved to file. These same commands would work for other predictions discussed in this chapter.

```
# Create training-based predictions for the entire data_s data frame
nnet_preds_data_s<- predict(nnet_model, data_s)

# Save to data_s
data_s$nnet_preds <- nnet_preds_data_s

# Save to file under the new filename "BostonCrime_Scaled.csv "
write.csv(data_s, file = "BostonCrime_Scaled.csv", row.names = FALSE)
```

7.10.4 Further tuning the nnet model outside caret

Employing nnet outside caret may lead to slightly different results, depending on the parameters employed. In particular, the random seed starting values can make a much larger difference than when employing nnet inside caret. By casting a wider parameter search, a higher observed-predicted R-squared may be obtained. This was the case for the example in this section, though here we used only onefold cross-validation whereas the caret approach in the previous section used tenfold cross-validation. We acknowledge that tenfold cross-validation, which is easy and automated under caret, which is a preferred approach to validating models than is using a single random train/test split of the data as in this section.

The `nnet()` program from the nnet package estimates a neural network with a single hidden layer. It optionally supports skip-layer connections, which are direct connections from the input to the output layer. A model with skip-layer connections reflects a sum of a linear model plus nonlinear neural model components. Below, the nnet model is run on the scaled "train_s" training data subset created in Section 7.10.1. To run the model, a number of parameters must be set:

- *decay=0* specifies no decay of weights between iterations and is the default Documentation examples use decay = 5e-4
- *entropy=FALSE* is the default, using least squares estimation
- *entropy=TRUE* uses maximum conditional likelihood estimation for logistic problems
- *linout=TRUE* must be the setting for regression problems
- *maxit=100* is the default maximum number of iterations
- *MaxNWts* sets the maximum number of weights that may be used in the solution Setting MaxNWts higher than the default (1000) may improve fit but is time-consuming
- *rang=0.7* sets initial random starting values between +/–0.7, which is the default Documentation suggest 0.5 but when inputs are large, set so that rang * max(|x|) is about 1
- `set.seed()` is not a parameter of `nnet()` but strongly affects its starting weights
- *size* is the number of neurons in the one hidden layer allowed. The size parameter can be 0 if skip-layer units are allowed
- *skip=FALSE* is the default and disallows direct connections between input to output layers
- *trace=TRUE* is the default, asking for trace information

The random seed, range of starting values (the rang parameter), size, and decay all impact the performance of `nnet()` models, sometimes substantially. The syntax below performs a grid search for the best seed, rang (because "range" is a reserved word), and size for the training data. The search below was for seeds from 1 to 200, rang from .1 to .9, and size from 1 to 10. For decay, we used 0.01, taking that value from the optimization of nnet for caret in the previous section (we could have added decay as a fourth loop of the grid search, but found results satisfactory without the extra computational time required). Yet other parameters might optimize the model even further.

```
# Loop to find the best random parameters by grid search
# R2 is R-squared, a performance metric
```

```
# We use size = 1, decay = .0001, as these were optimal values found using nnet under caret
# Initialize loop
bestrang=-1
bestsize=-1
bestR2 = -1
# Below we must use integers for indexes; later we divide rang by 10 to get fractional values.
maxrang= 9
maxseed = 200
maxsize = 10

# Start loop for seed
for(i in 1:maxseed) {
# Start inner loop for rang
for(j in 1:maxrang) {
# Start third loop for size
for(k in 1:maxsize){
set.seed(i)
j2 = j/10
nnetModel <- nnet::nnet(CRIM ~ CMEDV + ZN + INDUS + CHAS + NOX + RM + AGE + DIS +
RAD + TAX + PTRATIO + B + LSTAT, size=k, linout = TRUE, skip = FALSE, MaxNWts =
1000, entropy = FALSE, rang = j2, trace = FALSE, maxit = 100, decay = .0001, data =
train_s)

# Get nnet predictions for the test_s dataset based on the train_s dataset model above
# If this were a classification problem, set type = "class"
nnetPredsTest <- predict(nnetModel, newdata = test_s, type="raw")

# Skip ahead in loop if no variance in predictions
if (sd(nnetPredsTest) == 0){ next }

# Compute R2 for observed-predicted correlation
R2 <- (cor(nnetPredsTest, test_s$CRIM))^2

# Update the loop
if (R2>bestR2){bestseed <- i}
if (R2>bestR2){bestrang <- j}
if (R2>bestR2){bestsize <- k}
if (R2>bestR2){bestR2 <- R2}

# Keep the researcher informed of progress during lengthy looping
writeLines(paste("R2 = ", round(R2,3),"Best R2 =", round(bestR2,3),"Best seed: ",
bestseed,"Best size",bestsize, "Best rang: ", bestrang/10))
}
}
}

# Print loop results for the test dataset
[Partial output:]
bestR2
     [1,] 0.8876424
bestseed
     [1] 29
bestrang
     [1] 9
bestsize
     [1] 3
```

We see above that when nnet is run on the example data with seed = 29, rang = 9/10 = 0.9, and size = 3, we obtain an R-squared for the training data of 0.888. The training-based model explains 88.8% of the variance in the test (validation) data. This is higher than the corresponding caret-based nnet model in Section 7.10.2. The difference reflects the fact that the tuning done automatically by caret is more restricted than the grid search for best tuning parameters done in this section.

Below, we swap in these optimal parameters and retest the model, obtaining the exactly the same R-squared results. Had we somehow known these optimal parameter values we could have gone directly to this step, skipping the grid search.

```
set.seed(29)
nnetModel2 <- nnet::nnet(CRIM ~ CMEDV + ZN + INDUS + CHAS + NOX + RM + AGE + DIS +
RAD + TAX + PTRATIO + B + LSTAT, size=3, linout=TRUE, skip=FALSE, MaxNWts=1000,
entropy=FALSE, rang=.9, trace=FALSE, maxit=100, decay=  .0001, data=train_s)

nnetPredsTest2 <- predict(nnetModel2, newdata=test_s, type="raw")

R2 <- (cor(nnetPredsTest2, test_s$CRIM))^2
R2
[Output:]
        [1,] 0.8876424
```

7.11 A classification model of marital status using nnet

7.11.1 Setup

Where regression problems deal with continuous outcome variables, classification problems deal with categorical ones. The "nnet" package can handle both. In this section, we provide a classification example using nnet. Specifically, we see if nnet can classify survey respondents by their marital status, where the classes of marital status are 1 = married, 2 = widowed, 3 = divorced, 4 = separated, 5 = never married. Data are drawn for an older General Social Survey of 2,050 U.S. individuals on 21 variables, as found in the file "surveysample.csv" available in the student section of this book's Support Material (www.routledge.com/9780367624293). Classification essentially parallels previous regression examples, though more effort is required to properly label the levels of categorical variables.

The five packages below should be loaded.

```
library(nnet)         # the neural network package used in this section
library(caret)        # provides a training shell for nnet
library(ggplot2)      # creates the violin plot below
library(plyr)         # Load this before dplyr
library(dplyr)        # supports the %>% operator (for violin plots)
library(reshape2)     # contains the melt() command to get names for violin plots
```

```
# Read in the data and view the names of available variables.
setwd("C:/Data")
surveysample <- read.table("surveysample.csv", header = TRUE, sep = ",",
stringsAsFactors = TRUE)
View(surveysample)
names(surveysample)
[Output:]
   [1]  "id"        "wrkstat"  "marital"  "childs"
   [5]  "age"       "educ"     "degree"   "sex"
   [9]  "race"      "born"     "income"   "polviews"
   [13] "cappun"    "happy"    "hapmar"   "tvhours"
   [17] "agecat"    "childcat" "news1"    "news5"
   [21] "car1"
```

```
# Ask for the data's structure, showing all variables are integer in class
str(surveysample)
[Partial output:]
    'data.frame':      2050 obs. of  21 variables:
    $ id       : int  1 2 3 4 5 6 7 8 9 10 ...
    $ wrkstat  : int  2 5 5 5 1 5 2 1 5 5 ...
    $ marital  : int  3 1 1 1 1 1 4 2 1 2 ...
    . . .
    $ car1     : int  6 6 6 6 6 6 6 6 6 6 ...
```

The command below checks for missing values; no variable has missing values. Had there been missing values, we might consider data imputation, discussed in a supplement to Chapter 3 and elsewhere in this book.

```
apply(surveysample,2,function(x) sum(is.na(x)))
[Output:]
   id  wrkstat  marital   childs      age      educ   degree
    0        0        0        0        0         0        0
   sex     race     born   income polviews   cappun    happy
   0        0        0        0        0         0        0
   hapmar  tvhours   agecat childcat news1    news5     car1
   0        0        0        0        0         0        0
```

The outcome variable is "marital". It is an integer variable. To demonstrate classification, we need to convert its present coding to be a factor variable.

```
class(surveysample$marital)
[Output:]
      [1] "integer"

# Convert marital to be a factor
surveysample$marital<-as.factor(surveysample$marital)

# Rename factor levels (presently "1" through "5") to character equivalents
surveysample$marital <- plyr::revalue(surveysample$marital, c("1"= "married", "2" =
"widowed", "3" = "divorced", "4" = "separated", "5" = "never married"))

class(surveysample$marital)
[Output:]
      [1] "factor"

levels(surveysample$marital)
[Output:]
   [1] "married"        "widowed"        "divorced"        "separated"        "never
   married"

# Similarly, convert nominal variables to factor variables and rename levels
# We do not convert binary or ordinal variables
# Changes may not appear until View(surveysample) is refreshed.
surveysample$wrkstat<-as.factor(surveysample$wrkstat)
surveysample$wrkstat <- plyr::revalue(surveysample$wrkstat, c("1"= "full-time", "2" =
"part_time", "3" = "temp not working", "4" = "unemployed", "5" = "retired", "6" =
"school", "7" = "keeping house", "8" = "other"))
surveysample$race<-as.factor(surveysample$race)
surveysample$race <- plyr::revalue(surveysample$race, c("1"="white", "2" = "black",
"3" = "other"))
surveysample$car1 <- as.factor(surveysample$car1)
```

```
surveysample$car1 <- plyr::revalue(surveysample$car1, c("1"= "American", "2" =
"Japanese", "3" = "Korean", "4" = "German", "5" = "Swedish", "6" = "Other"))
```

7.11.2 The nnet classification model of marital status

As satisfactory performance was later achieved without scaling or normalizing the data, we skip that step for the surveysample example. Instead we proceed to classification of the "marital" variable using nnet as implemented by caret, starting by creating the training and validation datasets. We start by creating the train and test subsets or surveysample, placing two-thirds of the observations in train and one third in test.

```
set.seed(123)
index <- sample(1:nrow(surveysample),round(0.67*nrow(surveysample)))
train <- surveysample[index,]
test <- surveysample[-index,]

# Set a random seed and train the model using the training data
set.seed(123)
nnet_surveysample_model <- caret::train(marital ~  childs+age+educ+tvhours+degree+in
come+polviews+cappun+happy+ hapmar+race+wrkstat+car1, method='nnet', linout=TRUE,
entropy=FALSE, skip=FALSE, trace = FALSE, data = train)
```

We then list the model to confirm it is for the 1,374 observations in the train set. In the last line of output we view the optimal parameters estimated automatically by caret. These parameters are size = 5 and decay = 0.1. With these parameters, the best model by accuracy (percent classified correctly) is shown in red font.

```
nnet_surveysample_model
[Partial output:]
   Neural Network
   1374 samples
     13 predictor
      5 classes: 'married', 'widowed', 'divorced', 'separated', 'never married'
  . . .
  Resampling results across tuning parameters:
    size  decay  Accuracy   Kappa
    1     0e+00  0.5347742  0.1664184
    1     1e-04  0.5175049  0.1313776
    . . .
    5     1e-04  0.7361266  0.5791687
    5     1e-01  0.8188004  0.7330763
  Accuracy was used to select the optimal model using the largest value.
  The final values used for the model were size = 5 and decay = 0.1.
```

Variable importance may be obtained using caret's `varImp()` command exactly the same as for the regression model in Section 7.10. Note that nominal variables like wrkstat have been converted to dummy variables automatically. Unfortunately, level-specific importance is not available for classification models. Therefore, the coefficients in the level columns (e.g., "married") are all the same as for "Overall". That is, the "Overall" column is the only one needed to rank variables by importance. The three top variables by importance are age, hapmar, and educ, in that order.

```
varImp(object=nnet_surveysample_model)
[Partial output:]
  nnet variable importance
  variables are sorted by maximum importance across the classes
  only 20 most important variables shown (out of 24)
                        Overall married widowed divorced separated never married
age                     100.000 100.000 100.000  100.000   100.000       100.000
hapmar                   60.455  60.455  60.455   60.455    60.455        60.455
```

```
educ              50.417  50.417  50.417  50.417  50.417  50.417
income            24.859  24.859  24.859  24.859  24.859  24.859
wrkstatother      24.802  24.802  24.802  24.802  24.802  24.802
childs            22.319  22.319  22.319  22.319  22.319  22.319
.. .
happy              9.635   9.635   9.635   9.635   9.635   9.635
raceother          6.864   6.864   6.864   6.864   6.864   6.864
cappun             4.616   4.616   4.616   4.616   4.616   4.616
```

We now use the train-based model to predict the test data and verify that this is for the 676 cases in the test (validation) data. We then view the first ten predictions.

```
nnet_surveysample_preds_test <- predict(nnet_surveysample_model, newdata = test,
type="raw")

length(nnet_surveysample_preds_test)
[Output:]
      [1] 676

head(nnet_surveysample_preds_test,10)
[Output:]
  [1] married  divorced married  widowed  married  married
  [7] married  married married  divorced
  Levels: married widowed divorced separated never married
```

In order to view nnet model performance, below we then compute the "confusion table" for the 676 cases in the test (validation) sample. This table shows the correspondence of observed and predicted race. To create the table we use the `confusionMatrix()` command from the caret package. Here, this output shows high classification accuracy (Accuracy = 82.4%) for the nnet model as applied to the test_s data. The meaning of other measures shown below was discussed in Chapter 4.

```
confusionMatrix(nnet_surveysample_preds_test,test$marital)
[Output:]
  Confusion Matrix and Statistics

                  Reference
  Prediction       married widowed divorced separated never married
    married            311       0        0         0             1
    widowed              0      36       25         1             1
    divorced             1      16       85        11            20
    separated            0       0        0         0             0
    never married        0       8       30         5           125

  Overall Statistics

                 Accuracy : 0.824
                   95% CI : (0.7931, 0.8519)
      No Information Rate : 0.4615
      P-Value [Acc > NIR] : < 2.2e-16

                    Kappa : 0.7426
   Mcnemar's Test P-Value : NA

  Statistics by Class:

                       Class: married Class: widowed Class: divorced
  Sensitivity                  0.9968        0.60000          0.6071
  Specificity                  0.9973        0.95617          0.9104
  Pos Pred Value               0.9968        0.57143          0.6391
```

```
Neg Pred Value                 0.9973      0.96085         0.8987
Prevalence                     0.4615      0.08876         0.2071
Detection Rate                 0.4601      0.05325         0.1257
Detection Prevalence           0.4615      0.09320         0.1967
Balanced Accuracy              0.9970      0.77808         0.7588

                  Class: separated Class: never married
Sensitivity                0.00000               0.8503
Specificity                1.00000               0.9187
Pos Pred Value                 NaN               0.7440
Neg Pred Value             0.97485               0.9567
Prevalence                 0.02515               0.2175
Detection Rate             0.00000               0.1849
Detection Prevalence       0.00000               0.2485
Balanced Accuracy          0.50000               0.8845
```

While the researcher is often interested in the accuracy coefficient for the validation (test) data, it is also of interest to know accuracy for all 2,050 cases in the surveysample data frame. We do this below, finding that the model has 84.78% classification accuracy for the entire sample. There are 312 errors, which are seen below as all of the off-diagonal cases in the confusion matrix. Proportionately the most errors occurred for separated respondents, none of whom were classified correctly. In contrast, all but 1 of the 946 married respondents were classified correctly.

```
nnet_surveysample_preds_all<- predict(nnet_surveysample_model, newdata=surveysample,
type="raw")
confusionMatrix(nnet_surveysample_preds_all,surveysample$marital)
```

[Output:]

```
Confusion Matrix and Statistics

               Reference
Prediction      married widowed divorced separated never married
  married           945       0        0         0             1
  widowed             0     108       53         7             3
  divorced            1      49      222        39            45
  separated           0       0        0         0             2
  never married       0      13       75        24           463

Overall Statistics
                                          
               Accuracy : 0.8478          
                 95% CI : (0.8315, 0.8631)
    No Information Rate : 0.4615          
    P-Value [Acc > NIR] : < 2.2e-16       
                  Kappa : 0.7762          
 Mcnemar's Test P-Value : NA              

Statistics by Class:
                     Class: married Class: widowed Class: divorced
Sensitivity                  0.9989        0.63529          0.6343
Specificity                  0.9991        0.96649          0.9212
Pos Pred Value               0.9989        0.63158          0.6236
Neg Pred Value               0.9991        0.96700          0.9244
Prevalence                   0.4615        0.08293          0.1707
Detection Rate               0.4610        0.05268          0.1083
Detection Prevalence         0.4615        0.08341          0.1737
Balanced Accuracy            0.9990        0.80089          0.7777
                     Class: separated Class: never married
Sensitivity                 0.0000000               0.9008
Specificity                 0.9989899               0.9271
```

```
Pos Pred Value              0.0000000             0.8052
Neg Pred Value              0.9658203             0.9654
Prevalence                  0.0341463             0.2507
Detection Rate              0.0000000             0.2259
Detection Prevalence        0.0009756             0.2805
Balanced Accuracy           0.4994949             0.9139
```

Optionally, we may save the predictions to the surveysample data frame and may save it to a. csv comma-separated values file for later use.

```
# Save to surveysample as a variable named "nnet_preds"
surveysample$nnet_preds <- nnet_surveysample_preds_all

# Save to file using a new filename so as to preserve the original intact.
write.csv(surveysample, file = "surveysample2.csv", row.names = FALSE)
```

Note that the nnet package also contains the program `multinom()`. Not discussed here, this program fits multinomial log-linear models via neural networks.

7.12 Neural network analysis using "mlr3keras"

Neural network analysis is often implemented through Keras and TensorFlow in a Python environment. Through the "mlr3keras" package, however, models of this type may now be implanted within the R environment. An example of this approach is presented in an online supplement to Chapter 7, found in the student section of this book's Support Material (www.routledge.com/9780367624293), under the supplement title "Neural Network Analysis with ml3keras".

7.13 Command summary

For convenience for those wishing to try models out for themselves, this book's Support Material (www.routledge.com/9780367624293) contains a listing of the main commands used in this chapter. This listing may be handy for readers following along with the book using their home or office computers. For topics presented as an online supplement ("Analyzing Boston crime via neuralnet with caret"; "Neural Network Analysis with ml3keras"), the command summary is at the end of the supplement.

Endnotes

1. The "BostonHousing2" data frame is based on http://lib.stat.cmu.edu/datasets/boston_corrected.txt. Also, the data frame used here is slightly different from "boston.c" documented at https://www.rdocumentation.org/packages/spdep/versions/0.6-15/topics/boston
2. Adapted from https://www.ncbi.nlm.nih.gov/pmc/articles/PMC6262849/
3. Code in this section is partly adapted from https://datascienceplus.com/fitting-neural-network-in-r/, where a similar dataset but different dependent variable is used (median housing prices).

Chapter 8

Network analysis

PART I: OVERVIEW OF NETWORK ANALYSIS WITH R

8.1 Introduction

Network analysis has emerged as a common method in social science as well as within the R community. The purpose of network analysis is to examine a set of relationships among people, organizations, or other units of analysis. The units of analysis in network analysis are "nodes". The relationships are "edges", referring to the lines connecting nodes in a network graph. Edges may describe symmetric relationships (an undirected network) or asymmetric ones (a directional network). "Network analysis" is an umbrella term which covers a wide variety of specific approaches to the understanding of such connected sets of units. In R, there are likewise many possible packages to choose among. What is common to all forms of network analysis is emphasis on studying units of analysis as an interconnected set.

8.2 Data and packages used in this chapter

Data

This chapter employs the following datasets:

- CA_c.txt, FL_c.txt, LA_c.txt, NY_c.txt, TX_c.txt: These are cleaned text files used in Section 8.8, which contains instructions for downloading similar text data from gubernatorial websites.
- citycrime.csv: This crime dataset is used in Section 8.15.4. This small dataset contains eight variables on various types of crime in 15 American cities: CITY, POP, MURDER, RAPE, ROBBERY, ASSAULT, BURGLARY, LARCENY, and MVTHEFT.
- crime_r.csv: A dataset on 13 crime-related variables for 47 U.S. states for which data were available. "CrimeRate" may be the outcome variable. The data are a slightly adapted version of a dataset available from http://www.statstutor.ac.uk. Variables include:
  - CrimeRate: Crime rate (offences per million population); continuous
  - Youth: Young males (males age 18–24 per 1,000); discrete
  - Education: Average years of education time (max = 25); discrete
  - ExpenditureYear: Per capita expenditure on police; continuous
  - LabourForce: Males employed 18–24 per 1,000 population); discrete
  - Males: Males per 1,000 females; discrete
  - MoreMales: More males identified per 1,000 females; 1 = yes, 0 = no; binary
  - StateSize: State size in hundred thousand population; discrete

DOI: 10.4324/9781003109396-8

- YouthUnemployment: Males age 18–24 per 1,000 population; discrete
- MatureUnemployment: Males age 35–39 per 1,000 population; discrete
- HighYouthUnemploy: High if Youth >3*Mature; 1 = yes, 0 = no; binary
- Wage: Median weekly wage; continuous
- BelowWage: Families below half wage per 1,000 population; discrete

- DHHS: This dataset is contained in the package "UserNetR" and need not be independently downloaded or read from a. csv file. The data, in network format, define the "DHHS Collaboration Network", where DHHS is the U.S. Department of Health and Human Services. There are 54 nodes in the network, representing tobacco control leaders working in 11 agencies. There are 447 connections (edges) relating the 54 leaders. To install UserNetR, which must be installed from Github rather than CRAN, use:

```
library(remotes)
remotes::install_github("DougLuke/UserNetR")
library(UserNetR)
data(DHHS)
```

- ELEnet16: This network is used in an online supplement to Chapter 8 to illustrate network analysis of international trade flows, and to illustrate the "intergraph" package for conversion among network formats. This supplement is titled "Statnet Network Analysis Example with Intergraph Conversion" and is located in the student resources section for Chapter 8, in this book's Support Material (www.routledge.com/9780367624293). Data are automotive electrical goods transactions for 99 countries. The "ITNr" package contains the ELEnet16 world network example. No separate download or. csv file is needed.
- "flo": This is a matrix representing relationships among 16 families in the Medici era of the Italian Renaissance. Data are binary, such that the absence of a relationship between two families is coded 0 and is coded 1 if there is a relationship. The data are provided with the "network" package in R. No separate download is needed.
- hero-net1000.csv: The section on "Analysis of network communities" explains and uses this coappearance dataset, which is publicly available as explained in that section. Coappearances here refer to the appearance of the same Marvel character with another character in the same comic book. However, the public dataset is too large for convenient instructional use. The same section explains how to download the public data and subset out the first 1,000 rows. Alternatively, the file "hero-net1000.csv" is made available for download in the student Support Material (www.routledge.com/9780367624293).
- migration_nodes.csv and migration_edges.csv: These files contain World Bank data on world migration and are used in Section 8.10 to illustrate superimposing a network diagram on a global map.
- s50_data: These data are supplied with the RSiena network simulation package, which is described in Section 8.16.2. Data concern friendship patterns among adolescent girls. Downloading the data is described in Section 8.16.2, or data, which are in multiple files, may be found in the "s50" folder of this book's Support Material (www.routledge.com/9780367624293).
- senate8groups.csv: This is a dataset downloaded from the web, but that is also available as a. csv file. Its 100 rows represent 100 U.S. Senators as of 2005. Its 12 columns are State, Senator, PARTY, and eight ratings by eight generally progressive interest groups (ACLU, ADA, CDF, LCV, NAACP, NARAL, PTA, and SEIU). It is used to illustrate similarity networks.
- world.csv: The "world" dataset was used and described in Chapters 2 and 3. It contains data on literacy and 19 other variables on 212 nations of the world.

Packages

In addition to packages in the R system library, this chapter uses the following R packages which may need installation. For example, `install.packages("network")` prior to loading this package with the `library(network)` command.

```
library(CINNA)        # Supports measures of network centrality
library(cluster)      # For k-means clustering in this section
library(corrr)        # Used to create a correlation network
```

```
library(dplyr)           # Supports %>% piping, counting, select(), and more
library(diagram)         # To visualize simple networks/flow diagrams
library(DT)              # Provides an R interface to the JavaScript library DataTables
library(gtools)          # Used for permutations in directed network
library(htm2txt)         # Used to scrape example data from the web
library(igraph)          # A leading network visualization package
                         # igraph also calls the following packages: graphics, grDevices, magrittr, Matrix,
                           pkgconfig (>= 2.0.0), stats, and utils. The user does not need to install these
                           separately
library(intergraph)      # Utility to convert among different network packages
library(ITNr)            # Has the ELEnet16 world network example
library(linkcomm)        # A package to analyze clustering within network communities
library(magrittr)        # Forward-pipe operator, called by dplyr and igraph
library(maps)            # Leading map package in R, has a world map background
library(NetLogoR)        # An R version of the NetLogo ABM package
library(network)         # A leading package to create and modify network objects
library(plotrix)         # Utility with plotting functions like rescale()
library(quickPlot)       # Its Plot() function is an alternative to plot()
library(RColorBrewer)    # A color-selection utility
library(rpart)           # A leading decision tree package
library(RSiena)          # A network simulation package used in Section 8.16.2
library(sna)             # Installed with statnet
library(sparkline)       # A utility needed by visNetwork for tree diagramming
library(statnet)         # A suite for network visualization, used in Sections 8.12.3 and 8.13
library(tidyverse)       # A leading text analysis package
library(tm)              # The Text Miner package, used to convert imported text data
library(UserNetR)        # Has the DHHS data used in Section 8.12.3
library(visNetwork)      # A package for interactive network analysis
```

8.3 Concepts in network analysis

A network is a set of relationships connecting objects or people. Each object or person is a "node" or "vertex". Each relationship connecting two nodes is an "edge" or "arc". A network "community" is a cluster of edges (relationships), such that a given node may belong to one or multiple network communities depending on its relationships with other nodes. The "linkcomm" package, for example, uses hierarchical cluster analysis to establish network communities.

While most networks are "undirected", some are "directed". A directed network reflects the directionality of a relationship. For instance, in an undirected coappearance network, each pair of people who coappear in a given context of interest (e.g., a political event) are counted as coappearing, whether or not they were for or against the purpose of the event. In a directed coappearance network, if one person is "pro" and the other person in the pair is "con", then the countervailing of directions is taken into account. Specifically, for directional networks there is a third column containing weights for each pair of units. A weight of 1.0 or greater indications the pair share the same directionality. Weights less than 1.0 indicate opposing directionality. For opposing directionality, the default weight is 0.5, but the researcher may assign any weight. The default assumption for assigning 0.5 is that the researcher is counting number of appearances at, say, a political event as an indicator of "support", but if one of the two people in a pair is there for an opposing reason, then that coappearance should count only half.

"Centrality" is a measure of the importance of a node in a network. There are different definitions of centrality corresponding to different definitions of "importance". In the "Quick Start" section on "Analysis of network relationships" using the package "network", centrality is defined in terms of number of relationships (edges) associated with a node. A person with many relationships is considered more central than one with few. In the same section but using the "linkcomm" package, in contrast, centrality is defined in terms of the number of network communities to which a node belongs.

8.4 Getting data into network format

As one might expect, each network package may require input in a specific format. In this chapter we illustrate several formats. The most common "file format" is comma-separated values (.csv). A. csv file may be created by Excel and by many other programs. However, the actual content of a. csv file is apt to need to differ by "network format". Network data formats are discussed below. This listing is not comprehensive as there are yet other formats.

1. Binary relationship network format: This is illustrated in the in the "Quick Start" section on "Analysis of network relationships" using the package "network". In this format objects may or may not share a relationship with another. Typically the objects are people. A square matrix is produced in which rows and columns are the same people in the same order. A cell entry of "0" means there is no relationship between the row person and the column person and a "1" means there is. The diagonal, representing people with themselves, is filled with "0" entries.

2. Coappearance network format: This is illustrated in the "Quick Start" section on "Analysis of network communities" using the "linkcomm" package. In this format there are two columns, representing person or object 1 and person or object 2. Taking people as the example, when two people coappear in the same context of research interest, their names are entered in the first and second columns of the same row. Order does not matter. The researcher must be careful to always spell names the same. For instance, the context might be membership on boards of directors. If Smith and Jones both serve on the same board, then their names would appear in the two columns for a row. In the case of the linkcomm package, the package will detect duplicates and eliminate them. In directed networks one also has a third column representing a weighting factor in which numbers below 1.0 reflect opposing direction of the two people in a paired coappearance. In the case of the linkcomm package, the two columns are entered without a header (no column names).

3. Nodes-and-edges format: The "visNetwork" package is among those which require two rather than one data frame as input, specifically one for nodes and one for edges. This is illustrated in the later section on "Interactive network analysis with visNetwork". Nodes refer to the people or objects of interest. Edges refer to the connections between pairs of nodes. Under visNetwork, the nodes object has columns for the person id and the person name (though the id may be the name). The nodes object may also have columns for font.size and shape. The edges object has columns for "from" (originating node), "to" (node which is the object of the connection), connection labels (e.g., likes, dislikes, neutral), and connection colors. There may be other columns for special purposes, but these are the essential ones.

   Separate nodes and edges data frames are also associated with, among others, the "network" and "statnet" packages. While the file names do not matter, it is convenient to call the two data frames "edges" and "vertexes". The edges data frame has as its first two columns the "to" and "from" vertex id numbers, perhaps labeled V1 and V2. Then the edges data frame may well have additional columns for edge attributes. In the "DHHS" example later on in this chapter, there is a column for "collab". For federal agencies as rows, the collab variable was coded 0 through 4 for levels of inter-agency collaboration. That is, "collab" was the type-of-connection variable. Additional edge variables are possible. Then the "vertexes" data frame must have an id column as its first column and must have a column with the name "vertex.names". There may be additional vertex attribute columns. The DHHS example, for instance, has a column for "agency", containing codes for the ten federal agencies in the network.

4. Similarity matrix format: A similarity matrix has entities (e.g., people) as both rows and columns. Cell entries represent some measure of distance between one entity and another. This chapter's section on similarity networks uses a difference matrix, which is a type of similarity matrix. In a difference matrix, lower cell entries represent greater similarities. Assuming that difference values are normed from 0 to 100, then subtracting difference values from 100 converts the difference matrix into a sameness matrix in which high values represent similarity. Layout algorithms used in network visualization may treat a difference matrix differently from its sameness matrix counterpart, leading to different visualizations for equivalent data.

PART II: QUICK START ON NETWORK ANALYSIS WITH R

8.5 Quick start exercise 1: The Medici family network

To get a quick start in doing network analysis in R, we take as example the task of describing the network associated with the Medici family in medieval Italy. The Medici dataset is provided as an example network data matrix in the "network" package. The Medici data come as a binary network matrix. The rows and columns are the family names of 16 Italian families, only one of which is "Medici". The cell entries in the matrix are coded in binary form: 0 if there is no relationship shared between the row and column family and 1 if there is a relationship. While definitions of "centrality" vary, here we will define it as the number of relationships of a given family with other families in the network.

While we may anticipate that the Medici family will be the most central (it turns out that it is), our research objective is to determine the rank order of network centrality for the 16 families in the study. To accomplish our research objective we mainly use the "igraph" package, perhaps the most widely-used of all network packages for R. We also use the "network" package, which supplies the example data on the Medici network.

Here and in the remainder of the chapter we use package prefixes before commands which are not from a package in the R system library. For instance, rather than listing a command as "`graph.adjacency()`" it is instead listed as "`igraph::graph.adjacency()`". If no package prefix is needed, then that command is from the system library and no package installation is needed. Packages which are assumed to be installed in the user's computer are listed next, in the "Setup" section.

```
# Setup
library(igraph)
library(network)

# The data() function is from the "utils" package in R's system library.
# flo is a sample dataset in matrix form, supplied with the "network" package
data(flo)

# flo is a 16x16 matrix of leading families in medieval Florence, Italy.
# The names of 16 Italian families are both rows and columns in the matrix.
# Cell entries are 0 = no relationship or 1 = relationship connecting row and column families.
View(flo)
class(flo)
      [1] "matrix"
dim(flo)
      [1] 16 16

# Thus the cell connecting the Acciauoli (1) family
# and the Medici (9) family is a 1, meaning there is a relationship
# This can also be seen in spreadsheet view when using View() above.
flo[1,9]
  [1] 1
rownames(flo)
    [1] "Acciaiuoli"   "Albizzi"
    [3] "Barbadori"    "Bischeri"
    [5] "Castellani"   "Ginori"
    [7] "Guadagni"     "Lamberteschi"
    [9] "Medici"       "Pazzi"
   [11] "Peruzzi"      "Pucci"
   [13] "Ridolfi"      "Salviati"
   [15] "Strozzi"      "Tornabuoni"
```

We now convert the "flo" matrix into an igraph object, needed by later commands. Our data meet the definition of an "adjacency matrix": A square matrix with elements (cells) in the matrix indicating whether pairs of vertices (in this example, families) are adjacent or not in the graph. Here, adjacent means "shares a relationship". The mode is "undirected", meaning that the cell entries are the same for cell (i,j) as for cell (j,i). It is not "directed", which would mean the upper and lower triangles of the data matrix differ (e.g., John likes Jane in the lower triangle, but Jane does not like John in the upper triangle).

```
net <- igraph::graph.adjacency(flo, mode = "undirected", weighted = NULL)
class(net)
      [1] "igraph"
```

Below, the `degree()` command computes the degree (number of connecting edges) of each vertex (family). The more relationships, the higher the degree. Therefore, degree is one measure of family centrality in the network.

```
deg <- igraph::degree(net,mode="all")
class(deg)
      [1] "numeric"

# The "deg" object is a numeric vector containing the names of the 16 Italian families
# and their degree. The Acciaiuoli family has only 1 network connection.
# The Albizzi family has 3 network connections. Etc.
deg
    Acciaiuoli       Albizzi    Barbadori
             1             3            2
      Bischeri    Castellani       Ginori
             3             3            1
      Guadagni  Lamberteschi       Medici
             4             1            6
         Pazzi       Peruzzi        Pucci
             1             3            0
       Ridolfi      Salviati      Strozzi
             3             2            4
    Tornabuoni
             3
```

At this point we have enough to list families by network centrality, using the "deg" object as the criterion for centrality. This object is a numeric vector of the number of network connections (degree) by row object (families). The steps to compute centrality and list families by centrality are as follows:

```
# Convert original flo matrix to a data frame
# The add rownames as a column (variable), with family names
# Then add degree as another column
flo_df <- as.data.frame(flo)
flo_df$families <- rownames(flo_df)
flo_df$degree <- deg

# Optionally, reorder the data frame so families and degree are first
flo_df <- subset(flo_df, select=c(families, degree, Acciaiuoli:Tornabuoni))

# Sort on degree
order_degree <- order(-flo_df$degree)
order_degree

[Output:]
 [1]  9  7 15  2  4  5 11 13 16  3 14  1  6  8 10 12
```

Below, the “degree” column of the centrality data frame ranks families in descending order of network centrality, using degree centrality as the measure.

```
centrality <- flo_df[order_degree,][,1:2]
centrality
```

[Output:]

```
                 families degree
Medici             Medici      6
Guadagni         Guadagni      4
Strozzi           Strozzi      4
Albizzi           Albizzi      3
Bischeri         Bischeri      3
Castellani     Castellani      3
Peruzzi           Peruzzi      3
Ridolfi           Ridolfi      3
Tornabuoni     Tornabuoni      3
Barbadori       Barbadori      2
Salviati         Salviati      2
Acciaiuoli     Acciaiuoli      1
Ginori             Ginori      1
Lamberteschi Lamberteschi      1
Pazzi               Pazzi      1
Pucci               Pucci      0
```

```
# Note that centrality is a data frame
class(centrality)
      [1] "data.frame"
```

Above we see that the Medici family is most central to the network of 16 families and the Pucci family is least central (and in fact is unconnected). Other families rank in-between according to their degree in the listing above.

The next set of steps is to visualize this network as a network graph. We use the default `plot()` command in the graphics package in the R system library. However, as `plot()` is operating on an igraph object (here, “net”) it has igraph-related attributes. Placement of vertices is random. Using `set.seed()` assures the same graph is depicted on each run. In the parameter settings below, layout is the graph architecture, here set to the default, but other layouts are possible (e.g., layout_in_circle or layout_as_tree).

It would be possible to create a network graph with the simple command `plot(net)`. However, below we produce a more customized graph, partly so that the result looks better and partly for instructional reasons. Setting the parameter size to eight makes the largest circle big enough to hold the family name “Medici”. Size of the nodes representing families varies by degree = number of relationships). Parameter options in the `plot()` command are:

- layout (plot.layout) sets the layout (see help for a list of alternatives)
- vertex.shape has nodes as circles by default but “square” or other shapes are possible
- vertex.size is size of nodes, set to centrality_index, created below
- vertex.label.dist places the vertex label within its circle
- vertex.label.font = 4 is sets font as bold and italic
- vertex.color sets the vertex color
- vertex.label.cex sets the label size
- edge.color sets the connecting line color
- margin sets the distance of one vertex to another (a negative value is more distance, making the graph larger)
- xlab is the X-axis title (main= would put a title at the top)

To get different size vertexes in Figure 8.1, we key size to a new variable called “centrality_index”.

```
# Sort the centrality dataframe alphabetically by family name
# This makes it match the order of the original “flo” matrix, which was alphabetical.
```

```
sortedcentrality <- with(centrality, centrality[order(families), ])
# Experiment to find an aesthetic magnification factor
magnification_factor = 5
# Create the centrality_index, which is sorted degree times magnification
centrality_index <- sortedcentrality$degree*magnification_factor
```

Now create the plot which is Figure 8.1:

```
set.seed(123)
plot(net, layout = layout_with_fr, vertex.size = centrality_index, vertex.shape =
"circle", vertex.label.dist = 0.2, vertex.label.font = 4, vertex.color =
"lightblue", vertex.label.cex = 1.2, edge.color = "darkred", margin = -0.2, xlab =
"Relationship Network of Linkages Among 16 Italian Families")
```

Now create the same plot in circle layout. This is Figure 8.2.

```
set.seed(123)
plot(net, layout = layout_in_circle, vertex.size = centrality_index, vertex.shape =
"circle", vertex.label.dist = 0.2, vertex.label.font = 4, vertex.color =
"lightblue", vertex.label.cex = 1.2, edge.color = "darkred", margin = -0.15, xlab =
"Relationship Network of Linkages Among 16 Italian Families")
```

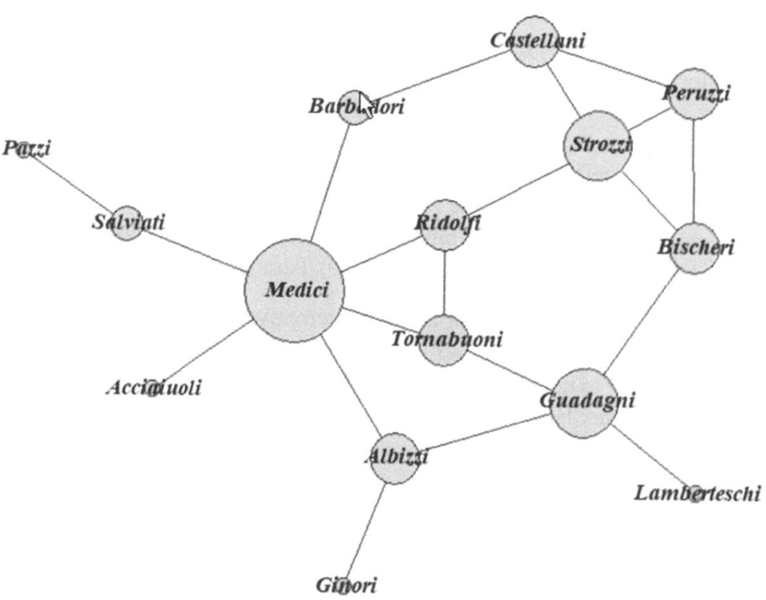

Figure 8.1 Medici Era Family Network

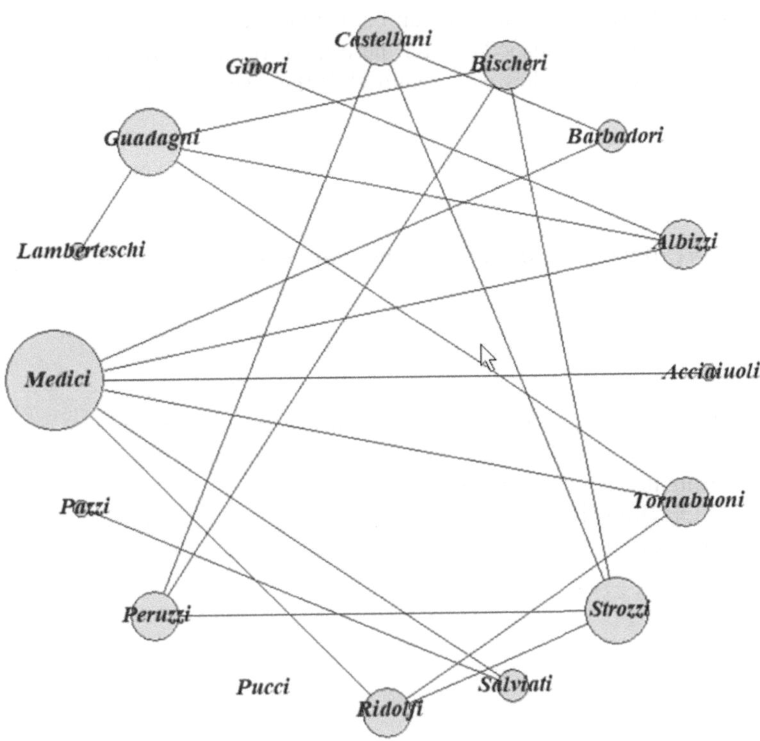

Figure 8.2 Medici Era Family Network, circle layout

8.6 Quick start exercise 2: Marvel hero network communities

In this exercise we illustrate some of the capabilities of the "linkcomm" package, which is assumed to have been installed. This package uses hierarchical clustering analysis to partition a network into "communities". Input data is a "coappearance" matrix. Such a matrix has two columns in which each row represents a person or object, which are nodes in the network. If a person appears in the same context with another, they are in the same data row and are linked by a network edge in the network graph. For directed networks, a third column provides weights indicating countervailing directions for the pair of people, in which numbers below 1.0 reflect degree of opposing direction (0.5 is default), as discussed earlier in this chapter.

The linkcomm package clusters by relationship (edges), not nodes (here, characters). In summarizing the uses and advantages of the package, its author notes that clustering by relationships makes it "possible for nodes to belong to multiple communities thereby revealing the overlapping and nested structure of the network and uncovering the key nodes that form connections across several communities" (Kalinka, 2020: 1).

The data used here are coappearances of Marvel heroes in the same comic book. Our research interest is in the treatment of female roles within the Marvel universe. The coappearance data we use is publicly available for download, but as it contains over half a million coappearances, its use is too time-intensive for instruction. Instead, after reading in the entire data, we create a subset of the first 1,000 coappearances and used that in this section. This sample is provided with this textbook as a file labeled "hero-net1000.csv". This should be saved to the local working directory.

While the reader is encouraged to use the "hero-net1000.csv", below we explain how this file was created. The full dataset in comma-separated value (csv) format can be downloaded from http://syntagmatic.github.io/exposedata/marvel/. From this website we downloaded the file "hero-network.csv", which we saved in our working directory. To create the sample file, the steps below were required. If the reader wishes, these steps may be skipped and the hero_net1000.csv file read instead.

```
# Step 1: Read in the saved hero_network.csv file, which does not have variable names in row 1
# This has over half a million hero co-occurrences
setwd("C:/Data")
heroes_df <- read.csv("hero-network.csv", header = FALSE, sep = ",")
class(heroes_df)
     [1] "data.frame"
nrow(heroes_df)
     [1] 574467

# Step 2: Create a new data frame with just the first 1000, for instructional purposes
# The row name in column V1 is comic character 1 and the name in column V2 is character 2,
# for two characters appearing in the same comic book.
hero_df <- heroes_df[1:1000,]
# Verify the attributes of hero_df
nrow(hero_df)
[Output:]
     [1] 1000
names(hero_df)
[Output:]
     [1] "V1" "V2"
head(hero_df, 3)
[Output:]
                     V1                    V2
  1        LITTLE, ABNER       PRINCESS ZANDA
  2        LITTLE, ABNER BLACK PANTHER/T'CHAL
  3 BLACK PANTHER/T'CHAL       PRINCESS ZANDA

# Step 3: Save hero_df as hero-net1000.csv
# Row 1 will have the variable names V1 and V2
write.csv(hero_df, file ="hero-net1000.csv", row.names = FALSE)
```

The setup for Quick Start Exercise 2, using the supplied hero-net1000.csv data, is described below. The needed linkcomm package is loaded, then the sample data are read in.

```
# Setup

library(linkcomm)
library(RColorBrewer)

setwd("C:/Data")
hero_df <- read.csv("hero-net1000.csv", header = TRUE, sep = ",")

# Verify the attributes of heroes_df
class(hero_df)
[Output:]
     [1] "data.frame"
nrow(hero_df)
[Output:]
     [1] 1000
head(hero_df,3)
```

[Output:]

```
                        V1                   V2
1         LITTLE, ABNER           PRINCESS ZANDA
2         LITTLE, ABNER BLACK PANTHER/T'CHAL
3 BLACK PANTHER/T'CHAL            PRINCESS ZANDA
```

For the remainder of this section on analysis of network communities, we must convert the data frame "hero_df" into linkcomm object (hence "_lo" in the object name). Linkcomm commands below use hierarchical cluster analysis to establish clusters, which are the "communities", based on coappearances. There are several hierarchical clustering method which might be used ("ward", "single", "complete", "average", "mcquitty", "median", or "centroid"). We use the default method, which is "average". A dendrogram of linkages is created by default based on hierarchical cluster analysis but is suppressed here. See the discussion of hierarchical cluster analysis and dendrograms in Chapter 2. Conversion from a data frame to a linkcomm object is accomplished by the `getLinkCommunities()` command:

```
# If plot = TRUE, a dendrogram of linkages will be displayed (not done here)
hero_lo <- linkcomm::getLinkCommunities(hero_df, hcmethod="average",
removetrivial=FALSE, plot=FALSE)
```

[Output:]

```
   Checking for loops and duplicate edges... 100.000%
   Found and removed 229 duplicate edge(s)
   Calculating edge similarities for 771 edges... 100.00%
   Hierarchical clustering of edges...
   Calculating link densities... 100.00%
   Maximum partition density =  0.696394
   Finishing up...4/4... 100.00%
```

Having created the listcomm object "hero_lo", we may list basic statistics pertaining to its community network architecture. Below, this output shows there are 771 edges connecting 87 nodes, grouped into eight communities. Grouping into communities was based on hierarchical clustering of edges.

```
hero_lo$numbers
```

[Output:]

```
      [1] 771  87   8
```

By way of illustration, we also list six of the pairings which were input. Note that a slash in a character name (e.g., "IRON MAN/TONY STARK ") indicates that single character has two names.

```
head(hero_lo$edgelist,6)
       [,1]                   [,2]
 [1,] "LITTLE, ABNER"        "PRINCESS ZANDA"
 [2,] "LITTLE, ABNER"        "BLACK PANTHER/T'CHAL"
 [3,] "BLACK PANTHER/T'CHAL" "PRINCESS ZANDA"
 [4,] "STEELE, SIMON/WOLFGA" "FORTUNE, DOMINIC"
 [5,] "STEELE, SIMON/WOLFGA" "ERWIN, CLYTEMNESTRA"
 [6,] "STEELE, SIMON/WOLFGA" "IRON MAN/TONY STARK "
```

Before proceeding, we can establish that the eight communities we have uncovered are distinct communities and that there are no communities which are actually nested as a subset of another. The `getAllNestedComm()` function may be used to see if there are nested communities. A community would be nested if all of its members were also members of a larger community. There are no nested communities in our set. The output "`list()`" signifies an empty set.

```
linkcomm::getAllNestedComm(hero_lo)
```

[Output:]

```
      list()
```

Next, we list the number of communities to which each hero belongs, in descending order. Here we list only the first six. We note that two female characters (Starshine and Scarlet Witch) are among the top six.

```
# There are 87 heroes in the 8 clusters (communities).
herolist <- hero_lo$numclusters
length(herolist)
[Output:]
   [1] 87
```

```
# We list the first 6 heroes
head(herolist,6)
[Output:]
   IRON MAN/TONY STARK
                     3
   STARSHINE II/BRANDY
                     3
   SCARLET WITCH/WANDA
                     2
            LORD CHAOS
                     2
   SILVER SURFER/NORRIN
                     2
        GALACTUS/GALAN
                     2
```

Above, the number under each character is the number of communities to which the hero belongs. The following table shows the frequency count for the 87 characters. Only two characters appear in three communities, 17 in two, and the majority in only one. Keep in mind, however, that our sample is 1,000 and this is a small fraction of the entire comic book database.

```
table(herolist)

  herolist
   1  2  3
  68 17  2
```

We next produce a basic plot in the form of a "community membership matrix". That is, we show which of the eight communities various heroes are in. This is done by adding the parameter `type = "members"` to the `plot()` command, which adapts plot details to fit the type of object being passed, which here is "hero_lo_", a linkcomm object. There are other types of plots also apart from "members":

- `#type = "graph"` plots a graph layout of the network with colored link communities
- `#type = "commsumm"` plots a bar graph or pie chart summarizing community modularity or connectedness for each community
- `#type = "dend"` plots a dendrogram with colored link communities
- `#type = "summary"` plots the dendrogram and partition density plot side-by-side

```
# We use the default layout for Figure 8.3
plot(hero_lo, type = "members")
```

Rather than discuss Figure 8.3, however, we create a fuller community membership matrix using the `plotLinkCommMembers()` function. This function gives more control over the plot. Critically, in the following code, `msize` is the number of heroes to display, in descending order of the number of communities to which they belong. We ask for 20 heroes. Also, `total=TRUE` causes display of row and column totals and `maxclusters` sets

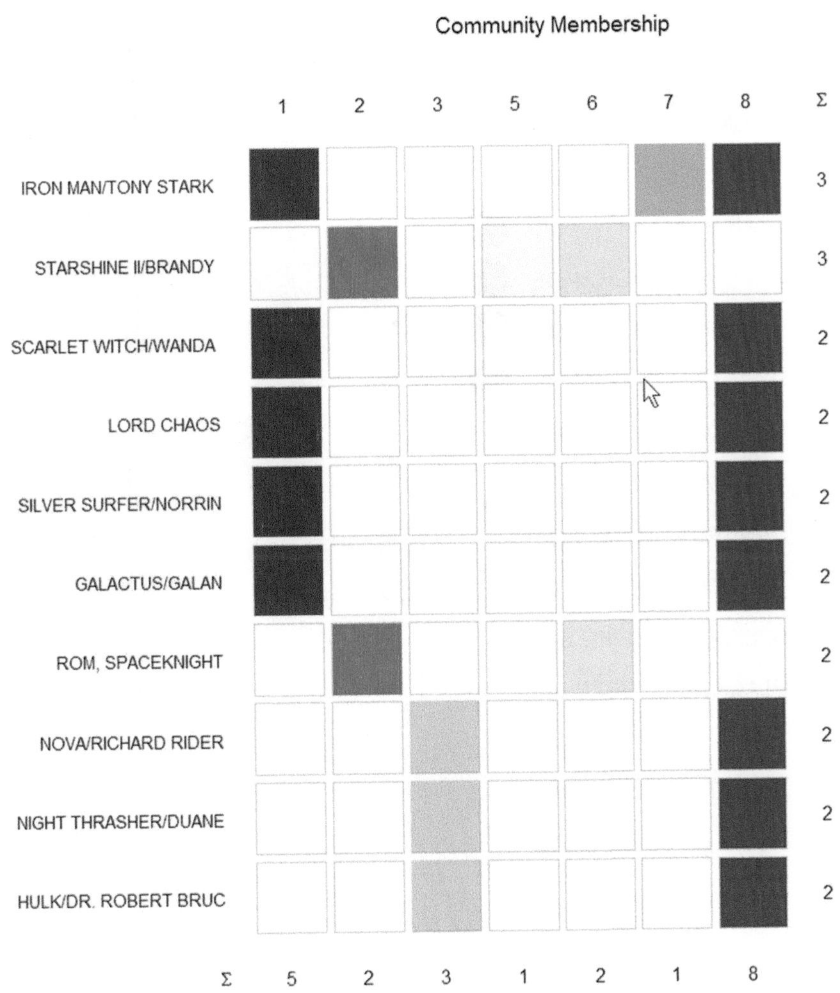

Figure 8.3 Community membership matrix, Marvel heroes

the maximum number of clusters to display. For these data, though, the solution created only eight communities (clusters) so that is the maximum here. Optionally, colors are set to the "Spectral" palette by the RColorBrewer utility rather than default, which is random color.

```
msize = 20
linkcomm::plotLinkCommMembers(hero_lo, nodes = head(names(hero_lo$numclusters),
msize), pal = RColorBrewer::brewer.pal(11, "Spectral"), shape = "circle", total =
TRUE, fontsize = 12, nspace = 3.5,maxclusters = 20)
```

The community membership matrix in Figure 8.4 gives some answers to research questions about the roles of women in the Marvel universe. We consider the top 20 characters in network importance, defining network importance as number of communities to which a hero belongs. Recall that our sample of 1,000 coappearances is a small fraction out of over half a million, so the findings here may well not be representative. Researchers could follow the same analytic process using the full database, however. For our sample of 1,000, we may make these observations:

- Women are underrepresented. There are only four women characters out of the top 20 pairs shown in Figure 8.4 (Starshine, Scarlet Witch, Leiko Wu, and Tigra).

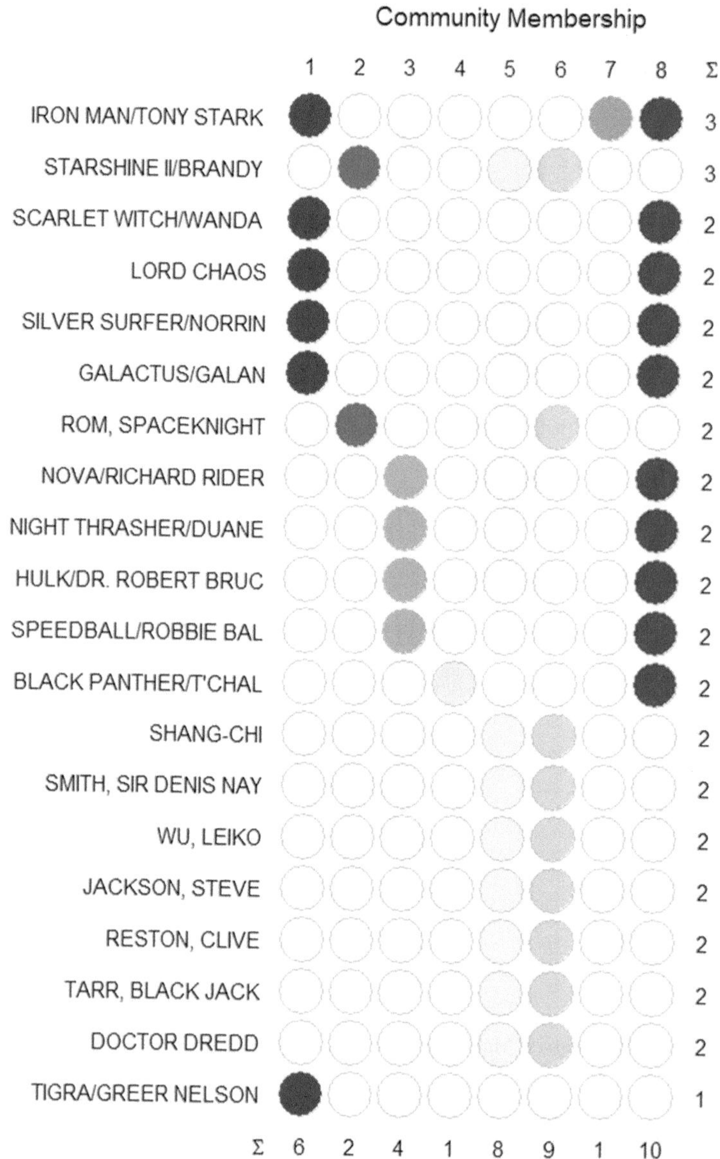

Figure 8.4 Community membership matrix, Marvel heroes, enhanced layout

- One female character, Starshine, is tied for first place in terms of number of network communities with which she is associated. One of these is the third-largest community (5).
- One female character, Tigra, ranks last, belonging to only one community.
- As might be expected, smaller communities are less likely to have female characters. Three communities have no female characters but these are small (4, 1, and 1 member or members each).
- The largest community (community 8) has ten members, with Scarlett Witch as its only female member. Scarlet Witch has done truly evil things, such as arranging the death of team-mates, but also is sometime is on the side of good. When she is not a flawed hero, she is a villain. Thus, the largest Marvel community (community 8) lacks a consistently heroic female role model.

We can compute a centrality score for each character to see if male or female characters are more central to the coappearance network on average. Here we limit consideration to the 20 most central characters. The higher the score, the more central the character to the coappearance network. The higher the centrality coefficient (cc), the more central the character. For computation of the centrality coefficient, see Golbeck (2013).

```
cc <- linkcomm::getCommunityCentrality(hero_lo)
head(round(cc,3),20)
[Output:]
   IRON MAN/TONY STARK  STARSHINE II/BRANDY  SCARLET WITCH/WANDA
                 3.803                3.547                2.767
            LORD CHAOS SILVER SURFER/NORRIN        GALACTUS/GALAN
                 2.767                2.767                2.767
      ROM, SPACEKNIGHT   NOVA/RICHARD RIDER NIGHT THRASHER/DUANE
                 2.852                2.814                2.814
  HULK/DR. ROBERT BRUC SPEEDBALL/ROBBIE BAL BLACK PANTHER/T'CHAL
                 2.814                2.814                2.951
             SHANG-CHI SMITH, SIR DENIS NAY            WU, LEIKO
                 2.385                2.385                2.385
       JACKSON, STEVE        RESTON, CLIVE     TARR, BLACK JACK
                 2.385                2.385                2.385
          DOCTOR DREDD   TIGRA/GREER NELSON
                 2.385                1.000
```

In terms of our research question about the roles of women in the Marvel universe, for these data we may note that although fewer, the average centrality of female characters is higher than for male characters (2.90 vs. 2.72). This reflects the centrality of Starshine being very high and her score being averaged across only three others, one of whom (Scarlet Witch) is also quite high.

In the next part of this section we graph the hero_lo network as a "Spencer circle".[1] The `shownodesin = 3` option calls for labeling only nodes with membership in three or more communities. For the sample data, this corresponds to heroes Iron Man and Starshine. If we set this parameter to `shownodesin = 1`, all nodes would be labeled except for some label conflicts. The numbers around the circumference of the circle are the communities, from 1 through 8. With node.pies = TRUE, characters (nodes) are shown as pie charts, with slices of the pie representing the percentage of relationships (edges) the character has in each community. If there are no slices, that character belongs to only one community. In the resulting Figure 8.5, insets have been added to increase the visibility of the node pie charts. Note that the figure will vary slightly with different random seeds.

```
set.seed(24)
plot(hero_lo,type="graph", layout="spencer.circle", shownodesin = 3, node.pies=TRUE)
   Ordering communities according to dendrogram...100%
   Calculating node co-ordinates for Spencer circle...100%
   Getting node community edge density...100%
   Getting node layout...
   Constructing node pies...100%
```

The Fruchterman-Reingold layout in Figure 8.6 below produces a rather similar network graph.[2] However, as it does not constrain the network to a circle, the layout may be more "natural" and informative. In this case it highlights there being two Marvel universes, not one, in terms of community membership based on coappearances in comic books. We set labeling for characters with membership in two or more communities. The result is shown in Figure 8.6.

```
set.seed(24)
plot(hero_lo, type="graph", layout= layout.fruchterman.reingold, shownodesin = 2,
node.pies=TRUE)
   Getting node community edge density...100%
   Getting node layout...
   Constructing node pies...100%
```

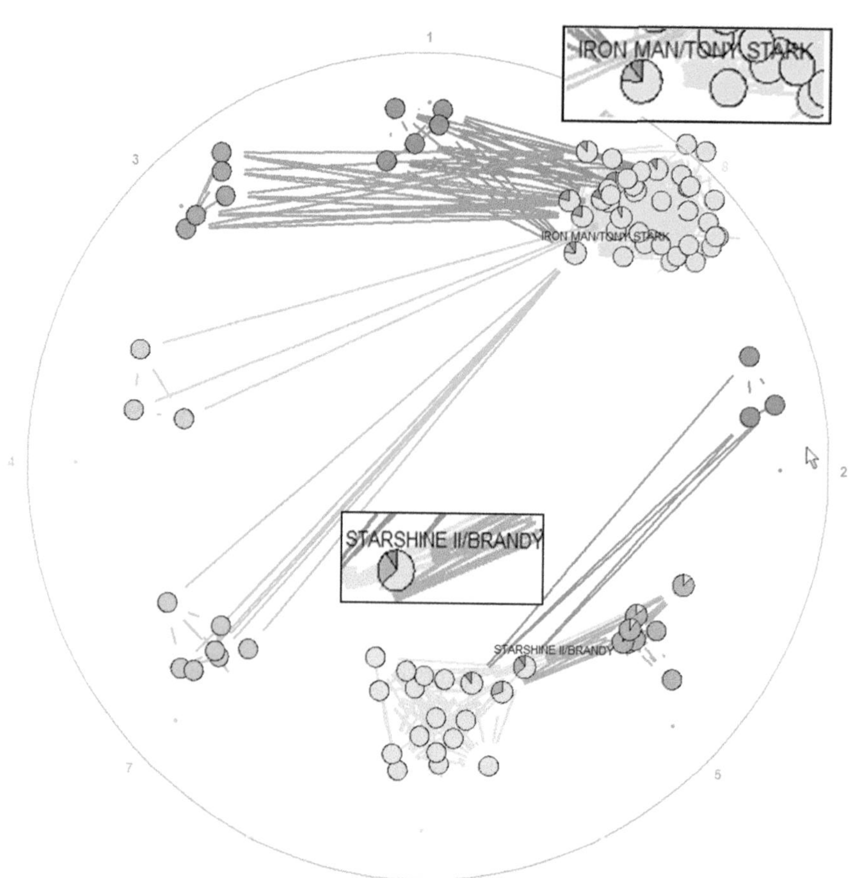

Figure 8.5 Marvel heroes coappearance network, Spencer layout

Figure 8.6 suggests that there are two distinct Marvel universes, at least for the sample of 1,000 coappearances we are using. The one on the left has five communities and includes Iron Man, but has two of the female characters we have discussed (Scarlet Witch, Tigra). The one on the left has three communities, and includes Starshine and Leiko Wu. Female characters, while relatively few in number, are not segregated off in their own universe of communities.

Finally, the reader may wish to experiment with the several other layouts available for linkcomm. Simply add one of the following after `layout=`: layout.circle, layout.fruchterman.reingold.grid, layout, graphopt, layout. kamada.kawai, layout.lgl, layout.mds, layout.reingold.tilford, layout.spring, layout.sphere, layout.svd, or layout. random.

PART III: NETWORK ANALYSIS WITH R IN DETAIL

8.7 Interactive network analysis with visNetwork

The "visNetwork" package creates undirected and directed network graphs relating people or other units of analysis by their connection type and group. In undirected mode, the connection is reciprocal, such that if A connects to B then we may be sure that B connects with A. In the research team example which follows the connections are undirected. Relationships are at three levels: "successful pair", "unsuccessful pair", and "never a pair", where success refers to a successful work project. If research staff member A has been paired with B and the result was successful, then A is a "successful pair" with B. It follows that B is also a "successful pair" with A.

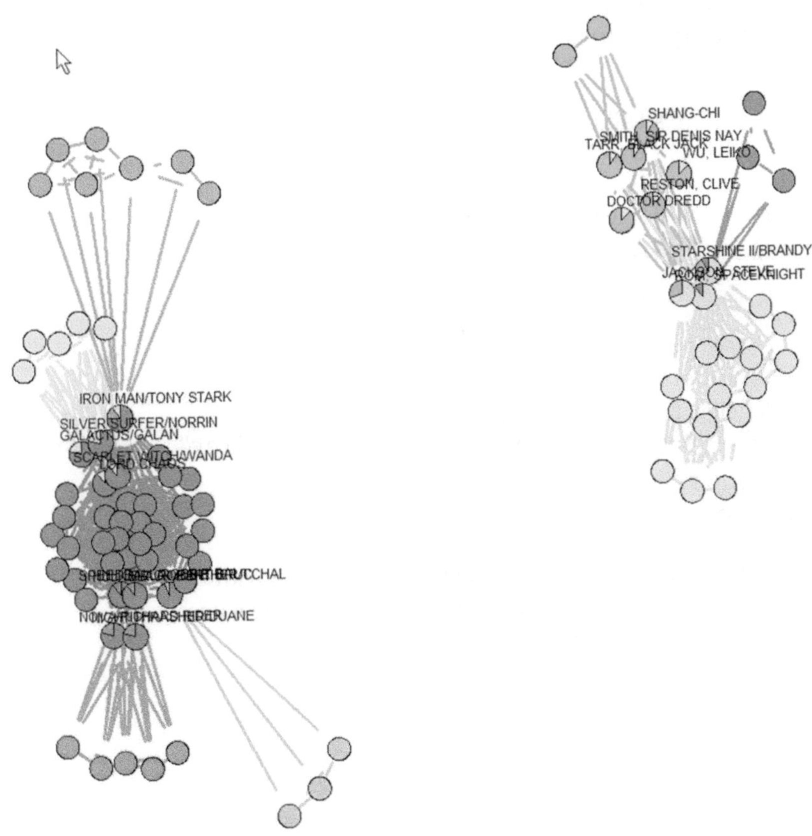

Figure 8.6 Marvel heroes coappearance network, Fruchterman-Reingold layout

In a directed network, in contrast, connections need not be reciprocal. Rather, a connection has a direction such that the type of connection of person A with person B is not necessarily the same as that of person B with person A. The classic sociometric network described by the famous sociologist Jacob Moreno (1951) is a directed network. Moreno's "sociograms" depicted which children in a classroom wished to be sitting next to which other children. While some pairings were reciprocal, others were not. For instance, Bob may wish to sit next to Mary, but Mary may not wish to sit next to Bob.

8.7.1 Undirected networks: Research team management

As our first example for this section we examine an undirected network using simulated data on a social science research team. The research objective is to aid the research team manager in staffing selected research tasks based on pairs of staff members who have teamed together in the past and who achieved successful outcomes. The "interactive" part of visNetwork is that an id selector appears in the network graph such that the team manager may select any staff member's id and view the network in a format which highlights connections pertaining to the selected individual. For instructional purposes, we limit the number of research members to only seven, though at the end we show a more complex network of 24 research team members. Following this, we also show a directed network example using the visNetwork package.

Networks under the visNetwork package require creation of two data frames: Nodes (units, here listing the staff members) and edges (relations, here listing the connections between pairs of staff members). The setup section below loads the needed packages, declares the working directory, sets a random seed, and creates the nodes and edges objects by direct data entry (not from a file).

```
# Setup
library(dplyr)          # Utility supporting %>% piping, counting, and more
library(gtools)         # Used for permutations in directed network
library(magrittr)       # Forward-pipe operator, needed by dplyr
library(tidyverse)      # A leading text analysis package
library(visNetwork)     # A package for interactive network analysis

setwd("C:/Data")        # Set the working directory
set.seed(123)           # Set a random seed

# Step 1
# First construct the nodes object. It is a data.frame of tibble type.
people<- c("Marlene", "Kendra", "Elena", "Marilyn", "Walter", "Calvin", "Clarence")

# Eliminate duplicates, if any
people<-unique(people)

# Create the nodes object, which is a data frame of tibble type populated with "people".
# with two columns: "id" and "label". Here we let id and label be the same names.
nodes <- dplyr::tibble(id = people)
nodes$label <- people
nodes
[Output:]
  # A tibble: 7 x 2
    id       label
    <chr>    <chr>
  1 Marlene  Marlene
  2 Kendra   Kendra
  3 Elena    Elena
  4 Marilyn  Marilyn
  5 Walter   Walter
  6 Calvin   Calvin
  7 Clarence Clarence
```

We now proceed to construct the "edges" object, which is more complex. Edges is a data frame of tibble type with four columns: "from", "to", "connection", and "color". The "connection" column could be named something else, such as "feelings", but then the R code below would have to make that switch. The "from" and "to" columns contain the names of two people. The "connection" column lists the type of connection, which in this example is "successful pair", "unsuccessful pair", and "never a pair". There may also be "NA" entries in the connection column, reflecting where data are absent. Each connection category corresponds to a given color.

The edges matrix could be created manually in a spreadsheet, exported to csv format, then read into R as a data frame. If created manually, the NA rows would be omitted. Also, since we are creating edges manually as an undirected network with only reciprocal relationships, the researcher should assure that there are no duplicate reciprocal rows (e.g., no from Mary to John if there is a from John to Mary). However, below we create simulated data for the edges object. Skip Step 2 if creating edges manually.

```
# Step 2: Create the pal object, a color palette tibble, with colors corresponding to edge types
pal <-
dplyr::tibble(connection = c("successful pair","unsuccessful pair", "never a pair"),
color = c("blue","red","darkgray"))

edges_legend <-  pal
edges_legend
```

[Output:]

```
# A tibble: 3 x 2
  connection         color
  <chr>              <chr>
1 successful pair    blue
2 unsuccessful pair  red
3 never a pair       darkgray
```

```
# Step 3: Create the edges data frame with simulated data
# First define all possible combinations of sample ids
set.seed(123)
edges <- combn(people, 2) %>%
# Transpose
t(.) %>%
# Convert the matrix to a tibble data frame
dplyr::as_tibble(.) %>%
# Set the "from" and "to" column labels
magrittr::set_names(c("from","to")) %>%
# Set "connection" as the column defining the nature of the connection
# Assign connection value at random using proportions below.
# If it is NA the connection has no data or does not exist (40% chance).
dplyr::mutate(connection = sample(c("successful pair","unsuccessful pair","never a
pair", NA), size = nrow(.), prob = c(0.2,0.2,0.2,0.4), replace = TRUE)) %>%
# If the connection is NA then the connection does not exist … filter for not NA.
dplyr::filter(!is.na(connection)) %>%
# Filter for only connections for the "from" person with other "to" people.
dplyr::filter(from != to) %>%
# Join the previously-created color palette (pal)
dplyr::left_join(pal)
# edges is a tibble-type data frame
class(edges)
      [1] "tbl_df"     "tbl"         "data.frame"
# View the first several edges
head(edges,6)
```

[Output:]

```
# A tibble: 6 x 4
  from    to      connection         color
  <chr>   <chr>   <chr>              <chr>
1 Marlene Elena   unsuccessful pair  red
2 Marlene Marilyn never a pair       darkgray
3 Marlene Walter  successful pair    blue
4 Marlene Calvin  successful pair    blue
5 Kendra  Elena   never a pair       darkgray
6 Kendra  Marilyn successful pair    blue
```

We now display the interactive network. For instructional reasons we proceed in steps, but the three steps could be collapsed to one by stringing them together with the %>% piping operators.

```
# Step 4
# Object g1 displays the network with id selection, reciprocal arrows, but no legend.
# Type g1 to view it.
g1 <- visNetwork::visNetwork(nodes, edges) %>%
     visNetwork::visEdges(arrows = 'to, from', arrowStrikethrough= FALSE,
smooth=TRUE) %>%
```

```
      visNetwork::visOptions(highlightNearest = TRUE, nodesIdSelection = TRUE,) %>%
      visNetwork::visLayout(randomSeed = 123) %>%
      visNetwork::visIgraphLayout()
# View g1
g1

# g2 displays the network with id selection, arrows, and a legend.
# Tip: Your display window must be wide enough for the legend to show properly
edges_legend <- pal %>%
rename(label = connection)
g2 <- visNetwork::visNetwork(nodes, edges) %>%
   visNetwork::visOptions(highlightNearest = TRUE, nodesIdSelection = TRUE) %>%
   visNetwork::visLayout(randomSeed = 123) %>%
   visNetwork::visIgraphLayout() %>%
   visNetwork::visLegend(addEdges = edges_legend)
# View g2
g2

# g3 displays the network with id selection, a legend, arrows, and icons.
g3 <- g2%>%
      visNetwork::addFontAwesome(name = "font-awesome") %>%
      visNetwork::visNodes(shape = "icon", icon = list(code = "f007", color =
"lightblue"))
# View g3, which is Figure 8.7
# The layout can be changed by grabbing and dragging nodes
g3
```

Then, by using the ID Selector in the upper left (or simply by clicking on a node), we can get a view, which highlights any particular person in the network. In Figure 8.8, we highlight Elena. One can see that Elena has mostly not been paired in a work team with anyone in the network.

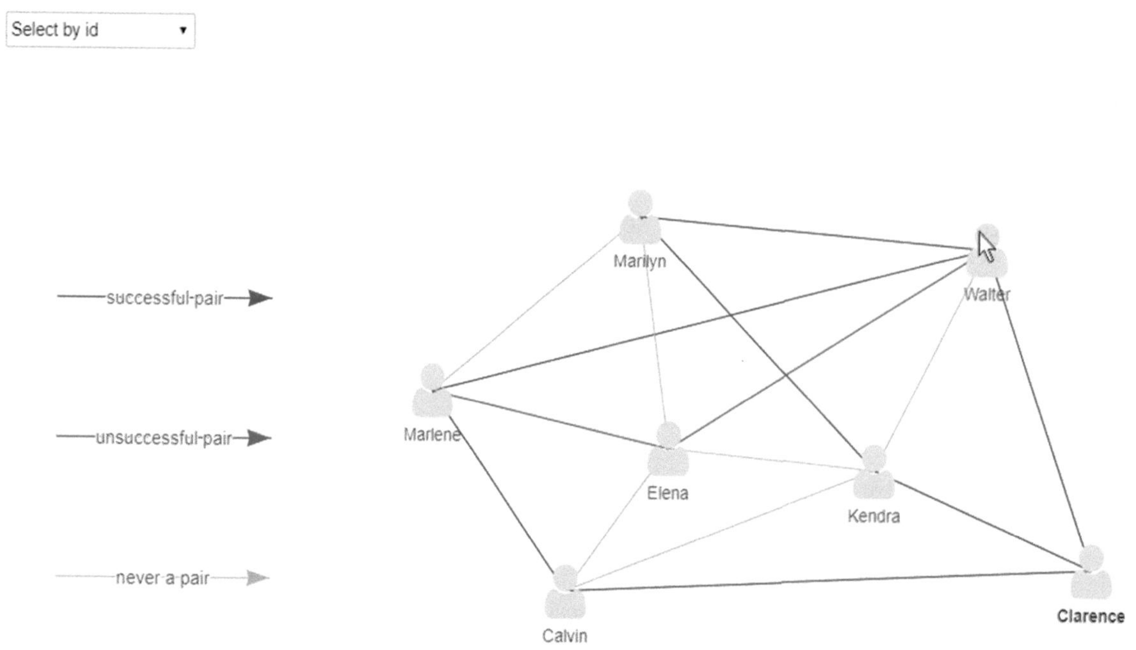

Figure 8.7 visNetwork interactive network, research staff example

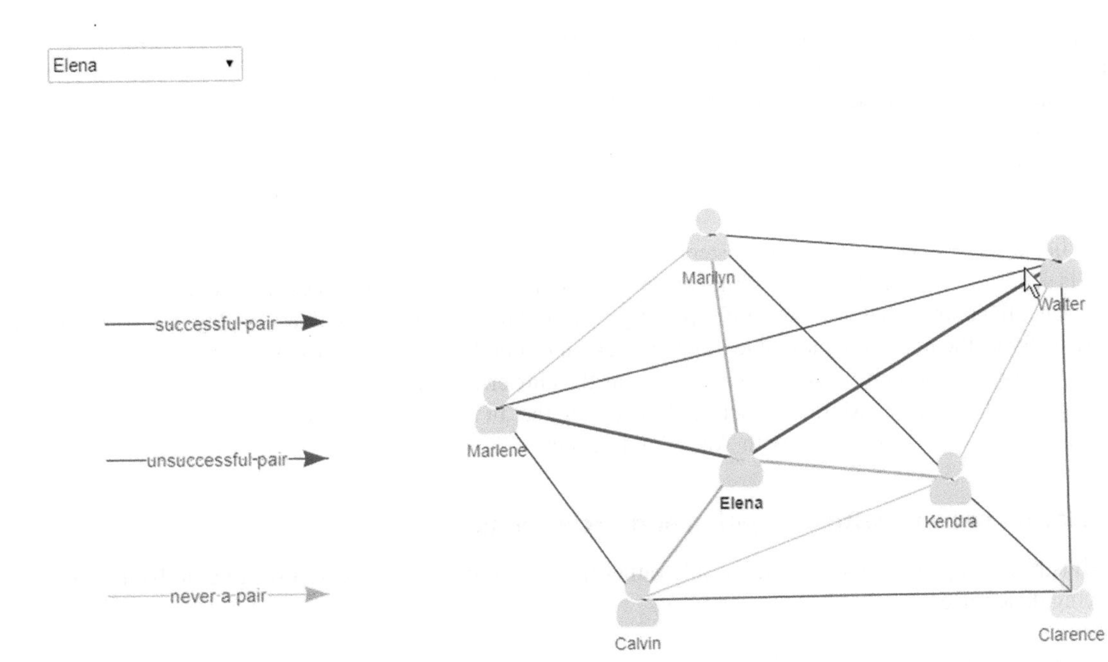

Figure 8.8 visNetwork interactive network, Elena selected

The two pairings that did occur (with Marlene and with Walter) had unsuccessful outcomes. Data are missing for Elena with regard to Clarence (hence no arrow).

We can save the current network to an html file in the default directory such as "C:/Data". Directing a browser to "file:///C:/Data/myvisnetwork.html" brings up the g3 network, complete with interactive selection by person id.

```
visNetwork::visSave(g3, file = "myvisnetwork.html")
```

8.7.2 Clustering by group: Research team grouped by gender

visNetwork can also aid in analysis by group. Its `visClusteringByGroup()` command color codes nodes (here, research staffers) by group (here, F or M gender). One may show the relation of individual female members to the male group as a group, as in Figure 8.9. One may also show the relation of individual female members to individual male members, color-coded by gender, as in Figure 8.10. Initially, the graph will just show the two groups, Group F and Group M. The analyst may double-click on a group to expand it to show individual nodes. If nodes are already expanded, the analyst may double-click on a node to contract nodes to show just their group. Also note that nodes may be dragged for better placement. Moreover, clicking on any node will select that person and highlight their connections.

```
# Start by inspecting nodes (the people)
View(nodes)
# In nodes, create a "group" column, assigning group letters based on order as just viewed
nodes$group <- c("F", "F","F","F","M","M","M")
# Create a visNetwork with group membership coded by color and shape.
visNetwork::visNetwork(nodes, edges) %>%
 visNetwork::visLayout(randomSeed = 123) %>%
 visNetwork::visGroups(groupname="F", color = "gold", shape = "circle") %>%
 visNetwork::visGroups(groupname="M",color="lightblue",shape="triangle") %>%
```

```
visNetwork::visClusteringByGroup(groups=c("F","M"), label = "Group : ", shape =
"ellipse",color="blue",force=FALSE, scale_size=TRUE) %>%
# The next line adds the nodes legend based on the connection column and colors in edges
visNetwork::visLegend() %>%
# The next line adds the edges legend
visNetwork::visLegend(addEdges = edges_legend, ncol=3, width = 0.6)
```

Figure 8.9 displays the visNetwork graph clustered by Gender, with the female group expanded and the male group not. Elena is selected. Among other things, the figure shows that Elena has one unsuccessful connection to the male group. Marlene, in contrast, has two successful pairings with the male group. Note that if trying this yourself, your image may differ as the nodes are moveable (double-click on Group F and drag nodes as desired).

Figure 8.10 displays the same network, with gender as the clustering variable, but with both the female and male groups expanded to node level. Marlene is selected, revealing that in terms of team experiences with males, her two successful team pair experiences were with Walter and Calvin.

8.7.3 A larger network with navigation and circle layout

Next we illustrate a large network (24 staff people rather than 7) for the same research staffing problem. These are the following differences:

- A circle layout is employed instead of the previous default, using the `visIgraphLayout(layout = 'layout _ in _ circle')` command
- Navigation buttons are added using the `visNetwork::visInteraction(navigationButtons=TRUE)` command. These add arrows for interactively enlarging or diminishing the size of the graph, and for moving right, left, up, and down. The navigation buttons are shown at the bottom of Figure 8.11.

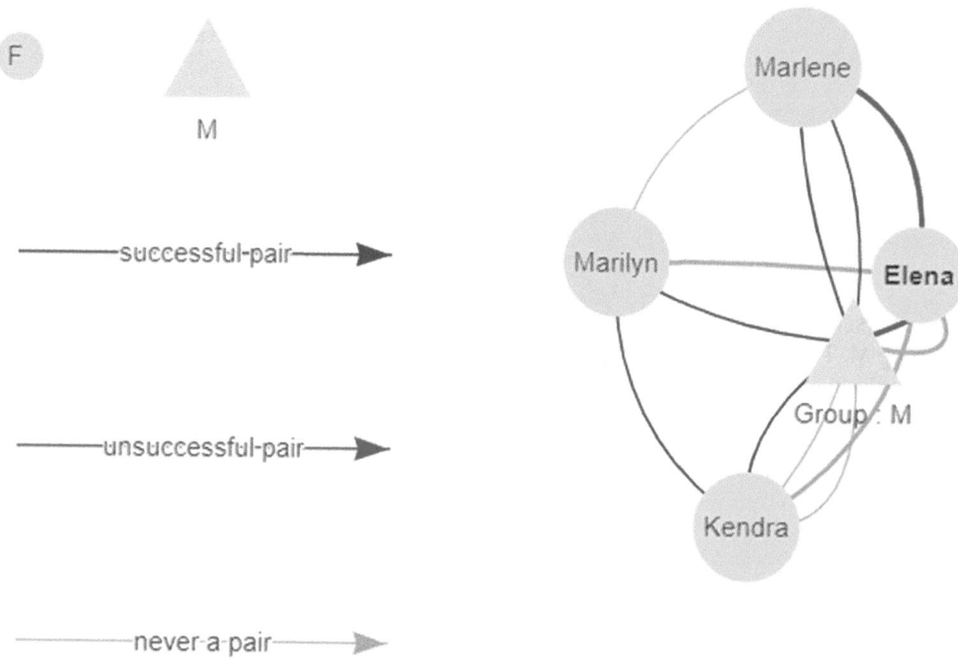

Figure 8.9 Group clustering: Group F expanded, Elena selected

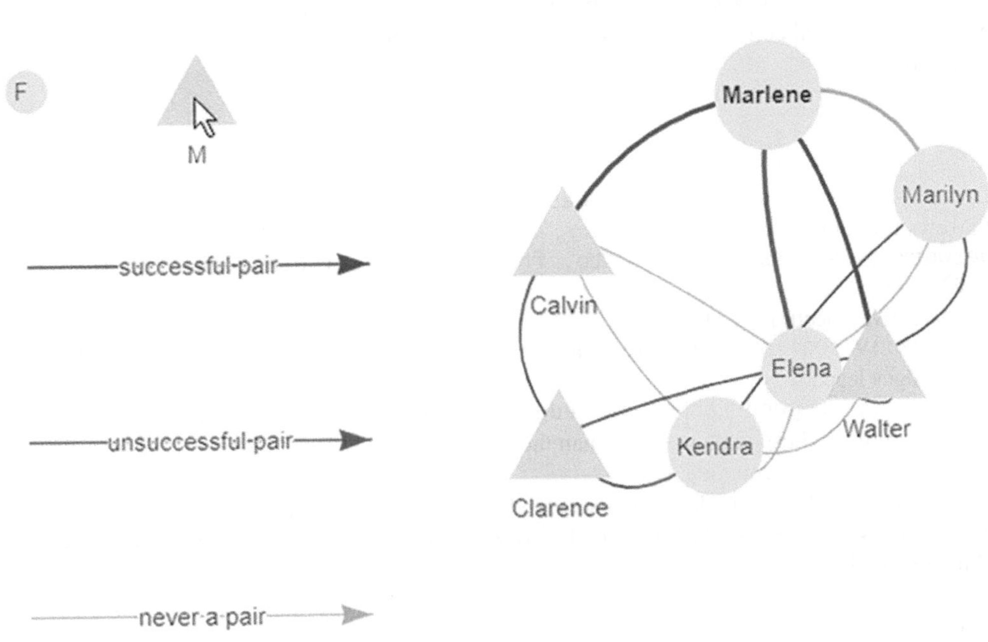

Figure 8.10 Group clustering: Both Groups expanded, Marlene selected

- After the graph is created, we use the drag functionality of visNetwork to drag the staff member with the most successful performance record to the center.

```
# Step 1
# First construct a larger nodes object with 24 research team members.
people<-c("Marlene","Kendra","Elena","Marilyn","Maggie","Carlie","Jenny","Leah",
"Ayanna", "Kaylee","Jane","Alisson", "Melvin", "Charles","Aydan","Leo", "Lamar","Aug
ustin","Donald","Reynaldo", "Ian","Walter","Calvin","Clarence")
# The following commands repeat the earlier subsection on undirected visNetwork graphs
# except font size and shape are specified. Labels will be inside circles.
# Node circle size will be set by length of the name (e.g., Leo is smallest).
people<-unique(people)
nodes <- dplyr::tibble(id = people,font.size=18,shape="circle")
nodes$label<- people
pal <-
dplyr::tibble(connection = c("successful pair","unsuccessful pair", "never a pair"),
color = c("blue","red","darkgray"))
set.seed(128)
edges <- combn(people, 2) %>%
t(.) %>%
dplyr::as_tibble(.) %>%
magrittr::set_names(c("from","to")) %>%
dplyr::mutate(connection = sample(c("successful pair","unsuccessful pair","never a
pair", NA), size = nrow(.), prob = c(0.2,0.2,0.2,0.4), replace = TRUE)) %>%
dplyr::filter(!is.na(connection)) %>%
dplyr::filter(from != to) %>%
dplyr::left_join(pal)
```

We now create the visNetwork network graph. Object g1 displays the network with id selection, reciprocal arrows, but no legend. Only reciprocal connections are shown. A later section shows a directed network where connections need not be reciprocal.

```
g1 <-
      # Create the base network
      visNetwork::visNetwork(nodes, edges) %>%
      # Set arrows for columns defining the edges
      visNetwork::visEdges(arrows = 'to, from', arrowStrikethrough= FALSE,
smooth=TRUE) %>%
      # Add interactive selection by id
      visNetwork::visOptions(highlightNearest = TRUE, nodesIdSelection = TRUE,) %>%
      # Add the edges legend
      visNetwork::visLegend(addEdges = edges_legend, ncol=3,width = 0.3)  %>%
      # Select a researcher-chosen layout rather than the default
      # The default layout is 'layout_nicely'
      # Other options include 'layout.davidson.harel' and 'layout_with_sugiyama',
      visNetwork::visIgraphLayout(layout='layout_in_circle', randomSeed = 123) %>%
      # Add navigation buttons
      visNetwork::visInteraction(navigationButtons=TRUE)
# Display g1, which is Figure 8.11
g1
```

In Figure 8.11, we see that Jane has the highest number of successful team pairings (8, compared to only 1 successful with Ayden). As Figure 8.11 makes apparent, the more network members, the harder to read the graph. This is

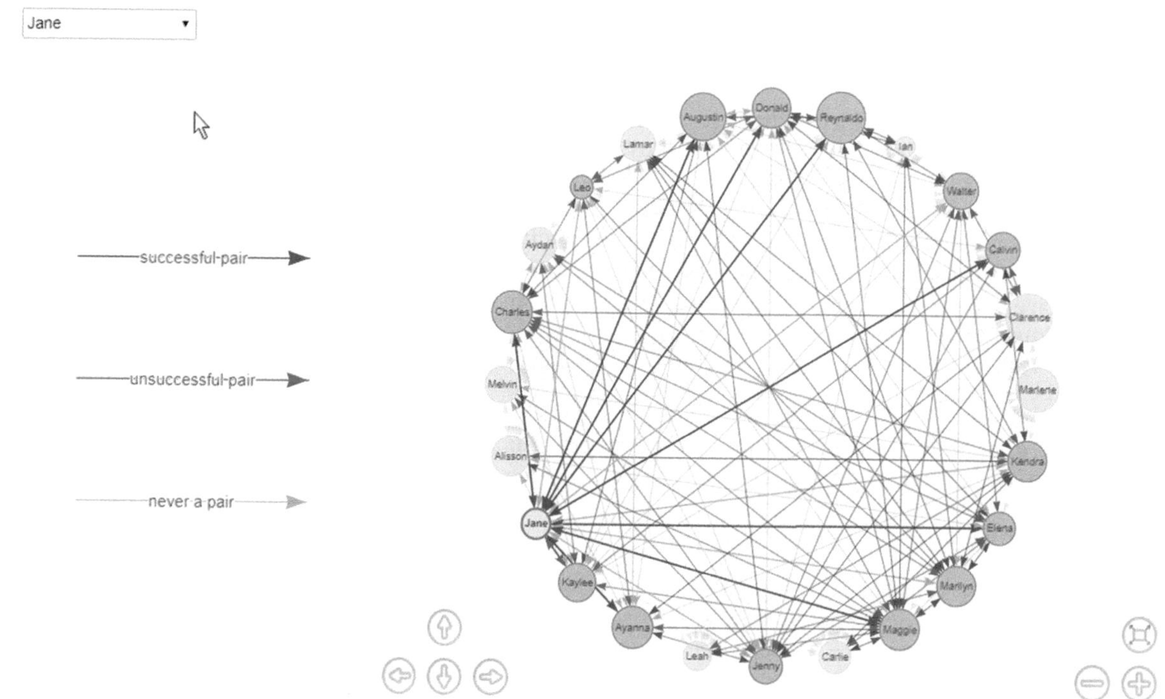

Figure 8.11 visNetwork with circle layout and navigation, Jane selected

where the interactivity of visNetwork helps greatly. Any given node, such as Jane, can be grabbed and moved, which both selects that node and highlights its connections, and also, by moving Jane to the left out of the circle, makes these connections even easier to identify and count.

8.7.4 Visualizing classification and regression trees: National literacy

The `visTree()` function of the visNetwork package creates attractive visualizations of classification and regression trees, discussed in Chapter 4. In that chapter we created the classification tree object "rparttree_class", which sought to classify 212 nations of the world as being high or low on national literacy rate. High was defined as being above-mean and low as below-mean. The predictors were a variety of demographic and other variables such as birthrate. The exact same model is created below, but results are graphed with the "visNetwork" package and shown in Figure 8.12. See Chapter 4 to compare other visualizations and for interpretation.

```
# Setup
setwd("C:/Data")
library(rpart)              # A leading decision tree package
library(sparkline)          # A utility needed by visNetwork
world <- read.table("world.csv", header = TRUE, sep = ",")

# Create the classification tree object, identical to Chapter 4
rparttree_class <- rpart::rpart(litgtmean ~ regionid+ population+areasqmiles+
poppersqmile+coast_arearatio+ netmigration+Infantdeathsper1k+ infdeaths+gdppercapita
lindollars +phonesper1000+arablepct+ cropspct+otherpct+birthrate+deathrate,
method="class", control=rpart.control(minbucket = 5), data=world)

# Visualize the solution using visNetwork's visTree() command
visNetwork::visTree(rparttree_class, edgesFontSize = 14, nodesFontSize = 16)
```

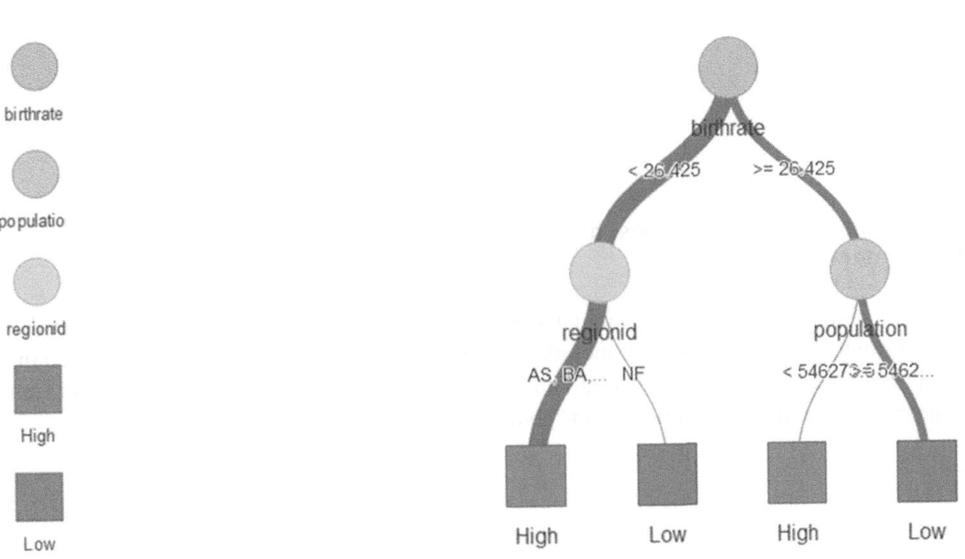

Figure 8.12 Literacy rate classification tree, visTree visualization

8.7.5 A directed network (asymmetrical relationships in a research team)

Previous sections on visNetwork have dealt with "undirected networks", define as one where the edges connecting nodes lack directionality. Put another way, edges in an undirected network are symmetrical. The relationship for which the edge stands does not have direction. Thus, in the previous examples, the relationship "successful pair" meant that when Kendra and Walter teamed as a pair in a project which was successful, this is the same as Walter and Kendra. The "from" person and the "to" person was arbitrary.

In contrast, a directed network (a.k.a., directed graph or digraph) is one where the edges do have a direction. For example, imagine a work group where each person rated each other person, with edges standing for "rates highly", "rates poorly", and "neutral". Kendra's rating of Walter may well not be the same as Walter's rating of Kendra. The relationships for which edges stand thus may be asymmetric. Two ways of depicting this are (1) to have two arrows connecting Walter and Kendra, one for the Kendra-rates-Walter direction and one for the Walter-rates-Kendra direction; or (2) to have a less cluttered graph, one may have only one arrow but the arrow tips are color coded to indicate the direction (rating) of the "to" person, with arrows being two-headed since Kendra and Walter are each the "to" person for the other. We illustrate both methods in this section.

Setup is largely the same as for an undirected visNetwork network:

```
library(dplyr)          # Utility supporting %>% piping, counting, and more
library(gtools)         # Used for permutations in directed network
library(visNetwork)     # A package for interactive network analysis
setwd("C:/Data")        # Set the working directory
```

Step 1
For simplicity of illustration, we go back to the 7-person research staff:

```
people<- c("Marlene", "Kendra", "Elena", "Marilyn", "Walter", "Calvin", "Clarence")
```

The following commands repeat the earlier subsection on undirected visNetwork graphs except font size and shape are specified. Labels will be inside circles. Node circle size will be set by length of the name (e.g., Leo is smallest).

```
# Create nodes
people<-unique(people)
nodes <- dplyr::tibble(id = people,font.size=16,shape="circle")
nodes$label<- people

# Set color codes
pal <-
dplyr::tibble(connection = c("rates highly","rates poorly", "is neutral"), color =
c("blue","red","darkgray"))
```

The next step is to create the edges object as a simulated data frame. In real life, step 2 would be skipped in favor of manually creating the data frame based on staff members' ratings of each other. This could be recorded in a spreadsheet and then exported as a. csv file, then read into an R data frame called "edges". The edges data frame would have these columns: "to", "from", "connection", and "color".

```
set.seed(123)

# To simulate a directed network, use permutations rather than combinations
edges <- as_tibble(gtools::permutations(length(people), 2, v=people, repeats.
allowed=FALSE))
names(edges) <- c("from","to")
```

```
edges$connection <- sample(c("rates highly","rates poorly", "is neutral", NA), size =
nrow(edges), prob = c(0.3,0.3,0.3,0.0), replace = TRUE)

edges <- edges %>%
dplyr::filter(!is.na(connection)) %>%
dplyr::left_join(pal)
# Step 3
```

We now create the visNetwork directed network graphs. Graph object g1 displays the network with id selection, directed arrows, but no legend. Type g1 to view it. A different random placement of nodes occurs each time you type g1. Nodes may be dragged for better placement but dragging will cause the underlying network physics algorithm to then adjust edges further.

```
set.seed(123)
g1 <-
# Create the network
visNetwork(nodes, edges, width="100%") %>%
# Set arrows for columns defining the edges
visNetwork::visEdges(arrows = 'to',length = 250) %>%
# Turn on id selection
visNetwork::visOptions(highlightNearest = TRUE, nodesIdSelection = TRUE)
g1
```

For graph g2, add the edges legend. Type g2 to view it.

```
edges_legend <- pal %>%
rename(label = connection)
g2 <-
    g1 %>%
    visNetwork::visLegend(addEdges = edges_legend,ncol=3,width = 0.30)  %>%
visNetwork::visOptions(highlightNearest = TRUE, nodesIdSelection = TRUE)
```

For graph g3, we add navigation buttons.

```
g3 <-
    g2 %>%
    visNetwork::visInteraction(navigationButtons=TRUE)
#Type g3 to view the network. This is Figure 8.13.
# Note nodes may be dragged, so the exact locations may differ.
g3
```

Graph g4 has the alternative double-headed arrow layout for a directed graph. We use one of several available layouts. Type g4 to view it. This is Figure 8.14.

```
g4 <-
    g3 %>%
    visNetwork::visIgraphLayout(layout= "layout_with_sugiyama")
```

In Figure 8.13, note that Kendra's rating of Marilyn is positive (blue) but Marilyn's rating of Kendra is negative (red), indicated by two connecting arrows respectively. In Figure 8.14, we see the same relationships, but asymmetry is indicated by different-colored tips on the two-headed edge arrows. The arrow from Kendra to Marilyn has a blue tip, indicating a positive rating. The same arrow but from Marilyn to Kendra has a red tip, indicating a negative rating. While we use "ratings" as the example here, the connection could be any sentiment. Sentiment analysis may well involve the creation of directed graphs.

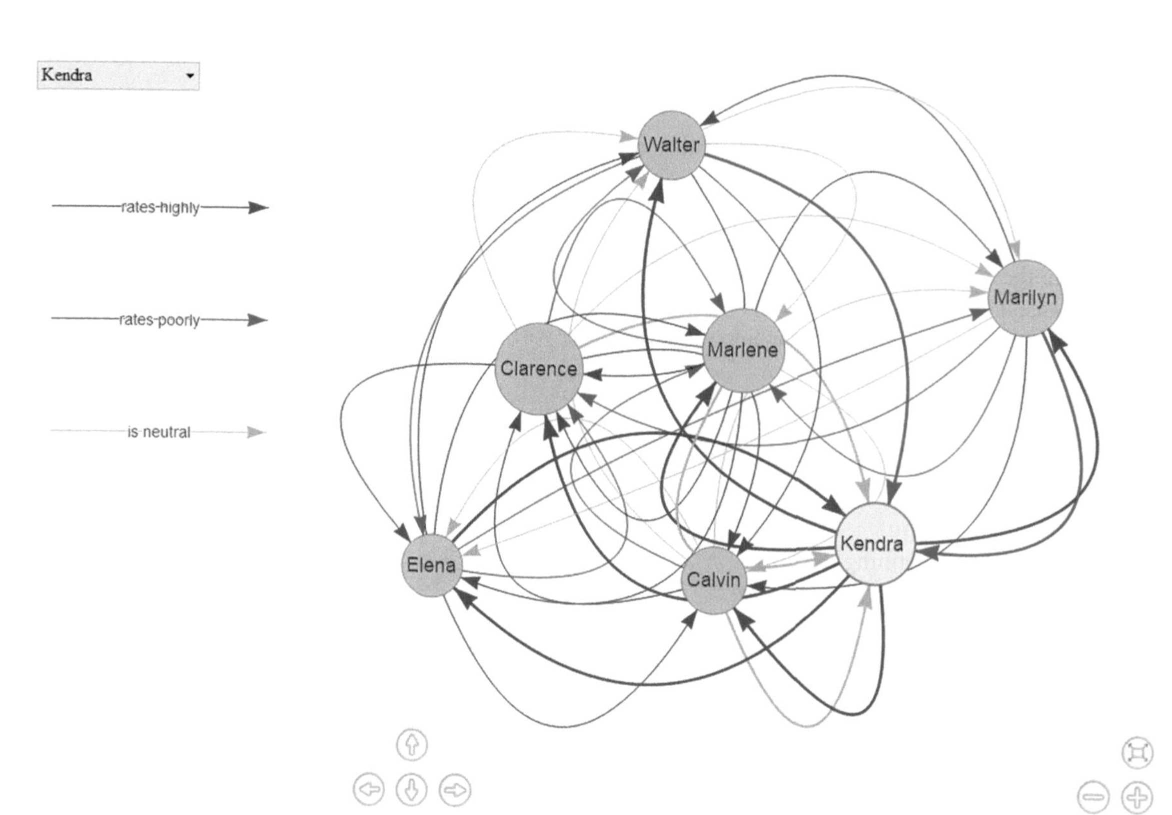

Figure 8.13 Directed network in visNetwork, two arrows per edge

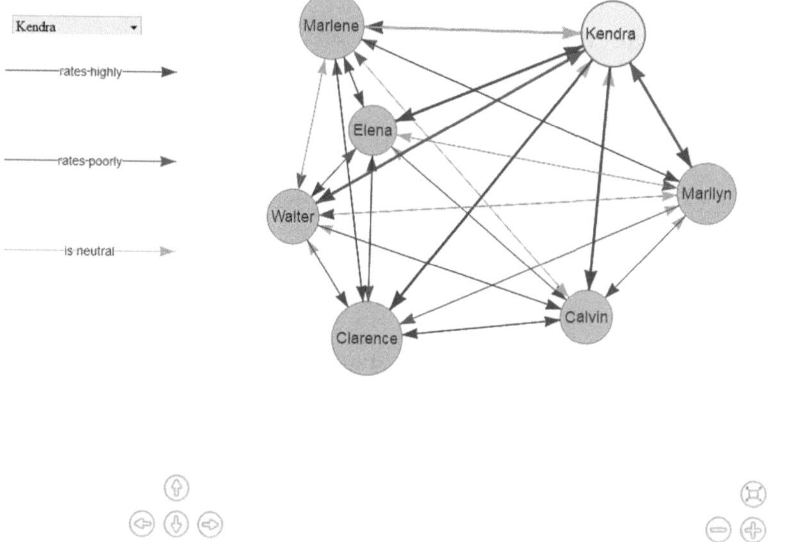

Figure 8.14 Directed network in visNetwork, double-headed arrows

8.8 Network analysis with igraph

The R package "igraph" is probably the most widely-utilized for visualization of networks. This package offers so many options and functionalities that only a few may be presented here. Basic features of igraph were presented in the earlier section of this chapter (see "Quick start exercise 1: Analysis of network relationships"). In this section, we present additional features and uses.

In the subsections which follow, these are the packages used:

```
library(CINNA)       # Supports measures of network centrality
library(cluster)     # For k-means clustering in this section
library(dplyr)       # Utility supports the select() command and more
library(DT)          # Provides an R interface to the JavaScript library DataTables
library(htm2txt)     # Used to scrape example data from the web
library(igraph)      # A leading network visualization package
                     # igraph also calls the following packages: graphics, grDevices, magrittr, Matrix,
                     pkgconfig (>= 2.0.0), stats, and utils. The user does not need to install these separately.
library(tm)          # The Text Miner package, used to convert imported text data
                     into "SimpleCorpus" format, then into "term document matrix"
                     (tdm) format.
```

8.8.1 Term adjacency networks: Gubernatorial websites and the covid pandemic

In this subsection we analyze a term adjacency network with igraph. Term adjacency simply means the co-occurrence of given terms in the same documents. For example data we use terms drawn from gubernatorial websites in five states. Term adjacency network analysis is a form of text analysis, discussed in Chapter 9, which in part uses the same gubernatorial website data.

The research question is an exploratory one: What terms co-occur in text material governors of selected states chose to employ on their official websites? As data were collected near a high point of the coronavirus (covid) pandemic of 2020–2021, we are particularly interested in what words co-occur with the term "covid". The term adjacency network method is an unsupervised one, meaning that results will flow entirely from found data.

Step 1: *Read website data into a term adjacency matrix*. We pull data from the gubernatorial websites of five selected states using the "htm2txt" package. Data were collected on June 4, 2020, near a high point in of the coronavirus pandemic. Gubernatorial website addresses were retrieved from https://www.nga.org/governors/addresses/. Web scraping is explained in much more detail in Chapter 9. For purposes of this chapter these steps create a "term adjacency matrix" in which rows and columns are terms (words) and cell entries are co-occurrences of the row term with the column term.

Specifically, if the reader collects similar data on a different date or for different states, results will differ. Therefore, if following along with this text, the reader may skip ahead to the section below on reading in the cleaned text files, which are supplied in the online Support Material (www.routledge.com/9780367624293) for this book.

```
# How the raw data were obtained:

CA <- htm2txt::gettxt("https://www.gov.ca.gov/")
FL <- htm2txt::gettxt("https://www.flgov.com/")
LA <- htm2txt::gettxt("https://gov.louisiana.gov/")
NY <- htm2txt::gettxt("https://www.governor.ny.gov/")
TX <- htm2txt::gettxt("https://gov.texas.gov/")

# For manual cleaning purposes, save the raw text files to the working directory.
# Actual cleaning is discussed in Chapter 9.
write.table(CA, file = "CA.txt", quote = FALSE, sep = "\n", col.names = FALSE)
write.table(FL, file = "FL.txt", quote = FALSE, sep = "\n", col.names = FALSE)
write.table(LA, file = "LA.txt", quote = FALSE, sep = "\n", col.names = FALSE)
```

```
write.table(NY, file = "NY.txt", quote = FALSE, sep = "\n", col.names = FALSE)
write.table(TX, file = "TX.txt", quote = FALSE, sep = "\n", col.names = FALSE)

# Read the cleaned text from the working directory back into R
# These text files are supplied on the Support Material (www.routledge.com/9780367624293) for this book.
setwd("C:/Data")
CA_C <- readLines('CA_C.txt')
FL_C <- readLines('FL_C.txt')
LA_C <- readLines('LA_C.txt')
NY_C <- readLines('NY_C.txt')
TX_C <- readLines('TX_C.txt')

# Convert from character vectors to a "capital-C" SimpleCorpus using the tm package.
library(tm)
governors_SimpleCorpus <- tm::SimpleCorpus(tm::VectorSource(unlist(lapply(c(CA_C,FL_
C,LA_C,NY_C,TX_C), as.character))))

# Convert from a SimpleCorpus to a term document matrix (tdm) using the tm package.
governors_tdm<- tm::TermDocumentMatrix(governors_SimpleCorpus, control =
list(removeNumbers = TRUE, removePunctuation=TRUE, stopwords = TRUE, stemming =
FALSE))
class(governors_tdm)
[1] "TermDocumentMatrix"    "simple_triplet_matrix"
```

The governors_tdm object is a matrix with 654 rows (words) and five columns (documents). The number of words is contingent on the date when webpages were retrieved. Below, the "tdm" object is a matrix version of governors_tdm. For instructional purposes, we subset just the first 25 words plus the 37th word, which is "covid". This creates a term document matrix (tdm2) with 26 terms. The full term document matrix is named "tdm" and the subset is "tdm2".

```
tdm <- as.matrix(governors_tdm)
x <- as.data.frame(tdm)
x2 <- x[c(1:25,37),]
tdm2 <- as.matrix(x2)
```

Finally, we convert to a term-term adjacency matrix (square) called "tdm_adj" for the full 654-word matrix and "tdm_adj2" for the 26-term instructional matrix. Each matrix has terms as rows and columns, with cell entries containing the number of co-occurrences of the row and column terms.

```
# Full adjacency matrix:
tdm_adj <- tdm %*% t(tdm)
dim(tdm_adj)
[Output:]
   [1] 654 654

# 26-term adjacency matrix
tdm_adj2 <- tdm2 %*% t(tdm2)
dim(tdm_adj2)
[Output:]
   [1] 26 26
```

Step 2: Display term frequencies. In this step we list word frequencies of co-occurrences in the 26-term instructional adjacency matrix (tdm_adj2). The instructional set is used because, being smaller, it is more easily viewed in Figure 8.15. The "DT" package displays an interactive matrix in Viewer area of RStudio. In the Viewer, click the up-arrow next to a word to sort frequencies by that word.

```
library(DT)
DT::datatable(tdm_adj2, class = 'cell-border stripe')
```

The interactive table resulting from the `datatable()` command above is shown in part in Figure 8.15, which has been sorted on "covid". This reveals that "covid" co-occurs five times with "action", ten times with "additional", and so on. This conforms with widespread reporting of California as a state leader in effective pandemic response. Other co-occurring terms (additional, action, benefit, can, bold, building) are suggestive of a proactive stance vis-à-vis the pandemic.

Step 3: *Create a network graph based on the term adjacency matrix.* Networks visualize matrices. While no truly additional information is contained in them, visualizations may throw more light on the nature of term co-occurrences. Here we use the "igraph" package to visualize the example network. We continue to use the smaller 26-term instructional term adjacency matrix.

Below we create and then simplify the "g" igraph object. In the process we simplify by removing loops (edges for which the two endpoints are the same vertex). We also simplify by eliminating multiple edges (edges having exactly the same two endpoints). Note: Don't remove multiple edges for directed graphs (the current example is undirected). This step does not actually create a network plot yet, just the igraph object.

```
g <- igraph::graph.adjacency(tdm_adj2, weighted=T, mode = "undirected")
g <- igraph::simplify(g, remove.multiple = TRUE, remove.loops = TRUE)

# Set colors. Recall "covid" is now the last (26th) term in the subset being used.
igraph::V(g)$color <- "lightblue"          # Default color
igraph::V(g)$color[26] <- "pink"           # Color for "covid"
```

Step 4: *Visualize the graph in alternative layouts.* In this step we visualize the "g" graph. With the full governors_tdm there would have been 654 words, making the network plot unreadably cluttered, though we could have discerned how many word clusters there were. Above, however, we limited our analysis to the first 25 words plus

Show 50 ▾ entries

	achieve	action	additional	advocate	agree	allowed
covid	5	10	13	5	5	5
announces	5	10	5	5	5	5
california	8	16	8	8	8	8
californians	5	10	5	5	5	5
additional	1	2	3	1	1	1
action	2	4	2	2	2	2
benefit	2	4	2	2	2	2
californias	2	4	2	2	2	2
can	2	4	2	2	2	2
bold	1	2	2	1	1	1
building	1	2	2	1	1	1
achieve	1	2	1	1	1	1
advocate	1	2	1	1	1	1
agree	1	2	1	1	1	1
allowed	1	2	1	1	1	1

Showing 1 to 26 of 26 entries

Figure 8.15 Term co-occurrence table

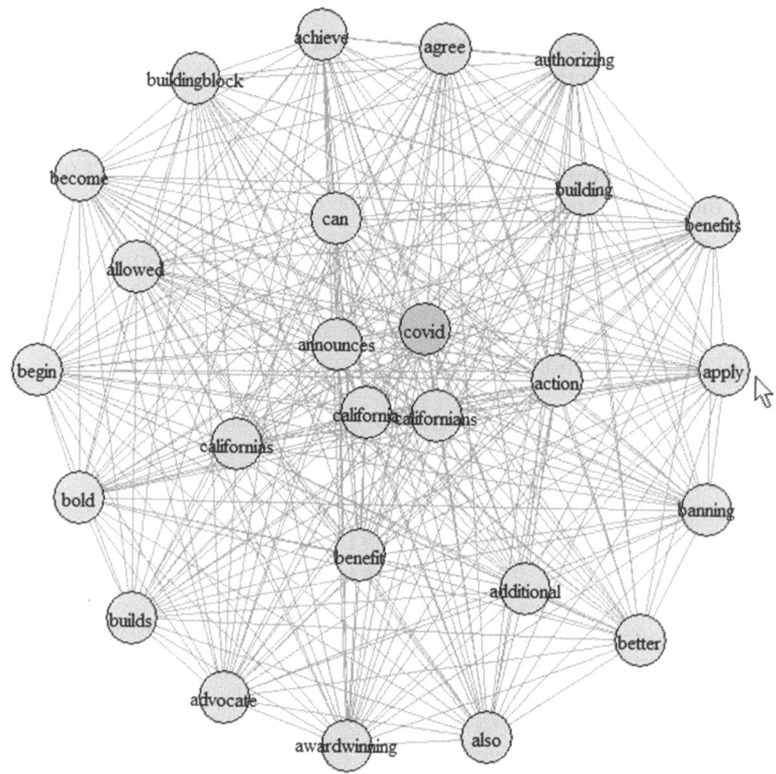

Figure 8.16 Term co-occurrence network, Fruchtenrman-Reingold layout

"covid". We plot the "g" graph in two layouts. First, the Fruchterman-Reingold layout places terms with higher co-occurrences more toward the center.

```
# The Fruchterman-Reingold layout
set.seed(1234)
igraph::plot.igraph(g, layout=layout.fruchterman.reingold)
mtext("Term co-occurrences, Fruchterman-Reingold layout",side=1)
```

In Figure 8.16, we see that the most central terms are covid, california, californians, and announces, followed by a second circle which includes the terms californias, benefits, additional, action can, allowed, and building. All others are peripheral in this layout. Contrast this layout with the Kamada-Kawai layout in Figure 8.17. This layout gives a more well-spaced graph in which terms with high co-occurrences appear toward the periphery, making them easier to spot.

A different view is obtained by using the "Kamada-Kawai" layout. Notice that the same color scheme is still in effect and does not need to be repeated.

```
set.seed(123)
plot(g, layout=layout.kamada.kawai, main = "Term co-occurrences, Kamada.Kawai
layout")
```

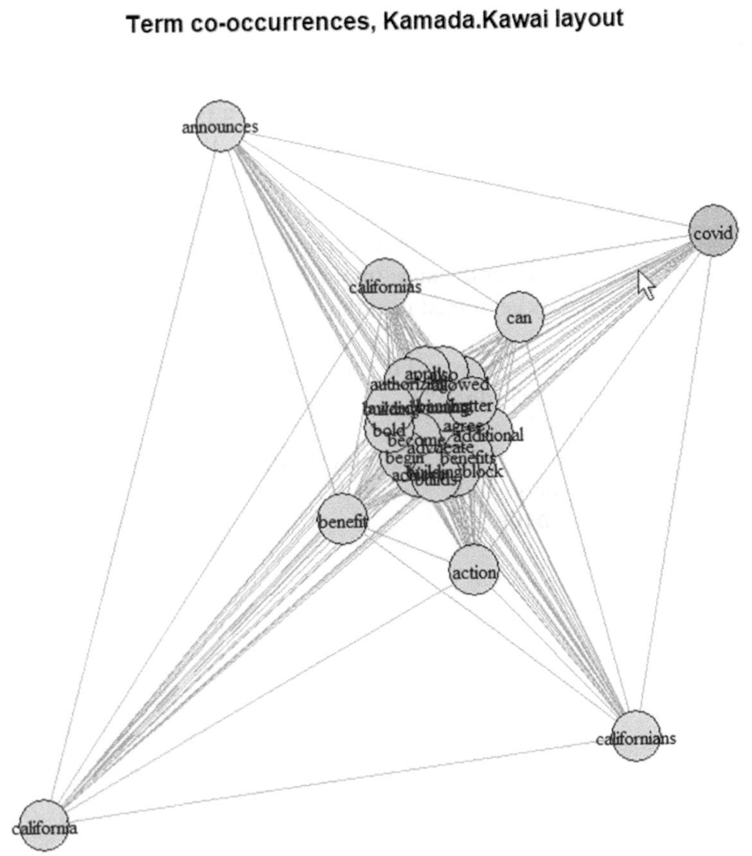

Figure 8.17 Term co-occurrence network, Kamada-Kawai layout

The presently possible igraph layouts are listed below. The layout term follows "layout=" on the igraph options list (e.g., igraph::plot.igraph(g, layout=layout_nicely). Note that not all layouts are compatible with all data (see help("layout")).

- layout_nicely # The default
- layout_as_bipartite
- layout_as_star
- layout_as_tree
- layout.fruchterman.reingold
- layout_in_circle
- layout.kamada.kawai
- layout_on_grid
- layout_on_sphere
- layout_randomly
- layout.reingold.tilford
- layout_with_dh
- layout_with_fr
- layout_with_gem
- layout_with_graphopt
- layout_with_kk

- layout_with_lgl
- layout_with_mds
- layout_with_sugiyama

Step 5: *Create a dendrogram based on hierarchical clustering.* Figure 8.18 shows the dendrogram for the current example using the 26-term instructional adjacency matrix. Cluster analysis was discussed in Chapter 2, along with explanation of how dendrograms are interpreted. Horizontal lines mark where terms or groups of terms were joined to make a cluster. Simplifying, the higher the joining line, the more unlike terms were being joined. Thus, Californians and announces were very similar in their co-occurrences, with California not much different. The term "covid" is joined to these three at a greater distance (more dissimilarity), but these four terms are different in co-occurrences from the others, which only get joined in at the very top of the graph.

```
# Both hclust() and rect.hclust() are part of the "stats" package in the R system library.
d <- dist(tdm_adj2, method = "euclidean")      # define distance matrix
fit <- hclust(d, method="ward.D")
plot(fit)                                      # display dendrogram
# Draw dendrogram with blue cluster borders
rect.hclust(fit, k=10, border="blue")
```

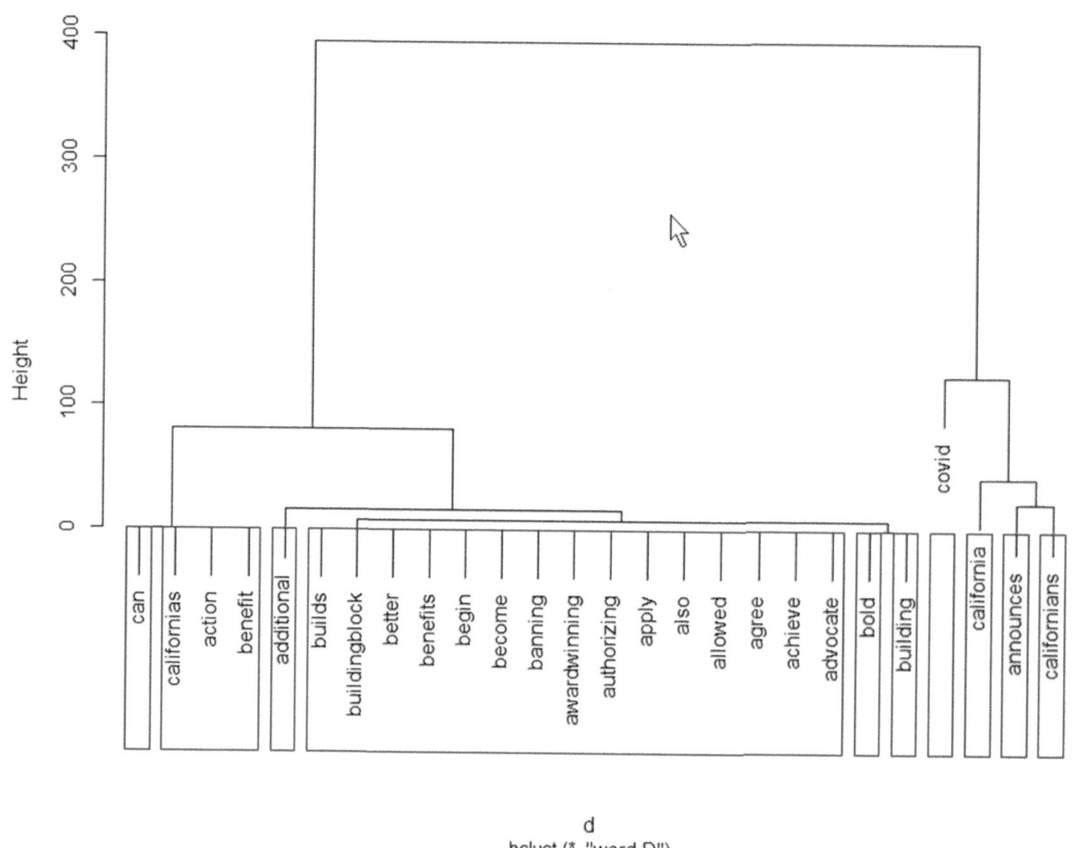

Figure 8.18 Dendrogram for term co-occurrences

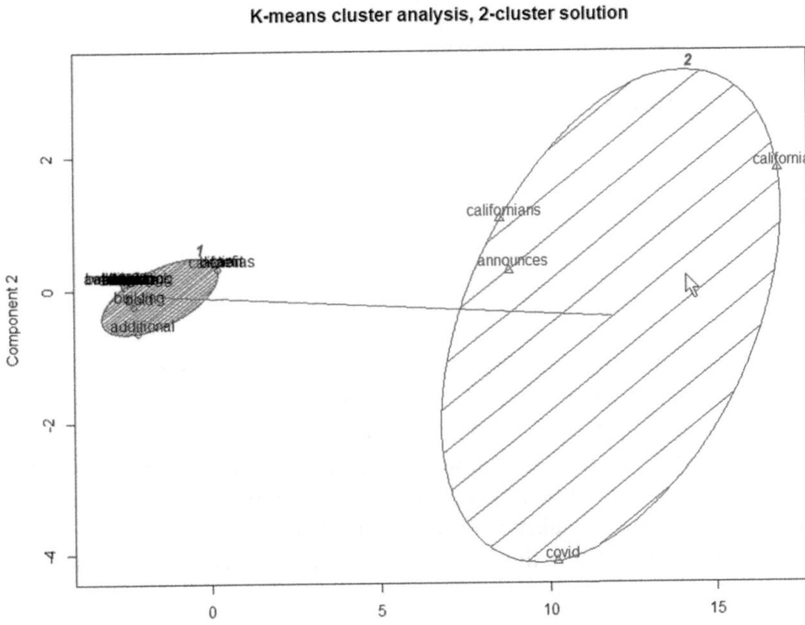

Figure 8.19 K-means clustering of term co-occurrences, 2-cluster solution

Step 6: *Create word clusters*. Figure 8.19 displays the results of k-means clustering of the terms in the example network. In this method of clustering, the researcher specifies the desired number of clusters. We specified two, corresponding roughly to the two groups of terms by co-occurrences shown in the dendrogram (Figure 8.17). Of course, the researcher could explore the 3-cluster, 4-cluster, or higher solutions not presented here. (Note: The reference in Figure 8.19 to the "two components explain 99.71% of the point variability" does not refer to the two clusters but to the two axes, which are the same for solutions of any number of clusters.)

```
# K-means clustering (2 clusters)
# Both kmeans() and clusplot() are part of the R system library.
fit <- kmeans(tdm_adj2, 2)
# Cluster Plot against first two principal components
# The cluster package is in the R System Library but may require loading on some machines.
library(cluster)
cluster::clusplot(tdm_adj2, fit$cluster, color=TRUE, shade=TRUE, labels=2, lines=1,
col.p = fit$cluster, main= "K-means cluster analysis, 2-cluster solution")
```

Finally, we create a list of words with their k-means cluster membership numbers. If terms overlap in the figure, the terms in each of the two clusters can be determined from this listing.

```
termlist <- fitted(fit, method = "classes")
termlist
[Output]
     achieve         action   additional
           2              2            2
    advocate          agree      allowed
           2              2            2
        also      announces        apply
           2              1            2
```

```
authorizing awardwinning       banning
          2            2             2
     become        begin       benefit
          2            2             2
   benefits       better          bold
          2            2             2
   building buildingblock       builds
          2            2             2
 california  californians  californias
          1            1             2
        can        covid
          2            1
```

In summary, with respect to our initial research questions, the test, table, and graphical output in this section serve well to explore what terms co-occur on the selected gubernatorial websites, based on the 26-term instructional term adjacency matrix. With respect to "covid" mentions in particular, we have confirmed that the "covid' term is a central one on gubernatorial websites on the day data were collected and is particularly associated with the state of California. Also, as shown in both network layouts and in the frequency table, other co-occurring terms (e.g., action, benefit, can) suggest a proactive stance was taken vis-à-vis the pandemic.

Limitations: We underscore the fact that in this instructional exercise, only a small subset of 26 of the 654 possible terms were analyzed. In Chapter 9, we discuss how terms to be analyzed might be limited to a smaller number of the most important ones. Also, words may be stemmed so that California, Californians, and Californias all appear as part of the stem "California".

8.8.2 Similarity/distance networks with igraph: Senate interest group ratings

In this section, we use igraph to visualize a similarity network, which is a type of distance network in which the distance metric is based on some measure of dissimilarity or similarity. In the subsequent section, we partition the 16-senator network into "communities", compute modularity as a performance score for the partition, and compute various centrality rankings for U.S. Senators, which are our focus. The similarities in question have to do with senators' rankings on roll-call votes as rated by a set of eight interest groups:[3] While all the groups are primarily progressive, senators' rankings are far from identical. The groups are:

- *ACLU* – American Civil Liberties Union
- *ADA* – Americans for Democratic Action
- *CDF* – Children's Defense Fund
- *LCV* – League of Conservation Voters
- *NAACP* – National Association for the Advancement of Colored People
- *NARAL* – National Abortion and Reproductive Rights Action League
- *PTA* – National Parent-Teacher Association
- *SEIU* – Service Employees International Union

In the original dataset, the eight groups form the columns, senators are the rows, and a cell entry is the group rating for a senator's set of roll-call votes selected by the row interest group. We then compute the absolute mean difference in scores between any two senators. Weighting is not necessary since scores for all interest groups are normed to the 0 to 100 range. Then we transpose the data matrix so senators are the columns (variables) and rows are the eight groups (the observations). For the transposed matrix, a distance matrix displays how similar one senator is to another in terms of interest group ratings taken as a set. Low values indicate greater similarity. To simplify the network graph, pairs with high distance are filtered out.

Why use a distance matrix rather than a correlation matrix as the measure of similarity or distance? For a very good reason! Consider the interest group rankings of Joe Biden, a liberal, and Jim Bunning, a conservative, in the "senate_df" data frame created further below. While Biden and Bunning are clearly far apart by any interest group measure, their ratings actually correlate quite highly (.71). This is because when one goes up, generally the other does as well. Two things which go up and down in tandem correlate highly, even though far apart. If we were interested in tandemness we would use a correlation matrix.[4] But as instead we are interested in similarity, we use a similarity matrix in which low values represent low distance and high values represent similarity.

Data are taken from 2005, an era in which both Joe Biden and Barack Obama were members of the U.S. Senate. Our social science research questions are, "In the network implied by interest group ratings from back in 2005, was Joe Biden close to members of the progressive wing of the Democratic Party, such as Hillary Clinton?" Considering a "strong link" to be one with a distance less than the mean, did Joe Biden have strong links mainly with Democrats or with members of both parties? The latter would imply more opportunity for Biden to play a bipartisan brokerage role.

In the following "Setup" section we read in the interest group rating data on all 100 U.S. Senators. However, for instructional simplicity and less cluttered graphs, we initially reduce this number to only 20 Senators. Later, we rerun some of the analysis for all 100 Senators.

Step 1: *Setup and data preparation*. First we set the working directory as usual, invoke the igraph library, and read in the senate ratings data. We also view the imported data frame and list out names of the variables it contains. We also subset the data into a data frame with only 16 Senators. We then transpose the data to make the senators the columns (variables) and make the interest groups the rows (observations). Finally, because the data contain missing values, we impute them. Better imputation with the "mice" package is discussed in Chapter 3, but here we use simple mean imputation.

```
setwd("C:/Data")
library(igraph)

senate_df <- read.table("senate8groups.csv", header = TRUE, sep = ",")

View(senate_df)

# Check to make sure each variable is of the expected data class
sapply(senate_df, class)
[Output]
      State     Senator       PARTY        ACLU
"character" "character" "character"   "integer"
        ADA         CDF         LCV       NAACP
  "integer"   "integer"   "integer"   "integer"
      NARAL         PTA        SEIU
  "integer"   "integer"   "integer"
```

For instructional purposes, we create a subset of two contrasting senatorial groups After dropping five cases with missing values, we pick the first ten (all Democrats) and the last ten (all Republicans). Below, we consider the "senate_sample" data frame of 20 Senators.

```
nrow(senate_df)
[Output:]
   [1] 100
```

Reduce to cases with no missing data.

```
data_complete <- senate_df[complete.cases(senate_df), ]
nrow(data_complete)
[Output:]
   [1] 95
```

Take a sample of the first and last ten cases. Drop the first three non-numeric columns (State, Senator, PARTY).

```
senate_sample <- data_complete[c(1:10,86:95),4:11]
nrow(senate_sample)
```

[Output:]
```
[1] 20
```

Add senator names as rownames

```
rownames(senate_sample)<- data_complete$Senator[c(1:10,86:95)]
```

Next, transpose with the `t()` function to make senators the columns (variables) and the eight interest groups the rows.

```
senate_t <- as.data.frame(t(senate_sample))
```

Check for missing values. There are none because we used only complete cases earlier, but this is one way to check.

```
sum(is.na(senate_t))
```
[Output:]
```
[1] 0
```

Step 2: Create the absolute difference matrix. For coding simplicity, we make "df" as a copy of senate_t, as this will be our data frame of interest.

```
df <- senate_t
```

We now compute a difference (not corr) matrix. Cell entries are absolute differences between mean ratings for a pair of senators. Start by getting the mean interest group ratings for each senator. The "dfmeans" object is a numeric vector.

```
dfmeans <- colMeans(df[sapply(df, is.numeric)])
```

Next get a matrix of absolute mean differences between senators. The resulting object, "diffs", is of class matrix, where senators are both rows and columns and cell entries are the absolute mean differences between any pair of senators. That is, the means are averages across all eight interest group ratings.

```
size <- length(dfmeans)
diffs <- abs(matrix(dfmeans, size, size, byrow=TRUE) - matrix(dfmeans, size, size,
byrow=FALSE))
```

The matrix operation above drops the row and column names, so we add them back in. After this step, diffs is a matrix with senator names as both row and column labels.

```
colnames(diffs)<-colnames(df)
rownames(diffs)<-colnames(df)
```

To preserve diffs, create a copy called "matrix1"

```
matrix1 <-  diffs
```

It is helpful to know the rownames for senators in matrix 1. Note, for example, that Joe Biden is row 7.

```
rownames(matrix1)
```
[Output:]
```
 [1] "Blanche Lincoln"     "Mark Pryor"
 [3] "Barbara Boxer"       "Dianne Feinstein"
 [5] "Christopher Dodd"    "Joseph Lieberman"
 [7] "Joe Biden"           "Tom Carper"
 [9] "Bill Nelson"         "Daniel Akaka"
[11] "Jim DeMint"          "John Cornyn"
[13] "Orrin Hatch"         "George Allen"
```

```
[15] "Jon Kyl"            "Saxby Chambliss"
[17] "Jim Bunning"        "Thad Cochran"
[19] "Kit Bond"           "Jeff Sessions"
```

Retain only differences of 43 or less (43 was approximately the mean difference). This has the effect of dropping less important edges from the network. Less important edges are edges connecting the least similar senators.

```
matrix1[matrix1 > 43] <- 0
```

Display the revised distance matrix

```
View(matrix1)
```

Step 3: *Create the igraph graph object, called "g"*. A distance matrix is a type of "adjacency matrix". The network is "undirected" because the distance coefficients are non-directional: Joe Biden's distance from Jeff Sessions it the same as for Jeff Sessions from Joe Biden. The diagonal, which contains distances of 0.000, is set to "FALSE" because we do not want these coefficients being interpreted as strong relationships.

Create the graph object "g". This step does not actually display the network plot yet.

```
g <- igraph::graph_from_adjacency_matrix(matrix1, weighted=TRUE, mode =
"undirected", diag=FALSE)
```

Now simplify by removing loops (edges for which the two endpoints are the same vertex). The `simplify()` function also eliminates multiple edges (edges having exactly the same two endpoints). Note: Do not remove multiple edges for directed graphs (the current example is undirected).

```
g <- igraph::simplify(g, remove.multiple = TRUE, remove.loops = TRUE)
```

Step 4: *Setup color scheme for the graph (network)*. We start by setting colors for senators in our 20-person sample. However, recall that in our sample, the first ten rows were all Democrats and the last ten were all Republicans. This can be verified by looking at the "PARTY" variable in the original data.

Set colors for the 20-Senator sample. The later section on "All 100 Senators" gives equivalent code for analyzing the entire sample. The color index numbers below correspond to row numbers in the 20-Senator graph (g, based on matrix1).

```
igraph::V(g)$color[c(1:6,8:10)] <- "lightblue" # Color for Democrats
igraph::V(g)$color[7] <- "green" # Color to highlight Joe Biden
igraph::V(g)$color[c(11:20)] <- "pink" # Color for Republicans (GOP)
```

Step 5: *Visualize the network*. There are many possible layouts for a network in igraph (see the listing in the previous section). We present two of the possible layouts: The popular Fruchterman-Reingold layout and the circle layout. Code for two additional layouts is also presented below (mds and grid layouts), but without figures reproduced here.

Figure 8.20 displays the similarity network based on interest group rating of 20 Senators. It employs the Fruchterman-Reingold layout, which places vertices (senators) that are less similar away from the center. Since difference scores which are less than the mean are suppressed in this diagram, senators with more edge connections tend to be more central. Isolates, who have no strong similarities with any other senator, are placed toward the periphery. Figure 8.20 shows two clusters, Republican and Democrat, with no strong ties between them.

Below is R code for the default plot (same as the command `plot(g)`). The exact configuration of the nodes and edges will vary according to the random seed. The user may wish to experiment with different seeds to obtain a plot which is wanted for the research purpose at hand. Here, setting seed to 12 showed Joe Biden clearly.

```
set.seed(12)
igraph::plot.igraph(g, layout=layout_nicely)
mtext("Similarity network, interest group rankings for Senators, Fruchterman-
Reingold layout",side=1)
```

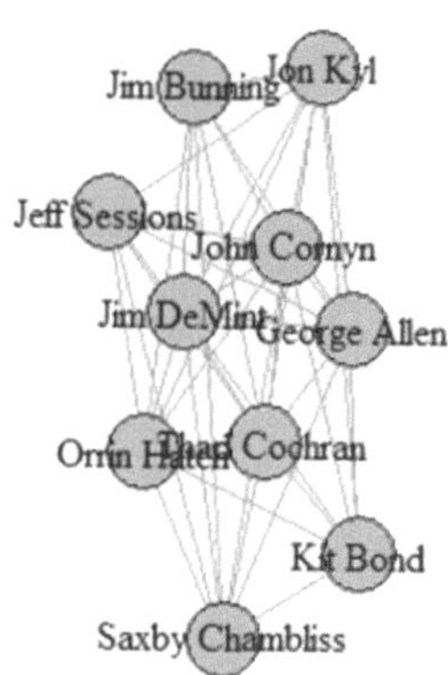

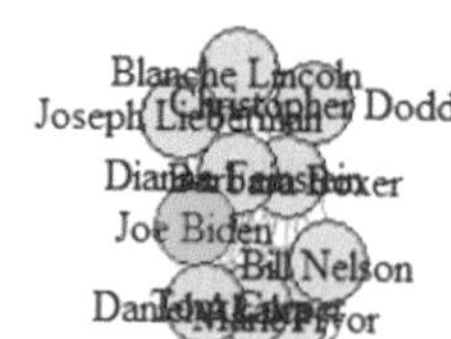

Similarity network, interest group rankings for Senators, Fruchterman-Reingold layout

Figure 8.20 Similarity network based on Senate interest group ratings, Fruchterman-Reingold layout

We now display the same network in circle layout, shown in Figure 8.21. As vertices (senators) are equally spaced about the circle, this layout does not show proximity of pairs of senators well. However, it more clearly shows the strong similarities (or absence thereof) between any two senators. Like Figure 8.20, the circle layout also shows the separation of the Republican and Democratic groups.

```
# The syntax below visualizes the "g" graph in circle layout
set.seed(123)
igraph::plot.igraph(g, layout=layout_in_circle)
mtext("Similarity network, interest group rankings for Senators, circle
layout",side=1)
```

Not displayed here in a figure, the R code for some alternative layouts is shown below:

```
igraph::plot.igraph(g, layout=layout.kamada.kawai)
mtext("Similarity network, interest group rankings for Senators, kamada.kawai
layout",side=1)

igraph::plot.igraph(g,layout= layout_with_mds, dist=matrix1, dim=2, size=88)
mtext("Similarity network, interest group rankings for Senators, mds layout",
side=1)

igraph::plot.igraph(g,layout= layout_on_grid)
mtext("Similarity network, interest group rankings for Senators, grid
layout",side=1)
```

8.8.3 Communities, modularity, and centrality

Our social science research questions, beyond those in the previous section, include the question, "Based on interest group ratings, how many subgroups ("communities") are identifiable in the similarity network? Which senators are

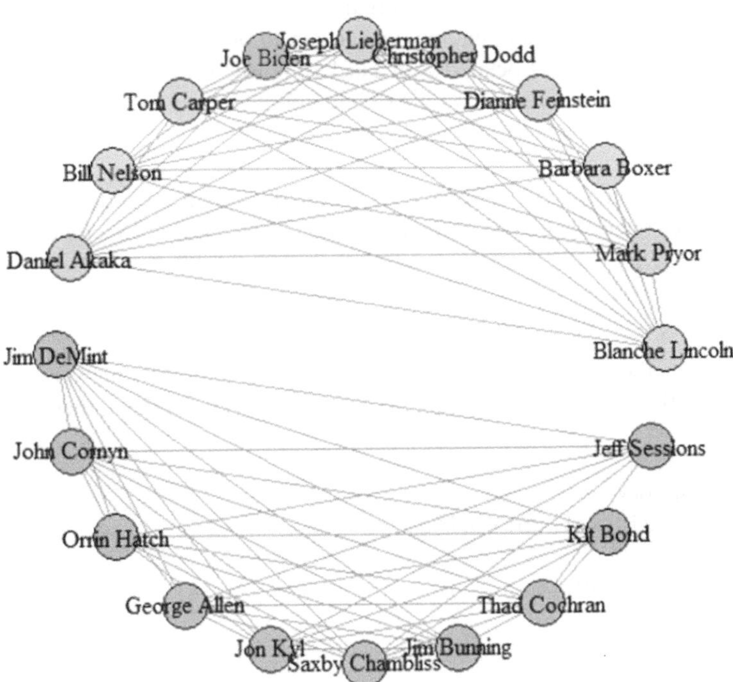

Similarity network, interest group rankings for Senators, circle layout

Figure 8.21 Similarity network based on Senate interest group ratings, circle layout

in the same community of Senators as Joe Biden? We first answer these questions for the 20-Senator sample, then in a subsequent section for the set of all 100 Senators.

Cluster analysis may be applied to the igraph "g" graph object, partitioning its vertices (senators) into clusters called "communities". We use the "cluster_optimal" method, but there are many alternatives. All return an object of class "communities". The label "cluster_optimal" is misleading. What is optimal depends upon the research context. The researcher is encouraged to try multiple clustering methods mentioned in the next paragraph, then assess which leads to the most insightful and useful clusters based on interpretability and theory.

Other methods include cluster_edge_betweenness, cluster_fast_greedy, cluster_label_prop, cluster_leading_eigen, cluster_louvain, cluster_optimal, cluster_spinglass, and cluster_walktrap. Different methods may result in different numbers of communities. In this section, we continue to use the "g" object for our analysis of the similarity network for 16 Senators based on eight interest group ratings. At the end we show results for all 100 Senators.

TEXT BOX 8.1 Analyzing organized criminal networks with the "igraph" package

Diviák, Coutinho, and Stivala (2020) studied organized crime networks using Canadian Law Enforcement data on 1,390 individuals known or suspect of organized crime involvement. It was known that men were responsible for much more organized crime than women, reflected in the fact that there were only 185 women in the sample. The research question was whether the structural position of women in organized crime networks was also secondary compared to men, with women holding positions of less influence and power. As a measure of structural position and influence, the authors used betweenness centrality as a metric. This metric was calculated using the "igraph" package in R. The igraph package was also used to visualize organized crime networks.

In spite of recent evidence that the gender gap in organized crime might be narrowing, the authors found that their network analysis suggested "an ongoing gender gap in organized crime, with women occupying structural positions that are generally associated with a lack of power. Overall, women are less present in the network, tend to collaborate with other women rather than with men, and are more often in the disadvantageous position of being connected by male intermediaries." (p. 547)

Source: Diviák, Tomáš; Coutinho, J. A.; & Stivala, A. D. (2020). A man's world? Comparing the structural positions of men and women in an organized criminal network. *Crime, Law and Social Change* 74(5): 547–569.

Communities

By the "optimal" clustering method, output below shows that the small similarity network may be partitioned into five communities (modules). Based on the same graph (g) as in the previous section, there are two communities of ten Senators each.

```
#Determining cluster communities
communities <- igraph::cluster_optimal(g)

# Print number and sizes of communities
igraph::sizes(communities)
[Output:]
   Community sizes
   1  2
   10 10
```

Modularity score

Modularity reflects how separated the different vertex types are from each other. For unweighted graphs, modularity is the fraction of the edges (connections) that fall within the given groups minus the expected fraction if edges were randomly distributed. Higher scores reflect more clear-cut partitioning. We can use the modularity score to see if another clustering method would partition better. Below, we compare the optimal method with the Louvain method, which has been reported to do well in other contexts. Note that the "communities" object just created above must be present.

```
igraph::modularity(communities, directed=FALSE)
[Output:]
      [1] 0.1885192
```

Below, we use the cluster_louvain method for clustering before computing modularity. For the current example, modularity remains the same.

```
communities_louvain <- igraph::cluster_louvain(g)
igraph::modularity(communities_louvain, directed=FALSE)
[Output:]
      [1] 0.1885192
```

While higher modularity is "better" partitioning, the modularity score should not be used to judge network model performance, only the relative performance of alternative clustering methods for the given data. A well-performing network model is one which accurately visualizes relationships, including communities, within the sample at hand. The modularity score in the present example is not high. High modularity would indicate connections are not only sparse between nodes in different communities but are also densely connected. For the current example, modularity is not high, which suggests that the model is satisfactory. Note that the modularity score is most useful for smaller samples (under 100).

Community membership

Listing the actual membership of each community is easily done with igraph's `membership()` function. For the sample of 20 Senators, there are only two communities. Joe Biden is in community 1, which is the Democratic community.

List members of each community

[Output:]

```
igraph::membership(communities)
```

[Output:]

```
   Blanche Lincoln         Mark Pryor      Barbara Boxer
                 1                  1                  1
  Dianne Feinstein Christopher Dodd Joseph Lieberman
                 1                  1                  1
         Joe Biden        Tom Carper        Bill Nelson
                 1                  1                  1
      Daniel Akaka        Jim DeMint        John Cornyn
                 1                  2                  2
      Orrin Hatch       George Allen            Jon Kyl
                 2                  2                  2
   Saxby Chambliss       Jim Bunning       Thad Cochran
                 2                  2                  2
          Kit Bond      Jeff Sessions
                 2                  2
```

List just members of community 1 (the Democratic community)

```
communities[1]
```

[Output:]

```
 [1] "Blanche Lincoln"  "Mark Pryor"
 [3] "Barbara Boxer"    "Dianne Feinstein"
 [5] "Christopher Dodd" "Joseph Lieberman"
 [7] "Joe Biden"        "Tom Carper"
 [9] "Bill Nelson"      "Daniel Akaka"
```

Determine which pairs of members have cross-community connections, if any. For the 20-Senator sample, there are none: All return FALSE

```
crossers <- igraph::crossing(communities,g)
crossers
```

[Partial output:]

```
          Blanche Lincoln|Mark Pryor
                               FALSE
       Blanche Lincoln|Barbara Boxer
                               FALSE
       . . .
              Thad Cochran|Kit Bond
                               FALSE
          Thad Cochran|Jeff Sessions
                               FALSE
```

Count number of cross-community relationships

```
sum(crossers)
```

[Output:]

```
      [1] 0
```

```
# List pairs with cross-community relationships
# In this example there are none. Change to "FALSE" to list all of them.
which(crossers=="TRUE")
[Output:]
      named integer(0)
```

For comparison, display graph communities, membership, and modularity score by a given clustering method (here, the walktrap method). The results below do not differ but for other data they could.

```
igraph::cluster_walktrap(g)
[Output:]
   IGRAPH clustering walktrap, groups: 2, mod: 0.19
   + groups:
     $'1'
      [1] "Jim DeMint"       "John Cornyn"
      [3] "Orrin Hatch"      "George Allen"
      [5] "Jon Kyl"          "Saxby Chambliss"
      [7] "Jim Bunning"      "Thad Cochran"
      [9] "Kit Bond"         "Jeff Sessions"

     $'2'
      [1] "Blanche Lincoln"  "Mark Pryor"
      [3] "Barbara Boxer"    "Dianne Feinstein"
     + ... omitted several groups/vertices
```

Plotting communities

Using `plot()` from the "graphics" package, part of the R system library, gives a different appearance to the graph by enabling customization of graph parameters. The plot is shown in Figure 8.22

```
# Set seed and set node colors
set.seed(123)
igraph::V(g)$color[c(1:6,8:20)] <- "lightblue" # Color for Democrats
igraph::V(g)$color[7] <- "green" # Color to highlight Joe Biden
igraph::V(g)$color[c(11:20)] <- "pink" # Color for Republicans (GOP)
# Plot from "graphics" package. Try experimenting with the settings.
# V and vertex refer to the nodes; mark refers to the community background.
# Edge refers to the connecting lines.
plot(communities,g, V(g)$color[1:20], vertex.size=10, vertex.label.dist=1.75, mark.
border="black", mark.col=c("lightblue", "pink"),mark.expand=30, ylim=c(-1.2,1))
# Title
mtext("Similarity network, communities plot for 20 Senators, plot() method",side=1)
```

Centrality

Centrality is one of the most common statistics in network analysis. It helps to identify the most important vertices (here, senators) in a network. However, "importance" may be defined in many ways and so there are many different types of centrality metric.

Degree centrality

"Degree centrality" is simply the number of connections (edges) held by any vertex (senators as nodes). Nodes with high degree centrality are very connected in the network, can quickly connect to other parts of the network, and are likely to hold the most information or other resources of value to other network nodes. Degree centrality is a "local measure" because it is based on the unadjusted count of edges. Its value is heavily dependent on the size of the network and it does not adjust for considerations pertaining to the rest of the network. For the current example, degree centrality is relative homogenous and high because there are two communities, each with all members

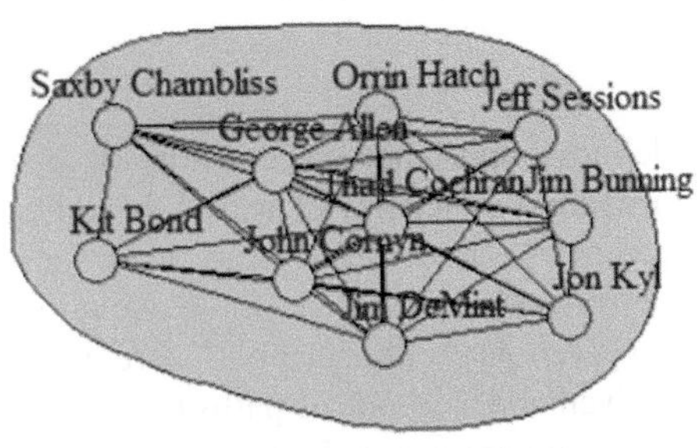

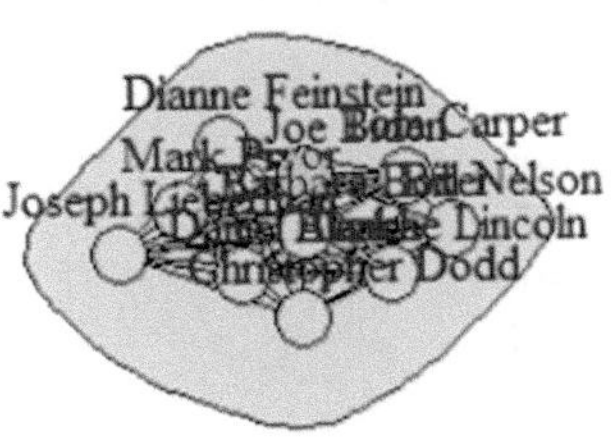

Similarity network, communities plot for 20 Senators, plot() method

Figure 8.22 Similarity network, communities plot for 20 senators, `plot()` method

tightly connected. All the Democrats are connected at degree centrality of 9. There is slightly more diversity in the Republican group, with various members having a degree centrality between 7 and 9.

```
igraph::degree(g)
```

[Output:]

```
   Blanche Lincoln         Mark Pryor      Barbara Boxer
                 9                  9                  9
  Dianne Feinstein Christopher Dodd Joseph Lieberman
                 9                  9                  9
         Joe Biden          Tom Carper       Bill Nelson
                 9                  9                  9
      Daniel Akaka          Jim DeMint       John Cornyn
                 9                  9                  9
       Orrin Hatch        George Allen           Jon Kyl
                 8                  8                  8
   Saxby Chambliss         Jim Bunning      Thad Cochran
                 8                  7                  9
          Kit Bond       Jeff Sessions
                 7                  7
```

Eigencentrality

Eigencentrality is similar to degree centrality, but is based not only on the number of links a node has but also on the number of links of nodes linked to it. That is, whereas degree centrality measures direct network connections, eigencentrality measures extended network connections. Eigencentrality is a common summary centrality metric.

Closeness centrality
"Closeness centrality" defines importance or centrality in terms of ability to influence the rest of the network quickly. As such it is a measure of efficiency of access. In some contexts, closeness centrality is also a measure of not depending on intermediaries for access. The closeness score is based on the reciprocal of the average length of the shortest edges to or from all other vertices in the network. That is, closeness centrality is the average length of the shortest paths for a given node. Shortest paths are called "geodesic paths" and thus closeness centrality is the mean distance of a given node's geodesic paths to other nodes. The lower the closeness centrality of a senator, the closer the senator is to other senators in the network, on average.

Closeness centrality is often used to find which node is most central within a community in the sense of being best place to influence the rest of the network quickly. For instance, in the output below it is seen that Barbara Boxer has the lowest closeness centrality and is only slightly more central than Joe Biden in community 1 (the Democratic community). Warning: Closeness centrality isn't well-defined for disconnected graphs, which are those with isolates (members not connected to any other member).

```
closeness.centrality <-  igraph::closeness(g, mode = "all")
sort(closeness.centrality)
```
[Output:]
```
   Barbara Boxer          Mark Pryor           Joe Biden
     0.003174603         0.003333333         0.003401361
    Daniel Akaka     Blanche Lincoln          Tom Carper
     0.003454231         0.003533569         0.003571429
Joseph Lieberman Christopher Dodd Dianne Feinstein
     0.003642987         0.003676471         0.003710575
     Bill Nelson        Thad Cochran         John Cornyn
     0.003710575         0.004675628         0.004708652
     Orrin Hatch        George Allen         Jim Bunning
     0.004725340         0.004725340         0.004730928
        Kit Bond       Jeff Sessions          Jim DeMint
     0.004730928         0.004730928         0.004787552
         Jon Kyl     Saxby Chambliss
     0.004787552         0.004787552
```

Betweenness centrality
"Betweenness centrality" usually refers to "node betweenness", calculated based on the number (not lengths) of shortest paths running through a vertex. Note that there is also "edge betweenness", calculated as the number of shortest paths using a given edge. Node betweenness centrality estimates the frequency with which a node lies on the shortest path connecting two other nodes. Higher values of betweenness centrality correspond to being more central and thus important to the flow of information or other influences through the network. Senators with high betweenness centrality have the potential to act as bridges connecting other pairs of senators. However, this potential may not be utilized. The notion of importance based on betweenness makes two debatable assumptions with respect to our example: (1) that every connection between a pair of senators is used with equal probability and weight; and (2) that information flows along the shortest path between two senators.

```
betweenness<- igraph::betweenness(g)
sort(betweenness)
```
[Output:]
```
     Mark Pryor     Barbara Boxer       John Cornyn
       0.000000          0.000000          1.000000
   Thad Cochran       Jim Bunning          Kit Bond
       1.000000          1.750000          1.750000
  Jeff Sessions       Orrin Hatch      George Allen
       1.750000          2.333333          2.333333
```

```
    Blanche Lincoln         Joe Biden            Jon Kyl
          4.000000           4.000000           6.333333
    Saxby Chambliss        Tom Carper      Daniel Akaka
          6.333333           7.000000           7.000000
  Christopher Dodd Joseph Lieberman         Jim DeMint
          9.000000           9.000000           9.250000
  Dianne Feinstein        Bill Nelson
         10.000000          10.000000
```

Other types of centrality
There are many more types of centrality than can be discussed here. For instance, the "igraph" package supports nine types. The "statnet" package supports ten types. Together, both packages support 14 types of centrality. The "CINNA" package may be used to compute 50 types of centrality and compare them. Where "g" is the igraph object used above, one may use CINNA's command below to list the types of centrality measure available under this package.

```
library(CINNA)              # Supports measures of network centrality
CINNA::proper_centralities(g)
```

[Partial output:]

```
    [1] "subgraph centrality scores"
    [2] "Topological Coefficient"
    [3] "Average Distance"
  . . .
   [48] "Local Bridging Centrality"
   [49] "Wiener Index Centrality"
   [50] "Weighted Vertex Degree"
```

8.8.4 Similarity network analysis: All senators

With 100 nodes, a network graph will become very cluttered. However, text output in terms of number of communities, community membership, and cross-community relationships may still be used without problems. Below we use almost exactly the same R code as for the 20-Senator sample except that the full senate_df data frame is used. See earlier comments on R syntax leading up to the full-Senate graph, which is Figure 8.23.

With the entire Senate, the network graph will become very cluttered. However, text output in terms of number of communities, community membership, and cross-community relationships may still be used without problems. Below we use almost exactly the same R code as for the 20-Senator sample except that the full senate_df data frame is used. See earlier comments on R syntax leading up to the full-Senate graph, which is Figure 8.23.

```
setwd("C:/Data")
library(igraph)
senate_df <- read.table("senate8groups.csv", header = TRUE, sep = ",")

# Reduce to cases with no missing data.
# For instructional simplicity, we will use only the 95 senators rated by all interest groups
data_complete <- senate_df[complete.cases(senate_df), ]
nrow(data_complete)
```

[Output:]

```
   [1] 95
```

```
# Drop the first three non-numeric columns (State, Senator, PARTY).
senate_numeric <- data_complete[,4:11]

# Next, transpose with the t() function to make senators the columns (variables) and the eight interest groups the rows.
senate_t <- as.data.frame(t(senate_numeric))
```

```
# Add senator names as column names
colnames(senate_t)<- data_complete$Senator

# Create the absolute difference matrix
df <- senate_t
dfmeans <- colMeans(df[sapply(df, is.numeric)])
size<- length(dfmeans)
diffs <- abs(matrix(dfmeans, size, size, byrow=TRUE) - matrix(dfmeans, size, size,
byrow=FALSE))
colnames(diffs) <- colnames(df)
rownames(diffs) <- colnames(df)

# For convenience, call the difference matrix "matrix1"
matrix1 <-  diffs
# Retain only differences of 43 or less (43 is still approximately the mean difference)
matrix1[matrix1 > 43] <- 0

# Create the graph object "g95".
g95 <- igraph::graph_from_adjacency_matrix(matrix1, weighted=TRUE, mode =
"undirected", diag=FALSE)
# Simplify
g95 <- igraph::simplify(g95, remove.multiple = TRUE, remove.loops = TRUE)

# For convenience, note Senator names in matrix1
rownames(matrix1)
     [1] "Blanche Lincoln"  "Mark Pryor"
     [3] "Barbara Boxer"    "Dianne Feinstein"
     [5] "Christopher Dodd" "Joseph Lieberman"
     [7] "Joe Biden"        "Tom Carper"
   . . .
    [93] "Thad Cochran"     "Kit Bond"
    [95] "Jeff Sessions"

# Setup color scheme for the 95 senators with complete data
# Parties can be read by listing data _ complete$PARTY
igraph::V(g95)$color <- "white" # Default color if not "R" or "D"
# Color for Dems:
igraph::V(g95)$color[c(1:6, 8:15,18:38,40:46)] <- "lightblue"
# Color to highlight Joe Biden
igraph::V(g95)$color[7] <- "green"
# Color for GOP
igraph::V(g95)$color[c(16:17, 47:95)] <- "pink"

# Display the network in Fruchterman-Reingold layout. This is Figure 8.23.
set.seed(123)
igraph::plot.igraph(g95, layout=layout_nicely)
mtext("Similarity network, interest group rankings for 95 Senators, Fruchterman-
Reingold layout",side=1)
```

As anticipated, the 95-Senator network graph is much more cluttered than that for just 20 Senators. Recalling that the graph highlights similarities, not differences, in spite of the clutter we can make the following main inferences visually:

- There are still just two main clusters, one for each major party. Even back in 2005, when the data were collected, the partisan divide was very strong.

Figure 8.23 Similarity network, interest group rankings for 95 Senators, Fruchterman-Reingold layout

- There are many lines connecting the two clusters, whereas in the 20-Senator network there were none. These are "crossings".
- There are a couple Republican senators (e.g., Olympia Snowe) who by interest group rating similarity are more associated with the Democratic than the Republican cluster.
- Ben Nelson, a Democrat, is located by similarity between the Republican and Democratic clusters. He may or may not have acted on this cross-cutting similarity status.

We now turn to a discussion of communities, modularity, crossings, and centrality for our analysis of the 95-member U.S. Senate sample. "Similarity" here refers to similarity in interest group ratings. We create a "communities" object using optimal clustering as before and find there are still just two communities, though much larger.

```
# The larger network will require more computing time.
communities <- igraph::cluster_optimal(g95)
igraph::sizes(communities)
[Output:]
   Community sizes
    1  2
   45 50
```

The modularity score when partitioning the network into communities was much higher: 0.395 for the full Senate compared to 0.173 for the 20-Senator sample. In a fuller analysis we would perhaps use the modularity score to investigate whether "optimal scaling" really is the best of the several available clustering methods, but we do not do so here.

```
# Modularity score
igraph::modularity(communities, directed=FALSE)
[Output:]
      [1] 0.3949977
```

Having established the community structure of the network, we can list out community membership. Joe Biden, as expected, is in community 1, but so is Olympia Snowe, a Republican.

```
igraph::membership(communities)
```
[Partial output:]
```
   Blanche Lincoln        Mark Pryor     Barbara Boxer
                 1                 1                 1
 Dianne Feinstein Christopher Dodd Joseph Lieberman
                 1                 1                 1
         Joe Biden        Tom Carper       Bill Nelson
                 1                 1                 1
 . . .
                 1                 1                 1
     Susan Collins     Olympia Snowe     Paul Sarbanes
                 1                 1                 1
  Barbara Mikulski        Ted Kennedy        John Kerry
                 1                 1                 1
 . . .
   Saxby Chambliss        Jim Bunning      Thad Cochran
                 2                 2                 2
          Kit Bond     Jeff Sessions
                 2                 2
```

If desired, we can also list all members a community by referring to the community index number (here, 1 or 2).

```
communities[1]
```
[Output not shown:]

By using the `crossing()` function we can pinpoint senators who have cross-community connections based on interest group rating similarity. The "crosspairs" object below lists the possible pairs of members who may or may not have cross-community connections. There are over two thousand possibilities. Looking through the list, one can see none of the crosspairs involved Joe Biden.

```
crosspairs <- igraph::crossing(communities,g95)
crosspairs
```
[Partial output from among 2,231 pairs]
```
  . . .
    Joe Biden|Tom Carper                Joe Biden|Bill Nelson
                   FALSE                                FALSE
  Joe Biden|Daniel Akaka              Joe Biden|Daniel Inouye
                   FALSE                                FALSE
  . . .
```

Of the 2,231 possible cross-community connections, we find only 67 actually exist, again indicating the strong partisan division of the U.S. Senate.

Count the number of cross-community relationships (the TRUE pairs)
```
sum(crosspairs)
```
[Output:]
```
    [1] 67
```

The "crossnames" object below reveals just which pairs of senators display cross-community similarities. Note, however, that cross-community does not mean cross-party. Many of the 67 crossers are associated with Ben Nelson, a Democrat who is in Community 2 (the predominantly Republican cluster), or with Olympia Snowe, a Republican who is in Community 1 (the predominantly Democratic cluster). For instance, the "Olympia

Snowe|Mike DeWine" pair counts as a crossing because Snow is in Community 1 and DeWine is in Community 2, but both are Republicans.

```
crossers <- which(crosspairs=="TRUE")
crossernames <- attributes(crossers)
crossernames
```

[Partial output:]

```
   $names
   . . .
   [29] "Olympia Snowe|Mike DeWine"       "Olympia Snowe|Arlen Specter"
   [31] "Olympia Snowe|Norm Coleman"      "Olympia Snowe|Gordon Smith"
   [33] "Olympia Snowe|John McCain"       "Olympia Snowe|George Voinovich"
   [35] "Olympia Snowe|John Sununu"       "Olympia Snowe|Lindsey Graham"
   [37] "Olympia Snowe|John Warner"       "Olympia Snowe|Kay Hutchison"
   . . .
   [45] "Harry Reid|Ben Nelson"           "Jeff Bingaman|Ben Nelson"
   . . .
   [61] "Maria Cantwell|Ben Nelson"       "Patty Murray|Ben Nelson"
   [63] "Jay Rockefeller|Ben Nelson"      "Robert Byrd|Ben Nelson"
   [65] "Robert Byrd|Mike DeWine"         "Russell Feingold|Ben Nelson"
   [67] "Herb Kohl|Ben Nelson"
```

We next investigate whether specific selected senators are on the "crossnames" list. Among selected noted Democrats, Senators Reid and Feinstein have crossnames with members of the predominantly Republican community but Senators Boxer and Biden did not. Closer inspection will show that for both Reid and Feinstein, their one crossing was with Ben Nelson, a Democrat who was nonetheless a member of predominantly Republican Community 2.

```
# grep() is a pattern-matching program in R's "base" package.
grep("Reid",crossernames)
      [1] 1
grep("Boxer",crossernames)
      integer(0)
grep("Feinstein",crossernames)
      [1] 1
grep("Biden",crossernames)
      integer(0)
```

We can also investigate who had the highest centrality in the network and also determine the centrality of a selected Senator, Joe Biden. We use "degree centrality", discussed earlier. For space reasons we do not investigate other types of centrality.

```
# Degree centrality scores
centrality <- igraph::degree(g95)
centrality
```

[Partial output:]

```
          Blanche Lincoln         Mark Pryor     Barbara Boxer Dianne Feinstein
                       46                 47                43               44
    Christopher Dodd Joseph Lieberman            Joe Biden        Tom Carper
                       45                 46                44               46
    . . . ...
    Evan Bayh          Tom Harkin    Mary Landrieu    Susan Collins
                       45                 41                47               51
    . . .
             Herb Kohl          Ben Nelson        Mike DeWine      Arlen Specter
                       45                 54                62               56
```

The "centrality" object above is a named numeric vector. That is, senator names are associated with each centrality value. We can find minimum and maximum values, and who has them, by the commands below. For instance, Mike DeWine, a Republican, has maximum degree centrality (62). DeWine is located at position 47 in the "centrality" vector.

```
class(centrality)
[Output:]
   [1] "numeric"
min(centrality)
[Output:]
   [1] 41
which.min(centrality)
[Output:]
   Dick Durbin
            12
max(centrality)
[Output:]
 [1] 62
which.max(centrality)
[Output:]
   Mike DeWine
            47
```

Centrality scores can also be obtained directly from the graph object, as illustrated below. For instance, Senator Biden, who is senator #7, has a degree centrality of only 44.

```
igraph::degree(g95)[7]
[Output:]
   Joe.Biden
         44
```

Findings

The two social science research questions posed at the outset were these:

1. Considering a "strong link" to be one with a distance less than the mean, did Joe Biden have strong links mainly with Democrats or with members of both parties? The latter would imply more opportunity for Biden to play a bipartisan brokerage role. Our similarity network analysis failed to show support for a bridging role for Senator Biden based on similarities. If he did in fact play a bridging role, it was in spite of lack of strong similarities with the Republican community.
2. In the network implied by interest group ratings from back in 2005, was Joe Biden close to members of the progressive wing of the Democratic Party, such as Hillary Clinton? This question is open for debate since pundits of the day sometimes cast Biden and Clinton as rivals. From output below, we see that while Clinton was in the list of ten most progressive senators by interest group rating, Joe Biden was not. However, Biden was ranked 13th.

```
# Create data frame of just Democrats
senateDems <- senate_df[senate_df$PARTY=="D",]

# Add a mean interest group rating to it. Use only numeric column 4:11.
senateDems$mean <- rowMeans(senateDems[,4:11])

# Create a data frame of the top-rated 15 Democratic senators
topRated <- senateDems[order(-senateDems$mean),]
top15 <- head(topRated,15)
```

```
library(dplyr)
dplyr::select(top15, c(Senator, mean))
[Output:]
              Senator   mean
    14       Dick Durbin 98.000
    16        Tom Harkin 98.000
    20     Paul Sarbanes 97.250
    3      Barbara Boxer 95.625
    22       Ted Kennedy 95.375
    32      Chuck Schumer 95.375
    37         Jack Reed 95.375
    33    Hillary Clinton 95.125
    29  Frank Lautenberg 95.000
    26        Mark Dayton 94.625
    30       Bob Menendez 94.625
    24   Debbie Stabenow 94.375
    8          Joe Biden 93.000
    11      Daniel Akaka 92.250
    21  Barbara Mikulski 92.125
```

8.9 Using intergraph for network conversions

This section treats data management issues when using network files. The "intergraph" package supports conversions between "igraph" and "network" network objects. This section uses the "DHHS" object as an example network object. DHHS is of class "network", used, for example, but the "network" and "statnet" packages. The DHHS data, which describe a network of officials in the U.S. DHHS, is used later in Sections 8.11 and 8.12. Operations paralleling those described further below may be performed for objects of igraph as well as network data classes.

With intergraph, the researcher may move from "igraph" or "network" objects to data frames and back. Output takes the form of creation of two data frames: Edges and vertexes. For the edges data frame, the first two columns are "to" and "from" the edge lists (by default labeled V1 and V2) and if there are any edge attributes, they are placed in subsequent columns. For the vertexes data frame, the vertex id is in column 1 (named id) and any edge attributes are in subsequent columns.

For objects of class "network", vertex attributes always include "vertex.names" and are retained but vertex ids from the source network object are not. Rather, the vertex data frame is created with vertex id as an integer sequence. The edge list is created using `as.matrix.network()` function and contains integer vertex ids.

For objects of class "igraph", vertex ids are integer sequences starting from 1. Optionally, igraph objects may have a vertex attribute called "name". If so, it is added to the vertex data frame being created. The edge list is created using the `get.edgelist()` function with argument names set to FALSE so that integer vertex ids are used.

```
# The UserNetR package contains the example network "DHHS"
# UserNetR, which must be installed from Github rather than CRAN, as follow:
library(remotes)
remotes::install_github("DougLuke/UserNetR")

# Setup and example network
# Close R and reinstall Intergraph to start clean
install.packages("intergraph")
library(intergraph)        # Utility to convert among different network packages
library(UserNetR)          # Has the DHHS data and more
data(DHHS)
class(DHHS)
[Output:]
      [1] "network"
```

```
# Optional for this section
setwd("C:/Data")
```

Intergraph's `dumpAttr()` function extracts graph edge and vertex information from a network object, including any edge or vertex attributes. Due to the length of output, here we list only the commands, not the corresponding output.

```
intergraph::dumpAttr(DHHS)              # List all network information
intergraph::dumpAttr(DHHS,"vertex")     # List vertex information
intergraph::dumpAttr(DHHS,"edge")       # List edge information
intergraph::dumpAttr(DHHS,"network")    # List network title, if directed, etc.
```

Another way to see the vertex and edge attributes in an object of class "network" (here, DHHS) is to use the `attrmap()` command.

```
x1 <- intergraph::attrmap(DHHS)
x1
[Output:]
    Network attributes:
      vertices = 54
      directed = FALSE
      hyper = FALSE
      loops = FALSE
      multiple = FALSE
      bipartite = FALSE
      title = DHHS_Collab
      total edges= 447
        missing edges= 0
        non-missing edges= 447
   Vertex attribute names:
       agency vertex.names
   Edge attribute names:
       collab
```

Conversion between networks of "igraph" and "network" classes is done using the `asIgraph()` and `asNetwork()` functions:[5]

```
# Setup (DHHS network and x assumed to still be in the environment)
class(DHHS)
[Output:]
   [1] "network"
```

To convert from a DHHS network object to an object called DHHS_igraph (an igraph object), it may be necessary to start from a fresh install of Intergraph, including restarting R.

```
install.packages("intergraph")
library(intergraph)
library(UserNetR)                  # Has DHHS network

DHHS_igraph <- intergraph::asIgraph(DHHS)
class(DHHS_igraph)
[Output:]
   [1] "igraph"

# Go back from igraph to network object
DHHS_network <- intergraph::asNetwork(DHHS_igraph)
class(DHHS_network)
```

[Output:]
```
[1] "network"
```

Using the “DHHS” network object (class “network”) as an example, conversion to an edges and vertexes list is accomplished using the `asDF()` function:

```
# From network object to vertex and edge list
DHHS_list <- intergraph::asDF(DHHS)
class(DHHS_list)
```
[Output:]
```
[1] "list"
```

```
str(DHHS_list)
```

[Output:]
```
List of 2
 $ edges    :'data.frame':    447 obs. of  4 variables:
  ..$ V1    : int [1:447] 1 2 2 2 2 2 3 3 3 3 ...
  ..$ V2    : int [1:447] 2 12 15 49 50 51 4 5 6 9 ...
  ..$ collab: num [1:447] 1 2 1 2 1 3 3 3 3 1 ...
  ..$ na    : logi [1:447] FALSE FALSE FALSE FALSE FALSE FALSE ...
 $ vertexes:'data.frame':   54 obs. of  4 variables:
  ..$ intergraph_id: int [1:54] 1 2 3 4 5 6 7 8 9 10 ...
  ..$ agency       : num [1:54] 0 0 1 1 1 1 2 2 2 2 ...
  ..$ na           : logi [1:54] FALSE FALSE FALSE FALSE FALSE FALSE ...
  ..$ vertex.names : chr [1:54] "ACF-1" "ACF-2" "AHRQ-1" "AHRQ-2" ...
```

```
# Display the list fields for the DHHS example
head(DHHS_list$vertexes,3)
```
[Output:]
```
  intergraph_id agency    na vertex.names
1             1      0 FALSE        ACF-1
2             2      0 FALSE        ACF-2
3             3      1 FALSE       AHRQ-1
```

```
head(DHHS_list$edges,3)
```
[Output:]
```
  V1 V2 collab    na
1  1  2      1 FALSE
2  2 12      2 FALSE
3  2 15      1 FALSE
```

Using the `as.data.frame()` function from R’s base package, we may easily convert from the lists in the object “DHHS_list” to two data frames, called “edges” and “vertexes”.

```
edges <- as.data.frame(DHHS_list$edges)
class(edges)
```
[Output:]
```
[1] "data.frame"
```

```
vertexes <- as.data.frame(DHHS_list$vertexes)
class(vertexes)
```
[Output:]
```
[1] "data.frame"
```

Finally, we can work in the other direction to create a network or igraph object from the edges and vertexes data frames just created above. Below we create a "network" class object with the `asNetwork()` command, but we could just as easily create an "igraph" object with the `asIgraph()` command. We are creating an undirected network because the "edges" object contained reciprocal relationships (the relation of agency A to B was the same as from B to A).

```
DHHS2 <- intergraph::asNetwork(edges, vertices=vertexes, undirected=TRUE)
class(DHHS2)
[Output:]
       [1] "network"
```

The "sna" package, which is loaded when "statnet" is installed, can be used for a quick-and-dirty visualization of the DHHS2 network object, with labels. The resulting figure is not shown here as there is a more detailed presentation of better statnet/sna plots in the statnet section. If the reader has been following along on their local computer, however, try these commands:

```
library(sna)
sna::gplot(DHHS2,displaylabels = TRUE)
```

We end this section with the code needed to save a network like DHHS to file, then load it back in a redisplay it.

```
# Needed packages
library(intergraph)
library(sna)
library(UserNetR)

# Load DHHS and plot the DHHS network
# gmode="graph" for undirected networks, "digraph" for directed (the default)
data(DHHS)
class(DHHS)
set.seed(123)
sna::gplot(DHHS,gmode="graph",displaylabels = TRUE)

# Convert DHHS (class = "network") to DHHS_list (class = "list")
DHHS_list <- intergraph::asDF(DHHS)

# Create the edges and vertexes data frames
edges <- as.data.frame(DHHS_list$edges)
vertexes <- as.data.frame(DHHS_list$vertexes)

# Write edges and vertexes to file
write.csv(edges, file = "DHHSedges.csv",row.names=FALSE)
write.csv(vertexes, file = "DHHSvertexes.csv", row.names=FALSE)

# Read edges and vertexes back in
EDGES <- read.csv(file = "DHHSedges.csv")
VERTEXES <- read.csv(file = "DHHSvertexes.csv")

# create the network object g
g <- intergraph::asNetwork(EDGES, vertices=VERTEXES, undirected=TRUE)

# Plot the g network
set.seed(123)
sna::gplot(g,gmode="graph",displaylabels = TRUE)
```

8.10 Network-on-a-map with the diagram and maps packages

Flow networks, such as the flow of migration among countries of the world, are a common social science focus. Immigration has become a hot "political football" in the United States. Many perceive the influx of immigrants as being particularly problematic for America. This is seen as an outcome of the lure of America's wealth compared to the rest of the world. But when we discuss the flows of millions of immigrants, how America-centric is the "big picture"? Our social science research purpose in this network exercise is to answer this question.

In this section, we use world migration data from the World Bank.[6] Limiting ourselves to country-to-country flows of one million persons or more, we create a flow network overlaid on a world map. We accomplish this using the "maps" package in R. This package contains various base maps, such as "world". It also contains the "world.cities" database, which lists 43,645 cities around the globe, with the longitude and latitude coördinates needed for mapping. For the actual network we use the "diagram" package, which is designed to visualize simple flow networks. It can be used in conjunction with maps such as "world".

In the migration network map we create, capital cities are used as the coordinates for their respective countries. The size of a country node is scaled to the total amount of in-migration for the given country. The connecting edges have arrows at midpoint, pointing toward the "to" country. The thickness of these edges is scaled to the amount of migration from the "from" country to the "to" country.

Two example datasets are supplied, located on the Support Material (www.routledge.com/9780367624293) for this book: migration_nodes.csv and migration_edges.csv. These were constructed based on the nodes-and-edges format described in an earlier section of this chapter. When read in with the `read.csv()` command, the resulting R objects are data frames. The nodes data frame has variables on 21 selected high-migration countries. The edges data frame has paths for all possible pairs of countries, though below we drop loops (same country to itself) and paths with migration less than one million.

We start by declaring the default director, loading needed packages, and reading in the nodes data from the. csv file into a data frame called migration_nodes_df, after which we rename it "nodes".

```
# Setup
setwd("C:/Data")
library(diagram)          # To visualize simple networks/flow diagrams
library(maps)             # Leading map package in R, has a world map background
library(plotrix)          # Utility with plotting functions like rescale()

migration_nodes_df <- read.csv("migration_nodes.csv", header = TRUE, sep = ",",
stringsAsFactors = TRUE)

# Make a copy
nodes <- migration_nodes_df
View(nodes)
# Verify that nodes is a data frame
class(nodes)
[Output:]
      [1] "data.frame"
```

Later we will want to color the nodes (vertices) so we create the object "nodecols" to use as a sequence of color codes for nodes. We add this to the nodes data frame as a variable called "nodecols".

```
nodecols <- as.integer(nodes$vertex.name)
nodes$nodecols <- nodecols
```

Attributes of nodes are listed below. Country names are in the "vertex.name" column. This and other columns in nodes are from the world.cities database in the maps package. Variables in this package include vertex.name (labeled country.etc in world.cities), lat, long, capital (labeled "name" in world.cities), and citypop (world.cities calls it "pop").[7] In our nodes object, "pop" is country population, drawn from public web sources. The immigration and emigration columns are from World Bank data and represent total in- and out-migration respectively.

```
names(nodes)
[Output:]
   [1] "vertex.name" "lat"     "long"      "pop"        "capital"
   [6] "citypop"     "immigration" "emigration"     "nodecols"
```

Before proceeding it is a good idea to verify that the data classes for all variables in the nodes object are as wanted and needed. The vertex.name and capital variables should be factors and all others should be numeric or integer. They are:

```
sapply(nodes,class)
## [Output:]
  vertex.name          lat        long         pop
     "factor"    "numeric"   "numeric"   "integer"
      capital      citypop immigration  emigration
     "factor"    "integer"   "integer"   "integer"
      nodecols
     "integer"
```

Now that the nodes object is created, we proceed to create the edges object. The first two columns in edges are two country name lists: The "from" and "to" vectors. Since there are 21 countries in our study, there are 21*21 = 441 possible pairs, which are pairs of countries. This includes loops (one country to itself), but we will eliminate loops later. Thus, each vector will have 441 rows.

We start with constructing the "to" vector, since that is easiest. The "to" vector is simply a country list repeated as many times as there are countries. We label this vector "to". Along the way, note that we store the number of countries in the variable "numnodes".

```
countries <- nodes$vertex.name
numnodes <- length(countries)
to <- rep(countries,numnodes)
```

Having computed numnodes we can set the color palette. We use the "grDevices" package for colors and fonts. This package is in the R system library and needs no installation. The "grDevices" package is used later in this exercise to send the map to a web browser. However, the line below should be included whether sending the map either to the Viewer or to the browser. The "rainbow" palette is one of the color ramps built into R.

```
grDevices::palette(rainbow(numnodes))
```

We now create the "from" vector. The "from" object is a factor vector in which each country name is repeated numnodes times. The "from" vector is created in a manner similar to the "to" vector, but the `each=` option assures grouping of country names (e.g., 21 instances of "Australia", then 21 instances of "Canada", etc.).

```
from <- rep(countries, each = numnodes)
```

The next seven steps create the edges dataframe.

1. Create the initial edges dataframe

   ```
   edges <- data.frame(from, to)
   ```

2. Merge into edges the geographic coordinates. The `merge()` function is from R's base package. This step adds columns for long.x, lat.x, long.y, and lat.y, where x is from and y is to.

   ```
   edges <- merge(merge(edges, nodes[, c("vertex.name", "long", "lat")], by.x =
   "from", by.y = "vertex.name"), nodes[, c("vertex.name", "long", "lat")], by.x =
   "to", by.y = "vertex.name")
   ```

```
View(edges)
class(edges)
[Output:]
    [1] "data.frame"
```

3. Now add additional columns to edges such as migration counts. Start by reading in migration_edges_df. The migration_count object is a data frame copy. The migration_edges_df is a data frame for the selected 21 countries as rows and columns. Cell entries are the migration count from the row country to the column country.

```
migration_edges_df <- read.csv("migration_edges.csv", header = TRUE, sep = ",")
migration_count <- migration_edges_df
View(migration_count)
```

4. Convert migration_count to a matrix, leaving off column 1, which is the country names. Recall that numnodes is the number of countries.

```
lastcol <- numnodes+1
migration_count_mat <- as.matrix(migration_count[2:lastcol])
View(migration_count_mat)
```

5. Now that it is a matrix we can convert it to a single vector to add migration count to edges. The migration object is an integer vector of length 441, the number of edges

```
migration <- as.vector(migration_count_mat)
# Add migration to edges
edges$migration <- migration
names(edges)
[Output:]
[1] "to"        "from"       "long.x"     "lat.x"
[5] "long.y"    "lat.y"      "migration"
```

6. Now remove loops (same country to itself) from edges. The original 441 edges are reduced to 420 after filtering out 21 loops

```
edges <- subset(edges, edges$to != edges$from)
```

7. Also remove edges with migration count less than one million. This reduces edges from 440 to only 11 for these data. The researcher can easily change the mincutoff constant below to explore other levels of migration flow.

```
mincutoff <- 1000000
edges <- subset(edges, migration >= mincutoff)
```

Before creating the actual map, we need to decide where it is to go. There are two major options. The first is to send it to the usual Viewer window in RStudio. The second is to create the map as a pdf file and send it to the default browser on the computer. We use the second option because it supports a much higher level of resolution. High resolution, in turn, allows the user to zoom in to view any area of the globe in detail. This enables visual unpacking of areas where edge density is high and might not be readable in Viewer mode. Once the researcher has selected the mode of output, it will be necessary to optimize for that mode the node label sizes, line widths, arrow sizes, and the size of the legend.

The grDevices package contains the `pdf()` command. This starts the driver for producing pdf graphics. A "g" (graph) object is created, later displayed with the `shell.exec()` command from the R base package.[8] The pdf map will be located in the C:\Users area (look at the browser header), but the browser offers a download button to save the map under a name and file folder of the researcher's choice. Comment out (add #) the next line when sending to the Viewer instead of the browser.

```
grDevices::pdf(g <- tempfile(fileext = ".pdf"), width = 40, height = 20)
```

Finally, we are ready to display the world map as a background. This is done with the `map()` command from the maps package. Below some possible parameters but there are others. Not all those below are necessary. This step sets map parameters but does not actually display the map yet. The map is sent to pdf by the `shell.exec()` command at the end.

```
maps::map('world',
    fill = TRUE,                    # Use filled symbols
    col = "gray95",                 # Foreground (country) color
    bg = "steelblue1",              # Background (ocean) color
    namefield = "vertex.name",      # Declare the name field if not "name"
    lty=1,                          # Type 1=solid line for country borders, 0 is none
    lwd =1,                         # Line width for country borders
    mar = rep(0, 4),                # Set margins
    wrap=c(-180,180,NA)             # Entire world without Antarctica
)
```

The next step is to place nodes on the map with the `points()` function from R's built-in graphics library. The nodes represent the countries but their coordinates are those of the capital city of the given country. Nodes are scaled to the migration column of the nodes object using the `rescale()` command from the "plotrix" package. Which variable is used for scaling is set by the sizevar value, which may be "immigration", "emigration", "pop" (country population), "citypoP", #, or any numeric column in the nodes object. Note that immigration is a country's in-migration for all countries, not just arrowed ones in the network.

```
sizevar <- nodes$immigration
# The col parameter sets colors, different for each country name.
# The pch parameter of 19 makes a filled circle the node symbol
# The cex parameter sets the node size
# sizefraction scales node sizes down if the largest is too large
# rescale's second parameter is the desired range, here scaling to the 1:8 range.
sizefraction <- 0.8
with(nodes, points(long, lat, col=as.integer(nodes$nodecols), pch=19, cex=sizefracti
on*plotrix::rescale(sizevar, c(1,8))))
```

We now label the countries (nodes) using the `text()` command from the graphics package in R's system library. If sending the map to the Viewer rather than the browser, cex = 0.8 is suggested.

```
text(nodes$long, y = nodes$lat, nodes$vertex.name, col="gray30",pos = 4, cex=2.0)
```

We now make edges the same color as the "from" country id in nodes. As part of this operation, the edges object gets the new column "edgecols". For example, the from USA to Mexico edge has col = 11 because Mexico is country 11 in nodes.

```
edges$edgecols <- as.integer(nodes$nodecols[match(edges$from, nodes$vertex.name)])
```

We also create a binned version of migration to use for graduated line widths. These cutpoints are based on the 11 edges remaining in the edges object but would vary by data and researcher preference. The binned version is labeled "migrcats", for migration categories.

```
migrcats <- as.integer(cut(edges$migration, breaks =  c(0,1000000,2000000,2500000,
3000000,35000000, 4000000,12000000), dig.lab = 6))
edges$migrcats <- migrcats
migrcats
[Output:]
    [1] 2 2 3 2 4 5 3 5 5 3 6
```

Now the edges are drawn as arrows on the map, using the `curvedarrow()` function of the "diagram" package. The R syntax uses the edges data frame but drops the first two columns, which are the from and to country names. This leaves the "from" coordinates in columns 1 and 2. The "to" coordinates are in columns 3 and 4. The migration variable is in column 5. Color codes are in column 6. The migration categories variable (migrcats), created above, then becomes column 7.

```
# Draw the arrows
# The curve parameter is the relative size of curving
# The arr.pos parameter is where the arrowhead goes (.5 is in middle, 1 is at end)
# arr.width and arr.length control the size of the arrowhead
# The lwd parameter is line width
# lwd can be reduced or increased by the linefactor multiplier
linefactor <- 0.80
apply(edges[, -(1:2)], 1, function(x) diagram::curvedarrow(to=x[3:4], from=x[1:2],
lcol=x[6], curve=.1, arr.pos = .5, arr.length=0.8, arr.width=0.3,
lwd=linefactor*x[7]))
```

After drawing the connecting arrows in the network, we add an edge legend. If sending the map to the RStudio Viewer instead of the browser, cex = 0.8 is suggested;

```
legend("bottomleft", lty = 1, legend = unique(edges$migrcats), lwd =
unique(edges$migrcats), bg="gray95", border="black",col = "red", title="Migration
Category",cex=2.5)
```

Finishing up (comment these lines out if sending the map to the Viewer).

```
# Turn off the pdf device
grDevices::dev.off()
# Send the map to the browser
shell.exec(g)
```

The pdf (browser) map is shown in Figure 8.24 with an inset for the corresponding map in the RStudio Viewer area. The former may be difficult to read here in a print textbook, but in the browser or in a graphics editor such as Adobe

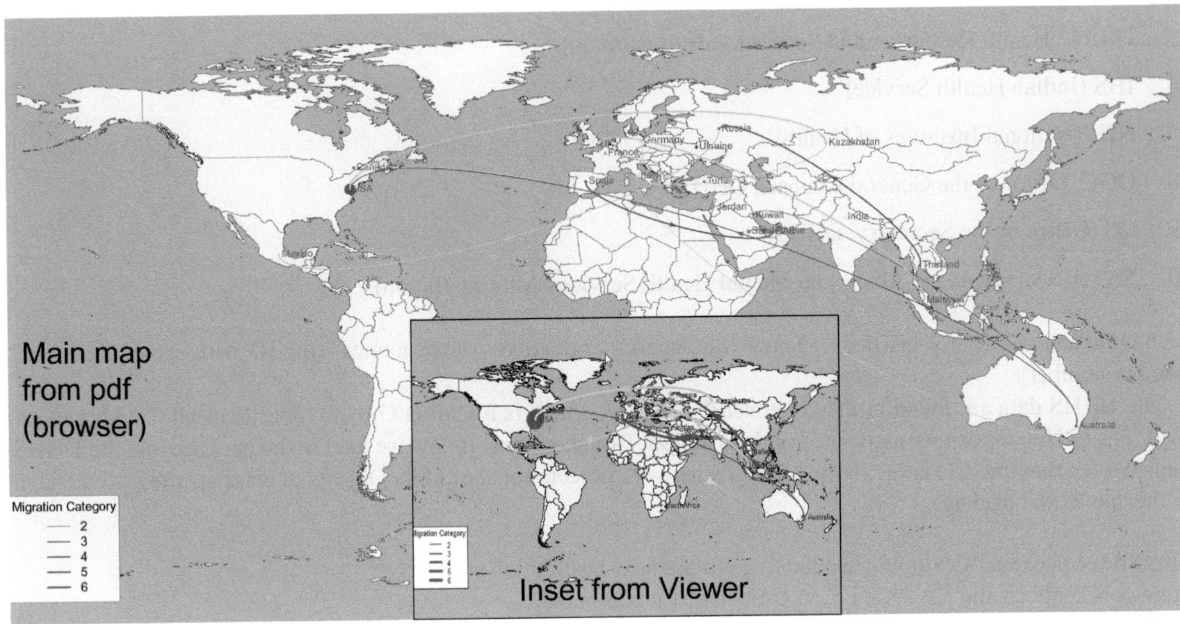

Figure 8.24 Migration network plotted on a world map

Photoshop, the pdf version is in very high resolution and one may zoom in to focus on any map area. When the network has more edges than in this example, being able to zoom in is essential. This is because in a larger network, the map viewed in its entirety will be unreadably cluttered. Thus, the pdf version may best be used interactively and the Viewer version used statically but limited to a small number of edges. The pdf/browser version is capable of output of publication quality.

8.11 Network analysis with the statnet and network packages

In this section, we analyze a network of U.S. federal inter-agency relationships using the statnet and network packages. "Statnet" is a suite of packages for network analysis. When it is installed, a set of related network packages such as "network" and "sna" are loaded. Statnet is used with network objects of class "network", which can be created by the "network" package. For more information on sna, see Butts (2008).

8.11.1 Introduction

The "DHHS" data used in this section is supplied by the package "UserNetR" as an object of class "network". Its full label is "DHHS Collaboration Network", where DHHS is the U.S. DHHS. Data are from 2005 and are described in and used by Leischow et al. (2020) and Harris et al. (2012). The network is an undirected network (connections are reciprocal, not directional). There are 54 nodes in the network, representing tobacco control leaders working in 11 agencies. There are 447 connections (edges) relating the 54 leaders.

These data were obtained from an evaluation of tobacco control leadership in the DHHS in 2005. The network data represent collaboration ties among 54 tobacco control leaders working in eleven different agencies. The agencies are coded as below:

0. ACF (Administration for Children and Families)
1. AHRQ (Agency for Healthcare Research and Quality)
2. CDC (Centers for Disease Control and Prevention)
3. CMS (Centers for Medicare and Medicaid Services)
4. FDA (Food and Drug Administration)
5. HRSA (Health Resources and Services Administration)
6. IHS (Indian Health Service)
7. NIH (National Institutes of Health)
8. OGC (Office of the General Counsel, DHHS)
9. OS (Office of the Secretary, DHHS)
10. SAMHSA (Substance Abuse and Mental Health Services Administration)

Each node has two characteristics: "agency" (the agency code) and "vertex.names" (the ID with agency code and member number).

The DHHS data are found in the "UserNetR" package, which is found on GitHub (not the usual CRAN repository). The gitHub repository associated with its author, Douglas Luke. Below we load in the package and the DHHS data. We see that the data come in the form of a network object, not a. cvs file. Objects of class network are created by the "network" package.

```
# Install the package "devtools", needed to go to the next installation step.
# devtools supports the install_github() command
install.packages("devtools")  # Skip if already installed on the user's machine
library(devtools)
```

```
install_github("DougLuke/UserNetR")
library(UserNetR)                    # Has the DHHS data and more
data(DHHS)
class(DHHS)
[Output:]
      [1] "network"
```

At this point we also load the other packages used in this section. We assume all are installed on the user's computer and do not require the prior `install.packages()` command. Note that installing statnet automatically loads supporting packages, including "sna" (a package supporting the `gplot()` command) and including the "network" package, and more. For instructional reasons, we load network and sna explicitly.

```
library(statnet)          # A leading suite for network visualization
library(network)          # Installed with statnet
library(sna)              # Social network analysis, also part of the statnet suite
```

The `View(DHHS)`command does not display the data in spreadsheet format since DHHS is a "network" object composed of a set of lists, not a "data.frame". However, if we convert DHHS to a sociomatrix, then its data may be viewed. Below we create "DHHS_sm" as a sociomatrix.

```
DHHS_sm <- network::as.sociomatrix(DHHS)
View(DHHS_sm)
class(DHHS_sm)
[Output:]
      [1] "matrix" "array
```

Type `View(DHHS _ sm)` to view the matrix, whose dimensions are 54 by 54. The 54 rows and columns are the instances of the agencies. For instance, some are NIH-1 through NIH-16), which are the 16 leaders/members from the National Institutes of Health. The Centers for Disease Control has 12 members, labeled CDC-1 through CDC-12. The Food and Drug Administration has only two members, FDA-1 and FDA-2, and so on. The cell entries in the matrix are all either 0 or 1, with 1 meaning the row and column members are connected in the network. Cells on the diagonal, representing members with themselves, are coded 0.

After the DHHS network object is loaded, the attributes "agency" and "vertex.names" may be revealed by using the `list.vertex()` command from the network package.

```
network::list.vertex.attributes(DHHS)
[Output:]
      [1] "agency"        "na"              "vertex.names"
```

For DHHS, the agencies (nodes) are connected by 447 edges. Edge data, which display five levels of collaboration, coded as below:

- 0 – No collaboration
- 1 – Share info only
- 2 – Collaborate informally
- 3 – Collaborate formally
- 4 – Collaborate formally on multiple projects

Each edge has one of these codes, stored under the edge characteristic "collab". The existence of attribute "collab" may be revealed by issuing the following command.

```
network::list.edge.attributes(DHHS)
[Output:]
      [1] "collab" "na"
```

The summary() command verifies the number of vertices and edges (54 and 447). It also gives the density coefficient, which may be useful in comparing networks. That the density for the DHHS network is .31 means that about 31% of potential connections in the DHHS network are actual connections. A network with a density of 1.0 would have an edge connecting every vertex (here, every network member) with every other.

```
# The print.adj=FALSE option limits output to just what is shown below.
summary(DHHS, print.adj=FALSE)
[Output:]
   Network attributes:
     vertices = 54
     directed = FALSE
     hyper = FALSE
     loops = FALSE
     multiple = FALSE
     bipartite = FALSE
     title = DHHS_Collab
    total edges = 447
      missing edges = 0
      non-missing edges = 447
   density = 0.312369
```

Also, the distribution of collaborations, not counting those with a collab code of 0 (no collaboration) may be shown in a table. Below, note that the %e% operator extracts attributes from an object of class "network".

```
table(DHHS %e% "collab")
[Output:]
     1   2   3   4
     163 111  94  79
```

The table above sums to 447 non-0 collaborations represented by edges in the network. Collaborations coded 2 or higher display informal or formal collaboration. Collaborations coded 3 or higher display formal collaboration. If we want, we may later use this information to trim the network to just display formal collaborations, for example.

In contrast to the binary-coded matrix DHHS_sm, we can ask for a sociomatrix with the cell entries representing the levels of collaboration between members, coded 0 through 4 as noted above. This is done with the syntax below, which adds the "collab" attribute. Later, connections of code 0 (no collaboration) will not show as connecting edges in the network.

```
DHHS_sm_collab<- network::as.sociomatrix(DHHS,attrname="collab")
class(DHHS_sm_collab)
[Output:]
      [1] "matrix"  "array"
```

We may now view the 54 members of the network:

```
colnames(DHHS_sm_collab)
[Partial output:]
   [1] "ACF-1"    "ACF-2"    "AHRQ-1"   "AHRQ-2"   "AHRQ-3"
   [6] "AHRQ-4"   "CDC-1"    "CDC-2"    "CDC-3"    "CDC-4"
   . . .
   [41] "NIH-14"   "NIH-15"   "NIH-16"   "OGC-1"    "OGC-2"
   [46] "OGC-3"    "OS-1"     "OS-2"     "OS-3"     "OS-4"
   [51] "OS-5"     "SAMHSA-1" "SAMHSA-2" "SAMHSA-3"
```

Next, we reduce the size of the network by creating a network object which only has collaborations of 3 or higher, which means only if formal collaboration is present. We rename the collaboration sociomatrix as "DHHS_sm_formal" so as to preserve the original, then zero-out collaborations less than collab=3, then convert back to an object of class "network" called "DHHS_formal".

```
# Create DHHS_sm_formal as a copy of DHHS_sm_collab
DHHS_sm_formal <- DHHS_sm_collab

# Recode all collaboration codes less than 3 as 0
DHHS_sm_formal[DHHS_sm_formal<3] <- 0

# Convert from sociomatrix back into a network object
DHHS_formal <- network::as.network(DHHS_sm_formal,
    directed=FALSE,
    matrix.type="a",
    ignore.eval=FALSE,
    names.eval = "collab")
class(DHHS_formal)
[Output:]
      [1] "network"

# Print summary
summary(DHHS_formal, print.adj=FALSE)
[Output:]
   Network attributes:
     vertices = 54
     directed = FALSE
     hyper = FALSE
     loops = FALSE
     multiple = FALSE
     bipartite = FALSE
    total edges = 173
      missing edges = 0
      non-missing edges = 173
    density = 0.1208945
   Vertex attributes:
    vertex.names:
     character valued attribute
     54 valid vertex names
   Edge attributes:
    collab:
      numeric valued attribute
      attribute summary:
      Min. 1st Qu.  Median    Mean 3rd Qu.    Max.
     3.000   3.000   3.000   3.457   4.000   4.000
```

From the summary above, one can see we have reduced the full DHHS network with its 447 edges representing all types of collaboration to one with 173 edges which represent formal collaboration only. This will make the visualized network easier to read and will emphasize formal collaboration.

We want to color code the edges by level of collaboration, so this step precedes actual plotting of the network. This is a three-step process:

1. First set the color palette for the two types of edges corresponding to collab=3 and collab=4 to which DHHS_formal is limited. The types are in the edge element "collab".

```
attributes(DHHS_formal)
[Output:]
   $names
   [1] "mel" "gal" "val" "iel" "oel"
```

```
$class
[1] "network"
```

The edge collab type value (here 3 for case 1, below) is in the "mel" attribute in the third element ($atl) then in the second subelement (collab) within the third element. This is revealed by inspecting the mel

```
head(DHHS_formal$mel,1)
[Output:]
  [[1]]
  [[1]]$inl
  [1] 2

  [[1]]$outl
  [1] 51

  [[1]]$atl
  [[1]]$atl$na
  [1] FALSE

  [[1]]$atl$collab
  [1] 3
```

2. With this knowledge we may create a vector called "edgevals" to hold the "collab" codes. First obtain a vector with the third element, then filter for the second subelement of the third element, which is the "collab" value.

```
List<- DHHS_formal$mel
edgevals <- sapply(List, '[[', 3)
edgevals <- edgevals[2,]
length(edgevals)
[Output:]
    [1] 173
class(edgevals)
[Output:]
   [1] "list"

# Convert from the list edgevals to the numeric vector edgetype
edgetype <- as.numeric(edgevals)
class(edgetype)
[Output:]
   [1] "numeric"

# Verify that edgetype is all 3s and 4s (the formal collaboration codes)

summary(edgetype)
[Output:]
   Min. 1st Qu.  Median    Mean 3rd Qu.    Max.
  3.000   3.000   3.000   3.457   4.000   4.000
```

3. Now create a corresponding color vector. Collab type 3 will be pink3, all others (which here is collab type 4) will be steelblue2.

```
edgecolors <-  ifelse(edgetype == 3, "pink3","steelblue2")
class(edgecolors)
   [1] "character"

edgecolors
[Partial output:]
  [1] "pink3"      "pink3"      "pink3"      "pink3"      "pink3"
. . .
[166] "pink3"      "pink3"      "steelblue2" "pink3"      "steelblue2"
[171] "steelblue2" "steelblue2" "pink3"
```

TEXT BOX 8.2 Analyzing social identification with sports teams using the "statnet" package

The "statnet" package was used by Graupensperger, Panza, and Evans (2020) to create networks for 35 sports teams and to compute outdegree centrality, indegree centrality, and team density as social network indices. Outdegree centrality measures self-reported connections with teammates. Indegree centrality was based on nominations from other team members, Team density was a group-level variable.

Using these metrics, the authors used multilevel modeling to test the relative effects of outdegree centrality, indegree centrality, and group-level team density on athletes' social identification strength. All three were found to be all positively related to social identification with their sport team. Team density was found to be related to social identification even after controlling for outdegree and indegree centrality. The authors concluded, "The current findings indicate that athletes who have greater social connections with teammates may form a stronger sense of social identification. Alongside theoretical contributions to a social identity approach to studying small groups, the current study highlights the utility of studying small groups using social network methodologies." (p. 59)

Source: Graupensperger, Scott; Panza, Michael; & Evans, M. Blair (2020). Network centrality, group density, and strength of social identification in college club sport teams. *Group Dynamics* 24(2): 59–73.

8.11.2 Visualization

Finally, the actual network plot of the formal DHHS network is done with the `gplot()` function of the "sna" package, which was installed when statnet was installed.

```
# Set graphical parameters for plotting wider margins for a larger, better spaced layout
op <- par(mar=rep(0,4))

# Include next line to divert output from the RStudio Viewer
# to a high-resolution pdf displayed in the default browser (not done here).
# Run the "g" graph object at the end as described in the network-on-a-map example.
# grDevices::pdf(g <- tempfile(fileext = ".pdf"), width = 40, height = 20)

# Plot the network. We present many of the options available, but not all are necessary.
# The plot is shown in Figure 8.25.
set.seed(123)
# Create a scaling factor for node size based on degree centrality
# The multiplier may require adjustment for different data
# ignore.eval=TRUE means degree is not weighted by values in a column
# gmode="graph" means the network is undirected; if directed, use "digraph"
# cmode="freeman" means degree is based on total, not "indegree" or "outdegree"
degscale <- .4 * sna::degree(DHHS_formal, ignore.eval=TRUE, gmode="graph",
cmode="freeman")

# Run the code creating "g" as a block, not line by line.
g <- sna::gplot(DHHS_formal,
    # "graph" mode is for undirected networks, "digraph" is for directed
    gmode="graph",
    # Mode sets layout ("fruchtermanreingold" is the default. Others include "kamadakawai",
    # "princoord", "eigen", "mds", "random", "circle", "circrand", or "rmds".
    mode="circle",
    # Don't use diagonal values (node to itself; this is the default and suppresses loops)
```

```
    diag = FALSE,
    # Allow user to move vertices for better placement (not the default)
    interactive = TRUE,
    # Don't display members who aren't formally collaborating with anyone (isolates).
    displayisolates = FALSE,
    # labels come from the vertex.names element of the nodes in a network class object.
    # For instance, the label "NIH-16" refers to member network member 16 from agency NIH.
    # The next commands turn labeling on, set the label color, and set label size.
    # label.pos = 5 sets the label on the vertex. However, 0 is the default (away from graph)
    # Set boxed.labels=TRUE to put a box around each node label.
    displaylabels = TRUE,
    label.col = "black",
    label.cex = 0.8,
    label.pos =  5,
    # %e% is a network extraction operator which here retrieves the edge element "collab"
    # Below we also set edge colors and line width. We do not use curved edges (the default).
    edge.lwf  %e% 'collab',
    edge.col  = edgecolors,
    edge.lwd = 1,
    usecurve = FALSE,
    # The scale option sets node size (default = .01). As the graph is dense we make it smaller.
    # For different node sizes, setup a size vector, then add vertex.cex=node_vector.
    # The next 3 settings are for node color, size, and number of vertex sides (50 is default)
    object.scale=.005,
    vertex.col="lightblue",
    vertex.cex= degscale,
    vertex.sides=20)

# Add legend Note cex= parameter may differ for RStudio Viewer vs. pdf in browser
# Note col= is here set for the particular two colors in the graph but will differ for different data.
legend("topright", lty = 1, legend = unique(edgevals), lwd=4,col =
c("pink3","steelblue2"), bg="gray98", border="black", title="Collaboration
Level",cex=1.0)

# Reset margins for future plots
par(op)
```

Figure 8.25 visualizes the interagency collaboration network, restricted to formal collaborations and based on the statnet, network, and sna packages. We have used the interactive feature of the network diagram to drag agencies out the three agencies with the highest degree centrality (OS-5, CDC-6, CDC-11) and two with very low degree centrality (FDA-1 and FDA-2). After dragging, click the "Finished" button to view the final graph.

The node OS=5, representing a tobacco control leader in the DHHS Office of the Secretary, is the most central person in the network. Also high in centrality is CDC-6 followed by CDC-11. FDA-1 and FDA-2 have only one edge, which is one connecting them in isolation from the rest of the formal network. Member OS-1 also has only one connection, which is to OS-5, but as it is a level 4 collaboration it is colored blue and indicates multiple collaborations. Edges in pink are single collaborations (level 3) edges in blue are multiple collaborations (level 4), as indicated in the legend. In general, all formal collaboration relationships among agency leaders are visualized in the network graph.

Degree centrality for each of the 54 actors in the formal interagency network may be listed as below:[9] The "!=0" condition causes `colSums()` to do column counts, not column sums. This is based on the simplest criterion for degree centrality, which is number of edges. It is close to the `kpset()` results from the "keyplayer" program, which can identify the top k members by various centrality criteria.[10]

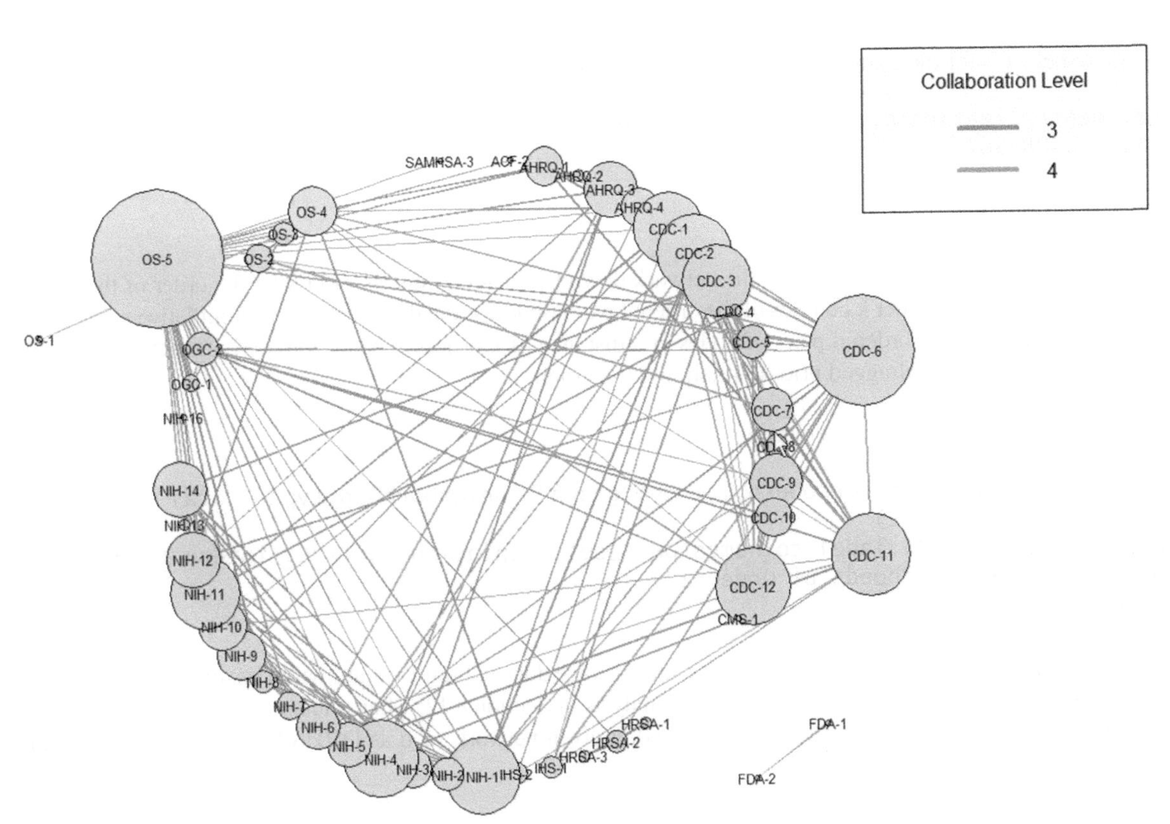

Figure 8.25 The DHHS formal collaboration network

```
sort(colSums(DHHS_sm_formal != 0))
```

[Output:]

```
    ACF-1     CMS-2    NIH-15     OGC-3  SAMHSA-1  SAMHSA-2
        0         0         0         0         0         0
    ACF-2     CMS-1     FDA-1     FDA-2    NIH-16      OS-1
        1         1         1         1         1         1
 SAMHSA-3    AHRQ-2     CDC-4    HRSA-1    HRSA-3    NIH-13
        1         2         2         2         2         2
    OGC-1     CDC-8    HRSA-2     IHS-1     IHS-2     NIH-8
        3         4         4         4         4         4
     OS-3     NIH-7      OS-2     CDC-5     NIH-2     OGC-2
        4         5         5         6         6         6
   AHRQ-1    AHRQ-4    CDC-10     NIH-3     CDC-7     NIH-5
        7         7         7         7         8         8
    NIH-6     NIH-9    NIH-10      OS-4    AHRQ-3     CDC-9
        8         9         9         9        10        10
   NIH-12    NIH-14     CDC-1     CDC-3    NIH-11     CDC-2
       10        10        13        13        13        14
   CDC-12     NIH-1     NIH-4    CDC-11     CDC-6      OS-5
       14        14        14        15        20        25
```

Though it is not explored here, the sna package has functions for many types of centrality metrics, including not only degree centrality but also betweenness, closeness, eigenvector, information, stress, load, and others. For instance, its `centralization()` command will return an overall centralization score for the network. The centralization score below is for the example graph based on normalized degree centrality.

```
sna::centralization(g,degree,mode="graph",normalize=TRUE)
 [1] 0.04085567
```

8.11.3 Neighborhoods

The sna package also supports breaking the network down by "neighborhoods". Let k be the order of the graph. A partial neighborhood of order k consists of the ordered pairs of nodes at a distance of k. A cumulative neighborhood of order k consists of the ordered pairs of nodes at a distance of k or less. The option `interactive=TRUE` means that nodes may be dragged prior to finalizing the graph.

```
# Just neighborhoods for k = 1, interactive
set.seed(123)
neigh_k1 <- sna::neighborhood(g,1,mode="graph", neighborhood.type="total",return.all=TRUE,partial=TRUE)
sna::gplot(neigh_k1, label=colnames(DHHS_sm),displaylabels=TRUE, interactive=TRUE, main=paste("Neighborhoods of Order 1"))
[Output is Figure 8.26]
```

The `neighborhood()` command from the sna package does not return a numbered list of neighborhoods with corresponding memberships. Compare sna clique analysis in Section 8.12, where clusters and cluster members may be listed. For the `neighborhood()` command, a given network such as DHHS has multiple neighborhoods

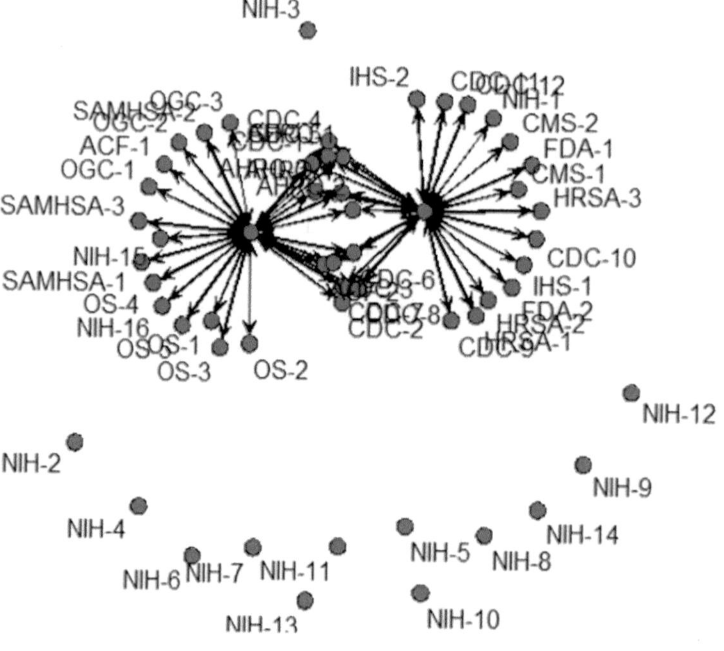

Figure 8.26 DHHS neighborhoods of order 1

based on the order values, as graphically depicted by the "neighpartial" object further below, which shows plots for orders 1 through 9. For a given order, such as order = 1 in Figure 8.26, neighborhoods can only be identified in a subjective way by "eyeballing" the plot. However, isolates (nodes not in any neighborhood) are well defined and their members may be listed.

```
# Get a list of isolates from Figure 8.26
isolates <- sna::isolates(neigh_k1)
# Convert list to a numeric vector
isolates <- unlist(isolates)
isolates
[Output:]
   [[1]]
   [1] 29 30 31 32 33 34 35 36 37 38 39 40 41
# List node names which are isolates
colnames(DHHS_sm)[c(isolates)]
[Output:]
   [1] "NIH-2"  "NIH-3"  "NIH-4"  "NIH-5"  "NIH-6"
   [6] "NIH-7"  "NIH-8"  "NIH-9"  "NIH-10" "NIH-11"
   [11] "NIH-12" "NIH-13" "NIH-14"
```

The subsequent commands produce different types of neighborhood plots but for space reasons no figures are shown.

```
# Partial neighborhoods to view trends across k = 1 through 9
# Replace "graph" with "digraph" if the network is directed.
set.seed(123)
neighpartial <- sna::neighborhood(g,9,mode="graph", neighborhood.
type="total",return.all=TRUE,partial=TRUE)
par(mfrow=c(3,3))
for(i in 1:9)
sna::gplot(neighpartial[i,,], label=colnames(DHHS_sm),
displaylabels=TRUE,main=paste("Partial Neighborhoods of Order",i))
[Output not shown]
```

```
# Cumulative neighborhoods across k = 1 through 9
# No labels so we can see trends across k distance from 1 to 9 better.
set.seed(123)
neighcum <- sna::neighborhood(g,9,mode="graph", neighborhood.type="total",return.
all=TRUE,partial=FALSE)
par(mfrow=c(3,3))
for(i in 1:9)
sna::gplot(neighcum[i,,], label=NULL,
displaylabels=FALSE,main=paste("Cumulative Neighborhoods of Order",i))
[Output not shown]
```

```
# Cumulative, just neighborhoods for k = 3, with labels
set.seed(123)
neighcumk3 <- sna::neighborhood(g,9,mode="graph", neighborhood.type="total",return.
all=TRUE,partial=FALSE)
par(mfrow=c(1,1))
for(i in 3:3)
sna::gplot(neighcumk3[i,,], label=colnames(DHHS_sm),
displaylabels=TRUE,main=paste("Neighborhoods of Order",i))
[Output not shown]
```

8.11.4 Cluster analysis

Using cluster analysis we can also produce a dendrogram based on comemberships. Dendrograms and the hierarchical clustering procedure on which they are based were discussed in Chapter 2.

```
# Compute weights reflecting formal collaboration
coweights <- network::as.sociomatrix(DHHS_sm_formal,"weights")

# Perform hierarchical cluster analysis based on coweights,
# which in turn are based on formal collaboration.

clustobj <- hclust(as.dist(1/(coweights+1)),method="average")

# Produce the dendrogram as a plot
plot(clustobj,xlab="Agency Actors",ylab="The more toward 1, the more unlike agencies
are clustered", main="Dendrogram of Agency Clustering by Formal Collaboration",
cex=0.9, col="darkblue")
```

The dendrogram in Figure 8.27 gives a different view of clustering of agencies in the DHHS formal comembership network. Agency actors are listed along the x-axis, connected at various levels by a horizontal crossbar. The higher

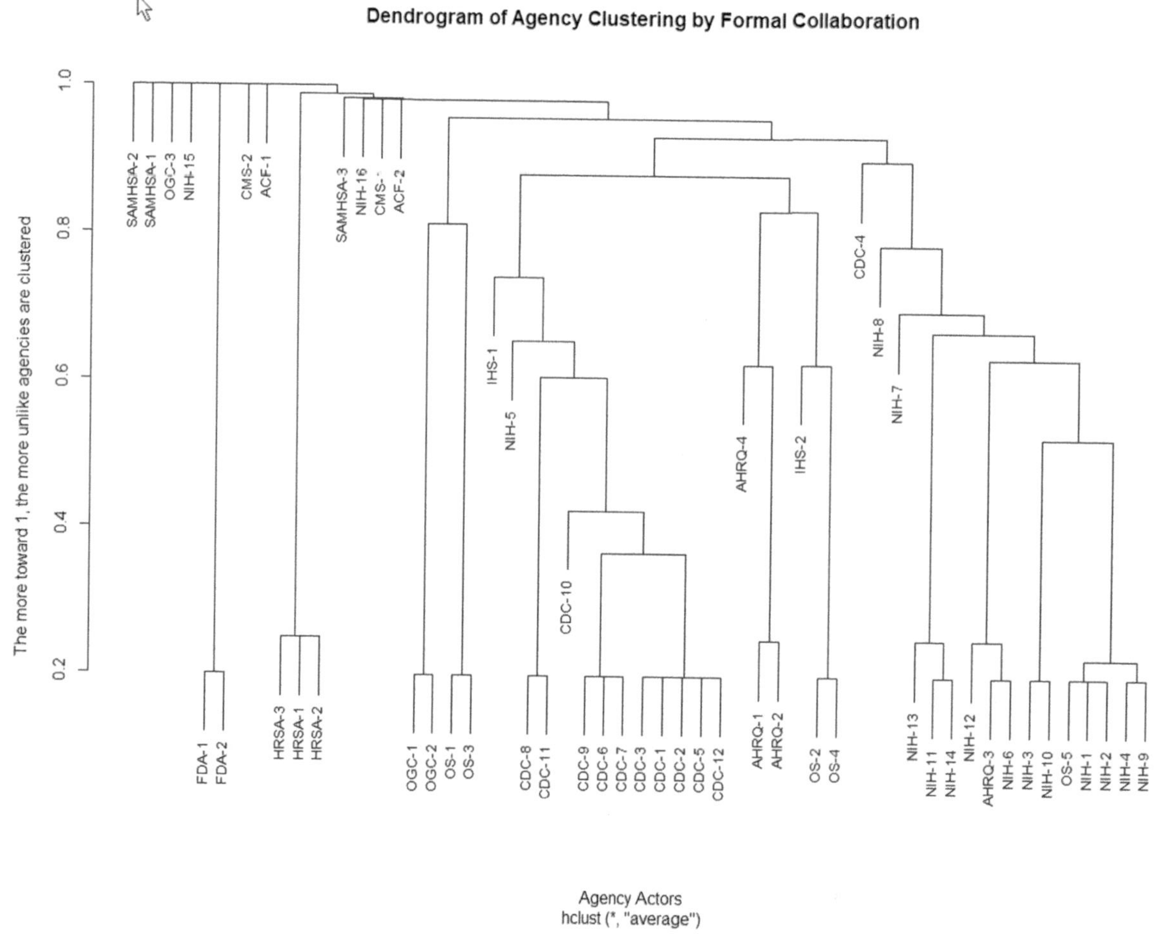

Figure 8.27 Dendrogram of clustering within the DHHS formal collaboration network

the crossbar is toward 1.0, the more unlike are the agencies being connected in the same cluster. For instance, actors NIH-11 and NIH-14 cluster toward the bottom, indicating high alikeness. Actor NIH-13 is also part of this cluster but at a higher distance, indicating this actor is a bit less like the first two with regard to comembership in formal collaborations. There is no specific optimal number of clusters. Rather, the researcher must decide what is optimal based on the specific research needs at hand, including judgment about the acceptable degree of tolerance for placing objects which are unlike to varying degrees in the same cluster.

8.12 Clique analysis with sna

The "sna" package, which is part of the "statnet" suite, along with the "network" package, has the `clique.census()` and other commands for the analysis of cliques within networks. A clique is a maximal set of mutually adjacent vertices. Vertices may represent organizations, agencies, individuals, or other units of analysis. In plain terms, a clique is a group of network actors who share some relationship such as liking each other, collaborating, engaging in communications or transactions, and so on. Any network will have many cliques, with isolates (cliques with one actor), to dyads (2-cliques, with a pair of actors), triads (3-cliques, with three actors), and so on. In the example below the highest level was a 7-clique (seven actors). At any clique level there may be multiple cliques. In the example, the level with the most cliques was that for 4-cliques, of which there were 22.

The example further below continues to use the "DHHS" formal network from the previous section. Some of the many types of social science questions that might be answered with clique analysis include those listed below.

- How many levels of cliques does a network have?
- How many cliques are at each level?
- How does the clique profile of one network compare to that of another in graphical terms?
- Who is in a particular clique (e.g., the highest level one)?
- What level of cliques is a given member in?
- How many cliques is a given member in?
- What other members are in the same clique as the given member?

Before addressing questions such as these for the DHHS formal network, we use a much-simplified network of only five agencies as an example. By keeping size small, it is easier to understand the tables created by sna's `clique.census()` command.

8.12.1 A simplified clique analysis

This initial section contains a simplified example to understand how to read cliques.census output from the sna package:

```
# Setup
setwd("C:/Data")
library(network)
library(sna)
```

Below we create an undirected matrix of Agencyl through Agency 5. We then list the matrix, which has two columns. Each row corresponds to a pair of agencies which has worked together on a project, making this an undirected network. A given pair may be listed more than once if the two agencies collaborated on more than one project.

```
# Data
agency_matrix <- matrix(c("Agency1", "Agency2", "Agency1", "Agency3", "Agency2",
"Agency3", "Agency1", "Agency2", "Agency1", "Agency4", "Agency2", "Agency4",
"Agency2", "Agency1", "Agency2", "Agency4", "Agency1", "Agency4", "Agency2",
"Agency1", "Agency2", "Agency3", "Agency1", "Agency3", "Agency2", "Agency4",
"Agency2", "Agency5", "Agency4", "Agency5"), ncol = 2)
```

```
agency_matrix
[Partial output:]
        [,1]      [,2]
    [1,] "Agency1" "Agency4"
    [2,] "Agency2" "Agency1"
   . . .
   [14,] "Agency1" "Agency4"
   [15,] "Agency2" "Agency5"
```

We then take the matrix (agency_matrix) and convert it to a network object using the `network()` command of the package of the same name.

```
net <- network::network(agency_matrix, directed=FALSE)
```

The next step in clique analysis is to take a census of network's cliques. This is done with the `clique.census()` command of the sna package. We use this command to create the object "census". The census object is of data class "list". The list components include $clique.count, which has the table of clique structure for the network. Setting tabulate.by.vertex to TRUE creates a variable in the first column of the table, called "Agg", discussed below. Another component of the census object is $clique.comemb, which shows comemberships for each agency. Comemberships are the basis for identifying cliques.

```
census <- sna::clique.census(net, tabulate.by.vertex=TRUE, enumerate=TRUE, clique.
comembership="bysize")

census
[Output:]
   $clique.count
     Agg Agency1 Agency2 Agency3 Agency4 Agency5
   1   0       0       0       0       0       0
   2   1       0       1       0       0       1
   3   2       2       2       1       1       0

   $clique.comemb
   [Partial output:]
     , ,  Agency1

       Agency1 Agency2 Agency3 Agency4 Agency5
     1       0       0       0       0       0
     2       0       0       0       0       0
     3       2       2       1       1       0
     . . .

     $cliques
     $cliques[[1]]
     NULL

     $cliques[[2]]
     $cliques[[2]][[1]]
     [1] 2 5

     $cliques[[3]]
     $cliques[[3]][[1]]
     [1] 1 2 4

     $cliques[[3]][[2]]
     [1] 1 2 3
```

Optionally, we may recall the names of the vertices (nodes) in the census network simply by using the `colnames()` command:

```
colnames(census$clique.comemb)
[Output:]
   [1] "Agency1" "Agency2" "Agency3" "Agency4"
   [5] "Agency5"
```

Below we bring the table of clique structure back up and put it into the object "comemb", which is of data class matrix. The Agg column shows there are 0 cliques with only 1 member, one clique with 2 members, and two cliques with 3 members. There are no cliques involving 4 or 5 agencies.

```
comemb <- census$clique.count
comemb
[Output:]
  Agg Agency1 Agency2 Agency3 Agency4 Agency5
1  0       0       0       0       0       0
2  1       0       1       0       0       1
3  2       2       2       1       1       0
```

Much the same information was in the $cliques component of the census object:

```
census$cliques
[Output with interspersed comments:]
   # There were no cliques of size 1, hence row 1 is all 0's (NULL)
   [[1]]
   NULL

   # There was one clique of size 2, with cases 2 (Agency2) and 5 (Agency5)
   # Therefore there is a "1" in both these columns in the table's row 2 and
   # Agg, which is the first column, is 1 since there is one clique of size 2.
   [[2]]
   [[2]][[1]]
   [1] 2 5

   # COMMENT: There were two cliques of size 3, thus 2 sets of 3-clique listings below
   # This is same as above in the Agg column of row 3 of the network clique structure table.
   # Clique 1 is cases 1, 2, and 4 (Agencyl, Agency2, Agency4 respectively)
   # Clique 2 is cases 1, 2, and 3 (Agencyl, Agency2, Agency3 respectively)
   # Agencies 1 and 2 were in both of the 3-cliques, Agencies 3 and 4 in only one,
   # and Agency 5 was not in any 3-clique.

   [[3]]
   [[3]][[1]]
   [1] 1 2 4

   [[3]][[2]]
   [1] 1 2 3
   # As the output ends here, there were no cliques of sizes 4 or 5.
```

8.12.2 A clique analysis of the DHHS formal network

We now turn to clique analysis of a more complex example, the DHHS formal network used as an example in the previous section. For the DHHS formal network, we find seven levels of cliques, within each level there may well be multiple agency sets.

As for the preceding simple five-agency example, clique analysis starts by taking a census of cliques in DHHS_formal, which is an object of class "network". The DHHS_formal data frame and DHHS_sm_formal sociomatrix were created above, but we repeat the essential commands for convenience:

```
library(UserNetR)        # Has the DHHS data and more
library(statnet)         # A leading suite for network visualization
library(network)         # Installed with statnet
library(sna)             # Installed with statnet

# Load DHHS data and convert it to a sociomatrix
data(DHHS)
DHHS_sm_collab<- network::as.sociomatrix(DHHS,attrname="collab")
# Create DHHS_sm_formal as a copy
DHHS_sm_formal <- DHHS_sm_collab
# Recode all collaboration codes less than 3 as 0, where 3 is the cutoff for formal collaboration
DHHS_sm_formal[DHHS_sm_formal<3] <- 0
# Convert from a sociomatrix back into a network object
DHHS_formal <- network::as.network(DHHS_sm_formal,
    directed=FALSE,
    matrix.type="a",
    ignore.eval=FALSE,
    names.eval = "collab")
```

The cliques list itself, here stored under the label "census", is of class "list" and has the objects listed below.

```
library(network)

census <- sna::clique.census(DHHS_formal, mode="graph", clique.comembership="sum")
class(census)
      [1] "list"
objects(census)
      [1] "clique.comemb" "clique.count"  "cliques"
```

With "census" created, we next investigate how many cliques there are in the DHHS formal network. Below, we find there are seven. This means that there are one or more cliques as large as 7 actors ("7-cliques").

```
length(census$cliques)
 [1] 7
```

We next create the comembership table, including the aggregate (Agg) variable, which is in column 1. This table is much larger than in the earlier simple example as DHHS has 54 agencies, not 5. In the "Agg" column we see the number of cliques of each level. For instance, there are twenty-two 4-actor cliques but only one 7-actor clique. AHRQ-2 belongs to one clique, but it is a 3-clique with two other members (AHRQ-1 and AHRQ-3). Thus, the comemb object shows the number of cliques with which a given member is associated, not the number of other network members with whom the given member is in a clique. The latter is shown in the DHHS_sm_formal data frame.

```
comemb <- census$clique.count
comemb
```

[Partial output:]

	Agg	ACF-1	ACF-2	AHRQ-1	AHRQ-2	AHRQ-3	AHRQ-4
1	6	1	0	0	0	0	0
2	10	0	1	0	0	0	0
3	13	0	0	1	1	2	0
4	22	0	0	5	0	6	5
5	11	0	0	0	0	0	0
6	7	0	0	0	0	0	0
7	1	0	0	0	0	0	0

```
   CDC-1 CDC-2 CDC-3 CDC-4 CDC-5 CDC-6 CDC-7
1    0     0     0     0     0     0     0
2    0     0     1     0     0     0     0
3    1     1     1     1     0     2     0
4    3     3     0     0     0    10     2
5    1     2     1     0     0     4     0
6    4     3     5     0     2     5     0
7    0     1     1     0     0     1     1
. . .
```

We can, of course, look at actual clique membership. To illustrate, we take the example of the one 7-member clique. The command below gives the list of the index numbers of the seven agencies in the 7-clique. The `unlist()` operation is needed to convert from list data type to integer data type (i.e., selected is an integer vector, not a list).

```
# First put the agency index number of the 7-clique into the object "selected":
selected <- unlist(census$cliques[7])
selected

[Output:]
     [1]  8  9 12 13 15 17 18

# Then list agency names corresponding to the index numbers in the clique
agencynames <- colnames(DHHS_sm_formal)
agencynames[selected]
   [1] "CDC-2"  "CDC-3"  "CDC-6"  "CDC-7"  "CDC-9"
   [6] "CDC-11" "CDC-12"
```

We may now plot the clique structure of the DHHS formal network. Moreover, we may compare its structure with the structure of a second network. Our social science motivation might be to compare clique sizes with what is known about optimal sizes for policy-making groups. While optimal size is a complex contextual issue, Kashian and Kohls (2009: 17), for example, found that the optimal size of planning commissions was 11. In general, sizes need to be large enough to represent diversity but small enough for reasoned discussion in the attempt to reach decision, if not consensus. In the data below, the largest formal clique in the context of DHHS tobacco control had seven members and the modal clique was only four. While this does not mean there is "something wrong" with interagency tobacco control collaboration, it is exploratory evidence raising questions about whether collaboration cliques are too concentrated in this arena. The counter-argument might be that small size reflects only division of labor and specialization. Regardless, clique analysis has served to highlight a potential issue for further research.

In the next part of clique analysis we graph the clique structure of the DHHS formal network. Visualization highlights the size issue. It is particularly valuable when not done for a single agency but for a comparison among agencies. For instance, does the clique structure seem to be a differentiating factor for networks, which achieve their goal and networks which do not? To illustrate how this comparison is made, we create a fictional second interagency network and overlay its clique profile on that of the DHHS formal clique profile. The steps involved in this visualization are below.

```
# Step 1. Put number of clique levels in "dimensions".
dimensions<-dim(comemb)
dimensions[1]
[1] 7

# Step 2. Create a clique size vector as the object "cliqueprofile"
# To do this we use Agg, which is column 1 of the dimensions object above.
cliquelevels<-dimensions[1]
cliqueprofile<-comemb[1:cliquelevels]
cliqueprofile
[1]  6 10 13 22 11  7  1

# Step 3. Set the maximum plot dimensions for any network being compared
# The maxlevels (maximum clique levels) and maxcliques (maximum number of cliques of any
```

```
# level in any network being plotted) variables should be set to the highest number in any
# network being compared.
maxlevels = 7
maxcliques = 22

# Step 4. Plot the clique profile for the DHHS formal network (Figure 8.28)
# Recall cex values set font and symbol sizes.
plot(cliqueprofile,col="red", pch=19,cex=2, xlab="Clique Size", ylab="Number of Cliques", cex.axis=1.5, cex.lab=1.5, cex.main=1.7,main="Profile Plot of Agency Cliques",xlim=c(1,maxlevels), ylim=c(1,maxcliques))
# Add connecting lines
lines(cliqueprofile,lwd=2, col="gray80")

# Step 5. Create a cliqueprofile vector for a second network (here, a fictional one)
# For an actual second network, cliqueprofile2 would be created in the same manner
# as for "comemb" above.
# "Plot" is not issued because the points and lines are to be overlaid on the DHHS plot.
cliqueprofile2 <- c(14, 10, 10, 6)
lines(cliqueprofile2,lwd=2, col="gray80")
points(cliqueprofile2,col="blue", pch=19,cex=2)

# Step 6. Add a legend
legend("topright", pch = 19, legend = c("DHHS Network", "Second Network"),
bg="gray95", border="black",col = c("red","blue"), title="Clique Profiles",cex=1.5)
```

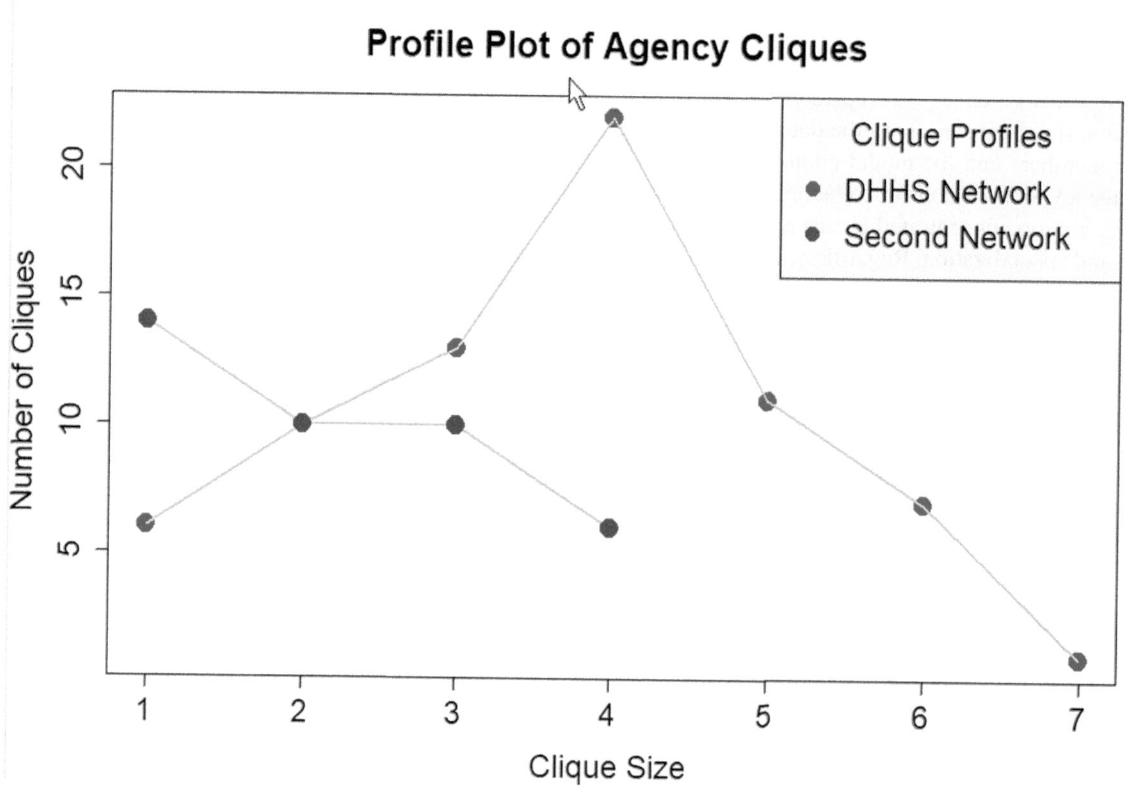

Figure 8.28 Profile plot of agency clique structures

Below we create a graph which visualizes the DHHS formal network with vertices (agency nodes) color-coded for the number of cliques to which each agency belongs. Cliques are computed by the sna package's `clique.census()` command, as earlier in this section. Thus, the "census" object contains the results of the `clique.census()` command and the "comemb" object reflects census$clique.count. The eight-step process for creating the clique comembership plot shown in Figure 8.29.

```
# Step 1. Create a vector of total clique memberships for each agency.
# This will be used to color-code the network vertices.
numcliques <- colSums(comemb)
# Strip off the first element of the vector, which is Agg sum, not an agency sum
numcliques <- numcliques[-1]

# Step 2. Divide numcliques into k equal-interval ranges (not equal number of cases)
# ranges has numcliques values, with k different labels
k <- 5
numranges <-  k

# Step 3. Put the range category for each node into "rangecat" (here, 1:5)
ranges <- cut(numcliques,k)
rangecat <- round(as.numeric(ranges))
rangelabels <- as.character(rangecat)

# Step 4. Optionally, view the cutpoints (cutpointstring can be added as text to the plot below)
cutpoints<-sort(unique(ranges))
cutpointstring <- paste(cutpoints,collapse = "/")
cutpointstring <- paste(k," Ranges: ", cutpointstring)
cutpointstring
[Output:]
   [1] "5  Ranges:  (0.973,6.4]/(6.4,11.8]/(11.8,17.2]/(17.2,22.6]/(22.6,28]"

# Step 5. Set the color palette
grDevices::palette(rainbow(numranges))

# Step 6. Plot the DHHS formal network created earlier but color-code by clique comembership.
# Notice that the network configuration is plotted on the basis of the DHHS_formal object
# while the clique count color coding is based on ranges, in turn based on comemb.
# Thus, comemb itself is not being plotted. The graph will differ for different random seeds.
set.seed(123)
g <- sna::gplot(DHHS_formal,
     gmode = "graph",
     mode = "fruchtermanreingold",
     diag=FALSE,
     coord=NULL,
     vertex.border="gray60",
     vertex.col= ranges,
     edge.col = "gray80",
     label.col = "black",
     usearrows=FALSE,
     displaylabels=TRUE,
     interactive=TRUE,
     main="Clique Comembership Plot")

# Step 7. Add a legend
legend("bottomright", pch = 19, legend = sort(unique(rangelabels)), bg="white", box.
col="white",col = sort(unique(numcliques)), title="Clique \n Comembership \n Range",
pt.cex=2, cex=1.2, ncol=2)
```

```
# Step 8. Add cutpoint information at bottom
mtext(cutpointstring,1)
```

Figure 8.29 comembership shows the DHHS formal network clique comembership network. Since the script above contained the option "interactive=TRUE", it was possible to drag nodes. We did this for the two agencies with the highest clique count to a more viewable position. These were OS-5 in the Office of the Secretary of DHHS and CDC-6, one of the tobacco control officers in the Centers for Disease Control. The main plot shows red points around the periphery, indicate low clique comembership. Other-colored points are more toward the central, dense part of the network. OS-5 and CDC-6, in comembership ranges 5 and 4 respectively, are very central to the network.

We may now answer the questions posed at the beginning of this section:

- How many levels of cliques does the DHHS formal network have?
- Answer: Seven (a 7-clique is the highest level).

```
nrow(census$clique.count)
[Output:]
   [1] 7
```

- How many cliques are at each level?
  Answer: From the cliqueprofile object, 6, 10, 13, 22, 11, 7, and 1 for levels 1–7, respectively.

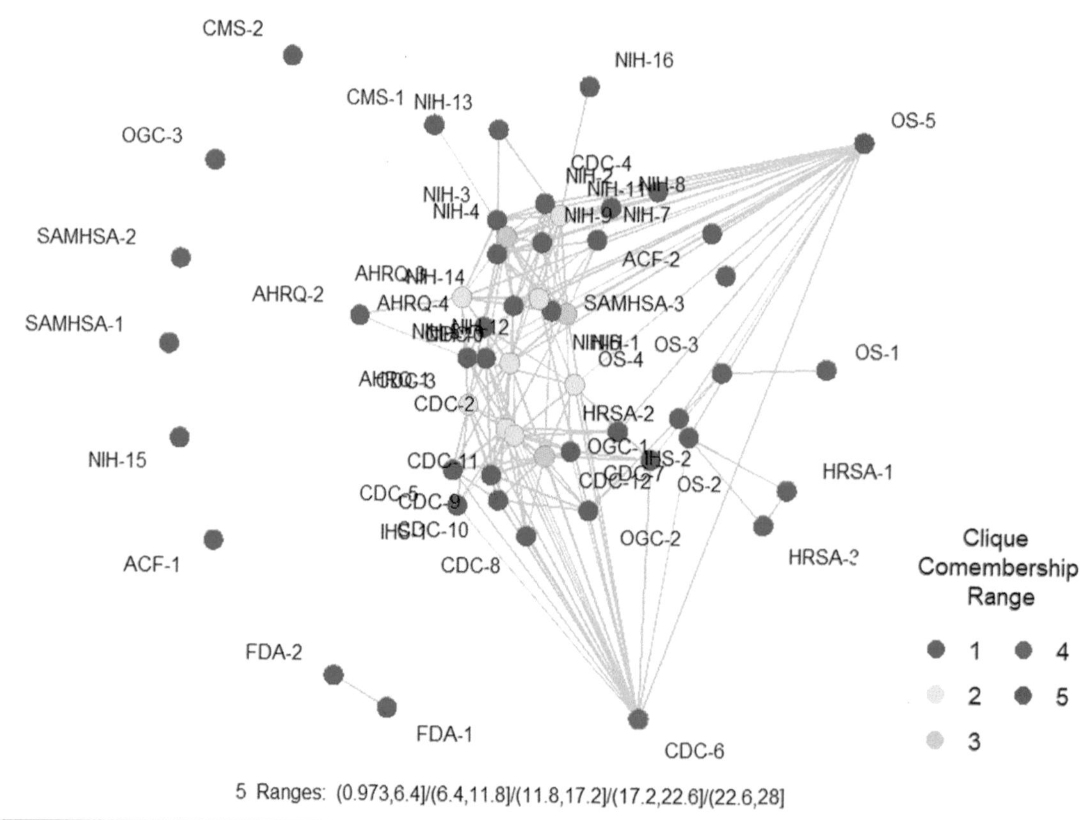

Figure 8.29 The DHHS formal collaboration clique comembership network

- How does the clique profile of one network compare to that of another in graphical terms?
  Answer: This was illustrated in Figure 8.28 (the profile plot).
- Who is in a particular clique (e.g., the highest level one)?
  Answer: CDC-2, CDC-3, CDC-6, CDC-7, CDC-9, CDC-11, and CDC-12, as found earlier in this section.
- What level of cliques is a given member in?
  Answer: This is found in comemb, the clique comembership table. For instance, agency actor AHRQ-2 was only in one clique, which was a 3-clique (level 3).
- With how many others is an actor in a clique of any size?
  Answer: This was given above for all members by the command

  ```
  colSums(DHHS_sm_formal != 0)
  ```

- What other members are in the same clique as the given member?
  Answer: The given member may be in multiple cliques and therefore have multiple sets of comembers. AHRQ-1, which was actor 3 (the third column of the DHHS_formal data frame) was in only one clique, which was a 3-clique. Looking in the "census" object, we see this one clique listing is:

  ```
  $cliques[[3]][[13]]
  [1] 3 4 5
  ```

  AHRQ-2 is actor 4 in the DHHS_formal data frame, and the same data frame shows the member id numbers 3 and 5 to be AHRQ-1 and AHRQ-5. Alternatively, the `which()` command will find the index number corresponding to a column name:

  ```
  which( colnames(DHHS_sm_formal)=="AHRQ-2" )
   [1] 4
  ```

- In addition, of course, we also created a clique profile plot comparing the profiles of two networks, and we created a network graph color-coded by agencies' range category of comemberships.

8.12.3 K-core analysis of the DHHS formal network

Coverage of this topic is available online in the Support Material (www.routledge.com/9780367624293) for this book, in its student resources section, with the supplement title "K-Core Analysis of the DHHS Interagency Collaboration Network." This section uses the sna package to show a different sort of breakdown of the DHHS network into "k-cores" rather than "cliques".

8.13 Mapping international trade flow with statnet and Intergraph

Coverage of this topic is available online in the Support Material (www.routledge.com/9780367624293) for this book, in its student resources section, where the title is "Mapping International Trade Flow With Statnet and Intergraph Conversion." In addition to presenting an illustration of different aspects of the "statnet" suite of packages using an example from economics and business, it also covers the "intergraph" package. The "intergraph" package is a valuable utility for network analysis, enabling the researcher to convert among network (from the network package also used by statnet and sna), igraph, data frame, and matrix R object formats.

8.14 Correlation networks with corrr

A correlation matrix is one of the most familiar data objects in social science. It is based on an input data matrix in which rows are people or other entities (e.g., cities or nations) and columns are variables. The correlation matrix itself is one in which both rows and columns are variables and cell entries are correlation coefficients of one type or another, usually Pearson correlation coefficients, which are used for continuous data. One use of a correlation matrix is in factor analysis to cluster variables for a set of entities, where clusters may represent underlying dimensions of the data. Alternatively, the original data may be transposed, making entities the columns and the variables the rows. Ordinarily the correlation matrix represents the correlation of a variable for a set of people or other entities. After transposition, however, the correlation matrix then represents the correlation of entities for a set of variables. Either way, a correlation network is a visualization of a correlation matrix. As such it is one of the most universally-applicable forms of network visualization in social science. Correlation matrices may be implemented under many R packages but in this section we discuss one designed specifically for the purpose, the "corrr" package.

We use the example file "crime_r.csv", described in Section 8.2. The outcome variable is "CrimeRate". The research question for this exercise is "What are the correlates of state-level crime rates?" More broadly, we presume the researcher is at the exploratory state of research and wishes to assess whether the supplied dataset contains variables, which may plausibly specify a model of state-level crime rates.

```
# Setup
setwd("C:/Data")
library(corrr)          # For analysis of correlation matrices
library(dplyr)          # Utility supporting %>% piping and more

# Read in the crime data as a data frame
setwd("C:/Data")
crime_df <- read.table("crime_r.csv", header = TRUE, sep = ",",
stringsAsFactors=TRUE)
class(crime_df)
      [1] "data.frame"
View(crime_df)

# Create the correlation matrix (class = matrix). Listwise deletion is specified by complete.obs.
mat1 <- cor(crime_df, method = "pearson", use = "complete.obs")
class(mat1)
       [1] "matrix"
head(mat1,2)
[Correlation matrix for first two variables:]
              CrimeRate       Youth  Education
   CrimeRate  1.00000000 -0.01887195  0.1280361
   Youth     -0.01887195  1.00000000 -0.3561723
             ExpenditureYear LabourForce     Males
   CrimeRate       0.6306089  0.10964944 0.1468304
   Youth          -0.4635777 -0.05652289 0.1029198
              MoreMales  StateSize YouthUnemploy
   CrimeRate 0.12856796  0.3200238   -0.03275446
   Youth     0.03216632 -0.1899728   -0.05750670
             MatureUnemploy HighYouthUnemploy       Wage
   CrimeRate     0.16538274        -0.2893501  0.4367869
   Youth         0.02082069        -0.1650532 -0.5522191
              BelowWage
   CrimeRate -0.06596506
   Youth      0.51778496
```

It is possible to use the `fashion()` command to prepare the correlation matrix for publication. This command removes leading spaces, replaces NAs with blanks, and rounds correlations to two decimal places. Note that this command uses the "%>%" piping operator from the dplyr package. Piping simply means here that the attributes of the mat1 correlation matrix object are passed to the `fashion()` command.

```
mat2 <- mat1 %>% corrr::fashion()
mat2
[Output not displayed here]
```

We now convert the correlation matrix from matrix format into a correlation matrix data frame (cor_df). Note: the `corrr:correlate()` command could have created a cor_df object by default, but that defaults to pairwise deletion, which is not the norm in social science, where each correlation is expected to have the same sample size (n). However, this can be overridden.

```
mat1_cordf <- corrr::as_cordf(mat1, diagonal=1)
mat1_cordf
class(mat1_cordf)
      [1] "cor_df"     "tbl_df"     "tbl"         "data.frame"
```

At this point we are finally ready to create the correlation network graph. Note that the corrr package automatically adds a legend. Note also that we only plot correlations of 0.2 or higher (Figure 8.30).

```
g  <-  corrr::network_plot(mat1_cordf, min_cor = 0.2, colors=c("darkgreen", "white", "royalblue2"), curved=TRUE)

# Display the graph
# NOTE: if arrows don't show in the RStudio Viewer, go to Plots > Zoom
plot(g)
```

The network plotting command in the "corrr" package places variables, which are more highly correlated on an absolute basis closer together. Also these variables are joined by stronger paths as indicated by being darker. Paths are colored by the sign of the relevant correlation (here, blue for positive correlations and green for negative). The proximity of variables is calculated using a multidimensional scaling algorithm.

In terms of the research questions for this section, the correlation network visualization suggests that state crime rates are best explained by per capita expenditure on police (ExpenditureYear), median weekly wage (Wage), and state population size (StateSize), in that order. These correspond to positive correlations of .631, .437, and .320, respectively. We would very likely want to include these variables in a more complete analysis. The cluster of variables to the right in the network graph, dealing with unemployment, males, and youth, may be less salient.

Limitations: Correlation is not causation. Binary relationships (correlations) may be altered when control variables are employed in multivariate analyses (e.g., regression). Moreover, what is true at the aggregate (state) level may not be true at the individual level. Longitudinal individual-level data in conjunction with multivariate and possibly multilevel analysis, including types discussed in Chapters 2 and 3, would be needed for actual confirmatory research. Still, the correlation network may lead to useful exploratory inferences about model selection for later research.

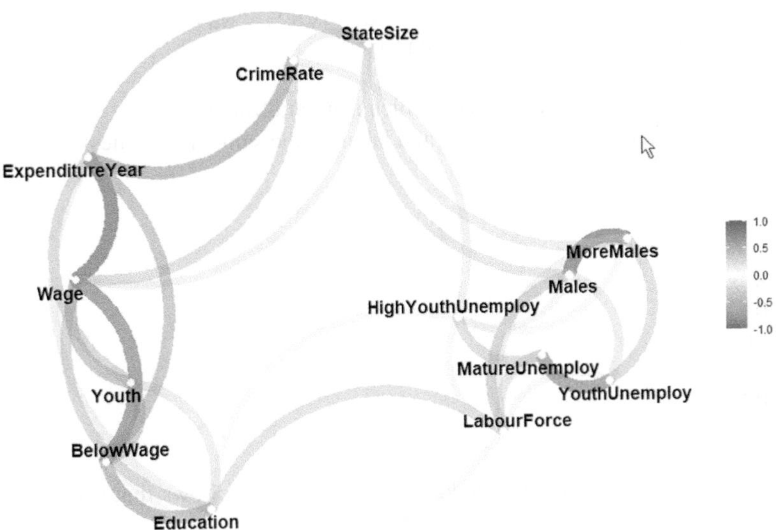

Figure 8.30 Correlation network of crime factors

8.15 Network analysis with tidygraph

8.15.1 Introduction

The "tidygraph: package" is the network visualization component of the "tidyverse" suite of tools, discussed more extensively in Chapter 9. It is useful for analyzing not only network objects but also graph and tree objects in R. A major feature of tidygraph is that it gives the network analyst direct use of commands associated with the widely-used "dplyr" package. In general, tidygraph may be thought of as providing an environment for integrating many network visualization tools, giving greater researcher control than some other packages. By the same token, its very power makes for more complex code, with separate commands pertaining to each aspect of network visualization. A major feature of tidygraph, on which we focus in this section, is tidygraph's support for a very large number of different centrality measures.

```
# Setup
setwd("C:/Data")                # Set the working directory
# Installation of tidyverse also loads tibble, dplyr, tidyr, stringr, readr, forcats, & purrr
library(tidyverse)              # Framework for tidygraph and other "tidy" components
library(tidygraph)              # A package to create and analyze network objects
library(ggraph)                 # Works with tidygraph to visualize networks
```

8.15.2 A simple tidygraph example

The `tbl _ graph()` command in tidygraph is used to create a tidygraph network based on two data frames, one for nodes and one for edges. Therefore, below we create the "nodes" and "edges" data frames first. The R code which does this is identical to what was done in this chapter's earlier section on research team membership networks with visNetwork, except we create a simulated network of 12 rather than 6 individuals. We seek to visualize a 15-member research network in which team members may have three types of connections: "S" = teaming together on a successful project, "U" = teaming together on an unsuccessful project, or "N" = never having teamed on a projected. Some data are NA (missing data on a given pair). We also seek in our visualization to represent the degree centrality of each member.

Step 1: Creating the nodes and edges data frames

```
# First construct the nodes object. It is a data.frame of tibble type with 12 names.
# As a preliminary, we populate the character vector "people" with names.
people<- c("Marlene", "Kendra", "Elena", "Marilyn", "Walter", "Calvin", "Clarence",
"Peter", "Mary", "Lincoln", "Jamal", "Caitlyn")

# Use the people vector to create the "nodes" object, which is a data frame
# with two columns: "id" and "label". Here we let id and label be the same (the names).
nodes <- dplyr::tibble(id = people)
nodes$label <- people
head(nodes,3)
[Output:]
  # A tibble: 3 x 2
    id      label
    <chr>   <chr>
  1 Marlene Marlene
  2 Kendra  Kendra
  3 Elena   Elena
```

Next we create the edges data frame with simulated data. The process follows that use for the earlier visNetwork example.

```
# First define all possible combinations of sample ids
set.seed(123)
```

```
# Create the pal object, a color palette tibble, with colors corresponding to edge types
pal <- dplyr::tibble(connection = c("S", "U", "N"), clabel = c("successful pair",
"unsuccessful pair", "never a pair"), color = c("blue", "red", "darkgray"))

# The combn() combinations function is from R's built-in "utils" package
# The t() transpose function is from R's "base" package.
edges <- combn(people, 2) %>% t(.) %>%
# Convert the matrix to a tibble data frame
dplyr::as_tibble(.) %>%
# Set the "from" and "to" column labels
magrittr::set_names(c("from","to")) %>%
# Set the "connection" column at random to the type of connection, or NA if no connection.
dplyr::mutate(connection = sample(c("S","U","N", NA), size = nrow(.), prob =
c(0.2,0.2,0.2,0.4), replace = TRUE)) %>%
# If the connection is NA then the connection does not exist … filter for not NA.
dplyr::filter(!is.na(connection)) %>%
# Filter out loops (the from person cannot be the same as the to person).
dplyr::filter(from != to) %>%
# Join the previously-created color palette (pal). This adds the "color" column to edges.
dplyr::left_join(pal)
# edges is a tibble-type data frame
head(edges,3)
[Output:]
  # A tibble: 3 x 5
  from    to      connection clabel            color
    <chr>   <chr>   <chr>      <chr>             <chr>
  1 Marlene Elena   U          unsuccessful pair red
  2 Marlene Marilyn N          never a pair      darkgray
  3 Marlene Walter  S          successful pair   blue
```

Step 2: Create the "researchnet" network from nodes and edges

We use tidygraph to create the network, labeled "researchnet". This object is of the data classes tbl_graph and igraph.

```
researchnet <- tidygraph::tbl_graph(nodes, edges, directed = FALSE)
class(researchnet)
      [1] "tbl_graph" "igraph"
```

Step 3: Plot the network with tidygraph

In the following plot of the research team network in tidygraph, we color-code nodes by their centrality. The tidygraph package supports many types of centrality measures. These are too numerous to discuss here but they are all described in the tidygraph online help pages. Each represents different definitions of node importance in a network. A few are setup to reflect importance of edges rather than nodes.

- centrality_alpha
- centrality_authority
- centrality_betweenness
- centrality_betweenness_communicability
- centrality_betweenness_current
- centrality_betweenness_network
- centrality_betweenness_rsp_net
- centrality_betweenness_rsp_simple
- centrality_closeness
- centrality_closeness_generalised

- centrality_closeness_harmonic
- centrality_closeness_residual
- centrality_communicability
- centrality_communicability_even
- centrality_communicability_odd
- centrality_decay
- centrality_degree
- centrality_edge_betweenness
- centrality_eigen
- centrality_expected
- centrality_hub
- centrality_information
- centrality_integration
- centrality_katz
- centrality_manual
- centrality_pagerank
- centrality_power
- centrality_random_walk
- centrality_subgraph
- centrality_subgraph_even
- centrality_subgraph_odd

Some of the most common centrality measures are these:

- *centrality_degree*: Nodes with more edges are more important.
- *centrality_betweenness*: Nodes with shortest paths passing through it are more important.
- *centrality_closeness*: Nodes which require fewer steps to reach all other nodes are more central and more important.
- *centrality_eigen*: By the eigenvector centrality criterion, an important node is connected to many other nodes which in turn are also connected to many others, and so on successively.
- *centrality_authority*: An asymmetrical version of eigenvector centrality, with a node ranked high if it receives connections from many important hubs.
- *centrality_hub*: An asymmetrical version of eigenvector centrality, with a node ranked high if it points to many high-ranking authorities.

A basic `plot()` command from R's built-in "graphics" package will visualize most of the information in the researchnet network quite easily, with a minimum of coding. Using edges$connection will give a network with one-character labels (S, U, or N).

```
plot(researchnet, edge.label = edges$connection)
```

Using edges$clabel will give a more cluttered graph with full labels such as "successful pair".

```
plot(researchnet, edge.label = edges$clabel)
```

Output for these plots is not shown here. Instead below we create a more sophisticated plot using the power of tidygraph and ggplot commands.

Below we plot the "researchnet" network in terms of degree centrality. Degree refers to a node's number of edges. It can be seen that Marlene, with nine edges, is the most central researcher by this criterion. Note that edges may be of any type – successful (labeled "S"), unsuccessful ("U"), or never on a team ("N"). To view just one of these, or to drop one, it would be necessary to filter for connection type when the "edges" object was created earlier. We do this further below. In Figure 8.31, degree centrality is shown in two ways: By node size and by node color, but both reflect the same information about degree centrality. Edges are labeled by connection type ("S", "U", or "N"). Marlene, Marilyn, and Elena are the most central network members, each with a degree centrality of 9.

```
set.seed(123)
researchnet %>%
  tidygraph::activate(nodes) %>%
  tidygraph::mutate(Degree_Centrality =
tidygraph::centrality_degree()) %>%
  ggraph::ggraph(layout = "graphopt") +
  ggraph::geom_edge_link(width = 1.1, colour = "lightgray",
label_colour="black", aes(label = edges$connection)) +
  ggraph::geom_node_point(aes(size = Degree_Centrality, color =
Degree_Centrality)) +
  ggraph::geom_node_text(ggplot2::aes(label =
label,hjust=2,vjust=2), repel = TRUE) +
  ggplot2::scale_color_gradient(low = "red", high = "blue") +
  ggplot2::theme(legend.position = "bottom")
```

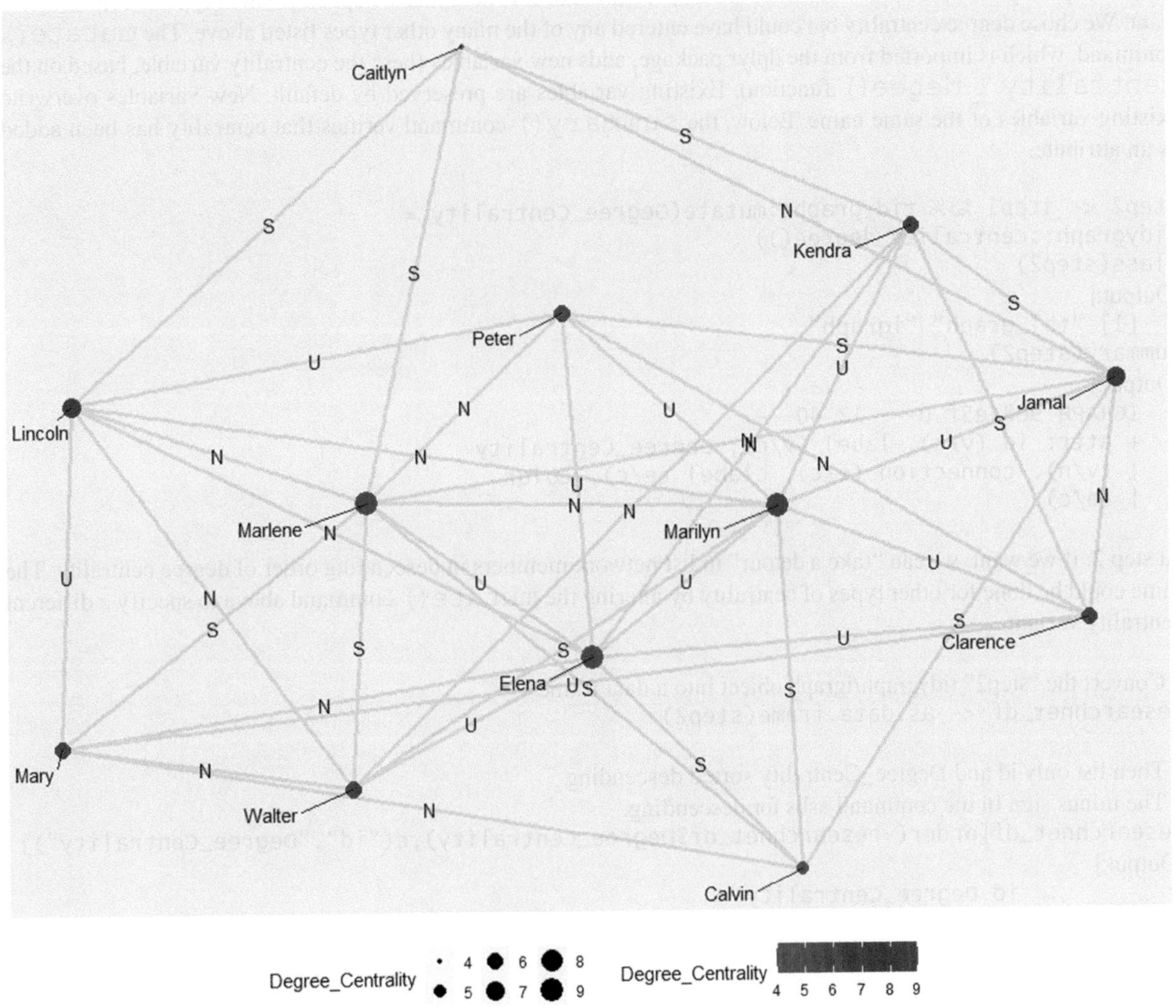

Figure 8.31 Researchnet in tidygraph with nodes proportional to degree centrality

We now explain the R code for making Figure 8.31. However, instead of stringing it all together with a series of "%>%" piping operators from the dplyr package, we create the same result in a series of steps. At each step we create an output object, such as stepl and step2.

Step 0:

Setting the random seed assures the same placement of nodes in the layout on each run. Also, keep in mind that a random seed was used when the edges object was created. Different random seeds lead to different network graphs.

```
set.seed(123)
```

Step 1:

Researchnet contains is a list-type object containing both nodes and edges. Step 1 activates the nodes table. However, as this is the default, this step is optional here.

```
step1 <- researchnet %>% tidygraph::activate(nodes)
class(step1)
      [1] "tbl_graph" "igraph"
```

Step 2:

The stepl object is passed to the `mutate()` command. It is here that we specify which type of centrality we want. We chose degree centrality but could have entered any of the many other types listed above. The `mutate()` command, which is imported from the dplyr package, adds new variables (here the centrality variable, based on the `centrality _ degee()` function). Existing variables are preserved by default. New variables overwrite existing variables of the same name. Below, the `summary()` command verifies that centrality has been added as an attribute.

```
step2 <- step1 %>% tidygraph::mutate(Degree_Centrality =
tidygraph::centrality_degree())
class(step2)
[Output:]
   [1] "tbl_graph" "igraph"
summary(step2)
[Output:]
   IGRAPH 9e84e5f U--- 12 40 --
   + attr: id (v/c), label (v/c), Degree_Centrality
   | (v/n), connection (e/c), clabel (e/c), color
   | (e/c)
```

At step 2, if we want, we can "take a detour" to list network members in descending order of degree centrality. The same could be done for other types of centrality by altering the `mutate()` command above to specify a different centrality variant.

```
# Convert the "step2" tidygraph/igraph object into a data frame
researchnet_df <- as.data.frame(step2)

# Then list only id and Degree_Centrality sorted descending
# The minus sign in the command asks for descending.
researchnet_df[order(-researchnet_df$Degree_Centrality),c("id","Degree_Centrality")]
[Output:]
           id Degree_Centrality
   1   Marlene                 9
   3     Elena                 9
   4   Marilyn                 9
   10  Lincoln                 7
   11    Jamal                 7
   2    Kendra                 6
```

```
5     Walter              6
7   Clarence              6
8      Peter              6
9       Mary              6
6     Calvin              5
12  Caitlyn               4
```

Step 3:

The step2 object is passed to the `ggraph()` command to produce the requested figure. Various ggraph and ggplot2 commands specify details about the plot. The layout may be any of those for igraph objects:

- `bipartite`: Minimize edge-crossings in a two-row (or column) layout for bipartite graphs.
- `star`: Place one node in the center and the rest equidistantly around it.
- `circle`: Place nodes in a circle in the order of their index. Consider using `layout_tbl_graph_linear()` with `circular=TRUE` for more control.
- `nicely`: Tries to pick an appropriate layout.
- `dh`: Uses Davidson and Harels simulated annealing algorithm to place nodes.
- `gem`: Place nodes on the plane using the GEM force-directed layout algorithm.
- `graphopt`: Uses the Graphopt algorithm based on alternating attraction and repulsion to place nodes.
- `grid`: Place nodes on a rectangular grid.
- `mds`: Perform a multidimensional scaling of nodes using either the shortest path or a user supplied distance.
- `sphere`: Place nodes uniformly on a sphere – less relevant for 2D visualizations of networks.
- `randomly`: Places nodes uniformly random.
- `fr`: Places nodes according to the force-directed algorithm of Fruchterman and Reingold.
- `kk`: Uses the spring-based algorithm by Kamada and Kawai to place nodes.
- `drl`: Uses the force directed algorithm from the DrL toolbox to place nodes.
- `lgl`: Uses the algorithm from Large Graph Layout to place nodes.

The `geom_edge_link()` command sets the width and color of the connecting lines (the edges) and also labels the edges by the "connection" column in the edges data frame. The `geom_node_point()` command sets node size and color to the value of the centrality coefficient for any given node. The `geom_node_text()` command sets the node labels to "label", which is the names of network members and which is an attribute of researchnet. The `scale_color_gradient()` command sets the node colors. The `theme()` command creates the legends, one for node size and one for node color, locating the legends at the bottom.

```
step2 %>%
  ggraph::ggraph(layout = "graphopt") +
  ggraph::geom_edge_link(width = 1.1, colour = "lightgray", label_colour="black",
aes(label = edges$connection)) +
  ggraph::geom_node_point(aes(size = Degree_Centrality, color = Degree_Centrality)) +
  ggraph::geom_node_text(ggplot2::aes(label = label,hjust=2,vjust=2), repel = TRUE) +
  ggplot2::scale_color_gradient(low = "red", high = "blue") +
  ggplot2::theme(legend.position = "bottom")
```

The steps above create a network plot identical to Figure 8.31.

It is possible to create a network graph depicting just one connection type, such as "S" successful pairings (edges) for researchnet. Graphing just one connection condition is simply a matter of filtering the edges object. The code below filters out the "S" (paired on a successful project) connection, so just the successful teams are shown in the network plot.

```
# Create "edges2" with just the successful pairs.
edges2<- edges[edges$connection=="S",]
```

```
# Create the "researchnet2" network with the same nodes but with the edges2 object.
researchnet2 <- tidygraph::tbl_graph(nodes, edges2, directed = FALSE)

# Plot identically as before, except using the researchnet2 network
# Also remember to switch edges to edges2.
set.seed(123)
researchnet2 %>%
  tidygraph::activate(nodes) %>%
  tidygraph::mutate(Degree_Centrality = tidygraph::centrality_degree()) %>%
  ggraph::ggraph(layout = "graphopt") +
  ggraph::geom_edge_link(width = 1.1, colour = "lightgray", label_colour="black",
aes(label = edges2$connection)) +
  ggraph::geom_node_point(aes(size = Degree_Centrality, color = Degree_Centrality)) +
  ggraph::geom_node_text(ggplot2::aes(label = label,hjust=2,vjust=2), repel = TRUE) +
  ggplot2::scale_color_gradient(low = "red", high = "blue") +
  ggplot2::theme(legend.position = "bottom")
```

The resulting network plot is not displayed here for space reasons, but shows Marlene and Calfin are the most central, each with a degree centrality of 4. Marlene, for instance, has connections to Mary, Walter, Caitlyn, and Calvin.

8.15.3 Network conversions with tidygraph

The tidygraph package also supports the `tbl _ graph()` function, which can convert other types of network objects into tidygraph format.

A partial list of source formats for conversions is shown in the listing below.

- From data.frame, list and matrix data [R base]
- From digraph network objects [igraph package]
- From network objects [network package]
- From dendrogram and hclust [stats package]
- From Node [data.tree package]

The conversion commands start with "as". Type `help(tbl _ graph)` for the full list.

```
# Example of converting a matrix to an object used by tidygraph and igraph:
# Bring in the "flo" matrix from the earlier example on the Medici family network
library(network)
data(flo)
class(flo)
      [1] "matrix"
# Convert
flonet <- tidygraph::as_tbl_graph(flo,directed=FALSE)
class(flonet)
      [1] "tbl_graph" "igraph"

# Example of converting a network object from the network package to an igraph object
# Bring in the "DHHS" network object from the earlier example on the interagency networks
library(UserNetR)
data(DHHS)
class(DHHS)
      [1] "network"
# Convert
DHHSnet <- tidygraph::as_tbl_graph(DHHS)
class(DHHSnet)
      [1] "tbl_graph" "igraph"
```

8.15.4 Finding community clusters with tidygraph

In Section 8.15.4, we illustrate the community mapping/grouping function of tidygraph. Our input data are eight variables on 15 American cities, contained in the file "citycrime.csv". In addition to tidygraph we also use the corrr package, discussed in the previous section, to produce the correlation matrix to be analyzed. The dplyr package is also used for its support of the "%>%" piping operator, by which attributes of an object are passed to the next operation in sequence.

Setup and data

```
setwd("C:/Data")
library(corrr)
library(dplyr)

citycrime_df <- read.table("citycrime.csv", header=TRUE,sep=",", stringsAsFactors =
TRUE)
class(citycrime_df)
      1] "data.frame"
names(citycrime_df)
  [1] "CITY"     "POP"        "MURDER"    "RAPE"     "ROBBERY"
  [6] "ASSAULT"  "BURGLARY" "LARCENY"   "MVTHEFT"
```

As the citycrime_df data frame has only numbered row names, we CITY as row names. This is important because later we will transpose the data, turning the row names into variable (column) names. That is, we will be correlating cities based on the set of variables listed above, in contrast to the usual correlation of variables based on a set of cities. The underlying research objective is to find the degree to which pairs of cities are peers in terms of the crime variables.

Add row names

```
row.names(citycrime_df) <- citycrime_df$CITY
```

Transpose
Leave off column 1, which is CITY, which is non-numeric and inappropriate for correlation.

```
citycrime_trans <- t(citycrime_df[,-1])
```

We next compute the correlation matrix. The default is Pearsonian correlation, with missing values dropped using `pairwise.complete.obs`. However, the example data had no missing values. The "-1" drops the first row, which is non-numeric CITY names.

```
citycrime_mat <- corrr::correlate(citycrime_trans[-1,])
citycrime_mat
```

[Output:]

```
      rowname SaintLouis Atlanta Baltimore Detroit  Miami
      <chr>        <dbl>   <dbl>     <dbl>   <dbl>  <dbl>
    1 SaintL~     NA       0.989     0.975   0.774  0.981
    2 Atlanta      0.989  NA         0.992   0.706  0.997
    3 Baltim~      0.975   0.992    NA       0.726  0.997
    4 Detroit      0.774   0.706     0.726  NA      0.719
    5 Miami        0.981   0.997     0.997   0.719 NA
    6 SaintP~      0.976   0.995     0.993   0.685  0.997
    7 Tampa        0.974   0.992     0.989   0.704  0.996
    8 Nashvi~      0.967   0.990     0.983   0.622  0.987
    9 Memphis      0.961   0.985     0.976   0.670  0.988
   10 Kansas~      0.985   0.997     0.985   0.678  0.993
   11 Philad~      0.983   0.990     0.986   0.721  0.985
   12 Stockt~      0.999   0.988     0.980   0.785  0.983
   13 Buffalo      0.974   0.996     0.988   0.679  0.996
   14 Washin~      0.973   0.941     0.941   0.879  0.938
   15 Raleigh      0.961   0.986     0.967   0.591  0.979
```

```
#   with 10 more variables: SaintPetersburg<dbl>, Tampa <dbl>,
#   Nashville <dbl>, Memphis <dbl>, KansasCityMo <dbl>,
#   Philadelphia <dbl>, Stockton <dbl>, Buffalo <dbl>,
#   WashingtonDC <dbl>, Raleigh <dbl>
```

At this point it is necessary to convert the data to "long format". This involves getting rid of the redundant upper triangle of correlations the `shave()` command from the corrr package, then using its `stretch()` command to convert to long format. We are left with a tibble data frame with three columns: x, y, and r. The x and y columns contain a pair of city names and r is their correlation.

```
# Create citycrime_cor as a long format correlation matrix
# The na.rm parameter removes NAs, such as those found on the diagonal,
citycrime_cor <- citycrime_mat %>% corrr::shave(upper = TRUE) %>% corrr::stretch(na.
rm = TRUE)

class(citycrime_cor)
    [1] "tbl_df"     "tbl"        "data.frame"
head(citycrime_cor,6)
  # A tibble: 6 x 3
    x          y                   r
    <chr>      <chr>           <dbl>
  1 SaintLouis Atlanta         0.989
  2 SaintLouis Baltimore       0.975
  3 SaintLouis Detroit         0.774
  4 SaintLouis Miami           0.981
  5 SaintLouis SaintPetersburg 0.976
  6 SaintLouis Tampa           0.974
```

Before proceeding, we filter the long form correlation matrix so that lesser correlations are removed. Specifically, retain correlations where r is greater than .799. Warning!: Since correlations are edges, if we filter aggressively so some cities have no correlations above the threshold then that city node will have no edges and will be dropped from the network. This in turn means the vector of city labels would need to change. This is not a problem with the current example but with other data it might require adjusting the labeling of points (cities) further below.

```
citycrime_cor <-  citycrime_cor  %>%  dplyr::filter(r > .799)
head(citycrime_cor, 6)
  # A tibble: 6 x 3
    x          y                   r
    <chr>      <chr>           <dbl>
  1 SaintLouis Atlanta         0.989
  2 SaintLouis Baltimore       0.975
  3 SaintLouis Miami           0.981
  4 SaintLouis SaintPetersburg 0.976
  5 SaintLouis Tampa           0.974
  6 SaintLouis Nashville       0.967

class(citycrime_cor)
    [1] "tbl_df"     "tbl"        "data.frame"
```

We are now at the point of creating the citycrime network. The citycrime_net object created below is a tidygraph tbl_graph object with 15 nodes and 92 edges. To see these counts, simply type `citycrime _ net`. The nodes are the cities and the edges are correlations between city pairs after filtering out those with r < .80.

```
set.seed(123)
citycrime_net <- tidygraph::as_tbl_graph(citycrime_cor, directed = FALSE)
class(citycrime_net)
    [1] "tbl_graph" "igraph"
```

Below is the R code to create a tidygraph plot of the city crime data. The “x2” variable below provides labels for the points (cities). For space reasons this particular lot is not displayed here but shows Detroit as an outlier in the citycrime network. It is similar to Figure 8.32 further below but without identification of communities of cities.

```
x2 <- citycrime_df$CITY
ggraph(citycrime_net) +
  ggraph::geom_edge_link() +
  ggraph::geom_node_point() +
  ggraph::geom_node_text(ggplot2::aes(label = x2), size = 3, repel = TRUE) +
  ggraph::theme_graph()
```

We now arrive at the primary purpose of this section, which is to plot the city crime network with cities color-coded by the “community” to which they belong. A community of cities is simply a cluster or grouping of cities based on some algorithm. The tidygraph package has many clustering routines to identify communities. Here we use the “group_spinglass” grouping algorithm. This creates the “community” variable, which is used for the number and colors of communities. Other grouping options will give differing solutions: To see options, type `help(group _ infomap)`. Below, we also use the “mds” layout, based on multidimensional scaling as discussed in Chapter 2. Alternative ggraph layouts were listed in Section 8.15.2. The result is shown in Figure 8.32.

```
# Community plot of citycrime
# The label2 variable is a vector of city names for labeling purposes.
set.seed(123)
label2<- citycrime_df$CITY
citycrime_net %>%
  tidygraph::activate(nodes) %>%
  dplyr::mutate(community = as.factor(tidygraph::group_spinglass(weights = NULL))) %>%
  ggraph(layout = "mds") +
  ggraph::geom_edge_link(width = 1, colour = "lightgray") +
  ggraph::geom_node_point(aes(colour = community), size = 5) +
  ggraph::geom_node_text(ggplot2::aes(label = label2), repel = TRUE) +
  ggraph::theme_graph()
```

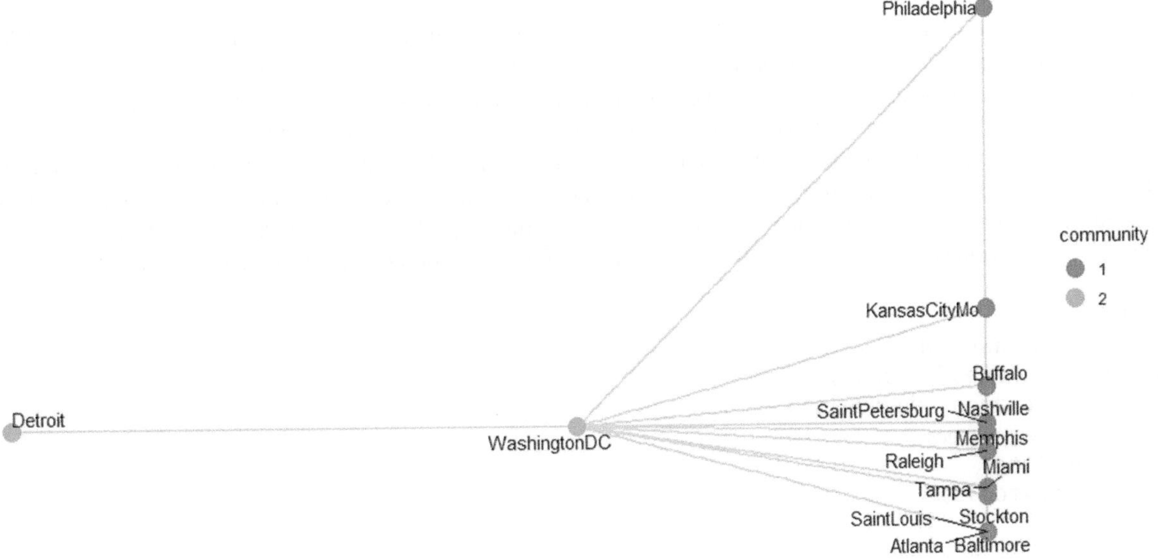

Figure 8.32 Tidygraph plot of city crime by community in mds layout

Figure 8.32 shows the tidygraph plot of the citycrime data. The layout is shown as constructed based on multidimensional scaling. The grouping function in tidygraph (here, `group _ spinglass()`) has identified two "communities" of cities. All cities are in community 1 except Detroit and Washington, DC, which are in community 2. Grouping these two cities together in the same community confirms their reputations as high-crime urban areas. While this seems plausible, other data inputs and other tidygraph grouping functions might reveal a different community structures.

8.16 Simulating networks

This chapter has focused on a few or the very large number of ways in R to visualize relationships connecting one actor to another. However, it is also possible to simulate the interaction of actors with a view toward understanding how their interrelationships evolve over time or in order to see the implications changes in various input levels on changes in network patterns and evolution. This brings a longitudinal perspective for network analysis. Such simulation falls in the category of "agent-based modeling" (ABM), which is a very large field of study in its own right, not necessarily explicitly linked to network analysis. Below we present only two ABM packages: SchellingR and RSiena.

8.16.1 Agent-based network modeling with SchellingR

The SchellingR package provides a simple illustration of ABM. Its purpose is to replicate the famous game-theoretic study by economist and sociologist Thomas C. Schelling demonstrating how neighborhood segregation evolves. Sometimes called the "tipping-point game", the simulation involves agents (actors) on a grid, which representing an urban area. The grid may be thought of as a type of network. The primary input is a hypothesized tipping point coefficient. Specifically, the coefficient is the minimum percentage of neighboring actors of the same race or group required by actors to be happy and not move. For instance, if the tipping threshold is 0.40, then as long as at least 40% of the actor's adjacent neighbors are of the same group, then the actor is "happy" and will not move.

Actors are placed on the grid at random then in an iterative process they move if unhappy. If they are "unhappy" then they move randomly to an open space. What Schelling demonstrated was that even when actors are posited to be relatively tolerant, striking neighborhood segregation is likely to occur over time (Schelling, 1971, 1978). In Schelling's terminology, micromotives at the individual level do not translate as one might expect into macrobehavior at the collective level.

The SchellingR package was authored by David Zimmerman to illustrate the actor-based modeling (ABM) simulation developed by Schelling in the 1970s.[11] The focus of the ABM is on urban migration and segregation. It visualizes the development of neighborhood network patterns and reports statistics for each iteration.

The setup step is more involved than the usual installation of a package located in the CRAN archives. Instead, installation is from a GitHub folder established by the package author. There are three steps to the setup: Install the "rlang" package, install the "devtools" package, then install the "SchellingR" package, in that sequence (assuming these are not already installed on the user's computer). The "rlang" package contains necessary utility functions. The "devtools" package contains more utilities, notably one for installation of a package from GitHub.

```
# Setup
# If not already installed:
install.packages("rlang")
install.packages("devtools")
# Invoke these packages
library(rlang)
library(devtools)

# Then install the SchellingR package
# Supporting packages are listed and you are encouraged to update all by typing "1"
devtools::install_github("DavZim/SchellingR")
```

[Output:]

```
Downloading GitHub repo DavZim/SchellingR@master
These packages have more recent versions available.
It is recommended to update all of them.
Which would you like to update?

 1: All
 2: CRAN packages only
 3: None
 4: dplyr      (0.8.5 -> 1.0.0) [CRAN]
 5: ggplot2    (3.3.0 -> 3.3.2) [CRAN]
 6: rlang      (0.4.5 -> 0.4.6) [CRAN]
 7: glue       (1.4.0 -> 1.4.1) [CRAN]
 8: ellipsis   (0.3.0 -> 0.3.1) [CRAN]
 9: pillar     (1.4.3 -> 1.4.4) [CRAN]
10: vctrs      (0.2.4 -> 0.3.1) [CRAN]
11: pkgload    (1.0.2 -> 1.1.0) [CRAN]
12: withr      (2.1.2 -> 2.2.0) [CRAN]
13: pkgbuild   (1.0.6 -> 1.0.8) [CRAN]
14: backports  (1.1.6 -> 1.1.8) [CRAN]
15: ps         (1.3.2 -> 1.3.3) [CRAN]
16: tidyselect (1.0.0 -> 1.1.0) [CRAN]
17: isoband    (0.2.0 -> 0.2.2) [CRAN]
18: scales     (1.1.0 -> 1.1.1) [CRAN]

Enter one or more numbers, or an empty line to skip updates:
1
```

```
# In this exercise we also use the following supporting utility package:
# The dplyr package supports piping, counting, creating tibbles, and more.
library(dplyr)

# For full functionality, these additional packages should be invoked.
# The user may need use install.packages() to install one or more first.
# When installing magick, when prompted ask to install from source to get the latest version.
# Note: At this time, emojifont is incompatible with RStudio. See online help for work-arounds.
library(colorspace)      # Used by gganimate
library(emojifont)       # Supports emojis for happy and not happy
library(gganimate)       # Supports animation and gif graphics
library(magick)          # Utility for combining gif images

# Invoke the Schelling actor-based model package
library(SchellingR)
```

After setup we turn to run the Schelling actor-based model. The simplest run of the model, accepting all defaults, is:

```
set.seed(123)
defaultmodel <- SchellingR::run_schelling()
```

This does not return any graphics but will return two data frames, "round" and "detailed", with output illustrated below. As random processes are involved, the exact values will differ each run unless the same random seed is used. The "round" data frame contains statistics aggregated by round (simulation iterations, which are simulated time periods) and includes the number of happy or unhappy agents and the number of moves. The "detailed" data frame contains data on the grid, the agents, and their neighbors. Below, note that the simulation runs until there are 0 unhappy agents or the maximum number of rounds is reached. For this default simulation and random seed, it took eight rounds past the starting state to reach a point where no agents were unhappy.

```
defaultmodel
[Output:]
   $round
   # A tibble: 9 x 4
     round happy_agents unhappy_agents number_moves
     <int>        <int>          <int>        <int>
   1     0           43             37            0
   2     1           62             18           37
   3     2           65             15           18
   4     3           70             10           15
   5     4           72              8           10
   6     5           77              3            8
   7     6           77              3            3
   8     7           79              1            3
   9     8           80              0            1

   $detailed
   # A tibble: 900 x 8
      round     x     y    id group n_same n_different happy
      <int> <int> <int> <int> <int>  <int>       <int> <int>
    1     0     1    10     0     2      1           1     1
    2     0     2    10     1     1      1           3     0
    3     0     3    10     2     2      1           2     0
    4     0     4    10     3     2      1           2     0
    5     0     5    10     0     0      0           0     0
    6     0     6    10     4     2      1           1     1
    7     0     7    10     5     2      2           0     1
    8     0     8    10     6     2      1           2     0
    9     0     9    10     7     1      1           2     0
   10     0    10    10     0     0      0           0     0
   # ... with 890 more rows
```

To go beyond the default model, SchellingR provides a number of model settings under user control. In addition, the random seed affects the simulation but is set separately in the usual way. The researcher may vary the settings listed below.

- number_of_groups: The number of racial, ethnic, or cultural groups to simulate. Default = 2.
- size: The number of cells on any side of the square grid. Default = 10.
- percent_empty: The percent of grid cells which are empty. Default = .2.
- threshold: The threshold above which agents are classed as happy. Default = .50.
- max_rounds: The maximum number of iterations the simulation is to run. Default = 100

Running the Schelling actor-based model with researcher-set parameters is simply a matter of plugging these values into the command. For the settings below, it requires 24 time periods (iterations) for all actors to be "happy" because at least 40% or more of their adjacent neighbors are of the same group. Since rounds are counted from round 0, the final round is round 23.

```
set.seed(123)
schell_40pct <- SchellingR::run_schelling(size = 50, percent_empty = 0.2, threshold =
0.40, number_of_groups = 3, max_rounds = 1000)

class(schell_40pct)
     [1] "list"
```

```
str(schell_40pct)
```
[Output:]
```
List of 2
 $ round   : tibble [24 x 4] (S3: tbl_df/tbl/data.frame)
  ..$ round          : int [1:24] 0 1 2 3 4 5 6 7 8 9 ...
  ..$ happy_agents   : int [1:24] 786 1035 1271 1457 1585 1685 1773 1838 1878
1916 ...
  ..$ unhappy_agents: int [1:24] 1214 965 729 543 415 315 227 162 122 84 ...
  ..$ number_moves   : int [1:24] 0 1214 965 729 543 415 315 227 162 122 ...
 $ detailed: tibble [60,000 x 8] (S3: tbl_df/tbl/data.frame)
  ..$ round       : int [1:60000] 0 0 0 0 0 0 0 0 0 0 ...
  ..$ x           : int [1:60000] 1 2 3 4 5 6 7 8 9 10 ...
  ..$ y           : int [1:60000] 50 50 50 50 50 50 50 50 50 50 ...
  ..$ id          : int [1:60000] 0 0 0 1 2 3 4 5 0 6 ...
  ..$ group       : int [1:60000] 2 0 0 2 3 2 2 2 0 3 ...
  ..$ n_same      : int [1:60000] 0 0 0 1 0 4 4 3 0 2 ...
  ..$ n_different: int [1:60000] 1 0 0 3 5 1 0 0 0 2 ...
  ..$ happy       : int [1:60000] 0 0 0 0 0 1 1 1 0 1 ...
```

```
schell_40pct
```
[Output:]
```
$round
# A tibble: 24 x 4
   round happy_agents unhappy_agents number_moves
   <int>        <int>          <int>        <int>
 1     0          786           1214            0
 2     1         1035            965         1214
 3     2         1271            729          965
 4     3         1457            543          729
 5     4         1585            415          543
 6     5         1685            315          415
 7     6         1773            227          315
 8     7         1838            162          227
 9     8         1878            122          162
10     9         1916             84          122
# ... with 14 more rows

$detailed
# A tibble: 60,000 x 8
   round     x     y    id group n_same n_different happy
   <int> <int> <int> <int> <int>  <int>       <int> <int>
 1     0     1    50     0     2      0           1     0
 2     0     2    50     0     0      0           0     0
 3     0     3    50     0     0      0           0     0
 4     0     4    50     1     2      1           3     0
 5     0     5    50     2     3      0           5     0
 6     0     6    50     3     2      4           1     1
 7     0     7    50     4     2      4           0     1
 8     0     8    50     5     2      3           0     1
 9     0     9    50     0     0      0           0     0
10     0    10    50     6     3      2           2     1
# ... with 59,990 more rows
```

After running the model we may visualize its results by plotting mean happiness per round. Behind the scenes, this calls on the "dplyr" and "ggplot2" packages. In the command below, if animate = TRUE, then the "gganimate" package must be installed. Also, if animate = TRUE, the "step" setting determines how many rounds the animation steps. Thus, step = 1 means each round is animated if animate = TRUE. This plot is shown in Figure 8.33, which shows that all segregation occurs quite rapidly before plateauing at a high level by about round 13, though all agents are not "happy" until round 24.

```
SchellingR::plot_development(schell_40pct, title=TRUE, animate=FALSE, step=1)
```

We can also use the detailed information to plot the grid at the first and last iteration.

```
SchellingR::plot_grid(schell_40pct, select_round = 1, title = TRUE)
SchellingR::plot_grid(schell_40pct, select_round = 23, title = TRUE)
```

Figure 8.34 shows that starting from a random distribution of actors from three groups at Round 0 one winds up with relative segregation at Round 23, even assuming relatively tolerant actor preferences, which require only that 40% of adjacent neighbors be of the same group. The researcher, of course, may play with alternative threshold levels to see the effect on segregation patterns and time to segregated status.

Watching the animated version across all 24 rounds (round 0 through round 23) is more informative but cannot be shown here on the printed page. The command, however, is:

```
SchellingR::plot_grid(schell_40pct, animate=TRUE, title = TRUE)
```

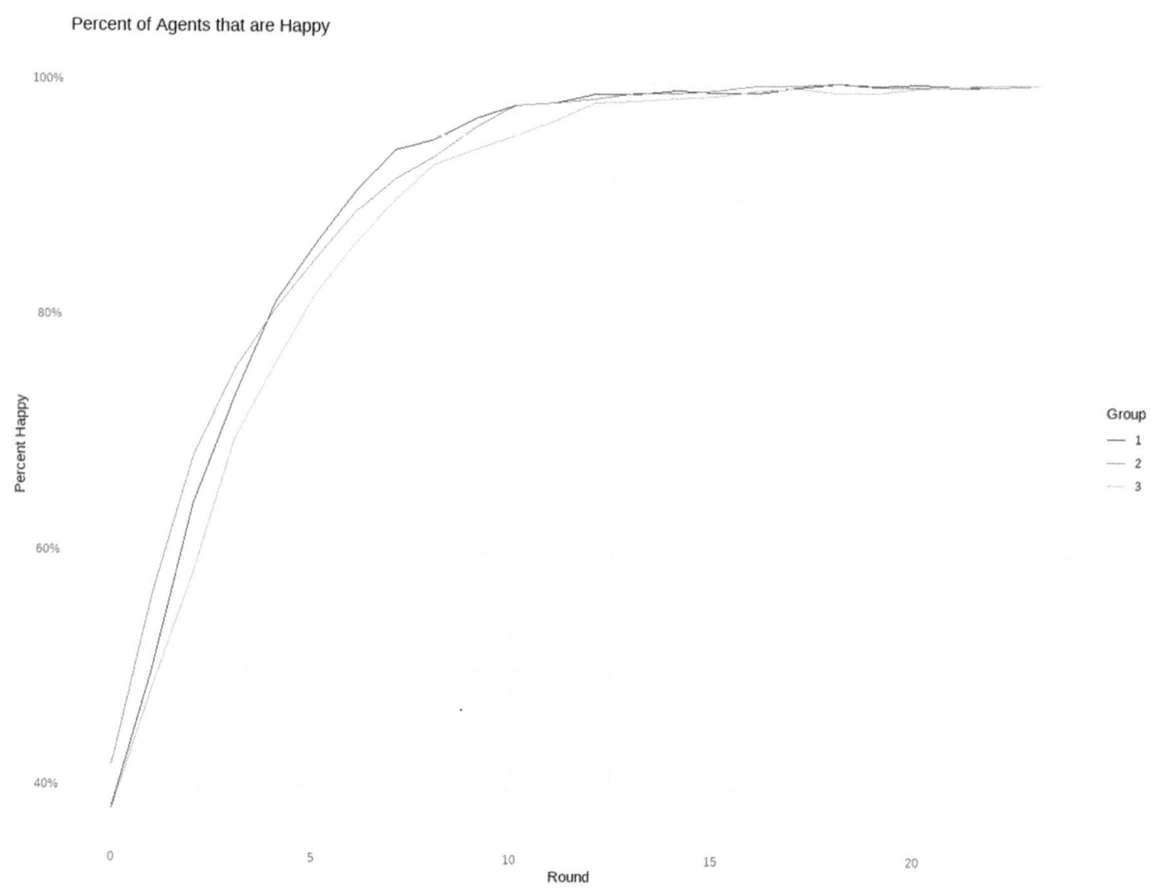

Figure 8.33 Development plot for the Schelling segregation model

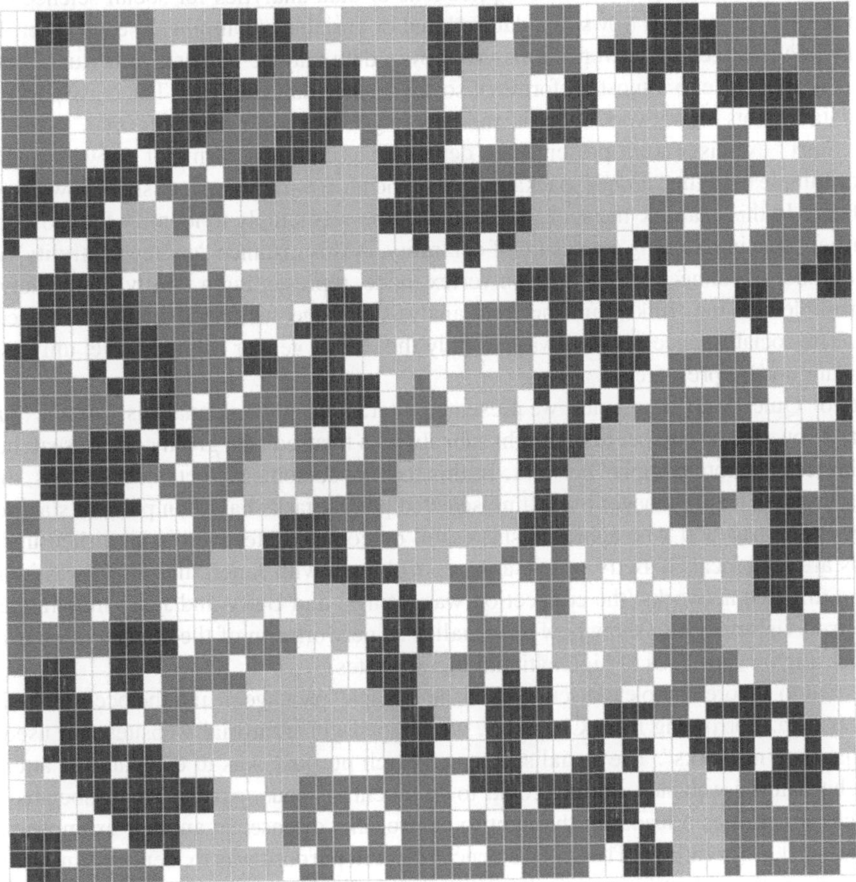

Figure 8.34 Schelling segregation model, 3 groups, threshold = 0.40, round 23

8.16.2 Agent-based network modeling with RSiena

Whereas SchellingR is a special-purpose ABM package, RSiena is a scripting language for actor-based networks. As such RSiena provides vastly more flexibility and control for the researcher but by the same token the learning curve is much higher. The development of RSiena is primarily associated with Tom A. B. Snijders (2001, 2011) and his colleagues (e.g., Snijders & Pickup, 2017) but has become a specialty in its own right with its own Siena web page at https://www.stats.ox.ac.uk/~snijders/siena/siena.html. The scripts page linked from there contains dozens of RSiena scripts and sample datasets, many tied to peer-reviewed articles. The manual is Ripley et al. (2021).

RSiena is presented in an online supplement titled "Agent-based network modeling with Rsiena". This supplement and its tutorial was written by Prof. Kate Albrecht (University of Illinois, Chicago) and is found in the "Readings and References" section of the student Support Material (www.routledge.com/9780367624293) for this book.

8.16.3 Agent-based network modeling with NetLogoR

NetLogo is a popular ABM package, albeit not one targeted specifically at network simulation. Coverage of NetLogo-type simulations is available online in the Support Material (www.routledge.com/9780367624293) for this book, in its student resources section, under the title "Agent-Based Network Modeling with NetLogoR". This supplement uses the "netlogoR" package to emulate the widely-used NetLogo program.

8.17 Summary

Network analysis is one of the most common applications of data analytics for social science data. A network is the relationship of units of analysis (rows in a dataset) and/or variables (columns) to each other. If data can fit in a matrix, they may be visualized in network terms. Moreover, data may be numeric or textual. At this general level, network analysis is applicable to almost all forms of social science data analysis. The early part of this chapter sets forth common data formats for network analysis and how to get data into network format.

Two "Quick Start" exercises were presented to demonstrate common forms of network analysis. The Medici family network example used the "igraph" package, one of the most widely used, to show how an adjacency network could be visualized. In this example the social science purpose was simply to identify the most central players in a network of families, thus introducing a measure of centrality, in this instance "degree centrality" where degree was defined by the number of connections for a given vertex (node, representing a family) in the network. The Marvel hero network example used the "linkcomm" network analysis package, which partitions and adjacency network into "communities". The social science purpose was to study the role of gender in the Marvel universe and the finding was that women are underrepresented.

After these two "Quick Start" examples, we presented interactive network analysis with the "visNetwork" package. Interactivity allows the researcher to highlight subnetworks focused on a given node (researcher in the example) within a much larger and more complex network. In this form of sociometric network analysis, the research objective was to aid a research team manager in staffing selected project tasks based on pairs of staff members who had teamed together in the past and who achieved successful outcomes. Later we distinguished undirected networks (all relationships are reciprocal: If Betty was in a successful team with Janet, then Janet was in a successful team with Betty) from directed networks (the connection was ratings, and Betty and Janet may rate each other differently). We also used visNetwork to show how to visualize as networks on of the decision tree examples discussed in Chapter 4, focusing on correlates of high national literacy rates.

Next we returned to a more complete discussion of the "igraph" package, using the occasion to illustrate network analysis with text data. Borrowing from Chapter 9, we scraped gubernatorial websites and used that text data to create "term adjacency networks". The social science research purpose was to evaluate the attention to the covid pandemic on gubernatorial websites, finding covid to be a central focus, particularly associated with the state of California, which was seen as a leader in the fight to control this disease. In another example, we used igraph to analyze Senate interest group ratings. The social science research purpose was to identify similarities between senators. We then used igraph to identify empirically "communities" of senators which defined the group structure of the U.S. Senate in terms of interest group ratings. Part of this presentation was explanation of the use of "modularity scores" to evaluate clustering of the network into communities. We also called attention to the "intergraph" package as a tool for converting network data from one package's format to another.

Turning to spatio-network analysis, we used the "diagrams" and "map" packages to overlay a network on a geographic map. Specifically we used World Bank data on nation-to-nation immigration flows to demonstrate a social science point: Contrary to American popular opinion, world migration is not US-centric.

Next we introduced another leading approach to network analysis, based on the "statnet" suite of tools, which include the "statnet", "network", and "sna" packages. Of particular focus was the use of these tools in clustering network nodes into "neighborhoods" and "cliques". A clique analysis was conducted on an interagency network of tobacco control officials associated with the DHHS. This enabled development of "clique comembership" tables and visualization of the "clique profile" for the DHHS network. This opened the door for comparative analysis of the clique profile of the DHHS network with a second interagency network. We also used the "statnet" and "intergraph" packages to map international trade flow.

To demonstrate that any correlation matrix may be visualized as a network of variables, we used the "Corrr" package. Correlation, of course, is limited by being bivariate rather than multivariate analysis. For this reason it is best used on an exploratory basis in the process of specifying a model for later multivariate analysis. However, on an exploratory basis the network visualization suggested that for the given data, state crime rates are best explained by per capita expenditure on police, median weekly wage, and state population size, in that order.

Network analysis with the "tidygraph" package was next in the order of presentation. Tidygraph is the network component of the "tidyverse" family of tools. These tools often center on text data and are treated further in Chapter 9. The tidygraph package afforded another was of identifying community clusters within a network. Again using data on city crime variables, the 15 cities studied could be clustered into two communities. All cities were in community 1 except Detroit and Washington, DC, which were in community 2, confirming the reputation of these two cities as high-crime urban areas.

In a final section, simulation of networks was treated. Network simulations are forms of ABM, in which a network consists of actors (nodes) and their relationships with others (edges), but with algorithmic rules which govern evolution across time, leading to different network configurations and visualizations in each time period. The "RSchelling" package was used to demonstrate the classic "tipping game" simulation of urban segregation. This game demonstrates that while individual actors may be relatively tolerant of having neighbors not in their group, over time the society-wide tendency is for the network of neighbors to evolve toward segregation. Also discussed was the package "RSiena", which is a complex R-based scripting language for creating simulations of actor-based networks based on stochastic algorithms (hence SAOM, stochastic actor-oriented modeling). The example, taken from the RSiena manual and the work of RSiena developer Tom Snijders and presented in the Support Material (www.routledge.com/9780367624293) to this book, focused on the evolution of friendship networks given tobacco and alcohol use as covariates. Finally, ABM simulations of the NetLogo type were discussed and illustrated in a supplement to this chapter, using the "NetLogoR" package.

8.18 Command summary

For convenience for those wishing to try models out for themselves, this book's Support Material (www.routledge.com/9780367624293) contains a listing of the main commands used in this chapter 8. This listing may be handy for readers following along with the book using their home or office computers. For topics presented as an online supplement ("K-core analysis of the DHHS interagency collaboration network", "Mapping international trade flow with statnet and Intergraph", "Network simulation with RSiena", and "Agent-based network modeling with NetLogoR"), the command summary is at the end of the supplement.

Endnotes

1. Spencer, R. (2010). http://scaledinnovation.com/analytics/communities/comlinks.html
2. As a plotting note, the `ewidth=` option sets edge line widths when `plot()` is used with a linkcomm object. If ewidth is set high so lines overlap, then the effect is to create colored background areas for each community, as would be the case with the command below. Or one may simply have somewhat thicker lines by setting `ewidth=2`. Plot output is not shown here but the reader is encouraged to try the command below locally if following along in RStudio. This strategy works for Spencer circle layouts also, but not as well due to communities being spread out along the circumference of a circle. Warning: Reset ewidth at the end by running a plot with ewidth=1.

   ```
   plot(hero_lo, type="graph", layout= layout.fruchterman.reingold, shownodesin = 2, node.
   pies=TRUE, ewidth=20)
   ```
3. Data source: https://electoral-vote.com/evp2009/Senate/senator_ratings-2005.html
4. For a correlation matrix:
   # Use correlations between variables "as distance"

   ```
   dd <- as.dist((1 - cor(senate_t_imputed))/2)
   round(1000 * dd) # (prints more nicely)
   plot(hclust(dd)) # to see a dendrogram of clustered variables
   ```
5. Other packages may have conflicts with the intergraph package. If the `asIgraph()` or other intergraph functions throw error messages, close R, load intergraph, and try again with a cleaner environment.
6. Warning: These data have been taken "as is" and are intended only for instructional use, not substantive research on immigration.
7. See https://www.rdocumentation.org/packages/maps/versions/3.3.0/topics/world.cities
8. The shell-exec command for PCs may, for Macs, be replaced by `system2("open",g)`.
9. The `degree()` function in the sna package computes degree centrality by a more complex algorithm but the node rankings are very close. This function returns the theoretical maximum absolute deviation (from maximum) conditional on size, which is used by sna centralization to normalize the observed centralization score.
10. The "keyplayers" package gets the top k players in an adjacency matrix like the DHHS_sm_formal network, using these parameters:

- size: Number of top players to identify.
- type: The type of centrality to use: "degree", "betweenness", "closeness", "ecent" (eigenvector centrality), "mreach. degree", "mreach.closeness", "fragment", or "diffusion".
- cmode: Needed if type is "degree" or an "mreach" type. For degree centrality, the options are "outdegree", "indegree", and "total". For undirected networks, use "total", which is the default.
- method: Indicates which grouping criterion should be used.
  - "add" indicates the "addition" criterion and is suggested for degree and eigenvector centralities as an alternative for "max".
  - "max" indicates the "maximum" criterion and is suggested for degree and eigenvector centralities.
  - "min" indicates the "minimum" criterion and is suggested for betweenness, closeness, fragmentation, and M-reach centralities. This is the default.
  - "union" indicates the "union" criterion and is suggested for diffusion centrality.
- Binary: If TRUE, the input matrix is binarized. If FALSE, the edge values are considered. The default is FALSE. In this example we accept the default to give more weight to level 4 (multiple formal collaborations) than level 3 (one formal collaboration).
- Other parameter settings exist but are not used in this example. See `help(kpset)`.

```
library(keyplayer)

# Calculate key players by their matrix column index numbers
# based on degree closeness defined additively
keyindex <- keyplayer::kpset(DHHS_sm_formal, size = 3, type = "degree", cmode =
"total", method = "add", binary=FALSE)

keyindex$keyplayers
[Output:]
      [1] 12 18 51

colnames(DHHS_sm_formal[,keyindex$keyplayers])

[Output:]
      [1] "CDC-6"  "CDC-12" "OS-5"
```

11. See https://github.com/DavZim/SchellingR#readme

Chapter 9

Text analytics

PART I: OVERVIEW OF TEXT ANALYTICS WITH R

9.1 Overview

"Text analysis" refers to qualitative or quantitative approaches to finding meaning in text documents. Qualitative analysis of text may be undertaken manually or manual methods may be enhanced by software such as Atlas.ti and NVivo, which make creating, editing, organizing, relating, and tallying text codes much easier. These non-R qualitative approaches are beyond the scope of this book. Moreover, at this writing, R itself has over one hundred packages for text analysis and natural language processing, far more than we can explore in a single chapter (for a listing, see https://cran.r-project.org/web/views/NaturalLanguageProcessing.html). Likewise, each package has many programs and functions, also too numerous for one chapter. Rather, our objective in this chapter is to provide the basis for a minimum level of text analytic literacy sufficient to do many common and useful forms of text mining and analysis.

Common text analysis tasks explained in this chapter include management and cleaning of text data, creating keyword-in-context dictionaries, creating bar charts of word frequencies, scraping web pages for text, scraping social media for text, creating multigroup word frequency charts, creating word clouds, creating word comparison clouds, creating word maps, doing sentiment analysis, conducting topic modeling, creating lexical dispersion plots, and analyzing bigrams and ngrams.

"Text analytics" refers specifically to quantitative approaches to text corpora and is what is treated in this chapter. Its many methods fall into three general categories: (1) text retrieval in digital format, (2) text preparation to get text data into a format needed for text analytics, and (3) applying text analytic procedures to the text data. There are a great many options at each step. Options are not standardized across text analytic procedures and only common combinations of retrieval-preparation-analysis steps can be presented in this relatively brief chapter.

Likewise, there are many software programs for text analytics outside the R world. Python is particularly noted for its procedures supporting one or another aspect of text analytics. There is a large and growing text and reference literature on text analytics in R. Books include Munzert et al. (2014); Silge and Robinson (2017); Aydin (2018); and Jockers and Thalkin (2020, Second Ed).

9.2 Data used in this chapter

The following data files are used in this chapter:

- CA_c.txt, FL_c.txt, LA_c.txt, MU_c.txt, TX_c.txt, and NYrow.txt. Cleaned text files captured from the Internet, used in Section 9.8.2.

DOI: 10.4324/9781003109396-9

- crude: This is a sample containing example articles from the Reuters news service. It is supplied as part of the "tm" (Text Miner) package. It is used to illustrate word clouds in Section 9.15.
- ISO8859.txt: Used in Sections 9.5.6 and 9.5.7 to illustrate the reading of text files.
- preambles.csv: This is a dataset of preambles to the constitutions of 155 countries of the world. The dataset was adapted from Kosuke Imai's website at https://raw.githubusercontent.com/kosukeimai/qss/master/DISCOVERY/constitution.csv
- tweets.csv: A small text dataset consisting of tweets by former President Donald Trump, used in Section 9.9.1 of this chapter.
- usconstitution.txt: The raw text of the U.S. Constitution. Text is in 872 lines, which have hard returns. Lines do not correspond to sentences.

9.3 Packages used in this chapter

Unless otherwise mentioned, functions cited in code in this chapter are from R's base, utils, and other automatically loaded packages. However, the following packages are used also in this chapter and may require being installed if not present in the researcher's environment. This is done with the `install.packages()` command, as in `install.packages("quanteda")`. Whether just installed or already present, they must be loaded with the `library()`command. After loading, the researcher may one type `help(name_of_package)` to obtain more information. If available, examples are obtained with the command `browseVignettes(package = "name_of_package")`.

- `library(broom)` # Convert objects from R into tidy tibble format
- `library(corrplot)` # Implements correlation plots
- `library(dendextend)` # Enhanced dendrograms for cluster analysis
- `library(dplyr)` # Utility w/`select()`, `rename()`, piping, more. It also calls the "magrittr" package, which supports the infix operator (%>%), which pipes what is on its left side, passing it to the first argument of the right-hand side.
- `library(ggplot2)` # The leading visualization/plotting package for R
- `library(ggraph)` # Here used for network plotting
- `library(graph)` # Installed from package "BiocManager"; see Section 9.17
- `library(grid)` # Here used for network arrows
- `library(gutenbergr)` # Archive of text sources
- `library(htm2txt)` # Retrieve a website's text, stripping html tags
- `library(igraph)` # A leading network diagramming package in R
- `library(janeaustin)` # Contains the works of Jane Austen
- `library(quanteda)` # One of the leading text analysis packages in R
- `library(RColorBrewer)` # Utility for color palettes
- `library(readr)` # Reads in .csv and other "rectangular" text files
- `library(readtext)` # Imports and handles a variety of text file formats
- `library(Rgraphviz)` # Installed from package "BiocManager"; see Section 9.17
- `library(rvest)` # One of the leading web scraping packages for R
- `library(scales)` # Supports the `percent_format()` function
- `library("SnowballC")` # Implements Porter's word stemming algorithm
- `library(stringr)` # Utilities for working with strings
- `library(textclean)` # Text cleaning utility
- `library(textreadr)` # A package used to read a .docx file
- `library(tibble)` # Create a tibble type dataset, often used with "tidy" formats.
- `library(tidyr)` # Tools to create and reshape tidytext data
- `library(tidytext)` # A leading text mining package
- `library(tm)` # The "Text Miner" package for text analysis
- `library(tokenizers)` # Parses text into words, sentences, other tokens

- `library(topicmodels)` # Has "AssociatedPress" sample of 2,246 articles
- `library(twitteR)` # Provides an interface to the Twitter web API
- `library(wordcloud)` # To create word clouds
- `library(xml2)` # Supports rvest (and is a dependency of it)

9.4 What is a corpus?

The term "corpus" is often used generically to refer to a collection of documents in a research project. It also may be used to refer specifically to documents in a corpus created by the "Text Mining in R" (tm) or the "Quantitative Analysis of Textual Data" (quanteda) packages in R. Documents may be taken from news reports, court cases, book excerpts, historical documents, official archives, political manifestos and platforms, social media feeds, web page scrapings, interview transcripts, or may derive from any number of other sources. The corpus may also contain multimedia items such as audio or video recordings but multimedia analysis is not treated in this chapter.

9.5 Text files

9.5.1 Overview

Large amounts of text and mixed data may already be available in file and archive form on the web. Using a browser to search for "environment AND .csv AND download", for instance, may lead to comma-separated values (.csv) files on environmental topics. Likewise, searching for "transportation AND .txt AND download" may lead to files in .txt format.

9.5.2 Archived texts

Text datasets are available in many archives. A few are cited below as illustrations.

- *Government documents*: More recent government documents may be downloaded in text and pdf formats from the Government Information Office at https://www.govinfo.gov/. Additional data and listing of links is at https://www.archives.gov/research/alic/reference/govt-docs.html. Search in your browser to find many other websites for public documents.
- *data_corpus_inaugural*: U.S. presidential inaugural addresses: These are contained in the "quanteda" text analysis package. Quanteda's dfm format is discussed further below.

  # Create a corpus in quanteda as a dfm object. Here we call in "corp".

  ```
  library(quanteda)
  corp <- quanteda::corpus_subset(data_corpus_inaugural, Year > 1970)
  ```

  Convert the corpus to a data frame. This facilitates adding more recent inaugural addresses which may not be present in the corpus as supplied.

  # The "text" column of inauguraldf will contain the actual text of inaugural speeches

  ```
  inauguraldf <-quanteda::convert(corp, to = "data.frame")
  ```

- *AssociatedPress:* This is a teaching example text dataset in the "topicmodels" package, first presented at the First Text Retrieval Conference (TREC-1), 1992. It is in the "DocumentTermMatrix" (dtm) format associated with the "tm" package. It contains the frequency of 10,473 terms in 2,246 documents. Silge and Robinson (2017: 71–73) used the AssociatedPress dtm file to illustrate a basic form of sentiment analysis, using code similar to that below. Assuming the packages listed below have been installed, the reader may copy this code and run it "as is" to see the results in bar chart form.

  ```
  library(topicmodels)
  library(tidytext)
  library(dplyr)
  library(ggplot2)
  ```

```
data("AssociatedPress")
class(AssociatedPress)
# Convert from dtm to tidy format data frame
AP_tidy <- tidytext::tidy(AssociatedPress)
# Convert from tidy format data frame to a data frame for sentiment analysis
AP_sentiments<-AP_tidy %>% dplyr::inner_join(tidytext::get_sentiments("bing"),
by = c(term="word"))
# Create a sentiment bar chart from a tidied sentiment analysis data frame using ggplot2
AP_sentiments %>%
  dplyr::count(sentiment, term, wt = count) %>%
  dplyr::ungroup() %>%
  dplyr::filter(n >= 200) %>%
  dplyr::mutate(n = ifelse(sentiment == "negative", -n, n)) %>%
  dplyr::mutate(term = reorder(term, n)) %>%
  ggplot2::ggplot(aes(term, n, fill = sentiment)) +
  ggplot2::geom_bar(stat = "identity") +
  ggplot2::ylab("Contribution to sentiment") +
  ggplot2::coord_flip()
```

- *Jane Austen's novels*: These are in the "janeaustenr" package and are used as the example for help (tidytext) and elsewhere. The help code is below for parsing words and sentences from Austen's "Pride and Prejudice" book, with additional explanation added. The "d" object created below is a tibble-type data frame. Further discussion is in the tokenization section. Again, assuming packages are installed, this block of code may be run "as is" to see the results.

```
library(janeaustenr)
library(dplyr)        # Calls the tibble package
library(readr)
library(tidytext)     # Calls the tokenizers package
d <- dplyr::tibble(txt = prideprejudice)
d
d %>%
  tidytext::unnest_tokens(word, txt)
d %>%
  tidytext::unnest_tokens(sentence, txt, token = "sentences")
```

- *Internet Archive*: The Internet archive at https://archive.org/ is home to the "Wayback Machine", which has collected over 500 billion web pages and other documents. For instance, enter a term such as "hearings" to find congressional hearings which may be downloaded as text, pdf files, or other formats. Not all documents may be downloaded. At this writing coverage is through 2016.
- Many other English-language text corpora, including the "Corpus of Supreme Court Decisions" and the "News on the Web Corpus", are available for download at https://www.english-corpora.org/corpora.asp. Some corpora cover to the present day and some do not.

9.5.3 Project Gutenberg archive

Project Gutenberg has assembled digital versions of over 60,000 public domain works as of 2021. Most are older works where copyright has expired or they were never copyrighted or they were donated to the public domain. Within the R environment at this writing, the "gutenbergr" package includes utilities for searching and downloading most of these works. Other texts may be available from https://www.gutenberg.org/. The primary utilities of the gutenbergr package are these:

`gutenberg _ download()`

Given a Gutenberg text id number, this program does the actual downloading. For instance, `gutenberg _ download(3)` downloads the text of the U.S. Constitution.

`gutenberg _ metadata()`

This program provides Gutenberg ids along with title, author, language, and other information about each work.

`gutenberg _ authors()`

This provides author information.

`gutenberg _ subjects()`

Lists works keyed to Library of Congress subjects.

`gutenberg _ metadata`

Used for searching and filtering the Gutenberg collection for works available as R datasets.

`gutenberg _ strip()`

Removes project Gutenberg metadata from the beginning of the work.

```
# Install gutenbergr and invoke needed other packages.
install.packages("gutenbergr")
library(gutenbergr)
library(dplyr)

# List the entire library
gutenberg_metadata
[Partial output:]
  A tibble: 51,997 x 8
     gutenberg_id title    author   gutenberg_autho~ language gutenberg_bookshe~
rightshas_text
          <int> <chr>      <chr>              <int> <chr>    <chr>              <chr>   <lgl>
   1          0  NA        NA                    NA en       NA                 Public~ TRUE
   2          1 "The Decl~ Jeffers~            1638 en       United States Law~ Public~ TRUE
   3          2 "The Unit~ United ~               1 en       American Revoluti~ Public~ TRUE
   4          3 "John F. ~ Kennedy~            1666 en       NA                 Public~ TRUE
   5          4 "Lincoln'~ Lincoln~               3 en       US Civil War       Public~ TRUE
   6          5 "The Unit~ United ~               1 en       American Revoluti~ Public~ TRUE
   7          6 "Give Me ~ Henry, ~               4 en       American Revoluti~ Public~ TRUE
   8          7 "The Mayf~ NA                    NA en       NA                 Public~ TRUE
   9          8 "Abraham ~ Lincoln~               3 en       US Civil War       Public~ TRUE
  10          9 "Abraham ~ Lincoln~               3 en       US Civil War       Public~ TRUE
  # ... with 51,987 more rows

# List ids and titles for a range of the library, such as the first 20 titles
gutenberg_metadata[1:20,1:2]
[Partial output:]
   # A tibble: 20 x 2
      gutenberg_id title
        <int> <chr>
    1     0 NA
    2     1 "The Declaration of Independence of the United States of America"
    3     2 "The United States Bill of Rights\r\nThe Ten Original Amendments to the Co~
    4     3 "John F. Kennedy's Inaugural Address"
    5     4 "Lincoln's Gettysburg Address\r\nGiven November 19, 1863 on the battlefiel~
    6     5 "The United States Constitution"
  . . .
   19    18 "The Federalist Papers"
   20    19 "The Song of Hiawatha"
```

```
# Search for given title. Make note of the gutenber_ids which are wanted.
# ID 5 is for the U.S. Constitution.
gutenberg_metadata %>% dplyr::filter(title == "The United States Constitution")
[Output:]
# A tibble: 1 x 8
  gutenberg_id title   author  gutenberg_autho~ language gutenberg_bookshe~ rights
has_text
         <int> <chr>   <chr>              <int> <chr>    <chr>              <chr> <lgl>
1            5 The Un~ United~                1 en       American Revoluti~ Publi~ TRUE
```

The gutenberg _ works() function operates similarly to Gutenberg _ metadata() but filters just for works in English with available text downloads, removing duplicates.

```
# Search all works
gutenberg_works()
[Output not shown but similar to that for Gutenberg _ metadata()

# Search by author
gutenbergr::gutenberg_works(author == "Jefferson, Thomas")
[Partial output:]
   # A tibble: 12 x 8
      gutenberg_id title    author  gutenberg_autho~ language gutenberg_books~
rights has_text
             <int> <chr>    <chr>           <int> <chr>    <chr>            <chr>  <lgl>
    1            1 The Dec~ Jeffer~          1638 en        United States L~ Publi~ TRUE
    2         5012 State o~ Jeffer~          1638 en        NA               Publi~ TRUE
   . . .
   11        45847 "The Wr~ Jeffer~          1638 en        NA               Publi~ TRUE
   12        50046 "The Wr~ Jeffer~          1638 en        NA               Publi~ TRUE

# Another way to search using the "stringr" package.
library(stringr)
gutenbergr::gutenberg_works(stringr::str_detect(author, "Jefferson"))
[Output is similar but is not shown here]

# Search by subject term and put results in a data frame called "temp".
# Search for terms at http://id.loc.gov/authorities/subjects.html
library(stringr)
temp  <- gutenberg_subjects %>% dplyr::filter(stringr::str_detect(subject, "Obama"))
temp
[Output:]
   # A tibble: 3 x 3
     gutenberg_id subject_type subject
            <int> <chr>        <chr>
   1        28000 lcsh         Obama, Barack, 1961- -- Inauguration, 2009
   2        28001 lcsh         Obama, Barack, 1961- -- Inauguration, 2009
   3        28971 lcsh         Obama, Barack, 1961- -- Inauguration, 2009
```

Actual downloading is done by the gutenberg _ download() function. The researcher may download one or multiple works based on Gutenberg id. For example, above we found that the id for the Declaration of Independence was 1 and for the U.S. Constitution was 5. We download each document separately (recall R will be case-sensitive to object names). The created objects are of class "data.frame", "tbl", and "tbl_df". Objects have two columns: "gutenberg_id" and "text". The "text" column has one line (not sentence) of the text file per row.

```
Declaration <- gutenbergr::gutenberg_download(1)
```

Unfortunately, the default mirror server may be down. If you get an error message from the command above, a new mirror must be listed. A list of available Gutenberg mirrors is at https://www.gutenberg.org/MIRRORS.ALL. After picking a new mirror, revise the download command to specify it:

```
Declaration <- gutenbergr::gutenberg_download(1, mirror = "http://mirrors.xmission.
com/gutenberg/")
```

In like manner we may download the U.S. Constitution.

```
Constitution <- gutenbergr::gutenberg_download(5, mirror = "http://mirrors.xmission.
com/gutenberg/")
# Download both documents to one object
# The "gutenberg_id" column of FoundingDocs differentiates the two documents.
FoundingDocs <- gutenbergr::gutenberg_download(c(1,5))

# For counting purposes, create a second data frame with a "title" column
# The "n" column in output is the number of lines in the work (same as nrow())
FoundingDocs2 <- gutenberg_download(c(1,5),meta_fields="title")
library(dplyr)
FoundingDocs2 %>% dplyr::count(title)
# Or sort descending by n: FoundingDocs2 %>% count(title, sort=TRUE)
[Output:]
   # A tibble: 2 x 2
     title                                                                n
     <chr>                                                            <int>
   1 The Declaration of Independence of the United States of America  2053
   2 The United States Constitution                                     627
   Other meta-datasets

# Convert to "tidy" format, one word per line
# FDwords is a data frame in tidy format
library(tidytext)
FDwords <- FoundingDocs %>% tidytext::unnest_tokens(word, text)

# View the contents of FDwords for a range of rows.
FDwords[1000:1005,]
[Output:]
   # A tibble: 6 x 2
     gutenberg_id word
            <int> <chr>
   1            1 a
   2            1 jurisdiction
   3            1 foreign
   4            1 to
   5            1 our
   6            1 constitution
```

9.5.4 Comma-separated values (.csv) files

The.csv files are the leading format for data exchange in R and between R and other platforms. While often used for exchange of numeric data, it is equally possible to use it for text data. The reading in and treatment of .csv files is illustrated in the section on tokenization later in this chapter.

9.5.5 Text from Word .docx files with the textreadr package

The "textreadr" package may be used to acquire text information from a variety of formats. Below we use its `read_docx()` function to read MS Word files. However, it also supports functions for other types of files:

`read.doc()`, `read_pdf()`, `read_html()`, `read_doc()`, and `read_transcript()`. Below we show how to read in a whole directory of .docx files into a data frame in R. We do not clean the imported text (see the separate section on cleaning). The Word .docx files used for this example were legal forms from https://www.courts.state.co.us/Forms/Forms_List.cfm and are not provided to the reader, who is encouraged to try this on their own directory of .docx files.

```
# Setup
library(textreadr)          # The package used to read a .docx file
library(tibble)             # A utility used here to add a column to a data frame
setwd("C:/mydocs")

# Read in a character vector of .docx files in the default directory, then list them.
# For the example used, the directory had 12 .docx documents.
# filenames will be a character vector sorted alphabetically.
# The list.files() function is in R's base package.
filenames <- list.files(path = "C:/mydocs", pattern = "*.docx", full.names=TRUE)

# Read in a single .docx file named "D1.docx" located in the working directory set above.
# doc1p is of class "character", meaning it is a character vector.
# It is of length 123 because each paragraph is an element within the character vector.
# For instance, doc1p[3] is the third paragraph.
doc1p <- textreadr::read_docx("C:/mydocs/Form 35.4 Pattern Interrogatories -
Domestic Relations.docx")
class(doc1p)
[Output:]
      [1] "character"
length(doc1p)

[Output:]
      [1] 123
doc1p
[Partial output:]
     [1] "FORM 35. 4  - Pattern Interrogatories (Domestic Relations)"
     [2] "[Reference to C.R.C.P. 16.2, 26 and 33.  These are not to be filed with
the court, except as may be ordered.]"
     . . .

# Collapse a character vector of paragraphs into a character vector document.
# The doc1p object would be suitable for paragraph-level analysis.
# However, for document-level analysis we need to collapse its 123 elements into 1 element.
doc1d <- paste(doc1p, collapse = '')
class(doc1d)
[Output:]
      [1] "character"
length(doc1d)
[Output:]
      [1] 1

# Read in all the .docx files in the working directory into an object called "docsall_matrix".
# Recall that length(filenames) is 12 for this example.
docsall_matrix <- ""
for(i in 1:length(filenames)){
  file <- textreadr::read_docx(filenames[i])
  doc <- paste(file, collapse = '')
  docsall_matrix <- rbind(docsall_matrix, doc)
}
```

```
# Remove the first row, which is a null (for docsall_matrix = "")
# This also leaves the rownames as 1:12 (there were 12 documents read in)
docsall_matrix <- docsall_matrix[-1,]

# Make the matrix into a data frame
docsall_df <- as.data.frame(docsall_matrix)

# Rename column 1 of the data frame to be "text"
colnames(docsall_df)[1] <- "text"

# Add rownames as a column in the matrix
docsall_df <- tibble::rownames_to_column(docsall_df, var="document")

# We wind up with a data frame of 12 rows, where each row is a former .docx document.
# The data frame has two columns: "document", which is document number from 1 to 12
# and "text", which contains the imported text.
class(docsall_df)
[Output:]
      [1] "data.frame"
nrow(docsall_df)
[Output:]
      [1] 9
names(docsall_df)
[Output:]
      [1] "document" "text"
```

We could now do most forms of text analysis with the imported .docx files. Below we show how to create a three-way comparative word cloud, comparing Documents 1, 4, and 8.

```
# Setup for word cloud based on the .docx documents now in docsall_df
library(quanteda)

# Convert document and text columns from factor to character in docsall_df
docsall_df$document <- as.character(docsall_df$document)
docsall_df$text <- as.character(docsall_df$text)

# Convert from data frame to a "small-C" corpus using the quanteda package.
docsall_corpus <- quanteda::corpus(docsall_df, docid_field = "document", text_field =
"text")

# Create better labels for the documents
# E.g., the rowname "text1" becomes "Document # 1".
doclabel <- paste("Document #", as.character(docsall_df$document))
names(docsall_corpus) <- doclabel
class(docsall_corpus)
[Output:]
      [1] "corpus"    "character"

# Convert corpus to document feature matrix (dfm) format needed by many quanteda tools.
# First define any desired custom stop words.
mystopwords <- c("a.the", "b.the","c.the","d.the")
pattern = c(quanteda::stopwords(language = "english"), mystopwords)

docsall_dfm <- quanteda::dfm(docsall_corpus, remove_numbers = TRUE, remove_punct =
TRUE, stem = TRUE, remove = pattern)
class(docsall_dfm)
```

```
[Output:]
    [1] "dfm"
   attr(,"package")
    [1] "quanteda"
```

```
# Create a comparison cloud. We ask for a three-way comparison cloud (rows 1, 4, and 8).
# max_words is the maximum number of words; minsize is the minimum length of any word.
# color= must have as many colors as the comparison (here, 3).
# rotation= is percent of words shown vertically.
set.seed(1)
docs <- c(1,4, 8)
quanteda::textplot_wordcloud(docsall_dfm[docs,], max_words = 200, minsize = 4, color =
c("blue", "darkgreen", "red"), rotation= .20, adjust=0.5, comparison = TRUE)
```

The result is shown in Figure 9.1, which shows contrasting word frequency usage across three legal documents used in this example. We can see what the documents are by typing filenames, which is an object created earlier when we read in the document files.

```
filenames
[Partial output:]
   [1] "C:/mydocs/Form 35.4 Pattern Interrogatories - Domestic Relations.docx"
   . . .
   [4] "C:/mydocs/JDF 1109 Temporary Orders Agreement.docx"
   . . .
   [8] "C:/mydocs/JDF 205 Motion to file without payment and supporting financial
affidavit .docx"
```

We see, for example, that Document 8 (which deals with finances) most frequently uses stemmed terms $, income, month, court, balance, and household. The later section on comparison clouds explores this form of text analysis in more detail, using a less arbitrary comparison which contrasts inaugural speech terms used by Presidents Obama and Trump.

9.5.6 Text from other formats with the readtext package

The "readtext" package may be used to acquire text information in raw text files (.txt), .csv files, tab-separated values (.tab, .tsv), PDF files (.pdf), Microsoft Word files (.doc, .docx), archive files (.zip, .tar, .tar.gz, .tar.bz), and JSON data. Here, however, we only have space to briefly demonstrate its use for .txt files.

The researcher may encounter text data in raw text file format, usually with the extension ".txt". To search for such files via Google, one could enter, for instance, [site:.gov filetype=".txt"] without brackets to see .txt files in the .gov domain. As an example in this section, we download the .txt file at https://www.w3.org/TR/PNG/iso_8859-1.txt. This raw text file is from the World Wide Web Consortium (W3C) and lists the graphical (non-control) characters defined by ISO 8859-1, also known as Latin-1. This and other encodings are discussed in a later section on "Character encoding" in this chapter. Knowledge of Latin-1 encoding is helpful in text analysis, so this text file is relevant to this chapter.

Go to the url above in Chrome. When there, right-click anywhere on the page and select "Save As". We saved this file to C:\Data under the name "ISO8859.txt" (this file is also provided at the Support Material (www.routledge.com/9780367624293) to this book). This file has an initial explanatory paragraph, then two columns of two fields each: A hex code and a brief text label in this format:

```
Hex Description                       Hex Description

20  SPACE
21  EXCLAMATION MARK                  A1  INVERTED EXCLAMATION MARK
...                                   ...
```

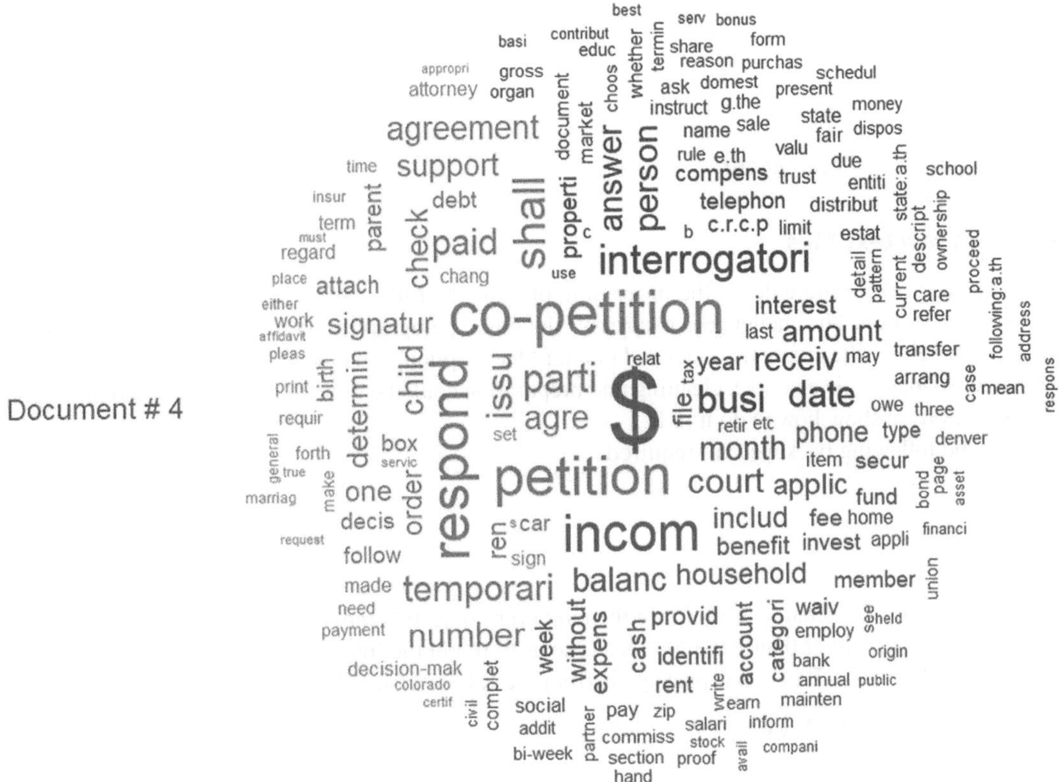

Figure 9.1 Word comparison cloud based on .docx files

Below we read in the ISO8859 text and convert it to Quanteda corpus format, discussed in a subsequent section on formats related to the quanteda package.

```
setwd("C:/Data")
library(readtext)

# Read in the text file
# If the first term were "*.txt", all txt files from the directory would be read in.
# isotext is a data frame with a "doc_id" column for the name of the source file, and
# a "text" column containing the contents.
# Thus isotext$text is a character vector with all the text data.
isotext <- readtext::readtext("ISO8859.txt",
  docvarsfrom = "filenames",
  docvarnames = "ISO8859",
  dvsep = " ",
  encoding = "ISO-8859-1")  # Latin-1 encoding
```

```
class(isotext)
[Output:]
      [1] "readtext"    "data.frame"

# This is easily converted into a quanteda corpus, discussed later in this chapter.
library(quanteda)
iso_corpus <-quanteda::corpus(isotext)
class(iso_corpus)
[Output:]
      [1] "corpus"     "character"
```

9.5.7 Text from raw text files

In this section, we illustrate in more detail the processing of a raw text file. We us the same ISO8859.txt file discussed in the previous section. The challenge is to strip off the initial paragraph and then to create a data frame with two columns, one for "Hex" (the character code) and one for "Description". Of course, every text file will contain a different challenge. Also, for this example, cleaning and preparation could be done in a word processor or a spreadsheet but in this section we show how to do it in R.

In this section, the following packages are required:

```
# Setup
library(stringr)
library(tidyr)

# First we read the file into an R character vector in the temporary object "temp"
# We use readLines() rather than readtext() so as to retain the line structure
# of the source table. The readLines() package is from the R base system library.

temp <- readLines('ISO8859.txt')
class(temp)
[Output:]
      [1] "character"
temp
[Output:]
[1] "The following are the graphical (non-control) characters defined by"
[2] "ISO 8859-1 (1987).  Descriptions in words aren't all that helpful,"
[3] "but they're the best we can do in text.  A graphics file illustrating"
[4] "the character set should be available from the same archive as this"
[5] "file."
[6] ""
[7] "Hex Description                          Hex Description"
[8] ""
[9] "20  SPACE"
[10] "21  EXCLAMATION MARK                    A1  INVERTED EXCLAMATION MARK"
. . .
[104] "                                        FF  SMALL LETTER Y WITH DIAERESIS"
# Strip off the first 8 rows of text, leaving only the data itself
isol <- temp[9:104]
isol
[Partial output:]
 [1] "20  SPACE"
 [2] "21  EXCLAMATION MARK                    A1  INVERTED EXCLAMATION MARK"
 [3] "22  QUOTATION MARK                      A2  CENT SIGN"
 [4] "23  NUMBER SIGN                         A3  POUND SIGN"
 [5] "24  DOLLAR SIGN                         A4  CURRENCY SIGN"
 [6] "25  PERCENT SIGN                        A5  YEN SIGN"
 . . .
```

```
# Break columns into separate rows
# Here, the two columns are separated by at least five spaces
# iso2 is of class matrix, with two columns of 96 rows each
iso2 <- stringr::str_split_fixed(iso1, "     ", 2)

# Strip leading and trailing blank spaces in the matrix. Interior whitespace is not removed.
# gsub is part of R's grep family in its "base" package
# Create trim function. This is just one method in R.
trim <- function( x ) {
  gsub("(^[[:space:]]+|[[:space:]]+$)", "", x)
}
# With use of the trim() function, leading and trailing spaces are removed.
iso2 <- trim(iso2)

# Convert to a data frame called "iso_df". It has two variables, V1 and V2
# V1 is column 1 of the matrix and V2 is column 2
# These correspond to the two columns in the source table
# The as.data.frame() function is from R's base package in the system library.
iso_df <- as.data.frame(iso2)

# Append column V2 to the end of column V1 so there is one list.
# The resulting one-column data frame replaces the old two-column iso_df
# The one column is named "iso8859chars"
# Each of its 2*96 = 192 rows is a character vector with both Hex and Description information
# The as.character() function is also from R's base package.

col1 <- as.character(iso_df$V1)
col2 <- as.character(iso_df$V2)
iso8859chars <- c(col1,col2)
iso_df <- data.frame(iso8859chars)
View(iso_df)

# For these data, it turns out rows 96 and 97 are blank so we get rid of them
# To keep "iso8859chars" as the column name we have to label it as such after this operation.
# The colnames() function is in the R base package.
# View() is in the utils package in the system library
iso_df  <- as.data.frame(iso_df[c(-96,-97),])
colnames(iso_df)[1] <- "iso8859chars"
View(iso_df)

# Separate Hex and Description elements of the iso8859chars column into separate columns.
# separate() automatically parses so8859chars into columns.
# The extra= argument in separate() assures everything else goes into "Description"
iso_df <- tidyr::separate(iso_df, col = iso8859chars, into = c("Hex",
"Description"),extra="merge")

# List the result
iso_df
[Partial output:]
      Hex     Description
   1  20      SPACE
   2  21      EXCLAMATION MARK
   . . .
   189  FE    SMALL LETTER THORN (Icelandic)
   190  FF    SMALL LETTER Y WITH DIAERESIS
```

At this point we have completed the challenge of converting raw text data into a corresponding R data frame. While every raw text source will be different, many of the operations outlined above should be useful in cleaning and preparing other text data.

PART II: QUICK START ON TEXT ANALYTICS WITH R

9.6 Quick start exercise 1: Key word in context (kwic) indexing

A kwic index is a type of concordance, listing words of research interest in the context in which they appear. That is, if "liberty" is the word of interest, then all instances of "liberty" will be listed, along with words, which appeared before and after "liberty". The listing may be for words, which appear in a single document or in multiple documents. The researcher may set the "window", which is the number of words before and after they key term. Below, for instance, the all instances of "free" and "liberty" are listed, along with a window of five words. There may be multiple keywords and output may be sorted by keyword, forming clusters of contexts for each. This may make it possible for the researcher to make generalizations about contexts of different keywords that otherwise would remain difficult to discern. Kwic indexes are also a useful supplement to word frequency tables, discussed in the next section, allowing the researcher to make informed qualitative statements regarding the context in which high-frequency words are used.

We start by loading the needed packages. Kwic indexing is done by the "quanteda" package, which is useful for many text analysis functions discussed later in this chapter. However, there are other available R packages for kwic, such as "PGRdup".[1]

```
# Setup
library(quanteda)          # Supports keyword-in-context via its kwic() function
library(gutenbergr)        # Houses the text data used here
setwd("C:/Data")           # Declare the working directory
options(width = 150)       # Set output width to be long enough to fit the index
```

The example to be used is a character vector containing two documents: The Declaration of Independence and the U.S. Constitution. These are the first and fifth documents in Project Gutenberg, as retrieved by the "gutenbergr" package described previously.

```
# FDbooks is a data frame whose columns are gutenberg_id, text, and title.
# Specifically, FDbooks is a tibble-type data frame. "FD" stands for "Founding Documents".
# The mirror= option may be omitted if the default mirror site is operational.
# Otherwise add a different mirror site such as that below (see earlier discussion).
FDbooks <- gutenbergr::gutenberg_download(c(1,5), meta_fields = "title", mirror =
"http://mirrors.xmission.com/gutenberg/")

class(FDbooks)
[Output:]
      [1] "tbl_df"      "tbl"         "data.frame"

# Create myvector as a character vector based on the "text" column of FDbooks
myvector<- FDbooks$text
class(myvector)
[Output:]
      [1] "character"

# myvector has 2,680 "documents", with one line per document
length(myvector)
```

[Output:]
```
[1] 2680
```

Here is an example line:
```
myvector[49]
```
[Output:]
```
[1] "When in the Course of human events, it becomes necessary for"
```

The `tokens()` function parses each line into individual words. Lines are still retained.
toks is of class "tokens"
```
toks <- quanteda::tokens(myvector)
```

Now set the search term or terms wanted. Note the use of an asterisk to make "free" a root word, so that any term beginning with "free" will be retrieved.

```
term <- c("liberty","free*")
```

We now create the kwic index and display its first dozen lines. The `window=` argument sets the maximum number of words on either side of the target word. Note that `kwic()` is case-insensitive by default.

```
mykwic <- quanteda::kwic(toks, pattern =  term, window = 5)
head(mykwic,12)
```
[Output:]
```
  [text26, 14]   they choose. Please feel |  free   | to
   [text59, 7]       among these are Life, | Liberty |,  and the pursuit of
  [text145, 4]         For abolishing the |  free   | System of English Laws in
  [text181, 3]                       of a |  free   | People.
  [text200, 7]      of Right ought to be |  Free   | and Independent States;
  [text204, 4]               and that as |  Free   | and Independent States, they
  [text234, 4]        or prohibiting the |  free   | exercise thereof; or abridging
 [text234, 11]  thereof; or abridging the | freedom | of speech,
 [text244, 12]       to the security of a |  free   | State,
  [text278, 7]       be deprived of life, | liberty |,  or property, without
 [text352, 13] party but a celebration of | freedom | ...
  [text375, 4]            the success of | liberty |.  This much we pledge
```

The bottom row above is the 375th line, with the search term in 4th position in that line.
We can see that line by asking for it by index number.

```
myvector[375]
```
[Output:]
```
[1] "the success of liberty. This much we pledge. . .and more."
```

It is also possible to index on multi-word expressions using the `phrase()` function.
```
myphrase <- quanteda::phrase("independent states")
mykwic2 <- quanteda::kwic(toks, pattern = c("free*",myphrase), window = 3)
head(mykwic2,7)
```
[Output:]
```
 [text26, 14:14].       Please feel |         free         | to
  [text145, 4:4] For abolishing the |         free         | System of English
  [text181, 3:3]               of a |         free         | People.
  [text200, 7:7]        ought to be |         Free         | and Independent States
 [text200, 9:10]        be Free and | Independent States | ;
  [text204, 4:4]        and that as |         Free         | and Independent States
  [text204, 6:7]        as Free and | Independent States |,  they have
```

Note that kwic objects like mykwic2 are of class "kwic" and "data.frame". They have the columns document, position, pre (the part before the keyword), keyword (the search term or terms), post (the part after), and pattern (e.g., free*).

```
class(mykwic2)
[Output:]
   [1] "kwic"        "data.frame"
# The command below converts to the generic class "data.frame"
mykwic2_df <- as.data.frame(mykwic2)
class(mykwic2_df)
[Output:]
   [1] "data.frame"
```

The command `View(mykwic2)` places results in the RStudio Viewer area because mykwic2 is a kwic-type data frame. In contrast, the command `View(mykwic2_df)` places results in the RStudio console (output) area because mykwic2_df is an ordinary data frame object.

Finally, if we wish we may sort by keyword (the search term or terms). In the example below the sort order will be instances of free, Free, freedom, Freedom, freely, and Independent States in that order.

```
mykwic2_df_sorted <- mykwic2_df[order(mykwic2_df$keyword),]
mykwic2_df_sorted
[Output not shown:]
```

9.7 Quick start exercise 2: Word frequencies and histograms

For word frequencies using the method described in this section, we assume an object in "tidy" format, created by `tidytext::unnest_tokens()`. This method is only one of many ways to create word frequency lists in R. Earlier in the "Project Gutenberg archive" section we created the tidy-format data frame "FDbooks", containing the founding documents "Declaration of Independence" and "United States Constitution". However, for word frequency tables we need a similar data frame but with a title field.

```
# Setup
library(dplyr)          # A utility with the piping function (%>%) and more
library(ggplot2)        # A leading visualization package
library(gutenbergr)     # Houses the text data used here
library(quanteda)       # Supports keyword-in-context via its kwic() function
library(tidytext)       # A leading text analysis package
setwd("C:/Data")        # Declare the working directory
```

We start by recreating FDbooks2, similar to FDbooks earlier but with a title field. FDbooks2 is a tibble-type data frame. Again, the first and fifth books from gutenbergr are selected. These are the Declaration of Independence and the Constitution. The columns in FDbooks2 are gutenberg_id, text, and title.

```
# The mirror= option may be omitted if the default mirror site is operational.
# Otherwise add a different mirror site such as that below (see earlier discussion).
FDbooks2 <- gutenbergr::gutenberg_download(c(1,5), meta_fields = "title", mirror =
"http://mirrors.xmission.com/gutenberg/")

class(FDbooks2)
[Output:]
   [1] "tbl_df"     "tbl"        "data.frame"
```

```
# Tokenize FDbooks2 to words using the tidytext package.
FDwords2 <- FDbooks2 %>% tidytext::unnest_tokens(word, text)

# Create word counts, stripping stop words
FDwords2_counts <- FDwords2 %>%
  dplyr::anti_join(stop_words, by = "word") %>%
  dplyr::count(gutenberg_id, title, word, sort = TRUE)
```

We now list results. The "n" column is the word count for the listed document title. Stop words were stripped using tidytext's built-in stop list. Results are sorted descending. Note "united" appears twice, once for each of the two documents.

```
FDwords2_counts
[Partial output:]
   # A tibble: 3,204 x 4
      gutenberg_id title                                                     word           n
      <int> <chr>                                                            <chr>      <int>
   1     1 The Declaration of Independence of the United States of ~ united        78
   2     5 The United States Constitution                                    united        56
   3     1 The Declaration of Independence of the United States of ~ people        53
   4     1 The Declaration of Independence of the United States of ~ constituti~ 45
   5     1 The Declaration of Independence of the United States of ~ law           44
   6     1 The Declaration of Independence of the United States of ~ time          43
   7     1 The Declaration of Independence of the United States of ~ laws          40
   8     1 The Declaration of Independence of the United States of ~ congress      39
   9     1 The Declaration of Independence of the United States of ~ government    38
  10     1 The Declaration of Independence of the United States of ~ president     38
```

We now create the bar plot of the ten most common words, not counting stop words. Warning: Widen the viewing area or zoom in RStudio to assure all words show for column titles. The result is shown in Figure 9.2.

```
# Set the desired number of bars
number_of_bars = 10

# If only one document, use:
#col _ labels<- c(head(FDwords2 _ counts,number _ of _ bars)$word)

# We use the code below for multiple documents
row1labels <- paste (c(head(FDwords2_counts$word, number_of_bars)))
row2labels <- paste (c(head(as.character(FDwords2_counts$gutenberg_id),
number_of_bars)))
row2labels<-paste("ID=",row2labels)
# sep="/n" inserts a linefeed between row 1 and row 2 labels
col_labels<- paste(row1labels,row2labels, sep="\n")

# Now produce the word frequency plot
barplot(height=head(FDwords2_counts, number_of_bars)$n, names=col_labels,
xlab="Words", ylab="Frequency", col = heat.colors(number_of_bars), main="Founding
Documents: Ten Most Frequent Words")
```

A different type of frequency plot is available in the "quanteda" package, which requires input as a document feature matrix (dfm) object. For this example, we use presidential inaugural speeches.

```
# Create a small-c corpus of inaugural speeches since 1990 as character vectors using quanteda
inaugurals_from_1990 <- quanteda::corpus_subset(data_corpus_inaugural, Year > 1990)
```

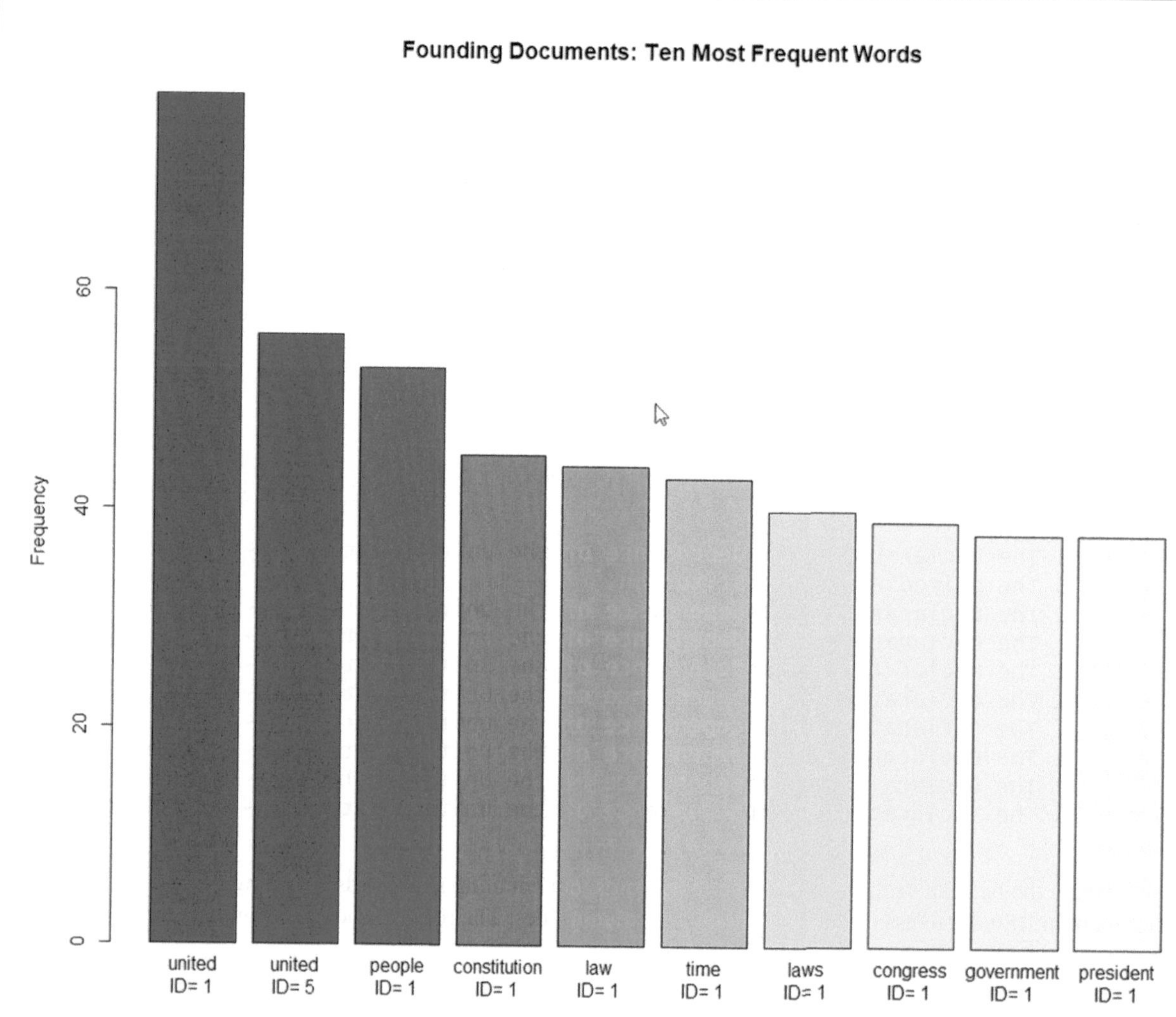

Figure 9.2 Word frequency bar chart for founding documents

```
# Convert corpus to document feature matrix (dfm) format needed by many quanteda tools.
# In addition to the preset stop words, the term "will" is also removed.
inaugurals_dfm <- quanteda::dfm(inaugurals_from_1990, remove_numbers = TRUE, remove_
punct = TRUE, stem = TRUE, remove = c("will",stopwords("english")))
```

We now compute needed word frequency statistics. The `textstat_frequency()` function computes term and document frequency summaries of the features in a dfm, optionally grouped by a docvars variable or another grouping variable. For example purposes, the plot is limited to the top 25 most frequent words.

```
inaugurals_features <- quanteda::textstat_frequency(inaugurals_dfm, n = 25)

# Sort in descending order of frequency.
# reorder() is part of the "stats" package in the R system library.
inaugurals_features$feature <- with(inaugurals_features, reorder(feature,
-frequency))
```

```
# Create the word frequency plot using the ggplot2 package.
ggplot2::ggplot(inaugurals_features,
   ggplot2::aes(x = feature, y = frequency, color="red", size = 2)) +
   ggplot2::geom_point() +
   ggplot2::theme(legend.position="none") +
   ggplot2::xlab("Word") +
   ggplot2::ylab("Word Frequency") +
   ggplot2::theme(axis.text.x = element_text(angle=90,hjust=1))
```

In Figure 9.3 we see, not surprisingly, that terms like American, Americans, us, and nation appear very frequently. What may be more interesting is what is not listed. If the plot above were redone for 100 terms we would find that "women" is ranked 100th, though "children" is 32nd. Terms, such as environment, earth, and global warming, are absent from the top 100 in presidential inaugural speeches.

It is also possible to track and compare multiple target terms across multiple documents. We do this next for the same inaugural speeches data, but for the combined frequency of the terms "women", "woman", and "children".

First get frequency grouped by "President", which is a column in the corpus below. The source, inaugurals_dfm, is a subset of inaugural speeches since 1990. This was created in the previous section. We use `textstat()` to create frequencies of target terms by president. These results are put in the object "freq_presgroup".

```
freq_presgroup <- quanteda::textstat_frequency(inaugurals_dfm, groups = "President")
```

Next we filter to get the category for women. The freq_women object has these columns: Feature, frequency, rank, docfreq, and group. It is of the classes "frequency", "textstat", and "data.frame". At this point, different search terms

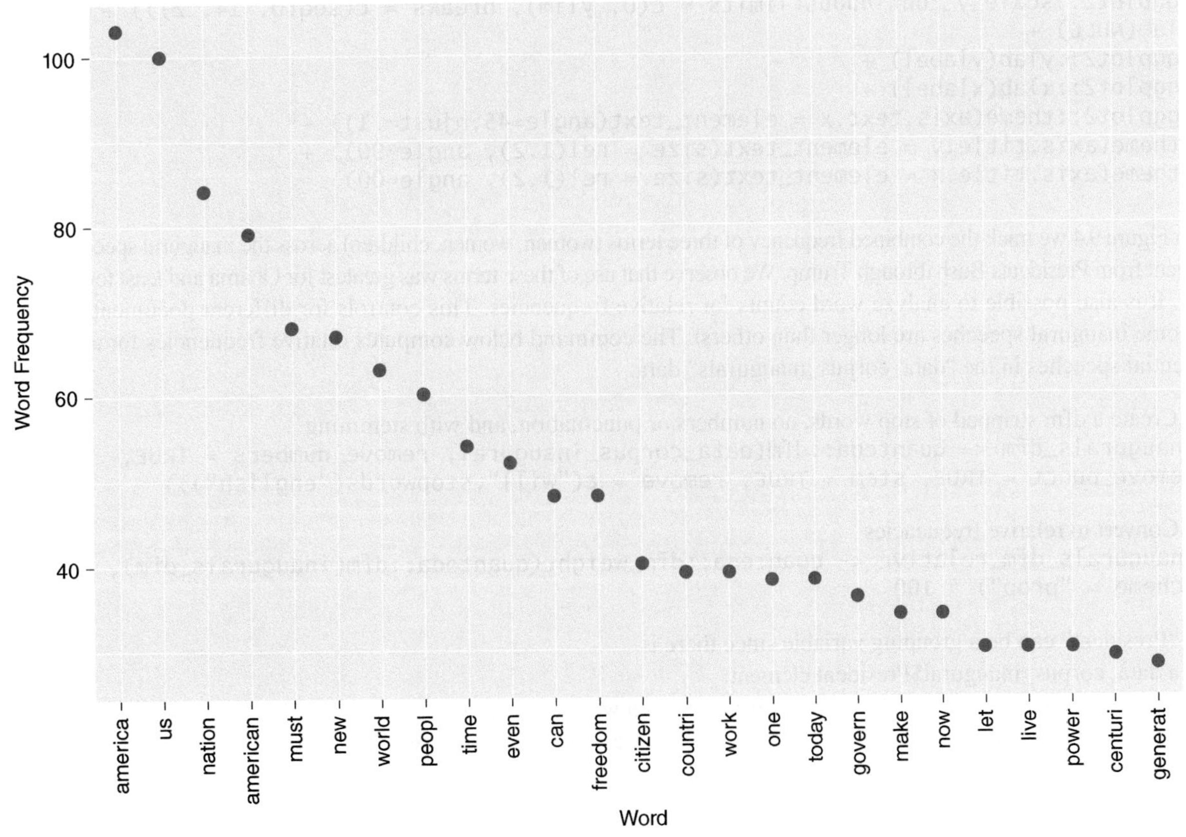

Figure 9.3 Word cloud for the "crude" data

might be substituted, but if so one must also change the axis label below. Note that stem words like "child*" should not be used in this context.

```
target <- c("woman","women","children")
freq_women <- subset(freq_presgroup, freq_presgroup$feature %in% target)
```

If the target has more than one term, we need to sum frequency by group. If there is only one term, skip this step and use the freq_women object, created above, in the ggplot code below. Otherwise use the `freq _ women2` object, which is also a tibble-type data frame. This object has two columns: group and total. The "group" column is the presidents for this example

```
freq_women2 <- freq_women %>%                # Specify data frame
  dplyr::group_by(group) %>%                 # Specify group indicator
  dplyr::summarise_at(vars(frequency),       # Specify column to sum
  base:: list(total = sum))                  # Specify sum function

# Create the axis labels
ylabel<- "Combined frequency of terms women, woman, children"
xlabel<- "Presidents"

# Create the plot. The upper limit of the y axis is ylim, which will vary by the data at hand.
ylim <- 14
ggplot2::ggplot(freq_women2,
 ggplot2::aes(x = group, y = total)) +
 ggplot2::geom_point(size=4, colour = "red") +
 ggplot2::scale_y_continuous(limits = c(0, ylim), breaks = c(seq(0, 14, 2))) +
xlab(NULL) +
 ggplot2::ylab(ylabel) +
 ggplot2::xlab(xlabel) +
 ggplot2::theme(axis.text.x = element_text(angle=45,hjust= 1)) +
 theme(axis.title.y = element_text(size = rel(1.2), angle=90)) +
 theme(axis.title.x = element_text(size = rel(1.2), angle=00))
```

In Figure 9.4 we track the combined frequency of three terms (women, women, children) across the inaugural speech document from Presidents Bush through Trump. We observe that use of these terms was greatest for Obama and least for Trump.

It is also possible to analyze word counts for relative frequencies. This controls for different document lengths (some inaugural speeches are longer than others). The command below computes relative frequencies for all presidential speeches in the "data_corpus_inaugurals" data.

```
# Create a dfm stripped of stop words, no numbers or punctuation, and with stemming
inaugurals_dfm <- quanteda::dfm(data_corpus_inaugural, remove_numbers = TRUE,
remove_punct = TRUE, stem = TRUE, remove = c("will",stopwords("english")))

# Convert to relative frequencies
inaugurals_dfm_relative <- quanteda::dfm_weight(quanteda::dfm(inaugurals_dfm),
scheme = "prop") * 100

# "President" can be a grouping variable since there is
# a data_corpus_inaugural$President element
# The topfeatures() function returns the top n words (here, 6)
quanteda::topfeatures(inaugurals_dfm_relative, n = 6, groups="President")
[Selected output from among output for all presidents]

  $Obama
        us     must   nation      can    peopl  america
  3.997642 2.330897 2.151711 1.787222 1.748937 1.725454
  ...
```

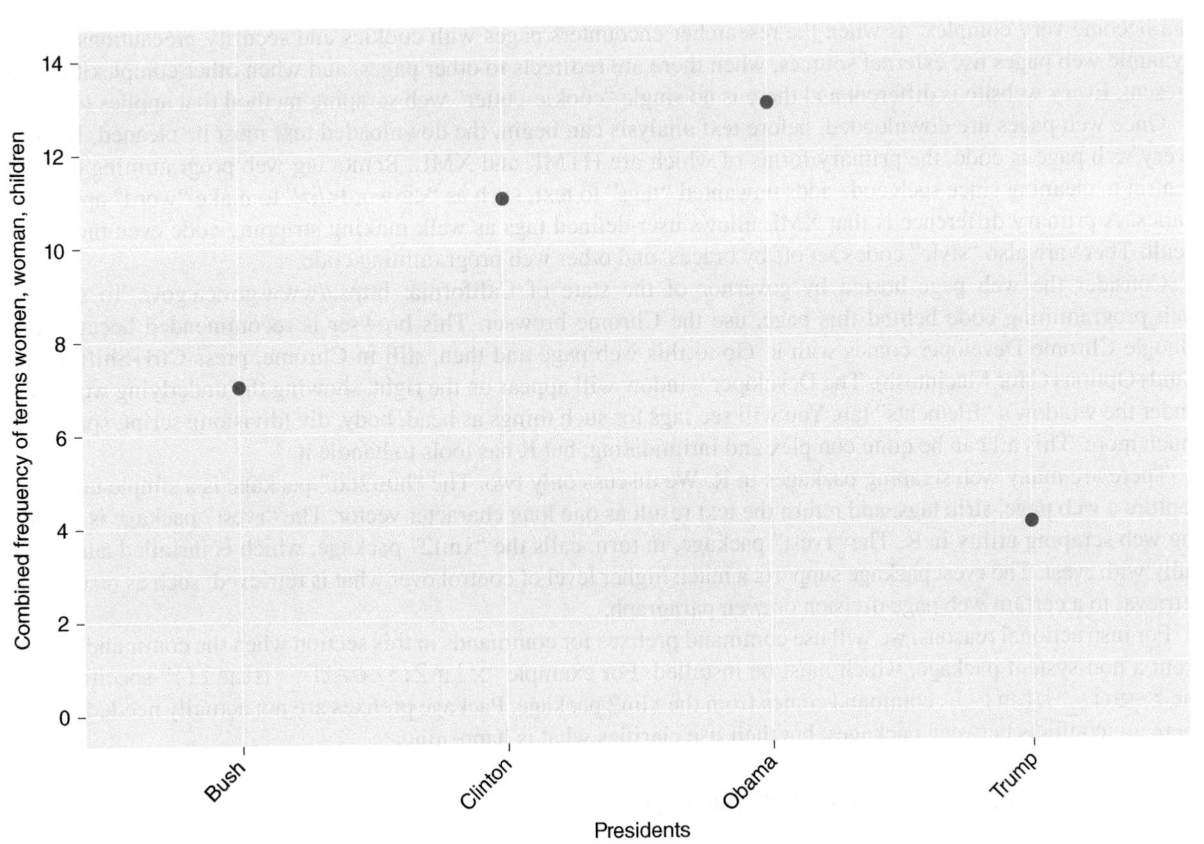

Figure 9.4 Word cloud for the U.S. Constitution

```
$Trump
 america american   nation  countri    peopl       one
2.664797 2.103787 1.823282 1.683029 1.402525 1.262272
...
$Kennedy
     let       us      can    power   nation     side
2.295552 1.721664 1.291248 1.291248 1.147776 1.147776
...
$Lincoln
      war      shall      union constitut      right    nation
 3.661626  2.510249  2.397968  2.365631  1.859377  1.788954
```

PART III: NETWORK ANALYSIS WITH R IN DETAIL

9.8 Web scraping

9.8.1 Overview

A great deal of text data, to say the least, is available via web pages. In this section, we deal with one type of text acquisition – web scraping, also called web mining or web harvesting. We do not deal here with harvesting graphics, video, or audio from the web. Moreover, our goal is just to provide an introduction, which means this section only scrapes (no pun intended!) the surface of a very large and complex topic. The simple examples which follow suggest that a great deal may be done even by the novice researcher. However, it should be emphasized that web scraping can become very complex, as when the researcher encounters pages with cookies and security precautions, when dynamic web pages use external sources, when there are redirects to other pages, and when other complexities are present. Every website is different and there is no single "cookie-cutter" web scraping method that applies to all.

Once web pages are downloaded, before text analysis can begin, the downloaded text must be cleaned. Behind every web page is code, the primary forms of which are HTML and XML. Removing web programming code is central to cleaning since such code adds unwanted "tags" to text, such as "<i>word</i>" to make "word" appear in italics. A primary difference is that XML allows user-defined tags as well, making stripping code even more difficult. There are also "style" codes set off by braces, and other web programming code.

Consider the web page hosted by governor of the state of California: https://www.gov.ca.gov/. To see the web programming code behind this page, use the Chrome browser. This browser is recommended because the Google Chrome Developer comes with it. Go to this web page and then, still in Chrome, press Ctrl+Shift+C (or Cmd+Option+C for Macintosh). The Developer window will appear on the right, showing the underlying web code under the window's "Elements" tab. You will see tags for such things as head, body, div (division), script, span, and much more. This all can be quite complex and intimidating, but R has tools to handle it.

There are many web scraping packages in R. We discuss only two. The "htm2txt" package is a simple utility to capture a web page, strip tags, and return the text result as one long character vector. The "rvest" package is a leading web scraping utility in R. The "rvest" package, in turn, calls the "xml2" package, which is installed automatically with rvest. The rvest package supports a much higher level of control over what is retrieved, such as restricting retrieval to a certain web page division or even paragraph.

For instructional reasons, we will use command prefixes for commands in this section when the command comes from a non-system package, which must be installed. For example "`xlm2::read_html()`" specifies that the `read_html()` command comes from the xlm2 package. Package prefixes are not actually needed unless there are conflicts between packages, but their use clarifies what is happening.

9.8.2 Web scraping: The "htm2txt" package

The "htm2txt" package provides a very simple-to-use basic approach to web scraping. It easily retrieves web pages and converts them to text, stripping out html tags. A given page is returned as a character vector. Multiple character vectors may be combined into a data frame. Here we combine five U.S. gubernatorial web pages scraped at the height of the coronavirus pandemic in 2020.

It must be emphasized that in creating our text data frame we skip over a very important step: Automated cleaning of the data. We purposely leave that to another section of this chapter. However, if the number of web pages is limited, as here, the researcher many manually clean the data in a word processor, eliminating unwanted text (e.g., menu items) and using search-find-replace to eliminate remaining codes (e.g., "/n" newline symbols). The manual method may in fact be preferable if feasible since algorithms for more automated cleaning are not perfect at knowing what the researcher considers "unwanted text". The more the researcher is interested in the narrative aspects of text, the more attractive the manual method. The more the researcher is interested in scraping numeric data, such as sports rankings or real estate prices, the more suitable automated methods are.

```
#Setup
library(htm2txt)      # Utility to retrieve a website's text, stripping html tags
library(tm)           # A leading text package; converts text into SimpleCorpus format
                      # Loading tm automatically loads package "NLP"
setwd("C:/Data")      # Set the working directory

# Read in gubernatorial web addresses (from https://www.nga.org/governors/addresses/)
# Taken 17 April 2020, at a height of the coronavirus pandemic
# Your content will differ since the date of retrieval will differ.
CA <- htm2txt::gettxt("https://www.gov.ca.gov/")
FL <- htm2txt::gettxt("https://www.flgov.com/")
LA <- htm2txt::gettxt("https://gov.louisiana.gov/")
NY <- htm2txt::gettxt("https://www.governor.ny.gov/")
TX <- htm2txt::gettxt("https://gov.texas.gov/")
```

For manual cleaning purposes, save the raw text files to the working directory.
```
write.table(CA, file = "CA.txt", quote = FALSE, sep = "\n", col.names = FALSE)
write.table(FL, file = "FL.txt", quote = FALSE, sep = "\n", col.names = FALSE)
write.table(LA, file = "LA.txt", quote = FALSE, sep = "\n", col.names = FALSE)
write.table(NY, file = "NY.txt", quote = FALSE, sep = "\n", col.names = FALSE)
write.table(TX, file = "TX.txt", quote = FALSE, sep = "\n", col.names = FALSE)
```

We clean the .txt files in our word processor, then resave as text files. The new files have a "c" added to indicate the cleaned versions (e.g., "CA_c.txt"). If using Microsoft Word for cleaning, here are considerations:

- Remove unwanted text such as menu choices, "read more", etc.
- Remove paragraph breaks (click the paragraph icon in the Paragraph section of the Home tab to view them). Warning: Leaving in extra paragraph marks, such as at the end of the document, will create unwanted extra documents in the corpus later on. However, there needs to be a single paragraph break at the end of the cleaned document.
- If tokenizing to words (as here), remove periods, question marks, and exclamation points. Do not do this if tokenizing to sentences.
- If tokenizing to words, you may wish to combine some words to keep them together to be treated as one word (e.g., convert "New York" to "NewYork"; "First Lady" to "FirstLady"). Likewise, examine dashes to see how terms with dashes should be handled.
- Remove other punctuation such as colons, apostrophes, commas, and double-dashes (use Ctrl-h in Word for replacing).
- Remove other extraneous symbols, such as the degree symbol. Consider removing numbers.
- You may need to convert foreign characters (e.g., the Latin n-tilde to n, the German o-umlaut to oe) if you get "invalid multibyte string, element" errors. Alternatively, consider a different encoding.
- When saving from Word at the end, select Unicode (UTF-8) encoding and leave unchecked "Insert line breaks".

Read the cleaned text from the working directory back into R.
For convenience, these txt files are also in the Data section of this book's Support Material (www.routledge.com/9780367624293).
```
CA_c <- readLines('CA_c.txt')
FL_c <- readLines('FL_c.txt')
LA_c <- readLines('LA_c.txt')
NY_c <- readLines('NY_c.txt')
TX_c <- readLines('TX_c.txt')
```

Optionally verify that the new objects are character vectors
```
class(CA_c)
```
[Output, verifying that a character vector is returned:]
```
      [1] "character"
```

Convert from character vectors to a "capital-C" SimpleCorpus using the tm package.
All txt files must be in the working directory.
```
governors_SimpleCorpus <- tm::SimpleCorpus(tm::VectorSource(unlist(lapply(c(CA_c,FL_
c,LA_c,NY_c,TX_c), as.character))))
class(governors_SimpleCorpus)
```
[Output:]
```
      [1] "SimpleCorpus" "Corpus"
```

Optionally, inspect governors_SimpleCorpus. Note that it contains the five state documents.
If there are more documents than five, unwanted paragraph markers were not eliminated.
```
inspect(governors_SimpleCorpus)
```

[Partial output:]
```
<<SimpleCorpus>>
Metadata:  corpus specific: 1, document level (indexed): 0
Content:  documents: 5
[1] Governor Gavin Newsom California values are not just a point of pride they
are the very fabric of our states history and our future California has been on
the leading edge of
. . .
```

```
# Convert from a SimpleCorpus to term document matrix (tdm) format using the tm package.
# Other conversions are discussed in a separate section of this chapter.
governors_tdm <- tm::TermDocumentMatrix(governors_SimpleCorpus, control =
list(removeNumbers = TRUE, removePunctuation=TRUE, stopwords = TRUE, stemming =
FALSE))
class(governors_tdm)
```
[Output:]
```
    [1] "TermDocumentMatrix"    "simple_triplet_matrix"
```

We now illustrate text analytic use of governors_tdm by creating word frequencies.

```
# Convert from tdm to matrix format
governors_matrix <- as.matrix(governors_tdm)

# Sort the matrix by word frequency
governors_matrix <- sort(rowSums(governors_matrix), decreasing=TRUE)

# Put the sorted matrix in a data frame
governors_df <- data.frame(word = names(governors_matrix), freq=governors_matrix)

# List out the 20 most frequent words with frequencies, descending
# Frequencies, of course, here reflect the combined web pages of the five gubernatorial sites.
head(governors_df, 20)
```
(Output:)
```
                    word freq
governor        governor   66
desantis        desantis   31
covid              covid   23
state              state   20
ron                  ron   20
abbott            abbott   17
florida          florida   15
will                will   14
program          program   13
newsom            newsom   12
new                  new   11
today              today   11
tallahassee tallahassee   11
order              order   10
announces      announces    9
firstlady      firstlady    9
small              small    9
california    california    8
executive      executive    8
fla                  fla    8
```

We see that on a day at a peak of the COVID-19 pandemic, the disease was the third most frequent term on gubernatorial web pages. Florida's Governor Ron DiSantis's last name, however, topped "COVID" in frequency. His was also the only first name on the top-20 list. Texas Governor Greg Abbott's last name frequency was sixth and California Governor Gavin Newsom's was tenth. The last names of New York's Andrew Cuomo and Louisiana's John Bel Edwards were absent from the most frequent terms list.

The purpose of the frequency listing above was only to demonstrate that information scraped from the web using the htm2txt method can be put to use in word frequency tables. Actually, once in one of the common text analysis formats, such as text-document (tdm) format, almost any of the analytic uses discussed later in this chapter could be employed. For instance, two gubernatorial web pages could be scraped by the htm2txt method, converted, and then contrasting word clouds could be created, to mention just one other use.

9.8.3 Web scraping: The "rvest" package

Web scraping associated with the htm2txt package is rudimentary, though possibly just what a given research purpose requires. Frequently, however, what is needed is to scrape a particular portion of a set of web page. For instance, Aydin (2018), in his book on web scraping, uses the rvest package to capture data on daily comment counts pertaining to a web page listing books. As another example, Keith McNulty has published a tutorial on using the rvest package to search "Billboard" web pages to retrieve song titles, artists, and song rankings, and insert this information into a data frame.[2] In general, more advanced programs such as rvest make it possible to retrieve selected elements from web pages from which to assemble data frames. Note also that the R world has many more packages useful for web scraping, including XML, xml2, rjson, RJSONIO, httr, RCurl, and selectr – many more than we can treat here.

9.8.3.1 A simple rvest web scraping example

In this subsection on web scraping, we present a simple example employing the widely used package "rvest".

```
# Setup
library(htm2txt)      # Utility to retrieve a website's text, stripping html tags
library(rvest)        # One of the leading web scraping packages for R
library(xml2)         # Supports rvest (and is a dependency of it)
setwd("C:/Data")      # Set the working directory

# Read in a url of interest. The resulting myurl object is of data class xml_node.
# This url is a page ranking the top 100 U.S. cities in descending order of population.
# Other variables to be retrieved from the listing are city name, state, and city website.
myurl <- xml2::read_html("https://www.baruch.cuny.edu/nycdata/world_cities/largest_
cities-usa.htm")

class(myurl)
[Output:]
      [1] "xml_document" "xml_node"
```

At this point we must identify the node in the web page containing the data we wish to retrieve. A recommended method is to use DevTools in the Chrome browser. This is shown in the Figure 9.5. The web page of interest is on the left and DevTools is on the right. Activate DevTools by typing Ctrl-Shift_C. The structure of the web page is shown in DevTools. When a node is selected in DevTools, the corresponding part of the web page lights up and allows the researcher to identify nodes of interest. In this case all the data columns are nodes of class "numbers".

```
# Read in a particular class of interest as class xml_nodeset
# The ".numbers" term points to all nodes of class "numbers".
mynode <- myurl %>% rvest::html_nodes(".numbers")
class(mynode)
[Output:]
      [1] "xml_nodeset"
```

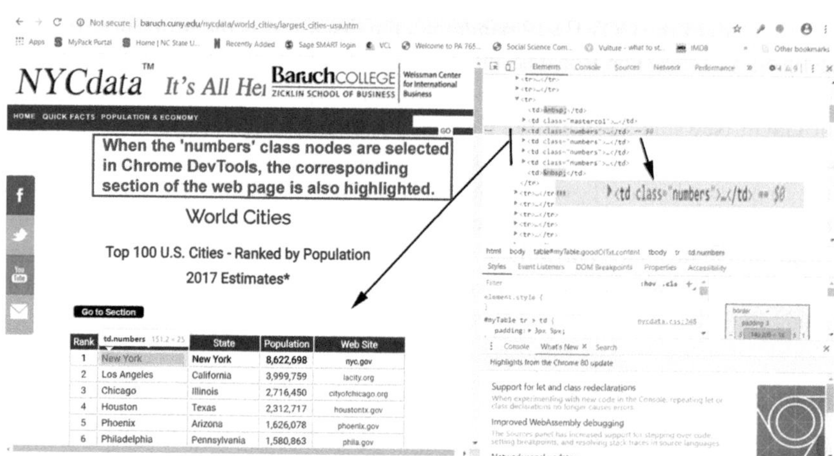

Figure 9.5 The example web page with Chrome DevTools open

```
# Scrape the text in the selected nodes into a character vector
myoutput <- mynode %>% rvest::html_text()
class(myoutput)
[Output:]
      [1] "character"

myoutput
[Partial output:]
  [1] "New York"                "New York"
  [3] "8,622,698"               "nyc.gov\r\n\r\n     "
  [5] "Los Angeles"             "California"
  [7] "3,999,759"               "lacity.org\r\n\r\n     "
  . . .
  [397] "Des Moines city"       "Iowa"
  [399] "217,521"               "\r\n\r\n    dmgov.org"
```

We cannot immediately use "myoutput" because each city has four rows, one for each variable, and there is only one column. In contrast, we want one row per city with separate columns for each variable. The method below creates a data frame of 1 column with 400 rows. We do not want this! We want separate columns for each variable.

```
mydf<- as.data.frame(myoutput)      # mydf is wrongly structured
```

To create a rightly-structured data frame we must read every fourth row into a separate vector, then add the vectors to a data frame as separate columns.

```
# Create a data frame to hold the 5 columns: Rank, city, state, population, website
# Initialize empty vectors
numrows = 100
rank <- rep(0, times=numrows)
city <- rep("", times=numrows)
state <- rep("", times=numrows)
population <- rep(0, times=numrows)
website <- rep("", times=numrows)

# Fill rank (by population), which is 1 to 100 since the original was already ordered this way
rank <- seq(1:100)

# Loop to fill other vectors from myoutput, in which every 4th row is a new city
# The four rows per city are: City, state, population, website
```

```
i =1
for (i in 1:numrows) {
   counter=i*4
   city[i]<- myoutput[counter-3]
   state[i]<- myoutput[counter-2]
   population[i]<- myoutput[counter-1]
   website[i]<- myoutput[counter]
}

# Strip "\r\n\r\n" and whitespace from the website vector
# We use the gsub() substitution command from R's base package
website <- gsub("\r\n\r\n ","",website)
website <- gsub(" ","",website)

# Add vectors to a new data frame called mydf.
mydf <- data.frame(rank,city,state,population, website)
head(mydf)
[Output:]
  rank         city        state population           website
1    1     New York     New York  8,622,698           nyc.gov
2    2  Los Angeles   California  3,999,759        lacity.org
3    3      Chicago     Illinois  2,716,450 cityofchicago.org
4    4      Houston        Texas  2,312,717      houstontx.gov
5    5      Phoenix      Arizona  1,626,078       phoenix.gov
6    6 Philadelphia Pennsylvania  1,580,863         phila.gov

#Optionally save the data frame to a comma-delimited file
write.csv(mydf, file = "mydata.csv", row.names = FALSE)
```

At this point we have successfully scraped the desired data from the Internet without downloading the entire page, as would have been the case had the htm2txt method discussed previously been used.

9.8.3.2 Scraping web elements with Chrome DevTools and the rvest package using XPaths

In this subsection, we take a different web page as an example and illustrate how to scrape a particular article from it. This is a web page on a county's response to the COVID-19 pandemic, mounted by Wake County Economic Development in Raleigh, NC, in February, 2021. We went to the web page shown below for "myurl", activated DevTools as before, then in DevTools highlighted the row in DevTools window that corresponds to "<article class="content_grid>". A section of the web page became highlighted. Then we right-clicked and from the DevTools context menu, selected Copy, then selected "Copy Full XPath". We pasted this below in the "xp =" line. While the reader is encouraged to try this on their own, content will have changed.

```
# Specify a url of interest
myurl <- "http://raleigh-wake.org/news-and-media/covid-19-resources"

# Read the url into an xml object
mynode <-xml2::read_html(myurl)
[Output:]
      [1] "xml_document" "xml_node"

# Use Chrome DevTools to find a particular section of the page
# Save its full XPath to xp
xp ="/html/body/div[2]/div/div/div/article"

# Save the section as an XML nodeset
myxml <- rvest::html_nodes(mynode,xpath=xp)
```

```
class(myxml)
[Output:]
      [1] "xml_nodeset"

# Convert from xm_nodeset to a simple character vector
mytext1 <- as.character(myxml)
class(mytext1)
[Output:]
      [1] "character"

# The selected article from the web page is now a character vector called mytext1
# It can be viewed simply by typing its name.
# It is not yet cleaned or saved to a file. That is discussed elsewhere in this chapter.
mytext1

[Partial output:]
   [1] "<article class=\"content grid\"><p>While there is not a clear path to know
   how or when to reopen your business, visit your favorite restaurant, or meet-up
   with friends, we can help provide resources so you can make the best decision for
   you. The well-being of Wake County and the region is a top priority for the
   Raleigh Chamber and Wake County Economic Development. Below, you will find a few
   resources that will help you decide how and when to continue moving forward.</p>
   . . .
```

9.8.3.3 Scraping a particular web element with Chrome DevTools and the htm2txt package

Using Chrome DevTools it is possible to scrap a particular web page element, which will contain the html code for that element. Then the htm2txt package may be used to strip the html code, leaving the plain text of the element. We illustrate for the NYC row of the same web page on city population rankings as used in Section 9.8.3.1.

Go to the web page ("https://www.baruch.cuny.edu/nycdata/world_cities/largest_cities-usa.htm"), activate DevTools as before, then in DevTools highlight the row in DevTools window (the "<tr>" html tag) that corresponds to the desired element. Here, this is the first row of the table, which is for NYC. Then right-click and from the DevTools context menu, select Copy, then select either "Copy Element" or "Copy OuterHTML". The captured element will then be in the Windows Clipboard. Paste it into a word processor, then save it as plain text, here as the file "NYrow.txt". For convenience, this text file is available in the Data section of the Support Material (www.routledge.com/9780367624293) for this text. Either way, place "NYrow.txt" in the working directory. Its contents with full of html code tags are as follows:

```
<tr>
  <td> </td>
  <td class="mastercol"><div align="center"><strong>1</strong></div></td>
  <td class="numbers"><div align="left" style="width:140px !important;"><strong>New
York</strong></div></td>
  <td class="numbers"><div align="left"><strong>New York</strong></div></td>
  <td class="numbers"><div align="center"><strong>8,622,698</strong></div></td>
  <td class="numbers"><div align="center"><strong><font size="2"><a href="http://
www.nyc.gov" target="_blank">nyc.gov</a></font></strong>
  </div></td>
  <td> </td>
</tr>
```

We then read NYrow.txt from the working directory back into R:

```
NYrow <- readLines('NYrow.txt')
```

We further strip out the html tags and display the result:

```
text <- htm2txt::htm2txt(NYrow)
text
[Output:]
   [1] "ï"¿"                                 ""
   [3] ""                                    ""
   [5] "1"                                   ""
   [7] "New York"                            ""
   [9] "New York"                            ""
  [11] "8,622,698"                           ""
  [13] "nyc.gov"                             ""
  [15] ""                                    ""
  [17] ""                                    ""
  [19] ""                                    ""
  [21] "/html/body/table[2]/tbody/tr[5]
```

Finally, we then retain in NYCrow the desired items:

```
NYCrow <- c(text[5],text[7],text[9],text[11],text[13])
NYCrow
[Output:]
   [1] "1"   "New York"   "New York"   "8,622,698" "nyc.gov"
```

NYCrow is a character vector, which could be added to a data frame. Below, however, we simply access its fourth element, which is the population of New York City.

```
class(NYCrow)
[Output:]
   [1] "character"

NYCrow[4]
[Output:]
   [1] "8,622,698"
```

9.9 Social media scraping

Twitter is but one of many well-known social media sources of text data. While direct retrieval from Twitter using the Twitter API as made available to researchers is possible, there are many restrictions. Twitter, for example, limits its retrieval to tweets in the last week and historical data is extremely limited. Typically only 3,200 tweets from a Twitter user's timeline are available, and only for the last 7–9 days. Even for current tweets, the Twitter API may not return all tweets but rather a sample. Moreover, the company imposes rigid privacy restrictions on release of data. Then the application for access to Twitter may take months to get a response and, if denied, appeal is not permitted.

It is also possible to obtain the archive of tweets pertaining to tweets you have sent from your own Twitter account. Go to https://twitter.com/settings/account. Click on "Your Twitter Data", then on the next screen under "Download your Twitter data", enter your Twitter password, then click "Confirm". On the next screen click "Request archive". Warning: You can make only one such request each 30 days. The response is not immediate but can take minutes to days.

Twitter restrictions and inconveniences have given rise to commercial services for Twitter text retrieval, including from Twitter itself. Some have access to Twitter's "firehose" level of capturing a Twitter stream and this is far richer than the API account an individual researcher may manage to obtain. For large-scale Twitter research, purchase from a commercial service is the norm. Such services vary considerably their search features, historical extent, and what can be delivered back to the researcher. Prices, generally aimed at corporate use, tend to be high, with the corollary that larger educational institutions may be able to license access while smaller ones cannot.

As the world of commercial Twitter access services is constantly changing with new companies entering and old ones exiting or merging. At this writing, some available services are these:

- Historical PowerTrack (https://developer.twitter.com/en/docs/tweets/batch-historical/overview) is from Twitter directly. It requires setting up an account with Twitter's enterprise sales team. It covers all publicly available tweets.
- Gnip had been a major commercial provider but is now part of Twitter's developer website at https://developer.twitter.com/en. Twitter has now added an academic research service at https://developer.twitter.com/en/solutions/academic-research/products-for-researchers.
- Brandwatch (https://www.brandwatch.com/), which in 2020 absorbed competitor CrimsonHexagon, provides access and online analytic tools for sentiment analysis of billions of historical social media observations. It claims to be the leading "digital consumer intelligence" service. It is heavily oriented toward commercial uses.
- Dialogfeed.com (https://www.dialogfeed.com/) aggregates multiple social media including Twitter, Facebook, Instagram, LinkedIn, Pinterest, YouTube, Weibo, and others. It is oriented toward reports for the individual's or company's own followings.
- Followersanalysis (https://www.followersanalysis.com/) is one of the most modestly priced services but it is oriented toward delivering 3,200 tweets per report and only for the individual or company's own Twitter following.

A third path, other than acquiring access to the Twitter API or purchasing data from a vendor, is to rely on one of the public collections of Twitter data. This is the path used in the example in this section. Two notable public collections are these:

- The Trump Twitter Archive (http://trumptwitterarchive.com/) is a free service which allows one to download small collections of tweets such as "741 tweets about Fake News". It covers several accounts for not only Donald Trump, but also Mike Pence, Hillary Clinton, and a few others. One may search by keyword or phrase for dates one selects. More details are in the example further below. Note that Twitter closed the Trump Twitter account on 8 January, 2021, but the archive is still operational at this writing.
- TweetSets (https://tweetsets.library.gwu.edu/) is maintained by George Washington University and is home to over 1.3 billion tweets at this writing. It may be used only for educational purposes and is free. The user can search on keywords and other parameters and will get back statistics for the set created, including a listing of top users, top mentions, top urls, and tweet type (original retweet, quote, reply). Actual text of the tweets is not available, however, except for a small set of sample tweets for the given search. Instead one may export tweet ids, mentions, top mentions, and top users.

9.9.1 Analysis of Twitter data: Trump and the *New York Times*

For the example in this section, we went to The Trump Twitter Archive (TTA) mentioned above. We entered as search terms [nytimes | "new york times"] but without the brackets. The vertical line signifies "or". We asked for the period from 1/1/2020 through 4/30/2020 and filtered out retweets. This generated a small dataset of 29 tweets in which President Trump mentioned one of these terms in the specified time period. When the "Export" button is clicked and then the "CSV" choice, a window opens with the results in .csv format. We cut and pasted this text into a word processor, then saved it under the filename "tweets.csv". For convenience, this file is available in the Data section of the Support Material (www.routledge.com/9780367624293) to this book. It should be put in the user's working directory.

After Twitter terminated Trump's Twitter Account, the Trump Twitter Archive changed and now defaults to saving in .json (Javascript Object Notation) format instead of the more widely-used .csv format. If the reader encounters this, the following steps apply.

1. In the Trump Twitter Archive, run your search with desired date or other filters.
2. Click the Export button. Search results will be put in a text box.
3. Copy the contents of the text box to your favorite text processor (one capable of saving plain text files without formatting). Save the file to a name ending in .json, such as trumptest.json.
4. On the web, go to https://json-csv.com/, which provides a free online json-to-csv converter. Upload trumptest.json, then, when prompted, click "DOWNLOAD CSV".
5. The file "trumptest.csv" will be saved to your Download folder. Copy it to the working directory you are using for R, such as "C:/Data".

6. Read the file into R: `trumptest <- read.csv('trumptest.csv', stringsAsFactors = FALSE)`. The trumptest object is a data frame.
7. The actual tweets will in the column labeled "text" (i.e., trumptest$text).
8. To use this file with the remainder of the R code in this section, copy trumptest to an object named "tweets": `tweets <- trumptest`. Output for the remaining coverage of this section will be the same as described below, with slight variations due to JSON file structure and due to date of retrieval of the tweets. Alternatively, however, the R code below uses the file "tweets.csv", which is available in the Data section of the Support Material (www.routledge.com/9780367624293) to this text.

The first line of tweets.csv lists the column names: source, text, created_at, retweet_count, favorite_count, is_retweet, and id_str. While there are a variety of forms of analysis that might be done using these variables, in this section we just focus on use of the "text" column, which contains the actual text of the tweets.[3]

```
# Setup
library(tm)            # Text Miner, a leading text analytics package in R
library(dendextend) # Supports enhanced dendrograms for cluster analysis
library(wordcloud)  # To create word clouds
library(dplyr)         # Supports glimpse() and other utility functions
setwd("C:/Data")       # Set the working directory

# Import Twitter data stored as a comma-separated values (csv) file
# Tweets are put into the object "tweets", which is of class "data.frame".
tweets <- read.csv('tweets.csv', stringsAsFactors = FALSE)

# View the structure of tweets
# We observe that the second column is "text", our main focus
dplyr::glimpse(tweets)
[Output:]
   Rows: 29
   Columns: 7
   $ source          <chr> "Twitter for iPhone", "Twitter for iPhone", "Twitte...
   $ text            <chr> "If you listened to the flawed advice of @paulkrugm...
   $ created_at      <chr> "01-19-2020 00:32:23", "01-19-2020 00:42:23", "01-1...
   $ retweet_count   <int> 1865, 1388, 18569, 11887, 3934, 25741, 19320, 35130...
   $ favorite_count <int> 6506, 4817, 78331, 47171, 16463, 121306, 78879, 120...
   $ is_retweet      <chr> "false", "false", "false", "false", "false", "false...
   $ id_str          <dbl> 1.218693e+18, 1.218695e+18, 1.218698e+18, 1.221427e...

# Print out the number of rows in tweets
# Output (not shown) confirms there are 29 rows (tweets), same as for glimpse()above.
nrow(tweets)

# Create a character vector from the text column of tweets,
# putting results in the object trump_tweets. This object is of class "character".
trump_tweets <- tweets$text

# View some of the character vector
head(trump_tweets)
[Partial output:]
   [1] "If you listened to the flawed advice of @paulkrugman at the @nytimes a
   newspaper that was going broke until I came along you would have entirely missed
   the RECORD BREAKING Stock Market (and other) numbers produced since Election Day
   2016. Sorry those are the FACTS...."
   . . .
```

```
[6] ""A lot of people feel defeated...Trump always wins. It seems like nothing
can stop him." Danny Villazon  @nytimes @DanaPerino @FoxNews  But isn't that what
you want from your President?"

# Convert trump_tweets from a character vector to a vector source
# trump_source is of classes "VectorSource", "SimpleSource", and "Source"
trump_source <- tm::VectorSource(trump_tweets)

# Make a volatile corpus called trump_vcorpus
# trump_corpus is of classes "VCorpus" and "Corpus"
trump_vcorpus <- tm::VCorpus(trump_source)

# How to display content of a given tweet (#22) in the trump_vcorpus
trump_vcorpus[[22]]$content
[Output:]
   [1] "So now the Fake News @nytimes is tracing the CoronaVirus origins back to
   Europe NOT China. This is a first! I wonder where the Failing New York Times got
   for this one? Are there any NAMED sources? They were recently thrown out of China
   like dogs and obviously want back in. Sad!"

# Clean the volatile corpus
# First create the function "clean_corpus", using multiple tm _ map() operations
# Note one may add additional stop words at this point.
clean_corpus <- function(corpus){
   corpus <- tm::tm_map(corpus, stripWhitespace)
   corpus <- tm::tm_map(corpus, removePunctuation)
   corpus <- tm::tm_map(corpus, content_transformer(tolower))
   corpus <- tm::tm_map(corpus, removeWords, c(stopwords("en"), "while","will",
"since", "can","amp"))
   return(corpus) }

# Then apply the cleaning function to trump_corpus
trump_vcorpus2 <- clean_corpus(trump_vcorpus)

# Create a "term document matrix" from the cleaned object which is trump_vcorpus2
trump_tdm <- tm::TermDocumentMatrix(trump_vcorpus2)

# Print trump_tdm data. We see there are 352 terms (words) in 29 documents (tweets).
trump_tdm
[Output:]
   <<TermDocumentMatrix (terms: 351, documents: 29)>>
   Non-/sparse entries: 663/9516
   Sparsity           : 93%
   Maximal term length: 18
   Weighting          : term frequency (tf)

# Also create a tdm limited to 25 words
# This is used later to produce a less cluttered dendrogram for cluster analysis of tweet terms
trump_tdm25 <-trump_tdm[names(tail(sort(rowSums(as.matrix(trump_tdm))), 25)),]
trump_tdm25
[Output:]
   <<TermDocumentMatrix (terms: 25, documents: 29)>>
   Non-/sparse entries: 175/550
   Sparsity           : 76%
   Maximal term length: 14
   Weighting          : term frequency (tf)
```

Compute inter-term distances for trump_tdm25 for purposes of cluster analysis
The resulting hc object is of class "hclust", standing for hierarchical clustering.
```
hc <- stats::hclust(d = stats::dist(trump_tdm25, method = "euclidean"), method =
"complete")
```

Plot a basic cluster analysis dendrogram
Dendrograms for cluster analysis were discussed in Chapter 2.
```
plot(hc)
```
[Output not shown, but a basic dendrogram is produced:]
Create a better dendrogram with the "dendextend" package
Convert from class hclust (which hc is) to class dendrogram (which hcd is)
```
hcd <- stats::as.dendrogram(hc)
```

Print the labels in hcd. The labels command is from R's "base" package.
```
labels(hcd)
```
[Output not shown but all 25 terms in hcd are listed]

Change the branch color to red for two terms of interest: "fake" and "news"
These terms must be in hcd (type `labels(hcd)` to check)
```
hcd <- dendextend::branches_attr_by_labels(hcd, c("fake", "news"), color = "red")
```

Plot hcd as a horizontal dendrogram with terms of interest in red. This is Figure 9.6.
```
plot(hcd, horiz=TRUE)
```

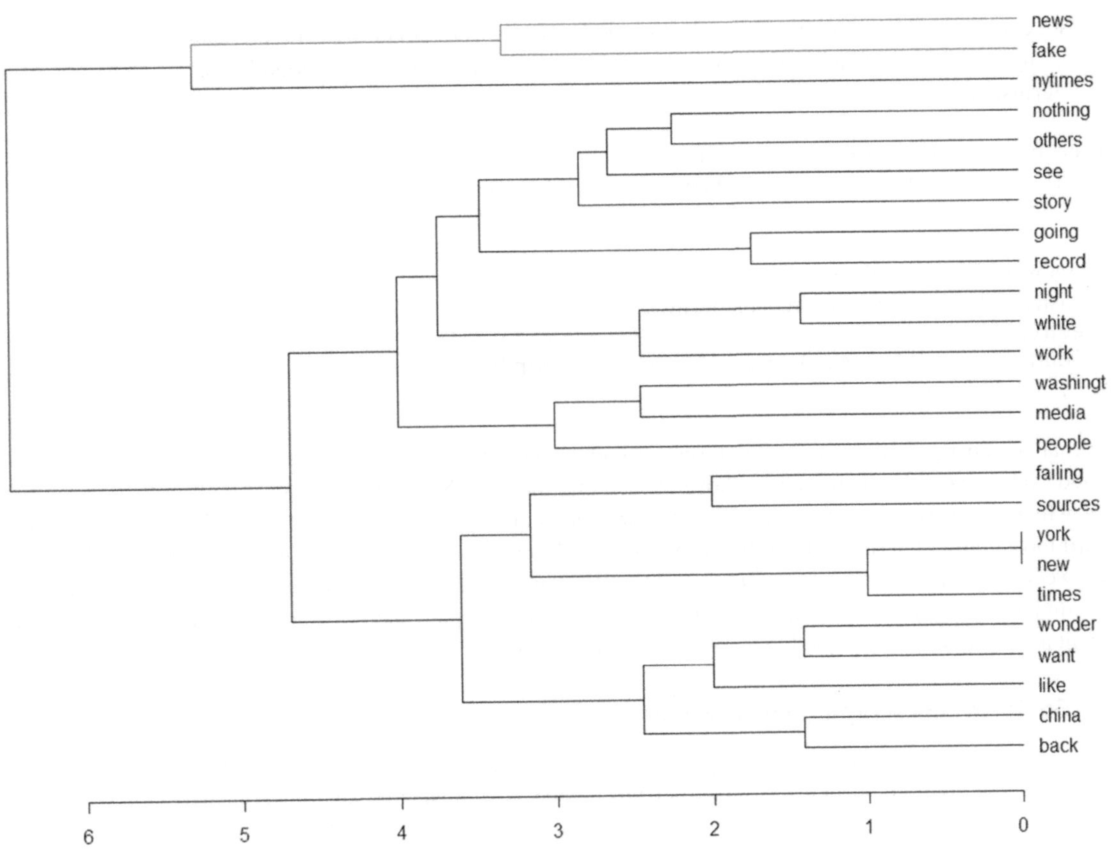

Figure 9.6 Dendrogram of tweets for the two-cluster solution

For the smaller set of 25 most frequent terms in the "tweets" dataset, the two-cluster solution shows one cluster containing "nytimes", "fake", and "news". The other cluster contains the other 22 terms. Note that here the individual words in New York Time are separate. In a more complex analysis we could have created a trigram keeping "New York Times" together. An even simpler way would have been to replace all instances of "New York Times" with "nytimes" during pre-processing. Nonetheless, the dendrogram above is supportive of the research hypothesis that President Trump continued to associate the New York Times with "fake news" in the 4-month period studied.

We can explore this further using word frequencies for all words in "tweets", not just the top 25. For this purpose we now go back to the trump_tdm object. Our objective is to compute term frequencies for frequency tables and barplots which may or may not show the association of New York Times with "fake news".

```
# Start by creating a matrix called trump_m
trump_matrix <- as.matrix(trump_tdm)

# The rowSums() in the matrix are term_frequency
term_frequency <- base::rowSums(trump_matrix)

# Sort term_frequency in descending order
trump_termfrequency <- base::sort(term_frequency, decreasing = TRUE)

# View the top 10 most common terms
trump_termfrequency[1:10]

# Make the list of top frequencies into a barchart. This is Figure 9.7.
barplot(trump_termfrequency[1:10], col = "lightblue", las = 2)
```

Finally, we can display the same frequency data in the form of a word cloud, which graphically highlights the association of "nytimes" with "fake" and "news". The difference is that in the word cloud below we show the 80 most frequent terms, not just 10.

```
# Convert from trump_termfrequeny to a data frame
trump_df <- data.frame( term = names(trump_termfrequency), num =
trump_termfrequency)

# Create a word cloud based on trump_df. This is Figure 9.8.
# Later-listed colors are for more frequent terms.
set.seed(23)
wordcloud(trump_df$term, trump_df$num, max.words = 80, colors = c("red", "darkred",
"blue", "darkblue"))
```

Recall that in setting up the "tweets" dataset we had requested "nytimes" and "New York Times" but had not requested "fake news". In the bar chart above we see that the New York Times terms are all in the top ten in frequency, which is hardly surprising since this was our tweet request. However, that "fake" and "news" are the second and third most common terms in the top ten (bar plot) and top 80 (word cloud) is evidence supporting the idea that Trump tweets associate the *New York Times* (and the *Washington Post*) with "fake news". We end our discussion of Twitter analysis here but note that many other techniques in this chapter, such as word correlations, word maps, and sentiment analysis might be applied to analysis of Twitter data.

9.9.2 Social media scraping with twitter

Twitter analysis is a large topic which easily could be a book unto itself. Though we only have space here to introduce it briefly, the "twitteR" package from author Jeff Gentry is at present the leading R package for Twitter analysis. The twitteR package is designed to provide access to the Twitter API within R, meaning that the researcher must have an account with API access. The package then allows users to select subsets of Twitter data of research interest.

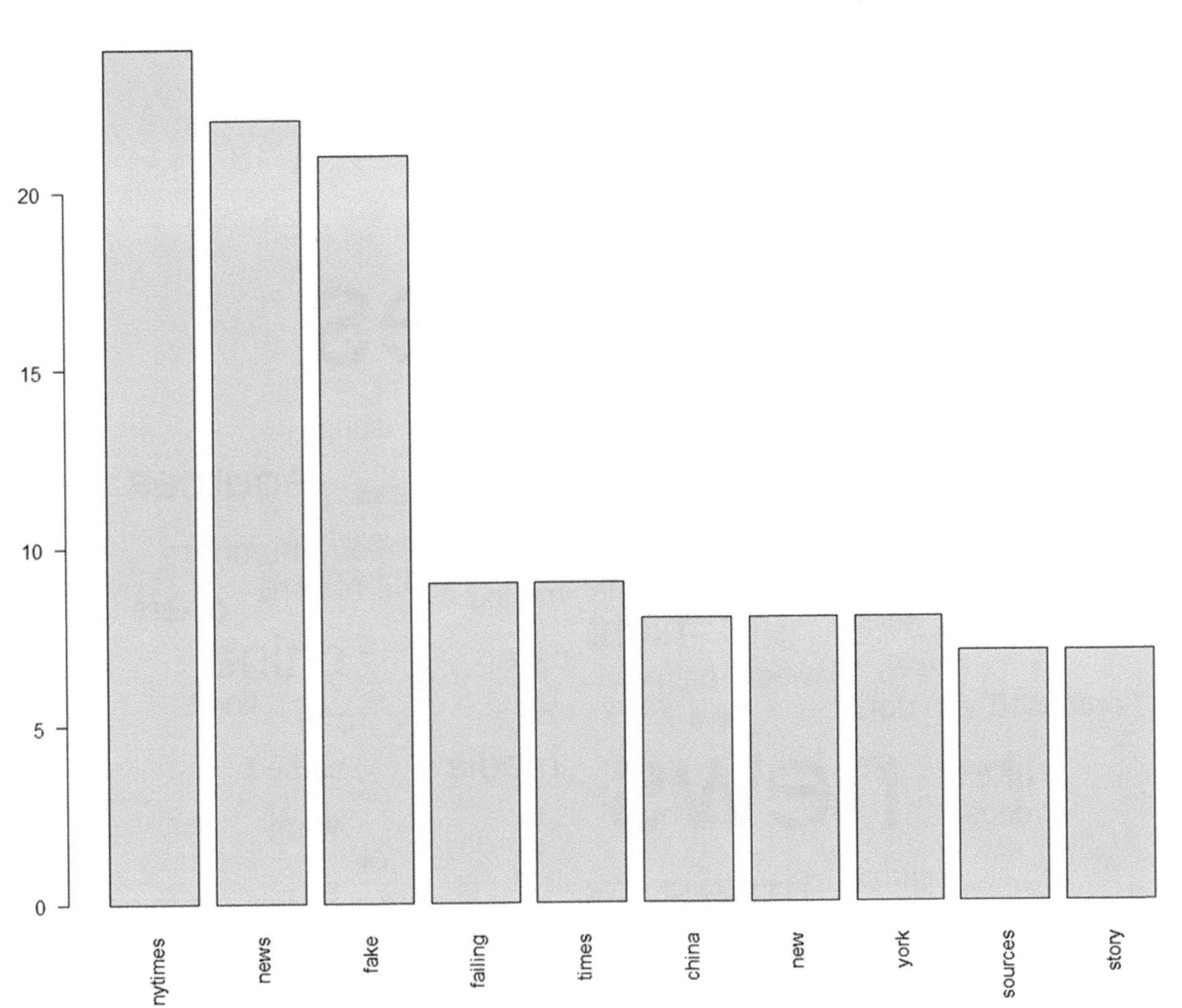

Figure 9.7 Bar plot of ten most frequent terms in Trump tweets

The Twitter API will only allow retrieval of a limited number of tweets for a limited number of days. Over time, of course, the researcher might accumulate a large database of tweets in spite of such limitations.

The researcher must acquire a developer account with Twitter, which will confer four needed codes: The API key, the API secret (secret key), the access token, and the access token secret. It is outside the scope of this chapter to detail the process of acquiring an account and, moreover, Twitter keeps changing the web address, procedures, and rules. However, by searching for "apply for a Twitter developer account" will return pages from Twitter and others with instructions on how to do this. Getting an account may take a day to months (about a week for the author). Tip: Read Twitter policies carefully and make sure your statements in the application conform to policies. The R code below assumes you have an account with valid codes.

```
# Setup
library(twitteR)

# Set up Twitter access codes from your developer account
# In this format but switch in the actual codes:
# setup_twitter_oauth("API key", "API secret", "Access token", "Access secret")
# Your code will look similar to that below, but these codes aren't valid. You must get your own.
```

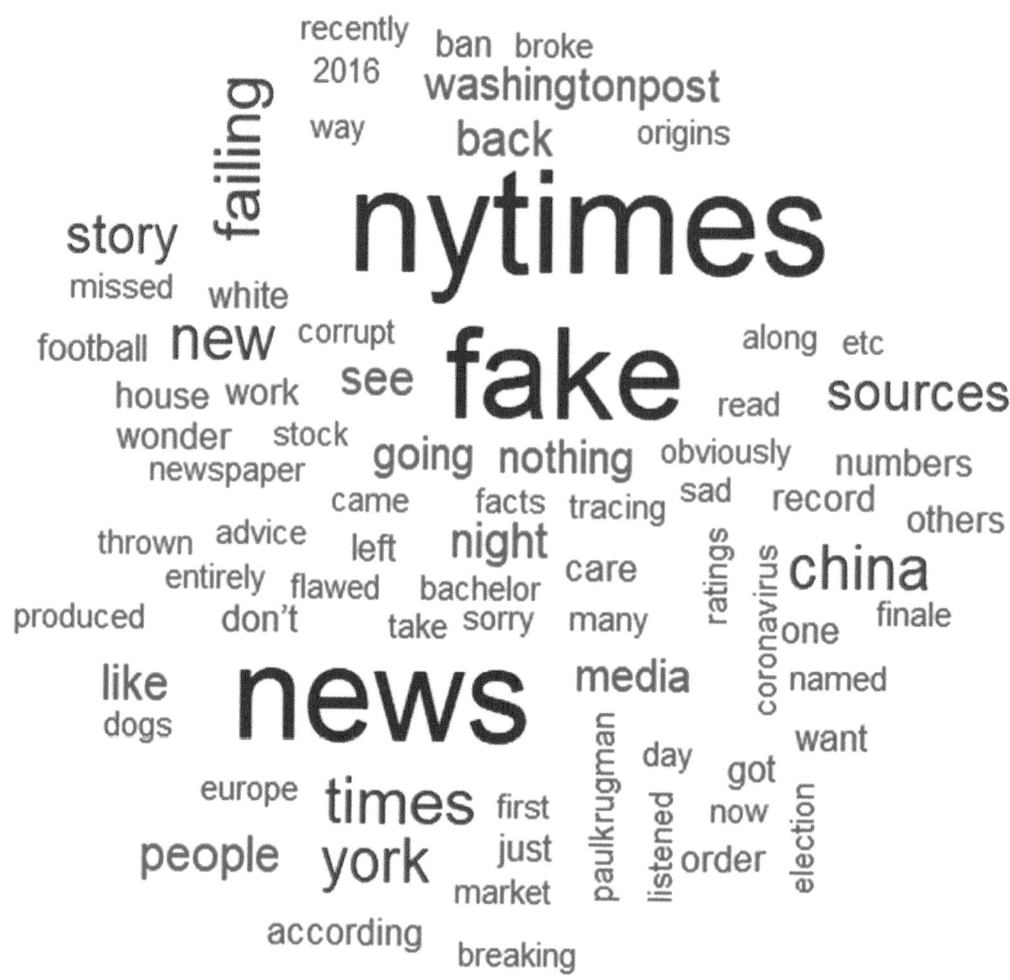

Figure 9.8 Word cloud of 80 most frequent terms in Trump tweets

```
setup_twitter_oauth("92H1XfbaPibHzPi1SgPAWGDUA",
"m0aeiQr0UNDUtDiQf5GEXgS63gUy5tsXJR7sEJME7qtZkQsv3R",
"1253742199373881844-890ld9qjoLmJR9d4lukTq8umQPckCr",
"jX8JvzHu8TcM11i4Gk9pQP5Ca96Vd5rmU41b9q1kKY0wp")
[Output:]
      [1] "Using direct authentication"

# Search for 50 tweets with "#COVID19" since 18 February 2020, filtering for English language.
# Put the date in yyyy-mm-dd format
# The tweets object is of type "list".
tweets = twitteR::searchTwitter('#COVID19', n=50, since='2020-02-18', lang='eng')

# Display tweet number6 (user handle changed).
tweets[6]
```

```
[Output:]
  [1] "Dorothy Imregon342: RT @Our_languages: Viruses don't distinguish between a
sneeze and a laugh. They're spread particularly through the #droplets we release
int…"

# Convert from list to a data frame with the "text" column as a character vector of tweets.
# Other conversions in format are possible, described elsewhere in this chapter.
tweets_df <- twitteR::twListToDF(tweets)

# List all the columns in the data frame
names(tweets_df)
[Output:]
  [1] "text"          "favorited"     "favoriteCount" "replyToSN"
  [5] "created"       "truncated"     "replyToSID"    "id"
  [9] "replyToUID"    "statusSource"  "screenName"    "retweetCount"
 [13] "isRetweet"     "retweeted"     "longitude"     "latitude"

# List the first two tweets in the data frame
head(tweets_df$text, 2)
[Output:]
 [1] "RT @CanadaTrade: On April 30, \U0001f1e8\U0001f1e6, Korea, Singapore,
 Australia and New Zealand signed a joint statement supporting concrete actions to
 keep…"
 [2] "RT @Our_languages: Viruses don't distinguish between a sneeze and a laugh.
 They're spread particularly through the #droplets we release int…"
```

The twitteR package has many more useful functions, such as `strip _ retweets()`, which filters out retweets. Under the "Packages" tab of RStudio, click on "twitteR", then select "User guides, package vignettes and other documentation" for a description of what the twitter package can do, which is much more than described here.

9.10 Leading text formats in R

9.10.1 Overview

In this section, we outline the primary text analysis formats used in R. Formats are associated with particular packages. To use a package's tools, the researcher usually needs the text to be in the package's preferred format. For instance, to use "tidytext" tools such as the tools to tokenize text into words, sentences, or other units, one first needs to convert text documents into "tidy format". There are other formats; of course, the most widely used being perhaps the "corpus format" associated with the "tm" (Text Miner) package, discussed in Section 9.10.3.

This subsection on text formats is admittedly on the dull-but-necessary side as it does not directly lead to the interesting deliverables of text analysis such as word clouds, word maps, topic analysis, or sentiment analysis. When the researcher comes to do these things, however, being in the right text format or converting to it is simply essential.

Text analysis format is different from file format. The reader will be aware that text may be in a variety of file formats such as.csv, plain text (.txt), Word (.docx or .doc), web formats (.html, .htm), spreadsheet format (.xls, .xlsx), R data.frame format, and many others. For some commands in R, text may be processed using its original file format. However, it is possible to get text from any original file format into the desired text analysis format as discussed in subsections below, though this may involve cleaning files first. Once a text object is in the desired text analytic format (e.g., tidytext format), text processing commands based on that text analysis format may be used directly even though the same commands might not be used on the original source file formats.

For more detail on the commands mentioned in this chapter, install the package containing the command of interest, load it with the `library()` command, then type `help(name _ of _ command)`.

In commands below, as elsewhere, we use package prefixes to make explicit which commands use which packages (e.g., `quanteda::corpus(data _ corpus _ inaugural)` for the `corpus()` command from the quanteda package).

9.10.2 Formats related to the "tidytext" package

A "token" is usually a word but may be a sentence or other unit of analysis, as discussed in the section on "Tokenization" further below. In tidy text format, a table or data frame has one token per document per row, usually a word. If there are multiple documents, each document is a set of rows, but each row has one token (e.g., one word) used in that document. Such tables/data frames are created by the `unnest _ tokens()` program of the tidytext package. After being put into tidy format, text may be processed by a number of other text-handling packages such as tidyr, dplyr, and ggplot2, as illustrated in later sections on types of text analysis.

While "tidytext" is the primary text mining package associated with tidy format, there are over 50 related packages. A list is available at https://cran.r-project.org/web/packages/available_packages_by_name.html. The followings are among them:

- tidyverse: Install and load tidyverse packages, with functions to list them, list current versions, and list conflicts.
- tidyr: Tidy messy data
- tidygraph: A tidy API for graph manipulation
- tidyxl: Read untidy Excel files
- tidycensus: Load US Census boundary and attribute data as "tidyverse"-ready data frames
- tidyfast: Fast tidying of data tables

Many commands may be used with text once it is in tidy format. To give a few instances, text in tidy format may be used to create a "sentiment lexicon" using the `inner _ join()` command from the dplyr package. The `summarize()` command,[4] also part of dplyr, creates summarized text, which may be visualized using the "ggplot2" package. The `gather()`, `separate()`, and `spread()` functions in the tidyr package may be used to restructure data, such as by moving variables into columns. Some later sections of this chapter illustrate the tidy format, such as the section on "Word frequencies and histograms". For further information, see also the text by Silge and Robinson (2017), which is subtitled, "A Tidy Approach". Other sections of this chapter, however, illustrate other text analytic formats.

A data frame is in tidytext format, loosely defined, if it has one token (e.g., word) per row. As discussed below, however, many tidytext operations require a stricter definition involving a tidytext tibble-type data frame with certain columns (document, term, count) as well as one term per row. Note that tidytext format is different from a "string", which is a character vector, though strings may be assembled into a data frame and might then be in tidytext format. Also in contrast to tidytext format, a "lower-c" corpus object (from the quanteda package) contains strings as character vectors but these are not tidytext. Tidytext format is also different from the document-term matrix (dtm) format, discussed in Section 9.10.4, which has one row per document and one column for each term.

To illustrate conversion using tidytext format, we use text data from Project Gutenberg, specifically the Declaration of Independence and the U.S. Constitution, as earlier.

```
# Setup
library(tidytext)    # One of the main text analysis programs for R
library(tm )         # A second major program, Text Miner
library(gutenbergr) # A public domain collection of many books and documents
library(dplyr)       # A utility package supporting count and many other operations

# Create FoundingDocs, which is an R data frame object.
# The mirror= option may be omitted if the default mirror site is operational.
# Otherwise add a different mirror site such as that below (see earlier discussion).
FoundingDocs <- gutenbergr::gutenberg_download(c(1,5), meta_fields = "title", mirror =
"http://mirrors.xmission.com/gutenberg/")

# Verify that it is a tibble-type data frame
class(FoundingDocs)
[Output:]
     [1] "tbl_df"     "tbl"        "data.frame"
```

```
# Show its first three rows
# We see the data are not stripped of Project Gutenberg's header lines.
head(FoundingDocs,3)
[Output:]
    gutenberg_id text                                  title
           <int> <chr>                                 <chr>
  1            1 "December, 1971  [Etext #1]"          The Declaration of Indepen~
  2            1 ""                                    The Declaration of Indepen~
  3            1 ""                                    The Declaration of Indepen~
  4            1 "The Project Gutenberg Etext~         The Declaration of Indepen~
```

We can type `View(FoundingDocs)` to manually inspect it in RStudio. When we do so, we find that rows 1–45 and 2054–2087 are Project Gutenberg header meta-information. We can also view or calculate that there are 2,680 rows in all:

```
nrow(FoundingDocs)
[Output number of rows]
    [1] 2680
```

We now create FoundingDocs2, a version without meta-information. If we wanted, we could have overwritten the original FoundingDocs instead. We ask for rows `46:2053` and `2088:2680`. Nothing after the comma means we are requesting all columns.

```
FoundingDocs2 <- FoundingDocs[c(46:2053, 2088:2680),]
head(FoundingDocs2, 6)
[Output:]
  # A tibble: 6 x 3
    gutenberg_id text                           title
           <int> <chr>                          <chr>
  1            1 "THE DECLARATION OF INDEPEND~  The Declaration of Indepen~
  2            1 ""                             The Declaration of Indepen~
  3            1 ""                             The Declaration of Indepen~
  4            1 "When in the Course of human~  The Declaration of Indepen~
  5            1 "one people to dissolve the ~  The Declaration of Indepen~
  6            1 "them with another, and to a~  The Declaration of Indepen~
```

Above, FoundingDocs2 contains lines (not words) associated with the U.S. Constitution and the Declaration of Independence. It has the columns gutenberg_id, text, and title. It is a data frame, just like FoundingDocs earlier. We now use FoundingDocs2 to create FDwords, which is in tidytext format. To do this we pipe FoundingDocs2 to dplyr's `count()` command and to tidytext's `unnest _ tokens()` command:

```
FoundingDocs2 %>% dplyr::count(title)
FDwords <- FoundingDocs2 %>% tidytext::unnest_tokens(word, text)
```

FDwords is a tibble-type data frame. Ordinary data frames are a subset of tibbles, which are a more versatile data format. Thus, "tbl_df" stands for "tibble data frame". It may be treated either as a tibble ("tbl") or as a data frame ("data.frame").

```
class(FDwords)
[Output:]
    [1] "tbl_df"     "tbl"         "data.frame"

# Look at the first 6 rows of FDwords and note its column names.
head(FDwords,6)
```

[Output:]
```
# A tibble: 6 x 3
  gutenberg_id title                                          word
         <int> <chr>                                          <chr>
1            1 The Declaration of Independence of the United ~ the
2            1 The Declaration of Independence of the United ~ declarat~
3            1 The Declaration of Independence of the United ~ of
4            1 The Declaration of Independence of the United ~ independ~
5            1 The Declaration of Independence of the United ~ of
6            1 The Declaration of Independence of the United ~ the
```

As there is one word per row (in the "word" column), FDwords is in tidy format. In general, data frames are in tidy format when created by the `unnest _ tokens()` command from the tidytext package, as here.

To convert from tidytext to a dtm or to a term-document matrix (tdm), both from the "tm" package, or to a document feature matrix (dfm) from the "quanteda" package, use the tidytext commands `cast(tdm)`, `cast _ dtm()`, and `cast(dfm)`. We use FDwords, the just-discussed tibble data frame in tidy format, as an example. Below we also distinguish between a broader and a stricter definition of a "tidy format data frame".

FDwords is a tidy-format tibble data frame with the columns gutenberg_id, title, and word. It is in tidy format in the sense that there is one row per word. However, it is not in tidy format in the same sense as FDwords_tidy_df created below. Note below that the columns differ between FDwords and FDwords_tidy_df, even though each has one row per word and are both tibble-type data frames.

The next several operations conclude this subsection by showing how to convert FDwords into any of several popular data analytic formats.

1. Create a character vector.

```
# Convert from a data frame to a character vector
# This assumes the column labeled "word" is the character variable of interest.
# The text variable of interest will vary.
FDwords_vector <- as.character(FDwords$word)
class(FDwords_vector)
[Output:]
      [1] "character"
```

2. From a character vector, create a "capital-C" Corpus using the tm package.

```
FDwords_Corpus <-
tm::SimpleCorpus(VectorSource(unlist(lapply(FDwords_vector, as.character))))
class(FDwords_Corpus)
      [1] "SimpleCorpus" "Corpus"
```

3. Convert from a "capital-C" Corpus to a dtm using the tm package.

```
FDwords_dtm<- tm::DocumentTermMatrix(FDwords_Corpus, control =
list(removeNumbers = TRUE, removePunctuation=TRUE, stopwords = TRUE, stemming =
TRUE))
class(FDwords_dtm)
```

4. Convert from dtm to strict-definition tidy-format data frame. FDwords_tidy_df has the columns document, term, and count. This is the type of "tidy format" object that is required by the `cast()` commands below.

```
FDwords_tidy_df<-tidytext::tidy(FDwords_dtm)
class(FDwords_tidy_df)
[Output:]
      [1] "tbl_df"     "tbl"        "data.frame"
```

5. Convert from a tidy text tibble-type data frame to back to tdm format.

```
FDwords_tdm <- FDwords_tidy_df %>% tidytext::cast_tdm(document, term,
count)class(FDwords_tdm)
```

```
[Output:]
        [1] "TermDocumentMatrix"    "simple_triplet_matrix"
```

6. Convert from a tidy text tibble data frame to back to dtm format, which is particularly associated with the tm package.

```
FDwords_dtm <- FDwords_tidy_df %>% tidytext::cast_dtm(document, term, count)
class(FDwords_dtm)
[Output:]
        [1] "DocumentTermMatrix"    "simple_triplet_matrix"
```

7. Convert from a tidy text tibble data frame to a document feature matrix (dfm) format, which is particularly associated with the quanteda package.

```
FDwords_dfm <- FDwords_tidy_df %>% tidytext::cast_dfm(document, term, count)
class(FDwords_dfm)
[Output:]
        [1] "dfm"
        attr(,"package")
        [1] "quanteda"
```

Not treated here, the tidytext package also has the similar command `cast _ sparse()`, which is for converting to a sparse matrix associated with the Matrix package, creating a "Matrix object".

9.10.3 Formats related to the "tm" package

The "tm" package is among the most widely used text analysis toolsets in R. It supports the reading in of file formats such as .csv, .txt, .pdf, and .xml. It also supports a variety of data preparation commands for such functions as stop words, stemming, and whitespace removal. Commonly, the "document feature matrix" (dfm) format is used with tm, but tm also supports export to the tdm format. Below we discuss the tm package and its use with some commands from the quanteda package discussed in the next section. The command prefixes "tm::" and "quanteda::" are not strictly needed if both packages are active, but this clarifies where functions are from.

The "tm" package creates a "Corpus" object, written in upper case, to distinguish it from a lower-case "corpus", which is associated with the quanteda package. A Corpus may be transformed to a dtm. However, as we discuss below, a Corpus comes in two very different flavors: VCorpus and SimpleCorpus. The "quanteda" package (another R package for quantitative analysis of text) creates lower-case "corpus", which also may be transformed into a document feature matrix (dfm) as well as to dtm and tdm formats as discussed below. Once in one of these formats, a text object may be converted to summarized text using the `cast _ dtm()` and `cast _ dfm()` commands from the "tidytext" package, illustrated in the previous section, after which text may be visualized using the ggplot2 package. Note that tdm and dtm formats are discussed and illustrated more extensively in the sections further below on "Common text file conversions" and on "Analysis: Word maps and word correlations", and elsewhere in this chapter.

In this section, we first read in example data for the dataset "crude", which comes with the "tm" package. This dataset contains twenty example news articles from the Reuters news service. It is of class "Corpus" ("capital-C"). The tm package also has the `readReut21578XML()` and `readReut21578XMLasPlain()` functions to read in Reuters XML documents.

```
#Setup
library(quanteda)
library(tm)
setwd("C:/Data")

# Read in the "crude" Corpus of texts and verify its class, which is a Corpus of type VCorpus.
data("crude")
```

```
class(crude)
[Output:]
      [1] "VCorpus" "Corpus"

# We can create a Corpus of type SimpleCorpus" also, for comparison.
# Note that corp1 is composed of document vectors, not the documents in raw form.
corp1 <- tm::Corpus(tm::VectorSource(crude))
class(corp1)
[Output:]
      [1] "SimpleCorpus" "Corpus"
```

In the example above, both crude and corp1 are a Corpus, though of different types (VCorpus and SimpleCorpus respectively). The VCorpus for crude is a “List of 20” as shown in RStudio’s environment listing, reflecting all 20 news articles. The corp1 SimpleCorpus version is a “List of 3”, only the first of which has content (it contains all 20 articles). Both have all the text, but in very different formats.

```
crude
[Output:]
  <<VCorpus>>
  Metadata:  corpus specific: 0, document level (indexed): 0
  Content:  documents: 20

corp1
[Output:]
  <<SimpleCorpus>>
  Metadata:  corpus specific: 1, document level (indexed): 0
  Content:  documents: 3
```

Below, we use an index to view a particular document, such as the first one. Use as.character to see the actual (but uncleaned) text.

```
crude[1]
[Output:]
  <<VCorpus>>
  Metadata:  corpus specific: 0, document level (indexed): 0
  Content:  documents: 1

as.character(crude[1])
[Output:]
   [1] "list('reut-00001.xml' = list(content = \"Diamond Shamrock Corp said that\\
  neffective today it had cut its contract prices for crude oil by\\n1.50 dlrs a
  barrel.\\n    The reduction brings its posted price for West Texas\\nIntermediate
  to 16.00 dlrs a barrel, the copany said.\\n    \\\"The price reduction today was
  made in the light of falling\\noil product prices and a weak crude oil market,\\\"
  a company\\nspokeswoman said.\\n    Diamond is the latest in a line of U.S. oil
  companies that\\nhave cut its contract, or posted, prices over the last two days\\
  nciting weak oil markets.\\n Reuter\", \n    meta = list(author = character(0),
  datetimestamp = list(sec = 56, min = 0, hour = 17, mday = 26, mon = 1, year = 87,
  wday = 4, yday = 56, isdst = 0), description = \"\", heading = \"DIAMOND SHAMROCK
  (DIA) CUTS CRUDE PRICES\", id = \"127\", language = \"en\", origin =
  \"Reuters-21578 XML\", topics = \"YES\", lewissplit = \"TRAIN\", cgisplit =
  \"TRAINING-SET\", oldid = \"5670\", places = \"usa\", people = character(0), orgs =
  character(0), exchanges = character(0))))"
  [2] "list()"
```

```
# We now try the same thing with corp1, a SimpleCorpus
corp1[1]
[Output:]
   <<SimpleCorpus>>
   Metadata:  corpus specific: 1, document level (indexed): 0
   Content:  documents: 1

as.character(corp1[1])
[Partial output:]
   [1] "list('reut-00001.xml' = list(content = \"Diamond Shamrock Corp said that\\
  neffective today it had cut its contract prices for crude oil by\\n1.50 dlrs a
  barrel.\\n    The reduction brings its posted price for West Texas\\nIntermediate
  to 16.00 dlrs a barrel
  [And so on, listing all the Reuters documents under corp1[1],  not just
  reut-00001.]
  . . .
  [2] "list(language = \"en\")"
  [3] "list()"
```

Both types of Corpus (VCorpus and SimpleCorpus) may be viewed with tm's `inspect()` command, also revealing different contents,

```
# Inspecting crude, a VCorpus
tm::inspect(crude)
[Partial output:]
  <<VCorpus>>
  Metadata:  corpus specific: 0, document level (indexed): 0
  Content:  documents: 20

  $'reut-00001.xml'
  <<PlainTextDocument>>
  Metadata:  15
  Content:  chars: 527
  . . .
  $'reut-00023.xml'
  <<PlainTextDocument>>
  Metadata:  15
  Content:  chars: 360

# Inspecting corp1, a SimpleCorpus
tm::inspect(corp1)
[Partial output, pre-cleaning:]
  <<SimpleCorpus>>
  Metadata:  corpus specific: 1, document level (indexed): 0
  Content:  documents: 3

  [1] list('reut-00001.xml' = list(content = "Diamond Shamrock Corp said that\\
  neffective today it had cut its contract prices for crude oil by\\n1.50 dlrs a
  barrel.\\n    The reduction brings its posted price for West Texas\\nIntermediate
  to 16.00 dlrs a barrel, the company said.\\n    \\"The price reduction today was
  made in the light of falling\\noil product prices and a weak crude oil market,\\"
  a company\\nspokeswoman said.\\n    Diamond is the latest in a line of U.S.
  . . .
  cs = "YES", lewissplit = "TRAIN", cgisplit = "TRAINING-SET", oldid = "12891",
  places = "argentina", people = character(0), orgs = character(0), exchanges =
  character(0))))
  [2] list()
```

We can use the quanteda package to create corp2, converting from the VCorpus crude to a the object corp2, which is a "lower-c" corpus. The corp2 object is composed of character vectors.

```
corp2 <- quanteda::corpus(crude)
class(corp2)
[Output:]
     [1] "corpus"    "character"
```

We can't inspect corp2 (a corpus) as we inspected crude or corp1 (both types of Corpus).

```
tm::inspect(corp2)
[Output:]
  Error in UseMethod("inspect", x) :
    no applicable method for 'inspect' applied to an object of class "c('corpus',
  'character')"
```

However, we can list a corpus like corp2 simply by typing its name, and see the actual text:

```
corp2
[Partial output:]
   Corpus consisting of 20 documents and 15 docvars.
   reut-00001.xml :
   "Diamond Shamrock Corp said that effective today it had cut i..."

   reut-00002.xml :
   "OPEC may be forced to meet before a scheduled June session t..."
   . . .
   reut-00007.xml :
   "Kuwait"s Oil Minister, in remarks published today, said ther..."
    [ reached max_ndoc ... 14 more documents ]
```

Other conversion operations are possible, described below.

1. Convert a VCorpus (like crude) to a tdm (like crude_tdm). Both tdm and dtm objects may be displayed with the `inspect()` command, as illustrated in the quanteda section below. The `inspect()` command works for objects of classes VCorpus, TermDocumentMatrix, or TextDocument. Since crude_tdm is of class TermDocumentMatrix, it may be inspected. Inspection reveals there are 20 documents but the display only shows a sample of terms and documents. This is the tdm file wanted for future analysis.

   ```
   crude_tdm <- tm::TermDocumentMatrix(crude, control = list(removePunctuation =
   TRUE, stopwords = TRUE))

   tm::inspect(crude_tdm)
   [Output:]
      <<TermDocumentMatrix (terms: 1000, documents: 20)>>
      Non-/sparse entries: 1738/18262
      Sparsity           : 91%
      Maximal term length: 16
      Weighting          : term frequency (tf)
      Sample             :
              Docs
      Terms    144 236 237 242 246 248 273 489 502 704
        bpd      4   7   0   0   0   2   8   0   0   0
        crude    0   2   0   0   0   0   5   0   0   0
        dlrs     0   2   1   0   0   4   2   1   1   0
        last     1   4   3   0   2   1   7   0   0   0
   ```

```
market   3   0   0   2   0   8   1   0   0   2
mln      4   4   1   0   0   3   9   3   3   0
oil     12   7   3   3   5   9   5   4   5   3
opec    13   6   1   2   1   6   5   0   0   0
prices   5   5   1   2   1   9   5   2   2   3
said    11  10   1   3   5   7   8   2   2   4
```

For instructional purposes, we repeat the operations above but using corp1 rather than crude. The corp1 object is a Corpus of type SimpleCorpus whereas crude is a Corpus of type VCorpus. Though both crude_tdm and crude_tfm2 are of data class TermDocumentMatrix, the contents are very different. Inspection of crude_tdm2 reveals only 3 documents, not 20. This is not the tdm file we want, but shows it as "the wrong way" to create a tdm file for text analysis.

```
crude_tdm2 <- tm::TermDocumentMatrix(corp1, control = list(removePunctuation =
TRUE, stopwords = TRUE))
```

```
inspect(crude_tdm2)
```

[Output:]

```
<<TermDocumentMatrix (terms: 1323, documents: 3)>>
Non-/sparse entries: 1325/2644
Sparsity           : 67%
Maximal term length: 22
Weighting          : term frequency (tf)
Sample             :
              Docs
Terms           1 2 3
  cgisplit     20 0 0
  character0   65 0 0
  crude        25 0 0
  mln          26 0 0
  oil          80 0 0
  opec         46 0 0
  prices       36 0 0
  said         53 0 0
  saudi        22 0 0
  year         23 0 0
```

2. We can convert a Corpus of type VCorpus into a dtm. The dtm format is also widely used in text analysis.

```
crude_dtm <- tm::DocumentTermMatrix(crude, control = list(weighting =
function(x) weightTfIdf(x, normalize = FALSE), stopwords = TRUE))
```

9.10.4 Formats related to the "quanteda" package

Quanteda is frequently used in social science for a variety of text analysis operations. For instance, in their analysis of biased social dissemination of political information, Bøggild, Aarøe, and Peterson (2021) used the "quanteda" package for text cleaning, writing, "To ensure that these results were not driven by simple filler words, we conducted an analysis of robustness in which we removed all filler words using the list of English stop words in the Quanteda R package. The results show that the findings replicate when filler words are removed" (p. 277).

Quanteda typically uses the document feature matrix (dfm) format. This format can be converted to dtm or a tdm format. Below we use the quanteda package in conjunction with the tm package to create a corpus with corresponding dfm, tdm, and dtm objects. In dfm format, there is one token (word, feature) per column and each row is a document. Similarly, in dtm or tdm formats, columns are tokens, and rows are the documents. The dfm format is associated with the "quanteda" package, which uses its `convert()` command to convert to a variety of other formats.

TEXT BOX 9.1 Analyzing the emergence of women political candidates with the "quanteda" package

Meredith Conroy and Jon Green (2020) studied how the emergence of women as political candidates in the United States was related to the "ethos" they presented. Two types of ethos were defined, "agentic" and "communal". The values in the agentic ethos include "status", "power", and "recognition". Values in the communal ethos include "compassion", "civility", and "honesty". A much longer listing of agentic and communal terms is found in Table 1 (p. 944) of the authors' article. Analyzing over ten thousand forms of potential candidates provided by the organization "Run for Something", the authors studies the vocabulary used by individuals who became candidates compared to those who did not. "Our results suggest", the authors concluded, "the candidate emergence path is still easier for women (and men) whose motives are congruent with agency, and therefore the 'masculine ethos' of politics" rather than the communal ethos. That is, differences in vocabulary were found to be greater between candidates and non-candidates than they were between men and women.

The authors provide full R code, including use of quanteda, at https://github.com/jgreen4919/takes_a_motive/blob/master/takes_a_motive_code.R

Source: Conroy, Meredith & Green, Jon (2020). It takes a motive: Communal and agentic articulated interest and candidate emergence. *Political Research Quarterly* 73(4): 942–956.

The following examples from quanteda use the "data_corpus_inaugural" dataset which comes with the quanteda package. This contains a listing of U.S. presidential inaugural addresses from George Washington to Donald Trump in 2017.

```
# Setup for this subsection
library(quanteda)        # quanteda is a major text analysis package for R
library(tidytext)        # tidytext is also a major text analysis package
library(tm)              # Text Miner (tm) is a third major text analysis package
library(dplyr)           # Utility supporting %>% piping and more
library(RColorBrewer)    # Utility for color palettes
setwd("C:/Data")         # Declare the working directory

# Inspect the data
quanteda::data_corpus_inaugural
[Partial output:]
   Corpus consisting of 58 documents and 4 docvars.
   1789-Washington :
   "Fellow-Citizens of the Senate and of the House of Representa..."
   . . .
   1809-Madison :
   "Unwilling to depart from examples of the most revered author..."
    [ reached max_ndoc ... 52 more documents ]

class(data_corpus_inaugural)
[Output:]
   [1] "corpus"    "character"

# As suggested by its name, data_corpus_inaugural is a lower-c corpus.
# We rename it as such, to inaugurals_corpus
inaugurals_corpus <- quanteda::data_corpus_inaugural
class(inaugurals_corpus)
[Output:]
      [1] "corpus"    "character"
```

Optionally, create a corpus just for years since 1970

```
inaugurals_corpus_since70 <- quanteda::corpus_subset(inaugurals_corpus, Year > 1970)
class(inaugurals_corpus_since70)
```

[Output:]

```
    [1] "corpus"    "character"
```

Summarize the corpus

```
summary(inaugurals_corpus)
```

[Partial output:]

```
  Corpus consisting of 58 documents, showing 58 documents:
              Text Types Tokens Sentences Year  President  FirstName        Party
   1789-Washington   625   1537        23 1789 Washington     George         none
   1793-Washington    96    147         4 1793 Washington     George         none
        1797-Adams   826   2577        37 1797      Adams       John   Federalist
        . . .
        2013-Obama   814   2317        88 2013      Obama     Barack   Democratic
        2017-Trump   582   1660        88 2017      Trump  Donald J.   Republican
```

The structure command reveals more information and is applicable to most objects.

```
str(inaugurals_corpus)
```

[Output not shown.]

We now convert inaugurals_corpus to from a corpus to document feature matrix (dfm) format, placing the result in "inaugurals_dfm". The dfm format is needed by many quanteda tools. The `dfm()` command not only does the conversion but also allows some text cleaning.

```
inaugurals_dfm <- quanteda::dfm(inaugurals_corpus, remove_numbers = TRUE, remove_
punct = TRUE, stem = TRUE, remove = stopwords("english"))

class(inaugurals_dfm)
```

[Output:]

```
   [1] "dfm"
  attr(,"package")
  [1] "quanteda"
```

We then look at the contents of inaugurals_dfm:

```
inaugurals_dfm
```

[Output:]

```
 Document-feature matrix of: 58 documents, 5,342 features (89.1% sparse) and 4 docvars.
            features
  docs       fellow-citizen senat hous repres among vicissitud incid life event fill
    1789-Washington      1     1    2      2     1          1     1    1     2    1
    1793-Washington      0     0    0      0     0          0     0    0     0    0
    1797-Adams           3     1    3      3     4          0     0    2     0    0
    1801-Jefferson       2     0    0      1     1          0     0    1     0    0
    1805-Jefferson       0     0    0      0     7          0     0    2     1    0
    1809-Madison         1     0    0      1     0          1     0    1     0    1
  [ reached max_ndoc ... 52 more documents, reached max_nfeat ... 5,332 more features ]
```

Quanteda provides a variety of functions applicable to dfm formatted objects:

1. Count the number of features in a dfm file (after removing stop words and after stemming).

   ```
   quanteda::nfeat(inaugurals_dfm)
   ```

   [Output:]

   ```
         [1] 5342
   ```

2. List the most frequent words in a dfm object.

   ```
   quanteda::topfeatures(inaugurals_dfm, 8)
   ```
   [Output:]
   ```
     will nation govern  peopl     us    can  state  great 
      931    675    657    623    478    471    450    373
   ```

3. Create a word cloud from a dfm object. Below, we could have specified colors with color = c("green", "red", "blue") but instead we use a palette from the RColorBrewer package. Palette choices are shown, for example, at https://www.r-graph-gallery.com/38-rcolorbrewers-palettes.html.

   ```
   quanteda::textplot_wordcloud(inaugurals_dfm, max_words = 150, minsize = 4,
   color = rev(RColorBrewer::brewer.pal(8, "Dark2")), rotation= .20, comparison =
   FALSE)
   ```
   [Output is not shown here since word clouds are illustrated in Sections 9.15 and 9.16.]

We now convert from "inaugurals_dfm" to the dtm format, placing results in the object "inaugurals_dtm". The dtm format is associated with the tm package. In the `convert()` command below, note that one may set the `to =` option not only to "tm", but also to "topicmodels", "stm", "triplelist", "lda", and other selections.

```
inaugurals_dtm <- quanteda::convert(inaugurals_dfm, to = "tm")

class(inaugurals_dtm)
```
[Output:]
```
      [1] "DocumentTermMatrix"    "simple_triplet_matrix"
```

Note that the dtm format contains word frequency counts.

```
inspect(inaugurals_dtm)
```
[Output:]
```
   <<DocumentTermMatrix (documents: 58, terms: 9399)>>
   Non-/sparse entries: 44735/500407
   Sparsity           : 92%
   Maximal term length: 21
   Weighting          : term frequency (tf)
   Sample             :
                  Terms
   Docs,              .       a and  in  of our that the  to
     1821-Monroe    271 130  76 141 136 197  60   59 360 146
     1837-VanBuren  174  89  59 150  76 198  60   60 252 139
     1841-Harrison  407 212 129 229 172 603  64  130 828 318
     1845-Polk      187 146  65 189  87 298 100   47 397 184
     1861-Lincoln   195 113  56 105  77 146  13   59 256 134
     1889-Harrison  167 152  65 192  80 240  76   66 360 133
     1897-McKinley  229 130  57 171  81 228  60   34 345 113
     1909-Taft      218 160 109 220 140 314  40   52 486 218
     1925-Coolidge  184 196  77 146  71 207  55   65 261 135
     1929-Hoover    106 158  49 122  83 250  75   39 288 100
```

Get number of documents in a corpus or dfm file
```
quanteda::ndoc(inaugurals_corpus)
```
[Output:]
```
     [1] 58
```
```
quanteda::ndoc(inaugurals_dfm)
```
[Output:]
```
     [1] 58
```

```
# Convert from lower-c corpus to upper-c Corpus of SimpleCorpus type, using the tm package.
inaugurals_SimpleCorpus <- tm::SimpleCorpus(VectorSource(unlist(lapply(inaugurals_
corpus, as.character))))

class(inaugurals_SimpleCorpus)
[Output:]
     [1] "SimpleCorpus" "Corpus"

summary(inaugurals_SimpleCorpus)
[Partial output:]
                   Length Class             Mode
  1789-Washington 2       PlainTextDocument list
  1793-Washington 2       PlainTextDocument list
  1797-Adams      2       PlainTextDocument list
  1801-Jefferson  2       PlainTextDocument list
  1805-Jefferson  2       PlainTextDocument list
  1809-Madison    2       PlainTextDocument list
  . . .
```

We now convert inaugurals_dfm to a data frame, placing the result in inaugurals_df. When converting from a dfm object as shown below, the `convert()` command creates a data.frame object without row.names, in which documents are rows, the first column is doc_id (containing the name of the document) and each subsequent column is a feature (word). When using the `convert()` command to convert from a corpus like inaugurals_corpus to a data frame; however, the first column in the data frame is doc_id, the second column is "text" (containing the actual text of the document), and subsequent columns are the document variables (here, Year, President, FirstName, and Party).

```
inaugurals_df <- convert(inaugurals_dfm, to = "data.frame")

class(inaugurals_df)
[Output:]
     [1] "data.frame"
```

We ask to view just the first three rows and first 5 columns of inaugurals_df:

```
# Rows are documents, columns are terms (words, features), cell entries are counts
inaugurals_df[1:3,1:5]
[Output:]
            document fellow-citizens  of the senate
  1 1789-Washington               1  71 116      1
  2 1793-Washington               0  11  13      0
  3      1797-Adams               3 140 163      1
```

Finally, we show how to create a tdm object from a SimpleCorpus by using via tm's `TermDocumentMatrix()` function.

```
inaugurals_tdm <- tm::TermDocumentMatrix(inaugurals_SimpleCorpus, control =
list(removeNumbers = TRUE, stopwords = TRUE, stemming = TRUE))
class(inaugurals_tdm)
     [1] "TermDocumentMatrix"    "simple_triplet_matrix"

inspect(inaugurals_tdm)
[Partial output; only a sample of documents and terms are shown:]
   Non-/sparse entries: 40386/549648
   Sparsity           : 93%
   Maximal term length: 22
```

```
Weighting          : term frequency (tf)
Sample             :
        Docs
Terms    1821-Monroe 1837-VanBuren 1841-Harrison 1845-Polk
  can              3           9            26        12
  govern          13          13            31        36
  great           29           7            24         7
  may             15          11            33        13
  must             2           5             9        12
  . . .
```

9.10.5 Common text file conversions

Below we list common text file conversions in addition to those mentioned in the three preceding sections on tidytext, tm, and quanteda. The listing below is hardly exhaustive as a very large number of types of conversion are possible. Moreover, conversion commands are often combined with text cleaning commands, introducing more syntax variants than can be presented below. Rather, this section is intended to be "just the basics" of text conversion.

For this subsection, the following packages must be installed and invoked:

```
library(quanteda)
library(tm)
```

To provide example text, we first create the character vector "HighCrime", containing police mission statements from five high-crime cities

```
HighCrime <- c("The mission of the Durham Police Department is to minimize crime,
promote safety, and enhance the quality of life in partnership with our community.",
"The Fayetteville Police Department is dedicated to improving the quality of life by
creating a safe and secure environment for the citizens we serve. We will always act
with integrity to reduce crime, create partnerships, and build trust while treating
everyone with respect, compassion and fairness.",
"Our Mission is to be the model of excellence in policing by working in partnership
with the community and others to: FIGHT crime and the fear of crime, including
terrorism; ENFORCE laws while safeguarding the constitutional rights of all people;
PROVIDE quality service to all of our residents and visitors; and CREATE a work
environment in which we recruit, train, and develop an exceptional team of
employees.",
"In partnership with the community, we will create and maintain neighborhoods
capable of sustaining civic life. We commit to reducing the levels of crime, fear,
and disorder through community-based, problem-oriented, and data-driven policing.",
"The mission of the Sacramento Police Department is to work in partnership with the
Community to protect life and property, solve neighborhood problems, and enhance the
quality of life in our City.")
```

```
# The data class of HighCrime is a character vector
class(HighCrime)
[Output:]
    [1] "character"
```

1. Convert from a character vector to a data frame. The data frame will have five rows, one per city. The column titled "HighCrime" will contain the actual mission statement text.

   ```
   HighCrime_df <- as.data.frame(HighCrime)
   ```

   ```
   class(HighCrime_df)
   [Output:]
       [1] "data.frame"
   ```

2. Convert from a data frame back to a character vector. For these data, HighCrime_vector will have five components, one for each city: `HighCrime_vector[1:5]`.

```
HighCrime_vector <- as.character(HighCrime_df$HighCrime)

class(HighCrime_vector)
[Output:]
      [1] "character"
```

3. Convert from a character vector to a "small-C" corpus using the quanteda package.

```
HighCrime_corpus <- quanteda::corpus(HighCrime)

class(HighCrime_corpus)
[Output:]
      [1] "corpus"    "character"
```

4. Convert from a character vector to a "capital-C" SimpleCorpus using the tm package.

```
HighCrime_Corpus <- tm::SimpleCorpus(tm::VectorSource(unlist(lapply(HighCrime,
as.character))))

class(HighCrime_Corpus)
[Output:]
      [1] "SimpleCorpus" "Corpus"
```

5. Convert from a character vector into a tdm object. To do this, first convert to a "capital-C" Corpus, as above, then to tdm format using the tm package, as shown below.

```
HighCrime_tdm<- tm::TermDocumentMatrix(HighCrime_Corpus, control =
list(removeNumbers = TRUE, removePunctuation=TRUE, stopwords = TRUE, stemming =
TRUE))

class(HighCrime_tdm)
  [Output:]
      [1] "TermDocumentMatrix"    "simple_triplet_matrix"
```

6. Convert from a "capital-C" SimpleCorpus to a dtm using tm.

```
HighCrime_dtm<- tm::DocumentTermMatrix(HighCrime_Corpus, control =
list(removeNumbers = TRUE, removePunctuation=TRUE, stopwords = TRUE, stemming =
TRUE))

class(HighCrime_dtm)
[Output:]
      [1] "TermDocumentMatrix"    "simple_triplet_matrix"
```

7. Convert from a dtm to tidy-format tibble-type data frame using the tidytext package.

```
HighCrime_tidy_df<-tidytext::tidy(HighCrime_dtm)

class(HighCrime_tidy_df)
[Output:]
      [1] "tbl_df"     "tbl"          "data.frame"
```

8. Convert from a "capital-C" Corpus to a data frame with a column called "text" containing the mission statements. This is the same as the object HighCrime_df created above.

```
HighCrime_df_fromCorpus <- data.frame(text = sapply(HighCrime_Corpus,
as.character), stringsAsFactors = FALSE)

class(HighCrime_df_fromCorpus)
[Output:]
      [1] "data.frame"
```

9. Alternative conversion from a SimpleCorpus to a data frame, specifying a function. The first parameter in `sapply()` is the Corpus but other object types are possible. The second parameter is the function to be applied to each element of the Corpus. Here it is the identity function, which is no change. The column label in the data frame will be "text".

```
HighCrime_df_fromCorpus <- data.frame(text=sapply(HighCrime_Corpus, identity),
stringsAsFactors=F)
```

```
class(HighCrime_df_fromCorpus)
[Output:]
      [1] "data.frame"
```

10. Convert from a "lower-c" corpus to a data frame. The text of the mission statements will be in a data frame column labeled "HighCrime_corpus".

```
HighCrime_df_fromcorpus <- as.data.frame(HighCrime_corpus)
```

```
class(HighCrime_df_fromcorpus)
[Output:]
      [1] "data.frame"
```

9.11 Tokenization

9.11.1 Overview

Tokenization is the process of splitting text into units of analysis. These units (tokens) may be characters, words, lines, sentences, paragraphs, tweets, documents, or other types such as "ngrams" and "shingles". An ngram is a sequence of n items, such as characters, syllables, or words. An ngram of words provides keyword in context data. A "shingle" is an ngram sequence where the items are characters or words. The product of tokenization in R is a data frame in which each element (row) is a string vector.

9.11.2 Word tokenization

Below we tokenize the "preambles" data frame into words and into sentences. We do this by tokenizing a .csv file into tidy format.

```
# Setup
library(tidytext)      # A leading text analysis package in R
library(tibble)        # Functions for tibble-type data frames
```

For example data, we read in the file "preambles.csv". This file is provided in the Data section of the Support Material (www.routledge.com/9780367624293) for this book. Its columns are country (a factor), year (an integer), and text (a factor). There are 155 observations (countries). The `read.csv()` and other functions shown in this section without a package prefix are from packages in the R system library and do not require installation.

```
preambles <- read.csv("c://Data/preambles.csv", header=TRUE, sep = ",",
stringsAsFactors=FALSE)
```

Tokenization of the preambles object by words is a two-step process. This assumes that preambles$text is of character rather than factor data class, by virtue of our using the stringsAsFactors = FALSE option above.

1. Add a document (element) id called "doc_id" to the preambles object. Below, `rownames()` returns 1, 2, 3, etc., as characters, making preambles$doc_id a character variable.

```
preambles$doc_id <- rownames(preambles)
```

2. Now tokenize by words. The wordlist object is a data frame.

```
wordlist <- preambles  %>%  tidytext::unnest_tokens(preambles,            text,,
token="words")
```

The actual words are in wordlist's column labeled "preambles". Other columns in wordlist are country, year, and doc_id. The wordlist data frame has over 45,000 rows since there is one row per word and the preambles for a given country have many words.

```
View(wordlist)
names(wordlist)
```
[Output:]
```
   [1] "country"   "year"      "doc_id"    "preambles"
```

By viewing the wordlist data frame we can spot that Afghanistan's words are rows 1–255, enabling us to print out these words, which in column 4, which is "preambles".

```
View(wordlist)
wordlist[1:255,"preambles"]
```
[Partial output:]
```
     [1] "in"              "the"              "name"
     [4] "of"              "allah"            "the"
  ...
    [37] "we"              "the"              "people"
    [40] "of"              "afghanistan"      "believing"
   . . .
   [250] "held"            "in"               "the"
   [253] "city"            "of"               "kabul"
```

We could also separate out the words for a particular country, such as Algeria:

```
justalgeriawords <- subset(wordlist, country == "algeria", select = c("preambles"))

justalgeriawords
```
[Partial output]
```
              preambles
   378              the
   379         algerian
   380           people
   . . .
   932                a
   933             free
   934          society
```

The justalgeriawords data frame has 557 rows (words).

```
nrow(justalgeriawords)
```
[Output:]
```
 [1] 557
```

The row numbering in justalgeriawords$preambles goes from row 1 = 378 to row 557 = 934, drawing on numbering in wordlist.justalgeria. Thus, the first word is "the" but its row number is 378:

```
justalgeriawords$preambles[1]
```
[Output:]
```
   [1] "the"
```

```
rownum <- rownames(justalgeriawords)
rownum[1]
[Output:]
   [1] "378"
```

We now tokenize by sentences rather than words. The sentencelist object we create is also a data frame. We do this by piping the contents of the preambles object to the tidytext command `unnest _ tokens()`.

```
sentencelist <- preambles  %>%  tidytext::unnest_tokens(preambles, text,,
token="sentences")
```

The actual sentences are in column 4, which is "preambles".

```
names(sentencelist)
[Output:]
   [1] "country"    "year"      "doc_id"     "preambles"
```

By viewing sentencelist we can spot that Algeria's sentences are rows 3–14, enabling us to print out these 12 sentences, which as noted, are in column 4, which is "preambles". Thus, we may use either the column label ("preambles") or the column index number (4) to call up the sentences. We use the label.

```
View(sentencelist)
sentencelist[3:14,"preambles"]
[Partial output:]
   [1] "the algerian people is a free people, decided to remain free."
   [2] "its history is a long chain of battles which have made algeria forever a
   country of freedom and dignity."
   . . .
   [12] "strong in its spiritual values, deeply ingrained, and its traditions of
   solidarity and justice, the people is confident of its capacities to work
   fully for the cultural, social and economic progress of the world, today and
   tomorrow."
```

Though we do not use it here immediately, we will be using commands from the "tidyverse" package, sometimes requiring the data be in "tibble" format. Below we create tibble versions of the preambles data frame.

```
# Create a new data frame labeled preambles2 so as to leave preambles intact.
# The new preambles2 object has 155 observations of the four variables (columns).
preambles2 <- preambles

# Rearrange columns so the first two are "doc_id" and "text".
preambles2 <- preambles2[, c(4,3,1,2)]
```

We then create a tibble version of preambles2 as used by tidyverse tools. The preambles_t object has 155 observations of 1 variable, which starts with txt.doc_id and txt.text but also contains the other variables (txt.country, txt.year). The preamble for Afghanistan is

```
preambles_t <- tibble::tibble(txt = preambles2)
preambles_t
[Output:]
   # A tibble: 155 x 1
   txt$doc_id $text                                               $country      $year
   <chr> <chr>                                                    <fct>         <int>
 1 1   In the name of Allah, the Most Beneficent, the Most Mer~ afghanistan    2004
 2 2   We, the people of Albania, proud and aware of our histo~ albania        1998
```

```
 3 3   The Algerian people is a free people, decided to remain~ algeria         1989
 4 4   The Andorran People, with full liberty and independence~ andorra         1993
 5 5   We, the people of Angola, through its lawful representa~ angola          2010
 6 6   WHEREAS the People of Antigua and Barbuda- a. proclaim ~ antigua_and_b~ 1981
 7 7   We, the representatives of the people of the Argentine ~ argentina       1853
 8 8   The Armenian People, recognizing as a basis the fundame~ armenia         1995
 9 9   The Azerbaijan people, continuing the traditions of man~ azerbaijan      1995
10 10  Whereas Four hundred and eighty-one years ago the redis~ bahamas         1973
# ... with 145 more rows
```

Retrieval from a tibble is different from retrieval from an ordinary data frame. For instance, to get all the information for row 1 (Afghanistan) above, issue the command below. Substituting 2 for the row number would retrieve similar data for Albania, and so on.

```
out <- preambles_t[1,,drop=TRUE]
out
```

[Partial output:]

```
    doc_id
  1      1

  text
  1 In the name of Allah, the Most Beneficent, the Most Merciful Praise be to
  Allah, the Cherisher and Sustainer of Worlds; and Praise and Peace be upon
  Mohammad, His Last Messenger and his
  . . .
  realities as well as requirements of time through our elected representatives in
  the Loya Jirga, dated January 3, 2004, held in the city of Kabul.
        country year
  1 afghanistan 2004
```

```
out$text
```

[Output not shown, but just has the preamble text for Afghanistan]

9.12 Character encoding

Character encoding defines how numeric values are assigned to characters, thereby allowing computers to represent characters on the screen or in print. Unfortunately, there are many possible encodings. While web browsers typically handle encoding-detection "behind the scenes", in text analysis it is often necessary that one's text corpora all have the same encoding. Consequently, the researcher may need to take action to prepare the text.

Standardization is governed by the International Organization for Standardization (ISO), the International Electrotechnical Commission (IEC), the Unicode Consortium, as well as other organizations. "Unicode" is the computer industry standard, supporting over 100,000 characters. It comes is 8-, 16-, and 32-bit versions, corresponding to UTF-8, UTF-16, and UTF-32 character encodings. Unicode version 12, released in 2019, corresponds to the ISO/IEC 10646:2017 standard. Other common encodings include ISO 646 (ASCII), ISO 8859 (most modern languages), MS-Windows-1252 (West European languages), EBCDIC (IBM implementations, now little used), and GB 18030 (Chinese government standard). All these have variants and updates.[5]

If working with English-language texts, researchers often standardize on UTF-8, of which ASCII is a subset. Most texts will already be UTF-8 encoded. If encoding is referred to as "Unicode", usually UTF-8 is meant. Perhaps second-most common is ISO-8859-1 encoding (also called Latin 1 (Latin alphabet 1, usually "latin1" in R), l1, IBM819, or Windows-28591), which is also an 8-bit system. Latin 1 is common in when East Asian languages are romanized and some websites use Latin 1. HTML 5 websites now default to Windows-1252. Windows-1252 encoding is sometimes mislabeled as ISO-8859-1 but there are differences.

No packages requiring installation are used in this section. As an example, we read in a raw text file from the working directory. The file "usconstitution.txt" is supplied in the Data section of the Support Material (www.routledge.com/9780367624293) for this book.

```
setwd("C:/Data")
x <- "usconstitution.txt"
```

Next we try to determine the character encoding for usconstitution.txt. The `Encoding()` command must be capitalized, is part of R's base package.

```
Encoding(x)   # Or use table(Encoding(x))
[Output:]
      [1] "unknown"
```

"Unknown" encoding means that the text is either ASCII or is "native encoding". US-ASCII is a subset of UTF-8 encoding and does not need converting if the project is working with Unicode UTF-8 encoding, as is usual. "Native encoding" refers to the encoding used on the researcher's local computer platform. Text strings in ASCII, UTF-8, and native encoding coexist and are handled automatically by R, which invisibly switches to native encoding for purposes of computer display or printing.

Below we give a few more examples based on the `Encoding()` command and the `enc2utf8()` conversion command, both part of R's base package.

```
# For some English-language text:
# That Encoding() reports it as "unknown" means it is UTF-8 or the ASCII subset of UTF-8
x1 <- "Some English text"
Encoding(x1)
[Output:]
     [1] "unknown"

# For some Russian-language text:
# While not ASCII, it is still UTF-8.
x2 <- c("Это какой-то текст на русском языке.")
Encoding(x2)
[Output:]
     [1] "UTF-8"

# For some text in latin1 (ISO-8859-1) character format.
# It is the French word "façile" but encoded in latin 1.
x3 <- "fa\xE7ile"
x3
[Output:]
    [1] "façile"
Encoding(x3)
[Output:]
     [1] "latin1"

# We can use the enc2utf8() conversion function to convert x3 from latin 1 to UTF-8.

x3b <- enc2utf8(x3)
x3b
[Output:]
    [1] "façile"
Encoding(x3b)
[Output:]
     [1] "UTF-8"
```

9.13 Text cleaning and preparation

Section 9.13 appears as a Chapter 9 online supplement in the Support Material (www.routledge.com/9780367624293) for this book. This section covers data cleaning with the "tm", "stringr", "textclean", and "grep" packages, and lists other related packages. Placement as a supplement is purely for space reasons. In fact, most text data requires pre-processing and is essential to text analysis. The supplement is titled, "Text cleaning and preparation".

9.14 Analysis: Multigroup word frequency comparisons

In this section, we illustrate word frequency tables/histograms where comparison of groups is involved. Along the way we also illustrate direct input of text to character vectors, transferring to "tidy" format, then creating word count objects and barplot visualizations. The research example is to compare the mission statements of police departments in the five highest and five lowest crime jurisdictions as part of a much larger study by Brad Holliday (2021). As another example of comparative word frequency analysis, one might use testimony by industry versus public interest groups on some issue before congressional hearings, using sources mentioned in the "Archived texts" section early in this chapter.

9.14.1 Multigroup analysis in tidytext

We start multigroup analysis by illustrating using the "tidytext" package.

```
# Setup

library(tidytext)
library(dplyr)
setwd("C:/Data")

# Create a character vector with mission statements from high crime cities
HighCrime<-c("The mission of the Durham Police Department is to minimize crime,
promote safety, and enhance the quality of life in partnership with our community.",
"The Fayetteville Police Department is dedicated to improving the quality of life by
creating a safe and secure environment for the citizens we serve. We will always act
with integrity to reduce crime, create partnerships, and build trust while treating
everyone with respect, compassion and fairness.",
"Our Mission is to be the model of excellence in policing by working in partnership
with the community and others to: FIGHT crime and the fear of crime, including
terrorism; ENFORCE laws while safeguarding the constitutional rights of all people;
PROVIDE quality service to all of our residents and visitors; and CREATE a work
environment in which we recruit, train, and develop an exceptional team of
employees.",
"In partnership with the community, we will create and maintain neighborhoods
capable of sustaining civic life. We commit to reducing the levels of crime, fear,
and disorder through community-based, problem-oriented, and data-driven policing.",
"The mission of the Sacramento Police Department is to work in partnership with the
Community to protect life and property, solve neighborhood problems, and enhance the
quality of life in our City.")

HighCrime
```

[Output not shown but typing the object name would list its contents.]

Next we make the HighCrime character vector into a "tidy" format data frame. The HighCrime_df data frame will have two columns: document_id and text.

```
HighCrime_df <- dplyr::data_frame(document_id=1:5, text=HighCrime)
```

We now tokenize the HighCrime_df data frame into words using tidytext's `unnest _ tokens()` command. HighCrime_df must have the column "text", containing the words to be tokenized.

```
HighCrime_words<-(HighCrime_df %>% tidytext::unnest_tokens(word, text))

HighCrime_words
```

[Partial output:]

```
   # A tibble: 205 x 2
       line word
      <int> <chr>
    1     1 the
    2     1 mission
    . . .
    9     1 to
   10     1 minimize
   # ... with 195 more rows
```

To create word counts HighCrime_words were piped to the `anti-join()` command, which strips stop words, the pipe to the actual `count()` command, asking for word sorting. The "n" column in the result is the word count.

```
HighCrime_wordcounts <- HighCrime_words %>%
  dplyr::anti_join(stop_words, by = "word") %>%
  dplyr::count(word, sort = TRUE)

HighCrime_wordcounts
```

[Output:]

```
   # A tibble: 75 x 2
     word              n
     <chr>         <int>
   1 community         5
   2 crime             5
   3 life              5
   4 partnership       4
   5 quality           4
   6 create            3
   7 department        3
   8 mission           3
   9 police            3
  10 enhance           2
  # ... with 65 more rows
```

Having created the word frequency table above, we now create a bar plot of the ten most common words for the high crime mission statements, not counting stop words. The plot is shown in Figure 9.9.

```
# First set the desired number of bars
number_of_bars = 10

# Second, set column labels
col_labels<- c(head(HighCrime_wordcounts,number_of_bars)$word)

# Now produce the word frequency plot.
# The barplot() function is in R's graphics package, which loads automatically.
barplot(height=head(HighCrime_wordcounts, number_of_bars)$n, names=col_labels,
xlab="Words", ylab="Frequency", col = heat.colors(number_of_bars), main="Mission
Statements for High Crime Cities: Ten Most Frequent Words")
```

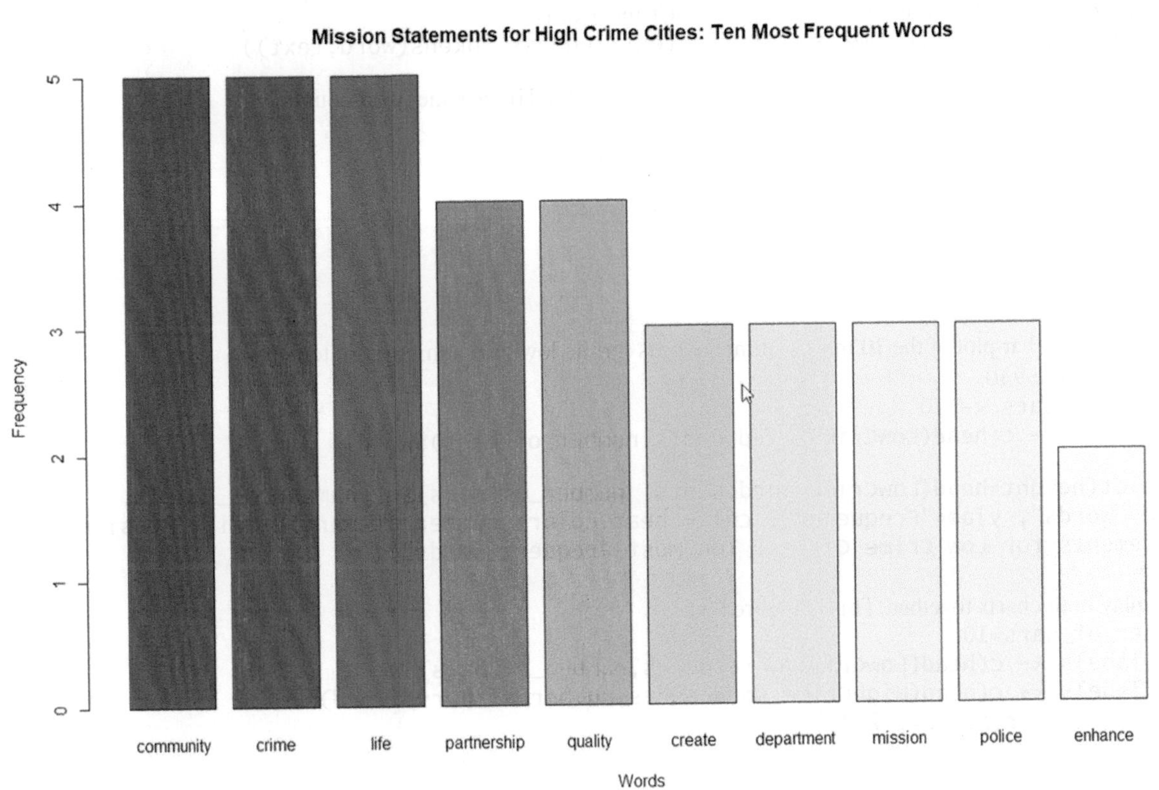

Figure 9.9 Word frequency bar chart for high-crime cities

```
# Repeat for lowest crime cities
# Create character vector with mission statements from low crime cities
LowCrime <- c("The Virginia Beach Police Department is committed to providing a safe
community and improving the quality of life for all people. We accomplish this by
delivering quality police services and enforcing laws with equity and impartiality.
In partnership with the community, we reduce crime through public education,
prevention, and awareness. In meeting this objective, we demand of ourselves the
highest professional standards and dedication to our core values.",
"We, the members of the Madison Police Department, are committed to providing high
quality police services that are accessible to all members of the community. We
believe in the dignity of all people and respect individual and constitutional
rights in fulfilling this mission.",
"Our mission is to serve as law enforcement leaders in protecting and assisting all
people in our community through effective problem solving, professional service, and
the relentless pursuit of those who victimize our citizens and compromise public
safety.",
"The mission of the Coronado Police Department is to ensure the safety and protect
and enhance the quality of life for all who live, work or visit our community by
delivering the highest quality police services.",
"To work in partnership with the community, enhance trust, protect with courage and
compassion, and empower victims of crime through excellence in service.")

# Make character vector into a "tidy" format data frame
LowCrime_df <- dplyr::data_frame(line=1:5, text=LowCrime)
```

Tokenize into words, place into data frame HighCrime_words
```
LowCrime_words<-(LowCrime_df %>% tidytext::unnest_tokens(word,text))
```

Create word counts, stripping stop words; put into data frame HighCrime_wordcounts
```
LowCrime_wordcounts <- LowCrime_words %>%
  dplyr::anti_join(stop_words, by = "word") %>%
  dplyr::count(word, sort = TRUE)
```

List word frequencies
```
LowCrime_wordcounts
```
[Output not shown]

Now create a bar plot of the 10 most common words for the low crime mission statements.
This is Figure 9.10.
```
number_of_bars <- 10
col_labels<- c(head(LowCrime_wordcounts,number_of_bars)$word)

barplot(height=head(LowCrime_wordcounts, number_of_bars)$n, names=col_labels,
xlab="Words", ylab="Frequency", col = heat.colors(number_of_bars), main="Mission
Statements for Low Crime Cities: Ten Most Frequent Words")
```

Display both charts together. This is Figure 9.11.
```
number_of_bars=10
col_labels1<- c(head(LowCrime_wordcounts,number_of_bars)$word)
col_labels2<- c(head(HighCrime_wordcounts,number_of_bars)$word)
graphics:: par(mfrow=c(2,1))
```

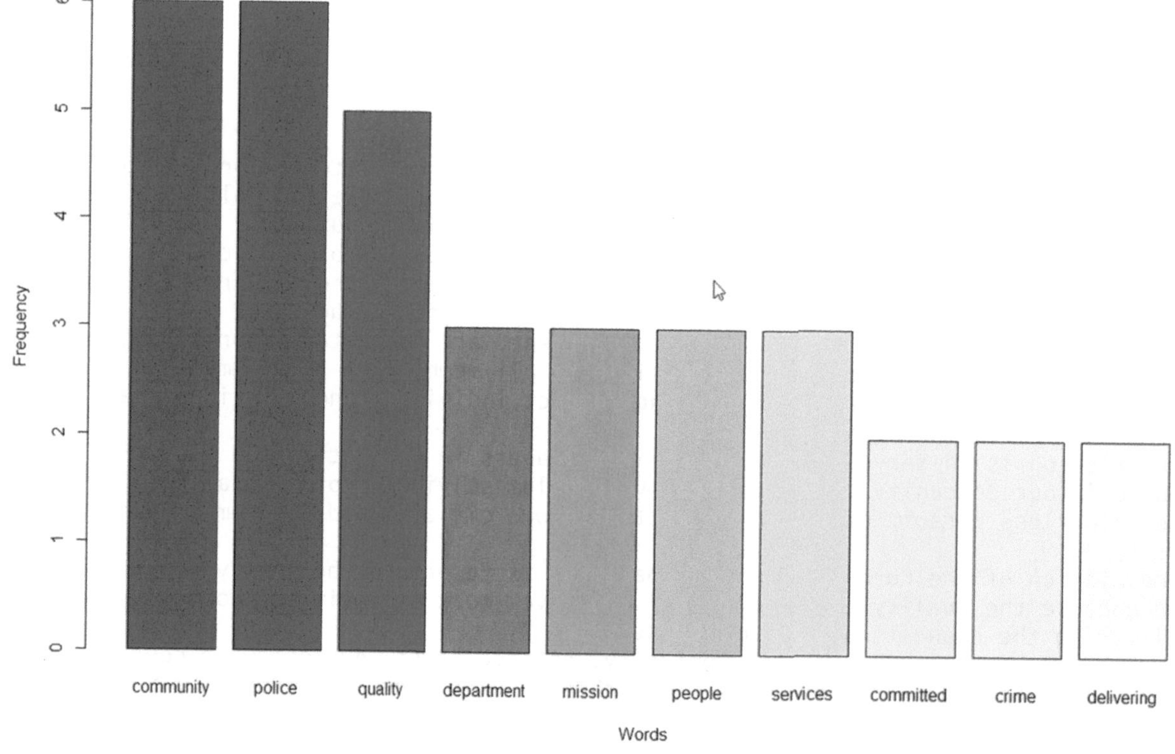

Figure 9.10 Word frequency bar chart for low-crime cities

```
graphics::barplot(height=head(LowCrime_wordcounts, number_of_bars)$n, names=col_
labels1, xlab="Words", ylab="Frequency", col = heat.colors(number_of_bars),
main="Mission Statements for Low Crime Cities: Ten Most Frequent Words")

graphics::barplot(height=head(HighCrime_wordcounts, number_of_bars)$n, names=col_
labels2, xlab="Words", ylab="Frequency", col = heat.colors(number_of_bars),
main="Mission Statements for High Crime Cities: Ten Most Frequent Words")

par(mfrow=c(1,1))  # reset
```

Top-listed words for low-crime cities absent from top-listed words for high-crime cities: People, services, committed, delivering. Top-listed words for high-crime cities absent from top-listed words for low-crime cities: Life, partnership, create, enhance.

9.14.2 Multigroup analysis with quanteda's `textstat _ keyness()` command

The "quanteda" package has a related approach to multigroup comparisons using a "keyness" score. A group of documents of primary interest is declared the "target'. The comparison is to all other documents. For the example below, the target is "HighCrime" (mission statements of police department in five high-crime cities) and the reference comparison is to documents associated with the "LowCrime" group of cities. These two groups refer to the HighCrime and LowCrime objects from the previous section.

Quanteda's `textstat _ keyness()` command computes a "keyness" score that measures the differential association of a term with a target group and a reference group. Higher scores reflect a term being mentioned more frequently in one group than another. There are four bases for scoring: "chi2" (the default); "exact" (Fisher's exact test); "lr" (the likelihood ratio); and "pmi" for pointwise mutual information. The ranking of terms depends

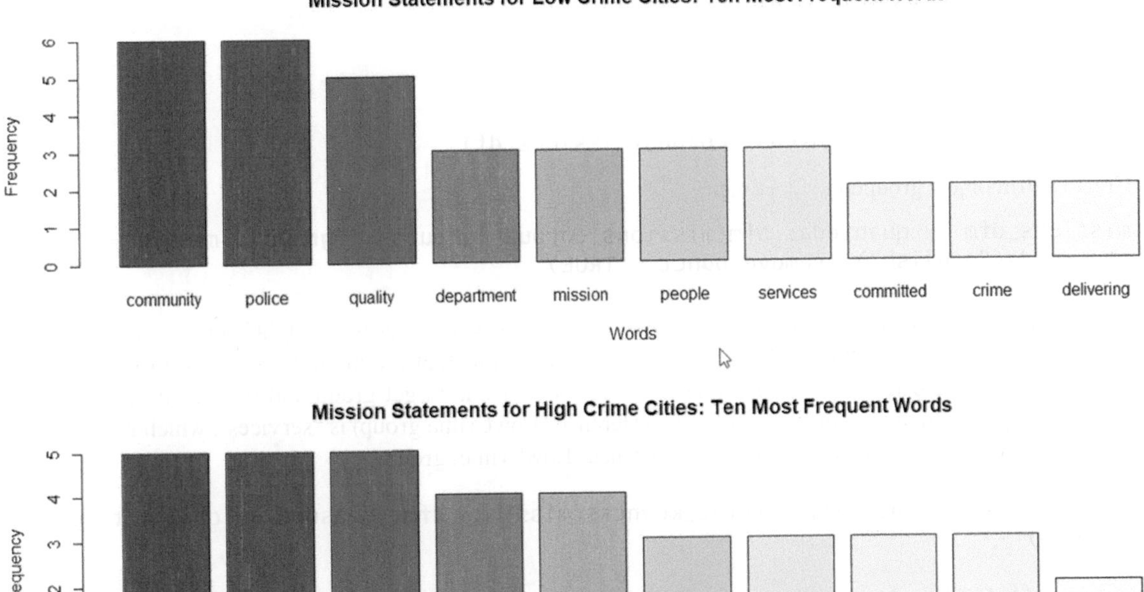

Figure 9.11 Word frequency bar chart for low vs. high crime cities

both on the frequency differential between target and reference groups and on the scoring measure used. For discussion of keyness scores, see Bondi and Scott (2010) and Stubbs (2010).

The "HighCrime" and "LowCrime" objects are character vectors representing police mission statements in high- and low-crime cities. As with many operations in quanteda, however, we have to get these objects into document feature matrix (dfm) format before multigroup keyness analysis can be accomplished with quanteda's `textstat _ keyness()` command. The HighCrime and LowCrime objects created in Section 9.14.1 are assumed to still be in the environment.

```
# setup
library(quanteda)
```

We start by creating data frames for the HighCrime and LowCrime cities. These are objects df1 and df2 respectively. Each has two columns: text and group. The text column contains the text of the mission statements. The group column is either "HighCrime" or "LowCrime".

```
df1 <- as.data.frame(HighCrime, stringsAsFactors = FALSE)
names(df1)[1] <- "text"
df1$group <- "HighCrime"
View(df1)

df2 <- as.data.frame(LowCrime, stringsAsFactors = FALSE)
names(df2)[1] <- "text"
df2$group <- "LowCrime"
View(df2)
```

There are three steps to create the needed document feature matrix (dfm) object.

1. Merge data frames vertically (add rows) into a new data frame. The `rbind()command` is from R's "base" package in the system library.

   ```
   missions_df <- rbind(df1,df2)View(missions_df)
   ```

2. Create a corpus from the data frame

   ```
   missions_corpus <- quanteda::corpus(missions_df)
   ```

3. Create a dfm object grouped by document

   ```
   missions_dfm <- quanteda::dfm(missions_corpus, groups = "group", remove =
   stopwords("english"), remove_punct = TRUE)
   ```

Having created the needed dfm object, we may now calculate keyness, setting "HighCrime" as target group. Results are placed in the object "result_keyness". Below, results show that the highest-scoring term for the target (HighCrime group) is "create", which is mentioned three times in the target group and 0 times in the reference (LowCrime) group. The highest-scoring term for the reference (LowCrime group) is "services", which is mentioned 0 times in the target group and three times in the reference (LowCrime) group.

```
result_keyness <- quanteda::textstat_keyness(missions_dfm, measure = "chi2", target =
"HighCrime")

# The command below lists the top 8 and bottom 8 terms by keyness.
rbind(head(result_keyness,8),tail(result_keyness,8))
```

[Output:]

```
      feature       chi2         p n_target n_reference
1      create  1.3694565 0.2419053        3           0
2       crime  0.6082805 0.4354360        5           2
```

```
3           life  0.6082805 0.4354360          5          2
4    environment  0.5135029 0.4736264          2          0
5           will  0.5135029 0.4736264          2          0
6       policing  0.5135029 0.4736264          2          0
7           fear  0.5135029 0.4736264          2          0
8    partnership  0.1804906 0.6709519          4          2
124     coronado -0.9955752 0.3183835          0          1
125       ensure -0.9955752 0.3183835          0          1
126         live -0.9955752 0.3183835          0          1
127        visit -0.9955752 0.3183835          0          1
128      courage -0.9955752 0.3183835          0          1
129      empower -0.9955752 0.3183835          0          1
130      victims -0.9955752 0.3183835          0          1
131     services -1.3334197 0.2481978          0          3
```

Estimated keyness, of course, may be plotted, as shown in Figure 9.12. The "n" column is the number of terms per group.

```
#If show_reference=FALSE, then only scores for the target group are displayed.
quanteda::textplot_keyness(result_keyness, color = c("red", "blue"),margin=0.2,
labelsize = 6, n=8, show_reference = TRUE, show_legend = TRUE)
```

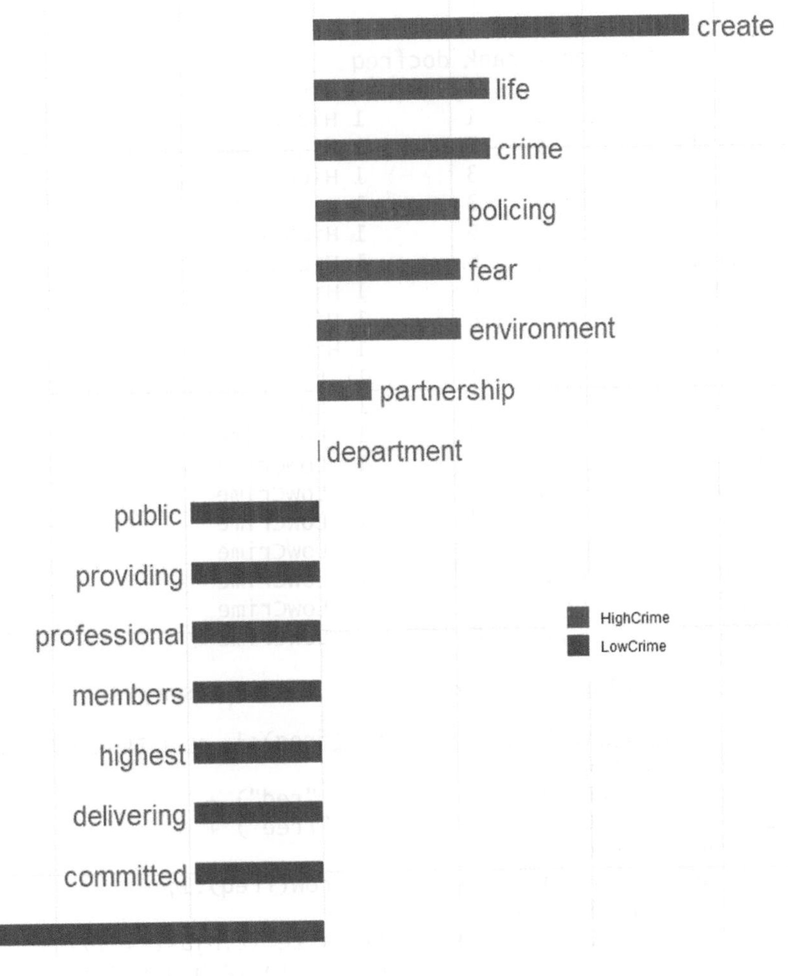

Figure 9.12 Word frequency keyness chart for low vs. high crime cities

In Figure 9.12, longer lines indicate terms where the frequency of words in HighCrime cities is greater than in LowCrime cities (red), or vice versa (blue). As the keyness measure is chi-square, the length of lines corresponds to the chi-square value, which in turn reflects observed frequency compared to expected frequency based on marginal frequency. We see, for instance, that "Services" is highest among LowCrime city police mission statements whereas this is not among the top eight terms for HighCrime cities. (Keep in mind this was a very small teaching dataset of only ten cities, not intended for substantive conclusions.) In the next section, keyness measures are compared with raw term frequency measures and the relevance of each to different types of research questions is noted.

9.14.3 Multigroup analysis with `textstat _ frequency()` in quanteda and ggplot2

Using quanteda's `textstat _ frequency()` command in conjunction with the ggplot2 data visualization package we can obtain another type of multigroup comparison plot. This section assumes that the missions_dfm object created in Section 9.14.2 is still present in the environment.

```
# Setup
library(quanteda)
library(ggplot2)

# Calculate and then view word frequencies by group (here, HighCrime vs. LowCrime)
freq <- quanteda::textstat_frequency(missions_dfm, n = 10, groups = "group")

freq
[Output:]
       feature frequency rank docfreq     group
1        crime         5    1       1 HighCrime
2         life         5    1       1 HighCrime
3      quality         4    3       1 HighCrime
4  partnership         4    3       1 HighCrime
5    community         4    3       1 HighCrime
6      mission         3    6       1 HighCrime
7       police         3    6       1 HighCrime
8   department         3    6       1 HighCrime
9       create         3    6       1 HighCrime
10     enhance         2   10       1 HighCrime
11      police         6    1       1  LowCrime
12   community         6    1       1  LowCrime
13     quality         5    3       1  LowCrime
14     mission         3    4       1  LowCrime
15  department         3    4       1  LowCrime
16      people         3    4       1  LowCrime
17    services         3    4       1  LowCrime
18       crime         2    8       1  LowCrime
19      safety         2    8       1  LowCrime
20     enhance         2    8       1  LowCrime
```

We then use the "ggplot" package to visualize the results in a comparison plot.

```
ggplot(data = freq, ggplot2::aes(x = nrow(freq):1, y = frequency)) +
    ggplot2::geom_point() +
    ggplot2::geom_point(size = 5, colour = "red") +
    ggplot2::facet_wrap(~ group, scales = "free") +
    ggplot2::coord_flip() +
    ggplot2::scale_x_continuous(breaks = nrow(freq):1,
          labels = freq$feature) +
    ggplot2::theme(axis.text=element_text(size=12,hjust = 1)) +
    ggplot2::theme(axis.title=element_text(size=14,hjust=0.5)) +
    ggplot2::labs(x = NULL, y = "Term frequency")
```

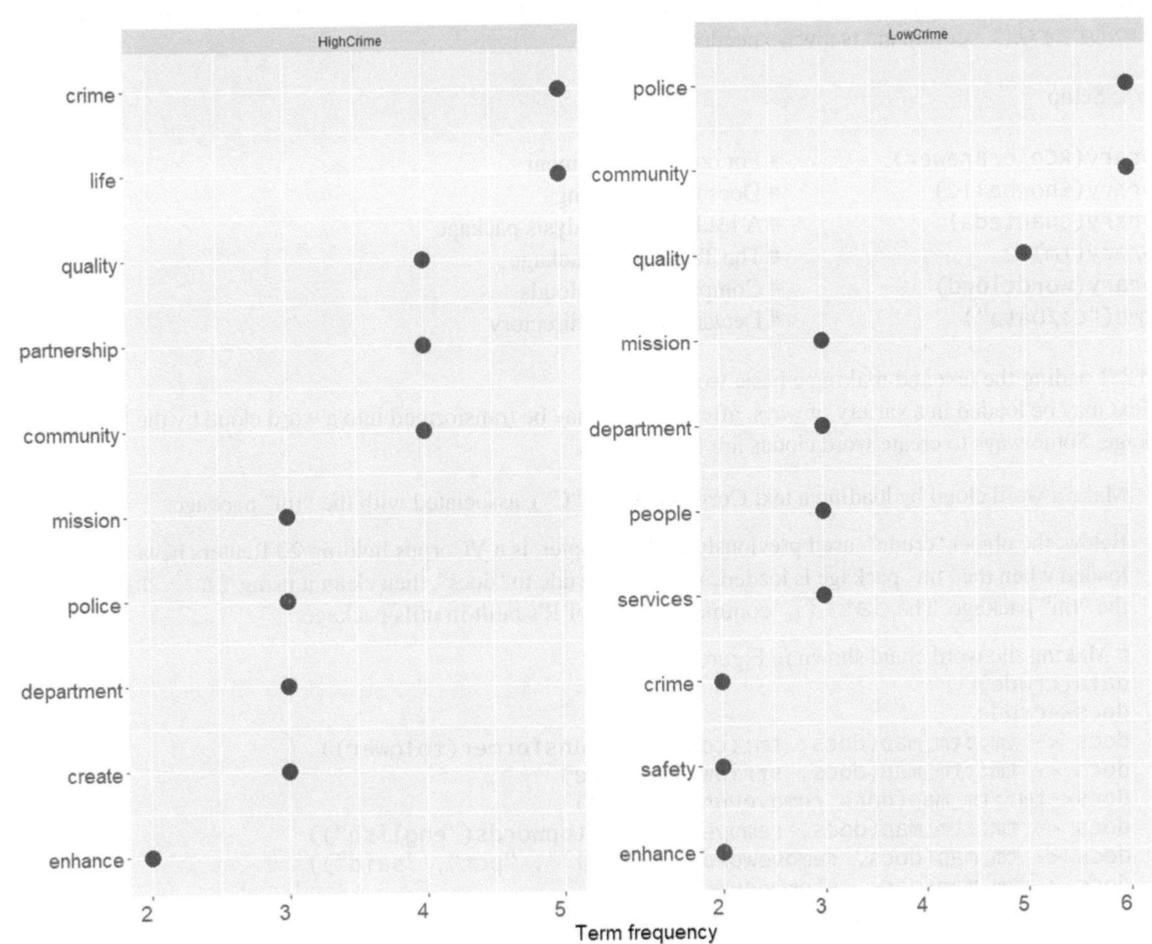

Figure 9.13 Term frequency by group

Where in the previous keyness plot the top term for the HighCrime cities was "create" and for LowCrime cities was "services", for the raw frequencies in Figure 9.13 the corresponding top terms were "crime" (HighCrime cities) and "police" (LowCrime cities). The difference is that the keyness rankings adjust for total word frequency in relation to group word frequency, then rank words in terms of what is observed and what would be expected. If the research question deals with the importance of term exposure then term frequencies by group should be the focus. If the research question deals with more-than-expected usage of terms, then keyness by group should be the focus.

9.15 Analysis: Word clouds

Word clouds are a visually compelling way of summarizing the focus of a document. When there are two or more documents, representing perhaps different organizations, the comparison of word clouds discussed in Section 9.16 can be an instructive contrast. Like other forms of text analysis, word clouds lend themselves to qualitative research, not requiring statistical analysis other than underlying word frequency counts.

There are several methods for creating word clouds in R, of which that discussed in this section is only one. Below we use the "wordcloud" package to generate word clouds. Supporting packages are "tm" (a popular text mining package), "SnowballC" (a utility for text stemming), and RColorBrewer (a utility for color palettes). As always, installation is only necessary if the package is not in the local R environment. However, invoking the package using the `library()` command is always needed.

Step 1: Setup

```
library(RColorBrewer)      # For color management
library(SnowballC)         # Does text stemming
library(quanteda)          # A leading text analysis package
library(tm)                # The Text Miner package
library(wordcloud)         # Composes word clouds
setwd("C:/Data")           # Declare working directory
```

Step 2: Loading the text and making a basic word cloud

Text may be loaded in a variety of ways, after which it may be transformed into a word cloud by the "wordcloud" package. Some ways to create word clouds are listed below.

1. Make a word cloud by loading a text Corpus (capital "C"), associated with the "tm" package.

   Below, the object "crude", used previously in this chapter, is a VCorpus holding 20 Reuters news articles. It is loaded when the "tm" package is loaded. We assign crude to "docs", then clean it using `tm _ map()` from the "tm" package. The `data()` command is part of R's built-in utils package.

   ```
   # Making the word cloud shown in Figure 9.14.
   data(crude)
   docs<-crude
   docs <- tm::tm_map(docs, tm::content_transformer(tolower))
   docs <- tm::tm_map(docs, stripWhitespace)
   docs<-tm::tm_map(docs,removePunctuation)
   docs <- tm::tm_map(docs, removeWords, stopwords("english"))
   docs <- tm_map(docs, removeWords, c("will", "pct", "said"))
   docs <- tm_map(docs, stemDocument)
   wordcloud::wordcloud(docs, min.freq=4, max.words = 75,
   rot.per=.2, colors=RColorBrewer::brewer.pal(6, "Dark2"))
   ```

   Comments on the syntax above:

   - The "crude" object is in Corpus format. We copy it into "docs" for convenience.
   - It is a good idea to move everything to lower case.
   - Then we strip white space and remove punctuation.
   - We remove stop words from tm's built-in English stop words list ("english" is lower case).
   - If we see other words we want to eliminate, we can apply removeWords for them.
   - Optionally we can stem the words. See `help(stemDocument)` for more information.
   - min.freq is minimum frequency for a word to appear in the cloud.
   - max.words is the maximum number of words to appear.
   - rot.per is the percentage of words to be vertical in the cloud.
   - colors set the color scheme. Using RColorBrewer is optional but versatile. To see RColorBrewer color codes, type `help(RColorBrewer)`.
   - Note one will get a different random arrangement of words each time the code is run.

2. Make a word cloud by loading a .txt text file from the Internet.

   The syntax for creating the word cloud is essentially similar (except we do not stem words), but the data are read in differently and must be converted to a Corpus by the `VectorSource()` function in tm.

   ```
   # Read in raw text of the U.S. Constitution from the Internet
   # readLines() is from R's built-in "base" package
   url <-
   "https://faculty.chass.ncsu.edu/garson/usconstitution.txt"
   ```

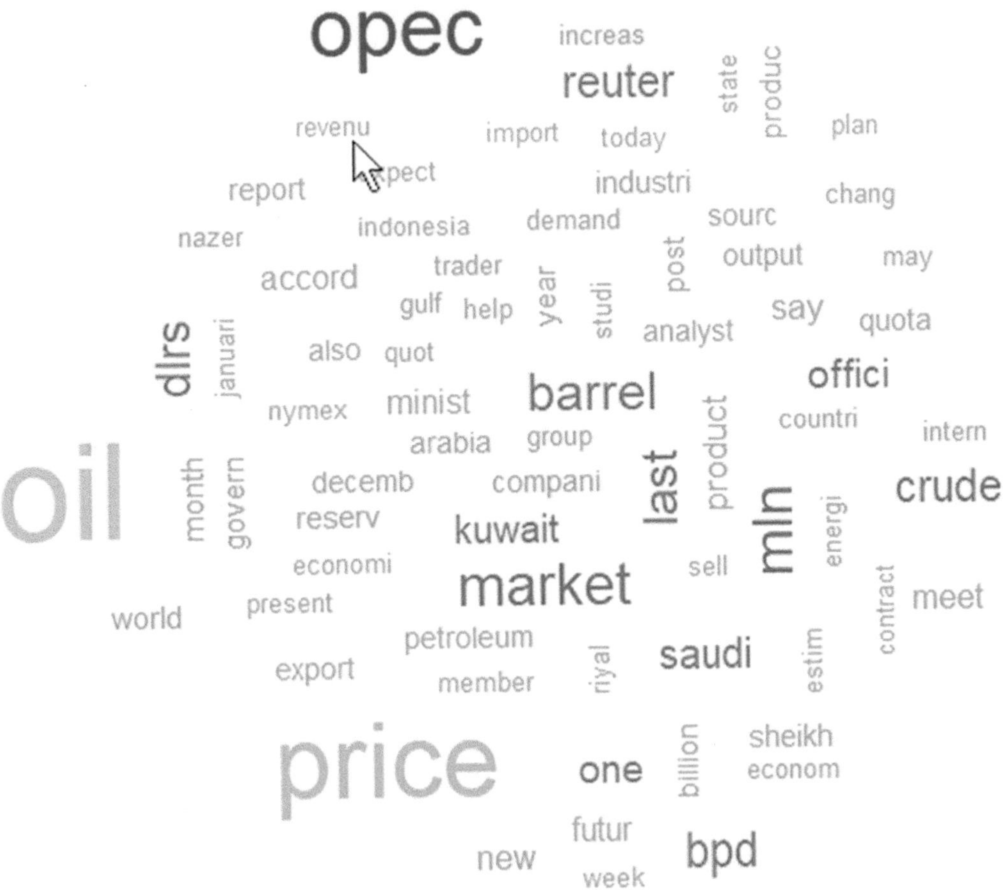

Figure 9.14 Word cloud for the "crude" data

```
text1 <- readLines(url)

# Convert to a tm-compatible SimpleCorpus called docs
docs <- tm::Corpus(tm::VectorSource(text1))

# Remove punctuation and stop words. Ignore warning messages*.
docs <- tm::tm_map(docs, tm::content_transformer(tolower))
docs <- tm::tm_map(docs, stripWhitespace)
docs<-tm::tm_map(docs,removePunctuation)
docs <- tm::tm_map(docs, removeWords, stopwords("english"))
docs <- tm_map(docs, removeWords, c("shall", "may"))
# Stemming words is omitted: docs <- tm _ map(docs, stemDocument)

# Create the word cloud shown in Figure 9.15.
wordcloud::wordcloud(docs, min.freq=4, max.words = 75, rot.per=.2,
colors=RColorBrewer::brewer.pal(6, "Dark2"))
```

* In code above, `VectorSource()` checks the number of document names in the Corpus, but with text read as a vector, there are no document names, causing an ignorable warning. Contrary to the warning, no documents were dropped.

Figure 9.15 Word cloud for the U.S. Constitution

3. Creating a word cloud from a term-document matrix.

   We start by creating a small-"c" corpus of character vectors in the "data_corpus_inaugural" object, which is loaded when the quanteda package is loaded. This is a collection of U.S. presidential inaugural addresses, discussed previously.

```
corp <- quanteda::corpus(data_corpus_inaugural)class(data_corpus_inaugural)
```

   [Output:]

```
      [1] "corpus"    "character"
```

Convert to a capital-"C" Corpus using the tm package.

```
corp_simple <- tm::SimpleCorpus(VectorSource(unlist(lapply(corp,
as.character))))
class(corp_simple)
[Output:]
   [1] "SimpleCorpus" "Corpus"
```

Convert to a term-document matrix (tdm) object with `TermDocumentMatrix()` options.

```
corp_tdm <- tm::TermDocumentMatrix(corp_simple, control = list(removeNumbers =
TRUE, removePunctuation=TRUE, stopwords = TRUE, stemming = TRUE))
class(corp_tdm)
[Output:]
    [1] "TermDocumentMatrix"    "simple_triplet_matrix"
```

Convert from a tdm object to a matrix, then sort it.

```
corp_matrix <- as.matrix(corp_tdm)
corp_matrix <- sort(rowSums(corp_matrix),decreasing=TRUE)
class(corp_matrix)
[Output:]
   [1] "numeric"
```

Finally, convert to a data frame

```
corp_df <- data.frame(word = names(corp_matrix), freq = corp_matrix)
class(corp_df)
[Output:]
    [1] "data.frame"
```

After these conversions, we may make word cloud shown in Figure 9.16 from the corp_df data frame. We don't do so here but could manually eliminate selected words (rows) from corp_df. Note its columns are word and freq. The rownames are the same as word.

```
wordcloud::wordcloud(words = corp_df$word, freq = corp_df$freq, min.freq = 100,
max.words=200, random.order=FALSE, rot.per=0.20, colors=RColorBrewer::brewer.
pal(8, "Dark2"))
```

4. Make a word cloud directly from a Corpus

   Using the same inaugural data, we can make a word cloud directly from a Corpus like corp_simple. This is another Corpus example, like those earlier, so the resulting figure is not shown. We use clean-up using `tm _ map()` from the "tm" package. Tip: Make sure the RStudio plotting window is large enough; otherwise the long word "government" will not be plotted.

```
docs <- corp_simple
docs <- tm::tm_map(docs, tm::content_transformer(tolower))
docs <- tm::tm_map(docs, stripWhitespace)
docs <- tm::tm_map(docs,removePunctuation)
docs <- tm::tm_map(docs, removeWords, stopwords("english"))
docs <- tm_map(docs, removeWords, c("will", "can", "upon"))
wordcloud::wordcloud(docs, min.freq=5, max.words = 75, rot.per=.2,
colors=RColorBrewer::brewer.pal(6, "Dark2"))
```

One could also search for a plain text .txt file on one's local computer. When issuing the command below, a "Select File" window will open from which one may select the file. The `file.choose()` function is from R's built-in "base" package. Once the text is read in, it may be converted to a Corpus and made into a word cloud as in the previous example.

```
text3 <- readLines(file.choose())
```

Figure 9.16 U.S. inaugural addresses: Words with frequency of 100 or more

9.16 Analysis: Comparison clouds

In Section 9.10.4 on formats related to the quanteda package, we gave an illustration of creating a word cloud using its `textplot _ wordcloud()` command. Here, however, we give a variant, which is comparison clouds. This was introduced in Section 9.5.5, Figure 9.1, where the textreadr package was used. Here in this section, we use inaugurals_dfm as an example. This contains presidential inaugural addresses from Washington through Trump. The inaugurals.dfm object was created in Section 9.5.5. In this dfm object, document 57 is the Obama inaugural and 58 is that of Trump.

```
# Recreate inaugurals_dfm as in Section 9.5.5.
inaugurals_corpus <- quanteda::data_corpus_inaugural
inaugurals_dfm <- quanteda::dfm(inaugurals_corpus, remove_numbers = TRUE, remove_
punct = TRUE, stem = TRUE, remove = stopwords("english"))
```

We now create a comparison cloud, shown in Figure 9.17. The max_words option is the maximum number of words. The minsize option is the minimum length of any word. The color option sets the first and second color in the comparison. The rotation option is the percent of words shown vertically.

```
quanteda::textplot_wordcloud(inaugurals_dfm[57:58,], max_words = 150, minsize = 4,
color = c("blue", "red"), rotation= .20, comparison = TRUE)
```

We see that important words for Obama included us, must, equal, know, time, generation, journey, and freedom. Important words for Trump included America, American, protect, nation, country, back, and dream (as in American

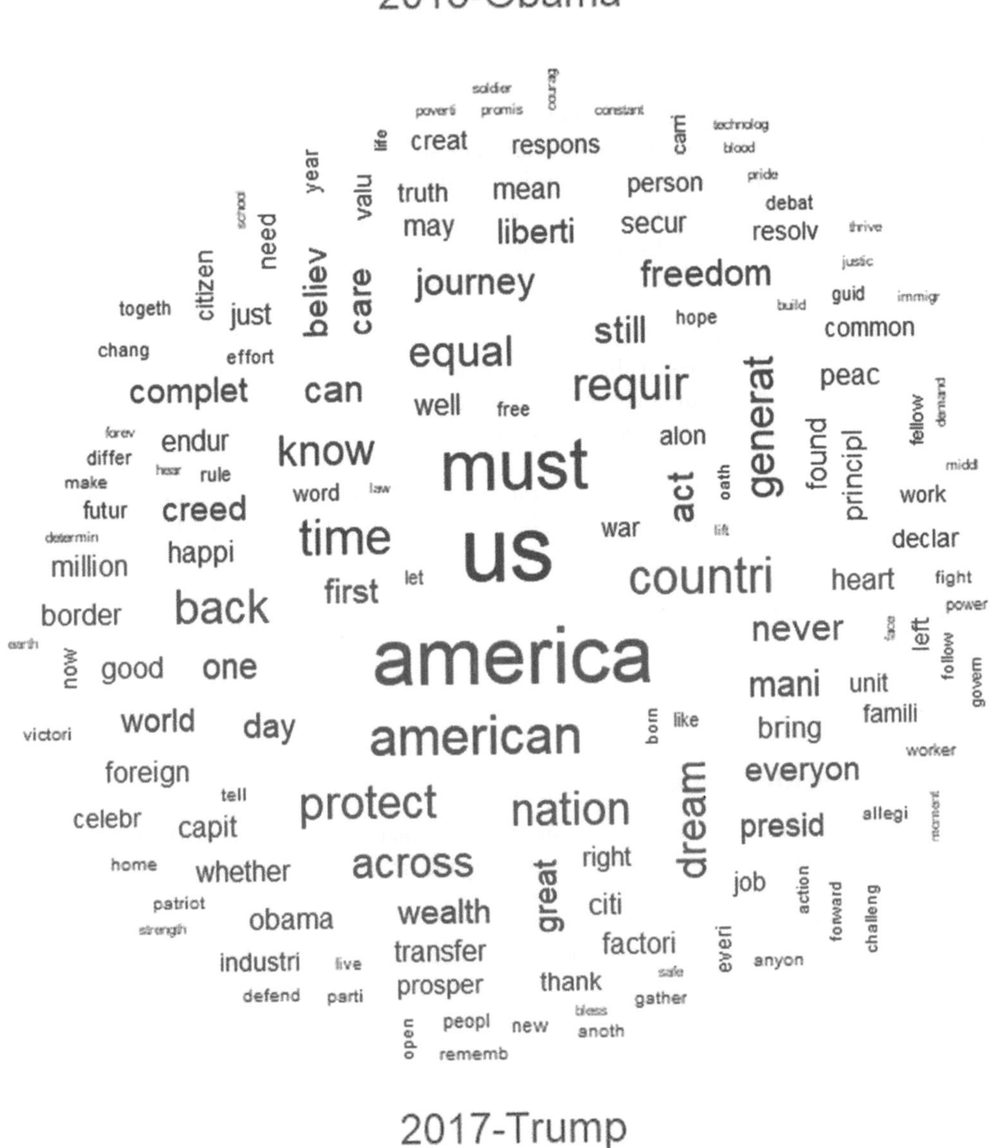

Figure 9.17 Obama/Trump comparison cloud

dream). To compare Washington and Trump instead, create a variable and use that for the range. For instance: docs <- c(1,58); inaugurals_dfm[docs,].

As illustrated in the endnote to this sentence, comparison clouds may also be implemented via the "wordcloud" package.[6]

9.17 Analysis: Word maps and word correlations

Once documents are in a tdm format, other commands from the "tm" package are available to find frequent terms and their associations. These can be used to compute word correlations and to create word maps.

```
# Setup (Rgraphviz must be installed via the "BiocManager" package, as below)
install.packages("BiocManager")
library(BiocManager)
BiocManager::install("Rgraphviz")

# For word maps
library(corrplot)          # For correlation plots
library(graph)             # Package to handle graph data structures
library(quanteda)          # A leading text analysis package
library(Rgraphviz)         # Plotting capabilities for R graphic objects
library(RColorBrewer)      # For color management
library(tm)                # A leading text analysis package

# For the word correlation chart and word correlations
library(dplyr)             # Utilities, including >%> piping
library(ggplot2)           # A leading visualization package
library(tidyr)             # Tools to create and clean tidy data
```

As example text, we again use the data_corpus_inaugural object from the "quanteda" package. This is a "small-c"corpus which contains U.S. presidential inaugural addresses, as discussed in Section 9.16 on comparative word clouds.

```
inaugurals_corpus <- quanteda::data_corpus_inaugural
class(inaugurals_corpus)
[Output:]
     [1] "corpus"    "character"
```

9.17.1 Working with the tdm format

To use many of the functions in the "tm" package, we must convert inaugurals_corpus to tdm format. A prior step here, however, is first to convert it to a "capital-C" Corpus using the tm package as shown below.

```
# Convert from a corpus to a Corpus.
inaugurals_Corpus <- tm::SimpleCorpus(tm::VectorSource(unlist(lapply(inaugurals_
corpus, as.character))))

class(inaugurals_Corpus)
[Output:]
     [1] "SimpleCorpus" "Corpus"
```

Having created a Corpus, we can convert the Corpus object into a tdm object. This is done with the `TermDocumentMatrix()` command. Stemming will make counts more accurate but terms will be stems, not the original words. We see below that there are 5,312 word stem terms in 58 documents. Had we set `stemming = FALSE`, then there would have been 9,091 words, with nation, nations, national, etc., all counted as different words.

```
tdm <- tm::TermDocumentMatrix(inaugurals_Corpus, control = list(removeNumbers =
TRUE, removePunctuation=TRUE, stopwords = TRUE, stemming = TRUE))
class(tdm)
```

[Output:]

```
[1] "TermDocumentMatrix"    "simple_triplet_matrix"
```

```
tdm
```

[Output:]

```
<<TermDocumentMatrix (terms: 5312, documents: 58)>>
Non-/sparse entries: 33590/274506
Sparsity           : 89%
Maximal term length: 17
Weighting          : term frequency (tf)
```

The same information about number of terms and documents can be obtained by using the `dim()` command.

```
dim(tdm)
```

[Output:]

```
[1] 5312   58
```

We can examine the tdm object by converting it to a matrix. Below, we look at seven rows (4354 to 4360) near the "state" stem, for only the first 4 of 58 columns. Values are the count of times the row word is used in the column document. Note that the stemming function in tm has collapsed state and states into the "state" stem but has left some other words starting with "state" as separate words. There are more sophisticated stemming programs than that built into the tm package. Note that in tdm format, documents are columns and words are rows.

```
m <- as.matrix(tdm)
m[4354:4360,1:4]
```

[Output:]

```
                Docs
Terms            1789-Washington 1793-Washington 1797-Adams 1801-Jefferson
  starv                        0               0          0              0
  state                        2               0         12              3
  statement                    0               0          0              0
  statesman                    0               0          0              0
  statesmanship                0               0          0              0
  statesmen                    0               0          0              0
  station                      2               0          1              1
```

9.17.2 Working with the dtm format

Similar to creating a tdm object above, we now convert a Corpus to dtm.

```
dtm <- tm::DocumentTermMatrix(inaugurals_Corpus, control = list(stemming=TRUE,
removePunctuation=TRUE, removeNumbers = TRUE, stopwords = TRUE))
class(dtm)
```

[Output:]

```
[1] "DocumentTermMatrix"    "simple_triplet_matrix"
```

The dtm format has 58 documents and 5,312 word stems, which is the same as the tdm format.

```
dtm
```

[Output:]

```
<<DocumentTermMatrix (documents: 58, terms: 5312)>>
Non-/sparse entries: 33590/274506
Sparsity           : 89%
Maximal term length: 17
Weighting          : term frequency (tf)
```

We may examine the dtm object by converting it to a matrix. Then we list the first 5 of 58 rows and a range of columns starting with "state". Values are the count of times the column word is used in the row document. Note that in dtm format, documents are rows and words are columns.

```
m2<-as.matrix(dtm)
m2[1:5,4355:4360]
```

[Output:]

```
                 Terms
Docs              state statement statesman statesmanship statesmen station
  1789-Washington     2         0         0             0         0       2
  1793-Washington     0         0         0             0         0       0
  1797-Adams         12         0         0             0         0       1
  1801-Jefferson      3         0         0             0         0       1
  1805-Jefferson     12         0         0             0         0       1
```

9.17.3 Word frequencies and word correlations

In this subsection, we seek to find frequent terms. Specifically, we list all terms used 150 times or more. Note that this requires the term-centric tdm format. It will not work with the document-centric "dtm" format. Later, in Section 9.17.6 we will create a word map of the most frequent terms.

```
tm::findFreqTerms(tdm, lowfreq = 150)
```

[Partial output:]

```
 [1] "america"   "american"  "can"       "citizen"
 [5] "constitut" "countri"   "duti"      "everi"
 [9] "free"      "freedom"   "good"      "govern"
[13] "great"     "hope"      "interest"  "law"
[17] "let"       "made"      "make"      "may"
[21] "must"      "nation"    "new"       "now"
[25] "one"       "peac"      "peopl"     "power"
[29] "principl"  "public"    "right"     "secur"
[33] "shall"     "state"     "time"      "union"
[37] "unit"      "upon"      "war"       "will"
[41] "world"     "year"
```

Next we compute word correlations, also called word associations. To do this we again use the term-centric tdm format. The tdm object has 5,312 word stems across 58 documents. Below we look for correlations of r >= .5 with the word stem "govern". Unlike output above, this listing is not limited to terms used 150 times or more but rather is limited to correlations of .5 or higher.

```
associations_tdm <- tm::findAssocs(tdm, terms = "govern", corlimit = 0.5)

associations_tdm
```

[Partial output, word stems by descending correlation with "govern":]

```
         state          system           oper          adopt
```

```
     0.77           0.76            0.75          0.74
    exist           duti            form        general
     0.74           0.73            0.73          0.73
  . . .

     feel          former    misconstruct        prevent
     0.50           0.50            0.50          0.50
   shield           void
     0.50           0.50
```

One also can get associations for more than one word stem at once.

```
tm::findAssocs(tdm, terms = c("govern", "state"), corlimit = 0.5)
```
[Output not shown. Two correlation lists are produced, one for "govern" and one for "state".]

It is also possible to find word stem correlations (associations) using the document-centric dtm format.

```
associations_dtm <- tm::findAssocs(dtm, terms = "govern", corlimit = 0.5)

associations_dtm
```
[Output is the same as for the tdm form, so is not shown here.]

Both tdm and dtm associations are the Pearsonian correlations of the search word stem ("govern") with the word stems listed in output above. For instance, the tdm correlation of "govern" and "state" is .77 in either tdm or dtm format. The correlation of .77 reflects the correlation of the frequencies of these two word stems across the 58 inaugural documents.

9.17.4 Correlation plots of word and document associations

The `corrplot()` command may be used to visualize word correlations. We may create correlation plots of terms, based on the "m2" object created above, which was the matrix version of the dtm version of the inaugural data. We want dtm format because columns are words, and columns are treated as variables for purposes of correlation. The corrplot's rows and columns will be the words. The problem, however, is that with 5,312 terms, any plot would be unmanageably large. Quite possible the user's computer would "hang" just trying to compute the solution. Therefore, it is necessary to subset a much smaller number of words. Below we create a subset of the first 30 words (m2subset) and use that instead for correlation data and for the plot, which is shown in Figure 9.18. High word correlations across the 58 inaugural speeches are abhor-abstract, abridge-absent, and absence-abode. The first 30 words from among 5,312 is an arbitrary set. More meaningful word associations would arise if words of greater research interest are selected.

```
m2subset <- subset(m2,subset=TRUE,select = 1:30)
cor_data <- cor(m2subset)
corrplot(cor_data, method = "square", type = "upper", tl.col = "black", order =
"hclust", col = brewer.pal(n = 5, name = "RdYlBu"))
```

Alternatively, it is possible to see which documents (here, inaugural speeches) are correlated across all 5,312 words considered. As there are only 58 documents, we do not need to subset but the plot would be crowded. We decide to look only at inaugural addresses since 1901. These are documents 29 through 58. This plot, shown in Figure 9.19, shows that words used by Obama 2013 were highly associated with words used by Obama 2009 and by Clinton 1997. Obama 2009 was highly correlated with Bush 1989 as well as with Clinton 1997. Trump 2017 was highly correlated with Reagan 1981 as might be expected, but also with Clinton 1997 and Obama 2009.

In code below, the RColorBrewer and corrplot libraries are used. The correlation plot is based on the earlier-created "m" object, which was the matrix version of the tdm version of the inaugural data. Since in

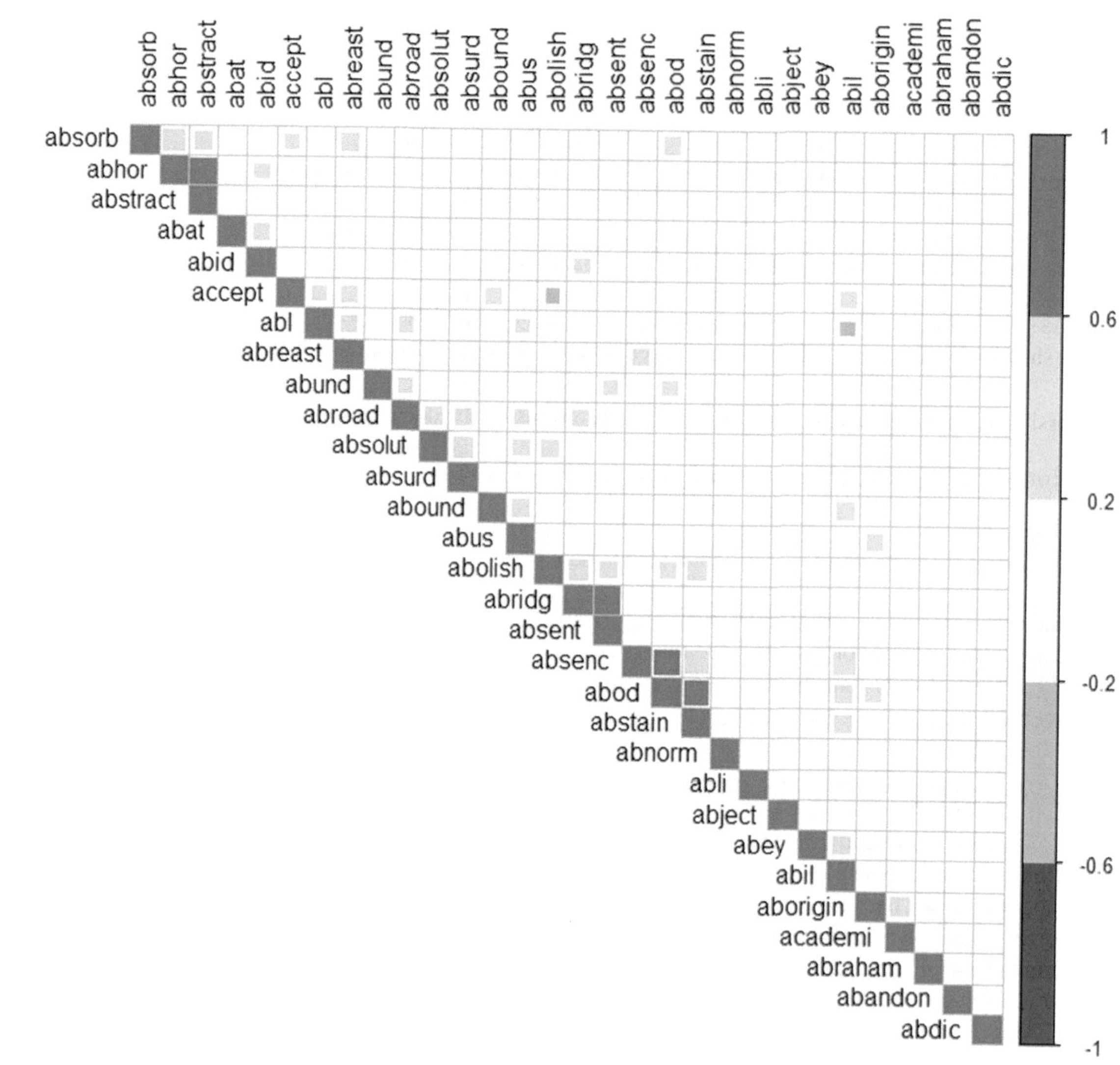

Figure 9.18 Correlation plot of the first 30 words across 58 inaugural addresses

tdm format the columns are the documents, treated as "variables", the corrplot's rows and columns are the documents.

```
msubset <- subset(m,subset=TRUE,select = 29:58)
cor_data <- cor(msubset)
corrplot::corrplot(cor_data, method = "square", type = "upper", tl.col = "black",
order = "hclust", col = brewer.pal(n = 5, name = "RdYlBu"))
```

The method below outlines how to print out word correlations of interest.

1. Convert tdm, created above, to a matrix. Note we do not want to convert tdm directly to a data frame.[7]

```
m <- as.matrix(tdm)
```

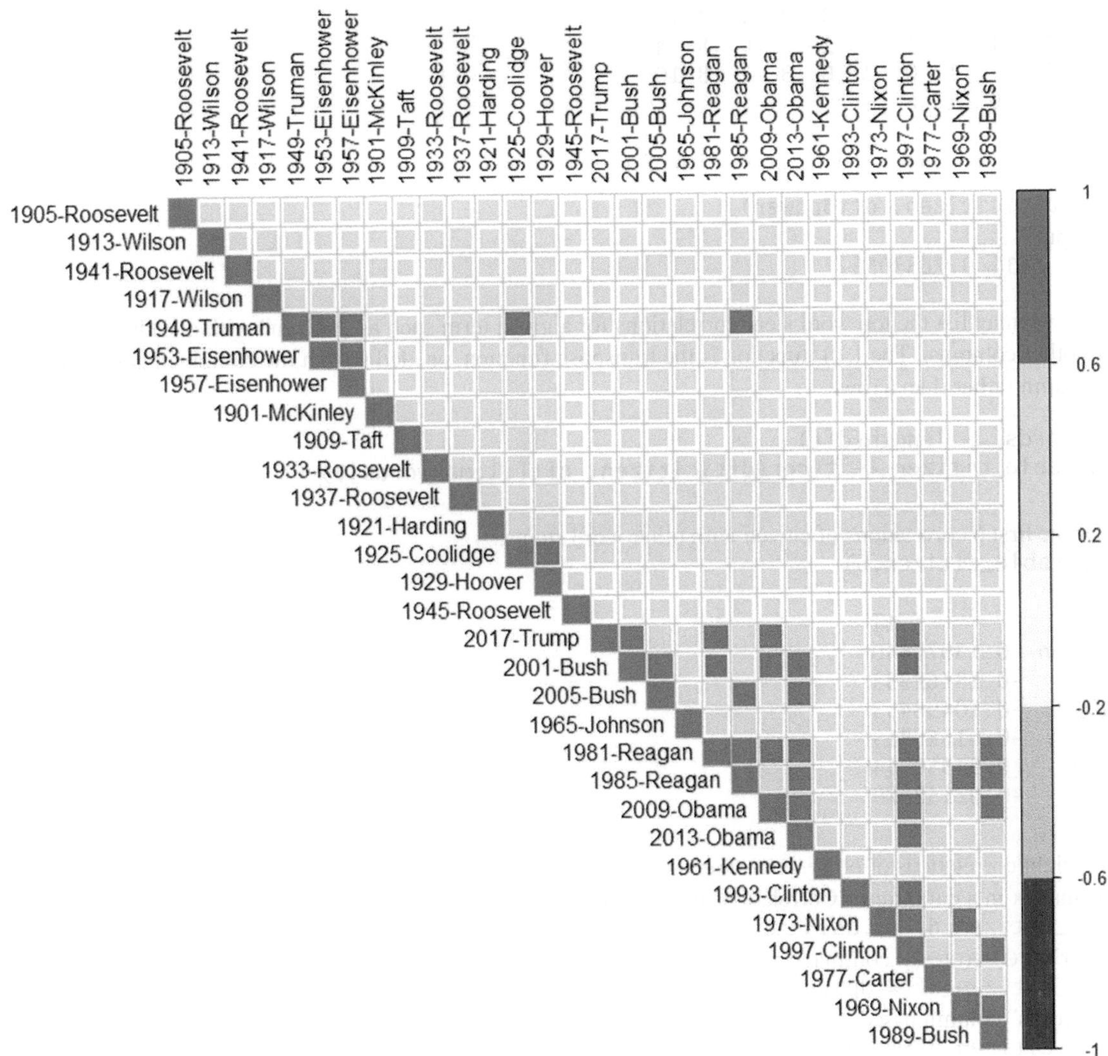

Figure 9.19 Correlation plot inaugural addresses since 1901 across 5,312 words

2. Transpose the matrix and then convert it to data frame dft, with words now as columns.

```
mt <- t(m)
dft <- as.data.frame(mt)
```

3. We may now compute the word count for any specified word stem such as “citizen”. The result gives it word count in each of the 58 documents.

```
dft$citizen
[Output:]
  [1]  4  1  3  5 10  0  3  9 14
 [10]  3  2  3  7 26 10  1  3  5
```

```
[19]  6  0  4  1  8  5 10  6  7
[28]  7  0  1  5  0  3  1  4 11
[37]  1  2  1  1  1  6  0  5  4
[46]  1  1  0  3  6  3  2  8 10
[55]  6  1  8  4
```

4. We can also compute a specific correlation of interest, such as the correlation of "citizen" with "power".

```
cor(dft$citizen, dft$power)
```
[Output:]
```
     [1] 0.7633055
```

5. Then we may list the top word stem correlations for a given term such as "citizen" with all other word stems (all other columns). The `t()` function is the transpose function, needed so that the computed correlations are a column rather than a row.

```
maxwords <- length(dft)
cortable_citizen <- t(cor(dft$citizen, dft[,1:maxwords]))
```

Look at the first 6 correlations of citizen with other word stems.
```
head(cortable_citizen,6)
```
[Output:]
```
                  [,1]
   abandon  0.13977640
   abat    -0.13462333
   abdic   -0.10493453
   abey    -0.01586815
   abhor    0.04350944
   abid    -0.02152870
```

List top eight correlations of other word stems with citizen
Put the matrix in a data frame. Correlations by default are in column "V1".
```
cortable_citizen_df <- as.data.frame(cortable_citizen)
```
Use dplyr's `rename()` command to rename the "V1" column to "correlation".
```
cortable_citizen_df = dplyr::rename(cortable_citizen_df, correlation = V1)
```
Add a "words" column based on rownames, which are the words
```
cortable_citizen_df$words <- rownames(cortable_citizen_df)
```
Sort correlations in descending order. The minus sign asks for descending order.
```
cortable_citizen_sorted <- cortable_citizen_df [with(cortable_citizen_df,
order(-correlation)), ]
```

We now list at the top eight word stem correlations. Note that the most correlated words are not the same as the most frequent words. For instance, "claim", which is the word stem most highly correlated with "citizen", will not be in the word map in Section 9.17.6 because it is not among the 30 most frequent words.

```
head(cortable_citizen_sorted,8)
```
[Output:]
```
           correlation   words
  citizen    1.0000000 citizen
  claim      0.7748056   claim
  charact    0.7641963 charact
  power      0.7633055   power
  dispos     0.7272110  dispos
  produc     0.7256399  produc
  exclus     0.7191399  exclus
  intend     0.7093824  intend
```

9.17.5 Plotting word stem correlations for word pairs

In this section, we create Figures 9.20 and 9.21, which plot word correlations for the selected terms "citizen" and "power". This is mainly done with the tidyr text analysis package and the ggplot2 visualization package. We assume that the "tdm" object, created in Section 9.17.1, is still in the R environment. Otherwise, recreate it with the commands below:

```
inaugurals_corpus <- quanteda::data_corpus_inaugural

inaugurals_Corpus <- tm::SimpleCorpus(tm::VectorSource(unlist(lapply(inaugurals_
corpus, as.character))))

tdm <- tm::TermDocumentMatrix(inaugurals_Corpus, control = list(removeNumbers =
TRUE, removePunctuation=TRUE, stopwords = TRUE, stemming = TRUE))

# Identify terms of interest (terms must be in the tdm file)
term1 <- "citizen"
term2 <- "power"

# Set the lower correlation bound: The higher, the simpler the later table.
corlimit <- 0.5

# Compute correlations for term1, which is "citizen".
# Note this method rounds to 2 decimals, whereas sortedwordcorrs above rounded to 3
# Ties will affect the word order.
corr1 <- findAssocs(tdm, term1, corlimit)[[1]]
corr1
[Partial output]
      claim        charact         power        dispos        produc
       0.77           0.76          0.76          0.73          0.73
     exclus         appear        intend      principl        defect
       0.72           0.71          0.71          0.71          0.70
 . . .
      excel            far        forbid         indic    necessari
       0.50           0.50          0.50          0.50         0.50
     period           ruin     sovereign
       0.50           0.50          0.50

# Compute correlations for term2, which is "power".
corr2 <- findAssocs(tdm, term2, corlimit)[[1]]
corr2
[Output not shown]

# Convert correlations into table format; corr1table is of class data.frame
# This is the table for term1, which is "citizen"
# The corr1table object has terms for rownames and has two variables (columns)
# Column 1 is "V1", also containing the terms
# Column 2 is "corr1", containing the correlations
corr1table <- cbind(read.table(text = names(corr1), stringsAsFactors = FALSE),
corr1)
# Use dplyr's rename() command to rename the "V1" column to "term", corr1 to "citizen".
corr1table = dplyr::rename(corr1table, word = V1, citizen = corr1)

# The same for term2, which is "power", but column 2 is "corr2".
corr2table <- cbind(read.table(text = names(corr2), stringsAsFactors = FALSE),
corr2)
```

```
# Use dplyr's rename() command to rename the "V1" column to "term", corr1 to "power".
corr2table = dplyr::rename(corr2table, word = V1, power = corr2)

# Join corr1table and corr2table to list stem word correlations with both "citizen" and "power".
term_corr_table <- full_join(corr1table, corr2table)
head(term_corr_table, 6)
[Output:]
     word citizen power
  1   claim    0.77  0.85
  2 charact    0.76  0.85
  3   power    0.76    NA
  4  dispos    0.73  0.85
  5  produc    0.73  0.79
  6  exclus    0.72  0.93
```

We now "gather" for plotting purposes. The `gather()` function of the tidyr package gathers columns into key-value pairs. Here the key value pair is citizen:power. The `term_corrs_gathered` object has 986 rows (2 correlations times 493 terms), listing the "citizen" terms first, then the "power" terms.

```
term_corrs_gathered <- tidyr::gather(term_corr_table, term, correlation,
citizen:power)
# List just the top and bottom three rows in term_corrs_gathered.
head(term_corrs_gathered,3)
       word    term correlation
  1   claim citizen        0.77
  2 charact citizen        0.76
  3   power citizen        0.76
tail(term_corrs_gathered,3)
   984 mischief power         0.5
   985  subsist power         0.5
   986   upward power         0.5

# Create the correlation chart for two terms of interest
# We get this ignorable warning message:
# "Warning message: Removed 131 rows containing missing values (geom_point),"
ggplot2::ggplot(term_corrs_gathered,
   aes(x = word, y = correlation, colour =  term) ) +
   geom_point(size = 3) +
   ylab(paste0("Correlation with the terms ", "\"", term1,  "\"", " and ",  "\"",
term2, "\"")) +
   theme_bw() +
   theme(axis.text.x = element_text(angle = 90, hjust = 1, vjust = 0.5))
```

The resulting Figure 9.20 shows that "power" tends to have more highly-correlated words than does "citizen", based on the original document (the Declaration of Independence and # the Constitution). However, there are too many words on the x-axis.

Because the x-axis has too many words, we next create a similar plot with fewer terms, using a four-step process.

1. Sort on the "correlation" column from term_corrs_gathered to get the index order.

   ```
   # The minus sign indicates to sort descending
   order.index <- order(-term_corrs_gathered$correlation)
   ```

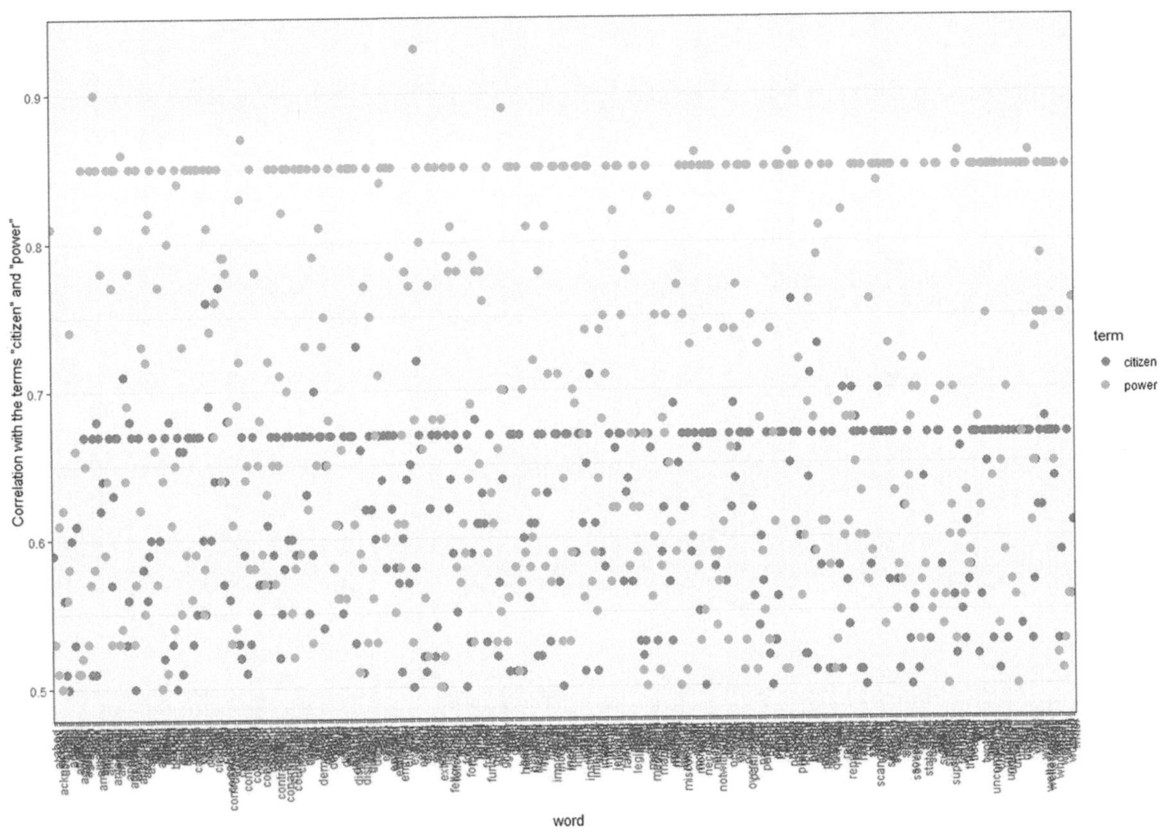

Figure 9.20 Word stem correlations for "citizen" and "power"

2. Create terms_sorted_all, which has all correlations in sorted order but would give the same cluttered plot as Figure 9.20.

```
terms_sorted_all <- term_corrs_gathered[order.index,]
```

3. For instructional purposes, we select some rows, which have both "citizen" and "power". Ordinarily we might select, say, the top 12 correlations, but for our example data, all would be correlations for "power" and none for "citizen". Therefore, we take a random sample of 20 words.

```
set.seed(123)
terms_sorted_selected <-
terms_sorted_all[sample(1:nrow(terms_sorted_all), 20),]
```

4. Plot terms_sorted_selected using the same syntax as for Figure 9.20, except we increase the symbol sixe, element size, element justification, and set the element angle to 45 degrees. This gives Figure 9.21.

```
ggplot2::ggplot(terms_sorted_selected,
   aes(x = word, y = correlation, colour =  term) ) +
   geom_point(size = 5) +
   ylab(paste0("Correlation with the terms ", "\"", term1,  "\"", " and ",
"\"", term2, "\"")) +
   theme_bw() +
   theme(axis.text.x = element_text(angle = 45, hjust = 0.5, vjust = 0.5,
size = 16))
```

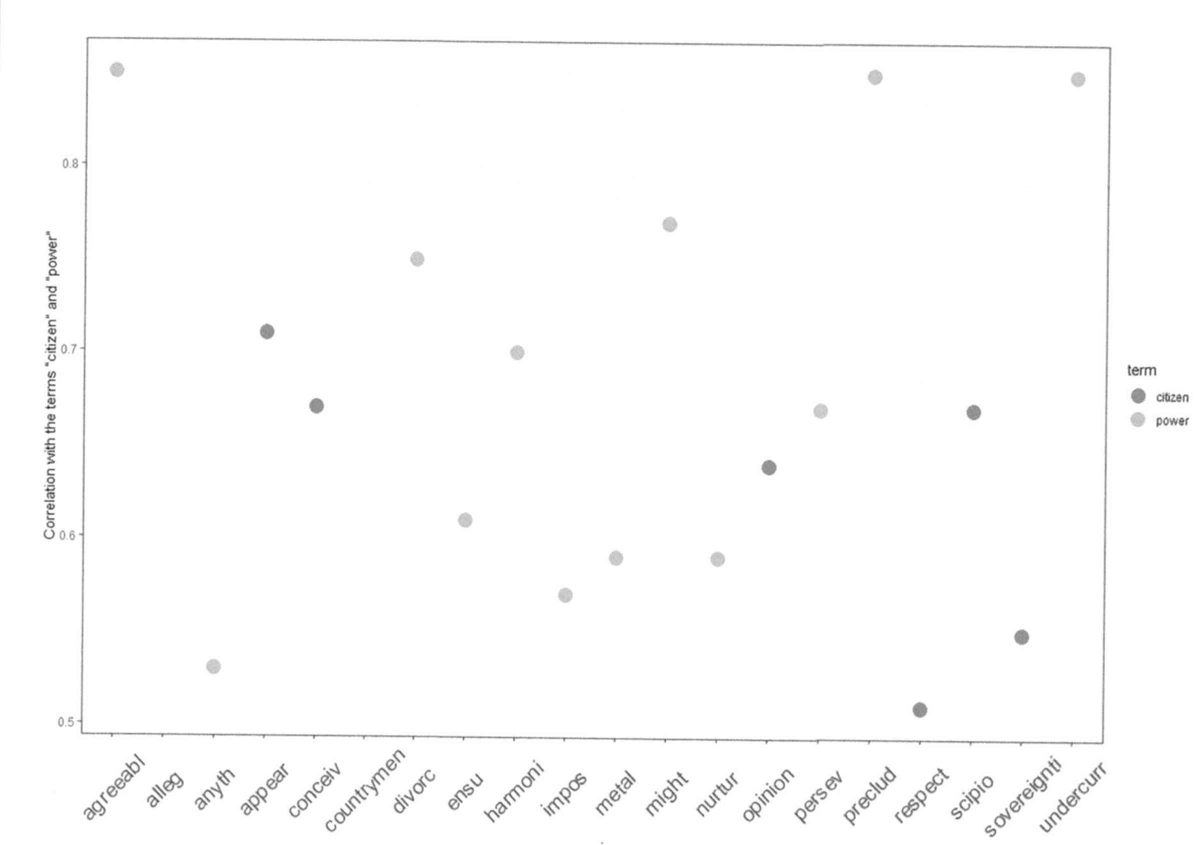

Figure 9.21 Correlations of 20 random words with "citizen" and "power"

9.17.6 Word correlation maps

Word correlation maps visualize relationships among the most frequently used words for all documents being considered. In this section, we continue to use as an example the collection of U.S. inaugural speeches used in the previous section. Specifically we use the "tdm" object created in Section 9.17.5. This is the text document matrix formatted version the data.

This section requires use of the package "Rgraphviz", which must be installed via the "BiocManager" package as explained at the start of Section 9.17. If following along, we assume the reader has done that and that the "tdm" object is active in local R environment. If not, repeat the instructions in Section 9.17.5 to recreate it.

```
# Setup
library(graph)          # Package to handle graph data structures
library(Rgraphviz)      # Plotting capabilities for R graphic objects
library(RColorBrewer)   # For color management
library(tm)             # A leading text analysis package

# Get word frequencies for 30 most frequent terms. Only these 30 words are in the plot.
freq.terms <- tm::findFreqTerms(tdm, lowfreq=150)[1:30]
```

A quick-and-dirty word map may be created with this simple command, shown in Figure 9.22. Note that there may well be other terms with high correlations with terms in the plot but which are not in the plot because they are not among the 30 most frequent terms.

```
plot(tdm, term=freq.terms, corThreshold=.50, weighting=FALSE)
```

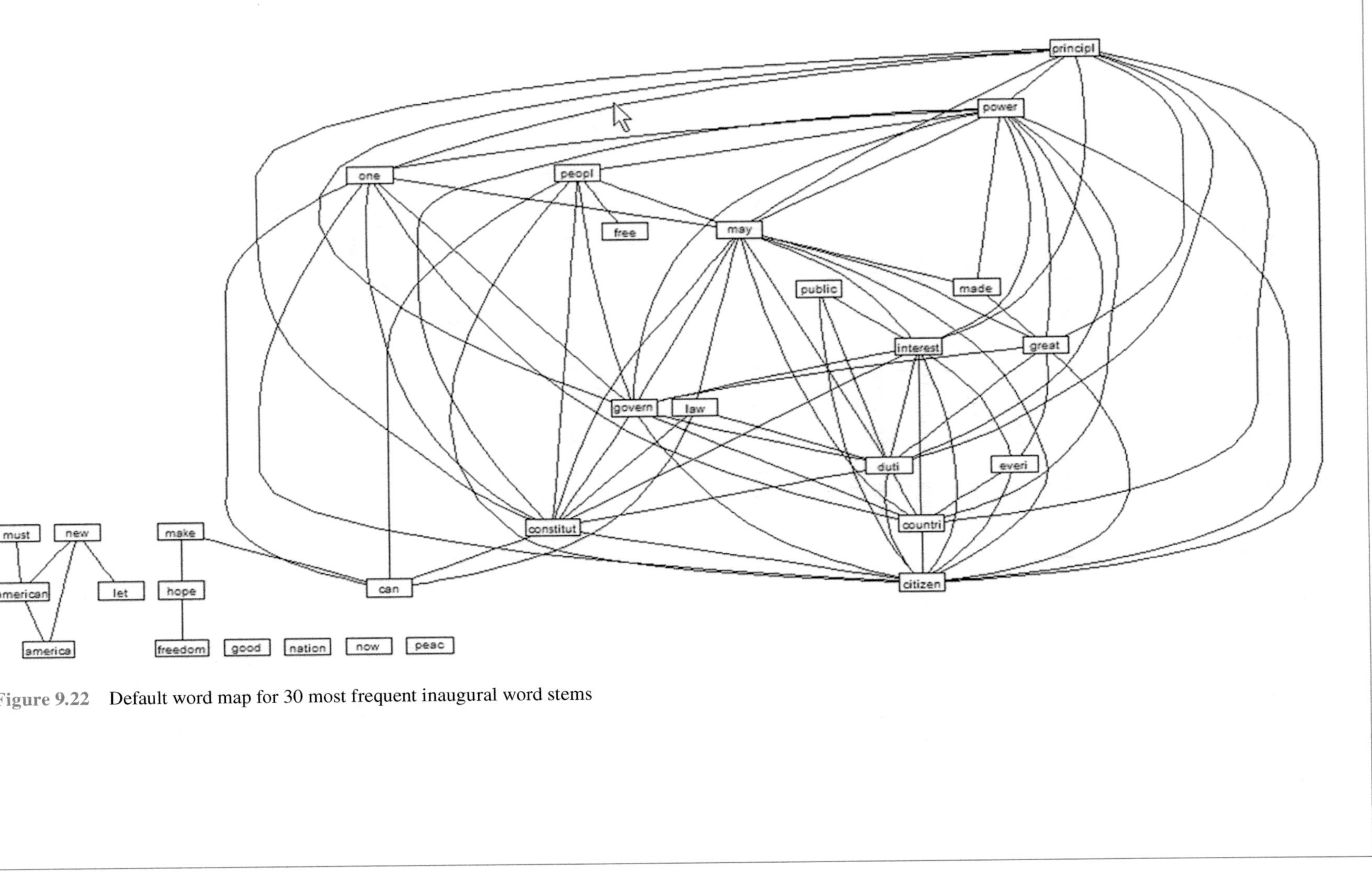

Figure 9.22 Default word map for 30 most frequent inaugural word stems

A better map with color coding of vertices (words) requires more code. Color coding highlights more central words. Below, we color code by number of vertices for a given word stem, so we count them first. The count is the number of word stem associations with a correlation greater than or equal to 0.5, which converge on a given word stem. After computing the vertex count object "vtxcnt", we sort vtxcount decreasing. Terms with higher vertex count correlate highly with more other terms and thus may be seen as representing terms with greater centrality for the set of documents.

```
vtxcnt <- rowSums(cor(as.matrix(t(tdm[freq.terms,])))>.5)-1
vtxcnt <- sort(vtxcnt,decreasing=TRUE)
vtxcnt
```

[Output:]

```
    citizen        may     power constitut      duti
         13         13        12        11        11
     govern   interest  principl   countri     great
         11         10        10         9         9
        one      peopl       can     everi       law
          8          8         5         4         4
   american       made       new    public   america
          3          3         3         3         2
       hope       make      free   freedom       let
          2          2         1         1         1
       must       good    nation       now      peac
          1          0         0         0         0
```

We then calculate the largest number of vertices for any word. The maximum is 13, for the term "citizen".

```
maxvtxcnt<-max(vtxcnt)
maxvtxcnt
```

[Output:]

```
[1] 13
```

For mapping purposes, we use the "RColorBrewer" package to get 13 corresponding colors using a yellow-orange-red color ramp. The "# grDevices" package is part of the R system library and is used to extend the number of color gradations. RColorBrewer on its own supports only nine color gradations. The mycols (my colors) object will have 13 shades of ramp colors, however. Colors are shown in hex code.

```
nb.cols<-maxvtxcnt
mycols<-grDevices::colorRampPalette(RColorBrewer::brewer.pal(9, "YlOrRd"))(nb.cols)
mycols
```

[Output of hex color codes]

```
 [1] "#FFFFCC" "#FFF3AE" "#FEE692" "#FED976" "#FEBF5A"
 [6] "#FDA546" "#FD8D3C" "#FC6330" "#F33C25" "#E31A1C"
[11] "#C90822" "#A80026" "#800026"
```

Then there are three steps involved in creating the final word correlation map:

1. Create the object vc with colors corresponding to vertex count.

   ```
   vc <- mycols[vtxcnt+1]
   ```

2. Assign names & shift colors by the count of terms tied for most vertices. This is 2 for this example. This assigns colors to words, as shown in output below.

   ```
   maxtop <-2
   names(vc) <- names(vtxcnt)
   for(i in 1:30) {vc[i]<-vc[i+maxtop]}
   last<-length(vc)
   vc[last]<-vc[last-maxtop]
   ```

```
vc
[Partial output:]
    citizen       may     power constitut      duti
  "#800026" "#A80026" "#A80026" "#A80026" "#C90822"
     govern  interest  principl   countri     great
  "#C90822" "#E31A1C" "#E31A1C" "#F33C25" "#F33C25"
  . . .
```

3. Map the word correlations. The result is shown in Figure 9.23. This complex map is admittedly hard to read in print, but shows up well on the computer. Also, it could be made simpler/smaller by increasing corThreshold (e.g., only mapping for r >= .7). A `weighting=TRUE option` would create lines of thickness keyed to correlation but, as all the requested correlations are high (.5 or greater), all lines would be thick. Tip: Select Zoom under the Plots tab to view the labeling more easily.

```
plot(tdm, terms = freq.terms, corThreshold = 0.5, weighting = FALSE, attrs =
list(node=list(width=1, fontsize=24, fontcolor = "black", shape="rectangle",fixe
dsize=FALSE)), nodeAttrs = list(fillcolor=vc))
```

Figure 9.23 employs stemming, connects word stems where the correlation is 0.50 or higher, and removes stop words. Darker shades of nodes in the resulting word correlation map reflect word stems with more high correlations (r >= .5) with other words as indicated by the connecting lines. "Citizen", at the top, is colored dark red and has 13 high correlations with other words in the map, including "constitute", "govern", and "power", all of which have several high correlations. At the other end of the spectrum, the word stem "free" has only one high correlation, which is to the word stem "peopl". "Freedom" is considered a separate word stem and also has only one high correlation, which is to "hope". "American" and "american" are highly related to "new".

9.18 Analysis: Sentiment analysis

9.18.1 Overview

Sentiment analysis also goes under such synonyms as sentiment mining, opinion mining, opinion analysis, and affect or emotion analysis. There are as many variations on sentiment analysis as there are researchers engaged in it. In general, however, sentiment analysis means that a text is tokenized into units (e.g., words), words are classified by the sentiment they connote (e.g., positive, negative), and the distribution of sentiments is tracked over time, compared between groups, or otherwise analyzed. In the example in this section, which is adapted from Silge and Robinson (2020), a publicly available dtm of over 10,000 words in over 2,000 Associated Press news articles is the basis for a simple type of sentiment analysis. The dtm format was discussed in Section 9.17.2. For further exploration, texts on sentiment analysis include Bing (2015), Pozzi and Fersini (2017), Cambria et al., eds. (2017), and Agarwal et al., eds. (2020).

9.18.2 Example: Sentiment analysis of news articles

This section illustrates one of a large number of approaches to sentiment analysis. It is assumed all the needed packages below have been installed previously and are available for loading.

```
# Setup
library(tidytext)        # A leading text analysis package for R
library(tidyr)           # Tools to create and reshape tidytext data
library(tm)              # Another leading text analysis package
library(topicmodels)     # Has the "AssociatedPress" sample of 2,246 AP articles
library(dplyr)           # Utility package with %>% piping, counting, and more
library(ggplot2)         # The leading visualization/plotting package for R
setwd("C:/Data")         # Set the working directory
```

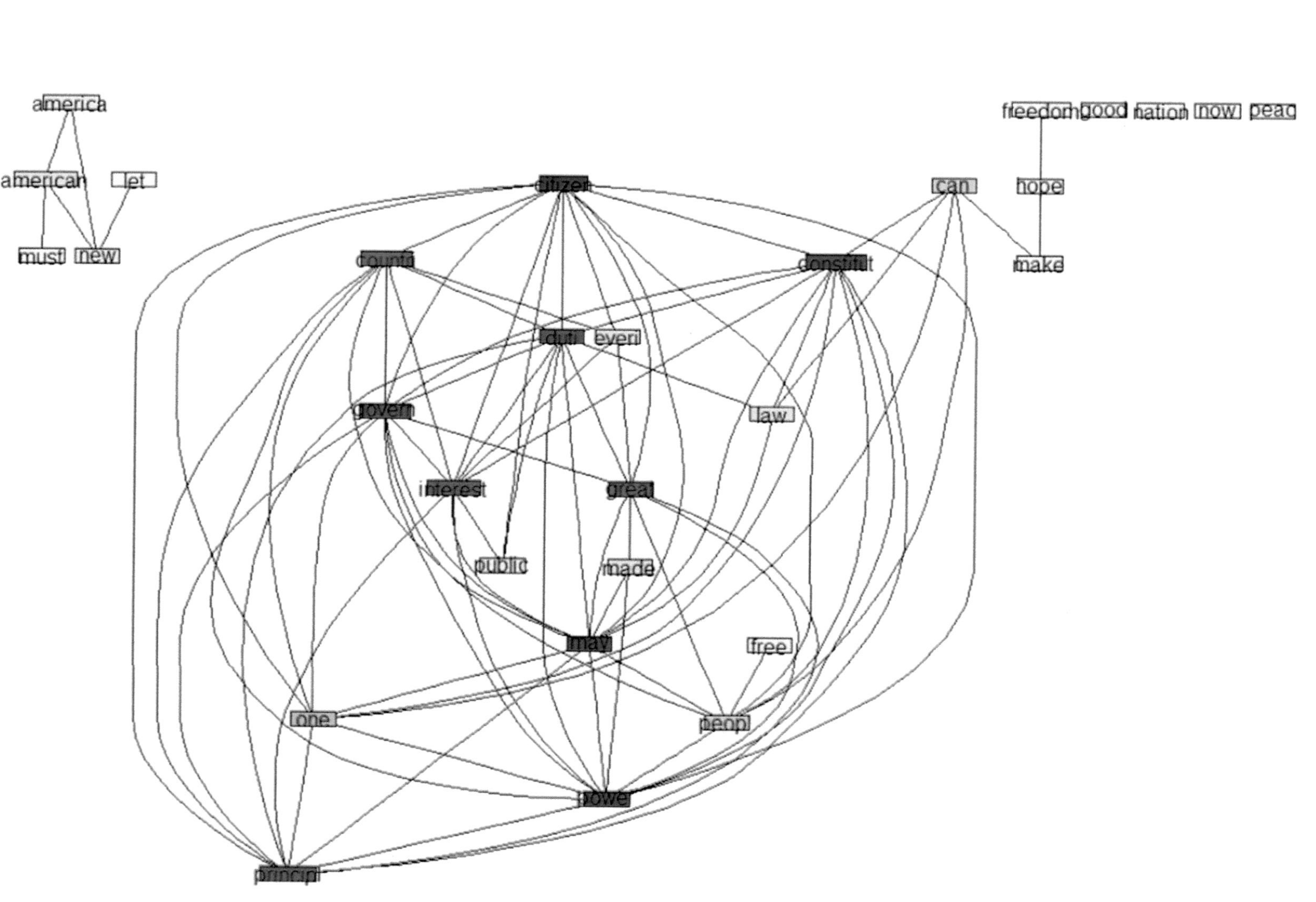

Figure 9.23 Color-coded word map for 30 most frequent inaugural word stems

After invoking the needed packages, the first step is to import the data. For clarity, we rename the original "AssociatedPress" object containing the text to be analyzed as "ap_dtm", with the "ap" part being the content (Associated Press articles) and the "dtm" part being the format, which is document text matrix format.

```
data("AssociatedPress", package = "topicmodels")
ap_dtm<-AssociatedPress
class(ap_dtm)
[Output]
      [1] "DocumentTermMatrix"    "simple_triplet_matrix"
```

Then, for informational purposes, we list the ap_dtm object to show it has 10,473 terms in 2,246 documents.

```
ap_dtm
[Output:]
   <<DocumentTermMatrix (documents: 2246, terms: 10473)>>
   Non-/sparse entries: 302031/23220327
   Sparsity           : 99%
   Maximal term length: 18
   Weighting          : term frequency (tf)
```

In this example we use an approach in which each row of our text data corresponds to a single term (word). Such an approach often involves, as here, converting our text object into "tidytext" format. The "ap_td" text object created below puts the text data into a tidytext tibble data frame in which each row is a term (word) and is considered a "document". A tibble is simply a versatile R data format which is used by the tidytext package. The more familiar data.frame format is a subtype of a tibble.

```
ap_td <- tidytext::tidy(ap_dtm)
class(ap_td)
  [Output]
      [1] "tbl_df"     "tbl"        "data.frame"
```

Below we list the first five rows of ap_td. The ap_td object has 302,031 rows, one term per row with a "count" variable entry for each. However, the variable ap_td$document has values ranging from 1 to 2,246, which is the number of articles in the AssociatedPress database.

```
nrow(ap_td)
[Output]
      [1] 302031

summary(ap_td$document)
[Output]
   Min. 1st Qu.  Median    Mean 3rd Qu.    Max.
      1     563    1113    1119    1682    2246
head(ap_td, 5)

[Output:]
  # A tibble: 6 x 3
  document term        count
       <int> <chr>      <dbl>
  1        1 adding         1
  2        1 adult          2
  3        1 ago            1
  4        1 alcohol        1
  5        1 allegedly      1
```

With our data in tidytext format, we are now ready to assign sentiments to each word in ap_td. This is done with the `get_sentiments()` command from the tidytext package. We use the infix (piping) operator from the dplyr package to pass information from ap_td to the `get_sentiments()` command. Which words are actually coded for sentiment and how they are coded is determined by the lexicon used. The `lexicon=` option names the sentiment lexicon to be used. At present, options are "bing", "nrc", "loughran", and "afinn". The "bing" lexicon is the default and is built into tidytext. Requesting any of the others will prompt the user to download that lexicon, which will be quite large. The "bing" lexicon categorizes words in a binary fashion into positive and negative categories, as shown below.

```
ap_sentiments <- ap_td %>%
dplyr::inner_join(tidytext::get_sentiments(lexicon="bing"), by = c(term = "word"))
```

The ap_sentiments object just created has 30,094 entries, one row per term per document. It is a tibble-type data frame. Note that ap_td has more than that number of words, but ap_sentiments only retains words which are in the lexicon. Most words are not retained because the "bing" lexicon is a tibble with only 6,786 terms. To see some of this word list, type `get _ sentiments("bing").` Because some terms are used in multiple documents, this adds 30,094 term uses. There are 2,190 unique documents in ap_sentiments.

```
nrow(ap_sentiments)
[Output]
      [1] 30094

class(ap_sentiments)
[Output]
   [1] "tbl_df"      "tbl"           "data.frame"

unique<-unique(ap_sentiments$document)
length(unique)
[Output]
      [1] 2190
```

It may be helpful to list some of sentiments in ap_sentiments. The first ones are all from document 1. For instance, document 1 used "killed" twice, adding 2 negative sentiment points to document 1.

```
ap_sentiments
[Output:]
   # A tibble: 30,094 x 4
      document term     count sentiment
         <int> <chr>    <dbl> <chr>
    1        1 assault      1 negative
    2        1 complex      1 negative
    3        1 death        1 negative
    4        1 died         1 negative
    5        1 good         2 positive
    6        1 illness      1 negative
    7        1 killed       2 negative
    8        1 like         2 positive
    9        1 liked        1 positive
   10        1 miracle      1 positive
   # ... with 30,084 more rows
```

Though we do not use it in this example, below is the listing had we used the "nrc" lexicon. Whereas the bing lexicon categorizes words by positive and negative sentiment, the nrc lexicon categorizes words by the sentiments positive, negative, anger, fear, disgust, anticipation, joy, trust, sadness, and surprise.

```
ap_sentiments

[Output:]
   # A tibble: 147,609 x 4
      document term     count sentiment
         <int> <chr>    <dbl> <chr>
    1        1 assault      1 anger
```

```
2        1 assault      1 fear
3        1 assault      1 negative
4        1 boy          4 disgust
5        1 boy          4 negative
6        1 building     1 positive
7        1 church       1 anticipation
8        1 church       1 joy
9        1 church       1 positive
10       1 church       1 trust
```

Similarly, below are listings using the "loughran" lexicon, which codes words into the sentiments of positive, negative, litigious, uncertainty, and constraining, We do not use this lexicon in the example.

```
ap_sentiments
```

[Output:]

```
# A tibble: 29,487 x 4
   document term          count sentiment
      <int> <chr>         <dbl> <chr>
1         1 allegedly         1 negative
2         1 allegedly         1 litigious
3         1 apparently        2 uncertainty
4         1 appeared          1 uncertainty
5         1 arrested          1 negative
6         1 assault           1 negative
7         1 believe           1 uncertainty
8         1 confiscated       1 negative
9         1 divorce           1 negative
10        1 felony            1 negative
```

Finally, below are word sentiments assigned by the "afinn" lexicon, which assigns a sentiment score rather than a label. Scores range from –5 to + 5. Negative scores indicate degree of negative sentiment while positive scores indicate degree of positive sentiment. There are no zero scores. The most recent "afinn" lexicon is available from the author at https://github.com/fnielsen/afinn/tree/master/afinn/data and is labeled "AFINN-111.txt" and codes 3,382 words rather than the 2,477 obtained when going at this writing via `get _ sentiments()`. This website has several versions of the afinn lexicon, including one for emoticons rather than words. The "textdata" package must be installed and loaded first. See the documentation for this package for further lexicon-related options. We do not use the afinn lexicon in the example below, however.

```
install.packages("textdata")
library(textdata)
get_sentiments("afinn")
```

[Output:]

```
# A tibble: 2,477 x 2
   word         value
   <chr>        <dbl>
 1 abandon         -2
 2 abandoned       -2
 3 abandons        -2
 4 abducted        -2
 5 abduction       -2
 6 abductions      -2
 7 abhor           -3
 8 abhorred        -3
 9 abhorrent       -3
10 abhors          -3
# ... with 2,467 more rows
```

After the detour above to illustrate sentiment categorization with different lexicons (and there are others not discussed), we return to the task of ranking documents (here, AP news articles) in order of positivity or negativity of the sentiments they contain. We use the "bing" lexicon. While in the example below we rank by negativity, ranking by positivity is a simple matter of changing the mutate command in the code syntax below to `mutate(sentiment = negative - positive)`.

The set of commands below creates an ordered ranking of documents by negativity score.

```
ap_arrange <- ap_sentiments %>%
  dplyr::count(document, sentiment, wt = count) %>%
  tidyr::spread(sentiment, n, fill = 0) %>%
  dplyr::mutate(sentiment = positive - negative) %>%
  dplyr::arrange(sentiment)
ap_arrange
```

[Output:]

```
  # A tibble: 2,190 x 4
     document negative positive sentiment
        <int>    <dbl>    <dbl>     <dbl>
   1     1251       54        6       -48
   2     1380       53        5       -48
   3      531       51        9       -42
   4       43       45       11       -34
   5     1263       44       10       -34
   6     2178       40        6       -34
   7      334       45       12       -33
   8     1664       38        5       -33
   9     2147       47       14       -33
  10      516       38        6       -32
  # ... with 2,180 more rows
```

However, to understand what is going on with this complex command, we take it step by step below, winding up with the same table.

Step 1: Count positive and negative sentiments by document. Each document has a negative and a positive count row.

```
ap_count<- ap_sentiments %>%
dplyr::count(document, sentiment, wt = count)
ap_count
```

[Output:]

```
  # A tibble: 4,159 x 3
     document sentiment     n
        <int> <chr>     <dbl>
   1        1 negative     11
   2        1 positive      9
   3        2 negative      8
   4        2 positive      5
   5        3 negative      9
   6        3 positive     11
   7        4 negative      8
   8        4 positive      6
   9        5 negative      1
  10        5 positive      2
  # ... with 4,149 more rows
```

```
# ap_count has 2,190 unique AP documents, same as ap_sentiments earlier
unique<-unique(ap_count$document)
length(unique)
```

[Output]

```
      [1] 2190
```

Document numbering in ap_count goes from 1 to 2,246, the count of articles in the AP data. However, above ap_count had 4,159 rows, not 2*2246 = 4,492 rows or 2*2190 = 4,380 rows.

Some documents had no positives or no negatives or both, reducing the count.

```
summary(ap_count$document)
```

[Output]

```
   Min. 1st Qu.  Median    Mean 3rd Qu.    Max.
    1.0   567.5  1133.0  1129.0  1690.0  2246.0
```

Step 2: We get negative and positive counts as columns with documents as rows. This is preparatory to subtracting them to get the spread (difference) by document. There are still 2,190 documents in ap_spread. Some additional documents with 0 count for both negative and positive have been dropped.

```
ap_spread<- ap_count %>%
  tidyr::spread(sentiment, n, fill = 0)
ap_spread
```

[Output:]

```
   # A tibble: 2,190 x 3
      document negative positive
         <int>    <dbl>    <dbl>
    1        1       11        9
    2        2        8        5
    3        3        9       11
    4        4        8        6
    5        5        1        2
    6        6        9       23
    7        7        5        4
    8        8        0        4
    9       10        5        3
   10       11        6        1
   # ... with 2,180 more rows
```

Step 3: We now calculate a sentiment spread score, which is the "sentiment" column in ap_mutate. All 2,190 remaining documents get a sentiment score. The score is here positive minus negative, giving a score in which higher negative numbers reflect greater negativity of the AP article, but this can be flipped.

```
ap_mutate<- ap_spread  %>%
  dplyr::mutate(sentiment = positive - negative)
ap_mutate
```

[Output:]

```
   # A tibble: 2,190 x 4
      document negative positive sentiment
         <int>    <dbl>    <dbl>     <dbl>
    1        1       11        9        -2
    2        2        8        5        -3
    3        3        9       11         2
    4        4        8        6        -2
    5        5        1        2         1
    6        6        9       23        14
    7        7        5        4        -1
    8        8        0        4         4
    9       10        5        3        -2
   10       11        6        1        -5
   # ... with 2,180 more rows
```

Step 4: Documents (rows) are sorted so that those with the highest negativity on sentiment spread appear at the top. All 2,190 remaining documents are in ap_arrange. AP document 1,251 has the most negative sentiment spread score. The output is the same table as that from the complex command with multiple pipes given earlier.

```
ap_arrange<- ap_mutate %>%
  dplyr::arrange(sentiment)
ap_arrange
```

[Output:]

```
# A tibble: 2,190 x 4
   document negative positive sentiment
      <int>    <dbl>    <dbl>     <dbl>
 1     1251       54        6       -48
 2     1380       53        5       -48
 3      531       51        9       -42
 4       43       45       11       -34
 5     1263       44       10       -34
 6     2178       40        6       -34
 7      334       45       12       -33
 8     1664       38        5       -33
 9     2147       47       14       -33
10      516       38        6       -32
# ... with 2,180 more rows
```

We now conclude this section by plotting the most frequent positive and negative terms across all AP articles. For this we go back to the ap_sentiments object created earlier with this command:

```
ap_sentiments <- ap_td %>%
  dplyr::inner_join(tidytext::get_sentiments(lexicon="bing"), by = c(term = "word"))
```

For space reasons, we do not elaborate on the eight steps contained within the R syntax below. Note, however, that the higher the cutoff (minimum number of instances of the term), the fewer terms will appear in the plot, which is shown in Figure 9.24.

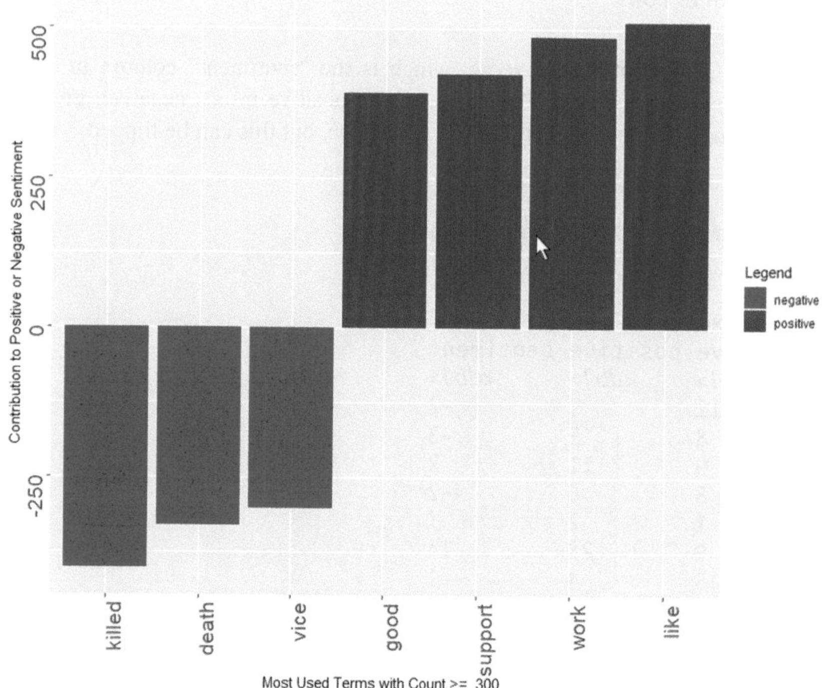

Figure 9.24 Sentiment contribution of high frequency AP words

```
fontsize <- 16
cutoff<- 300
xlabel<-paste("Most Used Terms with Count >= ",as.character(cutoff))
ap_sentiments %>%
 dplyr::count(sentiment, term, wt = count) %>%
 dplyr::filter(n >= cutoff) %>%
 dplyr::mutate(n = ifelse(sentiment == "negative", -n, n)) %>%
 dplyr::mutate(term = reorder(term, n)) %>%
 ggplot2::ggplot(aes(term, n, fill = sentiment)) +
 ggplot2::scale_fill_manual("Legend", values = c("positive" = "blue", "negative" =
"red")) +
 ggplot2::geom_bar(stat = "identity") +
 ggplot2::theme(axis.text=element_text(size=fontsize,angle = 90,hjust = 1)) +
 ggplot2::xlab(xlabel)+
 ggplot2::ylab("Contribution to Positive or Negative Sentiment")
```

Considering only terms used 300 times or more in the set of 2,190 AP articles, which remained in ap_sentiments, the term "killed" contributed most on the negative sentiment side and "like" on the positive side. To plot a larger number of words, simply enter a lower "cutoff" in the syntax above.

The AP corpus has 2,190 documents, which are Associated Press articles. We may use it to identify the documents rather than the words, as above, by sentiment score. Below, we rank these articles by sentiment. This is based on the "ap_arrange" object created above.

```
# For convenience, put ap_arrange into the object "docs".
docs <- ap_arrange

# Sort docs by the sentiments score, placing results in the object "docs2".
docs2 <- docs[order(-docs$sentiment),]

# List the five most positive documents by sentiment out of 2,190 documents.
head(docs2,5)
[Output:]]
  # A tibble: 5 x 4
    document negative positive sentiment
       <int>    <dbl>    <dbl>     <dbl>
  1      647        5       39        34
  2     1860        5       37        32
  3      210        2       30        28
  4     1370        7       35        28
  5     1482        7       35        28

# List the five most negative documents by sentiment out of 2,190 documents.
tail(docs2,5)
[Output:]
  # A tibble: 5 x 4
    document negative positive sentiment
       <int>    <dbl>    <dbl>     <dbl>
  1     1263       44       10       -34
  2     2178       40        6       -34
  3      531       51        9       -42
  4     1251       54        6       -48
  5     1380       53        5       -48

nrow(docs2)
[Output:]
   [1] 2190

# Put top and bottom five documents by sentiment into the docs10 object.
docs10 <- docs2[c(1:5, 2186:2190),]

plot(docs10$sentiment)
```

```
fontsize <- 16
cutoff<- 300

library(ggplot2)
docids <- as.character(docs10$document)
xlabel <- paste("Article Document Number, Five Most Positive and Negative Articles")
ylabel<-paste("Sentiment Score")
Color = ifelse(docs10$sentiment <0, "red","blue")
ggplot(data=docs10, aes(x=as.character(document), y=sentiment, color=sentiment)) +
geom_bar(stat="identity", width=1, color="white", fill=Color) +
ggplot2::xlab(xlabel) +
ggplot2::ylab(ylabel) +
scale_x_discrete(limits=docids) +
geom_text(aes(label=sentiment),vjust=1.0,color="red", size=5) +
theme(axis.text=element_text(size=12),title = element_text(size =14,face="italic"))
```

9.19 Analysis: Topic modeling

9.19.1 Overview

As with sentiment analysis, topic modeling means different things to different researchers. A common meaning of topic modeling includes analyses in which the frequency of use of a term or set of terms (e.g., "freedom", "power") is tracked over time, compared between groups, and otherwise analyzed. The first example below (Section 9.19.2) illustrates this form of topic modeling using the example of tracking the frequency of use of terms from U.S. presidential inaugural speeches over time. A second meaning of topic modeling refers to a text analog to factor analysis, in which topics which compose a set of documents are uncovered and classified through unsupervised learning methods. The primary such method is Latent Dirichlet Allocation (LDA). The second example below (Section 9.19.3) illustrates a simple form of LDA.

TEXT BOX 9.2 Topic modeling of radical activism with the "stm" and "tm" packages

As an example of topic modeling around the subject of radical activism, Zack Almquist and Benjamin Bagbozzi (2020) studied 1,020 texts associated with the North American Animal Rights League, including its primary publication, *No Compromise*. The purpose of the study was to provide "insights into the topical agenda of animal liberationists, and the relative attention paid toward networking, (non)violence, radicalization, and direct actions." The authors were able to document ideological and tactical shifts over time which, they argued, were predictive of future direct-action events. In an Online Appendix the authors also applied similar topic modeling to a distinct radical movement on the right: The Michigan Militia Corps.

The authors used a variety of R text analytic packages. These included the "tm" package discussed in this chapter. Also used centrally, mentioned but not discussed in this chapter, was the Structural Topic Model (stm) package, which supports estimation of topic models with document-level covariates, for model selection, visualization, and estimation of topic-covariate regressions. Other packages used included topicmodels, lda, SnowballC, and broom.

R script source: Almquist, Zack; Bagozzi, Benjamin, 2020, "Replication Data.zip", Replication Data for: Automated Text Analysis for Understanding Radical Activism: The Topical Agenda of the North American Animal Liberation Movement, https://doi.org/10.7910/DVN/GFWQCE/FVKTKL, Harvard Dataverse, V1. Click "Access File", then "Download" to download R scripts for most aspects of the article.

Source: Almquist, Zack W. & Bagbozzi, Benjamin E. (2020). Automated text analysis for understanding radical activism: The topical agenda of the North American Animal Liberation Movement. *Research and Politics* 7(2): 1–8.

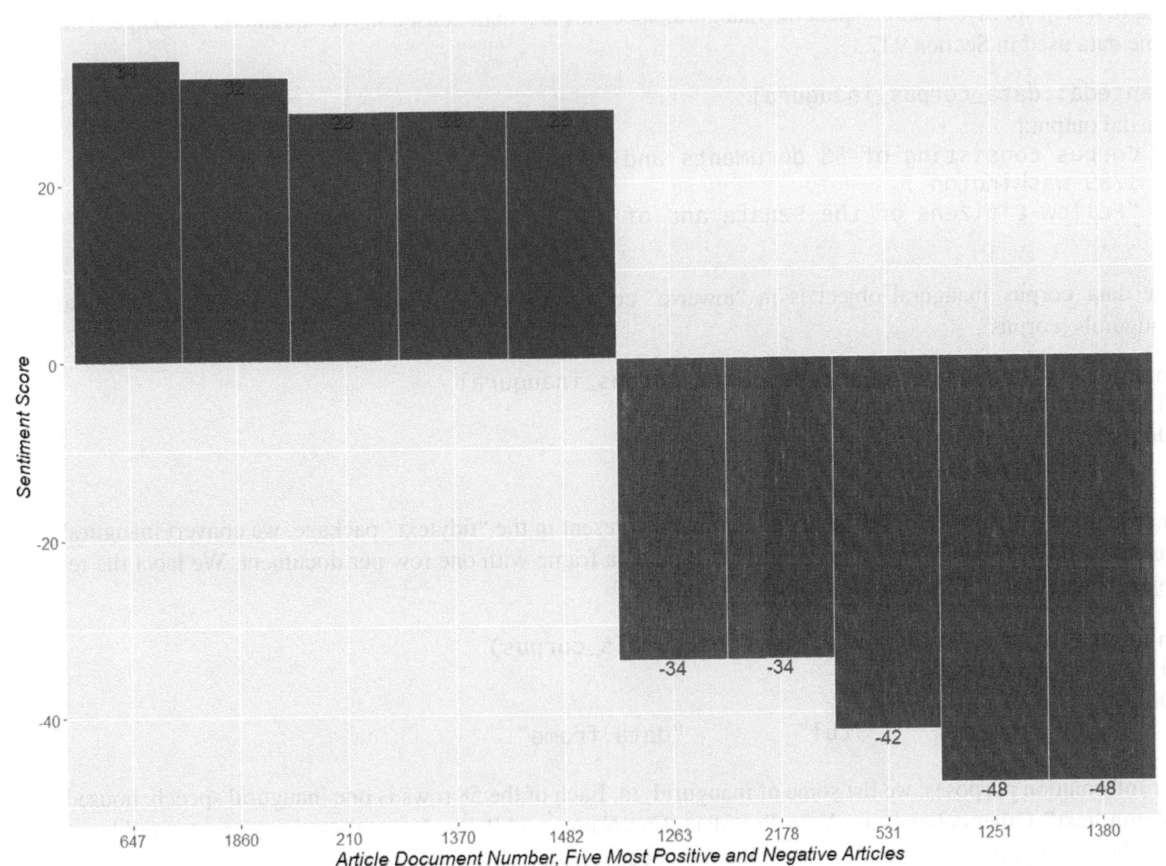

Figure 9.25 Five most positive and negative AP documents by sentiment score

9.19.2 Topic analysis example 1: Modeling topic frequency over time

In this section, a publicly available corpus consisting of the 58 U.S. presidential inaugural addresses from 1789 to 2017 is used as the focus for a simple type of topic analysis. Output, shown further below in Figures 9.25 and 9.26, reveals, for instance, how certain topic terms such as "America" and "Americans" have become noticeably more common in speeches over the years. This may reflect heightened appeals to patriotism.

Although the inaugurals data are from the "quanteda" package, much of the analysis is driven by commands from the "tidytext" package. As earlier, package prefixes are attached to commands to make the connection of command to package clear (e.g., `tidytext:: tidy()`). The example is adapted from Silge and Robinson (2020).

As with any analysis in R, we start by loading the packages we will be using in topic analysis.

```
library(ggplot2)    # The leading data visualization package in R
library(quanteda)   # A leading text analysis package in R
library(tidytext)   # A leading text analysis package for R
library(tidyr)      # Tools to create and reshape tidytext data
library(broom)      # Convert statistical analysis objects from R into tidy tibble format
library(scales)     # Supports the percent _ format() function
library(dplyr)      # Utility package with %>% piping, anti-join, and more
setwd("C:/Data")    # Declare the default directory
```

As a first step we invoke and inspect the inaugural speeches text data housed in the "quanteda" package. This is the same data used in Section 9.17.

```
quanteda::data_corpus_inaugural
```
[Partial output:]
```
   Corpus consisting of 58 documents and 4 docvars.
   1789-Washington :
   "Fellow-Citizens of the Senate and of the House of Representa..."
   . . .
```

The data_corpus_inaugural object is in "lower-c" corpus format. Again for clarity, we rename it as such, to inaugurals_corpus".

```
inaugurals_corpus <- quanteda::data_corpus_inaugural
class(inaugurals_corpus)
```
[Output]
```
      [1] "corpus"
```

In order to use the powerful text analysis commands present in the "tidytext" package, we convert inaugurals_corpus into a tidytext data frame. This is a tibble-type data frame with one row per document. We label the resulting object "inaugurals_td", where "td" stands for "tidy".

```
inaugurals_td <- tidytext::tidy(inaugurals_corpus)
class(inaugurals_td)
```
[Output]
```
      [1] "tbl_df"     "tbl"        "data.frame"
```

For information purposes, we list some of inaugural_td. Each of the 58 rows is one inaugural speech, housed in the column 'text". Other columns are Year, President, FirstName, and Party. As yet there is no count variable, nor have speeches been parsed into topics (words). We only need type the object's name to view some of its contents.

```
inaugurals_td
```
[Output:]
```
   # A tibble: 58 x 5
      text           Year President  FirstName Party
      <chr>         <int> <chr>      <chr>     <fct>
    1 "Fellow-Citi~  1789 Washington George    none
    2 "Fellow citi~  1793 Washington George    none
    3 "When it was~  1797 Adams      John      Federa~
    4 "Friends and~  1801 Jefferson  Thomas    Democr~
    5 "Proceeding,~  1805 Jefferson  Thomas    Democr~
    6 "Unwilling t~  1809 Madison    James     Democr~
    7 "About to ad~  1813 Madison    James     Democr~
    8 "I should be~  1817 Monroe     James     Democr~
    9 "Fellow citi~  1821 Monroe     James     Democr~
   10 "In complian~  1825 Adams      John Qui~ Democr~
   # ... with 48 more rows
```

Although inaugurals_td has been "tidied" into a format with one row per document, it is not yet in "tidytext" format, which has one row per word. This is done with tidytext's `unnest _ tokens()` command. We do this and label the resulting object "inaugurals_words". Note that a set of stop words, from the tidytext package, has been used to eliminate common words such as articles and prepositions. Note also that the %>% infix (piping) operator, from the "dplyr" package, is used to pass information contained in inaugurals_td to tidytext's `unnest _ tokens()` command.

```
inaugurals_words <- inaugurals_td %>%
  tidytext::unnest_tokens(word, text) %>%
  dplyr::anti_join(stop_words)
```

When we now list inaugurals_words we see that it is in tidytext format. There is one row per word. Since both "Year" and "word" are columns, we are in a position to track word usage over time. However, we have yet to have a "count" variable, also needed for this type of topic modeling. Again, we view contents by typing the object name.

```
inaugurals_words
```
[Partial output:]
```
  # A tibble: 50,156 x 5
      Year President  FirstName Party word
     <int> <chr>      <chr>     <fct> <chr>
   1  1789 Washington George    none  fellow
   2  1789 Washington George    none  citizens
   . . .
  10  1789 Washington George    none  filled
  # ... with 50,146 more rows
```

To get word counts, we rely on the `count()` command from the "dplyr" package. The end result is placed in a new object, here called "inaugurals_freq". This new object has not only columns (variables) for "Year" and "word", but also a new column "n" for whether a word is used in a given document (here, same as a given year). The "n" variable is binary, coded 0 or 1. All the objects below are tibble data frames. The series of five piping commands below could be collapsed into a single command, [8] but are not here for instructional reasons. Space does not allow listing each of the objects created, but the reader may wish to do so simply by typing their names.

1. Count words. The resulting "iw_count" object has columns for "Year", "word", and "n" (count) for 33,174 words. By comparison, " inaugurals_words" had "Year", " President", "FirstName", "Party", & "word" for 50,156 words.

```
iw_count <- inaugurals_words %>%
  dplyr::count(Year, word)
```

2. The "iw_complete" object has columns for "Year", "word", and "n" for 501,990 words.

```
iw_complete<- iw_count %>%
  tidyr::complete(Year, word, fill = list(n = 0))
```

3. The "iw_group" object has columns for "Year", "word", and "n" for 501,990 words grouped by year for 58 years.

```
iw_group<- iw_complete %>%
  dplyr::group_by(Year)
```

4. The "iw_mutate" object has columns for "Year", "word", "n", but also adds columns for "year_total" and "percent", for 501,990 words and 58 groups, which are years. This is 8,655 words for each of the 58 years. Each of the 8,655 words will be counted for each year, receiving 0 if not used that year.

```
iw_mutate <- iw_group %>%
  dplyr::mutate(year_total = sum(n),
                percent = n / year_total)
```

5. The "inaugurals_freq" object has columns for "Year", "word", "n", "year_total", and "percent" for 501,990 words, as shown below.

```
inaugurals_freq <- iw_mutate %>%
  dplyr::ungroup()
```

We now list some of inaugurals_freq, which has over half a million word rows! We list a specific limited range. The "year_total" value will be the same for each word in any given one of the 58 yearly groups but will differ between groups. The "percent" variable is the row word's percent of count for the year_total for that year. The inaugurals_freq tibble will be the basis for the topic models. Since we have not used word stems, each term is treated as a different word. Thus, output below shows that the word "decide" was used once in the 1789 inaugural, which was 1/529 = .00189 or 0.189%, where 529 was the sum of n for 1789.

```
inaugurals_freq[2000:2005,]
```
[Partial output:]
```
  # A tibble: 11 x 5
      Year word              n year_total percent
     <int> <chr>         <dbl>      <dbl>   <dbl>
  1  1789 decency           0        529 0
  2  1789 decent            0        529 0
  3  1789 decide            1        529 0.00189
  4  1789 decided           0        529 0
  5  1789 decides           0        529 0
  6  1789 deciding          1        529 0.00189
```

Below we take a "side trip" to see the word count (n) by inaugural year.

```
sumsByYear<- inaugurals_freq %>%  dplyr::group_by(Year) %>%
dplyr::summarise(Frequency = sum(n))

sumsByYear
```
[Partial output:]
```
  # A tibble: 58 x 2
      Year Frequency
     <int>     <dbl>
   1  1789       529
   2  1793        51
   . . .
   9  1821      1578
  10  1825      1153
  # ... with 48 more rows
```

Below we see that the inaugural year 1789 (Washington) used the fewest words and 2017 (Trump) the most, by far.

```
summary(sumsByYear)
```
[Output:]
```
         Year         Frequency
   Min.   :1789   Min.   :  51.0
   1st Qu.:1846   1st Qu.: 484.2
   Median :1903   Median : 765.0
   Mean   :1903   Mean   : 864.8
   3rd Qu.:1960   3rd Qu.:1130.5
   Max.   :2017   Max.   :2943.0
```

We now create the actual topic models. This set of models are logistic regression models for each word, but, as discussed below, a two-column DV is used, not the usual one-column binary variable. The "n" variable is passed from inaugurals_freq. The "models" output object is a tidy-format tibble data frame. The logistic regression command `glm()` is from the stats package in the R system library and the `sum()` and `cbind()` are from the base package. For instructional reasons the computation is in steps but may be collapsed into a single command.[9] All the objects below are tibble-type data frames.

Creating the "models" object for topic models is a five-step process:

1. The im_group object has 501,990 words in alphabetical order, with the columns Year, word, n, year_total, and percent.

   ```
   im_group <- inaugurals_freq %>% dplyr::group_by(word)
   ```

2. The im_filter object has the same columns but only for words with sum(n) > 50. The research could alter the "50" cutoff at this step, of course. Each of the object's 114 words appears in 58 rows, one per year, grouped by year, for a total of 6,612 rows.

```
im_filter <- im_group %>%
  dplyr::filter(sum(n) > 50)
```

3. The im_glm object, which has the results of logistic regression, has 228 rows with the columns word, term, estimate, std.error, statistic, and p.value. It has 114 groups, each representing a word. Each of the 114 words has two rows: One for the estimate of the logistic b coefficient for Year and one for the intercept.

```
im_glm <- im_filter %>%
  dplyr::do(tidytext::tidy(glm(cbind(n, year_total - n) ~ Year,. ,family =
"binomial")))
```

   Note that the `glm()` command embedded in the im_glm object enters both "n" and "year_total - n" as the dependent variable (DV). The DV is then predicted by Year. In R's `glm()` command, a binomial model may be specified defining the DV as a two-column response. In this situation, the weights returned by prior.weights are the total numbers of cases (factored by the supplied case weights, if any) and the component y of the result is the proportion of successes. That is, this is not the usual binary logistic regression model. Two more steps remain to get to the actual models.

4. The im_ungroup object also has 228 rows, with two rows per word. It has the same columns as im_glm. It has two rows per word but there is no group structure by Year.

```
im_ungroup <- im_glm %>% dplyr::ungroup()
```

5. Finally, the models object has 114 rows, one per word. It has the same columns as im_glm. The intercept row for each word is omitted, cutting the number of rows in half. That is, only rows in im_ungroup where "term" is "Year" (not "(Intercept)") are retained. The models object is a tibble data frame.

```
models <- im_ungroup %>% dplyr::filter(term == "Year")

# models is a tibble data frame
class(models)
[Output]
      [1] "tbl_df"      "tbl"           "data.frame"
```

Having created "models", we proceed to analyze it. First we list some of "models", which represent one equation for each of the 114 words. The dependent variables reflect both "n" and "year_total - n". The "estimate" column for each word's equation is the logistic b coefficient. Each word also has a standard error and a p value.

```
models
[Partial output:]
   # A tibble: 114 x 6
      word           term  estimate std.error statistic  p.value
      <chr>          <chr>    <dbl>     <dbl>     <dbl>    <dbl>
    1 act            Year   0.00636   0.00215      2.96 3.10e- 3
    2 action         Year   0.00209   0.00190      1.10 2.71e- 1
    3 administration Year  -0.00667   0.00184     -3.63 2.84e- 4
    4 america        Year   0.0200    0.00154     13.0  2.02e-38
    5 american       Year   0.00818   0.00127      6.43 1.32e-10
    6 americans      Year   0.0316    0.00346      9.14 6.22e-20
    7 authority      Year  -0.00585   0.00232     -2.53 1.15e- 2
    8 business       Year   0.00332   0.00199      1.67 9.48e- 2
    9 called         Year  -0.00222   0.00207     -1.07 2.83e- 1
   10 century        Year   0.0155    0.00242      6.41 1.45e-10
   # ... with 104 more rows
```

We now filter the "models" object for Year, sorting descending by the glm estimate (the logistic b coefficient). The `abs()` function is from the base package in the system library.

```
rankedmodels <- models %>%
   dplyr::filter(term == "Year") %>%
   dplyr::filter(term == "Year") %>%
   dplyr::arrange(dplyr::desc(abs(estimate)))

rankedmodels
```

[Partial output:]

```
   # A tibble: 114 x 6
     word      term  estimate std.error statistic  p.value
     <chr>     <chr>    <dbl>     <dbl>     <dbl>    <dbl>
   1 americans Year    0.0316   0.00346      9.14 6.22e-20
   2 america   Year    0.0200   0.00154     13.0  2.02e-38
   3 century   Year    0.0155   0.00242      6.41 1.45e-10
   4 live      Year    0.0140   0.00242      5.79 6.92e- 9
   . . .
```

While the table above has the same information, it is much easier to see the results of topic analysis by visualizing the time trends for the word models, shown in Figure 9.26. In each quadrant of the figure, "Year" is the x-axis and "percent" is the y-axis.

```
howmany<- 4            # How many top words to plot
ylabel <- paste("Word Frequency over Time: Top ", as.character(howmany), " Words")
```

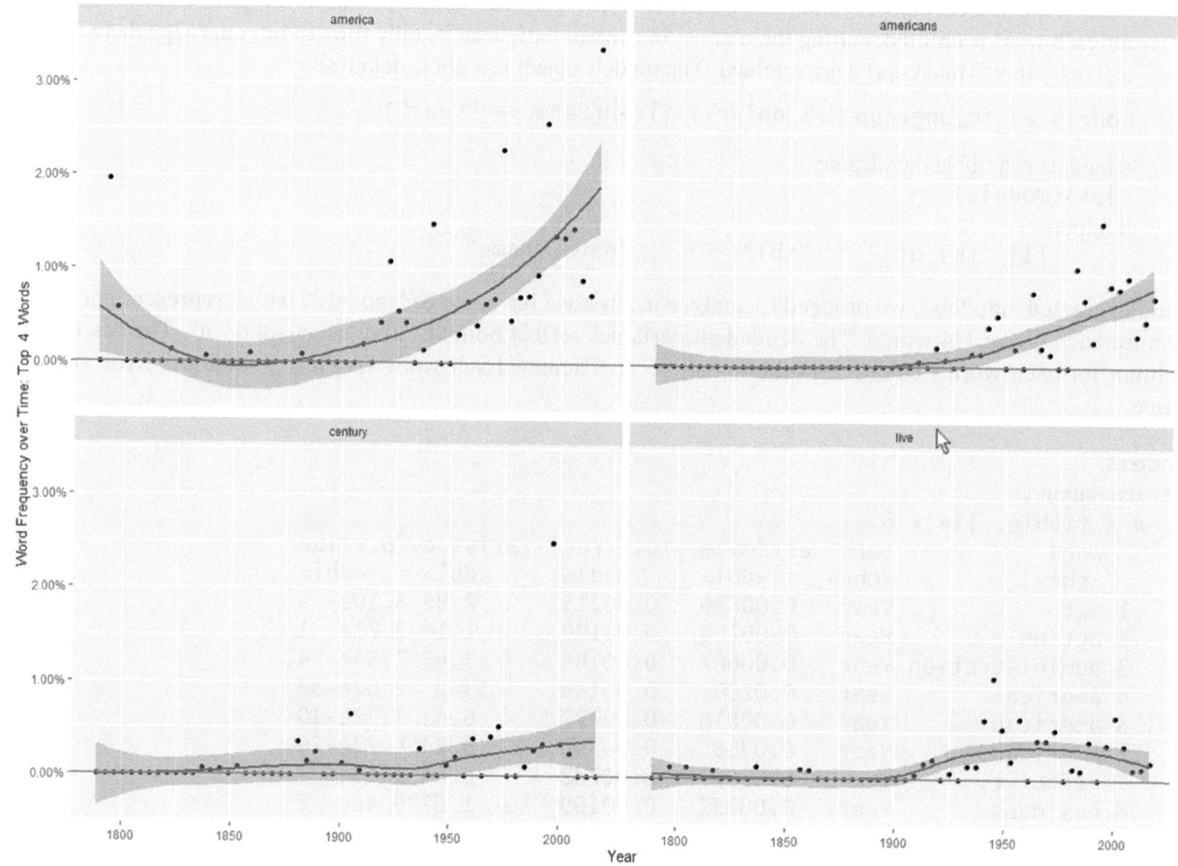

Figure 9.26 Inaugural speeches word frequencies, 1789–2017

```
rankedmodels %>%
  dplyr::top_n(howmany, abs(estimate)) %>%
  dplyr::inner_join(inaugurals_freq) %>%
  ggplot2::ggplot(ggplot2::aes(Year, percent)) +
  ggplot2::geom_point() +
  ggplot2::geom_smooth() +
  ggplot2::facet_wrap(~ word) +
  ggplot2::scale_y_continuous(labels=scales::percent_format()) +
  ggplot2::geom_hline(ggplot2::aes(yintercept=0), colour="violet", lwd=1) +
  ggplot2::ylab(ylabel)
```

As a final step in this example, we create a "volcano plot". Volcano plots as used here show significant changes over time in word use. This type of plot has effect size as the x-axis and significance on the y-axis. For these data, effect size is "estimate" and significance is an adjusted version of "p.value". The `p.adjust()` function is from the "stats" package in the R system library.

```
axisfontsize <- 16
models %>%
   dplyr::mutate(adjusted.p.value = p.adjust(p.value)) %>%
   ggplot2::ggplot(ggplot2::aes(estimate, adjusted.p.value)) +
   ggplot2::geom_point() +
  ggplot2::geom_text(ggplot2::aes(label = word), vjust = 1, hjust = 1, check_overlap =
TRUE) +
  ggplot2:: theme(text = ggplot2::element_text(size = axisfontsize)) +
  ggplot2::geom_hline(ggplot2::aes(yintercept=0.05), colour = "red", lwd=1) +
  ggplot2::geom_vline(ggplot2::aes(xintercept=0.0), colour = "blue", lwd=1) +
  ggplot2::xlab("Rate (slope) of Word Frequency Change over Time (estimate)") +
  ggplot2::ylab("Significance (adjusted p-value)")
```

In Figure 9.27, words corresponding to the 114 word regression models are plotted. The "estimate" variable represents logistic b coefficients and is the x-axis. The adjusted version of the "p.value" variable is the y-axis. Terms below the horizontal .05 red line display significant change over time. Terms near the vertical blue zero line display little change. Words to the left of the blue line are those for which frequency diminishes by Year, with "constitution" being the strongest example. Words with estimates nearer zero on the x-axis are more likely to have high values on p on the y-axis, indicating non-significance. This causes the hump in the plot, reminiscent to some of a volcano-shaped distribution, hence "volcano plot". Word frequency increases with passage of Year for terms to the right of the blue line, with "americans" exhibiting the strongest tendency in this respect. This may suggest a trend toward more patriotic or at least America-centric wording in more recent inaugural addresses.

9.19.3 Topic analysis example 2: LDA analysis

LDA[10] analysis is a mathematical algorithm which examines a document text matrix (text in dtm format was discussed in Section 9.17.2) and, for a researcher-specified k, establishes the k groupings which best partition the text data. These groupings are the "topics". LDA also calculates the probabilities of any given word being generated by each topic. The two central research topics addressed by LDA center on the extent to which a given word contributes to each topic and the extent to which a given topic contributes to each document. Words may contribute to multiple topics and topics may contribute to multiple documents, meaning that LDA is a type of "fuzzy set" analysis.

LDA is a form of unsupervised learning. This means that the LDA algorithm is not given topic examples beforehand but rather uncovers topics in a document without predetermination by the researcher. LDA for text data is loosely analogous to exploratory factor analysis (EFA) for numeric data. Both LDA and EFA are nondependent procedures (there is no "dependent variable") which arrange data into clusters, which are called "topics" in LDA or "factors" (or "components") in EFA. A given term in LDA has a probability of being generated by each topic, similar to each variable in EFA having a loading on each factor.

As with any analytic procedure, clearest results emerge with LDA when underlying relationships are strong. A classic illustration of LDA, for instance, uses as texts four strongly divergent novels, including *Twenty Thousand Leagues Under the Sea*, *War of the Worlds*, *Great Expectations*, and *Pride and Prejudice*. With four books, it is easy to posit that

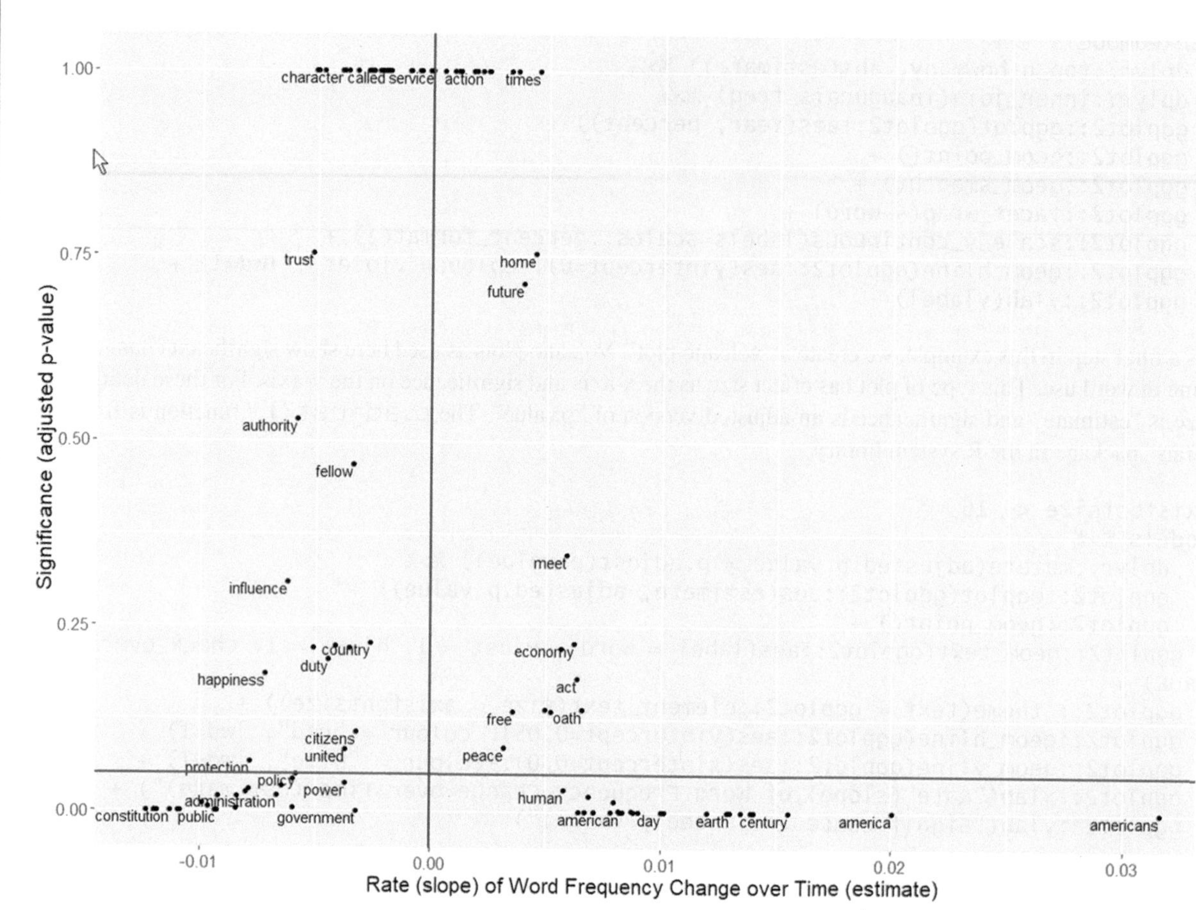

Figure 9.27 Volcano plot of word frequency change in inaugural speeches

a four-topic solution should be requested. And, indeed, when most common terms associated with each LDA topic are listed, the four sets of words do correspond to the novels. For instance, one cluster has as top words "captain", "nautilus", "sea", "nemo", and "ned", and thus represents the *Twenty Thousand Leagues Under the Sea* topic. This is something of a cherry-picked example. In practice, the researcher may find it challenging to find the appropriate number of topics (k) to request. It may be necessary to explore a spread of solutions with different ks to see which gives the most useful results.

The words which emerge under the requested topics may seem heterogeneous, making it difficult to assign a descriptive label each topic. This is analogous to EFA, where variables loaded on a given factor may be heterogeneous and it may be challenging to induce a name for the given factor. Put another way, the meaningfulness of topics identified by LDA depends on the coherence of the generated words. The best solution, as always, is a meaningful one, but no technique, including LDA, can assure meaningfulness. Random input will lead to arbitrary output not useful for interpretation.

```
# Setup for LDA
library(topicmodels)    # Supports LDA and CTM (correlated topics model) models
library(quanteda)       # A leading text analysis package in R
library(tm)             # Invoke Text Miner, another leading package
library(tidytext)       # A third leading text analysis package for R
library(tidyr)          # Utilities for tidytext
library(ggplot2)        # Leading package for visualization of results
library(dplyr)          # Utility package with %>% piping, anti-join, and more
setwd("C:/Data")        # Declare the default directory
```

In this section, we continue to use the U.S. presidential inaugural speeches texts as an example, calling it "inaugurals_corpus".

```
inaugurals_corpus <- quanteda::data_corpus_inaugural

class(inaugurals_corpus)
[Output:]
     [1] "corpus"
```

Before starting LDA we must convert the data into the needed document text format. This is a two-step process: (1) converting from corpus to dfm, and (2) converting from dfm to dtm.

1. Convert corpus from corpus to document feature matrix (dfm).

   ```
   inaugurals_dfm <- quanteda::dfm(inaugurals_corpus)

   class(inaugurals_dfm)
   [Output:]
         [1] "dfm"      attr(,"package")      [1] "quanteda"
   ```

2. Convert from dfm to document text matrix (dtm) format. Note that the option `to = "topicmodels"` would also result in a dtm object.

   ```
   inaugurals_dtm <- quanteda::convert(inaugurals_dfm, to = "tm")

   class(inaugurals_dtm)
   [Output:]
         [1] "DocumentTermMatrix"    "simple_triplet_matrix"
   ```

To illustrate LDA, we now ask for a four-topic LDA solution, using the dtm object we just created. The resulting object, "inaugurals_lda", is of data class LDA_VEM and is a topic model with four topics.

```
inaugurals_lda <- topicmodels::LDA(inaugurals_dtm, k = 4, control=list(seed=321))

class(inaugurals_lda)
[Output:]
   [1] "LDA_VEM"
   attr(,"package")
   [1] "topicmodels"
```

We now convert to one-word-per-row tidytext tibble data frame format. Columns will be topic, term, beta. LDA probabilities are listed under "beta". At this point, the "inaugurals_topics" data frame contains 37,440 words, many of them trivial words such as "of" and "the".

```
inaugurals_topics <- tidytext::tidy(inaugurals_lda, matrix = "beta")

class(inaugurals_topics)
[Output:]
     [1] "tbl_df"      "tbl"          "data.frame"
```

To make inaugurals_topics more useful, we remove common stop words, custom stop words, and punctuation. This is a two-step process:

1. Creating a list of custom (researcher-specified) stop words. The list of custom stop words could be much longer. A separate list of punctuation marks to be removed is also created.

   ```
   custom_stop_words <- dplyr::tibble(word = c("1", "addyourownword2"))

   punctuation <- dplyr::tibble(word = c(".", ",", "'", ":", ";", "?", "/", ")",
   "(", "-","-", "|", " ", "-", "_", "-","\"", "\\n"))
   ```

2. Remove tidytext's stop words, custom stop words, and punctuation. The cleaned text is put in the "inaugurals_topics" object, overwriting it.

```
inaugurals_topics <- inaugurals_topics %>%
      dplyr::anti_join(stop_words, by = c("term" = "word")) %>%
      dplyr::anti_join(punctuation, by = c("term" = "word")) %>%
      dplyr::anti_join(custom_stop_words, by = c("term"="word"))
```

We may now list words (term) by topic and by LDA probabilities (beta). Each word is listed once for each topic, so four times in this example. We see that "fellow-citizens" is most associated with topics 4 and 1 in that order. It is little associated with topic 2. This listing also suggests the need to rank words, of which there are over 35,000, by the beta coefficient.

```
head(inaugurals_topics,4)
[Output:]
  # A tibble: 4 x 3
    topic term               beta
    <int> <chr>             <dbl>
  1     1 fellow-citizens 3.55e- 4
  2     2 fellow-citizens 4.41e-54
  3     3 fellow-citizens 1.67e- 4
  4     4 fellow-citizens 5.56e- 4
```

It is more useful to list the top words by beta coefficient. The `top _ n()` function from the dplyr package does hit by returning top terms. Other commands below arrange words in rank order by beta coefficient. The output object, "inaugurals_top", is a tidy tibble data frame with the columns topic, term, and beta.

```
ntt <- 6          # Specify the number of top terms wanted
inaugurals_top <- inaugurals_topics %>%
     dplyr::group_by(topic) %>%
     dplyr::top_n(ntt,beta) %>%
     dplyr::ungroup()%>%
     dplyr::arrange (topic, -beta)

class(inaugurals_top)
[Output:]
     [1] "tbl_df"     "tbl"          "data.frame"
```

Below, the top six terms for each of the four topics are listed from highest to lowest beta (probability) grouped by topic. The `paste()` and `round()` commands are from the "base" package in R's system library.

```
paste(inaugurals_top$topic,inaugurals_top$term, round(inaugurals_top$beta,4))
[Output:]
    [1] "1 government 0.005"    "1 people 0.0029"       "1 power 0.0024"
    [4] "1 union 0.0023"        "1 country 0.0022"      "1 public 0.002"
    [7] "2 world 0.0049"        "2 people 0.0038"       "2 nation 0.0035"
   [10] "2 america 0.0035"      "2 freedom 0.0027"      "2 government 0.0024"
   [13] "3 people 0.0031"       "3 government 0.0026"   "3 war 0.002"
   [16] "3 peace 0.002"         "3 constitution 0.0019" "3 country 0.0019"
   [19] "4 people 0.0055"       "4 government 0.0049"   "4 country 0.0029"
   [22] "4 public 0.0027"       "4 constitution 0.0025" "4 congress 0.0022"
```

It is not easy to attach labels to the four topics. The first-listed word in each topic is the one most strongly loaded. Most-loaded words could be used as labels for the topics. Taking beta weights greater than .003, the topics are:

Topic 1: government
Topic 2: world-people-nation-america
Topic 3: people
Topic 4: people-government

This is not the well-differentiated topic model result of the type mentioned above with regard to the four contrasting novels. Rather it is analogous to a factor solution in exploratory factor analysis in which there are notable cross-loadings – a common occurrence in social science. Given this LDA result, the researcher might well explore a variety of solutions other than the four-topic solution. Also, the .300 cutoff could be changed. Rerunning the analysis is easy to do as it only involves changing "k" in the topicmodels command above. For instance, the two-topic solution with a cutoff of .004 has the advantage that the top words differ between topics (LDA 1 = "government", LDA 2 = "people"). Finally, note that beta has to do with frequency, so that the LDA 4 in the four-topic solution, which was identified above as "people-government", might be read as "people more often than government".

While perhaps interesting, overall the mixed results of LDA fail to support the existence a simple topic structure for U.S. presidential inaugural addresses. This is perhaps to be expected since all documents were presidential inaugural speeches, not contrasting novels as in the example mentioned earlier. Put another way, there is poor LDA fit. There are multiple ways of assessing LDA fit. The most popular is the "perplexity" criterion illustrated below. However, there are several R packages for computing and plotting perplexity, and there are a number of other LDA fit criteria apart from perplexity, such as that based on mean log likelihoods as developed in R by Ponweiser (2012).

The most common measure of how successful an LDA solution has been is "perplexity" (see Blei, Ng, & Jordan, 2003). While there is no agreed-upon "good model" level, when comparing models, the lower the perplexity, the better the LDA fit. While with all things statistical there are variations, a simple perplexity measure is supported by the "topicmodels" package. Below is the perplexity value for the k = 4 solution, for four topics.

```
topicmodels::perplexity(inaugurals_lda)
[Output]
      [1] 428.5711
```

The number "428.5722" is largely meaningless in itself. Rather, we must compare the perplexity of the k = 4 solution with perplexity for other k solutions. Perplexity for the entire dataset ("in-sample perplexity", as opposed to "cross-validated perplexity", which is also possible and which does not necessarily display lower values for increased number of topics), will tend to improve (perplexity will be lower) as k increases (there are more topics). However, improvement also tends to level off as each increase in k captures less important structures in the data.

Alternatively, rather than base k on the solution with the lowest perplexity, which is selection on a data-driven basis, the researcher may instead make a non-statistical judgment about the interpretability of a given solution and its usefulness for model development and theory-building. The fact that the literature shows little correlation of perplexity-based judgments with researcher-based judgments encourages use of this "eyeball" approach to picking the best number of topics.

To pick the number of topics to request (k) based on perplexity, one might plot the perplexity coefficients for various solutions, such as from k = 2 through k = 10. Then one chooses the k corresponding to the "elbow" in the plot, as in the use of scree plots in factor analysis. An example plot is shown in Figure 9.28. While the choice of the elbow is somewhat subjective, one might say that it occurs at k – 3.

Next we show how the most common terms within each LDA topic may be displayed. This listing is based on the object "inaugurals_topics", which was created and then cleaned earlier in this section, for the four-topic solution. The most common terms figure is Figure 9.29, created in the two steps below.

1. Group the ten top terms by topic, in descending order by LDA beta weight:

```
inaugurals_top_terms <- inaugurals_topics  %>%
   dplyr::group_by(topic) %>%
   dplyr::top_n(10,beta) %>%
   dplyr::ungroup()%>%
   dplyr::arrange(topic, -beta)
```

2. Plot the top terms as measured by LDA beta weights.

```
inaugurals_top_terms %>%
   dplyr::mutate(term=reorder(term,beta)) %>%
   ggplot2::ggplot(ggplot2::aes(term,beta,fill=factor(topic))) +
   ggplot2::geom_col(show.legend=FALSE) +
```

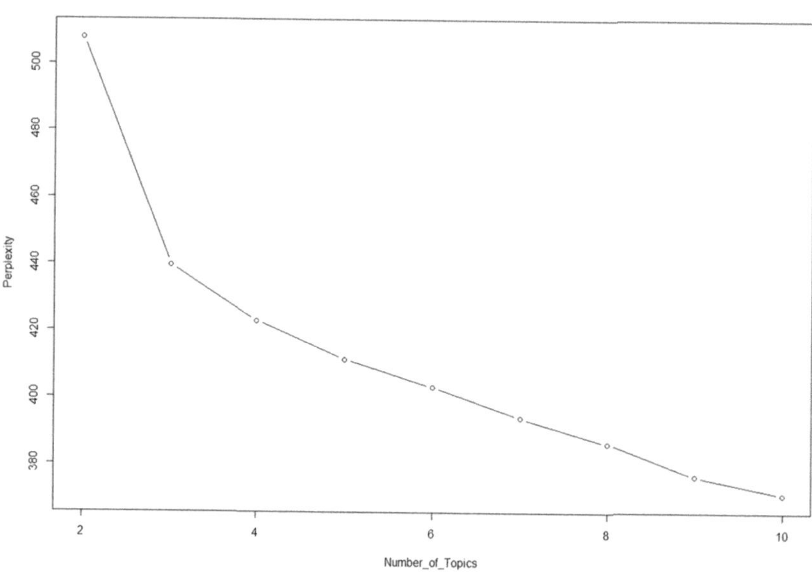

Figure 9.28 LDA perplexity plot

```
ggplot2::facet_wrap(~topic, scales="free") +
ggplot2::coord_flip() +
ggplot2::theme(text = element_text(size=rel(5), angle=00)) +
ggplot2::theme(axis.title.y = element_text(size = rel(3.5), angle=90)) +
ggplot2::theme(axis.title.x = element_text(size = rel(3.5), angle=00))
```

Finally, though there are many other aspects to LDA analysis which might be explored, for space reasons we end by presenting another useful figure. Figure 9.20 plots a listing of words which are most different (based on LDA beta weights) between a pair of LDA topics. For the k = 4 solution, we choose to compare topics 1 and 2, though any pair of topics might be compared in the same manner. We compute beta_spread based on term differences in topics 1 and 2. We also compute log_ratio as the log of the ratio of betas for topic2 to topic1.

```
beta_spread <- inaugurals_topics %>%
  mutate(topic = paste0("topic", topic)) %>%
  spread(topic, beta) %>%
  filter(topic1 >  .001 | topic2 > .001) %>%
  mutate(log_ratio = log2(topic2/topic1))

beta_spread
```

[Output:]

```
   tibble: 41 x 6
      term            topic1    topic2    topic3   topic4 log_ratio
      <chr>            <dbl>     <dbl>     <dbl>    <dbl>     <dbl>
    1 america       0.000138  0.00348   1.22e- 4 2.83e- 4      4.66
    2 american      0.000604  0.00180   3.47e- 4 1.23e- 3      1.57
    3 americans     0.0000234 0.00154   5.88e-11 2.03e-13      6.04
    4 citizens      0.00172   0.00132   1.45e- 3 1.08e- 3    -0.382
    5 constitution  0.00163   0.0000877 1.92e- 3 2.46e- 3     -4.22
    6 country       0.00218   0.00138   1.88e- 3 2.86e- 3    -0.657
    7 day           0.000213  0.00115   2.09e- 4 3.56e- 4      2.42
    8 democracy     0.000126  0.00111   2.45e- 8 7.87e-10      3.14
    9 duties        0.00111   0.000136  3.47e- 4 8.34e- 4     -3.03
   10 executive     0.00115   0.0000500 2.39e- 4 1.11e- 3     -4.52
   # ... with 31 more rows
```

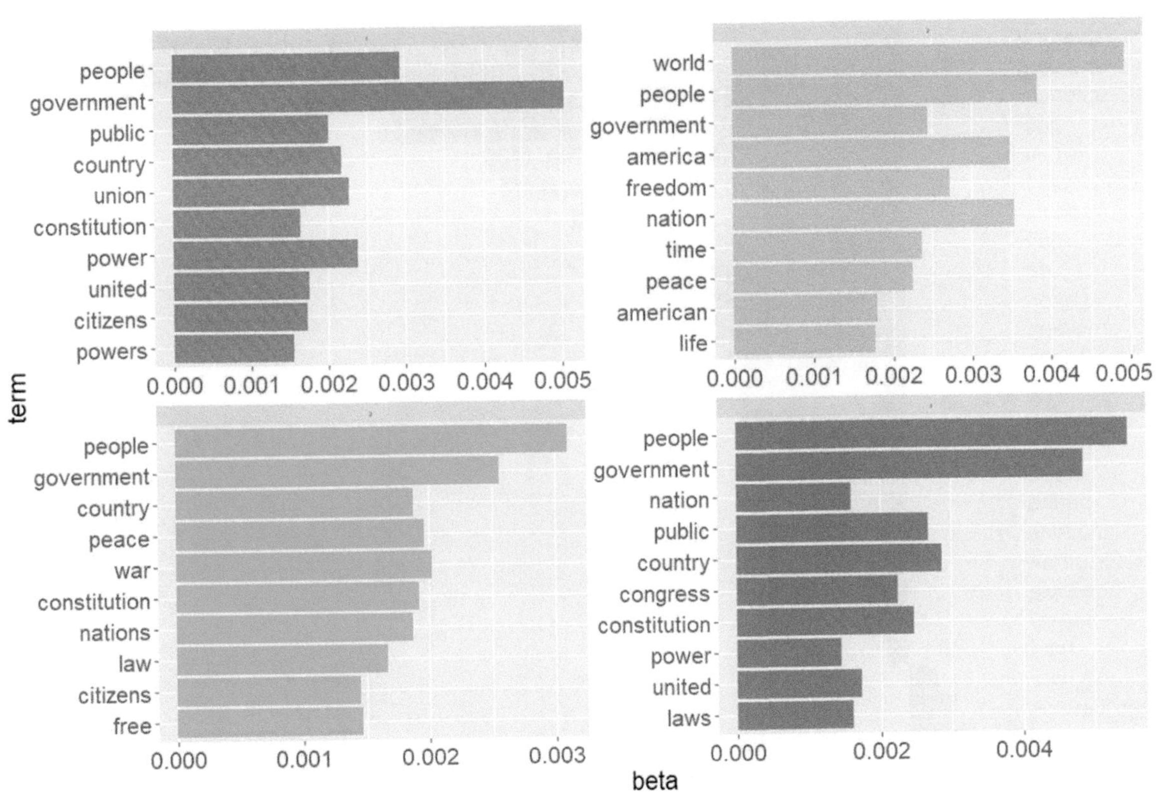

Figure 9.29 Most frequent terms by topic

Having computed beta_spread, we may visualize topic ratio differences by term, using a four-step process. This is useful in inferring differences in meaning between LDA factors.

1. Set colors and font size.

```
cbPalette <- c("red", "blue")
fontsize <- 16
```

2. Get the most frequent topics differentiated by spread in terms of betas.

```
topictop<-beta_spread %>%
    dplyr::top_n(25,beta_spread$log_ratio)
```

3. Order terms by their log ratios.

```
topicspread <- topictop %>%
   dplyr::mutate(term= stats::reorder(term, topictop$log_ratio))
```

4. Create the plot shown in Figure 9.30.

```
topicspread %>%
  ggplot2::ggplot(ggplot2::aes(term,log_ratio, fill = log_ratio > 0))+
  ggplot2::scale_fill_manual(values=cbPalette)+
  ggplot2::theme(axis.text=element_text(size=fontsize,hjust=1))+
  ggplot2::xlab("Term")+
  ggplot2::ylab("Top Terms with Odds of Being More from Topic 1 > 2 (red) or
Topic 2 > 1 (blue)") +
  ggplot2::geom_col(show.legend=FALSE) +
  ggplot2::coord_flip()+
   ggplot2::theme(axis.title.y = element_text(size = rel(1.4), angle=90)) +
   ggplot2::theme(axis.title.x = element_text(size = rel(1.4), angle=00))
```

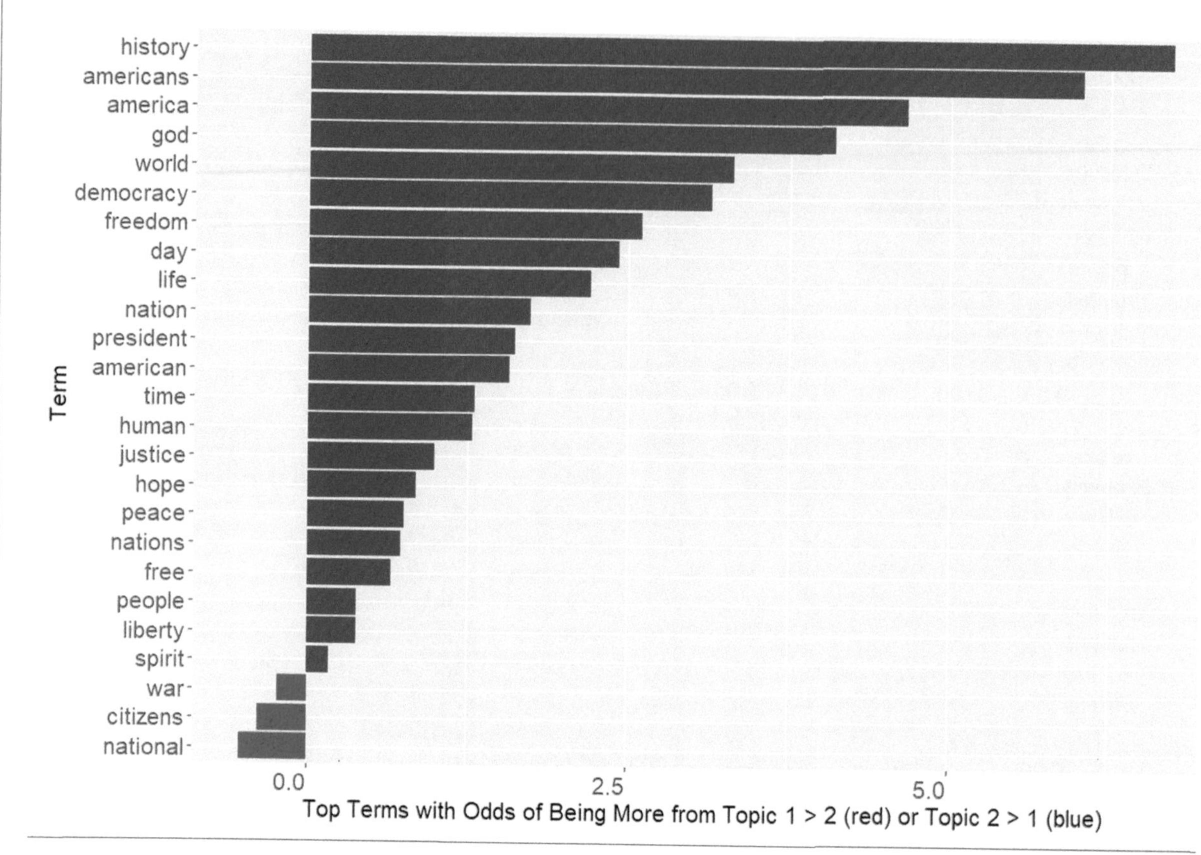

Figure 9.30 Most frequent terms differentiated between topics 1 and 2

9.20 Analysis: Lexical dispersion plots

Also called "x-ray" plots, lexical dispersion plots are another way of showing the relative frequency of word use across documents. Below, we take as two documents to compare the inaugural addresses from President Clinton (1997) through President Trump (2017), for the terms "equal" and "wealth". While the comparison could be accomplished with word frequency lists, the lexical dispersion plot conveys more information at a glance. The lexical dispersion plot is shown in Figure 9.31.

```
# Setup
library(quanteda)

# Create a small-c corpus of character vectors using quanteda
inaugurals_from_1990 <- quanteda::corpus_subset(data_corpus_inaugural, Year > 1990)

# Lexical dispersion plot comparing two terms across multiple documents
quanteda::textplot_xray(quanteda::kwic(inaugurals_from_1990, pattern = "equal*"),
quanteda::kwic(inaugurals_from_1990, pattern = "wealth"),scale="relative")
```

Figure 9.31 may be interpreted in these ways:

- The number of vertical lines for a given president (row) is the number of uses of the column term, either "equal" or "wealth". For instance, the term "equal" was used most frequently by President Obama, who did not use the term "wealth" at all. Trump mentioned wealth more often than any other recent president but stood alone in not mentioning equal or equality at all.

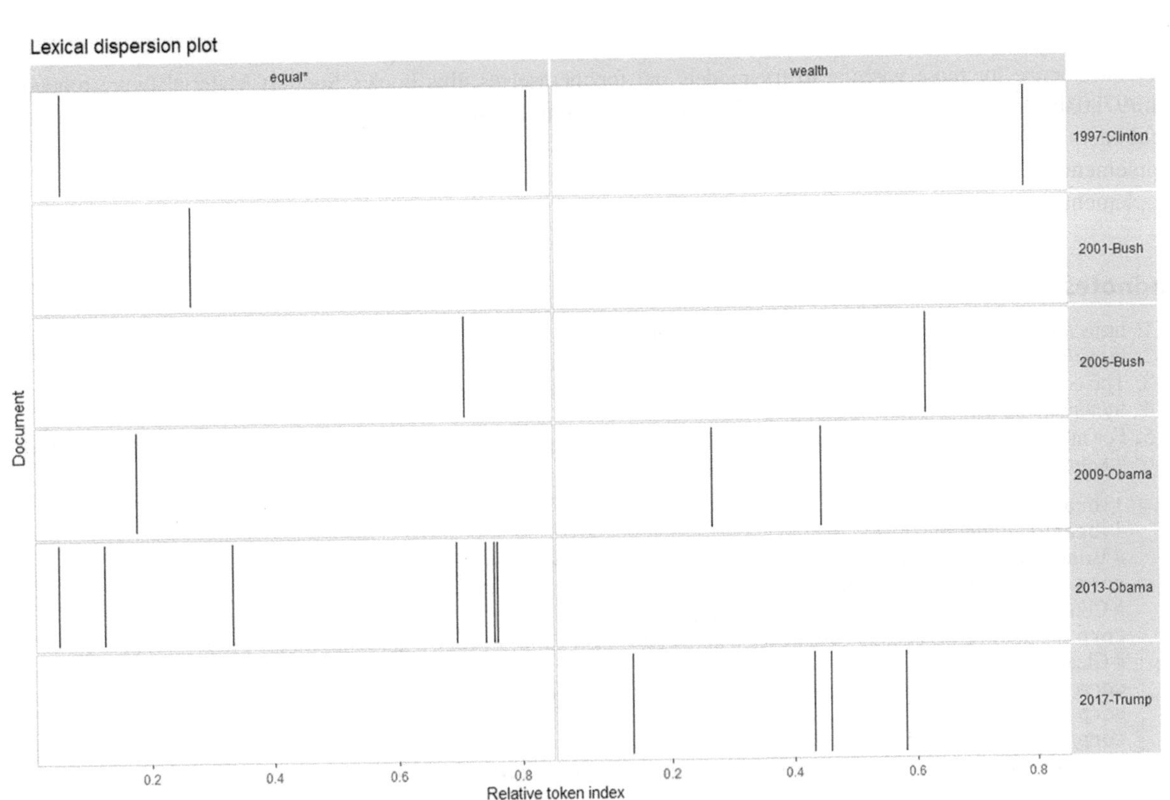

Figure 9.31 Lexical dispersion plots for "equal*" and "wealth"

- The placement of the vertical lines indicates the relative position in the term in the inaugural speech document, with early in the document being toward the left of the plot. For instance, President Clinton used the term "equal" at the beginning and end of his speech, but not in the middle.
- The x-axis is the "relative token index". The "token" is the word at the top of the column, either "equal" or "wealth". "Relative" means that even though speeches were of different lengths, they are displayed in the same width for every president. Thus, for instance, if the relative token index for a vertical line is 0.40, then that occurrence of the word occurred 40% of the way into the speech. Had there only been one document, the x-axis would have been the absolute token index. For multiple documents, one may override the relative token index default by using the `scale="absolute"` option in the `textplot _ xray()` command. Then, for instance, an absolute token index of 1,000 would mean that the given term occurred 1,000 words into the speech. However, the lengths of the plots for each president would differ.

9.21 Analysis: Bigrams and ngrams

Section 9.21 appears as a Chapter 9 online supplement in the Support Material (www.routledge.com/9780367624293) for this book. The supplement covers the important topic of use bigrams (two-word phrases), ngrams (strings of a researcher-set number of words), paragraphs, or other text units as a basis for text analysis. Placement as a supplement is purely for space reasons and does not indicate lesser importance of this topic. The supplement is titled, "Bigrams and ngrams".

9.22 Command summary

For convenience for those wishing to try models out for themselves, this book's Support Material (www.routledge.com/9780367624293) contains a listing of the main commands used in this chapter. This listing may be handy for readers following along with the book using their home or office computers. For topics presented as an online supplement ("Text cleaning and preparation", "Bigrams and ngrams"), the command summary is at the end of the supplement.

Endnotes

1. https://aravind-j.github.io/PGRdup/reference/KWIC.html
2. https://towardsdatascience.com/tidy-web-scraping-in-r-tutorial-and-resources-ac9f72b4fe47
3. The code in this section is adapted in part from https://rpubs.com/williamsurles/316682
4. Synonymous with `summarise()`.
5. For more about encoding, see https://www.rdocumentation.org/packages/stringi/versions/1.4.5/topics/stringi-encoding
6. # Setup

```
library(tm)
library(wordcloud)
# Bring in inaugurals speeches data as small-c corpus of character vectors
corp <- quanteda::corpus(data_corpus_inaugural)
# Convert to a "capital-C" Corpus using the tm package.
corp <- tm::SimpleCorpus(VectorSource(unlist(lapply(corp, as.character))))
# Cleaning steps
corp <- tm_map(corp, content_transformer(tolower))
corp <- tm_map(corp, removePunctuation)
corp <- tm_map(corp, removeNumbers)
corp <- tm_map(corp, function(x)removeWords(x,stopwords()))
# Convert to a term document matrix (tdm)
term.matrix <- tm::TermDocumentMatrix(corp)
# Convert to a matrix or class "matrix' (no longer a tdm)
term.matrix <- as.matrix(term.matrix)
# Select out just two columns (Obama, Trump)
term.matrix2 <- as.matrix(term.matrix[,57:58])
# Assign column labels
colnames(term.matrix2) <- c("Obama 2013","Trump 2017")
# Create the comparison cloud using the wordcloud package (not shown here)
wordcloud::comparison.cloud(term.matrix2,max.words= 50,random.order=FALSE,colors=c("blue",
"red"), match.colors=TRUE, title.size=1)
```

7. # Convert matrix to data frame: rows are words, columns are documents

```
# This is not what we want and is presented only for instructional purposes!
df <- as.data.frame(m)
```

8. # The syntax below shows how to collapse into a single command.

```
inaugurals_freq <- inaugurals_words %>%
  dplyr::count(Year, word) %>%
  tidyr::complete(Year, word, fill = list(n = 0)) %>%
  dplyr::group_by(Year) %>%  dplyr::mutate(year_total = sum(n),
         percent = n / year_total) %>%
  dplyr::ungroup()
```

9. # The syntax below shows how to collapse into a single command.

```
models <- inaugurals_freq %>%
  dplyr::group_by(word) %>%
  dplyr::filter(sum(n) > 50) %>%
  dplyr::do(tidytext::tidy(glm(cbind(n, year_total - n) ~ Year,. ,family = "binomial"))) %>%
  dplyr::ungroup() %>%
  dplyr::filter(term == "Year")
```

10. Pronounced – deer-ih-CLAY.

Appendix 1: Introduction to R and RStudio

Why R?

R is a language which is used for statistics, data analysis, text analysis, and machine learning. While it may be employed using simple commands to implement common procedures, such as linear regression, it is also a programming language, allowing the user to create original functions, programs, and packages. This has made R arguably the fastest-growing and leading statistical tool for researchers. Even if you do not wish to program yourself, you can take advantage of thousands of cutting-edge programs for an "alphabet soup" of applications, including agent-based modeling, Bayesian modeling, cluster analysis, correlation, correspondence analysis, data management, decision trees, descriptive statistics, economics, factor analysis, forecasting, generalized linear modeling, instrumental variables regression, logistic regression, longitudinal and time series analysis, machine learning models, mapping and spatial analysis, mediation and moderation analysis, multiple linear regression, multilevel modeling, network analysis, neural network analysis, panel data regression, path analysis, partial least squares modeling, power analysis, reliability analysis, significance testing, structural equation modeling, survey research, text analytics, and visualization of data – and many more. New state-of-the-art R packages are added daily in an ever-expanding universe of research tools, many created by leading scholars in their fields.

R is free and thus liberates the researcher from dependency on the willingness of his or her purchasing department to acquire new software. Moreover, it is platform-independent and may be used with any operating system. Also, R is open-source, with all source code available to those inclined to look "under the hood". Statistical algorithms are not locked in proprietary "black boxes". One benefit of being open source is that bug fixes and added features may be put forward from the R user community, members of which do not need to wait upon a vendor for new releases, which may be a year or more away.

R packages are available to import from and export to a variety of data sources, such as SPSS, SAS, Stata, and Excel, to name a few. Although R is quite full-featured in its own right, it also may be integrated with other programming environments, such as Python, Java, and C/C++. Starting with version 1.4, RStudio now offers access to Python tools and packages through its Python interpreter, the "reticulate" package, and as well as through other avenues. All of this is supported by a very large user community with a full array of mailing lists (through which help questions may be posed and answered), blogs, conferences, journals, training opportunities, and archives.

Installing R and RStudio

While it is perfectly possible to install R without using a graphical user interface, in this tutorial we recommend the most popular approach, which is using the free RStudio package. Installation of RStudio will also install the latest version of R. RStudio's functionality is summarized at https://www.rstudio.com/products/rstudio/features/. To install RStudio, follow the steps below.

1. To install RStudio, go to https://www.rstudio.com/products/rstudio/download/.
2. Click the "Download" button for the "Free" version of "RStudio Desktop".

3. Under "Installers for Supported Platforms", click "Download RStudio for Windows" or choose one of the other supported platforms, which include macOS and various flavors of Linux. Note that RStudio requires a 64-bit system. If yours is 32-bit, you will have to use an older version of RStudio.
4. After clicking to download, an executable file (.exe) will be downloaded to your computer. Depending on your browser and operating system, this file may be launched automatically or you may have to choose to run the .exe file manually.
5. When the .exe file is run, a setup wizard starts. Accept the defaults and click the "Finish" button at the end.
6. RStudio will now be in the Windows start menu. You can right-click its icon and choose to pin it to the taskbar if you wish.

It is a good idea to check from time to time to see if you have the current version of R and RStudio. In the RStudio menu system, select Help > About RStudio to see the RStudio version. Issue the command `version` to see the loaded version of R.

Installing RStudio will not automatically install RTools. However, installing some R packages requires RTools and so we recommend installing it. Go to https://cran.rstudio.com/bin/windows/Rtools/ and follow the download directions to install the 64-bit version.

While it is possible to install R without RStudio, we recommend the installation procedure above. RStudio will automatically use the most recent version of R installed on the user's computer. Typically this will be the version installed when RStudio is installed.

Example data

Further below we use a very small dataset called mydata.csv (comma-separated values format), mydata.sav (SPSS format), or mydata.dta (Stata format). These are supplied in the online Support Material (www.routledge.com/9780367624293) for this book. However, this dataset is small enough to enter into R manually, as shown below.

The dataset contains ten fictional cases, each with two variables: gender and happy. The "happy" variable is an ordinal item with values coded from 1 = very unhappy to 5 = very happy. Gender is a binary item coded male = 0 and female = 1. Actual data are listed below and may be pasted into any statistical package or spreadsheet, from which a comma-separated values (.csv) or other format dataset may be created.

happy	gender
4	0
1	0
3	0
5	0
3	0
3	1
2	1
4	1
5	1
1	1

The data may be read into an object called "mydata" from the supplied.csv file by running the R commands below. Note that lines beginning with the pound sign (#) are comments not acted upon by R. Note also that all three commands, including comments, can be cut and pasted as a batch into RStudio and run.

```
# Set the working directory (yours may differ)
setwd("C:/Data")
```

```
# Read the .csv file into the object "mydata".
mydata <- read.table("mydata.csv", header = TRUE, sep = ",")

# Verify that mydata is of data class "data.frame", the most common R format for storing data.
class(mydata)
[Output:]
   [1] "data.frame"
```

Alternatively, the mydata data frame may be created manually using the commands below. The assignment operator (<–) puts whatever is on its right-hand side into the object named on its left-hand side. The `c()` combine function combines values into a vector or list. Below it combines the ten values listed for each variable into numeric vectors called happy and gender.

```
# Create numeric vector objects for happy and gender
happy <- c(4,1,3,5,3,3,2,4,5,1)
gender <- c(0,0,0,0,0,1,1,1,1,1)

# Create a data frame called "mydata" from gender and happy.
mydata <- data.frame(happy,gender)

# View the contents of mydata. Note that "View" must be capitalized, unlike most R commands.
# The display of mydata will appear in RStudio in the upper left.
View (mydata)
```

In addition to viewing a data frame like mydata, we may summarize it. The `summary()` command provides basic descriptive statistics about variables in the data set.

```
summary(mydata)
[Output:]
         happy              gender
     Min.   :1.00     Min.   :0.0
     1st Qu.:2.25     1st Qu.:0.0
     Median :3.00     Median :0.5
     Mean   :3.10     Mean   :0.5
     3rd Qu.:4.00     3rd Qu.:1.0
     Max.   :5.00     Max.   :1.0
```

In this introduction to R, we also use a larger dataset, gssdata. The file "gssdata.csv" is supplied on the Support Material (www.routledge.com/9780367624293) to this text. Other .csv files used in this tutorial are cobb_survey.csv and world.csv. For illustrating importing SPSS data, we use mydata.sav. All are found in the Data section of this text's Support Material (www.routledge.com/9780367624293).

Quick start: Computing a correlation

As a quick start example, we will use RStudio to import an SPSS data file, then we will compute the correlation coefficient between "gender" and "happy". We assume the "mydata" object has already been created as in the previous section.

After starting RStudio, its basic user interface appears as shown in Figure Appl.1.

In Figure Appl.1, the R user interface is shown:

- The upper left area is where the results of the `View()` command will be displayed, revealing spreadsheet-style the contents of a data frame, for instance.
- The upper right area displays the Environment, History, Connections, and Tutorial, depending on which tab is selected. In the figure, the Environment tab is selected, showing objects currently in the R environment, such as the "mydata" data frame.

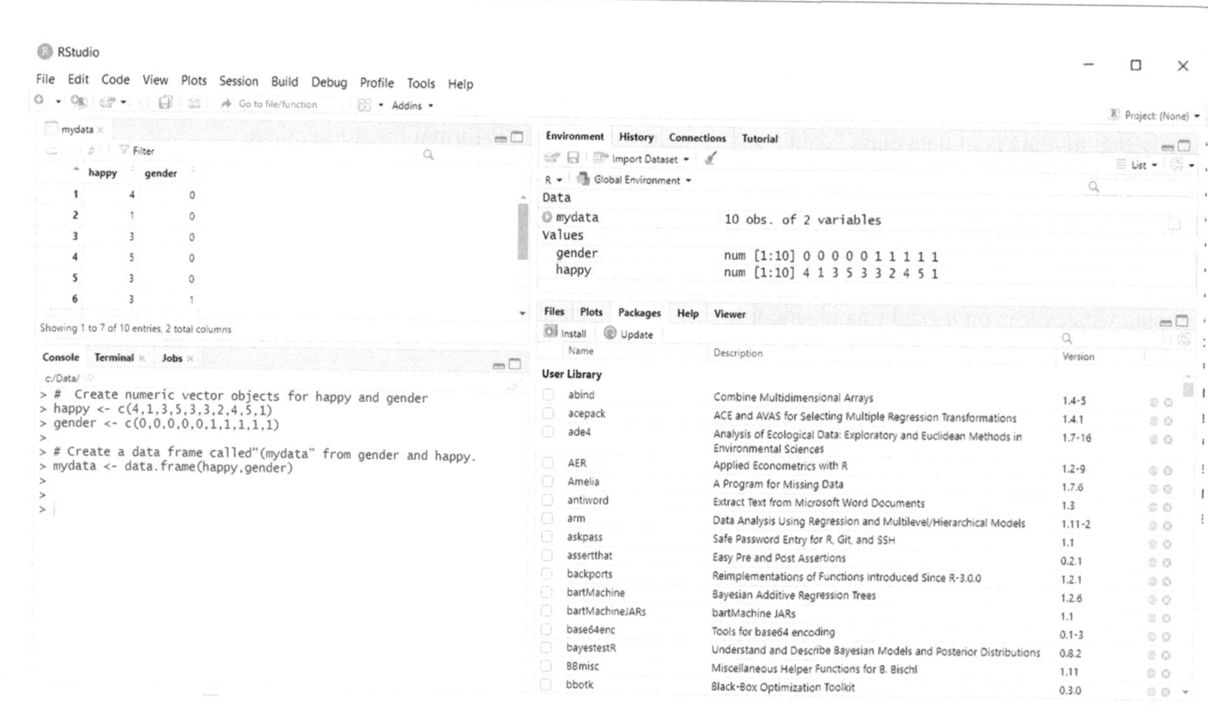

Figure App1.1 The Rstudio interface

- The lower left shows the area where commands may be entered and text output from commands, as well as error messages, are displayed.
- The lower right area displays Files, Plots, Packages, or the Viewer, depending on which tab is selected. In the figure, the Packages tab is selected, showing packages which have been installed on the local computer.

It is a good idea to do three things right at the start and one thing at the end of an RStudio session:

1. Select Session > New Session from the RStudio menu. This creates a new instance of RStudio with a cleared environment.
2. Choose Session > Set Working Directory. Many researchers make a practice of creating a separate file folder for each R project. Set the working directory to point to your project folder. This is the same as issuing the `setwd()` command used above.
3. At the end, select Session > Quit Session. Respond "Yes" when asked if you want to save your workspace image in a. RDATA file in your working directory.

To continue with the "quick start" example of computing the correlation of the variable gender and happy, make sure the example data are loaded in using one of the methods in Example data. The data frame object "mydata" should appear in the Environment tab of RStudio.

The correlation command in R is `cor()`. Because it is in the "stats" package, which is part of R's "System Library", it may be used directly without having to install a package and without having to use the `library()` command to activate it.

```
myoutput <- cor(mydata$happy,mydata$gender)

myoutput
[Output:]
   [1] -0.0727393
```

This simple example provides the following lessons:

- We are performing an operation on a data frame (mydata), which is the most common format in R for storing data.
- This is an example of using the assignment operator (<-) to assign the results of the right-hand side of the operator to the object named on the left-hand side.
- We may list results by typing the name of the output object, here myoutput. However, had we entered only the `cor()` expression on the right-hand side without any assignment, the results would also have been printed.
- R is case sensitive. Be careful to enter terms in the proper case. Most commands in R are lower case, but not all.
- Variable names are entered in long form, which is the name of the data frame (mydata), a dollar sign, then the name of the column (happy). If a command had a `data=mydata` option (not the case here and not supported by the `cor()` command), then the short variable name (e.g., happy) could be used. It is also possible to issue the command `attach(mydata)` before the correlation command, then issue the command `detach(mydata)` afterward. This allows the use of short variable names. However, attaching and detaching is derogated for reasons given in the FAQ at the end of this document. Many recommend using long form variable names in all circumstances, even if just for clarification of which variable comes from which data frame.
- When a data frame is the source, variables correspond to column names in the data frame.

The `cor()` command defaults to Pearsonian correlation. However, `cor()`, like most R commands, supports options. Type `help(cor)` to see the options. We may similarly type `help(name or command)` for almost any command. It is a good idea to check the options for any command if only to see what defaults are being used.

Among the options for `cor()` are the `method=` option to generate Kendall's correlation tau (used for ordinal variables) instead of Pearson's correlation r (used for continuous or binary variables).

```
myoutputKendall <- cor(mydata$happy,mydata$gender, method="kendall")
myoutputKendall
```

[Output:]
```
[1] -0.06405126
```

Another option for the `cor()` command is to omit mentioning of a pair of variables to correlate and instead entering just the name of the data frame. If variables in the data frame are numeric, we then get the correlation matrix of all variables. If saved to an object like "mycormatrix" below, the correlation matrix may be used as input to some other statistical command. Note that while we do not do so here, we could have added the option `method="kendall"` to get a matrix of Kendall's tau rather than Pearson's r coefficients

```
# Compute a correlation matrix, putting it in the object "mycormatrix".
mycormatrix <- cor(mydata)

# List the matrix.
mycormatrix
```
[Output:]
```
            happy      gender
happy   1.0000000 -0.0727393
gender -0.0727393  1.0000000
```

Importing data

It is hard to do anything without data. Acquiring data from some source is often one of the first tasks to be undertaken in a research project. Fortunately, R has the ability to import data from a very wide range of formats. RStudio provides menu options for common types of data importation. Thus, one may select File > Import Dataset > From SPSS to import an SPSS .sav data file. Other choices are From SAS, From Stata, From Excel, or From Text (for .csv files, for instance). RStudio will create the necessary code for you, displaying it in the lower right of the "Import Statistical Data" window. Browse to the file you wish to import, give it an output name, and click the "Import" button. Note that loading one data file does not erase others from memory, provided it is not of the same name.

There are multiple other ways to create or import data, listed below.

- **Manual data entry:** This was illustrated in Section 1.3, where we created the "mydata" data frame.
- **Excel data and .csv files:** One of the most common data storage strategies is to keep data in an Excel or similar spreadsheet, then share the data by saving it in.csv format. The .csv format is a type of "generic" data medium. A very large number of statistics and data management packages can read and write .csv data, including R.

If one chooses to keep data in Excel or some other non-R software, the researcher should keep in mind these general R data format requirements:

- One variable per column.
- All columns have the same number of rows.
- It is common for variable names to be in row 1.
- No interior spaces in variable names.
- Names are case-sensitive.
- Do not use reserved words in names like "integer" or "break". For a list of reserved words in R, type `help(reserved)`. Use of such terms may lead to unpredictable results.
- For missing data values, enter "NA" without the quote marks. If the original data contain some other missing code, such as –99, these cases must be recoded inside R. For example, the command below recodes –99 to NA missing for the variable happy:

  ```
  mydata$happy[mydata$happy==-99] <- NA
  ```

- For continuous data entered as vectors, enter an integer (e.g., 76) or a decimal value (e.g., 76.832). Note that the expression `newvar = 76L` will assure newvar is of type integer, not type numeric as would be for the expression `newvar2 = 76`.
- For categorical data may be entered as integer values such as 1L, 2L, and 3L. Use of 0 is permissible but not recommended. Factors may also be entered as text values (e.g., female, male) or logical values (e.g., T, F).

Assuming that a .csv file has been moved to one's working directory, the `read.csv()` command may be used to read in the data as shown below. The `read.table()` command functions in the same way. The `stringsAsFactors= option` is recommended (assuming this is consistent with the research purpose) but is not required. If set to TRUE (or T) then strings in the data will be of factor data class. If set to FALSE (or F) then strings in the data will be of character data class. This can make a difference for certain statistical procedures. The header=TRUE option specifies that row 1 contains the variable names, which is usual.

```
setwd("C:/Data")

mydata <- read.csv("mydata.csv", header=TRUE, sep = ",",          stringsAsFactors =
TRUE)
```

or:

```
mydata  <- read.table("mydata.csv", header = TRUE, sep = ",", stringsAsFactors =
TRUE)
```

Alternatively, It is possible to use a Windows-style file selection window to browse to the text file that is wanted (e.g., .txt, .csv) using the `file.choose()` command. The command below will enter the selected file into the object "mydata". Of course, what is chose must be mydata.csv to have the mydata content discussed above. This method gives the option of browsing to the correct file when it is not in the working directory.

```
mydata <- read.csv(file.choose(),header=TRUE, sep = ",", stringsAsFactors = TRUE)
```

Type `help(read.table)`, with or without the quotation marks, to view more options for this command, which is not restricted to .csv format.

Importing Stata .dta files

A commonly-used utility package in R is "haven", which is used for importing data in various formats, including Stata's .dta format. We must, of course, install and load the haven package before importing Stata files. This can be done by the RStudio menu method or by the command method.

The menu method is to select the "Packages" tab in RStudio, selecting "Install", as shown in Figure Appl.2. Most packages are installed from the CRAN repository, also shown in the figure, but there are other archives. Note that "install dependencies" is the default. This means that other packages needed by the haven package will also be installed.

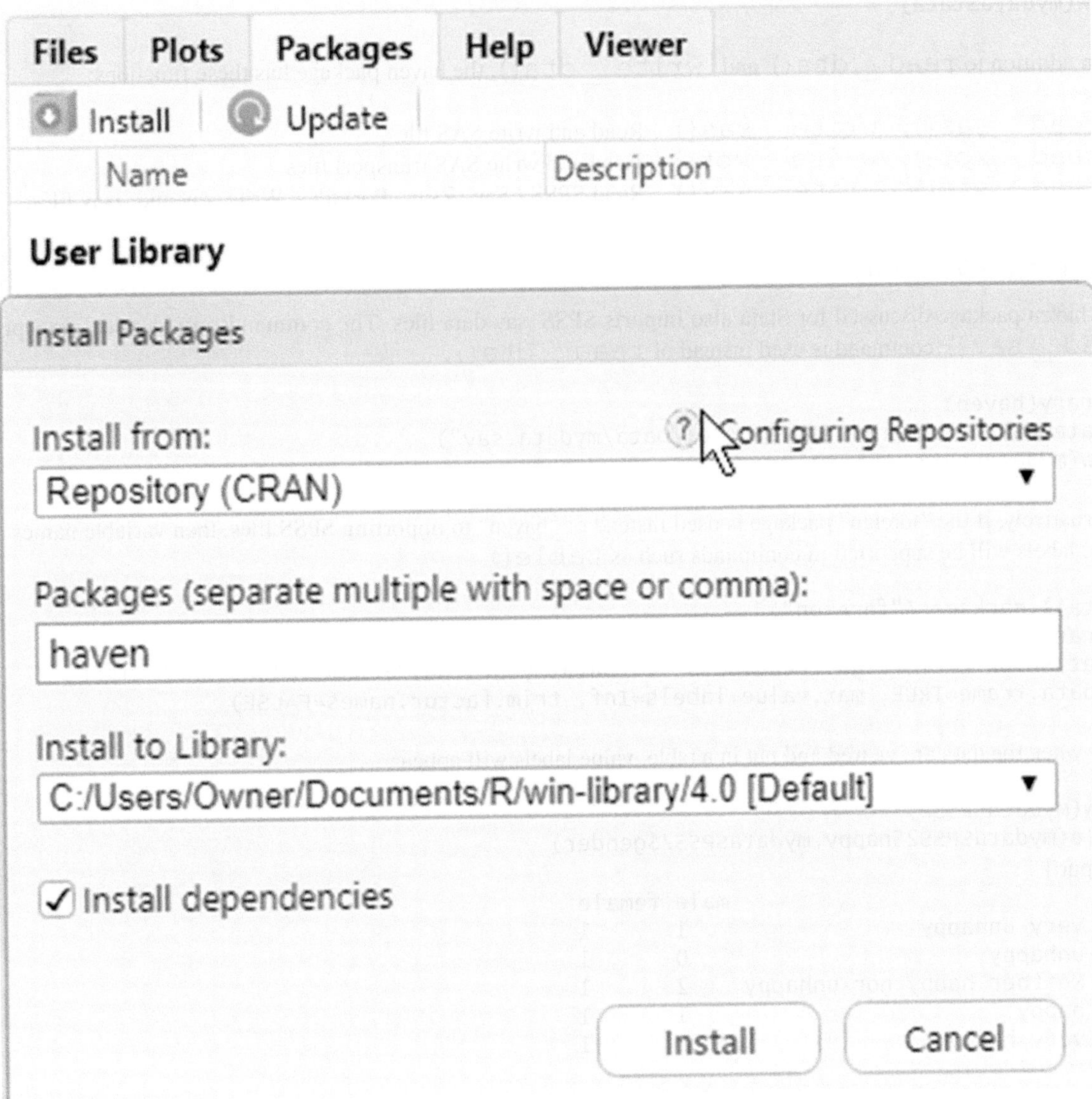

Figure Appl.2 RStudio install packages window

Alternatively, use the command method of installation below. Note that unlike the `library()` command, for `install.packages()` the package name must be within quote marks.

```
install.packages("haven")
```

Like all packages not in the R System Library, haven must be loaded after it is installed. This is done with the `library(haven)` command.

```
library(haven)
```

The command below reads in a Stata .dta file, which had been placed in the named folder.

```
mydataStata  <-  haven::read_dta("C:/Data/mydata.dta")
```

Then inspect the data:

```
View(mydataStata)
```

In addition to `read _ dta()` and `write _ dta()`, the haven package has these functions:

`read _ sas(), write _ sas()`	Read and write SAS files.
`read _ xpt(), write _ xpt()`	Read and write SAS transport files.
`read _ sav(), write _ sav()`	Read SPSS (.Sav, .Zsav, .Por) files. Write .sav and .zsav files.

Importing SPSS .sav files

The haven package discussed for Stata also imports SPSS .sav data files. The commands are identical, except the `read _ sav()` command is used instead of `read _ dta()`.

```
library(haven)
mydataSPSS <- haven::read_sav("C:/Data/mydata.sav")
View(mydataSPSS)
```

Alternatively, if the "foreign" package is used instead of "haven" to importing SPSS files, then variable names and value labels will be supported in commands such as `table()`.

```
install.packages("foreign")
library(foreign)
mydataSPSS2 <- foreign::read.spss("C:/Data/mydata.sav", use.value.labels=TRUE,
to.data.frame=TRUE, max.value.labels=Inf, trim.factor.names=FALSE)
```

Now when the data are viewed and put in a table, value labels will appear.

```
View(mydataSPSS2)
table(mydataSPSS2$happy,mydataSPSS2$gender)
```
[Output:]

```
                              male female
    Very unhappy                 1      1
    unhappy                      0      1
    Neither happy nor unhappy    2      1
    happy                        1      1
    very happy                   1      1
```

Warning: Before importing SPSS data, read the section further below on "Checking and handling missing data" as SPSS poses special problems when there are missing data. Specifically, R wants missing data to be coded NA, but SPSS allows a variety of other codings. This does not apply to the sample mydata.sav file, however.

In addition to `read.spss()` and `write.spss()`, the "foreign" package has these functions:

`read.dbf(),write.dbf()`	Read and write a DBF file
`read.dta(), write.dta()`	Read and write files in Stata format
`write.foreign()`	Write text files and code
`read.mtp()`	Read MiniTab files
`read.systat()`	Read Systat files
`read.xport()`	Read SAS export files and others

Importing SAS .sas7bdat files

Importing SAS files may also be done by an almost identical haven method, substituting the command read_sas(). We assume that the haven package has already been installed as described above.

```
library(haven)
mydataSAS <- haven::read_sas("C:/Data/mydata.sas7bdat")
View(mydataSAS)
```

SAS export files (.xpt format) may also be loaded with the "Hmisc" package. This is not illustrated here but information may be obtained using the following commands:

```
install.packages("Hmisc")
library(Hmisc)
help(sasxport.get)
```

Saving data

The commands for saving data largely parallel the commands discussed above for reading and importing data. In this section, we assume that the data frame object "mydata" is still in memory.

Remember to set the working directory to which you wish to save. For example:

```
setwd("C:/Data")
```

Saving to .csv format

The .csv format is the most common among R users, even more so than the native R format discussed below. To write the mydata data frame object in R to a .csv file: The `col.names=` option determines if column (variable) names are written to row 1 (TRUE is the default). The `row.names=` option determines if row names are written to column 1 (TRUE is the default).

```
write.csv(mydata, file = "mydata2.csv", col.names = TRUE, row.names = FALSE)
```

Saving to .txt format

To write to .txt plain text format (.txt), as in writing a web page to a raw, uncleaned text file, one may use the `write.table()` command below. The sep= option specifies what separator is to be used between values in any row of mydata. Here is a space.

```
write.table(mydata,"mydata2.txt", sep=" ",col.names = FALSE, row.names = FALSE)
```

However, ordinarily a data frame would have been written to a comma-separate values file rather than a text file. A better example would be saving a web page to a .txt file. This can be done easily using the "htm2txt" package, used here to capture the web page of the governor of California.

```
install.packages("htm2txt")
library(htm2txt)
CA <- htm2txt::gettxt("https://www.gov.ca.gov/")
write.table(CA, file = "myCA.txt", quote = FALSE, sep = "\n", col.names = FALSE)
```

Saving and reading in R format (.rds)

As in other statistical packages, data in memory in R will not be saved to disk unless the researcher explicitly asks to do so. R's native file format extension is .rds, as in mydata.rds. Ironically, this data format is eclipsed by the .csv format, even among R users. The `saveRDS()` and `readRDS()` functions are in the "base" package in the R System Library and can be accessed directly without installing any package.

```
# Save to .rds format
saveRDS(mydata, file = "mydata.rds")

# Read from .rds format
mydata <- readRDS("mydata.rds")
```

Adding value labels to data

Many data objects (datasets) in R are kept in a rectangular rows-and-columns format called a "data frame". The newer "tibble" format can handle more types of data. A data frame is a subset of a tibble, handling most numeric or character data you probably have been used to. In Section 1.3, we created a data frame called "mydata" from the numeric vectors "happy" and "gender" using the `data.frame()` command.

A data frame may be displayed as a table but unless data are imported from an external format which had value labels using a package like "foreign" which supports value labels, by default initially a data frame is apt to lack value labels for binary and categorical variables. Therefore, the table will lack value labels, making it difficult to read. This is shown in table output below.

```
table(mydata)
[Output:]
      gender
   happy 0 1
       1 1 1
       2 0 1
       3 2 1
       4 1 1
       5 1 1
```

The table above has no value labels. The `factor()` function may be used to assign value labels, here for the gender variable. The command below says to treat the gender variable in the mydata_df data frame as a factor with two levels, coded 0 and 1, and to substitute the labels "male" and "female" for these codes.

Warning: We start by making a copy of mydata. The copied data frame is "mydataLabeled". This is an important step because adding value labels will put the labels, which are character strings, in place of the numeric codes. If the labeled data are then saved to, say, mydata.csv, the original numeric codes will be lost.

```
mydataLabeled <- mydata

mydataLabeled$gender <- factor(mydataLabeled$gender,levels = c(0,1), labels =
c("male", "female"))
```

For ordinal variables, use the `ordered()` command. This is used to label for ordinal variables such as "happy", which is a Likert item with five levels. This command asks to take the "happy" variable, which has five levels coded from 1 through 5 and substitute the five listed labels to these codes.

```
mydataLabeled$happy <- ordered(mydataLabeled$happy,
   levels = c(1, 2, 3, 4, 5),
   labels = c("very unhappy", "unhappy",
     "neither happy nor unhappy", "happy", "very happy"))
```

Now we create a table of happy by gender. Output now has value labels.

```
table(mydataLabeled$happy,mydataLabeled$gender)
```
[Output:]
```
                            male female
   very unhappy                1      1
   unhappy                     0      1
   neither happy nor unhappy   2      1
   happy                       1      1
   very happy                  1      1
```

In summary, the method of adding value labels described above calls for maintaining two datasets: (1) the original one containing numeric codes, and (2) the value labeled version containing character labels. Either the labeled data frame is saved under a different name (e.g., "mydataLabeled.csv") or the labeling commands are saved as a text file to cut and paste as a batch of commands when needed. This achieves its purpose in producing output with value labels, such as the table above, but there is an alternative to this dual data frames approach.

Most functions in R do not use variable labels and even drop them. Though not discussed here, the package "expss" supports SPSS-style variable names and value labels. If variable names and value labels will be used more than briefly in the user's research, use of this package is recommended. The expss package integrates value labels support into base R functions and into functions from other R packages.

Inspecting data

As a research project unfolds, there are apt to be many R objects created. These are listed under the "Environment" tab in RStudio. For data frames and objects which can be coerced into a data frame (e.g., by `as.data.frame(mymatrix)` for the object "mymatrix"), data may be inspected by the `View()` command, which opens spreadsheet-like window in the upper left of the RStudio interface. Certain objects which are not a data frame, such as a text Corpus (discussed in Chapter 9), must be viewed with the `inspect()` command, not `View()`.

```
View(mydata)
```

A way to see a list of all objects in the environment is to issue the `objects()` command.

```
objects()
```
[Output:]
```
    [1] "CA"                "gender"
    [3] "happy"             "mycormatrix"
    [5] "mydata"            "mydataLabeled"
    [7] "mydataSAS"         "mydataSPSS"
    [9] "mydataSPSS2"       "mydataStata"
   [11] "myoutput"          "myoutputKendall"
```

Use the `class()` function to reveal the data class of any object. Here mydata is a data.frame while gender is an integer vector.

```
class(mydata)
[Output:]
        [1] "data.frame"
```

```
class(mydata$gender)
[Output:]
      [1] "integer"
```

We can also use the `sapply()` command to get the data class of all columns (variables) in a data frame. While mydata has only two columns, this method is even more useful when there are numerous variables. It is import to know the data class of each variable because some R functions will want a certain class of data as input. Also, this helps debug data class errors, as when a function gives an error message because it wanted integers such as 0 or 1, but a given variable was actually of character data class with values of "0" and "1". Another common problem occurs when a procedure wanted a variable of the factor class but the actual variable was of the character class. Bottom line: It is good to know what the data classes of your variables are. When you type `help(insert _ name _ of _ command)`, the resulting help page on RStudio will tell you what data class was wanted as input.

```
sapply(mydata, class)
[Output:]
        happy     gender
    "integer" "integer"
```

We can make sure all variables are of the desired data class at the time they are read into R by using the `colClasses=` option within the `read.csv()` command. While data classes may be assigned to columns after data are read in, it is more convenient to do so at the time of read-in, using the colClasses = option. For instance, if all variables were factors, with none meant to be of character type or numeric (even if coded with numerals), then we could read the data in this way:

```
gssdata  <-  read.csv("C:/Data/gssdata.csv", header=TRUE, sep = ",",
stringsAsFactors = TRUE, colClasses="factor")
```

Often, however, data are mixed in data type. This is the case for the example file "gssdata.csv", which is supplied on the Support Material (www.routledge.com/9780367624293) for this text. Below we read in the data, assigning columns their appropriate data classes. In this example, the first six columns are numeric, then 1 is factor, then 7 are numeric, then 5 are factors, then 4 are numeric, then 1 is factor, for a total of 24 columns. This is specified using the `rep()` replicate command nested within the `c()` combine command.

```
gssdata <- read.csv("C:/Data/gssdata.csv", header=TRUE, sep = ",", stringsAsFactors =
TRUE, colClasses = c(rep("numeric",6), "factor",rep("numeric",7), rep("factor",5),
rep("numeric",4), "factor"))
```

To verify the data classes of all columns we reissue the `sapply()` command, asking that it apply the class() command repeatedly to columns of the gssdata data frame.

```
sapply(gssdata, class)
[Output:]
       year          id     adults         age     attend
  "numeric"   "numeric"  "numeric"   "numeric"  "numeric"
     babies       bible       born      childs      class
  "numeric"    "factor"  "numeric"   "numeric"  "numeric"
     degree        fund    gender1       happy     hhrace
  "numeric"   "numeric"  "numeric"   "numeric"   "factor"
```

```
 hispanic   marital   partyid      relig   respnum
 "factor"  "factor"  "factor"  "factor" "numeric"
   satfin       sex  vetyears    wrkstat
"numeric" "numeric" "numeric"   "factor"
```

Each row in a data frame is an observation. The sample size is therefore the number of rows:

```
nrow(gssdata)
```

[Output:]

```
   [1] 1785
```

Each column in a data frame is a variable. The `length()` command returns the number of variables and the `names()` command returns their names.

```
length(gssdata)
```

[Output:]

```
   [1] 24
```

```
names(gssdata)
```

[Output:]

```
    [1] "year"     "id"       "adults"   "age"      "attend"
    [6] "babies"   "bible"    "born"     "childs"   "class"
   [11] "degree"   "fund"     "gender1"  "happy"    "hhrace"
   [16] "hispanic" "marital"  "partyid"  "relig"    "respnum"
   [21] "satfin"   "sex"      "vetyears" "wrkstat"
```

The `summary()` command is one of the simplest ways to inspect an object. The partial output below shows us that all data in gssdata are for the year 2012. For the numeric variable adults (in family), the minimum code is 1, the maximum is 6, and the median is 2. Mean age is 48.4 years. For the factor variable "bible", the frequency distribution is returned. Some 802 respondents are of code 2 on this variable. Above we saw that gssdata has 1,785 observations but below we see its maximum is 1,973, meaning that some id numbers are skipped.

[Partial output:]

```
         year              id              adults
    Min.   :2012   Min.   :   1.0   Min.   :1.000
    1st Qu.:2012   1st Qu.: 504.0   1st Qu.:1.000
    Median :2012   Median : 989.0   Median :2.000
    Mean   :2012   Mean   : 990.7   Mean   :1.885
    3rd Qu.:2012   3rd Qu.:1481.0   3rd Qu.:2.000
    Max.   :2012   Max.   :1973.0   Max.   :6.000

         age            attend           babies         bible
    Min.   :18.0   Min.   :0.000   Min.   :0.0000   1:590
    1st Qu.:34.0   1st Qu.:1.000   1st Qu.:0.0000   2:802
    Median :48.0   Median :3.000   Median :0.0000   3:367
    Mean   :48.4   Mean   :3.525   Mean   :0.1894   4: 26
    3rd Qu.:62.0   3rd Qu.:7.000   3rd Qu.:0.0000
    Max.   :89.0   Max.   :8.000   Max.   :4.0000
  . . .
```

More descriptive statistics may be obtained by using the `describe()` command found in the "psych" package. After installing and loading this package, type `help(describe)` for an explanation of the different statistical coefficients. Note that factor variables like bible are flagged with an asterisk.

```
install.packages("psych")
library(psych)
```

```
psych::describe(out.table <- gssdata, IQR = TRUE)
```
[Output:]
```
           vars    n    mean     sd median trimmed    mad
year          1 1785 2012.00   0.00   2012 2012.00   0.00
id            2 1785  990.66 566.22    989  990.84 724.99
adults        3 1785    1.88   0.83      2    1.78   0.00
age           4 1785   48.40  17.70     48   47.72  20.76
attend        5 1785    3.53   2.82      3    3.44   4.45
babies        6 1785    0.19   0.52      0    0.05   0.00
bible*        7 1785    1.90   0.77      2    1.86   1.48
 . . .
            min  max range skew kurtosis    se IQR
year       2012 2012     0  NaN      NaN  0.00   0
id            1 1973  1972 0.00    -1.20 13.40 977
adults        1    6     5 1.28     2.80  0.02   1
age          18   89    71 0.27    -0.82  0.42  28
attend        0    8     8 0.15    -1.43  0.07   6
babies        0    4     4 3.06     9.71  0.01   0
bible*        1    4     3 0.36    -0.67  0.02   1
 . . .
```

We may be interested in the highest and lowest observations on some variable, such as age. This requires us to sort the data frame with the `order()` command, then view the top and bottom observations with the `head()` and `tail()` commands, respectively. Of course, this assumes we sort descending, otherwise top and bottom are flipped. We see below that the top five cases are all age 89 and the bottom five are all age 18. The sorting variable was gssdata$age. The minus sign before it asked for a descending sort.

```
# Sort gssdata on age, descending, putting results in the data frame "gssdataSorted".
gssdataSorted <- gssdata[order(-gssdata$age),]

# List the top five observations.
head(gssdataSorted,5)
```
[Partial output:]
```
    year  id adults age attend babies bible born childs
200 2012 228      1  89      3      0     3    1      2
226 2012 256      1  89      7      0     1    1      8
231 2012 261      1  89      7      0     2    2      1
294 2012 334      1  89      2      0     3    1      1
369 2012 415      1  89      2      0     2    1      2
 . . .
```

```
# List the bottom five observations
tail(gssdataSorted,5)
```
[Partial output:]
```
      year   id adults age attend babies bible born childs
628   2012  702      3  18      2      0     3    1      0
828   2012  921      2  18      5      0     1    1      0
1251 2012 1388      1  18      0      0     2    2      0
1468 2012 1619      2  18      7      0     1    1      0
1522 2012 1679      3  18      3      0     3    1      0
```

Finally, we may also be interested in the value of a particular observation on a particular variable. Above, one of the youngest observations was observation 1522. This is the person with id = 1679. That person is in row 1522 of gssdata, the unsorted data frame, not in gssdataSorted! If we wanted to know this person's code on church attendance (the "attend" variable), we would ask for it as below. Note that the sequence in R is always row first, then column (the variable). We may ask for the "attend" column by its column number or by its name. The format is data frame name, begin bracket, row, column, end bracket.

```
gssdata[1522,5]
[Output:]
   [1] 3

gssdata[1522,"attend"]
[Output:]
   [1] 3
```

By way of summary, some useful data inspection commands in R are listed:

```
class(mydata)        # Shows data class (data frame, matrix, numeric, etc.)
dim(mydata)          # Shows dimension of mydata, here 10 rows,2 columns
head(mydata,10)      # Print the first 10 rows of mydata (if 10 exist)
ls()                 # Lists objects in the environment, like mydata
mode(mydata)         # Shows the data type of mydata
names(mydata)        # Shows the variable names in mydata
str(mydata)          # Shows structure of mydata in brief format
summary(mydata)      # Displays descriptive statistics for mydata as shown earlier
tail(mydata, n=10)   # Print the last 10 rows of mydata
View(mydata)         # Displays mydata as a spreadsheet-style table; capitalize "View"
```

R data structures

R supports many complex data structures, which is one reason for its popularity. A common novice problem in using R for statistics is error messages arising from using the wrong class of data object for the selected statistical command. For purposes here, however, we discuss only the very basics. In general, however, it is a good idea to type `class(myobject)` to be sure you know the data class of "myobject". Data frames, tibbles, vectors, factors, and other data structures are all "objects" in R parlance.

Data frames and tibbles

A "data frame" is what social scientists usually think of as a dataset. Each row is an observation. Each column is a variable, which may be a numeric vector, a factor (a categorical variable), a date, or other data types. Whatever the type, each has the same number of observations, thus forming a rectangular dataset. The data frame is the most common structure for storing data in R, which calls it a "data.frame". Note that a data frame is a type of matrix. Cells in the matrix may be retrieved by adding "[rownumber, columnnumber]" to the data frame object name, as discussed in Section 1.8. THUS:

```
# List the contents of a cell at row 1, column 1
mydata[1,1]
# List the contents of row 1
mydata[1,]
# List the contents of column 1
mydata[,1]
```

A "tibble" is a newer alternative to a data frames, providing greater functionality. A data frame is one type of tibble. Most operations one can do on data frames can be done on tibbles, but not necessarily vice versa.

Tibbles may be conceived as a superset of data frames and sometimes they are called "tibble data frames". When the `class()` command is used on a tibble object, one may something like that below. This object is of three types simultaneously: tibble data frame, tibble, and data.frame. The mytibble object may be used with programs that require any of these three types of input. There are also "tsibbles", which are tibbles for time series. For further discussion of tibbles, see https://cran.r-project.org/web/packages/tibble/vignettes/tibble.html

```
class(mytibble)
[Output:]
   [1] "tbl_df"     "tbl"          "data.frame"
```

Vectors

A "vector" is what social scientists usually think of as a variable, corresponding to a single column in a dataset. Usually "vector" means that it is a numeric vector, containing numeric data. However, a vector may also be a character vector. This is illustrated by the simple examples below.

```
x <- c(1,2,3)
x
[Output:]
          [1] 1 2 3

class(x)
[Output:]
          [1] "numeric"

x <- c("1","b","3")
class(x)
[Output:]
          [1] "character"
```

Occasionally one needs to know be sure that a variable is classed as an integer. An integer type has only whole numbers, in contrast to the default numeric vector type, which is double precision. To force a numeral to be read as an integer, add "L":

```
x <- c(1L, 2L, 3L)
# x is of data class integer
class(x)
[Output:]
   [1] "integer"

# Therefore the first element in x is an integer.
is.integer(x[1])
[Output:]
   [1] TRUE
```

Factors

A "factor" is what social scientists usually think of as a categorical variable, corresponding to a column in a dataset, containing alphanumeric data. It is different from a character vector. A character vector is simply a listing of words or characters (some or all of which may be numerals). Sometimes character vector elements are called "strings". In contrast, a factor has categories, called levels. The R program you are using may give an error message if you try to use a character vector instead of a factor, even though the contents "looks the same" to you. Fortunately, a character vector like "party" below can be coerced into being a factor like "partyFactor".

```
party <- c("Republicans", "Democrats", "Independents")
class(party)
[Output:]
        [1] "character"

partyFactor <- as.factor(party)
class(partyFactor)
[Output:]
        [1] "factor"
```

The command below converts all character variables in a data frame called "df" to factors.

```
df <- gssdata

df[sapply(df, is.character)] <- lapply(df[sapply(df, is.character)], as.factor)
```

It is also possible to separate a data frame into its atomic vectors, which may be numeric, character, or logical (illustrated further below). The `as.integer()` and `as.factor()` functions are examples. Once created in this way, note that simple names are used in commands. For instance, there is no mydata$happyInteger, only happyInteger.

```
happyInteger <- as.integer(mydata$happy)
genderFactor <- as.factor(mydata$gender)
```

Many arithmetic operations can be performed on atomic vectors.

```
sum(happyInteger)
[Output:]
   [1] 31
```

However, what works for a numeric vector does not necessarily work for a factor:

```
sum(genderFactor)
[Output:]
   Error in Summary.factor(c(1L, 1L, 1L, 1L, 1L, 2L, 2L, 2L, 2L, 2L), na.rm = FALSE)
   : 'sum' not meaningful for factors
```

The `is.vector()` function determines if an object is a numeric vector. The `is.factor()` function does the same for character vectors. The commands and output below assume happy and gender are numeric and character atomic vectors respectively and are also embedded in the data frame mydata. The embedded versions return "FALSE" because they are not atomic vectors. The `is.data.frame()` function checks if an object is a data frame.

```
# These two return TRUE
is.vector(happyInteger)
is.integer(happyInteger)
is.factor(genderFactor)
```

```
# These return FALSE
is.factor(happyInteger)
is.vector(mydata$happy)
is.factor(mydata$happy)
is.vector(genderFactor)
is.vector(mydata$gender)
is.factor(mydata$gender)
```

We see that although data frames (e.g., mydata) may contain numeric or factor data, they are not vectors or factors in data type until put on an atomic basis by a command such as this:

```
genderFactor2 <- mydata$gender
class(genderFactor2)
```

[Output: The mydata$gender variable is treated as integer because it was coded 0, 1]

```
    [1] "integer"
```

```
genderFactor3 <- as.factor(mydata$gender)
class(genderFactor3)
```

[Output: genderFactor3 is a factor because we used the `as.factor()` function to coerce mydata$gender into status as a factor]

```
    [1] "factor"
```

It is also possible to go the other way, creating a data frame from atomic vectors or factors. This was done using the `data.frame()` command as one way of creating mydata in Section 1.3.

Lists

The list data format allows mixing of data types such as vectors, factors, and logical vectors. However, due to this mixing, where one may use `View()` with data frames, `View()` does not work with lists. Below we create a list called "mylist" and demonstrate some of its properties.

```
# Create a numeric atomic vector called mpg:
mpg <- c(28, 25, 30, 34)

# Create a character atomic vector (factor) called brand:
brand <- c("Ford","Chevrolet","Honda", "Mazda")

# Create a logical atomic vector called owned:
owned = c(TRUE, FALSE, FALSE, TRUE)

# Combine the atomic vectors in a list called mylist:
mylist <-  list(mpg, brand, owned)

# Optionally, remove the original atomic vectors from the R environment:
rm(brand,mpg,owned)

summary(mylist)
```

[Output:]

```
        Length Class  Mode
   [1,] 4      -none- numeric
   [2,] 4      -none- character
   [3,] 4      -none- logical
```

```
# To better read the summary output, give names to list components.
# Make sure to use the same order as in the list() command above.
names(mylist) <- c("mpg", "brand", "owned")
```

Display named contents of mylist:
```
summary(mylist)
```
[Output:]
```
        Length Class  Mode
   mpg   4      -none- numeric
   brand 4      -none- character
   owned 4      -none- logical
```

We can print the contents of individual list elements like brand.
```
print(mylist$brand)
```
[Output:]
```
  [1] "Ford"       "Chevrolet" "Honda"      "Mazda"
```

The `lapply()` function in base R provides certain statistics repetitively. Below, we get the mean of all variables. However, as brand is of character data type, we cannot compute a mean and an error message is returned. For a logical variable like owned, a mean is returned using the numeric equivalents of 0 = FALSE and 1 = TRUE. It is 0.5 because half the cases were FALSE and half were TRUE.

```
lapply(mylist, mean)
```
[Output:]
```
  $mpg
     [1] 29.25

  $brand
     [1] NA

  $owned
     [1] 0.5

  Warning message:
  In mean.default(X[[i]], ...) :
    argument is not numeric or logical: returning NA
```

Most statistical commands will want the data to be in a data frame, not a list. We may convert the mylist list to a data frame called myframe. This assumes all list components are atomic vectors, which are numeric (synonym: double), character, logical, integer, complex, or raw in data type.

```
myframe <- as.data.frame(mylist)
View(myframe)
class(myframe)
```
[Output:]
```
   [1] "data.frame"
```

Changing from one data type to another

As we have seen above, in many cases it is possible to coerce data of one class to be of another class. Below, for instance, we take the tibble data frame "mydata" and create the matrix "mydata_matrix" object.

```
class(mydata)
     [1] "tbl_df"     "tbl"          "data.frame"

mydata_matrix <- as.matrix(mydata)
class(mydata_matrix)
     [1] "matrix" "array"
```

Selected conversion functions in the "base" package in the R system library are listed below. Other packages such as the "data.table" package have other conversion functions as well. For more information on these conversion functions, type `help(name of function)`, as in `help(as.Date)`.

Function	Convert to
`as.character()`	Character Vectors
`as.character.Date()`	Date Conversion to and from Character
`as.data.frame()`	Coerce to a Data Frame
`as.data.frame.Date()`	Date Class
`as.data.frame.table()`	Cross Tabulation and Table Creation
`as.Date()`	Date Conversion Functions to and from Character
`as.difftime()`	Time Intervals/Differences
`as.double()`	Double-Precision Vectors
`as.factor()`	Factors
`as.integer()`	Integer Vectors
`as.list()`	Lists – Generic and Dotted Pairs
`as.logical()`	Logical Vectors
`as.matrix()`	Matrices
`as.matrix.noquote()`	Class for 'no quote' Printing of Character Strings
`as.numeric()`	Numeric Vectors
`as.ordered()`	Factors
`as.table()`	Cross Tabulation and Table Creation
`as.vector()`	Vectors

Handling missing values

Most real-world data have missing values. Handling missing values is treated in an online supplement to Chapter 3 of this text, available on its Support Material (www.routledge.com/9780367624293). However, we can discuss some highlights here in this section. To illustrate, we use the file "cobb_survey.csv", also available on the Support Material (www.routledge.com/9780367624293), using it to create the data frame "cobb". The cobb data frame contains survey responses of 338 individuals (rows) on 88 items (columns).

```
cobb <- read.csv("C:/Data/cobb_survey.csv", header=TRUE, sep = ",", stringsAsFactors =
TRUE)
```

Missing values in R should be coded NA. If data have been imported from SPSS or some other package using different missing value codes, the researcher must convert to NA coding. Once missing values are properly coded NA, one may check for rows with missing data using the command below.

The `summary()` command displays descriptive statistics for all columns. If any column has missing values, such as "rvpos" below, the NA count is given.

```
summary(cobb)
```

[Partial output:]

```
          id           debwatch          rvpos
    Min.   :  1.00   Min.   :1.000   Min.   :1.000
    1st Qu.: 85.25   1st Qu.:1.000   1st Qu.:1.000
    Median :169.50   Median :1.000   Median :2.000
    Mean   :169.50   Mean   :1.429   Mean   :1.592
    3rd Qu.:253.75   3rd Qu.:2.000   3rd Qu.:2.000
    Max.   :338.00   Max.   :2.000   Max.   :2.000
                                     NA's   :76
```

The more complex command below gives a simple count of missing values by variable.

```
na_count  <- sapply(cobb, function(y) sum(length( which(is.na(y)))))
na_count
```

[Partial output:]

```
         id       debwatch          rvpos        rposvst          gsupv
          0              0             76             64            168
      bsupv       rposuhc       rposuhcs         rposdp       rstposdp
        144             32             34             43             33
```

It is also possible to get a long listing of all rows (observations) with at least one missing value. For the Cobb data, this is most of them. In syntax below, the exclamation point in R means "not", so we are checking for rows which are not complete cases, meaning rows which have missing data.

```
cobb[!complete.cases(cobb),]
```

[Partial output:]

```
    id debwatch rvpos rposvst gsupv bsupv rposuhc rposuhcs
1    1        2     2       1     1     2       1        1
2    2        1     1       1    NA     2       1        1
3    3        2     2      NA     2     1       1       NA
4    4        2     2       1    NA    NA       1        1
5    5        1    NA       2     2    NA       1        1
6    6        1     1       1     2     1       2        2
. . .
```

If missing data are found, one may create a new dataset in which rows with missing data have been dropped listwise. However, imputation of missing values is usually preferred. Data imputation is discussed in the "Missing Values and Data Imputation" supplement to Chapter 3 of this text, found on its Support Material (www.routledge.com/9780367624293). For the cobb data, we see below that 330 of the 338 observations are dropped, leaving only 8! This is clearly unacceptable and might prompt the researcher to go back and retain only variables with few missing values.

```
cobbComplete <- na.omit(cobb)

nrow(cobbComplete)
```

[Output:]

```
   [1] 8
```

We now turn to the question of what to do if imported data have missing values but do not use the "NA" code for them. SPSS, for instance, allows user-created missing values such as –99. If data are exported from SPSS or another package, R may not recognize the ways these other packages specify missing values. In R, missing data must be coded NA, without quotes.

We illustrate how to handle this problem for SPSS as an example.

- In SPSS, change all system-missing or user-missing values to some numeric value, such as minus 99. To do this, select Transform > Recode into same variables. In the Transform dialog, move all numeric variables into the variable list. Click Old and New Values. Check "System-missing or user-missing". Let the "New Value" be –99. Click Add. Click Continue, then OK. Only then export to .csv, which SPSS can read: File > Export > CSV Data. Save under some name such as "mytest.csv".
- Then in R, import mytest.csv as exported by SPSS. If exported from Excel, the .csv file will not have these problems. With export from Excel, blanks are converted to NAs and there is no naming glitch as described below.
- Note: mytest.csv is supplied with this text. It can be created by the user in SPSS. Syntax below is illustrative but your data will differ. The mytest object is like mydata, but with a couple –99 codes in the variable "happy".

Steps:

1. Import mytest.csv into R in the usual way.

```
setwd("C:/Data")

mytest <- read.csv("C:/Data/mytest.csv", header=TRUE, sep = ",", stringsAsFactors =
TRUE)
```

2. Change –99s to NAs

Before: No missings are reported because –99 not recognized as a code for missing.

```
is.na(mytest)
        happy  gender
 [1,]   FALSE  FALSE
 [2,]   FALSE  FALSE
 [3,]   FALSE  FALSE
 [4,]   FALSE  FALSE
 [5,]   FALSE  FALSE
 [6,]   FALSE  FALSE
 [7,]   FALSE  FALSE
 [8,]   FALSE  FALSE
 [9,]   FALSE  FALSE
[10,]   FALSE  FALSE
```

Replace –99s with NA. Note changes are not saved to file until you do so explicitly.

```
mytest[mytest == -99] <- NA
```

After: Missings are now recognized.

```
is.na(mytest)
        happy  gender
 [1,]   FALSE  FALSE
 [2,]   FALSE  FALSE
 [3,]   FALSE  FALSE
 [4,]   FALSE  FALSE
 [5,]    TRUE  FALSE
 [6,]   FALSE  FALSE
 [7,]   FALSE  FALSE
 [8,]    TRUE  FALSE
 [9,]   FALSE  FALSE
[10,]   FALSE  FALSE
```

Replacement may also be done with the “naniar” package. This command replaces a missing value code for data from an external source with NA, which R wants. Below we replace –99 values with NA values. (The xdf data does not have any –99 values, so here this just checks).

```
mytest2 <- read.csv("C:/Data/mytest.csv", header=TRUE, sep = ",",
stringsAsFactors = TRUE)

install.packages("naniar")
library(naniar)
mytest2 <- mytest2 %>%
naniar::replace_with_na_all(condition = ~.x == -99)
```

```
# Check result, which now has NA coding.
mytest2
[Output:]
   # A tibble: 10 x 2
     ï..happy gender
        <int>  <int>
   1        4      0
   2        1      0
   3        3      0
   4        5      0
   5       NA      0
   6        3      1
   7        2      1
   8       NA      1
   9        5      1
  10        1      1

# 3. A known glitch in SPSS csv export will/may mislabel the first variable.
#The code below illustrates and corrects the name of the first column.
names(mytest)
[Output:]
   [1] "ï..happy" "gender"

names(mytest)[1]<-"happy"

names(mytest)
[Output:]
   [1] "happy"  "gender"

# 4. Then write the corrected data frame to a .csv file, possibly with a new name
write.csv(mytest, file = "mytest2.csv", row.names = FALSE)
```

The `freq.na()` command from the "questionr" package will print a frequency table of missing values, such as in the cobb data frame.

```
install.packages("questionr")
library(questionr)
questionr::freq.na(cobb)
[Partial output:]
                missing %
. . .
defense             105  31
rposdef             104  31
pid2pt               92  27
rstdef               81  24
vouchers             77  23
. . .
```

Finding useful packages to install

After one has data in a usable format, the next step is to find a statistical or other package that will use it.

Packages in the R System Library do not need to be installed but others do. One may browse the R System Library by clicking on the "Packages" tab in RStudio. At the top of the listing will be the "User Library", which is packages you have installed thus far. Scroll below this and one will see the "System Library", which is a list of R's "built-in" packages such as base, utils, foreign, and graphics.

How do people find appropriate R packages to use? All kinds of ways. Here are a few ideas:

- Article search: Research articles that you encounter in conducting your literature review for your research project. R packages cited in such articles have proven to be useful to other researchers in your field. R syntax (code) for using the package may be available as a supplement to the article or by writing to the authors.
- Browser search: Because the R community is so large, the probability of finding useful package is high. For example, simply type "cluster analysis in R" (with quotes to keep these terms together) to find listings. There were over a quarter million hits for this popular topic! May hits link to articles which not only identify useful packages but also provide R code for using them.
- Archive search: While CRAN is not the only archive of R packages, it is the largest. One can find a listing of packages by name or date at https://cran.r-project.org/web/packages/. At this writing, there were over 200,000 packages available on CRAN, listed alphabetically by name or by publication date. A second major website is that of the R-Forge project at https://r-forge.r-project.org/.
- Blog search: While there are a great many R-oriented blogs, a notable one is r-Bloggers at https://www.r-bloggers.com/. This blog republishes blog posts of others and publicize popular packages, including code to use them. Every month it lists the "top 40" new R packages. RPubs (https://rpubs.com/) lists recent interesting examples.
- Ask on a list: Two popular lists which may be used to ask about new packages are stackoverflow (https://stackoverflow.com/), which also maintains an archive of past questions and answers; and R-Help (https://stat.ethz.ch/mailman/listinfo/r-help).
- Use the "sos" package described below to search by keyword, such as "reliability".

Unfortunately, R commands may be found on websites or in print without mention of the required package names. More confusingly, sometimes the same command term may be available in more than one package, not always with the same functionality. For instance, there are 11 packages, which use the command `reliability()` for differing purposes. If one is aware of a command (function) name one wants to use but is unsure which package contains it, or if one simply wants to search for functions containing a key word, there is an "sos" package to help. This package contains the `findFn()` function. For instance, to find all packages referring to "reliability":

```
install.packages("sos")
library(sos)
findFn("reliability",maxPages=1000,sortby="Function")
```

Two tables appear in one's browser. The one of greater interest is the browser page titled "Help pages for reliability". This page contains a table listing hundreds of reliability-related links. Look under the "Function" column to find the name of a command, then look across in the "Packages" column to see the package it comes from. For instance, the `reliability.plot()` command is in the "verification" package. Click on the link in the last column (the Description and Link column) of this row to see more information about this command.

Installing packages

Seeing if a package is already installed

Before trying to install a package, one may want to see if it is already installed. Let's say one is considering installing the "lme4" package, which is for linear mixed modeling (multilevel modeling). Simply use the `library()` command and if there is no error message, it has been installed.

```
# The package is already installed.
library(lme4)
```

[Output – only the prompt sign:]

```
>
```

The package is not already installed.

```
library(lme8)
```

[Output:]

```
Error in library("lme8") : there is no package called 'lme8'
```

One may use the `getoption()` command to see packages which are loaded automatically when R starts up. These are all in the R system library.

```
getOption("defaultPackages")
```

[Output:]

```
[1] "datasets" "utils" "grDevices"
[4] "graphics" "stats" "methods"
```

There are other packages in the R System Library which are not loaded automatically but which do not need to be installed. They are listed at the bottom of the listing from the "Packages" tab in RStudio in the "System Library" section. One, for example, is the "cluster" package, which has the built-in dataset "animals".

Before loading the cluster package, we cannot access animals,
even though cluster is in the R System Library.

```
head(animals)
```

[Output:]

```
Error in head(animals) : object 'animals' not found
```

We load cluster and then can access animals.

```
library(cluster)
```

```
head(animals)
```

[Output:]

```
    war fly ver end gro hai
ant   1   1   1   1   2   1
bee   1   2   1   1   2   2
cat   2   1   2   1   1   2
cpl   1   1   1   1   1   2
chi   2   1   2   2   2   2
cow   2   1   2   1   2   2
```

Optionally, view all currently installed packages, including their version numbers, dependencies, and other information using the `installed.packages()` function, also part of base R:

```
installed.packages()
```

[Output is too long to list here]

Sometimes the `library()` command will give an "Error in unloadNamespace" error if there are conflicts. For instance:

```
library(caret)
```

```
[Output:]
   Loading required package: lattice
   Error in value[[3L]](cond):
     Package 'lattice' version 0.20.38 cannot be unloaded:
    Error in unloadNamespace(package): namespace 'lattice' is imported by 'nlme',
    'Matrix', 'lme4' so cannot be unloaded
```

This error message means that the caret package is trying to unload and install the lattice package again but it can't because other packages (nlme, Matrix, lme4) already have lattice as a dependency. The solution is to close R and reload with caret first

```
library(caret)
[Output:]
   Loading required package: lattice
   Loading required package: ggplot2
library(nlme)
library(Matrix)
library(lme4)
```

Note that sometimes the unloadNamespace error cites a package you did not recall installing. The cited package is a dependency of a package which you did load. For instance gower is a dependency of recipes, which is a dependency of caret. The gower package may be cited in the error but you only recall loading caret. The remedy is the same as above: Restart and issue the `library()` commands again. You may have to load gower manually by the command `install.packages("gower")`, then restart and issue the `library()` commands again.

When loading a package, you may get conflict warnings such as that below.

```
library(caret)
[Output:]
   Loading required package: lattice
   Attaching package: 'caret'
   The following object is masked from 'package:purrr':
     lift
```

This means that both lattice and purr have the command `lift()`. If lattice was loaded most recently, then its version of `lift()` will be used. However, this can be overridden by using package prefixes. The command `purrr::lift()` assures that the purr version is used. Using package prefixes routinely may be easier than keeping track of such conflicts.

In summary:

- If a package is not in the R System Library, it must be installed. For packages in the CRAN archive (most packages), this is done with the `install.packages()` command. The package name within the parentheses must be within quote marks. Documentation for non-CRAN packages will contain different installation instructions.
- Packages not on the R System Library default list must then be loaded using the `library()` command.
- On loading a package, take note of error messages and warnings described above.
- Installing a specified package may install automatically other packages on which it depends ("dependencies").
- Once a package is installed and activated, one may type `help(name-of-command)` to get details about any of the package's commands and options.

Alternative to command-line installation as above, it is also possible in RStudio to click on the "Install" button for the "Packages" tab and an "Install Packages" window will appear, as shown in Figure Appl.3. In this figure, "rel" is the name of the package to be installed. Note that the default for the drop-down "Install from" text box is "Repository (CRAN)". While unusual, the alternative is "Package Archive File", used to install packages downloaded from the Internet in archived (.zip, .tar, .gz) formats. If this is the case, in the same dialog screen browse to and select the file address when you saved the archive (usually your download directory) and enter it in the "Package Archive" text box of RStudio.

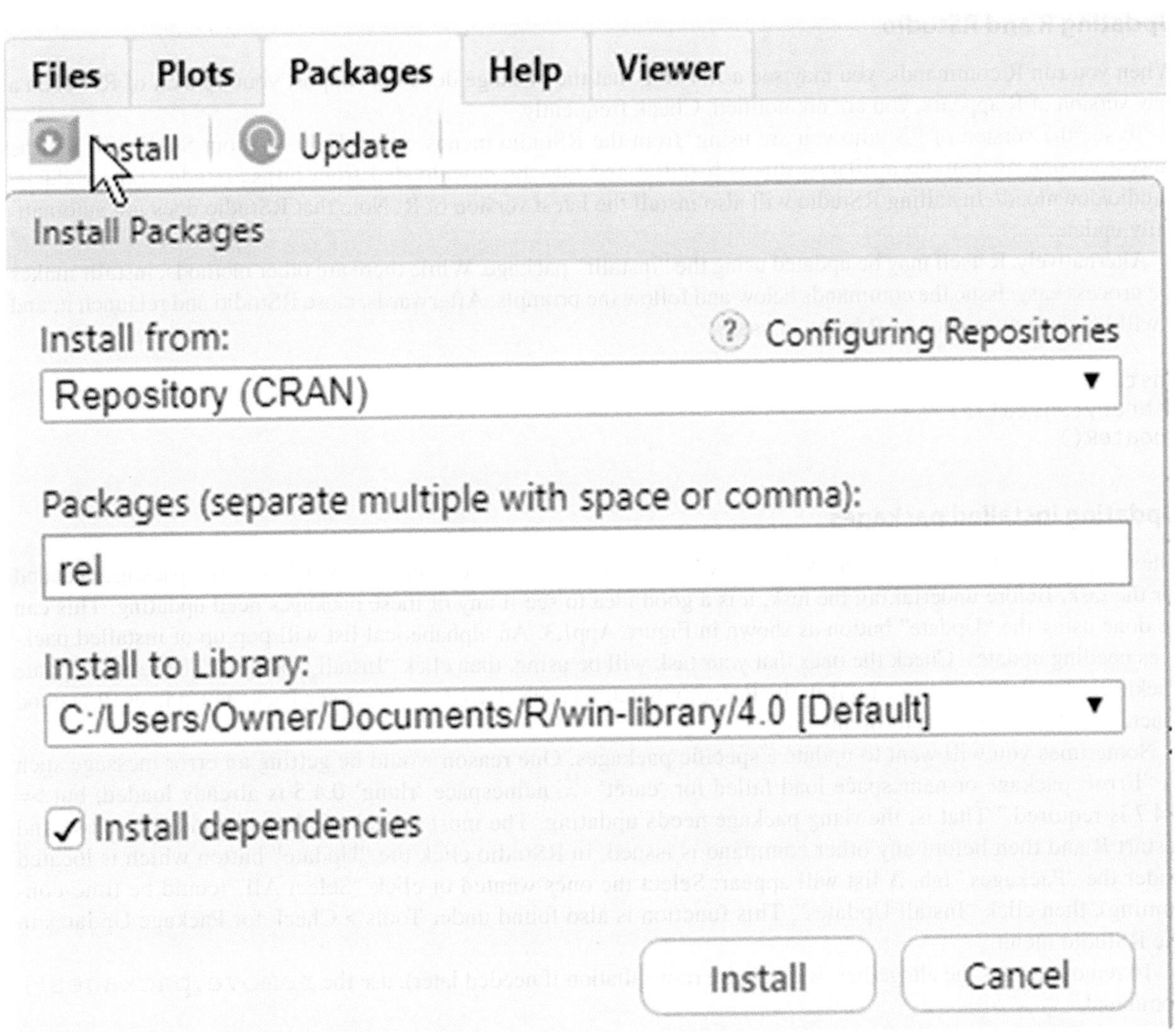

Figure App1.3 Install packages window in RStudio

Updating packages

Checking R and package version numbers

Because of possible incompatibilities and also for update purposes, occasionally one may need to know the version number of a package and/or the version number of R itself.

- To get version number of R, simply type `version.` At the time this command was issued, we were running R Version 4.0.4 on a Windows computer with 64-bit architecture:

  ```
  version
  ```
  [Partial output:]
  ```
  ...
  arch           x86_64
  ...
  version.string R version 4.0.4 (2021-02-15)
  ```

- To see the version number of any installed package, whether active or not, click on the "Packages" tab in RStudio and look in the "version" column.

Updating R and RStudio

When you run R commands, you may see a warning that the package does not support your version of R. When a new version of R appears, you are not notified. Check frequently.

To see the version of RStudio you are using, from the RStudio menus, select Help > About Studio. To see the newest version of RStudio available, this is listed at and may be downloaded from https://rstudio.com/products/rstudio/download/. Installing RStudio will also install the latest version of R. Note that RStudio does not automatically update.

Alternatively, R itself may be updated using the "installr" package. While there are other methods, installr makes the process easy. Issue the commands below and follow the prompts. Afterwards, close RStudio and relaunch it, and it will list the new version of R being in use.

```
install.packages("installr")
library(installr)
updateR()
```

Updating installed packages

The code for a task typically starts with a series of `library()` commands, which load the packages needed for the task. Before undertaking the task, it is a good idea to see if any of these packages need updating. This can be done using the "Update" button as shown in Figure Appl.3. An alphabetical list will pop up of installed packages needing updates. Check the ones that your task will be using, then click "Install Updates". The same "Update Packages" window will come up if in the RStudio menu, you select Tools > Check for Package Updates. It is good practice to do this at the start of any project.

Sometimes you will want to update a specific packages. One reason would be getting an error message such as "Error: package or namespace load failed for 'caret' .... namespace 'rlang' 0.4.5 is already loaded, but >= 0.4.7 is required." That is, the rlang package needs updating. The most reliable update method is to close and restart R and then before any other command is issued, in RStudio click the "Update" button which is located under the "Packages" tab. A list will appear: Select the ones wanted or click "Select All" (could be time-consuming), then click "Install Updates". This function is also found under Tools > Check for Package Updates in the RStudio menu.

To remove a package altogether (will require reinstallation if needed later), use the `remove.packages()` command.

```
remove.packages("installr")
```

Using, saving, and loading packages and sessions

- **Using R keyboard shortcuts:** From the RStudio menu, select Help > Keyboard Shortcuts Help (or type Alt-Shift-K) to view a listing of keystrokes used for scrolling and editing (e.g., the Esc (Escape) key aborts the R interpreter and returns to the R prompt to ">"). Keep in mind that R is case-sensitive (e.g., Ctrl + L is not the same as Ctrl + l).
- **Setting the working directory:** One of the first things usually done is to set the working directory. This declares where files are to be loaded or saved. For example, setwd("`C:/Data`"). Note that a forward slash is used in the path name. You can also type `getwd()` to list your current working directory.
- **Clearing RStudio:** As you work, your work environment may become cluttered. You may wish to start fresh. If you have just selected Session > New Session from the RStudio menu, this is not a problem as the work environment starts cleared in a new instance of RStudio. However, rerunning RStudio for the same session will not accomplish this as the saved environment is reinstated. Instead, consider using the following commands (but be careful!).

- *Clear the console*: Ctrl-L – This will clear the "Console" window in the lower left of RStudio, which is where commands are entered and where output appears. However, command history is not cleared. The up/down arrows may still be used to scroll through past commands. This is equivalent to selecting Edit > Clear Console from the RStudio menu.
- *Clear all datasets from the environment*: Select the "Environment" tab in RStudio and click the broom icon. Alternatively, select Session > Clear Workspace. As a third alternative, issue the command `rm(list=ls())`. All objects are removed from the "Global Environment" in the upper right of RStudio.
- *Clear history*: Select the "History" tab and click the broom icon. This will clear the history of all commands. The up/down arrow keys will no longer have effect until you enter more commands.
- *Clear datasets shown in upper left "View" window*: Click the "x" option for each dataset to close it. When RStudio is closed, answer "yes" when queried whether you wish to save the current environment. When RStudio is run again, it will not list the datasets that were closed. Datasets are not removed from saved files on disk. To clear a specific dataset use the `rm()` command. For example: `rm(mydata _ df)`. To clear all datasets, use `rm(list=ls())`.
- *Clear plots*: Select the "Plots" tab and click the broom icon.
- *Clear workspace*: Select Session > Clear Workspace, which removes all objects from the R environment.

- **Saving and loading your workspace:** Your workspace is your current R working environment, including any objects you have created, such as data frames and functions. At the end of any R session you will be prompted to save your workspace. If you respond affirmatively, the workspace as configured when you saved it will be saved. Then the next time you start R, it will be reloaded automatically. The workspace is saved in the current working directly with the default name ".RData". You can also give it a unique filename if you desire.
- **Saving and loading your command history.** R keeps a log of commands you have issued. You can use the up and down arrow keys to recall them, then click the Enter key to reissue the selected previous command. When you quit an R session, the command history is lost unless you save it. Below, the working directory is set, two commands used elsewhere in this tutorial are given, the `savehistory()` command is given, and the R session is terminated. History will be saved to "C:/Data/.RHistory".

```
setwd("C:/Data")
savehistory()
quit()
```

R is closed and then restarted. History will be empty so the up/down arrow keys will not scroll through previously used commands until the `loadhistory()` command loads the saved history of commands. The `history()` command displays these commands in the "History" tab of RStudio.

```
setwd("C:/Data")
loadhistory()
history()
```

It is also possible to save or load under specific filenames. Files go to the current working directory.

```
savehistory(file="Tutorial2.Rhistory")
loadhistory(file="Tutorial2.Rhistory")
```

- **Saving the RStudio session:** You may wish to save and even share your RStudio session. You may use any of the techniques listed below.

1. *Cut and paste commands and output.* You can drag the mouse over a section of output, which will include your commands too. Then type "Ctrl-C" to copy, go to Word or some other program, type "Ctrl-V" to paste.
2. *To save figures,* go to the Plots tab and click the down arrow for "Export", and select one of the choices there. Choices are Copying to Clipboard, Save as Image (any of 7 graphics formats), or Save as PDF.
3. *To save commands* without output, go to the "History" tab in RStudio and click on the save icon (a computer disk). The list of all your commands will be saved to a directory and filename you give, with the file

extension ".RHistory". To save just a portion of your history, go to the "History" tab and block out what you want. Click on the first line, scroll down to the last line, "Shift-click" to multi-select down to the last line, then cut and paste as in (1). You can also save history using the `history()` command and can retrieve it with the `loadhistory()` command. Files must have a. Rhistory extension.

4. *Save output with* `sink()`. The `sink()` command from R's "base" package can redirect output (and only output, not prompts, commands, comments, warnings, or plots) to a file. Output is not sent to the screen until you revert output back as shown below. This makes the `sink()` method useful if you want output only and if you have a prepared batch of commands to enter in the syntax section illustrated below. Note: The `capture.output()` command uses `sink()` and is very similar. The `file.show()` command displays the sunk output, which is a text file in the working directory. For example: `file.show("myoutput_sink.txt")`. Type `help(sink)` for more information and examples.

5. *Saving everything with RMarkdown.* RMarkdown is the most versatile way to save your work. It can save code, output, graphics, and more. It can save to html, Word, pdf, and other formats. What you save can be "live" such that viewers on the web could run your program with the same or other inputs. Scholars have written entire books in RMarkdown. This impressive versatility comes at the price of a nontrivial learning curve, however.

   There are many available tutorials on using RMarkdown. A few are:
   - "RMarkdown from RStudio: An Introduction", from RStudio, at https://rmarkdown.rstudio.com/lesson-1.html. This is the "Getting Started" button on the RStudio RMarkdown page at https://rmarkdown.rstudio.com/.
   - "Getting Started with RMarkdown", from the Coding Club at https://ourcodingclub.github.io/tutorials/rmarkdown/
   - "RMarkdown: The Definitive Guide", by Yihui Xie, J. J. Allaire, & Garrett Grolemund, at https://bookdown.org/yihui/rmarkdown/
   - "RMarkdown Cheat Sheet", from RStudio, at https://rstudio.com/wp-content/uploads/2016/03/rmarkdown-cheatsheet-2.0.pdf

6. *Save with a batch function.* Unlike `sink()`, in the batch method commands as well as output are saved, but still no plots. This method requires that you have saved all your commands as a batch in a text file with the extension ".r". For instance, save "mycommands.r" in the working directory. There are three steps, not counting creating the mycommands.r file and setting the working directory in the usual manner:

   (6a) Create the batch function
   ```
   batch <- function(x){
     stopifnot(is.character(x) & length(x)==1)
     system2(paste(R.home("bin"), "/R", sep=""),
         args=paste("CMD BATCH", shQuote(x)))
   }
   ```

   (6b) Use the batch function on your saved command file
   ```
   batch("mycommands.r")
   ```

   (6c) View the resulting file using the `cat()` command
   ```
   # The "mycommands.r.Rout" file is a text file in your working directory,
   cat(paste(readLines("mycommands.r.Rout"), collapse = "\n"))
   ```

Visualization and graphics in R

Data visualization is one reason researchers may choose R as their preferred statistical environment. This is an enormous area outside the scope of this tutorial. However, a great starting point is the website http://r-graph-gallery.com/. It presents hundreds of different graph types with examples and illustrative working code. Even mapping and animated graphs are treated. It illustrates visualization with many packages, including base (has `plot()`), graph, graphics (has `barplot()`), igraph, leaflet, and ggplot2.

The most widely used package for data visualization is ggplot2, which was used for many figures in the textbook. However, the versatility of ggplot2 may seem daunting to beginners. Some free tutorials on ggplot2 are found at https://www.tutorialspoint.com/ggplot2/index.htm and http://r-statistics.co/Complete-Ggplot2-Tutorial-Part1-With-R-Code.html to name just two. There are also many video tutorials on ggplot2, found by searching YouTube, Bing Videos, or similar websites.

Data management basics

For example purposes, we use the "mydata" object created earlier:

```
mydata <- read.table("mydata.csv", header = TRUE, sep = ",")
```

We start by making a copy called "xdf" and viewing it.

```
xdf <- mydata
View(xdf)
```

Data frame, delete a variable (column)

This command deletes column 1. Find column numbers by looking at your data in View, or by using the `names(xdf)` command. Alternatively, you may refer to the column by name.

```
xdf[1] <- NULL
```
or
```
xdf["happy"] <- NULL
```
Restore xdf:
```
xdf <- mydata
```

Data frame, rename a variable (column)

This command renames column 2, which is "gender":

```
colnames(xdf)[2] <- "sex"
View(xdf)
```
Restore xdf:
```
xdf <- mydata
```

Dummy variables, create

Sometimes on wishes to convert all categorical variables to sets of dummy variables. Below, "world" is the original data frame. The "worldDummy" object is the new frame with dummy variables (this frame may be named whatever you want). The last level will be the omitted reference level. For example, infdeaths in world is character-coded as Low or High. In worldDummy, there is only infdeaths.Low, with the High category being the reference category. Type names(worldDummy) to see all variable names.

```
# Set the working directory
setwd("c:/Data")

# Read in the text file called world.csv into a data object called "world"
world <- read.csv("C://Data/world.csv", header=TRUE, sep = ",")
```

```
# Make a copy of world, then create dummy variables.
install.packages("caret")
library(caret)
xdf2 <- world

# worldTypeDummyvars is of data class"dummyvars".
# The "~." specification asks for all variables in xdf2.
worldTypeDummyvars <- caret::dummyVars(" ~. ", data = xdf2,fullRank = T)

# worldDummyDf is a data frame (like world, but with dummy variables)
worldDummyDf <- data.frame(predict(worldTypeDummyvars, newdata = xdf2))
```

Where world had one column for the variable labeled "country". The worldDummy data frame has separate dummy variable columns for each country except the last (reference) country. The USA is now the dummy variable countryUSA, for instance. It has also converted to dummy variables the former region, infdeaths, and litgtmean variables. The infdeaths variable is now the dummy variable infdeathsLow, with the left-out High category being the reference.

```
names(worldDummyDf)
[Output not shown]
```

We can use the `table()` command on the original data (world) to see the levels of a categorical variable like infdeaths, and also the number of observations in each level. This also shows the order of the levels, here High = 0 and Low = 1.

```
table(world$infdeaths)
[Output:]
   High  Low
     71  141
```

The sum of the corresponding variable in the dummy version of the data is the same count as the "1" category – here 141 observations are "Low" on infdeaths and this is saved in the dummy variable infdeathsLow.

```
sum(worldDummyDf$infdeathsLow)
[Output:]
    [1] 141
```

Objects, testing if the same

The identical (object1, object2) command below returns TRUE if two R objects are the same. We use two data frame objects from the discussion above on dummy variables.

```
identical(world$deathrate, worldDummyDf$deathrate)
[Output:]
   [1] TRUE
```

Variables, binning

This command creates a categorical variable split on given cutpoints.

Here the bins will be 0-2, 3-7, and >7. First we get the descriptives for un-binned literacy.

```
summary(world$literacy)
[Output:]
      Min. 1st Qu.  Median    Mean 3rd Qu.    Max.
     17.60   75.55   92.50   83.28   98.00  100.00
```

```
world$literacy_categories <- cut(world$literacy, breaks = c(-1, 75.56, 83.29, 98.01, 100.1), right=TRUE, labels = c("Q1","Q2","Q3", "Q4"))
```

Below is the distribution of observations by bin.

```
summary(world$literacy_categories)
[Output:]
    Q1 Q2 Q3 Q4
    53 9 93 47
```

Dealing with error messages

Debugging: Things to check

- Use `class(name of object)` to see if your object is the right class for the command you are using. Consult `help(name of command)` to see what data type the command needs.
- Some programs need all vector variables to have the same number of elements. Use `length(name of vector variable)` on each variable to check.
- Check for missing values as some operations want complete cases data. Reduce to complete cases or impute missing data. See Section 1.10.
- *Common quotation mark error*: The novice user may encounter "Unexpected input" error messages when using quote marks. R wants straight quote marks, such as around "text". Unfortunately, word defaults to smart quotes: "text". To change this Word default, do this:

  1. On the File tab, click Options.
  2. Click Proofing, and then click AutoCorrect Options.
  3. In the AutoCorrect dialog box, do the following: Click the AutoFormat As You Type tab, and under Replace as you type, uncheck the option labeled "Straight quotes with smart quotes".
  4. Click OK.

- *Common minus sign error*: A similar error may occur when trying to type the minus sign. The symbol in Word is not the same as what R needs even though they look the same. **Avoid** cutting-and-pasting minus signs from Word and instead type the minus sign directly in RStudio.

  Pasted:
      4 – 1
          Error: unexpected input in "4 –"
  Typed in RStudio:
      4-1
          [1] 3

- *Plot margins error*: If your RStudio plot panel is too small for the plot you are creating, you may get the error message, "Error in `plot.new()`: figure margins too large". Correct this by making your plot panel window larger and rerunning the command which generated the plot. You can avoid this error by checking your margins with the `par("mar")` command. You should get: "[1] 5.1 4.1 4.1 2.1". Reset with `par(mar=c(5.1,4.1,4.1,2.1))`. For maximum margins enter `par(mar=c(1,1,1,1))`.
- *Installing packages, "not available" error message*: If you get an error message that a given package does not work with your version of R, in RStudio try selecting Tools > Install packages and install that way rather than with the `install.packages()` command. Most packages load automatically with the `install.packages()` command, or by using Tools > Install packages from the

RStudio menu. However, sometimes it is necessary to install Rtools using the commands below. After installing Rtools, try the `install.packages()` command again. Starting with R version 4.0, Rtools was replaced by rtools40. Instructions and links for installation are at https://cran.r-project.org/bin/windows/Rtools/.

- *RStudio logs for error messages*: RStudio keeps logs of errors, warnings, and exceptions. This may be useful for debugging purposes. You can access the names of the log files in RStudio by selecting Help > Diagnostics > Show Log Files. Log files are text files that can be loaded into a word processor, but only after the session is terminated and RStudio has closed the file. Right-click on a log name and select Properties to see where it is located on your computer. For more detail, select Help > Diagnostics > Write Diagnostics Report. Or issue the command `rstudioDiagnosticsReport()`. The file diagnostics-report.txt will be written to your Documents folder (e.g., C:/Users/Owner/Documents/rstudio-diagnostics/diagnostics-report.txt). It contains listings of attached base and other packages, system and platform information, R version and home path, environmental variables, loaded packages, installed packages, site profile with options settings, user preferences, the error log file, and more.

Getting data

Getting data for R projects is no different from getting data for any project. However, for purposes of learning R, R comes with sample data and demonstrations.

Many datasets are listed in the "datasets" package, which in the R System Library. To view some of the available datasets, simply type:

```
data()
```

To view datasets available in any package installed in the User or System Libraries:

```
data(package = .packages(all.available = TRUE))
```

One of the available datasets is USJudgeRatings. To load it into to a data frame called "judges":

```
judges <- data.frame(USJudgeRatings)
```

View the loaded dataset in the ordinary manner:

```
View(judges)
```

Get documentation on the dataset:

```
help(USJudgeRatings)
```

Use the dataset in a command. Below we create a bare-bones plot of judges' decision promptness by judges' worthiness of retention with a lowess smoothing line through the points:

```
plot(judges$DECI,judges$RTEN)
lines(lowess(judges$DECI, judges$RTEN))
```

Some packages have datasets not from the "datasets" package in the R System Library. For instance, the package "carData" has the "Arrests" data on marijuana possession arrests. You may need to install the package first: `install.packages(carData)` first.

```
library(carData)
class(Arrests)
     [1] "data.frame"
View(Arrests)
```

Getting help

Many packages have "vignettes" which describe how to use the package. The `vignette()` command is part of the "utils" package in the R System Library.

```
vignette(package="psych")
```

[Output:]

```
Vignettes in package 'psych':
intro            Introduction to the psych package
                 (source, pdf)
overview         Overview of the psych package for
                 psychometrics (source, pdf)
```

To access any vignette, click on the "Packages" tab in RStudio, browse to the package of interest, then click on the link "User guides, package vignettes and other documentation".

In the same vein, R packages also may come with built-in demonstrations. Only some statistical programs have demos. The `demo()` command is part of the "utils" package in the R System Library. For information, type `help(demo)`. To bring up a listing of the many demos in packages in the system library type:

```
demo()
```

Packages may have multiple demos. To list all demos in a particular package:

```
demo(package = "lattice")
```

To run a specific demo:

```
demo("intervals", package = "lattice")
```

To run an available demo in the `demo()` listing, such as that for one of the linear and generalized linear modeling demos from "An Introduction to Statistical Modelling" by Annette Dobson (available in the stats package), type:

```
demo(lm.glm)
```

Use the escape key to terminate any demo.

Cheatsheets are concise summaries of R commands in a given area. Some come with RStudio under the menu sequence Help > Cheatsheets. These pdf documents concisely summarize many widely used R packages and commands, with very brief illustrations of R code. For example, one is "Data Transformation Cheatsheet" and another is "Python with R and Reticulate Cheatsheet." A large number of cheat sheets are listed at https://www.rstudio.com/resources/cheatsheets/. From this page, one may subscribe to cheatsheet updates.

With the "cheatsheet" package you can download many more cheatsheets in pdf format in this way:

```
install.packages("cheatsheet")
library(cheatsheet)
# Save to a specified existing directory such as C:/References/R, but adding the folder "/cheats".
# Note: Use forward slashes.
# If the local path is only "cheats", it will be created in the Documents folder of your User area.
cheatsheet::get_all_cheatsheets(local_path = "C:/References/R/cheats", tidyverse_
only = FALSE)
```

View the cheatsheets, such as "base-r.pdf", as you would any other pdf document.

A searchable listing of thousands of R packages for statistical analysis is found at https://advanceddataanalytics.net/r-packages/.

From the R prompt, the following commands illustrate other ways to get help:

- Get basic information about file manipulation functions in R: `help(files)`
- Get basic information about R functions for base stats: `help(stats)`
- Get documentation listing commands available for the stats package: `library(help = "stats")`
- Get help for the cor (correlation) command, one of the commands in the stats library: `help(cor)`
- Use the search facility at https://rdrr.io/search

Similarly, you can also insert other package names in the `help()` command. For instance, `help(graphics)` gives help on the "graphics" package and `help(data)` gives help on the data function of the "utils" package, which includes help on loading data, formats supported, etc. To list all locally installed packages issue the command `installed.packages()`. Not all packages have help pages, however.

Sometimes `help()` fails, in which case the double-question mark method may be used, causing the R console to search more broadly, as illustrated below.

```
help(lme4)
```

> No documentation for 'lme4' in specified packages and libraries: you could try '??lme4'

```
??lme4
```

> Search Results
[Search results appear web-style in RStudio's lower right, with hypertext links.]

As a web search will show, there are many free tutorials available for learning R. One is the swirl package. It contains a variety of lessons, some of which are video-based, some are self-review tests, and some are hands-on exercises. User responses are tested for correctness and hints are given if appropriate. Progress is automatically saved so that a user may quit at any time and later resume, without losing work, by typing `swirl()`.

A note on using the `attach()` command

Note that an object in the View window is not necessarily in R's search path. The `attach()` function puts an object in the search path. When in the search path, variables like "happy" can be referenced with their simple name instead of their full name (i.e., by "happy" rather than "mydata$happy").

Why use of `attach()` is derogated: The `attach()` method does not update changes made to variables in the data frame, requiring the researcher to detach and then reattach. Also, in more complex projects the `attach()` method may find more than one object of the same name, requiring reverting to the more conservative practice of using full variable names. For these reasons, and for variable-naming clarity, the `attach()` method often is derogated. If it is used, remember to issue the `detach()` command at the end.

In summary:

- `attach()` is read-only and will always refer to the values in your data frame at the time you issued this command. It will not recognize subsequent changes.
- Do not use `attach()` if you have multiple objects with the same variable name such as income. The `attach()` command will only reference names in the most recently attached object.
- If you have an R script and come back to it later, it will be a lot easier to read if only long names have been used. Short names are bad programming practice. The `attach()` command is mainly for short exploratory or instructional purposes.
- Consider using `with` instead of `attach()`. The format is with (data frame name, command (you may use simple variable names). For example:

```
mydata <- read.table("mydata.csv", header = TRUE, sep = ",")
with(mydata, class(happy))
```

[Output:]
```
[1] "numeric"
```

- Remember to `detach()` at the end.

An example: Factor analysis in R

Factor analysis is a data reduction method typically used to cluster a larger number of variables into a smaller number of underlying dimensions, also called factors, components, or latent variables. Rather than attempting to model, say, 80 survey items as 80 individual variables, the researcher may be able to reduce the data to a more manageable nine underlying factors such as a factor for socioeconomic status (SES). Observations (data rows, often representing people) can be assigned factor scores (e.g., an SES score) and these can be used in any form of subsequent quantitative analysis, such as regression.

A second purpose of factor analysis, and the one used in this example, is to see if all the variables proposed for an additive scale seem to form a single dimension. Scales should be both reliable and unidimensional. To be shown reliable, a proposed set of scale variables should be above some cutoff (e.g., .80) on Cronbach's alpha or another reliability coefficient. Reliability measures, however, do not establish unidimensionality. That is one of the purposes of factor analysis.

We use the USJudgeRatings data, a sample dataset in the "utils" package from the R System Library. This dataset was discussed Section 1.18. These data contain 54 observations on 12 numeric variables. While not an original purpose of these data, for pedagogical reasons we imagine that a researcher wished to see if the 12 variables formed a single dimension, justifying using them additively to form a judicial performance scale. These variables are listed below:

CONT	Number of contacts of lawyer with judge
INTG	Judicial integrity
DMNR	Demeanor
DILG	Diligence
CFMG	Case flow managing
DECI	Prompt decisions
PREP	Preparation for trial
FAMI	Familiarity with law
ORAL	Sound oral rulings
WRIT	Sound written rulings
PHYS	Physical ability
RTEN	Worthy of retention

The commented R code below gives self-explanatory steps for running a factor analysis model in R.

Set the working directory as usual:

```
setwd("C:/Data")
```

Next set up the environment. Base packages not needing installing or invoking include utils and stats. Install packages containing all the functions to be used below. Some may already be installed in your R environment. Install needed packages not already on your local computer. The psych package contains the `principal()` function for PCA-type factor analysis: The corrplot package contains the `corrplot()` function for correlation plots:

```
install.packages("psych")
install.packages("corrplot")

library(psych)
library(corrplot)
```

Now load the sample dataset into the data frame "judges". The `data.frame()` and `summary()` commands are from the R "base" package. USJudgeRatings is a data frame in R's built-in "datasets" package. It is not a .csv file.

```
judges <- data.frame(USJudgeRatings)
summary(USJudgeRatings)
```

[Partial output of first four variables]

```
       CONT              INTG             DMNR              DILG
 Min.   : 5.700   Min.   :5.900   Min.   :4.300   Min.   :5.100
 1st Qu.: 6.850   1st Qu.:7.550   1st Qu.:6.900   1st Qu.:7.150
 Median : 7.300   Median :8.100   Median :7.700   Median :7.800
 Mean   : 7.437   Mean   :8.021   Mean   :7.516   Mean   :7.693
 3rd Qu.: 7.900   3rd Qu.:8.550   3rd Qu.:8.350   3rd Qu.:8.450
 Max.   :10.600   Max.   :9.200   Max.   :9.000   Max.   :9.000
 . . .
```

Optionally, run the correlation command `cor()` from R's built-in "stats" package to get a correlations. The "use" clause eliminates cases with missing values, as required by `cor()`.

```
cor(USJudgeRatings, use = "complete.obs")
```

[Partial output of correlation matrix for first four columns]

```
            CONT       INTG       DMNR      DILG
CONT  1.00000000 -0.1331909 -0.1536885 0.0123920
INTG -0.13319089  1.0000000  0.9646153 0.8715111
DMNR -0.15368853  0.9646153  1.0000000 0.8368510
DILG  0.01239200  0.8715111  0.8368510 1.0000000
CFMG  0.13691230  0.8140858  0.8133582 0.9587988
DECI  0.08653823  0.8028464  0.8041168 0.9561661
PREP  0.01146921  0.8777965  0.8558175 0.9785684
FAMI -0.02563656  0.8688580  0.8412415 0.9573634
ORAL -0.01199681  0.9113992  0.9067729 0.9544758
WRIT -0.04381025  0.9088347  0.8930611 0.9592503
PHYS  0.05424827  0.7419360  0.7886804 0.8129211
RTEN -0.03364343  0.9372632  0.9437002 0.9299652
```

```
# Optionally, put the correlation matrix in the object judgesmatrix
# Only use observations without missing values (listwise deletion)
judgesmatrix <- cor(USJudgeRatings, use = "complete.obs")
```

Optionally, create a correlation plot with variables arranged by the angular order of eigenvectors (AOE), which reveals correlation clusters. This is Figure Appl.4. We add the package name prefix to clarify the command's source package. Note that we use judgesmatrix, not USJudgeRatings. Output shows high intercorrelations among the variables. Note that the corrplot is not itself a test of unidimensionality, however.

```
corrplot::corrplot(judgesmatrix, method = "square", order="AOE")
```

We now obtain eigenvalues. These may be used to determine the number of factors to extract. The `eigen()` command is from R's base package. The `cor()` command is from the stats package. Both are in the R System Library. By the usual Kaiser criterion, factors with eigenvalues of 1.0 or higher are extracted. The first eigenvalue is highest, the last is lowest. Output below shows only the first to meet the Kaiser criterion. This could be taken as evidence of unidimensionality.

```
ev <- eigen(cor(judgesmatrix))

list(ev)
```

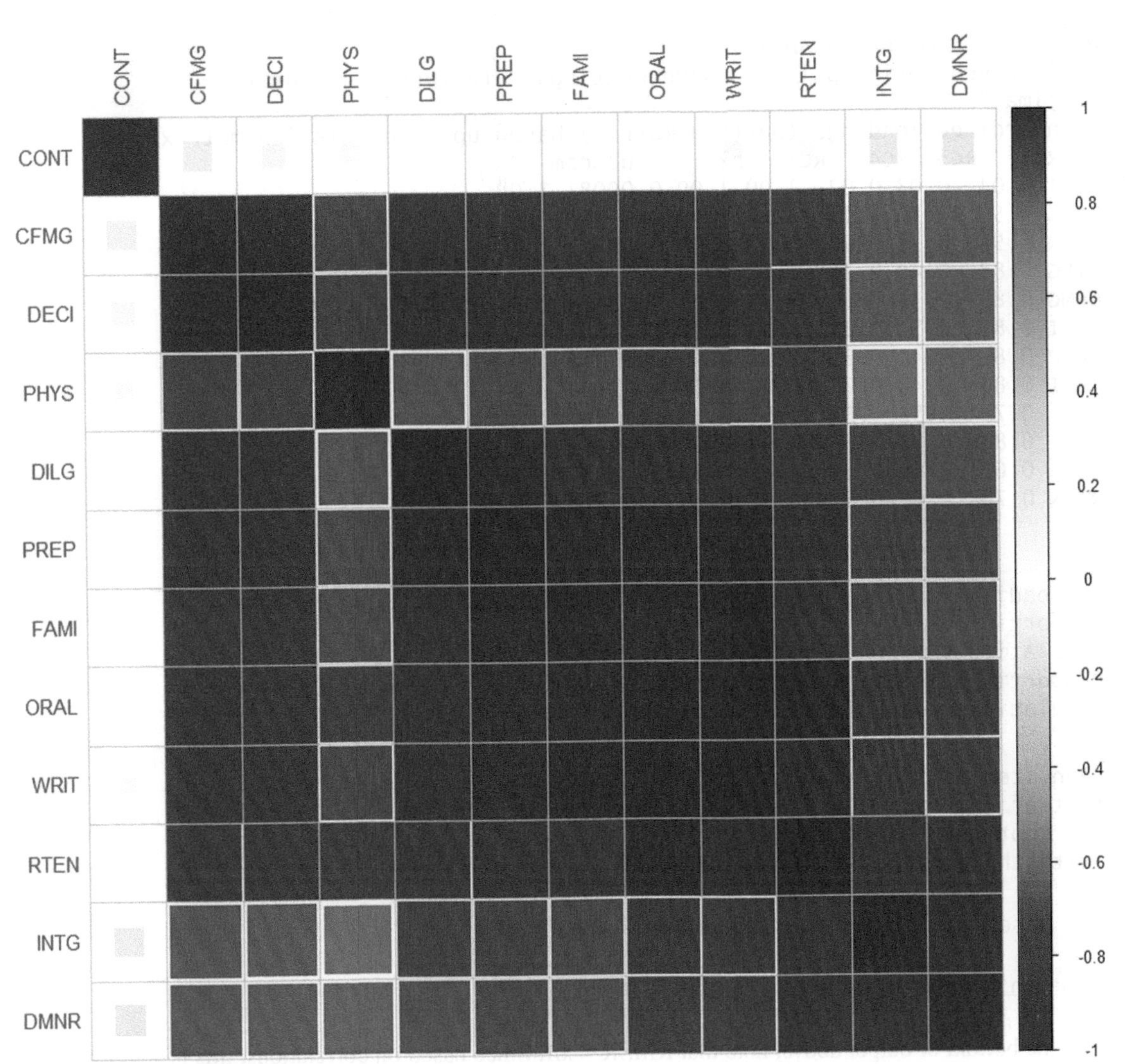

Figure Appl.4 Correlation plot of judgesmatrix

[Partial output:]

```
[[1]]
eigen() decomposition
$values
 [1] 1.158081e+01 3.070219e-01 9.286498e-02
 [4] 1.226513e-02 4.618167e-03 1.627413e-03
 [7] 4.748006e-04 2.514993e-04 4.078930e-05
[10] 1.647766e-05 4.777786e-06 1.434171e-16
```

However, we may explore further by running `principal()` for four factors. Four is all factors with scientific notation of "e-02" or higher. Results are sent to the object "out1".

```
out1 <- psych::principal(USJudgeRatings, nfactors=4, rotate="varimax")

out1
```

[Output:]

```
Principal Components Analysis
Call: psych::principal(r = USJudgeRatings, nfactors = 4, rotate =
"varimax")
Standardized loadings (pattern matrix) based upon correlation matrix
      RC1   RC3  RC4   RC2   h2      u2 com
CONT 0.04 -0.08 0.02  1.00 1.00 0.00081 1.0
INTG 0.58  0.79 0.14 -0.10 0.99 0.01153 1.9
DMNR 0.52  0.79 0.28 -0.12 0.98 0.01587 2.1
DILG 0.88  0.43 0.16  0.01 0.98 0.02473 1.5
CFMG 0.85  0.37 0.32  0.13 0.97 0.02661 1.7
DECI 0.87  0.33 0.31  0.08 0.97 0.02861 1.6
PREP 0.87  0.44 0.21  0.01 0.99 0.00948 1.6
FAMI 0.86  0.43 0.22 -0.03 0.98 0.02400 1.6
ORAL 0.79  0.52 0.31 -0.01 0.99 0.00905 2.1
WRIT 0.82  0.50 0.24 -0.04 0.99 0.01259 1.9
PHYS 0.62  0.36 0.69  0.05 0.99 0.00512 2.5
RTEN 0.70  0.61 0.37 -0.02 0.99 0.00721 2.5

                       RC1  RC3  RC4  RC2
SS loadings           6.52 3.09 1.17 1.04
Proportion Var        0.54 0.26 0.10 0.09
Cumulative Var        0.54 0.80 0.90 0.99
Proportion Explained  0.55 0.26 0.10 0.09
Cumulative Proportion 0.55 0.81 0.91 1.00

Mean item complexity =  1.8
Test of the hypothesis that 4 components are sufficient.
The root mean square of the residuals (RMSR) is  0.01
 with the empirical chi square  0.25  with prob <  1

Fit based upon off diagonal values = 1>
```

Interpretation of output for out1:

- At the bottom of output above, note that RMSR = .01. Since based on correlations, this is actually standardized RMSR. A value less than .05 is widely considered good fit and below .08 adequate fit.
- Note that factors are auto-labeled with an "RC" prefix, standing for "rotated component" By common rule of thumb, high loadings are => .7, low loadings are <=.3, and cross-loadings are –.4 and <.7. Cross-loadings imply overlap of factor meanings.
- PHYS and RTEN also load on RC1 but have cross-loadings with another factor. Likewise, INTG and DMNR load highly on RC3, but with cross-loadings. CONT alone loads highly on RC2, without cross-loadings.
- Of the 12 variables, 7 load highly on factor RC1 without cross-loadings. These are DILF, CFMG, DECI, PREP, FAMI, ORAL, and WRIT. These seven variables may be preferred as the basis for creating a unidimensional judicial performance scale.

We explore further by looking at a two-factor solution instead of the four-factor solution above. This output is sent to the object "out2".

```
out2 <- psych::principal(USJudgeRatings, nfactors=2, rotate="varimax")

out2
```

[Output:]

```
Principal Components Analysis
Call: psych::principal(r = USJudgeRatings, nfactors = 2, rotate = "varimax")
Standardized loadings (pattern matrix) based upon correlation matrix
      RC1   RC2   h2     u2 com
CONT 0.00  0.98 0.96 0.0390 1.0
INTG 0.92 -0.20 0.88 0.1197 1.1
DMNR 0.91 -0.22 0.88 0.1229 1.1
DILG 0.97  0.03 0.94 0.0599 1.0
CFMG 0.97  0.17 0.96 0.0410 1.1
DECI 0.96  0.12 0.94 0.0584 1.0
PREP 0.99  0.02 0.97 0.0287 1.0
FAMI 0.98 -0.01 0.95 0.0469 1.0
ORAL 1.00 -0.01 0.99 0.0091 1.0
WRIT 0.99 -0.04 0.98 0.0184 1.0
PHYS 0.89  0.08 0.81 0.1927 1.0
RTEN 0.99 -0.05 0.97 0.0258 1.0

                        RC1  RC2
SS loadings           10.13 1.11
Proportion Var         0.84 0.09
Cumulative Var         0.84 0.94
Proportion Explained   0.90 0.10
Cumulative Proportion  0.90 1.00

Mean item complexity =  1
Test of the hypothesis that 2 components are sufficient.

The root mean square of the residuals (RMSR) is  0.03
 with the empirical chi square  4.46  with prob <  1

Fit based upon off diagonal values = 1>
```

Interpretation of output for out2:

- In the two-factor solution above, model fit is still good (RMSR = .03).
- CONT loads highly on factor RC2, without cross-loadings.
- All 11 other variables load highly on factor RC1, without cross-loadings.
- This would justify using all variables except CONT in the judicial performance scale. Picking seven variables based on the earlier four-factor model would result in a more unidimensional scale than the 11 variables in the two-factor model, but the two-factor solution (include all variables except CONT) has good model fit.
- If the data were survey items (they aren't), the smaller seven-item scale might reduce subject fatigue and be preferred on that basis.

We now go on with additional exploration of the two-factor model. Obtain a scree plot of eigenvalues, shown in Figure Appl.5. This is an alternative to the Kaiser criterion for selecting number of factors to extract. The scree rule is to stop when the curve levels off. For these data, this alternative method would suggest a three-factor solution.

```
plot(out2$values, type = "l", col ="red", lwd=3, ylab = "Eigenvalue", xlab = "Number
of Factors")
```

We now print factor loadings for the two-factor solution. This prints a simplified version of the factor loadings matrix with loadings < .1 omitted. We see all measures except CONT load on the same factor (RC!). This suggests

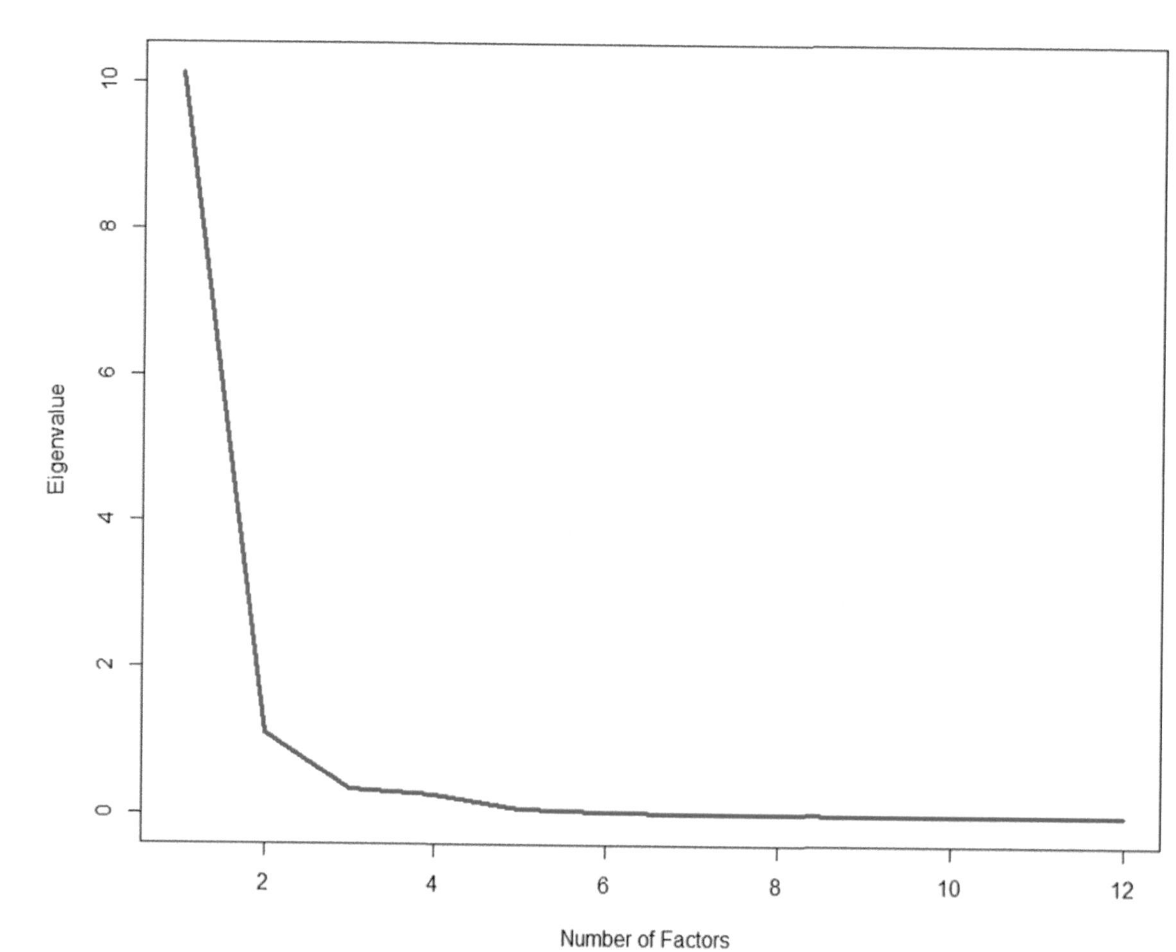

Figure App1.5 Scree plot

that if measures are combined in a scale, CONT should be omitted since it reflects a different factor (a different dimension of meaning).

```
loadings(out2)
```
[Output:]
```
   Loadings:
            RC1    RC2
   CONT           0.980
   INTG  0.916 -0.202
   DMNR  0.911 -0.218
   DILG  0.969
   CFMG  0.965  0.166
   DECI  0.962  0.124
   PREP  0.985
   FAMI  0.976
   ORAL  0.995
   WRIT  0.990
   PHYS  0.895
   RTEN  0.986
```

```
                 RC1    RC2
SS loadings     10.132 1.105
Proportion Var   0.844 0.092
Cumulative Var   0.844 0.936
```

We now calculate communalities. The communality coefficient measures the percent of variance in a given variable explained by all the factors jointly and may be interpreted as the "reliability" of the indicator. Higher is better. Here, all the measures are well explained by the factor model.

```
round(out2$communality,2)
```

[Output:]

```
CONT INTG DMNR DILG CFMG DECI
0.96 0.88 0.88 0.94 0.96 0.94
PREP FAMI ORAL WRIT PHYS RTEN
0.97 0.95 0.99 0.98 0.81 0.97
```

Next we calculate uniquenesses. Uniqueness is simply 1 – communality. Uniqueness is total variability minus the common variability represented by communality. Uniqueness is the percent of variance in a measure not explained by the factor model. The highest uniqueness is PHYS. That is, the factor model is working least well for PHYS, which on basis it might possibly be dropped from the scale.

```
round(out2$uniquenesses,2)
```

[Output:]

```
CONT INTG DMNR DILG CFMG DECI
0.04 0.12 0.12 0.06 0.04 0.06
PREP FAMI ORAL WRIT PHYS RTEN
0.03 0.05 0.01 0.02 0.19 0.03
```

One way to create a scale of judges' performance is to use factor scores. Below, based on the two-factor solution, we send factor scores for all observations to a list called judgescores. This object contains two columns, one for each of the two factors. We are mainly interested in RC1, which are scores on Factor 1, on which most of the items loaded heavily. Judge Aaronson, who is listed first, had a score of –.20 on RC1.

```
judgescores<- out2$scores

head(judgescores)
[Output for first six judges:]
                          RC1
   AARONSON,L.H.  -0.20325626
   ALEXANDER,J.M.  0.73838502
   ARMENTANO,A.J.  0.06754621
   BERDON,R.I.     1.13018700
   BRACKEN,J.J.   -2.15690547
   BURNS,E.B.      0.75323535
                          RC2
   AARONSON,L.H.  -1.7233115
   ALEXANDER,J.M. -0.8342428
   ARMENTANO,A.J. -0.2851121
   BERDON,R.I.    -0.5735352
   BRACKEN,J.J.    0.1532756
   BURNS,E.B.     -1.3463369
```

Finally, we plot variables in factor space. Below we select the two most important factors (there are only two):

```
load = out2$loadings[,1:2]
```

Set up the empty plot for Figure App1.6; `plot()` is part of the built-in "graphics" package

```
plot(load, type="n")
```

```
# Fill in the plot using variable labels; text() is part of the built-in "graphics" package
# We set colors with the color management package RColorBrewer,
# but you could skip it and just set col="red" or some other single color.
library(RColorBrewer)
text(load,labels=c("CONT","INTG","DMNR","DILG","CFMG","DECI","PREP", "FAMI","ORAL","
WRIT","PHYS","RTEN"), col=brewer.pal(n = 12, name = "Set1"))
```

The plot for the two-factor solution in Figure App1.6 shows CONT in a cluster by itself in the upper left of the plot, indicating it should not be part of an additive scale with the other variables. All other variables cluster are in the lower right corner. It is shown graphically that while these variables do cluster well and might be part of a judicial performance scale (the two-factor solution), some measures cluster more tightly than others.

Finally, we check if the 11 variables in the USJudgeRatings data frame (not including CONT) form a reliable scale by Cronbach's alpha, which was discussed in Chapter 2, Section 2.11.1. CONT was in column 1.

```
# Create judgevars as a data frame copy of USJudgeRatings, but with only columns 2–12.
judgevars <- USJudgeRatings[,2:12]
# Cronbach's alpha is computed by the alpha() command in the psych package,
# which is in the R System Library.
psych::alpha(judgevars, na.rm=TRUE, delete=TRUE, check.keys=TRUE)
```

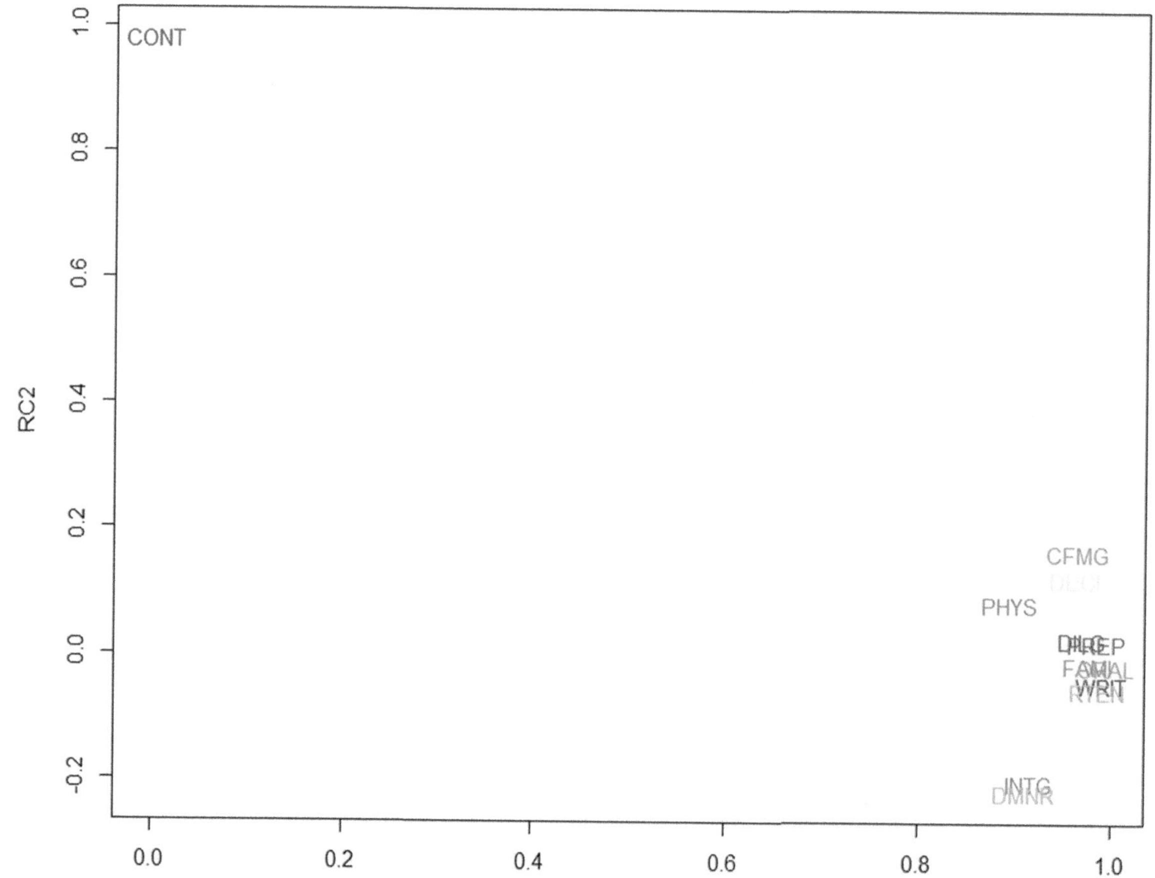

Figure App1.6 Factor space for the two-factor solution

[Partial output:]

```
Reliability analysis
. . .
  raw_alpha std.alpha G6(smc) average_r S/N    ase mean   sd median_r
      0.99      0.99       1      0.91 114 0.0021  7.6 0.91     0.94
  lower alpha upper     95% confidence boundaries
0.99 0.99 0.99
. . .
```

Interpretation of output

For the 11 items excluding CONT, Cronbach's alpha is well above .80, meaning these 11 items constitute a reliable scale. That in the two-factor solution all 11 were highly loaded on the same factor, without cross-loadings, means that they are also unidimensional. That the 11 items are reliable and unidimensional means that we could now proceed to constructing an additive scale composed of values on these items.

Side note: If Cronbach's alpha were computed for all 12 variables in USJudgeRatings, alpha would have been .97, considered good for scaling. However, as we have seen, the CONT variable really does not belong in the scale because it reflects a different dimension of meaning. Cronbach's alpha alone is too weak a criterion for forming a scale. Both alpha reliability and unidimensionality shown in factor analysis should always be used in item selection for scales.

The `summary()` command shows that the 11 items are roughly comparable in mean and range.

```
summary(judgevars)
```

[Output:]

```
      INTG             DMNR             DILG             CFMG
 Min.   :5.900   Min.   :4.300   Min.   :5.100   Min.   :5.400
 1st Qu.:7.550   1st Qu.:6.900   1st Qu.:7.150   1st Qu.:7.000
 Median :8.100   Median :7.700   Median :7.800   Median :7.600
 Mean   :8.021   Mean   :7.516   Mean   :7.693   Mean   :7.479
 3rd Qu.:8.550   3rd Qu.:8.350   3rd Qu.:8.450   3rd Qu.:8.050
 Max.   :9.200   Max.   :9.000   Max.   :9.000   Max.   :8.700
    DECI             PREP             FAMI             ORAL
 Min.   :5.700   Min.   :4.800   Min.   :5.100   Min.   :4.700
 1st Qu.:7.100   1st Qu.:6.900   1st Qu.:6.950   1st Qu.:6.850
 Median :7.700   Median :7.700   Median :7.600   Median :7.500
 Mean   :7.565   Mean   :7.467   Mean   :7.488   Mean   :7.293
 3rd Qu.:8.150   3rd Qu.:8.200   3rd Qu.:8.250   3rd Qu.:8.000
 Max.   :8.800   Max.   :9.100   Max.   :9.100   Max.   :8.900
      WRIT             PHYS             RTEN
 Min.   :4.900   Min.   :4.700   Min.   :4.800
 1st Qu.:6.900   1st Qu.:7.700   1st Qu.:7.150
 Median :7.600   Median :8.100   Median :7.800
 Mean   :7.384   Mean   :7.935   Mean   :7.602
 3rd Qu.:8.050   3rd Qu.:8.500   3rd Qu.:8.250
 Max.   :9.000   Max.   :9.100   Max.   :9.200
```

Having established the unidimensionality, reliability, and comparability of the 11 items, we could then create a judicial performance scale based upon them. This simplest approach to doing so is to average the scores on the 11 variables, then norm the results to range from 0 to 100.

Appendix 2: Data used in this book

boston_c.csv

The "boston_c" dataset is a corrected version of the "Boston" data frame found in the "MASS" package and is almost identical to the "BostonHousing2" data frame found in the "mlbench" package.[1] The original data were found in Harrison and Rubinfeld (1978). The dataset contains 21 variables (columns) for 506 rows (observations). Each observation is a Census tract in the Boston area. A given town may have multiple tracts. In Chapter 7, these data were read into a data frame labeled "BostonHousing", later converted to the data frame "BostonCrime". Variables, which are upper case, are listed below in column number order:

OBS	the observation id number
TOWN	the name of the town (a character variable)
TOWN.1	the id of the town in numeric form
TRACT	the tract number of the observation
LON	the longitude of the tract centroid
LAT	the latitude of the tract centroid
MEDV	the median value of owner-occupied homes in $1000s MEDV is censored: all values > 50 are set to 50
CMEDV	corrected MEDV (very minor corrections)
CRIM	the town's per capita crime rate
ZN	the percent or residential land zone for large lots (> 25k sq. ft.)
INDUS	the percent of non-retail business acres in a town
CHAS	dummy variable coded 1 = tract bounds Charles River, 0 = doesn't
NOX	nitrogen oxides concentration in parts per 10 million
RM	mean number of rooms per dwelling
AGE	percent owner-occupied units built prior to 1940
DIS	weighted mean of distances to five Boston employment centers
RAD	an index of accessibility to radial highways
TAX	the full-value property tax rate per $10,000
PTRATIO	the town's pupil-teacher ratio
B	1000(Bk – 0.63)^2 where Bk is the proportion of blacks by town
LSTAT	percent of population classed lower status

carinsure.csv

This small dataset of just six observations on five variables, listed below, is used in Chapter 3 to illustrate the Poisson regression model in generalized linear modeling.

```
Variable     Obs Unique    Mean          Min          Max        Label
-----------------------------------------------------------------------
clients              6       5          500          100         1200
claims               6       6     44.66667            1          101
carsize              6       3            2            1            3
age                  6       2          1.5            1            2
lnclients            6       5     5.969952      4.60517     7.090077
-----------------------------------------------------------------------
```

citycrime.csv

This is a dataset on 15 U.S. cities, with population and crime statistics as listed below. It is used in Chapter 8 to illustrate community analysis of networks using the "tidygraph" package.

Variable	Obs	Unique	Mean	Min	Max	Label
city	15	15	.	.	.	CITY
pop	15	15	1526.933	580	2076	POP
murder	15	14	21.47333	5	43.5	MURDER
rape	15	15	54.32667	26.5	78.6	RAPE
robbery	15	15	530.7333	205	785	ROBBERY
assault	15	15	920.4	339	1206	ASSAULT
burglary	15	15	1373.467	710	2244	BURGLARY
larceny	15	15	3992	2257	7039	LARCENY
mvtheft	15	15	1280.933	319	2687	MVTHEFT

cobb_survey.csv

This dataset provided with permission by Prof. Michael Cobb, pertain to the 2004 U.S. presidential elections and whether the respondent watched the presidential debates. The dataset contains 338 observations on 88 variables. It is used in Chapter 3 to illustrate missing values analysis and data imputation. The variables in the file, most of which are not used in this text, are these:

Variable	Obs	Unique	Mean	Min	Max	Label
id	338	338	169.5	1	338	
debwatch	338	2	1.428994	1	2	
rvpos	338	3	.	.	.	
rposvst	338	3	.	.	.	
gsupv	338	3	.	.	.	
bsupv	338	3	.	.	.	
rposuhc	338	3	.	.	.	
rposuhcs	338	3	.	.	.	
rposdp	338	3	.	.	.	
rstposdp	338	3	.	.	.	
rgposdp	338	3	.	.	.	
rbposdp	338	3	.	.	.	
rposss	338	3	.	.	.	
rstposss	338	3	.	.	.	
rgposss	338	3	.	.	.	
rbposss	338	3	.	.	.	
renveco	338	3	.	.	.	
rstenvec	338	3	.	.	.	
rgenvec	338	3	.	.	.	
rbenvec	338	3	.	.	.	
rposgun	338	4	.	.	.	
rstgun	338	3	.	.	.	
rggun	338	3	.	.	.	
rbgun	338	3	.	.	.	
rposdef	338	3	.	.	.	

(Continued)

```
Variable          Obs Unique      Mean           Min      Max     Label
-----------------------------------------------------------------------
rstdef               338        3              .        .          .
rgdef                338        3              .        .          .
rbdef                338        3              .        .          .
candtax              338        3              .        .          .
mostimp              338        7              .        .          .
gbhealth             338        3              .        .          .
gbsocsec             338        3              .        .          .
gbguns               338        3              .        .          .
gbenv                338        3              .        .          .
gbtax                338        3              .        .          .
gbdef                338        3              .        .          .
gbedu                338        3              .        .          .
goreint              338        5              .        .          .
gorelike             338        5              .        .          .
gorehon              338        5              .        .          .
gorecare             338        5              .        .          .
gorerdy              338        5              .        .          .
bushint              338        5              .        .          .
bushlike             338        5              .        .          .
bushhon              338        5              .        .          .
bushcare             338        5              .        .          .
bushrdy              338        5              .        .          .
interest             338        4              .        .          .
vote                 338        4              .        .          .
clinton              338        5              .        .          .
sex                  338        3              .        .          .
grade                338        6              .        .          .
race                 338        6              .        .          .
religion             338        6              .        .          .
news                 338        5              .        .          .
tv                   338        9              .        .          .
paper                338        9              .        .          .
pid                  338        6              .        .          .
ideo                 338        6              .        .          .
bushgore             338        3              .        .          .
pid3pt               338        4              .        .          .
pid2pt               338        3              .        .          .
ideo3pt              338        4              .        .          .
ideo2pt              338        3              .        .          .
healthc              338        5              .        .          .
death                338        5              .        .          .
socsec               338        5              .        .          .
envir                338        5              .        .          .
defense              338        5              .        .          .
vouchers             338        5              .        .          .
guns                 338        6              .        .          .
fac1_1               338       11              .        .          .
fac2_1               338       11              .        .          .
fac3_1               338       11              .        .          .
```

(Continued)

Variable	Obs	Unique	Mean	Min	Max	Label
fac4_1		338	11	.	.	.
fac5_1		338	11	.	.	.
fac6_1		338	11	.	.	.
fac7_1		338	11	.	.	.
fac8_1		338	11	.	.	.
fac9_1		338	11	.	.	.
debwatch_ind		338	1	0	0	0
rvpos_ind		338	2	.2248521	0	1
rposvst_ind		338	2	.1893491	0	1
gsupv_ind		338	2	.4970414	0	1
bsupv_ind		338	2	.4260355	0	1
rposuhc_ind		338	2	.0946746	0	1
rposuhcs_ind		338	2	.1005917	0	1
rposdp_ind		338	2	.1272189	0	1

courts.csv

This dataset is an adapted version of ICPSR Study No. 3987, "Determinants of Case Growth in Federal District Courts in the United States, 1904-2002", subset DS6: "Federal Court Panel Data on Drugs and Immigration, 1968-1998. " This dataset is maintained and distributed by the National Archive of Criminal Justice Data (NACJD), the criminal justice archive within ICPSR. It is used in Chapter 3 to illustrate panel data regression, which is a form of longitudinal analysis. The variables in the file are these:

Variable	Obs	Unique	Mean	Min	Max	Label
year		2786	31	1983.019	1968	1998
circuit		2786	12	.	.	.
district		2786	90	.	.	.
ndistrict		2786	90	45.51508	1	90
noj		2786	40	5.638582	1	28
pfpy		2786	772	271.9257	5	4420
totalcom		2786	1007	456.4961	24	3825
totalterm		2786	975	438.9483	23	3337
efficiency		2786	2044	.6411673	.0842	2.2532
drugs		2786	394	84.46841	0	1593
immigration		2786	233	28.4537	0	2240
civilfpj		2786	591	348.9548	62	3822
criminalfpj		2786	232	70.24156	7	1460
pendingpj		2786	688	397.6788	33	5532
trialstermpj		2786	572	402.2563	36	2951
trialstepj		2786	99	39.74767	5	131
crimftod		2786	124	4.806317	.1	18
civilftod		2786	35	9.42893	0	51
pdrugmm		2786	1996	.1969267	0	1.2273
zcivilfpj		2786	591	1.15e-09	-1.824156	22.07796
zcriminalfpj		2786	232	-3.82e-10	-1.039108	22.83481
zpendingpj		2786	688	-1.68e-10	-1.390106	19.57134
zpdrugmm		2786	1996	2.08e-09	-1.216471	6.364903
ztrialster~j		2786	572	7.77e-10	-2.604756	18.12626

edvars.csv

This is a subset of just four variables for 1,500 observations in the 1993 General Social Survey, used to illustrate calculation of reliability measures. The variables are these:

- educ Highest year of school completed
- degree Respondent's highest degree
- madeg Mother's highest degree
- padeg Father's highest degree

Descriptive statistics, produced by Stata's codebook, compact command, are:

Variable	Obs	Unique	Mean	Min	Max	Label
degree	1496	5	1.413102	0	4	R's Highest Degree
educ	1496	19	13.03743	0	20	Highest Year of School Completed
madeg	1352	5	.8365385	0	4	Mother's Highest Degree
padeg	1207	5	.9328915	0	4	Father's Highest Degree

hsbmerged.csv

This dataset is a version of the classic "High School and Beyond Survey" subsample data on 7,185 student-level observations with no missing values, grouped under 160 schools, and collected in 1982. These data are used by Raudenbush et al. (2011) in their seminal work on multilevel modeling. It is used to illustrate multilevel modeling in Chapter 3. Math achievement is the outcome variable. The variables are these:

Variable	Obs	Unique	Mean	Min	Max	Label
schoolid	7185	160	5277.898	1224	9586	
minority	7185	2	.274739	0	1	
female	7185	2	.5281837	0	1	
ses	7185	373	.0001434	-3.758	2.692	
mathach	7185	6031	12.74785	-2.832	24.993	
size	7185	149	1056.862	100	2713	
sector	7185	2	.4931106	0	1	
pracad	7185	73	.5344871	0	1	
disclim	7185	159	-.1318694	-2.416	2.756	
himinty	7185	2	.2800278	0	1	
meanses	7185	150	.0061385	-1.188	.831	

iris or iris.dta

This is a well-known teaching dataset used for a variety of classification problems. It is used in this volume to illustrate CHAID, exhaustive CHAID, and random forests, and also nnet classification in the chapter on neural networks. It is a built-in dataset in the "datasets" package, which loads automatically when R is launched. There are 150 observations on iris plants, which may be of species sertosa, versicolor, or virginica. The variable "Species" contains these labels in string form. The variable "Speciescode", used as the target variable, contains the same data numerically coded from 1 through 3. The potential classification (splitting, predictor) variables are SepalLength, SepalWidth, PetalLength, and PetalWidth.

Variable	Obs	Unique	Mean	Min	Max	Label
caseno	150	150	75.5	1	150	
SepalLength	150	35	5.843333	4.3	7.9	
SepalWidth	150	23	3.057333	2	4.4	
PetalLength	150	43	3.758	1	6.9	
PetalWidth	150	22	1.199333	.1	2.5	
Species	150	3	.	.	.	
Speciescode	150	3	2	1	3	

judges.csv

This data file is used to illustrate reliability analysis in Chapter 2. It contains the sports ratings of eight judges rating 300 athlete events on a scale from 0 to 10, though in reality the judges' scores ranged from 7 to 10. The variables as listed in Stata are these:

Variable	Obs	Unique	Mean	Min	Max	Label
judge1	300	31	8.485667	7	10	Italy
judge2	300	31	8.895333	7	10	South Korea
judge3	300	30	8.106333	7	9.9	Romania
judge4	300	29	8.955333	7.2	10	France
judge5	300	29	8.038667	7	9.8	China
judge6	300	31	8.836667	7	10	United States
judge7	300	31	8.153333	7	10	Russia
judge8	300	31	8.505	7	10	Enthusiast

mydata.csv

This is a very small dataset used in Appendix 1 ("Getting Started with R and RStudio") to illustrate simple R commands.

Variable	Obs	Unique	Mean	Min	Max	Label
happy	10	5	3.1	1	5	
gender	10	2	.5	0	1	

nycflights.csv

The nycflights dataset contains data on 897,629 flights by American Airlines (AA) and United Airlines (UA) in 2013. The outcome variable is arrival delay (arr_delay). Predictor variables are dep_delay, dep_time, arr_time, air_time, and distance. The data are modified and selected from the original "flights" dataset that is contained in the "nycflights13" package, which is available on CRAN. The nycflights.csv data are used in Quick Start Example 1 in Chapter 7.

nycflights_scaled.csv

This is the same dataset as nycflights.csv above, except the outcome variable is rescaled to range from 0 to 1 and all other variables are normalized to make them of comparable scale. The nycflights_scaled.csv data are also used in Quick Start Example 1 in Chapter 7.

protest.csv

This dataset focused on subjects who were asked to rate how much they liked a woman lawyer in the scenario (liking, on a 7-point scale) based on response to a protest action. The data are used in Chapter 2 to illustrate mediation and moderation analysis. Note that other versions of this dataset are in circulation and may not be equivalent to that supplied with this textbook. The variables are these:

Variable	Obs	Unique	Mean	Min	Max	Label
liking	129	23	5.636744	1	7	
respappr	129	23	4.866279	1.5	7	
protest	129	2	.6821705	0	1	
int_xw	129	29	3.505271	0	7	
group	129	3	1.992248	1	3	
int_ps	129	29	3.505271	0	7	
int_pr	129	19	3.631783	0	7	
sexism	129	28	5.116977	2.87	7	

ratification.dta

This data file contains data on the 13 original U.S. states. The variable Days is the time variable used for time-to-event, where the event is ratification of the Constitution. The failure (status) variable is Status, coded 1 for all states since all states eventually experienced the event. Potential splitting (classifier, predictor) variables explored in this example included Founded, Battles, EVotes, Size, Distance, and Rights. The codebook for this dataset is shown below.

Variable	Obs	Unique	Mean	Min	Max	Label
StateNam	13	13	.	.	.	
Days	13	13	288.3846	81	985	
VotePct	13	8	71.76923	52	100	Percent favoring ratif...
Status	13	1	1	1	1	
Founded	13	12	1650.077	1607	1732	Year state was founded
Battles	13	8	8.615385	0	67	Number of Revolutionar...
PopPct17	13	10	.0769231	.01	.2	
Pop1776	13	13	279884.6	59100	747500	
Vote1796	13	6	.6030769	0	1	Adams EV/Adams+Jeff EV
EVotes	13	11	9.769231	3	21	Electoral Votes 1792
Size	13	3	2	1	3	Size of state
Distance	13	13	238.5385	0	658	Miles to Philadelphia
Candidat	13	6	10.15385	0	69	EV for candidate from...
Rights	13	2	.5384615	0	1	Center of support for...

senateratings05.csv

This file contains three variables used to illustrate binary SVM classification. Data rows represent 99 U.S. Senators (one "Independent" was dropped from analysis) in 2005. Fields (columns) in the dataset are PARTY, ACLU, and NAACP. The PARTY variable serves as the binary outcome for classification purposes and is coded Dem or GOP. The ACLU and NAACP variables are interest group ratings ranging from 0 to 100, based on Senators' votes. Of the 99 ACLU ratings, 5 were imputed by mean substitution to avoid missing values. For this reason, this dataset is not recommended for substantive research.

```
. codebook, compact*

          Variable   Obs   Unique       Mean   Min    Max   Label
          ---------------------------------------------------------
          party       99        2          .     .      .   PARTY
          aclu        99       23   38.64646     0    100   ACLU
          naacp       99       18   49.25253     5    100   NAACP
          ---------------------------------------------------------
```

* Shown in Stata, which has converted all the original variable labels to lower case. They are upper case in the .csv file.

surveysample.csv

This contains data on 21 social variables for 2,050 U.S. individuals. The data are a subset from which missing values have been eliminated, adapted from but different from a General Social Survey sample provided by IBM SPSS for instructional purposes. Not appropriate for substantive research. It is used in Chapter 2 to illustrate various statistical procedures in R, in Chapter 3 to illustrate generalized linear models, and in Chapter 7 to illustrate neural network analysis.

```
Variable    Obs  Unique       Mean  Min   Max  Label
-----------------------------------------------------------------------------------
id         2050    2050     1025.5    1  2050  Respondent id number
wrkstat    2050       8   2.605366    1     8  Labor force status
marital    2050       5   2.529756    1     5  Marital status
childs     2050       9   1.730244    0     8  Number of children
age        2050      72   44.33707   18    89  Age of respondent
educ       2050      20    13.4761    0    20  Highest year of school completed
degree     2050       5   1.553171    0     4  Highest degree
sex        2050       2   1.546829    1     2  Gender
race       2050       3   1.266341    1     3  Race of respondent
born       2050       2   1.081463    1     2  Born in this country
income     2050      12      10.72    1    12  Total family income
polviews   2050       7   4.040488    1     7  Think of self as liberal or
                                                conservative
cappun     2050       2   1.274146    1     2  Favor or oppose death penalty
                                                fo...
happy      2050       3   1.823902    1     3  General happiness
hapmar     2050       4   .6336585    0     3  Happiness of marriage
tvhours    2050      17   2.243902   -1    20  Hours per day watching TV
agecat     2050       6   3.402439    1     6  Age category
childcat   2050       4    1.02439    0     3  Number of children(group
                                                category)
news1      2050       2   .3082927    0     1  Get news from newspapers
news5      2050       2   .3258537    0     1  Get news from internet
car1       2050       6   2.332195    1     6  Car maker, most recent car
-----------------------------------------------------------------------------------
```

test.csv

Used with the kind permission of NCSU doctoral student Yanan Yu, this dataset is used in Chapter 3 to illustrate handling of imported .csv files with missing data. Though this file has 408 cases, it has only 102 complete cases.[2] The dependent variable is "dpadopt", a binary variable coded 0 = did not adopt digital printing, 1 = did adopt.

Variable	Obs	Unique	Mean	Min	Max	Label
year	408	8	2014.5	2011	2018	
state	408	102	.	.	.	State
employment~e	408	28	.6550735	.18	.88	employment pct
povertyper~e	408	29	.3232353	.19	.47	poverty percentage
femaleperc~e	408	6	.5104657	.48	.53	female percentage
whiteperce~e	408	60	.6922794	.21	.94	white percentage
bachelorpe~e	102	79	.3112157	.199	.566	bachelor percentage
youthperce~e	408	10	.2118382	.18	.32	youth percentage
gdp	408	402	48748.95	28110	168030	GDP
digitalpri~n	408	2	.4681373	0	1	adopt dig printing

world.csv

This is a cleaned and modified version of a public domain dataset constructed by the U.S. government. It is used in Chapters 2, 3, 5, and elsewhere in this book. It contains data on 20 variables for 212 countries of the world. There are no missing values. This dataset is presented for pedagogical uses and may not be suitable for substantive research. The usual dependent variable was either literacy (national literacy rate as a continuous variable) or litgtmean (a binary version of literacy, coded 0 = below mean or 1 = above mean). No nation was exactly at the statistical mean. The variables are these:

Variable	Obs	Unique	Mean	Min	Max	Label
ID	212	212	106.5	1	212	ID
country	212	212	.	.	.	country
region	212	14	.	.	.	region
population	212	212	3.07e+07	7026	1.31e+09	population
areasqmiles	212	212	639138.6	2	1.71e+07	areasqmiles
poppersqmile	212	212	385.2902	.03	16271.5	poppersqmile
coast_area~o	212	138	18.85953	0	870.66	coast_arearatio
netmigration	212	150	-.0708491	-20.99	23.06	netmigration
Infantdea~1k	212	209	36.36311	2.29	191.19	Infantdeathsper1k
infdeaths	212	2	.	.	.	infdeaths
gdppercapi~s	212	128	9716.981	500	55100	gdppercapitalin...
literacy	212	140	83.27547	17.6	100	literacy
litgtmean	212	2	.	.	.	litgtmean
phonesp~1000	212	211	230.939	.17	1035.55	phonesper1000
arablepct	212	194	14.23896	0	62.11	arablepct

(Continued)

Variable	Obs	Unique	Mean	Min	Max	Label
cropspct	212	156	4.312028	0	48.96	cropspct
otherpct	212	201	81.44863	33.33	100	otherpct
birthrate	211	208	22.19024	7.29	50.73	birthrate
deathrate	211	191	9.321943	2.29	29.74	deathrate

Endnotes

1. The "BostonHousing2" data frame is based on http://lib.stat.cmu.edu/datasets/boston_corrected.txt. Also, the data frame used here is slightly different from "boston.c" documented at https://www.rdocumentation.org/packages/spdep/versions/0.6-15/topics/boston.
2. This is an instructional sample. In Yanan Yu's actual research dataset, there were many fewer missing values.

References

ACLU (2020). Untold number of people implicated in crimes they didn't commit because of face recognition. American Civil Liberties Union, *News and Commentary.* Retrieved 7/14/2020 from https://www.aclu.org/news/privacy-technology/the-untold-number-of-people-implicated-in-crimes-they-didnt-commit-because-of-face-recognition/.

Agarwal, Basant; Nayak, Richi; Mittal, Namita; & Patnaik, Srikanta, eds. (2020). *Deep learning-based approaches for sentiment analysis: Algorithms for intelligent systems.* New York, NY: Springer.

Aitkin, M.; Anderson, D.; Francis, B.; & Hinde, J. (1989). *Statistical modelling in GLIM.* Oxford: Oxford Science Publications.

Alexander, L.; Mulfinger, E.; & Oswald, F. L. (2020). Using big data and machine learning in personality measurement: Opportunities and challenges. *European Journal of Personality* 34(5): 632–648.

Anastasiadis, A. et. al. (2005). New globally convergent training scheme based on the resilient propagation algorithm. *Neurocomputing* 64: 253–270.

Angwin, J.; Larson, J.; Mattu, S.; & Kirchner, L. (2016). Machine bias: There's software used across the country to predict future criminals. And it's biased against blacks. *ProPublica* 23 May 2016. Available at http:/www.propublica.org/article/machine-bias-risk-assessments-in-criminal-sentencing.

Aydin, Olgun (2018). *R web scraping quick start guide: Techniques and tools to crawl and scrape data from websites.* Birmingham, UK: Pakt Publishing.

Ayers, J.; Caputi, T.; Nebeker, C.; & Dredze M. (2018). Don't quote me: Reverse identification of research participants in social media studies. *Digital Media* 1(1): 30. DOI: 10.1038/s41746-018-0036-2.

Azamathulla, H. Md. & Wu, F.-C. (2011). Support vector machine approach for longitudinal dispersion coefficients in natural streams. *Applied Soft Computing* 11(2): 2902–2905.

Baćak, Valerio & Kennedy, Edward H. (2019). Principled machine learning using the super learner: An application to predicting prison violence. *Sociological Methods & Research* 48(3): 698–721.

Bailey, Todd M. (2015). Convergence of Rprop and variants. *Neurocomputing* 159: 90–95.

Balakrishnan, Vimala; Khan, Shahzaib; Fernandez, Terence; & Arabnia, Hamid R. (2019). Cyberbullying detection on Twitter using Big Five and Dark Triad features. *Personality and Individual Differences* 141: 252–257.

Bates, D.; Maechler, M.; Bolker, B.; & Walker, S. (2015). Fitting linear mixed-effects models using lme4. *Journal of Statistical Software* 67: 1–48.

Bauduin, Sarah & McIntire, Eliot J. N. (2016). *Programming guide NetLogoR.* Published in "Vignettes from package 'NetLogoR'" when NetLogoR is installed.

Bauduin, Sarah; McIntire, Eliot J. B.; & Chubaty, Alex M. (2019). NetLogoR: A package to build and run spatially explicit agent-based models in R. *Ecography* 42(11): 1841–1849.

Beck, Marcus. (2018). NeuralNetTools: Visualization and analysis tools for neural networks. *Journal of Statistical Software* 85(11): 1–20.

Bennet, K. P. & Campbell, C. (2000). Support vector machines: Hype or hallelujah? *ACM SIGKDD Explorations Newsletter* 2(2): 1–13.

Bertsimas, Dimitris; Delarue, Arthur; Jaillet, Patrick; Martin, Sébastien (2019). Travel time estimations in the age of big data. *Operations Research* 67(2): 498–515.

Biggs, D.; de Ville, B.; & Suen, E. (1991). A method of choosing multiway partitions for classification and decision trees. *Journal of Applied Statistics* 18: 49–62.

Blei, David M.; Ng, Andrew Y.; & Jordan, Michael I. (2003). Latent dirichlet allocation. *Journal of Machine Learning Research* 3: 993–1022.

Bøggild, Troels; Aarøe, Lene; & Peterson, Michael Bang (2021). Citizens as complicits: Distrust in politicians and biased social dissemination of political information. *American Political Science Review* 115(1): 269–285.

Boker, Steven et al. (2011). OpenMX: An open source extended structural equation modeling framework. *Psychometrica* 76(2): 306–317. DOI: 10.1007/S11336-010-9200-6.

Bollen, Kenneth A. (1979). Political democracy and the timing of development. *American Sociological Review* 44: 572–587.

Bollen, Kenneth A. (1980). Issues in the comparative measurement of political democracy. *American Sociological Review* 45: 370–390.

Bollen, Kenneth A. (1989). *Structural equations with latent variables.* Wiley Series in Probability and Mathematical Statistics. New York, NY: John Wiley and Sons.

Bollen, Kenneth A.; Gates, Kathleen M.; & Fisher, Zachary (2018). Robustness conditions for MIV-2SLS when the latent variable or measurement model is structurally misspecified. *Structural Equation Modeling* 25(6): 848–859. DOI: 10.1080/10705511.2018.1456341.

Bollier, David (2010). *The promise and peril of big data.* Washington, DC: The Aspen Institute.

Bondi, M. & Scott, M., eds. (2010). *Keyness in texts.* Amsterdam, Philadelphia: John Benjamins.

Bonica, Adam (2018). Inferring roll-call scores from campaign contributions using supervised machine learning. *American Journal of Political Science* 62(4): 830–848.

boyd, danah & Crawford, Kate (2012). Critical questions for big data. *Information, Communication & Society* 15(5): 662–679.

Breiman, Leo (1996). Bagging predictors. *Machine Learning* 24(2): 123–140.

Breiman, Leo (2001). Random forests. *Machine Learning* 45(1): 5–32.

Breiman, Leo (2002). *Manual on setting up, using, and understanding Random Forests V3.1.* Berkeley, CA, USA: University of California – Berkeley. Available at https://www.stat.berkeley.edu/~breiman/Using_random_forests_V3.1.pdf. Refers to the FORTRAN version.

Breiman, Leo; Friedman, Jerome; Stone, Charles J.; & Olshen, R. A. (1984). *Classification and regression trees.* Wadsworth Statistics/Probability Series. Boca Raton, FL: Chapman and Hall/CRC.

Bretz, Frank; Hothorn, Torsten; & Westfall, Peter (2010). *Multiple comparisons using R.* Boca Raton, FL: CRC Press.

Brey, Philip (2007). The technological construction of social power. *Social Epistemology* 22(1): 71–95.

Broc, Guillaume & Gana, Kamel (2019). *Structural equation modeling with lavaan.* New York, NY: ISTE/Wiley.

Bugdol, Marcin D; Bugdol, Monika N; Lipowicz, Anna M; Mitas, Andrzej W; Bienkowska, Maria J; et al. (2019). Prediction of menarcheal status of girls using voice features. *Computers in Biology and Medicine* 100: 296–304.

Butts, Carter T. (2008). Social network analysis with sna. *Journal of Statistical Software* 24(6): 1–51. Available at https://www.jstatsoft.org/article/view/v024i06.

Cambria, Erik; Das, Dipankar; Bandyopadhyay, Sivaji; & Feraco, Antonio, eds. (2017). *A practical guide to sentiment analysis: Socio-affective computing.* Paranaque City, Philippines: Springer International.

Campbell, Charlie (2019). The fight for our faces: China shows the worrying future of the surveillance state. *Time* 194(24–25): 52–55. December 2–9, 2019.

CBS News (2020). Florida's COVID-19 dashboard manager fired, says she voiced concerns over manipulated data. Retrieved 7/14/2020 from https://www.cbsnews.com/video/floridas-covid-19-dashboard-manager-fired-says-she-voiced-concerns-over-manipulated-data/.

Charrad, Malika; Ghazzali, Nadia; Boiteau, Véronique Boiteau; & Niknafs, Azam (2014). NbClust: An R package for determining the relevant number of clusters in a data set. *Journal of Statistical Software* 61: 1–36.

Chiauzzi, Emil & Wicks, Paul (2019). Digital trespass: Ethical and terms-of-use violations by researchers accessing data from an online patient community. *Journal of Medical Internet Research* 21(2): e11985. Available at https://www.jmir.org/2019/2/e11985. DOI: 10.2196/11985.

Ciner, Cetin (2019). Do industry returns predict the stock market? A reprise using the random forest. *The Quarterly Review of Economics and Finance* 72: 152–158.

Citron, Danielle Keats (2007). Technological due process. *Washington University Law Review* 85(6): 1249–1313.

Cohen, W. W. (1995). Fast effective rule induction. pp. 115–123 in Prieditis, A. & Russell, S., eds. *Proceedings of the 12th International Conference on Machine Learning.* Burlington, MA: Morgan Kaufmann.

Cox, Trevor F. & Cox, M. A. A. (2000). *Multidimensional scaling,* Second edition. Boca Raton, FL: Chapman & Hall/CRC. Monographs on Statistics and Applied Probability (Book 88).

Crawford, K. (2017). The trouble with bias. Paper presented at the Thirty-First Conference on Neural Information Processing Systems, Long Beach, CA, December 4–9.

Croissant, Yves & Millo, Giovanni (2018). *Panel data econometrics with R.* New York City, NY: Wiley.

Cronbach, L. J. (1951). Coefficient alpha and the internal strucuture of tests. *Psychometrika* 16: 297–334.

Cronbach, L. J. & Gleser, G. C. (1964). The signal/noise ratio in the comparison of reliability coefficients. *Educational and Psychological Measurement* 24(3): 467–480.

DataRobot, Inc. (2019a). *The state of AI bias in 2019.* Boston, MA: DataRobot, Inc.

DataRobot, Inc. (2019b). DataRobot reports that nearly half of AI professionals are very to extremely concerned about AI bias. *Journal of Engineering* [Atlanta] 2 Dec 2019: 386.

Department of Homeland Security (2012). *The Menlo Report: Ethical principles guiding information and communication technology research.* Directorate of Science & Technology, August 2012.

Dhana, Klodian (2017). Graphical presentation of missing data; VIM package. Posted on 8 May 2017 to R-Bloggers. Retrieved 11/20.2019 from https://www.r-bloggers.com/graphical-presentation-of-missing-data-vim-package/.

Di, Zonglin; Gong, Xiaoliang; Shi, Jingyu; Ahmed, Hosameldin O. A.; & Nandi, Asoke K. (2019). Internet addiction disorder detection of Chinese college students using several personality questionnaire data and support vector machine. *Addictive Behaviors Reports.* Published online before print and retrieved 8/8/2019 from https://www.sciencedirect.com/science/article/pii/S2352853218301512.

Dittrich, D.; Kenneally, E.; & Bailey, M. (2013). Applying ethical principles to information and communication technology research: A companion to the Menlo Report, Tech. Report., U.S. Department of Homeland Security, October 2013.

Diviák, Tomáš; Coutinho, J. A.; & Stivala, A. D. (2020). A man's world? Comparing the structural positions of men and women in an organized criminal network. *Crime, Law and Social Change* 74(5): 547–569.

Dressel, Julia & Farid, Hany (2018). The accuracy, fairness, and limits of predicting recidivism. *Science Advances* 4(1). Available at https://advances.sciencemag.org/content/4/1/eaao5580.

Drozdenko, Ronald G. & Drake, Perry D. (2002). *Optimal database marketing: Strategy, development, & data mining*. Thousand Oaks, CA: Sage Publications. On classification performance measures, see "Optimal Database Marketing", Chapter 11.

Drucker, Harris; Burges, Christopher J. C.; Kaufman, Linda; Smola, Alexander J.; & Vapnik, Vladimir N. (1997). Support vector regression machines. *Advances in Neural Information Processing Systems* 9 (NIPS 1996): 155–161.

Du, Wei; Cheung, Huey; Goldberg, Ilya; Thambisetty, Madhav; Becker, Kevin; & Jonson, Calvin A. (2015). A longitudinal support vector regression for prediction of ALS score. *IEEE International Conference Bioinformatics* (November 2015): 1586–1590. DOI: 10.1109/BIBM.2015.7359912.

Durstewitz, Daniel; Koppe, Georgia; Meyer-Lindenberg, Andreas; National Library of Medicine (2019). Deep neural networks in psychiatry. *Molecular Psychiatry* 24(11): 1583–1598. DOI: 10.1038/s41380-019-0365-9.

Ehrlinger, John (2015). ggRandomForests: Random forests for regression. arXiv: 1501.07196v2 [stat.CO].

Ertam, F. & Aydin, G. (2017). Data classification with deep learning using Tensorflow. *IEEE, 2nd International Conference on Computer Science and Engineering*, Retrieved from https://ieeexplore.ieee.org/document/8093521.

Etli, Yasing; Asirdizer, Mahmut; Hekimoglu, Yavuz; Keskin, Siddik; & Yavuz, A. (2019). Sex estimation from sacrum and coccyx with discriminant analyses and neural networks in an equally distributed population by age and sex. *Forensic Science International* 303: online. DOI: 10.1016/j.forsciint.2019.109955.

Ettensperger, Felix (2020). Comparing supervised learning algorithms and artificial neural networks for conflict prediction: Performance and applicability of deep learning in the field. *Quality and Quantity* 54(2): 567–601.

Eubanks, Virginia (2019). *Automating inequality: How high-tech tools profile, police, and punish the poor*. New York City, NY: Picador/Macmillan.

Favaretto, Maddalena; De Clercq, Eva; & Elger, Bernice Simone (2019). Big Data and discrimination: Perils, promises and solutions. A systematic review. *Journal of Big Data* 6(1): 1–27.

Fawcett, T. (2003). ROC graphs: Notes and practical considerations for data mining researchers. *Tech report HPL-2003-4*. Palo Alto, CA: HP Laboratories.

Feinerer, I. & Hornik, K. (2018). tm: Text mining package. Retrieved from https://CRAN.R-project.org/package=tm.

Findler, Nicholas V. (1988). The debt of Artificial Intelligence to John von Neumann. *Artificial Intelligence Review* 2: 311–312.

Fisher, W. D. (1958). On grouping for maximum homogeneity. *Journal of the American Statistical Association* 53: 789–798.

Flach, P. A. (2003). The geometry of ROC space: Understanding machine learning metrics through ROC isometrics. pp. 194–201 in Fawcett, T. & Mishra, N., eds. *Proceedings of the 20th International Conference on Machine Learning* (ICML'03). Menlo Park, CA: AAAI Press.

Fleiss, J. L. (1981). *Statistical methods for rates and proportions*, Second edition. New York City, NY: Wiley.

Fletcher, Roger (1987). *Practical methods of optimization*, Second edition. New York, NY: John Wiley & Sons.

Fliss, Barbara; Luethi, Marcel; Fuernstahl, Philipp; Christensen, Angi M.; Sibold, Ken; Thali, Michael; & Ebert, Lars C. (2019). CT-based sex estimation on human femora using statistical shape modeling. *Journal of Physical Anthropology* 169: 279–286.

Fox, John (2006). Structural equation modeling with the sem package in R. *Structural Equation Modeling* 13: 465–486.

Frey, William R.; Patton, Desmond U.; & Gaskell, Michael B. (2020). Artificial intelligence and inclusion: Formerly gang-involved youth as domain experts for analyzing unstructured Twitter data. *Social Science Computer Review* 38(1): 42–56.

Friedman, Jerome H. (2001). Greedy function approximation: A gradient boosting machine. *The Annals of Statistics* 29(5): 1189–1232.

Garattini, Chiara; Raffle, Jade; Aisyah, Dewi N.; Sartain, Felicity; & Kozlakidis, Zisis (2019). Big data analytics, infectious diseases and associated ethical impacts. *Philosophy & Technology* 32(1): 69–85.

Garcia, D. M.; Schmitt, M. T.; Branscombe, N. R.; & Ellemers, N. (2010). Women's reactions to ingroup members who protest discriminatory treatment: The importance of beliefs about inequality and response appropriateness. *European Journal of Social Psychology* 40(5): 733–745.

Garcia, M. (2016). Racist in the machine: The disturbing implications of algorithmic bias. *World Policy Journal* 33(4): 111–117.

Garrido, Luis Eduardo; Abad, Francisco José; & Ponsoda, Vicente (2013), A new look at Horn's parallel analysis with ordinal variables. *Psychological Methods* 18(4): 454–474.

Garson, G. David (2012). *Loglinear analysis*. Asheboro, NC: Statistical Associates Publishers.

Garson, G. David (2013a). *Cox regression*. Asheboro, NC: Statistical Associates Publishers.

Garson, G. David (2013b). *Multidimensional scaling*. Asheboro, NC: Statistical Associates Publishers.

Garson, G. David (2013c). *Generalized linear models/Generalized estimating equations*. Asheboro, NC: Statistical Associates Publishers.

Garson, G. David (2014a). *Cluster analysis*. Asheboro, NC: Statistical Associates Publishers.

Garson, G. David (2014b). *GLM univariate: ANOVA and repeated measures*. Asheboro, NC: Statistical Associates Publishers.

Garson, G. David (2015). *GLM multivariate: MANOVA, MANCOVA, and canonical correlation*. Asheboro, NC: Statistical Associates Publishers.

Garson, G. David (2016a). *Scales and measures*. Asheboro, NC: Statistical Associates.

Garson, G. David (2016b). *Validity and reliability.* Asheboro, NC: Statistical Associates.

Garson, G. David (2016c). *Case study research and comparative qualitative analysis.* Asheboro, NC: Statistical Associates Publishers.

Garson, G. David (2017). *Mediation and moderation: Partial correlation and regression approaches.* Asheboro, NC: Statistical Associates Publishers.

Garson, G. David (2018a). *Structural equation modeling.* Asheboro, NC: Statistical Associates Publishers.

Garson, G. David (2018b). *Getting started with R and RStudio.* Asheboro, NC: Statistical Associates Publishers. Available free at http://www.statisticalassociates.com/gettingstartedwithR.pdf.

Garson, G. David (2020). *Multilevel modeling: Applications in the social sciences: Applications in SPSS, SAS, Stata, R, & HLM.* Thousand Oaks, CA: Sage Publications.

Gelman, Andrew & Hill, Jennifer (2006). *Data analysis using regression and multilevel/hierarchical models.* Cambridge University Press.

Gelman, Andrew; Jakulin, Aleks; Pittau, Maria Grazia; & Su, Yu-Sung (2008). A weakly informative default prior distribution for logistic and other regression models. *The Annals of Applied Statistics* 2(4): 1360–1383.

Gevrey, M.; Dimopoulos, I.; & Lek, S. (2003). Review and comparison of methods to study the contribution of variables in artificial neural network models. *Ecological Modelling* 160(3): 249–264.

Ghoddusi, Hamed; Creamer, Germán G.; & Rafizadeh, Nima (2019). Machine learning in energy economics and finance: A review. *Energy Economics* 81: 709–727.

Gilbert, Nigel & Troitzsch, Klaus G. (2005). *Simulation for the social scientist*, Second edition. London: McGraw Hill.

Glas, Alfina S.; Lijmer, Jeroen G.; Prins, Martin H.; Bonsel, Gouke J.; & Bossuyt, Patrick M. M. (2003). The diagnostic odds ratio: A single indicator of test performance. *Journal of Clinical Epidemiology* 56: 1129–1135.

Glauser, W. (2020). AI in health care: Improving outcomes or threatening equity? *Canadian Medical Association Journal* 192(1): E21–E22. DOI: http://dx.doi.org.prox.lib.ncsu.edu/10.1503/cmaj.1095838.

Golbeck, Jennifer (2013). *Analyzing the social web.* Elsevier/Morgan Kaufman.

Golden, Chase E.; Rothrock, Michael J.; & Mishra, Abhinav (2019). Comparison between random forest and gradient boosting machine methods for predicting listeria spp. *Food Research International* 122: 47–55.

Goodman, L. A. (1979). Simple models for the analysis of association in cross-classifications having ordered categories. *Journal of the American Statistical Association* 74(367): 537–552.

Granovetter, M. S. (1973). The strength of weak ties. *American Journal of Sociology* 78(6): 1360–1380.

Graupensperger, Scott; Panza, Michae; & Evans, M. Blair (2020). Network centrality, group density, and strength of social identification in college club sport teams. *Group Dynamics* 24(2): 59–73.

Grun, B. & Hornik, K. (2011). topicmodels: An R package for fitting topic models. *Journal of Statistical Software* 40(13): 1–30.

Günther, Frauke & Fritsch, Stefan (2010). neuralnet: Training of neural networks. *The R Journal* 2(1): 30–38. Retrieved 1/19/2020 from https://journal.r-project.org/archive/2010/RJ-2010-006/RJ-2010-006.pdf.

Hagen, Loni; Keller, Thomas E.; Yerden, Xiaoyi; & Luna-Reyes, Luis Felipe (2019). Open data visualizations and analytics as tools for policy-making. *Government Information Quarterly* 36. Available online 25 June 2019 at https://doi.org/10.1016/j.giq.2019.06.004.

Hagen, Loni; Neely, Stephen; Keller, Thomas E.; Scharf, Ryan; & Vasquez, Fatima Espinoza (2020). Rise of the machines? Examining the influence of social bots on a political discussion network. *Social Science Computer Review* 40(2), published online April 2020.

Halkidi, Maria; Batistakis, Yannis; & Vazirgiannis, Michalis (2002). Clustering validity checking methods: Part II. *ACM SIGMOD Record* 3(3): 19–27.

Hammer, Barbara & Villmann, Thomas (2002). Generalized relevance learning vector quantization. *Neural Networks* 15(8): 1059–1068.

Hargittai, Eszter (2020). Potential biases in big data: Omitted voices on social media. *Social Science Computer Review* 38(1): 10–24.

Harris, J. K., et al. (2012). Interpersonal influence among public health leaders in the United States Department of Health and Human Services. *Journal of Public Health Research* 1: 67–74.

Harrison, D. & Rubinfeld, D. L. (1978). Hedonic prices and the demand for clean air. *Journal of Environmental Economics and Management* 5: 81–102.

Hartigan, J. A. (1975). *Clustering algorithms.* New York City, NY: Wiley. Chapter 6.

Hastie, T; Tibshirani, R; & Friedman, J. (2013). *The elements of statistical learning*, Second edition. New York, NY: Springer.

Hauer, Tomas (2019). Society caught in a labyrinth of algorithms: Disputes, promises, and limitations of the new order of things. *Society* 56: 222–230.

Hayes, Andrew F. (2013, 2018). *Introduction to mediation, moderation, and conditional process analysis*, Second edition. New York, NY: Guilford Press.

Hekman, Susan (1997). Truth and method: Feminist standpoint theory revisited. *Signs* 22(2): 341–365.

Holliday, Bradley S. (2021). The relationship between police mission statements and organizational effectiveness: An exploratory study. Doctoral dissertation, North Carolina State University, Raleigh, NC.

Hothorn, Torsten (2018). *CRAN task view: Machine learning & statistical learning*. Version: 2018-08-05. CRAN-R Project. Available at https://cran.r-project.org/web/views/MachineLearning.html.

Hothorn, Torsten; Bühlmann, P.; Dudoit, S.; Molinaro, A.; & Van der Laan, M. J. (2006). Survival ensembles. *Biostatistics* 7(3): 355–373.

Hothorn, Torstein; Hornik, Kirk; &, Zeileis, Achim (2006). Unbiased recursive partitioning: A conditional inference framework. *Journal of Computational and Graphical Statistics* 15(3): 651–674.

Hothorn, Torsten; Hornik, Kurt; & Zeileis, Achim (2015). *ctree: Conditional inference trees*. Available at https://cran.r-project.org/web/packages/partykit/vignettes/ctree.pdf.

Hothorn, Torsten; Lausen, B.; Benner, A.; & Radespiel-Troeger, M. (2004). Bagging survival trees. *Statistics in Medicine* 23(1): 77–91.

Hothorn, Torsten & Zeileis, Achim (2015). partykit: A modular toolkit for recursive partytioning in R. *Journal of Machine Learning Research* 16: 3905–3909. Available at http://jmlr.org/papers/ v16/hothorn15a.html.

Howe, B.; Franklin, M.; Haas, L.; Kraska, T.; & Ullman, J. (2017). Data science education: We're missing the boat, again. In *2017 IEEE 33rd international conference on data engineering (ICDE)*: 1473–1474. DOI:10.1109/ICDE.2017.215.

Hunt, Robert M. (2005). A Century of Consumer Credit Reporting in America. FRB Philadelphia Working Paper No. 05-13. Accessed September 24, 2015. Available at http://ssrn.com/abstract¼757929 or http://dx.doi.org/10.2139/ssrn.757929.

Hunter, Floyd (1969). *Community power structure: A study of decision makers*. Chapel Hill, NC: UNC Press.

Ishwaran, H.; Kogalur, U. B.; Gorodeski, E. Z.; Minn, A. J.; & Lauer, M. S. (2010). High-dimensional variable selection for survival data. *Journal of the American Statistical Association* 105: 205–217.

Jacobs, Paige (2019). *Machine learning with Python*. Seattle, WA: Amazon Digital Services LLC.

Jacobucci, Ross (2018). Are decision trees stable enough for psychological research?: Notre Dame, IN, University of Notre Dame: Preprint. DOI: 10.31234/osf.io/f2utw.

James, G.; Witten, D.; Hastie, T.; & Tibshirani, R. (2013). *An introduction to statistical learning with applications in R*. New York, NY: Springer.

James, G.; Witten, D.; Hastie, T.; & Tibshirani, R. (2013; 2017). *An introduction to statistical learning with applications in R*, First edition 2013; 2017 edition. New York, NY: Springer.

James, G.; Witten, D.; Hastie, T.; & Tibshirani, R. (2017). *Data for an introduction to statistical learning with applications in R.*, 13th edition. New York, NY: Springer.

James, Gareth; Witten, Daniela; Hastie, Trevor; Tibshirani, Robert (2017). *Tree-based methods*. pp. 303–336 in James, Witten, Hastie, & Tibshirani (2017), supra.

Jamshidian, Mortaza & Jalal, Siavach (2010). Tests of homoscedasticity, normality, and missing completely at random for incomplete multivariate data. *Psychometrika* 75(4): 649–674.

Jamshidian, Mortaza & Jalal, Siavash (2014). MissMech: An R package for testing homoscedasticity, multivariate normality, and missing completely at random (MCAR). *Journal of Statistical Software* 56(6): 1–31.

Jenks, George F. (1967). The data model concept in statistical mapping. *International Yearbook of Cartography* 7: 186–190.

Jeong, Jinook & Yoon, Byung Ho (2010). The effect of pseudo-exogenous instrumental variables on Hausman test. *Communications in Statistics – Simulation and Computation*, 39(2): 315–321.

Jimenez, Egan & Daniels, Kendall (2020). Projecting the outcomes of people's lives with AI isn't so simple. *Virginia Tech Daily* (March). Retrieved 3/31/2020 from https://vtnews.vt.edu/articles/2020/03/Fralin-Life-Sci-AI-Predictive-Models-Brian-Goode.html.

Jockers, Matthew L. & Thalken, Rosamond (2020). *Text analysis with R for students of literature*, Second edition. Quantitative Methods in the Humanities and Social Sciences. New York, NY: Springer.

Kalinka, Alex T. (2020). The generation, visualization, and analysis of like communities in arbitrary networks with the R package 'linkcomm'. Published by cran-r-project.org and available at https://cran.r-project.org/web/packages/linkcomm/vignettes/linkcomm.pdf. Version of 11 March 2020.

Karatzoglou, Alexandros; Meyer, David; & Hornik, Kurt (2006). Support vector machines in R. *Journal of Statistical Software* 15(9): 1–28.

Karimi, Firoozeh; Sultana, Selima; Babakar, Ali Shirzadi; Suthaharan, Shan (2019). An enhanced support vector machine model for urban expansion prediction. *Computers, Environment and Urban Systems* 75: 61–75.

Kashian, Russell; & Kohls, Heather (2009). Committee size and smart growth: An optimal solution. *The Journal of Applied Business and Economics* 9(2): 11–20.

Kass, G. V. (1980). An exploratory technique for investigating large quantities of categorical data. *Applied Statistics* 29(2): 119–127.

Keerthi, S. S. & Lin, C.-J. (2003). Asymptotic behaviors of support vector machines with Gaussian kernel. *Neural Computation* 15(7): 1667–1689.

Kemper, Jakko & Kolkman, Daan (2019). Transparent to whom? No algorithmic accountability without a critical audience. *Information, Communication & Society* 22(14): 2081–2096. DOI: 10.1080/1369118X.2018.1477967.

Kirchner, Antje & Signorino, Curtis S. (2018). Using support vector machines for survey research. *Survey Practice* 11(1). Retrieved 8/8/2019 from https://www.surveypractice.org/article/2715-using-support-vector-machines-for-survey-research.

Kitamura, Tatsuru; Kitamura, Maki; Hino, Shoryoku; & Kurata, Koichi (2013). Predictors of time to discharge in patients hospitalized for behavioral and psychological symptoms of dementia. *Dementia and Geriatric Cognitive Disorders* 3(1): 86–95.

Knapp, Thomas R. (2013). *To pool or not to pool: That is the confusion*. Retrieved 9/15/2019 from http://www.statlit.org/pdf/2013-Knapp-To-pool-or-not-to-pool.pdf.

Kohonen, Teuvo (1997). *Self-organizing maps*. Berlin: Springer.

König, Hans-Helmut et al. (2013). Effects of multiple chronic conditions on health care costs: An analysis based on an advanced tree-based regression model. *BMC Health Services Research* 13: 219. Available at https://doi.org/10.1186/1472-6963-13-219.

Kraicer, Eve (2019). It's time to address the lack of gender diversity in the research tools landscape. Forum post of 7/2/2019 to https://ocean.sagepub.com. Retrieved 9/12/2019 from https://ocean.sagepub.com/blog/its-time-to-address-the-lack-of-gender-diversity-in-the-research-tools-landscape?utm_source=Adestra&utm_medium=email&utm_content=9P0129B&utm_campaign=not+tracked&utm_term=&em=263f69f5e6931113815d5aab746efa06a36c1532b1568bf8015ed60f80507e1b.

Kuhn, Max (2008), Building predictive models in R using the caret package. *Journal of Statistical Software* 28(5). Retrieved 9/29/2018 from http://www.jstatsoft.org/article/view/v028i05/v28i05.pdf.

Kuhn, Max (2013). Predictive modeling with R and the caret package. Albacete, Spain: R User Conference 2013. Retrieved 9/29/2018 from https://www.r-project.org/conferences/useR-2013/Tutorials/kuhn/user_caret_2up.pdf.

Kuhn, Max & Johnson, Kjell (2016). *Applied predictive modeling*, First edition 2013. New York, NY: Springer. Corrected second printing, 2016.

Kulkarni, Mayur (2017). Decision trees for classification: A machine learning algorithm. Post to "The Xoriant Blog" of 7 Sept. 2017. Retrieved 8/28/2018 from https://www.xoriant.com/blog/product-engineering/decision-trees-machine-learning-algorithm.html.

Kusner, Matt J. & Loftus, Joshua R. (2020). The long road to fairer algorithms: Build models that identify and mitigate the causes of discrimination. *Nature* 578: 34–36.

La Fors, Karolina; Custers, Bart; & Keymolen, Esther (2019). Reassessing values for emerging big data technologies: Integrating design-based and application-based approaches. *Ethics and Information Technology* 21(3): 209–226.

Landis, J. R. & Koch, G. G. (1977). The measurement of observer agreement for categorical data. *Biometrics* 33(1): 159–174.

Lang, M.; Binder, M.; Richter, J.; Schratz, P.; Pfisterer, F.; Coors, S.; Au, Q.; Casalicchio, G.; Kotthoff, L.; & Bischl, B. (2019). mlr3: A modern object-oriented machine learning framework in R. *Journal of Open Source Software*. DOI: 10.21105/joss.01903; available at https://joss.theoj.org/papers/10.21105/joss.01903.

Lantz, Brett (2013). *Machine learning with R*, Second edition. Birmingham, UK: PACKT Publishing/Open Source.

Lausen, B.; Sauerbrei, W.; & Schumacher, M. (1994). Classification and regression trees (CART) used for the exploration of prognostic factors measured on different scales. pp. 483–496 in Dirschedl, P. & Ostermann, R., eds., *Computational Statistics*. Heidelberg, Germany: Physica-Verlag.

Lawyers' Committee for Civil Rights under Law (2020). Facebook engages in online segregation and redlining through discriminatory advertising system, Lawyers' Committee argues. Press release, July 10, 2020. Source: https://lawyerscommitee.org.

Le, James (2018). *Decision trees in R*. New York City, NY: DataCamp.com. Retrieved 9/1/2018 from https://www.datacamp.com/community/tutorials/decision-trees-R.

LeCun, Yann; Bottou, Leon; Orr, Genevieve B.; & Muller, Klaus-Robert (1998). Efficient backprop. In Orr, G. & Muller, K., eds., *Neural Networks: Tricks of the Trade*. Springer.

Leinweber, D. J. (2007). Stupid data miner tricks: Overfitting the S&P 500. *Journal of Investing* 16(1): 15–22. Retrieved from https://proxying.lib.ncsu.edu/index.php/login?url=https://www-proquest-com.prox.lib.ncsu.edu/trade-journals/stupid-data-miner-tricks-overfitting-s-amp-p-500/docview/220762487/se-2?accountid=12725.

Leischow, S. J.; Luke, D. A., et al. (2010). Mapping U.S. government tobacco control leadership: Networked for success? *Nicotine & Tobacco Research* 12: 888–894.

Liaw, Andy (2003). rpart vs. randomForest. R-help at stat.math.ethz.ch mailing list. Apr 14 19:37:21 CEST 2003. Retrieved from https://stat.ethz.ch/pipermail/r-help/2003-April/032256.html.

Lin, Hsuan-Tien & Lin, Chih-Jen (2003). A study on sigmoid kernels for SVM and the training of non-PSD kernels by SMO-type methods. Technical report, Department of Computer Science, National Taiwan University, 2003. Retrieved 7/13/2019 from https://www.csie.ntu.edu.tw/~cjlin/papers/tanh.pdf.

Little, R. J. A. & Rubin, D. B. (1987). *Statistical analysis with missing data*. New York, NY: Wiley.

Liu, Bing (2015). *Sentiment analysis: Mining opinions, sentiments, and emotions*. New York, NY: Cambridge University Press.

Long, Jacob (2019). *A new package for panel data analysis in R*. Posted on 18 May 2019 to R-Bloggers. Retrieved 11/20/2019 from https://www.r-bloggers.com/a-new-package-for-panel-data-analysis-in-r/.

Lu, Weisheng (2019). Big data analytics to identify illegal construction waste dumping: A Hong Kong study. *Resources, conservation and recycling* 141: 264–272.

Lu, Zhengdong; Leen, Todd K.; & Kaye, Jeffrey (2009). Hierarchical Fisher kernel for longitudinal data. *Advances in Neural Information Processing Systems*. Proceedings, Advances in Neural Information Processing Systems (NIPS 21). Retrieved 12/1/2019 from https://www.microsoft.com/en-us/research/publication/hierarchical-fisher-kernel-for-longitudinal-data/.

Luke, Douglas A. (2015). *A user's guide to network analysis in R.* New York, NY: Springer.

Luts, Jan; Molenberghs, Verneke Geert; Van Huffel, Sabine; & Suykens, Johan A. K. (2012). A mixed effects least squares support vector machine model for classification of longitudinal data. *Computational Statistics & Data Analysis* 56(1): 611–628.

MacFeely, S. (2019). Big data and official statistics. pp. 25–54 in Strydom, S., & Strydom. M., eds. *Big data governance and perspectives in knowledge management.* Hershey, PA: IGI Global.

Mannes, A. (2020). Governance, risk, and artificial intelligence. *AI Magazine* 41(1): 61–69.

McNamee, Roger (2020). Facebook cannot fix itselt. *Time* 15 June 2020: 20–21.

Michell, L. & Amos, A. (1997). Girls, pecking order and smoking. *Social Science and Medicine* 44: 1861–1869.

Miguel-Hurtado, Oscar; Guest, Richard; Stevenage, Sarah V.; Neil, Greg J.; & Black, Sue (2015). Comparing machine learning classifiers and linear/logistic regression to explore the relationship between hand dimensions and demographic characteristics. *PLoS One* 11(1): 1–25. 2 November 2016.

Millar, A. (2002). *Subset selection in regression,* Second edition. Boca Raton, FL: Chapman & Hall/CRC Monographs on Statistics & Applied Probability.

Miller, Rupert & Siegmund, David (1982). Maximally selected chi-square statistics. *Biometrics* 38(4): 1011–1016.

Mittelstadt, Brent (2019). The ethics of biomedical 'big data' analytics. *Philosophy & Technology* 32: 17–21.

Moreno, Jacob Levy (1934). *Who shall survive?* New York, NY: Beacon House.

Moreno, Jacob Levy (1951). *Sociometry, experimental method and the science of society: An approach to a new political orientation.* New York, NY: Beacon House.

Muchlinski, D.; Siroki, D.; He, J.; & Kocher, M. (2016). Comparing random forest with logistic regression for predicting class-imbalanced civil war onset data. *Political Analysis* 24(1): 87–103.

Munzert, Simon; Rubba, Christian; Meissner, Peter; & Nyhuis, Dominic (2014). *Automated data collection with R: A practical guide to web scraping and text mining.* Chichester, West Sussex, UK: John Wiley & Sons.

Mora, Ricardo (2015). An implementation of CART in Stata. 2015 Spanish Stata Users' Group Meeting. Retrieved 9/7/2018 from https://www.stata.com/meeting/spain15/abstracts/materials/spain15_mora.pdf.

Muchlinski, D.; Siroky, D.; He, J.; & Kocher, M. (2016). Comparing random forest with logistic regression for predicting class-imbalanced civil war onset data. *Political Analysis* 24(1): 87–103.

Natekin, Alexey & Knoll, Alois (2013). Gradient boosting machines, a tutorial. *Frontiers in Neurorobotics* 7(21): 1–17. Published online 2013 Dec 4. DOI: 10.3389/fnbot.2013.00021.

Nersessian, David (2018). The law and ethics of big data analytics: A new role for international human rights in the search for global standards. *Business Horizons* 61(6): 845–854.

Neville, Padraic (1998). Growing trees for stratified modeling. *Computing Science and Statistics, Proceedings of the 30th Symposium on the Interface* 30: 528–533.

Nisbet, Robert; Elder IV, John; & Miner, Gary (2009). *Handbook of statistical analysis and data mining applications.* Burlington, MA, & London, UK: Academic Press.

Norval, Chris; & Henderson, Tristan (2020). Automating dynamic consent decisions for the processing of social media data in health research. *Journal of Empirical Research on Human Research Ethics* 15(3): 187–201.

Nova, David & Estévez, Pablo A. (2014). A review of learning vector quantization classifiers. *Neural Computing and Applications* 25(3): 511–524.

Obermeyer, Ziad; Powers, Brian; Vogeli, Christine; & Mullainathan, Sendhil (2019). Dissecting racial bias in an algorithm used to manage the health of populations. *Science* 366(6464): 447–453.

Olden, J. D. & Jackson, D. A. (2002). Illuminating the "Black Box": A randomization approach for understanding variable contributions in artificial neural networks. *Ecological Modelling* 154(1–2): 135–150.

Olden, J. D.; Joy, M. K.; & Death, R. G. (2004). An accurate comparison of methods for quantifying variable importance in artificial neural networks using simulated data. *Ecological Modelling* 178:389–397.

O'Neil, Cathy (2017). *Weapons of math destruction: How big data increases inequality and threatens democracy.* New York City, NY: Broadway Books/Crown Publishing Group.

O'Neill, Cathy (2020). 10 reasons to doubt the Covid-19 data: The pandemic's true toll might never be known. *Bloomberg News.* April 13. Retrieved 7/14/2020 from https://www.bloomberg.com/opinion/articles/2020-04-13/ten-reasons-to-doubt-the-covid-19-data.

O'Sullivan, David & Perry, George (2013). *Spatial simulation: Exploring pattern and process.* Hoboken, NJ: Wiley-Blackwell.

Pak, T. R. & Kasarskis, A. (2015). How next-generation sequencing and multiscale data analysis will transform infectious disease management. *Clinical Infectious Diseases* 61(11): 1695–1702.

Paluszyńska, Aleksandra (2017a). *Understanding random forests with randomForestExplainer.* Retrieved 5/22/2019 from https://cran.rstudio.com/web/packages/randomForestExplainer/vignettes/randomForestExplainer.html.

Paluszyńska, Aleksandra (2017b). *Structure mining and knowledge extraction from random forest with applications to The Cancer Genome Atlas project.* Master's Thesis, University of Warsaw, Faculty of Mathematics, Informatics and Mechanics. Retrieved 5/22/2019 from https://pdfs.semanticscholar.org/9263/120a2cd953780c80fb13a6263104c04acd91.pdf.

Papakyriakopoulos, Orestis; Carlos Medina Serrano, Juan; & Hegelich, Simon (2020). Political communication on social media: A tale of hyperactive users and bias in recommender systems. *Online Social Networks and Media* 15(Jan.). Available online at https://doi.org/10.1016/j.osnem.2019.100058.

Parasuraman, R. & Manzey, D. H. (2010). Complacency and bias in human use of automation: An attentional integration. *Human Factors* 52(3): 381–410.

Parikh, R. B.; Teeple, S.; & Navathe, A. S. (2019). Addressing bias in artificial intelligence in health care. *JAMA (Journal of the American Medical Association)* 322(24): 2377–2378. DOI: 10.1001/jama.2019.18058.

Pearson, M. A. & Michell, L. (2000). Smoke rings: Social network analysis of friendship groups, smoking and drug-taking. *Drugs: Education, Prevention and Policy* 7: 21–37.

Pearson, M. A. & West, P. (2003). Drifting smoke rings: Social network analysis and Markov processes in a longitudinal study of friendship groups and risk-taking. *Connections* 25(2): 59–76.

Pensacola News Journal (2020). DeSantis still hiding data on COVID-19 deaths. May 8, 2020. Retrieved 7/14/2020 from https://www.msn.com/en-us/news/us/editorial-desantis-still-hiding-data-on-covid-19-deaths/ar-BB13MTfU.

Petrozzino, Cathy (2020). Big data analytics: Ethical considerations make a difference. *Scitech Lawyer* 16(3): 14–21.

Pontius, R. G. & Millones, M. (2011). Death to kappa: Birth of quantity disagreement and allocation disagreement for accuracy assessment. *International Journal of Remote Sensing* 32: 4407–4429.

Ponweiser, Martin (2012). *Latent dirichlet allocation in R*. Diploma thesis. Vienna, Austria: Institute for Statistics and Mathematics, Vienna University of Economics and Business. Retrieved 4/14/2020 from http://epub.wu.ac.at/3558/1/main.pdf.

Pozzi, Federico Alberto & Fersini, Elisabetta Fersini (2017). *Sentiment analysis in social networks*. Cambridge, MA: Morgan Kaufmann (Elsevier).

Quinlan, J. Ross (1986). Induction of decision trees. *Machine Learning* 1(1): 81–106.

Quinlan, J. Ross (1990). Learning logical definitions from relations. *Machine Learning* 5: 239–266.

Quinlan, J. Ross (1994). *C4.5: Programs for machine learning*. Burlington, MA: Morgan Kaufmann Publishers.

Quinlan, J. Ross; Yang, Qiang; Yu, Philip S.; Zhihua, Zhou; & Hand, David Hand (2008). Top 10 algorithms in data mining. *Knowledge and Information Systems* 14: 1–37.

Raileanu, L. E. & Stoffel, K. (2004). Theoretical comparison between the Gini Index and Information Gain Criteria. *Annals of Mathematics and Artificial Intelligence* 41: 77–93.

Railsback, Steven F. & Grimm, Volker (2012). *Agent-based and individual-based modeling: A practical introduction*. Princeton, NJ: Princeton University Press.

Raudenbush, Stephen W.; Bryk, Anthony; Cheong, Yuk Fai; Congdon, Richard; & Du Toit, Mathilda (2011). *HLM 7: Hierarchical linear & nonlinear modeling*. Lincolnwood, IL: Scientific Software International.

Reades, Jonathan; De Souza, Jordan; & Hubbard, Phil (2019). Understanding urban gentrification through machine learning. *Urban Studies* 56(5): 922–942.

Revelle, William (2017). How to use the psych package for mediation/moderation/regression analysis. Retrieved 10/20/2019 from http://personality-project.org/r/psych/HowTo/mediation.pdf.

Rezaee, Zabihollah & Wang, Jim (2019). Relevance of big data to forensic accounting practice and education. *Managerial Auditing Journal* 34(3): 268–288.

Riccucci, Norma M.; Van Ryzin, Gregg G.; & Li, Huafang (2016). Representative bureaucracy and the willingness to coproduce: An experimental study. *Public Administration Review* 76(1): 121–130.

Riedmiller, M. (1994). *Rprop – Description and implementation details*. Technical Report. University of Karlsruhe.

Riedmiller, M. & Braun, H. (1993). A direct adaptive method for faster backpropagation learning: The RPROP algorithm. *Proceedings of the IEEE International Conference on Neural Networks* (ICNN), pp. 586–591. San Francisco.

Ripley, Brian D. (1996). *Pattern recognition and neural networks*. Cambridge, UK: Cambridge University Press.

Ripley, Ruth M.; Snijders, Tom A. B.; Boda, Zsófia; Vörös, András; & Preciado, Paulina (2020). *Manual for SIENA version 4.0* (version June 24, 2020). Oxford: University of Oxford, Department of Statistics; Nuffield College. Available at http://www.stats.ox.ac.uk/~snijders/siena/RSiena_Manual.pdf.

Ripley, Ruth M.; Snijders, Tom A. B; Boda, Zsófia; András Vörös, Andrea; & Preciado, Paulina (2021). *Manual for RSiena*. University of Oxford: Department of Statistics; Nuffield College. Available at http://www.stats.ox.ac.uk/~snijders/siena/RSiena_Manual.pdf.

Robila, M. & Robila, S. A. (2020). Applications of artificial intelligence methodologies to behavioral and social sciences. *Journal of Child and Family Studies* 29: 2954–2966.

Rodriguez, J. J.; Kuncheva, L. I.; Alonso, C. J. (2006). Rotation forest: A new classifier ensemble method. *IEEE Transactions on Pattern Analysis and Machine Intelligence* 28(10): 1619–1630.

Rogers, W. H. (1993). Comparison of nbreg and glm for negative binomial. *Stata Technical Bulletin* 16: 7.

Rousseeuw, P. J. (1987). Silhouettes: A graphical aid to the interpretation and validation of cluster analysis. *Journal of Computational and Applied Mathematics* 20: 53–65.

Rubin, D. B. (1987). *Multiple imputation for nonresponse in surveys*. New York, NY: Wiley.

Rubin, D. B. & Schenker, N. (1986). Multiple imputation for interval estimation from simple random samples with ignorable nonresponse. *Journal of the American Statistical Association* 81: 366–374.

Rumelhart, D. E.; Hinton, G. E.; & Williams, R. J. (1986). Learning representations by back-propagating errors. *Nature* 323: 533–566.

Ryan, Mark (2020). Agricultural big data analytics and the ethics of power. *Journal of Agricultural and Environmental Ethics* 33: 49–69.

Schelling, Thomas C. (1971). Dynamic models of segregation. *Journal of Mathematical Sociology* 1.2: 143–186.

Schelling, Thomas C. (1978). *Micromotives and macrobehavior.* New York City, NY: W. W. Norton.

Schneble, C. O.; Elger, B. S.; & Shaw, D. M. (2020). Google's Project Nightingale highlights the necessity of data science ethics review. *EMBO molecular medicine* 12(3). Available at https://doi.org/10.15252/emmm.202012053.

Selker, Ravi (2017). medmod – mediation and moderation in jamovi and R. A post on the R-bloggers and jamovi blogs. Retrieved 10/10/2019 from https://www.r-bloggers.com/medmod-mediation-and-moderation-in-jamovi-and-r/.

Seok, K. H.; Shim, J.; Cho, D.; Noh, G. J.; & Hwang, C. (2011). Semiparametric mixed-effect least squares support vector machine for analyzing pharmacokinetic and pharmacodynamic data. *Neurocomputing* 74(17): 3412–3419.

Shatnawi, Nawras & Qdais, Hani Abu (2019). Mapping urban land surface temperature using remote sensing techniques and artificial neural network modelling. *International Journal of Remote Sensing* 40(10). Published online: https://doi.org/10.1080/01431161.2018.1557792.

Shellenbarger, S. (2019). A crucial step for averting artificial intelligence disasters. *Wall Street Journal.* 10 February 2019. Available online at https://www.wsj.com/articles/a-crucial-step-for-avoiding-ai-disasters-11550069865.

Silge, Julia & Robinson, David (2017). *Text mining with R: A tidy approach.* Sebastopol, CA: O'Reilly Media.

Silge, Julia & Robinson, David (2020). Converting to and from Document-Term Matrix and Corpus objects. A vignette for the tidytext package published by cran.r-project.org. 2020=03-03. Retrieved 4/8/2020 from https://cran.r-project.org/web/packages/tidytext/vignettes/tidying_casting.html.

Sing, Tobias; Sander, Oliver; Beerenwinkel, Niko; & Lengauer, Thomas (2005). ROCR: Visualizing classifier performance in R. *Bioinformatics* 21(20): 3940–3941.

Sipior, Janice C. (2020). Considerations for development and use of AI in response to COVID-19. *International Journal of Information Management* 55: 1–6 (Article 102170).

Smith, Chris (2017). *Decision trees and random forests: A visual introduction for beginners.* Vancouver, Canada: Blue Windmill Media.

Snijders, Tom A. B. (2001). The statistical evaluation of social network dynamics. *Sociological Methodology* 31: 361–395.

Snijders, Tom A. B. (2011). Statistical models for social networks. *Annual Review of Sociology* 37: 131–153.

Snijders, Tom A. B.; Lomi, A.; & Torlo, V. (2013). A model for the multiplex dynamics of two-mode and one-mode networks, with an application to employment preference, friendship, and advice. *Social Networks* 35: 265–276.

Snijders, Tom A. B. & Pickup, Mark (2017). Stochastic actor-oriented models for network dynamics. *Annual Review of Statistics and Its Application* 4: 343–363. Reprinted pp. 221–227 in Nicoll; Montgomery, Alexander H.; & Lubell, Mark, eds., *Oxford Handbook of Political Networks.* New York, NY: Oxford University Press.

Snijders, Tom A. B.; van de Bunt, G. G.; & Steglich, C. (2010). Introduction to actor-based models for network dynamics. *Social Networks* 32: 44–60.

Somervuo, Panu & Kohonen, Teuvo (1999, 2004). Self-organizing maps and learning vector quantization for feature sequences. *Neural Processing Letters* 10(2): 151–159. A 2004 update is at http://cis.legacy.ics.tkk.fi/panus/papers/dtwsom.pdf.

Sousa, Maria José; Pesqueira, António Miguel; Lemos, Carlos; Sousa, Miguel; & Rocha, Álvaro (2019). Decision-making based on big data analytics for people management in healthcare organizations. *Journal of Medical Systems* 43(9): 290.

Souza, César (2010). Kernel functions for machine learning applications. Online publication. Retrieved 7/12/2019 from http://crsouza.com/2010/03/17/kernel-functions-for-machine-learning-applications/.

Srivastava, M. S. & Dolatabadi, M. (2009). Multiple imputation and other resampling schemes for imputing missing observations. *Journal of Multivariate Analysis* 100(9): 1919–1937.

Strasser, H. & Weber, C. (1999). On the asymptotic theory of permutation statistics. *Mathematical Methods of Statistics* 8: 220–250.

Strobl, Carolin; Boulesteix, Anne-Laure; Kneib, Thomas; Augustin, Thomas; & Zeileis, Achim (2008). Conditional variable importance for random forests. *BMC Bioinformatics* 9: 307.

Strobl, Carolin; Malley, J.; & Tutz, G. (2009). An introduction to recursive partitioning: Rationale, application, and characteristics of classification and regression trees, bagging, and random forests. *Psychological Methods* 14(4): 323–348.

Stubbs, M. (2010). Three concepts of keywords. pp. 1–42 in Bondi, M. & Scott, M., eds. *Keyness in texts.* Amsterdam, Philadelphia: John Benjamins.

Suykens, Johan A. K. & Vandewalle, Joos P. L. (1999). Least squares support vector machine classifiers. *Neural Processing Letters* 9(3): 293–300.

Tan, Timothy (2020). Back to basics: Assumptions of common machine learning models. Retrieved 11/10/2020 from https://towardsdatascience.com/back-to-basics-assumptions-of-common-machine-learning-models-e43c02325535.

Therneau, Terry M. & Atkinson, Elizabeth J. (2018). An introduction to recursive partitioning using the RPART routines. This is the file "longintro.pdf" which is installed in the "Users" directory when rpart is installed (e.g., 'C:/Users/David/Documents/R/win-library/3.5/rpart/doc/lonzgintro.pdf'). https://cran.r-project.org/web/packages/rpart/vignettes/longintro.pdf.

Thomson, Nicholas D. (2020). An exploratory study of female psychopathy and drug-related violent crime. *Journal of Interpersonal Violence* 35(3–4): 794–808.

Tingley, D.; Yamamoto, T.; Hirose, K.; Keele, L.; & Imai, K. (2014). mediation: R package for causal mediation analysis. *Journal of Statistical Software* 59(5): 1–38.

Tossas-Milligan, K. Y. & Winn, R. A. (2019). Breaking the cycle of health inequities: The bioethics of data. *Journal of Health Care for the Poor and Underserved* 30(5): 86–90.

Tseng, Fan-Hsun; Cho, Hsin-Hung; & Wu, Hsin-Te (2019). Applying big data for intelligent agriculture-based crop selection analysis. *IEEE Access, Special Section on Data Mining for Internet of Things*, 3 September 2019. DOI:10.1109/ACCESS.2019.2935564.

Twitter, Inc. (2011). One hundred million voices. From blog.Twitter.com, 12 September 2011. Retrieved 9/15/2019 from http://blog.Twitter.com/2011/09/one-hundred-million-voices.html.

United Nations (2011). *Guiding principles on business and human rights.* Available at http://www.ohchr.org/Documents/Publications/GuidingPrinciplesBusinessHR_EN.pdf.

van Putten, Wim (2002). Classification and regression tree analysis with Stata. Maastricht, Austria: NL Stata Users meeting, May 23. Retrieved 8/28/2018 from https://www.stata.com/meeting/2dutch/cart.pdf.

van Putten, Wim (2006). CART: Stata module to perform classification and regression tree analysis. *Statistical Software Components S456776*, Boston College Department of Economics.

Van Rijsbergen, C. H. (1979). *Information retrieval*, Second edition. Newton, MA: Butterworth-Heinemann.

Von Neumann, John (1958). *The computer and the brain.* New Haven, CT: Yale University Press.

Volpentesta, Tiziano (2020). *A text mining approach to strategy research: Demand-side strategy via topic modeling.* Beau Bassin, Mauritius: LAP LAMBERT Academic Publishing.

Wang, Dakuo et al. (2019). Human-AI collaboration in data science: Exploring data scientists' perceptions of automated AI. *Proceedings of the ACM on Human-Computer Interaction.* Vol. 3, Issue CSCW, Article No.: 211, November 2019.

Wang, Y. (2019). Comparing random forest with logistic regression for predicting class-imbalanced civil war onset data: A comment. *Political Analysis* 27(1): 107–110.

Watson, David (2019). The rhetoric and reality of anthropomorphism in artificial intelligence. *Minds and Machines* 29(3): 417–440.

White, Mark (2018). Using processr. A post to the RPubs block. Retrieved 3/4/2019 from http://rpubs.com/markhw/processr.

Wilensky, Uri & Rand, William (2015). *An introduction to agent-based modeling: Modeling natural, social and engineered complex systems with NetLogo.* Cambridge, MA: MIT Press.

Williams, Maxwell (2020). The trouble with facial recognition. *ACLU Magazine* Winter: 11–15. New York City, NY: American Civil Liberties Union.

Wohlstetter, Roberta & Schelling, Thomas C. (1962). *Pearl Harbor: Warning and decision.* Redwood City, CA: Stanford University Press.

Worsley, K. J. (1983). Testing for a two-phase multiple regression. *Technometrics* 25(1): 35–42.

Wykstra, Stephanie (2018). Can racial bias ever be removed from criminal justice algorithms? *Pacific Standard* July 12. Available at https://psmag.com/social-justice/removing-racial-bias-from-the-algorithm.

Yu, Zhuoxi; Qin, Lu; Cehn, Yunjing; & Parmar, Milan Deepak (2020). Stock price forecasting based on LLE-BP neural network model. *Physica A: Statistical mechanics and its applications.* Published online: https://doi-org.prox.lib.ncsu.edu/10.1016/j.physa.2020.124197.

Zarsky, Tal (2016). The trouble with algorithmic decisions: An analytic road map to examine efficiency. *Science, technology, & human values* 41(1): 118–132.

Zeileis, Achim; Hothorn, Torsten; & Hornik, Kurt (2008). *Party with the mob: Model-based recursive partitioning in R.* American Statistical Association, Institute of Mathematical Statistics, and Interface Foundation of North America. Retrieved 4/1/2019 from https://eeecon.uibk.ac.at/~zeileis/papers/Zeileis+Hothorn+Hornik-2008.pdf.

Zhang, H. & Pan, J. (2019). CASM: A deep-learning approach for identifying collective action events with text and image data from social media. *Sociological Methodology* 49(1): 1–57.

Zumbo, Bruno D.; Gadermann, Anne M.; & Zeisser, C. (2007). Ordinal versions of coefficients alpha and theta for Likert rating scales. *Journal of Modern Applied Statistical Methods* 6: 21–29.

Index

Page numbers in *italics* refer to figures.

9780367624279